ARTIFICIAL INTELLIGENCE APPLICATIONS AND INNOVATIONS

IFIP – The International Federation for Information Processing

IFIP was founded in 1960 under the auspices of UNESCO, following the First World Computer Congress held in Paris the previous year. An umbrella organization for societies working in information processing, IFIP's aim is two-fold: to support information processing within its member countries and to encourage technology transfer to developing nations. As its mission statement clearly states,

> *IFIP's mission is to be the leading, truly international, apolitical organization which encourages and assists in the development, exploitation and application of information technology for the benefit of all people.*

IFIP is a non-profitmaking organization, run almost solely by 2500 volunteers. It operates through a number of technical committees, which organize events and publications. IFIP's events range from an international congress to local seminars, but the most important are:

- The IFIP World Computer Congress, held every second year;
- Open conferences;
- Working conferences.

The flagship event is the IFIP World Computer Congress, at which both invited and contributed papers are presented. Contributed papers are rigorously refereed and the rejection rate is high.

As with the Congress, participation in the open conferences is open to all and papers may be invited or submitted. Again, submitted papers are stringently refereed.

The working conferences are structured differently. They are usually run by a working group and attendance is small and by invitation only. Their purpose is to create an atmosphere conducive to innovation and development. Refereeing is less rigorous and papers are subjected to extensive group discussion.

Publications arising from IFIP events vary. The papers presented at the IFIP World Computer Congress and at open conferences are published as conference proceedings, while the results of the working conferences are often published as collections of selected and edited papers.

Any national society whose primary activity is in information may apply to become a full member of IFIP, although full membership is restricted to one society per country. Full members are entitled to vote at the annual General Assembly, National societies preferring a less committed involvement may apply for associate or corresponding membership. Associate members enjoy the same benefits as full members, but without voting rights. Corresponding members are not represented in IFIP bodies. Affiliated membership is open to non-national societies, and individual and honorary membership schemes are also offered.

ARTIFICIAL INTELLIGENCE APPLICATIONS AND INNOVATIONS

IFIP TC12 WG12.5 - Second IFIP Conference on Artificial Intelligence Applications and Innovations (AIAI2005), September 7-9, 2005, Beijing, China

Edited by

Daoliang Li
China Agricultural University
China

Baoji Wang
China Agricultural University
China

Springer

Library of Congress Cataloging-in-Publication Data

A C.I.P. Catalogue record for this book is available from the Library of Congress.

Artificial Intelligence Applications and Innovations, Edited by Daoliang Li and Baoji Wang

p.cm. (The International Federation for Information Processing)

ISBN-10: (HB) 0-387-28318-8
ISBN-13: (HB) 978-0387-28318-0
Printed on acid-free paper.

Printed in the United States of America.

9 8 7 6 5 4 3 2 1 SPIN 11540335 (HC)
springeronline.com

Contents

Algorithms

Others

Foreword

The papers in this volume comprise the refereed proceedings of the Second International Conference on Artificial Intelligence Applications and Innovations (AIAI2005), in Beijing, China in 2005.

The conference is sponsored by the IFIP Technical Committee on Artificial Intelligence (Technical Committee 12) and its Working Group 12.5 (Artificial Intelligence Applications), and organized by China Agricultural University and Information Committee, Chinese Society of Agricultural Engineering.

A very promising sign of the growing importance of Artificial Intelligence techniques in practical applications is the large number of submissions received this time - more than 150. All papers were reviewed by at least two members of the Programme Committee. The best 93 were selected for the conference and are included in this volume. The international nature of IFIP is amply reflected in the large number of countries represented here.

The conference also featured a Symposium on partner make-matching about Professional Practice in Artificial Intelligence in European Commission funded and bilateral cooperation projects, it is expected about 140 participants will attend the event.

I should like to thank the program co-chair Professor Zongzhi Shi, Secretary in General Mr. Baoji Wang, Vice Chair of the organization committee Dr. Renjie Dong for all their efforts in organizing the conference. Our special thanks should also go to Prof. Max Bramer and Prof. John Debenham for their kind help in the each step of the conference organization, and all the members of our program committee for reviewing an unexpectedly large number of papers to a tight deadline. I should also like to thank Ms. Xiangyun Guo and Mr.

Wei Zhu for their assistance in editing this volume of proceedings.

This is the second in a new series of conferences dedicated to real-world applications of AI around the world. The wide range and importance of these applications is clearly indicated by the papers in this volume. Both are likely to increase still further as time goes by and we intend to reflect these developments in our future conferences.

Daoliang Li

Chair of programme committee, organizing committee

Steering Board

Co-Chairs

Maohua Wang (Member of Chinese Academy of Engineering, Beijing, China)
Zetian Fu (Vice president of China Agricultural University, Beijing, China)
Chunjiang Zhao (China National Engineering center for Information technology in Agriculture, China)

Organizing Committee

Chair

Daoliang Li (China Agricultural University， China)

Vice-chairs

Baoji Wang (China Agricultural University, China)
Renjie Dong (China Agricultural University, China)

Programme Committee

Co-Chairs

Daoliang Li (China Agricultural University, China)
Zhongzhi Shi (Chinese Institute of Computing Technology, CAS, China)

Members [in alpha order]

Agnar Aamodt (Norwegian University of Science and Technology, Norway)
Chunjiang Zhao (NERCITA, China)
Constantine D. Spyropoulos (Greek Computer Society, Greece)
Fangquan Mei. (Chinese Academy of Agricultural Sciences, China)
Renjie Dong (China Agricultural University, China)
Ioannis Paspaliaris (National Technical University of Athens, Greece)
John Debenham (University of Technology, Sydney, Australia)

Kostas Komnitsas (National T echnical University of Crete, Greece)
Maohua Wang (China Agricultural University, China)
Max Bramer (University of Portsmouth, UK)
Minzhan Li (China Agricultural University, China)
Minshu Li (Chinese academy of Science, China)
Ray Kemp (Massey University, New Zealand)
Tom Blackeman (VLM, Belgium)
Yanqing Duan (University of Luton, UK)
Yeping Zhu (Chinese academy of Agricultural Science, China)
Yiming Wang(China Agricultural University, China)
Zetian Fu (China Agricultural University, China)

Secretariat

Secretary-general
Baoji Wang (China Agricultural University, China)

Secretaries

Xiangyun Guo (China Agricultural University, China)
Wei Zhu (China Agricultural University, China)
Hu Wang (China Agricultural University, China)

A FUZZY SYSTEM FOR MULTIOBJECTIVE PROBLEMS

A Case Study in NP-Hard Problems

M. R. Gholamian, S. M. T. Fatemi Ghomi and M. Ghazanfari

Department of Industrial Engineering, Amirkabir University of Technology, 424 Hafez Avenue, Tehran, Iran, {Gholamian, Fatemi}@aut.ac.ir

Department of Industrial Engineering, Iran University of Science and Technology, Narmak 16844, Tehran, Iran, mehdi@iust.ac.ir

Abstract: In this study, an intelligent fuzzy system is used instead of mathematical models. The main core of the system is fuzzy rule base which maps decision space (Z) to solution space (X). The system is designed on noninferior region and gives a big picture of this region in the pattern of fuzzy rules. In addition, numerical examples of well-known NP-hard problems (i.e. multiobjective traveling salesman problem and multiobjective knapsack problem) are provided to clarify the accuracy of developed system.

Key words: Multiobjective decision making, Fuzzy Systems, NP-hard Problems

1. INTRODUCTION

A multiobjective problem is generally defined as follows [21]:

$$\text{Max } \mathbf{F}(\mathbf{x}) = (f_1(\mathbf{x}), f_2(\mathbf{x}) \ldots f_P(\mathbf{x})) \quad (1)$$
$$g_i(\mathbf{x}) \leq 0 \qquad i = 1, 2, \ldots, m \quad (2)$$
$$h_j(\mathbf{x}) = 0 \qquad j = 1, 2, \ldots, m' \quad (3)$$
$$\mathbf{x} \geq 0 \quad (4)$$

where $\mathbf{x}$ is the vector with n decision variables. $\mathbf{f}$: $R^n \rightarrow R^P$ are real valued functions which may be non-differentiable, discontinuous, non-smooth and generally difficult to express mathematically. On the other hand, $\mathbf{g}$: $R^n \rightarrow R^m$

and **h**: $R^n \rightarrow R^{m'}$ are also real valued functions. For simplicity, in this paper $f_1(\mathbf{x})$, $f_2(\mathbf{x})$... $f_P(\mathbf{x})$ are shown as z_1, z_2... z_p respectively.

In principle, multiobjective problems are very different than the single objective problems. In single objective problems, one attempts to obtain the best design or decision, which is usually the global minimum or maximum depending on the problem definition. In the case of multiobjective, there may not exist one solution which is the best (global minimum or maximum) with respect to all objectives; instead there exists a set of solutions which are superior respect to the rest of solutions in solution space when all objectives are considered but are inferior respect to other solutions in the space in one or more objectives. These tradeoff solutions are known as noninferior points [18]. In other word **x** is a noninferior solution if and only if:

$$\neg \exists x' \in R^n : \forall i \in \{1, \ldots, p\} \; F_i(x') \geq F_i(x) \;\wedge\; \exists i \in \{1, \ldots, p\} \; F_i(x') > F_i(x) \qquad (5)$$

To find such solutions, many mathematical and stochastic based methods are developed. In particular, the recent works are concentrated on multiobjective evolutionary algorithms [4]. But these approaches would not support unstructured or semi-structured problems. The approaches are founded on specified mathematical models and hence vagueness, imprecision and incompleteness can not be supported with these approaches [19].

In contrast, the knowledge based systems are traditionally used in such ill-structured cases of real world problems [10]. Specially, various rule based systems are developed in a wide range of ill-structured optimization problems. However, in multiobjective problems the applications are restricted to marginal or auxiliary of other implementation methods.

The systems are used along with Meta-heuristics and even classical approaches. For example Nabrzski and Weglarz [15] introduced a rule based system aside with a Tabu search method to control Tabu list, choose neighbors, define aspiration level and change attributes. EESA [13] and PAMUCII [5] are other samples of such rule based applications. In applications with classical methods for example Poulos et al. [16] used fuzzy rule based system to control incremental changes of weights in a weighting method for a warehouse multiobjective problem. As another work, Agrell et al. [1] developed a rule based decision support system aside with Tchebycheff interactive method to provide an agro-ecological and economic assessment of various types of land uses. Also, Rasmy et al. [17] developed fuzzy expert system to extract priorities and aspiration levels based on linguistic preferences and then convert multiobjective problems to equivalent goal programming model.

Fuzzy rule bases are also used to extract unstructured objective functions of decision maker [2]. The fuzzy rules are developed with linguistic variables in antecedent and linguistic objectives in consequents and then Tsukamoto's fuzzy reasoning method is used to determine crisp mathematical structure of objective functions. Similarly, Sugeno's fuzzy reasoning method with fuzzy decision making method are used as MANFIS network, which is an extension of the ANFIS network for fuzzy multiobjective problems to extract related single objective model and then this model is optimized via genetic algorithm [3].

As shown in all applications, the rule bases are used with marginal roles. In contrast, in this study the rule bases are used with an original role. Specially in this study, a system constituting fuzzy rule-base is used [8]. Since decision maker interface is goal space (Z) and the system must produce the solutions, system inferencing is developed as Z to X mapping and fuzzy logic is used to support uncertainty [11]. Meanwhile, since the knowledge base is generated in noninferior region, the system can be used as an analyzer for decision maker and he/she can analyze various levels of goals and observe related solutions. Then the system not only searches the noninferior region but also helps analyzer to make the best decisions in this region [7].

The rest of the paper is organized as follows. Section 2 introduces structure of the system and describes the steps of system development. To clarify the performance of developed system, two well-known numerical examples (i.e. multiobjective TSP problem and multiobjective knapsack problem) are brought in section 3. The fuzzy rule-based system is developed for each example and results are explained clearly. Finally section 4 is devoted to conclusions and recommendations for future studies.

2. SYSTEM STRUCTURE

The system structure developed in this paper is more attended to ill-structured problems; ones which traditional methods can not acquit them. Originally, the system vision is different. In this vision instead of attending to the elements of the problem and generating complex mathematical models, concentration is made on global rules which the problem is dominated and controlled with them. This is the reason of using rule bases in the structure of the system.

On the other hand, most of real problems are defined in uncertain conditions with inadequate information. This vagueness and imprecision is supported with fuzzy logic [6] and hence fuzzy rule base is suggested for the system.

In designing fuzzy rule-based systems, if familiar experts and elites exist, the rules can be extracted of them. But this operation may be bias of these specialists which will not be representative of real noninferior region.

Another way may be usage of historical data. When set of historical data exists, the information can be evaluated to extract noninferior subset as an estimation of real noninferior population. This operation can be performed with simple procedure developed for extraction of real noninferior set. The outline of this procedure is as follows:

```
Parameters: n: Size of target population,
      Ψ: Set of inferior population,
Υ: Set of noninferior population
Generate initial solutions of size N = {n * (1 + κ) | 0 ≤ κ ≤ 1}:
F = [f_1(x), f_2(x), ..., f_p(x)] ∈ R^p | x ∈ R^n & |F| = n;
Set Ψ = ∅; Υ = [F, x];
Noninferiority checking:
For each F = [f_1, f_2, ..., f_p] from 1 to N– 1,
  If F ∉ Ψ
    For each F' = [f'_1, f'_2, ..., f'_p] from |F| to N
      If F' ∉ Ψ
        If f_1 >= f'_1 & f_2 >= f'_2 & ... & f_p >= f'_p
          Υ = Υ - {F}; Ψ = Ψ + {F};
        Else if f'_1 >= f_1 & f'_2 >= f_2 & ... & f'_p >= f_p
          Υ = Υ - {F'}; Ψ = Ψ + {F'};
        end
      end
    end
  end
end
```

In the next step, the resulted noninferior points are used in designing of fuzzy rule base. Rules are defined based on Gaussian membership functions; because in general cases, most of the membership functions are converged to this typical smooth one [12]:

$$\mu_i([\mathbf{F}(\mathbf{x}),\mathbf{x}]) = \text{EXP}\left(\frac{-([\mathbf{F}(\mathbf{x}),\mathbf{x}]-[\mathbf{F}(\mathbf{x}_i),\mathbf{x}_i])^2}{2\sigma^2_{[\mathbf{F}(\mathbf{x}),\mathbf{x}]}}\right),\ [\mathbf{F}(\mathbf{x}),\mathbf{x}]\in R^{p+n},\ i=1,2,\dots n \quad (6)$$

where n is number of noninferior points and $\sigma_{[\mathbf{F}(\mathbf{x}),\mathbf{x}]}$ is defined as follows:

$$\sigma_{[\mathbf{F}(\mathbf{x}),\mathbf{x}]} = \left(\frac{\sum_i [\mathbf{F}(\mathbf{x}_i),\mathbf{x}_i]^2 \mu_i([\mathbf{F}(\mathbf{x}),\mathbf{x}])}{n} - \left(\frac{\sum_i [\mathbf{F}(\mathbf{x}_i),\mathbf{x}_i]\mu_i([\mathbf{F}(\mathbf{x}),\mathbf{x}])}{n}\right)^2\right)^{\frac{1}{2}} \quad (7)$$

Then, the fuzzy rules R: A → B are defined as follows [14]:

$$A_j = \int_{f(\mathbf{x})\in R^p} \left(\mu_j(f(\mathbf{x}))\middle| f(\mathbf{x})\right) \qquad j = 1, 2, \dots, p \quad (8)$$

$$B_i = \int_{\mathbf{x}\in R^n} \left(\mu_i(\mathbf{x})\middle|\mathbf{x}\right) \qquad i = 1, 2, \dots, n \quad (9)$$

Now, Mamdani inferencing system [12] is used on developed rules to constitute the fuzzy rule base. Let **z** as the input vector of decision space, then the rule R_r is fired as follows:

$$\tau_r = \bigwedge_{j=1}^{p} \mu_j^{r_j}(z_j) \mid A_j^{r_j} \ \&\ A_j^{r_j} = (\int_{\mathbf{z}\in R^p} \mu_j^{r_j}(\mathbf{z}) \mid \mathbf{z}) \subset A_j \quad (10)$$

and then, the inferred consequences are obtained as follows:

$$\mu_r^{Cons}(\mathbf{x}) = \tau_r \wedge \mu_i^{r_i}(x_i) \mid B_i^{r_i} \ \&\ B_i^{r_i} = (\int_{\mathbf{x}\in R^n} \mu_i^{r_i}(\mathbf{x}) \mid \mathbf{x}) \subset B_i \quad (11)$$

Finally, the aggregation is performed as follows:

$$\mu^{Cons}(\mathbf{x}) = \bigvee_{r=1}^{n} \mu_r^{Cons}(\mathbf{x}) \quad (12)$$

The t-norm and t-conorm operators either may be simple, such as standard, product, drastic and bounded operators or may be parametric such as Yager class, Schweizer & Sklar classes, Hamacher class and Dubois class [22].

Finally, the solutions must be defuzzified to obtain crisp trading values. In this part also parametric and non-parametric methods can be used.

Specially, SLIDE generalized defuzzification method [20] is applied as follows:

$$x^* = \frac{(1-\beta)\int\limits_{i\in L} x\,\mu_i^\alpha(x)dx + \beta \int\limits_{i\in H} x\,\mu_i^\alpha(x)dx}{(1-\beta)\int\limits_{i\in L} \mu_i^\alpha(x)dx + \beta \int\limits_{i\in H} \mu_i^\alpha(x)dx} \quad \alpha \in [0\,,\,\mathrm{Height}(\mu_i(x))],\ \beta \in [0, 1] \qquad (13)$$

where $L = \{i \mid \mu(x_i) < \alpha\}$ and $H = \{i \mid \mu(x_i) \geq \alpha\}$.

It should be attended that most of noninferior points are not sensible for decision maker and it is necessary to focus on the highlighted areas; the work which is not performed with traditional methods.

These sensible points are supported in the system at arrival to fuzzy rule-based system. In fact an activated area is given to the system instead of entire area. Focusing in activated area may be performed by decision maker. Generally managers and specialists continuously impact with various objectives of the firm such as price, quality, and delivery and hence can comfortably explain critical interval of changes in each objective [9]. This is one of the reasons that Z to X mapping is suggested for the system. In fact, the arrival to the system is what the decision maker knows (z) and the departure of the system is what the decision maker wants (x).

Now, suppose the situation that activation area is not sensible for decision maker; then this area must be obtained by the system. In existence of mathematical structure following payoff table can be produced with the optimal solutions.

Table 1: Payoff table of optimal solutions

	f_1	f_2	...	f_p
x_1*	$f_1(x_1^*)$	$f_2(x_1^*)$	...	$f_p(x_1^*)$
x_2*	$f_1(x_2^*)$	$f_2(x_2^*)$	...	$f_p(x_2^*)$
⋮	⋮	⋮	...	⋮
x_p*	$f_1(x_p^*)$	$f_2(x_p^*)$	...	$f_p(x_p^*)$

In above table, the positive ideal and negative-ideal solutions can be identified as follows:

$$A^+ = \left\{ V_j^+ \mid V_j^+ = \operatorname*{Max}_{i=1}^{p} \frac{f_j(x_i^*)}{\left\| f_j(x_i^*) \right\|^K} \right\} \qquad A^- = \left\{ V_j^- \mid V_j^- = \operatorname*{Min}_{i=1}^{p} \frac{f_j(x_i^*)}{\left\| f_j(x_i^*) \right\|^K} \right\} \qquad (14)$$

Then, similar to TOPSIS method, the following index gives decision maker an idea to determine the boundaries of activated areas:

$$I_i^* = \left\{ \frac{\left\|V_{ji} - V_j^+\right\|^{\kappa}}{\left\|V_{ji} - V_j^+\right\|^{\kappa} + \left\|V_{ji} - V_j^-\right\|^{\kappa}} \middle| V_{ji} = \frac{f_j(\mathbf{x}_i^*)}{\left\|f_j(\mathbf{x}_i^*)\right\|^{\kappa}} \right\} \tag{15}$$

When activation area is obtained, this area is atomized to set of grid points by splitting the intervals and producing ordered vector of goal values. This is the set of points which are given to fuzzy rule-based system as activation points. The generation of these points is integrated in the system as "Z Generator" gate.

Finally, the output of the system is projected in decision space in order to evaluate the resultant performance of the system

3. NUMERICAL EXAMPLES

In this section, to clarify the performance of fuzzy rule-based system, two well-known problems of multiobjective traveling salesman problem (MOTSP) and multiobjective knapsack problem (MOKP) are suggested and the system is developed for each of them. In this study, programs are developed with MATALB software on the Pentium personal computer.

3.1 Multiobjective TSP problem (MOTSP)

MOTSP is formulated in the following way. Let U = {1, 2... n} be the set of cities and $C^{(1)}$, $C^{(2)}$, ..., $C^{(p)}$ the distance matrices of cities. Also let $\mathbf{X} = \{x_{ij} \mid i, j \in U\}$ be the binary matrix of decision variables. Then the multiobjective TSP problem is formulated as follows:

$$\text{Min } \mathbf{F}(\mathbf{X}) = (\mathbf{C}^{(1)} * \mathbf{X}, \mathbf{C}^{(2)} * \mathbf{X} \ldots \mathbf{C}^{(p)} * \mathbf{X}) \tag{16}$$

Subject to:

$$\|\mathbf{X}_i\|_1 \;\&\; \|\mathbf{X}_j\|_1 = 1 \qquad \forall\, i, j \in U \tag{17}$$

$$\sum_{i \in V} \sum_{i \in U \setminus V} x_{ij} \geq 1 \qquad \forall\, V \subset U\ (V \neq \varnothing, V \neq U) \tag{18}$$

$$x_{ij} = [0, 1] \qquad \forall\, i, j \in U \tag{19}$$

Obviously, while single objective of this problem is NP-hard, the multiobjective ones, is also NP-Hard. The MOTSP solutions can be represented as a sequence of cities with related objective values. Let S be solution of the problem, then S can be represented as follows:

$$S = [f_1(U^O), f_2(U^O), \ldots, f_p(U^O), U^O] \tag{20}$$

where U^O is the ordered set of U based on the sequence of cities. Since only n! sequences of the cities can be generated, n! S solutions can be produced.

In this study, a bi-objective model is developed with opposite goals (Max profit and Min Risk) for 8 cities problem (because of restriction in illustration, 8 cities problem is selected). $\mathbf{C}^{(1)}$ and $\mathbf{C}^{(2)}$ are generated randomly with uniform distribution in the ranges of [0, 100] and [0, 10] respectively.

As the beginning, 5000 S solutions are generated. This is approximately %10 of total solutions. The operation is performed in the time 2.344^s. Then noninferior solutions are extracted using noninferior procedure. Interestingly from 5000 random points only 8 noninferior solutions are extracted in the time less than 0.01^s. In the next stage, fuzzy rules are developed. Membership functions are selected based on Gaussian functions with uniform variance on the activation area. The activation area of outputs is selected in the range [0, 8] to support city selection (The output must be rounded to obtain selected cities). The activation area of inputs is obtained as $240 \le z_1 \le 360$ and $1 \le z_2 \le 2.5$. The operators are selected by default in the Mamdani system and finally the following rule base is obtained:

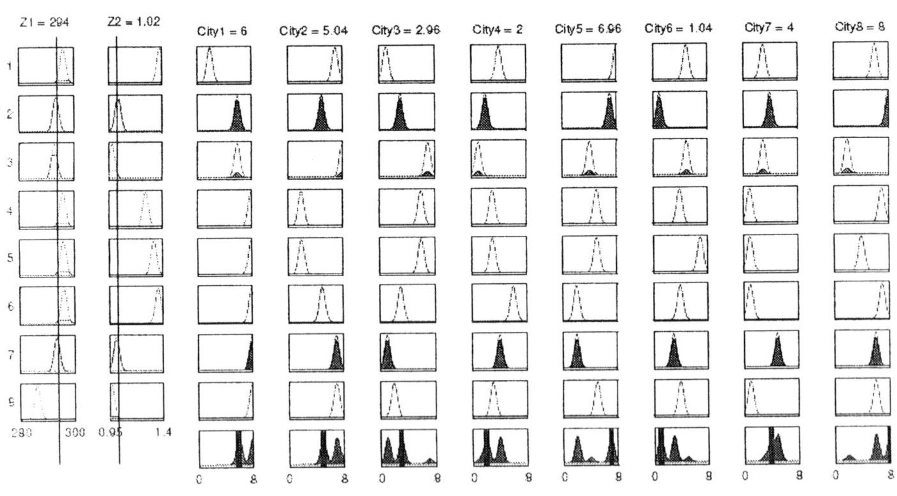

Figure 1. Fuzzy rule base of MOTSP problem

This rule base is constructed on noninferior region, and then changing the goal levels (z_1 and z_2) by simply sliding the red lines, caused other noninferior path solutions. In fact, the system let decision maker to analyze various solutions based on various decisional levels. While in traditional methods even in Meta heuristic ones, this analyzing needs a lot of repetitive calculations with huge time consumption, in this system decision maker can analyze various paths with various profit and distance and then select the pleasure ones easily and simply.

As an additional work, to examine the performance of developed system, the activated area (i.e. $240 \leq z_1 \leq 360$ and $1 \leq z_2 \leq 2.5$) is divided to the grids with the rates 1 and 0.1 respectively. Then each couple points of grid region is given to the system as input values ($z_1$and z_2) and on the other hand, the system generates outputs as a sequence of the cities immediately.

After rounding the solutions, a validation test is performed on the sequences and accordingly, 1831 solutions are accepted from 1936 ones (i.e. %94.58 of solutions). The checking process is performed in only 1.762^s.

The accepted solutions are projected in decisional space. The result was wonderful. While input space is complete grid points, the output projection space is quite adapted to the noninferior region; such as shown in the following Figure.

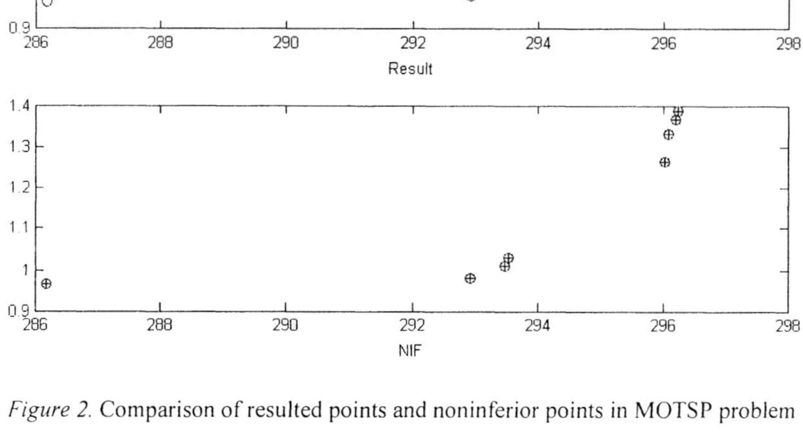

Figure 2. Comparison of resulted points and noninferior points in MOTSP problem

3.2 Multiobjective knapsack problem (MOKP)

MOKP is formulated in the following way. Let **g** be vector of element weights and $\mathbf{c}^{(1)}, \mathbf{c}^{(2)}, \ldots, \mathbf{c}^{(p)}$ vectors of element values. Then multiobjective knapsack problem is formulated as follows:

$$\text{Max } \mathbf{F}(\mathbf{y}) = (\mathbf{c}^{(1)}\,\mathbf{y}, \mathbf{c}^{(2)}\,\mathbf{y} \ldots \mathbf{c}^{(p)}\,\mathbf{y}) \tag{21}$$

$$\mathbf{g}\,\mathbf{y} \le \text{G} \tag{22}$$

$$\text{y} \in [0, 1] \tag{23}$$

where G is a scalar value corresponding to the knapsack size and y is the vector of variables.

Again, in this example a bi-objective model with opposite goals (Max confidence, Min cost) and 8 items is developed. The weights are generated randomly in the range [0, 1] and G is set to G $=\|g\|_1/2$. The vectors of element values are generated randomly; but in different ranges. $c^{(1)}$ is generated in the range [0, 1] while $c^{(2)}$ is generated in [0, 1000].

Similar to previous example, the work is begun with generation of random binary vector (y). Since the model is mono-constraint, the feasibility of random solutions is checked and only feasible ones are used. In this fashion, 1000 random feasible solutions are generated at 0.07^s. Then, using described noninferior procedure, 8 noninferior solutions are extracted in the time less than 0.01^s. The obtained noninferior points are used in rule construction.

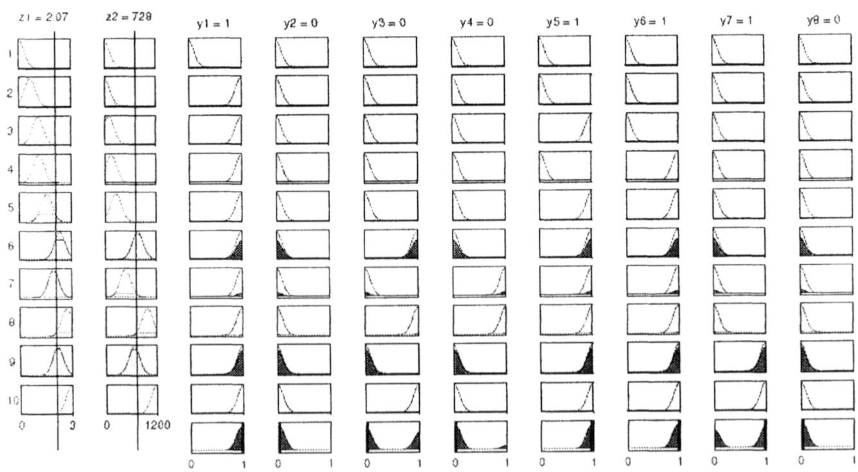

Figure 3. Fuzzy rule base of MOKP problem

Again Mamdani system is used with default operators and membership functions. While outputs range are obviously [0, 1], the inputs range are obtained by plotting initial feasible solutions as $0 \leq z_1 \leq 3.5$ and $0 \leq z_2 \leq 4000$. Finally the generated rule base is obtained as shown in Figure 3.

Such as shown, the outputs are always binary values and feasible in noninferior region. Then the system can be used as an analyzer of various goal levels and the related solutions. In fact, decision maker can select various subsets of elements based on the desired composition of goals in noninferior region without any additional computation efforts.

Similar to previous example, to show the performance of the system, a grid point set of activation area (i.e. $0 \leq z_1 \leq 3.5$ and $0 \leq z_2 \leq 3500$) is generated with step sizes 0.1 and 10 respectively and couple points (z_1, z_2) are given to the system. The outputs are produced immediately as binary vectors. Then, the feasibility test is performed on the solutions and all of 12636 solutions are accepted. The solutions are projected in decisional space as illustrated in the following figure. Such as shown, the solutions fall in the noninferior boundaries; while the inputs of the system were couple points from all of activation area.

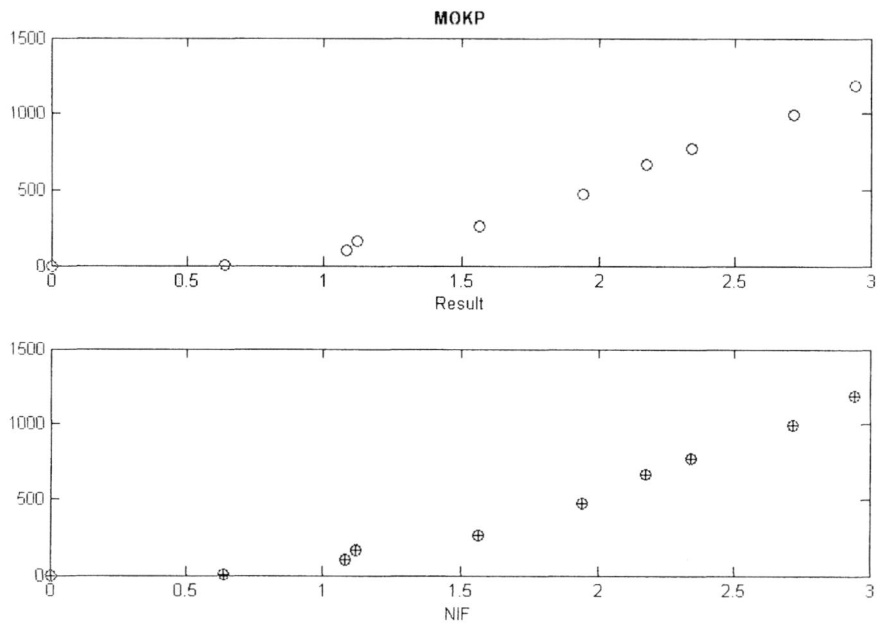

Figure 4. Comparison of resulted points and noninferior points in MOKP problem

4. FUTURE STUDIES

The system structure can also be suggested as another aspect of future study. Some of real problems have not been constructed in predefined domain theory and would not be explained with rules. In these situations, some features are defined for the problem and then an analogical inferencing system along with historical case base is used as case-based reasoning (CBR) system instead of rule-based reasoning (RBR) system. The system is more suitable for ill-structured problems and the problems which can not be represented with mathematical models.

REFERENCES

[1] Agrell PJ, et al. Interactive multiobjective agro-ecological land use planning: The Bungoma region in Kenya. European Journal of Operational Research, 2004, 158(1): 194~217

[2] Carlsson C, Fuller R. Multiobjective linguistic optimization. Fuzzy Sets and Systems, 2000, 115: 5~10

[3] Cheng CB, et al. Neuro-fuzzy and genetic algorithm in multiple response optimization. Computers and Mathematics with Applications, 2002, 44(12): 1503~1514

[4] Coello C, et al. Evolutionary Algorithms for Solving Multi-Objective Problems. Kluwer, New York, 2002

[5] Coelho RF, Bouillard P. PAMUC II for multicriteria optimization of mechanical designs with expert rules. In: Proceedings of the Congress on Evolutionary Computation (CEC2004). Portland, 2004, 1: 17~22

[6] Ghazanfari M, Kazemi Z. The principle of expert systems. IUST Publisher, Tehran, 2003

[7] Gholamian, MR, et al. A systematic design of multiobjective problem solutions with fuzzy rule based systems. In: Proceedings of the 6th International Multi-Objective Programming and Goal Programming conference (MOPGP'04). Hammamet, Tunisia, 2004

[8] Gholamian MR, Fatemi Ghomi SMT. A hybrid intelligent system for multiobjective decision making problem. In: Proceedings of the 33rd International Conference on Computers and Industrial Engineering (C&IE2004). Jeju, Korea, 2004

[9] Gholamian MR, Fatemi Ghomi SMT. A hybrid system oscillator for multiobjective supplier selection problem. In: Proceedings of the XVII-th International Conference on Multiple Criteria Decision Making. Whistler, British Columbia, Canada, 2004

[10] Gholamian MR, Fatemi Ghomi SMT. An empirical research in intelligent manufacturing: a frame based representation of AI usages in manufacturing aspects. In: proceedings of the 6th IFIP International Conference on Information Technology for Balanced Automation Systems in Manufacturing and Services (BASYS'04). Vienna, Austria, 2004

[11] Gholamian MR, et al. A hybrid system for multiobjective marketing problems- A case study in crude oil markets. Engineering Applications of Artificial Intelligence, 2005, 18(4): 495~509.

[12] Jang J-SR, Sun C-T. Neuro-Fuzzy and Soft Computing: A Computational Approach to Learning and Machine Intelligence. Prentice Hall, New Jersey, 1997

[13] Jwo WS, et al. Hybrid expert system and simulated annealing approach to optimal reactive power planning. In: IEE Proceedings of Generation, Transmission and Distribution. 1995, 142(4): 381~385.

[14] Kosko B. Fuzzy engineering. Prentice Hall, New Jersey, 1997

[15] Nabrzyski J, Weglarz J. On an expert system with multicriteria Tabu search for multiobjective project scheduling. In: Proceedings of the 6th International Conference on Emerging Technologies and Factory Automation. 1997, 287~291.

[16] Poulos PN, et al. A Pareto optimal genetic algorithm for warehouse multi-objective optimization. Engineering Applications of Artificial Intelligence, 2001, 14: 737~749

[17] Rasmy MH, et al. An expert system for multiobjective decision making: application of fuzzy linguistic preferences and goal programming. Fuzzy Sets and Systems, 2002, 127: 209~220.

[18] Steuer PE, Multiple criteria optimization: theory, computation and application. John Wiley & Sons, New York, 1986

[19] Van Veldhauizen D, Lamont GB. Multiobjective evolutionary algorithms: analyzing the state-of-the-art. Evolutionary Computation, 2000, 8(2): 125~147.

[20] Yager RR, Zadeh LA. Fuzzy sets, neural networks and soft computing. Van Nostrand Reinhold, New York, 1994

[21] Zeleny M. Multiple criteria decision making: Eight concepts of optimality. Human Systems Management, 1998, 17: 97~107

[22] Zimmmermann HJ. Fuzzy set theory and its applications. 3rd edn. Kluwer, Boston, 1996

AERO-ENGINE ADAPTIVE FUZZY DECOUPLING CONTROL

Xinyu Ren and Siqi Fan

School of Aero-engine Engineering, Northwestern Polytechnical University Xi'an 710072, China

Abstract: A new kind of multivariable adaptive fuzzy decoupling controller is present for Aero-engine, which consists of multivariable fuzzy decoupling control and fuzzy model reference learning control. A fuzzy inverse model is used to produce and adjust fuzzy rules online. The simulation results show that this controller is effective.

Key words: Aero-engine, fuzzy decouple, Adaptive Fuzzy Control

1. INTRODUCTION

Fuzzy control has emerged in recent years as a promising way to approach nonlinear control problems. An engine system is a non-linear distributed system with complex interactions between sensors and actuators, the dynamics of the system and the dynamics of the environment. Many researchers have investigated control of engines with a motivation towards applying fuzzy control techniques for improve engine performance.

Conventionally, fuzzy rules are established by a combination of knowledge, experience and observation and may thus not be optimal. However, a synthesis of fuzzy logic controllers to a large extent does not rely on sound mathematical principles. It is entirely based on the nature of problem in hand and the ability of the engineer to translate his experience into meaningful rules and fuzzy sets. Although this approach works well for simple problems, or problems with single input and single output, it is almost impossible to manually arrive at fuzzy controllers for more complex problems. Multivariable fuzzy decoupling control can be used to model the multivariable fuzzy controller using the decomposition of the control rule base into a set of simple rule bases. But there are some limitations to such a method including: the difficulties in developing an accurate intuition about how to best compensate for the unpredictable and significant system parameter variations that can occur while the engine flight environment changed and a lack of basic expertise in the decoupling rule–base.

In this paper, we investigate the possibility of consisting the multivariable fuzzy decoupling control and fuzzy model reference learning control for automatically synthesizing and tuning a fuzzy decoupling controller.

2 ADAPTIVE FUZZY DECOUPLING CONTROLLER

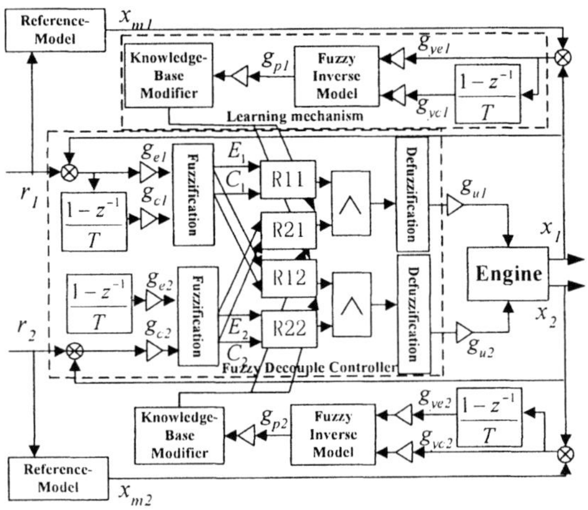

Figure 1. .Architecture for adaptive fuzzy decouple control

Figure 1 shows Architecture for multivariable adaptive fuzzy decoupling control, which consists of fuzzy decoupling controller, reference model and learning mechanism. where the $g_e, g_c, g_{ye}, g_y, g_u, g_p$ is the normalize gains, r_1, r_2 is the reference input, x_{m1}, x_{m2} the reference model output, x_1, x_2 is the plant output.

2.1 The Fuzzy Decoupling Controller

The inputs to the fuzzy controller are the error of the plant output and the reference input and change in error. In this paper, we have 11 fuzzy sets on the input universes of discourse, which is {-1,-0.8,-0.6,-0.4,-0.2,0,0.2,0.4, 0.6,0.8,1}.The knowledge-base for the fuzzy controller associated with the n process inputs is generated from **IF-THEN** control rules of the form:

$$\text{If } E_1^j \text{ and} \ldots \text{and } E_s^k \text{ and } C_1^l \text{ and} \ldots \text{and } C_s^m \text{ then } U_n^{j,\ldots,k,l,\ldots,m} \tag{1}$$

This fuzzy implication can be represented by a fuzzy relation:

$$R_n^{j,\ldots,k,l,\ldots,m} = (E_1^j \times C_1^l) \times \ldots \times (E_s^k \times C_s^m) \times U_n^{j,\ldots,k,l,\ldots,m} \tag{2}$$

The fuzzy controller decision mechanism for this control rule may be expressed by

$$U_n^{j,\ldots,k,l,\ldots,m} = (E_1^j \times C_1^l) \times \ldots \times (E_s^k \times C_s^m) \circ R_n^{j,\ldots,k,l,\ldots,m} \tag{3}$$

The number of rule base can become quite large (in the case of n variables in the premise of the m fuzzy set, the number of cross-products is m^n), multivariable control rules can be approximately decomposed into several sets of two-dimensional rules for each input. The decomposed multivariable control rules is as follows:

$$U_n^{j,\ldots,k,l,\ldots,m} = (E_1^j \times C_1^l) \circ R_{n1}^{jl} \wedge \ldots \wedge (E_s^k \times C_s^m) \circ R_{ns}^{k,m} \tag{4}$$

In this way, multivariable fuzzy controller can be divided into the aggregation of several simple fuzzy controllers, and the rule base number reduces to $(mn)^2$. Let $\mu_{E_iC_i}(e_i, c_i)$ denote the membership of the ith input variable of the subset, then the membership of formula (4) is as follows:

$$\mu_n^{j,\ldots k,l,\ldots,m} = \mu_{E_1C_1}(e_1, c_1) \wedge \ldots \wedge \mu_{EsCs}(e_s, c_s) \tag{5}$$

The "Center of gravity" method calculates the crisp output by:

$$u_n = \frac{\sum_{j,\ldots,k,l,\ldots,m} U_n^{j,\ldots,k,l,\ldots,m} \times \mu_n^{j,\ldots k,l,\ldots,m}}{\sum \mu_n^{j,\ldots k,l,\ldots m}} \tag{6}$$

2.2 The Reference Model

The reference model provides a capability for quantifying the desired performance of the process. The reference model may be any type of dynamical system either linear or nonlinear. It is use to characterize closed-loop specifications such as stability, rise time, overshoot and settling time. The performance of the overall system is computed with respect the error of the plant output and the reference model output. The desired performance of the controlled process is met if the learning mechanism forces the error to remain very small for all time. It is very important to make proper choice for a reference model so that the desired respond does not to dictate unreasonable performance requirements for plant to be control.

$U^{j,k}$		C^j										
		-5	-4	-3	-2	-1	0	+1	+2	+3	+4	+5
	-5	-1.0	-1.0	-1.0	-1.0	-1.0	-1.0	-0.8	-0.6	-0.4	-0.2	0.0
	-4	-1.0	-1.0	-1.0	-1.0	-1.0	-0.8	-0.6	-0.4	-0.2	0.0	+0.2
	-3	-1.0	-1.0	-1.0	-1.0	-0.8	-0.6	-0.4	-0.2	0.0	+0.2	+0.4
	-2	-1.0	-1.0	-1.0	-0.8	-0.6	-0.4	-0.2	0.0	+0.2	+0.4	+0.6
	-1	-1.0	-1.0	-0.8	-0.6	-0.4	-0.2	0.0	+0.2	+0.4	+0.6	+0.8
E^k	0	-1.0	-0.8	-0.6	-0.4	-0.2	0.0	+0.2	+0.4	+0.6	+0.8	+1.0
	+1	-0.8	-0.6	-0.4	-0.2	0.0	+0.2	+0.4	+0.6	+0.8	+1.0	+1.0
	+2	-0.6	-0.4	-0.2	0.0	+0.2	+0.4	+0.6	+0.8	+1.0	+1.0	+1.0
	+3	-0.4	-0.1	+0.1	+0.2	+0.4	+0.6	+0.8	+1.0	+1.0	+1.0	+1.0
	+4	-0.2	+0.1	+0.3	+0.4	+0.6	+0.8	+1.0	+1.0	+1.0	+1.0	+1.0
	+5	0.0	+0.2	+0.4	+0.6	+0.8	+1.0	+1.0	+1.0	+1.0	+1.0	+1.0

Figure 2. Rule base array table

2.3 The Learning Mechanism

As previously mentioned, the learning mechanism performs the function of modifying the knowledgebase of a direct fuzzy controller so that the closed-loop system behaves like the reference model. The learning mechanism consists of two parts: a fuzzy inverse model and a knowledge-base modifier. The fuzzy inverse model performs the function of mapping necessary changes in the process output, and decides how to change the plant command inputs so that this deviation goes to zero. The knowledge-base modifier performs the function of modifying the fuzzy controller's knowledge-base to affect the needed changes in the process inputs. The output of the fuzzy inverse model is represented by $p(kT)$. Then the output, $p(kT)$, is used to modify the controllers rule-base. The controller output that would have been desired is expressed by

$$\bar{u}(kT-T) = u(kT-T) + p(kT)$$

Assume that only symmetric membership functions are defined for the fuzzy controller's output so that $c_{ns}^{p,q}$ denotes the center value of the membership function associated with the rule-base $R_{n1}^{jl} \ldots R_{ns}^{k,m}$. Consider the effect that the above knowledge-base modification in Equation 6. Notice that only those fuzzy relations whose $\mu_n^{j,\ldots k,l,\ldots,m} > 0$ contribute to the previous control. For all active rules the modification of the output membership function centers will be

$$\bar{c}_{ns}^{p,q}(kT-T) = c_{ns}^{pq}(kT-T) + p_n(kT),$$

while all other rules stay unchanged. The intersection of the subset should be shifted $p_n(kT)$:

$$\bar{U}_n^{j,\ldots k,l,\ldots m}(kT-T) = U_n^{j,\ldots k,l,\ldots,m}(kT-T) + p_n(kT)$$

Substituting this new fuzzy set into Equation 5 we obtain

$$\bar{u}_n(kT-T) = u_n(kT-T) + p_n(kT) 。$$

It is worth mentioning that the entire rule base does not need to be modified every time step, but the rules that apply to the current situations are changed and stored. Therefore, when the plant returns to a familiar operating point, it does not need to re-adapt or re-tune. The controller will already know how to handle the process. This kind of controller is great for systems in which robustness issues are extremely relevant. Table 2 shows a knowledge-base array table. For our example, assume that $p_n(kT)$=0.1,only four items whose certainty is greater than zero are modified.

The selection of controller gains is an important step in the design progress, as the ability of the controller to track the reference model will heavily depend on particular choices of gains. Due to physical constraints for a given system, the range of values for the process inputs and outputs is generally known from a qualitative analysis of the process. As a result, we can select the controller gains g_e, g_{ye}, g_u, g_p so that each universe of discourse is mapped to the interval [-1,1]. Using standard fuzzy control design techniques or simple experiments choose g_c to map the universes of discourse of c (kT) to [1, 1]. A suitable selection of g_{yc} may be obtained by monitoring the response of the overall process with respect to the reference model response.

3. ENGINE CONTROL APPLICATIONS RESULTS

The verification of the effectiveness of this approach was carry out using a linear turbofan engine model, the dynamical behavior of the engine system can be described by using the state space model

$$\begin{bmatrix} \dot{n}_h \\ \dot{n}_l \end{bmatrix} = \begin{pmatrix} -1.1789 & -0.2119 \\ 2.4610 & -3.6797 \end{pmatrix} \begin{bmatrix} n_h \\ n_l \end{bmatrix} + \begin{pmatrix} 0.4642 & 0.0896 \\ 0.6888 & 0.4324 \end{pmatrix} \begin{bmatrix} m_f \\ A_e \end{bmatrix}$$

where the n_h is compressor rotor speed, n_l is fan rotor speed, m_f is core fuel flow and A_e is nozzle throat area. The system matrices are determined by linearization of non-linear physical model around design condition of Mach 0 and 0-km altitude.

For this application, the controller includes four fuzzy decoupling controllers and two fuzzy inverse models. Usually, the knowledge-base array shown in fig.2 can be employed for both fuzzy inverse models and fuzzy decoupling controllers. The normalizing controller gains are chosen to be g_e=[300,300], g_c=[13.,13.] and g_u=[0.012,0.012], and the normalizing learning mechanism gains are chosen to be g_{ye},=[400,400],g_{yc}=[7.4,7.4] and g_p=[0.012,0.012].

The design condition simulation results for the adaptive fuzzy decoupling controller of the aero-engine are shown in Figure 3 for n_h, and Figure 4 for n_l. Once again the FMRLC provided good system tracking with respect to the reference model. As a result, the system exhibits good steady state and transient response. The main attribute of the adaptive controller is its ability to accommodate system changes. We demonstrate this aspect of the adaptive fuzzy decoupling controller by changing the engine flight environment. Figure 5-Figure 8 shows the step response at Mach 1.3 and 12 km altitude and Mach 1.5 and 18km altitude. It is observed the system exhibits good tracking with the reference model even after engine flight environment changes significantly.

4 CONCLUDING REMARKS

The key advantages of the adaptive fuzzy decoupling controller are:

1. Providing an automatic method to synthesize a portion of the knowledge-base for the direct fuzzy controller while at the same time it ensures that the system will behave in a desirable fashion
2. Updating the knowledge-base in the fuzzy decoupling controller dynamically and continually in response to process parameter variations or disturbances. In this way if engine flight environment changes, the controller can make on-line adjustments to fuzzy decoupling controllers to maintain adequate performance levels
3. Decomposition of multivariable control rules into several sets of two-dimensional rules for each input, simplified the evolution of the rule base.

REFERENCES

1. M M Gupta. Multivariable structure of fuzzy control system, IEEE Transactions System Man and Cybernetics, 1986,16(16): 638-665
2. J B Kiszka, M M Gupta, G M Trojan. Multivariable fuzzy controller under Gödel's implication, Fuzzy Sets and Systems, 1990,34(3): 301-321
3. J R Layne, K M Passino. Fuzzy Model Reference Learning Control, Journal of Intelligent and Fuzzy Systems, 1996,4(1): 33– 47
4. G Kopasakia, Adaptive Performance Seeking Control Using Fuzzy Model Reference Learning Control and Positive Gradient Control, AIAA-97-3191, 1996,7.

5. Fang Zhongxiang, Wu Chihua. Application of Two-Variable Fuzzy-PI Control in an Aero engine, Journal of Propulsion and Power, 1998

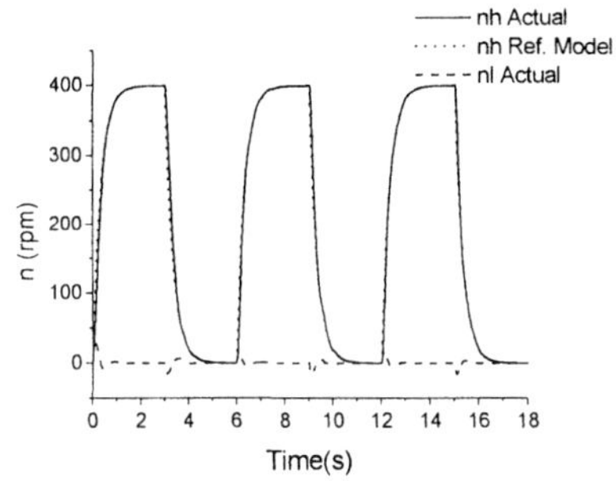

Figure. 3 Step response of n_h at Mach 0 and 0 km altitude

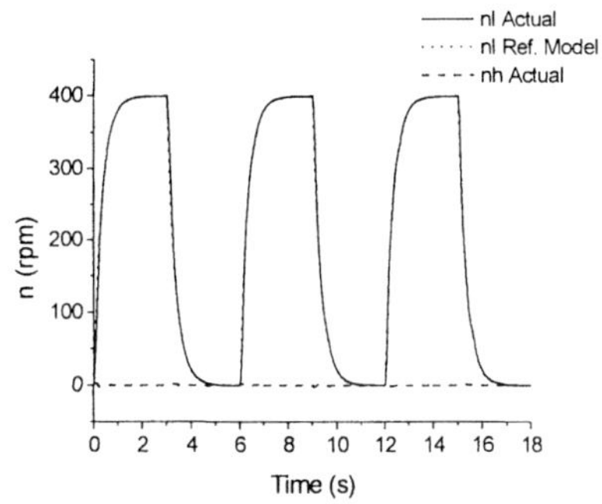

Figure. 4 Step response of n_l at Mach 0 and 0 km altitude

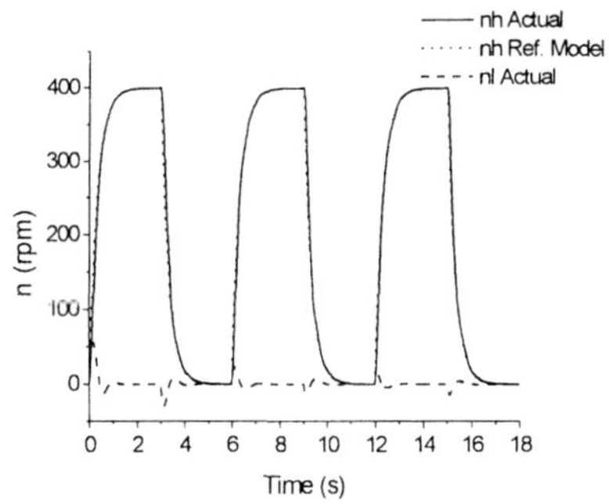

Figure. 5 Step response of n_h at Mach 1.3 and 12 km altitude

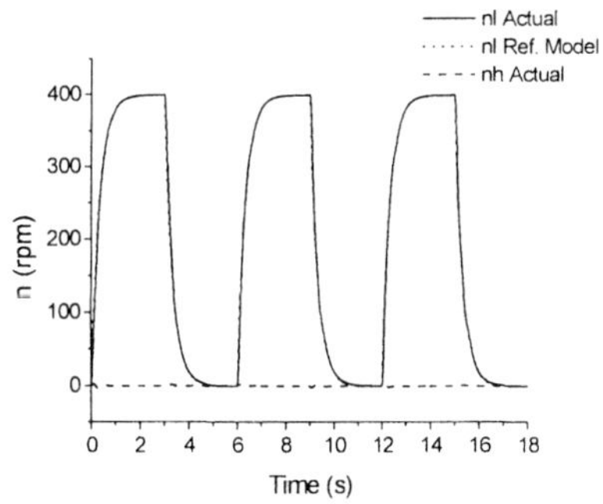

Figure. 6 Step response of n_l at Mach 1.3 and 12 km altitude

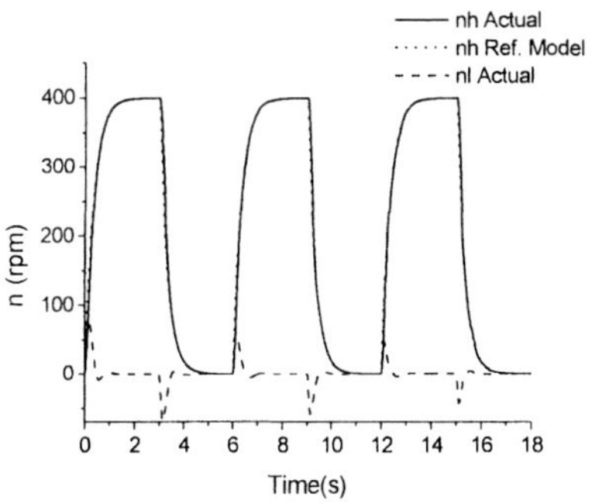

Figure. 7 Step response of n_h at Mach 1.5 and 18km altitude

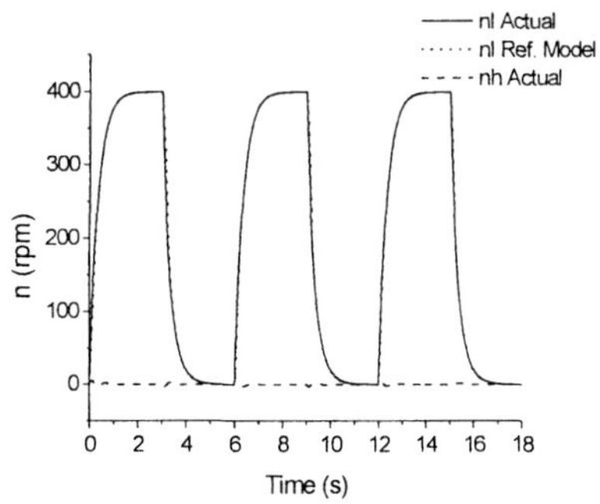

Figure. 8 Step response of n_l at Mach 1.5 and 18 km altitude

CONCEPTUAL MODELLING OF KNOWLEDGE-BASED SYSTEMS USING UML

Mohd Syazwan Abdullah[1,3], Richard Paige[1], Carl Thompson[2], Ian Benest[1], and Chris Kimble[1]

[1] *Department of Computer Science,* [2]*Department of Health Sciences,* [3]*Faculty of Info Tech*
[1,2]*University of York,, Heslington, York, United Kingdom,* [3]*Universiti Utara Malaysia, Sintok*
[1]*{syazwan, paige, idb, kimble}@cs.york.ac.uk ,* [2]*cat4@york.ac.uk,* [3]*pathma @uum.edu.my*

Abstract: Conceptual modelling is an important aspect in designing systems. However, the use of conceptual models in knowledge-based system (KBS) is limited as there is no particular consensus on which modelling language should be used and most of these systems are developed in a 'problem to code' manner. This paper focuses on the use ofa Unified Modeling Language (UML) Profile for conceptual knowledge modelling. The profile is created using the profile extension approach of UML and is based on the XMF (eXecutable Modelling Framework). An example of modelling a KBS based on the Ottawa Ankle Rule demonstrates the use of the profile.

Key words: conceptual modelling, knowledge-based system, UML Profile

1. INTRODUCTION

Knowledge-based systems (KBS) are developed using knowledge engineering (KE) techniques [1], which are similar to those used in software engineering (SE), but place an emphasis on knowledge rather than on data or information processing. As such, they inherently advocate an engineering approach to the process of developing a KBS. Central to this is the conceptual modelling of the system during the analysis and design stages of the development process. Many KE methodologies have been developed with an emphasis on the use of models and conceptual modelling, for example: CommonKADS [2], MIKE [3], Protégé [4], and KARL [3].

In first generation expert systems, the knowledge of the expert (or experts) was captured and translated into a set of rules. This was essentially a process of knowledge transfer [3]. The disadvantage of this approach is that the captured knowledge in the form of hard-coded rules within the system provides little understanding of how the rules are linked or connected with each other [2]. As a result, when the knowledge base needs updating, there is a substantial effort required to ensure that the knowledge base remains correct. KE is no longer simply a means of mining the knowledge from the expert's head [2]. It now encompasses *"methods and techniques for knowledge acquisition, modelling, representation and use of knowledge"* [2].

This paper demonstrates a systematic approach to modelling and designing KBSs in a purely object-oriented fashion through the use of UML's profile mechanism. The novelty of the system design lies in the profile that is used to create it. The profile is constructed using compliant standards for modelling software systems by adopting the XMF approach [12]. XMF uses standard modelling techniques taken from SE. It provides tool support for designing and verifying models as well as executing the models. It is one of the latest techniques in modelling and this work demonstrates the use of this approach. A case study on modelling a KBS based on the Ottawa Ankle Rule demonstrates the ability of the profile.

This paper is organised as follows: Section 2 generally describes the process of designing knowledge-based systems. Section 3 gives an overview of UML and the profile extension mechanism. Section 4 explains the XMF profile design approach and presents the abstract syntax model of the knowledge modelling profile and discusses the specialisation made to the existing meta-model of XMF. Section 5 illustrates how the profile can be used as part of the development of a KBS, while section 6 concludes and indicates the direction for future work.

2. DESIGNING KNOWLEDGE-BASED SYSTEM

Models are used to capture the essential features of real systems by breaking them down into more manageable parts that are easy to understand and to manipulate. Schreiber *et al* [2] argue that models are important for understanding the working mechanisms within a KBS; such mechanisms are: the tasks, methods, how knowledge is inferred, the domain knowledge and its schemas. A further benefit arising from the shift towards the modelling approach is that fragments of knowledge may be re-used in different areas of the same domain [3] making systems development faster and more efficient. In the past, most knowledge systems had to be developed afresh each time a new system was needed, and it could not interact with other systems in the organization.

Although a KBS is developed using knowledge engineering techniques, the modelling aspects of it are largely dependent on software engineering modelling languages. The development process of a KBS is similar to that used in any general system development; stages such as: requirements gathering, system analysis, system design, system development and implementation are common activities. The stages in KBS development are: business modelling, conceptual modelling, knowledge acquisition, knowledge system design and KBS implementation. Most of the modelling techniques adopt a mix of notations derived from different modelling languages such as: UML, IDEF, SADT, OMT, Multi-perspective Modelling and others. The object-oriented paradigm has influenced systems development activities in software engineering and this trend has also been reflected in knowledge engineering methodologies such as: CommonKADS [2], MOKA [6] and KBS in product configuration as described by Felfernig *et al.* [7].

As there is no standard way of modelling KBS, there is a need to extend the use of standardised software engineering modelling language, such as UML for knowledge modelling. This promotes the use of a common modelling language, so that the vision of integration, reusability and interoperability among enterprise systems can be achieved.

3. KNOWLEDGE MODELLING PROFILE

The Unified Modeling Language (UML) together with the Object Constraint Language (OCL) is the *de facto* standard for object modelling in software engineering as defined by the Object Management Group (OMG). The UML is a general-purpose modelling language that may be used in a wide spectrum of different application domains. The OMG [8] has defined two mechanisms for extending UML: profiles and meta-model extensions. Profiles are sometimes referred to as the "lightweight" extension mechanism of UML [9]. A profile contains a predefined set of Stereotypes, TaggedValues, Constraints, and notation icons that collectively specialize and tailor the UML for a specific domain or process. The main construct in this profile is the stereotype that is purely an extension mechanism. In the model, it is marked as <<stereotype>> and has the same structure (attributes, associations, operations) as defined by the meta-model that describes it. Nevertheless, the usage of stereotypes is restricted, as changes in the semantics, structure, and the introduction of new concepts to the meta-model are not permitted [10]. The "heavyweight" extension mechanism for UML (known as the meta-model extension) is defined through the Meta-Object Facility (MOF) specification [11] which involves the process of defining a new meta-model. Using this extension, new meta-classes and meta-constructors can be added to the UML meta-model. However, it is easier to create a profile using the "lightweight" extension as it is easier to use, easier to introduce new concepts through specialising existing meta-model and has better tool support compared with meta-model extension. It is unfortunate that both extensions are known as profiles. The work presented in this paper incorporates the "lightweight" extension mechanisms of UML using the XMF approach when designing the profile. A brief introduction of XMF is given in Section 4.

4. PROFILE DESIGN – THE XMF APPROACH

The XMF (eXecutable Meta-modelling Framework) is an object-oriented meta-modelling language, and is an extension to existing standards for meta-models such as MOF, OCL and QVT, which are also defined by OMG. XMF exploits the features of these standards and adds a new dimension that allows them to be executable using an associated XMT software tool. The most comprehensive use of these standards are seen in the UML in which its meta-models are described using MOF. Details of XMF can be found in [12]. The XMF approach to profile creation can be divided into three steps: the derivation of an abstract syntax model, a description of the semantics, and a presentation of the profile's concrete syntax. In this paper we only present the creation of the abstract syntax model of the profile. The knowledge modelling profile is supported by all UML tools.

4.1 Abstract Syntax Model

The abstract syntax of the knowledge modelling language has been derived using the modelling concepts reviewed from literature [1, 3-5] and the CommonKADS modelling language (CML) [2]. The modelling concepts are concept (class) that represents the category of things; inference, which performs the reasoning function of the KBS; transfer function used to transfer between the reasoning agent and external entities (system, user); task which defines the reasoning function; task method used to describe the realisation of the task through sub-function decomposition; static role used to specify the collection of domain knowledge (rules) that is used to make the inference; dynamic role which specifies the information flow (input/output) of meaningful facts between the working memory/data base and the inference; rule type which refers to the categorisation of domain knowledge; rule which are expressions that involve an attribute value of a concept; knowledge base that contains the collection of instances of domain knowledge in the form of rules; and fact base which are the collection of attribute instances of concepts stored in working memory or database, upon which the KBS reasoning will be based. The knowledge modelling profile has four packages: domain concept, knowledge base, rule type and inference.

The Domain Concept package within the profile describes the concept constructs of the profile that are related to knowledge elements. This package is shown in Fig.1.

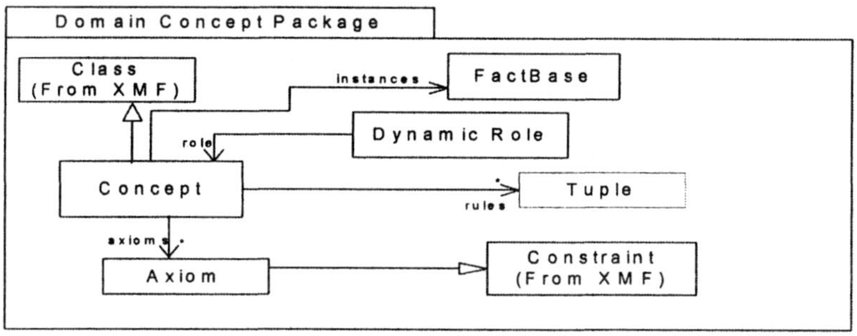

Figure 1. Domain Concept Package

The Knowledge Base package of the profile describes the modelling of a knowledge base that represents instances of knowledge elements (instances of rule type) within the domain concepts. These instances are important as they contain the actual knowledge on which the KBS reasoning process is based. Knowledge elements within the knowledge base are accessed by an inference through a static role. This package is shown in Figure 2.

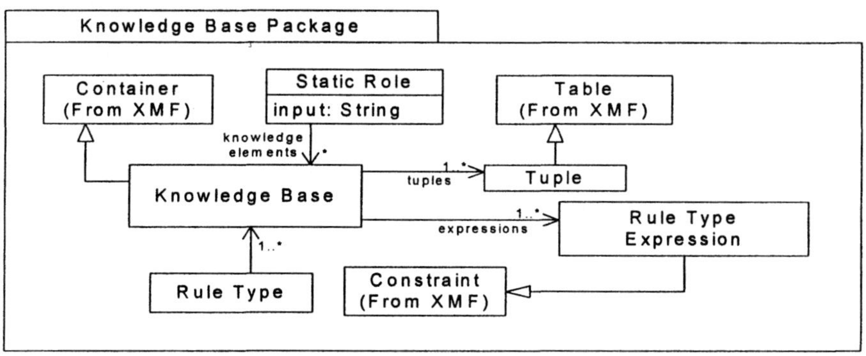

Figure 2. Knowledge Base Package

The Inference package of the profile describes the inference, inference method, task, task method, transfer function and both the static and dynamic knowledge roles. The inference package plays a pivotal role in designing the KBS as it defines the inference structure of the system, the type of knowledge used in the reasoning process and the task associated with the execution of the inference. An important point to note here is that the KBS is designed independently of the target implementation platform and inference engines, overcoming the difficulties of reusing implementation specific designs. This package is shown in Fig.3.

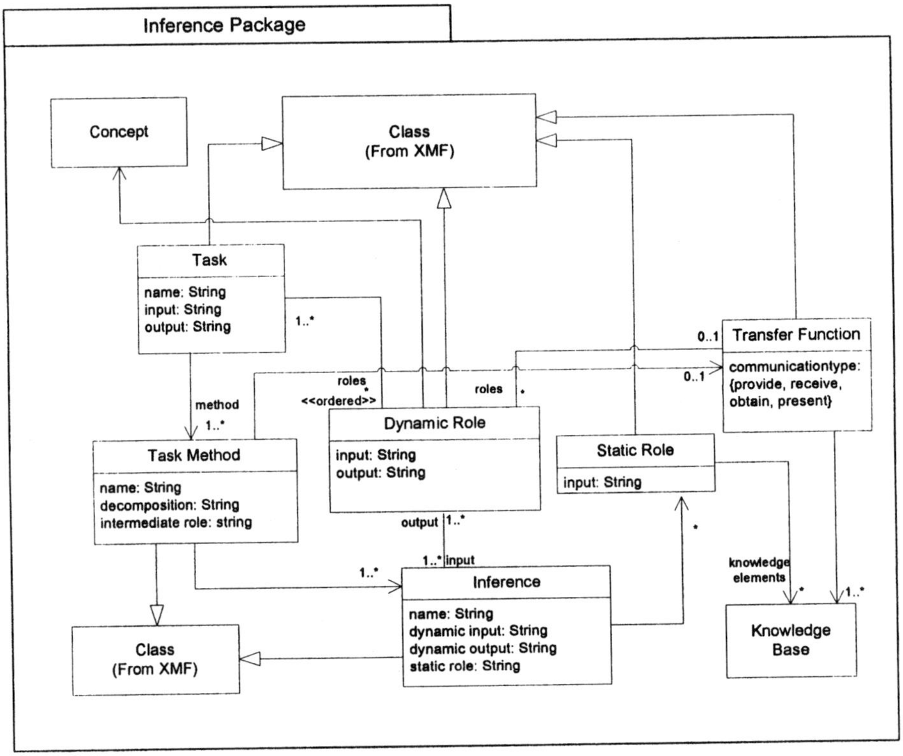

Figure 3. Inference Package

The Rule Type package (shown in Fig. 4) within the profile describes the modelling of rules. There are three types of rule: constraint rule, implication rule and decision table. A decision table is an addition to the used set of rule types. It is introduced here because certain rules are best expressed in the form of a decision table. This paper only concentrates on rule-based KBSs as it is the widely adopted KBS technology.

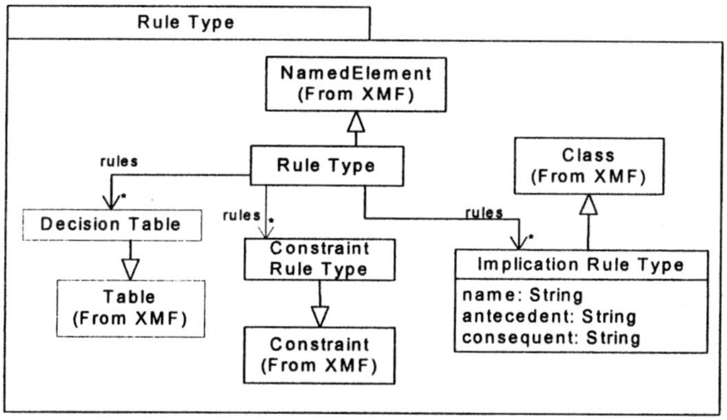

Figure 4. Rule Type Package

4.2 Model Specialisation

The knowledge modelling profile concept extends the existing meta-models of XMF by defining the profile's abstract syntax. There are five places where the profile can be viewed as an extension to XMF and these are: Class, Constraints, Named Element, Container and Table, all of which are central to the Core XMF meta-model.

The knowledge modelling class concept is viewed as a special class that is a subclass of the XMF Class. This enables the concept to inherit all the features of a class and allows it to define additional constraints such as "concepts do not have any operations or methods". The implication rule type, decision table and constraint rule type, are also examples of this. The inference package of the profile (which has the task, task method, inference, dynamic role, static role, and the transfer function concepts) can be viewed as a subclass of an XMF Class. This allows operations related to objects to be expressed, such as an execute inference call from the task method, the execution of the inference process and the access to knowledge in the knowledge base through the static role and at the same time allows the inference package elements to specify attributes. Rule Type is subclassed from NamedElement as all rule sets must have unique name.

The Constraint class is a subclass of the XMF meta-model that incorporates profile concepts such as axioms and rule type expressions. All these concepts need the ability to express constraints and this class allows for this. Knowledge base is a subclass of the Container class of XMF. It has a 'content' slot that is a table. This is a natural choice for a subclass as the knowledge base is actually a collection of tables grouped together in order to store rule type instances. The table class of XMF is extended to incorporate the profile's concepts of tuple.

5. 'OTTAWA ANKLE RULE' SYSTEM

The Ottawa ankle rules was devised by Stiell [13], as an assessment on ankle injury patients at Emergency Department. Physicians use these rules to rule out the possibility of having an ankle X-ray series or a foot X-ray series. The decision rule is based on assessment of the two different type of pain, bone tenderness and the inability to bear weight. Figure 6, adapted from [13] shows the major recommendation of the ankle rules.

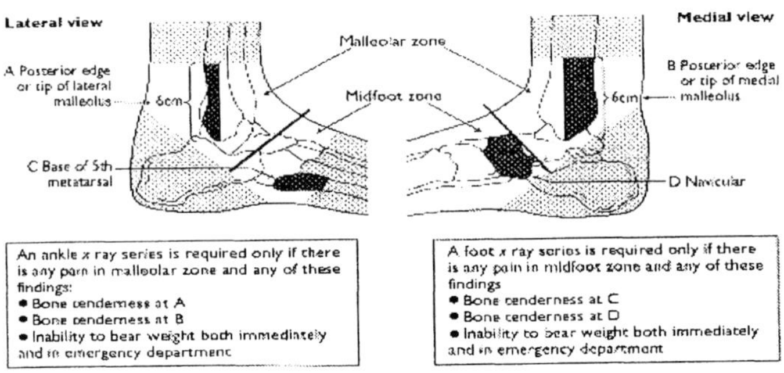

Figure 4. Ottawa ankle rule for use of radiography in acute ankle injuries (adapted from Stiell. *et al* [13])

Figure 5 shows the knowledge modelling profile used to represent the Ottawa ankle rules in a KBS. This example concentrates on showing the abstraction and matching process of the Ottawa application based on the modified task template of assessment task suggested by [2]. The profile packages used here are the domain concept, inference, knowledge base and rule type.

The task 'Assess Injury' will be realised by the task method 'abstract case' and 'match method'. The task method can be decomposed into other tasks or inferences. In this example of 'abstract case', it is decomposed into the inference "abstract". The concept patient has two attributes: name and pain area enumeration type. Here the assessment task will abstract all cases into two groups, based on the pain suffered by the patients. Patients will suffer pain, either in the malleolar zone or in the midfoot area. The purpose of this abstraction process is to provide useful categories of cases that need to be distinguished for assessment purposes. The inference will execute the task of abstracting the cases by adding case abstraction to the pain area data. The reasoning process will use the "pain abstraction knowledge" which is a static knowledge role. This knowledge is accessed from the knowledge base 'Ottawa ankle' and is based on the 'pain abstraction rule'. The next step is to match the whether an ankle or foot x-ray series is required based on the pain area. This is executed by the task method 'match method'. This method is decomposed into the transfer function 'obtain' and inference 'match'. The transfer function will obtain injury details from patient during consultation with the system based on the question regarding bone tenderness and inability to bear weight. The injury details will be used by the inference 'match' to make the decision on the different type of x-ray series to be performed on the patient. This inference will use the rule 'Ottawa ankle rules' to match the decision.

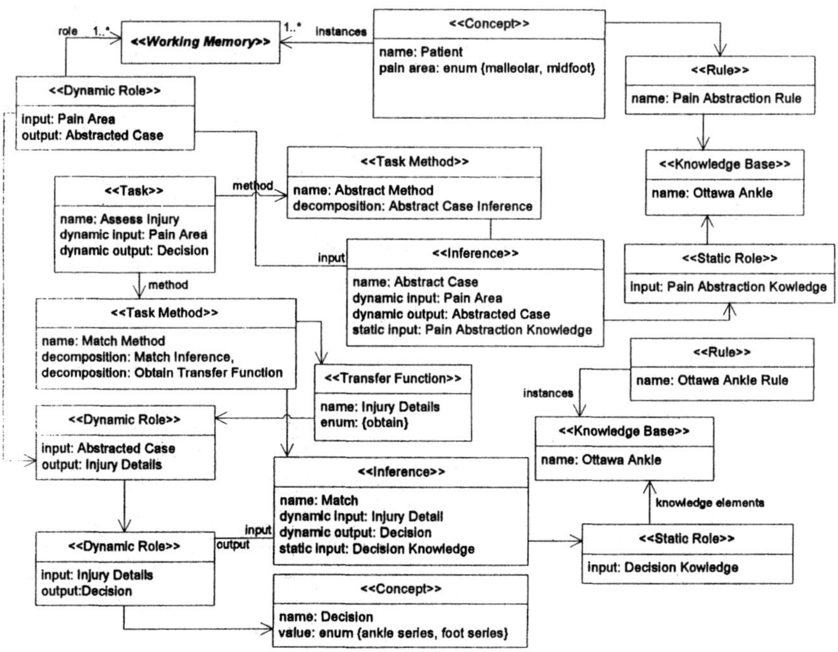

Figure 5. Ottawa Ankle Rule system model

6. CONCLUSION AND FUTURE WORK

Knowledge-based systems have evolved from being stand-alone machines to being part of the enterprise's group of systems. The process of constructing KBSs is similar to that required by other software systems, and conceptual modelling plays an important role in the development process. Software engineering has adopted UML as a standard for modelling, but the field of knowledge engineering is still searching for the right language. UML can be adopted for knowledge modelling by exploiting the profile extension mechanism. This paper has described the process of creating such an extension by basing the design of the profile on that of the XMF framework. This is a novel approach in profile design as the XMF approach is an extension to existing standards for meta-modelling such as MOF, OCL and QVT. The creation of the profile is important as it allows KBS to be designed using an object-oriented approach.

The future work involves the specification of the profile's semantics and construction of the concrete syntax model. Both activities involve the use of the XMT tool, and are in its final stage of development. The profile's ability to model the requirements of KBS has only be tested on two case studies adapted from [2] and [13]. Testing the profile in a number of real-world situations would be beneficial and would identify any limitations and assist in the refinement of the profile. Currently we are testing the profile on case studies from the Center for Evidence Based Nursing at the Department of Health Sciences at York.

REFERENCES

1. Studer, R., Benjamins, R.V., and Fensel, D.: *Knowledge Engineering: Principles and Methods.* Data & Knowledge Engineering, 1998. **25**: p. 161-197.
2. Schreiber, G., Akkermans, H., Anjewierden, A., de Hoog, R., Shadbolt, N., de Velde, W.V. and Wielinga, B.: *Knowledge Engineering and Management: The CommonKADS Methodology.* 1999, Massachusetts: MIT Press.
3. Angele, J., Fensel, D., Landes, D., Studer, R.: *Developing Knowledge-Based Systems with MIKE.* J of Automated Software Engineering, 1998. **5**(4): p. 389-418.
4. Grosso, W.E., Eriksson, H., Fergerson, R.W., Gennari, S., Tu, S., Musen, M.A.: *Knowledge Modelling at the Millennium (The Design and Evolution of Protege 2000).* 1999, Stanford Medical Institute.
5. Speel, P., Schreiber, A. Th., van Joolingen, W., and Beijer, G.: *Conceptual Models for Knowledge-Based Systems*, in *Encyclopedia of Computer Science and Technology.* 2001, Marcel Dekker Inc, New York.
6. Stokes, M., *Managing Engineering Knowledge: MOKA - Methodology for Knowledge Based Engineering Applications.* 2001, London, UK: Professional Engineering and Publishing Limited.

7. Felfernig, A., Friedrich, G.E., Jannach, D.: *Generating product configuration knowledge bases from precise domain extended UML models.* in *12 th International Conference on Software Engineering and Knowledge Engineering (SEKE'00).* 2000. Chicago, USA.
8. OMG: *Unified Modeling Language specification (version 1.4).* 2001.
9. OMG: *Requirements for UML Profile.* 1999.
10. Perez-Martinez, J.E.: *Heavyweight extensions to the UML metamodel to describe the C3 architectural style.* ACM SIGSOFT Notes, 2003. **28**(3).
11. OMG: *MOF Specification version 1.4.* 2002.
12. Clark, T., Evans, A., Sammut, P., Willians, J.: *Metamodelling for Model-Driven Development (draft): To be published.* 2005. (Accessible at www.xactium.com)
13. Stiell IG, McKnight RD, Greenberg GH, McDowell I, Nair RC, Wells GA, et al. Implementation of the Ottawa ankle rules. *JAMA* 1994;271:827-32.

DYNAMIC-FUZZY CONCEPTS

Junquan Li[1] Andrzej Buller[2] Yixin Yin[3]
1, 3School of Information Engineering, University of Science and Technology Beijing,Haidian Zone, Beijing 100083, China,
2 ATR International Network Informatics Laboratories,Kyoto,JapanE-mail: tq097rr@163.com; Andrzej Buller@atr.jp; yyx@ies.ustb.edu.cn

Abstract: This paper presents dynamic-fuzzy logic (DFL) and its usefulness in cognitive/affective modeling. Freud noted that hate changes into love and love into hate even without any alteration of the object. Vallacher and Nowak confirmed experimentally that people might change their judgment even in absence of new data of the object. Related mental phenomena can be modeled using fuzzy sets, provided that constant membership values are replaced with dynamic ones. As for definition of membership, instead of a real numbers in the interval [0, 1] Buller proposed a function mapping time onto this interval. This way a membership becomes a dynamic membership and fuzzy sets become dynamic-fuzzy. A cellular inference engine, called Working Memory, was used for dynamic-fuzzy calculus. Fuzziness of input data was represented there as streams of contradictory statements called memes. When two or more memes met in a cell, they may elastically collide, annihilate, or exchange/invert some of their codes.

Keywords: dynamic fuzziness, working memory, social judgment

1 INTRODUCTION

As Sigmund Freud noted, in a number of circumstances hate changes into love and love into hate. The changes are purely internal and an alteration of the object plays no part in them [7]. Robin Vallacher and Andrzej Nowak, based on experiments with human subjects, confirmed that when judging a perceived person or social situation people sometimes switch from highly positive feelings to highly negative ones even in the absence of new data about the object of interest [10]. Andrzej Buller [4] considered the question: 'Can we model this mental phenomenon using fuzzy sets?' and proposed to replace constant values of memberships to fuzzy sets with dynamic ones, or, in other words, instead of a real number in the interval [0; 1], to employ a function mapping time onto the interval. Fuzzy logic dealing with dynamic memberships to sets is called Dynamic-Fuzzy Logic (DFL).

The following example from the domain of social psychology (taken from [4]) explains the idea of dynamic membership. *Let us consider a situation wherein two subjects S' and S" one-day fall in love with the same person P. Among a number of possible plots of the subjects' feelings towards P, let us assume that the feelings of S' start from extreme love and then a linear decay of the fascination takes place towards complete indifference after three weeks, while S" feels constant and extreme love that after two weeks turns without any external reasons into a deep aversion. Let us try to describe the feelings of the subjects in terms of classic fuzzy sets. We could provide information on the subjects' feelings in a particular moment in time or an average value for a period of interest (e.g. three weeks). Let us introduce fuzzy sets* H', H", L', *and* L", *which contain people hated by S', people hated by S", people loved by S', and people loved by S", respectively. For the last day of the period of interest, the fuzzy-set-theoretic membership values can be provided as, say:* $\mu_{H'}(P)=0$, $\mu_{H''}(P)=0$, $\mu_{L'}(P)=1$, $\mu_{L''}(P)=0$. *Average values covering the full period of interest (three weeks) could be:* $\mu_{H'}(P)=0$, $\mu_{H''}(P)=0.33$, $\mu_{L'}(P)=0.5$, $\mu_{L''}(P)=0.67$. *Unfortunately, the provided figures are not too informative. In both cases the most essential knowledge about the subjects' mental states is lost. Hence, the idea of a replacement of constant membership values* $\mu_{H'}(P)$, $\mu_{H''}(P)$, ... *with functions of time, i.e.* $\mu_{H'}(P, t)$, $\mu_{H''}(P, t)$, ..., *respectively are suggested. These functions are dynamic memberships.*

It can be noted, that if for a period of interest, the values of the dynamic membership functions remained constant (or almost constant), the sets would be subject to classic fuzzy calculus. DFL was introduced to handle dynamic memberships. It is assumed in DFL that based on a set of functions describing dynamic memberships of objects e_1, e_2, ... to each of dynamic fuzzy sets D', D", ..., where plots of some of the functions are unknown, an updated set of the functions (i.e. a set containing the missing definitions) is to be produced [4]. A cellular inference engine, called Working Memory, was used for dynamic-fuzzy calculus. Fuzziness of input data was represented there as streams of contradictory statements called memes. When two or more memes met in a cell, an interaction took place [3][5][6].

2 DYNAMIC FUZZY CALCULUS

Buller et al. investigated several models of cellular- automata-based Working Memory [2][3][5][6]. In all of them fuzziness of input data was represented as streams of contradictory statements introduced in [1]. The following example (taken from [4]) explains the idea of dynamic-fuzzy calculus. *Let us consider milk as an example of an object of interest* θ*. Let us assume that* θ *is recognized as suitable for baby feeding if it is warm. When, based on perceived data, membership of* θ *to the classic fuzzy set* W*, where* W *denotes "warm drinks", is* $\mu_W(\theta)$*, a stream of identical copies of the statement "*$\theta \in W$*", as well as a stream of identical copies of the statement "*$\theta \in \neg W$*" are being directed to Working Memory. The statements have been christened memes. Notation "*$\neg W$*" is for "drinks that are not warm". The existence of the two contradictory meme streams represent a mother's uncertainty whether the milk is warm enough. Let us assume that the densities of the streams are* σ_t *("*$\theta \in W$*")* = σ*("*$\theta \in W$*")* = *const. and* σ_t *("*$\theta \in \neg W$*")* = σ*("*$\theta \in \neg W$*")* = *const., respectively, and such that* $\mu_W(\theta) = \sigma$*("*$\theta \in W$*")/(* σ*("*$\theta \in W$*")* + σ*("*$\theta \in \neg W$*")). The streams cause the Working Memory to become a space populated by a "society" of contradictory memes. Let us assume that a stream of identical copies of the meme "*$W \subset P$*", where* P *denotes the set of "drinks proper for baby feeding", is also directed to Working Memory. Dynamic fuzzy inferencing consists in interactions between memes populating Working Memory and production of output streams of memes "*$\theta \in P$*" and "*$\theta \in \neg P$*". The deduced* $\mu_P(\theta, t)$ *equals* σ_t*("*$\theta \in P$*")/(* σ_t *("*$\theta \in P$*")* + σ_t *("*$\theta \in \neg P$*"). The above example becomes more interesting when the streams of memes "*$\theta \in H$*", "*$\theta \in \neg H$*" and "*$\neg H \subset P$*", where* H *is a set of "hot drinks", are also involved.*

Since Working Memory is implemented as a cellular automaton, memes represented as binary words wander all over the cellular space. When two or more memes meet in a cell, an interaction takes place. Via trial and error, a set of meme interactions causing a psychologically plausible dynamics of simulated mental states has been obtained. The interactions are:

(i) *elastic collision between unrelated memes;*

(ii) *annihilation of contradictory memes,*
e.g. "$\theta \in W$", "$\theta \in \neg W$" → *null;*

(iii) *positive cross-over,*
e.g. "$\theta \in W$", "$W \subset P$" → "$\theta \in P$";

(iv) *negative cross-over,*
e.g. "$\theta \in \neg W$", "$W \subset P$" → "$\theta \in \neg P$".

Simulation experiments confirmed that even in case of constant streams of input memes, the densities of the resulting streams may vary in time. This phenomenon takes place especially when the populations of resulting contradictory memes have an equal or almost equal "birth rate". Instead of chaotic oscillations or a convergence to a "level of balance", a given population of memes may enjoy its quick victory (i.e. dominate Working Memory) and, after a period of time, suddenly lose to the population of contradictory memes. This dramatic change may refer to a case when a mother recognizes milk as warm enough for her baby, and when going to feed it, changes her mind and decides to warm the milk a little more.

Similar irregular oscillations of meme population was observed in a model of a subject's hesitation how to react to date proposal (Fig. 1), as well as in a model of a robot's hesitation whether to go to recharge batteries or to continue playing with an attractive toy [9]. Recently leaky neurons are investigates as units facilitating dynamics-fuzzy calculus applied to robotics [8].

3 CONCLUDING REMARKS

Dynamic membership offered by Dynamic- Fuzzy Logic (DFL) is a convenient concept to be used for modeling high-level mental functions including social judgment. On the other hand, the cellular Working Memory proposed in DFL-related papers does not seem to be the best way to process dynamic-fuzzy concepts because of big computational power required. Hence, further research on DFL should seek for simple neural networks capable of processing dynamic-fuzzy data.

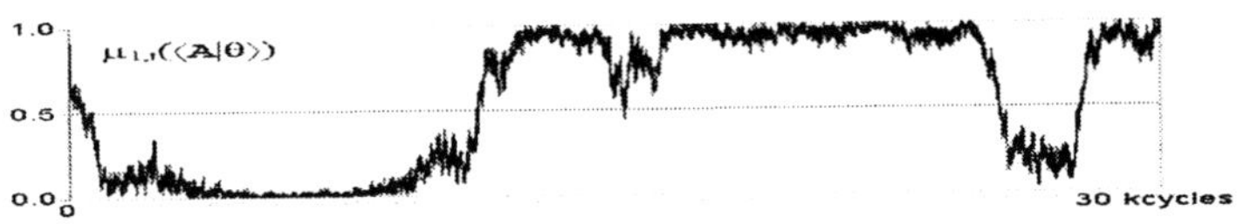

Fig. 1. Dynamics of meme populations in cellular Working Memory. Oscillating feelings of a simulated subject represented as dynamic-fuzzy membership of an object of interest (θ) to a dynamic fuzzy set **A** (adopted from [3]).

4 Acknowledgements

This research was supported by NSFC, China (Grant No.60374032). The authors thank Dr. Andrzej Buller and ATR.

REFERENCES

[1] A. Buller, Fuzzy Inferencing: A Novel, Massively Parallel Approach, Technical Report TR-95-027, Intnl. Computer Sci. Institute, Berkeley, CA, 1995.

[2] A. Buller, "Dynamic Fuzzy Sets for Cognitive Modeling", Proceedings, AROB 6th '01, Tokyo, 15-17 Jan., pp. 150-151, 2001.

[3] A. Buller, "Dynamic Fuzziness", Proceedings, 7th Pacific Rim Intnl Conf. on Artificial Intelligence (PRICAI-02), Tokyo, pp. 90-96, 18-22 August, 2002.

[4] A. Buller, "Fuzzy Sets with Dynamic Memberships", FSKD'02, 18-22 Nov., Singapore, pp. 564-565, 2002.

[5] A. Buller & K. Shimohara, "Decision Making as a Debate in the Society of Memes in a Neural Working Memory", J. of 3D Forum, 13 (3), pp. 77-82, 1999.

[6] A. Buller & K. Shimohara, "On the dynamics of judgment: does the butterfly effect take place in human working memory?", Artificial Life and Robotics, Vol. 5, No. 2, pp. 88-92, 2001.

[7] S. Freud, The Ego and the Id, W.W. Norton & Company, New York, pp. 41-42, 1923/1990.

[8] J. Li, A. Buller & J. Liu, "Robot's behavior driven by internal tensions regulated by pulsed para-neural networks", AROB 10th '05, Beppu, 4-6 Feb., 2005.

[9] J. Liu & A. Buller, "Tensions and conflicts: Toward a pleasure-seeking artifact", Proceedings, 5th IFAC Symposium on Intelligent Autonomous Vehicles (IAV'2004), 5-7 July, Lisboa, 2004.

[10] R.A. Vallacher & A. Nowak, "The Stream of Social Judgment", In: R.A. Vallacher & A. Nowak (Eds.) Dynamical Systems in Social Psychology, Academic Press: San Diego, pp. 251-277, 1994.

ONTO-THESAURI: AN EFFICIENT ONTOLOGY!

F. Vandamme[1]&[2], L. Wang[2], M. Vandamme[3] and P. Kaczmarski[3]
1LAE, Ghent University, Blandijnberg 2, 9000 Gent, Belgium
2BIKIT vzw, J. Plateaustraat 22, 9000 Gent, Belgium
3 VARTEC NV, Holstraat 19, 9000 Gent
Fernand.Vandamme@ugent.be, www.Ugent.be
Lin.Wang@bikit.org, www.bikit.org
Mike.Vandamme@vartec.behttp://www.vartec.be/
Peter.Kaczmarski@vartec.be

Abstract: There is an eternal problem for enterprise content management: "Everyday living is too fast, too busy, too complicated. More than at any time in history, it's important to have good information on just about every aspect of life. And, An onto-thesaurus based document and content management platform is very successful. It provides an improvement of recall and precision of information retrieval by ISO mono-lingual or multilingual thesauri indexing, homonymy resolution and onto-thesaurus.

Key words: onto-thesauri, knowledge retrieval, knowledge management, ontology

1. INTRODUCTION: HOW TO HAVE EFFICIENT KNOWLEDGE RETRIEVAL, WITH PRECISION:

There is an eternal problem for enterprise content management: "Everyday living is too fast, too busy, too complicated. More than at any time in history, it's important to have good information on just about every aspect of life. And, there is more information available than ever before. Too much in fact. There is simply no time for people to gather and absorb the information they need." Britton Hadden – 1929. The goal for the solution is improving retrieval recall and precision. In this paper we will introduce an onto-thesaurus approach.

2. A HIGH SUCCESSFUL SOLUTION: AN ONTO-THESAURUS ENHANCED WITH MULTILINGUAL QUALITY AND HOMONYMS DETECTION

An onto-thesaurus based document and content management platform is very successful. It provides an improvement of recall and precision of information retrieval by ISO mono-lingual or multilingual thesauri indexing, homonymy resolution and onto-thesaurus.

It includes following modules:

2.1 modules for (onto)-Thesaurus life cycle (see fig 1):

IKEM.ThesCreator™
IKEM.ThesEditor™
IKEM.ThesAnnot™

2.1.1 IKEM.ThesCreator™

Users can develop a (onto)-Thesaurus using document corpus/content by IKEM.ThesCreatorTM. It provides a simultaneous view of (onto-)thesaurus relations and document content, context of current thesaurus terms and context of full index terms. User can simultaneous updating of the (onto-) thesaurus

2.1.2 IKEM.ThesEditor™

The powerful thesaurus editor system supports ISO relations (mono & multi-lingual), homonym resolution, enhancement of ISO standard Relation, consistence checking, circular relations checking. It also supports intuitive graphical thesaurus development and support for multi-lingual & multi-domain

2.1.3 IKEM.ThesAnnot™

The IKEM.ThesAnnotTM can thread annotations of the thesaurus terms managed via a web service which support multiple user and discussion for maintenance of thesaurus.

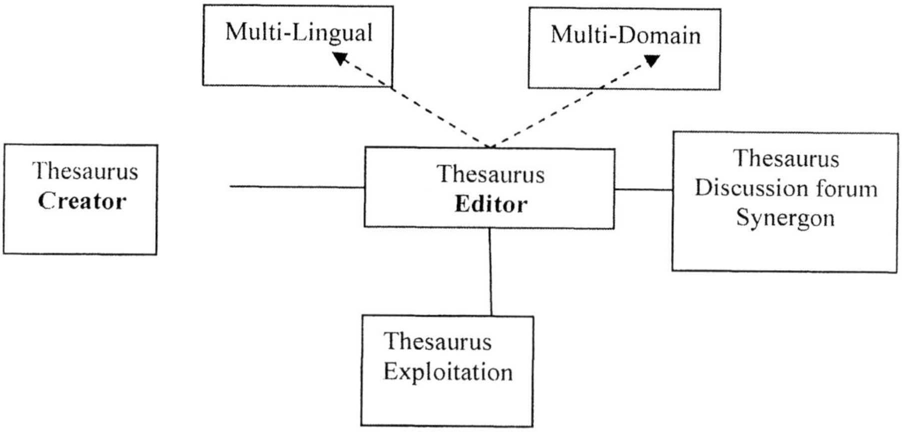

Fig 1. (onto)-Thesaurus life cycle

2.2 modules for (onto)-Thesaurus exploitation (see fig.2)

IKEM.DocSearch™ and IKEM.Query-Expansion™
IKEM.3D-Navigation™
IKEM.Onto-thesaurus™ and 3D-Search™

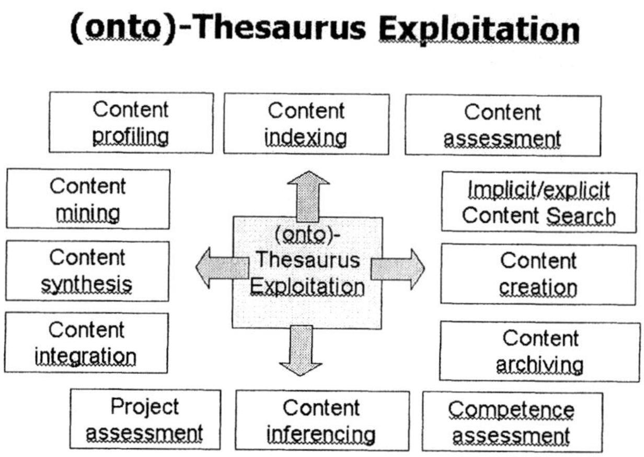

Fig.2 (onto)-thesaurus exploitation

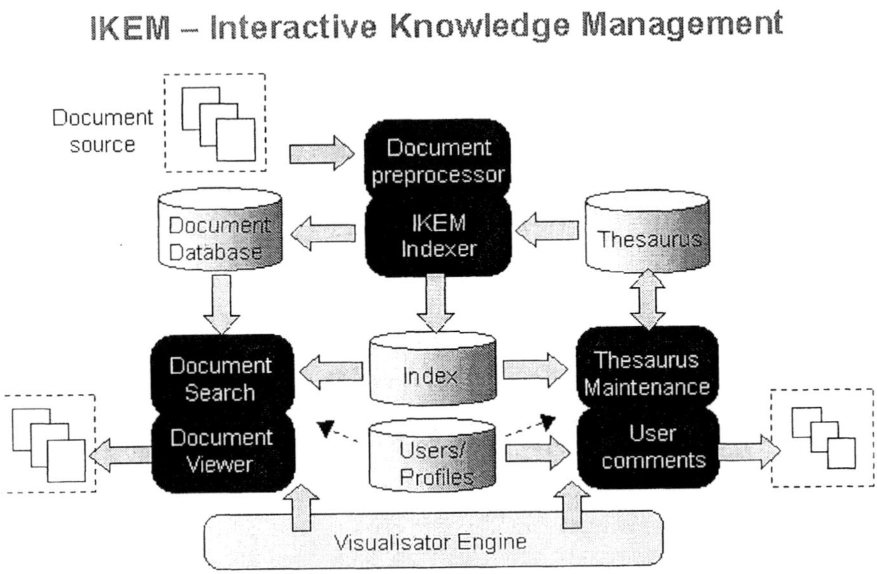

Fig. 3 IKEM platform for document and content management

2.2.1. IKEM.DocSearch™ and IKEM.Query-Expansion™

IKEM through web services supports user query in different languages, query expansion based on thesaurus and onto-thesaurus.

2.2.2 IKEM.3D-Navigation™

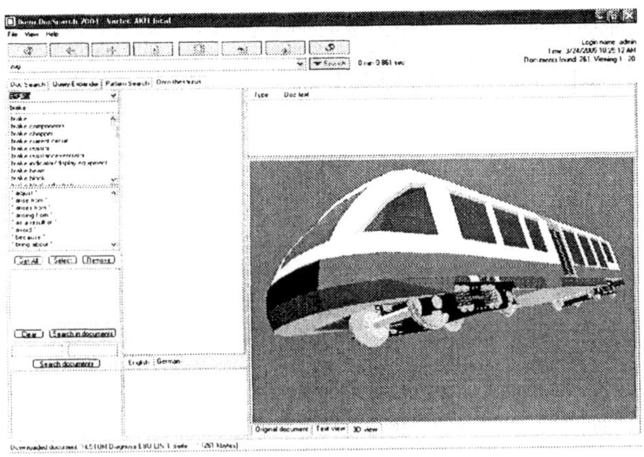

Fig 4 IKEM search via 3D space navigation

2.2.3 IKEM.Onto-thesaurus™ and 3D-Search™

IKEM offers users search by query extension and pattern search.

2.2.4 Application of thesaurus and onto-thesaurus for assessment

Assessment through project views:

a). Task view
 -dynamic overview of tasks as a function of time
 -can be linked with project- and task specification

b). Coordination view
 -early warnings regarding possible delays in project realisation

c). Cooperation view
 -using actor profiles to analyze the cooperation patterns

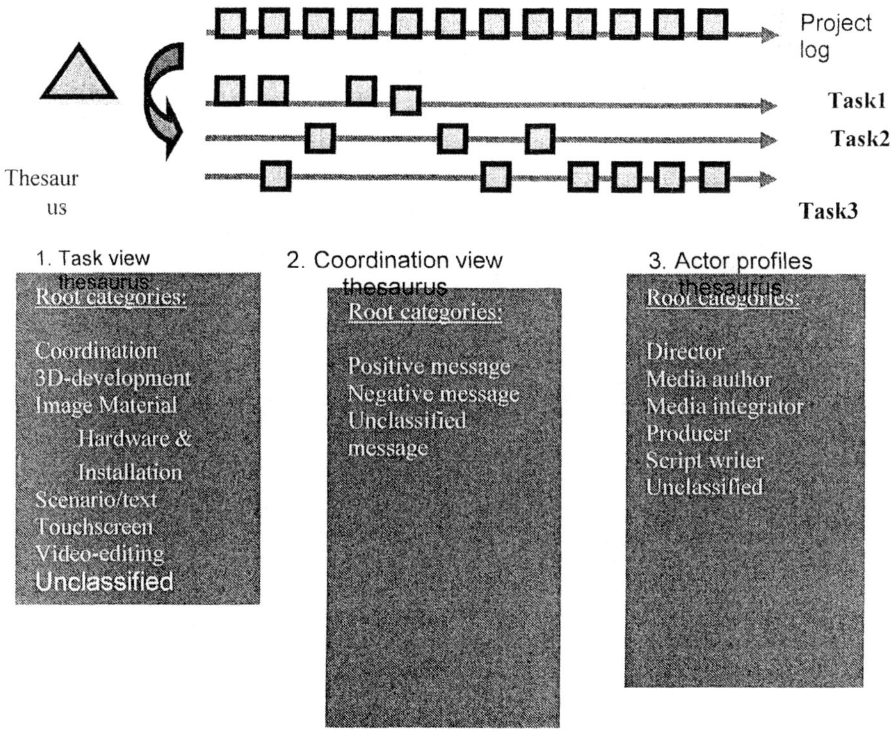

Fig .5 Assessment through project views

3. CONCLUSIONS

Thesauri & Onto-Thesauri based document and content management can enhanced retrieval recall & precision and Interactive Knowledge Management. Onto-thesauri approach have the benefit that they can be build semi-automatically and can be used for automatic indexing and search. They have the main benefits as ontology, but their performance is much higher. (see fig. 6)

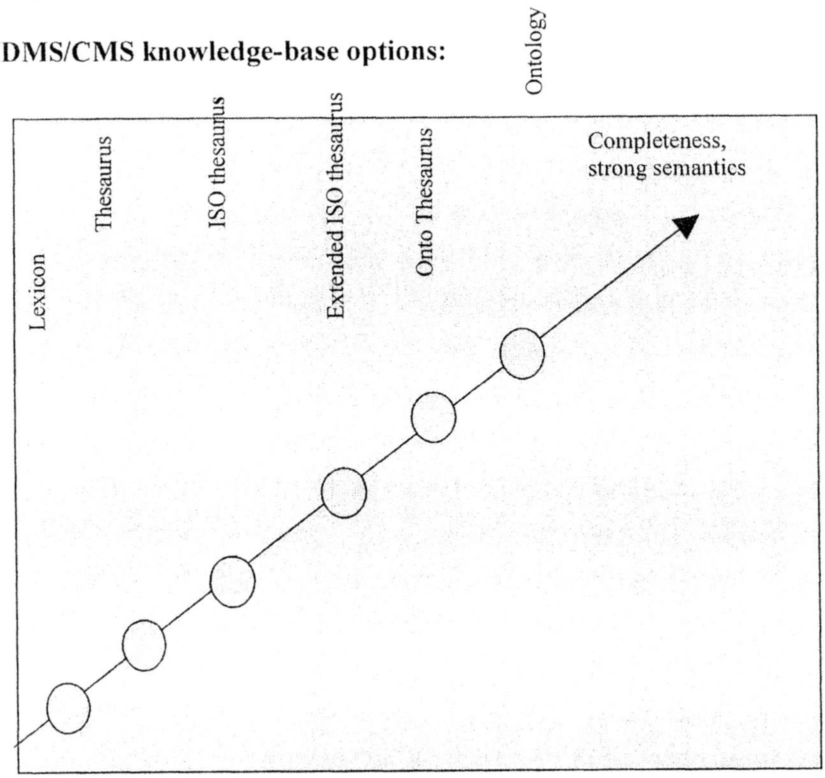

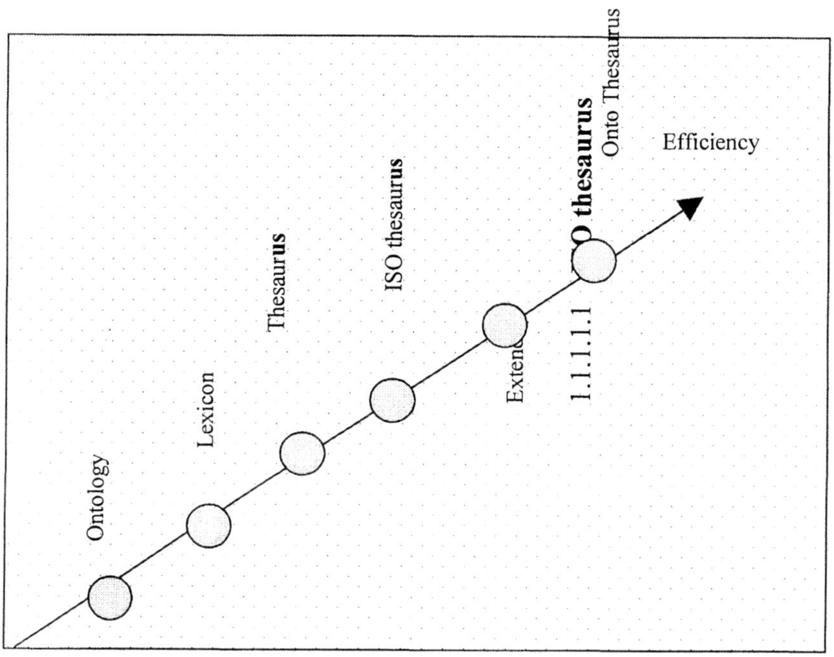

Fig. 6 DMS/CMS knowledge-base options

REFDERENCES

[1] Abuzir, Y., 2002, E-mail messages classification and user profiling by the use of semantic thesauri, Capita Selecta uit de Toegepaste Epistemologie, deel IX, Communication & Cognition, Gent

[2] Vandamme, F., 2001, Learning and Education, CC-AI, Vol. 18 n° 1/2, Communication & Cognition, Gent

[3]Vandamme, F., Simmons, S., 2001, Advanced Content Management (ACM) for Project Process Assessment and Control. A Knowledge Management Approach., CC-AI, Vol. 18 n° 3/4, Communication & Cognition, Gent

[4] Vandamme F., 2002, Knowledge Management and its vital components, Capita Selecta uit de Toegepaste Epistemologie, deel IX, Communication & Cognition, Gent

[5] Lin, W., Van Vosselen, N., Vandamme, F., 2004, Sustainability based project life-cycle management, Caleidoscoop of Knowledge Management, Communicatie & Cognitie, Gent.

[6] Vandamme, F., 2004, Gandhi and Knowledge management, introduction, Communication & Cognition, Vol. 37, nr. 1-2, pp. 3-4, Communication & Cognition, Gent

A HYBRID CONNECTIONIST-SYMBOLIC APPROACH FOR REAL-VALUED PATTERN CLASSIFICATION

Lina, Lim Tong Ming, Leow Soo Kar

Monash University Malaysia, No.2 Jalan Kolej, Bandar Sunway, 46150 Petaling Jaya, Selangor, Malaysia. Email: lynn81@gmail.com leow.soo.kar@infotech.monash.edu.my lim.tong.ming@infotech.monash.edu.my

Abstract: Knowledge-Based Artificial Neural Networks (KBANNs) offer a means for combining symbolic and connectionist approaches into a hybrid methodology capable of dealing with small datasets and requires shorter training time when compared to conventional artificial neural networks (ANNs). These approaches were developed mainly for binary-valued domain problems and when applied to real-valued data, many tedious transformation processes need to be undertaken before it could be used. In this paper we propose to extend KBANN to a Real Knowledge-Based Neural Network (RealKBNN) that is able to handle real-valued data directly, making it a more powerful and realistic methodology to be applied to real-world problem domains. Four real-valued datasets (one artificial, 2 medical and 1 classification datasets) were used to evaluate RealKBNN. The results showed that RealKBNN performs very well in terms of its ability to correctly classify unseen examples as well as its suitability for classification of scarce and complex real data.

Key words: Knowledge based Artificial Neural Networks, Hybrid systems, pattern classification

1. INTRODUCTION

Symbolic and connectionist approaches are two major techniques to machine learning. They began independently but in the mid 1990's researchers in these two areas started investigating ways of integrating both approaches [2] to explore if better generalization can be attained when correct background knowledge is available. Imperfect domain knowledge is fed to the integrated system and then revised by training with available examples. Knowledge learned by the system is extracted as revised knowledge. This revised knowledge can then be used to provide better insight and understanding of the problem at hand.

Current knowledge based neural network systems work mainly on binary inputs. However, real world applications rarely contain only binary data. The way to deal with real-valued domains is to convert real data into the binary form but this usually increases the number of inputs and prolongs the training time as well as degrading the generalization capability of the network.

In this paper, we present a proposed technique based on KBANN, to translate inference rules that accepts real-valued inputs into neural networks. The remainder of the paper is organized as follows: Section 2 provides a brief discussion of related work in Knowledge-Based Neural Networks (KBNNs). Following this, section 3 describes the proposed technique called RealKBNN. In section 4, we present the experimental details and results to evaluate the effectiveness and performance of RealKBNN. Finally, section 5 summarizes this paper.

2. RELATED WORK

Rule Based Neural Networks (RBNN) use prior knowledge if-then inference rules. Input data variables are mapped as input units, target concepts or final consequences are mapped as output units and intermediate concepts are mapped as hidden units. The initial domain rules determine how the concepts or units are linked and how the weights are allocated to the links. KBCNN [4], (Knowledge-based conceptual neural network), KBANN [9], Sordo's KBANN [6] (knowledge based artificial neural networks) are some examples of RBNN. KBANNs accept propositional and acyclic rules and their input features are either in nominal or binary format. This restricts KBANNs in many ways. One obvious restriction is that it is only suitable for binary input data and thus is limited in its applicability.

In an attempt to use KBANN for real-valued problems, Sordo et. Al. [7] modified KBANN to accept real-valued inputs by preserving all rule-to-network translation algorithms and applied it to scarce and complex problem domain like the P Magnetic Resonance Spectroscopy (MRS) data. Sordo's KBANN treated real-valued numbers as positive antecedents and set ω as the weight on all links from the real-valued input nodes. Using this technique, she reported some encouraging results.

3. REALKBNN

Our proposed approach, RealKBNN is based on KBANN. First, domain theory in the form of if-then-else rules for real-valued inputs is translated into the forms of neurons, weights and thresholds. The novelty of this technique is in its manipulation of weight and threshold parameters by eliminating the hidden layer encoding the conjunctive relationship. This step speeds up the training time and convergence time since eliminating a layer in the neural network reduces its complexity and lessens the amount of the computational work.

After the rules are translated, the neural network is formed and is then initialized with some predetermined parametric values. The initialized network is then refined to a final network to classify unseen examples. Figure 1 shows the RealKBNN framework.

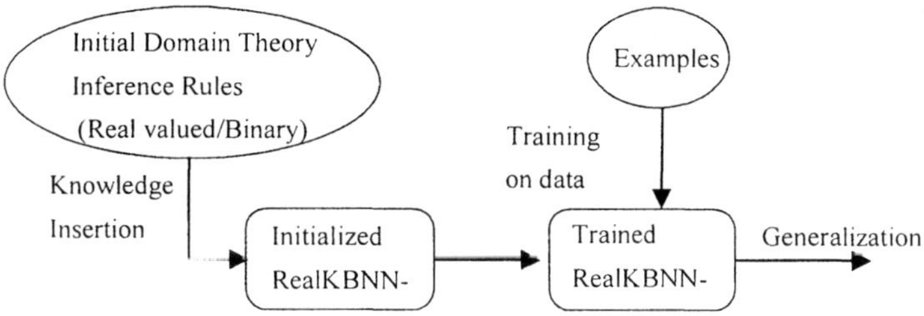

Figure. 1. RealKBNN Framework

In current knowledge refinement systems, the networks created may contain many layers depending on the domain knowledge rules used for creating the network. There are intermediate concepts in the domain knowledge and each concept is mapped as a node in the neural network and the intermediate concepts may be mapped as nodes in different layers according to the dependency of these concepts. This is a major problem because feed forward neural network learning algorithms are not good at training deep networks.

To overcome this drawback, the RealKBNN-net has only three layers, an input layer, a hidden layer and an output layer. The connection between the input layer and the hidden layer represents the conjunctive relationships while the connection between the hidden layer and the output layer represents the disjunctive relationships. For domain knowledge rules that consist of many intermediate concepts, some additional steps are required to rearrange or rewrite the propositional rules to eliminate these intermediate concepts and have a mapping only from input attributes to consequences that lead to the final results. The antecedents of a rule can be a set of arbitrary linear conditions on the input features. For instance, the precondition of a rule could be expressed as linear constraints on the values of the input feature. Likewise, the output of the rule can be a set of arbitrary linear conditions on the output activations. For simplicity, we consider only rules where the precondition is given by a set of intervals. An example of such rules is *"IF $A \le a$ and $B \le b$ then C"*

3.1 Theoretical Results

Before we describe the knowledge integration module of RealKBNN, we present some theoretical results to support the validity of RealKBNN. The following notation is used:

$F(x) = \frac{1}{\left(1+e^{-x}\right)}$, the standard logistic activation function.

- w_i^g the weight on links corresponding to "greater than-equal to" inequality dependencies.
- w_i^l the weight on links corresponding to "less than-equal to" inequality dependencies.
- Y_i the antecedent in Domain D_i corresponding to "greater than-equal to" inequality dependencies.
- y_i the real input value of the antecedent Y_i.
- b_i the right-hand side value of Y_i corresponding to "greater than-equal to" inequality dependencies.
- X_i the antecedent in Domain D_i corresponding to "less than-equal to" inequality dependencies.
- x_i the real input value of the antecedent X_i.
- a_i the right-hand side value of X_i corresponding to "less than-equal to" inequality dependencies.

Theorem 1. Mapping conjunctive rules of the form

"If $\underset{i}{\wedge}(X_i \le a_i) \underset{j}{\wedge}(Y_j \ge b_j)$ then C" into a neural network using:

(i) $w_j^g = -w_i^l = \omega > 0$ (1)

(ii) $\theta = \left(\sum_{i=1}^{n} a_i - \sum_{i=1}^{m} b_i \right) \omega$ (2)

creates a network that accurately encodes the rules.

Proof. This theorem is proved by showing that these mappings are correct in the following three situations:

(A) The unit encoding the consequent of the rule is active when all of the antecedents are satisfied.

(B) The unit encoding the consequent of the rule is inactive when none of the antecedents is satisfied.

(C) When the unit encoding the consequent of the rule is inactive, then at least one of the antecedents is not satisfied.

Case A: Assume that all of the antecedents are satisfied and show that the unit encoding the consequent is active. When all of the antecedents are true, it means that all the inputs satisfy their respective inequality conditions.
This implies: $x_i \leq a_i$, i = 1,...n and $y_j \geq b_j$, j = 1,....m
Summing both sides of all inequalities we get,

$$\sum_{i=1}^{n} x_i \leq \sum_{i=1}^{n} a_i \quad \text{i.e.} \quad \sum_{i=1}^{n} a_i - \sum_{i=1}^{n} x_i \geq 0 \tag{3}$$

$$\sum_{j=1}^{m} y_j \geq \sum_{j=1}^{m} b_j \quad \text{i.e.} \quad \sum_{j=1}^{m} y_j - \sum_{j=1}^{m} b_j \geq 0 \tag{4}$$

Thus, the activation function is given as

$$F\left(\sum_{i=1}^{n} x_i w_i^{l} + \sum_{j=1}^{m} y_j w_j^{g} + \theta\right) = F\left(\sum x_i(-\omega) + \sum y_i(\omega) + \left(\sum a_i - \sum b_j\right)\omega\right)$$

$$= F\left(\omega\left(\left(\sum a_i - \sum x_i\right) + \left(\sum y_j - \sum b_j\right)\right)\right)$$

$$= F(+ve\ value) > 0.5$$

Hence, the output unit is activated.

Case B: Assume that all antecedents of the rule are not satisfied and show that the unit encoding the consequent is inactive.
When all antecedents are false, it means that all the inputs do not satisfy their respective inequality conditions.
This implies: $x_i > a_i$, i = 1...n $\quad y_j < b_j$, j = 1...m

$$\forall_i (x_i > a_i) \text{ implies } \sum_{i=1}^{n} x_i > \sum_{i=1}^{n} a_i \quad \text{i.e.} \sum_{i=1}^{n} a_i - \sum_{i=1}^{n} x_i < 0 \tag{5}$$

$$\forall_j (y_j < b_j) \text{ implies } \sum_{j=1}^{m} y_j < \sum_{j=1}^{m} b_j \quad \text{i.e.} \sum_{j=1}^{m} y_j - \sum_{j=1}^{m} b_j < 0 \tag{6}$$

Hence, the activation function is as follows:

$$F\left(\sum_{i=1}^{n} x_i w_i^{\,l} + \sum_{j=1}^{m} y_j w_j^{\,g} + \theta\right)$$

$$= F\left(\sum x_i(-\omega) + \sum y_j(\omega) + \left(\sum a_i - \sum b_j\right)\omega\right)$$

$$= F\left(\omega\left(\left(\sum a_i - \sum x_i\right) + \left(\sum y_j - \sum b_j\right)\right)\right)$$

$$= F(\text{-ve value}) < 0.5$$

Hence, the output unit is deactivated.

Case C: Assume that the consequent of the rule is inactive, then the activation function is

$$F\left(\omega\left(\left(\sum a_i - \sum x_i\right) + \left(\sum y_j - \sum b_j\right)\right)\right) < 0.5$$

This implies that $\left(\omega\left(\left(\sum a_i - \sum x_i\right) + \left(\sum y_j - \sum b_j\right)\right)\right) < 0$

i.e. $(\sum_{i=1}^{n} a_i - \sum_{i=1}^{n} x_i) + (\sum_{j=1}^{m} y_j - \sum_{j=1}^{m} b_j) < 0$ since $\omega > 0$

Hence, at least one of the antecedents is not satisfied.
Case C of theorem 1 shows that by defining the threshold function as in (2), it eliminates the occurrence of false negative errors (type 1 errors). However, the function is unable to eliminate false positive errors (type II errors). Despite this fact, the threshold function performed creditably in our experiments and proved empirically to be somewhat powerful in translating the inequality rules into the neural network for training. Even though the rules translated are very rough rules, the network manages to learn and classify the output very accurately.

Theorem 2. Mapping disjunctive rules of the form "if $\vee_i X_i \geq 0.5$ then C" into a neural network using:

(i) $w_i = \omega > 0$ for $i = 1, 2, \ldots n$ (7)

(ii) $\theta = -\frac{\omega}{2}$ (8)

creates a network that accurately encodes the disjunctive rules.

Proof. This theorem is proved by showing that these mappings are correct in the following two situations:

(A) The unit encoding the consequent of the rule is active when at least one of the antecedents is satisfied.

(B) When the unit encoding the consequent of the rule is inactive, then none of the antecedents is satisfied.

Case A: Assume that at least one of the antecedents is satisfied and show that the unit encoding the consequent of the rule is active.

Let x_i be the input value of an antecedent, $i = 1....n$.

Let w_i be the weight associated with x_i.

The minimum activation value, to be considered as active is 0.5. Assume at least one of the antecedents x_p is active.

Given $x_i \geq 0$, $i = 1,2,...(p\text{-}1),(p+1),.......,n$ and , assume $x_p \geq 0.5$

Then $\sum_{i=1}^{n} x_i \geq 0.5$.

This implies $\sum_{i=1}^{n} x_i w_i - \frac{\omega}{2} = \sum_{i=1}^{n} x_i \omega - \frac{\omega}{2} > 0$

Therefore, $F\left(\sum_{i=1}^{n} x_i \omega - \frac{\omega}{2}\right) = F(+ve\ value) > 0.5$

Hence, the unit will be activated.

Case B: Assume that the unit encoding the consequent of the rule is inactive and show that none of the antecedents is active.

$$F\left(\sum_{i=1}^{n} x_i w_i + \theta\right) < 0.5$$

$$\sum_{i=1}^{n} x_i \omega - \frac{\omega}{2} < 0$$

$$\omega\left(\sum_{i=1}^{n} x_i - \frac{1}{2}\right) < 0$$

$$\sum_{i=1}^{n} x_i < 0.5$$

Thus, $\forall i$, $x_i < 0.5 \Rightarrow$ none of the antecedents is active.

3.2 Translating conjunctive rules

The weight and threshold values depend on the inequality ("$\leq$" or "$\geq$") of the antecedent to be inserted. For rules with "$\leq$" inequality, the weight ω is assigned a negative value (e.g. -4) and the threshold θ is equal to $\sum$ +(RHS constant of inequality) ω. As for rules with "$\geq$" inequality, it works the opposite way, the weight ω is given positive value (e.g. 4) while threshold value θ is set as $\sum$ –(RHS constant of inequality) ω. Figure 3 illustrates how conjunctive and disjunctive rules are translated into ANNs.

3.3 Translating disjunctive rules

Disjunctive rules are translated into a neural network by setting weights on the link corresponding to a disjunctive antecedent to ω. The threshold of the unit encoding the consequent is set to be $-\frac{\omega}{2}$. Figure 2 illustrates an example of the translation of the rules.

Figure 2. Conjunctive Rules Disjunctive Rules

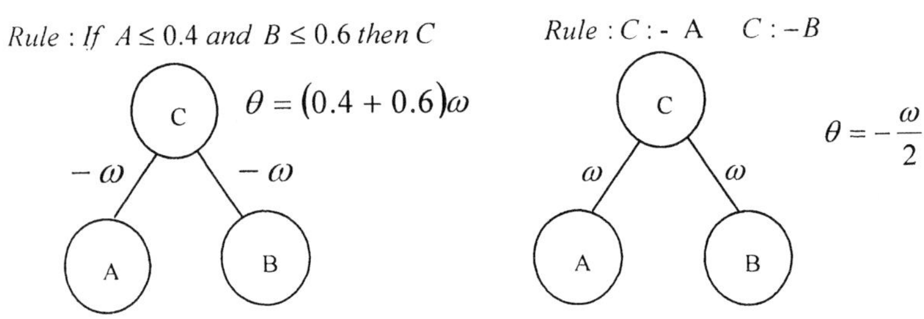

This is a reasonable strategy as the output is activated whenever one of the antecedents is true. After the rules are translated into the neural networks, the next step would be to refine the RealKBNN-net so that they are capable of predicting the unseen examples. Generally, learning in artificial neural networks means the process of modifying connection weights in order to achieve correct inference behavior [4]. In RealKBNN we use a generalized back-propagation algorithm as the learning algorithm.

4. PERFORMANCE OF REALKBNN

The performance of RealKBNN was evaluated using three groups of experiments operating on different datasets. The first experiment was conducted on the Wisconsin Breast Cancer Data (WBCD) set obtained from the UCI Repository [5]. The second test was run on an artificial dataset while the third experiment was run on the Iris data [3] and a Diabetes data set [8] obtained from the UCI Repository.

All the experiments were conducted using the hold-out method [1]. In short, the data is divided into two sets. One set whose elements were randomly selected, is used for training the classifier while the other set is reserved for testing the generalization capability of the trained classifier. Only 10% of the data is used as the training data while the other 90% were used for testing. This proportion was chosen to investigate how well RealKBNN can perform with scarce data

4.1 Wisconsin Breast Cancer Data

Table 1. Performance of RealKBNN on WBCD

Method	Accuracy	Training Cycle	MSE
RealKBNN	96.2%	7	0.083
KBANN	27.1%	7	0.670
SordoKBANN	35.3%	6	0.668
ANN	90.5%	158	0.093

The first experiment was conducted to evaluate RealKBNN's performance against 3 other methods, namely, KBANN, Sordo's KBANN (SordoKBANN) and the conventional ANN. The results showed that RealKBNN performed much better compared to the other three methods. KBANN was very inefficient in dealing with real-valued data showing only 27.1% compared to 96.2% average accuracy of RealKBNN. A small improvement was seen in Sordo's KBANN technique. It only improved the KBANN's performance by a mere 8%. The conventional ANN performed relatively well (90.5% average accuracy), but it was much more computationally expensive as it required 158 training cycles to converge while RealKBNN only needed 7 training cycles.

4.2 Artificial Data

Table 2. Performance on Artificial Data

Noise Level (%)	Accuracy	Training Cycle	MSE
0%	100%	6	0.01
10%	100%	6	0.098
20%	100%	6	0.201
30%	99.6%	6	0.289
40%	95.4%	6	0.417
50%	90.9%	6	0.5

The second experiment was conducted on an artificial dataser, which was generated to test the generalizability of RealKBNN. Table 2 presents the results of the experiment at different noise levels. The results showed that RealKBNN is a consistent and reliable system as it could learn from mistakes that were present in the training data. At the 30% noise level, RealKBNN can still learn perfectly and shows 100%

accuracy. Two other experiments were conducted on real-world classification problems, the Iris database and a Diabetes data set; both obtained from UCI repository. The objective of the experiments was to conduct a comparison of RealKBNN with other techniques available in the literature. For the Iris Data, RealKBNN performed credibly with an average accuracy of 96.3% when compared to the other methods. On the Diabetes Data, RealKBNN out performed all the other techniques achieving an average accuracy of 76.6%.

5. CONCLUSION

Overall, RealKBNN has dealt with real-valued data very successfully and is also a robust technique in dealing with noise levels present in data. Moreover, RealKBNN performed consistently in all experiments as many runs were conducted and the results produced were consistent with a low accuracy variance, error rates and training cycles. This observation is important especially when applied to real-world critical problems where system crashes or unpredictable response times or results cannot be tolerated.

REFERENCES

1. Anonymous (2004), "Lecture 13: Validation", Retrieved: September 24, 2004, from http://research.cs.tamu.edu/prism/lectures/iss/iss_l13.pdf.
2. Boz, O. (1995), "Knowledge Integration and Rule Extraction in Neural Networks", Ph.D Proposal, Lehigh University.
3. Fisher, R. A. (1936), "The use of multiple measurements in taxonomic problems", *Annual Eugenics*, vol. 7, Part II, pp. 179-188.
4. Fu, L-M. and Fu, L-C. (1990), "Mapping Rule-based Systems into Neural Architecture", *Knowledge-Based Systems.*, vol. 3, no. 1, pp.48-56.
5. Mertz, C. J. and Murphy, P. M. (2004), *UCI repository of machine learning databases*, Retrieved: July 25, 2004, from http://www.ics.uci.edu/pub/machine-learning-data-bases.
6. Sordo, M. (1999). "A Neurosymbolic Approach to the Classification of Scarce and Complex Data", Ph.D thesis, University of Sussex
7. Sordo, M., Buxton, H. and Watson, D. (2001) "A Hybrid Approach to Breast Cancer Diagnosis", In Wilde, D. and Jain (Eds), *Practical Applications of Computational Intelligence Techniques*, Kluwer.
8. Smith, J. W., Everhart, J. E., Dickson, W. C., Knowler, W. C. and Johannes, R. S. (1998), "Using the ADAP learning algorithm to forecast

the onset of diabetes mellitus", In *Proceedings of the Symposium on Computer Applications and Medical Care*, IEEE Computer Society Press, pp.261-265.

9. Towell, G. and Shavlik, J. W. (1994), "Knowledge-Based Artificial Neural Networks", *Artificial Intelligence*, vol. 70, no. 1-2, pp.119-165.

DESIGNING FUZZY LOGIC CONTROLLER FOR INVERTED PENDULUM

Haresh A. Suthar and Kaushal B. Pandya
Sardar Vallabhbhai Patel Institute of Technology, VASAD. Dist. Anand, Gujarat, India.

Abstract: In control system, if all the states of the system are measured, then by using state feedback control law we can control the system. As we know that value of feedback gain cannot be found easily, it requires trial and error method for suitable pole locations. In certain applications state variables cannot be measured because of cost considerations or lack of suitable transducers. In such cases, state variables that cannot be measured must be estimated from the ones that are measurable. A device, which estimates states, is known as 'observer' or 'state observer'. To design observer, person has to face mathematical complexities. Here without facing mathematical complexities control system can be controlled using Fuzzy Logic Approach.

1. INTRODUCTION

We have considered the problem of Inverted Pendulum, which is hinged to a moving cart; the main objective is to keep pendulum vertical and cart in its initial position irrespective of disturbances. Considering all the parameters involved in the problem the differential equations describing dynamics of the inverted pendulum and the cart are derived. System is simulated in MATLAB SIMULINK. Using Fuzzy Logic Toolbox in MATLAB system is controlled and satisfactory results are obtained.

2. PROBLEM OF INVERTED PENDULUM

The problem of stabilization of an inverted pendulum on a cart is considered.. The following Figure-1 Shows an Inverted pendulum with its pivot mounted on a cart. An external force drives the cart. The external force drives a pair of wheels of the cart. The force at a time t exerts a Torque T (t) on the wheels. The linear force applied to the cart is u (t); T (t)= R u (t) where, R is radius of the wheels.

The pendulum is unstable, but be kept upright by applying a proper control force u (t).

The dynamics of the inverted pendulum and the cart are described by the equations 1 & 2.

$$\ddot{\theta}(t)=\frac{ml(M+m)g}{\Delta}\theta(t)-\frac{ml}{\Delta}u(t) \qquad \ldots 1$$

$$\ddot{z}(t)=\frac{m^2l^2g}{\Delta}\theta(t)+\frac{(J+ml^2)}{\Delta}u(t) \qquad \ldots 2$$

Where,

Horizontal displacement of the pivot on the cart is z (t),

Rotational angle of the pendulum is θ (t).

The parameters of the system are as follows.

M= the mass of the cart,

L= length of the pendulum =2 x l,

m= the mass of pendulum and

J=the moment of inertia of pendulum with respect to center of gravity

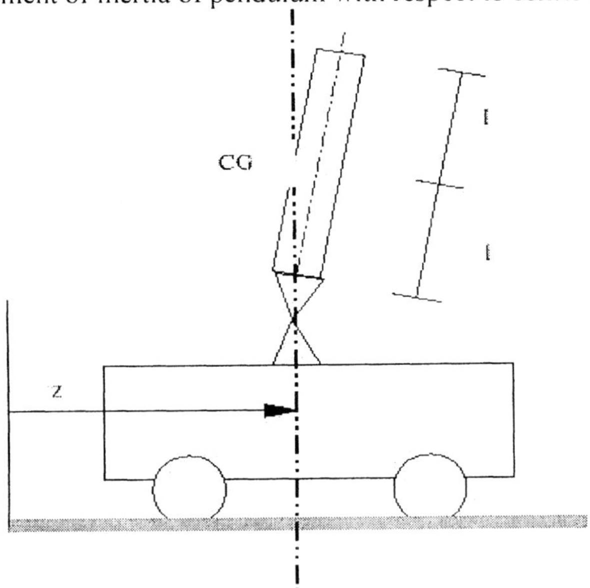

Figure-1: Inverted Pendulum System

Suppose that system parameters are M=1 kg, m = 0.15 kg , l = 1 m. Recall that g=9.81 m/sec^2.

$$J=\frac{1}{3}mL^2=\frac{4}{3}ml^2=0.2kg-m^2$$

$\ddot{\theta}(t) = 4.4537\ \theta(t) - 0.3947\ u(t)$ ...3

$\ddot{z}(t) = -0.5809\ \theta(t) + 0.9211\ u(t)$ ...4

Choosing the states $x_1 = \theta(t), x_2 = \dot{\theta}(t), x_3 = z(t), x_4 = \dot{z}(t)$. We obtain the following state model for the inverted pendulum on moving cart.

$\dot{X} = AX + Bu$ ...5

$$A = \begin{bmatrix} 0 & 1 & 0 & 0 \\ 4.4537 & 0 & 0 & 0 \\ 0 & 0 & 0 & 1 \\ -0.5809 & 0 & 0 & 0 \end{bmatrix} \qquad B = \begin{bmatrix} 0 \\ -0.3947 \\ 0 \\ 0.9211 \end{bmatrix}$$

The corresponding discrete state model of the above system is as under: $X(k+1) = AX(k) + Bu(k)$

where,

$$A = \begin{bmatrix} 1.0009 & 0.020006 & 0 & 0 \\ 0.0891 & 1.0009 & 0 & 0 \\ -0.0001162 & -7.746e-07 & 1 & 0.02 \\ -0.011621 & -0.0001162 & 0 & 1 \end{bmatrix} \qquad B = \begin{bmatrix} -7.8952e-005 \\ -0.0078963 \\ 0.00018422 \\ 0.018422 \end{bmatrix}$$

Move the cart from one location to another without causing pendulum to fall...

3. PROBLEM SOLUTION

As shown in Figure-2, when we apply disturbance signal to the system four state variables i.e. angle, rate of change of angle, distance traversed by the cart and velocity of the cart will be generated. At any instant k, the input to the system is u(k); and generated four state variables are $\theta(k), \dot{\theta}(k), z(k)$ and $\dot{z}(k)$. Two state variables $\theta(k)$ and $\dot{\theta}(k)$ are given to the fuzzy controller. Fuzzy controller generates next required velocity of the cart i.e. $\dot{\bar{z}}(k+1)$

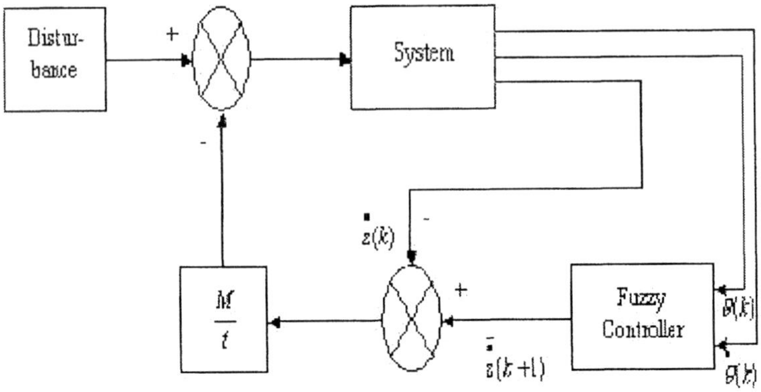

Figure 2 : Block Diagram

$\bar{\dot{z}}(k+1)$ can be obtained by applying proper force to the system i.e. $\bar{u}(k+1)$. Where,

$$\bar{u}(k+1) = M \times \bar{\ddot{z}}(k+1)$$

$$= M \times \left[\frac{\bar{\dot{z}}(k+1) - \dot{z}(k)}{t} \right]$$

t = time in which $\bar{\dot{z}}(k+1)$ is to be obtained.

Now it is required to design a Fuzzy Controller that can be done using FIS Editor in MATLAB.

4. DESIGN OF FUZZY CONTROLLER USING FIS EDITOR

As discussed in above block diagram, angle and rate of change of angle ($\theta(k) and \dot{\theta}(k)$) are the selected inputs of the Mamdani type of fuzzy controller and next required velocity of the cart ($\bar{\dot{z}}(k+1)$) is the output. Two input variables and one output variable along with their fuzzy levels and membership functions are as shown in the following Figure-3.

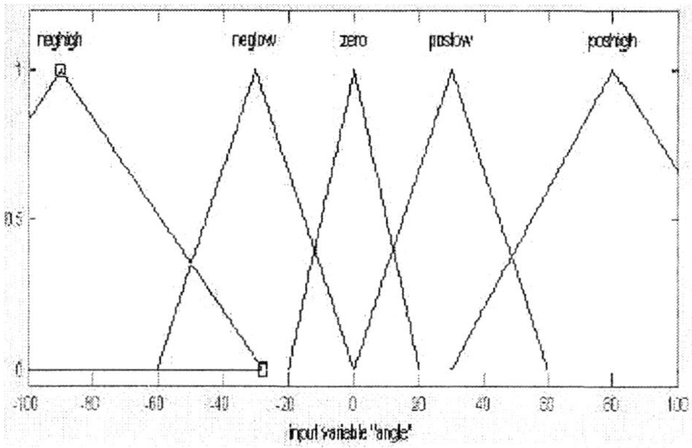

(a)

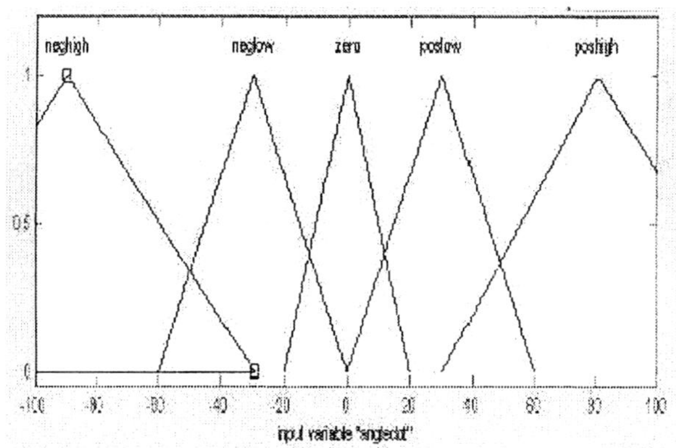

(b)

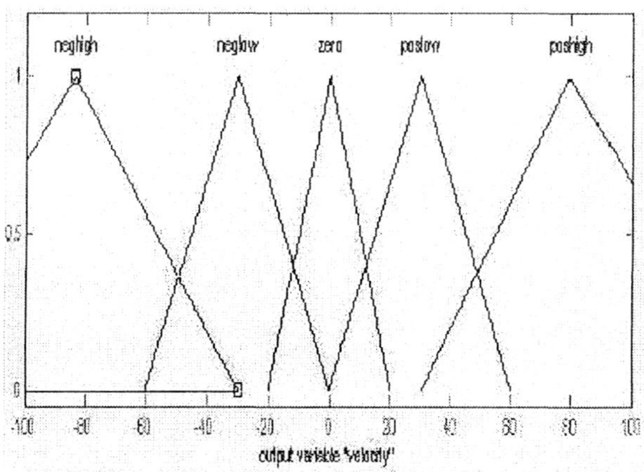

(c)

FIGURE-3: COMPLETE SET OF MEMBERSHIP FUNCTIONS WITH THEIR FUZZY LEVELS.

Depending upon the Fuzzy Levels selected for the inputs and output appropriate rules can be generated. Some of which are,

1) If *angle is zero* and *rate of change of angle is negative high* then next *required velocity is positive high.*
2) If *angle is positive* and *rate of change of angle is positive high* then next *required velocity is negative high.*

The Mamdani type Fuzzy Controller is designed in FIS Editor and then exported to workspace for simulation purpose. The system of inverted pendulum is simulated in MATLAB SIMULINK as shown in Figure-4. The Fuzzy Logic Controller of simulink uses the '.fis' file from the workspace.

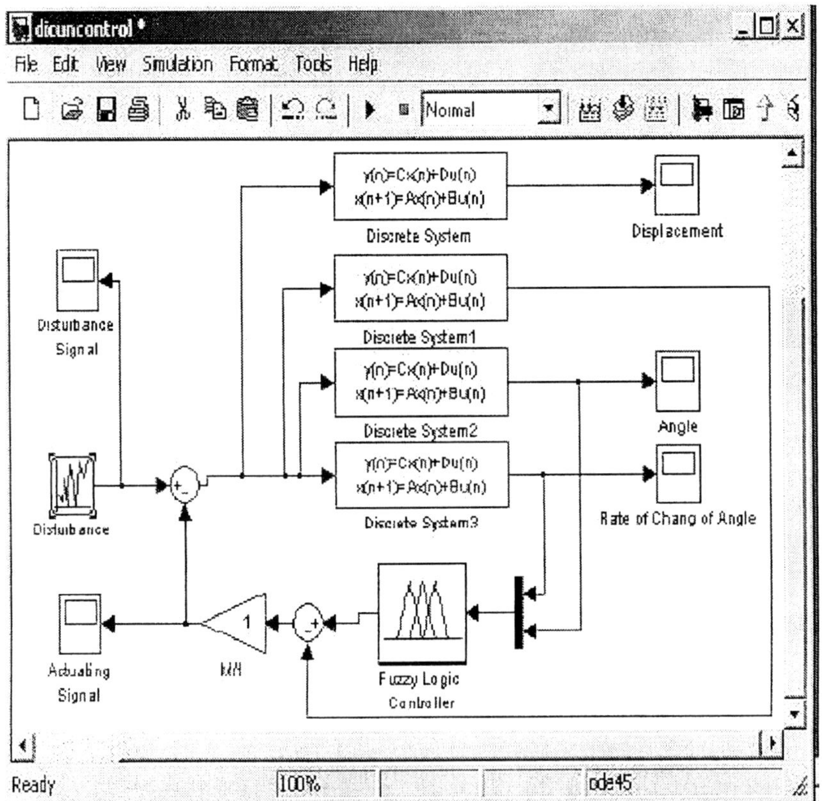

FIGURE-4: SIMULATION IN MATLAB

The simulation results along with disturbance input are taken which are as shown in following figures.

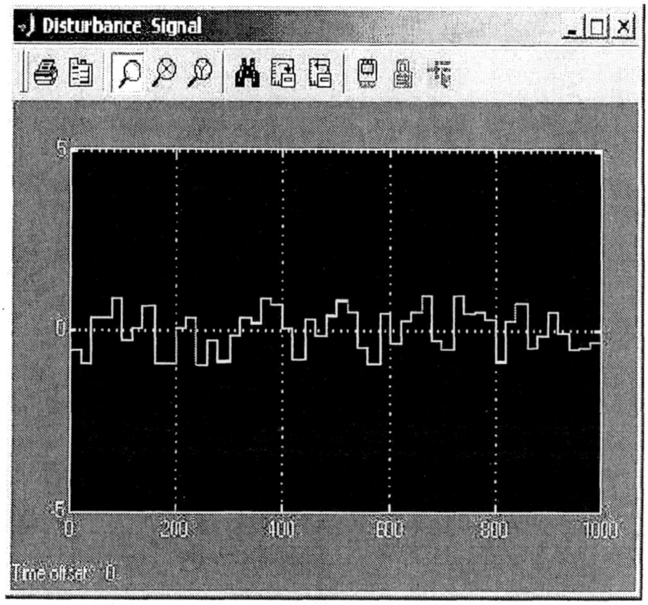
Disturbance Signal
5
0
-5
0
200
400
600
800
1000
Time offset: 0

(a)

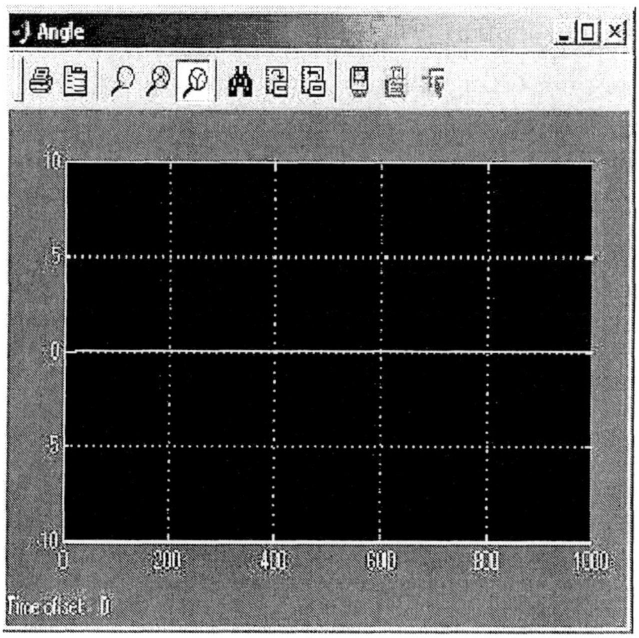
Angle
10
5
0
-5
-10
0
200
400
600
800
1000
Time offset: 0

(b)

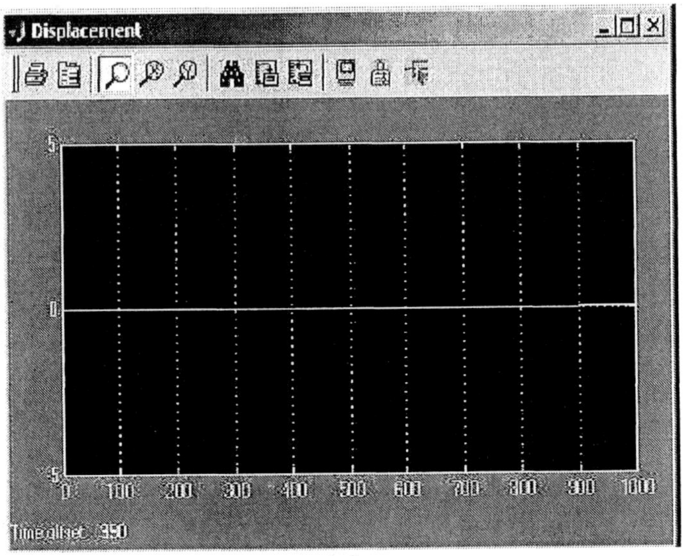

(c)
FIGURE-5: RESULTS

5. CONCLUSION

The next required velocity can be predicted from two inputs i.e. angle and rate of change of angle for that we have to design predictor. Predictor cannot be designed without facing mathematical complexities. Here, we tried to propose a non-mathematical approach to obtain next required velocity using fuzzy logic approach, which is used to obtain actuating signal to control the system. Problem of Inverted Pendulum is used as the test-bed to verify the effectiveness of the methodology and satisfactory results are obtained.

ACKNOWLEDGEMENT

The guidance and help of Prof. S. K. Shah (Faculty of Technology & Engineering, M.S.University of Baroda) is gratefully acknowledged.

REFERENCES

[1] Fuzzy Logic Toolbox of MATALAB 6.5.
[2] M.Gopal, E(1997). " Digital Control and State Variable Methods".
[3] Fene F. Franklin and J. David Powell. " Digital Control of Dynamic Systems.

LEARNING SEARCH PATTERN FOR CONSTRUCTION PROCUREMENT USING KEYWORD NET

Ren Jye Dzeng, Shyh Shiuh Wang

Department of Civil Engineering,National Chiao-Tung University, Taiwan

Abstract: As more and more procurement websites become available on the Internet, seeking information from websites has become an essential part of a contractor's procurement undertaking. Several e-markets, specifically for construction, have also been established, including bLiquid.com and ProcureZone. However, most websites provide only two primary ways of searching for information, namely by index/menu or by keyword. Instead of relying on the primitive search engines found in most procurement websites, a search guide system could help a user's keyword search by reducing the number of keywords required to find the desired information. Our research recognized that professional procurement experience helped users more effectively carry out website information searches, by using fewer keywords. We planned to capture such experience in order to guide inexperienced users in their search. The research goal was to improve search effectiveness by guiding the user's search using three approaches; namely correction, specification and extension. Based on these three approaches, this research applied the following guides: correction; specification-by-equivalence; specification-by-detail; extension-by-time; extension-by-location; extension-by-team; and extension-by-component. The paper will describe how we classified users for learning credibility, and the learning framework for recording expert users' search patterns. Twelve professionals, using 14 procurement packages, with 64 items in total, evaluated the proposed framework. It will be demonstrated that the proposed learning keyword guide facilitated a dynamic, customized menu and indexing system, and reduced the number of keywords required for the professionals to find the information they desired.

Key words: Construction procurement, information search, machine learning, e-commerce, knowledge acquisition

1. INTRODUCTION

Traditional contractors frequently maintain and send RFQs only to a few qualified suppliers for each type of procurement item by fax or telephone. Since the proliferation of the Internet in the second half of the 1990s, almost all electronic project document management systems have migrated to using the general Internet as their physical network, project-specific Web servers as their storage media and Web browsers as the main platform for buyer interfaces [1]. Several e-markets specifically for construction have also been established, including AEC Info [2], BuildPoint [3], bLiquid.com [4], Citadon, Inc. [5]. The proliferation of Web-based project management platforms and e-markets has given contractors more business opportunities and a wider selection of suppliers, but has also challenged contractors in managing the flood of electronic information.

Commercial construction procurement websites have aimed to provide all relevant procurement information on a single website to attract buyers with one-stop shopping. However, most websites provide only two primary ways of seeking information - by index/menu and by keyword. Most users who are unfamiliar with the content or indexing scheme of a website prefer keyword search. Keyword search may also be more efficient when too many indexes exist, the website hosts a large body of information, or a buyer does not know the specific procurement terms used by the website. Nevertheless, most buyers may have to use a trial-and-error process of inputting keywords to narrow down the search results to the desired information, even though they are professionally experienced.

General-purpose websites, such as portals like AltaVista [6] or Google [7] also offer information indexing and keyword search functionality. However, these sites deal with general-purpose Web pages, with unstructured data instead of domain-specific, structured data as found in the procurement websites, and perform a full-text search based on input keywords. They sort search results based on a pre-specified algorithm, and do not enable buyers to choose how to sort the results.

A construction procurement website must host various structured procurement information and also unstructured data like that found on general-purpose websites, to become a one-stop website that enables buyers to complete a procurement task. Hence, a predetermined indexing system is typically impractical. Also, each type of procurement item may require different specification fields, so establishing a generic data table and covering all items is difficult. The usefulness of applying several predetermined multiple fields becomes limited when on-line suppliers offer various construction items.

Until now, researchers have been developing intelligent guides and agents to help buyers navigate Web pages or find information concerning consumer-product e-marketplaces. However, even for the best knowledge of the authors, no intelligent guide has been developed specifically for the construction procurement website domain. Thus, this work presents an innovative guide system that captures the domain-specific keyword search patterns of expert buyers via a learning framework. When an inexperienced buyer inputs a search keyword, the guide may replace the keyword with correct or more specific ones, or add keywords that target related procurement items. An evaluation that involves 12 professionals and 64 procurement items demonstrates that the proposed guide system enables a dynamic, customized menu/index and reduces the number of keywords required by the professionals to find desired information in conventional websites that have no guide.

2. INFORMATION SETS

A search process generally comprises a series of search sessions. In each session, the buyer inputs a series of keywords to locate the information of interest, termed the target information set (I_{target}). The search result expected by the buyer when he inputs a keyword is termed the anticipated information set ($I_{anticipated}$). I_{target} differs from $I_{anticipated}$ because the buyer lacks confidence in controlling the search; this difference is governed primarily by the buyer's familiarity with the website. After a keyword is entered, the actual search result of the website is termed the result information set (I_{result}). $I_{anticipated}$ differs from I_{result} because the search is not executed as the buyer expects; this difference is influenced mainly by the design of the website. I_{result} differs from I_{target} when the search engine's interpretation of the input keyword differs from that of the buyer; this difference thus depends mainly on the buyer's experience of procurement, assuming that the website is professionally designed. Figure 1 presents the difference among information sets.

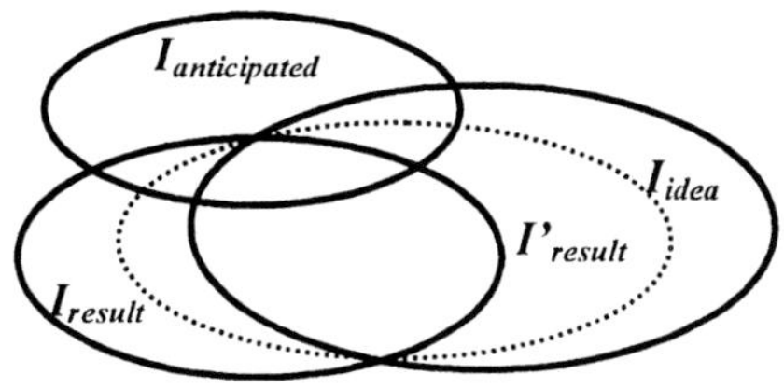

Figure 1 procurement in an open e-market

The following search scenario illustrates the information sets. A buyer wants to find suppliers of H-type steel and enters the search keyword, "H steel" on a procurement website. The search outcome includes all H-type steel suppliers' nationwide and other information on "H steel", including work specifications for H-type steel. In fact, the buyer is looking only for H-type steel manufacturers in the northern area. Therefore, the buyer must perform the search again by entering a specific keyword "H steel *State-A*" as *State-A* is the state of interest in the northern area. Browsing the URL (Unified Resource Locator) references of the search results, the buyer finally finds the suppliers of H-type steel with dimensions 400x400, 13mm and 21mm.

This scenario describes a search session that includes the process of inputting two keywords. I_{target} is "the list of suppliers in the northern area that sell H-type steel". $I_{anticipated}$ is "the list of suppliers of H-type steel" when the first keyword was entered, and "the list of suppliers in *State-A* that sell H-type steel" when the second keyword was entered. I_{result} includes all H-type steel suppliers nationwide along with work specifications, codes, buyer calls and news about H-type steel. I_{idea} is "the list of suppliers in the northern area that sell 400x400-13mm-21mm H steel".

The search effectiveness refers to the hit rate, the proportion of URL references in the search result that provide the target information. The search efficiency refers to the number of keywords that must be input to yield a satisfactory search result. This work focuses on improving search efficiency.

3. KEYWORD NET

The proposed guide system is based on a learning model that builds search guide knowledge by learning from the search patterns of expert buyers. Figure 2 illustrates a typical search for completing specifications for some procurement packages. The buyer inputs a keyword, K_{11}, to find information about a procurement item. The result shows no URL reference, and the buyer then realizes that he has just misspelled a word. He corrects the mistake by inputting another keyword, K_{12}. However, the result now contains too many URL references, so the buyer performs the search again by inputting a more specific keyword, K_{13}, and thus obtains satisfactory references. He inputs another keyword, K_{21} to find another item in the same procurement package. He repeats the process until he inputs keyword K_{24} and finds satisfactory references. The information found so far enables the buyer to complete the procurement documents for the first package. The buyer may still continue the search, starting with keyword K'_{11}, to complete specifications for other packages.

The processes from K_{11} to K_{13} and from K_{21} to K_{24} are two search sessions, each of which seeks information pertaining to an item. The process from K_{11} to K_{24} represents a series of keywords input to complete a procurement package. Such a process is called a learning session because the keywords in this session are related, and their relationships can be learned to support the corresponding proposed guides with appropriate annotation by expert users. Figure 3 presents a net example that connects related keywords using directed links, including *correction*, *equivalence*, *detail*, *time*, *location*, *team* and *component*.

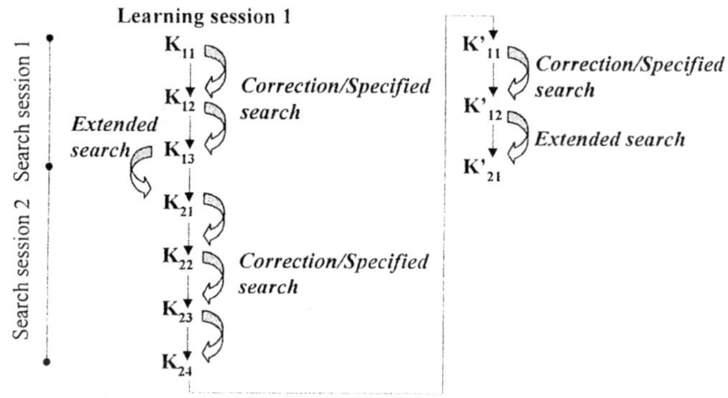

Figure 2 Search session and learning session

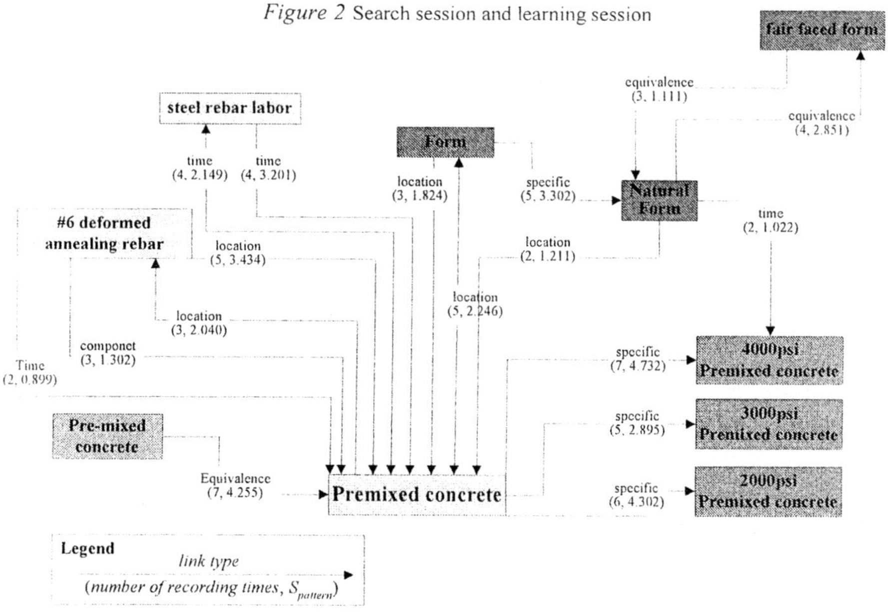

Figure 3 Example of keyword net

4. KEYWORD SEARCH PATTERN

In a learning session, an expert user annotates the relationship between two consecutive recorded keywords that have been input using the links. Each pair of linked keywords constitutes a keyword search pattern unit. Each unit includes a preceding keyword, a succeeding keyword, the type of link that connects two keywords and other log information, including the number of times that the pattern has been learned and the time since the last recording of the pattern.

Search patterns with the same pair of keywords may have a link recorded multiple times, multiple links of different types or bidirectional links of the same type. Appropriate ranking of suggested keywords, similar to the webpage ranking of Google [8], reduces the time the buyer needs to select one from them. The learned outbound links from a keyword point to keywords that the buyer might need in a subsequent search. The proposed guide system ranks suggested subsequent keywords by considering the number of links from the preceding keyword; the number of links to the succeeding keyword, the experience of the buyer who is annotating the link, and the number of times that the buyer has actually adopted the keyword suggested by the link. Suppose that a user adds a link between two keywords, K_1 and K_2. When the user inputs K_1 next time, the proposed guide uses Eq. (1) to calculate the rank of K_2.

$$\begin{aligned} & R\ (K_1, link, K_2, user, \Delta t) \\ & = w_1\left(S_{pattern}(K_1, link, K_2, user, \Delta t)\right) + w_2\left(S_{keyword}(link, K_2)\right) \\ & = w_1\left(p \sum_{(K_1, link, K_2)} (user) + q\left(1/\min \Delta t\right)\right) + w_2\left(\frac{Q_{link}(link, K_2)}{Q_{link}(link)}\right) \end{aligned} \tag{1}$$

$R(\ )$: rank of K_2 given K_1 as the initial input;
link: type of link that connects K_1 and K_2;
user: level of experience of the user (the default setting is 1 for expert user, 0.7 for experienced user, 0.4 for inexperienced user and 0.1 for novice user);
Δt: (the current date) – (the date when the link was recorded)
w_1, w_2: weights determined by the system user, $w_1 + w_2 = 1$, $0 \le w_1, w_2 \le 1$;
$S_{pattern}()$: strength of the pattern (K_1, *link*, K_2);
$S_{keyword}()$:strength of K_2 from the perspective of *link*;
p, q: weights determined by the system user, $p + q = 1$, $0 \le p, q \le 1$;
$Q_{link}(link, K_2)$: number of links of the *link* type to K_2;
$Q_{link}(link)$: total number of links of the *link* type in the keyword net;

Equation (1) comprises two parts - $S_{pattern}$ and $S_{keyword}$. $S_{pattern}$ concerns the importance of the pattern and the time since the pattern was learnt.

Table 1 shows the calculation of $S_{pattern}$ for pattern ("premixed concrete", *location*, "#6 deformed rebar"). The pattern comprises three *location* links, indicated by Fig. 3 and detailed by Links 1, 2, and 3 in the table. The most recent link was recorded by an expert user two days ago, and the oldest link was recorded by an expert user six days ago. Assuming $p = 0.7$ and $q = 0.3$, $S_{pattern}$ is 2.040 for "#6 deformed rebar". Table 1 also shows that $S_{pattern}$ for pattern ("premixed concrete", *location*, "form") is 2.246.

$S_{keyword}$ measures the importance of the succeeding keyword K_2 from the perspective of the link of interest. More links of the type to a keyword indicate a higher probability that the keyword is the next one to be needed by the user. The net in Fig. 3 comprises 18 (= 3+5+3+5+2) *location* links, of which three enter "#6 deformed annealing rebar" and five enter "form". Thus, "form" ($S_{keyword}$ = 5/18) is more likely than "#6 deformed annealing rebar" ($S_{keyword}$ = 3/18) to be the next *location*-related keyword required by the user.

Table 1. Spattern calculation for patterns

	"premixed concrete" location "#6 deformed rebar"			"premixed concrete" location "form"				
Link #	1	2	3	1	2	3	4	5
user	1	0.7	1	1	0.7	0.7	1	1
Δt	2	5	6	1	3	4	6	6
p×∑user	1.89			3.08				
q×(1/minΔt)	0.15			0.3				
Spattern	2.04			2.246				

Assuming w_1= 0.7 and w_2 = 0.3, R is 2.04×0.7+(3/18)×0.3=1.478 for "#6 deformed rebar" and 2.246×0.7+(5/18)×0.3=1.656 for "form". Hence, "form" is ranked higher than "#6 deformed rebar" in the list of suggested location-related keywords with respect to "premixed concrete".

5. SYSTEM IMPLEMENTATION AND EVALUATION

The system is implemented on the Microsoft Windows 2000 Server platform with Internet Information Server v5.0, using PHP [9] and MySQL [10]. The system database consists of three categories of procurement-related data, including suppliers, supply catalogs and specifications.

The evaluation described herein focuses on the potential reduction in the number of input keywords. The experiment conducted involved monitoring 12 procurement engineers as they performed procurement tasks for a US$

9,000,000 project to construct a school building, which involved 14 procurement packages (such as soil preparation and excavation) and a total of 64 procurement items (such as an excavator, unskilled laborers, Type IV Portland cement). Descriptions of the procurement items given to the participants were taken directly from the actual contract. The participants' procurement experience ranged from one to 11 years, and web search experience ranged from under one to seven years.

A pretest was performed to divide the project into two "equivalent" subprojects, which both required approximately the same number of input keywords, to reduce the learning effect. Fifteen graduate students participated in the pretest; each was required, for each procurement item, to complete the procurement task that includes finishing item specifications and RFQs, as well as finding contact information of three prospective suppliers. The quantity takeoff for each procurement item was given. Each participant could find information from the system only by inputting search keywords and browsing the resulting URL references. The items were then divided into two groups, namely Group-1 and Group-2, according to the average number of input keywords used for each item. The difference between the average numbers of input keywords for the two groups was less than 1%. Therefore, the two groups of items were assumed to require the same amount of search work.

In the following experiment, the 12 participating engineers used the system to complete the procurement tasks for the items in Group-1 without a guide, and for those in Group-2 with the guide. Only 12 engineers could participate in this experiment because each procurement task took a long time. Thus, the result may lack conclusive statistical meaning due to the limited number of samples. Nevertheless, the following statistics help to explicate the extent of the efficiency improvement of the guided search.

Table 2. Average number of search keywords used with and without guide

Group-1 (without guide)									
Procurement package	Site preparation	Survey	Excavation	2500psi concrete	Brick laying	Rebar assembly			Total
procurement items	4	3	2	9	4	4			26
keywords $\bar{x}$	18.58	15.67	10	33.17	17.08	27.5			122
σ	2.84	4.39	3.38	7.2	2.75	5.71			
Group-2 (with guide)									
Procurement package	Pebble pavement	Backfill	3200psi concrete	Form-work	Floor tiling	painting	Water-proofing	Wall tiling	Total
procurement items	3	1	8	5	6	5	5	5	38
keywords $\bar{x}$	6.83	1.75	12	19.58	12	13	10.42	14.25	89.83
σ	1.95	0.97	3.15	2.16	1.1	1.09	1.56	1.45	

Table 2 lists the average numbers of search keywords with and without the guide for each work package of Group-1 and Group-2. The number of procurement items in a work package ranges from one to nine. On average, the total number of keywords used in the procurement task is 122 for Group-1 (without the guide), and 89.83 for Group-2 (with the guide); these values represent a reduction in the number of keywords of 32.17 and 26%.

Table 3 shows cross analyses of data based on the participants' experiences. For instance, the average number of keywords used to complete the procurement task without the guide is 101.67 for the half of the participants with the most professional procurement experience, measured in years, and 142.33 for those who have less experience. With the guide, the average number of keywords used by more experienced participants is 75.67 and the number used by less experienced participants is 104.00. Thus, the guide reduces the number of keywords used by more experienced participants by 26 (26%), and by less experienced participants by 38.33 (27%).

Table 3. Comparison of reductions in numbers of keywords used by two groups of participants

		Group			
		More procurement-experienced	Less procurement-experienced	More Web-search-experienced	Less Web-search-experienced
Number of	No guide	101.67	142.33	121.67	122.23
keywords	With guide	75.67	104	88	91.67
Saving	# of keywords	26	38.33	33.67	30.67
	%	26%	27%	28%	25%

The findings in Tables 2 and 3 can be summarized as follows. First, procurement experience considerably reduced the number of keywords used in the search, but web-search experience did not. Engineers with more procurement experience used fewer keywords to complete the task without the guide than did less experienced engineers (101.67 vs. 142.33); but the number of keywords used by engineers with more experience of web-searches was approximately that used by those with less experience of web-searches (121.67 vs. 122.23).

Second, the guide reduced the number of input keywords by about 26%. The reduction was greater for engineers with less experience of procurement than those with more experience (38.33 vs. 26.00) because less experienced engineers used more input keywords originally; however, the difference between the percentage reductions was insignificant.

6. CONCLUSIONS

This work developed a guide system that suggests possible subsequent keywords based on a keyword initially input by a user. A subsequent keyword is predicted according to a learning net that connects the recorded keywords using links, which are annotated by expert users during their search. The system offers seven guides - *correction*, *specification-by-equivalence*, *specification-by-detail*, *extension-by-time*, *extension-by-location*, *extension-by-team* and *extension-by-component*. The order of the suggested keywords is calculated by considering the number of links from the input keyword; the number of links to the subsequent keyword that is being considered, the experience level of the user who annotates the link, and the number of times that the user has actually adopts the keyword that was suggested based on the link.

The evaluation experiment demonstrated that users with more procurement experience required fewer input keywords than those with less experience. The number of input keywords is independent of the users' experience of web-searches. The guide system reduced the number of keywords input without the guide by 26%.

ACKNOWLEDGEMENT

The authors would like to thank the National Science Council of Republic of China, for financially supporting this work under Contract No. NSC-92-2211-E009-064.

REFERENCES

1. B.C. Björk, "Electronic document management in construction- research issues and results," Electronic Journal of IT in Construction, vol. 8, pp. 105-117, 2003.
2. AEC Info (2004). Available: www.visualibrary.com.
3. BuildPoint (2003). Available: www.buildpoint.com.
4. bLiquid.com (2003). Available: bliquid.com.
5. Citadon, Inc. (2004). Available: www.citadon.com.
6. AltaVista (2004). Available: www.altavista.com.
7. Google (2004). Available: www.google.com.
8. P. Craven (2004). Google's PageRank explained and how to make the most of it. Web Workshop: http://webworkshop.net/pagerank.html.
9. PHP (2003) PHP: Hypertext Preprocessor. [Online]. Available: http://www.php.net
10. MySQL (2003). Available: http://www.mysql.com.

STRATIFIED SAMPLING FOR ASSOCIATION RULES MINING

Yanrong Li and Raj P. Gopalan
Department of computing, Curtin University of Technology Kent st. Bentley, WA 6102, Australia

Abstract: It is well recognized that mining association rules in a very large database is usually time consuming due to the I/O overhead in scanning the disk resident database. As one of the techniques for reducing the I/O overhead, sampling for mining association rules has been actively investigated during the last few years. Each sampling method and algorithm proposed in the literature has its own merits and demerits in terms of effectiveness and efficiency and none of them can claim to be the best. Which sampling method to use and how big the sample size should be for a given database are key issues in sampling for particular data mining tasks. In this paper a transaction size based stratified sampling method has been proposed, tested and compared with the simple random sampling method for mining association rules. It opens up the questions of how to stratify the datasets so that it can better suit the problem of association rule mining.

Key words: stratified random sampling, association rules, effectiveness.

1. INTRODUCTION

Since the concept of association rules was first introduced in 1993 by Agrawal et al[1], many algorithms and techniques for mining association rules in a static large database has been proposed in the literature. However mining a very large database for association rules is usually time consuming and the I/O overhead in scanning the database plays an important role in it.

While many algorithms have been developed to reduce the number of database scans from as many as the size of the longest frequent itemsets in [2, 3] to as small as two in [4] and one in [5](see[6] for more details of the up-to-date association rules mining algorithms and their performance on typical datasets), sampling is another approach to reduce the I/O cost for processing very large databases. Random sampling of large databases for association rules was first proposed in [3] and was followed by more studies in [7-11].

Toivenon et al performed theoretical analyses of sampling large databases for association rules based on binomial distribution and Chernoff bound in [3, 7]. They sampled a database using simple random sampling with replacement and determined the sample size based on Chernoff bounds where the sample size is a function of the desired error bound and the confidence level. A sample was used to find frequent itemsets that probably hold in the entire database and the results were verified with the rest of the database. Zaki et al applied simple random sampling without replacement to some datasets and mined association rule by using only samples [8]. Since the sample size was empirically chosen as a certain percentage of the original database, which is independent of the error bound, and confidence level, it is difficult to quantify the quality of the results for a chosen sample size. A two-phase sampling based algorithm for association rules, FAST-trim, was presented in [9]. A large initial random sample is selected in Phase I to estimate the support of each distinct item in the database and these supports are used in phase II to trim out the outliers in the initial sample to form a small final sample based on the distance function,

$$\boldsymbol{Dist}(\boldsymbol{S}_0, \boldsymbol{S}) = \frac{|\boldsymbol{L}_1(\boldsymbol{S}) - \boldsymbol{L}_1(\boldsymbol{S}_0)| + |\boldsymbol{L}_1(\boldsymbol{S}_0) - \boldsymbol{L}_1(\boldsymbol{S})|}{|\boldsymbol{L}_1(\boldsymbol{S}_0)| + |\boldsymbol{L}_1(\boldsymbol{S})|}$$

where S and S_0 denote the original sample and the final sample, and $L_1(S)$ and $L_1(S_0)$ denote the sets of frequent 1-itemsets in S and S_0. However, the question of how to determine the initial sample size to ensure its subset, i.e. the small final sample, can effectively approximate the complete frequent itemsets in the original database remains. On the other hand, since the goal of the trimming algorithm is to minimize the Dist (S0, *S)*, the accuracy of the final sample is expected to be nearly the same as the original sample. Zhang et al [10] and Li et al[12] obtained the sufficient sample sizes based on binomial distribution and central limit theorem that were smaller than in [7] for a given error bound and confidence level. A database is sampled by random sampling without replacement in [10] and with replacement in [12].

To the best of our knowledge, the sampling methods used for mining association rules in the literature are simple random sampling either with replacement or without replacement. In this paper, we explore the feasibility of using stratified random sampling for association rules mining. Ideally, if a dataset can be partitioned into groups with distinct features appropriate for a particular data mining task, then proportionally sampling each group will give the exact result as with the whole dataset. In this work, a dataset is partitioned into strata according to the size of each transaction, and simple random sampling is applied to each stratum. The accuracy of the proposed stratified sampling method is compared with that using the simple random sampling method. The results open up the question of how to stratify a dataset for a particular data mining task.

The rest of this paper is organized as follows. Section 2 provides the definitions of association rules. The stratified random sampling method for association rules is presented in section 3 and the experimental evaluation of the sampling method is shown in section 4. Section 5 contains the conclusion and pointers for further work.

2. TERMS AND DEFINITIONS

Let $I = \{I_1, I_2, \ldots, I_m\}$ be a set of m distinct items. A transaction T is a non-empty subset of I. A database D is a set of N transactions. A set of items is called an itemset, and an itemset with k items is called a k-itemset. The support p of an itemset X in D, is the proportion of the transactions that contains X as subset. An itemset is called a *frequent itemset* if its support $p \geq p_t$, where p_t is the *minimum support* specified by users. Otherwise, the itemset is *not frequent*.

The *transaction size* is defined as the number of distinct items in the transaction, and its values lies in [1, m]. The *density* of a dataset is defined as the average transaction size of the dataset divided by the total number of distinct items in the dataset. The domain of density is [0, 1]. A dataset with longer average transaction size has higher density and vice versa.

3. SAMPLING LARGE DATASET FOR ASSOCAIATION RULES

In the context of sampling large databases for association rules, a transaction database D of size N is the population that we want to study, and a sample is a subset of D that consists of n transactions selected from the population D. The sample size selection and transaction size based stratified sampling method are described below.

3.1 Sample Size Selections

The size of a sample will affect both efficiency and the effectiveness of the sampling based algorithms. If we sample a transaction database with replacement, for a given error bound e and a given confidence level $1-\alpha$, the sufficient sample size for estimating an itemset's support is [12] :

$$n \geq \frac{z_{\alpha/2}^2 p(1-p)}{e^2} \tag{1}$$

where p is the support of the itemset in the population and $z_{\alpha/2}$ is the Z value above which the area under the standard normal curve is $\alpha/2$. Since $p(1\text{-}p)$ has the maximum value of 1/4 when $p = 1/2$, if we choose

$$n \geq \frac{z_{\alpha/2}^2}{4e^2} \tag{2}$$

then we can simultaneously estimate the support of each itemset in the dataset with confidence $1-\alpha$ that the error will not exceed e (see [12]for more details).

3.2 Transaction Size Based Stratified Random Sampling

In stratified random sampling, the population of size N is partitioned into strata and a sample is selected by simple random sampling within each stratum [13]. Given a total sample size n, if the strata differ in size, proportional allocation could be used to maintain a steady sampling fraction throughout the population [13]. If stratum k has N_k units, the sample size allocated to it would be

$$n_k = \frac{n}{N} N_k \tag{3}$$

The principle of stratification is to partition the population in such a way that the units within a stratum are as similar as possible. For example, in the survey of a human population, stratification may be based on the geographic region, sex or socio-economic factors. In this paper, we partition a dataset according to transaction sizes.

The difference between the size of the longest transactions and the shortest transactions in a stratum is called the width of the stratum, which is denoted as w. If we partition the data in such a way that each stratum has the same width, then the partition method is called *equal-width partition*, otherwise it is called *unequal-width partition.* In equal-width partition, there will be $\lceil L_{max}/w \rceil$ strata for a dataset whose longest transactions' size is L_{max}. Transactions with size s will be partitioned to kth stratum, where $k = \lceil s/w \rceil$. For example, when $w = 2$, transactions with size s = 1 and s = 2 will go to 1st stratum, transactions with size s = 3 and s = 4 will go to 2nd stratum, and so on.

Given a minimum support, an error bound e, a confidence level $1-\alpha$, and the desired width of a stratum w, the transaction size based stratified sampling algorithm proceed as follows:

1. Initialize a sample $S = \{\}$;
2. Calculate the sufficient sample size n using equation (2);
3. Partition the dataset into $\lceil L_{max}/w \rceil$ strata based on the size of transaction;
4. Calculate sample size for each stratum using equation (3), sample the stratum by simple random sampling without replacement and add to S;
5. Run a standard association rules mining algorithm on S.

4. EFFECTIVENESS OF STRATIFIED SAMPLING

4.1 Measurement of Accuracy and Errors

The complete frequent itemsets discovered from the original database and its sample are denoted as $L(D)$ and $L(S)$, *respectively*. If an itemset exists in $L(S)$ but not in $L(D)$ then we call the itemset a *false positive.* If an itemset exists in $L(D)$ but not in $L(S)$, then we call this itemset a *false negative.* Therefore the number of false positives is $|L(S) - L(D)|$ and the number of false negatives is $|L(D) - L(S)|$. We use the same measure as in [9] to obtain the accuracy of sampling:

$$\boldsymbol{accuracy} = 1 - \frac{|\boldsymbol{L(D)} - \boldsymbol{L(S)}| + |\boldsymbol{L(S)} - \boldsymbol{L(D)}|}{|\boldsymbol{L(D)}| + |\boldsymbol{L(S)}|} \tag{4}$$

This measurement is sensitive to both false positives and false negatives. We also use the following two measurements to quantify the errors of sampling:

$$fp = |L(S) - L(D)| / |L(S)| \tag{5}$$

which represents the proportion of the false frequent itemsets in a sample, and

$$fn = |\, L(D) - L(S) \,| \,/\, |\, L(D) \,| \qquad (6)$$

which represents the proportion of the frequent itemsets in the original dataset that is missing in a sample.

4.2 Datasets Studied

We perform experiments on three datasets that are available at FIMI'03 (Frequent Itemsets Mining Implementations Repository)[14]. They are: (1) BMSPOS dataset, provided by Blue Martin Software, (2) Retail dataset, donated by Tom Brijs, which contains the (anonymized) retail market basket data from an anonymous Belgian retail store, and (3) Accidents dataset, donated by Karolien Geurts and contains (anonymized) traffic accident data. The density of the Accidents dataset is relatively higher than for the other two. The characteristics of these datasets are summarized in table 1, where N is the number of transactions in a database, T is the average transaction length, $|R|$ is the number of distinct items in the database and L_{max} is the size of the longest transactions. The histogram for each dataset is shown in Figure 1. To save space, transactions with size > 20 in BMSPOS and transactions with size > 27 in Retail, which only count for less than 5% of transactions, are not shown.

Table 1. Summaries of characteristics of datasets

Dataset Name	N	$\|R\|$	T	L_{max}	*Density(%)*
BMSPOS	515596	1657	7.5	164	0.45
Retail	88162	16570	13	76	0.08
Accidents	340184	468	34	51	7.26

4.3 Experimental Results

In this section we show the experimental results of the proposed stratified sampling method and compare its accuracy with the simple random sampling method in [12]. The sample size chosen is 16513, which corresponds to error bound of 0.01 and confidence level of 99%.

As mentioned before, a dataset is partitioned based on the transactions sizes. Given a w value, the dataset is partition into $k = \lceil L_{max} / w \rceil$ strata. The width of each stratum in the resulting strata is w except that the width of kth stratum may be less than w. Each stratum is sampled according to equation (2). The accuracy and errors of the proposed stratified sampling method were compared with that of the simple random sampling method. Figures 2-4 show some of the testing results on different datasets for different minimum support levels and different widths of stratum. In each figure, SR represents the result of simple random sampling.

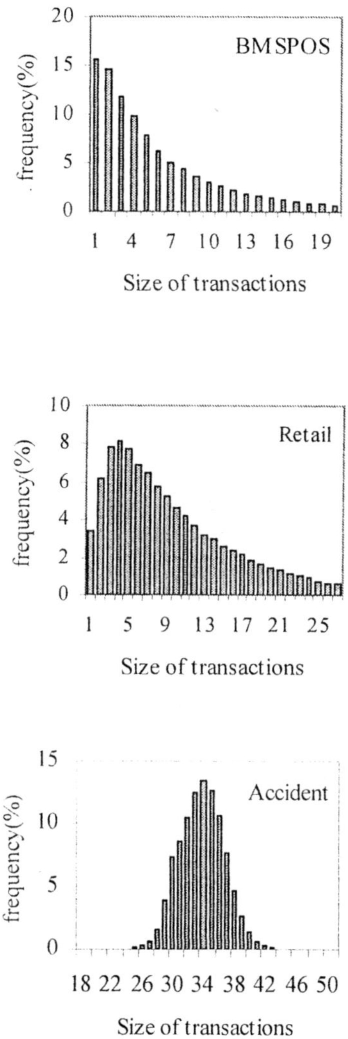

Figure 1. Histogram of transactions

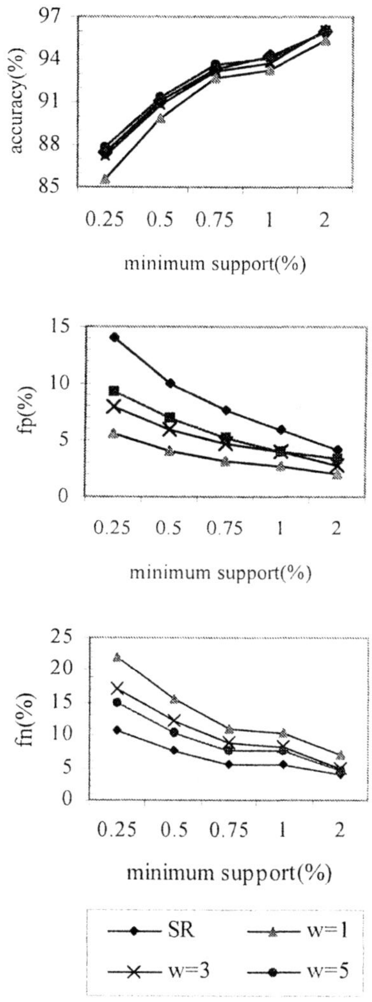

Figure 2. Testing results for BMSPOS

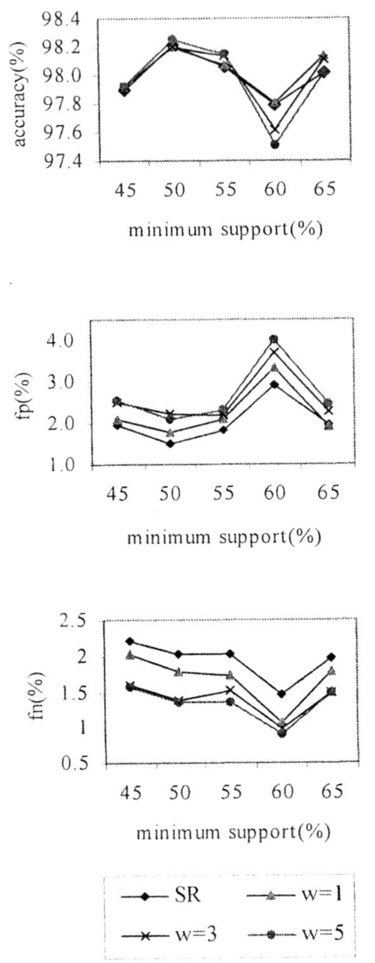

Figure 3. Testing results for Accidents

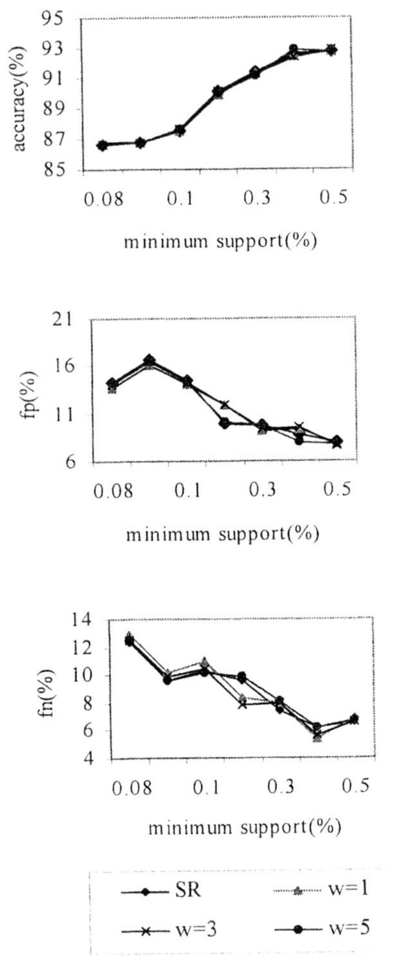

Figure 4. Testing results for Retail

For BMSPOS (Fig. 2), the accuracy of stratified sampling method increases while w increases. When $w = 5$, the accuracy of stratified sampling is slightly higher than that of simple random sampling. When we inspect the errors closely, we can see that *fp* increases as w increases and the *fn* decreases when w increases. The *fp* of stratified sampling is lower than that of simple random sampling and the *fn* of stratified sampling is higher than that of simple random sampling for all w values.

For the Accidents dataset (Fig. 3), the accuracy is very high since it is a relatively dense dataset and many transactions have the similar items. The accuracy does not vary too much while *w* changes (less than 1% for all minimum support levels). The trends of changes of *fn* and *fp* while w changes are the same as that for BMSPOS. In contrast to the results for BMSPOS, the *fp* of stratified sampling for Accidents is higher than that of simple random sampling while *fn* of stratified sampling is lower.

For Retail (Fig. 4), the accuracy and the errors (*fp* and *fn*) of stratified sampling method are almost the same as for the simple random sampling method at different *w* values. The values of *fp* and *fn* are not too different for most of the minimum support levels except 0.2%. It is noticed that sampling ratio of Retail is high, about 6 times higher than that of BMSPOS. much higher that of

We want to point out that transaction size based stratified sampling method will not be any different from the simple random sampling method for the dense datasets like Connect-4 that is also used for comparing algorithms at FIMI'03. In Connect-4, all the transactions have the same transaction size, and the proposed stratified sampling method will give exactly the same result as simple random sampling since all the transactions will be partitioned to a single stratum.

5. CONCLUSIONS AND DISCUSSIONS

Just as with other sampling methods, the proposed transaction size based stratified sampling may not suit all applications. The choice of a sampling method should depend on the characteristics of the dataset to be mined and the cost of errors in a given application. For a dataset like BMSPOS, if lower *fp* is desirable, the proposed stratified sampling will be a better choice than simple random sampling. Similarly, for applications where the lower *fn* is crucial, stratified sampling will perform better than the simple random sampling for dataset like Accidents. For some datasets such as Retail, both simple random sampling and stratified sampling are suitable. The open question for stratified sampling is how to partition the dataset so that each stratum has similar properties in relation to the association rules mining problem. We consider that the accuracy of stratified sampling may be improved if the stratification scheme is based on the similarity of transactions, i.e., the number of common items between transactions. We will continue our work to find better stratification schemes to improve the accuracy of stratified sampling.

REFERENCES

[1] R. Agrawal, T. Imielinski, and A. Swami, "Mining association rules between sets of items in large databases," presented at ACM SIGMOD Conference on Management of Data, Washington, D.C, 1993.

[2] R. Agrawal and R. Srikant, "Fast Algorithms for Mining Association Rules," presented at the 20th VLDB Conference, Santiago, Chile, 1994.

[3] H. T. Heikki Mannila, Inkeri Verkamo, "Efficient Algorithms for Discovering Association Rules," presented at AAAI Workshop on Knowledge Discovery in Databases (KDD-94), Seattle, Washington, 1994.

[4] J. Han, J. Pei, and Y. Yin, "Mining Frequent Patterns without Candidate Generation," presented at Proceedings of the 2000 ACM SIGMOD International Conference on Management of Data (SIGMOD'00), Dallas, TX, 2000.

[5] W. Cheung and O. R. Zaïane, " Incremental Mining of Frequent Patterns Without Candidate Generation or Support Constraint," presented at Seventh International Database Engineering and Applications Symposium (IDEAS 2003), Hong Kong, China, 2003.

[6] B. Goethals and M. J. Zaki, "Advances in Frequent Itemset Mining Implementations," *ACM SIGKDD Explorations*, vol. 6, pp. 109-117, 2004.

[7] H. Toivonen, "Sampling large databases for association rules," presented at 22th International Conference on Very Large Databases (VLDB'96), Mumbay, India, 1996.

[8] M. J. Zaki, S. Parthasarathy, W. Li, and M. Ogihara, "Evaluation of sampling for data mining of association rules," presented at 7th International Workshop on Research Issues in Data Engineering (RIDE '97) High Performance Database Management for Large-Scale Applications, Birmingham, UK, 1997.

[9] B. Chen, P. Haas, and P. Scheuermann, "A New Two Phase Sampling Based Algorithm for Discovering Association Rules," presented at SIGKDD '02, Edmonton, Alberta, Canada, 2002.

[10] C. Zhang, S. Zhang, and G. I. Webb, "Identifying Approximate Itemsets of Interest in Large Databases." *Applied Intelligence*, vol. 18, pp. 91-104, 2003.

[11] S. Parthasarathy, " Efficient Progressive Sampling for Association Rules," presented at IEEE International Conference on Data Mining, 2002.

[12] Y. Li and R. P. Gopalan, "Effective Sampling for Mining Association Rules," presented at 17th Australian Joint Conference on Artificial Intelligence, Cairns, Australia, 2004.

[13] S. K. Thomson, *Sampling*: John Wiley & Sons Inc., 1992.

[14] "Frequent Itemset Mining Dataset Repository," http://fimi.cs.helsinki.fi/data/.

THE INCOMPATIBLE KNOWLEDGE ELIMINATION IN KNOWLEDGE-INTEGRATION*

Ping Guo, Lian Ye, Li Fan
School of Computer Science, Chongqing University, Chongqing, 400044, P.R.China
E-MAIL: guoping@cqu.edu.cn

Abstract: Knowledge base is the foundation of intelligent system. It is very important to insure the consistency and non-redundancy of knowledge in knowledge base. The redundant, inclusive and incompatible knowledge must be processed in knowledge-integration due to variety of knowledge source. In this paper, we research the incompatible knowledge elimination approach in knowledge-integration based on rough set theory, and present a new knowledge-integration framework, which is effective to improve the efficiency of knowledge-integration.

Key words: rough set,knowledge base,knowledge integration framework

1. INTRODUCTION

In expert system and intelligent information system, the knowledge of knowledge base must be consistent, complete and unambiguous. Due to the difficulty of knowledge-acquisition, the knowledge come from different experts and exterior environment in the domain, so, it may have redundant, inclusive and incompatible knowledge. The purpose of knowledge-integration is to eliminate the redundancy, inclusion and contradiction in knowledge base.

Gaines and Shaw[1], Baral, Kraus and Minker [2] research integration technology of multiple knowledge, and mention that the knowledge-

* This work was supported by National Natural Science Foundation of China, NO. 50378093.

integration plays an important role in building expert system. Medsker, Tan and Turban[3] mention the benefits for developing an expert system by integrating multiple knowledge sources, (1) knowledge reuse, (2) knowledge is more valid, (3) knowledge is more comprehensive, (4) knowledge integration by computers facilitates faster and more inexpensive than that by manpower [4].

Wang, hong and Tesng[5,6,7] propose the knowledge-integration strategies based on genetic algorithm (GA) at the rule-set level in distributed-knowledge environment. The proposed knowledge-integration consists of two phases: knowledge encoding and integration. First, the knowledge is transformed into centralized inner representation and encoded as a fixed-length bit string. Second, the encoding set as initial population is taken to genetic operation. The integrated knowledge base can be obtained by decoding the population of last got.

In the paper, we research the incompatible knowledge elimination approach in knowledge-integration based on rough set theory. The remainder of this paper is organized as follows: stipulate the centralized representation patterns based on whole dictionary in section 2. In section 3, the knowledge set is divided into non-incompatible knowledge set and incompatible knowledge set based on RS classification method. In section 4, the contradiction elimination approach and strategy in incompatible knowledge set is discussed, and that the knowledge set obtained is non-contradiction is proved. A knowledge-integration framework to eliminate incompatible knowledge is presented in section 5. Conclusions are given in Section 6.

2. STIPULATION OF KNOWLEDGE REPRESENTATION

The knowledge from different knowledge sources has different representations. The stipulations for knowledge-integration are as follows:

(1) The whole dictionary is constructed. Knowledge is expressed by using consistent logic predication, variable and logic constant.

(2) All knowledge is denoted as form of production rule

$$r: p \rightarrow q \tag{1}$$

Logic precondition p and logic conclusion q are conjunction normal form.

After the vocabularies being centralized encoded, the knowledge in formula (1) is denoted as following pattern:

$$r': p_1 \wedge p_2 \wedge \ldots \wedge p_n \rightarrow q$$

Request: the all precondition of r' comprise the same amount of items (when cannot satisfy the request, add several code with value of true), and conclusion of r' is single predication or logic constant.

The integrated knowledge set is denote as U={ u_i }, u_i is denoted as:

$$u_i: p_{i1}\wedge p_{i2}\wedge\ldots\wedge p_{in}\rightarrow q_i \quad (2)$$

3. CLASSIFICATION OF KNOWLEDGE SET

Rough set is a common mathematical tool dealing with uncertain problem and uncertain knowledge. R in knowledge set U is constructed as follows:

R: $u_iRu_j \Leftrightarrow$ logic precondition of u_i= logic precondition of u_j, $\forall u_i, u_j \in U$
This is the relation R exists between u_i and u_j iff logic precondition of u_i and u_j are sameness.

That R is equivalence relation in U can be proved. The equivalence class U_R to U can be obtained by R. Each equivalence class is called a concept, viz. an item of knowledge (rule). Different elements belonging to one equivalence class cannot be distinguished to this concept.

The set of knowledge conclusion in U is denoted as Q,

$$Q=\{q_i|u_i\in U,\ q_i \text{ is logic conclusion of } u_i\}$$

The subset U_i of U can be defined by logic conclusion of knowledge:

$U_i=U(u_i)=\{u_j|u_j\in U$, logic conclusion of u_j, q_j = logic conclusion of u_i, q_i }

Definition 1. For any subset U_i of U,

$$\underline{Apr}_R(U_i)=\{u|u\in x\ \&\ x\in U_R\ \&\ x\subset U_i\}$$

$$\overline{Apr}_R(U_i)=\{u|u\in x\ \&\ x\in U_R\ \&\ x\cap U_i\neq\varnothing\}$$

$\underline{Apr}_R(U_i)$ and $\overline{Apr}_R(U_i)$ are called the lower-approximation set and the upper-approximation set of U_i respectively.

Definition 2. For any subset U_i of U,

$$BND_R(U_i)=\overline{Apr}_R(U_i)-\underline{Apr}_R(U_i)$$

Is called the boundary set of U_i.

Definition 3. For u_i, $u_j\in U$, if they have the same logic precondition and different logic conclusions, then they are called contradiction.

By lower-approximation set and boundary set of U_i, there is:

Theorem 1. The knowledge in $\underline{Apr}_R(U_i)$ is non-contradiction, and the knowledge in $\underline{Apr}_R(U) = \bigcup_i \underline{Apr}_R(U_i)$ is non-contradiction.

Proof:

First, we prove the knowledge in $\underline{Apr}_R(U_i)$ is non-contradiction.

For $\forall u_j$, $u_k\in \underline{Apr}_R(U_i)$, by definition 1, u_j, $u_k\in U_i$, so the logic conclusion of u_j and u_k is the same. There are two cases:

(1) When u_j and u_k belong to the same equivalence class of U_R, they have the same logic precondition, so non-contradiction.

(2) When u_j and u_k belong to different equivalence classes of U_R, they have different logic preconditions, so non-contradiction.
Therefore, the knowledge in $\underline{Apr}_R(U_i)$ is non-contradiction.

Second, for $\underline{Apr}_R(U)$, we only need to prove $\forall u_j \in \underline{Apr}_R(U_l)$ and $\forall u_k \in \underline{Apr}_R(U_m)$($U_l \neq U_m$)is non-contradiction. Due to $U_l \neq U_m$, viz. u_j and u_k have different logic conclusions. According to the definition 1, $\exists x$, $y \in U_R$, and $x \subset U_l$, $y \subset U_m$, so $u_j \in x$, $u_k \in y$ and $x \neq y$, otherwise $u_j \in x = y \subset U_m$ is incompatible with different logic conclusions of u_j and u_k. Therefore, u_j and u_k have different logic preconditions.

Summarize above, u_j and u_k not only have different logic preconditions, but also have different logic conclusions. So they are non-contradiction.

[♦]

Theorem 2. If $|BND_R(U_i)|>1$, the knowledge in $BND_R(U_i)$ has contradiction. $BND_R(U) = \bigcup_i BND_R(U_i)$. If $|BND_R(U)|>1$, the knowledge in $BND_R(U)$ has contradiction.

Proof:

First, we prove that the knowledge in $BND_R(U_i)$ has contradiction when $|BND_R(U_i)|>1$.

By definition 2, $\exists x \in U_R$, so as to $x \cap U_i \neq \varnothing$ and $x \not\subset U_i$, viz.$\exists u_j$, $u_k \in x$, so that $u_j \in U_i$, $u_k \notin U$. So u_j and u_k have the same logic precondition and different logic conclusions, u_j and u_k are contradiction. Viz. the knowledge in $BND_R(U_i)$ has contradiction.

Second, for $BND_R(U)$, only need to prove that there exists i so as to $|BND_R(U_i)|>1$ when $|BND_R(U)|>1$.

By $|BND_R(U)|>1$, there exists m so as to $|BND_R(U_m)|>0$. By the definition of $BND_R(U_m)$ to know: $\exists x \in U_R$, so that $x \cap U_m \neq \varnothing$ and $x \not\subset U_m$. Apparently, there exists $|x|>1$, viz. $|BND_R(U_m)|>1$.

Summarize above, the knowledge in $BND_R(U)$ has contradiction.

[♦]

We can prove, $\underline{Apr}_R(U) \cap BND_R(U) = \varnothing$. So U can be divided up:

$$U = \underline{Apr}_R(U) \cup BND_R(U) \tag{3}$$

By theorem 1 and theorem 2, the $BND_R(U)$ only need be processed to eliminate the incompatible knowledge in U.

4. INCOMPATIBLE KNOWLEDGE PROCESS IN BOUNDARY SET

By formula (3), it needs to eliminate the incompatible knowledge in boundary set $BND_R(U)$ to make non-contradiction of knowledge in U. There are several strategies for process [5,6,7,8]. A test dataset is introduced to eliminate the contradiction of knowledge in $BND_R(U)$ in this paper.

Definition 4. Assume the test object set Ω. That object $o \in \Omega$ is correctly predicted by knowledge u_i means the logic precondition of u_i is satisfied with o and logic conclusion of u_i is consistent with conclusion of o. Denote the object set correctly predicted by u_i as Ω_{u_i}. That object o is wrongly predicted by knowledge u_i means the logic precondition of u_i is satisfied with o but logic conclusion of u_i is inconsistent with conclusion of o. Denote the object set wrongly predicted by u_i as $\bar{\Omega}_{u_i}$.

Using test object set Ω, calculate the object set Ω_{u_i} and $\bar{\Omega}_{u_i}$ predicted by each item of knowledge u_i in $BND_R(U)$, and calculate the parameters:

$$A(u_i)=\begin{cases} 0 & \text{if } |\Omega_{u_i}|+|\bar{\Omega}_{u_i}|=0 \\ \dfrac{|\Omega_{u_i}|}{|\Omega_{u_i}|+|\bar{\Omega}_{u_i}|} & \text{if } |\Omega_{u_i}|+|\bar{\Omega}_{u_i}|\neq 0 \end{cases} \tag{4}$$

$$E(u_i)=\sum_{o\in\Omega}\frac{\Phi(u_i,o)}{\sum\limits_{u\in BND_R(U)}\Phi(u,o)} \tag{5}$$

Thereinto:

$$\Phi(u_j,e)=\begin{cases} \mathbf{1} & \text{if o is correctly predicted by } u_j \\ \mathbf{0} & \text{otherwise} \end{cases}$$

$$C(u_i)=\frac{|\Omega_{u_i}|+|\bar{\Omega}_{u_i}|}{|\Omega|} \tag{6}$$

The calculative result of formulas (4), (5), (6) is called accuracy, utility and coverage respectively. As to every item of knowledge, the ideal situation is the maximum of accuracy, utility and coverage. But these cannot usually be satisfied at the same time. Calculate the following integrative criterion:

$$f(u_i)=A(u_i)*E(u_i)*C(u_i) \tag{7}$$

The strategy for eliminating incompatible knowledge in $BND_R(U)$ by calculative result of formula (7) is: the calculative results of formula (7) are sorted in descending. If u_i and u_j are incompatible knowledge in $BND_R(U)$ and $f(u_i)$ is in front of $f(u_j)$ in order then delete u_j in $BND_R(U)$, else delete u_i.

The result set which is deleted incompatible knowledge in $BND_R(U)$ is denoted as $\underline{BND}_R(U)$, and denote

$$\underline{U}=\underline{Apr}_R(U)\cup\underline{BND}_R(U) \tag{8}$$

Theorem 3. The knowledge in $\underline{U}$ is non-contradiction.

Proof:

For $\forall u_j, u_k \in \underline{U}$, we divide three steps to prove the theorem.

(1) $u_j, u_k \in \underline{Apr}_R(U)$. By theorem 1, u_j is consistent with u_k.

(2) $u_j \in \underline{Apr}(U)$, $u_k \in \underline{BND}_R(U)$. Assume u_j and u_k are incompatible, viz.: u_j and u_k have the same logic precondition, but different logic conclusions.

By definition 1, $\exists$m and $x \in U_R$, so that: $u_j \in x$, $x \subset U_m$

Due to u_j and u_k having the same precondition and definition of U_R, exist $u_k \in x \subset U_m$. Viz., u_j and u_k have the same conclusion q_m. This is contradicted with assumption of different logic conclusions of u_j and u_k. So u_j and u_k are non-contradiction.

(3) u_j, $u_k \in \underline{BND}(U)$. u_j and u_k are non-contradiction by the construction procedure of $\underline{BND}(U)$.

Summarize above, the theorem is correct. [♦]

5. KNOWLEDGE-INTEGRATION FRAMEWORK

By the conclusion of above sections, the proposed framework for eliminating incompatible knowledge in knowledge-integration is shown in figure1. Decoding procedure is the inverse procedure of knowledge encode. The knowledge in $\underline{Apr}_R(U) \cup \underline{BND}_R(U)$ can be transformed into knowledge representation comprehensible by whole dictionary. The additive value of true in logic precondition of knowledge is deleted to predigest the knowledge representation.

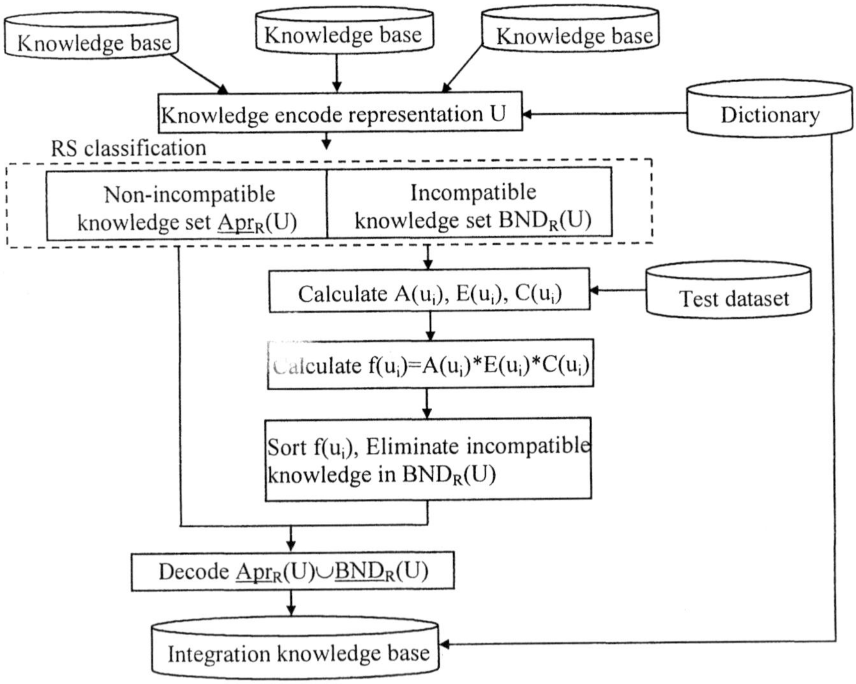

Figure 1. Knowledge-integration framework

6. CONCLUSION

It is one of pivotal problems in knowledge-integration research to eliminate the incompatible knowledge in knowledge base. In this paper, the knowledge in knowledge base is divided into two types by RS theory: non-incompatible knowledge set and incompatible knowledge set. To each item of knowledge in incompatible knowledge set, calculate the accuracy, utility and coverage of test data, provide a feasible approach to eliminate incompatible knowledge, and prove that the knowledge set acquired is non-contradiction. At the same tine, we present a framework to eliminate incompatible knowledge in knowledge base based on the theory.

REFERENCES

[1] Gaines, B. R., & Shaw, M. L. (1993). Eliciting knowledge and transferring it effectively to a knowledge-based system. IEEE Transaction on Knowledge and Data Engineering, 5 (1), 4–14.

[2] Baral, C., Kraus, S., & Minker, J. (1991). Combining multiple knowledge bases. IEEE Transactions on Knowledge and Data Engineering, 3 (2), 208–220.

[3] Yuan, Y., & Zhuang, H. (1996). A genetic algorithm for generating fuzzy classification rules. Fuzzy Sets and Systems, 84, 1–19.

[4] Medsker, L., Tan, M., & Turban, E. (1995). Knowledge acquisition from multiple experts: problems and issues. Expert Systems with Applica-tions, 9 (1), 35–40.

[5] Wang, C. H., Hong, T. P., & Tseng, S. S. (1997). Knowledge integration by genetic algorithms. Proceedings of the Seventh International Fuzzy Systems Association World Congress, 2, 404–408.

[6] Wang, C. H., Hong, T. P., & Tseng, S. S. (1998). A genetic fuzzy-knowledge integration framework. The Seventh International Conference of Fuzzy Systems, 1194–1199.

[7] Wang, C. H., Hong, T. P., & Tseng, S. S. (2000). Integrating membership functions and fuzzy rule sets from multiple knowledge sources, Fuzzy Sets and Systems, 112, 141–154.

[8] Wang, C. H., Hong, T. P., & Tseng, S. S. (2000). A Genetics-Based Approach to Knowledge Integration and Refinement. Journal of Information Science and Engineering, 17, 85-94.

[9] Mathias,K.E.&Whity,L.D.(1994),Transforming the Search Spacs with Gray Coding, Proc. of the 1st IEEE Intl. Conf. On Evolutionary Computation,Orlando,Florid,USA,IEEE Press,519-542.

[10] Wang, C. H., Hong, T. P., & Tseng, S. S. (2000). A Coverage-based Genetic Knowledge-integration strategy, Experty Systems with Applications,19(2000),9-17.

DESIGNING COOPERATIVE EMBEDDED SYSTEMS USING A MULTIAGENT APPROACH : THE DIAMOND METHOD

Jean-Paul and Michel Occello
Université Pierre-Mendès France, Laboratoire LCIS/INPG, F-26000 Valence, France

Abstract: Multiagent systems are well suited to specify requirements for open physical complex systems. However, up to now, no method allows to build software/hardware hybrid multiagent systems. This paper presents an original method for designing physical multiagent systems. It advocates a basic multiagent phase able to tackle functionnal and organizational issues, associated to a componential phase for the detailed design making easier the software/hardware partitionment.

Key words: Multiagent oriented method, embedded multiagent system, codesign.

1. INTRODUCTION

Complex artificial cooperative physical systems are involved in application domains as pervasive computing, intelligent distributed control or wireless computing. Physical systems have a physical reality which does not apply only to the entities but also to the environment in which they evolve. The system and its environment are strongly related. In this context, the system elements integrate generally a software part and a hardware part (electronic cards, sensors, effectors). The high dynamics, the great heterogeneity of elements and the openess make a multiagent approach highly profitable for these artificial complex systems. But the existing multiagent design lifecycles have to be modified to take into account software/hardware hybridation particularities.

This paper aims to present our approach called DIAMOND (Decentralized Iterative Multiagent Open Networks Design) for the design of open multiagent physical complex systems.

Our method can be qualified of codesign because it unifies the development of the hardware part and the software part : the partitioning step is pushed back at the end of the life cycle. A multiagent phase allows the management of collective features. A component phase is used to design the elementary entities of the system (the agents) and to facilitate the hardware/software partitioning.

2. OVERVIEW OF THE DIAMOND METHOD

The DIAMOND method is built to design physical multiagent system. Four main stages, distributed on a spiral cycle (fig. 1), may be distinguished within our physical multiagent design approach. The *definition of needs* defines what the user needs and characterizes the global functionalities. The second stage is a *multiagent-oriented analysis* which consists in decomposing a problem in a multiagent solution. The third stage of our method starts with a *generic design* which aims to build the multiagent system, once one knows what agents have to do without distinguishing hardware/software parts. Finaly, the *implementation* stage consists in partitioning the system in a hardware part and a software part to produce the code and the hardware synthesis.

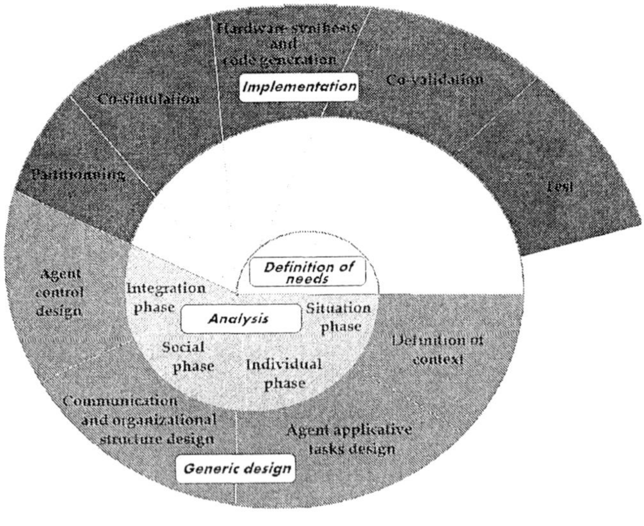

Figure 1. Our lifecyle

Most existing multiagent methods usually distinguish only analysis and design phases [2]. Very few methods deal with other phases. We can find for example a deployment phase in MASSIVE [8] or Vowels [10]. This deployment phase takes in our particular field a great importance since it includes the hardware/software partitioning. To cover the whole lifecycle, different formalisms are required to express different things at different levels [5], for this reason we adopt a cycle using four stages mixing different expressions using more or less formal paradigms and languages (agents, components, Finite State Machines, Hardware Definition Languages). The most current lifecycle used in multiagent methods is the classical cascade cycle. Even if some works attempt to introduce iterative cycle as Cassiopeia (W) [4] or Gaia [12], the proposal of a spiral life cycle is very original.

3. DEFINITION OF NEEDS

This preliminary stage begins by analysing the physical context of the system (identifying workflow, main tasks, etc...). Then, we study the different actors and their participative user cases (using UML use case diagrams), the services requirements (using UML sequence diagram) of these actors.

The second step consists in the study of the different modes of steps and stop. This activity is very significant because it will make it possible to structure the global running of the system. It is generally wishable that the system functions in autonomy. But working with physical systems imposes to know all the other possible behaviors precisely when the system starts, when it goes under maintenance, when we want to stop it.

This activity puts forward a degraded running of the system. It allows to specify the first elements necessary to the fault-tolerance, to identify of cooperative (or not) situations, to define states of recognition in order to analyze, for example, the self-organizational process of an application, to take into account the safety of the physical integrity of the users possibly plunged in the physical system.

We have defined fifteen different modes that we regroup in three families. The *stop modes* which are related to the different procedures for stopping (partially or completely) and to define associate recognition states. The *steps modes* which focus on the definition of the recognition states of normal functionning, tests procedure etc. The *failing operations modes* which concentrate to the procedure allowing to a human maintenance team to work in the system or to specify rules for degraded running.

4. MULTIAGENT-ORIENTED ANALYSIS

The multiagent stage is handled in a concurrent manner at two different levels. At the society level, the multiagent system is considered as a whole. At the individual level, the system's agents are build. This integrated multiagent design procedure encompasses five main phases discussed in the following.

Situation phase. The situation phase defines the overall setting, i.e., the environment, the agents, their roles and their contexts. This stems from the analysis stage. We first examine the environment boundaries, identify passive and active component and proceed to the agentification of the problem.

We insist here on some elements of reflexion about the characteristics of the environment [11,12]. We must identify here what is relevant to take into account from the environment, in the resulting application.

It's, first of all, necessary to determine the environment *accessibility* degree i.e. what can be perceived from it. We will deduce from which are the primitives of perception needed by agents. Measurements make possible to recognize states of the environment to interprete the state of the environment. They thus will condition the agent decisional aspect.

The environment can be qualified of *determinist* if it is predictible by an agent, starting from the environment current state and from the agent actions. The physical environment is seldom deterministic. Examining allowed actions can influence the agent effectors definition.

The environment is *episodic* if its next state does not depend on the actions carried out by the agents. Some parts of a physical environment are generally episodical. This characteristic has a direct influence on agent goals which aim to monitor the environment.

Real environment is almost always *dynamic* but the designer is the single one able to appreciate the level of dynamicity of the part of the environment in which he is interested. This dynamicity parameter as an impact on the agent architecture. Physical environments may require reactive or hydride architectures.

The environment is *discret* if the number of possible actions and states reached by the environment are finished. This criterion is left to the designer appreciation according to the application it considers. A real environment is almost always continuous.

It is then necessary to identify the active and passive entities which make the system. These entities can be in interaction or be presented more simply as the constraints which modulate these interactions. For each entities it is necessary to specify the role of these entities in the system. This phase makes it possible to identify the key components that we will use. Some of these active entities will become agents.

Individual phase. Decomposing the development process of an agent refers to the distinction made between the agent's external and internal aspects. Its external aspect deals with the definition of the media linking the agent to the external world, i.e., what and how the agent can perceive, what it can communicate and according to which type of interactions, and how it can make use of them.

The agent's internal aspect consists in defining what is proper to the agent, i.e. what it can do (a list of actions) and what it knows (its representation of the agents, the environment, the interaction and the organization elements [3].

In most cases, the actions are carried out according to the avaiable data about the agent's representation of the environment. Such a representation based on expressed needs has to be specified during specifications of actions. In order to guarantee that the data handled are actual ones, it is necessary to define the useful perception capabilities.

We can take to illustrate these phases the the EnvSys application described in [6]. Capabilities can be specified using a tree to show the different nested levels (see fig. 2). We specify the agent context with a context diagram (see fig. 2}.

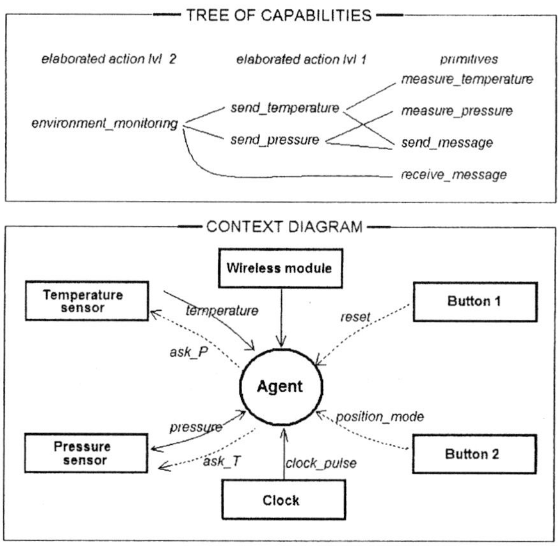

Figure 2. Primitives and actions scheme / Context diagram

Society phase. Interaction among agents are achieved via message passing. Such exchange modes are formalized by means of interaction protocols based on speech acts. Although common to all the agents, these interaction protocols are rather external to them.

Conflict resolution is efficiently handled by taking into account the relationships between the agents, that is, by constructing an explicit organizational structure.

Such an organization is naturally modeled through subordination relations that express the priority of one agent on another.

The main property of our organization is that it will be dynamic. In this kind of application no one can control a priori the organization. Relations between agents are going to emerge from the evolution of the agents'states and from their interactions. We are only going to fix the organization parameters, i.e. agents'tasks, agents'roles.

Integration phase. We need to analyse the possible influences upon the previous levels. Those influences are integrated within the agents by means of their communication and perception assessment capabilities (given in each agent's model). The decomposition masks the notion of agent's control, i.e., how it handles its focus of attention, its decisions, and link its actions. This dual aspect is based on the two previous ones. Via the integration of social influences within the agents, one will endow the multiagent system with some dynamics. According to the social analysis we must give to the agent the possibility to interact in order to choose its role.

5. THE GENERIC DESIGN

This stage is based on a component decomposition. We can easyly define component models as an architecture and an API that allows developers to define reusable segments of code that can be combined to create an application. So, a component is a reusable program building block, which is an identifiable part of a larger program. Component can be combined with others to build more complex functions. This phase offers an efficient process leading to a component decomposition by starting from the informal description of the multiagent system built during the previous stage.

The Problem Description Phase. This phase consists in identifying and delimiting the domain of the general problem, as well as identifying some specific aspects that should be taken into account. Althrough this phase is informal, it allows designers to clearly separate the various aspects embedded within the application. We must choose here the architecture of the different agents.

The agents are built following hybrid architectures, i.e. a composition of some pure types of architecture. Indeed, the agents will be of a cognitive type in case of a configuration alteration, it will be necessary for them to communicate and to manipulate their knowledge in order to have an efficient collaboration. On the other hand, in normal use it will be necessary for them to be reactive (stimuli/response paradigm) to be most efficient.

Agent applicative tasks design phase. We must construct the external shell of the agent i.e. elaborate the interface with the external world for each sensor and effector. It is time, here, to choose technological solution for them and complete the context diagram to specify all information about the signal. The next step is to design the internal shell of the agent. We begin by the elaborated actions (according to the task tree).

It is necessary for this stage to arrange the components to build the application : the architecture of the agent will be used as a pattern, at a very high level, for the component decomposition.

The components have an external and an internal description. Internal description can be an assembly of components or a formalism to describe a decisional.

6. IMPLEMENTATION STAGE

Partitionning Phase. The main use of the codesign technique appears in the software/hardware partitioning of the components defined in the third level. Also it is essential to study the different partitioning criteria.

A first level relates to agent parts for which the partitioning question doesn't exist i.e. sensors and effectors. Indeed some elements must be hardware as input/output peripherals such as for example the sensors and the actuators.

The second level relates to features for which there are several choices of implementation. We present below, those which can be considered to be relevant for the agents according to previous work we have made in this field [9,7] and codesign work:

The *cost* is present at all the stages of a system design life cycle. On very small series, we must decrease, as much as possible, the price of the software/hardware development and the hardware material. In the case of great series, we must reduce manufacturing costs.

The *performance* depends on the considered problem. A real-time application for which the robustness is a function of the occupation processor time is an example of system where this criterion is very important. A hardware partitioning is often privileged.

The *flexibility* plays in favor of the software. Software modifications have generally a less significant impact on the whole system than a hardware change. However, the flexibility of the EPLD (Electrical Programmable Logic Device) and other FPGA (Field Programmable Gate Array) increases quickly. For example, these architectures are reprogrammable in-situ : it is possible to modify their specifications without extracting them from the electronic chart.

From their nature, software systems are less *fault tolerant* than hardware components like EPLD. Indeed, microcontrolers use memories, stack structures with possible overflow etc. The *internal fault tolerance* will be thus a criterion which will play in favour of a hardware partitioning.

The *ergonomic contrainsts* gather all the system physical characteristics like weight, volume, power consumption, thermal release etc. Depending on the application, this criterion can be highly critical (case of the aeronautics embedded applications). One more time, the designer must appreciate correctly this criterion .

The *algorithmic complexity* has a great importance for some applications. The software part will be more important if tasks are very complex. In fact, it is very difficult to make hardware synthesis of highly cognitive features.

Co-simulation and co-validation Phases. This activity allows to simulate the collaboration between software part, hardware part and there interface.

Implementation Phase. At this level, each components are completely specified with a common graphic specification formalism for the hardware part and the software part. For each component, the designer has already selected if he wishes a hardware or a software implementation.

This level must ensure the automatic generation of the code for the components for which an implementation software has been selected (see fig. 3). The code is made in a portable language like Java or C++.

We use a Hardware Description Language which provides a formal or symbolic the components of a hardware circuit and it interconnections. In our method the hardware components is specified in VHDL [1]. The compilation of the codes and the hardware synthesis of the different VHDL specifications are carried out like illustrated on figure 3.

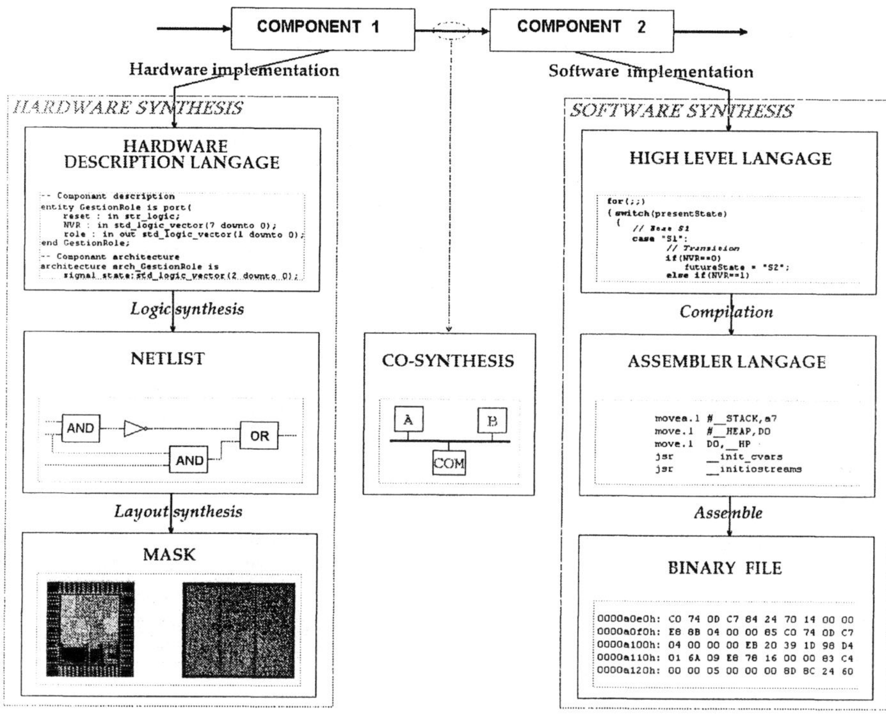

Figure 3. Software component synthesis and hardware component synthesis

7. CONCLUSION

We work currently on the tool associated with the method that we propose. It is created using the Java language. The part which relates to the creation of agents creation with components, manual partitioning and automatic generation of code are operationnal.

This work proposes some innovative contributions in term of hybrid software/physical multiagent life cycle. It integrates in particular all the phases of the development from the analysis to the implementation. It introduces a multi-paradigm spiral lifecycle. It proposes components used as tools for integration, allowing software or hardware derivation. Components are thus used in this approach as units of implementation but further as unit of design allowing the assembly.

REFERENCES

[1] Breuer, P. T., Madrid, N. M., Bowen, J. P., France, R. B., Larrondo-Petrie, M. M., and Kloos,. D. (1999). Reasoning about vhdl and vhdl-ams using denotational semantics. In DATE, pages 346-352.

[2] DeLoach, S. A., Wood, M. F., and Sparkman, C. H. (2001). Multiagent systems engineering. International Journal of Software Engineering and Knowledge Engineering, 11(3):231-258.

[3] Demazeau, Y. (1995). From interactions to collective behavior in agent-based systems. In European Conference on Cognitive Science, France.

[4] Drogoul, A. and Collinot, A. (1998). Applying an agent oriented methodology to the design of articial organizations: A case study in robotic soccer. Autonomous Agents and Multi-Agent Systems, 1(1):113-129.

[5] Herlea, D. E., Jonker, C. M., Treur, J., and Wijngaards, N. J. E. (1999). Specication of bahavioural requirements within compositional multi-agent system design. In MAAMAW, pages 8-27.

[6] J.P. Jamont and M. Occello (2004). Using organisational structures emergence for maintaining functional integrity in embedded systems networks. In Proceedings of IFIP Working Conference on Artificial Intelligence Applications and Innovations, pages 197-210, Kluwer Academic Publisher.

[7] J.P. Jamont and Occello, M. and A. Lagreze (2002). A multiagent system for the instrumentation of an underground hydrographic system. In Proceedings of IEEE International Symposium on Virtual and Intelligent Measurement Systems, Mt Alyeska Resort, AK, USA.

[8] Lind, J. (2001). Interative Software Engineering for multiagent systems: The MASSIVE Method, volume 1994 of LNCS/LNAI. Springer Verlag.

[9] Occello, M., Demazeau, Y., and Baeijs, C. (1998). Designing organized agents for cooperation in a real time context. In Drogoul, A., Tambe, M., and Singh, J., editors, Collective Robotics, volume LNCS/LNAI 1456, pages 25-73. Springer-Verlag.

[10] Ricordel, P.-M. and Demazeau, Y. (2000). From analysis to deployment: Amulti-agent platform survey. In Proceedings of the First International Workshop on Engineering Societies in the Agent World, pages 93-105, London, UK. Springer-Verlag.

[11] Russel, S. and Norvig, P. (1995). Articial Intelligence : a Modern Approach. Prantice-Hall.

[12] Wooldridge, M., Jennings, N. R., and Kinny, D. (2000). The gaia methodology for agent-oriented analysis and design. Autonomous Agents and Multi-Agent Systems, 3(3):285-312.

FFCAS: A FLEXIBLE AGENT-BASED SIMULATION FRAMEWORK FOR COMPLEX ADAPTIVE SYSTEMS

Ji Wu, Chaoqun Ye, Shiyao Jin
Collage of Computer Science and Technology,
National University of Defense Technology,410073 Changsha, China
{wwuji, cqyie, Syjin1937}@163.com

Abstract: Agent-based simulation methodology has shown merits to handle complex adaptive systems' spontaneity, non-linearity, uncertainty, relevancy and emergence. Based on the agent theory of modeling and simulation, this paper proposes a flexible, scalable and cross-domain framework for simulating complex adaptive systems. After discussion on the design of FFCAS, applications on FFCAS in different complex domains, and empirical results are presented as experimental validation.

Key words: multi-agent simulation, complex adaptive system, ecology, public attitude

1. INTRODUCTION

Complex adaptive systems (CASs) have been identified everywhere both in the nature and human world. For CASs' spontaneity, non-linearity, uncertainty, relevancy and emergence, it is hard to model and analysis complex system with mathematical and other formalized methods. Agent-based modeling and simulation methodology has shown good prospect in dealing with the CASs difficulties. Existing agent-based simulation applications can be seen in domains include computational economic[1], ecology[2], military strategy[3], and certain social science specific as our examples in public attitude etc.

So far, many tools have been developed to facilitate the modeling and developing for the CAS simulation application, such as popular SFI Swarm[4] which was implemented in Object C, Cormas[5] in Smalltalk, and RePast[6] in Java. Unfortunately, none of these testbeds meets in large-scale CAS problem. Thus, flexible, scalable agent-based framework for CAS simulation is in urge.

FFCAS (Flexible simulation Framework for Complex Adaptive System) is a Java-based CAS simulation, integration, and development framework. FFCAS currently runs on cluster of workstations (COW) environments. The FFCAS design gives special attention to perfect current agent-based conceptual model and simulating very large communities of agents. It exhibits a significant degree of flexibility in dealing with multi-domain problems, scalability in permitting simulation for more than 4,000 agents.

The rest of this paper is organized as follows. To facilitate our discussion, section 2 outlines the agent-based CAS model embedded in the framework. Section 3 introduces design considerations and architecture of the framework. In section 4, applications built on the framework are presented as validate demonstration. Section 5 describes recent related work and concludes this paper.

2. ENHANCED AGENT-BASED CASS MODEL

Based on traditional theory of agent-based modeling and simulation and empirical researches, we regard that a complex adaptive system can be defined as such a tuple:

$$CAS_{Model}=\langle Environment,\ Agents,\ Micro\ Rules,\ Macro\ Rules,\ External\ Stimulations\rangle. \quad (1)$$

Here *Environment* denotes set of system situations; *Agents* represent system entities which exhibit autonomy, adaptability and sociability; *Micro Rules* denote agents evolvement patterns, restraints of interactions between agents; *Macro Rules* denote evolvement and constraints on system macro levels; *External Stimulations* denote external effects which destroy system's original balance and reaches a new balanced state. There is no difference from traditional models except *Macro rules*. Most of traditional models only keen on the micro level regulation. They ignore system level regulation effects on system. In fact, evolutions of complex adaptive systems depend surely on the hybrid effects of micro and macro regulation.

Proofs can be found in typical CASs. Like Grassland-Ecological System[7], which describes the dynamic balance of numbers of species. Seldom traditional research considers the macro effects on the ecological system, like climate, grassland's or animals' growth cycles, and other specie's aggression. Anther case is theory of plate tectonics. Plate motions and collisions can be modeled in agent theory: plate is modeled as agent group while each agent represents unit area plate, and each agent's properties include altitude, crust stress, tenacity etc. When see into the continent plates' collision, agents at the plate boundaries and fragile zones will tune their properties to exhibit the collision consequence such as altitudes ascend or descend; agent groups at fragile parts may depart from the plates to form new plates or islands.

Figure 1 demonstrates notion of the macro rules involved agent based CAS model. In phase I, target CAS was run with primitive agents, which evolved according to micro rules and external stimulations. Target CAS transfer from Phase I to Phase II, part of agents in the environment evolves to new types agents; and by effects of macro rules, environment at macro level also evolve. Namely, target CAS evolves according to hybrid effects of each agent's evolution and macro level evolution. In phase III, agents and environment advance continuously, and for the reason that primitive agents can not adapt to the new environment, they will eliminate to the end; on the contrary, evolutionary agent will thrive for their adaptabilities to the evolved environment.

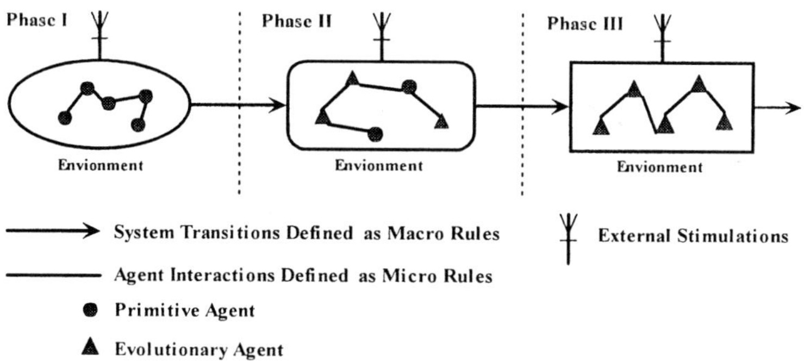

Figure 1. The Enhanced Macro Rules Involved Agent-Based CAS Model

3. FFCAS: AGENT-BASED SIMULATION FRAMEWORK FOR CAS

As discussed in section 1 and section 2, we can identify that requirements of CAS simulation platform may include two folds. One is perfecting the kernel model of CAS embedded in the platform and the other is matching growing scale of simulation computation. Here, when presents design criteria of FFCAS, we mainly keen on two aspects: one is specifications initiated from the above macro rules involved agent-based CAS simulation model; the other is on process efficiency and computation decentralizing. We call these two design starts are model-driven and computation-driven design criteria.

3.1 Model-Driven Design

UML class diagram is used to depict the FFCAS design derived from the above conceptual model. All elements of the agent-based CAS model in tuple (1) are exhibited and abstracted to classes. These classes and their connections are depicted as Figure 2.

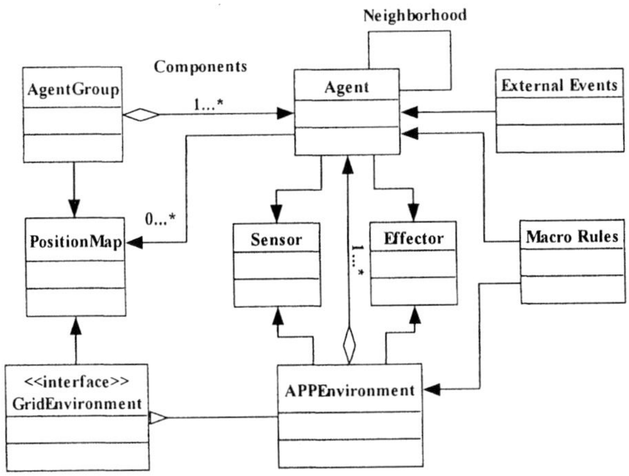

Figure 2. Class Diagram for the Framework

- **Agent** class is the basic element of the CAS. Its properties specify simulation related social and natural features; its methods generally implement agent's functions of environment data processing, decision, and motion. Connections among agents specified interactions and social relationship like neighborhood among them.
- **Agent group** class is a container for all agents. The class is constructed in purpose of providing a schedule console for all agents' activities.
- **GridEnvironment** class and **APPEnvironment** class implement CAS environment. And **GridEnvironment** class is constructed for exchange data between environment model and the display class namely **PositionMap**.
- **PositionMap** class is in charge of collecting statistics from agents and environment then display running information in a grid map.
- **Sensor** class and **Effector** class implement agent's sensor and action.

- **External events** class implements parameter variation on agents' properties resulted from external stimulations.
- **Macro Rules** class implements parameter variation both agents' properties and environment's parameters resulted from macro rules.

3.2 Computation-Driven Design

Java was chosen for FFCAS implementation for its excellent multi-threads techniques. As had been discussed in lecture, when Java program constructed as multi-thread mode, the program will execute in a parallel mode, and memory management and computation resource will be disposed at once a thread end. While other OO languages implemented program may run in a serial mode and instead of thread, process is used to run a program instance, which is memory consumed and uncontrollable. Other advantages of Java lie in its capabilities in modularization, platform-independence and openness.

Figure.3 presents the FFCAS's distributed computational architecture on 2 workstations. Each *agent* run as a thread and all these threads are put in the *agent hash table*. Schedule on agent threads completes in the *agent group* thread loop. Agent group, *environment* and *position map* are implemented as parallel threads. Agent threads and environment thread can be partitioned into multiple computation nodes. And synchronization and time management of three main threads, i.e., agent group, environment, position map, are maintained by simulation engine.

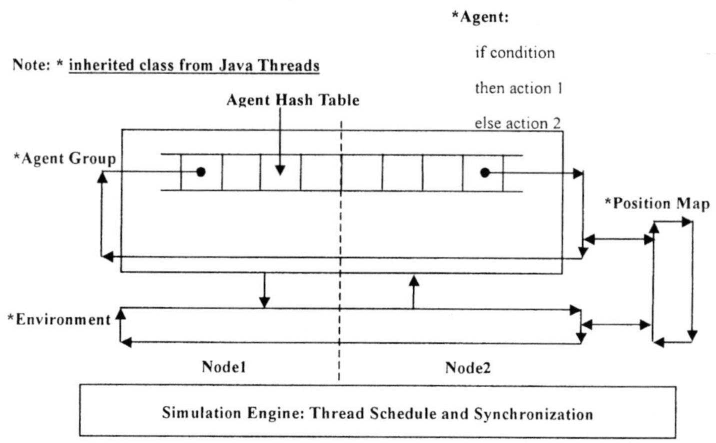

Figure 3. Distributed Computational Architecture of FFCAS

With this design framework, FFCAS has flexibility in model general CASs, for only common features were abstracted to the framework.

Secondly, mu!ti-threads implemented framework ensures computing efficiency, no matter the domain applications run on one machine or cluster. Thirdly, scalability is acquired for the partitions of the agent hash table and environment model, and display and synchronization are detached running so they wouldn't bother the computation decentralized.

4. CASE VALIDATION

Applications in different domains have been implemented on FFCAS for validation. Inter-domain flexibility, reusability and scalability of FFCAS is approximately measured in Table 1. Column 1 lists two different domains of FFCAS's application — Grassland Ecology System (GES), Pubic Attitude System (PAS) — thus providing some evidence of FFCAS's generality. Column 2 measures percent reuses of FFCAS codes across domain. There is 40% reuse in GES from the initial framework. While in building up PAS, reuse was improved to 60% for agent interacting in neighborhood, stimulation effects had been encoding and work was saving. Column 3 list agent numbers and Column 4 list the Grid Size in the two applications. In PAS, more than 4,000 agents and grid with size of 150 × 100 are implemented. GES was run on 2 computing nodes and PAS on 4.

Table 1. Flexibility, reusability, and scalability data of FFCAS

Domain	Reuse	Agent Number	Grid Size	Computing Node
GES	40%	328	64×64	2
PAS	60%	4192	150×100	4

Grassland Ecological System (GES) simulate the dynamic balance on numbers of wolf—rabbit—grass pane. Cormas has implemented it as platform demo named ECEC[5]. We extended this work for comparative purpose. Extended GES simulations were run with about 328 agents (200 rabbits, and 128 wolves are initiated) and 820 grass pane, on a 64×64-cell grid. A COW of two nodes is used to support the GES running. Each type of agent runs on their strategy, i.e., grass panes are eliminated by rabbits and regenerate in their growth law. And rabbits survive on grass, and stay in any state of stuff, hungry and dead. Wolves survive on hunting rabbits, stay in any one of the same three states as rabbits. When in stuff state, animals jog on the grid in random manner; in hungry state, they search out for food, if not access food, their energy index continues decreasing. When energy index lower than zero, animal starves and is eliminated from the grid.

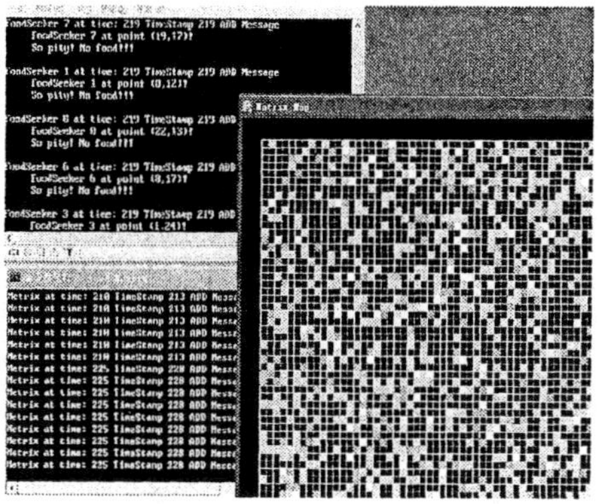

Figure. 4 Simulation scenario of FFCAS applied to Grassland Ecological System. Rabbits (red cells) stroll about in the grid and feed on grass pane (yellow cell), wolves (white cell) pursue rabbits, and environment will control the regeneration rules of grass pane according to the grassland growth law, climate. Two command windows list agent interaction messages between two distributed nodes.

The second example is Public Attitude System (PAS), as in Figure.5. Public attitude denotes the mass thinking and tendency on certain public event, such as approve, dispose or neutral. Empirical research works show that public attitude on certain event on each citizen's faith and faith environment around him/her. And faith immigration, namely, attitude change on the event, will happen when there are positive or negative feedbacks on the event. And final degree of the effects depend on citizen's social properties include age, gender, occupation, economic status.

PAS simulation was run with about 4192 agents (about 1048 approval agents, 838 disproval agents, and 1886 neutral agents are initiated) on a 150 $\times$ 100-cell grid. A COW of four nodes is used to support the PAS running. The running strategy is that, i.e., agents each with certain belief were initiated using poll data, each of them interacted with their neighbors and belief was interfered by the environment around him/her and slowly tuned their own believes to the mean level. When a external stimulation which maybe a positive or negative feedback was scheduled, agents' believes transfer, and to what effect extent depends on agents' social properties such as age, gender, social status etc.

We choose the Grassland Ecological System and Public Attitude System as demonstration of FFCAS, for GES was regarded as member of the first generation multi-agent model, while PAS represents novel domain of agent-based simulation — social process simulation. In our developed cases, classical agent-based simulation application is extended in agents scale, more complex heuristic and enhanced model description relevant to the enhanced agent-based CAS model. While PAS shows FFCAS's flexibility and scalability in supporting large scale social process simulation.

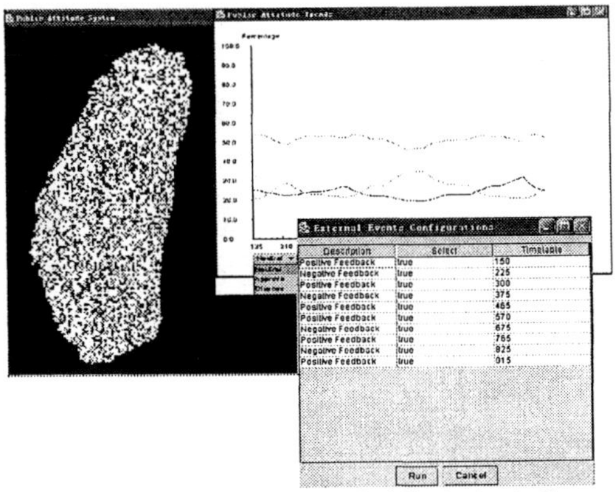

Figure. 5 Simulation scenario of FFCAS applied to Public Attitude System. Approval citizens (blue cells), Disposal citizens (green cells) and Neutral citizens (white cells) are initiated in the spatially-explicit environment. Citizen with certain belief tune their belief value according to its neighborhood and external feedbacks which are listed in the external event panel. In curve panel, number variations of three types of agents are demonstrated in real time.

5. RELATED WORK AND CONCLUSION

Many tools have been developed to facilitate the modeling and development for the CAS simulation app, such as popular SFI Swarm , Cormas and RePast. They implemented abound tools and facilities for CAS simulation. For example, Cormas contains flexible agent and environment modeling facilities, display tools that include graphs and movies, and flexible data capture, and a CAS application can be built with small amount of encoding. However, these single processor depending platforms can not meet the rapid growth of scale of CAS simulation.

Other endeavors to improve the scalability of CAS platform include: building multi-agent simulation on the HLA/RTI[10], JADE[11], and other simulation middleware. However, each of them has to be improved before they can afford simulating a scalable CAS application. We know that HLA/RTI is not specifically agent-based, and agent-oriented services (message passing, agent communication languages, middleware services, addressing, coordination infrastructures, etc.). are not intrinsic part of HLA/RTI. JADE is a specific platform for simulating communications between small amount agents, it specifies none concept of environment, evolve rules which are kernel of CAS simulation. Despite their shortages, we consider that in future CAS simulation work, high performance communication component and excellent services middleware will improve performance of current existing platform.

FFCAS is a Java-based CAS simulation, integration, and development framework. FFCAS currently runs on single workstation, and in cluster of workstations (COW) environments. The FFCAS design gives special attention to perfecting current agent-based conceptual model and simulating very large communities of agents. It exhibits a significant degree of flexibility in dealing with inter-domain problems, scalability in permitting simulation for more than 4,000 agents.

This paper presents FFCAS design criteria and our approach to a number of critical tradeoff. FFCAS shows novelty in breadth, flexibility and scalability, implements a enhanced macro rules involved agent-based CAS model and finally give results from the use of FFCAS in real experiments in realistic CAS domains. The framework offers a bridge for theory integration where gaps and contradictions become evident.

REFERENCES

1. http://www.econ.iastate.edu/tesfatsi/ (2005)
2. Craig, W., R.(ed.): Flocks, Herds, and Schools: A Distributed Behavioral Model. Computer Graphics, Vol.21, (1987) 25-34
3. Michael, B., Adam E.(ed): CROCADILE-An Open, Extensible Agent-based Distillation Engine. Information & Security, Vol.8, (2002) 17-51
4. http://www.swarm.org (2005)
5. http://cormas.cirad.fr/ (2005)
6. Nick C. RePast: the REsursive Porous Agent Simualtion Toolkit. http://repast.sourceforge.net (2005)
7. Pepper, J.W., Smuts B.B.: The Evolution of Cooperation in An Ecological Context: An Agent-Based Model. Dynamics of Human and Primate Societies: Agent-Based Modeling of Social and Spatial Processes, Oxford University Press, Oxford(2000) 45-76
8. Wooldridge M, Jennings N R, Kinny D.: The Gaia Methodology for Agent-Oriented Analysis and Designs. Journal of Autonomous Agents and Multi-Agent Systems. Vol.3, (2000) 285-312
9. Tambe, M.: Towards Flexible Teamwork. Journal of Artificial Intelligence Research, Vo.7, (1997) 83-124
10. Wang, F., Turner, S., J., Wang, L.: Integrating Agents into HLA-Based Distributed Virtual Environments, The 4th Workshop on Agent-Based Simulation, (2003) 9-14

POSITIVE EFFECTS OF PROACTIVE COMMUNICATION IN MAS

Félix Ramos
CINVESTAV GDL Lopez Mateos Sur 590 Guadalajara Jalisco México

Abstract: This paper presents an adaptive communication in MAS. To achieve its objectives agents must send and receive information. Most used mechanism of communication in MAS is broadcast but this is quite expensive and prohibited in some sort of applications mainly because the very poor quality of the service. In this paper we describe trough a real problem the positive effects of proactive communication in Multi-Agent systems. Even if in this paper we show an example, results can be extended to different problems where negotiation is important.

Key words: Proactive communication, Multi-agent System, Load Sharing, QoS.

1. INTRODUCTION

This paper presents an adaptive communication control in a MAS distributed in geographically. To achieve its objectives agents must send and receive information, a problem is how to make efficient the communication, that is make communication only when necessary and just to whom must be communicated. Today most used mechanism of communication in MAS is broadcast, because it is useful in different phases of a team work [5], for instance the discovery of services and the negotiation process. But broadcast is quite expensive and prohibited in some sort of critic applications because the very poor quality of the service and security problems.

Nowadays several systems use services provided in an ad hoc fashion at fixed locations. Then one first approach is communicating well defined from the beginning. This approach is not well suitable for dynamic systems like those of Internet where more services are available day after day. Another approach is to establish communication among agents taking into account the distance among services. In general statistic methods have no god experimental results as shown in other studies for assignment of request in Internet [2] because they ignore the network's path dynamic conditions. There are dynamic strategies for assignment of request in internet is taken into account the maximum of parameters like network properties distance replica and load of services [1,3, 4, 5, 6, 7].

The objective of our work is to study how proactive communication can improve the communications cost and improve quality of service. Our solution includes an Agent's knowledge model; this model offers the possibilities specify the relevant metrics to be used as quality of the service and reduce communication cost. In this paper we show using an example of load sharing how proactive communication is useful to reduce communication cost and improve the quality of service. The main contributions of our method of Dynamic Request Placement approach using proactive communication among agents are:

--The ability of agents to adapt to the dynamic behavior of Internet and user preferences; this allows agents to adapt the response time estimation to the QoS requirement of user's requests

--The experimentation in a realistic scenario where actual Internet conditions are considered as high variability, self similarity, hourly effects and servers load.

1.1 Quality of Service

The International Organization for Standards (ISO) [17] defines QoS as a concept for specifying how good the offered networking services are [9]. Generally, QoS parameters are performance measures and the set of parameters for a chosen service deter-mines what will be measured as QoS. We concentrate on the QoS perceived by users specified in terms of:

-- Network Performance, describing the requirements that the network services must guarantee, it might be expressed as end-to-end delay,

-- Service Performance: characterized for the requirements that the Web service must guarantee expressed as the Web service response time.

2. SYSTEM ARCHITECTURE

In this section is devoted to describe the system's architecture, the agent structure, the knowledge model used and the request placement techniques under examination used among this our proactive communication.

2.1 System Architecture

We consider as in Internet a set of servers each with his own identity and whose service is replicated through common redundancy mechanisms as mirroring or caching. Figure 1 depicts the model of architecture we proposed in [8] showing how a set of Service Agents provides a number of services with a defined QoS.

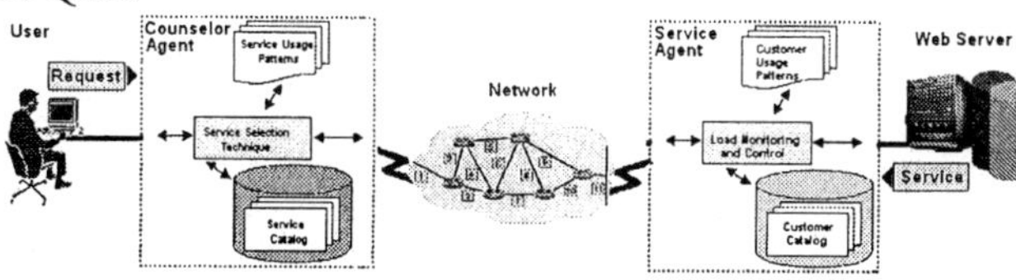

Fig. 1. System's Architecture.

Each agent in the system is an independent self-contained, concurrently executing thread of control encapsulating a perceived system state. Agents communicate with its environment and with other agents via a common communication protocol. The Internet is the environment where agents inter-operate to improve QoS in the case presented in this paper reducing response times perceived by users and load balancing Service Agents. The description of the community of agents is:

1) Counselor Agent: As depicted in Figure 1, a counselor agent is constituted of an interface to get the request and a service solver. Each Counselor Agent implements a Service Discovery mechanism, a communication manager to be able to communicate with other agent using common models and communication protocols. The basic implementation of a counselor Agent uses a MPI (Message Passing Inter-face), a user interface to intercept requests from users and deliver received responses, a Service Directory to resolve service requests, a Knowledge Model to update the QoS service repository. Finally at the core of the counselor agent it's the Request Placement Strategy to make dynamic placement decisions to a selected server depending on the selected technique.

2) Service Agent: A Service Agent is located on each Web Server and is responsible for controlling access client requests and service load levels by means of monitoring QoS. It's also responsible for appropriately market QoS negotiation protocols avoiding a suboptimal load balance due to the Counselor Agents behavior trying to optimize its individual QoS obtained from popular Web services. Figure 1 illustrates the Service Agent component structure inside we have the QoS information Scheduler who is responsible for the dissemination of QoS information to Counselor Agents in order to enforce load balancing. As part of the Service Agent component structure there's also a QoS passive monitor. Finally, the main component of the service Agent is the Ser-vice Manager who incorporates all the necessary components to control access to services, load balancing and forwarding of responses to Counselor Agents.

2.2 Service Discovery Mechanism

When users request a service, the Counselor Agent checks its knowledge base (i.e. service directory) to determine whether or not it is aware of the existence of the re-quested service. If, based on its knowledge, the Counselor Agent knows about the requested service then it will contact the corresponding Ser-vice Agent directly. But if the Counselor agent can't determine the existence of the requested service, it will start a Service Discovery mechanism to obtain the currently available services and update its knowledge base. The Service Discovery mechanism is implemented based on two popular spanning tree techniques:

-- MST. Multiple Spanning Tree, and

-- NPR. Non Predetermined Root methods described in [9].

2.3 Knowledge Model

The Knowledge Model objective is to maintain and estimate of services QoS in the Service Directory in order to improve whole QoS of the system. The Knowledge Model is based on statistical information of the use of Web services. For each service it stores, as a time series, the identity of the Service Agent, the QoS, and time validity for the perceived QoS. This last parameter enables Counselor Agents to consider old information when it becomes obsolete. An example of the knowledge base of a Counselor is displayed in figure 2.

The background to store QoS as a time series is bounded to the well known daily effect on Web services [9], bandwidth and latencies depends on time of day and day of week. This means that each Counselor Agent stores its QoS parameters as a time series, which is sampled at different hours, and deduces a function representing the QoS by interpolation dealing with large skew, long tails and high variability. Figure 2 shows such QoS as a function of day and time of the day. Whenever a new response is received for an allocated request, the QoS is stored at specific time H of day D, this new value is used to update the Counselor Agent knowledge as follows considering the memory of the agent.

$$q_{x(D,H)} = \mu * \left(q_{x-1(D,H)}\right) + \left(1 - \mu\right)q \quad (1)$$

Where μ is comprised between 0 and 1, and represents the Agent capability to keep a reference of past measured QoS. Additionally when service information has not been updated before some delay V, it is considered obsolete. In that case, a Counselor Agent must start a new learning phase based on relevant knowledge.

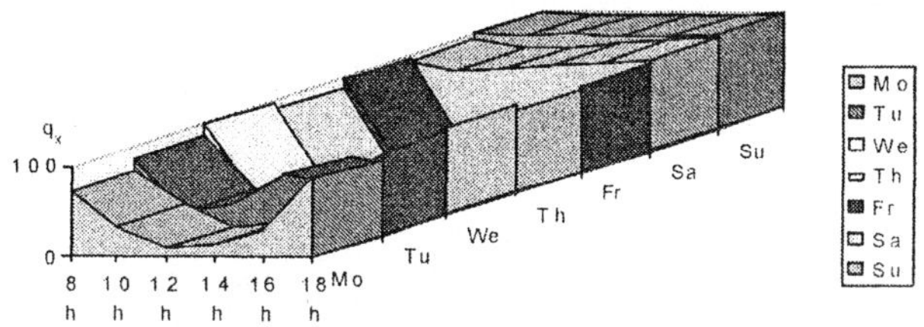

Fig. 2. QoS as a time series function.

2.4 Dynamic Server Selection Strategies

In this section we describe the techniques used to demonstrate how proactive communication is useful to improve the quality of service. The problem of finding a request placement technique that improves system QoS perceived by the system users has been extensively investigated analytically, empirical, and via simulation [4, 10, 11]. We can classify the request placement techniques in the literature into static, statistical and dynamic. Static techniques have proved to be useful to well parameterized architectures so are not useful for the sort of systems we are interested in. On the other hand, dynamic placement strategies use small probes as key in the negotiation process to detect the current network and service conditions in order to make a decision based on the current perceived.

We focused in showing by simulation that proactive communication is the key in the dynamic techniques to improve QoS because it is a factor for adapting automatically changes in necessities of clients and servers. The contribution of this study is the comparison in performance of three algorithms concurrently getting different services from different servers hosting a Web page instead of getting all the required services from a Web Page in the same server. The difference among the algorithms is that they use different knowledge levels and negotiation mechanisms. First technique rather does not use knowledge we name this random strategy. The second use a simple mechanism like free market and third one use knowledge of both clients and servers to create a proactive communication.

2.5 Random Technique

The first strategy, we refer as RND, lies under the basic idea that Counselor Agents take advantage of the Service Discovery mechanism and the resulting Service Directory uniformly assigning the requests to servers randomly. A first guess is that this technique can overload some servers.

2.6 Market-based Technique (MKT)

The MKT is the second strategy we use to compare and show how proactive communication improves the QoS. This technique is based on the contract net negotiation protocol. Using contract net in our example, for every Web service request Counselor Agents starts a QoS negotiation process [12]. Three steps distinguish such process: first a request-for-bidding is launched to all Service Agents proposing the service. Second, Service Agent replies are evaluated; these replies are also used by the Counselor Agent to refresh its knowledge on the QoS of the service requested. Finally, the contract is awarded to the Service Agent comprising the best QoS. Obviously this strategy is general and simple, but quite expensive. Therefore this technique is modified to consider only a subset of N Service Agents whose historical information does not reflect a poor QoS. Consequently the modified version of MTK reduces the communication cost for large number of candidate Service Agents.

2.7 Bilateral Technique (BIL)

The third technique tries to solve some drawbacks of last one by means of improving the quality of information a Counselor Agent has. The proactive communication among Counselor Agents and Service Agents allows have fresh information to take best decisions. The proactive communication behaves next way: more a client request a specific service, there exist more strong relations among the corresponding Counselor and Service agents. Also memory and learning skills are part of the mechanism necessitated for in our proactive communication. The basic algorithm is composed of two parts one of Counselor Agent the second of Service Agent both described next:

On the reception of a service request from users, if the Counselor Agent has no actual information about the QoS of Service Agents, it sends a request-for-bidding to select the Service Agent that has the best QoS from responses, the Counselor agent learns about the QoS of responsive Service Agents. Otherwise, the Counselor Agent uses its knowledge and allocates the request on the Service agent with the best QoS.

The Service Agents behave as follows: When a Counselor Agent receives a request-for-bidding; it makes its offer and stores the sender identity. From that moment it will send QoS offers to register Counselor Agents according to three criteria: the date of the last request for bid, the date of its last request allocation, and the number of requests that the Counselor Agent has awarded to it. In this way is implemented the proactive communication, that is, a Service Agent will offer its service to frequent clients, while the others will be less often addressed. This proactive communication, ensure that Service Agents provide Counselor Agents with accurate knowledge of the QoS of services it frequently re-quest, and this, without perturbing the whole system with useless offers.

3. SYSTEM AND WORKLOAD MODEL

In this section we present the model of workload we use to make experiments with the strategies described before. To analyze the performance of dynamic request placement techniques over wired networks, we work at the logical IP-network level. The model then consists of realistic IP hosts and routers, abstracted LANs, and wide-area links, but ignores the details of link-level transmission beyond gross characterizations of the bandwidth and transmission delays on long-distance. The simulation model for the three Dynamic Request Placement techniques introduced in section 2 has been implemented through an extension we have made to the SIDE [13] package, designed for describe network configurations and specify distributed programs organized into event-driven threads.

3.1 Web traffic model

Although no solid, abstract description of Internet traffic exists. We use the best, of the salient characteristics of such traffic. The traffic that drives our experiments is based on the "Behavioral model" of web browsing developed by H.K. Choi [14]. Choi's model is an application-level description of the critical elements that characterize how HTTP protocols are used. A motivation for choosing Web-like traffic to drive these experiments was the assumption that properly generated traffic would exhibit highly variable and bursty demands on Web services.

3.2 System Model

A model in SIDE [16] consists of a number of source files. The basic unit of execution is called a process and it looks like a specification of a finite state machine. A process always runs in the context of some station, which conceptually represents a logical component of the controlled/modeled system. In our simulation each Client is modeled as a process at some station owing a copy of the presented Web Traffic Model to generate Web requests, such requests are forwarded by an interface to the Counselor Agent process and waits for the Web-request to be retrieved. Counselor Agents process implements one of the three techniques to decide where to send the received requests, allocated requests are sent to Service Agents through the network interface. The network connections have different structures to represent available network bandwidths present in the Internet links and also have different distribution of transmission delays, finally the network topology is defined by a connectivity function. Service Agent process run in the context of Web server stations and receive requests that accept or reject them depending on service load and in the case of Bilateral implementation it sends its QoS offers to clients accordingly to the mechanism presented in section 2. Likewise the process model of Web servers is an abstraction of actions that occur at the session level layer of the HTTP protocol. We model a Web server as a set of resource queues. Service times are based upon two types of re-quested objects: static and dynamic objects. Service time for static objects is proportional to its size, and dynamic objects require extra time drawn from a Hyper Geometric Distribution representing objects that requires to be processed at Web server before the response is sent to the client.

4. EXPERIMENTAL SETUP

In this section we describe the scenario within which experiments of the three strategies have been carried out. We use SIDE as a platform to simulate the described strategies. Every simulation experiment for a given configuration has consisted of 1200 measurement sessions. Connection failures are set to occur in 0.5% to 0.7% of the measurements, and are independent of both client and time-of-day. Read failure rates are typically even smaller, ranging from 0.05% to 0.2%. The values for the Web traffic model that drives client Web-request generation are shown in Table 1.

TABLE 1
WEB TRAFFIC MODEL PARAMETER STATISTICS

Parameter		Mean	S.D.	Distribution
Request Size		360.4	106.5	Lognormal
Obj. Size	Main	10710	25032	Lognormal
	In-line	7758	126168	Lognormal
Parsing time		0.13	0.187	Gamma
In-line objects		5.55	1.14	Gamma

Viewing time	39.5	92.6	Gamma
Temporal locality	1.5	0.80	Lognormal
Service popularity			Zipf

There are two kinds of objects: The file containing an HTML document is referred to as main object and the objects linked from the Hypertext Document are referred to as In-line objects. Parsing time is the time spent parsing the HTML code in order to determine the layout of a page after fetching the main object. Viewing time is the inactive interval between Web-requests. Temporal locality is the number of sequential Web-requests addressed to the same server. Finally to address the issue of popular Web services and client preferences a Zipf distribution is implemented as an extension to the original Work load model in [18].

In our simulations we characterize how the proposed strategies perform in a range of topologies. We rely on INET [15] network-generation tools and intuition about the nature of networks to produce subject network topologies.

We focus on two type of simulation scenarios in our work: The so called Inet-tool scenarios, and real-world scenarios, for space reasons we show only a representative real-world scenario, the Net-mx model (mx stands for México) a large network model that is representative of an existing backbone (see Fig. 3) The Net-mx scenario is very complex, takes a long time to simulate and the results are harder to understand compared to the Inet-tool scenarios, nevertheless, it is a model of an early state of the network that connects all Mexican research institutes and the results of simulations with this model can be regarded as a test case to evaluate real network behavior.

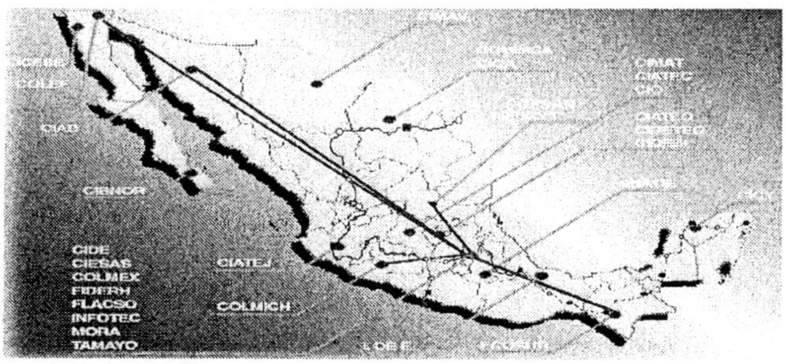

Fig. 3. The Net-MX topology.

In the scenario of Fig 3, five Web services has been considered with a replication level of 3 giving 15 available services distributed randomly, Table II shows the values for the hyper-exponential distribution parameters defining service time at Web servers for dynamic objects requested by clients. Five services were chosen because it is a large enough number to make the task of correct service selection hard enough for the Agents to learn service values within the time frame of the experiment.

TABLE II
PARAMETERS CONSIDERED IN THE WEB-SERVICE MODEL

Parameter	Type	Mean	Frequency
Service Time	High	0.7	0.01
	Med	0.1	0.14
	Low	0.0 .001	0.85

5. RESULTS

In order to evaluate the advantages of proactive communication, we compare the bilateral technique that uses proactive communication against the MKT and Random strategies. Obviously the MKT technique use memory about QoS of Services so in some way it is mix strategy. We consider four metrics to evaluate the effectiveness for each technique we measure:

-- The median of user response times experienced by users to complete a Web-request for 500K size (large Web-requests).

-- The CDF (cumulative probability function) of user response times.

-- The overhead of each technique given by its communication cost derived from QoS information collection and dissemination and technique negotiation mechanisms.

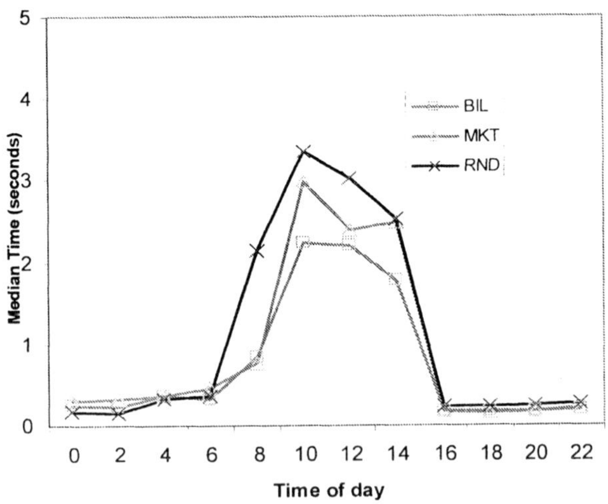

Fig. 4. Time of Day Effects.

We found very positive the inclusion of proactive communication in this problem of load sharing. In Fig. 4, we report the responsiveness of the three techniques, for large 500K Web-requests, we see that BIL outperform MKT and RND for bigger Web-request, due to the feedback mechanism of BIL technique and the amortization request-bidding over baggers requested Web pages. Differences between request placement techniques are far pronounced during busy daytime hours than for quieter periods (see Fig. 4), reflecting the network load on the techniques, and the periodicity of hourly effects. MKT technique always perform worse than BIL and better than RND, with minor exceptions curves do not cross, implying that as QoS perceived changes clients need not to use a different technique to achieve optimal performance.

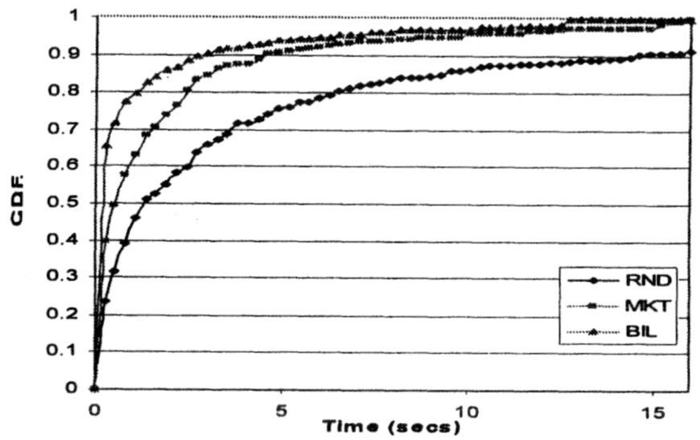

Fig. 5. Median Response Time Cumulative Probability Function.

We compare in Fig. 5, the performance of the three techniques using the total response time of allocated requests and the overhead induced by negotiation techniques implemented by such techniques in Fig. 6; we can see that selecting with RND technique has the lowest performance although it does not produce any overhead as compared with MKT whose performance is higher because its QoS actualization mechanism, but it incurs in high overhead too, then the most cost-effective strategy is BIL whose performance is high and overhead remains relative low in comparison with RND and MKT.

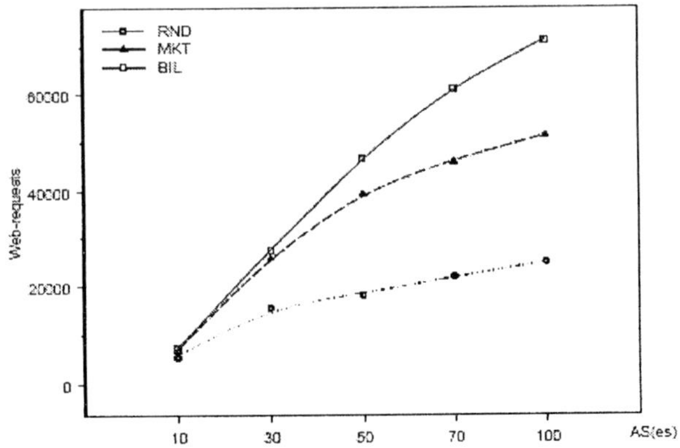

Fig. 6. Request Placement Technique overhead.

The result of the comparison in a total qualitative agreement goes in the sense that the relationship among the improvement of QoS perceived by users of the contrasted curves is preserved. In the quantitative side, the figures presented in this paper show slower response times that those conducted before, the reason being the workload model described in [16] on which experiments where conducted are based on a Non-Homogenous-Poisson Process, showing low variability and uniform response times.

6. CONCLUSION AND FUTURE WORK

The experimental results demonstrate the positive role of proactive communication in the load sharing problem. Positive obtained results are due to proactive communication allows keeping updated the information that agents keep about most common counterparts (services).

Also we think that random selection technique would be sufficient when the primary goal is load balancing and when the clients do not have QoS constraints. On the other hand the Bilateral dynamic technique we have developed, would be useful in an environment in which QoS-aware clients that have different requirements accessing servers that display significant variability in their response times. Although our proactive based technique was mainly developed to improve QoS perceived by Web service's users, we are sure that results obtained for proactive communication can be generalized to different problems where negotiation is an important aspect in the solution of the problem.

REFERENCES

[1] J. Guyton and M. Schwartz. Locating nearby copies of replicated internet servers. In Proceeding of ACM SIGCOMM' 95, 1995.

[2] E. Zegura, M. Ammar, Z. Fei, and S. Bhattacharjee, Application-layer anycasting: a server selection architecture and use in a replicated web service, IEEE/ACM Transactions on Net-working, vol. 8, no. 4, pp. 455–466, Aug. 2000.

[3] M. Crovella and R. Carter. Dynamic server selection in the internet. In Proceeding of IEEE Workshop on the Architecture and Implementation of High Performance Communication Subsystems, 1995.

[4] Crovella and R. Carter, Dynamic Server Selection Using Bandwidth Probing inWide-Area Networks, In Proceedings of IEEE INFOCOM, 1997.

[5] M. Rabinovich, I. Rabinovich, R. Rajaraman, and A. Aggarwal. A Dynamic Object Replication and Migration Protocol for an Internet Hosting Service. In Proc. 19th Int'l Conf. on Dis-tributed Computing Systems, pp. 101–113, Austin, TX, June 1999. 18 IEEE.

[6] S. Krishnamurthy, W. H. Sanders, M. Curier, Performance Evaluation of a QoS-Aware Framework for Providing Tunable Consistency and Timeliness, Proc. of The 10th IEEE International Workshop on Quality of Service (IWQoS 2002), May 2002.

[7] S. Krishnamurthy, W. H. Sanders, M. Curier, Performance Evaluation of a Probabilistic Replica Selection Algorithm, Proc. of The Seventh IEEE International Workshop on Object-Oriented Real-Time Dependable Systems (WORDS 2002), Jan. 2002.

[8] F. F. Ramos, "Placement dynamique de requêtes multiagents dans les systèmes d'information globaux", PhD thesis, Université de Technologie de Compiègne, juin 1997.

[9] M. Bui, F. Butelle, C. Lavault, (2003). A Distributed Algorithm for Constructing a Mini-mum Diameter Spanning Tree. Journal of Parallel and Distributed Computing.

[10] S.G. Dykes, K. A. Robbins, C.L. Jeffery, "An Empirical Evaluation of Client-Side Server Selection Algorithms", in IEEE INFOCOM 3:1361-1370, 2000.

[11] M. H. Balter, M.E. Crovella, C.D. Murta, "On Choosing a Task Assignment Policy for a Distributed Server System", in Parallel and Distributed Computing 59:204-228, 1999.

[12] G. R. Smith, "The contract net protocol: high-level communication and control in a distributed problem solver", IEEE Trans. on Computer, 12(29), Dec. 1981, pp.1104-1113

[13] P. G. Burzynsky, Protocol Design for Local and Metropolitan Area Networks, Prentice Hall, 1996

[14] H. K. Choi, J. O. Limb, "A Behavioral Model of Web Traffic", Proceedings of the Seventh Annual International Conference on Network Protocols, 1999.

[15] K. Calvert, M. Doar, and E. W. Zegura, "Modeling internet topology, " IEEE Communications Magazine, June 1997. [10] C. Jin, Q.Chen, S. Jamin, "Inet: Internet Topology Genera-tor," University of Michigan Technical Report, CSE-TR-433-00, September 2000.

[16] Felix F. Ramos, Liming Chen and Marc Bui. A Comparison of Two Dynamic Request Placement Strategies in Large Distributed Information Systems. In International Workshop on Database and Expert Systems Applications of DEXA 1999 IEEE Computers Society. Florida, on September 1999.

[17] ISO, "Quality of Service Framework", ISO/IEC JTC1/SC21/WG1 N9680, International Standards Organization, UK, 1995.

IMPLEMENTATION OF AN APPLICATION ONTOLOGY

A Comparison of Two Tools

Robert Harrison and Christine W. Chan*

Faculty of Engineering, University of Regina, Regina, Saskatchewan, Canada, S4S 0A2

Email: harrisor@uregina.ca, Christine.Chan@uregina.ca

Abstract: This study presents two implementations of an application ontology for the problem domain of selection of remediation technologies for petroleum contaminated sites. The objective of this work is to study design of ontology modeling systems by comparing two implementations of the same application ontology, one on Protégé and another on a prototype Ontology Modeler developed in-house at Energy Informatics Laboratory of University of Regina, Canada. The two tools both aim to document and represent static knowledge of an application domain. The knowledge acquisition and ontology construction phases are discussed and a comparison of the two implementations is also presented.

Key words: Ontology construction, selection of remediation for petroleum contamination

1. INTRODUCTION

A major cost in building knowledge-based systems is construction of the knowledge base. If several application systems on the same domain are to be constructed, the effort needed to build the knowledge bases for the different systems is often duplicated. This effort is often substantial due to the tacit nature of expertise; and the process of acquiring knowledge for building the knowledge bases is known to be a major bottleneck in the development process. A possible solution for the problem is to share any knowledge on a given problem domain that has been acquired among

* Author to whom all correspondence should be addressed.

systems. Four different approaches have been adopted within the Knowledge Sharing Effort sponsored by Air Force Office of Scientific Research, Defense Advanced Research Projects Agency, the Corporation for National Research Initiatives, and the National Science Foundation [1]. Similar to the objective of the "shared, reusable knowledge based working group" [1], the work reported here aims to overcome the barriers to sharing that arise from lack of consensus across knowledge bases on vocabulary and semantic interpretations in domain models. This approach results in fostering the evolution of sharable ontologies for particular domains, as well as in developing tools and infrastructure needed to facilitate creation and reuse of domain-oriented ontologies.

The objective of this work is to study design of ontology modeling tools by comparing implementations of an ontology developed on Protégé with that on a prototype tool called the Ontology Modeler, constructed at Energy Informatics Laboratory of University of Regina, Canada. Both ontology modeling tools are used for implementation of the same application ontology. A comparison of two implementations of the same application ontology would shed light on the types of features that are useful in an ontology modeling tool, and lay the groundwork for construction of an enhanced version of the Ontology Modeler. The application problem domain used is that of remediation selection for petroleum contaminated sites.

2. BACKGROUND

The Knowledge Acquisition (KA) research community has emphasized for many years knowledge level modeling. This involves knowledge acquisition and analysis of a domain by means of various modeling efforts such as the KADS methodology [2], the generic task approach [3], and components of expertise approach [4]. Within the framework of knowledge-level modeling, two major lines of research have developed. One refines the existing knowledge-level frameworks and emphasizes their formalizations. For example, ML2 has been developed as a formal implemented language based on the KADS methodology [5]. Another line of research aims at developing knowledge level models for a range of tasks and domains in order to uncover generic components, problem solving methods, and ontologies that enable reuse across applications. The objective of the effort is to facilitate knowledge acquisition by providing domain-independent generic models which can guide knowledge engineers in the construction of knowledge models for a particular domain. Specifically, this effort at knowledge modeling can proceed along one of two axis: (1) problem solving methods, and (2) domain ontology. Briefly, a problem solving method can be seen as an abstract model which provides a means of identifying at each step, candidate actions in a sequence of actions that accomplish some task within a specific domain [6]; while an ontology defines the vocabulary of representational terms with agreed upon definitions in human and machine readable forms [7]. The ontology of a system consists of its vocabulary and a set of constraints on the way terms can be combined to model a domain. All knowledge systems are based on an ontology, which can be implicit or explicit [1].

Ontological analysis as a knowledge modeling technique was first introduced in [8]. Since then, other researchers have emphasized the importance of creating an ontology of a domain [7]. For example, the CommonKADS methodology suggested knowledge categorization in the model of expertise to consist of the two major types of domain theory and control knowledge, the latter includes inference, task, and strategic knowledge (see e.g. Flores-Mendez et al.[5]). In other words, there are four categories of knowledge: domain, inference, task, and strategy. In this paper only the domain knowledge of the sample application domain is represented in the two ontology modeling tools.

3. APPLICATION PROBLEM DOMAIN: SELECTION OF REMEDIATION METHODS FOR PETROLEUM CONTAMINATED SITES

The problem domain involves a selection task. Automation of engineering selection is important for the petroleum industries in which decision for a desired remediation technology at a contaminated site is critical for ensuring safety of the environment and the public. A variety of remediation methods/technologies are available. However, different contaminated sites have different characteristics depending on pollutants' properties, hydrological conditions, and a variety of physical (e.g. mass transfer between different phases), chemical (e.g. oxidation and reduction), and biological processes (e.g. aerobic biodegradation). Thus, the methods selected for different sites vary significantly. The decision for a suitable method at a given site often requires expertise on both remediation technologies and site hydrological conditions.

Most of the remediation technologies are too complex and not easily comprehensible for managers and engineers in industries and government.

Therefore, a decision support system (DSS) for supporting decision-making on site remediation techniques is useful.

4. KNOWLEDGE ACQUISITION FOR DEVELOPMENT OF DECISION SUPPORT SYSTEM

The problem domain in this study involves a vast amount of knowledge and decision tools related to site remediation practices. Factors relevant for treating a site contaminated by petroleum products include information on the site hydrogeology, subsurface contamination, and contaminant transport and conversion. An ontology of the domain can provide the basis for such a system.

Knowledge acquisition involved both interviewing the expert as well as consulting published materials and databases about the hundreds of remediation methods on the market. During the interviews, the expert introduced and explained the concepts and tasks of the problem domain to the knowledge engineer. The process of interviews continued until the knowledge engineer was satisfied that the material was sufficiently clarified. In addition to the human expert, a secondary knowledge source was the commercial database of several hundreds of remediation methods. The database includes descriptions of the remediation methods and the conditions in which they are suitable. Through knowledge acquisition, the domain expert specified the considerations for selection of remediation technologies to include: (1) contaminated site, (2) site hydraulic condition, (3) estimated volume of contaminated soil and groundwater, (4) density of the immisible petroleum contaminant, (5) the immisible contaminants present as free phase or residual phase, and (6) concentration range of chemicals in soil and groundwater. Based on the knowledge acquired and analyzed during knowledge acquisition, an application ontology was configured and implemented on the two tools of Protégé and Ontology Modeler.

5. IMPLEMENTATION OF REMEDIATION SELECTION ONTOLOGY ON PROTEGE

Protégé is an ontology editing tool created by researchers at Stanford University [9]. It is an open-source system programmed in Java. Protégé has been under development for a number of years with the most recent release being version 3.0.

The Remediation Selection ontology was implemented in Protege through an iterative process of creating a class and then its slots (properties). In Protégé, classes are created and modified through the **Classes** tab. On the left-hand side of the **Classes** tab, there is the **Class Browser**. The **Class Browser** contains a **Class Hierarchy**, which lists the classes contained in the ontology. Initially, the **Class Hierarchy** only contains the class *THING* and its subclass *SYSTEM-CLASS*, which are both required by Protégé. *THING* is the root class of every class in Protégé and *SYSTEM-CLASS* defines base elements such as Class, Slot, Facet, etc. The Remediation Selection ontology's *Media* class is used as an example of how to create classes, slots, and relations.

A class is created by selecting the parent class (in the case of *Media*, the parent is *THING*) in the class hierarchy and then clicking on the **Create Class** button. A window will appear enabling the user to input information about the class. The *Media* class has three sub-classes: *Soil*, *Water*, and *Soil_GroundWater*. Sub-classes are created in the same manner as classes. The class hierarchy for *Media* and its sub classes is shown in Figure 1.

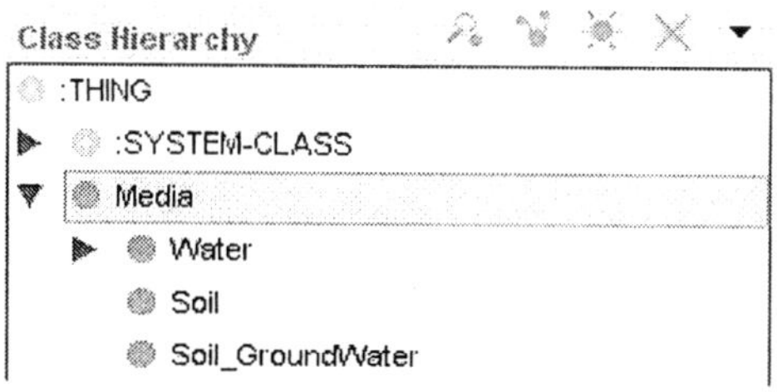

*Figure 1.*Protege Class Hierarchy

The slots for a class are shown in the **Template Slots** window in the **Classes** tab. To create a slot, select a class (eg. *Media*) and then click on the **Create Slot** button. A slot editor window will appear enabling the user to input all the details of the slot. The *Media* class has the slot *site_size*. Details of entering all the *site_size* information is described below. Figure 2 shows the slots window when all the information for the *site_size* slot is entered.

1. In the Name field, type "site_size".

2. *site_size* has three allowed values: small, medium, and large. These values are created by selecting **Symbol** from the **Value Type** field and then using the **Create Value** button.
3. For *site_size*, leave the **Cardinality** fields with the default values.
4. Documentation for the slot goes in the **Documentation** box.
5. The **Default Values** box is for setting one of the allowed values to be the default value for all of the classes and instances that use or inherit the slot. To set the default allowed value to *small*, click on the **Add Value** button above the **Default Values** box, and select *small.*
6. The **Domain** box contains the domains to which this slot belongs. In this case, *site_size* belongs to the *Media* domain.
7. When all information for the slot are entered, click on the **X** in the upper-right corner to close the slot window.

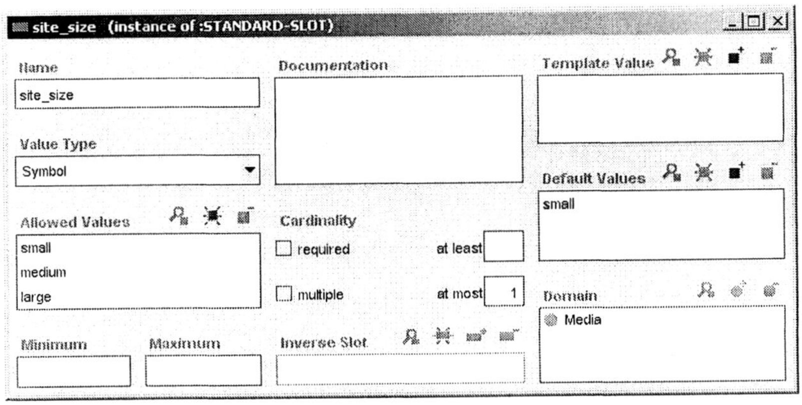

*Figure 2.*Editing site_size slot in Protege

6. DISCUSSION ON THE PROTÉGÉ IMPLEMENTATION

Protégé was not expressive enough and some domain knowledge cannot be entered into the system. For example, *Contaminant.Chemical_Contaminant* has the slot *contamination_weight*, which has different values for each chemical type. When the chemical type is *Benzene_B*, the *contamination_weight* is 0.5. However, the interface does not support input of this sort of knowledge. It is left to the user to ensure that they are using the correct *contamination_weight* with their chosen chemical.

The interface of Protégé can lead the user to incorrectly classify knowledge. For example, the attribute of *contamination_weights* has the values of { 0.5, 0.2, 0.15, 0.15 }, which are floating point values. But, when the user tries to set the value type to float, only the minimum and maximum value constraints can be set, and the value type was set instead to symbol. However, a symbol is not an accurate representation of these values which are really floating point values. The same problem also occurs for multiple integer values.

Protégé can support only parent-child relationships between classes, and other relationships such as the association relationships cannot be defined. For example, the *Media* class has association relationships with the *Remediation*, *Contaminant*, and *Experiment* classes, but these relationships cannot be defined because they are not a parent or child of each other.

7. DESIGN OF THE ONTOLOGY MODELER

The objective of the new ontology modeling system, Ontology Modeler, is to develop a prototype ontology modeling application that provides a visualization of the ontologies and an interface that enables the user to easily manipulate the ontology data. The system was developed with Microsoft Visual C# .Net 2002. The representation of classes and slots in Ontology Modeler is shown in Figure 3.

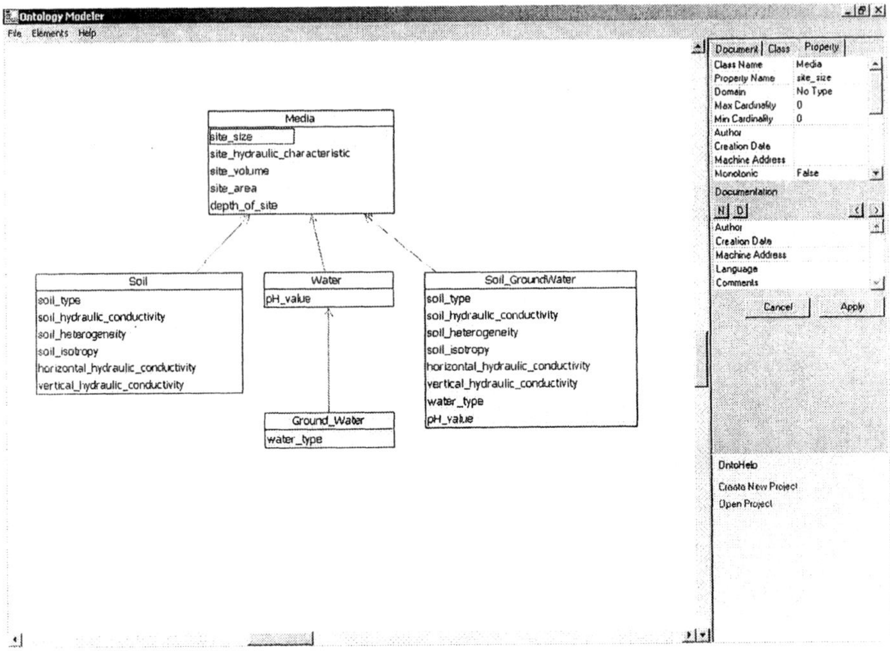

Figure 3. Ontology Modeler

7.1 Ontology Representation

The ontologies in Ontology Modeler are represented in the Generic Ontology Representation [10]. The Generic Representation is an object-oriented ontology representation that provides a level of abstraction that makes it easier to manipulate and manage the ontologies. The three main Generic Representation elements discussed in this paper are the document, class axiom, and the data property axiom. A class axiom is similar to a class and a data property axiom is similar to a slot. A document is a structure that contains the ontology's class axioms and data property axioms.

7.2 Ontology Visualization

Ontology visualization can either improve the ontology development process or hinder it, depending on the visualization technique used. One visualization technique is to use a tree structure. Trees, such as the Class Hierarchy in Protégé, are not sufficient for displaying classes with multiple inheritance because they can only show single inheritance. Protégé compensates for this limitation of the tree, by supporting multiple inheritance in a Superclasses pane. However, with this feature, managing the class hierarchy becomes cumbersome because a class in the Class Hierarchy must be selected first and then the user needs to remember to look at the Superclasses window to see all the parents of a class. It can be concluded that using a tree to visualize an ontology hinders the ontology development process.

A more effective method of visualizing ontologies is to use a graph because it can show multiple inheritance. Due to the similarities between ontologies and object-oriented design, the UML (Trademark of Object Management Group, Inc.) class diagrams are adopted for displaying classes and their properties, and relationships between classes.

The classes of an ontology are displayed in the Viewer, which is the main viewing window. As shown in Figure 3, the top compartment of a class contains the name of the class. The lower compartment of a class contains the names of the properties of the class. Inheritance relationships between classes are shown by lines with arrows pointing to the parent. Clicking on a class will select the class. Classes can be moved by dragging them with the mouse.

7.3 Ontology Editing

The user can modify ontologies with the use of the Viewer and perform the following operations: (1) Add/Delete class axioms, (2) Add/Delete properties, (3) Modify class and property names, and (4) Add/Delete inheritance relationships between classes. However, not all ontology information can be displayed and modified graphically. To support the modification of non-graphical data, the InfoWindow, at the upper-right corner of the screen, can be used. The InfoWindow uses a tabbed user interface, which enables the user to quickly and easily switch between different ontology information types. There are three tabs: Document, Class, and Property. The Document tab contains information defined by the Document class, the Class tab contains information defined by the ClassAxiom class, and the Property tab contains information defined by the DataProperty class. The information contained within the tabs is displayed in a grid for viewing and editing the information. When the user clicks on a class or property in the Viewer, the appropriate tab is displayed and is filled with the information of the clicked class or property. This feature enables the users to focus on their task and not worry about changing tabs or searching through lists of classes or properties.

8. IMPLEMENTATION OF REMEDIATION SELECTION ONTOLOGY ON ONTOLOGY MODELER

Similar to the development process using Protégé, the Remediation Selection ontology was implemented in Ontology Modeler through an iterative process of creating a class and then its properties. To create a class, click Elements->Class and then click in an empty space in the viewer. To change the class name, to *Media*, for example, (1) click Elements->Select, (2) double click on the class, and (3) type to change the name of the class to "Media". Documentation for the *Media* class was created by (1) in the Class tab, click **N** to create new documentation, (2) in the Comments field, type "Media is an object consisting of note 1", and (3) click Apply.

When a class has been created, its properties are created. Properties can be modified through both the main viewer and the Properties tab. The steps for creating the *site_size* property of the *Media* class are listed as follows:

1. With **Elements->Select** enabled, click on the *Media* class.
2. Right-click on *Media* and left-click on **Add Property**.
3. Double-click on the added property.
4. Type to change the name of the property to "site_size".
5. Click outside of the class to save changes.
6. Additional information about the property, such as domain and cardinality, can be input through the **Property** tab.

To show the child-parent relationship between two classes, the user has to draw an arrow pointing from the child class to the parent class. This is performed by selecting **Relation** from the **Elements** menu and then clicking on the child class, *Soil*, and then clicking on the parent class, *Media*.

9. COMPARISON OF TWO IMPLEMENTATIONS: STRENGTHS AND WEAKNESSES

Both Protégé and Ontology Modeler are able to graphically display an ontology. Protégé's tree hierarchy is inadequate for dealing with multiple inheritance. Protégé contains the plugins, OntoViz and Jambalaya, for visualizing ontologies as a graph. However, both plugins have problems. OntoViz gave Java errors while creating a graph and the interface for Jambalaya is not user friendly. To create new nodes and arcs in Jambalaya, a user needs to use the Class Hierarchy, which suffers from the multiple inheritance problem described above. Ontology Modeler's ontology visualization is an improvement over Protégé's in that it uses a graph and it allows the user to modify and manipulate the classes and relations directly, rather than performing manipulation operations through a separate window. Additionally, the visualization is enhanced with the use of the UML. Neither Protégé nor the current version of Ontology Modeler support association relationships between classes.

Poor labeling is a problem in Protégé. Protégé uses Open Knowledge Base Connectivity (OKBC) for handling the representation of the ontologies [11]. OKBC elements include *:THING*, *:SYSTEM-CLASS*, and *:Documentation*. While these OKBC elements appear in the class and slot hierarchy, they are not a part of the ontology, and should be transparent to the user. The Ontology Modeler uses the Generic Representation, which enables a language neutral user interface to be developed. This is more user-friendly.

Some labels are confusing in the Edit Slot window of Protégé. For a novice user, the difference between the Template Value box and the Default Values box is unclear. The behavior of both boxes is identical as they can both set a default value. The user would only become aware of the differences through trial and error or by reading the online documentation.

Protégé can express more types of data and support representation of more elements of the Remediation Selection ontology. For example, the *site_size* property of the *Media* class has the values of *small*, *medium*, and *large*, which are represented in Protégé. It is not possible to specify these values in Ontology Modeler.

Documenting the knowledge elements is an important feature and both Protégé and Ontology Modeler support documentation of ontology elements. In comparison, Ontology Modeler has better documentation facilities because in addition to comments, it supports the user in recording the author, date, and language of the comments.

10. CONCLUSION AND FUTURE WORK

The objective of this work is to study design of ontology modeling tools by comparing Protégé with a prototype tool called the Ontology Modeler. A comparison of two implementations of the same application ontology reveals that ontology visualization, support for a wide variety of data types, and the user interface are important features of an ontology modeling tool. This study lays the groundwork for construction of an enhanced version of the Ontology Modeler. Ontology visualization can be further improved by using 3D graphics as more information can be displayed in a 3D environment. Adding support for the object property axiom, a Generic Representation element, will enable users to define more complex properties. Ontology learning techniques can be applied to refine the quality of the generated ontologies. Ontology Modeler will also be enhanced with an ontology management system.

ACKNOWLEDGEMENTS

The generous support of a Strategic Grant from Natural Sciences and Engineering Research Council is gratefully acknowledged. The contributions of current and former students of Energy Informatics Laboratory in this work are also gratefully acknowledged.

REFERENCES

[1] R. Neches, R. Fikes, T. Finn, T. Gruber, R. Patil, T. Senator, and W. R. Swartout, "Enabling Technology for Knowledge Sharing", *AI Magazine*, **12**(3) (Fall 1991) 37-56.

[2] G. Schreiber, J. Breuker, B. Bredeweg, and B. Wielinga, "Modeling in knowledge based systems development", in Boose, J. ,Gaines, B., Linster, M., (eds) *Proceedings of the European Knowledge Acquisition Workshop* (EKAW '88), June 19-23, 1988, Gesellschaft fur Mathematik und Datenverarbeitung, MBH.

[3] B. Chandrasekaran, "Generic tasks in knowledge-based reasoning: high-level building blocks for expert systems design", *IEEE Expert* **1**(3) (1986) 23-30.

[4] L. Steels, "Components of Expertise", *AI Magazine* **11**(2) (1990) 29-49.

[5] R.A. Flores-Mendez, P. van Leeuwen, and D. Lukose, "Modeling expertise using KADS and MODEL-ECS", in *Proceedings of Banff Knowledge Acquisition Workshop '98*, Banff Canada, October 1998.

[6] J. McDermott, "Preliminary steps toward a taxonomy of problem-solving methods", ed. S. Marcus, *Automating Knowledge Acquisition for Expert Systems*, (Boston, MA: Kluwer Academic, 1988) 225-255.

[7] T. Gruber, "A translation approach to portable ontology specifications", in *Proceedings of the seventh Banff Knowledge acquisition Knowledge-Based Systems Workshop '92*, Banff Canada, October 11-16, 1992, paper no.12.

[8] J.H. Alexander, M.J. Freiling, S.J Shulman, S. Rehfuss, and S.L. Messick, "Ontological analysis: An ongoing experiment", International Journal of Man-Machine Studies **26**(4), 473-485.

[9] Protégé, http://protege.stanford.edu.

[10] R. Harrison, D. Obst and C. Chan, "Design of an Ontology Management Framework", accepted for ICCI 2005, Irvine, California, August 8-10, 2005.

[11] N. F. Noy, R. W. Fergerson, and M. A. Musen, "The knowledge model of Protege-2000: Combining interoperability and flexibility", *2nd International Conference on Knowledge Engineering and Knowledge Management (EKAW'2000)*, Juan-les-Pins, France, 2000.

TRANSLATING ONTOLOGIES TO DEFAULT LOGIC

Yu Sun[1] and Yuefei Sui[2]
[1,2]*Key Laboratory of Intelligent Information Processing, Institute of Computing Technology, Chinese Academy of Sciences, Beijing, 100080, P.R.China;* [1]*Institute of Computer Science and Information Technology, Yunnan Normal University, Kunming, 620092, P.R.China.*

Abstract: The translation of inheritance nets to default logic has been discussed by Etherington [9], Touretzky [10], etc. Ontologies and inheritance nets are similar in some aspects and based on methods of translating inheritance nets to default logic, a translation of ontologies to default logic with a priority order on defaults is given. Hence, properties of an ontology and the revision of ontologies can be studied in terms of default logic. Ontologies are assumed to be trees under the subsumption relation between concepts and have deduction rules to infer what are not explicitly stated. The statements in ontologies are translated to facts of default theories of the ontologies and the default inheritance of properties are represented by normal defaults with a priority order on them due to the intuition that subclasses overriding superclasses. For an ontology with a tree structure, it is consistent if and only if the default theory of the ontology has a unique extension.

Key words: ontology, default logic, priority order, extension

1. INTRODUCTION

Ontologies are important in sharing and reusing knowledge [1,2].An ontology is "an explicit specification of a conceptualisation" [4], where the conceptualisation is an abstract model of some phenomenon in the world through specifying the concepts relevant to that phenomenon.

In an ontology, classes (concepts) consist of individuals: all the individuals of a class have some common properties. A set of relevant concepts and their relationships in an ontology are the conceptualizations [5]

used to represent the world. Concepts are described by sets of properties true for all the individuals of the class, where the properties are important for the knowledge representation and for distinguishing a concept from the others. Usually properties that are generally true for that concept are also represented. Concepts in an ontology are hierarchically organized through the isa (subsumption) relation to form the ontology's main structure which is further enriched by properties, and by relationships relating concepts.

Our ontology consists of a set of concepts and properties; and three relations: the subsumption relation between concepts; the inheritance and default inheritance relation between concepts and properties. Hence, default logic can be used to study the properties of ontologies. Moreover, in the building and maintaining of ontologies, new information will be added to ontologies continually and ontology revision is necessary. Approaches to belief revision where consistent sets of formulas are changed after adding contradictory information have been treated extensively in the literature [12]. In order to be able to apply the results of belief revision, we need to represent ontologies as sets of formulas. The default theories of ontologies yield such sets. Then based on such sets, we can use the methods of belief revision to study ontology revision. In this paper, we attempt to study the translation of ontologies to default logic.

Similar works [9,10,11] have been investigated by researchers in translating inheritance nets to default logic. Inheritance nets [8] are means for representing taxonomic knowledge. In the inheritance language, there are strict links; default links; and three kinds of objects: categories, individuals and properties. There are some approaches translating inheritance nets to default logic. Etherington and Reiter [9] translated the inheritance nets with exceptions to default logic in which strict links are translated to facts, and defeasible links with exceptions to semi-normal defaults. Unlike Etherington and Reiter's method, in [10], all the links among properties were represented by normal defaults; the links between individuals and properties were represented as facts. A partial order on defaults was defined to decide which inference path was more preferable. In [11], it was assumed that all links were defeasible. Hence, all links were represented uniformly as facts of the corresponding default theory. The defaults only expressed closed world assumption between properties and individuals.

Our ontologies and inheritance nets are similar in that they both consist of two kinds of objects: concepts and properties; and there are strict and defeasible relations among these objects. But they are different. The structure of an inheritance net is a net and there are many connections among concepts and properties. However, an ontology in this paper includes a set of concepts which forms the main structure of the ontology under subsumption relation which is not defeasible. That is, the main structure of an ontology is a tree and not a net. Concepts are described by sets of properties, that is, ontologies distinguish concepts from properties. Similar to the default theories of inheritance nets, ontologies can be translated to default logic.

In this paper, we translate all the statements in ontologies to facts and the default inheritance of properties from concepts to their sub-concepts are represented by normal defaults in default logic. There is a priority order on these defaults due to the intuition similar to that of inheritance nets: subclasses override superclasses. Thus, a translation of ontologies to default logic with priority order on defaults is given. For an ontology with a tree structure under the subsumption relation, the ontology is consistent if and only if the default theory of the ontology has a unique extension.

The paper is organized as follows: in section 2, we give the basic concepts of default logic; the presuppositions and deduction rules for ontologies are discussed in section 3. In section 4, a method of translating ontologies to default logic with priority order on defaults is proposed. We conclude the paper with conclusion and future works.

2. DEFAULT LOGIC

Default logic introduced by Reiter [3,6] is one of the most famous formalism for non-monotonic reasoning and its most apparent property is default reasoning produce reliable conclusions but not the irrevocable ones.

Given a first order language L, a default rule δ is an expression of the form $p: q \ / \ r$, where p, q and r are formulas in L, which are called the *prerequisite*, *consequence* and *justification* of the default. The intuitive explanation of δ is that if p is provable and it is consistent to assume q, then infer r. A default theory is a pair (W,D), where W is a set of sentences in L, called the facts, and D is a set of defaults. An extension is a maximal consistent set of conclusions that can be drawn from a default theory. We call δ a normal default if $q=r$ and (W,D) a normal default theory if D is a set of normal defaults.

In a default theory, there are situations that it is reasonable to give some defaults higher priority order than others. We call a default theory (W,D) a prioritized default theory, denoted by $(W, D, <)$, if there is a priority order $<$ on the defaults in D. $(W, D, <)$ is a normal prioritized default theory if D is a set of normal defaults. Then, we give the definition of the extensions for prioritized default theories [7].

Definition 1. *Given a prioritized default theory* $(W, D, <)$, Γ *is an operator on sets of sentences such that for any set* S *of sentences,* $\Gamma(S)$ *is smallest satisfying the following conditions:*

(1) $W \subseteq \Gamma(S)$;

(2) *$Th(\Gamma(S))=\Gamma(S)$, that is, $\Gamma(S)$ is logically closed;*

(3) *if $p{:}q/r \in D$, $p\in\Gamma(S)$, $\neg q\notin S$ and there is no $\delta'=p'{:}q' / r'\in D$ such that $p'\in\Gamma(S), \neg q'\notin S$ and $\delta'<\delta$, then $r\in\Gamma(S)$, where $\delta'<\delta$ means that δ' has higher priority than δ.*

A set E of sentences is an *extension* of $(W, D, <)$ iff $\Gamma(E)=E$ for some operator Γ satisfying 1,2 and 3.

Given a prioritized default theory $(W, D, <)$, let Γ be an operator defined above and S be a set of sentences, then

(1) a default $\delta= p{:}q / r\in D$ is priority-free applicable to $\Gamma(S)$ with respect to S, if $p\in\Gamma(S)$ and $\neg q\notin S$. For convenience, we say δ is priority-free applicable with respect to S.

(2) a default $\delta= p{:}q / r \in D$ is applicable to $\Gamma(S)$ with respect to S, if $p\in \Gamma(S)$ and $\neg q\notin S$ and there is no default $\delta'=p'{:}q' / r'\in D$ such that $p'\in\Gamma(S), \neg q'\notin S$ and $\delta'<\delta$. For convenience, we say δ is applicable with respect to S.

Then, we given two propositions about the extensions of normal prioritized default theories.

Proposition 1. *Given a normal prioritized default theory $(W, D, <)$, there is at least one extensions.*

Proposition 2. *Let E, E' be two extensions of a normal prioritized default theory $(W, D, <)$, if $E\neq E'$, then $E\cup E'$ is inconsistent.*

For the proof of the above propositions, see [3].

3. ONTOLOGIES

In this section, we discuss the presuppositions for ontologies and the deduction rules in ontologies.

The presuppositions about ontology ***O***:

1. The objects in ***O*** are classified into four classes: categories, attributes denoted and attribute values. We call category objects concepts denoted by $C, D, \ldots$; a combination of attributes and attribute values of the form $[a{:}v]$ property which represent that the value of attribute a is v.

2. There is one kind of relation between concepts: the subsumption relation *isa*; two kinds of relations between a concept and a property: the inheritance relation *prop* and the default inheritance relation *dprop*.

We assume that a concept C has value v at attribute a, denoted by *prop*$(C,[a{:}v])$, means that every sub-concept of C has property $[a{:}v]$, that is, $[a{:}v]$ is a universal property of C ; a concept C defautly has value v at attribute a, denoted by *dprop*$(C,[a{:}v])$, means that defaultly every sub-concept of C has property $[a{:}v]$, that is, $[a{:}v]$ is a default property of C;

and C is a sub-concept of D, denoted by *isa*(C, D), means that for any property [*a*:*v*], if *prop*(D,[*a*:*v*]), then *prop*(C,[*a*:*v*]).

In another words, *isa* relates two concepts: *isa*(C, D) ("the dog is an animal", *isa*(dog, animal)) and *prop* relates a concept and a property: *prop*(C,[*a*:*v*]) ("Birds have two legs," *prop*(bird, [*legs*:2])); and *dprop* relates a concept and a property defaultly: *dprop*(C,[*a*:*v*]) ("Cars defaultly have 4 wheels,"*dprop*(car, [*wheels*:4])).

We assume there is only one value for an attribute defined in a concept.

3. For convenience, we assume that all the concepts form a tree under the subsumption relation, that is, if a concept C is subsumed by two concepts D and F then either $D = F$ or one of D and F is subsumed by another, where $D = F$ if and only if D instantiates the same set of properties as F does. Because as a classification of all the individuals in the real world, a tree-like structure is a better choice.

Definition 2. *An ontology* ***O***=(U, *isa*, *prop*, *dprop*, O), *where*

(1) U is a set of concepts and properties;

(2) *isa is a binary relation on concepts in* U. *We assume that isa is a partial order;*

(3) *prop and dprop are binary relations on concepts and properties in* U; *and*

(4) O *is a set of statements of the form*

isa(C, D) | $\neg$ *isa*(C, D) | *prop*(C, [*a*:*v*])| $\neg$ *prop*(C, [*a*:*v*])| *dprop*(C, [*a*:*v*]), *where* C, D,[*a*:*v*]$\in U$, and *isa*, *prop*, *dprop* are relations between concepts and between concepts and properties respectively.

In ontologies, all the universal properties of a super-concept are inherited to its sub-concepts. A sub-concept inherits all default properties of a super-concept unless they are overridden in the sub-concepts. That is, for a concept D and its default property [*a*:*v*], if a is redefined in a sub-concept C of D, then the new statement *prop*(C,[*a*:*v*']) or *dprop*(C,[*a*:*v*']) overrides the statement *dprop*(D,[*a*: *v*]). In this case, the default property [*a*:*v*] is not inherited from D to C.

With multiple inheritance, there can be conflicting statements, that is, default properties for a same attribute may be declared in more than one super-concepts. In this case, default properties declared in a more specific super-concept is inherited to its sub-concepts, for example, if *isa*(C,D), *isa*(C,F), *isa*(D,F), *dprop*(D, [*a*:*v*]), and *dprop*(F, [*a*:*v*']) ($v\neq v'$) and a is not redefined in C, then we have *dprop*(C,[*a*:*v*]), that is, C inherits the default property [*a*:*v*] from D since *isa*(D,F).

Based on what has been discussed above, we give the following deduction rules. Deduction rules in ontologies include inheritance rules, default inheritance rules, transitivity rules and subaltern rules.

The inheritance rule, if *isa(C,D)* and *prop(D, [a:v])* are provable, then infer *prop(C, [a:v])*, is denoted by *isa(C,D), prop(D,[a:v]) / prop(C,[a:v])*; the default inheritance rule, if *isa(C,D)* and *dprop(D,[a:v])* are provable and it is consistent to assume *dprop(C,[a:v])*, then infer *dprop(C,[a:v])*, is represented by *isa(C,D),dprop(D,[a:v]): dprop(C,[a:v]) / dprop(C,[a:v])*; the transitivity rule, if *isa(C,D)*, and *isa(D,F)* are provble, then infer *isa(C,F)*, is represented by *isa(C,D), isa(D,F) / isa(C,F)*. For the relation between *prop* and *dprop*, we have the following subaltern rule: *prop(C,[a:v]) / dprop(C,[a:v])*, which means that if a property is a universal property of a concept then it is a default property of the concept.

An ontology has the deduction rules to infer statements not explicitly represented in the ontology.

For the inheritance of default properties, in order to solve the conflicts caused by multiple inheritance, there is a priority order on defaults due to the intuition that sub-concepts overrides super-concepts. That is, give two defaults

δ= *isa(C,D)* , *dprop(D,[a:v]): dprop(C,[a:v]) / dprop(C,[a:v])*, and

δ'= *isa(C,F)* , *dprop(F,[a:v']): dprop(C,[a:v']) / dprop(C,[a:v'])*, then $\delta<\delta'$ if *isa(D,F)* is provable; for example, from the facts *isa(tweety, penguin)*, *isa(penguin,,bird)*, *dprop(penguin,[fly:no])* and *dprop(bird,[fly:yes])*, we can infer the statement *dprop(tweety,[fly:no])*.

For the consistency of a set of statements in an ontology or derived from an ontology, we give the following definition:

Definition 3. *A set of statements M is consistent if and only if there do not exist concepts C , D and properties [a:v],[a:v'] such that*

(1) *isa(C,D)* , $\neg$*isa(C,D)* $\in$ *Th(M)*;

(2) *prop(C,[a:v]), prop(C,[a:v'])* $\in$ *Th(M)*;

(3) *prop(C,[a:v]),* $\neg$*prop(C,[a:v])* $\in$ *Th(M)*;

(4) *dprop(C,[a:v]), dprop(C,[a:v'])* $\in$ *Th(M)*;

(5) *prop(C,[a:v]), dprop(C,[a:v'])* $\in$ *Th(M); where* $v\neq v'$, *and Th(M) is the logical closure of M, that is, the set of statements inferred from M by the deduction rules.*

We say an ontology ***O*** is consistent if and only if *O* is onsistent.

4. TRANSLATING ONTOLOGIES TO DEFAULT LOGIC

In this section, we propose the translation of ontologies to default logic, then study the properties of the default theories of ontologies.

Definition 4. *Given an ontology* ***O***, *we call a normal prioritized default theory (O, D, <) the default theory of* ***O*** , *if*

(1) $D=\{isa(C, D), dprop(D,[a:v]): dprop(C,[a:v]) / dprop(C,[a:v]) \mid C, D, [a:v] \in U, dprop(D,[a:v]) \in O\}$;

(2) $<$ *is a priority order on the defaults in D such that for any two defaults* $\delta_1 = isa(C, D), dprop(D,[a:v]): dprop(C,[a:v]) / dprop(C,[a:v])$, $\delta_2 = isa(C, F), dprop(F,[a: v']): dprop(C,[a: v']) / dprop(C,[a:v'])$, *we have* $\delta_1 < \delta_2$, *if* $isa(D, F)$.

Let $Th^+(O)$ be the first order logical closure of O which is the set of statements inferred from O by the deduction rules except the default inheritance rules.

We say $Th^+(O)$ is consistent if and only if there do not exist concepts C, D, properties $[a:v]$ and $[a:v']$ such that (1) $isa(C,D)$, $\neg isa(C,D) \in Th^+(O)$; (2) $prop(C,[a:v]), prop(C,[a:v']) \in Th^+(O)$; (3) $prop(C,[a:v]), \neg prop(C,[a:v]) \in Th^+(O)$; (4) $dprop(C,[a:v]), dprop(C,[a:v']) \in Th^+(O)$; (5) $prop(C,[a:v]), dprop(C,[a:v']) \in Th^+(O)$.

Definition 5. *A statement* θ *is a theorem of an ontology* ***O****, if and only if* θ *can be inferred from the deduction rules.*

Definition 6. *An ontology* ***O*** *is a tree under the subsumption relation isa if there are no concepts* $C, D, F \in U$ *such that* $D \neq F$, $\neg isa(D,F)$, $\neg isa(F,D)$, $isa(C,D)$ *and* $isa(C,F)$.

Using the above propositions, we have the following theorem:

Theorem 1. *Given an ontology* ***O*** *, if* ***O*** *is a tree and* $Th^+(O)$ *is consistent then the normal prioritized default theory of the ontology* $(O, D, <)$ *has a unique extension.*

Proof. Since all the defaults in D are normal defaults, the default theory has at least one extensions (Proposition 1). Assume that there are two distinct extensions E and E', we prove that $E \cup E'$ is consistent. Since E and E' are extensions, then $\Gamma(E)=E$ and $\Gamma(E')=E'$. From Definition 3, there are the following five kinds of cases that may make $E \cup E'$ inconsistent:

(1) $isa(C,D) \in E$, $\neg isa(C,D) \in E'$; in this case, since the derivation of $isa(C,D)$ and $\neg isa(C,D)$ is not concerned with defaults, then $isa(C,D)$, $\neg isa(C,D) \in Th^+(O)$ which is impossible since O is consistent.

(2) $prop(C,[a:v]) \in E$, $prop(C,[a:v']) \in E'$; where $v \neq v'$; for the same reason as case one, this case is impossible.

(3) $prop(C,[a:v]) \in E$, $\neg prop(C,[a:v]) \in E'$; for the same reason as case one, this case is impossible.

(4) $dprop(C,[a:v]) \in E$, $dprop(C,[a:v']) \in E'$; in this case, it is impossible that $dprop(C,[a:v]), dprop(C,[a:v']) \in Th^+(O)$, since O is consistent; if one of $dprop(C,[a:v])$ and $dprop(C,[a:v'])$ is in $Th^+(O)$ and the other is derived from some default, then let $dprop(C,[a:v]) \in Th^+(O)$ and there is $\delta = isa(C,D), dprop(D,[a:v']): dprop(C,[a:v']) / dprop(C,[a:v'])$ applicable with respect to E'. The applicatin of δ produces $dprop(C,[a:v']) \in E'$ which contradicts with $dprop(C,[a:v]) \in Th^+(O)) \subseteq E'$. If there exists some defaults

δ_1 applicable with respect to E and δ_2 applicable with respect to E', let δ_1= *isa*(C,D) , *dprop*(D,[a:v]): *dprop*(C,[a:v]) / *dprop*(C,[a:v]), δ_2= *isa*(C,F) , *dprop*(F,[a:v']): *dprop*(C,[a:v']) / *dprop*(C,[a:v']), producing *dprop*(C,[a:v]) $\in E$ and *dprop*(C,[a:v']) $\in E'$. In the process of constructing extension E, before the using of δ_1, δ_1 and δ_2 are priority-free applicable with respect to E since *isa*(C,D), *isa*(C,F) $\in Th^+(O)) \subseteq \Gamma(E)$, *dprop*($D$,[$a$:$v$]), *dprop*($F$,[$a$:$v'$]) $\in O \subseteq \Gamma(E)$ and there is no v_1 such that $v_1 \neq v$, $v_1 \neq v'$ and *dprop*(C,[a:v_1])$\in E$.

Similarly, in the process of constructing E', before the using of δ_2, δ_1 and δ_2 are priority-free applicable with respect to E'. Hence, if there is no subsumption relation between D and F, then C has two parent concepts which contradicts with the assumption that ***O*** is a tree. Otherwise, *isa*(D,F) or *isa*(F,D) , then we have $\delta_1 < \delta_2$, or $\delta_2 < \delta_1$ which means that δ_2 is not applicable with respect to E' or δ_1 is not applicable with respect to E and contradicts with the above assumption.

(5) *prop*(C,[a:v]) $\in E$, *dprop*(C,[a:v']) $\in E'$; in this case, *dprop*(C,[a:v]) $\in E$ by the subaltern rule, and for the same reason as case (4), this case is impossible.

Hence, $E \cup E'$ is consistent and from the contraposition of proposition 2, we have $E=E'$ contradictory with our assumption E and E' are two distinct extensions of (O, D, <). Therefore, (O, D, <) has only one extension. □

The above theorem shows that the set of statements inferred from the default theory of ***O*** is consistent if ***O*** is a tree under *isa* and $Th^+(O)$ is consistent.

From the definition 4,5 and theorem 1, we have the following proposition:

Proposition 3. *Given an ontology **O** with a tree strcuture under isa relation, if $Th^+(O)$ is consistent, then $E=Th(O)$, where E is the unique extension of the default thory (O,D, <) of **O**.*

From theorem 1 and the definitions of consistency of ***O*** , we have the following proposition:

Proposition 4. *Given an ontology **O** with a tree strcuture under isa relation, **O** is consistent if and only if (O, D, <) has a unique extension.*

5. CONCLUSION AND FUTURE WORKS

We provide a method of translating ontologies to default logic with the following properties:

(1) for an ontology ***O*** , given concepts C, D, $F \in U$, and a property [a:v] $\in U$, if the statements formed from C, D, [a:v] by *isa*, *prop*, and *dprop* relations are in O, then they are facts in the default theory of ***O*** ;

(2) if *dprop(D,[a:v])*$\in$*O*, then the default rule *isa(C,D)* , *dprop(D,[a:v])*: *dprop(C,[a:v])* / *dprop(C,[a:v])* is in *D*; the priority order < on the defaults of *D* is due to the intuition that sub-concepts overrides super-concepts.

(3) for an ontology ***O*** with tree structure under *isa* relation, ***O*** is consistent if and only (*O, D*, <) has exactly one extension.

Future works includes: the study of the properties of ontologies in terms of default logic, the revision of default theories and ontology revision based on the default theories of ontologies.

NOTES

The work is partially supported by the National NSF of China (No. 60373042, 60273019 and 60037017), the NSF of Yunnan Province(No. 2004F0017Q), and the Education Bureau Youth Fund of Yunnan Province (No. 03Y312D and 04Y769D).

REFERENCES

[1] ValentinaTamma, A. and Trevor, J. SupportingInheritance Mechanisms in Ontology Representation. In *Proc. of the 12th International Conference on Knowledge Engineering and Knowledge Management*, pages 140-155, 2000.

[2] Guarino, N. and Welty, C. Ontological Analysis of Taxonomic Relationship. In *Proc. of International Conference on Conceptual Modelling*, pages 210-224, 2000.

[3] Besnard, P. *An introduction to default logic*, Springer-Verlag, Berlin, 1989.

[4] Gruber,T. A Translation Approach to Portable Ontology Specifications. In *Knowledge Acquisition,* 5(2):199-220, 1993.

[5] Genesereth, M. R., Nillson, N. *LogicalFoundations of Artificial Intelligence*, Morgan Kauffman, 1987.

[6] Reiter, R. A Logic for Default Reasoning. In *Artificial Intelligence*, 13:81-132, 1980.

[7] Antoniou, G. Priorities in Default Logic Revisited. In *Proc. of 4th Congress of the Italian Association forArtificial Intelligence*, Springer, pages 152-162,1995.

[8] Touretzky, D. S. *The Mathematics of InheritanceSystems*, Morgan Kaufmann, Pitman, London, 1986.

[9] Etherington, D. Reiter, R. On Inheritance Hierarchies with Exception. In *Proc. of AAAI-83*, William Kaufman, Los Altos, CA, pages 104-108, 1983.

[10] Touretzky, D. Implicit Ordering of Defaults in Inheritance systems. In *Readings in Nonmonotonic Reasoning*, Morgan Kaufmann, Los Altos, CA, pages 106-109, 1987.

[11] Ingrid, N. Translating Inheritance Nets to Default Logic, http://www.ubka.uni-karlsruhe.de/cgi-bin/psgunzip/ira/1994/25/25.pdf, 1994.

[12] Bochman, A. A foundational theory of belief and belief change. In *Artificial Intelligence*, 108(1-2):309-352, 1999.

FUZZY TIMED OBJECT-ORIENTED PETRI NET

Hua Xu and Peifa Jia
State Key Laboratory of Intelligent Technology and Systems, Tsinghua University, Beijing, 100084, P. R. China

Abstract: The goal of this work is to extend a model of timed object-oriented Petri nets (TOPN) to allow modeling and analyzing dynamic systems with timing effect on system information. In the proposed Fuzzy timed object-oriented Petri net (FTOPN), we attach temporal fuzzy sets to each transition objects accounting for the aging of information. In particular, we investigate a new way to represent and deal with timing effect in dynamic systems. FTOPN also supports learning similar to that in fuzzy timed Petri net (FTPN). Finally, we use FTOPN to model a real decision making model of our cooperative multiple robot system (CMRS) to demonstrate its following benefits: independent training for its supporting object abstraction and size reconfiguration for its object granularity control function.

Key words: Petri nets; Fuzzy sets; Object-oriented method; Timing effect; Learning

1. INTRODUCTION

Petri nets [1], [2] have been widely used to model various discrete event systems [3]. Characterized as concurrent, asynchronous, distributed, parallel, nondeterministic, and/or stochastic [1], Petri nets have gained more and more applications. However, when they are used to analyze and model practical systems in different fields, models may be too complex to be analyzed. These years, object-oriented concepts have been introduced into Petri nets and object-oriented Petri nets (OPN) are presented such as HOONet [4], OBJSA [5], COOPN/2 [6] and LOOPN++ [7], which are suggested on the base of colored Petri Net (CPN) [8]. Then for providing the ability of modeling time critical systems, timed hierarchical object oriented Petri net (TOPN) [9] is proposed on the base of HOONet [4]. It supports temporal description and object-oriented concepts. Modeling features in TOPN support abstracting complex systems, so the corresponding models can be simplified effectively.

On the other hand, although Petri nets can be used to model and analyze different systems, they fail to model the timing effects in dynamic systems. Recently, fuzzy timed Petri net (FTPN) [10] has been presented and it has solved this modeling problem, which is on the base of temporal fuzzy sets and Petri nets. However, similar to the general Petri Nets, FTPN may also meet the complexity problem, when it is used to model complex dynamic systems.

In this paper, fuzzy timed object-oriented Petri net (FTOPN) is proposed on the base of TOPN and FTPN, whose aim is to solve the timing effects and other modeling problems of dynamic systems. This paper is organized as the following. In Section 2, the preliminary notions of TOPN are reviewed. Section 3 presents our FTOPN. Section 4 discusses the learning of FTOPN. In section 5, FTOPN is used to model the decision making procedure of our cooperative multiple robot system (CMRS) to demonstrate its model abstraction and reconfiguration benefits. Finally, the conclusion and future work can be found in section 5.

2. PRELIMINARY NOTIONS OF TOPN

Formally TOPN is a four-tuple (OIP, ION, DD, SI), where (OIP,ION,DD) is an ordinary object Petri net-"HOONet" [4] and *SI* associates a *static (firing)* temporal *interval* SI: $\{o\}\rightarrow[a, b]$ with each object o, where *a* and *b* are rationals in the range $0\leq a\leq b\leq+\infty$, with $b\neq+\infty$. The four parts in TOPN have different function roles. *Object identification place* (OIP) is a unique identifier of a class. *Internal timed object net* (ION) is a net to depict the behaviors (methods) of a class. *Data dictionary* (DD) declares the attributes of a class in TOPN. And *static time interval function* (SI) binds the temporal knowledge of a class in TOPN. There are two kinds of places in TOPN. They are common places (represented as circles with thin prim) and abstract places (represented as circles with bold prim). Abstract places are also associated with a static time interval. Because at this situation, abstract places represent not only firing conditions, but also the objects with their own behaviors. So, abstract places (TABP) in TOPN also need to be associated with time intervals. One problem to be emphasized is that the tokens in abstract places need to have two colors at least. Before the internal behaviors of an abstract place object are fired, the color of tokens in it is one color (represented as hollow token in this paper). However, after fired, the color becomes the other one (represented as liquid token in this paper). At this time, for the following transitions, it is just actually enabled. There are three kinds of transitions in TOPN. The timed primitive transition (represented as rectangles with thin prim) (TPIT), timed abstract transition (represented as rectangles with bold prim) (TABT) and timed communication transition (represented as rectangles with double thin prim) (TCOT).

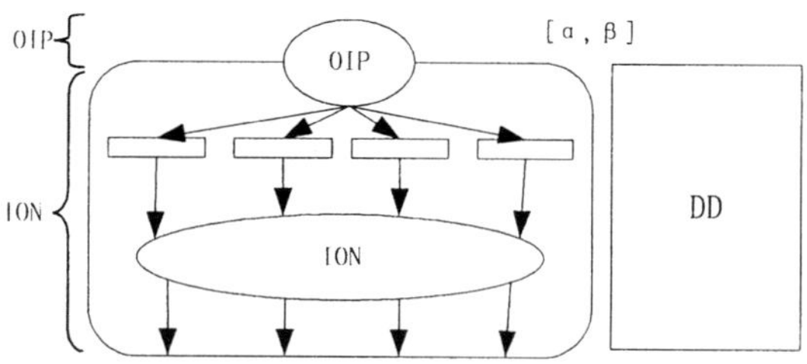

Figure 1. The General Structure of TOPN

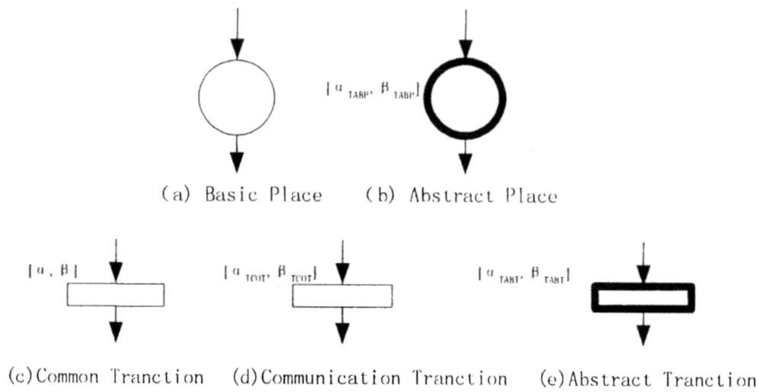

Figure 2. Places and Transactions in TOPN

Static time intervals change the behavior of TOPN just similar to a time Petri net in the following way. If an object *o* with SI(*o*)=[*a*, *b*] becomes enabled at time I_0, then the object *o must be* fired in the time interval [I_0+*a*, I_0+*b*], unless it becomes disabled by the removal of tokens from some input place in the meantime. The *static earliest firing time* of the object *o* is *a*; the *static latest firing time* of *o* is *b*; the *dynamic earliest firing time* (EFT) of *t* is I_0+*a*; the *dynamic latest firing time* (LFT) of *t* is I_0+*b*; the *dynamic firing interval* of *t* is [I_0+*a*, I_0+*b*].

The state of TOPN (Extended States-"ES") is a 3-tuple, where ES=(M, I, path) consists of a marking M, a firing interval vector I and an execution path. According to the initial marking M_0 and the firing rules mentioned above, the following marking at any time can be calculated. The vector--"I" is composed of the temporal intervals of enabled transitions and TABPs, which are to be fired in the following states. The dimension of I equals to the number of enabled transitions and TABPs at the current state. The firing interval of every enabled transition or TABP can be got according to the calculation formula of EFT and LFT in TOPN [9].

For enabling rules in TOPN, two different situations exist. A transition t in TOPN is said to be enabled at the current state (M, I, path), if each input place p of t contains at least the number of *solid tokens* equal to the weight of the directed arcs connecting p to t in the marking M. If the TABP object is marked with a *hollow token*, it is enabled. At this time, its ION is enabled. After the ION has been *fired*, the tokens in TABP are changed into *solid ones*.

We say that an object *o* is *fireable* in state (M, I, path) if it is enabled, and if it is legal to fire *o* next. This will be true if and only if the EFT of *o* is less than or equal to the LFT of all other enabled transitions. Of course, even with strong time semantics, *o*'s being fireable in state (*M*, I, path) does not necessarily mean that *t will* fire in the time interval I.

3. FUZZY TIMED OBJECT-ORIENTED PETRI NETS

Similar to FTPN [10], fuzzy set concepts are introduced into TOPN [9]. Then FTOPN is proposed, which can describe fuzzy timing effect in dynamic systems.

Definition 1: FTOPN is a six-tuple, FTOPN= (OIP, ION, DD, SI, R, I) where

1) Suppose OIP=(oip, pid, M_0, status), where oip, pid, M_0 and status are the same as those in HOONet [4] and TOPN [9].
   - oip is a variable for the unique name of a FTOPN.
   - pid is a unique process identifier to distinguish multiple instances of a class, which contains return address.
   - M_0 is the function that gives initial token distributions of this specific value to OIP.
   - status is a flag variable to specify the state of OIP.
2) ION is the internal net structure of FTOPN to be defined in the following. It is a variant CPN that describes the changes in the values of attributes and the behaviors of methods in FTOPN.
3) DD formally defines the variables, token types and functions (methods) just like those in HOONet [4] and TOPN [9].

4) SI is a static time interval binding function, SI: {OIP}→Q^*, where Q^* is a set of time intervals.
5) R: {OIP} → r, where r is a specific threshold.
6) I is a function of the time *v*. It evaluates the resulting degree of the abstract object firing. □

Definition 2: An internal object net structure of TOPN, ION = (P,T,A,K,N,G,E,F,M_0)

1) P and T are finite sets of places and transitions with time restricting conditions attached respectively.
2) A is a finite set of arcs such that $P\cap T=P\cap A=T\cap A=\Phi$.
3) *K* is a function mapping from P to a set of token types declared in DD.
4) N, G, and E mean the functions of nodes, guards, and arc expressions, respectively. The results of these functions are the additional condition to restrict the firing of transitions. So they are also called *additional restricting conditions.*
5) F is a special arc from any transitions to OIP, and notated as a body frame of ION.
6) M_0 is a function giving an initial marking to any place the same as those in HOONet [4] and TOPN [9]. □

Definition 3: A set of places in TOPN is defined as P=PIP∪TABP, where

1) Primary place PIP is a three-tuple: PIP =(P,R,I), where
   - P is the set of common places similar to those in PN [1], [2].
2) Timed abstract place (TABP) is a six-tuple: TABP= TABP(pn, refine state, action, SI, R, I), where
   - pn is the identifier of the abstract timed place.
   - refine state is a flag variable denoting whether this abstract place has been refined or not.
   - action is the static reaction imitating the internal behavior of this abstract place.
3) SI, R and I are the same as those in *Definition 1*.□

Definition 4: A set of transitions in TOPN can be defined as T= TPIT∪TABT∪TCOT, where

1) Timed primitive transition TPIT = TPIT (BAT, SI), where
   - BAT is the set of common transitions.
2) Timed abstract transition TABT= TABT (tn, refine state, action, SI), where
   - tn is the name of this TABT.
3) Timed communication transition TCOT=TCOT (tn, target, comm type, action, SI).
   - tn is the name of TCOT.
   - target is a flag variable denoting whether the behavior of this TCOT has been modeled or not. If target="Yes", it has been modeled. Otherwise, if target="No", it has not been modeled yet.

- comm type is a flag variable denoting the communication type. If comm type ="SYNC", then the communication transition is synchronous one. Otherwise, if comm type="ASYN", it is an asynchronous communication transition.

4) *SI is* the same as that in *Definition 1*.
5) *refine state* and *action* are the same as those in *Definition 3*. □

Similar to those in FTPN [10], the object t fires if the foregoing objects come with a nonzero marking of the tokens; the level of firing is inherently continuous. The level of firing ($z(v)$) assuming values in the unit interval is governed by the following expression:

$$z(v) = (\mathop{T}_{i=1}^{n}(r_i \rightarrow x_i(v'))\, sw_i)\, t\mathrm{I}(v) \tag{1}$$

where T (or t) denotes a t-norm while "s" stands for any s-norm. "v" is the time instant immediately following v'. More specifically, $x_i(v)$ denotes a level of marking of the ith place. The weight w_i is used to quantify an input coming from the ith place. The threshold r_i expresses an extent to which the corresponding place's marking contributes to the firing of the transition. The implication operator (→) expresses a requirement that a transition fires if the level of tokens exceeds a specific threshold (quantified here by r_i).

Once the transition has been fired, the input places involved in this firing modify their markings that is governed by the expression

$$x_i(v)=x_i(v')t(1-z(v)) \tag{2}$$

(Note that the reduction in the level of marking depends upon the intensity of the firing of the corresponding transition, $z(v)$.) Owing to the t-norm being used in the above expression, the marking of the input place gets lowered. The output place increases its level of tokens following the expression:

$$y(v)=y(v')sz(v) \tag{3}$$

The s-norm is used to aggregate the level of firing of the transition with the actual level of tokens at this output place. This way of aggregation makes the marking of the output place increase.

The FTOPN model directly generalizes the Boolean case of TOPN and OPN. In other words, if $x_i(v)$ and w_i assume values in {0, 1} then the rules governing the behavior of the net are the same as those encountered in TOPN.

4. LEARNING IN FTOPN

The parameters of FTOPN are always given beforehand. In general, however, these parameters may not be available and need to be estimated just like those in FTPN[10]. The estimation is conducted on the base of some experimental data concerning marking of input and output places. The marking of the places is provided as a discrete time series. More specifically we consider that the marking of the output place(s) is treated as a collection of target values to be followed during the training process. As a matter of fact, the learning is carried in a supervised mode returning to these target data.

The connections of the FTOPN (namely weights w_i and thresholds r_i) as well as the time decay factors α_i are optimized (or trained) so that a given performance index $\boldsymbol{Q}$ becomes minimized. The training data set consists of (a) initial marking of the input places $x_i(0),\ldots,x_n(0)$ and (b) target values—markings of the output place that are given in a sequence of discrete time moments, that is target(0), target(1),..., target(K).

In our FTOPN, the performance index $\boldsymbol{Q}$ under discussion assumes the form of the following sum:

$$Q=\sum_{k=1}^{K}(target(k)-y(k))^2 \tag{4}$$

where the summation is taken over all time instants (k =1, 2,..., K).

The crux of the training in FTOPN models follows the general update formula being applied to the parameters:

$$\mathbf{param}(\text{iter}+1)=\mathbf{param}(\text{iter})-\gamma\nabla_{\mathbf{param}}\boldsymbol{Q} \tag{5}$$

where γ is a learning rate and $\Box_{\mathbf{param}}\boldsymbol{Q}$ denotes a gradient of the performance index taken with respect to all parameters of the net (here we use a notation **param** to embrace all parameters in FTOPN to be trained).

In the training of FTOPN models, marking of the input places is updated according to the following form:

$$x_i^{\sim}=x_i(0)T_i(k) \tag{6}$$

where $T_i(k)$ is the temporal decay. And Ti(k) complies with the following form. In what follows, the temporal decay is modeled by an exponential function,

$$T_i(k)=\begin{cases}\exp(-\alpha_i(k-k_i)) & if \quad k>k_i, \\ 0 & others\end{cases} \tag{7}$$

The level of firing of the place can be computed as the following:

$$z=(\mathop{T}_{i=1}^{n}\ ((r_i\rightarrow x_i^{\sim})sw_i)) \tag{8}$$

The successive level of tokens at the output place and input places can be calculated as:

$$y(k) = y(k\text{-}1)\boldsymbol{s}z,\ x_i(k) = x_i(k\text{-}1)\boldsymbol{t}(1\text{-}z) \tag{9}$$

We assume that the initial marking of the output place y(0) is equal to zero, y(0)=0. The derivatives of the weights w_i are computed as follows:

$$\frac{\partial}{\partial w_i}(target(k) - y(k))^2 = -2(target(k) - y(k)\frac{\partial y(k)}{\partial w_i}) \tag{10}$$

where i=1,2,..., n. Note that y(k+1)=y(k)**s**z(k).

5. A MODELING EXAMPLE

In cooperative multiple robot systems (CMRS), every robot is controlled according to different system information such as other robot states, its own states and task assignment. As the information may not be available from all sensors or sources at the same time moment, the one that occurs earlier needs to be discounted over time as becoming less relevant. That is to say, information timing effects exist in this kind of dynamic systems. However, in the control of every robot system, every kind of information is required simultaneously. As the information readings could come at different time instants and be collected at different sampling frequency, we encounter an inevitable timing effect of information collected by the system and sensors. It becomes apparent that its relevance is the highest at the time moment when the system sensor captures it but then its relevance has to be discounted over the passage of time. This is an effect of aging that has to be viewed as an integral part of the model. So FTOPN is used to model our CMRS. At the same time, FTOPN can reduce the model complexity and can model complex decision making processes in different levels, because of the OO abstraction concept supported in FTOPN. It triggers interest in the class of the FTOPN.

5.1 CMRS Example

In our experiment, there are two cooperative robots. FTOPN is used to model the information fusion process in the decision making of scheduling robot in every robot. Because the model is hierarchical, only the highest level of the model is depicted in Figure.3.

In the model of Figure.3, 3 place objects are used to represent 3 kinds of information to be fused. Each kind of information may include different detailed contents. For example, “other robot state” may include other robots’ working state, location, speed, movement direction, etc al. So every kind of information is also an abstract object. On the other hand, the relative firing temporal interval is [a, b] of the object. The information should be sampled and processed in this relative interval. So does command sending. If the relative time exceeds it, the information should be sampled again and task should be reassigned. In the model, one transaction object represents the information fusion process. The timing effect on the fusion is depicted in Figure.4. The information "other robot state" and "own state" complies with the rule in Figure.4 (1). The other information complies with Figure.4 (2). After the fusion, a new command will be sent in this relative interval. The command to be sent is also a place object, which include robot schedule and control commands.

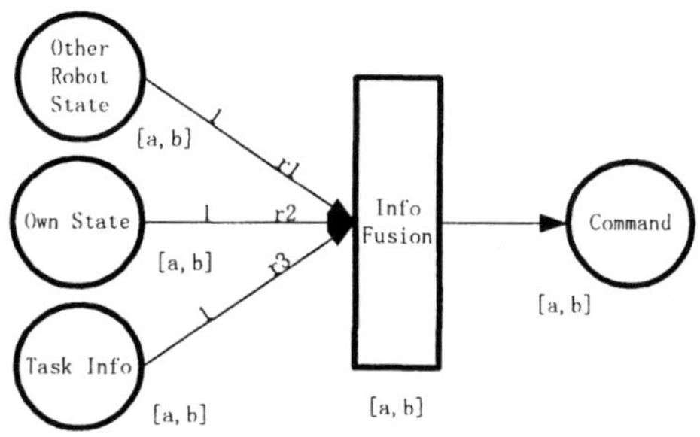

Figure3. The FTOPN Model

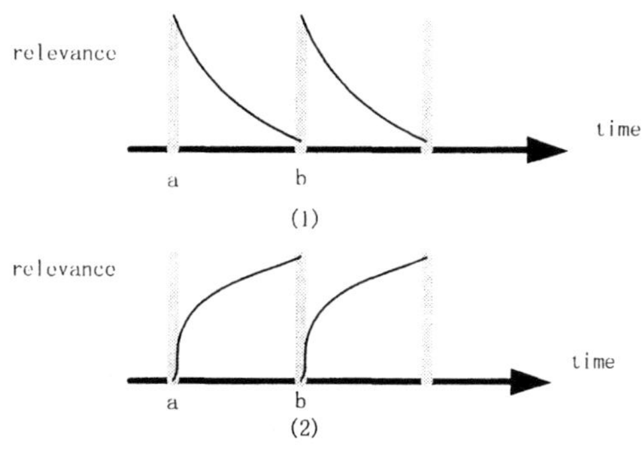

Figure 4. The Relevance

What's more, all the objects in Figure.3 can also be depicted in details by FTOPN. For example, the object—"Other Robot State" in Figure.3 can also be modeled concretely with FTOPN. The detailed model of the object is depicted in Figure.5. It is also an independent fuzzy reduction process. According to the modeling and analysis requirements, the detailed model can be unfolded directly in the model of Figure.3. At the same time, its training can be conducted independently. It can also be reduced independently and the reduction results will be used as the believing effect of the corresponding object in the higher level of the FTOPN model in Figure.3.

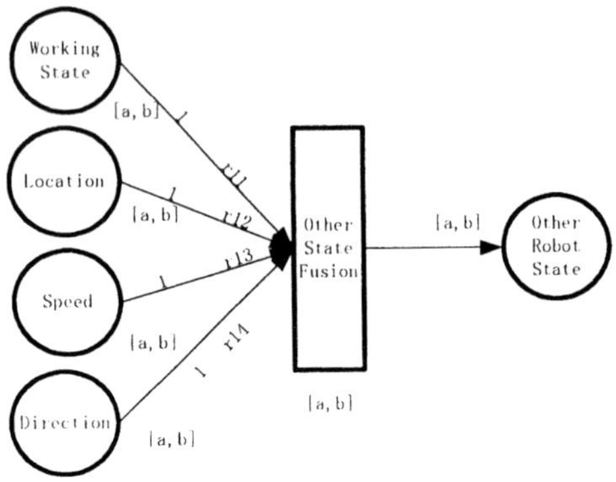

Figure 5. The Object-"Other Robot State" Model

After completing the FTOPN model, the learning algorithm of FTOPN can be used to train our model and adjust it to fulfill the practical requirements.

5.2 Application Analysis

From the view of the former FTOPN modeling example, objects in FTOPN model can be abstracted. They can be modeled and represented in other levels independently. At the same time, the training and fuzzy reduction can also be conducted independently. So for the abstraction concepts supported, the model complexity has been reduced effectively because of abstraction concepts in FTOPN. And the fuzzy reduction procedures have been simplified. Essentially, hierarchical modeling idea in FTOPN is to control model size by abstracting objects in FTOPN model. In nature, OO abstraction concepts are used to control fuzzy knowledge granularity in FTOPN. Because OO concepts are supported in FTOPN, the abstract objects can be unfolded or abstracted in FTOPN model flexibly. Our modeling focus can also be paid upon the important parts.

A comparative analysis between FPN, PN and neural network is conducted in [11]. Table.1 summarizes the main features of the fuzzy timed Object-oriented Petri nets and contrast these with the structures with which the proposed constructs have a lot in common, namely FPN and TFPN. It becomes apparent that FTOPN combine the advantages of both FPN in terms of their learning abilities and the glass-style of processing (and architectures) of Petri nets with the abstraction of OO concepts.

Table.1 Object Petri nets, Fuzzy Petri nets and Fuzzy Time Object-oriented Petri nets: a comparative analysis

Characteristics	Object Petri nets	Fuzzy Petri Nets	Fuzzy Timed Object Oriented Petri nets
Learning Aspects	From non-existent to significantly limited (the same as those of common Petri nets).	Significant learning abilities parametric optimization of the connections of the net. Structural optimization can be exercised through a variable number of the transitions utilized in the network.	Significant learning abilities as well as FPN. Distributed learning (training) abilities are supported in different independent objects on various system model levels.
Knowledge Representation Aspects	Glass Box or black box style knowledge representation supporting as a result of abstracting a given problem (problem specification) onto the structure of the net in different levels. Well-defined semantics of places and transitions	Transparent knowledge representation (glass box processing style) the problem (its specification) is mapped directly onto the topology of the fuzzy Petri net. Additionally, fuzzy sets deliver an essential feature of continuity required to cope with continuous phenomena encountered in a vast array of problems (including classification tasks)	Glass Box Style (Transparent Knowledge Representation) and Black Box Processing is supported at the same time. The problem (its specification) is mapped directly onto the topology of FTOPN. Knowledge representation granularity reconfiguration reacts on the reduction of model size and complexity.

6. CONCLUSIONS AND FUTURE WORKS

Timing effect is a usual phenomenon in dynamic systems especially in time critical systems. In order to model, analyze and simulate this kind of systems, this paper proposes fuzzy timed object-oriented Petri net (FTOPN) on the base of TOPN [9] and FTPN [4]. Temporal fuzzy sets are used in FTOPN to describe the timing effect and evaluation levels can be got according to the information arriving time and specific fuzzy relevance function. What's more, compared with FTPN (or FPN) models, the model size and reduction complexity of FTOPN models can be reduced by controlling object granularity because of supporting OO concept in FTOPN. Every abstract object in FTOPN can train and reduce independently according to the modeling and analysis requirements for OO concepts supported in FTOPN. The validity of this modeling method has been demonstrated by using it in the simulation of the decision information fusion process in our CMRS.

State analysis needs to be studied in the future. Xu [9] has proposed an extended State Graph to analyze the state change of TOPN models. With the temporal fuzzy sets introduced into TOPN, the certainty factor about object firing (state changing) needs to be considered in the state analysis.

ACKNOWLEDGEMENTS

This work is jointly supported by the National Nature Science Foundation for Youth Fund (Grant No: 60405011) and China Postdoctoral Foundation for China Postdoctoral Science Fund (Grant No: 20040350078).

REFERENCES

1. Tadao Murata, "Petri Nets: Properties, Analysis and Applications", Proceedings of IEEE, Vol.77, No.4, April 1989, pp.541-580
2. James L. Peterson, Petri Net Theory and the Modeling of Systems, Prentice-Hall, 1991
3. John O.Moody, Panos J. Antsaklis, Supervisory Control of Discrete Event Systems Using Petri Nets, Kluwer Academic Publishers, 1998:1-4
4. Jang-Eui Hong, Doo-Hwan Bae, Software Modeling And Analysis Using a Hierarchical Object-oriented Petri net, Information Sciences 130(2000), 133-164
5. E. Battiston, F.D. Cindio, G. Mauri, OBJSA Nets: a class of high-level nets having objects as domains, in: APN'88, Lecture Notes in Computer Science, vol. 340, 1988, pp. 20±43.
6. Biberstein, D. Buchs, An object-oriented specification language based on hierarchical algebraic Petri nets, in: Proceedings of the IS-CORE Workshop Amsterdam, September 1994 (and TR: EPFL-DI 94-76)
7. C. Lakos, C. Keen, LOOPN++: a new language for object-oriented Perti nets, Technical Report R94-4, Networking Research Group, Univesity of Tasmania, Australia, April 1994.
8. Kurt Jensen, Coloured Petri Nets: Basic Concepts, Analysis methods and Practical Use, 1992, Berlin: Springer,1:65-85
9. Hua Xu, Studies on Timed Hierarchical Object-oriented Petri Net and Its Application, Doctor Thesis, Tsinghua University, 2003
10. Pedrycz, Witold; Camargo, Heloisa: Fuzzy timed Petri nets, Fuzzy Sets and Systems Volume: 140, Issue: 2, December 1, 2003, pp. 301-330
11. Witold Pedrycz, Generalized fuzzy Petri nets as pattern classifiers, Pattern Recognition Letters 20 (1999):1489－1498

MODELING MULTI-AGENT SYSTEMS WITH HIERARCHICAL COLORED PETRI NETS

Bingxian Ma [1,2]
[1](Institute of Computing Technology, Chinese Academy of Sciences, Beijing, China, 100080;
[2](The Graduate School of the Chinese Academy of Sciences, Beijing, China, 100039)

Abstract: A new approach to model multi-agent systems with hierarchical colored Petri nets is introduced. Every agent has its colored Petri net system, when agents are composed into a MAS, we get hierarchical colored Petri net system of the multi-agent system, properties of the hierarchical colored Petri net system, such as reachability, deadlock detection and avoidance, fairness can be used to analyze dynamic properties of the multi-agent system.

Key words: agent, multi-agent system, hierarchical colored Petri nets

1. INTRODUCTION

Multi-agent systems (MASs, [1,2]) provide robust and scalable approach for the solution of complex problems. In a MAS, different agents are organized working together to achieve the project, Each individual agent is organized to be a specialist for a particular task of the MAS, but none has the capability of performing all the tasks required of the project. Agents will cooperate and interact with others to achieve the project. MASs are obviously dynamic systems, composing heterogeneous agents running to achieve users demands. The technologies of modeling and analyzing of MAS are very important for the using of agents technology, which is not a new idea. Many works ([2,3,4,5,6])have been done to model and analysis the inter-relationships among agents, while their methods are not good at modeling the distributed and concurrent events in a MAS at the system level.

Petri nets ([7,8]) are applicable to a variety of fields and systems, especially suitable for systems with distributed and concurrent events ,and have been used to model and analyze MASs. [9]firstly modeled single agent behaviors with Petri nets, [10]uses predicate/transition nets model and analysis multi-agent behaviors, a single Pr/T net is used to model the whole multi-agent problem, especially multi-agent plans.[3] using system net, agent nets and connectors nets model the mobile agents environment, mobile agent and connectors. [11] use agents based G-net (a extended G-net([3])) model agents, which have explicit asynchronous communication interface and support formal reasoning of agents behaviors. Colored Petri nets([12]) ,combining the advantages of Petri nets and high level programming languages, are suit to model complex systems with concurrent and dynamic behaviors. [4,5,6]use colored Petri nets model the sociality, conversation and interaction between agents in multi-agent systems. These works mostly are about just one aspect property of a MAS.

How to embed Petri nets technologies into the dynamic running processes and get full-sided analysis of a MAS are the problems that we are interested in. In this paper, we will set out a new approach to model MAS with hierarchical colored Petri nets. Each agent has its colored Petri net system, when composed into a MAS we can get its hierarchical colored Petri net system of the MAS, through which we are able to get the dynamic properties of the MAS, including qualitative and quantitative properties.

The remainder of this paper is structured as follows: In section 2 we briefly present related concepts and theories about this paper, in section 3, we model and analyze MAS with hierarchical colored Petri net system; we conclude current workings and present further work in section 4.

2. AGENT AND HIERARCHICAL COLORED PETRI NETS

Agents are mostly used to denote a hardware or (more usually) software-based computer systems that enjoy the following properties ([1,2]): autonomy, social ability, reactivity, and pro-activeness. MAS is an approach for the solution of complex problems. In a MAS, different agents are organized work together to achieve the project, Each individual agent is organized to be a specialist for a particular task of the MAS, but none has the capability of performing all the tasks required of the project. Agents will cooperate and interact with others to achieve the project. For the smoothly running of the MAS, effective formal model and analysis methods and tools are essentially.

Colored Petri nets (CP-nets,[12]) attaching a color to each token and a color set to each place allows us to use fewer places than would be needed in a PT-net without losing any properties. The basic idea behind Hierarchical Colored Petri nets (HCP-net) is to allow the modeler to construct a large model by combining a number of small CP-nets into a larger net which is similar to the situation in which a programmer constructs a large program from a set of modules and subroutines. It is always possible to translate a HCP-net into a non hierarchical CP-net-which in turn can be translate into an ordinary Petri net ,which means that the theoretical modeling powers of these three classes of Petri nets are same.

3. MODELING MULTI-AGENT SYSTEMS WITH HIERARCHICAL COLORED PETRI NETS

We set up a new approach to model MASs with HCP-nets technology. Firstly, the structure of an agent is based on BDI theories ([1,2]) and its behaviors can be modeled with a non-hierarchical CP-net, the structure of an agent is:

Agent Profile	Description of the agent, name, goals, intentions, beliefs.
Agent Process Model	Description of the agent how to work, modeled with colored Petri nets.
Agent Information Table	Registers agents that cooperate with the agent recently.

The process model is a non-hierarchical CP-net that used to model agent's behavior logic mechanism, with which we can get the agent's states transformation and behaviors schedules to achieve a goal. Agent information tables will help we effectively organizing a dynamic MAS.

Secondly, MAS can be modeled with its HCP-net system, each agent within it is denoted as Figure1 in the prime page and process models of agents are sub-pages of the HCP-net system. The MAS is described at system level and agent level. At system level, the structure of MAS is modeled with the prime page (a non-hierarchical CP-net), agents are presented with their substitution of transitions, we can get the relationships among agents and monitor the MAS from the running of its HCP-net system. At agent level, each agent is particular modeled in this level and we can get each agent's behaviors and states transitions to achieve its goals, It is just as the way that model a large-scale system at macro- and micro- levels with hierarchical modeling technologies.

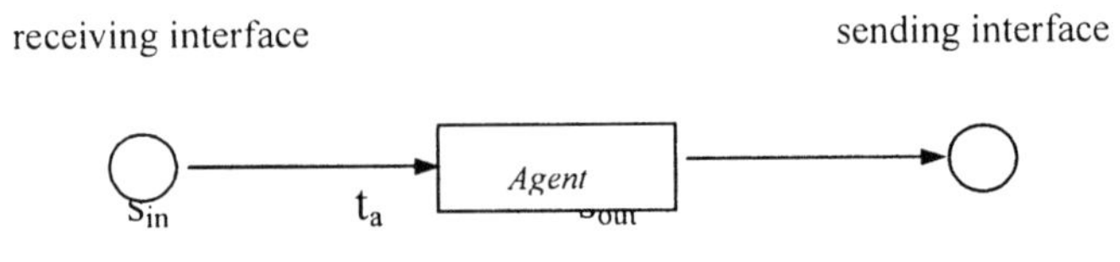

Figure1 Substitution transition of agent

Note: The HCP-net system of a MAS is bounded Petri nets system.

Because users would not waiting for a system running absoluteness long time without any outcome, when the system running longer than their expect time, they will abandon or adjust it.

The analysis of MAS can be transformed into its Petri net system properties analysis, including qualitative and quantitative properties, more than just partially about coordination or negotiation between agents([4,5,6]), such as:

1)Reachability: when MAS set out to deal with a goal, the system must reaches a state that denotes the goal had been achieved(goal state). From initial state to goal state, the system involving several states transformations from one to another. Markings of the HCP-net are able to exactly describe the system's states. M_0, the initial marking of the HCP-net corresponds with initial state of the MAS, and M_1 corresponds with the goal state. If M_1 can be reached from M_0, it means the goal can be achieve; else the goal can not be achieved and we should do some adjustment for the MAS.

2) Deadlock detection and avoidance. Through coordination, agents within MAS can work together to ensure coherent action. Conflict resolution is essential for coordinated agent behaviors. When the HCP-net system of MAS running into a deadlock, it means conflicts resolution is needed in the MAS. Reasons and resolution methods to deadlock states of the HCP-net system can be applied to resolve or avoid conflicts in the MAS.

3) Fairness. Fairness property describes the dependences among transitions in the HCP-net, accordingly, the dependence among agents in the MAS.

4 CONCLUSION AND FURTHER WORK

We have dealt with the approach to model MAS with its HCP-nets system. Each agent has its colored Petri net system and when agents are composed into a MAS, we get its HCP-net system. Properties of the HCP-net system, such as reachability, deadlock detection and avoidance, fairness, can be used to analyze dynamic properties of the MAS.

Our future work reminded to be done includes: a) dynamic organizing procedure of a MAS based on the agent structure in section 3; b) conflicts detection and avoiding in the MAS with Petri nets methods.

REFERENCE

[1] Wooldridge, M., and Jennings, N, "Intelligent agents: theory and practice", The Knowledge Engineering Review. 1995.

[2]Shi Zhongzhi, Intelligent agents and its Applications, Science Press, 2000(in Chinese)

[3] A.Perkusich and J.de Figueiredo , "G-net: A Petri Net Based Approach for Logicaal and Timing Analysis of Complex Software Systems " ,.Journal of systems and Software, 39(1):39-59,1997

[4] Danny Weyns & Tom Holvoet " A Colored Petri Net for a Multi-Agent Application." .Aarhus, Denmark – August 27, 2002..MOCA '02.

[5] D.Moldt and F.Wienberg. " Multi-Agent-Systems based on Coloured Petri Nets " , Proceedings of the 18th international Conference ICATPN'97, Toulouse, France,1997.

[6] R. Cost et al., Modeling Agent Conversations with Colored Petri Nets,, IJCAI '99, Stockholm, Sweden, 1999.

[7] T. Murata : "Petri nets: Properties, Analysis and Application" .Proceedings of the IEEE Vol.77 no.4(April 1989),541-580.

[8]Yuan Chongyi,Theories of Petri Nets, China Publishing House of Electronics Industry ,1998, (in Chinese)

[9] T. holvoet. "Agents and Petri nets." Petri net news letter, (49):3-8 Oct-1995

[10] D. Xu, R. A. Volz, T. R. Ioerger, and J. Yen, "Modeling and Verifying Multi-Agent BehaviorsUsing Predicate/Transition Nets," Proc. of the 14th International Conference on Software Engineering and Knowledge Engineering, Italy, July 2002.

[11] H. Xu and S. M. Shatz, "An Agent-based Petri Net Model with Application to Seller/Buyer Design in Electronic Commerce," ISADS 2001, March 2001, Dallas, Texas, USA.pp.11-18.

[12] Jensen,K.: Colored Petri Nets. Basic Concepts ,Analysis Methods and Practical Use. Volume 1,Basic Concepts. Monographs in Theoretical Computer Science .Berlin, Heidelberg, New York:Springer-Verlag,2nd corrected printing 1997,ISBN:3-540-60943-1.

SOFT MODELING OF KNOWLEDGE SYSTEMS THROUGH FUZZY PETRI NETS

Felipe Lara-Rosano
Centre for Applied Sciences and Technological Development, National University of Mexico
e-mail: lararf@servidor.unam.mx

Abstract: Knowledge in the social and human Sciences cannot be modeled with old time mathematical modeling techniques. In this situation, it would be very useful to have modeling approaches capable to express the richness of social reality, including its vagueness and uncertainty. Aiming at this objective, a soft modeling approach is proposed, implemented as a generalized fuzzy Petri net. This model can be then used to make inferences and to solve problems related to the complex system.

Key words: Complex systems, soft models, fuzzy Petri nets, knowledge-based systems, knowledge representation.

1. INTRODUCTION

Real problems in the social and human environments in a modern world are characterized by a great economic polarisation of societies, aggresive global markets, environmental problems, natural resources depletion, violence and crime outbursts, etc. These complex problems cannot be approached with old time mathematical modeling techniques. In the 50's and 60's the Expert Consultation Techniques were introduced as valid heuristic methods to analyze and to handle social problems [1]. These techniques are based not on trying to model mathematically the complex real world, but to extract the conceptual logical model that an expert or a panel of experts have about it, that permits them with remarkable efficiency to solve real world problems in their speciality domains. This conceptual logical model is expressed in terms of rules of behavior of the system elements, as a Knowledge Base, that is a collection of logical propositions whose relationships model the knowledge that experts have about a certain topic.

One of the principal issues in building Knowledge Bases is related to modeling real situations characterized by uncertainty [2]. This uncertainty may be produced by following factors: [3]:

a) It is impossible to assign the whole truth or the whole falsity to propositions, even to those taken as premises or starting points of a logical discourse [4].

b) The logical support of a premise or condition for determining a given conclusion or result is uncertain, that is, we can define a conditional belief value of a conclusion given a premise.

c) The premises contain fuzzy terms.

A way to model this fuzzy logic model is the fuzzy production rule. The components of a fuzzy production rule are:

a) A conclusion whose belief value is to be estimated.

b) The premises and their belief values.

c) The logical combination of the premises, generally expressed in a normal form as a disjunction of conjunctions.

d) The uncertain implication relating the belief value of the conclusion with the premises.

The logical belief functions should be drawn from a specific fuzzy logic. In a former paper Lara-Rosano [3] proposed the Logic of Lukasiewicz as the most suitable one to handle uncertainty according to a set of logic-mathematical criteria.

In this paper a Fuzzy Petri Net approach is proposed to model linguistic conceptual models, using linguistic belief values for the propositions, as well as a linguistic weight for the contributions of premises to the belief value of the conclusion. This kind of model can be used to make inferences and to solve problems related to the complex system.

2. LINGUISTIC BELIEF PETRI NETS

Arguments in favor of modeling fuzzy conditional rules by Fuzzy Petri Nets (FPN) can be found in some papers [5], [6]. We assume that the fuzzy knowledge-based logical system is described by fuzzy belief networks with conditional rules and the system modeling is realized by mapping these rules into a Linguistic Belief Petri Net (LBPN). model

Definition 1: A ***Linguistic Belief Petri Net*** (LBPN) is a 7-tuple

$$\text{LBPN} = [P, T, I, O, \alpha, \Lambda, W] \tag{1}$$

where $P = [p_1, p_2, \ldots, p_n]$ denotes a set of places associated with uncertain propositions, $T = [t_1, t_2, \ldots, t_m]$ denotes a set of transitions associated with fuzzy implications, $I(O)\colon T \rightarrow P^{\infty}$ is the input (output) function, a mapping from sets of places to transitions (transitions to set of places). $\alpha: P \rightarrow [0,1]$ is a certainty association function which assigns a linguistic truth value represented as a trapezoidal fuzzy number in [0, 1] to each place, $\Lambda\colon P \rightarrow [0,1]$ is a certainty threshold association function which assigns a real value λ_i from zero to one to each place i $\Lambda = [\lambda_1, \ldots \lambda_t, \ldots, \lambda_\mu]$, For any transition **t**, if all the trapezoidal fuzzy numbers representing the linguistic certainty factors α associated with the tokens of all its input places have elements greater than their thresholds λ, then the transition is enabled and fires. $W\colon T \rightarrow [0,1]$, are a set of weights that assigns a linguistic truth value represented as a trapezoidal fuzzy number in [0, 1] to the transition arcs of a net. For a transition **t**, $w_j \in W$ indicates the linguistic belief value of the implication (rule) for the jth output place, that is, how much the premises impact the belief values of the jth output place, if the transition fires. To map linguistic conditional rules into LBPN, we map propositions as places; the logical implication functions ``THEN" between antecedent and consequent propositions as transitions; the impact of belief values of antecedents over the consequent as arcs.

3. INFERENCE WITH LINGUISTIC BELIEF PETRI NETS

A LBPN is an inference engine. The inference engine is activated by firing transitions. A transition **t** fires instantly as soon as it is enabled. **t** is enabled if all its input places have tokens whose certainty factors are greater than their thresholds.

Let I(t)= $[p_{i1}, p_{i2}, \ldots, p_{in}]$, with the corresponding thresholds: $\lambda_1, \lambda_2, \ldots, \lambda_v$ and let O(t)= $[p_{o1}, p_{o2}, \ldots, p_{om}]$ with the corresponding output weights: $w_{O1}, w_{O2}, \ldots, w_{Om}$,

Definition 2: $\forall$ **t** $\in$ T, ***t is enabled and fires*** if $\forall\ p_{ij} \in I(t)$, the linguistic (trapezoidal fuzzy number) certainty value $\alpha(p_{ij})$ has an interval $[\alpha_{kij}(p_{ij})]$ such that all its values $\alpha_{kij} \geq \lambda_j$, j =1,2, ... ,n After firing **t**, the token in p_{ij} is removed, and a token with a membership certainty function $w_{ok}[\min_j\{\alpha_{kij}(p_{ij})\}]$ is put into each of its output places p_{ok}, k=1,2, ..., m. If a place p_{ok} has more than one input transition and more than one of its input transitions fire, then the new certainty factor of p_{ok} is the new token which is produced by the transition with the maximum output weight, because it has the maximal evidence.

In order to describe the fuzzy reasoning algorithm more clearly, we make some other remarks.

Let P the set of places. Let divide P into three parts: P_I, P_{int} and P_O such that $P = P_I \cup P_{int} \cup P_O$ and $P_I \cap P_{int} \cap P_O = \varnothing$. Furthermore $P_I = \{p \in P \mid \bullet p = \varnothing\}$, $P_{int} = \{p \in P \mid \bullet p \neq \varnothing \text{ and } p\bullet \neq \varnothing\}$, $P_O = \{p \in P \mid p\bullet = \varnothing\}$. Then $p \in P_I$ is called an **initial premise**, $p \in P_{int}$ is called a **hidden proposition**, $p \in P_O$ is called a **conclusion**.

4. FUZZY REASONING ALGORITHM

Step 1. Put a token on initial premises P_I .and define initial transitions T_I

Step 2. Find the enabled transitions T_e from T_I. That is where $\forall\ p_{ij} \in P_I$ the linguistic (trapezoidal fuzzy number) certainty value $\alpha(p_{ij})$ has an interval $[\alpha_{kij}(p_{ij})]$ such that all its values $\alpha_{kij} \geq \lambda_j$, j =1,2, ... ,n

Step 3. Fire all enabled transitions T_e and calculate new certainty membership functions which are produced by fired transitions according to Definition 2.

Step 4. Make token transmission. Take a token from the input places of a fired transition. Assume p is one of the output places of a fired transition

4.1 If p has only one input transition, then add a token to p with the certainty membership function w_{ok} [$\min_j\{\alpha_{kij}(p_{ij})\}$] which is produced by its input transition;

4.2 If If p has more than one input transition and more than one of its input transitions fire, then the new certainty membership function of p is the new token which is produced by the transition with the maximum output weight, because it has the maximal evidence.

Step 5. Let T = T-T_e, and define the next transitions T_t and the places with tokens P_t.

Step 6. Go to Step 2 and repeat, until $T_e = \varnothing$

EXAMPLE

Let following knowledge base:

A = "There is fever"
B = "There is throat pain"
C = "The leukocyte count is too large"
D = "There is a throat infection"
E = "The patient must stay at home"

Implication $\mathbf{t_1}$: = "If the patient has fever (more than 38°C) and there is throat pain, then the patient should stay at home with "high" certainty (μ_1= "high").

Implication $\mathbf{t_2}$: = "If the patient has fever (more than 38°C) and there is throat pain and the leukocyte count is too large, then the certainty of a throat infection is very high (μ_2= "very high")..

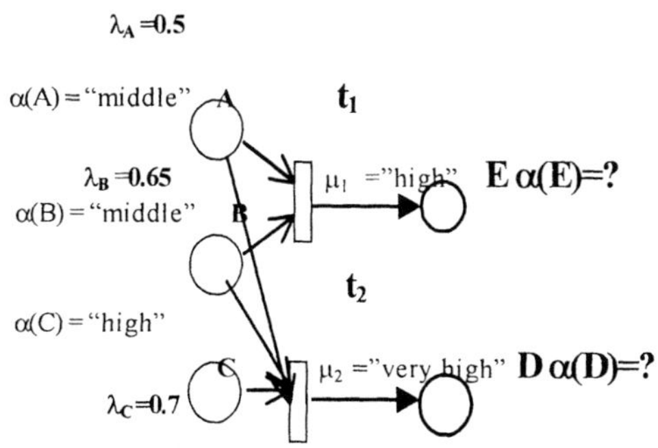

Figure 1 Linguistic Belief Petri Net corresponding to Example

Let the following facts:

The certainty α(A) of **A** is "middle". Its threshold is 0.5

The certainty α(B) of **B** is "middle". Its threshold is 0.65

The certainty α(C) of **C** is "high". Its threshold is 0.7

It is asked the certainty value α(E) of **E** = "The patient must stay at home" and α(D) of **D** = "There is a throat infection".

Let following linguistic terms and their corresponding fuzzy numbers.

Linguistic terms	Trapezoidal Fuzzy Numbers
Absolutely false	(0, 0, 0, 0)
Low certainty	(0, 1, 2, 3)
Middle certainty	(2, 4, 6, 8)
High certainty	(7, 8, 9, 1)
Very High certainty	(9, 1, 1, 1)

This table can be represented in Fig 2

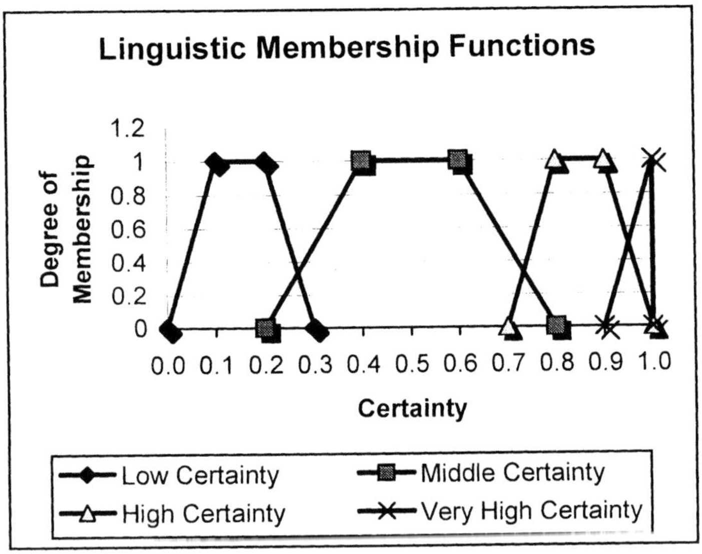

Figure 2. Trapezoidal Membership Functions of Linguistic Certainty Values

Step 1. Initial premises are A, B and C. $P_t = A \cup B \cup C$. $T_t = [t_1, t_2]$

Step 2. $\alpha(A)$ = “middle” and its fuzzy membership has values greater than its thresholod 0.5 In the same way $\alpha(B)$ = “middle” and its fuzzy membership has values greater than its threshold 0.6 then transition t_1 is enabled. Also $\alpha(C)$ = “high” and its fuzzy membership has values greater than its threshold 0.7 then transition t_2 is enabled too.

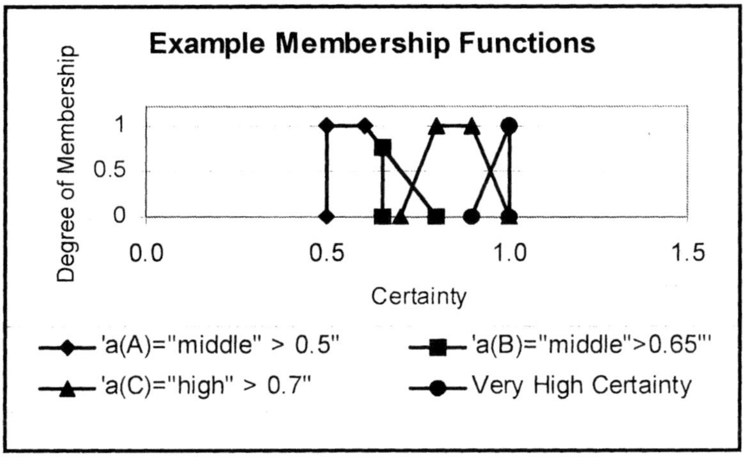

Figure 3. Trapezoidal Membership Functions of Example Certainty Values

Step 3. Transition t_1 fires. After firing t_1 a membership certainty function "high" ⊗ [min {("middle" > 0.5), ("middle" > 0.65)}] is calculated for E. The way to calculate this is membership function is to consider that "high" is represented by (0.7, 0.8, 0.9, 1), "middle" > 0.5 is represented by (0.5, 0.5, 0.6, 0.8), "middle" > 0.65 is represented by (0.65, 0.65, 0.65, 0.8). Therefore, the certainty membership function associated with t_1 and E is (0.7, 0.8, 0.9, 1) ⊗ [min {(0.5, 0.5, 0.6, 0.8), (0.65, 0.65, 0.65, 0.8)}] = (0.7, 0.8, 0.9, 1) ⊗ (0.65, 0.65, 0.65, 0.8) = (0.455, 0.520, 0.585, 0.8).

In the same way, transition t_2 fires. After firing t_2 a membership certainty function "very high" ⊗ [min {("middle" > 0.5), ("middle" > 0.65), ("high" > 0.7)}] is calculated for D.

Its value is given by (0.9, 0.9, 1, 1) ⊗ [min {(0.5, 0.5, 0.6, 0.8), (0.65, 0.65, 0.65, 0.8), (0.7, 0.8, 0.9, 1)}] = (0.9, 0.9, 1, 1) ⊗ [(0.5, 0.5, 0.6, 0.8)] = (0.45, 0.45, 0.6, 0.8).

Step 4. A token is taken from inputs A, B and C. E receives one token with trapezoidal certainty function (0.455, 0.520, 0.585, 0.8). D receives one token with trapezoidal certainty function (0.45, 0.45, 0.6, 0.8).

Step 5. Let $T = T\text{-}T_e = \varnothing$ There is no more transitions T_t . The places with tokens P_t .are E and D.

Step 6. Go to Step2 . There are no more enabled transitions $T_e = \varnothing$. The conclusions are: **E** = "The patient must stay at home" with trapezoidal certainty function (0.455, 0.520, 0.585, 0.8) that could be translated into linguistic terms as ***"Probably the patient must stay at home"*** and **D** = "There is a throat infection" with trapezoidal certainty function (0.45, 0.45, 0.6, 0.8) that could be translated into linguistic terms as ***"It could be that the patient has a throat infection".*** Their graphics are represented in Figure 4.

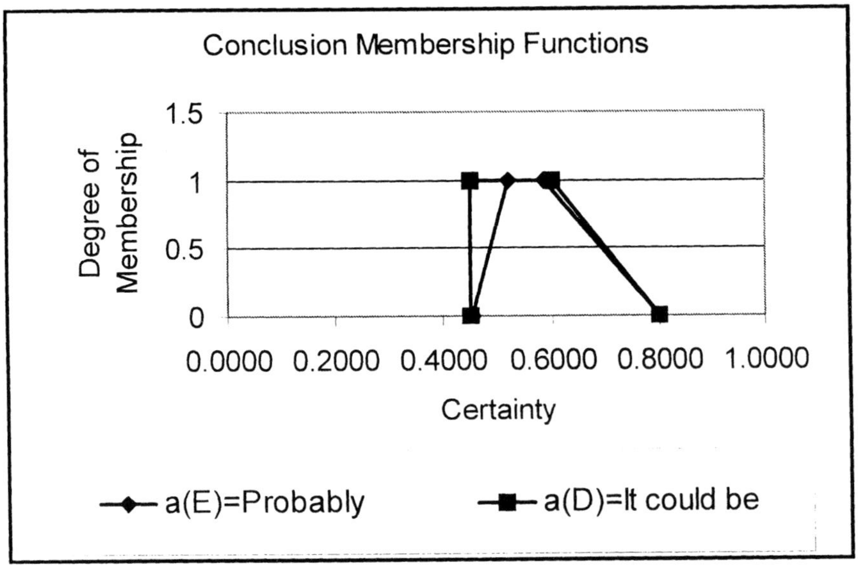

Figure 4 Certainty Functions of the Conclusions

5. CONCLUSION

Expert Consultation Techniques are based not on trying to model the real world, but to extract the conceptual model that an expert or a panel of experts have about it, that permits them with remarkable efficiency to solve real world problems in their speciality domains. Aiming at this objective, a fuzzy logical knowledge based model was proposed, implemented as a generalized fuzzy Petri net model, to make inferences and to solve problems.

6. REFERENCES.

[1] Linstone, H. A. & Turoff, M. (1972). "The Delphi Method". New York: Universe Books.

[2] Yager R R, (1992) "Expert Systems using Fuzzy Logic" in Yager R R & Zadeh L A (eds) *"An Introduction to Fuzzy Logic Applications in Intelligent Systems"*. Boston: Kluwer Academic Publishers.

[3] Lara-Rosano F. (1989) "Uncertain Knowledge Representation through Fuzzy Knowledge Networks based on Lukasiewicz Logic", in *Advances in Computer Science*, George E. Lasker (ed), Windsor, Canada: IIAS, ISBN 0-921836-031: 32-38

[4] Zadeh L A (1965) "Fuzzy Sets", *Information and Control,* 8: 338-353

[5] Yeung D.S. and Tsang E.C.C. (1994) "Fuzzy knowledge representation and reasoning using Petri nets", *Expert Systems & Applications*,7: 281-290

[6] Xiaoou Li & Lara-Rosano F. (2000) "Adaptive Fuzzy Petri Nets for Dynamic Knowledge Representation and Inference", *"Expert Systems with Applications"*, 19(3): 235-241 .

AN IMPROVED 3D FACE SYNTHESIS BASED ON MORPHABLE MODEL

Chengzhang Wang, Baocai Yin, Qin Shi, Yanfeng Sun
Beijing Municipal Multimedia and Intelligent Software Key Lab, Beijing University of Technology, Beijing 100022, China

Abstract: A novel model matching method based on improved genetic algorithm is presented in this paper to improve efficiency of matching process for 3D face synthesis. New method is independent from initial values and more robust than stochastic gradient descent method. Improved genetic algorithm has strong global searching ability. Crossover and mutation probability are regulated during optimization process to improve precision and convergence speed of the algorithm. Experimental results show our new model matching method has good performance on 3D face synthesis.

Key words: Morphable model, 3D face synthesis, Genetic Algorithm

1. INTRODUCTION

Modeling human faces has challenged researchers in computer graphics since its beginning. Since the pioneering work of Parke [1], various methods have been reported for modeling the shape and texture of faces and for animating them [2, 3]. In past several years, a novel face modeling method, the morphable model is proposed by T. Vetter [4]. Matching the model to given facial images, even a single image, realistic 3D face model of the person could be synthesized automatically by combination of prototypic faces. The method based on the morphable model is automatic and gives light on the difficult problems of facial research, illumination and poses evaluation. Stochastic gradient descent method is generally used to implement model matching process presently [4]. However, this method depends too much on initial values and to be time consuming. Convergence of the method is hardly well either [5]. Novel model matching method need to be studied to improve efficiency of the morphable model.

We will introduce the morphable model in following section. Model matching method based on improved genetic algorithm will be presented in section 3. In section 4, 3D face synthesis results are presented using the proposed method. Conclusions are presented in section 5.

2. MORPHABLE MODEL

3D face synthesis system based on the morpable model is composed of two components. One is model construction. The other is model matching process. To construct the morphable model, prototypic 3D faces are acquired firstly by CyberWare 3D Face Scanner [6]. After computing correspondence between the prototypes, every prototypic 3D face can be represented by a shape vector and a texture vector. Technique of PCA (principal component analysis) is used to give the final morphable model format [4]:

$$S_{model} = \overline{S} + \sum_{i=1}^{m} \alpha_i s_i \quad T_{model} = \overline{T} + \sum_{i=1}^{m} \beta_i t_i$$

Matching the morphable model to given facial images is the process of face synthesis. By model matching process, reconstructed 3D face is obtained by combination operation. Object function is defined as follows [4]:

$$E = \sum_{(x,y)} [I_{input}(x,y) - I_{model}(x,y)]^2$$

3. MODEL MATCHING BASED ON IMPROVED GENETIC ALGORITHM

Genetic algorithm is one of the modern optimization methods [7]. Improved genetic algorithm is proposed to solve model matching process.

3.1 Genetic Operator

Floating encoding and roulette selection method are adopted in this work. Evaluation function is designed by the formula: $F(X) = C_{max} - E$, if

$E < C_{max}$. $F(X) = 0$, otherwise. Crossover operator is designed as follows: Suppose two individuals of a paired group in parent generation $X_1 = (x_1^{(1)}, \cdots, x_n^{(1)})$, $X_2 = (x_1^{(2)}, \cdots, x_n^{(2)})$. n random numbers α_i are generated within space interval (0,1). Individuals in child generation after implementing crossover operation are $Y_1 = (y_1^{(1)}, \cdots, y_n^{(1)})$, $Y_2 = (y_1^{(2)}, \cdots, y_n^{(2)})$, $y_i^{(1)} = \alpha_i x_i^{(1)} + (1-\alpha_i) x_i^{(2)}$, $y_i^{(2)} = \alpha_i x_i^{(2)} + (1-\alpha_i) x_i^{(1)}$. Nonuniformity mutation operator is adopted in this paper. Suppose $k-th$ component of $X = (x_1, \cdots, x_n)$ is selected to implement mutation operation. Individual in child generation after implementing mutation operation is $X' = (x_1, x_2, \cdots, x_k', \cdots, x_n)$. Muted gene x_k' is calculated by the formula: $x_k' = x_k + \Delta(t, b_k - x_k)$, if $rnd(2) = 0$. $x_k' = x_k + \Delta(t, x_k - a_k)$, otherwise. Where $\Delta(t,z) = z \cdot (1 - r^{(1-t/T)^{\lambda}})$, $\Delta(t,z) \in [0, z]$.

3.2 Regulation of Crossover and Mutation Probability

In this paper, fitting density difference of adjacent two generations is used to estimate varying tendency of convergence. The following technique is adopted to regulate crossover and mutation probability.

Suppose set of the $i-th$ generation fitting density is: $F_i = \{F_{i1}, F_{i2}, \cdots, F_{in}\}$. Mean of sample F_i is $E(F_i) = \frac{1}{n}\sum_{j=1}^{n} F_{ij}$. Standard deviation of sample F_i is $S_{F_i}^2 = \frac{1}{n}\sum_{j=1}^{n}(F_{ij} - E(F_i))^2$. Covariance of sample F_i and F_j is $S_{F_iF_j} = \frac{1}{n}\sum_{k=1}^{n}(F_{ik} - E(F_i))(F_{jk} - E(F_j))$. Correlation coefficient of sample F_i and F_j is $R_{F_iF_j} = \frac{S_{F_iF_j}}{S_{F_i} S_{F_j}}$. When number of current evolution generation is less than half of the largest number of evolution generation, crossover probability is regulated. If $R_{F_iF_i}$ decreases more than 0.1, crossover probability is increased by 0.1. Crossover probability is set to initial value otherwise. When number of current evolution generation is more than half of the largest number of evolution generation, mutation probability is regulated. If $R_{F_iF_i}$ increases more than 0.03, mutation probability is increased by 0.03. Mutation probability is set to initial value otherwise.

4. EXPERIMENTAL RESULTS AND DISCUSSIONS

To construct the morphable model, 200 prototypic 3D faces are selected. 24.7 minutes is needed to reconstruct a 3D face with 2GHz Pentium 4 processor using our new algorithm (our improved genetic algorithm) while the conventional method (stochastic gradient descent method) needs 33.8 minutes to do the same. Synthesis results are shown in Figure 1. Left column is input image, second column is result of new matching method and last column is result of conventional one.

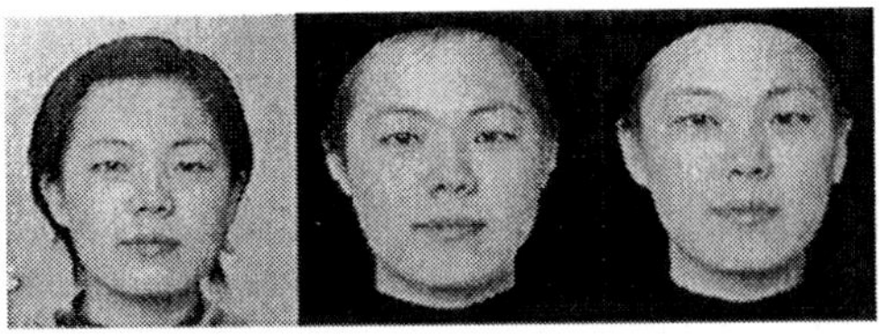

Figure. 1 Results of reconstructed 3D faces

3D faces reconstructed using two methods are compared with 3D face of same person scanned by the Cyberware. Relative error of corresponding vertexes on two types of 3D face model is defined as the criteria to compare synthesis precision. Error at each vertex is the sum of ratios of coordinate difference to the scale of corresponding coordinate axis along X, Y and Z axis. Figure 2 shows synthesis error decreased by our new algorithm compare to the conventional one.

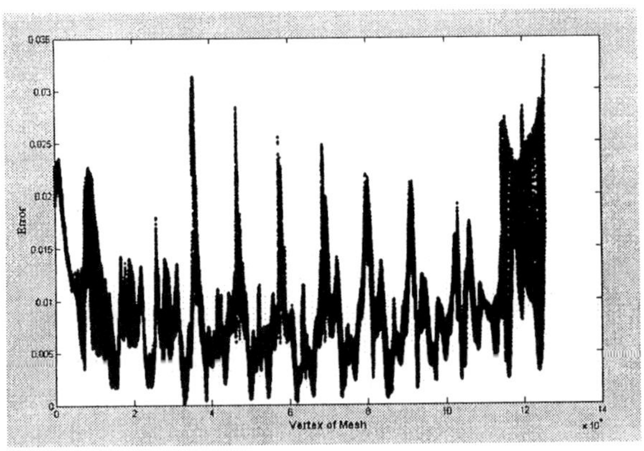

Figure. 2 Decreased error

Experimental results show that our new model matching method based on improved genetic algorithm performs appealing on 3D face synthesis.

Time consumed by our improved genetic algorithm is less than stochastic gradient descent method under the same conditions. As shown in Figure 1, 9.1 minutes is saved to synthesize a 3D face using our new model matching method. 3D face synthesis precision is improved by our new model matching method. As shown in Figure 2 maximum synthesis error can be decreased by 3.3 percent

5. CONCLUSIONS

In this paper, we propose a novel model matching method based on improved genetic algorithm for 3D face synthesis. Our new method overcomes weaknesses of stochastic gradient descent method. Regulation of crossover and mutation probability during optimization process improves precision and convergence speed of the algorithm. Experimental results show our new matching method based on improved genetic algorithm improves convergence speed, precision and can be applied effectively to solve the model matching problem for 3D face synthesis.

ACKNOWLEDGEMENTS

This work is supported by the Beijing Educational Committee Project of China (2002KJ001, KM200310005025), the National Natural Science Project of China (60375007).

REFERENCES

[1] Parke F. I. A Parametric Model of Human Faces. PhD thesis, Salt Lake City: University of Utah, 1974.

[2] Pighin F, Hecker J, et al. Synthesizing realistic facial expressions from photographs. In Proceedings of SIGGRAPH'98, Orlando, Florida: ACM Press, 1998: 75-84.

[3] Lee W S, Thalmann N M. Fast Head Modeling for Animation. Journal Image and Vision Computing, 2000, 18 (4): 355-364.

[4] Blanz V, Vetter T. A morphable model for the synthesis of 3D faces. In Proceeding of SIGGRAPH'99, Los Angeles: ACM Press, 1999: 187-194.

[5] Fletcher, R., Practical Methods of Optimization, Vol. 1: Unconstrained Optimization, John Willy and Sons, Chichester, 1980.

[6] Cyberware Laboratory Inc, http://www.cyberware.com

[7]Ozcan E., Onbasioglu E., Genetic algorithms for parallel code optimization. Congress on Evolutionary Computation, 19-23 June, 2004, 2(2): 1375-1381.

ANT-BASED DOCUMENT CLUSTERING AND VISUALIZATION

Yan Yang, Fan Jin, and Yongquan Jiang
School of Computer and Communication Engineering, Southwest Jiaotong University, Chengdu, P. R. China

Abstract: This paper discusses the document clustering and visualization process: analyzing documents index, clustering document, and visualizing exploration. It focuses on ant-based clustering algorithm and some significant improvements. Clusterings are formed on the plane by ants walking, picking up or dropping down projected document vectors with different probability. It is shown that the similar documents appear in spatial proximity, whereas unrelated documents are clearly separated in visual space.

Key words: ant-based algorithm, document clustering, visualization

1. INTRODUCTION

Document clustering is valuable tool in exploratory data mining, data analysis and web search. In order to help users orient the returning of thousands of documents in web search, it has proven useful to cluster documents according to contents-similarity and to visualize the clustered document data.

The ant-based clustering algorithm is inspired by the behavior of ant colonies in clustering their corpses and sorting their larvae. Deneubourg et al. [1] first proposed a basic model that allowed ants to randomly move, pick up and drop objects according to the number of similar surrounding objects so as to cluster them. Then Lumer and Faieta [2] extended Deneubourg's model from robotic implementation to exploratory data analysis (LF algorithm). Some improvements have later been proposed, such as the CSIM （a document clustering algorithm based on swarm intelligence and k-means） by Wu and Shi [3], and the ant–based clustering ensemble algorithm by Yang and Kamel [4].

Clustering visualization aims at representing the clusterings using graphics to help users visually perceive clusterings. The Self-Organizing Map (SOM) is widely used as a data visualization method that performs a non-linear mapping from a high-dimensional data space to a lower dimensional visualization space. A color coding method to express the approximate cluster structure of the SOM model vectors was presented by Himberg [5]. Distance mapping, a new visualization method to envision the results trained by SOM, was studied by Liao et al. [6]. The ant-based algorithm also projects data objects onto 2-dimensional visual space. Clusterings are visually formed on the plane. Handl and Meyer proposed an improved ant-based clustering and sorting as the core of a visual document retrieval system for web searches [7].

In this paper, an improved ant-based clustering and visualization for document is used to meet users' search needs. Documents are clustered according to contents-similarity. The similar documents appear in spatial proximity, whereas unrelated documents are clearly separated in visualization space.

Section 2 of this paper describes steps of the documents index analysis. Section 3 discusses the ant-based document clustering algorithm and its modification. Finally, Section 4 gives an example of visualization and follows by a conclusion in Section 5.

2. DOCUMENT INDEX ANALYSIS

In order to cluster a document collection, the key task is to represent the documents. One of the most common representation techniques in information retrieval is vector space model, also called document indexing [8]. It usually is of the following step:

2.1 Cleaning

An important part of any text processing is the cleaning of a document. Cleaning a document is to get rid of unwanted elements of the document. The procedure for document cleaning in this algorithm includes removing tags, removal of stop-words, and stemming of words.

After removing tags, the textual contents are extracted ignoring the textual structure and organization. Stop-words are frequent words that carry no information such as "the", "and", "of", etc. It is often useful to eliminate these words. Finally, word stemming is the process of converting different forms of a word into one canonical form, called terms. Words like "walk", "walker", "walked", "walking" are all converted to a single word "walk". The Porter stemming [9] is a popular algorithm for this task.

2.2 Indexing

In the vector space model, each document is represented by a vector of words d. Each element of the vector reflects a particular word, or term, associated with the given document. In the term space, $d_i = \{w_{i1}, w_{i2}, \ldots, w_{in}\}$, where $w_{ij}, j = 1, \ldots, n$ is the weight of term j in document i. The most common ways of determining the weight w_{ij} are based on the assumption that the best indexing terms are those that occur frequently in individual documents but rarely in the remainder of the collection. A well-known approach for computing term weights is the TF-IDF-weighting. The weight of a term j in a document i is given by:

$$w_{ij} = tf_{ij} \times \log(N / df_j) \tag{1}$$

where tf_{ij} is the term j frequency in the document i, or the number of occurrences of the term j in a document i. N is the total number of documents and df_j is the document frequency, that is the number of documents in which the term j occurs at least once. The inverse document frequency (*idf*) factor of this type is given by $\log(N / df_i)$. In order to account for documents of lengths, each document vector is normalized.

Once the documents are represented as vectors, the similarity between two documents can be measured. The most common measure of similarity is the cosine measure, which is defined as:

$$Sim(d_i, d_j) = \frac{\sum_{k=1}^{n} (w_{ik} \cdot w_{jk})}{\sqrt{\sum_{k=1}^{n} (w_{ik})^2 \cdot \sum_{k=1}^{n} (w_{jk})^2}}. \tag{2}$$

2.3 Reducing Dimensionality

When documents are represented as vectors, as described above, they belong to a very high-dimensional feature space because of one dimension for each unique term in the collection of documents. In order to reduce the dimension of the feature vector, the Document Frequency Thresholding is performed. Some terms whose document frequency are less than the predetermined threshold or appear in over 90% of the documents are removed. Further, only a small number of n terms with the highest weights in each document are chosen as indexing terms.

3. IMPROVED ANT-BASED DOCUMENT CLUSTERING

The ant-based document clustering algorithm is based on the basic LF model proposed by Lumer and Faieta [2] and the CSIM model given by Wu and Shi [3]. First, document vector are randomly projected onto a plane. Second, each ant chooses a vector at random, and picks up or drops down the vector according to picking-up or dropping probability with respect to the similarity of current document within the local region by probability conversion function. Finally, clusters are collected from the plane.

Let us assume that an ant is located at site r at time t, and finds a document vector $\mathbf{d}_i$ at that site. A measure of the average similarity of document vector $\mathbf{d}_i$ with the other vector $\mathbf{d}_j$ present in its neighborhood is given by:

In order to cluster a document collection, the key task is to represent the documents. One of the most common representation techniques in information retrieval is vector space model, also called document indexing [8]. It usually is of the following step:

$$f(d_i) = \max\left\{0, \frac{1}{s^2} \sum_{d_j \in Neigh_{s\times s}(r)} \left[1 - \frac{1 - Sim(d_i, d_j)}{\alpha(1 + (v-1)/v_{max})}\right]\right\} \tag{3}$$

where $Neigh_{s\times s}(r)$ denotes a square of $s\times s$ sites surrounding site r. α is a factor that defines the scale of similarity between document vectors. Too Large values of α will result in making the similarity between the vectors larger and forces vectors to lay the same clusters. When α is too small, the similarity will decrease and may in the extreme result in too many separate clusters. On the other hand, the parameter α also adjusts the cluster number and the speed of convergence. The bigger α is, the smaller the cluster number, while the faster the algorithm converges.

The parameter v denotes the speed of the ants. Fast moving ants form clusters roughly on large scales, while slow ants group document vectors at smaller scales by placing vectors with more accuracy. In our algorithm, v is chosen as random value between 1 and v_{max}, where v_{max} is the ants' maximum speed.

Probability conversion function is a function of $f(\mathbf{d}_i)$ that converts the average similarity of a document vector into the probability of picking-up or dropping for an ant. The picking-up probability for a randomly moving ant that is currently not carrying a document to pick up a document is given by:

$$P_p = 1 - sigmoid(f(\mathrm{d}_i)) \tag{4}$$

The dropping probability for a randomly moving loaded ant to deposit a document is given by:

$$P_d = sigmoid(f(\mathrm{d}_i)) \tag{5}$$

Instead of using the quadric function by Lumer and Faieta [2], here we use the sigmoid function, which only needs one parameter to be adjusted in the calculation. The sigmoid function has a natural exponential form:

$$sigmoid(x) = \frac{1}{1 + e^{-\beta x}} \tag{6}$$

where β is a slope constant and can speed up the algorithm convergence if it is increased. Thus we choose larger parameter β to help ants to drop faster the outliers (with high dissimilarity to all other neighborhood) at the later stage of algorithm.

Now, we can give the description of the improved ant-based document clustering algorithm in Figure 1.

The time complexity of the improved ant-based clustering algorithm is approximately $O(Mn \times ant\_number \times (s^2 + near\_num))$, where *Mn* is the maximum number of iteration, *ant_number* is the number of ants, *s* is the side length of local region, and *near_num* is the average number of document vectors within the local region [3].

4. VISUALIZATION

The role of clustering visualization is to assist users in insight of the clustered document data. Usually, simplified graphical and pictorial forms are preferred representations of clusters over numbers. Users can find it more intuitive to identify patterns that exist in data by using visual cues. There are many research efforts such as dotmap, distance mapping, and U-matrix for visualization [6], [10], [11]. Some of them focus on document visualization by SOM [5], [11], [12].

The ant-based clustering algorithm is capable of mapping high-dimensional data onto 2-dimensional visualization space. We investigate it as an alternative from SOM. Figure 2 illustrates an example of 200

1. Initialize the number of ants: *ant_number*, maximum number of iteration: *Mn*, side length of local region: *s*, maximum speed of ants moving: v_{max}, and other parameters: α, β.
2. Project the document vectors on a plane, i.e. give a pair of coordinate (x, y) to each vector randomly.
3. Each ant that is currently unloaded chooses a document vector at random.

   for $i = 1, 2, \ldots, Mn$

   for j = 1, 2, …, *ant_number*

   4.1 compute the similarity of a document vector within a local region by formula (3), where v is chosen as random value between 1 and v_{max};

   4.2 If the ant is unloaded, compute picking-up probability P_p by formula (4). If P_p is greater than a random probability, and this vector is not picked up by the other ants simultaneously, then the ant picks up the vector, labels itself as loaded, and moves the vector to a new position; else the ant does not pick up this vector, and reselect another vector randomly;

   4.3 If the ant is loaded, compute dropping probability P_d by formula (5). If P_d is greater than a random probability, then the ant drops the vector, labels itself as unloaded, and reselects a new vector randomly; else the ant continues moving the vector to a new position.
5. for $i = 1, 2, \ldots, N$ // for all document vectors

   5.1 If a document vector is isolated, or the number of its neighbor is less than a given constant, then label it as an outlier;

   5.2 Else give this vector a cluster sequent number, and recursively label the same sequent number to those vectors who is the neighbors of this vector within local region.

Figure 1. The improved ant-based document clustering algorithm

documents with 8 clusters, each document having single topic from the Reuters-21578 collection [13]. The *x*-axis and the *y*-axis of the U-matrix indicate a document vector's position on the plane, and the *z*-axis is the average similarity of document vector from its adjacent ones. We can visually observe 8 clusters almost separated, whereas the similar documents appear in close proximity.

In order to represent better visualization of cluster document populations, Figure 3 gives a landscape format. Documents are grouped into clusters around the similarity represented by mountain peaks on the landscape. The height of the surface above the plane is proportional to the numbers of documents at that position on the plane. Furthermore, a topic corresponding to its cluster can be labeled as landmarks easily.

5. CONCLUSION

In this paper we introduced an improved ant-based clustering and

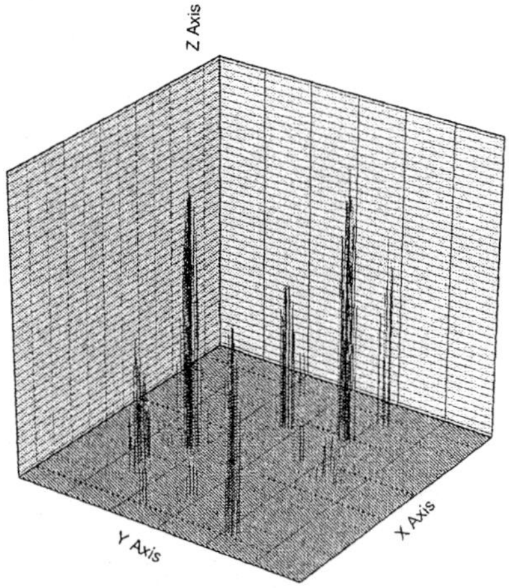

Figure 2. U-matrix of 200 documents clusterings algorithm, and a clusters map is generated to visualize the document populations.

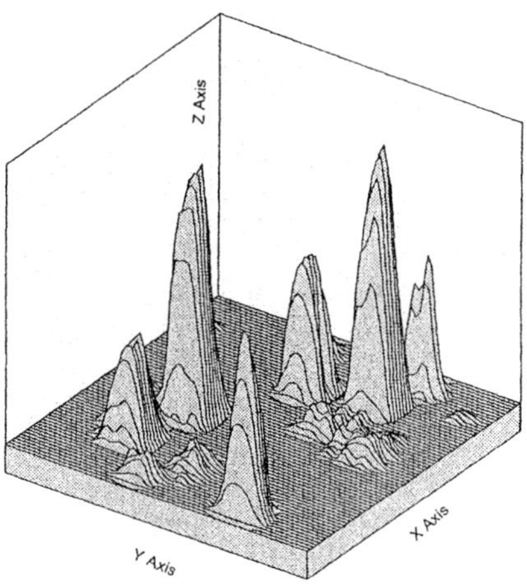

Figure 3. Landscape map of 200 documents clusterings

visualization simply. For future work, our approach can operate as a core mechanism of search engine. When users specify a query, matching documents returned by search engine are clustered based on a document index analysis and ant-based clustering algorithm, and a clusters map is generated to visualize the document populations.

ACKNOWLEDGEMENTS

This work was partially funded by the Key Basic Application Founding of Sichuan Province (04JY029-001-4) and the Science Development Founding of Southwest Jiaotong University (2004A15).

REFERENCES

1. Deneubourg, J. L., Goss, S., Franks, N., Sendova-Franks, A., Detrain, C., Chretien, L.: The Dynamics of Collective Sorting: Robot-like Ant and Ant-like Robot. In Meyer, J. A., Wilson, S. W. (eds.): Proc. First Conference on Simulation of Adaptive Behavior: From Animals to Animats. Cambridge, MA: MIT Press (1991) 356-365
2. Lumer, E., Faieta, B.: Diversity and Adaptation in Populations of Clustering Ants. Proc. Third International Conference on Simulation of Adaptive Behavior: From Animals to Animats 3. Cambridge, MA: MIT Press (1994) 499-508
3. Wu, B., Zheng, Y., Liu, S., Shi, Z.: CSIM: a Document Clustering Algorithm Based on Swarm Intelligence. IEEE World Congress on Computational Intelligence (2002) 477-482
4. Yang, Y., Kamel, M.: Clustering Ensemble Using Swarm Intelligence. IEEE Swarm Intelligence Symposium (2003) 65-71
5. Himberg, J.: A SOM Based Cluster Visualization and Its Application for False Coloring. Proceedings of the IEEE-INNS-ENNS International Joint Conference on Neural Networks (IJCNN 2000), Vol. 3 (2000) 587-592
6. Liao, G., Chen, Y., Shi, T.: Research on Visualization of SOM Network. Computer Engineering and Application (2003) 35-37
7. Handl, J., Meyer, B.: Improved Ant-based Clustering and Sorting in A Document Retrieval Interface. 7th International Conference on Parallel Problem Solving from Nature (2002) 221-230
8. Salton, G., Wong, A., Yang, C.: A Vector Space Model for Automatic Indexing. Communications of the ACM, vol. 18(11) (1975) 613-620
9. Porter, M. F.: An Algorithm for Suffix Stripping. Program, vol. 14(3) (1980) 130-137
10. Morris, S., Yong, C. D., Wu, Z., Salman, S., Yemenu, D.: DIVA: A Visualization System for Exploring Document Databases for Technology Forecasting. Computers & Industrial Engineering, Vol. 43 (2002) 841-862
11. Jin, H., Shum, W. H., Leung, K. S.: Expanding Self-organizing Map for Data Visualization and Cluster Analysis. Information Sciences, Vol.163 (2004) 157-173
12. Sangole, A., Knopf, G. K.: Visualization of Randomly Ordered Numeric Data Sets Using Spherical Self-organizing Feature Maps. Computers & Graphics, Vol.27 (2003) 963-976
13. http://kdd.ics.uci.edu/databases/reuters21578/reuters21578.html

LOCAL LINEAR EMBEDDING WITH MORPHABLE MODEL FOR FACE RECOGNITION

Xiaoming Bai, Baocai Yin, Qin Shi, Yanfeng Sun
Beijing Municipal Multimedia and Intelligent Software Key Lab, Beijing University of Technology, Beijing 100022, China

Abstract: In this paper, we use local linear embedding and linear discriminant analysis for face recognition. Local linear embedding method is used to nonlinearly map high-dimensional face images to low-dimensional feature space. To recover space structure of face images, we use 3D morphable model to derive multiple images of a person from one single image. Experimental results on ORL and UMIST face database show that our method make impressive performance improvement compared with conventional Fisherface method.

Key words: Local linear embedding, Fisherface, Morphable model, Face recognition.

1. INTRODUCTION

PCA and LDA are two powerful tools utilized for data reduction and feature extraction in face recognition [1]. However face images are regarded as a nonlinear manifold in high-dimensional space [2], linear methods are bounds to ignore essential nonlinear structures that contains in manifold. Nonlinear reduction methods [3, 4] are presented to implement data reduction. LLE [2] performs with effective results. To recover structure of embedding manifold in low-dimensional space, a large number of training images taken from different viewpoints under different illumination conditions are needed to approximate distribution of manifold. These images are usually hardly available in real-world applications. Morphable model is proposed by Vetter [5]. Matching model to given facial images, 3D face could be reconstructed automatically. Reconstructed 3D face can be viewed from different viewpoints and under different illumination conditions.

Remainder of the paper is organized as follows: Section 2 explains LLE algorithm and its parameter selections. Section 3 describes method to derive multiple images from a single image with morphable model. Section 4 describes face recognition system based on LLE with morphable model. Section 5 presents experimental results. Section 6 gives conclusions.

2. LLE ALGORITHM

Main principle of LLE algorithm is to preserve local relation of data set in both embedding and intrinsic space [2]. LLE maps data set in high-dimensional space globally to low-dimensional space. Dimensionality d of intrinsic space, number of neighbors k and regularization parameter r are to be set [7].

To estimate k, we perform PCA on data set X and get the t largest eigenvalue $\lambda_j^{(i)}$, which satisfy $e \le \sum_{j=1}^{t} \lambda_j^{(i)} \Big/ \sum_{j=1}^{D} \lambda_j^{(i)}$; Sample x_i and its t-neighbor constructs a subspace X_i. PCA is performed on every X_i to get the $l^{(i)}$ largest eigenvalue $\mu_j^{(i)}$, which satisfy $e' \le \sum_{j=1}^{l^{(i)}} u_j^{(i)} \Big/ \sum_{j=1}^{t} u_j^{(i)}$; Lastly, we estimate $k = \max_{i=1\ldots n}\{l^{(i)}\}$. To estimate local dimensionality, we perform PCA on each k-neighbor of sample x_i to get the $p^{(i)}$ largest eigenvalues $\gamma_j^{(i)}$, which satisfy $e'' \le \sum_{j=1}^{p^{(i)}} \gamma_j^{(i)} \Big/ \sum_{j=1}^{k} \gamma_j^{(i)}$. Then we compute mean value of the $p^{(i)}$ and let $d = \frac{1}{n}\sum_{i=1}^{n} p^{(i)}$. For computation of regularization parameter r, we use same method as d. For each k-neighbor of sample x_i, $\sigma_i^2 = \frac{1}{k-d}\sum_{j=d+1}^{k} \gamma_j^{(i)}$ and $r = \frac{1}{n}\sum_{i=1}^{n} \sigma_i^2$.

3. DERIVING MULTIPLE IMAGES FROM A SINGLE IMAGE

Basic theory of morphable model is linear combination of object class [6]. Given an input facial image, through model matching process, 3D face model of specific person can be reconstructed. New illumination model can be applied to 3D face model to generate multiple images under different lighting conditions [6]. Figure 1 illustrates some example images derived from a single image. Left column is a single image of a person. Right columns are multiple images derived from the single image by rotating and adding new lighting to the 3D face model.

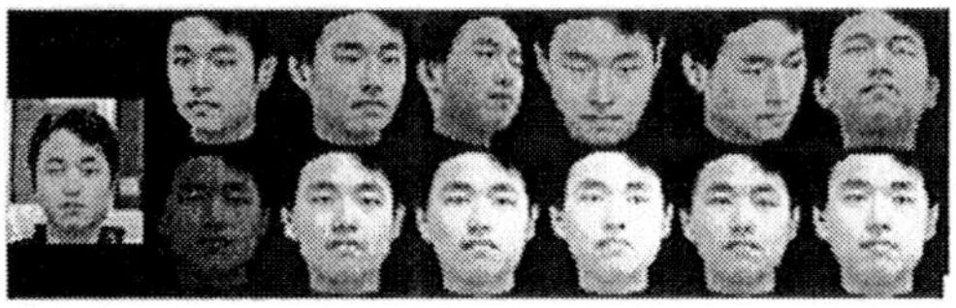

Figure.1 Multiple images derived from a single image

4. LLE BASED FACE RECOGNITION

LLE algorithm needs samples cover full manifold and FLD method can not be applied to face recognition problems where only one training image per person is available. Multiple training images per person are needed to compute within-class scatter matrix. Morphable model is applied into face recognition system to derive multiple samples from a single example image. Framework of our face recognition system is as shown in figure 2. The part above broken line is to derive multiple images from a single image. All images derived from the single image consist into the training sample set.

5. EXPERIMENTAL RESULTS

To verify effectiveness of the proposed approach, we also develop Fisherface method as benchmark according to [8]. Performance of these approaches are evaluated and compared using the Recognition Rate (RR) standard definded as $R(j) = \frac{N_j}{N}$. Where N is total number of test sample set, N_j is number of test images recognized correctly in the top j candidate.

Experiments are conducted on ORL and UMIST database. ORL database [9] contains 40 distinct persons with ten images per person. Images are taken at different time instance, with varying lighting conditions, facial expressions and poses. In our experiments, the approximately frontal examples with neutral expression of each subject in database are chosen as example images to form training set. 20 novel face images derived from example image of each subject using method described in section 3 are utilized as training sample images for each person. Performance curves of our method and benchmarks are shown in figure 3. The rank-1(first-choice) recognition rate of Fisherface method is 75.1%, while our proposed method is 83.7%.($k = 37$ $d = 57$ $r = 1.3 \times 10^{-4}$)

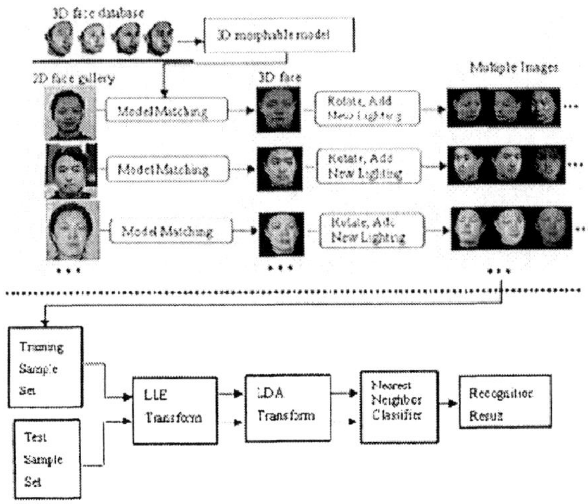

Figure. 2. Framework of face recognition system

UMIST database [10] is a multi-view database, consisting of 575 images of 20 people, each covering a wide range of poses from profile to frontal views. For each subject, one normal face is chosen as example image to form training set. 45 novel face images derived from example image of each subject using method described in section 3 are utilized as training sample images for each person. Performance curves of our method and benchmark are shown in figure 3. The rank-1 recognition rate of our method is 88.7%, Fisherface method is 80.6%.($k = 45$ $d = 23$ $r = 1.2 \times 10^{-4}$)

6. CONCLUSIONS

In this paper, LLE and LDA are combined for face recognition. Low-dimensional manifold structure of face space is obtained by LLE. LDA is used to implement classification on description space. 3D morphable model is utilized to derive multiple images from a single example image to form training set for LLE+LDA. Experiments on ORL and UMIST face database demonstrate impressive performance of our method.

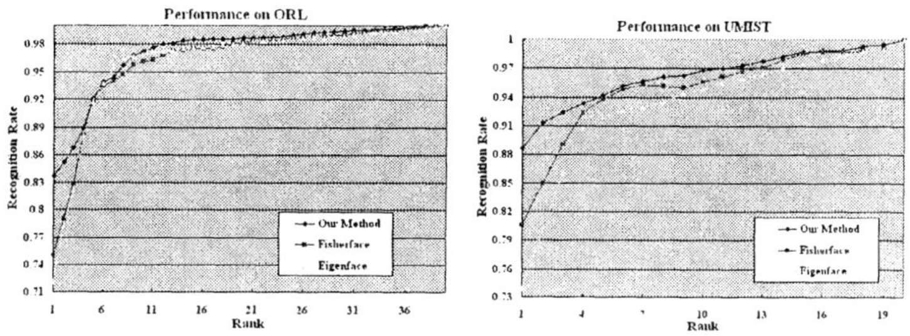

Figure.3 Performance Comparisons on ORL and UMIST Database

ACKNOWLEDGEMENTS

The authors would like to thank AT&T Laboratories Cambridge for providing the ORL face database and Dr. D. Graham and Dr. N. Allinson for providing the UMIST face database. This work is supported by the Beijing Educational Committee Project of China (2002KJ001, KM200310005025), the National Natural Science Project of China (60375007).

REFERENCES

[1] R. Chellapa, C. Wilson, S. Sirohey, Human and machine recognition of faces: a survey, Proceedings of the IEEE, 1995, 83(5):705-741.

[2] Sam. T. Roweis, L. K. Saul, Nonlinear Dimensionality Reduction by Locally Linear Embedding, Science, Vol 290, 2000: 2323-2326.

[3] T. Hastie, Principal curves and surfaces, Laboratory for computational Statistics Stanford University, Dept. of Statistics Technical Report 11, 1984.

[4] J. B. Tenenbaum, de Silva, V. & Langford, J. C, A global geometric framework for nonlinear dimensionality reduction, Science, Vol 290, 2000: 2319-2323.

[5] Blanz V, Vetter T. A morphable model for the synthesis of 3D faces. In Proceeding of SIGGRAPH'99, Los Angeles: ACM Press, 1999: 187-194.

[6] Yongli Hu, et al, An Improved Morphable Model for 3D Face Synthesis, International Conference on Machine Learning and Cybernetics, Vol. 6, 2004: 4362-4367.

[7] De Ridder, et al, Locally linear embedding for classification, Technical report PH-2002-01, Dept. of Imaging Science & Technology, Delft University of Technology, 2002: 1-15.

[8] P. N. Belhumeur, et al, Eigenfaces vs. Fisherfaces: Recognition using class specific linear projection, IEEE Trans. Pattern Anal.Machine Intell, Vol. 19, May 1997: 711-720.

[9] ORL face database. AT&T Laboratories, Cambridge, U. K. [Online]. Available: http://www.cam-orl.co.uk/facedatabase.html

[10] D. B. Graham and N. M. Allinson, Characterizing virtual eigensignatures for general purpose face recognition, in Face Recognition: From Theory to Applications, H. Wechsler, P. J. Phillips, V. Bruce, F. Fogelman-Soulie, and T. S. Huang, Eds., 1998, vol. 163, NATO ASI Series F, Computer and Systems Sciences, pp. 446–456.

SEMANTIC NETWORK AND CONCEPT MAPPING IN XHY ITEMS

Xingfu Wang[1] and Guohui Liu[2]

1. School of Computer Science, Chongqing University, 400030, Chongqing, China.
2. Institute for Languages, Cognition and Information Processing, Chongqing University, 400030, Chongqing, China

Abstract: Semantic network is a popular knowledge representation. The authors in this article apply it to analyze the literary language, *xiehouyu*(riddle-pun in English) —a unique feature in Chinese literature and daily communication, for the purpose of seeking the activation and mapping of riddle's function to the true meaning of this genre. The key concept in the riddle in *xiehouyu* items is well-known information, and generally it has the similarity to the other concept in the riddle therefore forming the dual relationship of mapping between them, thus the simile of this specific langue is formed by comparing the similarities of the two concepts and the metaphor of it is formed by extending the literal meaning of the answer.

Key words: semantic network; *xiehouyu*; concept mapping; metaphor; spreading activation

The application of Artificial Intelligence(AI) in Natural Language Processing(NLP) is brilliant and outstanding, and semantic network becomes a popular knowledge representation[1]. Semantic network is the idea of arranging concepts into a hierarchical taxonomy and using this for semantic processing. It is well established in some consultation systems to distinguish animals or mineral cores, for instance, the attempts to represent the knowledge and reasoning processes of experts in the geological domain; and literary concepts are rarely represented in this way. The authors try to describe the spreading activation of semantic network in *xiehouyu* items with a series of examples containing the word "monk" in the riddle and expects to deal with this specific genre with metaphor by depicting the complex relationships.

1. SEMANTIC NETWORK AND X*IEHOUYU*

Semantic network was first introduced by Quillian [2] based on the so-called "associative memory model": the notion that human memory is organized on the basis of association, that humans represent the real-world through a series of associations. In comprehending the transmitted information the hearer depends on his searching and choosing a suitable knowledge network in his memory [3], thus establishing an optimal relation with what has been said. More precisely a semantic network "is defined as a type of knowledge representation that formalises objects and values as nodes and connects the nodes with arcs or links that indicate the relationships between the various nodes: A data structure for representing declarative knowledge. It can be argued that the nodes can also represent concepts, and the arcs the relations between concepts, thereby forming semantic networks"[4].

Minsky's Frames [5] sought to provide the default information for transforming an image of a scene into a linguistic description. Though semantic networks sought to provide a similar foundation for natural language understanding. Its primary motivation was the economy principle stating that items are stored without redundancy and could be realized in computer environments on reasoning.

Chinese culture has a long history and its literature works contain unique accumulated features. In the development of Chinese culture some genres such as idioms, proverbs, and *xiehouyu* items were created. In this article the authors prefer the spelling of *xiehouyu* because its unique features in Chinese even though some scholars used "rest-ending sayings", "post-pause expressions", "example-explanation sayings", "enigmatic folk similes"[6], "two-part allegorical sayings" or "riddle-puns"[7]. And the authors put *xiehouyu* for short in the title of this article. It's hard for people to decompose a text into single elements in hopes of finding equivalents in the target language. We should keep in mind that the content expressed grammatically in one language may be expressed lexically in another language. If no grammatical forms are available in the target language, the translator must look for lexical means to render the same semantic content. Therefore the translation here is not of vital importance, the purpose is to demonstrate this genre in English. The similarities in two languages would permit the semantic equivalence translation but the difference in them would create the unique genres in them.

Xiehouyu is a unique Chinese fixed expression and is a popular form with common people. *Xiehouyu* is defined as "a two-part allegorical saying, of which the first part, always stated, describes a riddle, while the second part, sometimes unstated, carries a message as an answer to the riddle."[8] The form of this genre in the *xiehouyu* dictionaries is usually linked with a dash, with the first part usually being a metaphor and the second part mainly the further explanation to the first part, and the dash being equal to the predicators "is" or "are". In this article the first and second parts are called the riddle and the answer. The explanatory function of *xiehouyu* requires the allegorical part being a well-known and outstanding concept[9]. There are 37 *xiehouyu* items containing the word 'monk', and this outnumbers those items containing 'Confucius' by eleven, thus forming the mostly used concept in this genre. The common items are the following:

1) A bald enters a temple—to make up the number (both a bald and a monk has an egghead)
2) To borrow a comb from a monk—to baffle the person (a monk has no hair, therefore no comb)
3) A flea on a monk's head—explicit (a monk has no hair, thus a flea on his head is explicit)
4) Monks do not eat bean curd—a strange thing (monks are vegetarians)
5) A monk is under an umbrella—unruly (in Chinese hair's pronunciation is the same as rule's)
6) Monks fight against each other—no evidence for others to make good use of (hair was usually combed into pigtails in ancient China and they are easily grasped by the opponent)
7) A bachelor meets a monk— two bachelors
8) Monks divide up temple property and live apart—to do what is unnecessary (temple is similar to business in Chinese pronunciation)

'Monk' is a well-known concept in Chinese with many explicit features. An unlimited feature set of 'monk' could be depicted as this:{monk |a shaven head, reciting Buddhist scripture, a vegetarian, living in temples, a bachelor, being charitable}. When we put these concepts into a semantic network, we can easily get the complex relationship among them when used in *xiehouyu* items and the feature "shaven head" is another spreading activation node for further concepts(see Figure 1):

According to the theory of knowledge graph, the ontology of word graph contains 8 dual relation groups and 4 n relation groups [10]. In Figure 1 we sought out 3 categories of dual relation, they are: 1)SUB: demonstrating the containment of concepts in the set. 2)ALI: showing the similarity of two things. 3)PAR: presenting the attributes and intension of a concept or entity.

In Figure 1, the nodes on the inner circle show the subordinate relations of the basic features to the word 'monk', while the concepts on the outer circle show the similarities comparing with the basic semantic concepts on the inner circle, thus a direct mapping is formed by comparing the similarities between them and the metaphors in *xiehouyu* items are produced by this way.

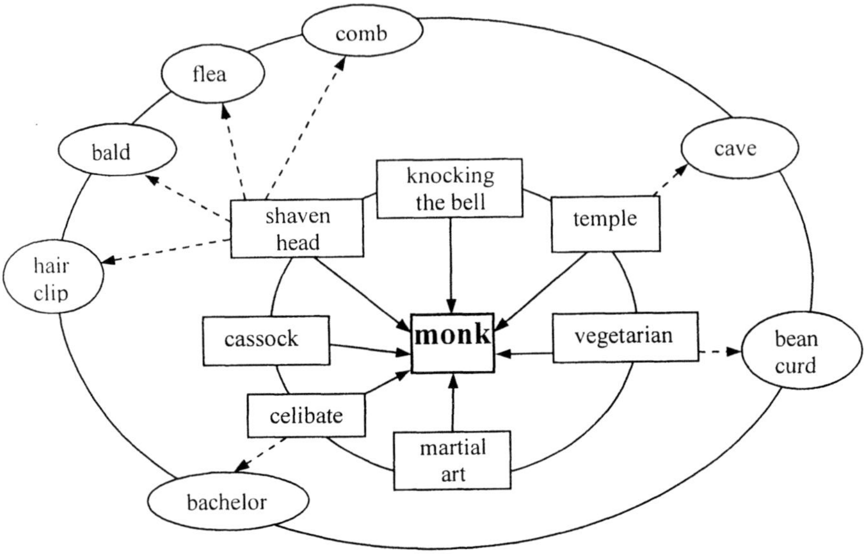

Figure 1. Semantic Network of 'Monk' in Chinese *Xiehouyu* Items

The core element and its activated features could be described as a generative formula according to the semantic containment and attribute of them, as the relation between the core 'monk' and features on the inner circle in Figure 1:

IF a person is a monk THEN he has a shaven head
IF a person is a monk THEN he lives in a temple
IF a person is a monk THEN he is a celibate
IF a person is a monk THEN he recites the Buddhist scripture
IF a person is a monk THEN he should do charitable things

But a generative formula would not be correct with the two parts changing their places, that is to say, the explanation of the above items would be a one-way cause and effect; hence the following formula is not appropriate or reasonable:

* IF a person has a shaven head THEN he is a monk

But if we put more than one of the subordinate concepts of 'monk' in the set together, the key concept 'monk' could be created:

IF a person has a shaven head AND lives in a temple

AND is single
AND recites the Buddhist scripture
AND ...

THEN this person is a monk.

The above generative formula demonstrates the basic elements of the word 'monk'. An important element in the feature set is the attribute element or governing element, the other important elements are subordinate element, functional element, and composing element [11]. In the *xiehouyu* items containing 'monk' there are no explicit features either in the riddle or in the answer because the key element of monk itself contains the basic features. In literary language the elements would not appear in the items because one feature of *xiehouyu* items is that they are short and concise, the usage of the basic elements would be superfluous, for example there would be no item as * '*Shaven* monks fight against each other—no evidence to be grasped by the opponent'.

2. DOUBLE MAPPING OF CHINESE RIDDLE-PUNS—*XIEHOUYU*

The simile of a riddle-pun is formed by the direct mapping between the riddle and the answer, and the indirect mapping between the surface meaning and the implicate meaning of the answer creates the metaphor of this genre. The two terms of direct mapping and indirect mapping are for communication and here we borrow them for the explanation of relations among different concepts of *xiehouyu* items.

The expression of *xiehouyu* is commonly used with the second part unreleased, as the name states, when people could use general knowledge to comprehend it. This is the literary meaning of this genre. But when we take the economy principle of language into consideration, in the expressions of *xiehouyu* we could omit the riddles because the direct mapping exists between the riddle and the second part. But the indirect mapping between the surface meaning and the implicate meaning of the second part demonstrates the unique function of this riddle-pun and the dynamics of *xiehouyu* items. The indirect mapping is a means of metaphor, and it enriches people's abstract thinking. The indirect mapping establishes a joint point between the known entity and the abstract concept and let people handle new concepts with what they have known, thus a mapping across two cognitive domains is formed, just as the name of *xiehouyu* tells. If the first part—the riddle—was not presented, this genre would not be unique any more and the indirect mapping would not be sought out, which would not be concord with the feature of Chinese people's exaggeration of language.

When people uses *xiehouyu* they just take the surface structure of the riddle as a clue for information processing, combined with background and the language context, forming a new cognition to explain the specific meaning of the riddle-pun. The semantic relation between the riddle and the answer is not isolated, but a correlated and mutually governed one.

The condition of a riddle-pun is that the riddle and the second part contain some explicit or implicit semantic relation. According to J. Oller [12] deduction, the deduction of *xiehouyu* items could be explained quite clearly.

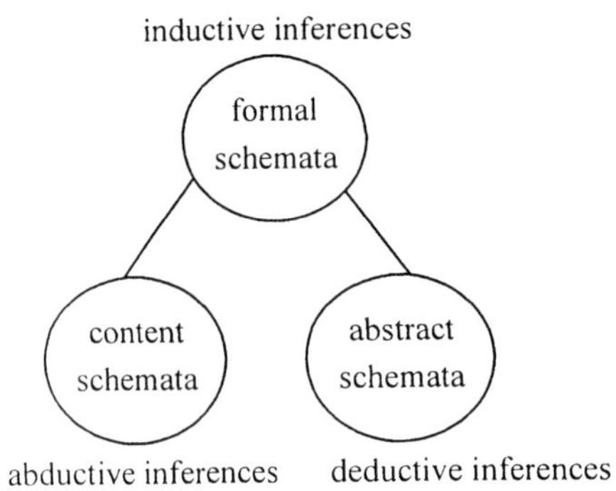

Figure 2
Oller's Three Classifications of Schemata

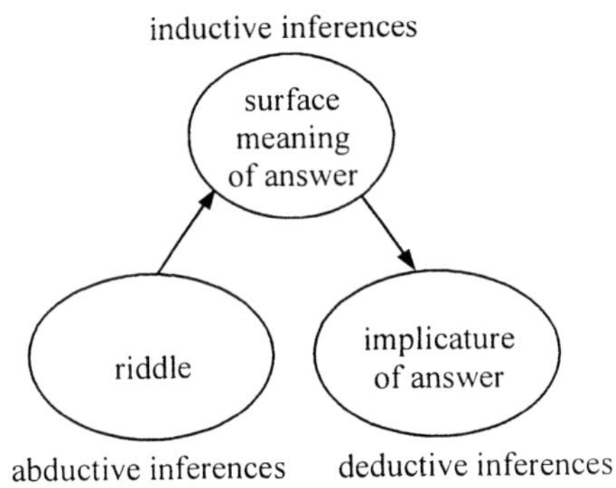

Figure 3 Xiehouyu's Deduction

Oller's three classifications of schemata are content, formal and abstract. Content schemata are defined as being based on "abductive judgments about particular facts and states of affairs". Formal schemata are the result mainly of inductive connections established across distinct states of affairs that are indexed as being similar in some respect. They seem to be developed from more distant connections of states of affairs that are somewhat similar. The third classification of abstract includes pure symbols and inductive integration. Abstract schemata carry the inductive integration to the completely general level of pure symbols. Abduction is recognizing a distinct representation; however induction is done if the recognition is more personal. The abstraction is an expansion of a single reference to act as a type through deduction. Following the classification of induction and deduction, we could easily depict the relation in the deductive direction among the three elements of *xiehouyu* items in Figure 3.

With deduction, a higher level of integration is achieved beyond the inductive level. Here in the item the conceptualization of the abstract concept in the answer reaches such a degree of integration and completeness that if the definition of the symbol in the riddle is sufficient, the inferences drawn from it would be equally valid and correct.

Semantically something unusual between two domains is a premise for metaphor, and this difference is essential for the indirect mapping in the genre of *xiehouyu*. For example, the item 'monks fight against each other—no pigtail to be grasped by the opponent' is not only a description that monks have no pigtails for the opponent to grasp, but an extension that a person has no evidence for others to make good use of. In this item, 'monks fight against each other' is the content scheme of intuition; 'no pigtail to be grasped by the opponent' is the formal scheme of deduction; and the extended 'no evidence for others to make good use of' is the highest abstract scheme of cognition.

If we take the riddle as **A**, the surface meaning of the answer is **a** and it shows the relation with the riddle because **a** is the small letter of **A,** and the implicate meaning of answer is **b**. Therefore the deductive relation from **A→a…→b** is what we usually seek out in this genre. The concept mapping of **b** deriving inderectly from **A** is implicate but attached. The relation between the riddle and the surface meaning of the answer is a simile because the hyphen could be depicted as '**be**', and the relation between the surface meaning of the answer and its implicature is a metaphor, therefore this genre contains two parts of speech and this is the reason why it stands out from other styles.

Generally speaking, we could summarize four major types of mapping in *xiehouyu* items:

A→a…→a'

A→a…→b

A→b…→b'

A→b…→c

All these formulae demonstrate the relation among the two concepts in the riddle and the concept of the answer in a *xiehouyu* item concerning the answer's weak and indirect mapping on the literal sense of the key concept in the riddle. And the formulae will be discussed in another essay.

The source category and target category of *xiehouyu* cognition could be built up from the relevant semantic network. In most *xiehouyu* items, the riddle is the source category and the answer to the riddle is the target category. In the above items containing 'monk' , the key concept 'monk' does not have its trace in the answer, this phenomenon shows that that the concept of 'monk' has projected on the target category. Even though the main idea is on the second part of the riddle, it does not say that the riddle is redundant. What is the function of using *xiehouyu* items in some contexts? The authors think that the presence of the riddle is for the converting of surface information into the deep message—that is, the true meaning conveyed by the answer. This projection would deepen the hearer's processing effort, thus borrowing an entity to refer to the intended one is the rational way in Chinese literature. This cognitive process makes *xiehouyu* items different from other fixed expressions in Chinese.

The phenomenon of *xiehouyu* items could be explained from a different angle. The direct mapping between the riddle and the answer could be regarded as an example of summarizing, but not an automatic one. This is not a complete summarizing because the real intention of a *xiehouyu* riddle is not the truth-value of the answer. *Xiehouyu* items supply us good examples for summarizing because the two concepts in the riddle are used in their true meaning, though in the answer the extended or prolonged semantic concepts are projected.

Hence the riddle is a combination of two concepts, among them the word 'monk' has decreased to be a referent and the answer is the extension of the key concept 'monk' and it goes beyond the surface meaning of the words. We want to find out how close the relation between the key concept and the secondary concept in the riddle should be for the activation of relevant knowledge, or how close the riddle and the answer are for the information receiver to create a new abstract concept in their mind. Of course it needs much effort for us to find out.

So we could safely say that the usage of the riddle in expressing our mind is not to show off the literacy of ancient Chinese, it provides the hearer relevant information to comprehend the true intention of the riddle, by this the hearer could manipulate the script to activate the required information. The concepts in the riddle are only the containers and their purpose is to create a visual image in the receiver's mind, so that he could remember the true meaning more impressively. Therefore if the information processor could not deal with the riddle and activates the relevant concepts and deduces the purpose of riddle-pun, the efficiency of *xiehouyu* items fails to covey the meaning in Chinese traditional way.

3. COGNITIVE MODEL REFLECTED IN *XIEHOUYU*

Metaphor is not only a way to construct a new cognitive model after the cognitive model of specific matters, it also converts the inner structure and relation of the whole cognitive model to the new source, this conversion is called the mapping from the source model onto the target model[13]. This metaphorical cognitive model would attach relevance to different categories, and it is also the effective way to simplify a language, thus reducing the difficulty of cognitive procession.

It is generally considered that in Chinese a *xiehouyu* item depicts a dynamic situation and presents the aesthetic function of this genre[14].

Xiehouyu is mainly an oral speech, and people prefer to it because it is rich and colorful to reflect people's humorous character in their daily language. This genre demonstrates Chinese peoples' cognitive means in language, which is a treasured accumulation of Chinese wisdom and culture.

The genre of *xiehouyu* could reflect Chinese people's thinking in borrowing a thing for analogy and extracting similarity from a category, this genre also shows the entertaining and amusing style in Chinese language. The metaphor and analogy of *xiehouyu* is peerless as for the other Chinese genres. Mr. Wen Duanzheng's study shows that the first part of *xiehouyu*—the riddle, is secondary in semantic expression but a primary role in figure of speech, which would visualize the expression [15].

As stated in the above, the common way of forming a *xiehouyu* items is that it compares the similarities with other concepts. The basic category of riddle's concepts is expanded in the answer and this expansion activates people's cognition of the relevant concepts. The expanded cognitive ability would provide base for the enrichment of the definitions of concepts, and the analogy between two different concepts would also improve people's cognitive ability. The mutual development of the two concepts contrasted promote people's cognitive ability and enrich people's cognitive models about the world, during the analogical cognition Chinese culture is accumulated with colorful figures of speech.

Yao Xiyuan[16] believes that Chinese people have the tradition to use euphemism in saying and to talk in a roundabout way, and the reserved manner in language is an important principle in Chinese. In ancient sayings there are 'to borrow a nearby thing to refer to a remote idea is an eloquent expression' and 'something unreleased in the sentences and texts is the style of eloquent speakers', these sayings could be safely quoted to explain the reasons for the popularity of the genre of *xiehouyu*. Most *xiehouyu* items are good examples to reflect the fact that the riddle is a description of the familiar, visualized and concrete things, though the answer is a referent to a more abstract concept. This expression of clarifying a reserved and abstract understanding is reasonable and language economy for cognitive construal is concord with people's average cognitive models in Chinese.

4. CONCLUSION

We take the examples of the core element of 'monk' to analyze the semantic network and the mapping of different concepts in *xiehouyu* items, and we find that the riddle is not redundant but assistance to the comprehension of the true meaning of this genre. The riddles are only an onset for the information processing of it and the answers are the intended activated information. The answers could be regarded as results in summarizing and we can use them for reference in NLP. We hope that this genre could help us to seek out more effective cognitive models for NLP.

REFERENCES

[1] Wang Yongqing. Principles and Methods of Artificial Intelligence. Xi'an: Xi'an Jiaotong University Press. 1998

[2] Quillian M.R., "*Semantic Memory*", in Semantic Information Processing, M. Minsky (Ed.), MIT press, Cambridge, Mass, 1968: 227~270

[3] Song Enmin, Guo Zhiyang, Xu Zewei. A Computer System for Chinese Sentence Comprehension. Journal of Huazhong University of Science & Technology. 1994(1) : 44~50

[4] http://www.computing.surrey.ac.uk/ai/PROFILE/prospector.html

[5] Minsky M. "A Framework for Representing Knowledge", in The Psychology of Computer Vision, P. Winston, Ed., McGraw Hill, New York, 1975: 211~277.

[6] Guo, Jianzhong. Theory and Practice of Enigmatic Folk Similes in Chinese. Chinese Translators Journal 1996 (02) : 12~15

[7] Gries, P. Hays. China's New Nationalism: Pride, Politics, and Diplomacy Publisher: University of California Press. 2004

[8] The Contemporary Chinese English Dictionary (Chinese-English Edition). Beijing: Foreign Language Teaching and Research Press. 2002: 2118.

[9] Zheng Guiyou. Defaming Buddhists of Chinese Riddle-puns and Buddhism in China. Journal of Yanbian University. 1994(3): 100~104

[10] Zhang Lei, Li Xueliang, Liu Xiaodong. Knowledge graph analysis of logic words in natural language processing. Journal of Chinese Information Processing. Vol.15 No. 6: 53~58

[11] Zhang Mingming. On the Role of Semanteme and Sememe in Semantic Understandings. Journal of Northeastern University (Social Science). 2003(5) :385~387

[12] Oller, J.W. (1995). Adding abstract to formal and content schemata: Results of recent work in Peircean semiotics. *Applied Linguistics,* 16(3): 273~306.

[13] Zhao Yanfang. Survey of Cognitive Linguistics. Shanghai: Shanghai Foreign Languages Press. 2000: 105

[14] Li Xia. Analysis of Semantic Function in Proverbs and Riddle-puns, Forum of Folk Literature, 1998(3) : 52~54

[15] Li shuyan. Review of *Study of Dialects and Vulgarism,* Journal of Chinese Study, 2004(1): 56~59

[16] Yao Xiyuan. On Idiomatic Phrases. Journal of Hebei University. 1994(3): 85~91

A KIND OF CONTINUOUS DIGIT SPEECH RECOGNITION METHOD

Wenming Cao

1Institute of Intelligent Information System, Information College, Zhejiang University of Technology, Hangzhou 310032, China

Abstract: In the light of descriptive geometry and notions in set theory, this paper re-defines the basic elements in space such as curve and surface and so on, presents some fundamental notions with respect to the point cover based on the High-Dimension Space(HDS) point covering theory, finally takes points from mapping part of speech signals to HDS, so as to analyze distribution information of these speech points in HDS, and various geometric covering objects for speech points and their relationship. Besides, this paper also proposes a new algorithm for speaker independent continuous digit speech recognition based on the HDS point dynamic searching theory without endpoints detection and segmentation. First from the different digit syllables in real continuous digit speech, we establish the covering area in feature space for continuous speech. During recognition, we make use of the point covering dynamic searching theory in HDS to do recognition, and then get the satisfying recognized results. At last, compared to HMM-based method, from the development trend of the comparing results, as sample amount increasing, the difference of recognition rate between two methods will decrease slowly, while sample amount approaching to be very large, two recognition rates all close to 100% little by little. As seen from the results, the recognition rate of HDS point covering method is higher than that of in HMM-based method, because, the point covering describes the morphological distribution for speech in HDS, whereas HMM-based method is only a probability distribution, whose accuracy is certainly inferior to point covering.

Keywords: High-Dimension Space, High-Dimension Space Covering Theory, Continuous Speech of Speaker-Independent

1. INTRODUCTION

In the recent years, Wang Soujue[1-4] proposed a point covering theory in high dimensional space (HDS), which uses the HDS descriptive geometry as tools, maps multidimensional digital signals to be points in HDS, and discuss relationship among multidimensional digital signals via analysis of point distribution and geometric object characteristics in HDS. Since this method is simple and feasible, and is able to accelerate computation by parallel operation, it has get remarkable achievements in many application fields [5-14].

In the light of descriptive geometry and notions in set theory, this paper redefines the basic elements in space such as curve and surface and so on, presents some fundamental notions with respect to the point cover based on the HDS point covering theory, finally, as an example, considers points generated by mapping part of speech signals to HDS to analyze distribution information of these speech points in HDS and various geometric covering objects for speech points and their relationship. Besides, this paper also proposes a new algorithm for speaker independent continuous digit speech recognition on the basis of the HDS point dynamic searching theory without endpoints detection and segmentation. First from the variant digit syllables in real continuous digit speech, we establish the covering area in feature space for continuous speech. During recognition, we make use of the point covering dynamic searching theory in HDS to do recognition, and then get the satisfying recognition results. At last, compared to HMM-based method, from the development trend of the comparing results, as sample amount increases, the difference of recognition rate between two methods will decrease slowly, while sample amount approaching to be large enough, two rates all close to 100% little by little. As seen from the results, the recognition rate of HDS point covering method is higher than that of in HMM-based method, because, the point covering describes the morphological distribution of speech in HDS, whereas HMM-based method is only a probability distribution, whose accuracy is certainly inferior to point covering.

2. SPEECH MORPHOLOGICAL ANALYSIS IN HDS

2.1 Cover

For geometry objects a and β, $\alpha \subset \beta$ in n-D space, β is said to be a cover of a or a is covered by β, β is the covering graph, a is the covered graph.

If for subspaces a and β, congruent transformation $P:\alpha\rightarrow\gamma$ exists, let $\gamma\subset\beta$, we say β can cover a or a can be covered by β. If after covering, $\gamma=\beta$, say **congruent cover**.

If a is the set of discrete points in n-D space, the feasibility using points to do congruent cover is almost zero. In order to process it quickly, we adopt fixed graph to cover it, say one cover which has the minimum volume of cover graph is the minimum cover of this graph, if using triangle to do covering, say minimum triangle cover, if sphere, say minimum sphere cover. If points in the set of covering points have been distributed to the border line of covering graph, that is, the covering graph cannot be shrank, we call it as vertex cover. This type of cover for the point set is said to be the point cover, vertex cover is one of point covers, which is the minimum point cover in the same class graph with different size.

Since signal is usually some discrete points in the computer signal processing, we focus on the point cover in HDS, therefore, if no special declaration, the cover below is the point cover.

2.2 Speech distribution in HDS

- A continuous single digit segment in feature space is distributed inside a flat and slender hyper-rectangular, tone and rhyme in different pronunciation on two ends, the transient region in the middle:

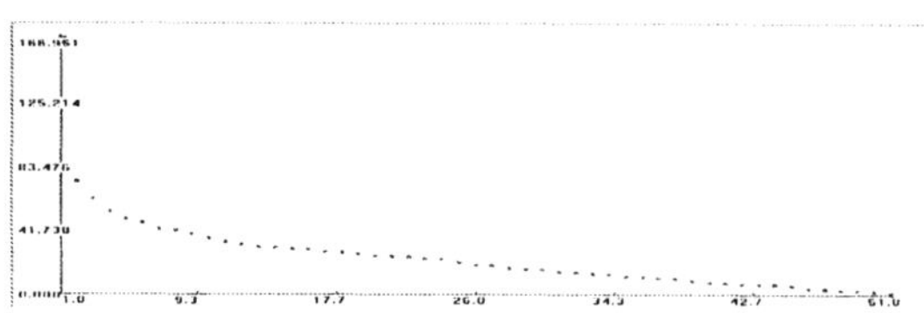

Fig. 1 PCA for a continuous digit "qi" in space, where horizontal axis is 51 mutually orthogonal axes from 52 points via PCA, vertical ordinate is axes length.

Distribution of the same speech segment from different speakers is much sparser in feature space, which might be covered by covering product of the surface jointed by multi-plane and hypershpere.

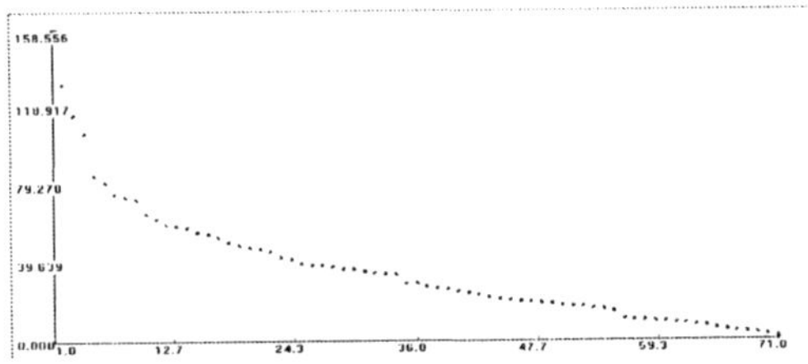

Fig. 2. PCA in feature space for the same digit speech "qi" from 24 speakers, each one choose 3 points totally 72 points. Horizontal axis is the position of 71 principal axes, vertical ordinate is the length of every principal axis

- What kind of cover should we use for speaker-independent speech recognition? The answer is to adopt the local covering principle, use the above-mentioned curve or surface to do the one by one cover for points in space, and then establish the covering area for one such speech by the cover product of surface and hypersphere. Thus the computation complicacy is reduced and the distribution of speech points might be depicted much realer. In the case of covering same amount of points completely, we apply a covering method of a smaller-volume manifold product (product of surface and hypersphere), so that probability of points in other classes which are dropped to this covering area would be reduced. The different continuous words are also continuously distributed in feature space. the graded procedure exists from one to another feature area, this sort of transformation is just the interface of the different speech, which is unobvious, just like the interface of continuous speech in time domain (the co-articulation effect of continuous speech), the dividing line but the pronounce area is not clear, we therefore easily find the speech covering area in the transformation domain, that is the foundation of the dynamic searching based on point covering.

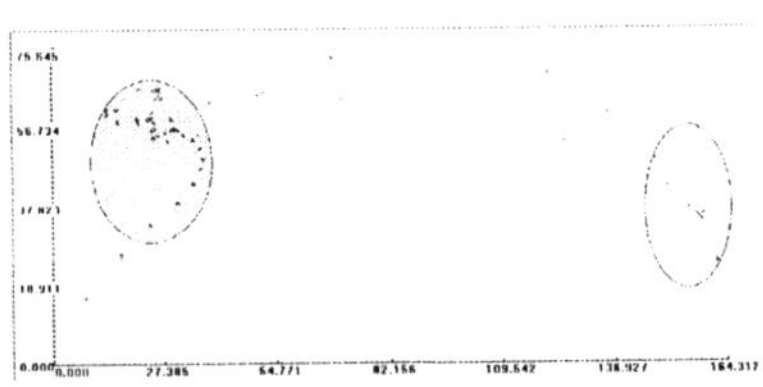

Fig 3. Distribution in the feature space of two continuous words "yi qi". The former solid points are the speech points of "yi", the latter hollow points are of "qi", the horizontal axis is the link line of two points with the farthest

distance, vertical ordinate is the vertical distance from point to horizontal axis.

2.3 Covering method for different classes of speech

As the above statement, the covering method for speech in the different classes is summarized as follows:

. construct the speech sample points in the covering area, select one representative point in continuous single digit speech (In Fig. 8b, one point in the transient area from tone to rhyme, choose one middle point with the clear pronunciation and strong periodicity in syllable without tone), this point is distinguishable in the time domain, i.e., its pronunciation can be recognized clearly by ears.

Apply the local covering principle, let covering basic element be the plane, the covering set is just a curve, hence the computation load is reduced and also the covering area is more approximate to the speech point distribution.

Assume dimensionality of the space in which speech points are via space mapping be N, use the covering product of surface and (N-2)–D hypersphere for the last covering area, the threshold of covering product is the radius of hypershpere.

Use neuron computer CASSANN-II to compute, the number of covering basic elements is co-determined by the sample number in the covering area within the built current network and the training algorithm of neural network.

Select the threshold of covering product between the average distance from points in one class to the center of its own covering area and the minimum distance from points in other classes to the central axis plane.

3. EXPERIMENTAL RESULT AND DISCUSSION

3.1 Statistical result and discussion in the experiment

The continuous speech sample used by built network is from 28 people. Select randomly 10 sample points in each digit class for each person, 280 sample points in each class, which builds up the digital neural network covering area in this class, experimental result is given in Tab. 1.

Table 1 Recognition result of randomly selected sample network

	Set A	Set B	Sum
Recognizable digit amount	225	32	256
digit amount of accuracy recognition	191	20	211
digit amount of misrecognition	18	8	26
Accuracy recognition rate	85.27%	62.5%	82.42%

The continuous speech sample used by built network is from 24 people, everyone picks up 10 sample points, but which is only by simple screening, these sample points by direction tracing to the source, the original speech segment is the digit read which can be recognized by ears. Applying 240 sample points to created network for the digit of each class, Tab.5-6 is the experimental result.

Tab.2 Recognition result of built sample network by screening

	Set A	Set B	Sum
Recognizable digit amount	200	64	264
Digit amount of accuracy recognition	177	52	229
Digit amount of misrecognition	14	6	20
Accuracy recognition rate	88.5%	81.25%	86.74%

3.2 Comparing result and discussion with HMM model

Under the case of fewer training samples, the speech recognition approach based on the HDS point covering theory is much better than HMM-based approach:

Firstly, in theory, the traditional HMM model is based on statistical model, whose accuracy completely depends on accuracy of probability statistics, and accuracy of probability statistics depends on massive data. Therefore, once the number of one type model is limited, algorithm accuracy based on statistical model is sure to be suspected. Method using neural network model building based on HDS point covering theory, by the efficient information melting ability of neural network and morphological analysis method and with a small amount of samples, can find the covering area in HDS for one type sample, thus the high recognition rate is obtained.

Secondly, during experiments, train the same training sample (according to the number of training sample in each class, there are five groups 48,96,144,192,240 to attend comparison) via HDS point covering and

HMM model method, then recognize the same recognized sample by these two methods respectively. Results are showed in table 3-9

Tab 3 Optimal state amount used by HMM model building and Gauss density function amount

Training sample amount	48	96	144	192	240
State amount	4	5	5	5	5
GDF	4	3	6	4	6

Tab.4 Comparison of recognition rate for speech of every class when 48 training samples in each class

digit	point covering method	HMM
ling	0.863931	0.7927
yi	0.923221	0.8408
er	0.852252	0.8054
san	0.978462	0.9154
si	0.969474	0.8895
wu	0.952712	0.9249
liu	0.849257	0.7495
qi	0.940202	0.8289
ba	0.936508	0.8825
jiu	0.917793	0.8423
yao	0.940828	0.7707

Tab. 5 Comparison of recognition rate for speech of every class when 96 training samples in each class

Digit	Point covering	HMM
ling	0.887689	0.8099
yi	0.973783	0.8783
er	0.861261	0.8288
san	0.989231	0.9369
si	0.957895	0.9453
wu	0.986092	0.9527
liu	0.921444	0.7771
qi	0.977921	0.8381
ba	0.968254	0.9079
jiu	0.967342	0.8795
yao	0.967456	0.9379

Tab.6. Comparison of recognition rate for speech of every class when 144 training samples in each class

Digit	Point covering	HMM
ling	0.946004	0.8963
yi	0.973783	0.9382
er	0.888288	0.8937
san	0.987692	0.9538
si	0.973684	0.9547
wu	0.968011	0.9555
liu	0.921444	0.8641
qi	0.966881	0.8684
ba	0.946032	0.927
jiu	0.977477	0.9324
yao	0.961538	0.9497

Tab.7. Comparison of recognition rate for speech of every class when 192 training samples in each class

Digit	Point covering	HMM
ling	0.952484	0.8531
yi	0.973783	0.9644
er	0.918919	0.8775
san	0.986154	0.9646
si	0.972632	0.9579
wu	0.987483	0.9805
liu	0.942675	0.8705
qi	0.973321	0.8657
ba	0.984127	0.946
jiu	0.974099	0.9279
yao	0.985207	0.9527

Tab. 8. Comparison of recognition rate for speech of every class when 240 training samples in each class

Digit	Point covering	HMM
ling	0.961123	0.9006
Yi	0.986891	0.9494
Er	0.933333	0.9045
san	0.989231	0.9738
Si	0.981053	0.9695

Wu	0.973574	0.9777
Liu	0.974522	0.896
Qi	0.965961	0.8896
Ba	0.993651	0.946
Jiu	0.974099	0.9313
yao	0.985207	0.9482

Tab.9. Comparison of overall recognition rate under the variant training sample amount in each class

Training sample amount in each class	Point covering	HMM
48	0.927203	0.8441
96	0.955939	0.8859
144	0.959907	0.9221
192	0.970033	0.9245
240	0.974001	0.9357

4. CONCLUSION

Research for HDS geometric theory and its application in the continuous digit speech recognition, making an investigation on a new sort of approach, experiments show it is promising for solving stability of Speaker-independent continuous speech recognition system. In those cases, e.g., microphone close to speakers and under circumstance with parts of road background noise etc., the word recognition rate still reach 86.74% (which is close to the result based on HMM method), however, for the speech recognition from untrained speakers, its recognition rate is still 81.25% (impossible for HMM method to have better stability like this). The method present here is no need to go through endpoints detection and segmentation, the recognized speech can be directly projected to the built covering area, and by a dynamic searching algorithm along time axis to find recognition results. This algorithm is simple and feasible, with fast computation speed, and can solve the contradiction of the processed signals in HDS having the same dimensionality necessarily and signals of same class having the irregular length on the time, i.e., solve difficulty about the continuous speech signal having the different length under the signal sequence at variant speech speed. This method differs from the conventional pattern matching and dynamic time warping, and the optimal route searching, so that it is a new research direction based on HDS covering theory.

REFERENCES

1. Wang ShouJue, Bionic(Topological) Pattern Recognition——A New Model of Pattern Recognition Theory and Its Applications, ACTA ELECTRONICA SINICA, 2002, 30(10): 1417-1420
2. Wang ShouJue, Wang Bianan, Analysis and Theory of High-Dimension Space Geometry for Artificial Neural Networks, ACTA ELECTRONICA SINICA, 2002,30(1): 1-4
3. Wang ShouJue, A new development on ANN in China – Biomimetic pattern recognition and multiweight vector neurons, LECTURE NOTES IN ARTIFICIAL INTELLIGENCE 2003,2639: 35-43
4. Wang Shoujue, Xu Jian, Wang Xianbao, Qin Hong, Multi-camera Human-face Personal Identification System Based on the Bionic Pattern Recognition, ACTA ELECTRONICA SINICA,2003,31(1): 1-3
5. Cao WM, Hao F, Wang SJ, The application of DBF neural networks for object recognition, INFORMATION SCIENCES, MAR 22 2004, 160 (1-4): 153-160
6. Shi Jingpu, Chen Ji, Chen Xiaodong, Chen Chuan, Wang Shoujue, The Speaker Verification System Based on Neurocomputer and Its Application, ACTA ELECTRONICA SINICA, 1999,27(10):27-29
7. Wang Shoujue, Li Zhaozhou, Wang Bonan, Deng Haojiang, Feed-forward Neural Network Modeling for Noise Rejection, JOURNAL OF CIRCUITS AND SYSTEMS, 2000, 5(04):21-26
8. Deng Haojiang, Wang Shoujue, Xing Cangju, Li Qian, Research of Text-Independent Speaker Recognition Using Clustering Statistic, JOURNAL OF CIRCUITS AND SYSTEMS, 2001,6(03):77-8
9. Xing Cangju, Qu Yanfeng, Wang Shoujue, Face Detection on Gray-Scale Static Image with Complex Background, JOURNAL OF COMPUTER-AIDED DESIGN & COMOPUTER GRAPHICS,2002, 14(05):401-403
10. Qu Yangfeng, Li Weijun, Xu Jian, Wang Shoujue, Fast Multi-Pose Face Dection in A Complex Background, OURNAL OF COMPUTER-AIDED DESIGN & COMOPUTER GRAPHICS, 2004,16(01):45-50
11. Deng Haojiang, Wang Shoujue, Du Limin, Text-Independent Speaker Verification on Using Priority Ordered Radial Basis Function Networks, JOURNAL OF ELECTRONICS AND INFORMATION TECHNOLOGY, 2003, 25(09):1153-1159
12. Wenming Cao Feng hao and Shoujue Wang, An adaptive controller for a class of nonlinear system using direction basis function. ACTA Journal Of Electronics 2002, 23: 43-48.
13. Xu, Jian, Li, Weijun, Qu, Yanfeng, Qin, Hong, Wang, Shoujue, Architecture Research and Hardware Implementation on Simplified Neural Computing System for Face Identification, Proceedings of the International Joint Conference on Neural Networks, 2003, 2:948-952

A NEW HYBRID HMM/ANN MODEL FOR SPEECH RECOGNITION

Xiaojing Xi[1] , Kunhui Lin[1], Changle Zhou[2],Jun Cai[2]
1. Software School of XiaMen University, China
2. Department of Computer Science XiaMen University, China

Abstract: Because of the application of the Hidden Markov Model (HMM) in acoustic modeling, a significant breakthrough has been made in recognizing continuous speech with a large glossary. However, some unreasonable hypotheses for acoustic modeling and the unclassified training algorithm on which the HMM based form a bottleneck, restricting the further improvement in speech recognition. The Artificial Neural Network (ANN) techniques can be adopted as an alternative modeling paradigm. By means of the weight values of the network connections, neural networks can steadily store the knowledge acquired from the training process. But they possess a weak memory, not being suitable to store the instantaneous response to various input modes. To overcome the flaws of the HMM paradigm, we design a hybrid HMM/ANN model. In this hybrid model, the nonparametric probabilistic model (a BP neural network) is used to substitute the Gauss blender to calculate the observed probability which is necessary for computing the states of the HMM model. To optimizing the network structure in and after the training process, we propose an algorithm to prune hidden nodes in a trained neural network, and utilize the generalized Hebbian algorithm to reconfigure the parameters of the network. Some experiments show that the hybrid model has a good performance in speech recognition.

Key words: HMM; ANN; BP; removing hidden nodes algorithm; generalized Hebbian algorithm

1. INTRODUCTION

Speech recognition is mainly to let the machine understand what human says which means under various situations, the machine can recognize the content of the speech accurately, and then execute the various intentions of the human according to the information. HMM has made great success in every field of speech processing, but it has many restrictions. The neural network memories and stores the information for a long time well by using the weight values, but the memory ability of instantaneous responding to the input model is weaker. So, it has difficulty to model the time variable. As both the HMM and the ANN have advantages and disadvantages, so we propose the hybrid HMM/ANN model to which has been attached importance by many research institutions, such an ICSI, SRI, SVR and so on. The performances of some speech recognition systems researched by them have overmatched the traditional HMM system. In this paper, we apply BP neural network to calculate the observation probability needed by the states of the HMM instead of the GM. In this hybrid model, we apply Continuous Destiny Hidden Markov Model (CDHMM) to build modeling for the short-time speech components, and calculate the observation probability of the CDHMM by using the ANN with the ability to classify the signal. In addition to, for optimization of the hybrid model, we proposed an algorithm to remove hidden nodes in a trained neural network, and optimize the parameters of the network by using the generalized Hebbian algorithm.

2. THE HYBRID HMM/ANN MODEL

The speech signal is a typical dynamic pattern sequence, the time relativity of the frame and the neighbor frame is very strong, so, if we want to apply the ANN to speech recognition, we must resolve the memory problem of instantaneous outputs. So we combine the ANN to the developed method HMM and form a Hybrid system, in which ANN may preprocess the data as former-end of HMM, or rear-process as back-end of HMM.

2.1 The combination of the HMM and the ANN

The combination of ANN and HMM has many ways, such as realizing the HMM using the ANN directly, the combination of the speech frame layer, the combination of the speech layer, the combination of the tone-phase layer, the combination of the sub-layer and so on. In this paper, we search after a new hybrid model instead of realizing the HMM by the ANN directly, the new hybrid model can optimize the HMM model and also can make use of the advantages of each technology: the time modeling of the HMM and the acoustic modeling of the ANN, specially, we calculate and estimate the observation probability by the ANN.

There are many methods to design and train the neural network. The simplest way is that we map the speech vector of one frame into observation probability; the network is trained from one frame to the next frame. This is the training for the network of the frame layer.

In the method of tone-phase layer, the input of the network comes from the whole speech phase instead of a speech frame or a fixed speech window. So it can utilize the correlation of the whole speech frames in the speech phrase better, and also we can use other information easily, for example the time-length, but we must divide the speech into speech phase firstly, and then the neural network can calculate the divided speech phase. Among these different combination methods, the experiment shows that the combination of the frame layer fits the characteristics of ANN and HMM better.

2.2 The application and algorithm of the hybrid model

In hybrid model, the acoustic modeling is completed by the ANN, the time-field modeling depends on the traditional HMM, and there are two kinds of methods to finish the acoustic modeling:

The first method is the predictive network, the input is the feature vectors of several continuous frames, the output is the prediction value of the next frame, we distribute a predictive network for every phoneme, and we select the network with minimal predictive error by comparing the predictive errors of the network of every phoneme matching with the currently speech segment, so it embodies the time-field correlation of the neighbor speech frames.

The second method is classifying network. In this network, the input is still the feature vectors of several continuous frames, but the output is mapped directly into the states of HMM. The n output nodes represent n sorts, the input nodes are mapped into one sort among the n sorts. The classifying network is easy, intuitionistic and distinguishable in essence, modularity in design, and it can organize bigger system, and has the advantages of prefect mathematical explanations, so it can be integrated into the statistical recognition frames easily.

In this paper, the hybrid model that is unlike the traditional HMM/ANN model adopts the classified network to estimate the posterior probability. So we may adopt context-sensitive input pattern as the input of the neural network, it takes the time correlation of the speech vectors into account. The posterior probability of the output of the neural network is $p(q_i \mid X_{t-d}^{t+d})$ while the likelihood probability destiny needed by the states of the HMM is $p(x_t \mid q_i)$, according to the Bayes rules, we deduce the measure likelihood destiny probability from the posterior probability $p(q_i \mid X_{t-d}^{t+d})$,

$\frac{p(x_t \mid q_i)}{p(x_t)} = \frac{p(q_i \mid x_t)}{p(q_i)}$, in the recognition, because $p(x_t)$ is the same to all paths, so measure likelihood function doesn't influence the recognition result. Because the classifying network embodies the essence of the hybrid model, we utilize it to constitute the speech recognition system. When the hybrid model recognizes the speech that is calculated by ANN scale observation probability of the states of HMM, The course is divided into two steps: The first step: computing all states' scale observation probability at t;

The second step: calculating the accumulating probabilities of the active paths, removing the superfluous nodes according to these probabilities and then ensuring the active paths at t

For every frame speech vector, we may calculate the output vector $g_i(x_i)$、$g_{j|i}(x_t)$、$u_{i,j}(x_t)$ of every node network (BP network)by posteorder traversal, when traverse to the root node, we can get the output collective,

$$u(x_i)=\sum_i g_i(x)\sum_j g_{j|i}(x_t)*u_{i,j}(x_t)$$

The output collective is the estimation of the posterior probability. That the posterior probability divided by the transcendent probability is the measure likelihood probability $\frac{p(q_i \mid X_{t-c}^{t+c})}{p(q_i)}=\frac{p(X_{t-c}^{t+c} \mid q_i)}{p(X_{t-c}^{t+c})}$

In the algorithm of frame synchronization in Viterbi path searching, for every frame speech vector, we may add up the measure observation probability to the path probability of every active path

$$a_{\lambda_m,q_k}(x_t)=\max_{i\in pre(q_k)}\{a_{\lambda_m,q_k}(x_{t-1})+\log(a_{i,k})+\log(p(q_i \mid x_t))-\log(p(q_i))\}$$

$a_{\lambda_m,q_k}(x_t)$ is the optimum path accumulative probability, when reaching the state q_k of the model λ_m at t, pre(q_k) is the set including all the prior nodes in the searching networks, $a_{i,k}$ is the state transition probability from the prior node i to the node j. According to the computing structure of the accumulative probability of the currently active path, we may remove some paths whose accumulative probability below a threshold, and then, get the every speech vector frame of active paths at t+1, and continue according to the above steps until the end of the pronounce sentences. At last, we trace back according to the optimum path until we find the model sequence of HMM matching to the pronounce sentence, and the result is the preferred result of the acoustics model.

2.3 Optimization of the hybrid model

2.3.1 Optimization of the number of hidden nodes

The first problem needed to be considered is how to confirm the number of the hidden nodes

1. The increasing algorithm of hidden nodes: By increasing the number of hidden nodes to improve the frame recognition ratio during the training.
2. The removing algorithm of hidden nodes: By removing the superfluous hidden modes and the weight values during the training.

After comparing and analyzing, we put forward a new method to confirm the number of the hidden nodes.

1. Getting the number of the clustering centers by analyzing the self-organizing data iteratively, and assigning a hidden node for a pair of clustering centers in different sorts. So to the input mode these hidden nodes form multidimensional space. In this space, the input nodes form decision-making curved surface easily, so we get the number of the hidden nodes N suited not only for training but the removing after training.
2. Training the BP network with n hidden nodes

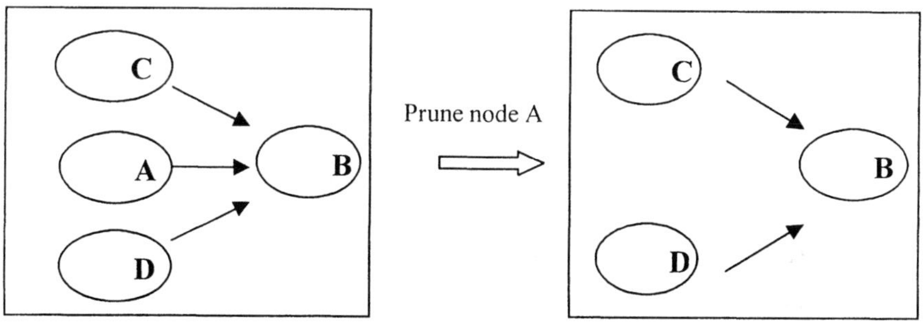

Fig1 A novel algorithm for hidden nodes pruning

. Removing the redundancy nodes by iteration algorithm, and then adjust the weight value of the remainder nodes on condition that keeping the intrinsic input, at last we get the optimum nodes number of the network, as the Fig1 shows, after removing the node A, we adjust the weight value of the remainder nodes to make the pure input unchanged defined by the least-mean-square, i.e. as for all the models in the training set

$$\sum_{j\in\{A,C,D\}} w_{j,B} y_j(n) = \sum_{j\in\{C,\ D\}} (w_{j,B} + \delta_{j,B}) y_j(n) \quad \forall n \in \{1,2...N\}$$

The $w_{j,B}$ is the weight value from the node j to B, $\delta_{j,B}$ is the residual error from the node j to B, $y_j(n)$ is the output of the node n-th, which is equivalent to a linear equation

$$\begin{bmatrix} y_C(1) & y_D(1) \\ M & M \\ y_C(N) & y_D(N) \end{bmatrix} \begin{bmatrix} \delta_{C,B} \\ \\ \delta_{D,B} \end{bmatrix} = w_{A,B} \begin{bmatrix} y_A(1) \\ M \\ y_A(N) \end{bmatrix}$$

With the LMS iterative algorithm we can get the optimized result of the linear equation under the least-mean-square condition. Because LMS algorithm resolves the above equation, the remained difference decreases with the decreasing of the iterative times monotonously, we can determine which nodes should be removed by calculating the initial remained difference of every node, the computing amount is very small, and the checking of the redundancy nodes is very easy.

2.3.2 The second improvement: the initialization of the weight parameters of network

Before training the network, every weight should be assigned a value. It is an important issue in ANN, which affects directly to the convergence of the training results. The main idea of the training is seeing out the study mechanism to initialize the weight values of Network using transcendental knowledge. In this paper, these classes are divided by the neural network, we utilize the Hebb algorithm to init the weight values, and the experiments show the good results.

Its principle: we set the hidden nodes as linear, as for the input mode x_i $i = 1,2,\ldots,k-1$,the weight value matrix brought by between the input nodes and the hidden nodes is $V_{k-1} = [v_{1,k-1}, v_{2,k-1}, v_{3,k-1}, \ldots, v_{n_k,k-1}]$, for x_k we update the weight matrix according to the Oja rule $V_k = V_{k-1} + a_0(I - V_{k-1}V_{k-1}^T)x_k x_k^T V_{k-1} = V_{k-1} + a_0(x_k - V_{k-1}\bar{h}_{k-1}^T)\bar{h}_k^T$,in this formula, $\bar{h}_k = V_{k-1}^T x_k$, every weight vector is given by the following formula $v_{i,k} = v_{i,k-1} + a_0 \bar{h}_{i,k}(x_k - \sum_{i=1}^{n_k} \bar{h}_{1,k} v_{i,k-1})$

For the generalized Hebbian study rule, in the formula

$V_k = V_{k-1} + a_0(x_k - V_{k-1}L_d(\bar{h}_k^T))L_h(\bar{h}_k^T)$

$L_h(\bar{h}_k^T) = [L_h(\bar{h}_{1,k}), L_h(\bar{h}_{2,k}), \ldots, L_h(\bar{h}_{n_k,k})]$ is the function of the output $\bar{h}_k$.Every weight vector $v_{i,k}$ can be gotten as follows:

$$v_{i,k} = v_{i,k-1} + a_0 L_h(\bar{h}_{i,k})(x_k - \sum_{i=1}^{n_k} L_d(\bar{h}_{i,k})v_{i,k-1})$$

The stop rule: if $n_k > n_i$, the stop rule is based on the decrease of error

E_v $$E_v = \sum_{k=1}^{m} \left\| \bar{x}_k - \sum_{i=1}^{n_k} L_d(\bar{h}_{l.k}) v_i \right\|^2, \bar{h}_k = V^T x_k$$

The form of the learning function can be defined as $\varphi(z) = \frac{d\rho^2(z)}{dz}$, $\rho(.)$ is the inspiring function, the initialization of the parameters of network can be divided into two parts, one is the weight values initialization between the input nodes and hidden nodes and the other is the weight values initialization between the hidden nodes and the output nodes. At first we initialize the connective weight value between the input nodes and the output nodes by using the generalized Hebbian algorithm and then init the connect weight values of the output layer by the supervisory training algorithm $v_i, i = 1,2,..., n_k$, the detailed process is as follows:

1. Initialize V with random values; Select $L_d(.)$、$L_h(.), a_0, \beta$; Set v=1;
2. Calculate $v_i, i = 1,2,..., n_k$, $\bar{h}_k = V_{k-1}^T x_k$, $v_i, i = 1,2,..., n_k$ and $\bar{x}_k = \sum_{i=1}^{n_k} L_d(\bar{h}_{i,k}) v_i$ according to the formula for every k=1, 2, ...m
3. Determine the stop rule by using the previous phase
4. if v>1 then $E_v^{rel} = \frac{E_v^{old} - E_v}{E_v^{old}}$ else set $E_v^{old} = E_v$;
5. if v=1 or $E_v^{old} > E_v$ then set v=v+1 else loop to the step 2

And then using the supervisory training algorithm to initialize the connective weight values of the output layer $w_i, i = 1,2,..., n_0$, and initialization the weight values and using the sample couple $(y_k, h_k^{\exists}), k = 1,2,..., m$ to initialize the weight values between the hidden layer and output layer. The whole process is divided into three parts as follows: A. Generalized training rule:

$$\lambda E + (1-\lambda)E' = \lambda \sum_{k=1}^{m} \sum_{i=1}^{n_0} \phi_2(e_{i,k}) + (1-\lambda) \sum_{k=1}^{m} \sum_{i=1}^{n_0} \phi_1(e_{i,k})$$ in this

formula, $\phi_2(e_{i,k}) = \frac{1}{2} e^2_{i,k}$ $\lambda : 1.0 -> 0.0, \lambda = \lambda(E) = \exp\left(-\frac{\mu}{E^2}\right)$, if the output of the network is Binary value, and the value is +1 or -1 then $\phi_1(e_{i,k}) = y_{i,k}(y_{i,k} - y_{i,k}^{\exists})$

B. Updating the weight values basing on the grads decreasing

$w_{i,k} = w_{i,k-1} + \alpha\delta^{0}_{i,k} h^{3}_{k}$

C. The program for initializing the connective weight of the output layer

(1) Initialize W with random values

Select α, μ, Set $\lambda = 1, E_w = 0$, and $v = 1$

(2) For each k=1, 2, ...,m Calculate $y^{3}_{i,k} = \sigma(w_i^T h^{3}_{k}), i = 1,2,\ldots,n_0$,

Evaluate $\delta^{0}_{i,k}, i = 1,2,\ldots,n_0$ Update $w_i, i = 1,2,\ldots,n_0$

Calculate $y^{3}_{i,k} = \sigma(w_i^T h^{3}_{k}), i = 1,2,\ldots,n_0$,

Set $E_w = E_w + \frac{1}{2}\sum_{i=1}^{n_0}(y_{i,k} - y^{3}_{i,k})^2$ Calculate

$\lambda = \lambda(E) = \exp(-\frac{\mu}{E^2})$ if v>1 then $E_w^{rel} = \frac{E_w^{old} - E_w}{E_w^{old}}$ $E_w^{old} = E_w$

If v=1 or $E_w^{old} > E_w$; then set v=v+1 and go to (2)

3. EXPERIMENT RESULT

The experiment shows that the recognition performance of the hybrid HMM/ANN excels the traditional HMM with the same number of parameter and the input characters. In order to implement the same recognizing performance, the HMM system has to use more parameters and more complex model structure. As for the same continuous speech database, the recognition error ratio of the Context-free traditional HMM for the testing sentences is 11%, using MLP output as the posterior probability estimation and with almost the same number of parameters, the error ratio is 5.8%, while using the hybrid model preferred in this paper, the error ratio is 4.1%. Meanwhile, the hybrid model has acquired upstanding effect in unspecific person recognition of and the key words detection.

REFERENCES

[1] Xiongwei Zhang, Liang Chen, and Jinbin Yang Modern Speech technology and applications, China Machine Press 2003.8 ISBN.7-1111-12795-1 219-222

[2] Jinhui Xie, Hidden Markov Model and its applications in speech processing, HuaZhong University Press, 1995.4 ISBN 7-5609-1094-7/TN.34 103-113

[3] Changning Huang, Ying Xia, Monograph of speech information processing [A], TSingHua University Press, 1996.4 ISBN7-302-01929-0/TP.879 489-508

[4] Tingyue Zhuang, Yunhe Pan and Fei Wu, Web-based Multimedia Information Analysis and Retrieve TsingHua Unversity Press 2002.9 ISBN 7-302-05584-X/TP.3299 122-272

THE IMPLEMENTATION OF ONLINE TRANSDUCTIVE SUPPORT VECTOR MACHINE

ZHANG Xihuang,XU Wenbo
School of Information Engineering, Southern Yangtze University
214122 Wuxi, Jiangsu, P.R.China

Abstract: For many learning tasks, samples are collected over a long period of time. The distribution of the data set is likely to change. And only a little labeled training data is available at beginning of SVM training. So the collected data could not represent the whole data set. SVM should be able to adapt to such changes and situation. In order to achieve an acceptable performance with fewer labeled training samples at beginning of SVM studying, after studying transductive inference method, an Online tranductive SVM based on feedback is well organized based on TSVM. To deal with the expending size of support vector window, the $\xi\alpha$ Estimators is introduced, which will maintain the window on the training data by automatically adjustment, The estimated generalization error is minimized. The approach is both theoretically well founded as well as effective and efficient in practice. Two experiments show OTSVM is effective

Key words: support vector machine; transductive inference; $\xi\alpha$ estimator; online tranductive

1. INTRODUCTION

A major concern with machine learning and supervised learning techniques such as support vector machine (SVM) is based on very complete, absolute, and strict theories [1,2,3,4]. But it is not suitable for the situation where data is collected over an extended period of time, or the data is likely to change over time. In many on-line applications this introduces the problem that the distribution of the data is likely to change over time. To meet this problem changed over time, a traditional machine leaning system should be able to adapt to such changes. A second problem in many real world applications is that only little labeled training data is available. Since only few labeled training samples are provided, users often take partial feedback, which could be able to achieve a good performance.

After introduce the basic support vector machine (SVM) principle, This paper improve the transductive inference method which could detect and handle concept changes with support vector machines extending the approach by using unlabeled data to reduce the need for labeled data [5,6,7]. The approach has a clear theoretical motivation and does not require complicated parameter tuning. At last, by the adjustment approach of sample window, an on-line SVM is suggested. The experiments on Hoovers Data set show that the on-line SVM approach effectively selects an appropriate window size and results in a low predictive error rate. In case of few labeled samples, the use of unlabeled data can also be expected to improve the performance of the on-line SVM. When the amount of unlabeled data is used, the performance of the system could be in an ideal level.

2. SUPPORT VECTOR MACHINES

Support vector machines are based on the structural risk minimization principle from statistical learning theory. In basic form, SVM learn linear decision rules. SVM learning can be well analyzed by using the feature vector space.

Let z be a set of training samples

$z = (x1,y1),(x2,y2),\cdots(xn,yn),xi \in Rm,\ yi \in \{-1,+1\}$

where $xi \in Rm$ is an m-dimensional input vector and $yi \in \{-1,+1\}$ is the label of xi.

According to Vapnik's theory about support vector machine. The solution of SVM could be described as the following optimized problem

$$\begin{aligned} &Min\,W(\alpha) = \frac{1}{2}\|w\|^2 + C\sum_{i=1}^{l}\xi_i \\ &s.t\ \ y_i(w\cdot x_i + b) \geq 1-\xi_i,\ \xi_i \geq \quad 0 \leq \alpha_i \leq C,\ \ \sum_{i=1}^{l}\alpha_i y_i = 0 \end{aligned} \tag{1}$$

Here, ξi is a relax parameter and C is an impact factor. $y = (w \cdot x + b)$ describes the plane to classify the samples[1,4].The solution of above problem is also given by Vapnik[1,4].

3. TRANSDUCTIVE INFERENCE LEARNING

The algorithm of transductive inference learning based on support vector machine is that both the labeled and unlabelled samples are used in the process of learning. If the distributed information of unlabelled samples is carried into the new classifier, the new classifier will be trained better because the data characteristic of the whole samples space is depicted well. At present the transductive inference leaning based on support vector machine is at the preliminary stage. The representative one is TSVM[5,6,7,8].

The following labeled training samples are

$(x1,y1),(x2,y2),\cdots(xn,yn),x \in Rm,\ yi \in \{-1,+1\}$

and another group of unlabelled samples with the same distribution are

$x1^*,x2^*,\ \cdots xk^*$. The training process of TSVM is the generalization of the training process of support vector machine. It can be described as the following optimized problem:

$$
\begin{aligned}
&Mini\ (y_1^*,\ldots,y_k^*,w,b,\xi_1,\ldots\xi_n,\xi_1^*,\ldots\xi_k^*) \\
&\frac{1}{2}\|w\|^2 + C\sum_{i=1}^{n}\xi_i + C^*\sum_{j=1}^{k}\xi_i^* \\
&s.t:\forall_{i=1}^{n}: y_i[w\cdot x_i + b] \geq 1-\xi_i \quad \forall_{j=1}^{k}: y_j[w\cdot x_j^* + b] \geq 1-\xi_j^* \\
&\quad \forall_{i=1}^{n}:\xi_i \geq 0 \quad \forall_{j=1}^{k}:\xi_j^* \geq 0
\end{aligned}
\tag{2}
$$

where C and $C^*$are the parameters that can be adjusted by users. The $C^*\xi i^*$is called as an impact factor in the object function. The training process of TVSM is the same as the process resolving the above-mentioned optimization question.

The main idea of the training algorithm consists of several steps. Firstly the N labeled samples makes the initialized classifier. And secondly, the k unlabeled samples is labeled by the initial classifier. At last, in succession, the final classifier will be obtained by training both the N original labeled samples and k labeled samples.

When $k=1$, the training algorithm of TVSM needs to be adjusted apparently.

Theorem: In the algorithm of TSVM, when $k=1$, if the labeled samples are classified by using the initial classifier, the classified result makes sure that the object function is minimum in the formula (2).

Prove: Let x^* is classified by the initial classifier with label +1,so x^* is in the +1 region of the division plane. The correspond loose variable $\xi+{}^*>0$. If x^* were labeled as the value −1, the corresponding loose variable should be $\xi+{}^*>0$.

$$
\begin{cases}
\left[w\cdot x^* + b\right] = 1-\xi_+^* \\
-\left[w\cdot x^* + b\right] = 1-\xi_-^*
\end{cases}
$$

$$\xi_+^* + \xi_-^* = 2$$

Since x^* is in the region of the current division plane +1, and $\xi+{}^*<1$,

$\xi_-^* = 2-\xi_+^* > 1$

i.e. $\xi_+^* < \xi_-^*$ or $C^*\xi_+^* < C^*\xi_-^*$

That is to say, when x* is in the region of the current division plane +1, the value of formula (2) using the plus label will be less than the one using the

-1 labels. Therefore, the less value of the objective function will be obtained when using the classified result of the initial classifier.
The theorem indicates that the training process of Joachims's TSVM in case of $k=1$ is valid. Apply the formula of $k=1$ to Joachims's TSVM continuously, you can get the online tranductive vector machine. However, the number of n supporting the vector will be increased constantly too. It will do harm to both calculating and the dynamic performance of the support vector machine.
In order to reduce the degree of calculation complexity of online tranductive vector machine, and to improve the dynamic performance, the redresses to the number of support vector must be considered.

4. ESTIMATING AND SUPPORT VECTOR WINDOW ADJUSTING

The concept of support vector window is introduced to select proper support vector quantity in OTSVM. The $\xi\alpha$ estimator could resolve the problem of selecting the proper support vector window. The $\xi\alpha$ estimator method [6,7,8] is based on LOO and has considered the selection of parameters during the estimating process. This method largely reduces the workload of computation.
We can know from last section that two $\xi\alpha$ vectors are gained after SVM training. ξ is the vector of training losses at the solution of the SVM training problem. α is the solution of the SVM training problem. Let $d=\|\{i: (\alpha iR\Delta 2 + \xi i) \geq 1\|$ record the number of vector which $(\alpha iR\Delta 2 + \xi i) \geq 1$, where $R\Delta 2$ coud be 1. Then $\xi\alpha$ estimator will be

$$Err^n_{\xi\alpha}(h_L) = \frac{\|\{i : (\alpha_i R^2_\Delta + \xi_i) \geq 1\}\|}{n} = \frac{d}{n} \tag{3}$$

$\xi\alpha$ estimate can be gained from every training. In terms of ξα estimate you can judge the quality of SVM. In the same way you can compute the ξα estimate value of SVM in different sample sets. The algorithm to choosing the size of the window in the sample set could be written briefly as following:
Let there are two vector sets $\{x0,x1,x2, \cdots xn\}$ and $\{x0,x1,x2, \cdots xn \cdots xm\}$, here m>n, Steps of the algorithm are:
step1: Input t two vector sets
step2: Calculate

$$Err^n_{\xi\alpha}(h_L) = \frac{\|\{i : (\alpha_i R^2_\Delta + \xi_i) \geq 1\}\|}{n} = \frac{d}{n}$$

and

$$Err_{\xi\alpha}^{m}(h_L) = \frac{\left\|\{i : (\alpha_i R_\Delta^2 + \xi_i) \geq 1\}\right\|}{m} = \frac{d}{m}$$

step3: If *Errnξα (hL)< Errmξα (hL)* then *n* is the corresponding size of vector window.

else *m* is the corresponding size of vector window.

The above algorithm could be applied to the design of online tranductive SVM based on feedback.

5. THE DESIGN AND IMPLEMENTATION

Samples could only represent a little part and the past. So it is necessary to modify the SVM classifier while using the initial classifier. This is the idea of Online tranductive SVM(OTSVM) design based on feedback. Considering labeled samples are not usually acquired at random, and samples have been handled with some representative character. So there is no reason to take the distribution of its label as a basis to estimate the whole samples. And that if there are samples which are acquired at random, it is inaccurate to use that samples for computing because the small number of samples. In this section we will apply *ξα* estimator to accomplish the design of dymanic SVM classifier based on feedback and the transductive inference learning [9,10,11]. In this OTSVM, the possibel labels for unlabeled samples are given by the initial SVM classifier. Then the the newer labelled samples are take part in the new training with initial labelled smples. In this process, OTSVM adjusts the division plane dynamically. The theorem certified in this article ensures the validity and rationality of this dynamic classifier, and the *ξα* estimator shows the selection of window in samples rationalitily.

In the design of OTSVM we introduced *Wmin* and *Wmax* to ensure the range of support vector which is selected rationality.

After synthesizing the transductive inference learning and the ξα estimator, the algorithm of OTSVM classifier would be :

Step1: select the labeled samples set *V0*, set the value of *Wmin* and *Wmax*

Step2: initial learning is done to the labeled samples set *V0*,. An original classifier *F0* and support vector *SV0*, will be gotten.

Step3: *W=number_of[SV0]*

Step4: for (i=1;i< numbers of samples tested; i++)

{ Step5: input the unlabelled tested sample *xi**

Step6: adopt classifiers *Fi-1* to classify unlabelled and tested sample *xi**, we will get the label value *yi**;

Step7: *Vi=SVi-1 U (xi*, yi*)*

Step8: calculate *ξα* estimate and the value of support vector window

Step9: If $W \leq Wmin$ then $W = Wmin$;if $W \geq Wmax$ then $W = Wmax$

Step 10: adjust *SVi-1*, then we get *SVi*.

Step 11: reorganize the classifier *Fi-1*, and then we get a new classifier *Fi*}
Step 12: end

6. THE EXPERIMENTS AND CONCLUSION

We have adopted the data set of experiment from Hoovers sets [12]. The data gather over 10800 Web pages from the Internet.

6.1 Experiment 1

The purpose of the experiment is to test the effect of different numbers of initial samples to OTSVM and simultaneously to draw the effect of classification from comparing it with the traditional SVM.
In Hoover's data set, four groups of label samples are used as training sets to train initial OTSVM. The number of +1 labeled samples and -1 labeled samples are 30, 50, 80 and 100 in each group respectively. The samples were classified by hand in advance. And 160 random samples used to test set are classified by hand too. The classification result of 160 random samples will be a test criterion and attend to train and study in OTSVM.

Table1: the performance of OTSVM with different initial samples

	OTSVM		SVM	
group	accurate rate	recall rate	accurate rate	recall rate
1 (30)	68.3	88.6	65.7	84.7
2 (50)	82.8	89.4	71.8	87.8
3 (80)	86.2	95.7	78.4	92.8
4 (100)	87.4	94.7	79.9	91.1
average	81.2	92.1	73.9	89.1

Table 1 shows the result of experiment. The first group of training set contains 30 label samples, the second contains 50 labeled samples, the third contains 80 labeled samples and the fourth contains 100 labeled samples. The result of classification and training from the 160 test samples indicated that: more initial training sample sets may improve classification performance; the average accurate rate of OTSVM is higher than that of SVM; the function of improving classification effect of OTSVM is not obvious when the number of initial samples is large enough (the 3rd&4th group).

6.2 Experiment 2

The purpose of this experiment is to test the effect of different initial samples to OTSVM and simultaneously to observe the study progress process of OTSVM. There are four groups; each group has 80 labeled samples in training set (labeled by hand in advance). Selected 200 random samples are classified by hand too. The result of classification by hand will be a test criterion and will attend to train and study.
Table 2 shows the results of studying method of OTSVM in the condition of the same number of initial training sample set(the result of SVM is not listed due to the limited space). The result of classification from 200 testing samples indicates that the study capability of OTSVM will be increased in the process of classification and the accurate rate will be improved too.

Table2: the result on different sample set with same number of samples and the change of performance in OTSVM training *(AR= accurate rate; RR= recall rate)*

	OTSVM							
group	AR* 1-50	RR** 51-100	AR 51-100	RR 51-100	AR 101-150	RR 101-150	AR 151-200	RR 151-200
1	83.4	92.1	86.7	93.4	89.4	93.6	91.1	94.4
2	76.5	89.4	81.7	95.2	84.5	92.4	87.3	96.5
3	81.9	94.8	83.9	91.4	88.7	97.3	92.7	95.7
4	82.7	94.2	84.1	92.7	87.6	94.7	90.8	97.2
average	81.1	92.6	84.1	93.2	87.6	94.5	90.5	96.0

We should pay more attention to the second group of the experiments. The data shows that its accurate rate is obviously lower than common SVM in the testing of former 50 data(The common SVM accurate rate is 79.1% and 92.1%). By the deep analysis of the data, there are some data distribution departures, which will cause low accurate rate. Fortunately, the accurate rate will continuously increase along with the continuously studying and adjustment of OTSVM. The fact shows that OTSVM may reduce the departure of label sample distribution departures and offset of support vector set.
We can draw the conclusion from the above two experiments that OTSVM is based on training samples and gradually changed in the process of classification and studying. Every testing sample will affect the training of OTSVM, which comes from the corporate function of the classification process and training. Training will not be finished if the classification does not end. Obviously, this kind of method can adapt to the more general data distribution regulation and then it has the attribute of extending. We also can deduce it from the experiment that the excursion trend of classification plane

direct to the right orientation that improves the capability of OTSVM in the process of classification and training.
Although we use the $\xi\alpha$ estimator, the amount of calculation of arithmetic is still very large. It may have some relatively convenient methods. By sorting αi, the method we chose supports vector in the experiment also lead to a good result. But it should be proved strictly in theory.

REFERENCES

[1] Vapnik V. The Nature of Statistical Learning Theory. New York: Springer-Verlag, 1995

[2] Stitson MO, Weston JAE, Gammerman A, Vovk V, Vapnik V. Theory of support vector machines. Technical Report, CSD-TR-96-17, Computational Intelligence Group, Royal Holloway: University of London, 1996

[3] Cortes C, Vapnik V. Support vector networks. Machine Learning, 1995,20:273~297

[4] Vapnik V. Statistical Learning Theory. John Wiley and Sons, 1998

[5] Branson K. A naive Bayes classifier using transductive inference for text classification. 2001. http://www-cse.ucsd.edu/

[6] Joachims T. Transductive inference for text classification using support vector machines. In: Proceedings of the 16th International Conference on Machine Learning (ICML). San Francisco: Morgan Kaufmann Publishers, 1999. 200~209

[7] Chen YS, Wang GP, Dong SH. A progressive transductive inference algorithm based on support vector machine. Journal of Software, 2003,14(3): 451~460

[8] Klinkenberg. Ralf Using Labeled and Unlabeled Data to Learn Drifting Concepts. http://www-ai.cs.uni-dortmund.de/ (2001)

[9] Ralf Klinkenberg ,Thorsten Joachims. Detecting concept drift with support vector machines. Proceedings of the Seventeenth International Conference on Machine Learning (ICML),San Francisco, 2000. Morgan Kaufmann

[10] James Allan. Incremental relevance feedback for information filtering. In H. P. Frei, editor, Proceedings of the Nineteenth ACM Conference on Research and Development in Information Retrieval, pages 270–278, New

[11] Nigam, K., McCallum, A. K., Thrun, S., & Mitchell,T. M. (2000). Text classi_cation from labeled and unlabeled documents using EM. Machine Learning,39, 103-134

[12] www.hoovers.com

AN INTELLIGENT RETRIEVAL FRAMEWORK IN SEMANTIC WEB BASED ON AGENTS

Lin Xu and Bo Peng
College of Information and Electricity Engineering,CAU,100083

Abstract: Semantic Web is a research project of the World Wide Web Consortium (W3C), which aims to solve the problem of that the Web data is hard to process automatically because of the lack of semantic. The objective of this project is to implement the intelligent reasoning and processing automatically for the information published in the Web. Agent, as an intelligent object, is particularly suitable for lots of applications which are implemented in the Semantic Web. Based on the research of WWW and Intelligent Agent, this paper combined with some technologies, such as Information Search, Knowledge Representation, Modeling of Ontology, then proposed and implemented a Multi-Agent System Framework on the basis of Ontology semantic information retrieval, which includes four parts: information collecting, storing, querying and semantic reasoning.

Key words: Semantic Web; Intelligent Agent; Ontology; Intelligent Retrieval; Multi-Agents system

1. INTRODUCTION

The Web was designed as an information space, with the goal that it should be useful not only for human-human communication, but also that machines would be able to participate and help. One of the major obstacles to this has been the fact that most information on the Web is lack of semantic, that the notion of the Semantic Web has been introduced. "The Semantic Web is an extension of the current web in which information is given well-defined meaning, better enabling computers and people to work in cooperation.", according to Tim Berners-Lee, the founder of the Semantic Web.

At XML 2000 Tim Berners-Lee, Director of the Wide Web Consortium, outlined his vision for the Semantic Web and explained the layered architecture that developed in the next ten years (Figure1).

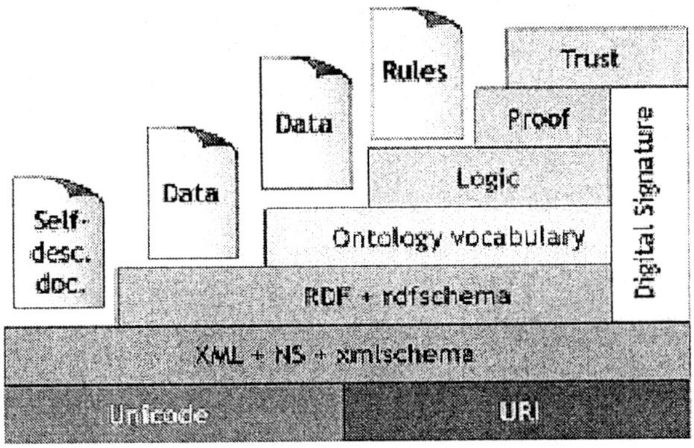

Figure1. The architecture of the Semantic Web

(1)The bottom of the Semantic Web is made up of Unicode and URIs(Uniform Resource Identifiers). Unicode is a character encoding system, like ASCII, designed to help developers who want to create software applications that work in any language in the world. URIs stand for Uniform Resource Identifiers, URIs are short strings that identify resources in the web, such as documents, images, downloadable files, services and so on. The Semantic Web can involve all resources and different languages with the help of Unicode and URI.

(2)The second layer of the Semantic Web is XML+NS（Name Space）+XML Schema. XML is a standard format for serializing data using tags. The NS（Name Space）of an element, is the scope within which it is valid. The XML+NS（Name Space）+XML Schema layer keeps the principles of SGML(Standard for General Markup Language) in place but its spec is thin enough to wave.

(3)The third layer consists of RDF and RDF Schema. RDF(Resource Description Framework) provides a way of describing resources via metadata. It restricts the description of resources to triplets. RDF Schema is a schema defines the terms that will be used in the RDF statements and gives specific meanings to them. RDF and RDF Schema layer is weak in some special area, so the Ontology layer is needed.

(4)The fourth layer is Ontology, the Ontology is designed to standardize means that can be used on the Web.

(5)Logic is the fifth layer, it is an inference engine that could explain how it followed the semantic links that it did.

(6)The next step in the architecture of the Semantic Web is trust and proof. Very little is written about them, which is a shame since it will become very important in the future.

The RDF/RDF Schema layer and the Ontology layer are the core of the architecture. The description information of Web exists in the form of metadata, it must be more intelligent if the metadata is collected and stored because of the semantic.

From the above descriptions, it is evident that applying the semantic in web retrieving is necessary. Agent, as an intelligent object, is particularly suitable for lots of applications which are implemented in the Semantic Web. So based on the research of WWW and Intelligent agent, this paper combined with some technologies, such as Information Retrieval, Knowledge Representation, Modeling of Ontology, then proposed and implemented a Multi-Agent System Framework on the basis of Ontology semantic information retrieval.

2. THE ARCHITECTURE OF THE INTELLIGENT RETRIEVAL FRAMEWORK

The Intelligent Retrieval Framework described the metadata of web by RDF models, which used for web resource only, to show details of the web. In order to store and query the RDFdata, an appropriate relational database will be ok, also the RDFdata can be treated as XML data. OWL, the Web Ontology Language, is a semantic markup language for publishing and sharing ontologies on the World Wide Web, also it is used in the Intelligent Retrieval Framework to support the knowledge reasoning.

The main function modules include the collecting agent to collect the information of Web metadata, the storing agent to store the metadata, the reasoning agent to deduce from the semantic correlation on the basis of Ontology and the querying agent to search by the results of the reasoning agent. Besides, it includes a database storing the Web metadata and an Ontology existed in the form of OWL files which supported special field knowledge for the reasoning agent. The architecture of the Intelligent Retrieval Framework is showed as Figure 2.

The flow of the Intelligent Retrieval Framework can be divided into the following four steps:

(1)Collect the information of Web metadata: the collecting agent draws out information from the metadata of the Semantic Web, and the metadata is expected to be stored by the storing agent after filtered by the collecting agent.

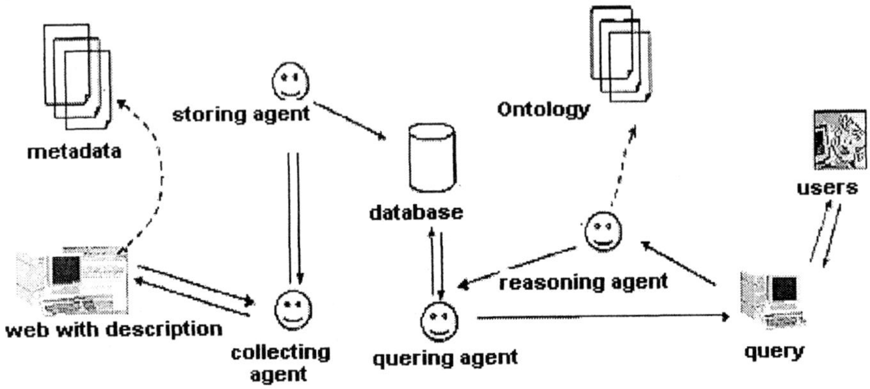

Figure 2. The architecture of the Intelligent Retrieval Framework

(2)Store the metadata: after receiving the metadata from the collecting agent, the storing agent store the metadata into database in an appropriate way.

(3)Intelligent reasoning on the basis of Ontology: when the Ontology is set up, the reasoning agent deduces the key words, or by semantic mapping, or by semantic correlation extending. Then the results that deduced by the reasoning agent would be accepted as a request by the querying agent.

(4)Intelligent querying based on semantic: the querying agent accepts a request from the reasoning agent, then searches the database that stored metadata by semantic. Finally, it returns the results that coincided with users.

3. THE IMPLEMENTATION OF THE INTELLIGENT RETRIEVAL FRAMEWORK

There are several modules in the Intelligent Retrieval Framework, but the core is the four agents: the information collecting agent, the storing agent, the reasoning agent and the querying agent.

3.1 The information collecting agent

The collecting agent collects description information of the Semantic Web metadata, and then hands the metadata to the storing Agent. Generally speaking, the description information of metadata is described in the form of RDF data at present, and the direct way is to insert the RDF data into Web, and often insert into the titles of HTML as XML syntax. Moreover, the RDF data can be stored in the form of files when there is a lot of metadata, and the links of the files would be provided on the Web for other agents or applications.

The collecting agent runs in the platform of JADE, and searches the semantic Web in a given route. It can filter the content of web automatically, draw out the description metadata of the Semantic Web, crawl from one web to another to affirm that the link is effective and delete the link that exist in name only.

3.2 The storing agent

By the communication between agents, the collecting agent passes the web metadata to the storing agent. The storing agent then recovers the metadata in the form of RDF data, after that, it stores the metadata in a proper way.

By and large, there are three methods to store the RDF data nowadays: XML/RDF file layout, RDF database, relational database. The XML/RDF file layout will be ok if there is little data, however, considering augmentability, the mode of querying, efficiency and other factors, it is a better choice to store the RDF data by RDF database or relational database when there is a lot of fact data. Relational database is the most popular application of database at present. However, because it is lack of semantic in relational database, it must be first convert RDF data model into relational model.

Statement is a basic description of a fact, and it is the minimal effective data unit in RDF data model. As a result, the table of storing statement is the most important part in database schema. (Table 1).

Table 1. RDFSatemens table

Column name	Type	Comments
Subject	Id-ref	
Predicate	Id-ref	
Object	Id-ref	
Object_isliteral	Smalllint	flags whether "object" is in literal or resource table
Model	Id-ref	
isreified	smllint	flags whether this statement is reified

Besides the RDFSatemens table, other tables are also needed, such as: RDFResourses table, RDFLiterals table, NameSpace table and LocalName table. The structure of these tables are simple, so omit them here.

RDF is a modeling language based on XML, so the RDF data is an especial XML data in some sense. It is the best way to store the RDF data by Middleware according to the characters of RDF data model. By mapping between XML documents and database, middleware completes the conversion. The typical Middleware product is XML-DBMS, and the Intelligent Retrieval framework in this paper also uses XML-DBMS to implement the conversion between RDF data and Mysql database with three steps: write a mapping document, a filter and java codes.

3.3 The reasoning agent

In order to search on the basis of semantic, not only the information of retrieved metadata is needed, but also the reasoning ability. The core of the reasoning agent is intelligent reasoning, it includes semantic mapping and semantic correlation extending in reasoning step.

During the course of semantic mapping, the key words are analyzed. Meanwhile, the querying agent judges the meaning of the key words by Ontology, and then selects the most accurate meaning from that several possible meanings. This method can improve the accuracy of the retrieval results for the key words that have several meanings. Traditional searching tools cannot discriminate different meanings of the same word, so it retrieves only by key words. But in the Retrieval Framework of this paper, every meaning of the key word is defined exactly by the Ontology, and mapping only one URI.

In the course of semantic correlation extending, not only the key words, but also other words that related to the key words are all obtained because of the Ontology. For example, the querying Agent can search one sub concept by subclass relation though this sub concept is not in the list of the key word.

At the end of the reasoning process, the reasoning agent delivers the results to the querying agent in the form of ACLMessage objects, some of the results are gained by semantic mapping, and some of them by semantic correlation extending.

3.4 The querying agent

The querying agent communicates with the reasoning agent, and receives the results from the reasoning agent. After that, the reasoning agent retrieves from the RDF database that storing metadata of the web, and returns the optimum result to users. Considering the features of RDF models, it is best for users to search by one special RDF searching language.

RDQL is one of the RDF searching languages of Jena, it resembles the "select" language of SQL, and it treats RDF data as triple, at the same time, it ignores Schema or Ontology information. RDQL provides one graph pattern to map data, and its graph pattern is a RDF statement. Users can search the unknown part of the statement according to the restriction of some parts of the statement.

RDQL can use solely, also can be embed in java codes. In this Retrieval Framework, RDQL language is used in the querying agent, and then it was encapsulated as a Query object. After that, the object was called, and users can get searching results in the form of ResultBinding variables, which can be stored and fetched easily by their names. Every model is a Web Unit in the RDF database, and their URL and title can be acquired easily when the model is retrieved. The querying agent returns this message to users, and the whole searching process finishes.

4. CONCLUSION

The semantic Web is the tendency of web in the future. Researches and applications on the Semantic Web will be useful for solving the bottleneck, which restricts the development of web nowadays, and also it can speed up the course of web application. Based on the research of WWW and Intelligent Agent, this paper combined with some technologies, such as Information Retrieval, Knowledge Representation, Modeling of Ontology, then proposed and implemented a Multi-Agent System Framework on the basis of Ontology semantic information retrieval. The purpose is to arise discussion of the Semantic Web and build a nice future for it together.

REFERENCES

[1]Tim Berners-Lee, J Hendler, O Lassila. The semantic web[J]. New York: Scientific American, 2001,284(5): 34~43.

[2]Tim Berners-Lee. Semantic Web-XML2000-Slide "Architecture" [EB/OL]. http://www.w3.org/2000/Talks-xml2k-tbl/Overview.html.

[3]T R Gruber. A translation approach to portable ontology specifications. Stanford University Knowledge system laboratory ,Tech Rep: Logic-92-1, 1992, Frank Manola, Eric Miller. RDF Primer. W3C Working Draft 23 January 2003[EB/OL]. http://www.w3.org/TR/2003/WD-rdf-primer-20030123/.

[4]Dan Brickley, R.V. Guha. RDF Vocabulary Description Language 1.0: RDF Schema. W3C Working Draft 23 January 2003[EB/OL]. http://www.w3.org/TR/2003/WD-rdf-schema-20030123/.

[5]Deborah L. McGuinness, Frank van Harmelen. OWL Web Ontology Language Overview. http://www.w3.org/TR/owl-features/Dave Reynolds.Jena relational database interface – introduction. 12 May 2001[EB/OL]. http:// www.hpl.hp.com/semweb/doc/RDB/rdb-intro.html.

[6]Ronald Bourret, XML and Databases[EB/OL], http://www.rpbourret.com/xml/XMLAndDatabases.htm.

[7]Michael K. Smith, Chris Welty, Deborah L. McGuinness. OWL Web Ontology Language Guide. http://www.w3.org/TR/owl-guide/

[8]Miller E. The Semantic Web.Technical Report, Eleventh International World Wide Web Conference (WWW2002), in Honolulu, Hawaii, USA, 2002.

[9]McBride B. RDF architecture.Technical Report, Eleventh International World Wide Web Conference (WWW2002) in Honolulu, Hawaii, USA, 2002.

[10]Hendler J. OWL: A Web Ontology Language. Technical Report, Eleventh International World Wide Web Conference (WWW2002) in Honolulu, Hawaii, USA, 2002.

A HYBRID ANT-BASED CLUSTERING ALGORITHM

Marianne Chong and Mylini Munusamy
Monash University Malaysia, No. 2, Jln Kolej, Bandar Sunway, 46150 Petaling Jaya, Selangor, Malaysia

Abstract: This research examines the ant-based clustering method as an alternative to k-means algorithm. Of particular interest is the AntClust which is modeled after the nestmate recognition system of real ants. We propose an algorithm called the Hybrid Ant-based Clustering Algorithm (HACA) which is a hybrid approach for unsupervised clustering problems. This algorithm combines the features of AntClust and k-means. HACA employs three different strategies – the blacklist strategy, the sniffing strategy and the nests fusion method, to improve the performance of the algorithm. We have conducted experimental investigations to demonstrate the effectiveness of HACA and the results have shown the advantages of the three strategies proposed as well as the improved performance of HACA compared to two other algorithms.

Key words: ant-based clustering, k-means algorithm,

1. INTRODUCTION

Clustering is an unsupervised task that seeks to identify natural groupings in data. The k-means algorithm is a traditional clustering algorithm that is commonly used where the advantages are its simplicity and speed. However, the shortcomings of k-means are that there is a need to supply an initial partition of the data set, the tendency to converge at a local optimum if the initial partition provided is not good and the assumption that all the clusters are of spherical shape. As a solution to these problems, various algorithms based on the behavior of real ants have been proposed. Ant-based algorithms have the advantages of not requiring an initial partition of the data set, being able to identify clusters of arbitrary shapes because of the bottom-up approaches of the algorithms as well as having a stochastic nature that allows the exploration of the data set. A hybrid algorithm that combines the clustering approach of k-means algorithm and an ant-based algorithm would counterbalance the advantages and disadvantage of both approaches.

In this research we propose a hybrid ant-based clustering algorithm (HACA) for unsupervised clustering problems. This algorithm combines the ant-based clustering algorithm with the k-means algorithm. As a measure of the performance of the algorithm, we have conducted experiments using differing data sets. Additionally, we also compared HACA against AntClust [8] and k-means.

The rest of the paper is organized as follows. The next section presents a brief literature review of various ant-based clustering algorithms. Section 3 discusses the AntClust [8] algorithm followed by a description of HACA and the three strategies that we have proposed to improve the algorithm. Section 4 details the experimental investigations that we have conducted to demonstrate the effectiveness and performance of HACA. Finally, Section 5 concludes this paper.

2. RELATED WORK

Various works on ant-based clustering algorithms that have been proposed based on either corpse clustering and larval sorting behaviors or the self-assembly behavior of real ants. The use of artificial ants for data clustering was first pioneered by Deneubourg et al [1] where they proposed a model based on the behaviors of corpse clustering and brood sorting in real ant colonies. This model is based on the idea of picking and dropping isolated objects at location where more objects of the same type are present. Lumer and Faieta [10] generalized Deneubourg's model for application on exploratory data analysis where they introduced a function to accommodate the clustering and sorting of complex objects. There are also algorithms that make use of artificial pheromone for ant clustering and sorting such as TermitAnt [14].

Additionally, there are hybrid algorithms that combine the Lumer and Faieta [13] algorithm with traditional clustering algorithms such as k-means and fuzzy c-means. The AntClass [11] is a hybrid algorithm that combines the Lumer and Faieta [10] algorithm with the k-means algorithm. This algorithm provides the initial partition for the k-means algorithm whilst the k-means algorithm refines the clustering results from the ant-based clustering algorithm. Schockaert et al. [13] proposed a simplified version of AntClass combining fuzzy IF-THEN rules that allows an ant to pick up either an object or a heap. The main advantage of ant-based algorithms is that it is able to generate a reasonably good clustering of the data set without any prior information about the data set.

3. HACA

We propose a hybrid approach called HACA that combines the features of the AntClust algorithm [8] with the k-means algorithm to counterbalance the advantages and disadvantages of both approaches.

3.1 AntClust

AntClust is an ant-based clustering algorithm that is modeled after the nestmate recognition system where the ants are used to represent items to be clustered (see Figure 1). The nestmate recognition system is described as a phenomenon that is "typically manifested by rejecting alien intruders" [8].

During the meeting phase, two ants are randomly picked at each iteration and a meeting is simulated between them. The outcome of the meeting is dictated by one of six behavioral rules. After the meeting phase, the nests formed are filtered in the nests deletion phase and only the meaningful nests are retained. Each artificial ant is coded as a set of parameters consisting of a $Label_i$, $Genome_i$, $Template_i$, M_i, M_i^+, and A_i.

The label $Label_i$, denotes the belonging nest and is initialised to 0 at the start of the algorithm. The label changes throughout the meeting phase until the ant finds the nest that best matches its genome. The genome $Genome_i$, corresponds to an item in the input data set and enables an ant to generate its own odour. It is used to learn and update its template. During meetings, ants compare their genome to evaluate the similarity between themselves. The template $Template_i$, is the acceptance threshold for an ant. This is one of two thresholds that are used to determine acceptance or rejection when an ant meets with another ant – the similarity between the genomes of the two ants has to be higher than $Template_i$ and $Template_j$ in order for acceptance to occur. $Template_i$ is learned during the initialisation period, in which an ant meets with a specified number of other ants, and each time evaluates the similarity between their genomes. After $Template_i$ has been learned, it is updated following every meeting realised by the ant regardless of the outcome, as the similarities observed may have changed.

```
Initialisation of the ants:
∀ ants i ∈ [1, N]
    Genome_i ← i^th object of the data set
    Label_i ← 0
    Template_i is learned during N_App iterations
    M_i ← 0, M_i^+ ← 0, A_i ← 0
Nb_Iter ← 75 * N
Simulate Nb_Iter meetings between two randomly chosen ants
Delete the nests that are not interesting with a probability P_del
Re-assign each ant that has no more nest to the nest of the most similar ant
```

Fig. 1. The AntClust Algorithm

The estimator M_i, indicates the proportion of meetings with nestmates and consequently enables an ant to have an estimation of the size of its nest. It increases each time an ant meets another ant with the same label, and decreases otherwise. The estimator M_i^+, reflects the proportion of positive meetings with nestmates. As positive meetings happen only when there is acceptance between ants, M_i^+ indicates the strength of an ant's integration in its own nest through acceptance from its nestmates. It is similar to M_i but with the additional condition that the nestmates accepted each other. M_i increases when there is acceptance between an ant and an encountered nestmate, and decreases otherwise. The age A_i, keeps track of the number of meetings that an ant has had. It is used to update the values of the maximal and mean similarities, and thus the value of $Template_i$. A_i increases each time an ant meets another ant. These parameters evolve according to a set of behavioural rules, as shown in Figure 2.

Once the ants have learned their templates, two ants at a time are picked to meet. These meetings are used to generate the nests that will define the final clusters. The first step in a meeting is the evaluation of similarity between the pair of ants. Then, each ant compares the evaluated similarity against its own template (i.e. the acceptance threshold). This comparison is also known as the principle of acceptance and rejection between two ants [12]. The outcome of this comparison (i.e. acceptance or rejection) and the current state of each ant are used to determine the correct rule to apply to the meeting, as shown in Figure 2. Briefly, the actions taken depending on the rules are: Rule 1 results in the creation of a new nest that consists of both the ants; Rule 2 joins the nestless ant with the nest of the other ant; Rule 3 increments the estimators M and M^+ for both ants; Rule 4 ejects the less integrated ant from the nest; Rule 5 absorbs the ant from the smaller nest into the bigger nest; and Rule 6 is the default rule where no action is taken.

The advantages of AntClust are that it does not need any initial knowledge of the data set such as the number or shape of the expected clusters in order to converge; this is unlike many other clustering algorithms such as k-means that require an initial partition of the data set prior to execution. It is able to find a partition that is as close as possible to the natural partition of the data set regardless of artificial or real data sets. It is able to find clusters of various shapes and sizes since AntClust adopts a

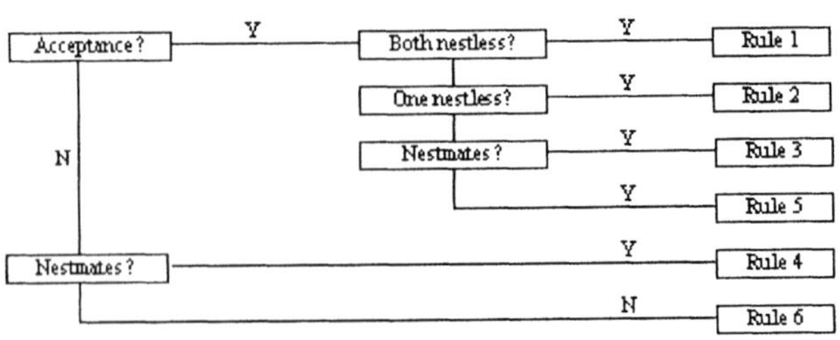

Fig. 2. The process of deciding which behavioral rule to apply

bottom-up approach towards clustering, that is, the clusters are formed from interactions between the ants. It shows favourable scaling behaviour to large and complex data sets. It is easily adapted to any type of data such as numeric or binary provided a suitable similarity measure is defined that takes two items as input and outputs a similarity value between 0 and 1.

3.2 HACA

Although AntClust has its advantages, there is a weakness of this approach. The stochastic nature of AntClust results in an inconsistency of the solutions obtained. Subsequent runs of the algorithm on the data set are likely to produce different clusters than in previous runs. HACA attempts to solve this problem with simple methods that will also improve the performance of the algorithm by producing more accurate classifications. Figure 3 shows the algorithm for HACA where we have introduced a blacklist strategy, a sniffing strategy and the nests fusion method. Apart from introducing these strategies, we have also made modifications to the *Template* and estimator M parameters. We will describe these strategies in the following sections.

3.2.1 Blacklist Strategy

The objective of this strategy is to reduce the number of meetings that is required for HACA to converge. Lenoir et al [9] suggested that the mechanism of recognition relies on detecting difference rather than similarities, therefore an ant has a more pronounced reaction towards its enemies than towards it own nestmates. In this strategy, every ant has the ability to remember information from past meetings with other ants,

```
Initialisation of the ants:
∀ ants i ∈ [1, N]
   Genome_i ← i^th object of the data set
   Label_i ← 0
   Template_i is learned during N_App iterations
   M_i ← 0, M_i^+ ← 0, A_i ← 0
   Blacklist_i ← empty
Nb_Iter ← ½ * α * N
Simulate Nb_Iter meetings between two randomly chosen ants, i and j
   Check that j ∉ Blacklist_i
   If no acceptance then
      Predict whether to blacklist ants
Compute for each nest j ∈ [1, Nb_nest], the probability to be deleted P_del(j)
Test the probability P_del(j) for each nest j ∈ [1, Nb_nest] against β
Delete the nests whose tests are unsuccessful
Perform sniffing on the remaining nests
Re-assign each nestless ant to the nest of the most similar ant to itself
Merge similar nests together
```

Fig. 3. High-level description of HACA.

particularly if it is a negative meeting. These ants are the blacklisted ants. Using these stored identities, an ant can be prevented from making an unnecessary meeting with a blacklisted ant, thus reducing the number of meetings. These meetings are unnecessary because there is little contribution towards the formation of the clustering structure. The incorporation of the blacklist strategy into HACA is likened to keeping a distributed memory of exploration that not only optimises the algorithm in terms of efficiency, but also facilitates the algorithm's response to changing conditions because it can now make use of previous knowledge learnt.

3.2.2 Sniffing Strategy

The nests that are formed using AntClust may contain ants that are not necessarily similar to each other. In fact, it is even possible that some of the ants in the same nest have nothing in common with one another. Additionally, if high-dimensional data is used, this problem is further aggravated as there are more chances for items to be misclassified. We propose a sniffing strategy as an attempt to overcome this weakness. The aim of the sniffing strategy is to maximise the similarity of ants in a nest by removing misplaced ants that exist in the nest. This is done by enforcing central coordination in the algorithm at the nest level. We take advantage of the principle of acceptance and rejection between ants as well as the ejection of ants from a nest in our strategy. A few ants, called "sniffer ants" that are the most integrated in their nest will be in-charge of the quality control in their nest. This sniffing strategy is inspired by the "elitist ants" introduced by Dorigo et al [3].

3.2.3 Nests Fusion Method

We found that the performance of AntClust over consecutive runs on the same data tends to vary [8]. Therefore, we have proposed the nests fusion method as an attempt to minimise the problem of inconsistent clusters with a better estimation of the number of expected clusters in the data set. It compensates for the inadequacies of Rule 5 and the nest deletion method. This method adopts a centroid-based approach, similar to the k-means algorithm. The difference is that nests fusion deals with collections of items as opposed to k-means which deals with individual items.

3.3 Advantages of HACA

We briefly describe some of the advantages of HACA. HACA combines the strengths of bottom-up clustering of AntClust with the top-down clustering of k-means. Bottom-up clustering is good at identifying small clusters, however it provides sub-optimal performance for identifying large clusters. Conversely, top-down clustering is good at identifying a few large clusters, but poor at smaller clusters. Hence, HACA is able to identify clusters of all sizes. The blacklist strategy enables HACA to run on less iterations per data set compared to AntClust. The artificial ants in HACA have the memory to remember the enemies that they have encountered before so that repeat meetings with enemies are avoided. The sniffing strategy functions to find misplaced ants that are then ejected so that they can be re-assigned at a later stage. With the three strategies proposed, HACA is more deterministic as each strategy introduces some degree of deterministic behaviour into the algorithm that reduces the stochastic nature of ant-based clustering algorithms. In the next section, we will describe the experiments that we have conducted to evaluate the effectiveness of HACA.

4. EVALUATION OF HACA

We briefly describe the setup of experiments conducted. All experiments have been conducted using data sets whose classifications are known. We have conducted experiments of the three proposed strategies individually and as a whole algorithm. The experiments were conducted using artificial and real data sets. The artificial data sets used are the 40D-60C data [2], Banana data [2, 5] and the Square data [6] and the real data sets include Iris [7], Soybean [7], Thyroid [7], Wisconsin [7] and Ruspini [12].

We evaluate the algorithm based on the two main criteria – accuracy and consistency. We measure accuracy using two evaluation functions – F-Measure [6, 15] and C-Success. The C-Success is adapted from the clustering success by Labroche et al [8] where we have simplified the measure with a reversal of the values used. The consistency is measured as a relative measure where we evaluate the consistency of HACA's performance over consecutive runs in comparison to other clustering algorithms on the same data sets. Additionally, we have also conducted experiments to determine the optimal values for the parameters used in HACA.

4.1 Overall Performance

We have conducted six individual tests on the eight test data sets as mentioned above. The information collected from each run includes the F-Measure, the C-Success and the mean clusters formed. Figure 4 shows the clustering quality results for each individual strategy.

All three strategies demonstrate similar results in terms of F-Measure and C-Success, especially on the 40D-6C, Square, Iris and Wisconsin data sets. The nests fusion strategy showed the best results in estimating the number of expected clusters for all data sets. It also showed consistent results at estimating close to the correct partitioning over consecutive runs. These results are expected of the nests fusion strategy as its purpose is to join highly similar clusters together. Overall, we found that the nests fusion method gives the best results, followed by the blacklist strategy and the sniffing strategy.

4.2 Comparison against AntClust and k-means

We also compare HACA against the two clustering algorithms it evolves from: AntClust and k-means. Thus providing us with the opportunity to find out how successful the hybrid approach is compared with its predecessors. Our implementation of k-means is based on the batch version, where cluster centers are only recomputed after the assignment of all the data items. In this experiment, we have set the initial partition to be the correct number of clusters corresponding to each data set. As for AntClust, we have implemented AntClust based on the paper by Labroche et al [8]. We have evaluated the clustering methods over the eight test data sets, where for each data set we perform fifty independent runs for each method and compute the F-Measure, C-Success and the mean number of clusters found. The results are summarized in Figure 5.

From the results, we may conclude that HACA performs well on all the data sets, both artificial and real, despite having the disadvantage of not being provided with prior knowledge of the data set. It also reveals that HACA performs better than AntClust on all data sets. This confirms the effectiveness of the three strategies proposed. The strategy that contributes the most significant difference in performance between AntClust and HACA is the nests fusion method as it enhances the ability of HACA to estimate the number of expected clusters in the data set. In comparing the number of clusters found by HACA as opposed to AntClust, we found that the number of clusters found by HACA for all the data sets is closer to the correct

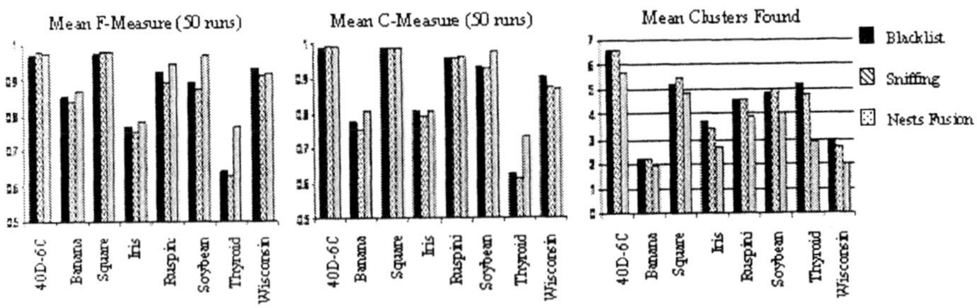

Fig. 4. Mean F-Measure, C-Success and mean clusters for blacklist, sniffing and nests fusion. .

partitioning than that found by AntClust. As for the consistency of the algorithms' performance, HACA's consistency is comparable to k-means where the values of standard deviation for all the data sets are not much larger than those of k-means.

Our experimental evaluations have shown that HACA is capable of generating quality clustering on both artificial and real data sets. In our comparisons, HACA performed better on all data sets, particularly compared to AntClust. The consistency of HACA is generating quality solutions consecutive runs is comparable to k-means for which the number of clusters is provided.

5. CONCLUSION

We have presented our investigation of the use of ant-clustering algorithms for the clustering problems. In particular, we have proposed a new hybrid algorithm that has been developed as a solution for clustering problems. This algorithm, Hybrid Ant-based Clustering Algorithm (HACA), combines the approaches of AntClust [8] and a standard k-means algorithm. In particular, we have introduced three strategies to improve the algorithm – the blacklist strategy, the sniffing strategy and the nests fusion method. This is done to reduce the stochastic nature of the ant-based approach. To evaluate the performance of HACA, we have conducted experimental investigations to determine the effectiveness of the proposed strategies. Additionally, we have also compared the performance of the HACA against AntClust and k-means. The results in both experiments have demonstrated the effectiveness of the three strategies as well as have shown HACA to perform better.

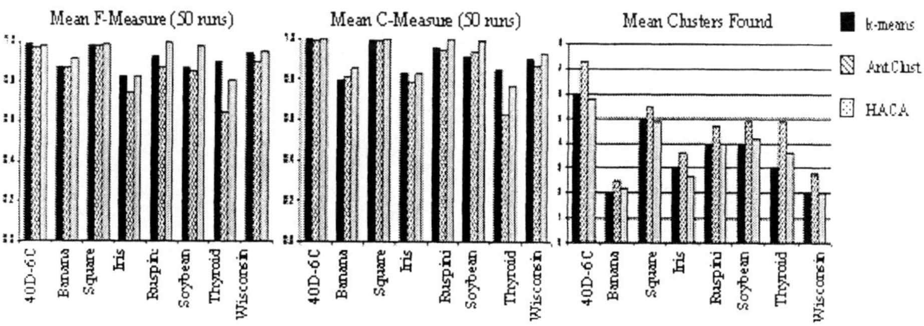

Fig. 5. Mean F-Measure, C-Success and number of clusters for k-means, AntClust and HACA.

REFERENCES

1. Deneubourg, J.-L., Goss, S., Franks, N., Sendova-Franks, A., Detrain, C., & Chretian, L. (1991), "The Dynamics of Collective Sorting: Robot-Like Ant and Ant-Like Robot", In: Meyer, J. A., and Wilson, S. W., (eds) *Proceedings First Conference on Simulation of Adaptive Behavior: From Animals to Animals*, MIT Press, Cambridge, MA, pp. 356-365.
2. Dimitriadou, E., Weingessel, A., & Hornik, K. (1999), "A voting-merging clustering algorithm", Working Paper 31, SFB "Adaptive Information Systems and Modeling in Economics and Management Science", Available: http://www.wu-wien.ac.at/am.
3. Dorigo, M., Maniezzo, V., & Colorni, A. (1996), "The Ant System: Optimization by a Colony of Cooperating Agents", *IEEE Transactions on Systems, Man, and Cybernatics-Part B*, vol. 26, no. 1, pp. 1-13.
4. Fred, A. L. N. (2001), "Finding Consistent Clusters in Data Partitions", *Proceedings of the 2nd International Workshop on Multiple Classifier Systems*, July 2-4 2001, LNCS, vol. 2096, Springer-Verlag Heidelberg, London, pp. 309-318
5. Frossyniotis, D., Pertsekalis, M., & Stafylopatis, A. (2002), "A Multi-clustering Fusion Algorithm", In: Vlahavas, I. P. & Spyropoulos, C. D. (eds.) Proceedings of the Second Hellenic Conference on AI: Methods and Applications of Artificial Intelligence, April 11-12, 2002, LNCS, vol. 2308, Springer-Verlag Heidelberg, London, UK, pp. 225-236
6. Handl, J., Knowles, J., & Dorigo, M. (2003), "Ant-based clustering: a comparative study of its relative performance with respect to K-means, average link and 1D-SOM", Technical Report TR/IRIDIA/2003-24. IRIDIA, Universite Libre de Bruxelles, Belgium, Available: http://dbkweb.ch.umist.ac.uk/handl/.
7. Hettich, S. & Bay, S. D. (eds) (2000, April 26 – last update), "The UCI KDD Archive", (*University of California, Irvine*), Available: http://kdd.ics.uci.edu
8. Labroche, N., Monmarché, N., & Venturini, G. (2003), "AntClust: Ant Clustering and Web Usage Mining", *Genetic and Evolutionary Computation Conference*, July 12-16 2003, Lecture Notes in Computer Science, vol. 2723, Springer-Verlag Heidelberg, London, UK, pp. 25-36.
9. Lenoir, A., Fresneau, D., Errard, C., & Hefetz, A. (1999), "Individuality and Colonial Identity in Ants: The Emergence of the Social Representation Concept", In: Detrain, C., Deneubourg, J.-L., and Pasteels, J., (eds) *Information Processing in Social Insects*, Birkhäuser Verlag Basel, Switzerland, pp. 219-237.
10. Lumer, E., & Faieta, B. (1994), "Diversity and Adaptation in Populations of Clustering Ants", *Proceedings Third International Conference on Simulations of Adaptive Behavior: From Animals to Animals 3*, MIT Press, Cambridge, MA, pp. 499-508.
11. Monmarché, N., Slimane, M., & Venturini, G. (1999), "AntClass: discovery of clusters in numeric data by an hybridization of an ant colony with the Kmeans algorithm", *Technical Report 213*, Laboratoire d'Informatique, E3i, University of Tours, France.
12. Ruspini, E. H. (1970), "Numerical methods for fuzzy clustering", *Information Science*, vol. 2, no. 3, pp. 319–350. Results summarised in Kaufman and Rousseeuw (1999).
13. Schockaert, S., De Cock, M., Cornelis, C., & Kerre, E. E (2004), "Efficient Clustering with Fuzzy Ants", In: Ruan, D., D'Hondt, P., De Cock, M., Nachtegael, M., Kerre, E. E., (eds), *Applied Computational Intelligence*, World Scientific Press, pp. 195-200.
14. Sherafat, V., de Castro, L. N., & Hruschka, E. R. (2004), "TermitAnt: An Ant Clustering Algorithm Improved by Ideas from Termite Colonies", In: Pal N. R., Kasabov, N., Mudi, R. K., Pal, S., and Parui, S. K., (eds) *11th International Conference on Neural Information Processing*, November 22-25 2004, LNCS, vol. 3316, Springer-Verlag Heidelberg, London, UK, pp. 1088-1093.
15. Witten, I. H. & Frank, E. (2000), *Data Mining: Practical Machine Learning Tools and Techniques with Java Implementations*, Morgan Kaufman Publishers, USA.

A HYBRID METHOD FOR EXTRACTING CLASSIFICATION RULES

Chuanli Zhuang [1,2], Zetian Fu [1,2], Daoliang Li [2*]

1. *College of Economics & Management, China Agricultural University, 100083, Beijing,China*
2. *Key Laboratory of Modern Precision Agriculture System Integration, College of Engineering, China Agricultural University 100083, Beijing,China*

Abstract: Neural networks is considered the most powerful classifier and rough set theory is thought of the best to reduce attributes and to generate rules. The combination of neural networks and rough set is very useful for knowledge acquires. Integrating of the advantages of two approaches and having solved the data continuous problem, this paper presents a hybrid method to extract classification rules. There are three models in our method, in first model, neural networks was employed to classify the data sets. In the second model, the continuous attributes are discretized and the self-organizing neural network was applied to ensure result consistent before and after the discretization. In the third model, rough sets theory was used to reduce attributes and generate the rules. The proposed approach was applied on abandoned mine wastes data and the extracted rules was testified based on the analysis of case studies, the result show that the method was reasonable.

Key words: extracting rules, rough sets, self-organizing artificial neural networks, discretization, classification

1. INTRODUCTION

One of the important issues in development expert system is knowledge acquisition from expert. Recently, in order to automate this problem,

* Corresponding author: tel: +86-10-62736717, Fax: +86-10-62737679, E-mail: dliangl@cau.edu.cn

machine-learning techniques have been developed to extract knowledge from database. Among proposed approaches deriving rules from training examples is most common. Given a set of examples a learning program tries to induce rules that describe each class.

Neural networks are considered the most powerful classifier for their low classification error rates and robustness to noise. There are some kinds of neural network. Self-organizing is a special kind of neural networks without teaching. It has the function of self-organizing. Through training by itself, it can classify the input samples automatically. But neural networks lack explanation facilities for their knowledge. The knowledge is buried in their structures and weights. It is often difficult to extract rules from a trained neural network.

Rough sets theory, a mathematical tool to deal with vagueness and uncertainty of information, was first introduced by Pawlak in the 1980's. It has been applied in a lot of applications such as machine learning, knowledge discovery, and expert system since then and has been proved to be very effective. It constitutes a framework for inducing minimal decision rules. These rules in turn can be used to perform a classification task. However, it only deals with the classificatory of data tables and it required the data continuous.

The combination of rough sets and neural networks is very nature for complementary features. In this paper, integrating of the advantages of two approaches, we present a hybrid method to extract classification rules. Different from those previous works, the neural network in this method was used twice; it is not only a classifier but also a checker. First time, neural networks is used as a classifier to classify the data set, second, the self-organizing neural networks is applied as a checker to testify the consistent of discrete result besides classification. After this the rough set can work well to reduce attribute and generate rules.

The remainder of this paper is organized as follows: in section 2, we make a brief description about rough set theory and the definition of classification accuracy and coverage based on this theory. Extracting classification method is described in Section 3. A sample was presented in section 4, and finally concluding remarks are given in section 5.

2. THE THEORY OF ROUGH SETS

2.1 Information system

An information system is a 4-tuple $S = \{U, A, V, f\}$,where U is a finite set of objects, called the universe; A is a finite set of attributes, $V = U_{a \in A} V_a$ is a domain of attribute a. and $f : U \times A \to V$, called an information function such that $f(x,a) \in V_a$, $\forall a \in A, \forall x \in U$.

In the classification problems an information system is also seen as a decision table assuming that $A = C \bigcup D$ and $C \bigcap D = \phi$,where C is a set of condition attribution and D is a set of decision attributes

2.2 indiscernibility

Let $S = \{U, A, V, f\}$ be an information system, every $P \subseteq A$, generates a indiscernibility relation

$ind(P)$ on U ,which is defined as follows:

$ind(P) = \{(x,y) \in U \times U : f(x,a) = f(y,a), \forall a \in P\}$, $U / ind(P) = \{C_1, C_2 \cdots C_K\}$ is a partition of U by P ,every C_i is an equivalence class. For $\forall x \in U$,the equivalence class of x in relation $U / ind(P)$ is defined as follows:

$$[x]_{IND(P)} = \{y \in U : f(y,a) = f(x,a), \forall a \in P\}$$

2.3 P_ lower approximation & P_upper approximation

Let $P \subseteq A$, $X \subseteq U$, the P _lower approximation of X (denote by $P_*(X)$) and the P _upper approximation of X (denote by $P_*(X)$) are defined as follows:

$$P_*(X) = \{Y \in U : [y]_{ind(P)} \subseteq X\},$$

$P^*(X) = \{Y \in U : [y]_{ind(P)} \bigcap X \neq \phi\}$ $P_*(X)$ is the set of all objects from U which can be certainly classified as elements of X employing the set of attributes P. $P^*(X)$ is the set of objects of U which can be possibly classified as elements of X using the set of attributes P.

Let $P, Q \subseteq A$, the positive region of classification $U / IND(Q)$ with respect to the set of attributes P ,or in short P -positive region of Q is defined as :

$$POS_P(Q) = \bigcup_{X \in U / IND(Q)} \underline{P}X$$

$POS_P(Q)$ contains all objects in U that can be classified to one class of the classification $U / IND(Q)$ by attributes P . The dependency of Q on P is defined as:

$$\gamma_P(Q) = \frac{card(POS_P(Q))}{card(U)}$$

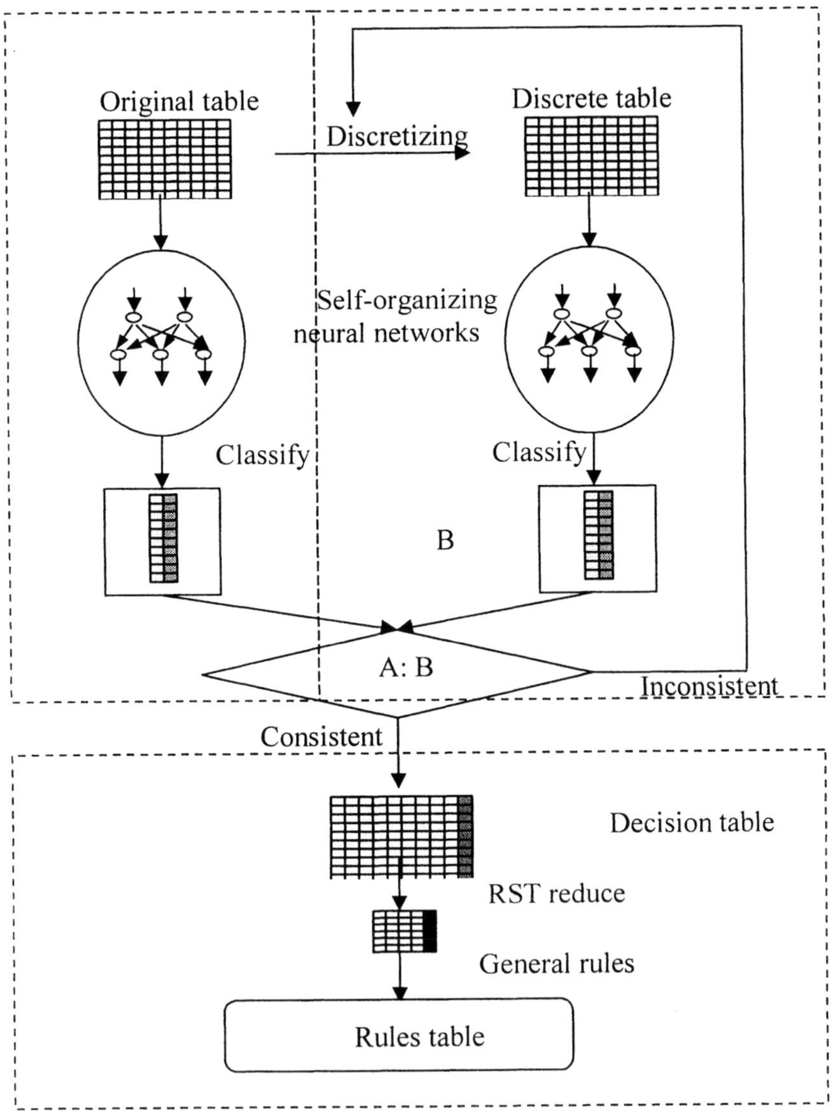

Fig. 1show the procedures of our approach

2.4 reduct

An attributes a is said to be dispensable in P with respect to Q,if $\gamma_P(Q) = \gamma_{P\text{-}\{a\}}(Q)$; otherwise a is indispensable attribute in P with respect to Q.

Let $S = \{U, C \cup D, V, f\}$ be a decision table, the set of attributes P ($P \subseteq C$) is a reduct of attributes C, which statisfies the following conditions:

$\gamma_P(D) = \gamma_C(D)$ and $\gamma_P(D) \neq \gamma_{P'}(D), \forall P' \subset P$. A reduct of condition attributes C is a subset that can discern decision classes with the same discriminating capability as C, and none of the attributes in the reduct can be eliminated without decreasing its discriminating capability.

2.5 Classification accuracy and coverage

If the equal-classes of $U/ind(C)$ and $U/ind(D)$ are presented by X_i, γ_j, defines decision rules as: r_{ij} : $X_i \to \gamma_j$, $\gamma_j \cap X_i \neq \phi$.And Classification accuracy and coverage is defined as:

$$\mu(X_i, \gamma_j) = \frac{card(\gamma_j \cap X_i)}{card(X_i)}$$

$$\eta(X_i, \gamma_j) = \frac{card(\gamma_j \cap X_i)}{card(\gamma_j)}$$

Where $card(A)$ denotes the cardinality of a set A , $\mu(X_i, \gamma_j)$ denotes a classification accuracy of X_i as to classification of γ_j, $\eta(X_i, \gamma_j)$ denotes a classification coverage of X_i as to classification of γ_j, respectively.

3. METHODOLOGY

Our hybrid method of extracting classification Rules of non-decision attribute data sets consists of three major models:

Model 1: Classification

Using the clustering function of self-organizing neural networks, the category of each data is acquired. The goal of this step is to obtain the decision attribute of data sets. If the data sets have decision set, this model can be skipped. There are four kinds of self-organizing algorithms. They are self-organizing competitive learning (SCL) neural networks, self-organizing feature map (SFM) neural networks and the frequency-sensitive competitive learning (FSCL) neural network. There is some software to implement implement the algorithm of self-organizing neural networks, such as artificial neural networks (ANN) toolbox of Matlab, ANN toolbox of Microsoft Office programmer, etc.

Model 2: discreteness

To reduce and extract rules from decision table by rough set, the attribute of each data in decision table should be discrete. This step is to discretize the continuous attributes. Firstly, Using discretizing algorithm, the discrete table is obtained then using self-organizing neural networks to testify the result consistent before and after the data discretized attribute. If they are consistent, then the decision table was obtained by combining the discrete table with the classification and goes to mode 3, else rediscretize the condition attributes. The usually discrete algorithms are equal-distance, equal-frequency, naïve scalar and semi-naïve scalar, etc.

Model 3: reduce the decision table and general rules

The last model is to generate the rules. Applying rough set theory, a reduct of decision table is obtained and the final knowledge-a rule set is generated from the reduced decision table.

4. APPLICATION

In this section, an example is given to show how the proposed methodology can be used to generate the classification rules from data set without decision attributes. Table 1 shows the climate-geography features of 12 abandoned mine wastes. There is no appropriate classification for them yet. There are 8 attributes Annual average temperature (℃), Annual Sunshine hours(h/a), Annual rainfall (mm), Accumulated temperature (℃), Percent of sand (%), Altitude (m), Annual precipitation (mm), Annual average wind velocity, denoted by a, b, c, d, e, f, g and h respectively.

Table 1. Original table

Area	a	b	C	d	e	f	g	h
SZ	6.9	2779	440	2476	30	1400	1570	3.6
YQ	10.9	2767	576	3325	72	1500	1362.5	2.8
TF	6.8	2350	650	3400	18	250	1667	3.6
HQ	13.3	2307	631	4391	56	480	2072	3.5
TL	0.1	2850	383	2525	68	1200	1784	3.7
QA	10.1	2782	735	3200	44	400	1100	2.5
HN	3.1	2427	475	2750	39	260	900	3.6
FS	6.5	2386	800	2800	12	230	1600	3.5

YKS	7.3	3100	385	3000	35	1100	2000	3.7
JZ	14.9	2300	604	4700	76	500	800	2.9
CF	5.0	2950	368	2400	40	1050	2100	3.7
LC	7.3	2518	663	3600	62	1058	1614	4.0

The followings are the deatil

Step 1. As a matter of convenience, we have normalized the input data firstly.

$x_{ij} = \frac{x'_{ij} - x_j^{\min}}{x_j^{\max} - x_j^{\min}}$ $i = 1 \cdots 8, j = 1 \cdots 12$. Where x'_{ij} is non-normalized elements of input table 1, $x_j^{\max}$, $x_j^{\min}$ are maximal and minimal non-normalized elements of $j-$**column**, respectively. Using self-organizing competitive learning function newc() to build a self-organizing neural networks. Set 8 input neurons and 3 output neurons, Kohonen learning rate and Conscience learning rate defined as default. The result was show in table 2

Table 2 the result of classification

Category	Colliery discard land
I	SZ、TL、YKS、CF、
II	YQ、HQ、JZ、LC
III	TF、QA、HN、FS

The classification is reasonable in view of the similar geographical feature of each category.

Step 2

Using the equidistance algorithm to discretize each attribute in table 1, the distance equal the one third of range. The discretization table (table 3) was obtained.

Table 3 the result of distcreted data

Area	a	b	c	d	e	f	g	h
SZ	2	2	1	1	1	3	2	3
YQ	3	2	2	2	3	3	2	1
TF	2	1	2	2	1	1	3	3
HQ	3	1	2	3	3	1	3	3
TL	1	3	1	1	3	3	3	3
QA	3	2	3	2	2	1	1	1
HN	1	1	1	1	2	1	1	3

FS	2	1	3	1	1	1	2	3
YKS	2	3	1	1	2	3	3	3
JZ	3	1	2	3	3	1	1	1
CF	1	3	1	1	2	3	3	3
LC	2	1	3	2	3	3	2	3

Using self-organizing to classify these 12 discreted data, the result is same as the before. So combing the condition attributes with the result of classification, the decision table obtained (table4).

Table 4. The decision table

Area	a	b	c	d	e	f	g	h	class
SZ	2	2	1	1	1	3	2	3	1
YQ	3	2	2	2	3	3	2	1	2
TF	2	1	2	2	1	1	3	3	3
HQ	3	1	2	3	3	1	3	3	2
TL	1	3	1	1	3	3	3	3	1
QA	3	2	3	2	2	1	1	1	3
HN	1	1	1	1	2	1	1	3	3
FS	2	1	3	1	1	1	2	3	3
YKS	2	3	1	1	2	3	3	3	1
JZ	3	1	2	3	3	1	1	1	2
CF	1	3	1	1	2	3	3	3	1
LC	2	1	3	2	3	3	2	3	2

Step 3 reduce decision table and generate rules

using ROSE software which developed by Professor S. Wilk and the staff of Institute of Computing Science of Poznan University of Technology , set the least RHS accuracy 50% and least RHS coverage 100%, the rules table was acquired(table 5).

Table 5. rules table

rules	accuracy, coverage
rule 1. (b = 3) => (class = 1)	[75%, 100%]
rule 2. (a = 2) & (c = 1) => (class = 1)	[50%, 100%]
rule 3. (a = 1) & (f = 3) => (class = 1)	[50%, 100%]
rule 4. (a = 1) & (g = 3) => (class = 1)	[50%, 100%]
rule 5. (c = 1) & (f = 3) => (class = 1)	[100%, 100%]
rule 6. (c = 1) & (g = 3) => (class = 1)	[75%, 100%]
rule 7. (d = 1) & (f = 3) => (class = 1)	[100%, 100%]
rule 8. (d = 1) & (g = 3) => (class = 1)	[75%, 100%]

rule 9. (e = 2) & (f = 3) => (class = 1)	[50%, 100%]
rule 10. (e = 2) & (g = 3) => (class = 1)	[50%, 100%]
rule 11. (f = 3) & (g = 3) => (class = 1)	[75%, 100%]
rule 12. (d = 3) => (class = 2)	[50%, 100%]
rule 13. (a = 3) & (b = 1) => (class = 2)	[50%, 100%]
rule 14. (a = 3) & (c = 2) => (class = 2)	[75%, 100%]
rule 15. (a = 3) & (e = 3) => (class = 2)	[75%, 100%]
rule 16. (b = 1) & (e = 3) => (class = 2)	[75%, 100%]
rule 17. (c = 2) & (e = 3) => (class = 2)	[75%, 100%]
rule 18. (c = 2) & (h = 1) => (class = 2)	[50%, 100%]
rule 19. (d = 2) & (e = 3) => (class = 2)	[50%, 100%]
rule 20. (d = 2) & (f = 3) => (class = 2)	[50%, 100%]
rule 21. (d = 2) & (g = 2) => (class = 2)	[50%, 100%]
rule 22. (e = 3) & (f = 1) => (class = 2)	[50%, 100%]
rule 23. (e = 3) & (g = 2) => (class = 2)	[50%, 100%]
rule 24. (e = 3) & (h = 1) => (class = 2)	[50%, 100%]
rule 25. (a = 2) & (f = 1) => (class = 3)	[50%, 100%]
rule 26. (b = 1) & (d = 1) => (class = 3)	[50%, 100%]
rule 27. (b = 1) & (e = 1) => (class = 3)	[50%, 100%]
rule 28. (c = 3) & (f = 1) => (class = 3)	[50%, 100%]
rule 29. (d = 2) & (f = 1) => (class = 3)	[50%, 100%]
rule 30. (d = 1) & (f = 1) => (class = 3)	[50%, 100%]
rule 31. (e = 1) & (f = 1) => (class = 3)	[50%, 100%]
rule 32. (e = 2) & (f = 1) => (class = 3)	[50%, 100%]
rule 33. (e = 2) & (g = 1) => (class = 3)	[50%, 100%]

Step 4 rules testify

Author collected the data of other three abandoned mine wastes from the web. This data is incomplete. However it can be classified by the rules. the result was show in table 6

Table 6. the results of test

Area	FX	HLH	JC
a	7.5(2)	0.2(1)	11.2(3)
b	2750(2)	3163(3)	2563(1)
c	540(2)	381.5(1)	650(2)
d	3400(2)	-	4000(2)
e	30(1)	-	-
f	500(1)		-
g	1746(3)	1543.8(2)	1558(3)

h	3.7(3)	-	-
Rules	25,29,31	1	13,14
Class	3	1	2

5. CONCLUSION

In this paper, we have presented a hybrid approach to extract classification rules through integrating the advances of self-organizing neural networks and rough sets. Using the clustering function of self-organizing neural networks, the method classifies the data all continuous attributes discretized by some discrete algorithms in succession, then using self-organizing neural testify the similarity of result of classification. At last the rules and the rudect was obtained using rough sets theory if the similarity is accepted.

The difficult problem of extracting classification rules of neural networks is solved through this hybrid method though the black box mechanism of neural network classification.

Discrete algorithms are used to make the self-organizing neural networks and rough set be applied effective. Using self-organizing networks to testify the result of discretization, this method can ensure the rules extracted from the discrete decision table consistent with original data.

The application of extracting classification rules on abandoned mine wastes case show that the method was reasonable and effective.

Although the proposed method works well in extracting classification rules, there are is still much work to be done in this field. Our method need to try some time on find the discretization algorithm to obtain the right one. In the future we will attempt to find the appropriate discrete algorithm quickly.

ACKNOWLEDGEMENTS

The authors would like to thank Guo Xiangyun, Wang Ying and Zhu Xiang for their helpful to collect data and constructive comments.

REFERENCE

[1]. Xu Dong, WuZheng. Analysis and design for ANNbased on MATLAB6.x. *Xidian University Press*.2002

[2]. Wen Xin, ZhouLu, etc. Design for ANN Based on MATLAB. Science press, 2001

[3]. Xie Hongqua, ChenQiuji. A Research on Mine Land Reclamation Conditions with the Help of SOM Internet Principle[J]. Journal of Beijing vocational technical institute of industry NO.1. Vol. 3 Jan 2004,31-33

[4]. Xiangdong Ma, Qiang Fu. Applying Self-Organizing Competition Artificial Neural Networks to Classify the Soil[J]. Nature and Science, 1(1), 2003,

[5]. V.V Gafiychuk etc. Analysis of Data Clusters Obtained by Self-organizing Methods[J]. Physica A 341(2004) 547-555

[6]. Renpu Li, Zheng-ou Wang, mining classification rules using rough set and neural networks [J],European journal of operation research 157 (2004) 439-448

[7]. Zhang wenxiu, etc. theory and method of rough sets [M] science publisher 2003.1

[8]. Tzung-Pei Hong , etc. Learning rules from incomplete training example by rough sets expert system with application 22(2002) 265-293

[9]. T.-P. Hong, etc. Learning a coverage set of maximally general fuzzy rules by rough sets. Expert system with application 19(2000) 97-103

[10]. Shusaku Tsumoto. Extract of experts' decision rules from clinical databases using rough set model.intelligent data analysis, 2(1998)215-227

[11]. Hilario lÒpez García,Iván Machón González. Self-organizing map and clustering for wastewater treatment monitoring. Artificial intelligence. 17(2004)215-225

A NEW INCREMENTAL CORE-BASED CLUSTERING METHOD

Alina Câmpan and Gabriela Şerban

Department of Computer Science, "Babes-Bolyai" University, 1 M. Kogalniceanu Street, Cluj-Napoca, Romania

Abstract: Clustering is a data mining activity that aims to differentiate groups inside a given set of objects, with respect to a set of relevant attributes of the analyzed objects. Generally, existing clustering methods, such as *k-means* algorithm, start with a known set of objects, measured against a known set of attributes. But there are numerous applications where the attribute set characterizing the objects evolves. We propose an incremental, *k-means* based clustering method, *Core Based Incremental Clustering* (*CBIC*), that is capable to re-partition the objects set, when the attribute set increases. The method starts from the partitioning into clusters that was established by applying *k-means* or *CBIC* before the attribute set changed. The result is reached more efficiently than running *k-means* again from the scratch on the feature-extended object set. Experiments proving the method's efficiency are also reported.

Key words: data mining, clustering, k-means

1. INTRODUCTION

Unsupervised classification, or clustering, as it is more often referred as, is a data mining activity that aims to differentiate groups (classes or clusters) inside a given set of objects. The inferring process is carried out with respect to a set of relevant characteristics or attributes of the analyzed objects. The resulting groups are to be built so that objects within a cluster to have high similarity with each other and low similarity with objects in other groups. Similarity and dissimilarity between objects are calculated using metric or semi-metric functions, applied to the attribute values characterizing the objects. A large collection of clustering algorithms is available in the literature. [6] and [7] contain comprehensive overviews of existing techniques.

A well-known class of clustering methods is the one of the partitioning methods, with representatives such as the *k-means* algorithm or the *k-medoids* algorithm. Essentially, given a set of n objects and a number k, $k \leq n$, such a method divides the object set into k distinct and non-empty partitions. The partitioning process is iterative and heuristic; it stops when a "good" partitioning is achieved. A partitioning is "good", as we said, when the intra-cluster similarities are high and inter-cluster similarities are low.

Generally, these methods start with a known set of objects, measured against a known set of attributes. But there are numerous applications where the object set is dynamic, or the attribute set characterizing the objects evolves. Obviously, for obtaining in these conditions a partitioning of the object set, the clustering algorithm can be applied over and over again, beginning from the scratch, every time the objects or attributes change. But this can be inefficient. What we want is to propose an incremental, *k-means* based clustering method, named *Core Based Incremental Clustering* (*CBIC*), that is capable to efficiently re-partition the object set, when the attribute set increases. The method starts from the partitioning into clusters that was established by applying *k-means* or *CBIC* before the attribute set changed. The result is reached more efficiently than running *k-means* again from the scratch on the feature-extended object set.

2. THEORETICAL MODEL

Let $\{O_1, O_2, \ldots, O_n\}$ be the set of objects to be classified. Each object is measured with respect to a set of m initial attributes and is therefore described by an m-dimensional vector $O_i = (O_{i1}, \ldots, O_{im}), O_{ik} \in \Re$, $1 \leq i \leq n,\ \ 1 \leq k \leq m$. Usually, the attributes associated to the objects are standardized, in order to ensure an equal weight to all of them ([7]).

The measure used for discriminating objects can be any *metric* function, d. We used the *Euclidian distance*:

$$d(O_i, O_j) = d_E(O_i, O_j) = \sqrt{\sum_{l=1}^{m} (O_{il} - O_{jl})^2}\ .$$

Let $\{K_1, K_2, \ldots, K_p\}$ be the set of clusters discovered in data by applying the *k-means* algorithm. Each cluster is a set of objects, $K_j = \{O_1^j, O_2^j, \ldots, O_{n_j}^j\},\ \ 1 \leq j \leq p$.

The centroid (cluster mean) of the cluster K_j is denoted by f_j, where

$$f_j = \left(\frac{\sum_{k=1}^{n_j} O_{k1}}{n_j}, \ldots, \frac{\sum_{k=1}^{n_j} O_{km}}{n_j} \right).$$

The measured set of attributes is afterwards extended with s ($s \geq 1$) new attributes, numbered as *(m+1), (m+2),…, (m+s)*. After extension, the objects' vectors become $O_i^{'} = (O_{i1}, \ldots, O_{im}, O_{i,m+1}, \ldots, O_{i,m+s})$, $1 \leq i \leq n$.

We want to analyze the problem of recalculating the objects' grouping into clusters, after attribute set extension and starting from the current partitioning. We aim to obtain a performance gain with respect to the partitioning from scratch process.

We start from the fact that, at the end of the initial clustering process, all objects are closer to the centroid of their cluster than to any other centroid. So, for any cluster j and any object $O_i^j \in K_j$, inequality (1) below holds.

$$d_E(O_i^j, f_j) \leq d_E(O_i^r, f_r), \forall j, r, 1 \leq j, r \leq p, r \neq j \tag{1}$$

We denote by $K_j^{'}, 1 \leq j \leq p$ the set containing the same objects as K_j, after the extension. By $f_j^{'}, 1 \leq j \leq p$ we denote the mean (center) of the set $K_j^{'}$. These sets K_j, $1 \leq j \leq p$, will not necessarily represent clusters after the attribute set extension. The newly arrived attributes can change the objects arrangement into clusters, formed so that the intra-cluster similarity to be high and inter-cluster similarity to be low. But there is a considerable chance, when adding one or few attributes to objects, and the attributes have equal weights and normal data distribution, that the old arrangement in clusters to be close to the actual one. The actual clusters could be obtained by applying the *k-means* classification algorithm on the set of extended objects. But we try to avoid this process and replace it with one less expensive but not less accurate. With these being said, we agree, however, to continue to refer the sets $K_j^{'}$ as clusters.

We therefore take as starting point the previous partitioning into clusters and study in which conditions an extended object $O_i^{j\,'}$ is still correctly placed in its cluster $K_j^{'}$. For that, we express the distance of $O_i^{j\,'}$ to the center of its cluster, $f_j^{'}$, compared to the distance to the center $f_r^{'}$ of any other cluster $K_r^{'}$.

Theorem 1. When inequality (2) holds for an extended object $O_i^{j\,'}$ and its cluster $K_j^{'}$

$$O_{il} \geq \frac{\sum_{k=1}^{n_j} O_{kl}}{n_j}, \forall l \in \{m+1, m+2, \ldots, m+s\} \tag{2}$$

then the object $O_i^{j'}$ is closer to the center $f_j^{'}$ than to any other center $f_r^{'}$, $1 \leq j, r \leq p, r \neq j$.

Proof. We prove below this statement.

$$d^2(O_i^{j'}, f_j^{'}) - d^2(O_i^{j'}, f_r^{'}) = d^2(O_i^j, f_j) + \sum_{l=m+1}^{m+s} \left(\frac{\sum_{k=1}^{n_j} O_{kl}}{n_j} - O_{il} \right)^2 -$$

$$- d^2(O_i^j, f_r) - \sum_{l=m+1}^{m+s} \left(\frac{\sum_{k=1}^{n_r} O_{kl}}{n_r} - O_{il} \right)^2$$

Using the inequality (1), we have:

$$d^2(O_i^{j'}, f_j^{'}) - d^2(O_i^{j'}, f_r^{'}) \leq \sum_{l=m+1}^{m+s} \left(\frac{\sum_{k=1}^{n_j} O_{kl}}{n_j} - O_{il} \right)^2 - \sum_{l=m+1}^{m+s} \left(\frac{\sum_{k=1}^{n_r} O_{kl}}{n_r} - O_{il} \right)^2 \Leftrightarrow$$

$$d^2(O_i^{j'}, f_j^{'}) - d^2(O_i^{j'}, f_r^{'}) \leq \sum_{l=m+1}^{m+s} \left(\frac{\sum_{k=1}^{n_j} O_{kl}}{n_j} - \frac{\sum_{k=1}^{n_r} O_{kl}}{n_r} \right) \cdot \left(\frac{\sum_{k=1}^{n_j} O_{kl}}{n_j} + \frac{\sum_{k=1}^{n_r} O_{kl}}{n_r} - 2 \cdot O_{il} \right)$$

If the inequality (2) holds for every new attribute of $O_i^{j'}$, then the inequality above becomes:

$$d^2(O_i^{j'}, f_j') - d^2(O_i^{j'}, f_r') \le -\sum_{l=m+1}^{m+s} \left(\frac{\sum_{k=1}^{n_j} O_{kl}}{n_j} - \frac{\sum_{k=1}^{n_r} O_{kl}}{n_r} \right)^2 \Leftrightarrow$$

$$d^2(O_i^{j'}, f_j') - d^2(O_i^{j'}, f_r') \le 0.$$

Because all distances are non-negative numbers, it follows that:

$$d(O_i^{j'}, f_j') \le d(O_i^{j'}, f_r') \, \forall r, 1 \le r \le p, r \ne j.$$

We have to notice that the inequality (2) imposes only intra-cluster conditions. An object is compared against its own cluster in order to decide its new affiliation to that cluster.

3. CORE BASED INCREMENTAL CLUSTERING

We will use the property enounced in the previous paragraph in order to identify inside each cluster $K_j', 1 \le j \le p$, those objects that have a considerable chance to remain stable in their cluster, and not to move in other cluster as a result of the attribute set extension. We will say that these objects form the *core* of their cluster.

Definition 1.

(a) We denote by $StrongCore_j = \{O_i^{j'} \mid O_i^{j'} \in K_j', O_i^{j'}$ satisfies inequalities set (2)$\}$ the set of all objects in K_j' satisfying inequality (2) for each new attribute l, $m+1 \le l \le m+s$;

(b) Let $sat(O_i^{j'})$ be the set of all new attributes l, $m+1 \le l \le m+s$ for which object $O_i^{j'}$ satisfies inequality (2). We denote by $WeakCore_j = \left\{ O_i^{j'} \mid O_i^{j'} \in K_j', |sat(O_i^{j'})| \ge \frac{\sum_{k=1}^{n_j} |sat(O_k^{j'})|}{n_j} \right\}$ the set of all objects in K_j' satisfying inequality (2) for at least so many new attributes that all objects in K_j' are satisfying (2) for, in the average.

(c) $Core_j$ = $StrongCore_j$ iif $StrongCore_j \neq \emptyset$, otherwise, $Core_j$ = $WeakCore_j$. $OCore_j = K_j^{'} - Core_j$ is the set of out-of-core objects in cluster $K_j^{'}$;

(d) We denote by *CORE* the set $\{Core_j,\ 1 \le j \le p\}$ of all clusters cores and by *OCORE* the set $\{OCore_j,\ 1 \le j \le p\}$.

For each new attribute l, $m+1 \le l \le m+s$, and each cluster $K_j^{'}$ there is at least one object that satisfies the inequality (2) in respect to the attribute l. Namely, the object that has the greatest value for attribute l between all objects in $K_j^{'}$ certainly satisfies the relation (the maximum value in a set is greater or equal than the mean of the values in the set). But it is not sure that there is in cluster $K_j^{'}$ any object that satisfies relation (2) for all new attributes $m+1,\ldots,m+s$. If there are such objects ($StrongCore_j \neq \emptyset$), we know that, according to **Theorem 1**, they are closer to the cluster center $f_j^{'}$ than to any other cluster center $f_r^{'}$, $1 \le r \le p,\ r \neq j$. Then, $Core_j$ will be initialized with $StrongCore_j$ and will be the seed for cluster j in the incremental algorithm. But if $StrongCore_j = \emptyset$, than we will choose as seed for cluster j other objects, the most stable ones between all objects in $K_j^{'}$. These objects ($WeakCore_j$) can be less stable than would be the objects in $StrongCore_j$. This is not, however, a certain fact: the objects in the "weaker" set $WeakCore_j$ can be as good as those in $StrongCore_j$. This comes from the fact that **Theorem 1** enounces a *sufficient* condition for the objects in $K_j^{'}$ to be closer to $f_j^{'}$ than to any other $f_r^{'}$, but not a *necessary* condition too.

The *cluster cores*, chosen as we described, will serve as seed in the incremental clustering process. All objects in $Core_j$ will surely remain together in the same group if clusters do not change. This will not be the case for all core objects, but for most of them, as we will see in the results section.

We give next the *Core Based Incremental Clustering* algorithm. We mention that the algorithm stops when the clusters from two consecutive iterations remain unchanged or the number of steps performed exceeds the maximum allowed number of iterations.

Algorithm Core Based Incremental Clustering is

Input: - the set $X = \{O_1,\ldots,O_n\}$ of m-dimensional objects,
- the set $X^{'} = \{O_1^{'},\ldots,O_n^{'}\}$ of (m+s)-dimensional extended objects to be clustered, $O_i^{'}$ has the same first m components as O_i,
- the metric d_E between objects in a multi-dimensional space,
- p, the number of desired clusters,
- $K = \{K_1,\ldots,K_p\}$ the previous partitioning of objects in X,
- *noMaxIter* the maximum number of iterations allowed.

Output:- the re-partitioning $K' = \{K'_1, \ldots, K'_p\}$ for the objects in X'.
Begin
  For all clusters $K_j \in K$ **do**
    Calculate $Core_j = (StrongCore_j \neq \emptyset)\ ?\ StrongCore_j : WeakCore_j$
    $K'_j = Core_j$,
    Calculate f'_j as the mean of objects in $Core_j$
  EndFor
  While (K'_j changes between two consecutive steps) and
      (there were not performed *noMaxIter* iterations) **do**
    For all clusters K'_j **do**
      $K'_j = \{O'_i \mid d(O'_i, f'_j) \leq d(O'_i, f'_r), \forall r, 1 \leq r \leq p, 1 \leq i \leq n\}$
    EndFor
    For all clusters K'_j **do**
      $f'_j =$ the mean of objects in K'_j
    EndFor
  EndWhile
End.

The algorithm starts by calculating the old clusters' cores. The cores will be the initial clusters for the iterative process. Next, the algorithm proceeds in the same manner as the classical *k-means* method does. We mention that the computation of the core of a cluster C depends only on the current cluster (does not depend on other clusters).

4. EXPERIMENTAL EVALUATION

In this section we present some experimental results obtained by applying the *CBIC* algorithm described in section 3.

For this purpose, we used a programming interface for non-hierarchical clustering described in ([1]). We have to mention that using this interface we can simply develop non-hierarchical clustering applications for different kind of data (objects to be clustered). As it is shown in our experiments, the objects to be clustered are very different (patients, wine instances).

As a case study, for experimenting our theoretical results described in section 2 and for evaluating the performance of the *CBIC* algorithm, we consider some experiments that are briefly described in the following subsections. We have to mention that all data were taken from the website at "http://www.cormactech.com/neunet".

4.1 Quality Measures

As a quality measure we take the movement degree of the core objects and of the extra-core objects. In other words, we measure how the objects in either $Core_j \in CORE$, or $OCore_j \in OCORE$, remain together in clusters after the algorithm ends.

As expected, more stable the core objects are and more they remain together with respect to the initial sets $Core_j$, better was the decision to choose them as seed for the incremental clustering process. Also, as the experiments will show, the movement degree was always smaller for the core objects than for the extra-core objects.

We express the *core stability factor* as:

$$CSF(CORE) = \frac{\sum_{j=1}^{p} \frac{|Core_j|}{no\ of\ clusters\ where\ the\ objects\ in\ Core_j\ ended}}{\sum_{j=1}^{p} |Core_j|} \quad (4)$$

The worst case is when each object in $Core_j$ ends in a different final cluster, and this happens for every core in *CORE*. The best case is when every $Core_j$ remains compact and it is found in a single final cluster. So, the limits between which *CSF* varies are given below, where the higher the value of *CSF* is, better was the cores choice:

$$\frac{p}{\sum_{j=1}^{p} |Core_j|} \leq CSF(CORE) \leq 1 \quad (5)$$

Accordingly, the *out-of-core stability factor*, *OCSF(OCORE)*, is defined similar to *CSF(CORE)*, replacing the sets $Core_j$ with $OCore_j$.

For comparing the informational relevance of the attributes we used the *information gain* (*IG*) measure ([9]).

4.2 Experiment 1. Cancer

The objects to be clustered in this experiment are patients: each patient is identified by 9 attributes [3]. The attributes have been used to represent instances. Each instance has one of 2 possible classes: benign or malignant. In this experiment there are 457 patients (objects).

4.3 Experiment 2. Dermatology

The objects to be clustered in this experiment are also patients: each patient is identified by 34 attributes, 33 of which are linear valued and one of them is nominal. There are 366 objects (patients).

The aim of the clustering process is to determine the type of Eryhemato-Squamous Disease [4].

4.4 Experiment 3. Wine

These data are the results of a chemical analysis of wines grown in the same region in Italy but derived from three different cultivars. The analysis determined the quantities of 13 constituents found in each of the three types of wines [5].

The objects to be clustered in this experiment are wine instances: each is identified by 13 attributes. There are 178 objects (wine instances).

4.5 Results

In this section we present comparatively the results obtained after applying the *CBIC* algorithm for the experiments described in the above subsections. We mention that the results are calculated in average, for six executions.

Table 1. Comparative results

Experiment	Cancer	Dermatology	Wine
No of objects	457	366	178
No of attributes (m+s)	9	34	13
No of new attributes (s)	4	3	4
No of k-means iterations for (m+s) attributes	6.2857	11.57	7
No of k-means iterations for m attributes	6	11.85	9.37
No of CBIC iterations for (m+s) attributes	7	6.14	6.8
CSF(CORE)	0.9	0.8406	0.5244
OCSF(OCORE)	0.5	0.7008	0.4194

From Table 1 we observe that using the *CBIC* algorithm the number of iterations for finding the solution is, in the average, smaller, and also the cores' stability factor, *CSF(CORE)*, is high. We mention that for every running of each experiment, $CSF(CORE) \geq OCSF(OCORE)$. So, every time, the stability of the objects chosen to be part or cores was greater than the stability of out-of-core objects.

In Table 2 we present, for each experiment, the attributes in decreasing order of their information gain (*IG*).

Table 2. The decreasing order of attributes in respect to the information gain measure

Experiment	Order of attributes	*IG* of new attributes / *IG* of old attributes (%)
Cancer	2 3 **6** 7 5 4 **8** 1 **9**	64,7%
Dermatology	22 21 23 1 **34** 30 28 13 26 7 17 9 29 10 16 11 25 15 6 27 4 20 **32** 8 5 24 3 31 12 2 19 18 14 **33**	7,6%
Wine	7 **10 12 13** 6 1 2 **11** 9 4 5 3 8	57%

From Table 2 it results that the importance of the added attributes influences the number of iterations performed by the *CBIC* algorithm for finding the solution. For example, in the "cancer" experiment where the information brought by the added attributes was close to that of the initial ones, the number of iterations performed by *CBIC* is also close to the number of iterations performed for all the attributes.

5. CONCLUSIONS AND FUTURE WORK

Further works can be done in the following directions: to apply the incremental algorithm on precise problems, from where the need for such an incremental algorithm originated; to study how the theoretical results described for non-hierarchical clustering could be applied/generalized for other clustering techniques.

REFERENCES

[1] Serban, G.: A Programming Interface for Non-Hierarchical Clustering, Studia Universitatis "Babes-Bolyai", Informatica, XLX(1), 2005, to appear.

[2] Serban, G., Campan, A.: Core Based Incremental Clustering, Studia Universitatis "Babes Bolyai", Informatica, XLXI(2), 2005, to appear.

[3] Wolberg, W., Mangasarian, O.L.: "Multisurface method of pattern separation for medical diagnosis applied to breast cytology", Proceedings of the National Academy of Sciences, U.S.A., Volume 87, December 1990: 9193-9196.

[4] Demiroz, G., Govenir, H. A., Ilter, N.: "Learning Differential Diagnosis of Eryhemato Squamous Diseases using Voting Feature Intervals", Artificial Intelligence in Medicine.

[5] Aeberhard, S., Coomans, D., de Vel, O.: "THE CLASSIFICATION PERFORMANCE OF RDA" Tech. Rep. no. 92--01, Dept. of Computer Science and Dept. of Mathematics and Statistics, James Cook University of North Queensland, 1992.

[6] Jain, A., Dubes, R, "Algorithms for Clustering Data", Prentice Hall, Englewood Cliffs, New Jersey, 1998.

[7] Han, J., Kamber, M., "Data Mining: Concepts and Techniques", Morgan Kaufmann Publishers, 2001.

[8] http://www.cormactech.com/neunet, "Discover the Patterns in Your Data", CorMac Technologies Inc, Canada.

[9] Quinlan, J. R., "C4.5: Programs for Machine Learning, Morgan Kaufmann", 1993.

AN ALGORITHM FOR MADM BASED ON SUBJECTIVE PREFERENCE

Feng Kong, Hongyan Liu

Department of Economics and Management, North China Electric Power University, Baoding, P.R.China, 071003

Abstract: In multi-attribute decision making (MADM) problems, as human judgments are often vague and complex, it is usually difficult for decision makers to estimate an exact or crisp value for his preferences. Further, the decision maker's subjective preferences affect the decision result directly. However, there are only a few researches on fuzzy MADM which took into account the decision maker's preferences. This paper put forward a new algorithm for fuzzy MADM, which takes into account the decision maker's preferences. This method makes our new algorithm more reasonable and the results in more agreement with the decision maker's intentions.

Key words: Fuzzy MADM; subjective preference; fuzzy weights; ideal solution

1. INTRODUCTION

In Multi-attribute Decision Making (MADM) problems, the decision maker is often faced with the problem of selecting among alternatives that have conflicting attributes. For example, in site selection problems, attributes such as prices, transportation, costs of operations, and the prospects of products are often considered in the selection of a satisfactory place. For some of these attributes, we can give exact assessments; while for others, we cannot. Since human judgments and preferences are often vague and complex, and decision makers cannot estimate their preferences with an exact scale, we can only give linguistic assessments instead of exact assessments. So fuzzy set theory is introduced into MADM, Fuzzy MADM is put forward to solve such uncertainty problems.

No matter what method is used to solve Fuzzy MADM problems, weights of attributes reflecting the relative importance of the attributes must be determined. There are many approaches to determine the weights of attributes. We can divide those approaches into subjective approaches and objective ones. The former selects weights according to the preference information of decision makers, such as the eigenvector method, weighted least square method, Delphi method, and mathematical programming models etc. The latter determines weights by solving mathematical models automatically without any consideration of the decision maker's preferences, for example, the entropy method, multiple objective programming, etc. Weights determined by subjective approaches can reflect the subjective judgments of decision makers, thus makes the rankings of alternatives in Fuzzy MADM problem have more arbitrary factors. The objective approaches select weights through mathematical calculation, which neglects subjective judgment information of decision makers. Since either subjective approaches or objective approaches have their advantages and disadvantages, an integrated or combined method seems more desirable in the determination of attribute weights. Thus, this paper tries to give a new weight determination approach to retain the merits of both subjective and objective approaches: to determine weights by solving mathematical models automatically and at the same time take into consideration the decision maker's preferences.

In this paper, the weights of attributes and the assessments of alternatives are described as fuzzy numbers. We put forward a new approach, which integrated the subjective and objective information, to determine the weights of attributes. In Section 2, we will give some introductions to fuzzy numbers. In Section 3, a combined approach to determine attributes weights is put forward. An algorithm for fuzzy MADM based on decision maker's subjective ideal solution is explored in detail and numerical example is illustrated in Section 4, with the conclusion in Section 5.

2. FUZZY NUMBERS

The fuzzy sets theory, introduced by Zadeh (1965) to deal with vague, imprecise and uncertain problems, has been used as a modeling tool for complex systems that can be controlled by humans but are hard to define precisely.

In this paper, we use triangular fuzzy numbers to illustrate our approach, though our approach fit with all types fuzzy numbers. Triangular fuzzy number is a special kind of fuzzy sets. A triangular fuzzy number can be denoted as: $N = (a,b,c)$. The membership function of triangular fuzzy numbers is:

$$\mu(x) = \begin{cases} \dfrac{x-a}{b-a}, & a \le x \le b; \\ \dfrac{c-x}{c-b}, & b \le x \le c; \\ 0, & else \end{cases} \tag{1}$$

Particularly, when $a = b = c$, trapezoidal fuzzy numbers become crisp numbers. That is, crisp numbers can be considered as a special case of fuzzy numbers.

The left and right fuzzy sets of a fuzzy number, *N*, can be denoted respectively as N_L and N_R, and their membership functions are respectively defined as:

$$\mu_{N_L}(x) = \sup_{x=y+z, z\le 0} \mu_N(y) \tag{2-a}$$

$$\mu_{N_R}(x) = \sup_{x=y+z, z\ge 0} \mu_N(y) \tag{2-b}$$

Given any two fuzzy numbers $\widetilde{N} = (a_1, b_1, c_1)$, $\widetilde{M} = (a_2, b_2, c_2)$ and a real number λ , some main operations of fuzzy numbers can be expressed as follows:

$$\widetilde{N} + \widetilde{M} = (a_1 + a_2, b_1 + b_2, c_1 + c_2) \tag{3}$$

$$\widetilde{N} \times \widetilde{M} = (a_1 \times a_2, b_1 \times b_2, c_1 \times c_2) \tag{4}$$

$$\widetilde{N}^{\lambda} = (a_1^{\lambda}, b_1^{\lambda}, c_1^{\lambda}) \tag{5}$$

3. A COMBINED APPROACH TO DETERMINE ATTRIBUTES WEIGHTS

Classical Fuzzy MADM problems usually assume that there are *m* feasible alternatives, A_1, A_2, A_3,..., and A_m, with each of the alternatives having *n* attributes, f_1, f_2, f_3,..., and f_n, and the weight of each attribute being $w_1, w_2, w_3, \ldots$, and w_n . The goal of decision-making is to find the most satisfactory one among the m alternatives. The decision problem can be expressed as the following:

$$D = \begin{bmatrix} y_{11} & y_{12} & \cdots & y_{1n} \\ y_{21} & y_{22} & \cdots & y_{2n} \\ \cdots & \cdots & \cdots & \cdots \\ y_{m1} & y_{m2} & \cdots & y_{mn} \end{bmatrix} \tag{6}$$

$$W = (w_1, w_2, \ldots, w_n)$$

where y_{ij} represents the uncertain assessments of the j-th attribute of the i-th alternative. They can be either fuzzy numbers or linguistic words.

Assume that all values for each attribute are scaled between 0 and 1 to have the same range of measurement. This is achieved by normalizing elements in the decision matrix using the following formulas:

For benefit criteria, $y_j^+ \geq \sup(\tilde{y}_{1j}, \tilde{y}_{2j}, \ldots, \tilde{y}_{mj})$; $y_{j-}^- \leq \inf(\tilde{y}_{1j}, \tilde{y}_{3j}, \ldots, \tilde{y}_{mj})$.

$$\tilde{x}_{ij} = \left(\frac{a_{ij} - y_j^-}{y_j^+ - y_j^-}, \frac{b_{ij} - y_j^-}{y_j^+ - y_j^-}, \frac{c_{ij} - y_j^-}{y_j^+ - y_j^-} \right), i = 1,2,\ldots,m \tag{7}$$

For cost type criteria, $y_j^+ \leq \inf(\tilde{y}_{1j}, \tilde{y}_{3j}, \ldots, \tilde{y}_{mj})$; $y_{j-}^- \geq \sup(\tilde{y}_{1j}, \tilde{y}_{3j}, \ldots, \tilde{y}_{mj})$.

$$\tilde{x}_{ij} = \left(\frac{y_j^+ - c_{ij}}{y_j^- - y_j^+}, \frac{y_j^+ - b_{ij}}{y_j^- - y_j^+}, \frac{y_j^+ - a_{ij}}{y_j^- - y_j^+} \right), i = 1,2,\ldots, m \tag{8}$$

where, $\tilde{x}_{ij}$ represents the scale in the decision matrix after normalization, which belongs to $[0,1]$. Therefore, after normalization, the values of each criterion of both the ideal solution and negative ideal solution are respectively: $x_j^+ = (1,1,1) = 1$, and $x_j^- = (0,0,0) = 0$.

The linguistic terms can be expressed in corresponding triangular fuzzy numbers as Table 1 show [3][4][5][6].

Table 1. Linguistic terms and triangular fuzzy numbers

Linguistic terms	Corresponding Fuzzy numbers
Very bad (VB)	(0,0,0.1)
Bad (B)	(0,0.1,0.3)
Medium bad (MB)	(0.1,0.3,0.5)
Medium (M)	(0.3,0.5,0.7)
Medium good (MG)	(0.5,0.7,0.9)
Good (G)	(0.7,0.9,1.0)
Very good (VG)	(0.9,1.0,1.0)

3.1 Determination of Subjective Weights

Suppose the decision maker give his pairwise comparison vector, V, on the attribute set [1][10][11][12][13][14].

$$V = (v_{11}, v_{12}, \ldots, v_{1n}) \tag{9}$$

where, v_{1j} is a fuzzy number comparison scale, $v_{1j} = (v_{1j}^l, v_{1j}^m, v_{1j}^r) \in [0,1]$, which represent the relative importance of the first attribute with respect to the j-th attribute. The fuzzy comparison scales can be obtained from the decision maker.

There is v_{11}=(0.5,0.5,0.5). The first attribute is considered to be of equal importance with the j-th attribute, if v_{1j} =0.5; the first attribute is more important than the j-th attribute, if $v_{1j} > 0.5$; and the first attribute is not so important as the j-th attribute, if $v_{1j} < 0.5$.

Using the fuzzy numbers normalization method of Dubois and Prade (1982) [9], calculate the subjective weights of the attributes:

$$W_j^s = (W_j^{sl}, W_j^{sm}, W_j^{sr}),\ j = 1,2,\ldots,n$$

$$W_j^{sm} = \frac{\dfrac{1}{v_{1j}^m} - 1}{\sum_{k=1}^{n}(\dfrac{1}{v_{1k}^m} - 1)},\ k = 1,2,\ldots,n \tag{10}$$

$$W_j^{sl} = \frac{\dfrac{1}{v_{1j}^l} - 1}{\dfrac{1}{v_{1j}^l} - 1 + \sum_{k \neq j}(\dfrac{1}{v_{1k}^r} - 1)}, \tag{11}$$

$$W_j^{sr} = \frac{\dfrac{1}{v_{1j}^r} - 1}{\dfrac{1}{v_{1j}^r} - 1 + \sum_{k \neq j}(\dfrac{1}{v_{1k}^l} - 1)}. \tag{12}$$

3.2 Determination of Objective Weights

As we know, entropy theory is another important theory to study the problem of uncertainty. Entropy weight is a parameter that describes how much different alternatives approach one another in respect to a certain attribute. The greater the value of the entropy, the smaller the entropy weight, then the smaller the differences of different alternatives in this specific attribute, and the less information the specific attribute provides, and the less important this attribute becomes in the decision making process. In this paper we give a Fuzzy Entropy Weight.

For crisp numbers, the calculation of the entropies is very straightforward. Usually we will use the following formula :

$$E(i) = -K\sum_{i=1}^{m} x_{ij} \ln x_{ij} \tag{13}$$

where K is a constant.

While for fuzzy numbers, we could not use the above formula to calculate the entropies of fuzzy numbers directly. Generally, we would first transform the fuzzy numbers into crisp numbers, and then calculate their respective entropies. Although there are many methods to transform fuzzy numbers, most of these methods did not take into account the decision-maker's preferences for the degree of uncertainties. Kong (2004)[20] gave a formula that took into account these factors:

$$F(x_{ij}) = m(x_{ij}) - \beta\sigma(x_{ij}) \tag{14}$$

$$m(x_{ij}) = \frac{\int x\mu(x_{ij})dx}{\int \mu(x_{ij})dx}, \quad \sigma(x_{ij}) = \left[\frac{\int x^2\mu(x_{ij})dx}{\int \mu(x_{ij})dx} - m^2(x_{ij})\right]^{1/2};$$

where $F(x_{ij})$ represents the ranking index of the j-th attribute of the i-th alternative, β represents the decision-maker's uncertainty-aversion coefficient, when $\beta > 0$, the decision maker is uncertainty-averse, when $\beta < 0$, the decision maker is uncertainty-loving, and when $\beta = 0$, the decision maker is uncertainty-neutral.

Next, normalize $F(x_{ij})$ according to the following equation:

$$f_{ij} = \frac{F(x_{ij})}{\sum_{i=1}^{m} F(x_{ij})} \tag{15}$$

Then, the fuzzy entropies of the attributes can be calculated with the following:

$$\widetilde{E}_j = -K\sum_{i=1}^{m} f_{ij}\ \ln f_{ij} = -\frac{1}{\ln m}\sum_{i=1}^{m} f_{ij}\ \ln f_{ij}\,. \tag{16}$$

Now, calculate the fuzzy entropy weight with the following equation:

$$W_j^o = \frac{(1-\widetilde{E}_j)}{\sum_{j=1}^{n}(1-\widetilde{E}_j)} \tag{17}$$

3.3 Calculation of the Combined Fuzzy Weights

Derive the combined fuzzy weight according to:

$$W_j = (W_j^s)^{\alpha} \cdot (W_j^o)^{\gamma} \tag{18}$$

where α, and γ represents the relative importance of the subjective weights and the objective weights to decision makers respectively, $\alpha + \gamma = 1$.

Combined fuzzy weight tells us that, if the values of an attribute in different alternatives do not differ much from one another, then the attribute will not be so important in the decision making process, though this attribute may seem very important to the decision-maker. Only those attributes which are both important to the decision-maker and whose values in different alternatives differ significantly can play important roles in decision-making processes. Combined fuzzy weight is such an indicator that not only shows how much important an attribute is to the decision-maker, but also shows how much different the values of the attribute in different alternatives are.

4. THE NEW ALGORITHM FOR FUZZY MADM BASED ON SUBJECTIVE PREFERENCES

4.1 Algorithm for MADM

Considering the different importance of each attribute, we should assign corresponding weights to the normalized fuzzy decision matrix to make it become: $\widetilde{R} = \left[\widetilde{r}_{ij}\right]_{m\times n}$, where

$$\widetilde{r}_{ij} = \widetilde{x}_{ij} \times \widetilde{w}_j \tag{19}$$

and the weighted values of each attribute of both the ideal solution and negative ideal solution respectively is:

$$\tilde{r}_j^{+} = x_j^{+} \times \tilde{w}_j = \tilde{w}_j \text{ , } \tilde{r}_j^{-} = x_j^{-} \times \tilde{w}_j = 0 \text{ .}$$

It is obvious that, the more the value of each attribute approaches the value of the ideal solution, and at the same time, the more faraway they are from the negative ideal solution, the better the alternative is. In fuzzy MADM, this approach can be represented by the distance between the crisp numbers (the values of ideal solution and negative ideal solution) and fuzzy numbers (the values of criteria of alternative), and it is affected by the decision maker's subjective preference.

The distance between each criterion of an alternative and the corresponding one of the ideal solution, can be derived according to the weighted Hamming fuzzy distance:

$$d_{ij}^{+} = \rho d_H(r_{jL}^{+}, r_{ijL}) + (1-\rho) d_H(r_{jR}^{+}, r_{ijR}) \tag{20}$$

where d_H represents the relative Hamming distance of the fuzzy set, ρ represents the coefficient of the decision maker's uncertainty preference, $0 \le \rho \le 1$. When $\rho > 0.5$, the decision maker is uncertainty-averse, when $\rho < 0.5$, the decision maker is uncertainty-loving, and when $\rho = 0.5$, the decision maker is uncertainty-neutral.

The same, we can derive the distance between the same criteria of the negative ideal solution and each alternative:

$$d_{ij}^{-} = \rho d_H(r_{jL}^{-}, r_{ijL}) + (1-\rho) d_H(r_{jL}^{-}, r_{ijR}) \tag{21}$$

The distance between each alternative and the ideal solution is given by:

$$D_i^{+} = \left\| (d_{i1}^{+}, d_{i2}^{+}, \ldots, d_{in}^{+}) \right\| = \sqrt{\sum_{j=1}^{n} (d_{ij}^{+})^2} \tag{22}$$

and the distance between each alternative and the negative ideal solution is given by:

$$D_i^{-} = \left\| (d_{i1}^{-}, d_{i2}^{-}, \ldots, d_{in}^{-}) \right\| = \sqrt{\sum_{j=1}^{n} (d_{ij}^{-})^2} \tag{23}$$

A closeness coefficient is defined to determine the ranking order of all alternatives. The closeness coefficient of each alternative is calculated by:

$$C_i = \frac{D_i^+}{D_i^+ + D_i^-} \tag{24}$$

The bigger its value, the better the alternative.

4.2 A numerical illustration

Now a firm has four feasible alternative plans, A_1, A_2, A_3 and A_4, to develop a new product. The firm evaluates each of the four alternatives in four aspects, risk, profit, prospect, and development. See the following Table 2 for the details of the evaluations.

Table. 2 Evaluation of the four alternatives

	Risk	Profit (10,000$)	Prospect	Development
A_1	High	(80,90,100)	Medium	Very difficult
A_2	Very low	(20,30,40)	Medium	Very easy
A_3	Medium	(60,75,80)	Good	Difficult
A_4	Low	(80,85,95)	Very Good	Easy

Now we show the steps of the decision-making.

Step 1: The decision maker gives his pairwise comparison vector, V, on the attributes,

$$V = (v_{11}, v_{12}, v_{13}, v_{14})$$
$$v_{11}=(0.5,0.5,0.5);\quad v_{12}=(0.4,0.45,0.5);$$
$$v_{13}=(0.7,0.75,0.8);\quad v_{14}=(0.5,0.55,0.6)$$

Then calculate the subjective fuzzy weights of attributes according to equations (5)~(7),

$$W_1^s=(0.252,0.271,0.289); W_2^s=(0.269,0.301,0.337);$$
$$W_3^s=(0.161,0.181,0.201); W_4^s=(0.219,0.247,0.276).$$

Step 2: Calculate the objective weights.

First, transform the fuzzy linguistic terms into triangular fuzzy numbers according to Table 1. Then derive the normalized decision matrix as in Table 3. Suppose, $y_2^+=1000000$ and $y_2^-=0$.

Table 3 The normalized fuzzy decision matrix

	Risk	Profit	Prospect	Development
	(0.9,1,1)	0.8,0.9,1)	(0.3,0.5,0.7)	(0,0.1,0.1)
A_2	(0,0.1,0.1)	(0.2,0.3,0.4)	(0.3,0.5,0.7)	(0.9,1,1)
A_3	(0.3,0.5,0.7)	(0.6,0.75,0.8)	(0.7,0.9,1)	(0,0.1,0.3)
A_4	(0,0.1,0.3)	(0.8,0.85,0.95)	(0.9,1,1)	(0.7,0.9,1)

Then calculate the objective weights according to equations (9)~(12), let $\beta = 2$.

$$W_1^o = 0.465,\ W_2^o = 0.061,\ W_3^o = 0.064,\ W_4^o = 0.409.$$

Step 3: Calculate the fuzzy combined weights by equation (13), we get:

$$W_1 = (0.342,0.355,0.367); W_2 = (0.128,0.136,0.144)$$

$$W_3 = (0.102,0.105,0.114); W_4 = (0.299,0.318,0.336).$$

Step 4: Calculate closeness of the alternatives according to equation (19)~(24), ρ=0.7:

$$C_1 = 0.584;\ C_2 = 0.279;\ C_3 = 0.473;\ C_4 = 0.437.$$

Thus the order of the alternatives is: $A_1 \succ A_3 \succ A_4 \succ A_2$. That is, alternative A_1 is the optimal one.

5. CONCLUSIONS

Fuzzy sets theory can be applied to deal with multi-attribute decision making problems under uncertainty and imprecise environment. In this paper, we made some improvement on the fuzzy MADM method by taking into account the decision maker's subjective preferences. This method makes our new algorithm more reasonable and the results in more agreement with the decision maker's intentions.

ACKNOWLEDGEMENTS

This paper is supported by Doctorial Foundation of North China Electric Power University.

REFERENCES

[1] C.L. Hwang, K. Yoon. Multiple criteria decision making method and applications. Springer, Berlin Heidelberg, 1981.

[2] M. Delgado, F. Herrera, et al. Combining numerical and linguistic information in group decision making. Journal of information sciences, 1998, 107: 177~194.

[3] Ching-Hsue Cheng, Yin Lin. Evaluating the best main battle tank using fuzzy decision theory with linguistic criteria evaluation. European Journal of Operational Research, 2002, 142: 174~186.

[4] F. Herrera, E. Herrera-Viedma, J.L. Verdegay. Linguistic Measures Based on Fuzzy Coincidence for Reaching Consensus in Group Decision Making. International Journal of Approximate Reasoning, 1997, 16: 309~334.

[5] Chen-Tung Chen. Extension of the TOPSIS for group decision making under fuzzy environment". Fuzzy Sets and Systems, 2000, 114: 1~9.

[6] Liu Shulin, Qiu Wanhua, Studies on the Basic Theories for MADM. System Engineering-Theory & Practice. 1998, 1: 38~43.

[7] Liou T S, Wang M J J. Ranking fuzzy numbers with integral value. Fuzzy sets and systems, 1992, 50: 247~255.

[8] R. J. Li and E. S. Lee, Comparison of Fuzzy numbers based on the probability measure of fuzzy events. Comp. Math. Applic, 1987, 15: 887~896.

[9] R. Csutoraa, J.J.Buckleyb. Fuzzy hierarchical analysis: The Lambda-Max method. Fuzzy Sets and Systems, 2001, 120: 181–195.

[10] J.J. Buckley, T. Feuring, Y. Hayashi, Fuzzy hierarchical analysis revisited. European Journal of Operational Research, 2001, 129: 48~64.

[11] N. Bryson, Group decision-making and the analytic hierarchy process: Exploring the consensus-relevant information content. Computer & Operations research. 1996, 23: 27~35.

[12] J.S. Dyer, A clarification of "Remarks on the analytic hierarchy process". Management Science, 1990, 36: 274~275.

[13] T.L. Saaty Highlights and critical points in the theory and application of analytic hierarchy process. European Journal of Operational Research, 1997, 74: 426~447

[14] T.L. Saaty, Rank generation, preservation, and reversal in the analytic hierarchy process. Decision Sic., 1987, 18: 157~177.

[15] Fong-Gong Wu, Ying-Jye Lee, Ming-Chyuan Lin, Using the fuzzy analytic hierarchy process on optimum spatial allocation. International Journal of Industrial Ergonomics, 2004, 33: 553–569.

[16] Zhang jijun. Fuzzy analytic hierarchy process, Chinese Journal of Fuzzy systems and mathematics, 1999, 14: 81~89.

[17] R. J. Li. FMCDM: Theories and Applications. Beijing, Science Press, 2002.

[18] Kong feng, Liu hongyan. Fuzzy Entropy-Weight Algorithm for Multiple Attribute Decision Making Based on Uncertainness Preference. Proceedings of the Seventh International Conference on Industrial Management, Beijing, 2004: 616~621.

[19] Carlsson C, Fuller R.. Fuzzy multiple criteria decision making: recent developments. Fuzzy sets and Systems, 1996, 78: 139~153.

[20] E. S. Lee and R. J. Li. Comparison of Fuzzy numbers based on the probability measure of fuzzy events. Comp. Math. Applic. 1987, 15: 887~896.

[21] R. M. Tong, P.P Bonissone. A linguistic approach to decision making with fuzzy sets. IEEE Trans. System Man Cybernet, 1980, 10: 716~723.

[22] J. Buckley. Ranking alternatives using fuzzy numbers. Fuzzy sets and systems, 1985, 15: 21~34.

AN ALGORITHM FOR MINING ASSOCIATION RULES WITH WEIGHTED MINIMUM SUPPORTS

Yuchiang Li[1], Chinchen Chang[1, 2], and Jiehshan Yeh[3]

[1] *Department of Computer Science and Information Engineering, National Chung Cheng University, Chiayi 621, Taiwan*

[2] *Department of Information Engineering and Computer Science, Feng Chia University, Taichung 407, Taiwan*

[3] *Department of Computer Science and Information Management, Providence University, Taichung 433, Taiwan*

Abstract: Most existing algorithms employ a uniform minimum support for mining association rules. Nevertheless, each item in a publication database, even each set of items, is exhibited in an individual period. A reasonable minimum support threshold has to be adjusted according to the exhibition period of each *k*-itemset. Accordingly, this paper proposes a new algorithm, called WMS, for mining association rules with weighted minimum supports in publication databases. WMS discovers all frequent itemsets which satisfy their individual requirement of minimum support thresholds. WMS applies the group closure property to prune futile itemsets, to reduce the number of candidates generated, and thus to generate the candidate sets efficiently.

Key words: data mining, association rules, multiple minimum support

1. INTRODUCTION

Data mining techniques are typically used to gather hidden but potentially useful information from data in data warehouses. Such techniques have come to constitute an important field of research [6]. Mining association rules is one of the core tasks in solving many data mining problems. The Apriori algorithm [4] is the most famous means of mining association rules. The mining of association rules can be divided into two sub-problems: (1) to find all *frequent itemsets* that occur more frequently than the minimum support threshold, and (2) to use these frequent itemsets to generate association rules. Other efficient methods have been studied to discover frequent itemsets in the past [1, 2, 8, 12].

Existing Apriori-like algorithms assume that all itemsets have a uniform minimum support. In practice, however, some items are important, but have low support. The straightforward approach is to lower the minimum support threshold to find these important but rare items. However, a lower minimum support may yield an excess of useless rules. The method of multiple minimum supports allows users to specify different minimum supports of different items, to discover rules that involve both frequent and rare items [11].

Available mining methods cannot efficiently handle a *publication-like* database. A publication database is also a transaction database wherein each item contains an individual exhibition period [9]. Two essential problems of the current model are as follows. (1) The exhibition period of each item is neglected, and (2) the support of each item is not evaluated on an equitable basis. For example, Fig. 1 refers to a publication database in a bookstore. Items $\{A\}$ and $\{B\}$ are exhibited from 2000 to the end of 2003. However, item $\{E\}$ is exhibited only in 2003. Classic mining techniques use an identical minimum support threshold and ignore the exhibition period of each item. The PPM algorithm has been proposed to solve this problem [9].

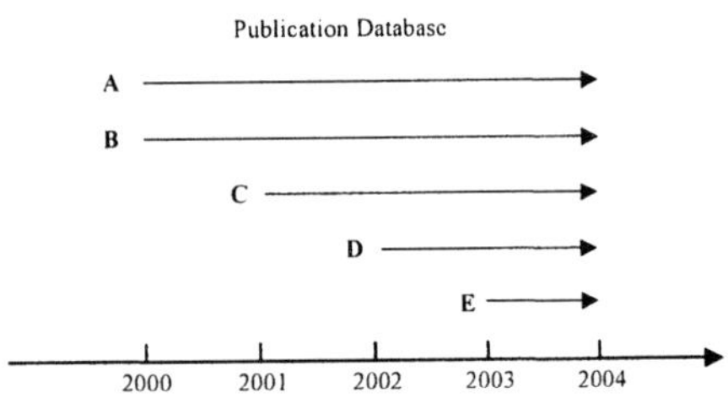

Figure 1. A publication database contains five items

LPMiner employs a linear function to tackle the problem of support that declines with the length of the itemsets. However, the linear function does not take into account the exhibition period of each item. Furthermore, the itemsets with equal length have the same minimum support threshold [13]. The PPM algorithm considers the exhibition period of each item, but it does not deal with the problem of support decrease with the length of itemsets. Moreover, the algorithm assumes that the termination times of all items are identical, but does not reflect on the exhibition period of each k-itemset. Therefore, this work proposes a novel weighted minimum supports (WMS) method that considers the individual exhibition period of each k-itemset.

Longer itemsets normally have shorter exhibition periods. Hence, WMS fulfills the requirement that the minimum support thresholds should be lower for longer itemsets. The reasonable exhibition period of a k-itemset is defined as the exhibition period shared by its k individual items. WMS also enables the exhibition period of each item to have a distinct cut-off date. This work focuses on generating frequent itemsets in the publication database.

2. RELATED WORK

Given a transaction database, the mining of association rules is defined to discover the important rules that relate *items*. In 1993, Agrawal *et al.* first defined such mining formally as follows [3]. Let $I = \{i_1, i_2, ..., i_m\}$ represent a set of items (*itemset*). Each transaction T is also an itemset such that $T \subseteq I$. Let DB be the transaction database, which is a set of transactions. Let X be an itemset; X is contained in T if and only if $X \subseteq T$. An association rule is used in the form $X \Rightarrow Y$, where $X \subseteq I$, $Y \subseteq I$ and $X \cap Y = \phi$ (For example, $I=\{A, B, C, D, E\}$, $X=\{A, C\}$, $Y=\{B, D\}$). An rule $X \Rightarrow Y$ has two essential properties, called *support* and *confidence*. The support of the rule $X \Rightarrow Y$, defined as $Sup(X \cup Y)$, is defined as the percentage of the transactions in DB that contain $X \cup Y$. The confidence of the rule $X \Rightarrow Y$, denoted as $Conf(X \Rightarrow Y)$, is c% when c% of the transactions in DB that contain X, also contain Y. The mathematical expression of confidence is $Conf(X \Rightarrow Y) = Sup(X \cup Y)/Sup(X)$. Given the minimum support (*minSup*) and minimum confidence (*minConf*) thresholds for the transaction database DB, the mining of association rules discovers all rules whose support, and the confidence in which, are greater than the two minimum thresholds, respectively. An itemset is called a frequent itemset when its support is above the *minSup* threshold.

Given a user-specified *minSup*, the Apriori algorithm takes advantage of the downward closure property to filter some infrequent itemsets beforehand [4]. The downward closure property is that any subset of a frequent itemset must be frequent; otherwise the itemset is infrequent. In each pass, Apriori constructs a candidate set of frequent itemsets. Then, the algorithm scans the entire transaction database to determine the frequent itemsets. A candidate k-itemset (an itemset with k items) is joined from two arbitrary frequent (k-1)-itemsets, whose first k-1 items are identical. If $k \geq 3$, Apriori uses the downward closure property to prune some infrequent itemsets. All remaining k-itemsets constitute candidate k-itemsets. The process is repeated until no candidate can be generated.

Apriori employs a single minimum support threshold for whole transaction database. In reality, the minimum support may not be uniform. In 1998, Cai *et al.* developed the notion of the multiple minimum support thresholds to reflect the importance of each item [5]. In 1999, Liu *et al.* described an algorithm that exhibits the sorted closure property to solve the problem that the downward closure characteristic cannot be employed in the multiple minimum supports scenario [11].

Example 2.1 Consider the three items $\{A\}$, $\{B\}$, and $\{C\}$ in a database. The individual minimum support threshold of each item is as follows.

$minSup(A) = 5\%$, $minSup(B) = 10\%$, and $minSup(C) = 15\%$.

The *minSup* threshold of an itemset is defined as the lowest support value among all items in the itemset. If the support of the itemset $\{B, C\}$ is 8%, then it is under both $minSup(A)$ and $minSup(B)$. $\{B, C\}$ is discarded because of downward closure. However, itemset $\{A, B, C\}$ may be frequent because $minSup(A)$ is 5%. The sorted closure property is used to solve the problem by sorting in order of ascending minimum support.

In 2000, Wang *et al.* presented a "pushing support constraints" method to "push" support constraints into the generation of the Apriori itemset to conserve the essence of Apriori and determine the minimum support for each itemset durning running time [15]. Recent research has developed numerous other mining association rules with multiple minimum supports [7, 9, 10, 13, 14]. In this work, the WMS algorithm is also a variant of mining association rules with multiple minimum supports.

3. WEIGHTED MINIMUM SUPPORTS (WMS)

The main idea behind the previous multiple minimum supports techniques is the assigning of an individual minimum support threshold to each item. Although the techniques can yield interesting itemsets with low support, they do not account for the lower support threshold of long itemsets. Short itemsets tend to be interesting when they have high support, whereas long itemsets may be of interest but occur relatively infrequently. To solve this problem, the LPMiner algorithm incorporates a support-constraining function, which reduces the support threshold as the length of the itemset increases. However, the minimum support thresholds of equally long itemsets are identical in LPMiner. This study proposes the Weighted Minimum Supports (WMS) algorithm, in which for each itemset, the minimum support is individually weighted, according to its period of exhibition.

3.1 Common Exhibition Period

In a publication database, the exhibition period of each individual itemset may be different, so measurements based on the assumption that all itemsets have an identical "life cycle" are biased. In this work, the exhibition period of each itemset is defined as a span of time granularities. Let a transaction database *DB* logically be divided into *n* partitions of unit time granularity (month, quarter or year, for example). The symbol db^{t_1,t_2} indicates the continuous portion of the database from partition P_{t_1} to partition P_{t_2}, where $t_2 \geq t_1 \geq 1$ and $t_1, t_2 \in N$. A *k*-itemset $I=\{i_1, i_2, \ldots, i_k\}^{t_1,t_2}$ denotes that the exhibition period of $\{i_1, i_2, \ldots, i_k\}$ is from P_{t_1} to P_{t_2}. For the entire database, given a *minSup*, the weighted minimum support (*WminSup*) threshold of each 1-itemset is $minSup*|db^{t_1,t_2}|/|DB|$, where $|db^{t_1,t_2}|$ indicates the number of transactions of db^{t_1,t_2} and $|DB|$ represents the number of transactions of *DB*. The weighted minimum support threshold of a *k*-itemset is derived from the common exhibition period of all *k* items in the *k*-itemset. Consider the *k* 1-itemsets $\{i_1\}^{t_{11},t_{12}}$, $\{i_2\}^{t_{21},t_{22}}$, …, $\{i_k\}^{t_{k1},t_{k2}}$; the start time of the exhibition of the *k*-itemset $\{i_1, i_2, \ldots, i_k\}$ is $t_1 = \max\{t_{11}, t_{21}, \ldots, t_{k1}\}$ and the end time is $t_2 = \min\{t_{12}, t_{12}, \ldots, t_{k2}\}$. The period in which these *k* individual items occur at the same time is from t_1 to t_2. If $t_2 < t_1$, then the *k*-itemset does not appear in *DB*.

Example 3.1 Consider a database that contains five individual items. Figure 2 illustrates the exhibition periods of these five 1-itemsets. The common exhibition period of $\{B\}^{2000,2001}$, $\{C\}^{2001,2003}$ and $\{D\}^{2001,2002}$ is the exhibition period of $\{B, C, D\}$. Therefore, the start time of $\{B, C, D\}$ is max{2000, 2001, 2001} = 2001 and the end time is min{2001, 2003, 2002} = 2001. $\{B, C, D\}^{2001,2001}$ denotes that the exhibition period of $\{B, C, D\}$ is one year, 2001.

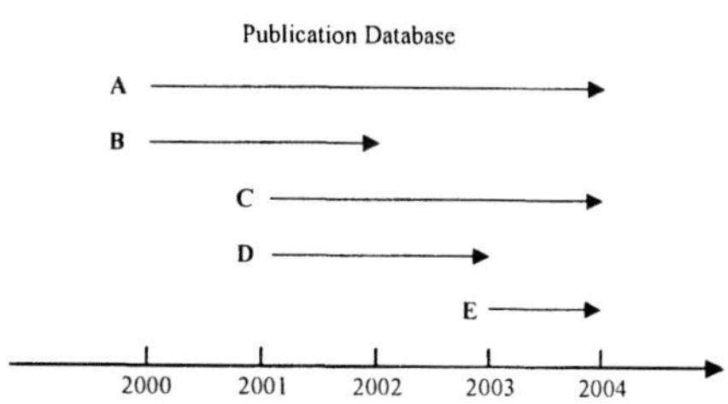

Figure 2. Exhibition period of each 1-itemset

The duration of the exhibition period of an itemset is turned into the minimum support weight. Users can effectively express various minimum support requirements for different rules, in light of the individual weight of each itemset. The use of weighted minimum supports can enable itemsets with long exhibition periods to have higher minimum supports and those short exhibition periods itemsets to have lower minimum supports.

3.2 Candidate Generation

In [11], Liu *et al.* used the sorted closure property to solve the problem of mining with multiple minimum supports. However, in this work, the sorted closure property does not be applied.

Example 3.2 Consider three items $\{A\}$, $\{B\}$ and $\{C\}$ in a transaction database, with exhibition periods $\{A\}^{1,4}$, $\{B\}^{1,3}$, and $\{C\}^{3,4}$, respectively. The distributions of the records in the database stretch over four time units. Assume that all partitions include the same number of transactions. The minimum support for the entire database is 40%. Thus, $WminSup(A)$ = 40%, $WminSup(B)$ = 30%, $WminSup(C)$ = 20% and $WminSup(BC)$ = 10%. If the support of itemset $\{B\}$=15%, then the itemset is discarded using sorted closure. The occurrence count is below the minimum of all 1-itemset *WminSup* values, so the potentially frequent itemset $\{BC\}^{2,2}$ is pruned by using the sorted closure property.

A publication database is logically divided into n partitions with unit time granularity. *WminSup* of each partition can be derived easily from the user-defined *minSup*. The minimum *WminSup* is the minimum among all of these *WminSups*. If the percentage of occurrences of a k-itemset is below the minimum *WminSup*, then all of its supersets must be infrequent. Hence, the k-itemset can be pruned. A superset of a k-itemset becomes a frequent itemset if the number of supports of the k-itemset exceeds the minimum *WminSup*. Sorted closure is irrelevant to WMS. Too many candidate itemsets will be generated if the minimum *WminSup* is the only pruned threshold. Therefore, this study describes another property, called the Group Closure Property (GCP), used to prune the number of candidate itemsets and generate the candidate set efficiently.

Group Closure Property (GCP)

Consider a database with n grains of time. The total number of distinct continuous exhibition periods is $n(n+1)/2$. Accordingly, each k-itemset can be assigned to one of the $n(n+1)/2$ groups such that each k-itemset in the same group has an identical exhibition period. That is, each k-itemset in the same group has an identical *WminSup*. After the k-th pass, WMS employs the minimum *WminSup* value to delete useless candidates. The remaining k-itemsets form a set RC_k. The set C_{k+1} is generated from RC_k. Let $WminSup(g_i)$

denote the *WminSup* value of the group g_i, and let *WminSup*($g_i \cap g_j$) denote the *WminSup* value of the common exhibition period of the two groups g_i and g_j, the generation of C_{k+1} proceeds as follows.

1. Sort the groups in order of descending *WminSup*. *Gr*(first) denotes the set of groups which is sorted, where *Gr*(first) = $\{g_1, g_2, \ldots, g_{n(n+1)/2}\}$. Select a group $g_i \in$ *Gr*(first) in order.
2. Compute the common exhibition period of g_i with each other group g_j, where $i < j$. WMS sorts other groups in order of increasing *WminSup*($g_i \cap g_j$) value; it discards groups that do not share common exhibition period. *Gr*(second) represents the set of groups which is sorted.
3. Select a group $g_j \in$ *Gr*(second) in order.
4. As required by the *WminSup*($g_i \cap g_j$), delete the k-itemsets in g_i whose occurrence counts are smaller than *WminSup*($g_i \cap g_j$).
5. Join each k-itemset in g_i with each k-itemset in g_j, whose occurrence counts are above the *WminSup*($g_i \cap g_j$) requirement, to generate candidate (k+1)-itemsets.
6. Select the next g_j and return to Step 4 until all groups have been chosen.
7. Delete all infrequent k-itemsets in g_i. Output frequent k-itemsets. Join each frequent k-itemset in g_i with each other to generate (k+1)-itemsets.
8. Select the next g_i and return to Step 2 until all groups have been selected.

In Step 4, if the number of occurrences of the k-itemset in g_i is smaller than *WminSup*($g_i \cap g_j$), then any superset of the k-itemset that has not yet be generated must be infrequent, because *Gr*(second) is sorted in order of increasing *WminSup*($g_i \cap g_j$). In Step 5, the candidate (k+1)-itemset is not produced if the support value is under the *WminSup*($g_i \cap g_j$) threshold. The method of joining artibrary two candidates is the same as that in Apriori. In Step 7, all k-itemsets which are in the same group exhibit the downward closure property.

Example 3.3 Consider a database in which the distribution of transactions stretches over four time grains. Assume that each partition contains the same number of transactions. The minimum support for the entire database is 40%. Let g^{t_1,t_2} expresses the group whose exhibition period is from t_1 to t_2. The first column in Table 1 lists the ten groups in the *Gr*(first) sequence from top to bottom. The second column presents the corresponding *Gr*(*second*) sequences. Assume that the support value of itemset $\{A, B\}^{1,4}$ is 15%. First, $\{A, B\}$ is joined with other 2-itemsets that in the group $g^{1,1}$ to generate the 3-itemset candidates. According to the group order $g^{2,2}$, $g^{3,3}$, ..., $g^{2,4}$, $\{A, B\}$ joins with other 2-itemsets until the process arrives at group $g^{1,2}$. Because, *WminSup*($g^{1,4} \cap g^{1,2}$) = 20% exceeds 15%, so $\{A, B\}$ is deleted from $g^{1,4}$ after the group $g^{1,2}$ is selected.

The pseudo-code for generating candidates is as follows.

Procedure candidate-gen(RC_{k-1})

```
01 Gr(first) = sort(G, WminSup(g_i ∈ G));  // G is the set of all groups
02 for each group g_i ∈ Gr(first) do
03    G = {g_j ∈ Gr(first) | i < j};
04    for each g_j ∈ G do
05       if WminSup(g_i ∩ g_j) = 0;
06          delete g_j;  endif  endfor
07    Gr(second) = sort(G, WminSup(g_i ∩ g_j) ≠ 0);
08    for each c_i ∈ g_i do
09       if c_i.count < WminSup(g_i ∩ g_j)
10          delete c_i;  endif
11       for each c_j ∈ g_j do
12          if c_j.count < WminSup(g_i ∩ g_j)
13             next;  endif
14          apriori-join(c_i, c_j);
15       endfor
16    endfor
17    for each c_i ∈ g_i do
18       if c_i.count < WminSup(g_i)
19          delete c_i;  endif  endfor
20    for each c_i ∈ g_i do
21       for each (c_j ≠ c_i) ∈ g_i do
22          apriori-join(c_i, c_j);  endfor
23    endfor
24 endfor
```

Table 1. Example of the Gr(first) sequence and the Gr(second) sequence

Gr(first)	Gr(second) sequence, in order of increasing $WminSup(g_i \cap g_j)$
$g_1 = g^{1,4}$	$\{g^{1,1}, g^{2,2}, g^{3,3}, g^{4,4}, g^{1,2}, g^{2,3}, g^{3,4}, g^{1,3}, g^{2,4}\}$
$g_2 = g^{1,3}$	$\{g^{1,1}, g^{2,2}, g^{3,3}, g^{3,4}, g^{1,2}, g^{2,3}, g^{2,4}\}$
$g_3 = g^{2,4}$	$\{g^{2,2}, g^{3,3}, g^{4,4}, g^{1,2}, g^{2,3}, g^{3,4}\}$
$g_4 = g^{1,2}$	$\{g^{1,1}, g^{2,2}, g^{2,3}\}$
$g_5 = g^{2,3}$	$\{g^{2,2}, g^{3,3}, g^{3,4}\}$
$g_6 = g^{3,4}$	$\{g^{3,3}, g^{4,4}\}$
$g_7 = g^{1,1}$	None
$g_8 = g^{2,2}$	None
$g_9 = g^{3,3}$	None
$g_{10} = g^{4,4}$	None

In Lines 14 and 22, the join function is the same as the join step in Apriori. This function joins two distinct (k-1)-itemsets whose first k-2 items are identical. Lines 8 to 16 generate candidate k-itemsets when arbitrary two (k-1)-itemsets are in different groups, whereas from Lines 17 to 23 relate to the case in which all (k-1)-itemsets appear in the same group. In Line 22, although the itemsets in the same group satisfy the property of download closure, the exhibition periods of the subset of a frequent k-itemset may be different with the k-itemset. Thus, omit the pruning step following the joining step. The candidate generation function deletes in advance (k-1)-itemsets whose supersets must be infrequent. Then, the candidate k-itemsets are generated. The pruning step is implemented only before the joining step, unlike in Apriori, whose pruning step is implemented only after the joining step. Lines 9-10, 12-13 and 18-19 are the pruning steps.

3.3 Weighted Minimum Supports

The WMS algorithm is based on a level-wise technique like Apriori. WMS passes over the database k or k+1 times to generate all frequent k-itemsets. In the first pass, each item is a candidate 1-itemset. WMS scans the database to count the supports of each candidate 1-itemset and determines whether these 1-itemsets are frequent. If the support values of the 1-itemsets are greater than or equal to the minimum *WminSup*, then these 1-itemsets are added to the set RC_1. In the pass k, C_k is generated from RC_{k-1}; then WMS scans the database to count the supports of each candidate k-itemset and determines whether they are frequent. The WMS algorithm pseudo-code is stated as follows.

Algorithm WMS

```
01 G = group();
02 C_1 = {All 1-itemsets};
03 count(C_1);   // scan DB
04 RC_1 = {c ∈ C_1 | c.count ≥ minimum WminSup};
05 F_1 = {c ∈ RC_1 | c.count ≥ WminSup(c.group)};
06 for (k = 2; RC_{k-1} ≠ φ; k++) do
07     C_k = candidate-gen(RC_{k-1});
08     count(C_k);   // scan DB
09     RC_k = {c ∈ C_k | c.count ≥ minimum WminSup};
10     F_k = {c ∈ RC_k | c.count ≥ WminSup(c.group)};
11 endfor
12 Answer = ∪_k F_k;
```

In Line 1, all itemsets are assigned to their corresponding groups, according to the distinct exhibition period of the itemsets. In Line 7, the set RC_{k-1} is used to generate candidate k-itemsets. WMS exploits the group closure property to prune some useless candidates and generate the candidate k-itemsets. Lines 3 and 8 scan the database and count the support value of the candidate k-itemsets.

4. CONCLUSIONS

In a publication database, each itemset has an individual exhibition period. Mining association rules on publication databases with a uniform minimum support is unpractical. The reasonable exhibition period of a k-itemset is the common exhibition period of its k individual items. The sensible minimum supports of distinct k-itemsets should be adjusted in the light of their exhibition periods. This investigation introduced a novel approach, WMS, for mining association rules with weighted minimum supports that consider the exhibition period of each itemset in a publication database. WMS also accounts for the distinct end time of the exhibition period of each item. The proposed method mines frequent itemsets whose percentage of occurrences exceeds the individual *WminSup* threshold. WMS eliminates some useless itemsets using the group closure property to avoid generating an excess of candidates. In the future, we will consider the extension of the WMS algorithm to multiple level association rules.

REFERENCES

[1] R. C. Agarwal, et al. A tree projection algorithm for generation of frequent itemsets. *Journal of Parallel and Distributed Computing*, 2000, 61(3): 350~361

[2] C. C. Aggarwal and P. S. Yu, Mining associations with the collective strength approach. *IEEE Trans. Knowledge and Data Engineering*, 2001, 13(6): 863~873

[3] R. Agrawal, et al. Mining association rules between sets of items in large databases. 1993 *ACM SIGMOD Intl. Conf. on Management of Data*, Washington: 207~216

[4] R. Agrawal and R. Srikant, Fast algorithms for mining association rules. *20th Intl. Conf. on Very Large Data Bases*, 1994, Santiago: 487~499.

[5] C. H. Cai, et al. Mining association rules with weighted items. *1998 Intl. Database Engineering and Applications Symposium*, Cardiff: 68~77

[6] M. S. Chen, et al. Data mining: An overview from a database perspective. *IEEE Trans. Knowledge Data Engineering*, 1996, 8(6): 866~883

[7] F. L. Chung and C. L. Lui, A post-analysis framework for mining generalized association rules with multiple minimum supports. *6th ACM SIGKDD Intl. Conf. on Knowledge Discovery and Data Mining Workshop on Post-Processing in Machine Learning and Data Mining*, 2000, Boston: 9~14

[8] J. Han, et al. Mining frequent patterns without candidate generation. 2000 *ACM-SIGMOD Intl. Conf. on Management of Data*, Dallas: 1~12

[9] C. H. Lee, et al. Progressive partition miner: An efficient algorithm for mining general temporal association rules. *IEEE Trans. Knowledge Data Engineering*, 2003, 15(4): 1004~1017

[10] C. L. Liu and F. L. Chung, Discovery of generalized association rules with multiple minimum supports. *4th European Conf. on Principles of Data Mining and Knowledge Discovery*, 2000, Lyon: 510~515

[11] B. Liu, et al. Mining association rules with multiple minimum support. *1999 ACM SIGKDD Intl. Conf on Knowledge Discovery and Data Mining*, San Diego: 337~341

[12] J. S. Park et al. An effective hash-based algorithm for mining association rules. *1995 ACM*-SIGMOD *Intl. Conf. on Management of Data*, San Jose: 175~186

[13] M. Seno and Karypis, LPMiner: An algorithm for finding frequent itemsets using length-decreasing support constraint. *2001 IEEE Intl. Conf. on Data Mining*, San Jose: 505~512

[14] M. C. Tseng, et al. Maintenance of generalized association rules with multiple minimum support. *Joint 9th IFSA World Congress and 20th NAFIPS Intl. Conf.*, 2001, Vancouver: 1294~1299

[15] K. Wang, et al. Pushing support constraints into association rules mining. *IEEE Trans. Knowledge Data Engineering*, 2003, 15(3): 642~658

AN IMPROVEMENT ON SAATY'S AHP

Feng Kong, Hongyan Liu
Department of Economics and management, North China Electric Power University, Baoding, P.R. China, 071003

Abstract: AHP is a commonly used method in analyzing multi-factor evaluation or multi-attribute decision-making problems. However, AHP has some serious logistic mistakes. Since it cannot maintain the independence of alternatives, AHP cannot lead to an ordering of alternatives that is consistent with their ordering before the values of the assessments or the quantity of alternatives change. Therefore, using a numerical illustration, the mistake of traditional AHP is found out. An improvement on AHP which can keep the consistency of the alternatives' ordering results is put forward in this paper.

Key words: AHP; Mistake; Improvement

1. INTRCDUCTION

Analytic Hierarchy Process (AHP) is a system analysis method put forward by professor Saaty in the 1980s. It is a connection of quantitative and qualitative analysis method and is commonly used to study multi-objective or multi-attribute problems in many fields.

By quantifying the process of thinking and subjective judges of human beings, computation could be greatly reduced; meanwhile, AHP strives to maintain the consistency of the decision-maker's process of thinking and the principles of decision-making and therefore tries to solve satisfactorily the complex social and economic problems which could not be fully quantified. This method has now been a key component of the science of decision-making. Although this method is widely applied, it has its mistakes. Besides the usually cited problems of inconsistency in comparison matrixes resulted from the definitions of Saaty's 1-9 scales [1]~[6], we find one serious mistake in AHP: it is Logic wrong in calculating the final priority weights of alternatives. As a result, decision results derived by applying this method could seriously deviate from the one the decision maker actually desires. Furthermore, the new priority ranking of the alternatives will be completely different from the old when the group of evaluation alters.

In this paper, Section two explains the principles and calculation of AHP. Section three proves the logical mistake in AHP theoretically and numerically. Section four gives corrections to AHP and gives a new correct comprehensive ranking method. And section five concludes.

2. THE TRADITIONAL AHP

For a typical hierarchy, the overall goal is situated at the highest level; element (attributes) with similar nature are grouped at the same interim levels and decision variables (alternatives) are situated at the lowest level. See Figure. 1. By means of pairwise comparisons of the elements using the scales as suggested by Saaty, reciprocal matrixes for all clusters can be formulated. In order to measure the level of consistency of a reciprocal matrix, a consistency test has been proposed. After finding the maximum eigenvalue and the corresponding eigenvector of each reciprocal matrix in each cluster, together with some manipulations in matrix algebra, a ranking of the alternatives can be obtained.

The steps of AHP are:

Step 1: Set up a hierarchy model:

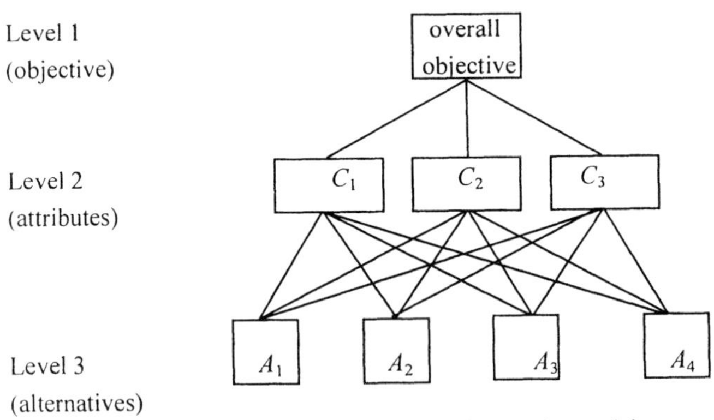

Figure. 1 The hierarchy model

Step 2:Set up the comparison matrix of each level.

$$A = \begin{pmatrix} a_{11} & a_{12} & \cdots & a_{1m} \\ a_{21} & a_{22} & \cdots & a_{2m} \\ \vdots & \vdots & \cdots & \vdots \\ a_{m1} & a_{m2} & \cdots & a_{mm} \end{pmatrix}$$

where, a_{ij} is an exact number representing the scale for the relative importance of the *i*-th sub-element over the *j*-th sub-element.

Usually we can use the Saaty's scale for pairwise comparison as follow:

Table. 1 The Saaty's scale for pairwise comparison

Saaty's scale	The relative importance of the two sub-elements
1	Equal importance
3	Moderate importance of one over another
5	Strong importance
7	Very strong importance
9	Extreme importance

Step 3: Consistency test

If the comparison matrix is "perfectly consistent", the scale of comparison matrix should be satisfied with:

$$a_{ii} = 1;\ a_{ij} = \frac{1}{a_{ji}};\ a_{ij} = \frac{a_{ik}}{a_{jk}},\ i, j, k = 1, 2, \ldots, m \tag{1}$$

In AHP, the decision maker should be consistent in the preference ratings give in the pairwise comparison matrix. Before using the scale, the comparison matrix should be checked for consistency. The focus of this paper is not the consistency of the comparison matrix. So all comparison matrixes in this paper are consistent matrix.

Step 4: Calculation of priority weights of each level

According to Saaty (1980), the priority weight of each level can be derived from the normalized eigenvector of corresponding matrix as follow:

$$AW = \lambda_{\max} W \tag{2}$$

where, $\lambda_{\max}$ and W represent the maximum eigenvalue and the corresponding normalized eigenvector of comparison matrix A. We have:

$$\sum_{i=1}^{n} W_i = 1 \tag{3}$$

Step 5: Calculation of final priority of alternatives

According to above the priority weights of each level, we can get the final priority of alternatives by using matrix algebra:

$$W_i = \sum_{j=1}^{m} W_j^c W_i^j, \quad i = 1,2,\ldots,n \tag{4}$$

where, W_i represents the final priority weight of the i-th alternative; W_j^c represents the priority weight of the j-th attribute; W_i^j represents the priority weight of the i-th alternative for the j-th attribute.

Obviously there should be:

$$\sum_{i=1}^{n} W_i = \sum_{i=1}^{n}\sum_{j=1}^{m} W_j^c W_i^j = 1 \tag{5}$$

3. THE MISTAKE OF TRADITIONAL AHP

We will find the Logic mistake of AHP through following analysis and illustration.

3.1 Numerical Illustration of AHP

A firm will make a decision. In this decision problem, the firm has five alternatives,A_1, A_2, A_3, A_4, A_5. The firm would evaluate the five alternatives from three attributes, C_1, C_2, C_3. Next, we will apply AHP to evaluate the above five alternatives.

First, set up the AHP hierarchy model as Fig. 2 shows:

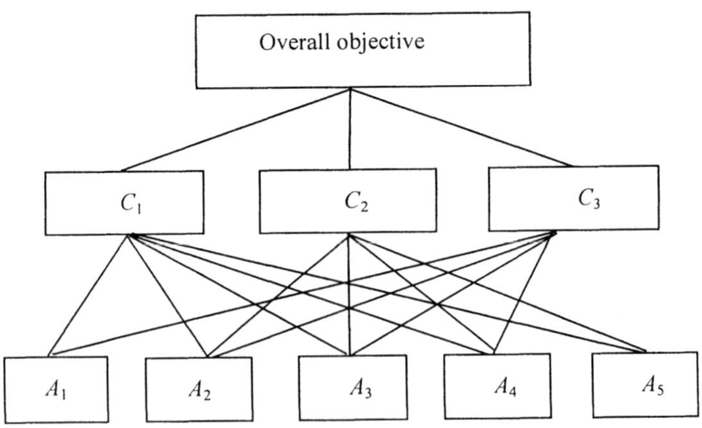

Figure. 2 The hierarchy model of the firm

Now, set up the comparison matrix to show the importance of the alternatives, and calculate the priority weights of the attributes, W_j^c. The calculation results are shown in Table. 2.

Table. 2 For the overall objective, the relative importance (weights) of attributes

Overall Objective	C_1	C_2	C_3	W_j^c
C_1	1	1/5	1/3	0.111
C_2	5	1	5/3	0.556
C_3	3	3/5	1	0.333

For each attribute, construct the comparison matrixes at the alternative level (All are strictly consistent matrixes), and calculate the priority weights of each alternative relative to attribute k, W_j^k (k=1, 2, 3). The calculation results are shown in Table. 3~5.

Table. 3 For C_1, the relative priority weight of alternatives

C_1	A_1	A_2	A_3	A_4	A_5	W_i^1
A_1	1	3	5	4	7	0.519
A_2	1/3	1	5/3	4/3	7/3	0.173
A_3	1/5	3/5	1	4/5	7/5	0.104
A_4	1/4	3/4	5/4	1	7/4	0.13
A_5	1/7	3/7	5/7	4/7	1	0.074

Table. 4 For C_2, the relative priority weight of alternatives

C_2	A_2	A_3	A_4	A_5	W_i^2
A_2	1	1/7	1/3	1/5	0.063
A_3	7	1	7/3	7/5	0.438
A_4	3	3/7	1	3/5	0.188
A_5	5	5/7	5/3	1	0.313

Next, calculate the final priority weights of the alternatives, W_i :

$$W_i = \sum_{j=1}^{3} W_j^c W_i^j$$

Table. 5 For C_3, the relative priority weight of alternatives

C_3	A_1	A_2	A_3	A_4	W_i^3
A_1	1	1	3	3	0.375
A_2	1	1	3	3	0.375
A_3	1/3	1/3	1	1	0.125
A_4	1/3	1/3	1	1	0.125

The results are shown in Table. 6.

Table. 6 The final priority weights of alternatives

Attribute / Alternative	C_1	C_2	C_3	W_i	Ranking results
	0.111	0.556	0.333		
A_1	0.519	0	0.375	0.183	2
A_2	0.173	0.063	0.375	0.179	4
A_3	0.104	0.438	0.125	0.296	1
A_4	0.13	0.188	0.125	0.16	5
A_5	0.074	0.313	0	0.182	3

The final ranking of the alternatives is:

$$A_3 > A_1 > A_5 > A_2 > A_4 \text{。}$$

3.2 The Logic Mistake in AHP

Now if, for certain reasons, alternative A1 could not be carried out any more, the ranking of the remaining four alternatives should be:

$$A_3 > A_5 > A_2 > A_4 \text{。}$$

However, if now we apply AHP to evaluate the following four alternatives once again, we will derive a completely different ranking order. The calculation results are shown in Table.7, 8, 9 and 10, with the weights of the alternatives being the same as in Table. 2.

Table. 7 For C_1, the relative priority weights of alternatives

C_1	A_2	A_3	A_4	A_5	W_i^1
A_2	1	5/3	4/3	7/3	0.36
A_3	3/5	1	4/5	7/5	0.216
A_4	3/4	5/4	1	7/4	0.27
A_5	3/7	5/7	4/7	1	0.154

Table. 8 For C_2*, the relative priority weights of alternatives*

C_2	A_2	A_3	A_4	A_5	W_i^2
A_2	1	1/7	1/3	1/5	0.063
A_3	7	1	7/3	7/5	0.438
A_4	3	3/7	1	3/5	0.188
A_5	5	5/7	5/3	1	0.313

Table. 9 For C_3*, the relative priority weights of alternatives*

C_3	A_2	A_3	A_4	W_i^3
A_2	1	3	3	0.6
A_3	1/3	1	1	0.2
A_4	1/3	1	1	0.2

Table. 10 The final priority weights of alternatives

Attribute / Alternative	C_1	C_2	C_3	W_i	Ranking results
	0.111	0.556	0.333		
A_2	0.36	0.063	0.6	0.275	2
A_3	0.216	0.438	0.2	0.334	1
A_4	0.27	0.188	0.2	0.201	3
A_5	0.154	0.313	0	0.191	4

The new ranking of the remaining alternatives become: $A_3 > A_2 > A_4 > A_5$, which is greatly different from the previous ranking of $A_3 > A_5 > A_2 > A_4$.

Now we assume it is A_3, instead of A_1 that could not be carried out any more. According to AHP, we can get the weights of the remaining four alternatives as shown in Table.11.

Table. 11 The final priority weights of alternatives

Attribute / Alternative	C_1	C_2	C_3	W_i	Ranking results
	0.111	0.556	0.333		
A_1	0.579	0	0.429	0.207	4
A_2	0.193	0.111	0.429	0.226	3
A_4	0.145	0.333	0.143	0.249	2
A_5	0.083	0.556	0	0.318	1

According to AHP, the ranking of the remaining four alternatives is: $A_5 > A_4 > A_2 > A_1$. This ranking is greatly different from the previous ranking of $A_1 > A_5 > A_2 > A_4$.

3.3 Analysis The Mistake in AHP

The key to judge whether AHP is mistaken is to see whether equation (3)~(5) holds. That is, whether there is need to normalize the sub-elements of the eigenvector of the matrix.

It is right to normalize the weights of the attributes, although actually, the ranking of the alternatives won't be affected whether we do the normalization or not. However, it is not correct to normalize the priority weights of the alternatives. For example, assume the decision matrix of a multi-attribute decision making problem is:

$$A = \begin{Bmatrix} 0.6 & 0.02 \\ 0.2 & 0.06 \end{Bmatrix}$$

where x_{ij} represents the utility that the decision maker derives from alternative i with respect to attribute j. The weights of the attributes both are 0.5.

If the decision maker did not know the values in the decision matrix, when he makes decisions by applying AHP, for the two attributes, he will give the following two comparison matrixes:

$$D_1 = \begin{Bmatrix} 1 & 3 \\ 1/3 & 1 \end{Bmatrix}, \quad D_2 = \begin{Bmatrix} 1 & 1/3 \\ 3 & 1 \end{Bmatrix}$$

Calculating the weights of the alternatives with respect to the two attributes respectively, we have: $W^1 = \{3/4, 1/4\}^T$, $W^2 = \{1/4, 3/4\}^T$

Then the final priority weights of the alternatives are: 1/2. That is, the two alternatives are the same to the decision maker. However, from the decision matrix, it is obvious that alternative 1 is more desirable than alternative 2. The cause of this discrepancy lies in the fact that the utilities of the alternatives in respect to attribute 2 have been enlarged relative to that in respect to attribute 1. For example, the utility for alternative 1 in respect to attribute 2, relative to attribute 1, has been enlarged from 1/30 to 1/3, and the utility for alternative 2 in respect to attribute 2, relative to attribute 1, has been enlarged from 3/10 to 3. In all, the fundamental cause of this discrepancy lies in the logic mistake in AHP in the respect of normalization and final priority weight calculation.

Further suppose the alternative the firm has is more than five. Suppose the firm has another X-5 ($X > 5$) alternatives: $A_6, A_7, \ldots, A_X$, and the weights of these alternatives all are zero except for one attribute, e.g., C_1 (or C_2, C_3). Suppose the weights of the X-5 alternatives are the same for attribute C1, and are equal to the weight of alternative A_1, or any other alternative, with respect to attribute C_1.

Now give the comparison matrix. The elements in the matrix, a_{ij} ($i, j = 1,2,3,4,5$), do not vary with the number of alternatives. That is,

$$W_1^1 = W_6^1 = \ldots = W_X^1 \circ$$

According to equation (3), there is:

$$\sum_{i=1}^{X} W_i^1 = 1 \tag{6}$$

Therefore, when the number of alternatives increases, although the relative values of the priority weights (a_{ij}) of the alternatives with respect to attribute C_1 remain the same, the absolute values decrease with the number of alternatives. That is, when the number of alternatives increases, there are more alternatives whose weights are not zero in respect to attribute C_1, with the sum of the weights still being 1. Hence, the final priority weight varies with the number of alternatives. When the number of alternatives decreases, the opposite will occur. Thus, we can see that AHP could not keep the independence of alternatives since the priority weights are affected by other alternatives.

However, from intuition, we know that alternatives should be independent. For example, in the overall evaluations of students, student *i* is better than student j, no matter whether they are evaluated in the whole class or in the whole grade or in the whole school. It is unbelievable if student *i* is better than *j* when evaluated in the whole class but obvious worse than *j* when evaluated in the whole grade. While the latter conclusion is right what we would reach when applying AHP.

4. IMPROVEMENT ON AHP

The cause of the mistake in AHP lies in the fact that it could not maintain the independence of alternatives. Therefore, it is of crucial importance to keep the relative utility of the attributes constant in order to correct AHP.

To show the correct calculation steps for AHP, we take the previous example once again.

(1) Set up a hierarchy model as the previous example shows.

(2) Set up the comparison matrix, here we do not set up the comparison matrix on the attribute level any more, we only set up the comparison matrix on the alternative level for a given attribute.

(3) Select an alternative for which the weight of no attribute is zero as the benchmark, and then give the comparison matrix for the attributes in the benchmark alternative.

Select alternative A_3 as the benchmark. Calculate the weights of the alternatives, α_3^j. See Table.12.

Table. 12 Relative weights of the attributes of the benchmark alternative A3

A_3	C_1	C_2	C_3	α_j^3
C_1	1	1/7	1	0.111
C_2	7	1	7	0.778
C_3	1	1/7	1	0.111

(4) Let the relative total utility of the benchmark alternative be 1, i.e., $U_* = 1$. Calculate the relative total utility of the other alternatives.

$$U_i = \sum_{j=1}^{n} \alpha_*^j \frac{W_i^j}{W_*^j} \tag{7}$$

Where * represents the benchmark alternative and n represents the number of alternatives.

(5) Rank the alternatives according to the relative total utilities of the alternatives.

As for our previous example, the relative total utilities of the alternatives are as follows.

Table. 13 Ranking of the alternatives (the benchmark being A3)

Alternatives \ Attribute	C_1	C_2	C_3	U_i	Ranking result
A_1	0.556	0	0.333	0.889	2
A_2	0.185	0.111	0.333	0.63	4
A_3	0.111	0.778	0.111	1	1
A_4	0.139	0.333	0.111	0.583	5
A_5	0.079	0.556	0	0.635	3

The ranking of the alternatives is: $A_3 > A_1 > A_5 > A_2 > A_4$.

If alternative A1 could not be implemented any more for certain reasons, calculate the relative total utilities of the remaining alternatives once again, with the benchmark still being A_3. The calculation results are shown in Table.14.

The ranking of the remaining alternatives is: $A_3 > A_5 > A_2 > A_4$.

There is no change in the ranking of the remaining alternatives when alternative A_1 is taken off.

Table.14 Ranking of the alternatives (the benchmark being A_3)

Attribute / Alternative	C_1	C_2	C_3	U_i	Ranking results
A_2	0.185	0.111	0.333	0.63	3
A_3	0.111	0.778	0.111	1	1
A_4	0.139	0.333	0.111	0.583	4
A_5	0.079	0.556	0	0.635	2

Now, if it is not alternative A_1, but A_3, that could not be implemented any more, we could recalculate the relative total utilities of the remaining alternatives, with another alternative as the benchmark, for example, A_2. Note that now the comparison matrix that shows the relative weights of the attributes of the benchmark alternative for the total utility has changed. The ranking of the alternatives is shown in Table.15.

Table.15 Ranking of the alternatives (the benchmark being A_2)

Attribute / Alternative	C_1	C_2	C_3	U_i	Ranking results
A_1	0.882	0	0.529	1.412	1
A_2	0.294	0.176	0.529	1	3
A_4	0.221	0.529	0.176	0.927	4
A_5	0.126	0.880	0	1.008	2

The ranking of the remaining alternatives is: $A_1 > A_5 > A_2 > A_4$.

There is no change in the ranking of the remaining alternatives when alternative A_3 is taken off.

5. CONCLUSIONS

The paper shows that the prevalent AHP has a serious mistake that makes the alternatives dependent on others, so that when there is one alternative taken off or more alternatives considered, there will be discrepancy of the other alternatives as compared with before.

Our improvement on AHP, however, could maintain the independency of alternatives, so that when the number of alternatives changes, the ranking of the other alternatives remain the same as before. Although our method does not calculate the weights of the attributes, this idea or information is already reflected in the calculation of the final priority ranking indexes, or the calculation of the relative weights of the attributes of the benchmark alternative for the total utility.

REFERENCES

1. Saaty, T.L., The analytic hierarchy process, McGrawHill, New York.1980.
2. Bryson, N. Group decision-making and the analytic hierarchy process: Exploring the consensus-relevant information content, Computer & Operations research, 1996, 23: 27-35.
3. Guo, Yajun. Sensibility and Practice Analysis of Comprehensive Evaluation Resultt, Journal of Management Science in China, 1998,1(3): 28-35.
4. Dyer, J.S. A clarification of "Remarks on the analytic hierarchy process" Management Science, 1990, 36: 274-275.
5. Saaty, T.L., Highlights and critical points in the theory and application of analytic hierarchy process, European Journal of Operational Research, 1997,74: 426-447
6. Saaty, T.L., Rank generation, preservation, and reversal in the analytic hierarchy process, Decision Sci., 1987,18: 157-177.
7. Weiss, E.N., Rao, V. R. AHP design issues for largescale systems, Decision Sci, 1986,18: 43-61.

DECISION MAKING WITH UNCERTAINTY

Qing Zhou[a], Wei Peng[b,]
[a]the Software Institute, Zhongshan University, Guangzhou,Guangdong, 510275, P.R. China
Email address: lnszq@zsulink.zsu.edu.cn
[b]Sci. and Tech. Institute of GRC, 2 Gonghexi Rd., Guangzhou, Guangdong, 510060, P.R.China
Email address: pengwei99@tom.com

Abstract: In this paper we discuss decision making based on incomplete knowledge. Asthe results of our decisions have always some uncertainties in these cases, we developeda method to measure the advantages brought by those possible solutions of our problem,which makes our decision making problem easier. Our proposal is entirely formulizedwithin the so called classical two valued logic, so it has a solid foundation. Basic notionsof various items are defined formally; formulas of supporting degree and safe supporting degree for decision making are discussed in details. Uncertainty of a proposition is clearly defined and the evaluation of such an uncertainty is clearly presented within our proposal without anything else. With the right evaluation of uncertain evidences, decision making with uncertain evidences is considered, which is also completely done within our proposal. Examples in the paper are comprehensively exhibited, which show that our proposal is reasonable and can be implemented by computers.

Key words: Reasoning under Uncertainty, Decision Support Systems

1. INTRODUCTION

In this paper we propose an auto-decision making system which is based on the knowledge we have and entirely formulized within the classical logic. Also the proposal in the paper can completely be implemented by computers.

The "decision making" problem can be described as following: We have a problem p, which could be our goal, or a difficulty we have to overcome. To reach our goal or overcome the difficulty, we have a few choices $c_1, \dots,$

c_n, which are supposed to be the possible solutions on the problem. The decision making problem is to find the best solution from the choice set $C = \{c_1; :::; c_n\}$.

In literature a number of research papers have been published in the area of decision making. Many of them use probability theory to work in this area, but probability is not always reliable in our practice. So other approaches are desirable.

From our view point, the knowledge on the problem *p* is often more reliable than experiments or past experiences, so we attempt to use it in our proposal. To this end, let us take a look at what we should do when we have to make a decision.

Suppose we have a choice set $C = \{c_1; :::; c_n\}$ and we have to make a decision for the problem *p*. As the result of our decision is about what will happen in the future and all the knowledge we have is about what have already happened by now, there are always uncertainties on what will exactly happen. This makes decision making di±cult. To reach the best solution a common way often taken by experts is:

i) gather information on the problem as complete as possible;

ii) make "what ... if ..." analysis for every $c_i \in C$ based on the knowledge gathered, i.e. use the knowledge we have in the specific area and the information gathered to see what advantages we can have from c_i for each c_i;

iii) compare the results of the above analysis for all c_i, and take the one as the decision which can bring us the most advantages than all others in *C*.

We will describe such a process formally and develop a method to select the best choice from the choice set C: For this purpose, a few notions are essential. First we have to have knowledge in the specific field in which the problem p is involved. Then we need information on p, which is called evidence in this paper. These knowledge and evidences can usually be formulized into a first order logical system. So in this paper we develop our proposal within a first order reasoning system and divide the axiom set of the first order reasoning system into two parts: the corpus of knowledge and the evidence set, for convenience.

References

[1].Doyle, J., Maintenance and Belief Revision, in Belief Revision, Ed. by P. G¨ardenfors, Cambridge University Press, 1992.

[2].Kanal, L., Lemmer, J.F., Uncertainty in Artificial Intelligence, North-Holland, Amsterdam, New York, Oxford, Tokyo, 1986.

[3].Zhou, Q., The Concept of Uncertain Reasoning and its Supporting Degree, Intelligent Systems,Proceedings of the ISCA 9th International Conference, 2000.

[4].Russell, S., Norvig, P. Artificial Intelligence - A Modern Approach, Chapter 16 "Making Simple Decisions", Prentice Hall, 1995.

APPLICATION OF PARTICLE SWARM OPTIMIZATION TO THE MIXED DISCRETE NON-LINEAR PROBLEMS

Satoshi KitaYama, Koetsu Yamazaki, Masao Arakawa
Dept. of Human & Mechanical Systems Engineering, Kanazawa University
2-40-20, Kodatsuno, Kanazawa, 920-8667, Japan
kitagon@t.kanazawa-u.ac.jp

Abstract: Particle Swarm Optimization is applied to the mixed discrete non-linear problems (MDNLP). PSO is mainly a method to find a global or quasi-minimum for a non-convex optimization problem of continuous design variables. To handle the discrete design variables, penalty function is introduced. By using penalty function, it is possible to treat all design variables as the continuous design variables. Through typical structural optimization problem, the validity of proposed approach for MDNLP is examined.

Key words: Particle Swarm Optimization, Global Optimization, Mixed Discrete Non-Linear Problems, Penalty Function Approach

1. INTRODUCTION

Particle Swarm Optimization (PSO), which mimics the social behavior, is an optimization technique developed by Kennedy et al [1]. It has been reported that PSO is suitable for the non-convex function of the continuous design variables. Few researches of PSO have been reported, with regard to the discrete design variables problems [2], [3]. These researches handle the discrete design variables as the continuous design variables, directly. That is, firstly all design variables may be considered as the continuous design variables. After optimum is calculated, the round-off or cut-off techniques are used. However some problems are included into these approaches. (See Fig.1 (a), (b))

Fig.1 (a) shows a case by the round-off. Point A and B represents the discrete design variables. In this case, Point B is chosen as the neighborhood of x_L by the round-off. However, the objective function at Point B makes a change for the worse, compared with the objective function at Point A[4].

Another case shown in Fig.1 (b) is well known. That is, all constraints are not satisfied by the round-off or the cut-off. [5]

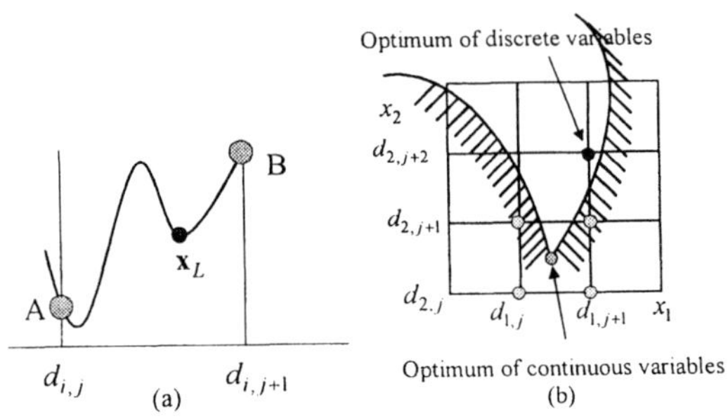

Fig.1 Optimum nature of discrete optimization

We consider that all design variables should be handled as the continuous design variables when we apply PSO to the discrete design variables problems. That is, the discrete design variables should be transformed into the continuous design variable by any methods [6].

In this paper, penalty function approach for the discrete design variables is used. By using penalty function, it is possible to handle the discrete design variables as the continuous design variables. The validity of proposed approach is examined through typical benchmark problem.

2. PARTICLE SWARM OPTIMIZATION

Particle Swarm Optimization (PSO), which is one of the meta-heuristic methods, is developed for the non-convex function of continuous design variables, and PSO does not utilize the gradient information of function like Genetic Algorithm (GA). In the PSO, each particle updates their position and velocity by a simple addition and subtraction of vector during search process, and finally some particles find global or quasi-optimum. Some models of PSO have been proposed. Among of them, most popular model may be called g-best model [7].

The position and velocity of particle d are represented by $\boldsymbol{x}_d^k$ and $\boldsymbol{v}_d^k$, respectively. k represents k-th iteration. The position and velocity of particle d at k+1 iteration are calculated by the following equations.

$$\boldsymbol{x}_d^{k+1} = \boldsymbol{x}_d^k + \boldsymbol{v}_d^{k+1} \tag{1}$$

$$\boldsymbol{v}_d^{k+1} = w\boldsymbol{v}_d^k + c_1 r_1(\boldsymbol{p}_d^k - \boldsymbol{x}_d^k) + c_2 r_2(\boldsymbol{p}_g^k - \boldsymbol{x}_d^k) \tag{2}$$

In Eq.(2), w is called as inertia term. c_1 and c_2 are parameters. r_1 and r_2 are random number between [0,1]. c_1=c_2=2 are often used[7]. $\boldsymbol{p}_d^k$, which is called as p-best, represents the best position of particle d till k-th iteration, and $\boldsymbol{p}_g^k$, which is called as g-best, represents the best position in the swarm till k-th iteration. The inertia term in Eq. (2) gradually decreases as follow.

$$w = w_{\max} - (w_{\max} - w_{\min}) / k_{\max} \times k \tag{3}$$

In Eq. (3), $w_{\max}$ and $w_{\min}$ represent the maximum and minimum value of inertia, respectively. $w_{\max} = 0.9$ and $w_{\min} = 0.4$ are generally recommended[8].

3. MDNLP BY PARTICLE SWARM OPTIMIZATION

3.1 Problem definition

In general, the Mixed Discrete Non-Linear Problem (MDNLP) is described as follow. [6]

$$f(\boldsymbol{x}) \rightarrow \min \tag{4}$$

$$x_{i,L} \le x_i \le x_{i,U} \quad i = 1, 2, \cdots, m \tag{5}$$

$$x_j \in D_j \quad D_j(d_{j,1}, d_{j,2}, \cdots, d_{j,q}) \quad j = 1, 2, \cdots, n \tag{6}$$

$$g_k(\boldsymbol{x}) \le 0 \quad k = 1, 2, \cdots, ncon \tag{7}$$

where $\boldsymbol{x}$ represents the design variables, which consist of the continuous and discrete design variables. $f(\boldsymbol{x})$is the objective function to be minimized, and $g_k(\boldsymbol{x})$ is the behavior constraints. $ncon$ is the number of behavior constraints. x_i represents the continuous design variables, and m is the number of continuous design variables. $x_{i,L}$ and $x_{i,U}$ denote the lower and upper bound of continuous design variables. On the other hand, x_j represents the discrete design variables, and n is the number of discrete design variables. D_j is the set of discrete values for the j-th discrete design variables. $d_{i,j}$ is the j-th discrete value for the i-the discrete design variables. q represents the number of discrete values. The lower and upper bound of the discrete design variables is given by $d_{j,1}$ and $d_{j,q}$, respectively.

3.2 Penalty function

In this paper, the following penalty function is used. [9]

$$\phi(\boldsymbol{x}) = \sum_{i=1}^{n} \frac{1}{2} \left[\sin \frac{2\pi \{x_i - 0.25(d_{i,j+1} + 3d_{i,j})\}}{d_{i,j+1} - d_{i,j}} + 1 \right] \tag{8}$$

where $d_{i,j}$ and $d_{i,j+1}$ represent the discrete design variables. x_i is the continuous design variables between $d_{i,j}$ and $d_{i,j+1}$. Then the augmented objective function is constructed as follow, by using above penalty function.

$$F(\boldsymbol{x}) = f(\boldsymbol{x}) + s\phi(\boldsymbol{x}) + r\sum_{k=1}^{ncon} \max[0, g_k(\boldsymbol{x})] \tag{9}$$

s in Eq.(9) denotes the penalty parameter for the penalty function of the discrete design variables, and r also denotes the penalty parameter for the penalty function of the behavior constraints. By using Eq. (8), it is possible to handle all design variables as the continuous design variables. MDNLP is transformed into the following problem.

$$F(\boldsymbol{x}) \rightarrow \min \tag{10}$$

$$x_{i,L} \leq x_i \leq x_{i,U} \quad i = 1, 2, \cdots, m \tag{11}$$

$$d_{j,1} \leq x_j \leq d_{j,q} \quad j = 1, 2, \cdots, n \tag{12}$$

In the following discussion design variables are sup[illegible]ed to be the discrete design variables for the simplicity. In the case of the mixed design variables, we discuss section 3.8.

3.3 Characteristics of penalty function

The value of penalty function of Eq. (8) is small at the neighborhood of discrete value. On the other hand, the value of penalty function of Eq. (8) is large, turning from discrete value. When $\boldsymbol{p}_g^k$, which represents the best value of the objective function in the swarm till the k-the iteration, satisfies the following equation, the discrete value resides in the neighborhood of $\boldsymbol{p}_g^k$.

$$\phi(\boldsymbol{p}_g^k) \leq \varepsilon \tag{13}$$

ε in Eq. (13) represents small positive value. As a result, we have to update the penalty parameter s for the discrete design variables in Eq. (9) until Eq. (13) is satisfied. In order to examine the effect of the penalty parameter s, let us consider a following simple problem.

$$f(x) = x^4 - \frac{8}{3}x^3 - 2x^2 + 8x \rightarrow \min \tag{14}$$

$$x = \{-1, 0, 1, 2\} \tag{15}$$

In this simple problem, objective $f(\boldsymbol{x})$ and augmented objective function $F(\boldsymbol{x})$ are shown in Fig. 3. Penalty parameter s in Fig. 3 is set as s=10.

From Fig.3, it is apparent that the augmented objective function becomes non-convex. As a result, to find optimum of the discrete design variables is transformed to finding global minimum of augmented objective function. Additionally, the discrete value is given by the point, at which the relative error becomes small between $f(\boldsymbol{x})$ and $F(\boldsymbol{x})$. Then we use the following equation as terminal criteria.

$$\frac{\left|F(\boldsymbol{p}_g^k)-f(\boldsymbol{p}_g^k)\right|}{\left|F(\boldsymbol{p}_g^k)\right|}\leq\varepsilon \tag{16}$$

Considered that PSO does not use the gradient information of function, it is difficult to satisfy Eq. (13) strictly. As a result, Eq. (16) is used.

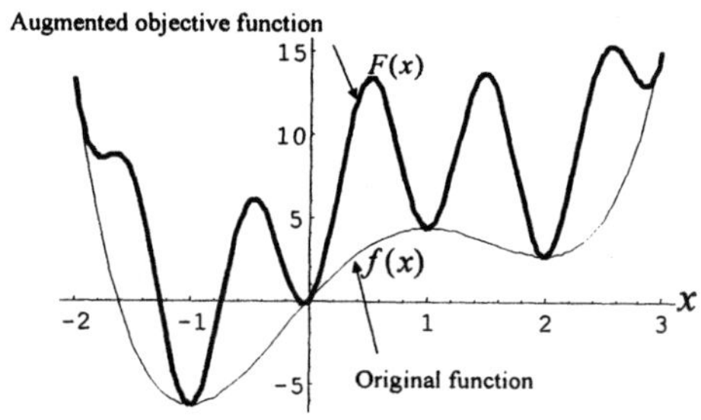

Fig. 3 Objective and augmented objective function

Behaviors of the augmented objective function for various penalty parameter s are shown in Fig. 4.

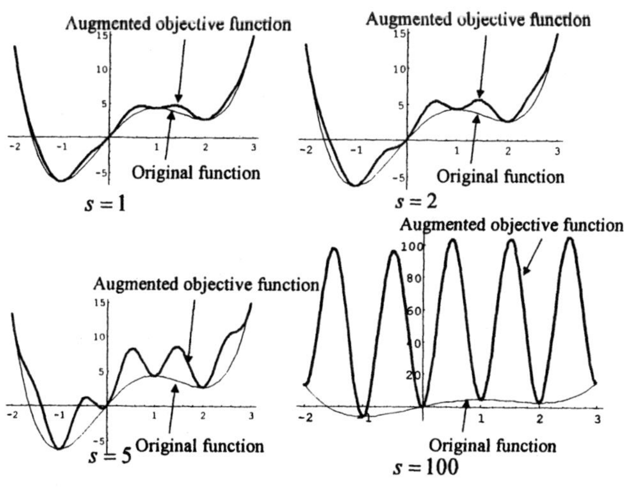

Fig. 4 Augmented objective function for various penalty parameters

3.4 Initial penalty parameter *s*

Penalty parameter s in Eq. (9) is determined as follows. Initial search point $\boldsymbol{x}_d$ of particle d is determined randomly. Then the value of penalty function represented by Eq. (8) is calculated to each particle.

$$s_d = 1+\phi(\boldsymbol{x}_d) \qquad d=1,2,\cdots,agent \tag{17}$$

where s_d represents the penalty parameter of particle *d*. *agent* is the number of particles. Initial penalty parameter $s_{initial}$ is determined as follow.

$$s_{initial} = \min\{s_1, s_2, \cdots, s_{agent}\} \tag{18}$$

At the initial stage to search optimum, we actively transform the augmented objective function into non-convex function. And local minima are generated at the neighborhood of discrete value.

3.5 Update of penalty parameter

Suppose that s^k denotes penalty parameter s at k-th iteration. Following equation is used to update penalty parameter s.

$$s^{k+1} = s^k \times \exp(1 + \phi(p_g^k)) \tag{19}$$

The behavior of the augmented objective function by updating penalty parameter s is shown in Fig.5. In Fig.5, solid line shows the augmented objective function at k-th iteration, and dot line shows the augmented objective function at k+1-th iteration.

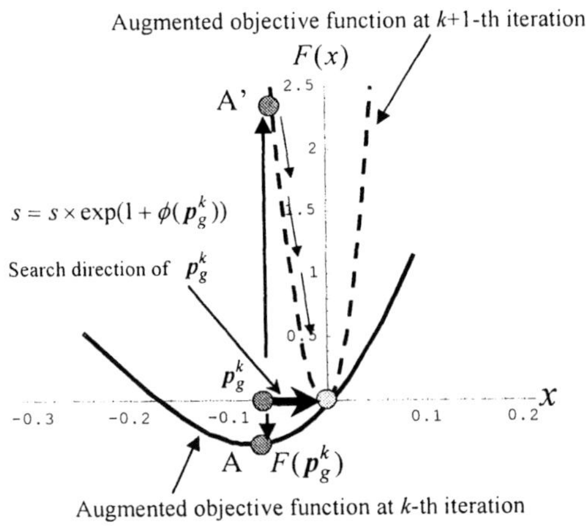

Fig. 5 Update of penalty parameter

As shown in Fig.5, an augmented objective function at k+1-th iteration becomes hard non-convex function, compared with an augmented objective function at k-th iteration. For example, A in Fig.5 corresponds to the point p_g^k at k-th iteration. By updating penalty parameter s, p_g^k corresponds to the point A' on the dot line, which represents the augmented objective function at k+1-th iteration. As a result, it is expected that p_g^k moves to the direction in Fig. 5. Finally, it is also expected that p_g^k will satisfy Eq. (16).

3.6 Initialization of penalty parameter

When Eq. (16) is satisfied, the discrete value around the neighborhood of p_g^k resides. Then in order to find another discrete value, initial penalty parameter obtained by Eq. (18) is utilized. This is because the augmented objective function becomes hard non-convex function, by updating penalty parameter s. As a result, it is considered that p_g^k fail to escape from local minimum. For such occasions, we relax the augmented objective function by initializing penalty parameter when p_g^k which satisfies Eq. (16) can be obtained. As a result, it is expected that p_g^k can escape from local minimum.

3.7 Difference between traditional and proposed method

In this paper, the penalty function for the discrete design variables is the same as Shin et. al.[9]. However, its approach is very different. Shin et. al. searched optimum by handling all design variables as the continuous design variables at the initial search stage. In this stage, penalty parameter s in Eq. (9) is set as zero. Then the penalty function for the discrete design variables was introduced after optimum was obtained. This is because the augmented objective function becomes non-convex when penalty parameter s is introduced at the initial search stage.

On the other hand, we actively introduce the penalty parameter s at the initial search stage. Obviously the augmented objective function becomes non-convex function. However, this is not serious problem because PSO is applied to this non-convex augmented objective function. We also introduced the new update scheme of penalty parameter s, which was expressed by Eq. (19). In the past researches [5], [9], the constant positive number is used to update the penalty parameter. This means the update scheme of penalty parameter depends on the problem. However, the penalty parameter s always changes in our approach. This is because the value of the penalty function $\phi(p_g^k)$ is utilized. Finally, we newly introduced the initialization of the penalty parameter s. By initializing the penalty parameter s, it is possible to relax the augmented objective function. As a result, it is expected that p_g^k can escape from local minimum.

3.8 In the case of mixed design variables

In case of mixed design variables, component of p_g^k can be expressed as follow.

$$p_g^k = (x^{cont}, x^{discrt})^T \tag{20}$$

where x^{cont} represents the components of the continuous design variables, and x^{discrt} also represents the components of the discrete design variables. Then, the components of the continuous design variables x^{cont} in p_g^k are neglected when we consider the terminal criteria given by Eq. (16). That is, only the components of the discrete design variables x^{discrt} in p_g^k are considered when we consider the terminal criteria by Eq. (16).

4. ALGORITHM

The algorithm of PSO for MDNLP is described.

(STEP1) Number of particles, and maximum search iteration k_{max} are determined. Set k=1. (k represents iteration) Set initial position and velocity of each particle, randomly.

(STEP2) Calculate the value of penalty function by Eq. (8) for each particle.

(STEP3) Calculate the penalty parameter s for each particle, using Eq. (17).

(STEP4) Initial penalty parameter $s_{initial}$ is determined by using Eq. (18).

(STEP5) Calculate the augmented objective function for each particle.

(STEP6) Calculate g-best and p-best.

(STEP7) Check the terminal criteria by Eq. (16). If Eq. (16) is satisfied, the penalty parameter s is initialized. Otherwise the penalty parameter s is updated by Eq. (19).

(STEP8) The inertia term is updated by Eq. (3).

(STEP9) The velocity and position is updated by using Eq.(1) and Eq.(2).

(STEP10) Iteration is increased as $k= k+1$.

(STEP11) Check the iteration. If $k \le k_{max}$, go to STEP 2. Otherwise, the algorithm will terminate by considering $\boldsymbol{p}_g^k$ as optimum.

5. OPTIMUM DESIGN OF PRESSURE VESSEL

Let us consider the optimum design of pressure vessel as shown in Fig.6. This problem is one of the most famous MDNLP, and many researches have been done [10-15]. Several results are shown in Table 1. From Table 1, it is considered that it is very difficult to find optimum solution though this problem consists of only 4 design variables.

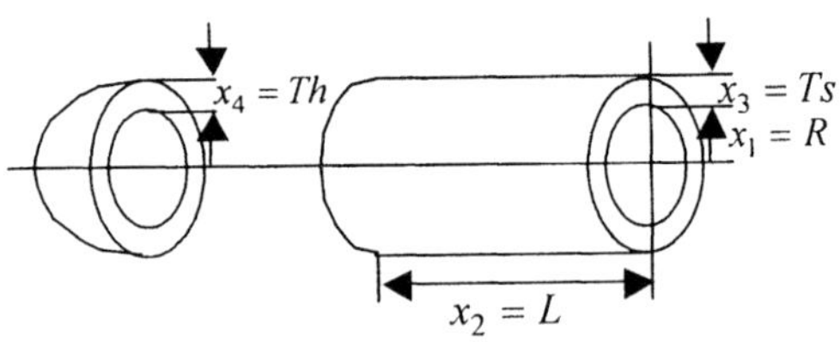

Fig.6 Optimum design of pressure vessel

Design variables are 1) Radii R (continuous design variables), 2) Length L (continuous design variables), 3) Thickness Ts (discrete design variables), and 4) Thickness Th (discrete design variables). Objective function is to minimize the cost, and is given as follow.

$$f(\boldsymbol{x}) = 0.6224x_1x_2x_3 + 1.7781x_1^2x_4 + 3.1661x_2x_3^2 + 19.84x_1x_3^2 \to \min \quad (21)$$

On the other hand, behavior and side constraints are given as follows.

$$25 \le x_1 \le 150 \tag{22}$$
$$25 \le x_2 \le 240 \tag{23}$$
$$0.0625 \le x_3, x_4 \le 1.25 \tag{24}$$
$$g_1(\boldsymbol{x}) = 0.0193 x_1 / x_3 - 1 \le 0 \tag{25}$$
$$g_2(\boldsymbol{x}) = 0.00954 x_1 / x_4 - 1 \le 0 \tag{26}$$
$$g_3(\boldsymbol{x}) = x_2 / 240 - 1 \le 0 \tag{27}$$
$$g_4(\boldsymbol{x}) = \left(1296000 - \frac{4}{3}\pi x_1^3\right) \Big/ \pi x_1^2 x_2 - 1 \le 0 \tag{28}$$

x_3 and x_4 are discrete design variables, and are integer multiples of 0.00625 inch. Behavior constraints from Eq. (25) to Eq. (28) are handled as penalty function as shown in Eq. (9). $r = 1.0 \times 10^8$ is used.

The number of particle is set as 100, and the number of maximum search iteration is set as 5000. 10 trials are performed with different random seed. The best result during 10 trials is shown in Table 1.

Table 1 Comparison of results

	Sandgren [11]	Qian [12]	Kannan [10]	Hsu [13]	Lewis [14]	Kitayama	Arakawa [15]
R[inch]	47.000	58.312	58.291	N/A	38.760	38.684	38.858
L[inch]	117.701	44.522	43.690	N/A	223.299	224.096	221.402
Ts[inch]	1.125	1.125	1.125	N/A	0.750	0.750	0.750
Th[inch]	0.625	0.625	0.625	N/A	0.375	0.375	0.375
g1	-0.194	0.000	0.000	N/A	-0.003	-0.004	0.000
g2	-0.283	-0.110	-0.110	N/A	-0.014	-0.016	-0.011
g3	-0.510	-0.814	-0.818	N/A	-0.070	-0.066	-0.078
g4	0.054	-0.021	-1.109	N/A	-1.519	0.000	0.000
Objective[$]	8129.800	7238.830	7198.200	7021.670	5980.950	5875.254	5850.770

6. CONCLUSIONS

In this paper PSO is applied to MDNLP. Penalty function has been introduced, in order to handle the discrete design variables. To utilize penalty function, it is possible to handle all design variables as the continuous design variables. The augmented objective function becomes non-convex function, by introducing penalty function. Considering that PSO is naturally suitable for the non-convex function of the continuous design variables, the penalty function approach may be valid. Additionally, we proposed how to determine the penalty parameter for the penalty function of the discrete design variables. Through typical benchmark problem, the validity has been examined.

ACKNOWLEDGEMENT

Authors would like to say many thanks to Prof. H. Yamakawa, (Waseda University in Japan), and Prof. H. Nakayama (Konan University in Japan), who gave us the useful and contributive comments.

REFERENCES

1. Kennedy, J., Eberhart, R.C., "*Swarm Intelligence*", Morgan Kaufmann Publishers, (2001).
2. Venter, G., Sobieski, J.S., "*Particle Swarm Optimization*", 9-th AIAA/USAF/NASA/ISSMO Symposium on Multidisciplinary Analysis and Optimization Conference, (2002), AIAA2002-1235.
3. Venter G., Sobieski J.S., "*Multidisciplinary Optimization of a Transport Aircraft Wing using Particle Swarm Optimization*", 9-th AIAA/USAF/NASA/ISSMO Symposium on Multidisciplinary Analysis and Optimization Conference, (2002), AIAA2002-5644.
4. Rao, S.S, "Engineering Optimization Theory and Practice", Wiley InterScience, (1996).
5. Fu, J.F, Fenton, R.G., Cleghorn, W.L, "*A Mixed Integer-Discrete Continuous Programming and its Application to Engineering Design Optimization*", Engineering Optimization, (1991), Vol. 17, pp.263-280.
6. Arora J.S, Huang M.W., "*Methods for Optimization of Nonlinear Problems with Discrete Variables: A Review*" ,Structural Optimization, (1994), 8, pp.69-85.
7. Parsopoulos, K.E., Vrahatis, M.N., "*Recent Approaches to Global Optimization Problems through Particle Swarm Optimization*", Natural Computing, (2002), Vol.1, pp.235-306.
8. Fukuyama, Y., "*A Particle Swarm Optimization for Reactive Power and Voltage Control Considering Voltage Security Assessment*", IEEE Trans. Power Syst., (2000), Vol.15-4, pp-1232-1239.
9. Shin, D.K, Gurdal, Z, Griffin O.H., "*A Penalty Approach for Nonlinear Optimization with Discrete Design Variables*", Engineering Optimization, (1990), Vol.16, pp-29-42.
10. Kannan, B.K., Kramer, S.N., "*An Augmented Lagrange Multiplier Based Method for Mixed Integer Discrete Continuous Optimization and Its Applications to Mechanical Design*", Journal of Mechanical Design, (1994), Vol.116, pp.405-411.
11. Sandgren,E., "*Nonlinear and Discrete Programming in Mechanical Design Optimization*", Journal of Mechanical Design, (1990), Vol.112, pp.223-229.
12. Qian, Z., Yu, J., Zhou, J., "*A Genetic Algorithm for Solving Mixed Discrete Optimization Problems*", DE-Vol.65-1, Advances in Design Automation, (1993), 1, pp.499-503.
13. Hsu Y.H., Sun, T.L.,Leu, LH., "*A Two Stage Sequential Approximation Method for Non-linear Discrete Variable Optimization*", ASME/DETC/DAC MA, (1995), pp.197-202
14. Lewis, K., and Mistree, F., "*Foraging-Directed Adaptive Liner Programming: An Algorithm for Solving Nonlinear Mixed Discrete/Continuous Design Problems*", ASME/DETC/DAC, (1996), Paper No. 1601, in CD-ROM.
15. Arakawa, M., Hagiwara, I., "*Nonlinear Integer Discrete and Continuous Optimization Using Adaptive Range Genetic Algorithm*", ASME/DETC/DAC, (1997), Paper No. 3728, in CD-ROM.

DESIGN AND IMPLEMENT COST-SENSITIVE EMAIL FILTERING ALGORITHMS

Wenbin Li[1,2], Chunnian Liu[1] and Yiying Chen[2]
1. Beijing University of Technology, Beijing 100022,China
2. ShiJiaZhuang University of Economics,ShiJiaZhuang 050031,China

Abstract: The growing problem of unsolicited bulk e-mail, also known as "spam", has generated a need for reliable anti-spam e-mail filters. We introduce seven filtering algorithms: Naive Bayesian (NB), Decision Tree (DT), AdaBoost, ANN, SVM, VSM and KNN. Design considerations and implementation issues of these filters are discussed, such as how to get cost-sensitive NB, SVM, VSM, KNN. Using two relatively large amounts of real personal E-mail data, a comprehensive comparative study based on a cost-sensitive measure we approved was conducted using above seven filters. The study includes the effect of feature subset size, training-corpus distribution, issues that have not been explored in previous experiments. The comparative results show that cost-sensitive filters such as NB, SVM, VSM and KNN have fewer count of misclassifying legitimate when relative parameters, feature subset size and training dataset's distribution are reasonable.

Key words: Spam E-mail, E-mail Filter, Cost-Sensitive

1. INTRODUCTION

It's known that spam Emails has generated a need for reliable anti-spam email filters. Filtering spam-email is a problem of text categorization (TC), it's said that it's the problem of automatically assigning predefined categories {spam, legitimate} to new emails [11]. So many researches addressed email filtering by casting it in the general framework of TC. However, email filtering is different from TC. Firstly, mistakenly treating a legitimate message as spam can be a more severe error than treating a spam message as legitimate, so filter should take this unbalanced misclassification cost into account. Secondly, the main barrier to seeing automated mail filtering becoming commonplace is the resolution issues regarding the implementation of mail filters and their integration into e-mail clients [4, 8]. Some of the important issues regarding mail filters include speed efficiency, database size and the collection of supervised training data. Time-consuming training or classification can degrade the interface. A large database to store the classification model may limit the user base. Also, a mail filter is only likely to be used if no additional effort is required to reap the benefits.

This paper is a comprehensive comparative study of email filtering algorithms. The focus is on cost-sensitive evaluation and effecting issues of filters. Seven methods were evaluated, including Naive Bayesian (NB),Decision Tree (DT), AdaBoost, Artificial Neural Network (ANN), Support Vector Machine (SVM), Vector Space Model (VSM) and K-Nearest Neighbor (KNN). In fact, some researches have done such works before [2, 9], but their studies are not full-scale on the one hand, on another hand, they didn't discuss specified problems in email filter.

The remainder of the paper is organized as follows. Section 2 discusses benchmark corpus and cost-sensitive evaluating measures. Section 3 presents our design and implementation of above seven filters. The experiments and results are presented in Section 4. Section 5 concludes the paper.

2. CORPUS, COST-SENSITIVE EVALUATING METHOD

Research on text categorization has benefited significantly from the existence of publicly available, manually categorized document collections, like the Reuters corpus, that have been used as standard benchmarks. Producing similar corpora for anti-spam filtering is more complicated, because of privacy issues. Publicizing spam messages does not pose a problem, since spam messages are distributed blindly to very large numbers of recipients, and, hence, they are effectively already publicly available. Legitimate messages, however, in general cannot be released without violating the privacy of their recipients and senders.

One way to bypass privacy problems is to experiment with legitimate messages collected from freely accessible newsgroups, or mailing lists with public archives. Ling-Spam, the earliest of our benchmark corpora, follows this approach. It consists of 481 spam messages received by the first author, and 2412 legitimate messages retrieved from the archives of the Linguist list, a moderated and, hence, spam-free list about linguistics. The SpamAssassin public mail corpus is similar to Ling-Spam, in that its legitimate messages are publicly available. It contains 1897 spam and 4150 legitimate messages, the latter collected from public fora or donated by users with the understanding that they may be made public. An alternative solution, adopted in pu1, is to release benchmark corpora that each consists of messages received by a particular user, after replacing each token by a unique number throughout the corpus.The mapping between tokens and numbers is not released, making it extremely difficult to recover the original text. PU1 contains 480 spam and 610 legitimate messages.

Table 1. Cost Matrix

	Actual Legitimate	Actual Spam
Predict Legitimate	c_{00}	c_{01}
Predict Spam	c_{10}	c_{11}

Table 2. Contingency Table

	Actual Legitimate	Actual Spam
Predict Legitimate	f_{00}	f_{01}
Predict Spam	f_{10}	f_{11}

This paper used Ling-Spam, PU1 as experimental data set. (downloaded from http://www.mlnet.org/cgi-bin/mlnetois.pl/?File=datasets.html).

Becaue email filtering is a cost-sensitive classification decisions with two-class, so PRECISION and RECALL can't reflect efficiency a filter h well and truly, because between high precision and high recall exists a trade-off. So we define the "Spam ->Legitimate Error Rate" SLER(h) and "Legitimate -> Spam Error Rate" LSER(h) of a filter h as follows:

$$SLER(h) = c_{01} * f_{01} /(c_{01} * f_{01} + f_{11}) \quad (1)$$

$$LSER(h) = c_{10} * f_{10} /(c_{10} * f_{10} + f_{00}) \quad (2)$$

"Error Rate" ER(h) and "Correct Rate" CR(h) are:

$$ER(h)=SLER(h)+LSER(h) \quad (3)$$

$$CR(h)=2-ER(h) \quad (4)$$

Here, c_{01}, c_{10} is give in cost matrix shown as Table 1. Parameters f_{01}, f_{01}, f_{00}, f_{11} is given in Table 2 which provides a convenient display of the prediction behavior for Email filtering. Each cell of table 2 represents of the four possible outcomes of a prediction for an example. The diagonal cells count how often the prediction was correct. The off-diagonal entries show the frequency of prediction errors. The sum of all cells equals the total number of predictions.

3. DESIGN AND IMPLEMENT COST-SENSITIVE FILTERS

The following lists the basic design decisions for the experiments in this paper.

- Words are chosen as the basic representational units. Words are defined as non-whitespace strings enclosed by whitespace characters.

- Only those words occurring in the training data are considered as potential features. And feature selection method is Information Gain(IG)[10].
- Stemming, stopwords is not used.
- NB, DT, AdaBoost, ANN, and SVM use the binary vector representation, while KNN and VSM adopt TF-IDF [6] vector representation.

3.1 NB

Given a new (unseen) document d, C= {c_0 = "legitimate", c_1 = "spam"}, classification of d is performed by computing the posterior probability of each class, given d, by applying Bayes' rule:

$$P(c_j \mid d;\theta) = P(c_j \mid \theta)P(d \mid c_j;\theta) / P(d \mid \theta) \tag{5}$$

The classifier simply selects the class with the highest posterior probability. Note that P(d|b_) is the same for all classes, thus d can be classified by computing:

$$c_d = \arg\max_{c_j \in C} P(c_j \mid \theta)P(d \mid c_j;\theta) \tag{6}$$

By making the Naive Bayes assumption, we can compute the probability of a document given a class from the probabilities of the words given the class [1] (V is feature set, $B_i \in \{0,1\}$ indicates whether word w_i occurs at least once in d):

$$P(d \mid c_j;\theta) = \prod_{i=1}^{|V|}(B_i P(w_i \mid c_j;\theta) + (1 - B_i)(1 - P(w_i \mid c_j;\theta))) \tag{7}$$

Here, $P(w_i|c_j;\theta)$ can be estimated as the fraction of training documents in c_j that contain w_i(D={d_1, ..., d_m} is the set of training emails):

$$P(w_i \mid c_j;\theta) = \prod_{i=1}^{|V|} \frac{\sum_{K=1}^{|D|} B_{ik} P(c_j \mid d_k)}{\sum_{k=1}^{|D|} P(c_j \mid d_k)} \tag{8}$$

And $P(c_j \mid \theta)$ are estimated as the fraction of training documents in c_j:

$$P(c_j \mid \theta) = \frac{\sum_{K=1}^{|D|} P(c_j \mid d_k)}{|D|} \tag{9}$$

NOTE: In order to get cost-sensitive NB, we think d is a spam if and only if $P(c_1 \mid d;\theta) / P(c_1 \mid d;\theta) + P(c_0 \mid d;\theta) > 0.99$, or else d is a legitimate mail.

3.2 DT and AdaBoost

Decision tree is a widely used data mining technique for classification and prediction. C4.5, a typical and effective method of building decision trees, was used in our work to build a Email filter. It's used with the default parameter settings and with rule post-pruning turned on. **NOTE:** DT algorithm is not easy to handle a large number of textual features. A straightforward way is to limit the number of textual features that are considered by the filter when a tree is built.

The purpose of boosting is to find a highly accurate classification rule by combining many weak hypotheses (assume it's h_t, 1<=t<=T), each of which may be only moderately accurate. It's assumed the existence of a separate procedure called the"Weak Learner" for acquiring the weak hypotheses. The boosting algorithm finds a set of weak hypotheses by calling the "Weak Learner" repeatedly in a series of T rounds. These weak hypotheses are then linearly combined into a single rule called the combined hypothesis (assume it's H). AdaBoost takes as input a training set $(x_1,c_1),\ldots,(x_n,c_n)$ where $x_n \in X$, and $c_i \in C=\{c_0=\text{"legitimate"}, c_1=\text{"spam"}\}$, its output is:

$$H(x) = sign(\sum_{t=1}^{T} a_t(h_t(x))) \quad (10)$$

H is a weight majority vote of the T weak hypotheses where α_t is the weight assigned to h_t, [5] discussed many methods for choosing α_t. **NOTE:** The "Weaker Learner" in our implementation is DT algorithm. The maximum depth of the DT is limited to one ten of the total number of frequent words.

3.3 ANN and SVM

This paper implements the back propagation ANN algorithm [7].The following lists main implemented details:

- Network has 3 layers: 1) Input layer: node number is ||V||+1 (V is feature subset); 2) Hidden layer: node number is half of input nodes; 3)Output Layer: only one node.
- We use sigmoid function as the activation function both in hidden layer and output layer.

Support vector machines are well founded from Statistical Learning Theory. They minimize the structural risk, instead of empirical risk as in most learning methods. SVM makes no assumptions of the distribution of the data. Support vector machines have been proven to be a very powerful classification method for high dimensional data set, e.g. in hand-written digits recognition, face recognition, object recognition and so on. In its simplest linearly separable case, a support vector machine is a hyperplane that separates a set of positive examples and negative examples correctly. Support vector machine can be generalized to linearly no separable case via introducing the concept of "soft-margin"; and constructs nonlinear classifiers via kernel functions. Kernel functions map the training examples into a higher dimensional feature space and SVM constructs a optimal separating hyper plane in the higher dimensional feature space that is corresponding to a nonlinear classifier in the input space. Examples of kernel functions are polynomials, Gaussian, and Radial Basis Functions. In experiments of this paper, we choose polynomials function.

In our application, we would like to penalize errors on legitimate examples stronger than errors on spam examples. This can be achieved using cost factors c_{10} and c_{01} to adjust the cost of false legitimate mails vs. false spam mails. Such cost factors can be directly incorporated into the SVM [3]. **NOTE:** In our experiments, we adopt $c_{10} = 1.5$ and $c_{01} = 0.5$.

3.4 KNN and VSM

Let χ be a set. We define:

DEFINE 0. For every email $x \in \chi$, a vector representation $\vec{x} = \langle w_1', w_2', \ldots w_{\|V\|}' \rangle$, where w_i' is the value of feature f_i, it's computed as follows (tf_i is the number of times feature f_i occurs in x, N is the total number of emails in corpus, N_i is total number of emails f_i appears in):

$$w_i' = tf_i * \log(N / N_i + \alpha) \tag{11}$$

We normalize $\vec{x} = \langle w_1', w_2', \ldots w_{\|V\|}' \rangle$ as follow:

$$\langle w_1, \ldots, w_{\|V\|} \rangle = \langle w_1', \ldots, w_{\|V\|}' \rangle / (\max(w_1', \ldots, w_{\|V\|}') * \sum_{j=1}^{\|V\|} w_j'^2) \tag{12}$$

For $x,y \in \chi$, assume $\vec{x} = \langle w_{x1}', w_{x2}', \ldots w_{x\|V\|}' \rangle$ and $\vec{y} = \langle w_{y1}, w_{y2}, \ldots, w_{y\|V\|} \rangle$, distance between x and y is:

$$D(x,y) = \sum_{i=1}^{\|V\|} (w_{xi} * w_{yi}) / \sqrt{\sum_{i=1}^{\|V\|} w_{xi}^2 \sum_{i=1}^{\|V\|} w_{yi}^2} \tag{13}$$

DEFINE 2. $D(\bullet,\bullet) : \chi \times \chi -> IR$ is a distance if, $\forall$ X, Z $\in \chi$: D(X,Z) ≥ 0, D(X, Z)=D(Z,X) and D(X,Z) $\leq$ D(X,V)+D(V,Z).

DEFINE 3. A metric space is a pair $(\chi, D(\bullet,\bullet))$, where χ is a distance on χ.

Let $\Gamma = (x_1, c_1), \ldots, (x_n, c_n)$ be a training set, $x_i \in X$, $X \in$ separable metric space χ, $c_i \in C = \{c_0 = \text{"spam"}, c_1 = \text{"legitimate"}\}$. Assume x is a sample to be labeled, let $(x_1', c_1'), \ldots, (x_n', c_n'))$ be the training samples arranged in increasing order of distance from X, we assign class c_j' to x, where

$$j' = \arg\max_{j} \sum_{i=1}^{k} 1_{c_i' = j'} \tag{14}$$

NOTE: In order to get cost-sensitive KNN, we can do that: In the k nearest neighbors of x, there are a spam mails and b legitimate mails, if and only if a/(a+b)> λ (λ = 0.99), we think x is a spam.

The VSM algorithm is very simple as well as effective. Let $X_0 = \{ \vec{x}_{01},\ldots,\vec{x}_{0m} \}$ be vector set of the legitimate training data, $X_1 = \{ \vec{x}_{10},\ldots,\vec{x}_{1m} \}$ be vector set of the spam training data. We can get centric vector $\vec{c}_{x_0}$ of X_0:

$$\vec{c}_{x_0} = \sum_{i=1}^{m} \vec{x}_{0i} / m \tag{15}$$

Similarly, we can get centric vector $\vec{c}_{x_1}$ of X_1. Let $\vec{x} = \{w_1,\ldots,w_{\|V\|}\}$ is a sample to be classified, we compute $D(\vec{x},\vec{c}_{x_1})$ and $D(\vec{x},\vec{c}_{x_1})$, if $D(\vec{x},\vec{c}_{x_1})$ > $D(\vec{x},\vec{c}_{x_1})$, we think $\vec{x}$ is "spam", else $\vec{x}$ is "legitimate". **NOTE:** In fact, in order to get cost-sensitive VSM algorithm, we can classify $\vec{x}$ into "spam" if and only if $D(\vec{x},\vec{c}_{x_1})$ - $D(\vec{x},\vec{c}_{x_1}) > \lambda$. However, it's difficult to specify the value of λ, so we classify $\vec{x}$ into "spam" if and only if $D(\vec{x},\vec{c}_{x_1})$ / ($D(\vec{x},\vec{c}_{x_1})$ + $D(\vec{x},\vec{c}_{x_1})$) $> \lambda$ ($\lambda = 0.6$)

*Table 3. Effect of varying the size of feature subset. Results1 for PU1 and Ling-Spam. *: Out of memory. @: Training time is too long (above 1 hours).x ratio of feature selection, y: size of feature subset. In each cell, a:b:c is result of a filter h, a is error count for loeitimate, b is error count for spam, c is value of ER(h).*

PU1					
Filter x(y)	0.05%(10)	0.25%(52)	0.5%(105)	1%(211)	2%(423)
NB	1:46:0.131	1:40:0.11	1:36:0.106	2:27:0.098	1:34:0.102
DT	83:2:0.496	33:13:0.33	14:9:0.170	11:12:0.15	*
AdaBoost	85:1:0.495	21:19:0.27	15:18:0.21	17:12:0.21	*
ANN	10:20:0.17	12:16:0.18	4:13:0.082	5:6:0.07	3:9:0.06
SVM	5:28:0.14	1:37:0.109	0:38:0.10	0:39:0.10	0:50:0.121
KNN(K=120	180:0:1	180:0:1	180:0:1	4:40:0.162	0:90:0.2
VSM	24:9:0.252	12:10:0.16	8:20:0.150	6:18:0.121	2:27:0.098
Ling-Spam					
Filter x(y)	0.05%(10)	0.25%(52)	0.5%(105)	1%(211)	2%(423)
NB	0:49:0.170	0:50:0.174	0:52:0.179	0:53:0.182	0:54:0.184
DT	22:23:0.35	2:15:0.087	*	*	*
AdaBoost	28:10:0.32	3:25:0.140	*	*	*
ANN	1:28:0.121	0:7:0.029	@	@	@
SVM	0:45:0.159	0:46:0.162	0:53:0.182	0:52:0.17	0:52:0.179
KNN(K=120	119:0:1	18:10:0.24	7:10:0.127	0:84:0.261	0:81:0.254
VSM	10:7:0.145	4:9:0.087	1:13:0.066	0:18:0.07	0:15:0.059

4. EXPERIMENTAL RESULTS

Table 3 shows the effect of varying the size of feature subset. We do experiments on PU1 and Ling-Spam dataset respectively. For PU1, we use 346 mails of spam and 430 examples of legitimate for training; testing mails of spam contain 134, non-spam testing mails contain 180. For Ling-Spam, count of training mails of spam is 357, count of legitimate mails for training is 2293; testing mails of spam and legitimate is 124 and 119.

Table 4. Effect of varying the count of training examples. Results for PU1 and Ling-Spam.: Out of memory. @: Training time is too long (above 1 hour). x0: training emails count of spam, y0: training emails count of legitimate, x1: testing emails count of spam, y1: testing emails count of legitimate, z: size of feature subset. In each cell, a:b:c is result of a filter h, a is error count for legitimate, b is error count for spam, c is value of ER(h). x0:y0:x1:z1(z) in each case is as follows: case 1: 10:430:134:180 (146) ,case 2: 100:430:134:180 (168); case 3: 200:430:134:180 (190); case 4: 346:430:134:180 (211); case 5: 346:10:134:180 (119); case 6:346:100:134:180 (144); case 7: 20:2293:124:119 (531); case 8: 100:2293:124:119 (542); case 9: 357:2293:124:119 (283); case 10: 357:357:124:119 (219); case 11: 357:10:124:119 (96); case 12: 357:100:124:119 (138)*

PU1						
Filter	Case 1	Case 2	Case 3	Case 4	Case 5	Case 6
NB	0:106:0.23	0:47:0.115	0:36:0.091	2:27:0.098	101:0:0.53	6:23:0.137
DT	2:90:0.266	5:35:0.161	13:28:0.23	11:12:0.15	134:2:0.63	32:7:0.297
AdaBoost	0:90:0.2	5:35:0.161	10:21:0.18	17:12:0.21	100:0:0.53	30:5:0.275
ANN	0:134:1	1:28:0.086	3:19:0.08	5:6:0.072	176:0:0.66	23:4:0.222
SVM	0:134:1	0:83:0.187	0:57:0.13	0:39:0.098	176:0:0.66	10:14:0.15
KNN	26:91:0.70 K=10	0:128:0.26 K=60	0:128:0.26 K=120	4:40:0.162 K=120	180:0:1 K=10	8:22:0.157 K=120
VSM	14:23:0.22	6:20:0.128	5:20:0.116	6:18:0.121	7:14:0.119	9:8:0.120

Ling-Spam						
Filter	Case 7	Case 8	Case 9	Case 10	Case 11	Case 12
NB	9:8:0.120	0:54:0.185	0:53:0.182	0:39:0.141	11:26:0.25	0:42:0.15
DT	*	*	*	2:12:0.075	95:2:0.579	9:80.139
AdaBoost	*	*	*	3:5:0.058	79:3:0.531	14:6:0.179
ANN	@	@	@	1:2:0.021	119:0:1	3:2:0.044
SVM	0:123:0.34	0:116:0.33	0:52:0.179	0:21:0.08	119:0:1	1:8:0.046
KNN	0:123:0.34 K=10	0:123:0.34 K=60	7:10:0.127 K=1	0:124:1 K=120	34:2:0.306 K=06	2:9:0.062 K=60
VSM	1:92:0.325	0:44:0.156	1:13:0.066	0:0:0	6:8:0.106	3:7:0.066

From table 3, we can see that: (1) Most filters's performance increase with an increasing size of feature subset; (2) When increase feature subset's size, cost-sensitive filters (SVM, NB, KNN, VSM) decrease the count of misclassifying legitimate (but increase the count of misclassifying spam sometimes), while DT, AdaBoost and ANN didn't have this characteristic; (3)DT, AdaBoost is not fit to large feature subset; (4)Although ANN has good performance, it's not available for email filtering because of its long training time. (5)Design of SLER(h), LSER(h) and ER(h) is reasonable, it reflect a filter's performance well and truly.

Table 4 shows the effect of varying the count of training examples. For PU1 and Ling-Spam dataset, we all select 1% features from original feature space. These results show us: (1)Filter h always errs in class _ with fewer training examples, because h know little information about ε ; (2)Most filters are very sensitive to unbalance dataset, while VSM is not so depend on dataset's distribution.

In addition, we investigated training time and filtering time of all filters. According to our all experiments, we sort these filters un-strictly: (1)Training time: {KNN} $\prec$ {NB, VSM} $\prec$ {SVM} $\prec$ {DT,AdaBoost}_{ANN}; (2)Testing time: {NB, SVM, VSM, ANN} $\prec$ {DT,AdaBoost} $\prec$ {KNN}.

5. CONCLUSION

Experiments suggest that our cost-sensitive evaluation method is good. The comparative results show that cost-sensitive filters we implemented such as NB, SVM, VSM and KNN have fewer count of misclassifying legitimate when relative parameters, feature subset size and training dataset's distribution are reasonable. It's noticeable that a filter with a low error rate on legitimate has high error rate on spam, so we will design a new method with low SLER(h) as well as low LSER(h) in the future.

ACKNOWLEDGEMENTS

(Partially) supported by the NSFC major research program: "Basic Theory and Core Techniques of Non-Canonical Knowledge" (60496322) .

REFERENCES

[1] A. McCallum and K. Nigam. A comparison of event models for naive bayes text classification. In M. Sahami, editor, Learning for Text Categorization: Proceedings of the 1998 AAAI/ICML Workshop, Madison, WI, 1998. AAAI Press, (1998) 41-48

[2] Androutsopoulos, I., Koutsias, J., Chandrinos, K. V., Spyropoulos, C. D. An Experimental Comparison of Naive Bayesian and Keyword-Based Anti-Spam Filtering with Personal E-mail Messages. Nicholas J. Belkin, Peter Ingwersen, Mun-Kew Leong.In Proc. of the 23 rd Annual International ACM SIGR Conference on Research and Development in Information Retrieval, Athens, Greece, 2000.ACM, (2000) 160-167

[3] Harris Drucker, Vladimir N. Vapnik, IEEE TRANSACTION ON NETWORK, VOL. 10.

NO. 5, SEPTEMBER 1999, Support Vector Machines for Spam Categorization

[4] Jason D. M. Rennie. ifile: An Application of Machine Learning to E-Mail Filtering. M. Grobelnik, D. Mladeni c, and N. Milic-Frayling.In Proc. KDD-2000 Text Mining Workshop, Boston, MA, USA,2000. University of Alberta,2000.

[5] Robert E. Schapire. Drifting games. Machine Learning. (June 2001) 43(3):265-291

[6] Thorsten Joachims. Learning to Classify Text Using Support Vector Machines.Kluwer Academic Publishers, (2001) 21-22

[7] T. M. Mitchell. Machine Learning. McGraw-Hill, 1997

[8] Wenbin Li, Ning zhong and Chunian Liu. Design and Implementation of an Email Classifier. 2nd International Conference on Active Media Technology, May 29-31, 2003. ACTIVE MEDAIA TECHNOLOGY, World Science, (2003) 423-430

[9] Y. Diao, H. Lu, and D. Wu. A Comparative Study of Classification Based Personal Email Filtering. Takao Terano, Huan Liu, Arbee L. P. Chen.In Proc. PAKDD-2000, Kyoto,Japan,2000.Springer, (2000) 408-419

[10] Yiming Yang and Jan O. Pedersen. 1997. A comparative study on feature selection in text categorization. In Proc. 14th International Conference on Machine Learning (ICML-97), 412C420

[11] Zhong, N., Matsunaga, T., Liu, C. A Text Mining Agents Based Architecture for Personal E-mail Filtering and Management, Proc. Third International Conference on Intelligent Data Engineering and Automated Learning (IDEAL 2002), LNCS 2412, Springer, 337-346.

FUZZY LOGIC MODEL FOR MULTI – PURPOSE MULTI - RESERVOIR SYSTEM

Mynepally.Anjaneya Prasad and S.Mohan

Environmental and Water Resources Division, Indian Institute of Technology Madras Chennai – 600 036 India

Abstract: Reservoirs are built usually to serve multiple purposes. viz. irrigation, municipal and industrial water supply, hydro-power and flood control. Due to high variability of annual rainfall and conflicting demands on scarce water resources, the study and operation of reservoir systems has assumed great significance to meet the short term and long-term requirements. The reservoir managers do not find previous techniques of complex optimization models are difficult to adopt practically. New methods have to be developed which are simple to understand and can be effectively adopted for the existing systems. Any reservoir problem is usually site specific in nature and hence any general modeling methodology cannot be directly applied to study the system behavior. Artificial intelligence approaches are now being adopted to effectively simulate the reservoir system based on the experience of human knowledge and expertise. These methods are simple to understand for the reservoir managers and also may be acceptable since the model is being developed with the output and opinion of experts who are really operating the reservoir system. The Fuzzy rule based systems are very much suitable for inferring developed operating policies. In the present work a rule based fuzzy model is attempted for long-term operation a multi reservoir system. The present model was developed on monthly basis for operation and the model was demonstrated with a case of two serial reservoirs on River Godavari sub system located in South India when they are operated individually. The recent artificial intelligence tools like Genetic programming, Artificial Neural networks and Fuzzy logic are increasingly used as soft computing techniques to address modelling issues. The main advantage of these techniques lies in handling noisy data, addressing non - linear and dynamic systems. These tools also useful when it is difficult to explain the physical relationship are not fully understood in order to enhance the performance of the system.

The present paper is aimed to present a fuzzy logic methodology for long-term reservoir operation. In this method a monthly fuzzy rule based model was developed based on the historical operation. The performance of the model was tested with calibrated period and validation period.

Keywords: Reservoirs, System, long-term operation, Fuzzy logic, Artificial intelligence, soft computing techniques.

1. INTRODUCTION

The purpose of this paper is to develop a fuzzy rule-based method for constructing reservoir operation rules. A case study of two serially connected reservoirs is used to illustrate the approach when the reservoirs are operated on individual basis. In fuzzy rule base system the operating rules are inferred from historical operation and hence the experience of operator can be in-built into the system. Fuzzy sets provides by means of translating linguistic descriptors into usable numerical values. Probability law does not bind the uncertainty and vagueness. Savic and Simonovic (1991) used fuzzy set method to model for a chance constrained reservoir operation for selecting risk levels. Shrestha et al (1996) proposed that inputs to the reservoir operating principles (e.g. initial storage, inflows, and demands), as well as outputs (historical releases) could be described by fuzzy relations. These fuzzy inputs and are combined to produce fuzzy output relation, which can be combined and defuzzified to get crisp output. Panigrahi and Mujumdar (2000) attempted a fuzzy rule based model for a single reservoir operation. In their methodology they adopted a Stochastic Dynamic Programming (SDP) for framing rule base. Cheng Chuntain (1999) adopted a fuzzy optimal model for real time flood operation for multi-reservoirs. Jolma et al attempted a fuzzy logic model for operation of five lakes. They attempted based on general knowledge to mimic human operator and presented two types of approaches based on case-based reasoning and a rule based reasoning. Durbovin et al (2002) presented a real time reservoir operation model based on total fuzzy similarity and compared with fuzzy inference method known as Sugeno-style fuzzy inference.

The present paper is aimed to present a fuzzy logic methodology for long-term reservoir operation. In this method a monthly fuzzy rule based model has been developed based on the historical Operation and the rules were derived for the two reservoirs on Godavari river system in South India

2. FUZZY RULE BASED SYSTEM

A fuzzy rule based model is a mathematical model based on a fuzzy rule system. In a fuzzy rule system if '$\Re$'is defined as a set of rules which consists of set of input variables or premises, $A_{i,k}$ in the form of fuzzy sets with membership functions $\mu_{Ai,k}$ and a set of consequences B_i also in the form of fuzzy sets.

For example, in a reservoir operation system, the premises may be of storage at the beginning of time period, inflows and the consequences of these variables are releases. Based on expert opinion or from historical operation the rules can be constructed. In the present study the historical operation was taken for the development of rule base. The combined response of the rule surface is a fuzzy output, which is transformed into a single crisp value called defuzzification.

2.1 Fuzzification of inputs

Any reservoir performance depends on its operation policies, which in turn depend on the inputs like inflows and storage apart from system losses. Hence it is important that the deriving operational rules for enhancement of performance plays important role for the managers of reservoir. In the present study the inputs to the system are Inflows during the time period 't' and Storage at the beginning of time period 't'. These are taken as fuzzy inputs and releases as fuzzy outputs to the model. Since inflows in any period are uncertain and the Storages are also uncertain due to variation of inflows and some times vague due to poor operation. These uncertainties and vagueness can be handled effectively by fuzzy logic modeling. The input values are always crisp numerical values limited to the universe of discourse of the input variable and the result of Fuzzification is called fuzzy degree of membership, which varies from 0 to 1. The problem lies in construction of membership function so as to capture the meaning of all the associated operations in the linguistic terms. The construction of membership function was attempted by several researchers to capture expert opinion, use of optimal models and more recently from the historical operation itself so that the knowledge of operators can be taken for building the model which is acceptable to the reservoir managers. In the present study the historical operation was taken for modeling.

Fig 1 shows the transformation of inflow variable into fuzzy variable as an example. For an inflow value of 30 M m^3 units the membership value is 0.8 when the variable lies in one class of input flows viz. Inflow is Low. Suppose if the input value is lying in two classes of inputs like inflow Low and Medium, the membership of both is considered and using centroid approach a single crisp membership value is calculated by the model.

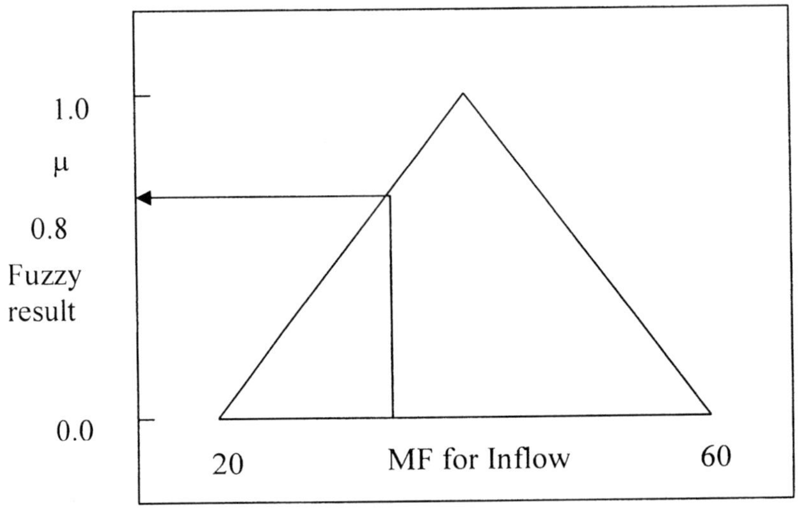

Fig 1. Fuzzy transformation of Input Inflow

2.2 Formation of fuzzy rule base

The fuzzy rule base was formed based on the historical operation and intuition or logically after studying the historical operation. From the historical operation a matrix of rule base was prepared based on the range of input parameters for all the months individually. Wherever the historical values were not available in any fuzzy range, the linguistic rules were developed based on logic and intuition. A fuzzy rule base may be in the form as follows.

If the storage is ***med***, and inflow is ***high*** for the period 't', then the release is ***med.***

2.3 Aggregation

Aggregation is the unification of output of each rule by joining them. If an input value correspond to both the membership functions, fuzzy rule corresponding to both the rules are invoked. Here each rule invokes after implication, specifies one fuzzy output set. Then two fuzzy output sets are then unified to get single output fuzzy set.

3. DEFUZZIFICATION METHOD

The result obtained from the implication is in the form of a fuzzy set. This is defuzzified to get a crisp output. In the present study the most common defuzzified centroid method was adopted. In the centroid method of defuzzification the real value is computed by the equation given in 1.

$$G = \frac{\sum_{i=1}^{n} y_i \, m_B(y_i)}{\sum_{i=1}^{n} m_B(y_i)} \tag{1}$$

where G is the centroid of the truncated fuzzy output set B. $m_B(y_i)$ is the membership value of element y_i in the fuzzy output set B, and n is the number of elements. In this centroid method of defuzzification all values of output is used

The entire methodology applied for the model is shown in fig 2

4. APPLICATION OF FUZZY MODEL TO RESERVOIRS CONSIDERED

In the present study 31 years of historical data of inflow, storage and releases were collected at the reservoir. From this data 23 years of data was used for building the model and 8 years of data was used to test the model on monthly basis. A typical membership function for input and output variable is presented in fig.3. Similarly the membership functions for inflows, Storage and releases for Sri Rama Sagar reservoir were also developed for all months. The basic mass balance equation was used to simulate the performance of reservoirs is given in equation 2.

$$S_n^{t+1} = S_n^t + I_n^t - R_n^t - O_n^t - E_n^t \tag{2}$$

where

S_n^{t+1} *Storage at the beginning of time period* $(t+1)$

S_n^t *Storage at the beginning of time period* (t)

I_n^t *Inflow during the time period* (t)

R_n^t Re*lease during the time period* (t)

O_n^t *overflow at the during of time period* (t)

E_n^t *Evaporation loss during the time period* (t)

5. PERFORMANCE OF NIZAMSAGAR RESERVOIR

The Nizamsagar project is a multipurpose project catering to Irrigation, Hydropower and Water supply to the near by town. The reservoir has a capacity of 504 M m^3 and a canal powerhouse with an installed capacity of 4 MW. The fuzzy simulation model was calibrated with 31 years of monthly data and validated with 8 years of data. To test the performance of this multi-purpose reservoir it was simulated for 5 years. For the computation of demands for irrigation Penman-Montieth method was adopted using cropwat software. The comparative performance of model with that of historical for irrigation is shown in fig 4 and fig 5 for Rabi and Kharief seasons. Fig 6 shows seasonal performance for water supply. Fig 7 shows the annual performance of Hydropower. The storage comparison for the period of simulation is shown in fig 8.

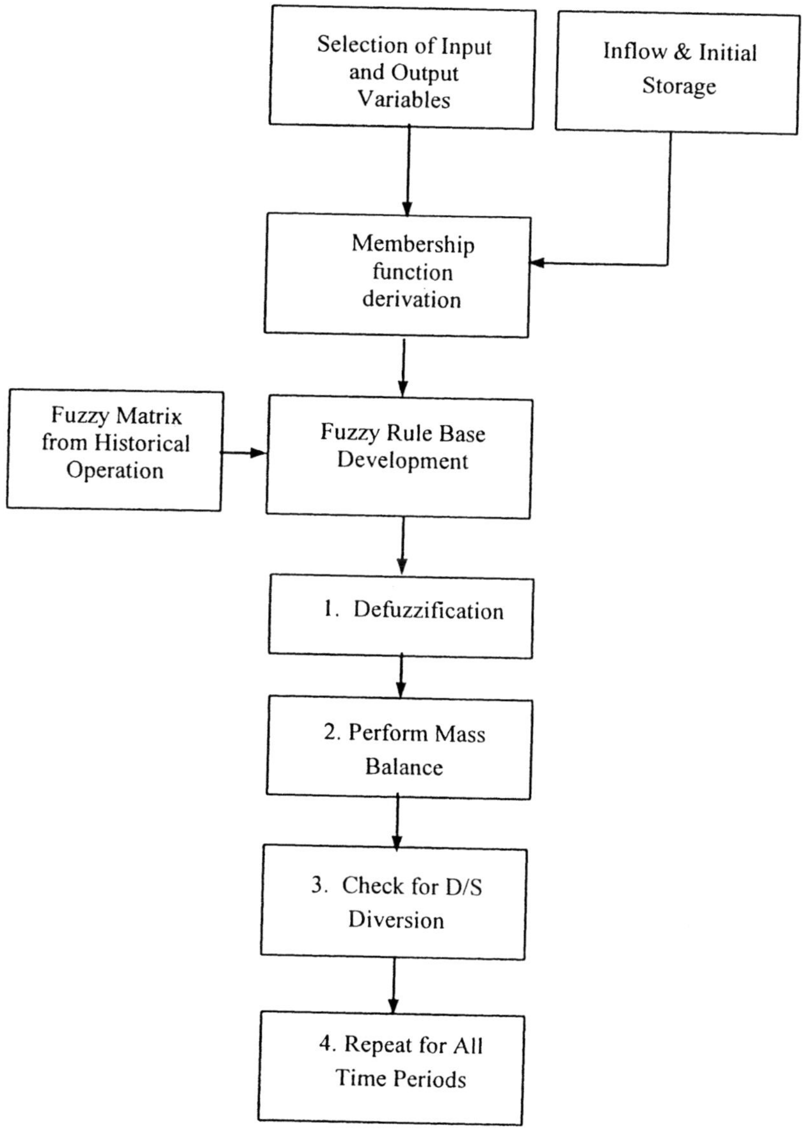

Fig 2 Flow Diagram of Fuzzy Logic Model for Reservoir Operation

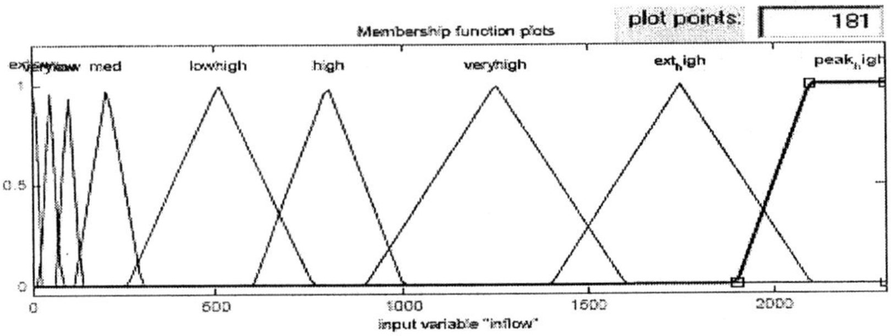

Membership function for Inflow during "August" at Nizamsagar

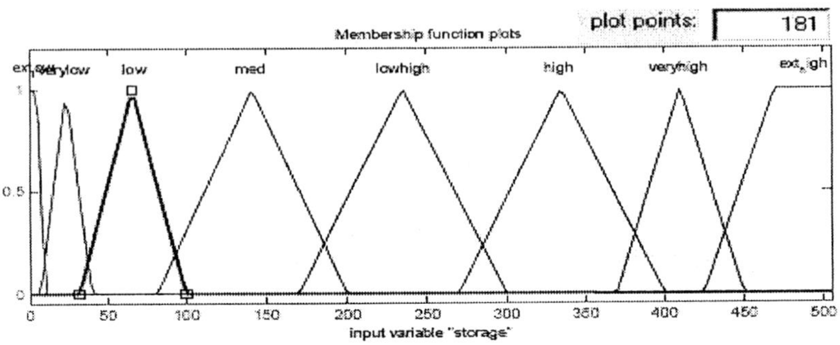

Membership function for Storage during "August" at Nizamsagar

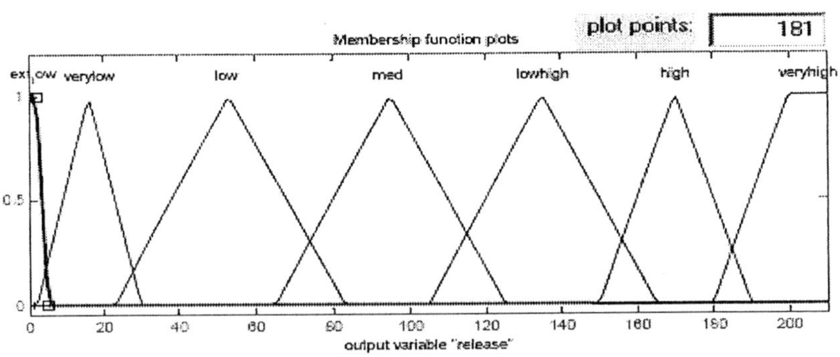

Membership function for Release during "August" at Nizamsagar

Fig 3 Membership functions for Input and Output Variables during "August" at Nizamsagar

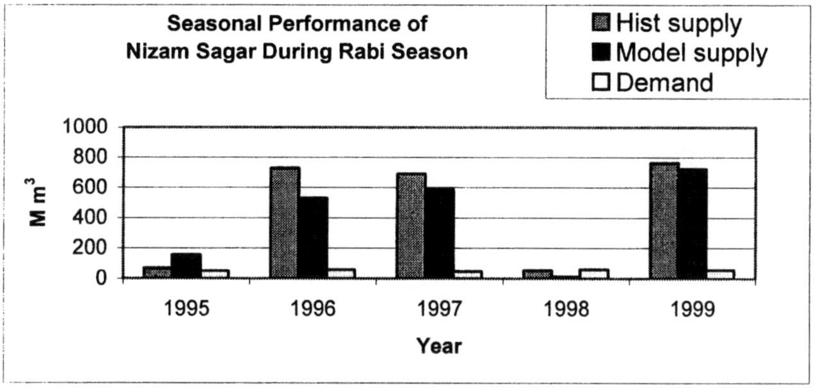

Fig 4 Nizamsagar Reservoir Rabi Performance

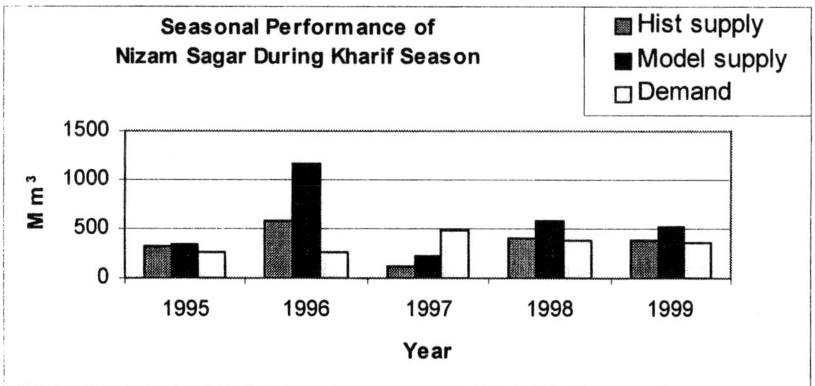

Fig 5 Nizamsagar Reservoir Kharif Performance

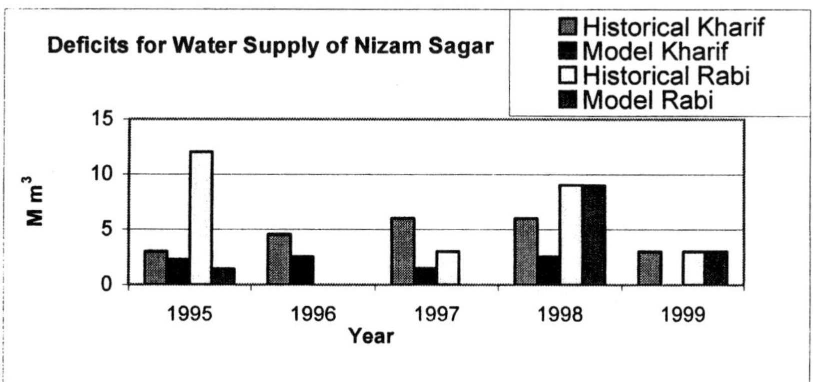

Fig 6. Performance of Nizamsagar for water supply

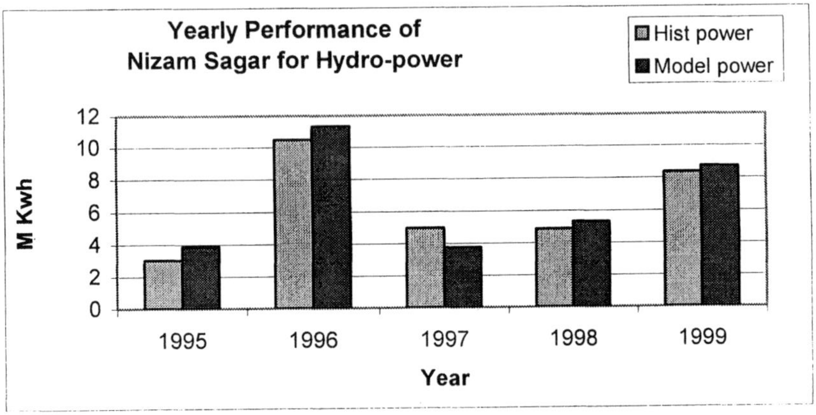

Fig 7. Performance of Annual Hydropower Production at Nizamsagar

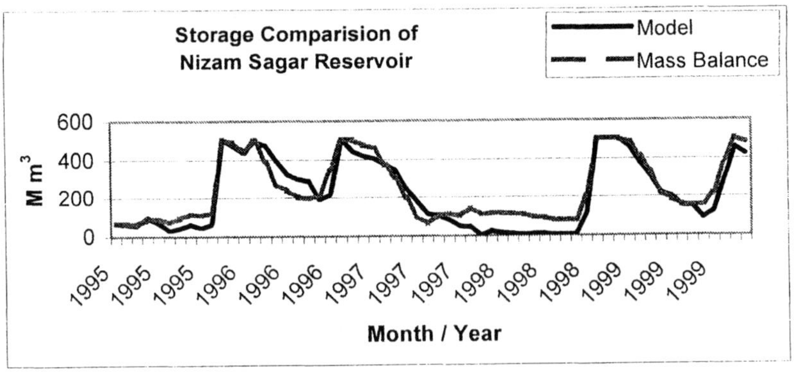

Fig 8. Variation of Storage Comparison at Nizamsagar

6. PERFORMANCE OF SRIRAMSAGAR RESERVOIR

The Sriramsagar project is a major multipurpose project catering to Irrigation, Hydropower and Water supply and industrial supply. The reservoir has a capacity of 3155 M m^3 and a canal powerhouse with an installed capacity of 27 MW. The fuzzy simulation model was calibrated with 24 years of monthly data and validated with 6 years of data. To test the performance of this multi-purpose reservoir it was simulated for 5 years. For the computation of demands for irrigation Penman-Monteith method was adopted using cropwat software. The comparative performance of model with that of historical for irrigation is shown in fig 9 and fig 10 for Rabi and Kharief seasons. Fig 11 shows seasonal performance for water supply. Fig 12 shows the annual performance of Hydropower. The storage comparison for the period of simulation is shown in fig 13.

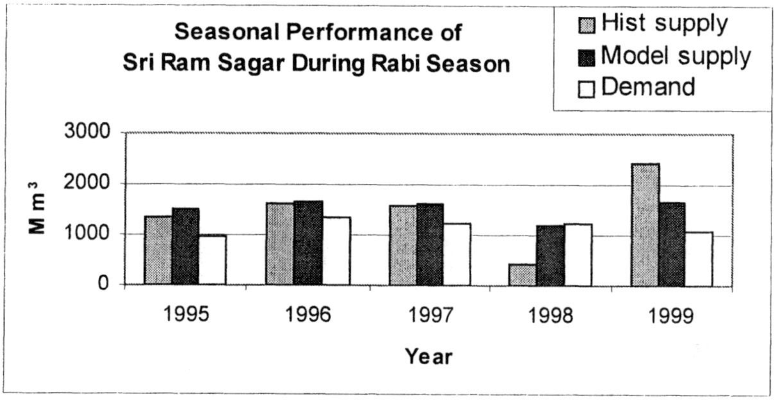

Fig 9 Sriramsagar Reservoir Rabi Performance

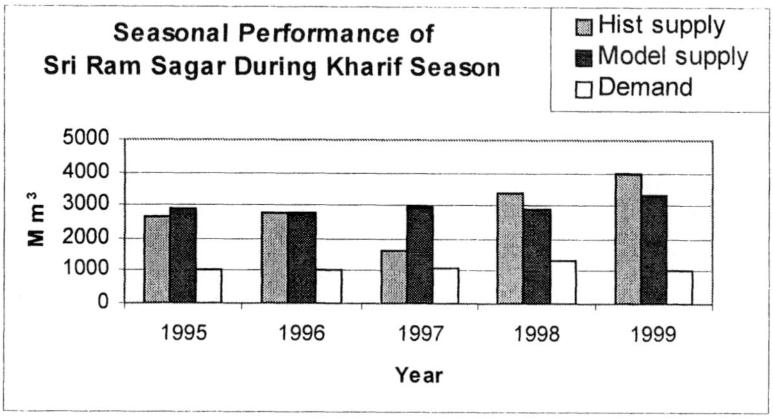

Fig 10 Sriramsagar Reservoir Kharief Performance

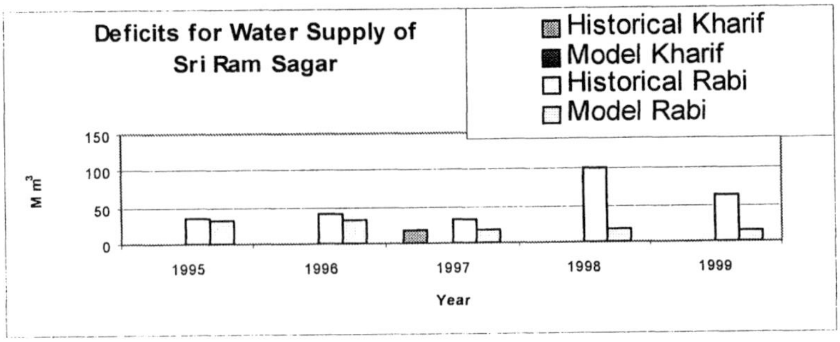

Fig 11 Sriramsagar Reservoir Performance for Water Supply

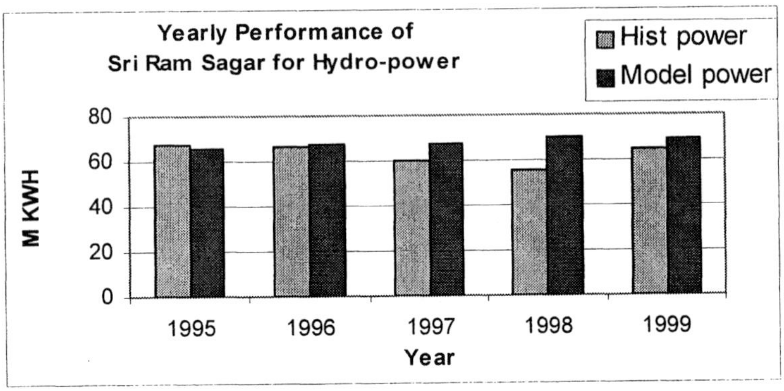

Fig 12 Sriramsagar Reservoir Annual Hydro Power Performance

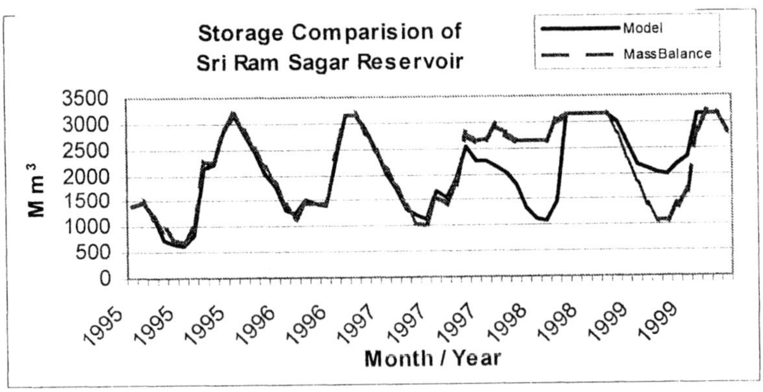

Fig 13. Variation of Storage Comparison at Sriramsagar

7. RESULTS AND CONCLUSIONS

A fuzzy rule based model for multi purpose multi reservoir operation in long term was presented. The advantage of fuzzy rule based system that it utilizes the knowledge of a reservoir operator and avoids complex optimization procedure hence it may be more acceptable to the reservoir managers. Since the input operators are in linguistic terms it is easy to adopt and operation. The methodology was demonstrated with a case study of Nizamsagar and Sriramasagar reservoirs on Godavari system in Andhra Pradesh, India. The result shows the potential application of mapping the reservoir manager's expertise in simulating the two reservoirs studied. At Nizamsagar model failed 10 months to meet full water supply compared to 17 times historically for the period of simulation. Similarly it was found that at Sriramsagar model failed 6 months to meet full water supply compared to 12 times historically for the period of simulation. The annual hydropower production is improved by about 4% to 21.6% in four years compared to historical hydropower production at Nizamsagar reservoir and at Sriramasagar it was improved by 1.6% to 20.3% in four years. Irrigation performance seasonal wise was shown in figs 4 to 7 and 9 to 12 shows improvement in Kharief and Rabi seasons.

REFERENCES

[1] Cheng Chuntian (1999) Fuzzy optimal model for the flood control system of the upper and middle reaches of Yangtze River, Hydrological Sciences Journal Vol. 44 No 4. 573 - 585

[2] Labadie (2004) Optimal Operation of Multi Reservoir Systems: State-of-The-Art Review Journal of Water Resource Planning and Management Vol. 130 No. 2 pp 93-111

[3] Panigrahi & Mujumdar (2000) Reservoir operation modeling with fuzzy logic, Journal of Water Resource Management No. 14 pp 89-109

[4] Shrestha et al (1996) A Fuzzy Rule based Reservoir operation, Journal of Water Resource Planning and Management Vol. 122 No 3. pp 262-268

[5] Savic and Simonovic (1991) Slecting risk levels in Chance-Constrained Reservoir Operation Modeling: A Fuzzy Set Approach, Journal of Water Resource Management No. 4 pp 251-271.

[6] Tanja Dubrovin et al (2002) Fuzzy Model for Real-Time Reservoir Operation, Journal of Water Resource Planning and Management Vol. 128 No 1 pp 66-73

FUZZY NEURO-BDI

Haibo Liu, Guochang Gu, Jing Shen
College of Computer Science and Technology, Harbin Engineering University, Harbin 150001, China

Abstract: The typical BDI (Belief-Desire-Intention) model of agent is not efficiently computable and the strict logic expression is not easily applicable to the domain with uncertainties. In this paper, a fuzzy neuro-BDI model is proposed. The model is a fuzzy neural network composed of five layers: input (beliefs & desires), fuzzification, commitment, fuzzy intention, and defuzzification layer. In the model, the fuzzy commitment rules and neural network are combined to form intentions from beliefs and desires. The model is demonstrated by solving dog-sheep problem, and the simulation result is satisfactory.

Key words: fuzzy neural network, BDI, agent

1. INTRODUCTION

BDI (Belief-Desire-Intention) model represents an abstraction of human deliberation based on a theory of rational actions in the human cognition process [1]. Singh [2] and Rao & Georgeff [3] have developed logic theories involving multiple worlds and logical formalisms. The logic theories greatly strengthen the usability of BDI and are viewed as critical compositions in the BDI family. Although the BDI model has become almost a norm in the area of Multi-Agent Systems (MAS) during the last 15 years, several problems still remain. One of the key problems is the gap that exists between theory and practice. The BDI model is not efficiently computable and the strict logic expression is not easily applicable to the domain with uncertainties. These uncertainties are related with the perception of the uncertain environments, the action of other agents, and the knowledge of the intelligent agents. In order to maximize the power of BDI, it is necessary to further develop BDI into a more effective model to deal with uncertainties. There were many researches attempted to solve these kinds of problems, and mostly by using the probabilistic and stochastic methods [4][5][6]. The intelligent agent must find optimal solutions from given user's goals and the environments that the agent explores. But, based on the previous researches, it is impossible to handle Beliefs, Desires, and Intentions represented with fuzzy linguistic values that comprise of uncertainties in human language and knowledge. To solve this problem, we propose a fuzzy neuro-BDI (FNBDI) model in this paper. The model is a fuzzy neural network composed of five layers: input (beliefs & desires), fuzzification, commitment, fuzzy intention, and defuzzification layer. In FNBDI, the fuzzy commitment rules and neural network are combined to form intentions from beliefs and desires.

2. MODELING

The proposed fuzzy neuro-BDI model shown in Figure 1 is a fuzzy neural network composed of five layers as follows.

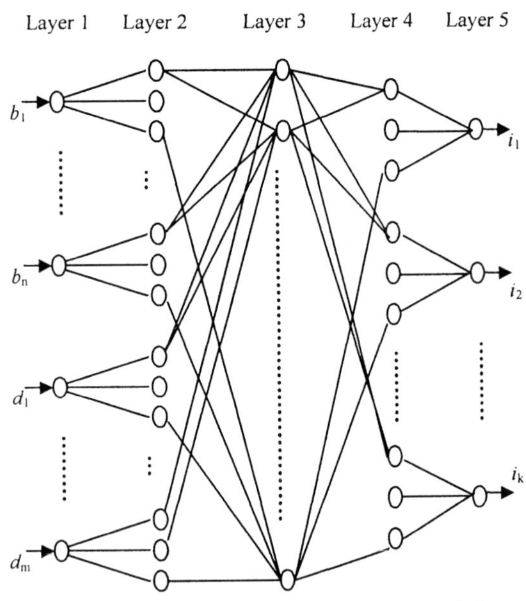

Figure 1. Fuzzy neuro-BDI model

Layer 1: Input layer. The nodes in first layer just directly transmit input values to next layer. The input variables include beliefs and desires ($\boldsymbol{B}$, $\boldsymbol{D}$). $\boldsymbol{B}=(b_1, b_2,\ldots, b_n)$ denotes the input vector of beliefs that is the information an agent has about the world, other agent, and itself. $\boldsymbol{D}=(d_1, d_2,\ldots, d_m)$ denotes the input vector of desires that are the states that agent wish to bring to meet the demands of human user. There are $N_1=n+m$ nodes in this layer. The output of layer 1 is

$$\boldsymbol{O}^1=(o_1^1, o_2^1, \ldots, o_{N_1}^1)=(b_1, b_2, \ldots, b_n, d_1, d_2, \ldots, d_m) \tag{1}$$

Layer 2: Fuzzification layer. Each fuzzy variable of the second layer appearing in the premise part is represented with a condition node. Each of the outputs of the condition node is connected to commitment nodes in the third layer to constitute a condition specified in some rules. Note that the output links must be emitted from proper linguistic terms as specified in fuzzy rules. This layer performs the first inference step to compute matching degrees. The output of this layer is

$$\boldsymbol{O}^2=(o_1^2, o_2^2, \ldots, o_{N_2}^2)=((\mu_{11}(b_1),\mu_{12}(b_1),\ldots,\mu_{1T1}(b_1)),(\mu_{21}(b_2),\mu_{22}(b_2),\ldots,\mu_{2T2}(b_2)),\ldots,(\mu_{(n+m)1}(d_m), \mu_{(n+m)2}(d_m),\ldots, \mu_{(n+m)T(n+m)}(d_m))) \tag{2}$$

where μ_{pq} is the membership degree of the qth linguistic term in the pth variable for $\boldsymbol{O}^1$, T_p is the number of linguistic term for the pth variable of $\boldsymbol{O}^1$. There are $N_2=\sum_{p=1}^{n+m} T_p$ nodes in this layer. Several functions such as the triangular function, trapezoidal function, and so on can be adopted as the membership functions μ of linguistic terms.

Layer 3: Commitment layer. Each neuron in this layer corresponds to a single fuzzy commitment rule. The links in this layer are used to perform precondition matching of fuzzy logic rules. Hence, the rule nodes should perform the fuzzy AND operation. In our model, the commitment rules are defined by domain expert's fuzzy knowledge previously as form of

R_h: IF b_1 IS B_1 AND b_2 IS B_2 AND … AND b_n IS B_n AND d_1 IS D_1 AND d_2 IS D_2 AND … AND d_m IS D_m THEN g_1 IS G_1 AND g_2 IS G_2 AND … AND g_l IS G_l

where B_x, D_y, and G_z are linguistic terms of the variable b_x, d_y and g_z corresponding to belief, desire, and subgoal, respectively. There are $N_3=\prod_{p=1}^{n+m} T_p$ nodes in layer 3. The output of this layer is

$$\boldsymbol{O}^3=(o_1^3, o_2^3, \ldots, o_{N_3}^3) \tag{3}$$

where o_h^3 is the firing strength of fuzzy commitment rule R_h:

$$o_h^3=\mu_{1h}\times\mu_{2h}\times\ldots\times\mu_{(n+m)h} \tag{4}$$

where μ_{jh} is the membership degree of the corresponding linguistic term of the jth variable in $\boldsymbol{O}^1$, the linguistic term appears in the conditions of R_h, The $\times$ in Eq.(4) is a fuzzy product operator which can be defined as a various forms such as *min*(). Note that the output links must be emitted to proper linguistic terms as specified in fuzzy rules.

Layer 4: Fuzzy intention layer. There are $N_4=\sum_{p=1}^{N_5} S_p$ nodes in this layer, where $N_5=k$ is the number of nodes in layer 5, S_p is the number of linguistic term for the pth variable of intentions. The neurons in this layer have weighted connections with the neurons in layer 3. The weight vector can be denoted by matrix $\boldsymbol{W}$ with $N_4 \times N_3$ elements that are adjusted during training.

$$\boldsymbol{W}=\begin{bmatrix} w_{11} & w_{12} & \cdots & w_{1N_3} \\ w_{21} & w_{22} & \cdots & w_{2N_3} \\ \vdots & \vdots & \ddots & \vdots \\ w_{N_4 1} & w_{N_4 2} & \cdots & w_{N_4 N_3} \end{bmatrix} \tag{5}$$

Note that if there is no connection between the ith nodes in layer 4 and the jth nodes in layer 3 then $w_{ij}=0$. The output of layer 4 is

$$\boldsymbol{O}^4=(o_1^4, o_2^4, \ldots, o_{N_4}^4), \text{ where } o_i^4=\sum_{j=1}^{N_3} o_j^3 w_{ij} \tag{6}$$

where Σ is a fuzzy sum operator which can be defined as a various forms such as *max*().

Layer 5: Defuzzification layer. There are k nodes in this layer, i.e., $N_5=k$, and the output intention vector is denoted as $\boldsymbol{I}=(i_1, i_2, \ldots, i_k)$ which can be calculated according to Eq.(7).

$$i_p=Centroid(Y_p, \rho_p), \quad p=1..k \tag{7}$$

where the function *Centroid*() denotes the centroid defuzzification process, Y_p and ρ_p are output domain and membership degree of the pth variable of intention. Without loss of generality, we assume that the output domain $\boldsymbol{Y}=\{Y_1, Y_2, \ldots, Y_p\} \in \boldsymbol{R}^k$.

A various learning algorithm may be applied to adjust the weights $\boldsymbol{W}$ and modify the input/output membership functions μ and ρ.

3. SIMULATION

We consider the dog-sheep problem [7] in a 9×9 grid. The dog can occupy one of the 81 positions and so can the sheep. Therefore, there are 6561 states in the system. The aim of the dog is to make the sheep go to the pen that is the (0,0) position for the sheep. $\boldsymbol{x}(t)$ is state vector given by $\boldsymbol{x}(t)=[x_s(t)\ y_s(t)\ x_d(t)\ y_d(t)]$ which stand for the coordinate of the sheep position and the dog position at time instance t. For the 9×9 dog sheep problem, we have $\forall t\ x_s(t) \in \{0..8\}$, $y_s(t) \in \{0..8\}$, $x_d(t) \in \{0..8\}$, $y_d(t) \in \{0..8\}$. However, the dog and the sheep cannot have the same location on the grid as their initial positions. There is a cost of one unit for each step (horizontal or vertical or diagonal) of a dog as well as of a sheep. The desire of the dog is to move the sheep to the pen (x_p, y_p) i.e. to the (0,0) coordinate, with the least cost c. We say the sheep is in an equilibrium state when given a time instant t' the condition, $\forall t \geq t'$, if $x_d(t)=x_d(t')$ and $y_d(t)=y_d(t')$ then $x_s(t)=x_s(t')$ and $y_s(t)=y_s(t')$, is satisfied. The dog can only move when sheep is in an equilibrium state. The dog can only move one step in one time instant and that step can be in vertical or diagonal direction. The sheep can also only move one step in horizontal, vertical or diagonal direction. The sheep moves based on the rules proposed Kachroo *et al.* [7] but the coordinates in the conditions should be modified to fit the scale of 9×9 grid. The dog moves based on the intentions formed by the FNBDI.

For this dog-sheep problem, we constructed an FNBDI with 7 inputs $(x_s(t), y_s(t), x_d(t), y_d(t), x_p=0, y_p=0, c=0)$ and 2 outputs $(x_d(t+1), y_d(t+1))$. Figure 2 shows the fuzzy sets of fuzzy input-output variables. For the desire variables (x_p, y_p, c) are invariants, we only have 81 fuzzy commitment rules, part of which are shown in Table 1.

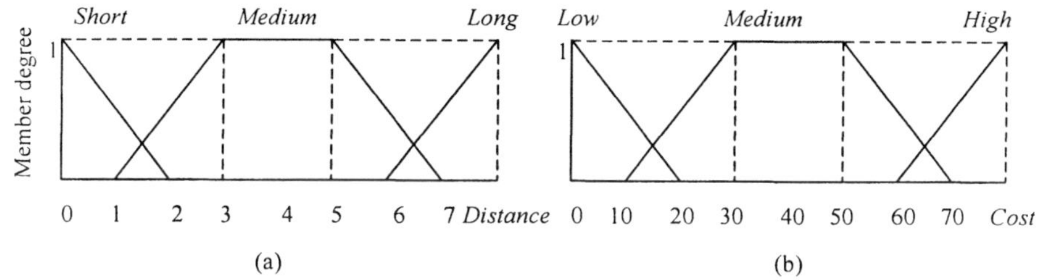

Figure 2: (a) Fuzzy sets for variable $x_s(t)$, $y_s(t)$, $x_d(t)$, $y_d(t)$, x_p, y_p, $x_d(t+1)$, and $y_d(t+1)$; (b) Fuzzy sets for variable c.

Table 1: Part of fuzzy commitment rules (*S*: *Short*, *M*: *Medium*, *L*: *Long* or *Low*, *H*: *High*)

Rule	$x_s(t)$	$y_s(t)$	$x_d(t)$	$y_d(t)$	x_p	y_p	c	$x_d(t+1)$	$y_d(t+1)$
1	*S*	*S*	*S*	*S*	*S*	*S*	*L*	*S*	*S*
2	*S*	*S*	*S*	*M*	*S*	*S*	*L*	*S*	*S*
3	*S*	*S*	*S*	*L*	*S*	*S*	*L*	*S*	*M*
4	*S*	*S*	*M*	*S*	*S*	*S*	*L*	*S*	*S*
...		...				...		...	
81	*L*	*L*	*L*	*L*	*S*	*S*	*L*	*L*	*L*

We make use of a mixture of back propagation and least mean square estimation to adjust the connection weights and modify the input/output membership functions. The training data is generating by the dynamic programming (DP) solution used in [7]. We trained the FNBDI using the ANFIS command in MATLAB by specifying the training epoch number to 20 and setting the default values to other training options. Then we replaced the dynamic programming solution with our trained FNBDI solution to form the moving intentions of the dog. As a simulation result, Figure 3 shows pursuit-evasion tracks of the dog and the sheep. Note that the tracks produced by FNBDI solution superposes that produced by DP, which indicate that the FNBDI solution can solve dog-sheep problem satisfactorily.

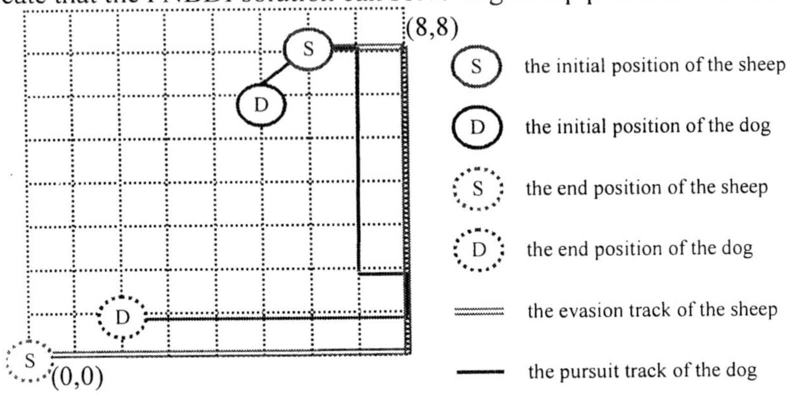

Figure 3: The pursuit-evasion tracks of the dog and the sheep.

4. CONCLUSIONS

In this paper we modeled an FNBDI and demonstrated how to apply it and how about the application by solving dog-sheep problem. The FNBDI extends the typical modal-logic-based BDI with fuzzy inference capability that is very useful for dealing with large-scale problems with uncertainties.

REFERENCES

1. Bratman M E. Intentions, Plans, and Practical Reason. Cambridge: Harvard University Press, 1987
2. Singh M P, Asher N M. Towards a formal theory of intentions. Proceedings of the European Workshop JELIA-90, Amsterdam, Netherlands, 1991: 472-486
3. Rao A S, Georgeff M P. Modelling Rational Agents within a BDI-Architecture. Proceedings of the Second International Conference on Principles of Knowledge Representation and Rcasoning, Cambridge, USA, 1991:473–484
4. Poole D. The Independent Choice Logic for Modelling Multiple Agents Under Uncertainty. Artificial Intelligence, 1997,94(1-2): 5-56
5. Kaelbling L P, Littman M L, Cassandra A R. Planning and Acting in Partially Observable Stochastic Domains. Artificial Intelligence, 1998,101(1-2): 99-134
6. Xuan P, Lesser V R. Handling Uncertainty in Multi-Agent Commitments. UMASS Computer Science Technical Report, University of Massachusetts Amherst, 1999
7. Kachroo P, *et al.* Pursuit Evasion: The Herding Non-cooperative Dynamic Game. Journal of Integrated Design & Process Science, 2002,6(1): 31-42

IMPROVING THE PARTICLE SWARM OPTIMIZATION ALGORITHM USING THE SIMPLEX METHOD AT LATE STAGE

Fang Wang, and Yuhui Qiu

Intelligent Software and Software Engineering Laboratory, Southwest-China Normal University, Chongqing, 400715, China

Abstract: This article proposes a hybrid Particle Swarm Optimization (PSO) based on the Nonlinear Simplex Method (NSM). At late stage of PSO running, when the promising regions of solutions have been located, the algorithm isolates particles which are very close to the extrema and applies the NSM to them to enhance the local exploitation. Experimental results on several benchmark functions demonstrate that this approach is very effective and efficient, especially for multimodal function optimizations. It yields better solution qualities and success rates compared to other methods taken from the literature.

Key words: particle swarm optimization, simplex method, multimodal function

1. INTRODUCTION

From the beginning of 90's, a new research field called Swarm Intelligence (SI) arose [1, 2]. These new optimization techniques focus on analogies of swarm behavior of natural creatures, which suggest that the main ideas of intelligent individual's socio-cognition can be effectively applied to develop efficient algorithms for optimization tasks. Ant Colony Optimization (ACO) is the most well known SI algorithm and is mainly used for combinatorial optimization tasks [3]. The Particle Swarm Optimization algorithm is another SI technique, which is mainly used for continuous optimization tasks and has been originally proposed by R.C. Eberhart and J. Kennedy [4] based on the analogy of swarm of bird and fish school. PSO exhibits good performance in solving hard optimization problems and engineering applications, and compares favorably to other optimization algorithms [5, 6].

Since its introduction, numerous variations of the basic PSO algorithm have been developed in the literature [7] to improve its overall performance. Hybrid PSO algorithms with determinate methods, such as the nonlinear simplex method, are proved to be superior to the original techniques and have many advantages over other techniques, because these hybrid procedures can perform the exploration with PSO and the exploitation with determinate methods [8]. Generating initial swarm by the NSM might improve, but is not satisfying in multimodal function optimization [9]. Applying the NSM as an operator to the swarm during the optimization may increase the computational complex considerably.

In this paper, the Nonlinear Simplex Method is adopted at late stage of PSO algorithm when particles fly quite near to the extrema. Experimental results on several famous test functions demonstrate that this is a very promising way to increase the convergence speed and the success rate significantly. We briefly introduce some background knowledge of the PSO algorithm in section 2. In section 3 the proposed algorithm is described, and experimental design and correlative results are given. The paper closes with some conclusions and ideas for further work in Section 4

2. THE PARTICLE SWARM OPTIMIZATION ALGORITHM

In the original PSO formulae, particle i is denoted as $Xi=(x_{i1},x_{i2},\ldots,x_{iD})$, which represents a potential solution to a problem in D-dimensional space. Each particle maintains a memory of its previous best position, $Pi=(p_{i1},p_{i2},\ldots,p_{iD})$, and a velocity along each dimension, represented as $Vi=(v_{i1},v_{i2},\ldots,v_{iD})$. At each iteration, the P vector of the particle with the best fitness in the local neighborhood, designated g, and the P vector of the current particle are combined to adjust the velocity along each dimension, and that velocity is then used to compute a new position for the particle.

The evolutionary equations of the swarm are [6]:

$$v_{id} = w*v_{id}+c1*rand()*(p_{id}-x_{id})+c2*Rand()*(p_{gd}-x_{id}) \quad (1)$$

$$x_{id} = x_{id}+v_{id} \quad (2)$$

Constants c1 and c2 determine the relative influence of the social and cognition components (learning rates), which often both are set to the same value to give each component equal weight. A constant, V_{max}, was used to limit the velocities of the particles. The parameter w, which was introduced as an inertia factor, can dynamically adjust the velocity over time, gradually focusing the PSO into a local search.

Maurice Clerc has derived a constriction coefficient K, a modification of the PSO that runs without V_{max}, reducing some undesirable explosive feedback effects [10]. The constriction factor is computed as:

$$K = \frac{2}{\left| 2 - \varphi - \sqrt{\varphi^2 - 4\varphi} \right|}, \quad \varphi = c_1 + c_2, \ \varphi > 4 \tag{3}$$

With the constriction factor K, the PSO formula for computing the new velocity is:

$$v_{id} = K*(v_{id}+c1*rand()*(p_{id}-x_{id})+c2*Rand()*(p_{gd}-x_{id})) \tag{4}$$

Carlisle and Doziert investigated the influence of different parameters in PSO, selected c1=2.8, c2=1.3, population size as 30, and proposed the Canonical PSO [11, 12].

3. THE PROPOSED ALGORITHM AND EXPERIMENTAL RESULTS

The basic simplex method was presented by Spendley et al in 1962, which is an efficient sequential optimization method for function minimization tasks, and then improved by Nelder and Mead, to what is called the Nonlinear Simplex Method (NSM) [13]. It needs only values and not derivatives of the objective function. In general, the NSM is considered as the best method if the figure of merit is "get something to work quickly".

At late stage of PSO running, promising regions of solutions have been located. Applying the NSM operator for many steps to enhance exploitation search at this stage is capable of improving the solution quality and convergence rate.

We propose a hybrid Nonlinear Simplex Method PSO (NSMPSO), which isolates a particle and apply the NSM to it when it reaches quite close to the extrema (within the diversion radius). If the particle "lands" within a specified precision of a goal solution (error goal) during the NSM running, a PSO process is considered to be successful, otherwise it may be laid back to the swarm and start the next PSO iteration.

The diversion radius is computed as:

$$DRadius = ErrorGoal + \delta \tag{5}$$

$$\delta = \begin{cases} 100 * ErrorGoal, & if \ ErrorGoal <= 10^{-4} \\ 0.01 * ErrorGoal, & otherwise \end{cases} \tag{6}$$

Table 1. The rate of success, mean function evaluations for each test function

Test Functions	Rate of success			Mean function evaluations		
	NSMPSO	NS-PSO	CPSO	NSMPSO	NS-PSO	CPSO
$Rastrigin_2$	1	0.84	1	2851.1	5573.3	3181.8
Levy $No.3_2$	1	0.83	1	2532	4827	2853.3
$Schaffer_2$	0.74	0.57	0.645	7872.6	9906.8	9119.7
$Rosenbrock_2$	1	0.845	0.97	7372.5	9421.8	8450.3
$Griewank_2$	0.805	0.685	0.735	8353.7	9397.6	8985.9
Levy $No.8_3$	1	0.995	1	2644	2045	2327.6
$Freudenstein_2$	0.98	0.52	0.975	5342.5	9321.1	4349.6
$Goldstern_2$	1	0.94	1	2714.1	3601.2	2955.4
$Sphere_{10}$	1	1	1	8138.3	5723.4	6306.8
$Rosenbrock_{10}$	0.855	0.945	0.84	5480.9	3552	5461.6
$Rastrigin_{10}$	0.965	0.83	0.96	5379.8	5929.5	5094.3
$Griewank_{10}$	0.885	0.8	0.845	8969.5	7084.1	7332.3
$Sphere_{30}$	1	1	1	78671	13789	15448
$Rosenbrock_{30}$	0.805	0.94	0.795	16783	10697	16576
$Rastrigin_{30}$	0.99	1	1	9100.4	3475.5	8511.3
$Griewank_{30}$	1	1	0.995	19388	8999.1	10801

*Note:

The subscript of each test function denotes its dimension.

NSMPSO: the proposed algorithm.

NS-PSO: another NSM hybrid PSO proposed by Parsopoulos and Vrahatis [9].

CPSO: the Canonical PSO, Carlisle A [12].

In a NSM process, an initial simplex is consists of the isolated particle i and other D vertices randomly generated with the mean of X_i and standard deviation of 0.02 times X_{max}.

The benchmark functions [14] on which the proposed algorithm has been tested and compared to other methods in the literature, as well as the equation of each one and the corresponding parameters are listed in Table 1. For all test functions 200 experiments have been done and the maximum number of PSO iterations is set to be 500, swarm size is 60 for 30-dimension functions and 30 for others. Parameters used in the NSM are: α=1.0, γ=2.0, $\beta^+ = \beta^-$=0.5. An each time when the NSM operator is applied, it searches 50 steps. Programming environment is: Matlab 7.0, PentiumIV 2.8GHz CPU, 512M RAM, Windows2000 Professional OS.

Table 2. The average optima and total CPU time for each test function

Test Functions	Average optima			Total CPU time		
	NSMPSO	NS-PSO	CPSO	NSMPSO	NS-PSO	CPSO
$Rastrigin_2$	4.8541e-9	0.42783	4.9856e-9	14.266	27.156	14.906
Levy $No.3_2$	-176.54	-163.17	-176.54	12.578	22.688	12.813
$Schaffer_2$	-0.99755	-0.99334	-0.99664	29.188	35.484	31.047
$Rosenbrock_2$	4.9915e-9	0.76162	0.002373	30.578	36.422	31.781
$Griewank_2$	1.0012	1.003	1.0016	44.016	49.141	44.813
Levy $No.8_3$	6.4267e-9	5.8974e-9	6.0348e-9	14.656	10.891	11.188
$Freudenstein_2$	0.97969	80.237	1.2246	16.078	31.875	14.516
$Goldstern_2$	3	2240.1	3	9.8906	12.859	9.8125
$Sphere_{10}$	8.8273e-9	8.2146e-9	8.2073e-9	38.828	23.125	24.656
$Rosenbrock_{10}$	31.146	461.95	20.688	22.922	15.266	22.547
$Rastrigin_{10}$	9.6321	10.14	9.7158	29.547	32.625	27.641
$Griewank_{10}$	9.0987	9.1038	9.1003	55.156	42.25	43.156
$Sphere_{30}$	9.2039e-5	9.3474e-5	9.2407e-5	494.11	67.594	68.609
$Rosenbrock_{30}$	2009.3	100.63	2856.7	81.484	56.281	80.047
$Rastrigin_{30}$	97.418	95.818	97.752	65.109	27.574	60.75
$Griewank_{30}$	29.098	29.094	29.094	156.08	71.609	81.547

In table 1 and 2, the rate of success, mean function evaluations, average optima and total CPU time for each test function are given. From the table we can see that the overall performance of NSMPSO algorithm is superior to other published algorithms in terms of success rate, solution quality and convergence speed, especially on multimodal functions such as Levy No.3, Schaffer, Rosenbrock and Griewank. As to high dimension function optimizing, NSMPSO operates appreciably inferior to NS-PSO due to its computational expense, but is still equal to the Canonical PSO algorithm.

4. CONCLUSIONS AND FUTURE WORK

A new hybrid Particle Swarm Optimization algorithm is proposed in this paper, which applies the Nonlinear Simplex Method at late stage of PSO running when the most promising regions of solutions are fixed. We implement wide variety of experiments on well-known benchmark functions to test the proposed algorithm. The results compared to other 3 published methods indicate that this method is reliable and efficient, especially for continuous multimodal function optimizations.

Future work may focus on accelerating the convergence for high dimension problems, developing practical applications of this hybrid approach in neuro-fuzzy network optimization, and extending the approach to constrained multi-objective optimization.

REFERENCE

[1] Bonabeau E, Dorigo M, andTheraulaz G. Swarm Intelligence: From Natural to Artificial Systems. Oxford Press, 1999

[2] Kennedy J, and Eberhart R C. Swarm Intelligence. Kaufmann Publishers, Morgan, 2001

[3] Deneubourg J L, Goss S, Franks N, Sendova-Franks A, Detrain C, and Chr´etien L. The dynamics of collective sorting: Robot-like ants and ant-like robots. Proceedings of the First International Conference on Simulation of Adaptive Behaviour: From Animals to Animats 1, 1991, MIT Press, Cambridge, MA: 356-365

[4] Kennedy J, and Eberhart R C. Particle swarm optimization. Proceedings of IEEE International Conference on Neural Networks, 1995, Piscataway, NJ: 1942-1948

[5] Shi Y, and Eberhart R C. Parameter selection in particle swarm optimization. Evolutionary Programming VII: Proceedings of the 7th Annual Conference on Evolutionary Programming, 1998, New York: 591-600

[6] Shi Y, and Eberhart R C. Empirical study of particle swarm optimization. Proceedings of the IEEE Congress on Evolutionary Computation, 1999, Piscataway, NJ: 1945-1950

[7] Parsopoulos K E, and Vrahatis M N. Recent approaches to global optimization problems through particle swarm optimization. Natural Computing, 2002, Vol. 1: 235-306

[8] Shu-Kai S. Fan, Yun-Chia Liang, and Erwie Zahara. Hybrid Simplex Search and Particle Swarm Optimization for the Global Optimization of Multimodal Functions. Engineering Optimization, 2004, 36(4): 401-418

[9] Parsopoulos K E, and Vrahatis M N. Initializing the particle swarm optimizer using the nonlinear simplex Method. Advances in Intelligent Systems, Fuzzy Systems, Evolutionary Computation, 2002, WSEAS Press: 216-221

[10] Clerc M. The swarm and the queen: towards a deterministic and adaptive particle swarm optimization. Proceedings of the IEEE Congress on Evolutionary Computation, 1999: 1951-1957

[11] Carlisle A, and Dozier G. An off-the-shelf PSO. Proceedings of the Workshop on Particle Swarm Optimization, 2001, Indianapolis

[12] Clerc M, and Kennedy J. The particle swarm-explosion, stability, and convergence in a multidimensional complex space. IEEE Transactions on Evolutionary Computation, 2002, 6(1): 58-73

[13] Nelder J, and Mead R. A simplex method for function minimization. Computer Journal, 1965, Vol. 7: 308-313

[14] Levy A, Montalvo A, Gomez S, et al. Topics in Global Optimization. Springer-Verlag, New York: 1981

INTERNET INTELLIGENT PLATFORM- AGRIP

Maoguang Wang, Jiewen Luo, Fen Lin, Zhongzhi Shi
Insitute of Computing Technology,Chinese Academy of Sciences Beijing, China
luojw@ics.ict.a.cn

Abstract: In information age, both governments and enterprises need intelligent platform to provide dynamic, real-time intelligent information processing service. This paper describes an **A**gent **Gr**id based **I**ntelligent **P**latform AGrIP to support service layer information processing. AGrIP integrates a comprehensive set of tools to compose a whole platform that will enable straightforward management of large-scale information from Internet and then apply data mining, case base reasoning and expert system to aid practical enterprise applications.

Key words: Intelligent Platform, Agent, Grid

1. INTRODUCTION

The "Grid" is an emerging infrastructure that connects multiple regional and national grids to create a universal source of computing power—the work "Grid" was chosen by analog with the electric power grid, which provides pervasive access to power. The resource management is central to the operation of a grid. Agent technology is one of the ways to meet these requirements in such grid environment. In the past decade, attempts to apply intelligent agents in realizing the Grid vision have been made by academic researchers during the past few years. The most interesting work in the literature might be the Agent Grid concept proposed under the DARPA ISO's Control of Agent-Based Systems (CoABS) program. The agent grid is a specific construct or mechanism within that layer for making services and resources available. Hence we can view the Grid as a number of interacting agents. In terms of the idea we have built a system of agent-based grid intelligent platform (AGrIP). It is based on the multiagent platform MAGE and integrated various middleware for intelligent information processing.

The rest paper is organized as follows. Section 2 will discuss the architecture and main characteristics of intelligent platform. Section 3 describes the multiagent environment MAGE [1]. Section3 introduce the middleware of the platform. And section 4 summarized the paper and gives a conclusion.

2. ARCHITECTURE

In this section, we introduce the architecture of AGrIP. As the figure 1 shows, AGrIP, from bottom to up, consists of three layers: MAGE integrated platform layer, middleware layer and application layer. At bottom, MAGE is a multiagent environment, which applies the wrap techniques to provide integration support. In the middle layer, the functional software is wrapped by agents and can cooperate with other to together complete complex applications. The functional software mainly includes the intelligent search engine GHunt, multi-strategy data mining tool MSMiner, case base reasoning tool CBR, multimedia retrieval tool MIRES and expert system OKPS etc. To summarize, it has the following characteristics.

Open. As a platform, not a toolbox, it should support HTML, XML, WML files etc, in order to support the mobile devices and low-band applications. Moreover, the platform should provide integration patterns for business intelligence and outer applications seamlessly. Likewise, it is a service engine based on web, not a client/server tool driven by end-users.

Distributing It can integrate heterogeneous data sources and deal with different file formats, granularities, dimensions and distributed documents stored in the business or decision-support systems.

Scalable. It should integrate external application systems and run on the high performance SMP machines, supporting the cluster technologies such as load-balance, fail-over, the connection pools, in order to support a great deal of transaction processes.

Self-adaptive. It can adapt to the front users according to the specified preferences, which only show the relevant functionalities when the authorized users use it.

Timely. It can provide the needed efficient and timely data to the users and business applications considering its distributing abilities and rich ontology or metadata.

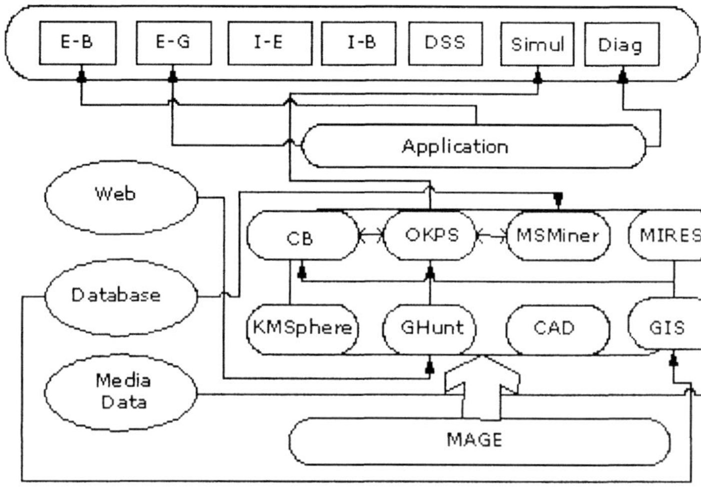

Figure1 The architecture of AGrIP

3. MULTIAGENT ENVIRONMENT-MAGE

MAGE is a multiagent environment with a collection of tools supporting the entire process of agent-oriented software engineering and programming. It is designed to facilitate the rapid design and development of new multiagent applications by abstracting into a toolkit the common principles and components underlying many multiagent systems. The idea was to create a relatively general purpose and customizable toolkit that could be used by software users with only basic competence in agent technology to analyze, design, implement and deploy multiagent systems.

MAGE has the following features:

(1) It utilizes standardized technology and standardized specification wherever feasible, for examples our MAGE is FIPA compliant, and agent interaction is based on FIPA-ACL.

(3) It provides friendly and easy-to-use human-computer interface by the visual programming paradigm and the pick-and-choose principle.

(4) It supports an open and flexible design so that it is easily to extend, thus users can easily add to the library different kind of components.

(5) It supports the entire development process of agent-based software engineering and programming: AUMP [4] (Agent Unified Modeling Platform) for system analysis and design, VAStudio (Visual Agent

Studio) for implementation, and MAGE deplorers for deployment and management.

3.1 MAGE platform architecture

MAGE is designed to be compliant with FIPA, and MAGE framework in which MAGE agents exist and operate is comply with FIPA Agent Management Specification. Figure 2 is the architecture of MAGE framework. It is a logical reference model for the creation, registration, location, communication, migration and retirement of agents. From Figure 2 we can see that MAGE platform consists of the following components, each representing a capability set.

Agent Management System (AMS) is a mandatory component of MAGE. The AMS exerts supervisory control over access to and use of MAGE platform. Only one AMS exists in MAGE. The AMS maintains a directory of AIDs (agent identifiers) which contain transport addresses (amongst other things) for agents registered in MAGE. The AMS offers white pages services to other agents. Each agent must register with an AMS in order to get a valid AID.

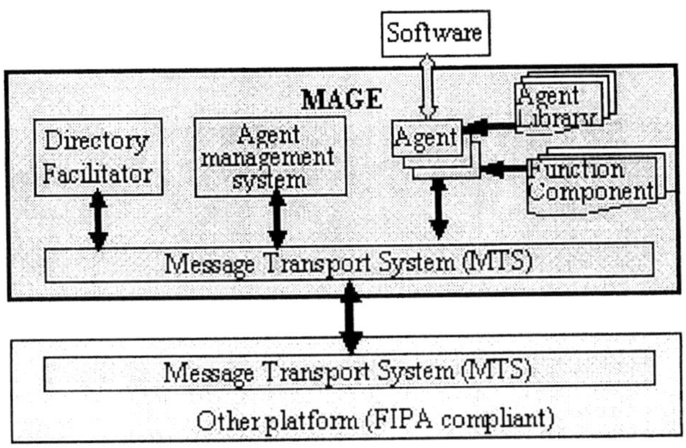

Figure 2. MAGE platform architecture

Directory Facilitator (DF) is a mandatory component of MAGE. The DF provides yellow pages services to other agents. Agents may register their services with the DF or query the DF to find out what services are offered by other agents. Multiple DFs may exist within MAGE and may be federated.

Message Transport Service (MTS) is the default communication method between agents on different agent platforms.

Agent is the fundamental actor in MAGE, which combines one or more service capabilities into a unified and integrated execution model that may include access to external software, human users and communications facilities. An agent may have certain resource brokering capabilities for accessing software.

Software describes all non-agent, executable collections of instructions accessible through an agent. Agents may access software, for example, to add new services, acquire new communications protocols, acquire new security protocols/algorithms, acquire new negotiation protocols, access tools that support migration, etc.

4. MIDDLEWARE MODULES

The section will describe two main middleware modules, intelligent search engine Ghunt and multi-strategy data mining tool MSMiner. They are seamlessly integrated in the AGrIP system.

4.1 Intelligent Search Engine-GHunt

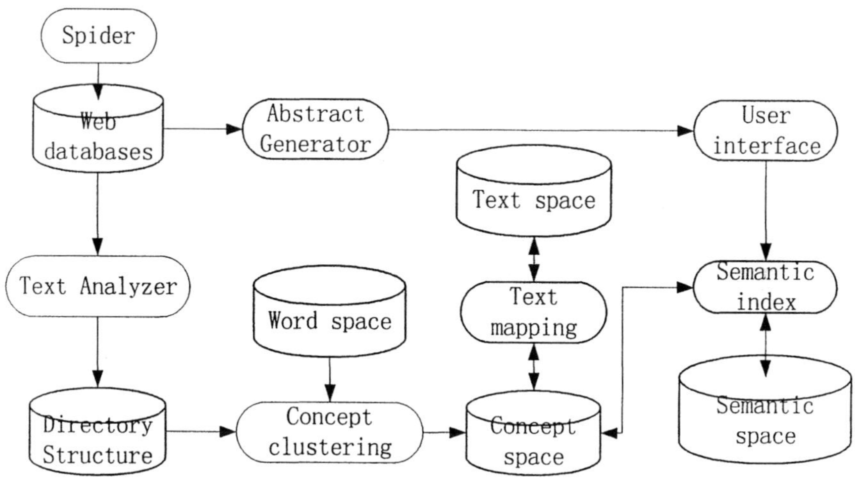

Figure 3 GHunt processing

In this section, we describe the intelligent search engine GHunt [3]. At first, GHunt is an independent tool for information retrieval, which is not integrated in the AGrIP platform. From the function aspect, it is an all-sided solution for information retrieval on the Internet. When it runs on the internet, a parallel, distributed and configurable Spider is used for information gather; a multi-hierarchy document classification approach combining the information gain initially processes gathered web documents;

a swarm intelligence based document clustering method is used for information organization; a concept-based retrieval interface is applied for user interactive retrieval. Since huge original information is crucial in a decision support system, it was integrated as a module of the AGrIP platform, which provides a powerful information collection function.

4.2 Data mining tool-MSMiner

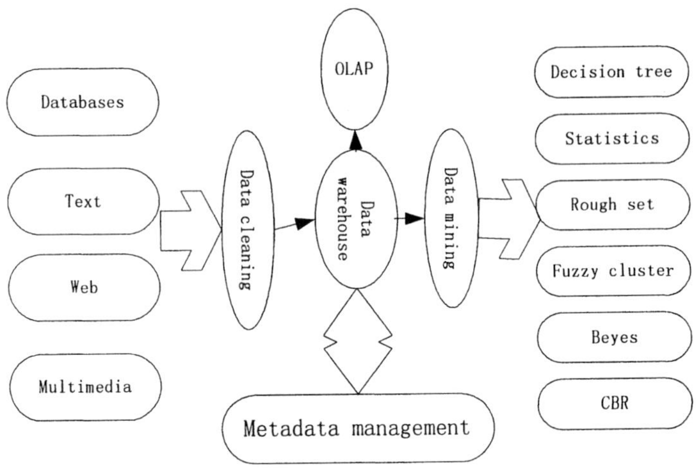

Figure 4. MSMiner

MSMiner [2] is a generic multi-strategy data-mining tool. The functions of the system include database access, data modeling, data preprocessing, data mining, and data visualization. In addition to this, emphasis has been put on the extensibility characteristics of the system. As multi-strategy data mining software, MSMiner not only provides convenient tools to develop new data mining algorithms, but also includes many build-in algorithms such as SOM and C4.5. MSMiner has an open interface for adding data preprocessing function and can access a variety of databases such as SQL Server, Oracle, and Informix. It can collect information from web, text, database and multimedia database. After data cleaning, they are stored in the data warehouse for data mining. Since it is a multi-strategy data mining tools, we integrated machine learning, rough set, CBR and Statistics techniques in the algorithms library which provides a strong data mining for decision support.

5 APPLICATIONS

AGrIP is now as the foundation platform for city emergency inter-act system. The process is as follows. Firstly, it searches the information through the Ghunt from the Internet and stores them in the database. And then, we use the MSMiner in the platform for data mining and acquire rules. These rules are applied for reasoning about the future cases. After getting decisions about the emergency, we apply the MAGE as the integrated platform to distributed the decision information to concrete department for actions.

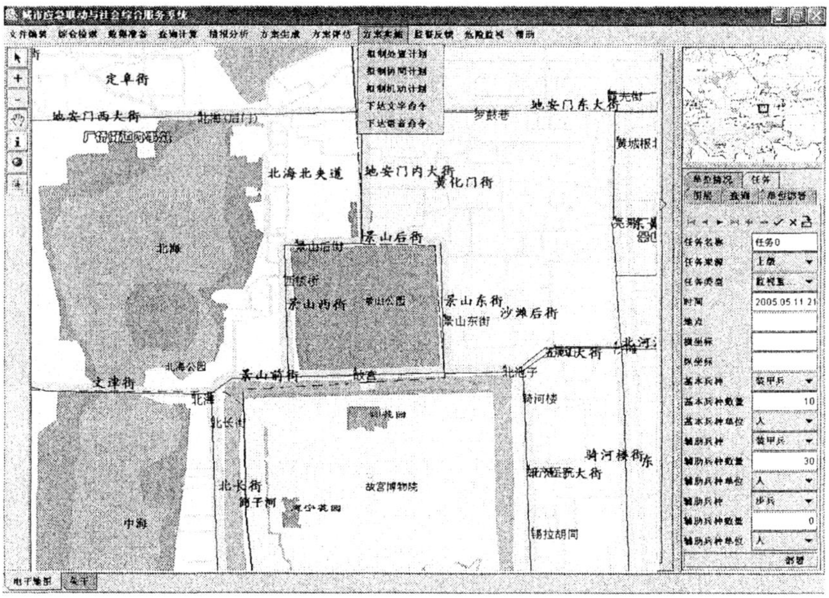

Figure 5 Grid-Based Emergency Inter-Act System

5. CONCLUSIONS

Establishing grids is an important undertaking in developing scalable infrastructures. In this paper we have proposed a model for agent-based grid computing from the implement point of view. Based on the model AGrIP has been constructed using MAGE, which is a multiagent environment platform.

Due to the very generic nature of the grid computing, we can involve the research on it from different level, such as operating system layer, information layer, knowledge layer, and service-oriented layer. Agent-based grid intelligent platform AGrIP focuses on service-oriented layer in terms of current exist running environment. AGrIP will be a useful platform for research on agent-based grid computing.

ACKNOWLEDGMENTS

This work is supported by the National High-Tech Programme of China (Grant No. 2003AA115220), the National Basic Research and Development Plan of China (Grant No. 2003CB317000) and the Youth Research Fund of CUMT(Grant No. 0D4489).

REFERENCE

[1] Zhongzhi Shi, Haijun Zhang, Yong Cheng, Yuncheng Jiang, Qiujian Sheng, Zhikung Zhao: MAGE: An Agent-Oriented Programming Environment. IEEE ICCI 2004: 250-257

[2]. Zhongzhi Shi, Youping Huang, Qing He, Lida Xu, Shaohui Liu, Liangxi Qin, Ziyan Jia, Jiayou Li. MSMiner-A Developing Platform for OLAP. Decision Support Systems, 2005

[3] Zhongzhi Shi, Qing He, Ziyan Jia and Jiayou Li. Intelligence Chinese Document Semantic Indexing System. International Journal of Information Technology and Decision Making, Vol.2, No.3, 2003: 407-424.

[4] Intelligent science web www.intsci.ac.cn

IRIS RECOGNITION ALGORITHM BASED ON COMPLEX GEOMETRICAL SHAPE COVER

Hao Feng[1], Wenming Cao[2,3], Shoujue Wang[3]
[1]Jiaxing College Jiaxing, zhejiang, 314001,China, [2]The College of Information Engineering, ZheJiang University of Technology, Hangzhou, 310014, China,[3]Lab of Artificial Neural Networks, Institute of Semiconductors, CAS, Beijing, 100083, Chinacsann@zjut.edu.cn

Abstract: In this my paper, we present a kind of Iris Recognition based on Complex Geometrical Shape Cover. From the cognition science point of view, we constructed a Complex Geometrical Shape for iris recognition. In this method, irises are trained as "cognition" one class by one class, and it doesn't influence the original recognition knowledge for samples of the new added class. The results of experiments show the correct rejection rate is 98.9%, the correct cognition rate and the error recognition rate are 95.71% and 3.5% respectively. The experimental results demonstrate that the correct rejection rate of the test samples excluded in the classes of training samples is very high. It proves the proposed method for iris recognition is effective.

Key words: Iris recognition, Complex Geometrical Shape Cover, HDS.

1. INTRODUCTION

With the appearance of information science field such as computer media signal processing etc., researchers get to look for various methods for processing multidimensional signal, the multidimensional signal processing theory therefore arises. However modern signal processing techniques, mostly depending on the complicated mathematical formulas, look for an optimum object by means of iteration and fitting etc. These methods have some disadvantages including huge computation load, non direct-viewing, hard to be understood, moreover often trapping at local minima.

In the recent years, Wang Soujue[1-4] proposed complex geometrical shape cover method, which uses the high dimensional space descriptive geometry as tools, maps multidimensional digital signals to be points in HDS, and discuss relationship among multidimensional digital signals via analysis of point distribution and geometric object characteristics in HDS. Since this method is simple and feasible, and is able to accelerate computation by parallel operation, it has get remarkable achievements in many application fields [4,5-14].

In the light of descriptive geometry and notions in set theory, this paper redefines the basic elements in space such as curve and surface and so on, presents some fundamental notions with respect to the point cover based on the HDS point covering theory, finally, as an example, considers points generated by mapping part of speech signals to HDS to analyze distribution information of these iris sample in HDS , in this paper also proposes a new algorithm for iris recognition on the basis of the HDS point dynamic searching theory.

The remainder of this paper is organized as follows. Section 2 describes the theory of multi weights neurons. Section 3 introduces iris recognition algorithm based on Complex Geometrical Shape Cover and multi-weighted neuron. Experiments results and experimental analysis is effective.

2. THE THEORY OF MULTI WEIGHTS NEURONS

As we said in the former, the method used by BPR is "Complex Geometrical Shape Cover Recognition Method". The present neurons are based on single-weight vector which can only reach the simple and regular shapes. In fact, the real shapes of some a pattern in the feature space, such as a given person's face images, are irregular and complicated, so we developed a novel theory of multi-weight vector neurons which can reach the complicated shapes and meet the need of BPR.

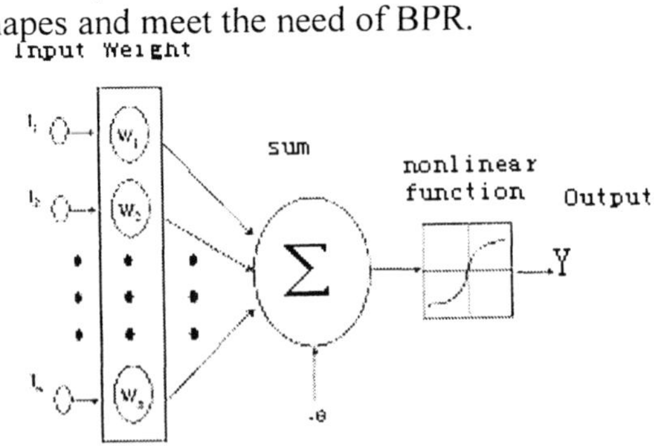

Fig1. Sigle weight neuron model

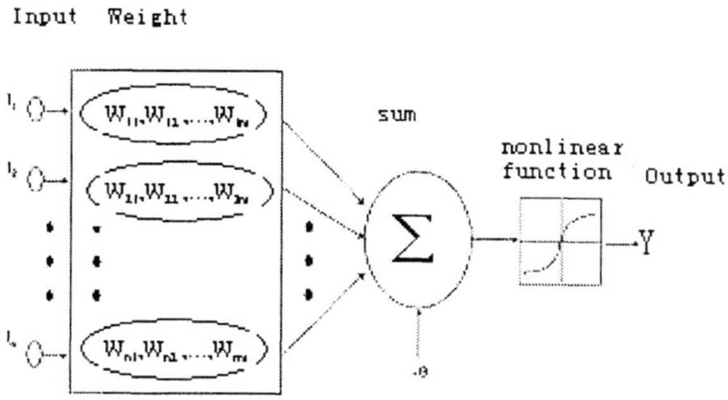

Fig 2.Multi Weight Neuron Model

According to the theory of BPR, the different samples of the same class are connected, then we can know all of the same class samples should be in a irregular and connected region. The aim of pattern recognition is to find this region or use a geometry shape to approximate to it as possibly. DBF is one typical method which use "hypersphere" to approximate real shape[6][7][18], however, few real shapes decided by the same class samples exactly are hypersphere. In our theory, all samples of the same class should be included in the shape covered by neuron, so when this shape is different from the real shape, it must be bigger than the real one and it not only covers samples of this class but also covers other class samples which should not be covered, then the error recognition rate will increase. Differently, the different approximation will result in different error recognition rate.

Generally, the expression of a multi-weight vectors neuron is:

$$Y = f[\Phi(W_1, W_2, ..., W_m, X)] \qquad (1)$$

$W_1, W_2, ..., W_m$ are m weights vectors and are decided by a group of study samples vectors $S_1, S_2, ..., S_m$; X is the input vector; Φ is a function decided by a multi weight neuron; f is step function, which is equal to 1 when x<=k and equal to 0 when x>k.

3. THE APPLICATION FOR IRIS RECOGNITION OF MULTI WEIGHTS NEURONS

In recent years, with the development of information technology and the increasing need for security, intelligent personal identification has become a very important and urgent problem. The emerging biometric technology can solve the problem, which takes the unique, reliable and stable biometric features (such as fingerprints, iris, face, palm-prints, gait etc.) as identification body. This technology has very high security, reliability and effectivity. As one of the biometric technology, iris recognition has very high reliability. Comparing with other biometric identification technology, the fault acceptance rate and the fault rejection rate of iris recognition are very low. The technology of iris recognition has many advantages, i.e., stability, non-invasiveness, uniqueness. All there desirable properties make the technology of iris recognition has very high commercial value. Based on the above reasons, many researchers have applied themselves to this field. Daugman used multi-scale quadrature wavelets to extract texture-phase structure information of iris to generate a 2048-bit iriscode and compared the difference between a pair of iris representations by computing their Hamming distance via the XOR operator [8],[9]. Wildes et al. represented the iris texture with a Laplacian pyramid constructed with four different resolution levels and used the normalized correlation to determine whether the input image and the model image are from the same class [10]. Boles et al. calculated zero-crossing representation of 1D wavelet transform at various resolution levels of a virtual circle on an iris image to characterize the texture of the iris. Iris mating was based on two dissimilarity functions [11]. As follow, Section3.1 describes Image preprocessing of iris-- Iris localization, Localization of the inner boundary, Localization of the outer boundary, Iris normalization and enhancement. Section 3.2 introduces iris recognition algorithm based on multi weight neuron, Experiments results and experimental analysis.

3.1 Image preprocessing

Iris image preprocessing is mainly composed of iris localization, iris normalization and enhancement.

Iris localization namely is the localization of the inner boundary and the outer boundary of a typical iris can approximately be taken as circles. It is the important part of the system of iris recognition, and exact localization is the premise of the iris identification and verification.

The original iris image has some character of the gray-scale distribution. The iris is darker than the sclera, and the pupil is greatly darker than the iris. From the histogram, we can clearly see that the low gray-scale mainly converges at the first peak value. Therefore, we adopt the binary transform to localize the inner boundary. From the image after binary transform, we find that the areas of zero gray-scale are almost the areas of the pupil and eyelash. Therefore, we reduce the influence of the eyelash by erode and dilation.

$$xpupil = xbegin + \frac{dia\max}{2},\ ypupil = ybegin,\ rpupil = \frac{dia\max}{2}。$$

Where *xpupil* and *ypupil* denote the center coordinates of the pupil, and *rpupil* denotes the radius of the pupil. after erode and dilation

When the quality of the image is reliable, this algorithm can localize the pupil quickly and exactly. Otherwise, we can correct the method as follow:

1. We can reduce the searching area by subtracting the pixels on the edge of the image.

2. We can get k chords, which are less than a certain threshold near the longest chord, and take the average value of center coordinates of k chord as the center of the pupil.

3.2 Localization of the outer boundary

The exact parameters of the outer boundary are obtained by using edge detection (Canny operator in our experiments) and Hough transform. The image after Edge detection includes some useless points. For eliminating the influence, we remove the useless points between the areas of $\left[30^\circ, 150^\circ\right]$ and $\left[225^\circ, 315^\circ\right]$ according to the center of the pupil. Then, Hough transform [14] is adopted to localize the outer boundary.

3.3 Iris normalization and enhancement

Irises from different people may be captured in different size, and even for irises from the same eye, the size may change because of illumination variations and other factors (the pupil is very sensitive to lighting changes). Such elastic deformation in iris texture will influence the results of iris recognition. For the purpose of achieving more accurate recognition results, it is necessary to compensate for such deformation. In our experiment, every point of the iris image is mapped to the polar coordinates by the following formula.

$$\begin{cases} x(r,\theta) = (1-r)x_p(\theta) + rx_s(\theta) \\ y(r,\theta) = (1-r)y_p(\theta) + ry_s(\theta) \end{cases}$$

In which, ($x_p(\theta), y_p(\theta)$) and ($x_s(\theta)\ y_p(\theta)$) denote the point of intersection with the inner boundary and the outer boundary respectively.

In our experiment, the sector areas ($\left[130^\circ, 230^\circ\right]$ and $\left[310^\circ, 410^\circ\right]$) are intercepted for normalization according the pupil center. In this way, one hand, it is simple; on the other hand, the segment texture information is enough to identify the different persons. Then, the iris ring is unwrapped to a rectangular texture block with a fixed size (64×256), and the rows correspond to the radius and the columns correspond to the angles. The normalized iris image still has low contrast and may have non-uniform brightness caused by the position of light sources. All these may affect the feature analysis. Therefore, we enhance the normalized image by means of histogram equalization. Such processing compensates for non-uniform illumination, as well as improving the contrast of the image.

3.4 Iris recognition algorithm based on Complex Geometrical Shape

Complex Geometrical Shape , $pSi3$ neuron, can be described as follow:

$$Y = f[\Phi(X, W_1, W_2, W_3) - Th] \quad 2$$

$$\Phi(X, W_1, W_2, W_3) = \left\| X - \theta_{(W_1, W_2, W_3)} \right\| \quad 3$$

In which, $\theta_{(W_1,W_2,W_3)}$ denotes the finite area, which is enclosed by three points(W_1 、 W_2 、 W_3), and it is a triangle area. Namely, $\theta_{(W_1,W_2,W_3)}$ can be represented as follow:

$$\theta_{(W_1,W_2,W_3)} = \{Y | Y = \alpha_2[\alpha_1 W_1 + (1-\alpha_1)W_2] + (1-\alpha_2)W_3, \alpha_1 \in [0,1], \alpha_2 \in [0,1]\} \quad 4$$

Then, $\Phi(X, W_1, W_2, W_3)$ - Th actually is the Euclid distance from X to the triangle area of the $pSi3$ neuron. The model of activation function is:

$$f(x) = \begin{cases} 1, & x \le Th \\ -1, & x > Th \end{cases} \quad 5$$

In multi-dimensional space, we use every three sample's points of the same class to construct a finite 2D plane, namely, a triangle. Then several 2D spaces can be constructed, and we cover these planes by the $pSi3$ neuron to approximate the complicated "shape", which is formed by many sample points of the iris in multi-dimensional space.

3.5 Construction of Complex Geometrical Shape

Step 1: Let the sample points of the training set are $\alpha = \{A_1, A_2, \cdots, A_N\}$. In which, N is the number of the total sample points. To figure out the distance of every two points, the two points having the least distance are defined as B_{11} and B_{12}. Let B_{13} denotes the nearest point away from B_{11} and B_{12}, and B_{13} must doesn't in the line formed by B_{11} and B_{12}. In this way, B_{11} 、 B_{12} and B_{13} construct the first triangle plane represented as θ_1, which is covered by a $pSi3$ neuron, the covering area is:

$$P_1 = \{X | \rho_{X\theta_1} \le Th, X \in R^n\} \quad 6$$

$$\theta_1 = \{Y \mid Y = \alpha_2[\alpha_1 B_{11} + (1-\alpha_1)B_{12}] + (1-\alpha_2)B_{13}, \alpha_1 \in [0,1], \alpha_2 \in [0,1]\} \quad 7$$

Where $\rho_{X\theta_1}$ denotes the distance from X to θ_1.

Step 2: Firstly, The rest points contained in P_1 should be removed. Then, according to the method of step1, define the nearest point away from B_{11}、B_{12} and B_{13} as B_{21}. Among B_{11}、B_{12} and B_{13}, two nearest points away from B_{21} are denoted as B_{22} and B_{23}. And B_{21}、B_{22} and B_{23} construct the second triangle defined as θ_2, which is covered by another $pSi3$ neuron. And the covering area is described as follow:

$$P_2 = \{X \mid \rho_{X\theta_2} \le Th, X \in R^n\} \quad 8$$

$$\theta_2 = \{Y \mid Y = \alpha_2[\alpha_1 B_{21} + (1-\alpha_1)B_{22}] + (1-\alpha_2)B_{23}, \alpha_1 \in [0,1], \alpha_2 \in [0,1]\} \quad 9$$

Where $\rho_{X\theta_2}$ denotes the distance from X to θ_2.

Step 3: Remove the rest points contained in the covering area of the front $(i-1)$ $pSi3$ neurons. Let B_{i1} denotes the nearest point from the remained points to the three vertexes of the $(i-1)th$ triangle. Two nearest vertexes of the (i -1) triangle away from B_{i1} are represented as B_{i2} and B_{i3}. Then, B_{i1}、B_{i2} and B_{i3} construct the ith triangle, defined as θ_3.

In the same way, θ_3 is covered by a $pSi3$ neuron. The covering area is

$$P_i = \{X \mid \rho_{X\theta_3} \le Th, X \in R^n\} \quad 10$$

$$\theta_3 - \{Y \mid Y = \alpha_2[\alpha_1 B_{i1} + (1-\alpha_1)B_{i2}] + (1-\alpha_2)B_{i3}, \alpha_1 \in [0,1], \alpha_2 \in [0,1]\} \quad 11$$

Step 4: Repeat the step 3 until all sample points are conducted successfully. Finally, there are m $pSi3$ neurons, and their mergence about covering area is the covering area of every iris' class.

$$P = \bigcup_{i=1}^{m} P_i \quad 12$$

3.6 Iris recognition algorithm

Taking Th=0 under recognition, the $pSi3$ neuron can be described as follow:

$$\rho = \left\| X - \theta_{(W_1,W_2,W_3)} \right\| \quad 13$$

The output ρ is the distance from X to the finite area $\theta_{(W_1,W_2,W_3)}$.

The distance from X to the covering area of the ith class iris is:

$$\rho_i = \min_{j=1}^{M_i} \rho_{ij}, \ i = 1, \cdots, 80 \quad 14$$

In which, M_i denotes the number of the $pSi3$ neuron of the ith iris, ρ is the distance from X to the covering area of the jth neuron of the ith class' iris.

The X will be classified to the iris class corresponding to the least ρ_i. Namely, the classification method is:

$$j = \min_{i=1}^{80} \rho_i , \quad j \in (1, \cdots, 80) \qquad 15$$

3.7 Experimental results

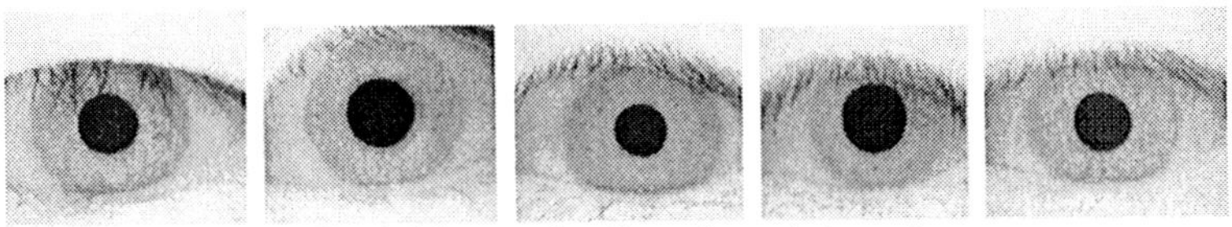

Fig.3 iris samples from the training set

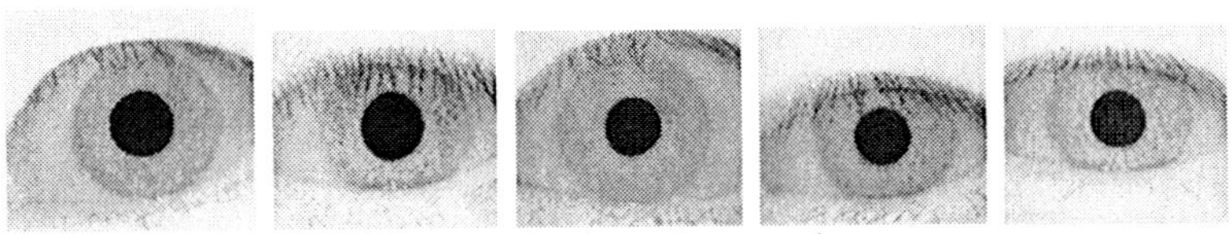

Fig.4 iris samples from the second test set

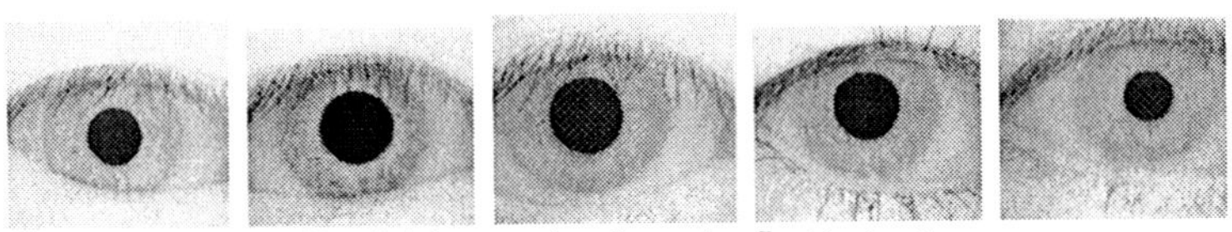

Fig.5 iris samples from the first test set

Images of CASIA (Institute of Automation, Chinese Academy of Sciences) iris image database are used in this paper. The database includes 742 iris images from 106 different eyes (hence 106 different classes) of 80 subjects. For each iris class, images are captured in two different sessions and the interval between two sessions is one month. The experiment processes and experiment results are presented as follow:

(1) In our experiment, 3 random samples from each class in the frontal 80 classes (hence, 240 samples) are chosen for training, and a *pSi*3 neuron of multi weight neuron is constructed for the 3 samples. Five samples from the training set are shown in Fig.3. Then, the entire iris database is taken as test sample set. In which, 182 (26×7) samples, which don't belong to the classes of training samples, are referred to the first sample set. The remainder of total 560 (80×7) samples is referred to the second sample set. Fig.4 shows five samples from the second test set and Fig.5 shows five samples from the first test set.

(2) The correct rejection rate=the number of samples which are rejected correctly in the first sample set/the total number of the first sample set. The correct cognition rate=the number of samples which are recognized corrected in the second sample set / the total number of the second sample set. The error recognition rate= (the number of samples which are

recognized mistakenly in the first sample set +the number of samples which are recognized mistakenly in the second sample set) / the total number of the second sample set.

(3) For total 742 test samples, 180 samples are rejected correctly and the other 2 samples are recognized mistakenly in the first test sample; and 536 samples are recognized correctly and the rest 24 samples are recognized mistakenly in the second test sample. Therefore, the correct rejection rate is 98.9%(180/182), the correct cognition rate and the error recognition rate are 95.71%(536/560) and 3.5%((2+24)/742) respectively.

3.8 Experimental analysis

We can conclude from the above experimental results that:

(1) Irises are trained as "cognition" one class by one class in our method, and it doesn't influence the original recognition knowledge for samples of the new added class.

(2) Although the correct cognition rate is not very well, the result of the correct rejection rate is wonderful. In our experiment, the correct rejection rate is 98.9%, namely, the iris classes that don't belong to the training test can be rejected successfully.

(3) The iris recognition algorithm based on neuron of multi weight neuron is applied in the experiment and the total samples of every class construct the shape of 1D distribution. Namely, it is the network connection of different neuron.

(4) In above experiment, if the image preprocessing is more perfectly, the experimental results maybe better.

To sum up, it proves the proposed iris recognition algorithm based on multi-weighted neuron is effective.

4. CONCLUSION

Biomimetic Pattern Recognition using the analysis method of ANN, which is based on a novel all-purposed mathematic model of Multi weight neurons, is proposed in this Paper. It is a fire-new theoretics of Pattern Recognition. As the base, we have proposed a new model of Multi weight neuron and implemented it in the new CASSANDRA-II neurocomputer.

This method of pattern recognition is more effective and efficient than traditional pattern recognition. And it's application is very broad, besides "multi-camera human-face personal identification system" and "speech recognition", "Iris recognition" we also apply Biomimetic Pattern

Recognition to identify objects (such as naval ship, tank, bus, bow, horse, sheep) from different directions on horizontal plane or sea level, etc.

From above analysis, the theory of Biomimetic Pattern Recognition using ANN and the method of multi weight neuron has created a new hopeful way for Pattern Recognition. This method is being improved and developed, and will be used practically into more science fields in future.

National Natural Science Foundation of China: 60135010

REFERENCES:

1. Wang Shou-jue, "Biomimetic (Topological) Pattern Recognition —— A New Model of Pattern Recognition Theory and Its Applications" (in Chinese), ACTA ELECTRONICA SINICA, Vol.30, No.10, pp.1417-1420, Oct.2002
2. Wang Shou-jue, "Analysis and Theory of High-Dimension Space Geometry to Artificial Neural Networks", ACTA ELECTRONICA SINICA, Vol.30, No.1, pp.1-4, Jan.2002
3. WANG Shoujue, Biomimetics Pattern Recognition, Neural Networks Society (INNS, ENNS, JNNS) Newsletter, Vol.1 No.1, 3-5, March 2003
4. WANG Shoujue, WANG Bainan, Analysis and Theory of High-Dimension Space Geometry for Artificial Neural Networks (in Chinese), Acta Electronica Sinica, Vol.30 No.1, Jan 2002
5. WANG Shoujue, XU Jian, WANG Xianbao, QIN Hong, Multi-camera Human-face Personal Identification System Based on the BIOMIMETIC PATTERN RECOGNITION (in Chinese), Acta Electronica Sinica, Vol. 30 No. 1, Jan 2002
6. Wang Shoujue, Shi Jingpu, Chen Chuan, Li Yujian. Direction-Basis-Function Neural Networks [A].#58 Session:4.2, IJCNN'99.[C] [6]
7. Wang Shou-jue, "Discussion on the Basic Mathematical Models of Neurons in General Purpose Neurocomputer", ACTA ELECTRONICA SINICA, Vol.29, No.5, pp.577-580, May.2001
8. J.Daugman, Biometric Personal Identification System Based on Iris Analysis [P]. U.S. Patent 5291560, 1994.
9. J.Daugman, High Confidence Visual Recognition of Persons by a Text of Statistical Independence, IEEE Trans. Pattern Anal. Mach. Intell. 15(11) (1993) 1148-1161.
10. R.Wildes, Iris Recogniton: An Emerging Biometric Techonology, Proc. IEEE 85(1997) 1348-1363.
11. W.Boles, B. Boashash, A Human Identification Technique Using Image of the Iris and Wavelet Transform, IEEE Trans. Signal Process. 46(4) (1998) 1185-1188.
12. Wang Shoujue, Li Zhaozhou, Chen Xiangdong, Wang Bainan, Discussion on the Basic Mathematical Models of Neurons in General Purpose Neurocomputer, ACTA ELECTRONICA SINICA. 2001, 29(5): 577-580
13. Wenming Cao, Feng Hao, Shoujue Wang: The application of DBF neural networks for object recognition. Inf. Sci. 160(1-4): 153-160 (2004)
14. T. Risse, Hough Transform for Line Recognition, Computer Vision and Image Processing, 1989, 46, 327-345, 1989

MULTI-POPULATION EVOLUTIONARY ALGORITHM FOR SOLVING CONSTRAINED OPTIMIZATION PROBLEMS

Ziyi Chen and Lishan Kang

State Key Laboratory of Software Engineering, Wuhan University, Wuhan 430072, Hubei, China

Abstract: A novel multi-population evolutionary algorithm (MPEA) is presented, which can solve the constrained function optimization problems rather efficiently. The MPEA adopts three populations with different multi-parent crossover operators. So each population emphasizes particularly on different searching regions and the complementarity of these three crossover operators can enhances the diversity of individuals, which improves the search ability of the MPEA dramatically. And during the MPEA runs, the three populations exchange the best solution in each generation to adjust its search direction to the possible optimum solution. Experiments have been carried on several benchmark functions to test the performance of the presented MPEA. Numerical results show that MPEA is highly competitive with other algorithms in effectiveness and generality.

Key words: evolutionary algorithm,constrained function optimization,multiple populations, Multi-parent crossover operator

1. INTRODUCTION

Researchers have developed many evolutionary algorithms to solve the constrained optimization problems.For example, DE[1],HDE[2],MIHDE[3] ,GENOCOP[4],etc. Meanwhile, many strategies have been adopted to improve the performance of evolutionary algorithms [5-8]。

These algorithms are basically single population evolutionary algorithms. Such single population evolutionary algorithms are powerful and perform well on a wide variety of problems. However, better results can be obtained by introducing multiple subpopulations. Every subpopulation evolves over a few generations isolated before one or more individuals are exchanged between the subpopulation[9][10] .The multi-population evolutionary algorithm models the evolution of a species in a way more similar to nature than the single population evolutionary algorithm. The key task of solving constrained function optimization problems is to design universal evolutionary operator with high efficiency and scheme out suitable strategy to handle the constraints .

A novel multi-population evolutionary algorithm(MPEA), which handles the constrained function optimization problems, is presented in this paper. Three populations are created at the beginning of the MPEA run and each population uses different multi-parent crossover operators. The complementarity among three crossover operators enhances the diversity, which makes the MPEA more likely to find the global optimum than other single population evolutionary algorithms. And during the MPEA runs, different populations exchange their best solutions in each generation in order to enhance its search performance. The new approach is compared against other evolutionary optimization techniques in several benchmark functions. The results obtained show that the new approach is a general, effective and robust method. Its performance outperforms some other techniques.

2. DESCRIPTION OF ALGORITHM (MPEA)

2.1 Constrained function optimization

Without loss of generality, we assume that the objective function $f(x)$ is minimized. The maximization problem can converted into a minimization problem according to the duality principle. The nonlinear programming problem is generally described as follows:

$$\begin{array}{ll} \textit{Minimize} & f(x), x=(x_1,x_2,\ldots,x_n)\in R^n \\ \textit{Subject to} & h_i(x)=0, i=1,2,\ldots,n_1 \\ & g_j(x)\le 0, j=1,2,\ldots,n_2 \\ & \text{where } X^l \le x=(x_1,x_2,\ldots,x_v)\le X^u \end{array} \quad (1)$$

The domain space of problem: $D = \{x \mid X^l \le x \le X^u\}$.
For most difficult real world problems, the objective function , constraints $g_j(x)$ and $h_k(x)$ are nonlinear .

2.2 The flow of MPEA

Algorithm MPEA

BEGIN

Initialize three different populations randomly : p_1, p_2, p_3 :
$p_j=\{X_{j1}, X_{j2},\dots, X_{jN}\}$, $X_{ji} \in \text{D}; 1 \le j \le 3, 1 \le i \le N$

$generation = 0$;

$X_{j,best} = \arg \underset{1\le i\le N}{Min} f(X_{ji}); 1 \le j \le 3$

$X_{j,worst} = \arg \underset{1\le i\le N}{Max} f(X_{ji}); 1 \le j \le 3$

WHILE not $\left(\left(abs\left(f(X_{1,best}) - f(X_{1,worst})\right) \le \varepsilon\right)\right.$ and

$\left(abs\left(f(X_{2,best}) - f(X_{2,worst})\right) \le \varepsilon\right)$ and

$\left.\left(abs\left(f(X_{3,best}) - f(X_{3,worst})\right) \le \varepsilon\right)\right)$ do

BEGIN

FOR k=1 to 3 do BEGIN

Select M individuals randomly from population p_k and create a new individual X by Multi-Parent Crossover Operator(C_k)

FOR j=1 to 3 do BEGIN

IF $better(X, X_{j,worst})$ THEN $X_{j,worst} = X$;

```
        END FOR;
```

$$X_{k,best} = \arg \underset{1 \le i \le N}{Min} f(X_{k,i});$$

$$X_{k,worst} = \arg \underset{1 \le i \le N}{Max} f(X_{k,i});$$

```
      END FOR;
```

$generation = generation + 1$;

```
    END;
  END WHILE;
  Output results;
END;
```

Where N is population size , ε is the precision of results , $X_{j,best}$ is the individual with lowest fitness value in population p_j , $X_{j,worst}$ is the individual with highest fitness value in population p_j . M is fixed as 4 。 C_1 is Reflect Operator , C_2 is Compact Operator, and C_3 is Expand Operator.

2.3 Algorithm Analysis

MPEA uses three different populations and every population use different Multi-parent crossover operators . Furthermore, every population adopts the steady elimination strategy to generate only one new individual in each generation. When one population generates a new individual, other populations will compare the new individual with the worst individual in their own population. If the new one is better than the worst, supersedes the latter. We use real-valued encoding without a mutation operator. The main idea of MPEA is that it searches the domain space to find the feasible region at first, then approaches the possible global optimum in the feasible region which have been found.

2.3.1 Handling the constraints —Two-time Evolution

Commonly, the equality constraints are so strong that the estimate of the feasible region is very hard, which leads to the impossibility to search the domain space at first to find the feasible region and approach the global optima in the following. The method of Two-time evolutionary is to transform those equality constraints to inequality constraints, then find a appropriate penalty parameter using evolutionary computation .

The flow of Two-time Evolutionary:

Step 1: transform equality constraints

$$h_i(x) = 0, i = 1,2,...,n_1 \text{ to}: -\delta \le h_i(x) \le \delta \;\; i = 1,2,.....n_1 ,$$

where δ is a positive parameter. Generally, we set δ =0.01。Thus, there are $2n_1 + n_2$ inequality constraints:

$$g_j^*(x) \le 0, j = 1,2,...2n_1 + n_2$$

We can define:

$$w_j(x) = \begin{cases} 0 & \text{if } g_j^*(x) \le 0 \\ g_j^*(x) & otherwise \end{cases}, \qquad j = 1,2,...2n_1 + n_2 \quad (2)$$

$$W(x) = \sum_{j=1}^{2n_1+n_2} w_j(x)$$

Therefore, a dualistic relation *better* can be defined as follow::

$$better(x', x'') = \begin{cases} true & \text{if } W(x') < W(x'') \\ false & \text{if } W(x') > W(x'') \\ true & \text{if } (W(x') = W(x'')) \wedge (f(x') \le f(x'' \\ false & \text{if } (W(x') = W(x'')) \wedge (f(x') > f(x'' \end{cases} \quad (3)$$

It means that the individual x' is better than x'' when $better(x', x'')$ is true . The feasible solutions will be *better* than the infeasible solutions when such method of handling the constraints adopted.

Step 2: the objective function $f(x)$ will be act as fitness function to start evolutionary using the algorithm MPEA, the evolutionary will be stopped when

$$(abs(f(X_{best}) - f(X_{worst})) \le \varepsilon) .$$

Where ε is also a small positive parameter . Since we only need the orders of magnitude of the global optima, we set ε =0.01 。After the algorithm stops, we can gain a relative good function value f^* 。

Step 3:

$$F(x) = f(x) + r\sum_{i=1}^{n_1} abs(h_i(x)) \quad (4)$$

will be act as the objective function to start evolutionary again , where $r = k \times f^*$ 。 The best result found at this time is the global optimum of the original problem. We have obtained rather good results in all experiments with setting $k = 10$. The reason lies that the value of objective function is larger than the value of penalty in the neighboring region of the optimum, but the value of the objective function has little distinction from penalty in the orders of magnitude .

2.3.2 Multi-Parent Crossover Operator

Multi-parent crossover operators, which mean that more than two parents are involved when generating offspring, are a more flexible version, generalizing the traditional two-parent crossover of nature. Much attention has been paying on them in the field of evolutionary computation. There are various Multi-parent crossover operators with good performance for the Real-Coded evolutionary Algorithms[11][12]. Because of the complexity of the feasible region, it is impractical that a single Multi-parent crossover operator can solve various problems. So we design three different Multi-parent crossover operators which have complementary features: Reflect Operator , Compact Operator,. Expand Operator .These Multi-Parent crossover operators generate offspring by linear non-convex combination of M parental vectors. Figure 1 shows how to generate a new individual using these three Multi-Parent crossover operators.

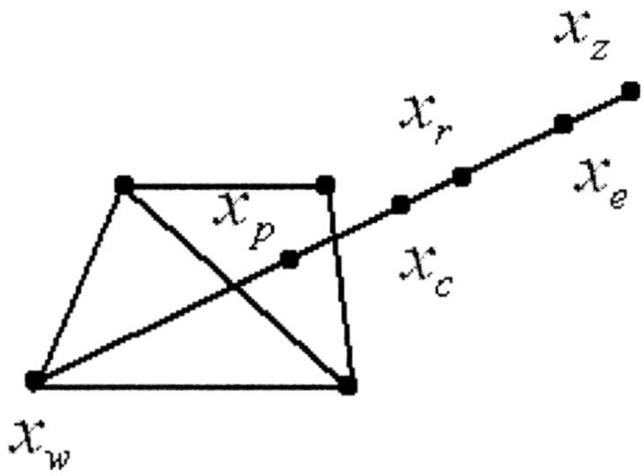

Figure. 1. Multi-Parent Crossover Operators

Their flows are as follows:

1) M individuals $x_j, j = 1,2,...,M$ are randomly selected in the population.

2) find the worst individual x_w in these M individuals (by comparing with the value of their fitness).

3) we call the centroid of the remanent M-1 individuals as x_p

$$x_p = \frac{\sum_{j=1}^{M} x_j - x_w}{M - 1} \tag{5}$$

4) find the reflecting point x_r of x_w corresponding to x_p:

$$x_r = 2 \times x_w - x_p \tag{6}$$

We call this Crossover Operator as **Reflect Operator** (generate a new individual x_r).

5) find the reflecting point x_z of x_p corresponding to x_r:

$$x_z = 2 \times x_p - x_r \tag{7}$$

6) Select a point x_c from x_p to x_r randomly,, We call this Crossover Operator as **Compact Operator** (generate a new individual x_c).

7) Select a point x_e from x_z to x_r randomly,, We call this Crossover Operator as **Expand Operator** (generate a new individual x_e).

8) In these multi-parent crossover operators, *M* is fixed to 4. Many numerical tests have been made to find a good value of *M*. The results show that it is a good choice with setting M=4.

These three Multi-Parent Crossover Operators have the following important features:

- New individual generated will near the region where individuals have high fitness value, so there is rather larger probability that the new individual has higher fitness value than that of the worst individual in the population. Thus, MPEA can speedup the constringency because of the strong direction of these multi-parent crossover operators. In fact, these operators can instruct their search direction using statistical information.

- These three crossover operators have complementary features .On the one hand, the numerical tests show that Reflect Operator is the main operator in our algorithm which can keep a good balance between exploration and exploitation. On the other hand, Compact Operator will stress on exploitation which can improve the speed of constringency . Meanwhile, Expand Operator will stress on exploration , then MPEA has lower possibility to be trapped in local optima .
- It is difficult to estimate which operators will more suitable to solve some type problems when we lack of the background of problems , so we hope that MPEA will gain higher generality because of the combination of multiple different operators .

3. EXPERIMENTS AND RESULT

We have developed software based on the algorithm MPEA and have made many numeric experiments .Six test problems are selected .Problem 2 to 6 are found in [14] and problem 1 to 6 in [13] . In these problems, the constraints include linear constraints , nonlinear constraints, inequality constraints and equality constraints .

In [14], Michalewicz compares the performance of six different methods on the five problems 2 to 6 .The result here is compared to the result for the best method found in [14]. In [13], Deb proposes a novel method to handle constraints ,and he tested his method on nine different problems of which test problem 1 to 6 are a subset . The results obtained by the proposed method in this paper are compared to the results obtained by Deb on all these six test problems . For each of the problems, 20 independent runs are performed and the best, worst and average results are recorded.

3.1 Benchmark problems

1 Minimize :

$$G_1(x) = 5.3578547x_3^2 + 0.8356891x_2x_5 + 37.293239x_1 - 40792.1 \tag{8}$$

Subject to:

$$0 \le 85.334407 + 0.0056858x_2x_5 + 0.00026x_1x_4 - 0.0022053x_3x_5 \le 92$$

$$90 \le 80.51246 + 0.0071317x_2x_5 + 0.0029955x_1x_2 + 0.0021813x_3^2 \le 110$$

$$20 \le 9.300961 + 0.0047026x_3x_5 + 0.0012547x_1x_3 + 0.0019085x_3x_4 \le 25$$

where $78 \le x_1 \le 102, 33 \le x_2 \le 45, 27 \le x_i \le 45, i = 3,4,5$

2 Minimize

$$G_2(x) = 5x_1 + 5x_2 + 5x_3 + 5x_4 - 5\sum_{i=1}^{4} x_i^2 - \sum_{i=5}^{13} x_i \tag{9}$$

subject to $2x_1 + 2x_2 + x_{10} + x_{11} \le 10$, $2x_1 + 2x_3 + x_{10} + x_{11} \le 10$, $2x_2 + 2x_3 + x_{11} + x_{12} \le 10$, $-8x_1 + x_{10} \le 0$, $-8x_2 + x_{11} \le 0$, $-8x_3 + x_{12} \le 0$, $-2x_4 - x_5 + x_{10} \le 0$, $-2x_6 - x_7 + x_{11} \le 0$, $-2x_8 - x_9 + x_{12} \le 0$,

Where the bounds are $0 \le x_i \le 1$, $i = 1,2,...,9$, $0 \le x_i \le 100, i = 10,11,12$ and $0 \le x_{13} \le 1$ 。

3 Minimize

$$G_3(x) = x_1 + x_2 + x_3 \tag{10}$$

subject to: $1 - 0.0025(x_4 + x_6) \ge 0$, $1 - 0.0025(x_5 + x_7 - x_4) \ge 0$, $1 - 0.01(x_8 - x_5) \ge 0$, $x_1x_6 - 833.33252x_4 - 100x_1 + 83333.333 \ge 0$, $x_2x_7 - 1250x_5 - x_2x_4 + 1250x_4 \ge 0$, $x_3x_8 - 1250000 - x_3x_5 + 2500x_5 \ge 0$

where $100 \le x_1 \le 10000, 1000 \le x_i \le 10000, i = 2,3, 10 \le x_i \le 1000, i = 4,5,...,8$

4 Minimize

$$G_4(x) = (x_1 - 10)^2 + 5(x_2 - 12)^2 + x_3^4 + 3(x_4 - 11)^2 + 10x_5^6 + 7x_6^2 + \\ -4x_6x_7 - 10x_6 - 8x_7 \quad \textbf{(11)}$$

subject to :

$127 - 2x_1^2 - 3x_2^4 - x_3 - 4x_4^2 - 5x_5 \geq 0$

$282 - 7x_1 - 3x_2 - 10x_3^2 - x_4 + x_5 \geq 0$, $196 - 23x_1 - x_2^2 - 6x_6^2 + 8x_7 \geq 0$,

$-4x_1^2 - x_2^2 + 3x_1x_2 - 2x_3^2 - 5x_6 + 11x_7 \geq 0$

where $-10 \leq x_i \leq 10, i = 1,2,...,7$

5 Minimize:

$$G_5(x) = e^{x_1 x_2 x_3 x_4 x_5} \quad \textbf{(12)}$$

subject to: $\sum_{i=1}^{5} x_i^2 = 10$, $x_2x_3 - 5x_4x_5 = 0$, $x_1^3 + x_2^3 = -1$

where $-2.3 \leq x_i \leq 2.3, i = 1,2, -3.2 \leq x_i \leq 3.2, i = 3,4,5$

6 Minimize:

$$G_6(x) = x_1^2 + x_2^2 + x_1x_2 - 14x_1 - 16x_2 + 4(x_4 - 5)^2 + (x_5 - 3)^2 \\ + 2(x_6 - 1)^2 + 5x_7^2 + 7(x_8 - 11)^2 + 2(x_9 - 10)^2 + (x_{10} - 7)^2 + 45 \quad \textbf{(13)}$$

Subject to

$105 - 4x_1 - 5x_2 + 3x_7 - 9x_8 \geq 0, -10x_1 + 8x_2 + 17x_7 - 2x_8 \geq 0$

$$8x_1 - 2x_2 - 5x_9 + 2x_{10} + 12 \geq 0 ,$$
$$-3(x_1 - 2)^2 - 4(x_2 - 3)^2 - 2x_3^2 + 7x_4 + 120 \geq 0 ,$$

$$-5x_1^2 - 8x_2 - (x_3 - 6)^2 + 2x_4 + 40 \geq 0 ,$$
$$-x_1^2 - 2(x_2 - 2)^2 + 2x_1x_2 - 14x_5 + 6x_6 \geq 0,$$

$$-0.5(x_1 - 8)^2 - 2(x_2 - 4)^2 - 3x_5^2 + x_6 + 30 \geq 0,$$

$$3x_1 - 6x_2 - 12(x_9 - 8)^2 + 7x_{10} \geq 0,$$

where $-10 \leq x_i \leq 10, i = 1,2,...,10$

3.2 Setting of parameters in MPEA

Control parameters are set as follows:
Population Size: 50 .
The number of independent runs is 20 .
The amount of parents in Multi-Parent crossover operators :M=4
Computing precision: 10^{-14}

3.3 Analysis of Results

Table 1. The comparison of this algorithm and the algorithms in the [13] and [14]

problem	Study	Best	Average	Worst	Known best result
G_1	MPEA	-31025.560	-31025.560	-31025.560	-30665.5
	[13]	-30665.5	-30665.5	-29846.7	
	[14]	No data	No data	No data	
G_2	MPEA	-15	-15	-15	-15
	[13]	-15	-15	-13	
	[14]	-15	-15	-15	
G_3	MPEA	7049.2480	7051.2780	7068.6440	7049.330923
	[13]	7062.2	7220.0	10230.8	
	[14]	7378.0	8206.2	9653.0	
G_4	MPEA	680.630	680.630	680.630	680.6300
	[13]	680.634	680.642	680.651	
	[14]	680.642	680.718	680.995	
G_5	MPEA	0.05395	0.1125	0.44025	0.053950
	[13]	0.05395	0.24129	0.50776	
	[14]	0.054	0.064	0.577	
G_6	MPEA	24.3062	24.3062	24.3062	24.3062091
	[13]	24.372	24.409	25.075	
	[14]	25.486	26.905	42.358	

1) From the Table 1, we can see that the experimental results using the new algorithm are surprisingly good. For the six benchmark problems , the results of MPEA are better than those using the algorithms proposed in the [13][14] in the best results , average results and worst results, which shows the good performance of the new algorithm in generality, effectiveness and stability.For the problems G_2 , G_4 , G_5 , G_6 the best results gained by MPEA are same with the known best results .

2) For the problems G_1 , the known best result is -30665.5 . While our new best result that is -31025.560 and the optimum point is （ 78.00000000000003 ， 33.00000000000001 ， 27.07099710517606 ， 44.99999999999996 ， 44.96924255010539）。

3) For the problems G_3, the known best result is -7049.3307 . While our new best result is 7049.2480 and the optimum point is : (579.30669022708838 , 1359.97068853270640 , 5109.97064176874688 , 182.01770006567686 , 295.60117432924806 , 217.98229993432710 , 286.41652573643283, 395.60117432924902）。

4) Generally, the setting of parameters in MPEA is very simple , thus the performance of our algorithm is independent on the value of parameters which is crucial to one algorithm's generality .
5) MPEA can also solve function optimization problems without constraint. Some typical test problems are solved by this algorithm. The results show that MPEA can solve unconstrained function optimization problems with high stability and performance .

4. CONCLUSIONS

This paper presents a novel multiple populations evolutionary algorithm (MPEA) to handle the constrained function optimization problems. The MPEA have three populations and each population adopts different multi-parent crossover operators. Because of the complementarity among three crossover operators, the diversity of all individuals in each generation is enhanced so that the MPEA is more likely to find the global optimum than other single population evolutionary algorithms. At the same time, different populations exchange their best solutions in each generation during the MPEA runs to direct its search, which improves its search performance ulteriorly. The new approach is compared against other evolutionary optimization techniques in several benchmark functions. The results obtained show that the new approach is a general, effective and robust method.

ACKNOWLEDGEMENTS

This research is supported by the National Natural Science Foundation of China (No. 60473081,60133010, 40275034).

REFERENCES

[1] Storn R And Price K.,Minimizing the real functions of the ICEC'96 contest by differntial evolution.IEEE Conf.on Evolutionary Computation.Nagoya.1997,842~844.

[2] Chiou J P and Wang,P S.A hybid method of differential evolution with application to optimal control problems of a bioprocess system. IEEE Conf. On Evolutionary Computation .Anchorage .1998,627~631

[3]Yun-Chien Lin,Feng-Shen Wang,and Kao-shing Hwang.a hybrid method of evolutionary algorithms for mixed-integer nonlinear optimization problems.Proceedings of the 1999 congress on Evolutionary Computation.Washington,D.C.OSA:IEEE Service Center,1999,3:2159~2169

[4]Michalewicz Z,Nazhiyath G.Genecop III: A Co-evolutionary Algorithm for Numerical Optimization Problems with Nonlinear Constraints.Proc. of 1995 IEEE Int'l. Conf. on Evolutionary Computation(ICEC'95).Perth,Australia,IEEE Press,1995, 647~651

[5] Renders,J.-M. and H.Bersini(1994). Hybridizing genetic algorithms with hill-climbing methods for global optimization : Two possible ways. In Z. Michalewicz, J.D.Schaffer, H.-P.Schwefel, D.B.Fogel,and H.Kitano(Eds.), Proceedings of the First IEEE International Conference on Evolutionary Computation,pp,IEEE Press,1994.312~317.

[6] Runarsson TP, Yao X. Stochastic ranking for constrained evolutionary optimization. IEEE Transactions on Evolutionary Computation, 2000,4(3):284~294.

[7]Deb K, Joshi D, Anand A. Real-Coded evolutionary algorithms with parent-centric recombination. Technical Report, KanGAL Report No.2001003, Kanpur: Indian Institute of Technology, 2001.

[8] Efr´en Mezura-Montes & Carlos A. Coello Coello:Adding a Diversity echanism to a Simple Evolution Strategy to Solve Constrained Optimization Problems. In *Proceedings of the 2003 Congress on Evolutionary Computation (CEC'03)*, IEEE Press, ADFA, UNSW, Canberra, Australia, 8-12 December 2003. pp. 6-13

[9] Tanese R.Distributed Genetic Algorithms.Proc. of the 3rd Int'l. Conf. on Genetic Algorithms. Morgan Kaufmann,Los Altos,1989

[10] Potts J C,Giddens T P,Yadav S B.The Development and Evaluation of an Improved Genetic Algorithm Based on Migration and Artificial Selection .IEEE Trans.on SMC,24(1),1994.73~86

[11] K. Deb and R.B. Agrawal: *Simulated Binary Crossover for Continuous Search Space*, Complex Systems, 9, 115-148(1995).

[12]Guo T,Kang L S: A new *Evolutionary Algorithm for Function Optimization.*Wuhan University Journal of Natural Sciences,1999,4(4) (In Chinese)

[13] K. Deb. An Efficient Constraint Handling Method for Genetic Algorithms. *Computer Methods in Applied Mechanics and Engineering*, 2000.186(2/4):311~338

[14] Z.Michalewicz: Genetic Algorithms,Numerical Optimization,and Constraints, In L.Eshelman (Ed.),Proceedings of the 6th International Conference on Genetic Algorithms,Morgan Kaufmann,San Francisco,1995.151~158

RECONSTRUCTION OF FREEFORM SURFACE BY SUPPORT VECTOR REGRESSION

Ling Jing and Ling Zhen
Science of College, China Agriculture University, Beijing,100083,China

Abstract: Reconstruction and manufacturing of existing freeform surfaces are of paramount importance for reverse engineering. The paper presents support vector regression (SVR) to reconstruction of computer models for existing freeform surfaces. Through examples, the effective is compared among different methods, and the influence of kernels to the precision is discussed. The results show that SVR is better than the algorithms given in [3] and [4], when it is used to reconstruct freeform surface.

Key words: reverse engineering, freeform surface, support vector regression, kernel

1. INTRODUCTION

One of the main issues in reverse engineering is to generate models or design representations based on the existing products[1-2]. There are a variety of engineering applications. For example, in the automobile, shipbuilding, or aircraft industries, designers may create a physical model based on the functional requirements and analysis. The model does not have a mathematical representation. For simple geometry, it is not difficult to generate such a representation in terms of drawings although it is very time consuming. If the model has very complex surface such as freeform surface, the development of such design representations or models becomes difficult.

A neural network approach is presented in [3]. To evaluate the effectiveness of the approach, a known non-uniform B-spline surface was

Supported by the National Nature Science Foundation of China (No. 10371131)

used for generating a number of samples for training the networks. There 4-layered neural networks were designed and trained using a modified back propagation algorithm. Taking advantage of the global minimum property of Simulated Annealing Procedure, a new technique[4] is proposed to accept a temporally failed training result in accordance to probability. This method is able to jump out of the local minimum and converge to the global minimum in some cases, but easily leads to the problem of over-fitting .

Support vector machines have become a subject of intensive study. They have been applied successfully to classification and also to regression. In this paper we use support vector machines in the field of the reconstruction of freeform surfaces and we find that they show an excellent performance.

In the following sections we will introduce the basic principles of ε-support vector regression (ε-SVR) and ν-support vector regression (ν-SVR) in reconstruction of freeform surfaces. The experimental section considers a comparison of ε-SVR, ν-SVR and other methods. Furthermore we compare the influence of different types of kernel function. A brief discussion concludes the paper.

2. ε-SVR AND ν-SVR

In order to model and machine an existing freeform surface, the freeform surface is first digitized by sampling a number of points. Our task is to find a regression function based on the digitized sample points—the training points.

Suppose the training data are given by a training set S of labeled inputs

$$S = \{(U_1, P_1), (U_2, P_2), \cdots, (U_l, P_l)\} \tag{1}$$

For $i = 1, \cdots, l$, the input $U_i = (u_i, v_i) \in R^2$ is the parameter of digitized point $P_i = (x_i, y_i, z_i) \in R^3$ of the freeform surface.

A parametric surface $p(u,v)$ can be decomposed into three surfaces $x(u,v), y(u,v)$ and $z(u,v)$ if the surface is a function of the parametric variables *u* and *v*. To reconstruct the surface in terms of points, we are interested in the relationships between the parametric variables *u*, *v* and the coordinate values of *x*,*y* and *z*. Thus, SVR process is designed as three separate process corresponding to the three functions $x(u,v), y(u,v)$ and $z(u,v)$ .We will only describe the process to find $x(u,v)$ below.

The input $U = (u,v)$ is first mapped to a feature space by a function Φ. Assume that regression function $x(u, v)$ takes the following form:

$$f(U) = (w \cdot \Phi(U)) + b \tag{2}$$

where $\Phi: R^2 \to H$, H is a Hilbert space, $w \in H, b \in R$. Let the loss function is the ε-insensitive loss function

$$c(U,x,f(U)) = \tilde{c}(f(U)-x) = |x-f(U)|_{\varepsilon} = \max\{0,|x-f(U)|-\varepsilon\} \quad (3)$$

Where $\varepsilon > 0$. This function ignores errors that are within a certain distance of the true value.

Suppose that ε is given in priori, the primal problem is[5-6]:

$$\min_{w,b,\xi,\xi^*} \quad \tau(w,b,\xi_i,\xi_i^*) = \frac{1}{2}\|w\|^2 + C \cdot \frac{1}{l}\sum_{i=1}^{l}(\xi_i + \xi_i^*)$$

$$s.t. \quad \begin{cases} (w \cdot \Phi(U_i)) + b - x_i \le \varepsilon + \xi_i \\ x_i - (w \cdot \Phi(U_i)) - b \le \varepsilon + \xi_i^* \quad (i = 1,\dots,l) \\ \xi_i, \xi_i^* \quad \ge 0 \end{cases} \quad (4)$$

where $\xi = (\xi_1, \xi_2, \cdots, \xi_l)^{\mathrm{T}}, \xi^* = (\xi_1^*, \xi_2^*, \cdots, \xi_l^*)^{\mathrm{T}}$. $C \geqslant 0$, $\varepsilon > 0$ are constants . In order to solve problem (4), SVR introduces its dual problem

$$\min_{\alpha_i,\alpha_i^*} \quad \frac{1}{2}\sum_{i,j=1}^{l}(\alpha_i^* - \alpha_i)(\alpha_j^* - \alpha_j)K(U_i,U_j) + \varepsilon\sum_{i=1}^{l}(\alpha_i^* + \alpha_i) - \sum_{i=1}^{l}(\alpha_i - \alpha_i^*)x_i$$

$$s.t. \quad \begin{cases} \sum_{i=1}^{l}(\alpha_i - \alpha_i^*) = 0 \\ \alpha_i, \alpha_i^* \in [0, C/l], \quad (i = 1,\dots,l) \end{cases} \quad (5)$$

Where $\alpha = (\alpha_1, \alpha_2, \cdots, \alpha_l)^{\mathrm{T}}, \alpha^* = (\alpha_1^*, \alpha_2^*, \cdots, \alpha_l^*)^{\mathrm{T}}, K(U_i, U_j) = (\Phi(U_i), \Phi(U_j))$ is the kernel function. After getting the solution α and α^* of problem (5), we obtain the decision function as

$$f(U) = \sum_{i=1}^{l}(\alpha_i^* - \alpha_i)K(U_i,U) + b = \sum_{SV}(\alpha_i^* - \alpha_i)K(U_i,U) + b \quad (6)$$

Where b is determined by KKT conditions. SV means the support vectors.

It must be pointed out that if U_i satisfies to $|f(U_i) - x_i| < \varepsilon$, α_i, α_i^* must be zero by the KKT conditions. This means w in (2) relies only on the U_i with $\alpha_i - \alpha_i^* \neq 0$. We call these points the support vectors, this property makes SVR be applied in pre-handle the data in reverse engineering.

Although the parameter ε does control the sparseness of the solution, it does this only in a rather indirect way. Lacking a priori information about the accuracy of the x-values, it can be difficult to come up with a reasonable value of ε a priori. Instead, one would rather specify the degree of sparseness and let the algorithm compute ε from the data. This is the idea of the ν-SVM[5-6], a modification of the original ε-SVM. In the ν-SVM the size of ε is not defined a priori but is itself a variable. Its value is traded off against model complexity and slack variables via a constant ν :

$$\min_{w,b,\xi,\xi^*,\varepsilon} \quad \tau(w,b,\xi_i,\xi_i^*,\varepsilon) = \frac{1}{2}\|w\|^2 + C(\nu\varepsilon + \frac{1}{l}\sum_{i=1}^{l}(\xi_i + \xi_i^*))$$

$$s.t. \quad \begin{cases} (w \cdot U_i) + b - x_i \le \varepsilon + \xi_i \\ x_i - (w \cdot U_i) - b_i \le \varepsilon + \xi_i^* \\ \xi_i, \xi_i^* \ge 0 \quad , \quad \varepsilon \ \ge 0 \end{cases} \tag{7}$$

where $C > 0$, $0 \le \nu \le 1$ are constants. The dual problem of problem (7) is

$$\min_{\alpha_i,\alpha_i^*} \quad \frac{1}{2}\sum_{i,j=1}^{l}(\alpha_i^* - \alpha_i)(\alpha_j^* - \alpha_j)K(U_i,U_j) - \sum_{i=1}^{l}(\alpha_i^* - \alpha_i)x_i$$

$$s.t. \quad \begin{cases} \sum_{i=1}^{l}(\alpha_i - \alpha_i^*) = 0 \\ \alpha_i, \alpha_i^* \in [0, C/l] \\ \sum_{i=1}^{l}(\alpha_i + \alpha_i^*) \le C \cdot \nu \end{cases} \tag{8}$$

We will use the term errors to refer to training points lying outside of the ε -tube, and the term fraction of errors/SVs to denote the relative numbers of errors/SVs, i.e. divided by l. This has been proved that ν can be used to control the fraction of support vectors (and hence the sparsity of the solution's expansion) and the fraction of outliers (i.e. the amount of confidence that we have in the data).

3. RECONSTRUCTION OF SURFACE

The example in [3-4] is now used to evaluate the effectiveness of SVR. Applying $\varepsilon - SVR$ and $\nu - SVR$, the reconstruction of the existing surface is realized by first training a series of points from a mathematically known surface in [3], the results were severed as models to generate all the points that are needed. The input is the two parametric variables $U = (u, v)$ of sample point. The output is the point of reconstruction surface. The expected output is the accurate point calculated using the NURBS equations. Then, we calculated a number of testing points using other set of $U = (u, v)$, the points and the differences between the points output from the predicting and the points generated by the NURBS equations indicated the performance of the different ways.

In learning process, the kernel form is chosen as:

$$K(U_i, U_j) = ((U_i \cdot U_j) + 1)^5$$

For the sake of simplicity, only the x-coordinate result is generated by different methods in *Table 1*. There x_1 is accurate value in the known surface, x_2 and x_3 are the results in [3] and [4], x_4 is given by $\varepsilon - SVR$ with the capacity constant $C = 225$ and $\varepsilon = 0.01$, and x_5 is obtained by $\nu - SVR$ with the capacity constant $C = 225$ and $\nu = 0.9$.

Table 1. x-coordinate generated by different methods

u	v	x_1	x_2	x_3	x_4	x_5
1.000000	1.000000	11.500000	11.447000	11.487403	11.5035	11.5099
1.000000	1.100000	12.264167	12.275300	12.266978	12.2589	12.2529
1.000000	1.200000	13.053333	13.102600	13.042305	13.0473	13.0398
1.000000	1.300000	13.862500	13.928400	13.870028	13.8597	13.8562
1.000000	1.400000	14.686677	14.752000	14.706395	14.688	14.6902
1.000000	1.500000	15.520833	15.572800	15.547921	15.5252	15.5322
1.000000	1.600000	16.360000	16.390100	16.391150	16.365	16.3744
1.000000	1.700000	17.199167	17.203300	17.232766	17.202	17.2113
1.000000	1.800000	18.033333	18.011800	18.048636	18.0321	18.0386
1.000000	1.900000	18.857500	18.815000	18.875552	18.8518	18.8539
1.000000	2.000000	19.666667	19.612400	19.717749	19.6586	19.6558
1.000000	2.100000	20.457167	20.403300	20.427167	20.4511	20.444
1.000000	2.200000	21.230667	21.187200	21.215274	21.2287	21.2192
1.000000	2.300000	21.990167	21.963600	21.989935	21.9918	21.9826
1.000000	2.400000	22.738677	22.732100	22.736344	22.7418	22.736
1.000000	2.500000	23.479167	23.492200	23.483185	23.481	23.4815
1.000000	2.600000	24.214667	24.243400	24.299485	24.2126	24.2212
1.000000	2.700000	24.948167	24.985300	24.964167	24.9409	24.9571
1.000000	2.800000	25.682667	25.717500	25.667085	25.671	25.6911
1.000000	2.900000	26.421167	26.439700	26.417486	26.4092	26.4242
1.000000	3.000000	27.166667	27.151500	26.945260	27.1625	27.1571
1.100000	1.000000	11.500000	11.446900	11.430027	11.5029	11.5105
1.100000	1.100000	12.264167	12.275200	12.269364	12.2588	12.2529
1.100000	1.200000	13.053333	13.102600	13.044518	13.0475	13.0394
1.100000	1.300000	13.862500	13.928400	13.871958	13.8603	13.8555
1.100000	1.400000	14.686677	14.752000	14.708116	14.6889	14.6893
1.100000	1.500000	15.520833	15.572800	15.549450	15.5262	15.5312
1.100000	1.600000	16.360000	16.390200	16.392507	16.3661	16.3735
1.100000	1.700000	17.199167	17.203400	17.233973	17.2032	17.2104
1.100000	1.800000	18.033333	18.011900	18.030717	18.0334	18.0379
1.100000	1.900000	18.857500	18.815200	18.899829	18.8531	18.8534
1.100000	2.000000	19.666667	19.612500	19.718640	19.66	19.6555
1.100000	2.100000	20.457167	20.403500	20.424773	20.4526	20.444
1.100000	2.200000	21.230667	21.187400	21.216083	21.2303	21.2194
1.100000	2.300000	21.990167	21.963900	21.990731	21.9935	21.983
1.100000	2.400000	22.738677	22.732400	22.747147	22.7436	22.7367
1.100000	2.500000	23.479167	23.492500	23.514025	23.4829	23.4824
1.100000	2.600000	24.214667	24.243700	24.300312	24.2147	24.2224

1.100000	2.700000	24.948167	24.985600	24.995192	24.9432	24.9585
1.100000	2.800000	25.682667	25.717900	25.668068	25.6736	25.6926
1.100000	2.900000	26.421167	26.440100	26.418542	26.412	26.4259
1.100000	3.000000	27.166667	27.152000	26.946396	27.1655	27.1589
max-error			0.0659	0.221407	0.011967	0.0144
min-error			0.004133	0.000232	3.3e-5	0.001967
average-error			0.034621	0.033148	0.004391	0.008415

The last three rows in *Table 1* indicate the maximum error, minimum error and the average error between the predicted value and the true value. The results show that the SVR approach is more effective than the methods used in [3] and [4].

4. DISCUSSION THE KERNEL

The use of the kernel function is the key of SVR to the reconstruction of the freeform surface. In order to observe the influence of different forms of kernel to approximate surface, different kernels are used , and the related results are showed in *Table 2*.Here we use $\varepsilon-SVR$ with the capacity constant $C=225$ and $\varepsilon=0.01$.

Table 2. the influence of different kernels

kernel function		max-error	min-error	average-error
dot kernel		0.371167	0.0005	0.179011
polynomial kernel	d = 2	0.1468	0.002	0.054185
	d = 5	0.018367	0	0.007824
radial kernel	$\gamma=2$	0.792433	0.0033	0.185621
	$\gamma=4$	0.634733	0.001267	0.142206
hyperbolic kernel	$a=1, b=1$	251.4227	2.1898	94.74889
	$a=0.0001, b=1$	0.294233	0.008967	0.110213
	$a=0.0001, b=0.0001$	0.283133	0.012667	0.107197

5. CONCLUSION

One of challenges in reverse engineering is to reconstruct computer representations of existing surfaces, based on digitized points. The problem becomes even more difficult when a surface is partially damaged or worn. Surface fitting is an obvious technique, however, to fit an existing surface, appropriate surface equations are first selected, and then the equations are evaluated to determine whether the approximation is acceptable. Selecting and evaluating the models remain difficult tasks. It will be difficult to use the surface fitting technique if the surface is partially damaged or worn or incompleted.

In this work we show that SVR can be used to reconstruction the freeform surfaces in reverse engineering. It not only gives the formula of the freeform surface but also predicts the position of input parameters which aren't be solved in [3-4].

The parameters ε and ν provide the user to construct freeform surface and control the errors at the same time. How to given the appropriate forms of kernel function is worth studying for the future.

REFERENCES

[1] Bolle R M, Vemuri B C. On three-dimensional surface reconstruction methods. IEEE Transactions on Pattern Analysis and Machine Intelligence, 1991, 13 (1): 1~13

[2] Varady T, Martin R R, and Cox J. Reverse engineering of geometric models-an introduction. Computer Aided Design, 1997, 29 (4): 255~268

[3] Gu P, Yan X. Neural network approach to the reconstruction of freeform surface for reverse engineering. Computer-Aided Design, 1995, 27: 59~64

[4] Wang K, Zhang C M, Neural network method to reconstruct the freeform surface. Journal of Computer-Aided Design & Computer Graphics, 1998, 10 (3): 193~199

[5] Nello Cristianini and John Shawe-Taylor. An introduction to Support vector machines. Cambridge University Press,Cambridge,UK,2000

[6] Deng N Y, Tian Y J. The new method in data mining— Support Vector Machine. Science Press, Beijing, China, 2004

THE DIGITAL IMAGE EXPERIMENT PLATFORM BASED ON EVEN LINER GRAMMAR

Limin Ao [1,2] Bo Li [2] Yongsheng Chen [2]

1. College of Information and Electrical Engineering, China Agricultural University, Beijing 100083, China

2. Department of Information Engineering, Northeast China Institute of Electric Power Engineering, Jilin 132012, China

Abstract: This paper describes a digital image processing experiment platform which is on the theory basis of the Even Linear Grammar. The platform is based on the Automatization of COM, which can increase the reusability of the image processing methods. In the image processing process, an Image Processing Process Tree (IPPT) is generated, which can make the image analysis easy.

Key words: syntax-directed, COM, IPPT, Reusable, Dynamically Construct

1. INTRODUCTION

In the process of image processing, in order to achieve our goal, we have to do many experiments and research, even to modify or design arithmetic to meet our need. In existing image processing software, Photoshop can't modify or add arithmetic; Matlab can do this, but everything must be preestablished, it is impossible to add some arithmetic into a program dynamically, and it can't record the middle results.

This paper is trying to describe an image processing platform which is based on constructed language and Syntax-directed Method.

Even Liner Grammar [1] is used to describe a constructed language. We can program using constructed language.

In general, an image-processing program is composed of some common image-processing methods. We can make use of the structure of attribute grammar to reconstruct the image processing methods to be semantic functions of attribute grammar.

One of the ways to increase the reusability of the image processing method is to use COM.

COM [2] is short for Component Object Model. COM allows the COM components communicate alternately in a uniform way.

2. EVEN LINER GRAMMAR AND SYNTAX-DIRECTED METHOD

Let F be an alphabet. A ELG(Even Liner Grammar) whose form is G=(N,Σ,P,X) is a context-free grammar. Its productions have the form like:

$$A \rightarrow uBv \quad \text{or} \quad A \rightarrow w$$

Thereinto, A, B $\in$ N; u, v, w $\in$ Σ*; $|u| = |v|$. Grammar G is a linear grammar. N is a non-terminal symbols set, Σ is the terminal symbols set, P is the set of productions and X is the started non-terminal symbol.

The definition of the language based on Grammar G:

$$L = L(G) = \{s \mid s \in \Sigma^*, X \overset{*}{\Rightarrow} s\}$$

Thereinto, the form $X \overset{*}{\Rightarrow} s$ expresses that the string s can be inferred from the started non-terminal symbol X by a serious of productions.

Takada expresses his viewpoint in literature [3]: the inference of ELG can be come down to the inference of DFA(Deterministic Finite Automata).

Takada's thinking:

There is an alphabet F and a ELG G=(N,Σ,P,X). Sign every production in P with a single letter in F. Let $f=f_1f_2...f_k \in F^*$. the form $X \Rightarrow f_G\omega$ expresses that the string ω can be inferred by the productions $f_1f_2...f_k$ from the started non-terminal symbol X of G .Let C be a language on the alphabet F, then the language generated by the Grammar G on the control set C can be defined as:

$$L_C(G) = \{\omega \in \Sigma^* \mid X \overset{*}{\Rightarrow} f_G\omega, f \in C\}$$

So every sentence in the control set C corresponds to the inference process of a sentence in $L_C(G)$.

Takada proves that:

Any Even Liner Language L can be generated by a universal ELG G^0 on a control set C which is a regular language. L and G^0 are all on an alphabet Σ. That is to say, for any ELL(Even Liner Language) L, there is a form like:

$$L = L_C(G^0) = \{\omega \in \Sigma^* \mid X^0 \overset{*}{\Rightarrow} f_{G^0}\omega, f \in C\}$$

Thereinto, C is a regular grammar, G^0 is defined as

$$G^0 = (\{X^0\}, \Sigma, P^0, X^0).$$

$P^0=\{X^0 \rightarrow aX^0b|a,b \in \Sigma\} \cup \{X^0 \rightarrow ab|a,b \in \Sigma\} \cup \{X^0 \rightarrow a|a \in \Sigma\} \cup \{X^0 \rightarrow \varepsilon\}$[1].

Takada's thinking is used in this experiment platform.

Syntax-directed Method is the typical method to analyze the meaning of a sentence. The Syntax-directed Method is used in this experiment platform alternately in the image processing process. The platform uses the Syntax-directed Method to determine the style of the operation, so as to construct an Image Processing Process Tree (IPPT) dynamically. A node in IPPT is an image. If there is a path between two nodes, it means that one image is acquired form the other image by some image processing method. The methods used in the IPPT can form a program. So the program represents the image processing process.

3. BRIEF INTRODUCTION OF COM

What COM (Component Object Model) provides is not only the criterion for components alternation, but also the alternation environment.

a) Specialities of COM

Theoretically speaking, COM is a criterion about C/S.

COM has the specialities of Language Independence, Robust Versioning, Local Transparency and Object Orientation.

b) Automatization

Automatization is a special example of COM. It is based on COM, but its use is much wider than COM. Automatization provides normal attempering measures for the transmission of parameters and return values between different processors or different computers.

c) Later Binding

Later Binding is one of the important characteristics of Automatization. That is, the client program doesn't check the data type of the parameters when it is programmed, but check when the component is used.

4. THE THEORY BASIS OF THE IMAGE PROCESSING PROCESS

In the experiment platform, along with the image processing process, a image processing process tree (IPPT) can be constructed. The root of the tree is the original image, the middle nodes are the images generated in the processing process, and the branches are the processing functions used in the platform. Users of the platform can easily know how an image is generated in the platform by along the branches of IPPT.

Let R_1 be the original image, R_2, R_3,…, R_n be the generated images in the image processing process, f_1, f_2, …, f_n be some function in the processing process. Then, there is a IPPT:

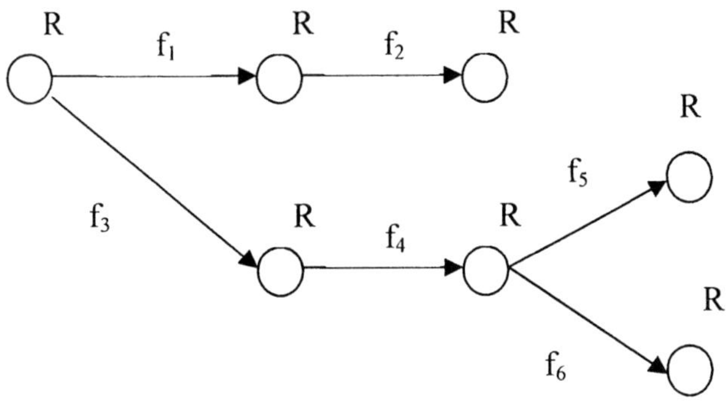

Figure 1. An IPPT

As figure1 shows, the original image R_1 can generate a serious of images by the image processing process. Supposing R_7 is the image that the user wants. The user can know how R_7 is acquired by analyzing the IPPT. And the user can save the process of generating R_7 as one operation, so as to simplify the operation process when it is used next time.

At the same time, every image generated in the processing process can be used as a root node to generate another IPPT, and the tree can go on and on.

Formalize the image processing process:

Another image will be generated if an image is processed by a specific arithmetic. And the generated image can be processed again. Let X,X',X'' represent an image, and a,b,…represent some specific image processing arithmetic, then the image processing process can be expressed as:

$$X \rightarrow aX', \quad X' \rightarrow bX''.$$

To the image experiment platform, image is just data, and an image processing arithmetic is just an operation.

So the image processing process can be described as: $X \rightarrow \alpha X$.

Thereinto, X is some image, α is some image processing arithmetic.

So every operation in the experiment platform can be considered as an application of regular grammar. RLG is a kind of regular grammar. Let a operation in the platform be f_i.

Thereout, we can define a regular language C, its corresponding regular grammar is: $G_C = (N_C, \Sigma_C, P_C, X_C)$. Thereinto, $N_C = \{X_C\}$, $\Sigma_C = \{ f_1, f_2, ..., f_k \}$, $P_C = \{ X_C \rightarrow f_i X_C \mid f \in \Sigma_C \} \cup \{ X_C \rightarrow f_i \mid f_i \in \Sigma_C \}$

The image experiment platform provides the function to save a serious of image processing operations to be one operation. That is to say, define a new operation f, let $f = f_1 f_2 ... f_k$. if F^* is the set of all the combinations of the arithmetic in the platform, then $f \in F^*$. And f can be inferred in regular language C, so $f \in C$.

On the other hand, the operation result can be described in 3 ways: the image data will be written into database, the DDB data to display the image in the screen, and the record about the current operation generated in the image processing process. So an operation f_i can be described as $X \rightarrow \alpha X' \beta$, thereinto, X is the original image, X' is the generated image, α is the image data written into the database, and β is the operation record. $|\alpha|=|\beta|=1$. When we get the image we want, it's not necessary to process any more. We just need to save the image data into database and record the information about the current arithmetic. In that case, the operation can be described as

$$X \rightarrow \alpha\, \beta \text{ or } X \rightarrow \alpha.$$

Thereout, we can get an ELG G^0, which is suited to this image processing experiment platform:

$$G^0 = (\{X^0\}, \Sigma, P^0, X^0)$$

Thereinto, $P^0=\{X^0 \rightarrow \alpha X^0 \beta | \alpha, \beta \in \Sigma\} \cup \{X^0 \rightarrow \alpha\beta | \alpha, \beta \in \Sigma\} \cup \{X^0 \rightarrow \alpha | \alpha \in \Sigma\}$.

According to Takada's proof, ELG G^0 can generate ELL $L_C(G^0)$ on the control set C.

$$L_C(G^0) = \{\omega \in \Sigma^* \mid X^0 \overset{*}{\Rightarrow} f_{G^0} \omega, f \in C\}$$

ω is a combination of the operation results.

Analyze the IPPT in figure1:

The production set of ELG G^0 is:

f_1: $R \rightarrow \alpha_1 R \beta_1$

f_2: $R \rightarrow \alpha_2 R \beta_2$

f_3: $R \rightarrow \alpha_3 R \beta_3$

f_4: $R \rightarrow \alpha_4 R \beta_4$

f_5: $R \rightarrow \alpha_5 R \beta_5$

...

f_n: $R \rightarrow \alpha_n R \beta_n$

If the number of image processing functions in the platform is n, the number of production as above is n. In the production, the non-terminal symbol is X. At the same time, X is the started non-terminal symbol.

α_i and β_i are the terminal symbols in the productions. α_i represents the image data written into database, β_i represents the current operation record.

We plight here, when it is not necessary for an image to be processed more, we use the production $X \rightarrow \alpha$ to acquire the image data.

So, we need to define a production f_0: $R \rightarrow \alpha$.

So in figure 1, different path represents different processing process.

The inference process of R_3 :

$$R \overset{f_1}{\Rightarrow} \alpha_1 R \beta_1 \overset{f_2}{\Rightarrow} \alpha_1 \alpha_2 R \beta_2 \beta_1 \overset{f_0}{\Rightarrow} \alpha_1 \alpha_2 \alpha \beta_2 \beta_1$$

The inference process of R_6 :

$$R \overset{f_3}{\Rightarrow} \alpha_3 R \beta_3 \overset{f_4}{\Rightarrow} \alpha_3 \alpha_4 R \beta_4 \beta_3 \overset{f_5}{\Rightarrow} \alpha_3 \alpha_4 \alpha_5 R \beta_5 \beta_4 \beta_3 \overset{f_0}{\Rightarrow} \alpha_3 \alpha_4 \alpha_5 \alpha \beta_5 \beta_4 \beta_3$$

The inference process of R_7 :

$$R \overset{f_3}{\Rightarrow} \alpha_3 R \beta_3 \overset{f_4}{\Rightarrow} \alpha_3 \alpha_4 R \beta_4 \beta_3 \overset{f_6}{\Rightarrow} \alpha_3 \alpha_4 \alpha_6 R \beta_6 \beta_4 \beta_3 \overset{f_0}{\Rightarrow} \alpha_3 \alpha_4 \alpha_6 \alpha \beta_6 \beta_4 \beta_3$$

Supposing that R_7 is the image we want. We can know that R_7 is acquired from R_1 via the image processing arithmetic f_3,f_4,f_6. Let $f_G^{\,0}= f_3f_4f_6$, then the inference process of R_7 can be described as:

$$R_1 \overset{*}{\Rightarrow} f_{G^0} R_7$$

$f_G^{\,0}$ can be inferred by the regular Grammar C, so $f_G^{\,0} \in C$.

So it is can be considered that the inference process of R_7 is a sentence in $L_C(G^0)$ which is generated by ELG G^0 on the control set C.

So we can say that the image experiment platform is an application of ELL $L_C(G^0)$.

5. THE IMPLEMENT OF THE PLATFORM

5.1 System Framework of the Platform

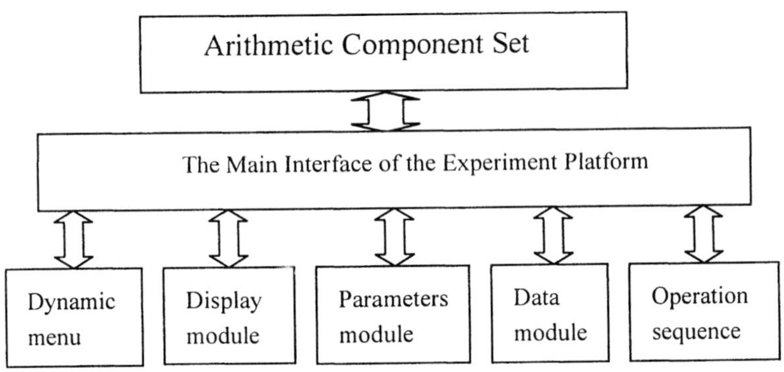

Figure 2. System Framework

The system framework is showed in figure 2. The ability of every component is:

(1) Arithmetic component set (P^0): the set of the arithmetic about image processing including the arithmetic you programmed yourself.

(2) The dynamic menu module: implement the function to generate dynamic menus from the methods in COM components.

(3) Display module: to display the image in a new window, this is generated in the image processing process.

(4) Parameters acquired module: to acquire the information about parameters from the database, and generate a parameter dialog dynamically which is used to implement the alternation between the user and the program.

(5) Data-saving and data-query module: to save the data acquired from the experiment process, so as to the data can be query later. In fact, the data saved is the IPPT generated in the image processing process.

(6) Save and execute the operation sequence: this module can save a serial of operations to be one operation, and then execute it.

That is equal to define a new operation f, and let f = f_1, f_2,...f_n , f_i is an operation.

5.2 The design and implement of the interface of COM server

In order to meet the demand of the platform, the design of the interface of the COM server must fit the condition below:

(1) The odd interface methods must have the same parameter form, and so as the even interface methods. By this way, the platform can process the method in two common ways.

(2) Every arithmetic in this platform is implemented in two interface methods. The odd method is used to retrieve the string which describes the function of arithmetic, and the even method implement the function of the arithmetic.

For example:

```
interface ILinear : IDispatch
{   [id(1), helpstring("gray linear truncation")] HRESULT
GetHelpString_1([out,retval]VARIANT *lResult);
    [id(2), helpstring("gray linear truncation ")] HRESULT
    GrayLinearOff([in]unsigned char *ArrayGray, [in]long nWidth, [in]long
    nHeight, [in]float *pfset, [out,retval]VARIANT *lResult);
    ...... }
```

The methods id(1) and id(2) complete the “gray linear truncation” function together. The method id(2) implement the arithmetic, and the method id(1) retrieves the string “gray linear truncation” which will be used as the name of a menu item in the platform.

5.3 The Retrospect Ability of the Platform

The processing object of every operation in the platform is the image displayed in a child window. And the image generated by the operation will be displayed in a new child window. So the contrast between the two images will be much more pronounced, the original image can be reprocessed again.

In this way, every node in the IPPT generated in the image processing process can be processed as a root node.

5.4 Save the Function Sequence

Implement the ability like: define a new operation f, let f= f_1, f_2,… f_n.

The platform implements the ability by record the information about every operation.

For example:

In order to find the boundary of a target area, we should operate like this:

① gray linear truncation, generating image 1, record as "Linear_Off 100 255 0 255";

② finding the edge of image 1, generating image 2, record as "Sobel";

③ turning image 2 to white-black image :image 3, the threshold is 128. record as "Two_Value 128";

④ edge trace image 3, record as "Edge_Trace" .

Save the operations above in a file named "Get_object_edge.serial".

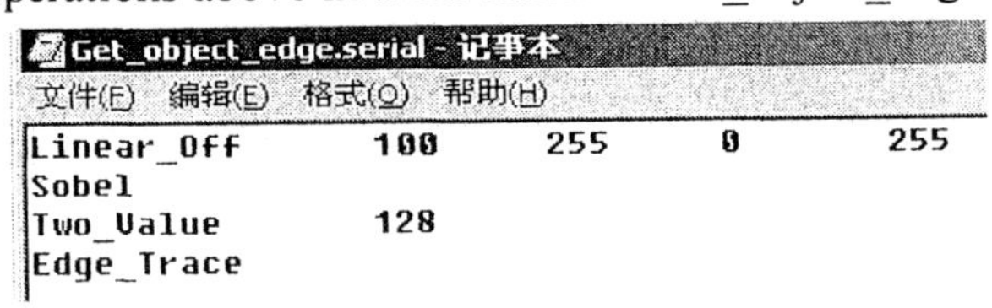
Get_object_edge.serial - 记事本
文件(F) 编辑(E) 格式(O) 帮助(H)

Linear_Off	100	255	0	255
Sobel				
Two_Value	128			
Edge_Trace				

Figure 3. Get_object_edge.serial

If it is needed to perform the operation above again, the user just need to execute the Get_object_edge.serial. And the content in the file can be modified to be the appropriate content. This ability makes the operation more agile.

6. CONLUSION

The Image Processing Experiment Platform has powerful expansibility; it provides a reliable experiment platform for image processing.

REFERENCE

[1] ZHANG Rui-Ling. Grammatical Inference: Retrospect and Prospect. Journal of software. 1999, 10(8): 850 ~ 860

[2] Dale Rogerson. COM Technology Inside. Beijing: Publishing House of Tsinghua University, 1999

[3] Takada Y. Grammatical inference for even linear languages based on control sets. Information Processing Letters, 1988,28(4):193～199

AN OPERATOR BASED ADAPTIVE GENETIC ALGORITHM

Koh Sueyi, Leowsoo Kar, Loke Kar Seng
koh.sue.yi@gmail.com,{leow.soo.kar,loke.kar.seng}@infotech.monash.edu.my
Monash University Malaysia, No.2 Jalan Kolej, Bandar Sunway, 46150 Petaling Jaya, Selangor, Malaysia.

Abstract: Genetic Algorithms (GAs) are a robust heuristic search technique capable of taking on a broad range of optimization problems. In most GAs, components and parameters are predetermined and remain static throughout its run. In this paper, it is hypothesized that a GA's performance and robustness can be enhanced through the 'online' adaptation of the operators and an operator based adaptive genetic algorithm (AGA) based on these concepts is designed and implemented. A number of permutation based problems were selected to evaluate the performance of AGA.

Key words: adaptive genetic algorithm, permutation based optimisation problems

1. INTRODUCTION

Genetic algorithms have been known to be a robust technique in finding optimal or near solutions to many large and complex optimization problems. However, its parameter settings are required to be tuned for the specific problem at hand in order for it to perform efficiently and effectively during its search for an acceptable solution in a reasonable amount of time. While there exist a number of methods that can and have been used to predetermine such settings before running it on a problem, the problem specific nature of some of these settings coupled with the mutual dependence of these settings on one another still render the tuning of a GA to be a tedious process. Additionally, some research has indicated that the use of more than the usual one crossover and one mutation operator during the run of the GA can be beneficial. This however, results in more parameters being needed to be tuned. In this paper, an operator based adaptive genetic algorithm is presented with the aim of combining the benefits of having more operators available while decreasing the amount of parameter tuning required.

2. RELATED WORK

For a GA to be efficient, it has to be configured with settings suitable to the problem at hand. The most commonly used method is empirically through hand tuning. DeJong [2], Grefenstette [4], Davis [3] and David et al. [5] used this technique to find some recommended settings that were 'good' for a set of numerical function optimization problems, known as the DeJong test suite. Using a traditional algorithm with a fixed population size, they worked out 'good' parameter values for single point crossover and bit mutation.
Recently, Maruo et al. [15] used an approach of self-adapting parameters to relieve the burden of hand tuning. However, due to the number of components and the mutual dependence of these components on one another, finding the appropriate settings was still a tedious task.

Another approach [6] adaptively varies the settings. It involves the utilization of information gained about the state of the GA during its run, This information may be about the population as a whole, individuals in the population or components of the GA. This knowledge is then used to vary 'online' its settings. Based on how the adaptive mechanism is employed, the approaches in this category can further be split into three subcategories, namely, the rule based approach, [9], the co-evolutionary approach generations [6, 8] and the evolutionary approach.[10]

3. THE ADAPTIVE GENETIC ALGORITHM

The proposed GA consists of two genetic algorithms, an operator level (OL) GA and a problem level (PL) GA. The PL GA is used to search the problem space for good or optimal solutions to the problem at hand, while the OL GA synchronously selects the operators to be applied in the PL GA based on the status and requirements of the search. A list of 17 operators is selected for this purpose [11]. To evaluate the operator level population, the encoded operators in each chromosome are utilized on one generation of the PL GA with the same PL population. After which, feedback on the performance of each chromosome in the form of a resulting PL population is returned to the OL GA and each OL chromosome is assigned a fitness value based on its relative performance to the other OL chromosomes. Among the resulting PL populations, the one that resulted from the OL chromosome with the highest fitness value is selected to be the next PL GA population for the next generation of the OL GA.

Both the OL GA and PL GA use the same selection and replacement technique. The selection technique is used to select chromosomes or parents for recombination, while the replacement strategy refers to how individuals from the present population are selected to live on in the population used in the next generation. In Figures 1 and 5, they are denoted by the term Select and Perform_replacement respectively. After some experimentation, the tournament selection technique with the number of competitors set to 2 and the steady state with elitism strategy were selected as the selection technique and replacement strategy respectively.

In the next two subsections, the main components of the operator level GA and the problem level GA are described in detail.

3.1 Operator Level Genetic Algorithm

```
OL_GA (end_condition)
BEGIN
    Generate population
    Generate plPopulation
    PLEvaluate plPopulation
    /* evaluate operator level GA's population returns
    best resulting PL population */
    plPopulation = Evaluate (population, plPopulation)
    WHILE end_condition has not been reached
        best_chromosome = Get_fittest_chromosome (population)
          Initialise children of size num_children_required
          num_children_required = crossover_rate * population_size
          num_parents_required = Get_num_parents_required (crossover_operator)
          num_children_produced = Get_num_children_produced (crossover_operator)
          num_children = 0
          WHILE num_children < num_children_required
            parent_chromosomes = Select (population, num_parents_required )
            child_chromosomes =
              Perform_crossover_operation (parent_chromosomes)
                /* ensure that children does not go out of bounds during Append */
            Append child_chromosomes to children
            Increment num_children by num_children_produced
          ENDWHILE
          new_population = Perform_replacement (population, children)
          num_mutations_required = mutation_rate * population_size
          num_mutations = 0
          WHILE num_mutations < num_mutations_required
           Randomly_select chromosome from new_population
           Perform_mutation_operation (chromosome)
           Increment num_mutations
          ENDWHILE
          Replace last chromosome in new_population with best_chromosome
          plPopulation = Evaluate (population, plPopulation)
          Evaluate_population (population)
          population = new_population
    ENDWHILE
END
```

Fig. 1. Pseudo Code of the Operator Level GA

3.1.1 Chromosomal Representation

The OL GA employs a permutation based encoding for its chromosomes. Based on this encoding, each chromosome is comprised of all the available operators in the search space and it is the positions of the genes in the chromosome that determine which operators are passed down to the PL GA. A typical operator level chromosome is shown below:

8	3	14	5	15	16	6	1	9	17	7	2	12	11	13	4	10

Fig. 2. Example of an Operator Level Chromosome

The value of each gene denotes the operator being represented by it. The first n genes denote the operators that are to be passed to the PL GA, where n is a predetermined variable set before the run. Should $n = 5$, for example, the operators represented by values 8, 3, 14, 5 and 15 are passed to the PL GA to be utilized during its search.

3.1.2 Operators

Following classic style genetic algorithms, the operator level GA of AGA uses a standard set of one crossover operator and one mutation operator. Noting that only the first n encoded operators in the OL chromosome will be utilized during the evaluation of the OL chromosome, perhaps positional information can be said to be the primary information that needs to be captured. With this observation, it was decided that the Coin Toss operator [11] would play the role of the crossover operator, and Random Create Coin Toss operator would play the role of the mutation operator, where the use of this mutation operator ensures that each gene in each locus of the chromosome has a chance of being mutated. After some arbitrary testing, the rates are set to be 0.8 and 0.2 for the crossover and mutation respectively.

3.1.3 Evaluation Function

In AGA, the adaptation mechanism is the OL GA and the object to be adapted is the configuration of the PL GA. The OL GA evaluates the performances of the various configurations of the PL GA through the evaluation of the OL chromosomes. Thus, in AGA, communications between the OL GA and the PL GA occur in the operator level evaluation function, known as **Evaluate** in *Fig 1.* Because it is the settings of the PL GA that guide the search through the PL search space, and it is the evaluation function of the OL GA that guides the forming of the sets of operators used in the PL GA through the assignment of fitness values to these sets of operators, it can be said that the OL GA's evaluation function is one of the main components whose performance is vital to the overall performance of the AGA. The interaction between the two levels of AGA is illustrated in *Fig. 3*.

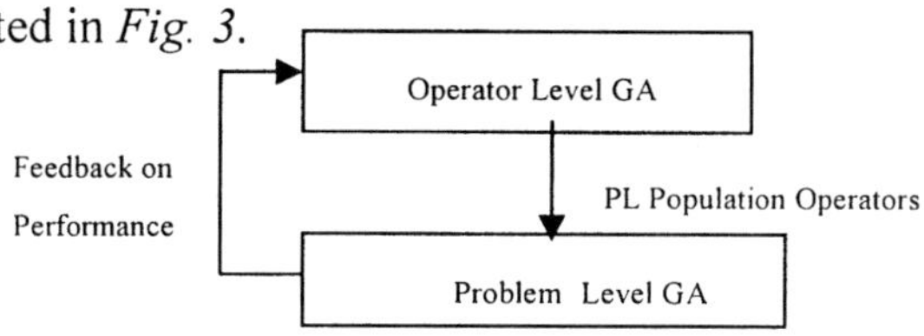

Fig. 3 Interaction between the Operator Level and Problem Level of the AGA

The pseudo code of the Evaluate function is given in *Fig. 4* and a detailed discussion of this function can be found in [11].

```
Population Evaluate (population: Population, plPopulation: Population)
BEGIN
   Initialise the array temp_plPopulations to be of size population_size
   FOR each chromosome in population
      operators = Decode_operators (chromosome, num_operators)
         PL_GA_set_operators (operators)
         pop = plPopulation
         /* num_generations in AGA is set to one */
         FOR (num = 0; num < num_generations; num+1)
         pop = PL_GA_Evolve (pop)
      ENDFOR
      Append pop to temp_plPopulations
   ENDFOR
   /* Calculate_and_assign_fitnesses returns best problem level population
  index based on the fitness values assigned by the fitness function */
   best_plPopulation_index =
         Calculate_and_assign_fitnesses (population, temp_plPopulations)
   best_plPopulation = temp_plPopulations[best_plPopulation]
   /* Updates the number of children produced by each of the operators in
    the problem level GA for during the evolution of best_plPopulation */
   Update_PL_operator_children_produced (best_plPopulation_index)
   RETURN best_plPopulation
END
```

Fig. 4. Pseudo Code of Evaluate in OL GA

Seven fitness functions for the OL GA were formulated to properly gauge and capture the desired properties of the performances of the various configurations on the PL GA, or in other words, the fitness values of the chromosomes in the population of the OL GA. The candidate fitness functions are shown below:

$$Fitness\_Function\_1_{OL} = R(f_b) \quad (1)$$

$$Fitness\_Function\_2_{OL} = R(BC) \quad (2)$$

$$Fitness\_Function\_3_{OL} = \begin{array}{l} R(BC)\times Weight_{BC} + R(f_{sd})\times Weight_{sd} \\ + R(f_m)\times Weight_m \end{array} \quad (3)$$

$$Fitness\_Function\_4_{OL} = \begin{cases} R(f_b) & f_b > prev.f_b \\ R(f_{sd}) + R(f_m), & f_b \le prev.f_b \end{cases} \quad (4)$$

$$Fitness\_Function\_5_{OL} = \begin{cases} R(BC) & f_b > prev.f_b \\ R(f_{sd}) + R(f_m) & f_b \le prev.f_b \end{cases} \quad (5)$$

$$Fitness\_Function\_6_{OL} = \begin{cases} R(f_b) & f_b > prev.f_b \\ R(f_{sd}) + R(BC) & f_b \le prev.f_b \end{cases} \quad (6)$$

$$Fitness\_Function\_7_{OL} = \begin{cases} R(BC) & f_b > prev.f_b \\ R(f_{sd}) + R(BC) & f_b \le prev.f_b \end{cases} \quad (7)$$

where $R(x)$ returns the rank of x associated with the chromosomes in the OL population,. A rank of 1 is the lowest rank and the rank value equal to the *population_size* is the highest rank. f_b is the fitness of the best candidate solution found in the associated PL GA's population; *BC* stands for Better Children, and is used to denote the number of child chromosomes that have been produced during a particular configuration that have better fitness values than the parents involved in creating them; f_{sd} is the standard deviation of the fitness values of the chromosomes in the associated PL population; f_m is the mean of the fitness values of the chromosomes in the associated PL population; $Weight_{BC}$, $Weight_m$ and $Weight_{sd}$ are the weights assigned to *BC*, f_m and f_{sd} respectively, where they are set to $Weight_{BC} = 1.0$, $Weight_{sd} = 0.8$ and $Weight_m = 0.8$; and $prev.f_b$ refers to the fitness of the best PL chromosome found during the previous OL generation. For a detailed description of the 7 fitness functions the reader is referred to [11].

3.2 Problem Level Genetic Algorithm

The primary purpose of the problem level genetic algorithm is to find good solutions to the problem at hand. At the same time, it is also used to evaluate the OL GA chromosomes and return feedback about the performances of the settings encoded in these chromosomes for the current state of the PL search. In order to serve these purposes, during each generation of the OL GA, each OL chromosome is decoded and the PL GA is configured with these decoded operators that are then used in its search of the current search space in the form of a PL population. How this search is conducted is illustrated in the pseudo code of the PL_GA_Evolve function of the PL GA shown below in *Fig 5.* The operators to be used for the current search, known as *operators* in *Fig 4*, are set just before this PL_GA_Evolve function is called in the Evaluate function of the OL GA.

```
Population PL_GA_Evolve (plPopulation)
BEGIN
   Initialise children of size num_children_required
   FOR each operator in operators
      num_parents_required = Get_num_parents_needed (operator)
      num_children_produced = Get_num_children_produced (operator)
      number = Get_num_children_to_be_produced_by_operator (operator)
      num = 0
      WHILE (num < number)
         parents = Select (plPopulation, num_parents_required)
         child = Perform_Operation (operator, parents)
         PLEvaluate (child)
         Append child to children
         Increment num by num_children_produced
      ENDWHILE
   ENDFOR
   new_population = Perform_replacement (plPopulation, children)
   evaluate_population (new_population)
   RETURN new_population
END
```

Fig. 5. Pseudo Code of (PL)_GA_Evolve

Get_num_children_to_be_produced_by_operator is a function used to calculate the allotted number of children that are to be produced by the specified operator. This is calculated by getting the number of children needed to be produced in total per PL generation and evenly dividing them among the operators, operators, to be used in that generation. Should there be leftover children from the division, these are then distributed to the first occurring operators from the OL chromosome. As for the number of children to be produced in each generation, this is defined by a predetermined rate expressed as a fraction of the PL population size and is set before the start of the application of the AGA. In the implementations of the AGAs, this parameter is arbitrarily set to a value of 0.9.

3.2.1 Operator Settings

As mentioned in section 3.1.1, the operators to be used in the PL GA are determined by chromosomes in the OL GA population, with the number of operators to be deciphered from each chromosome to be used, predetermined before the run of the GA. With this parameter set, the rate for each operator is also indirectly determined, since each operator is assigned an equal number of children for it to produce from the number of children to be produced each generation. Hence, when compared to a classic GA that requires the crossover and mutation operators and rates to be retuned for different problems in the same domain, the proposed AGA, which only requires the number of operators to be used retuned, can be said to be more easily applied on different problems in the same domain.

3.2.2 Reproduction Strategy

In classic GAs, the crossover operator creates child chromosomes, while the mutation operator modify the existing chromosomes present in the new generation's population that may or may not have been produced by a crossover operator. However, because of the inability of distinguishing between crossover and mutation operators in a relatively problem independent GA such as this as well as for simplicity's sake, it was decided to have all operators produce children, such that a modified chromosome is also considered a child chromosome.

4. EVALUATION OF THE PERFORMANCE OF AGA

Seven AGAs with fitness functions corresponding to those described in 3.1.3 are implemented. Henceforth, the AGA that utilizes Fitness_Function_1OL will be referred to as (1), the AGA that utilises Fitness_Function_2OL will be referred to as (2) and so on. For all variations of the AGA, the OL population size is set to 20 and the PL population size is set to 50.

To provide benchmarks against which the proposed variations of the AGA may be tested against, a classic GA (RGA), and a variation of the AGA to act as a control (Control) are designed and implemented. To allow for fairer testing, RGA uses most of the same components as the problem level GA of the AGA, while Control uses the same components as the AGAs except that no evolutionary procedures and evaluations are performed in the OL GA. Hence, RGA provides a benchmark against classic GAs and Control provides a benchmark to gauge the effectiveness of the role of the OL GA.

The tuning process for the AGAs and Control consists of predetermining the number of operators to be used in the PL GA in the range of 1 to 9, while for RGA, this consists of finding the optimal crossover and mutation rates in the range of 0.5 to 1.0 and 0.0 to 0.5, in steps of 0.1, respectively.

4.1 Experimental Results

A number of experiments were conducted on a variety of problem sets [11]. The results of two problem sets are presented in this paper. The following describes the details of the tables; in the first column "RGA" refers to the regular GA, "Control" refers to the control adaptive genetic algorithm and (1), (2), (3), (4), (5), (6) and (7) represent the proposed adaptive genetic algorithms; the second column Opt shows the number of times the corresponding algorithm found optimal solutions; B.B.Fitness is an acronym for best best fitness and is the fitness of the overall best solution found among the set of tests; Mean.B.Fitness refers to mean best fitness and is the mean of the fitness values of the best solutions found for the set of tests of that particular problem; SD.B.Fitness is the standard deviation of the fitness values of the best solutions found during the set of tests for that problem; M.Time refers to the average amount of time taken to run the set of tests, where each algorithm is run on a particular instance of a problem until it finds the optimal or until it reaches the time limit; and under the column rank, states the rank of the algorithms according to their performance evaluation and in relation to one another, where a rank of 1 signifies the best performing algorithm and 9, the worst.

Table 1. Summary of the Performances of the GAs on the Knb150 Problem

Algo	Opt	B.B.Fitness	M.B.Fitness	SD.B.Fitness	M.Time	Rank
RGA	0	0.070819	0.070825	3.43E-06	120.00	7
Control	0	0.070893	0.070946	2.64E-05	120.04	9
(1)	0	0.070825	0.070838	8.97E-06	120.06	8
(2)	7	0.070818	0.070818	1.19E-07	107.73	3
(3)	10	0.070818	0.070818	0	95.541	1
(4)	1	0.070818	0.070818	1.97E-07	119.94	4
(5)	1	0.070818	0.070819	3.88E-07	119.75	5
(6)	0	0.070818	0.070819	4.22E-07	120.05	6
(7)	7	0.070818	0.070818	2.98E-08	111.28	2

Table 2. Summary of the Performances of the GAs on the Eil51 Problem

Algo	Opt	B.B.Fitness	M.B.Fitness	SD.B.Fitness	M.Time	Rank
RGA	0	431	453.5	12.4036285	90.0037	9
Control	0	427	436.4	6.696267617	90.0193	8
(1)	1	426	435.2	4.643274706	82.5172	2
(2)	0	427	433.7	5.020956084	90.0123	4
(3)	0	427	435.4	4.923413450	90.0167	6
(4)	2	426	434	4.582575695	82.7868	1
(5)	0	427	433.7	5.866003750	90.0129	5
(6)	1	426	435.3	5.984145720	82.0365	3
(7)	0	427	435.8	3.841874542	90.0166	7

Tables 1 and 2 shows the results of the experiments on the Knb150 problem set [12] and a 51 city travelling salesman problem (Eil51), [13]. From these tables we see that the AGAs outperform both the RGA and Control algorithms. In TSP problem, out of the 7 AGAs, 3 of them (AGA 1, 4 and 6) managed to find optimal solutions, whereas the RGA and control AGA failed to do so. Furthermore, the other 4 AGAs (2,3,5 and 7) performed better in terms of the consistency of the solutions found (lower standard deviations)

5. CONCLUSION

The results of the experiments showed that AGA is an effective approach in enhancing the performance of a GA. It consistently outperformed a regular GA throughout the various test problems, demonstrating the versatility of the adaptation mechanisms. Further, based on the different performances of the various AGAs in relation to one another on the different test problems, it was found that different adaptation mechanisms are better suited to different problems. The results also showed that the previously feared high overhead of such an approach was unfounded, since the proposed AGAs were able to find better solutions in a shorter time.

REFERENCES

1. Tuson, A. L. (1995), "Adapting Operator Probabilities in Genetic Algorithms", Unpublished M.Sc. thesis, Department of Artificial Intelligence, University of Edinburgh.
2. DeJong, K. A. (1975), "An Analysis of the Behavior of a Class of Genetic Adaptive Systems", University of Michigan, Ph.D. Dissertation.
3. Davis, L. (1991), "Handbook of Genetic Algorithms", Van Nostrand Reinhold.
4. Grefenstette, J. J. (1986), "Optimization of control parameters for genetic algorithms," in IEEE Trans. On Systems, Man, and Cybernetics.
5. David, J., Caruana, R. A., Eshelman, L. J. and Das, R. (1989), "A study of control parameters affecting online performance of genetic algorithms for function optimisation", in Proceedings of the Third International Conference on Genetic Algorithms, Morgan Kaufmann Publishers.
6. Spears, W. M. (1995), "Adapting crossover in a genetic algorithm", in Proceedings of the 5th Conference on Evolutionary Programming, Cambridge MIT Press
7. Herrera, F and Lozano, M. (1996), "Adaptation of Genetic Algorithm Parameters Based on Fuzzy Logic Controllers", in Genetic Algorithms and Soft Computing, Physica-Verlag.
8. Tuson, A. L. and Ross, P. M. (1998), "Adapting Operator Settings in Genetic Algorithms. Evolutionary Computation", 6(2)
9. Hatta, K., Matsuda, K., Wakabayashi, S. and Koide, T. (1997), "On-the-fly crossover adaptation of genetic algorithms," in Proceedings of IEE/IEEE Genetic Algorithms in Engineering Systems: Innovations and Applications, pp.197-202.
10. Chen, S. and Liu, Y. (2001), "The application of multi-level genetic algorithms in assembly planning", Journal of Industrial Technology, 17(4)
11. Koh S. (2004) "An Operator Based Adaptive Genetic Algorithm for Permutation Based Optimization Problems" MIT Thesis, Monash University Malaysia.
12. Leow, S. K. and Koh, S. (2004), "Using the Invariant Optimal Assignment of a k-out-of-n: G system to Test the Effectiveness of Genetic Algorithms", in 8th IEEE International Conference on Intelligent Engineering Systems.
13. TSPLIB (2000), "TSPLIB – Travelling Salesman Problem Library", Available: http://www.iwr.uni-heidelberg.de/groups/comopt/software/TSPLIB95/, 24/5/2004
14. Burkard, R. E., Çela, E., Karisch, S.E. and Rendl, F. (2002), "QAPLIB – A Quadratic Assignment Problem Library", Available: http://www.seas.upenn.edu/qaPLib/, 12/6/2004.
15. Marcos H. M, Heitor S. L., Myriam R D. (2005), "Self-Adapting Evolutionary Parameters: Encoding Aspects for Combinatorial Optimization Problems" G.R. Raidl and J. Gottlieb (Eds.): EvoCOP 2005, LNCS 3448, pp. 154-165

GENETIC ALGORITHM-BASED DYNAMIC INTRAOPERATIVE TREATMENT PLANNING FOR PROSTATE BRACHYTHERAPY

Lei Fu, Yan Yu and Haisong Liu
Departments of Radiation Oncology, University of Rochester, Rochester, NY, U.S.A

Abstract: This paper reports on the use of a genetic algorithm (GA) for dynamic intraoperative treatment planning (DITP) with stepwise replanning for the prostate implant. The study applied a simple needle and seed reconstruction model to simulate the seed displacement. The simulation of DITP consists of an initial plan and four re-optimized plans. The results show that, on average, the total number of seeds required by each re-plan increased. The average maximum urethral dose and maximum rectal dose showed a slight increase during the first two replanning steps, but increased substantially during the latter two replanning steps. Several issues are discussed regarding the limitation and future improvement of GA-based DITP.

Key words: Prostate, Brachytherapy, Treatment planning, Intraoperative, Genetic algorithm, Robotics, Dosimetry

1. INTRODUCTION

Prostate brachytherapy is a method of treating early prostate cancer using permanent implantation of radioactive sources. Traditionally, the implantation pattern was preplanned days or weeks before surgery. In recent years, intraoperative preplanning and interactive planning are gaining popularity because of their advantages over the preplanned technique. Furthermore, a number of institutions are currently performing and refining dynamic intraoperative treatment planning (DITP), which was defined by the American Brachytherapy Society as continuous update of the treatment plan in the operating room (OR) [1]. Potentially, DITP can address and compensate for defects in the dosimetry due to deflection of needles and displacement of seed positions, and due to changes in prostate size and shape. The major limitation of DITP is the difficulty in localizing the seeds in relation to the prostate in real time. Memorial Sloan-Kettering Cancer Center used the technique of fusion of ultrasound and fluoroscopy to achieve seed reconstruction [2,3]. They recently presented an intraoperative dynamic dose optimization (IDDO) algorithm that can theoretically perform the DITP. IDDO re-optimizes the plan 2, 3, or 4 times during the implant based on the simulated shifted seed positions. They analyzed the sensitivity and effect of the IDDO procedure with respect to the total number of re-optimizations performed, and reported that IDDO treatment planning can improve post-implant dose coverage and conformity and reduced irradiation to urethra and rectum [2].

In our center, a robotic system for assisting prostate brachytherapy is under development. It will provide the possibility of DITP because of improvements in active, on-demand image acquisition and seeds detection. Our inverse planning system applies needle and seed spacing optimizations using a genetic algorithm (GA), which is different from the integer programming technique used in MSKCC's 3D treatment plan system.

In this paper, a simulation of DITP is presented using a model of seed displacement based on clinical observation in our center. This simulation consists of an initial plan and four re-optimized plans. Each re-optimized plan is based on the previous simulated position of seeds. Our study focuses on the dosimetric analysis and comparison of each re-optimization step.

2. METHODS AND MATERIALS

2.1 Simulation of seeds displacement

The implementation of DITP requires dosimetric information based on the actual positions of seeds already implanted. Some center applied Monte Carlo models to simulate post-implant needle reconstruction [4]. The seed displacement statistics varies among centers because of different implantation techniques.

According to our clinical observation, we created a simple but effective model to simulate the displacement of implanted seeds. In this model, post-implant seed displacements were decomposed into needle displacements and seed displacements relative to the needle. If x_{pi}, y_{pi}, z_{pi} are the coordinates of the *i*th seed of a n-source planning needle (there are total *m* needles to be displaced), and x_{qi}, y_{qi}, z_{qi} are the coordinates of simulated post-implant source, the transformations from planning to post-implant are applied as follows:

1. Needle translation δxj, δyj.

$$x_{qi} = x_{pi} + \delta x_j,$$

$$yqi = ypi + \delta yj, \qquad i=1,\ldots,n,\ j=1,\ldots,m$$

2. Angulation. The angles αj and β_j respectively formed by the needle and the insertion axis z in the coronal and sagittal planes.

$$z_{qi}=z_{pi} / (1+\tan(\alpha_j)^2+ \tan(\beta_j)^2)^{1/2},$$

$$x_{qi} = z_{pi} \bullet \tan(\alpha_j) + x_{pi},$$

$$yqi = zpi \bullet \tan(\beta j) + ypi, \qquad i=1,\ldots,n,\ j=1,\ldots,m$$

3. Random noise of seeds relative to the needle: Δx_i, Δy_i, Δz_i

$$x_{qi} = x_{qi} + \Delta x_i,$$

$$y_{qi} = y_{qi} + \Delta y_i,$$

$$z_{qi} = z_{qi} + \Delta z_i, \qquad i=1,\ldots,n,$$

The actual seed positions were identified from CT images, which were obtained one day after the implant procedure. The actual seed positions were automatically matched with the original planed seed positions using a deterministic annealing point-match algorithm. The mean and standard deviation of parameters δx_j, δy_j, αj, β_j, Δx_i, Δy_i, *and* Δz_i were collected from 15 patients. They were, respectively, 0±0.13cm, 0±0.14cm, 0±4.4°,

0.08°±5.5°, 0±0.04cm, 0±0.05cm, and 0±0.26cm. We used this model to obtain simulated individual seed displacement to approximate practical cases. The mean and standard deviation in x, y, z of individual seed displacement are 0.15cm, 0.17cm, 0.26cm, respectively.

2.2 Genetic algorithm optimization

Our treatment planning software employs GA as the optimization engine because of its conceptual simplicity, the ease of programming, and the small number of parameters to be defined. In this algorithm, grid coordinates x and y, angles α and β represent the solid angle position of each needle, and each needle position can be set to 1 or 0, which indicates if this position will be selected in the plan. This is an improvement based on our previous GA software, where only the grid coordinates x and y represent each needle position. Therefore, current software can generate traditional parallel needle dosimetry, as well as conical dosimetry and hybrid dosimetry where both parallel needles and angulated needles are applied.

There are two steps of optimization in the GA software: the needle optimization and seed spacing optimization. First, the needle optimization was performed by using one of a few selected seed spacing rules [5,6]. Nominally, seeds were 1 cm apart center-to-center in the same needle, and 0.5 cm spacing was permitted at the apex or base to best fit the length of the needle path in the prostate. This restriction in the original algorithm was introduced to permit use of ready-loaded needles or stranded seeds, which were typically provided in this fashion. All needles that intersected the prostate boundary become the chromosomes. During the GA optimization, the selected seed loading rule was applied to calculate the seed coordinates, and then the seed positions were used to calculate the dose, from which the fitness function was evaluated. The fitness function is essentially a weighted summation of the dosimetric outcomes. After a certain number of iterations (200 generations were used in our study), an optimal needle pattern was obtained.

Second, seed spacing optimization is performed based on this needle pattern [7]. Assuming 0.5 cm minimum nominal spacing and increment of seeds within each needle, all possible seed positions within the optimal needle pattern constitute the GA chromosomes. Using the same fitness function, an optimal seed position can be obtained.

2.3 Simulation of intraoperative treatment planning

The simulated DITP consists of one initial optimized plan and four intraoperative optimized plans.

First, the GA-based inverse planning software was used to obtain an initial optimized dosimetry. Based on this result, about ¼ of the total number of needles were selected for "simulated implantation". The seeds in these needles were displaced using the model described above in this paper. The needles were selected in the following order: right periphery of prostate, then left periphery of prostate, and lastly posterior to anterior. The left or right periphery is defined as the left or right ¼ width of the prostate in the transverse view.

Second, the remaining volume of the prostate was re-optimized using the same inverse planning algorithm. In this step the positions of the seeds already deposited in the prostate were included in the dosimetry calculation. The possible remaining positions were those that were certain distance away from the implanted seeds. This distance is a variable parameter in our software, and we used 2.5mm in this study according to the parameter test results, which will be discussed later in this paper.

Third, the above method of seed displacement and re-optimization was repeated twice. Each time 1/3 and ½, respectively, of the remaining needles and seeds were displaced. The positions of the seeds that were already displaced in the previous step were kept unchanged.

Lastly, all the remaining needles and seeds were displaced and the implant was re-optimized to see if any additional seed need to be placed.

2.4 Test cases

Ten unselected prostate seed implant cases were used in this study. All necessary data were acquired in a previous study [8]. The prostate volume ranges from 15 to 66 cm^3. For each case, two types of seeds and different prescription doses were tested: iodine-125 with initial air kerma strength of 0.5 U and a prescription dose of 145Gy, and palladium-103 with initial air kerma strength of 2.5 U and a prescription dose of 115Gy. Only one case, which is the smallest prostate, used 2.2 U per seed.

Each simulation was repeated three times to obtain the average results, because the random displacement of seeds tends to influence the final dosimetric results.

The following data were recorded for dosimetric analysis: the number of seeds used, maximum urethral dose (MUD), and maximum rectal dose (MRD). The change of the number of seeds is computed as the ratio of the total number of seeds used in each step (including those seeds already implanted) to the number of seeds used in the initial plan. We are interested in the change in the number of seeds, which indicates the change of S10mPD (total air kerma strength to deliver 10 Gy minimum peripheral dose). Any increase of S10mPD also indicates worsening of dose uniformity.

3. RESULTS

Table 1 shows the change in the number of seeds comparing the initial plan with each re-optimized plan. In general, the average number of seeds increased during the DITP simulation. The variation in the percentage change of seeds needed is also substantial. (The number in the parentheses in the tables shows the variation from minimum to maximum across ten cases.)

Table1. Change of number of seeds, comparing each re-optimization with initial plan

Seed type	Percentage change of number of seeds	Re optimization 1	Re optimization 2	Re-optimization 3	Re-optimization 4
I-125	Mean	-1 (--7 ~ 5)	1 (-8 ~ 15)	5 (-5 ~ 23)	11 (0 ~ 37)
	Standard Dev.	4	7	8	11
Pd-103	Mean	3 (-2 ~ 7)	6 (-2 ~ 18)	11 (3 ~ 25)	21 (7 ~ 35)
	Standard Dev.	3	5	7	9

Figures 1 and 2 illustrate the percentage change of number of seeds in each re-optimization step for the 10 cases, using seed type I-125 and Pd-103 respectively. Both results show the same trend of considerable variation among cases. However, Pd-103 produces more change of seeds than I-125.

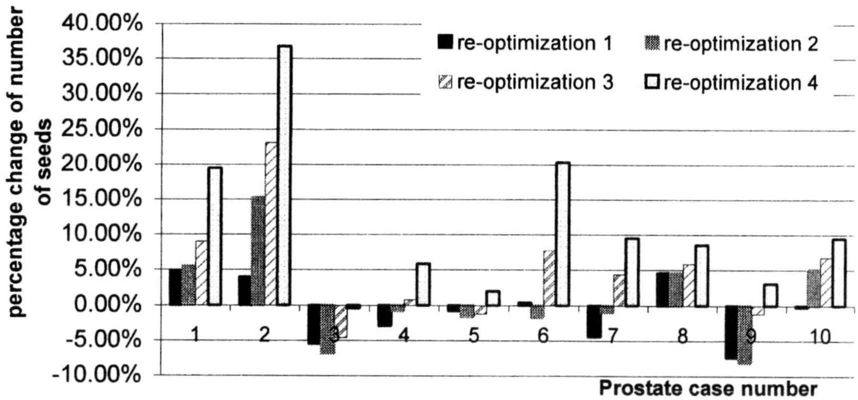

Figure 1. Change number of seeds in each re-optimization for 10 cases; using I-125

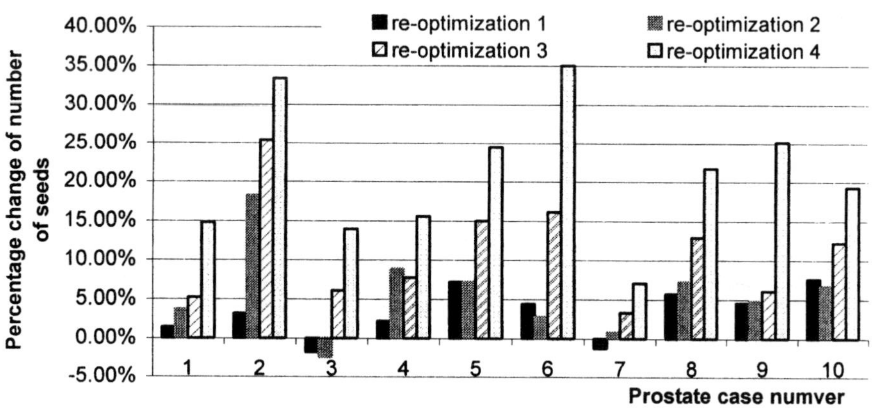

Figure 2. Change number of seeds in each re-optimization for 10 cases; using Pd-103

Table 2 and Table 3, respectively, show the change of MUD and MRD comparing the initial plan with each re-optimized plan. The average MUD and MRD also increased during re-optimization, particularly in the third re-optimization. Recall that during the third optimization, about 3/4 of the total seeds were displaced. These seeds include some located in the center of the prostate, which have relatively large influence to the MUD and MRD. At the last optimization, all of the seeds were displaced and the uniformity of prostate dosimetry became worst. The results also suggest that iodine and palladium have similar effects on the change of MUD and MRD, although I-125 displayed somewhat better test results than Pd-103.

Table 2. Change of MUD, comparing each re-optimization with initial plan

Seed type	Percentage change of number of seeds	Re-optimization 1	Re-optimization 2	Re-optimization 3	Re-optimization 4
I-125	Mean	-4 (-19 ~ 11)	-4 (-20 ~ 25)	3 (-9 ~ 73)	17 (-9 ~ 73)
	Standard Dev.	9	12	20	29
Pd-103	Mean	1 (-8 ~ 8)	-1 (-12 ~ 13)	9 (-15 ~ 25)	28 (7 ~ 60)
	Standard Dev.	6	8	10	14

Table 3. Change of MRD, comparing each re-optimization with initial plan

Seed type	Percentage change of number of seeds	Re-optimization 1	Re-optimization 2	Re-optimization 3	Re-optimization 4
I-125	Mean	0(-13 ~ 17)	2 (-14 ~ 29)	10 (-8 ~ 38)	16 (-7 ~ 52)
	Standard Dev.	10	12	13	17
Pd-103	Mean	8 (-5 ~ 24)	21 (0 ~ 66)	35 (0 ~ 94)	42 (-1 ~ 99)
	Standard Dev.	10	23	28	30

4. DISCUSSION

Although the average change in the number of seeds, MUD and MRD shows consistent results, the individual dosimetry results vary considerably among patients. The results may be influenced by the prostate shapes and volumes chosen, as well as the random Gaussian distribution of seed displacement. We suggest implanting seeds from right to left periphery, and then from posterior to anterior. Although the seed positions in the periphery may be altered intraoperatively due to prostate edema and tissue movement, the inverse planning system can still optimize the seed positions in the center of the prostate to ensure that dose to the urethra and rectum is minimized as much as possible.

The results indicate that DITP may require more seeds and more needles than the preplan. In current clinical practice, approximately 10% extra seeds are ordered as a safety margin. Our study shows that the first three re-optimizations require about 5% (I-125) and 11% (Pd-103) extra seeds on average. However, it varies significantly among patients.

We obtained individual seed displacement from the simulation results of ten cases. The standard deviation in the x, y, z directions are 0.15cm, 0.17cm,

0.26cm, respectively. This is the same as the results of seed reconstruction from matching planned seed positions to CT identified seed positions. In this study, the CT images were retrieved one day after the prostate brachytherapy in the OR. Edema of the prostate one day after brachytherapy may be more pronounced than that during brachytherapy or several days after brachytherapy [9]. DITP is a procedure in the OR so the standard deviation of seed displacement would be different from what we obtained in this study.

Intraoperative edema of the prostate is another factor that cannot be neglect in DITP. Many researchers are studying the effects of prostate edema on post-implant dosimetry. It was found that edema can result in a wide range of volume increases [10], and both the magnitude and duration of edema vary considerably among patients [11]. In this study we assume the prostate shape to be unchanged and only consider the effect of seed displacement on the re-optimization. In the future we will include prostate edema as observed in the OR at the re-optimization intervals.

The first step of needle optimization in the planning engine eliminates the needles that are near already implanted seeds. We found that the distance used to gauge needles will affect the optimization results. Because the template grid spacing is 5mm and the standard deviation of seed displacement is 1.5mm and 1.7mm in x, y direction, we chose 2.5mm as the gauge. We also tested 1mm and 4mm and found that for the smaller prostate the 4mm distance is too restrictive causing loss of some potential seed positions, and for the larger prostate the 1 mm may create too many potential seed positions so that the GA-based inverse planning engine would not produce optimal results in a limited number of generations (200).

Our simulated DITP divides the whole procedure into four re-optimization procedures. The demand for re-optimization depends on practical situations in the OR, such as the observed edema and deformation of the prostate and the detected seed displacement. Our robotic system is designed to obtain real-time information including prostate imaging and implanted seed positions, and to update the dosimetry on-the-fly. Based on this information, the clinicians will decide if it is necessary to re-optimize the dosimetry.

5. CONCLUSION

Simulated DITP based on a modified GA inverse planning engine generated increased average number of seeds, increased urethral dose and rectal dose during four re-optimization steps. Two types of seeds were tested and I-125 produced relatively lower average number of seeds, urethral dose and rectal dose than Pd-103. There was significant variability among the test cases.

ACKNOWLEDGEMENT

Work supported by NCI grant R01 CA091763.

REFERENCES

[1] Nag S, el al. Intraoperative planning and evaluation of permanent prostate brachytherapy: report of the American Brachytherapy Society. Int J Radiat Oncol Biol Phys. 2001, 51(5):1422~1430.

[2] Lee EK, el al. Intraoperative dynamic dose optimization in permanent prostate implants. Int J Radiat Oncol Biol Phys. 2003, 56(3):854~861.

[3] Todor DA, el al. Intraoperative dynamic dosimetry for prostate implants. Phys Med Biol. 2003, 48(9):1153~1171.

[4] Taschereau R, el al. Monte Carlo simulations of prostate implants to improve dosimetry and compare planning methods. Med Phys. 1999, 26(9):1952~1959.

[5] Yu Y, el al. A genetic algorithm for the optimization of prostate implants. Med Phys. 1996, 23(12):2085~2091.

[6] Yu Y, et al. Automated treatment planning engine for prostate seed implant brachytherapy. Int J Radiat Oncol Biol Phys. 1999, 43(3):647~652.

[7] Fu L, el al. Bouquet brachytherapy: feasibility and optimization of conically spaced implants. Brachytherapy. 2005, 4(1):59~63

[8] Messing EM, et al. Intraoperative optimized inverse planning for prostate brachytherapy: early experience. Int J Radiat Oncol Biol Phys. 1999, 44(4):801~808.

[9] Dogan N, el al. Effect of prostatic edema on CT-based postimplant dosimetry. Int J Radiat Oncol Biol Phys. 2002, 53(2):483~489.

[10] Yamada Y, el al. Impact of intraoperative edema during transperineal permanent prostate brachytherapy on computer-optimized and preimplant planning techniques. Am J Clin Oncol. 2003, 26(5):e130~e135.

[11] Waterman F.M, et al. Edema associated with 125I or 103Pd prostate brachytherapy and its impact on post-implant dosimetry: An analysis based on serial CT acquisition. Int J Radiat Oncol Biol Phys 1998, 41(4):1069~1077.

NONLINEAR ERROR CORRECT OF INTELLIGENT SENSOR BY USING GENETIC ALGORITHMS AND CUBIC SPLINE INTERPOLATION

Lin Lei, Houjun Wang and Yang Bai

School of Automation Engineering, University of Electronic Science and Technology of China, Chengdu,610054 China

Abstract: The new technique in this paper is investigated to correct the nonlinear measurement error of intelligent sensor by use of genetic algorithms and cubic spline interpolation. The principle is using the advantage of both genetic algorithms and cubic spline function to reduce the iteration times and improve measurement precision of intelligent sensor. The way is through selecting genetic algorithms with appropriate design parameter and cubic spline function to build error correction model. The coefficients of the cubic spline function can be figured out by matrix operation. Then use genetic algorithms to fit the first part data, yielding optimization function and optimization coefficients. Simulation result and practice application show this technique is available compared with traditional way such as least-squares method.

Key words: GA, nonlinear error correction, cubic spline, optimization

1. INTRODUCTION

In system of industry control or automatic detection, the majority signals of electric voltage or electric current of sensors are the nonlinear. To nonlinear signal usually has two kinds of handling ways, one kind of ways is preparing the data form in advance according to the curve characteristic, then the adoption checks the form method to proceeds to handle to the signal of sensor; another method is nonlinear curve be divided into some a value for, each segment is linear or looking like for linear, according to the signal adopting kind getting, then find out the homologous linear zone, then makes use of the formula method handle to the signal. These two kinds of methods are all to orders the curvilinear cent segment to do in procedure, certainly data form can't be changed again. Obviously, above two kinds of methods contain a premise, that is this type of sensor signal of the curve a result for can having first, or saying getting of the same kind sensor must have good consistency, very much will have the error margin, even that gauge can't apply because the error margin is very big.

Aim at the problem as above, in this text we puts forward using genetic arithmetic combinative cubic spline interpolation method. Genetic Algorithms (GA) is especially suitable in solving complex and nonlinear problems, which are difficult for traditional searching algorithms. In practice intelligent sensor, nonlinear error of intelligent sensor is the source of most system. For the shortcoming of the nonlinear problem solving way existed presently, we present a new way combined genetic algorithms and cubic spline to correct nonlinear error. Spline interpolation function is in common use and important among those convergent and steady interpolation function. The cubic spline function with 2-order continue derivative is used under the condition of satisfying project design demands usually. It can be proved that the resolution of interpolation problems S (x) exists uniquely under the condition of above three boundary conditions.

2. NONLINEAR ERROR CORRECTION MODEL

In general, x expresses the physics parameters to be measured and y expresses the value measured by sensor. For n groups experiment data (x_i, y_i) (i=1,2,..., n), we can adopt m term polynomial as the approximate function to describe these data: $y' = a_0 + a_1x + a_2x^2 + \cdots + a_mx^m = \sum_{j=0}^{m} a_jx^j$ (1)

Where, $A = (a_0, a_1, a_2, \cdots, a_m)^T$ are $m+1$ coefficients to be confirmed. Let δ_i be the error between the result figured out by formula (1) and y_i at x_i. And import n pairs measure data (x_i, y_i) into formula (1), yielding n equations: $\delta_i = y_i - y_i' = y_i - \sum_{j=0}^{m} a_jx^j$ (2)

Where i = 1, 2...n. The goal is to get the optimum estimate value $A' = (a_0', a_1', \cdots, a_m')^T$ under the condition of the least-squares sum of δ_i.

The individual fitness mapped from object function should be non-negative. And the optimization direction should be the fitness increases direction. We use ER, the least-squares sum of δ_i, as the object function in the process of dealing with nonlinear error.

$$ER = \sum_{j=1} [\sum a_j x^j - y_j]^2 \tag{3}$$

The mapping relation between f_i and object function ER is:

$$f_i(x) = \begin{cases} C_{max} - ER, & ER < C_{max} \\ 0\ , & others \end{cases} \tag{4}$$

C_{max} is an integer, which is maximum estimate value of $f(x)$.

Then use model as above to correct nonlinear error of sensor on-line. If the result of comparing with the value decided by model and real-time measurement by sensor, two of deviation beyond the reach of the normal motion scope that rule, precede again line revise. And this process can finish automatically by microprocessor in sensor.

3. THE COMBINATION OF GENETIC ALGORITHMS AND CUBIC SPLINE

Taking advantage of the GA and cubic spline function, we can reduce the iteration times and decrease the nonlinear error to zero at the boundary especially. The curve is very smooth at the joint of GA and cubic spline, and the correction precision will reach to a high level.

When we acquire a lot of measurement data by intelligent sensor in real measurement system. These data are divided into three parts unequally. Two points of intersection (X_1, Y_1) and (X_2, Y_2) will occur. We use GA to fit the first part data, yielding optimization function: $Y_0=A_0+B0X+C_0X_2+D_0X_3$

A_0, B_0, C_0 and D_0 will be confirmed through many times of iteration of improved GA. The square sum of nonlinear error will be minimum. The second part data are fitted by cubic spline function. The coefficients of the cubic spline function can be figured out by matrix operation. This segment cubic spline function is: $Y_1=A_1+B_1X+C_1X_2+D_1X_3$

$$\begin{bmatrix} 1 & x_1 & x_1^2 & x_1^3 \\ 0 & 1 & 2x_1 & 3x_1 \\ 0 & 0 & 2 & 6x_1 \\ 1 & x_2 & x_2^2 & x_2^3 \end{bmatrix} \begin{bmatrix} A_1 \\ B_1 \\ C_1 \\ D_1 \end{bmatrix} = \begin{bmatrix} A_0 + B_0 x_1 + C_0 x_1^2 + D_0 x_1^3 \\ B_0 + 2C_0 x_1 + 3D_0 x_1^2 \\ 2C_0 + 6D_0 x_1 \\ y_2 \end{bmatrix} \tag{5}$$

we get the third cubic spline function: $Y_2 = A_2+B_2X+C_2X_2+D_2X_3$. According to the end point (X_3,Y_3) of data , the matrix as follows:

$$\begin{bmatrix} 1 & x_2 & x_2^2 & x_2^3 \\ 0 & 1 & 2x_2 & 3x_2^2 \\ 0 & 0 & 2 & 6x_2 \\ 1 & x_3 & x_3^2 & x_3^3 \end{bmatrix} \begin{bmatrix} A_2 \\ B_2 \\ C_2 \\ D_2 \end{bmatrix} = \begin{bmatrix} A_1 + B_1x_2 + C_1x_2^2 + D_1x_2^3 \\ B_1 + 2C_1x_2 + 3D_1x_2^2 \\ 2C_1 + 6D_1x_2 \\ y_3 \end{bmatrix} \tag{6}$$

The value of A_2, B_2, C_2 and D_2 can be figured out through matrix operation. Thus, three fitting curves have been figured out, and connected smoothly in turn. At the same time, the square sum of nonlinear error is minimum, satisfied the precision demand.

4. GENETIC ALGORITHMS DESIGN

The parameter of genetic algorithms has bigger influence on our correction algorithm, so we must design these parameters very well.

We adopt real number to encode the chromosome. Real number encoding mode can save the operation time, which has higher precision and explicit physics meaning. adopt 2 member sign gene table S={＋, －}and 11 member numerical value gene table V={0, 1, 2, 3, 4, 5, 6, 7, 8, 9, •}to encode chromosome, where "•" expresses radix point. Letters with subscript can express every chromosome, where subscript expresses sequence of location. The sign gene takes part in the mutation operation. The sign "＋" can mutates only to "－", and the sign "－" can mutates only to "＋". Adopting this encoding rule, invalidation pattern will not occur in chromosome individuals no matter what selection、crossover or mutation operation.

The fitness distribute strategy adopted in this paper is based on sorting. The population is sorted according to the object value. Sorting method imported with population uniformity scale supplies a simple and effective way to control the selection pressure. The robustness of sorting method is better than that of proportion method.

We give attention to global and local searching ability through selecting high crossover probability and mutation probability synthetically. Such pair of operation has both cooperation and competition. The design and realization of crossover operator relates to special problem. We adopt simple single point crossover operator at here. The defining domain is determined by vector $A=(a_1,a_2,\cdots,a_i,\cdots a_n)T$ and $B=(b_1,b_2,\cdots,b_i,\cdots b_n)T$. In order to make sure $D_n=A\times B$, namely the solution domain is protruding domain, we make any chromosome X0 satisfy $\forall i\in\{1,2,\cdots n\}$, $a_i \le x_{i0} \le b_i$. Let the two chromosomes to be crossed in parent generation are: $X= (x_1,x_2,\cdots,x_i\cdots x_n)^T$,

$Y=(y_1,y_2,\cdots,y_i\cdots y_n)^T$.For any i, if $x_i \le y_i$ (or else, exchange x_i and y_i), thus the cross algorithms defined as follows: $C = A \oplus B$

$$C_i=\begin{cases}\alpha a_i+(1-\alpha)x_i & \mathrm{mod}(\theta,4)=0\\ \alpha x_i+(1-\varepsilon)y_i & \mathrm{mod}(\theta,4)=1 or 2\\ \alpha y_i+(1-\alpha)b_i & \mathrm{mod}(\theta,4)=3\end{cases} \quad (i=1,2,\cdots,n) \qquad (7)$$

where, α is a random real number satisfied $\alpha\in[0, 1]$and θ is a random nonnegative integer. In above formula, the probability, which the value of child is between parents, equals to that of other two instances, so that better convergence speed can be achieved when the solutions are inner points.

According to the characteristics of protruding combination, if $X, Y\in D_n$, $C\in D_n$, what can make sure the searching proceed in certain space. Therefore, the cross operation of evolution GA can assure the solutions to be better and better and make the evolution GA has more strong global convergence ability that can deal with not only inner point problem but also the problem with solutions located near the boundary.

Improved mutation operation is: $C=\nabla_\theta X$ (8)

$$C_i=\begin{cases}\alpha a_i+(1-\alpha)x_i & \mathrm{mod}(\theta,2)=0\\ \alpha x_i+(1-\alpha)b_i & \mathrm{mod}(\theta,2)=1\end{cases} \quad X\in D_n, \quad \forall x_i\in X \qquad (9)$$

α is a random real number; satisfied with $0\le\alpha\le1$, and θ is a random non-negative integer.

5. SIMULATION RESULTS

The example of nonlinear error correction is based on thermocouple temperature intelligent sensor in this paper. The GA approach equation of the first segment is: $F(X)=3.4977+2.5038X+1.4984X_2+0.5002X_3$ (10)

The sum of error square is 3.2804e-006, and the maximum relative error is 9.9781e-005. Simulation software is programmed by MATLAB language. We can get the coefficients of the approximation equation of the second segment through importing the coefficients of the first segment into this program. The coefficients of the third segment, the fourth segment, ⋯, the sixteenth segment may be deduced by analogy. Here, the square sum of error of total group data is 5.4039e-006, and the curve of simulation shows in Fig1.In Fig1, horizontal coordinate is temperature(℃), vertical coordinate is voltage(unit is μV).

In addition, the result of this method is better than least squares method and the best uniform approximation compared with traditional ways, and the precision is better than that of genetic algorithms purely.

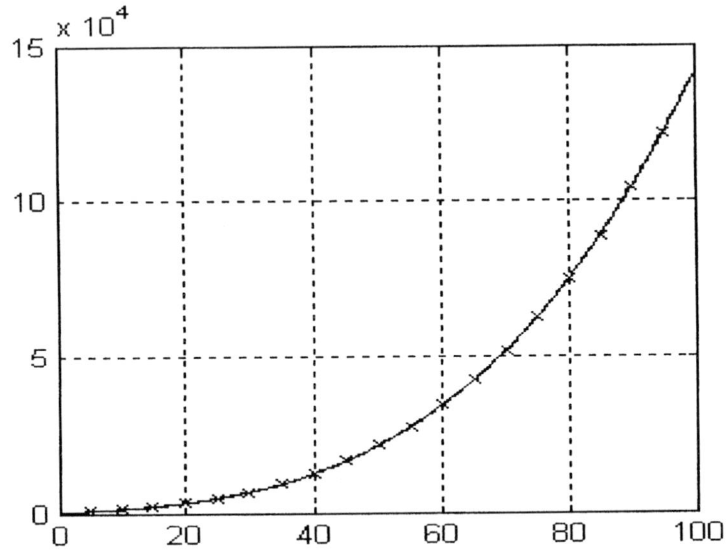

Figure 1. Facilities

6. CONCLUSIONS

We researched the ability of combination GA and cubic spline interpolation to correct nonlinear error of intelligent sensor. Data information that makes use of the hour of normal movement in sensor can reflect the normal measurement data of sensor. Like this correction curve or importations that establishes output the relation since solved the inconsistent of the sensor, increases measurement accuracy again. The simulation and practice application show the feasibility of combination genetic algorithms and cubic spline interpolation to correct nonlinear errors of sensor, put forward to the sensor measurement data in the text not the line error margin revises the technique, for all kinds of signals are all containing good result, having the application the value.

REFERENCES

[1]Li Qing-Yang, Guan Zhi, Bai Feng-Shan, numerical value compute theory, Beijing: Tsinghua university Publishing House, 2000.

[2]Wang Xiao-Ping, Cao Li-Ming, genetic algorithms —theory、application and software realization, Xi'an: Xi'an Jiaotong university Publishing House, 2002.

[3]Zhou Ming, Sun Shudong, genetic algorithms theory and application, Beijing: national defense industry Publishing House, 1999.

SOLVING NETWORK TESTBED MAPPING PROBLEM WITH GENETIC ALGORITHM

Yi Liu, Kaiping Xiao and Yanping Li
Department of Computer, Xi'an Jiaotong University, Xi'an, Shannxi, 710049, China E-mail: Liuyi97@263.net

Abstract: To provide remote service and auto-configuration mechanisms, network emulation testbed needs to map the logic-topology, which the researchers require, to the testbed physical-topology. This network testbed-mapping problem is discussed and formulated in this paper; an evaluation function is also defined in which both the number of network links and bandwidth are considered. This paper also gives a solution for considering delay-node. Based on the model, a solver for the problem using Genetic Algorithm is implemented. Evaluation result shows that the genetic algorithm can find near-optimal solutions in reasonable time.

Key words: network emulation, genetic algorithm, network testbed

1. INTRODUCTION

Experiment plays an important role in researches of various network technologies. Considering the cost and complexity of network experimentations in live networks, network simulation and emulation are widely used. Meanwhile, traditional simulation tools, such as widely used ns-2, are more available and economical, due to their ease of installation, management and relatively low resource requirements. Unfortunately, simulation-based experiments may be deemed less convincing, due to their lack of fidelity to real-world environments. Compared to the live network and simulation, emulation provides a good trade-off between fidelity and cost.

The goal of network emulation is to build an environment nearing real-world network, which researchers require in an experimental network. The primary difference between emulation and simulation is: simulators are totally implemented in software, in which network topologies and links are simulated; as a contrast, emulators are commonly built on one or several inter-connected LANs, in which network topologies are implemented by setting virtual LAN (VLAN) on network switches, and network links directly correspond to physical links in the LAN, delay-nodes are inserted to emulate low-speed network links. A number of recently proposed testbeds have clearly demonstrated the advantage and promise of this approach, such as Emulab/Netbed, ModelNet, vBET, and PlanetLab.

To provide remote service and auto-configuration mechanisms, network emulation testbed needs to map the logic-topology, which the researchers require, to the testbed physical-topology. In this paper, we explore this network testbed mapping problem. After building a model of the problem, this paper implements a solver for the problem using Genetic Algorithm. Finally, the solver is evaluated and results are discussed.

The rest of this paper is organized as follows. Section 2 gives an overview of network testbed mapping problem. Section 3 builds a model of the problem. Section 4 solves the problem using genetic algorithm, a well-known general-purpose method for solving difficult problems. Section 5 evaluates the solver using 100 randomly generated samples. Section 6 concludes the paper.

2. OVERVIEW OF NETWORK TESTBED MAPPING PROBLEM

The kernel of the network emulation testbed is to simulate the network environment, which researchers require in an experimental network. One of the key challenges to the testbed is how to construct required network topology on the physical topology of the experimental environment. This work can be done either manually or automatically. When it is done by the system automatically, the system must have the ability to map the logic-topology that researchers require to the physical topology of the testbed, and the mapping process is called "network testbed mapping problem" [1] or "network mapping problem" [3].

The mapping process includes two aspects: mapping of nodes (hosts & routers) and mapping of network links. The first one determines which physical nodes are used to emulate the logic-nodes. The assigned physical node must satisfy the hardware requirements of the logic-topology, such as processor speed of host, or packet routing delay of routers, etc. The second aspect, mapping of network links is relatively complex since it involves the use of the delay node sometimes. For example, to simulate 64 Kbps link on a 100Mbps network, delay nodes must be inserted between two ends of the 100Mbps link, by running dedicated emulation software on the delay node, the emulated link can have the same characteristics with 64Kbps link, such as bandwidth, transport delay and packet loss rate. Another example to use delay node is emulating long delay links such as satellite communications in a LAN.

Figure-1 gives a simple mapping example. There are three hosts and one router in experimenter's logic-topology. The physical topology includes one switch and four PCs, each of them has three network interfaces. Figure-1(c) shows the mapping result: all the nodes in logic-topology are mapped to the PC nodes, network links are emulated by configuring VLANs on the switch. The real lines in Figure-1 represent used links while the dotted lines represent unused links. Three VLANs are configured in this mapping, to emulate links between router and node 1,2 and 3 respectively. VLANs will isolate these three links form each other.

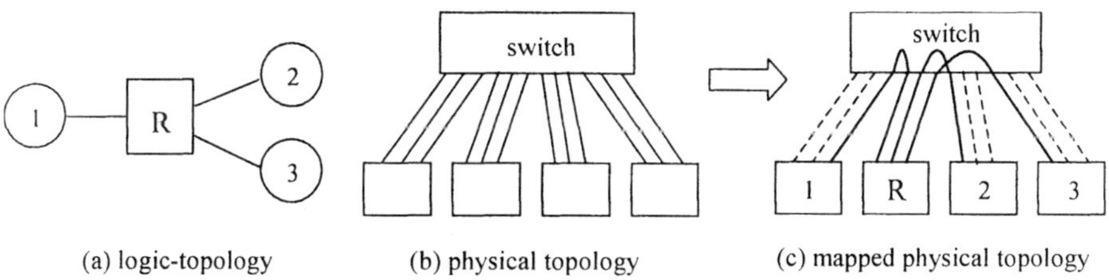

Figure 1. A Simple Mapping Example

To utilize resources more efficiently, emulation testbed should support as many experiments as possible simultaneously. This requires that the mapping of network topology should use as few resources as possible for an experiment, in order to reserve as many resources as possible for future experiments.

Network testbed mapping problem is finally turns to partitioning of graph. With different kinds of restrictions, the problem becomes NP-hard[7].

The main related researches about network testbed mapping problem include: [2] implements a solver using simulated annealing algorithm without considering the delay node; [3] presents a heuristic algorithm based on process allocating algorithms from parallel processing, with the aim of traffic-based load balancing among nodes.

3. MODELING OF THE PROBLEM

3.1 Modeling of the problem

The network topology in network testbed mapping problem can be expressed by graphs, in which vertices represent hosts & routers and graph edges represent network links.

Let graph *GP* and *GL* represent the physical topology of the testbed and experimenter's logic-topology respectively.

Graph *GL* is composed of node set $\{NL_i\}$ and link set $\{EL_{jk}\}$, $i,j,k=0,1,...,n-1$. A node, which corresponding to a host or a router, is represented by a tuple with each item reflects one configuration-parameter of the node. As a example, we use 4-tuple $<pl, ml, dl, ll>$ to represent a node in this paper, where *pl* is the processing capability, *ml* is the memory space, *dl* is the hard disk space, *ll* is the delay of routing. An element E_{jk} in link set represents an edge between node NL_j and NL_k, while the bandwidth of the network link is represented by the edge's weight *W*.

Similarly, graph *GP* is composed of the node set $\{NP_i\}$ and the link set $\{EP_{jk}\}$, $i,j,k=0,1,...,m-1$. The node in the graph is represented by the 4-tuple $<pp, mp, dp, lp>$.

According to the definitions above, the mapping from logic-topology *GL* to physical topology *GP* can be described as follows:

(1) **Mapping of nodes**: each node NL_i in *GL* is mapped to a NP_j in *GP*, and hardware configuration requirements of NL_i are satisfied by NP_j. That is:

$$f(NL_i) = NP_j,\ i=0,1,...n-1, j=0,1,...m-1$$
$$\text{and } pl_i \leqslant pp_j,\ ml_i \leqslant mp_j,\ dl_i \leqslant dp_j,\ ll_i \geqslant ll_j$$

(2) **Mapping of links**: there are two situations as follows.

- Network link EL_{ij} in *GL* is mapped to network link EP_{kl} in *GP*, while the two ends of EL_{ij} are mapped to two ends of EP_{kl}, and bandwidth requirement is satisfied by EP_{kl}. That is:

$$g(EL_{ij}) = \{EP_{kl}\}$$
$$\text{and } f(NL_i) = NP_k,\ f(NL_j) = NP_l \quad i,j=0,1,...n-1;\ k,l=0,1,...m-1$$

- Network link EL_{ij} in *GL* is mapped to multiple chained links in *GP*, while the two ends of EL_{ij} are mapped to two ends of those chained links, and each of those chained links satisfies bandwidth requirement of EL_{ij}. Nodes in the middle of the chain are all switching nodes. That is:

$$g(EL_{ij}) = \{EP_{kl}, EP_{lo},..., EP_{xy}\}$$
$$\text{and } f(NL_i) = NP_k,\ f(NL_j) = NP_y \quad i,j=0,1,...n-1;\ k,l,o,...x,y=0,1,...m-1$$

(3) **Evaluation method of a mapping**:

As discussed in section 2, a mapping of network topology should use as few resources as possible for an experiment. According to this principle, the evaluation method can be defined as follows.

Supposing for a mapping scheme, the set of used network links in *GP* is:

$U = \{EP_{ij}, EP_{jk}, ..., EP_{xy}\}$ $i,j,...,x,y=0,1,...m-1$

The evaluation value of the mapping scheme can be calculated according to:

$$E = (\alpha \times NU) + (\beta \times \sum W_{ij}) \quad (3\text{-}1)$$

Where *NU* is the element number of set *U*; W_{ij} is the link's weight in set *U*; α and β are scaling values satisfying $\alpha + \beta = 1$, which are used to achieve trade-off between number of network links and bandwidth.

In fact, the two restrictions of network-link number and bandwidth are independent each other, and may have conflicts sometimes. For example, there is no absolute standard to judge which of the following two mapping schemes is better: using three 10Mbps links to emulate a logic link, or using one 100Mbps link. Commonly, it needs the network administrator to make the decision according to various situations.

Considering this, the scaling values α and β are added. When α is comparably bigger and β is smaller, the evaluation function tends to choose the result that uses less links and vice versa. In most situations, network administrator is more willing to reserve more links for future experiments, so usually $\alpha > \beta$.

In all the mapping schemes, the one that has the smallest evaluating value *E* according to the expression (3-1) is the best solution.

3.2 About the delay node

The delay node is not considered by the modeling of the problem in section 3.1, which is used to emulate a low speed (such as Dial-Up networking) or long delay network link (such as Satellite communication) on a high-speed network. The delay node connects two network interfaces, and by using dedicated emulation software, it can forward packets between network interfaces, while adjusts transmission delay and packet lost to emulate the specified network link. Adding delay nodes dynamically during the mapping process will make the problem more complex, so many related works ignore it.

The problem can be solved by a pre-processing to the logic-topology before the mapping. In the pre-processing step, each link in logic-topology is checked, those low speed and long delay network links are substituted with "high speed link + delay node + high speed link" in sequence, and the pre-processed topology can be used in the following mapping process.

4. SOLVING THE PROBLEM WITH GENETIC ALGORITHM

Genetic Algorithm (GA) is a computing model which simulating genetic choice and natural elimination in the biological evolution process. It treats each possible solution of the problem as one individual in the population, and codes each individual in the form of a string. Then a fitness function is used to calculate a fitness for each individual, which is used to evaluate the individual. At the beginning of the algorithm, several possible individuals are selected randomly to form the original population; secondly, based on each individual's fitness, they are operated using the gene (selection, crossover, mutation) to generate the new population.

Based on the model in section 3, we implements a solver for the network testbed mapping problem using genetic algorithm. The implementation detail is as follows:

(1) **Coding**: a simple coding scheme is used in which each octet corresponds to a physical node, and the value of the octet represents which logic-node it is mapped. For example, to map 9 logic-nodes to 12 physical nodes, the coding result have 12 octets, the code 1 5 2 3 4 -1 6 -1 7 8 9 –1 means physical node 1 is used for logic-node 1, physical node 2 is used for logic-node 5, etc. Value –1 means the physical node is unused.

(2) **Fitness function**: same with the evaluation function in expression (3-1).

(3) **Selection mechanism**: selection means the process of copying individuals to the new population according to the fitness of them. The bigger the fitness is, the higher the possibility of the individual been copied and therefore has more offspring. Selection mechanisms being widely used include: roulette wheel selection, elitist model, expected value model, stochastic tournament, ranking, and mixing. In our implementation, roulette wheel selection is used, in which the possibility for an individual being selected is directly determined by its fitness in the population.

(4) **Crossover**: for sequence coding, crossover can't be simply done in one-point crossover or multi-point crossover. As Figure-2 shows, for two parent individual A and B, if position 2 and 6 are chosen as the cross point, the resulted children of regional crossing are shown in Figure-2(b), in which logic-node 1 and 3 are mapped twice in child A, while logic-node 2 and 7 are not mapped to any physical node. The same problem also exists in child B. therefore, it is not a reasonable mapping method.

Solution to the problem we used is: after position 2 and 6 are chosen as the cross point, we put B's crossing region in front of A and put A's crossing region in front of B, then we have A1 and B1, finally, overlapped genes are deleted from A1 and B1 and child A2 and B2 are generated. As shown in Figure-2(c), both children A2 and B2 are legal mapping results.

Parent A: 1 3| 5 7 2 4 |6 8 9
Parent B: 2 6| 3 1 4 5 |8 9 7

(a) Parent

Child A : 1 3 |3 1 4 5 |6 8 9
Child B : 2 6 |5 7 2 4 |8 9 7

(b) Children from one-point crossover

A1: 3 1 4 5 |1 3 5 7 2 4 6 8 9
B1: 5 7 2 4 |2 6 3 1 4 5 8 9 7

Child A2: 3 1 4 5 7 2 6 8 9
Child B2: 5 7 2 4 6 3 1 8 9

(c) Revised crossover

Figure 2. Crossover

(5) **Mutation**: mutation randomly changes value of octets in some individuals in a small probability. Exchange mutation is used in our implementation, in which two positions of an individual are selected and their values are exchanged. For example, for individual A, if position 3 and 6 are randomly selected, new individual A1 will be generated by exchanging values of position 3 and 6, as shown in Figure-3.

A: 1 3 5^ 7 2 4^ 6 8 9
A1: 1 3 4^ 7 2 5^ 6 8 9

Figure 3. Mutation

A: 1 3 5^ 7 2 4^ 6 8 9
A1: 1 3 5^ 4 2 7^ 6 8 9

Figure 4. Evolution inversion

(6) **Evolution inversion**: to improve the regional searching capability of genetic algorithm, evolution reversion is used in our implementation. As shown in Figure-4, for individual A, if position 3 and 6 are selected as the inversion points, octets from position 3 to 6 are exchanges and new individual A1 are generated.

5. EVALUATION AND COMPARISON

The algorithm is evaluated using 100 randomly generated logic-topologies. The node number in logic-topologies varies from 4 to 16. The physical-topology used in evaluation is composed of 24 nodes, each of which have three network interfaces installed, and all connected to backplane switches.

For all the logic-topologies, optimal solutions are exhaustively searched and compared with genetic algorithm solutions. Furthermore, the exhaustive searching algorithm is improved by eliminating unnecessary searching steps, this improved algorithm cost much less time than the old.

For all the solutions, evaluation value E is calculated using expression (3-1), where scaling value α and β are fixed to 0.8 and 0.2.

Parameters for our implementation of genetic algorithm include: population size=300, number of iterations in each generation=200, crossover probability=0.85, and mutation probability=0.005.

Figure-5 gives the error rate of genetic solutions, which is calculated by comparing value E of genetic and optimal solutions. As Figure-5 shows, with number of nodes increases, error rates increases slowly and stays at about 10%. This demonstrates that genetic algorithm can find near-optimal solutions.

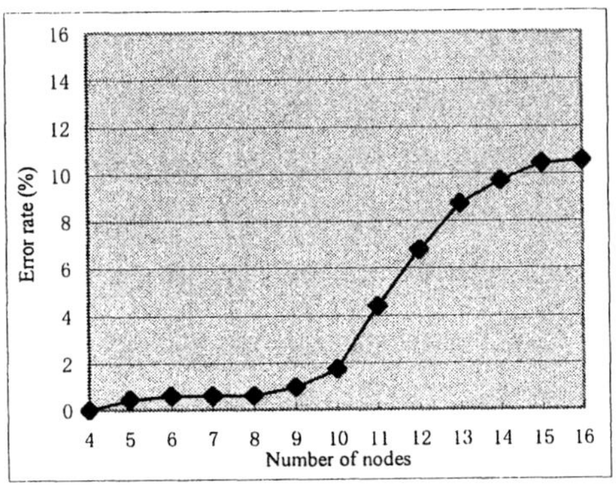

Figure 5. Error Rates of Genetic Solutions

Table 1. Average cost of algorithms

Number of nodes	Exhaustive searching	Improved exhaustive	Genetic algorithm
4	0 s	0 s	1.0 s
5	0 s	0 s	1.4 s
6	0 s	0 s	2.0 s
7	0 s	0 s	2.4 s
8	0.4 s	0 s	2.6 s
9	11.2 s	0 s	3.6 s
10	76.6 s	0.6 s	4.2 s
11	734 s	2.6 s	4.4 s
12	8817 s	7.6 s	4.6 s
13	114628 s	128 s	5.2 s
14	1604803 s	225 s	5.4 s
15	24072048 s	587 s	6.4 s
16	5885687808 s	2046 s	7.4 s

Tested on Windows XP with Intel P4 2.4GHz processor

Table 1 gives the computation cost of genetic, exhaustive-searching and improved exhaustive-searching algorithms. The data shows that scalabilities of genetic algorithms are preferable.

6. CONCLUSION

To provide remote service and auto-configuration mechanisms, network emulation testbed needs to map the logic-topology, which the researchers require, to the testbed physical-topology. In this paper, we explore this network testbed mapping problem. After building a model of the problem, this paper implements a solver for the problem using Genetic Algorithm. The evaluation result shows that the solver can find near-optimal solutions in reasonable time.

REFERENCES

[1] Brian White, et.al, An Integrated Experimental Environment for Distributed Systems and Networks, In Proceedings of the Fifth Symposium on Operating Systems Design and Implementation, Dec 2002.

[2] Robert Ricci, et.al, A Solver for the Network Testbed Mapping Problem, ACM SIGCOMM Computer Communication Review, Apr 2003.

[3] Xin Liu, Andrew A. Chien, Traffic-based Load Balance for Scalable Network Emulation, In Proceedings of Super Computing 2003 (SC'03), Nov 2003.

[4] Amin Vahdat, et.al, Scalability and Accuracy in a Large-Scale Network Emulator, In Proceedings of the Fifth symposium on Operating Systems Design and Implementation, Dec 2002.

[5] K. Fall, Network Emulation in the Vint/NS Simulator, In Proceedings of the Fourth Symposium on Computers and Communications, 1999.

[6] Larry Peterson, et.al, A Blueprint for Introducing Disruptive Technology into the Internet, First ACM Workshop on Hot Topics in Networks (HotNets-I), Oct 2002.

[7] D. Anderson. Theoretical Approaches To Node Assignment, Dec 2002. Unpublished manuscript. http://nms.lcs.mit.edu/papers/andersen-assign.ps

[8] Chen Guo-liang, et.al, Genetic Algorithm and Its Applictions, China Posts & Telecom Press, 1996.

VASTUDIO –A GENERIC TOOLKIT FOR MULTI-AGENT DEVELOPMENT

Jiewen Luo, Zhongzhi Shi, Fen Lin, Maoguang Wang
Institute of Computing Technology, Chinese Academy of Sciences, 100080 Beijing, China
{luojw, linf, wangmg, shzz}@ics.ict.ac.cn

Abstract: In this paper, we propose a hierarchical agent development toolkit-VAStudio. It is composed with legacy component layer, behavior layer, agent layer and society layer. Through the structure, it can facilitate software reuse and rapidly develop multi-agent system. We use it as the main developing toolkit for various multi-agent applications, which include the agent based, distributed data mining and flood decision support system etc.

Key words: Agent, MAGE, AUML, Toolkit, VAStudio

1. INTRODUCTION

Intelligent agent technology has been raised as the primary technology in the intelligent Internet and mobile computing. Agent is the rational entity with big-granularity, high-intelligence and autonomy characteristics, and multi-agent system (MAS) is composed of a number of agents capable of communicating, coordinating, cooperating and even competing with each other. Up to now, it has been applied in some industry domains such as transportation control, emergency management. However, there still exist many challenges to construct complex agent-based industry applications because of lacking uniform methods and proper integrated development platform. Most of current platforms focus on the multi-agent run-time environment and neglect the development environment. In order to conquer this problem, we develop a toolkit named VAStudio to provide an integrated, user-friendly environment for system developers.

The rest paper is organized as follows. Section 2 introduces the multi-agent development process. Section 3 describes the hierarchical architecture of VAStudio. Section 4 demonstrates its GUI and its main functions. Section 5 presents two application developed by VAStudio. Section 6 summarizes the paper and gives a conclusion.

2. DEVELOPMENT PROCESS

Our development process is as follows. When facing a problem and thinking it beneficial from the multi-agent paradigm, we first analyze the problem and model it using the AUML [4]. After that, we implement the model through the toolkit VAStudio. And then, the implemented agent programs run on the multi-agent environment MAGE to concrete applications. The process is as figure 1. The next we briefly introduce VAStuido's companion systems: AUML and MAGE.

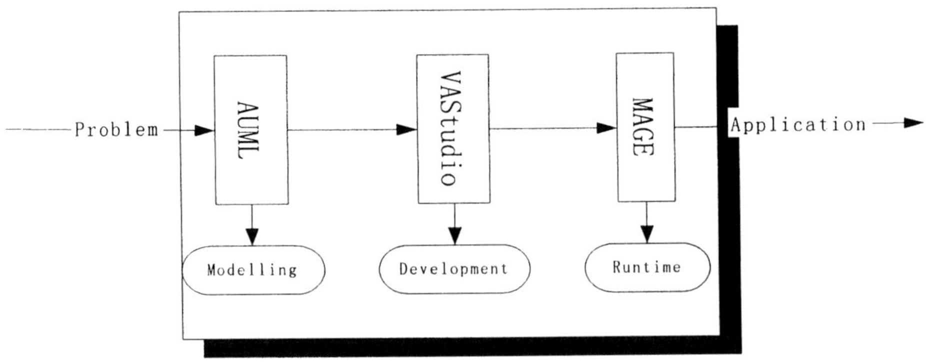

Figure 1. Multi-Agent Development process

2.1 AUML

Multi-agent Systems are complex software. Building such complex systems software requires using adequate engineering methods. In the UML standard published by OMG, the abstract syntax are expressed by a class diagram that represents the relationships between the model elements, and the static semantics are described by constraints in OCL. Diagrams are very clear and easy to understand by the UML users, but they are hard to process by computers. We combine the attributed graph and the Meta representation to formalize the abstract syntax of AUML. This formal abstract syntax and static semantics meets the requirements of AUML supporting tool designing and model checking.

2.2 MAGE

MAGE [1] is a multi-agent run-time environment From Fig. 4 we can see that it consists of four main components, that is, Agent Management System (AMS), Directory Facilitator (DF), Agent, and Message Transport System (MTS). The AMS maintains a directory of AIDs (agent identifiers), which contain transport addresses (amongst other things) for agents registered in MAGE. The DF provides yellow pages services to other agents. MTS is the default communication method between agents on different agent platforms. Agent is the fundamental actor in MAGE, which combines one or more service capabilities into a unified and integrated execution model that may include access to external software, human users and communications facilities.

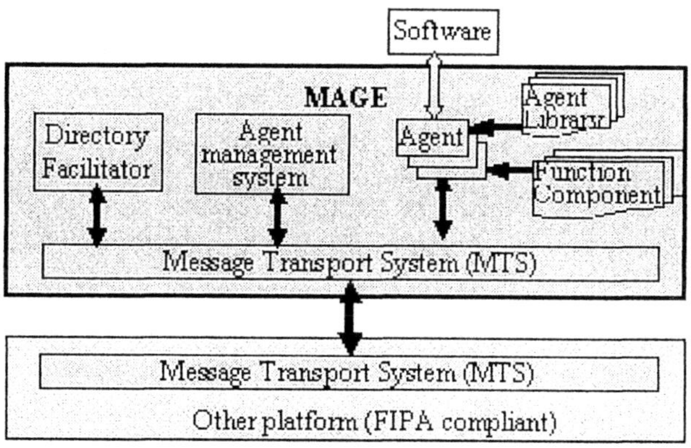

Figure.2 Runtime platform-MAGE

3. HIERARCHICAL STRUCTURE OF VASTUDIO

After introduce the development process, this section will describe the hierarchical architecture of the VAStudio in detail. From software engineering perspective, the reusable classes are main components of new software and programmers prefer to integrate the existing modules for rapid development. Hence, we adopt a hierarchical design pattern in VAStudio development phase. Figure 3 shows VAStudio's structure, which is composed with four different layers: the legacy component layer, behavior layer, agent layer and the society layer. The lower layers supply the fundamental materials for upper ones to construct more abstract and complex instances.

Legacy component layer includes connectors and entity components. The entity components are independent existence and can be applied directly. For example: procedures, functions, DLL and java Beans etc. Connectors are used for guaranteeing connection, which includes pipe, cache, and message transmission etc. We can describe them as follows.

<EntityComponent>:: = <Entity Name> <EntityType><EntityDescription>
<EntityResource><OperateProcedure><OperateEnvironment>
<EntityType> :: = Procedure | Function | Java Bean | DLL
<EntityResource> :: = Variable | Class | <EntityComponent>
<LinkComponent> :: = <LinkName> <LinkType> <LinkDescription>
<Connectors><Precondition><Postcondition>
<LinkType> :: = PipeLine | ProcedureCall | RPC | MessagePassing |

Figure. 2 Legacy component descriptions

According to specification, behaviors are the basic components to build agents. In VAStudio, we apply the template to build basic framework of every behavior, which has one or more actions in the program bodies. Moreover, the base Behavior Class that provides common interfaces for subclasses has been implemented and stored in the template library. It can be conveniently inherited by every child Behavior to implement various applications.

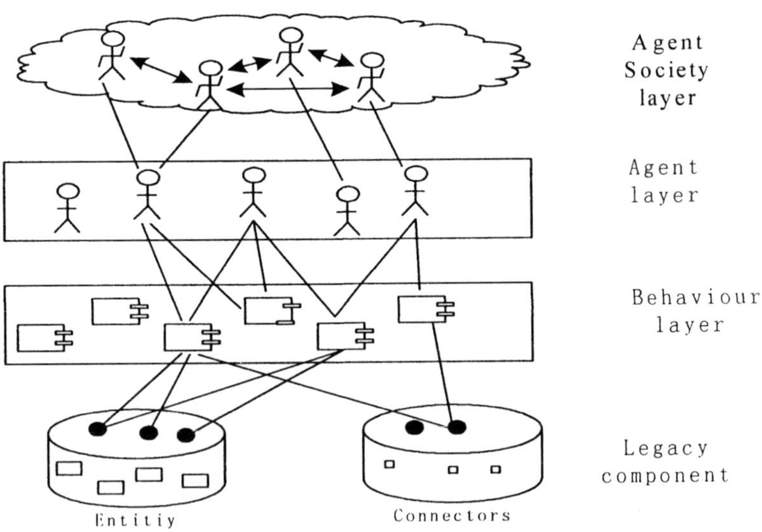

Figure 3. Hierarchical Structure of VAStudio

Although behaviors are components having concrete actions, they cannot execute as independent entities. They are used by autonomous, intelligent and mobile agents. In VAStudio, agents that wrap concrete behaviors can be moved to distributed data sites for independent run and can communicate and collaborate with their peers for complex multi-agent application.

The highest layer of the structure is agent society that provides a platform for controlling multi-agent interaction. In this layer, we can monitor the message transmission, agent collaboration process.

4. VASUTIDO ENVIRONMENT

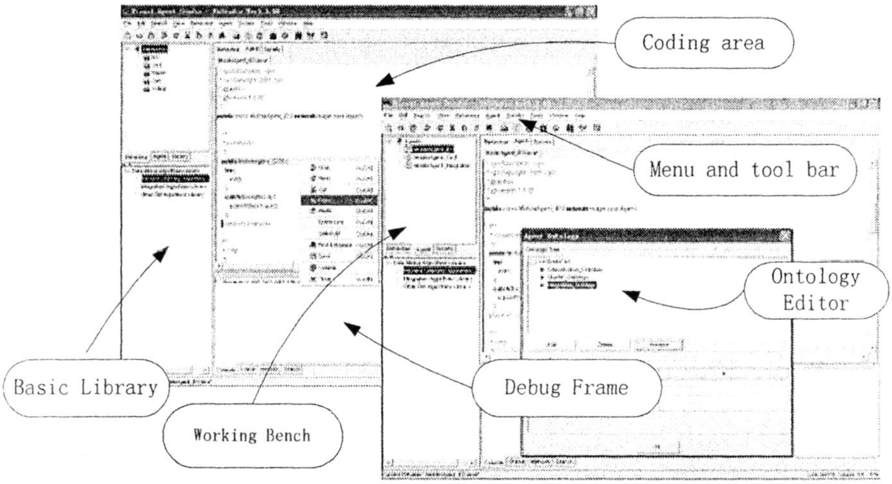

Figure 4. Graphical user interface of VAStudio

VAStudio is a multi-agent development platform. We summarize its main function and characteristics as follows.

(1) Software reusable. VAStudio can support software reuse including functions, procedures, classes and java Bean etc.

(2) ADL Description. VAStudio provides an effective description method and uses the ADL (Agent Description Language) for dynamic deployment.

(3) Powerful tool sets. It provides many useful tools for users to develop applications, which include code editor, ADL analyzer and ontology editor etc.

(4) GUI. VAStudio uses the visual Wizard to help builders step by step, which makes users feel easier to develop.

(5) Java. VAStudio is developed completely by Java language, which has good ability to cross-heterogeneous platforms.

As figure 4 shows, GUI is composed with the five main parts: the visual coding area, basic library, debugs frame, working bench and menu-tool bar. Visual coding area offers an ideal window for java-oriented programmers to implement agent-based applications. Considering some programmers not familiar with agent theory, we provide the Behavior, Agent and Society building Wizard like most business software to help them quickly master multi-agent development process. Working bench record the recent classes and packages. It is composed by three overlap frames, which includes the recent behaviors, agent and society. The menu and tool bar provide the basic support for various manipulations. And the debug frame records the bugs of the recent programs and give suggest how to correct them. One of the most important components is basic library. It stores the basic legacy components which support system builders to rapidly implement their applications. From the figure, we also show the ontology editor, it provides a wizard to visually develop agent ontology, which is much important for multi-agent interaction.

5. APPLICATIONS

5.1 Agent-Based Distributed data mining

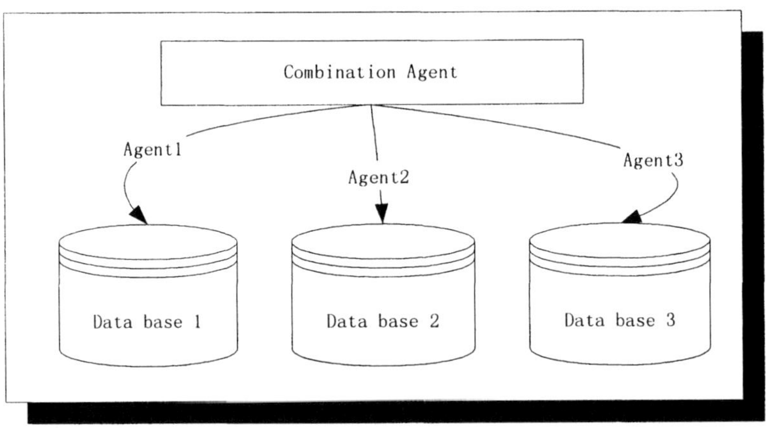

Figure. 5 Agent based distributed data mining

Recent years, many researchers are investigating to apply the multi-agent paradigm for distributed data mining. Although many models and techniques are introduced such as meta leaning and wrapping-agent, there is few mature development environments for this kind of application. In order to narrow the gap of theory and practice, we build the data-mining algorithms and store them in the basic library. These algorithms include classifiers and clusters and some of them are imported from Weka [5]. Through the visual agent development environment, user can easily to wrap the algorithms to agents and dispatch them to remote hosts for distributed data mining.

5.2 Flood decision support system

We use sense network to monitor rivers, which transmit the real-time information to mobile agents. After collecting flood information, the agents sent the message to the central control office where has flood information analysis software wrapped by agents. At the same time, we use the agent spiders to collect former cases and store them in the case bases. Combining with the expert system software OKPS and data mining software MSMiner [2], we can acquire the proper decisions.

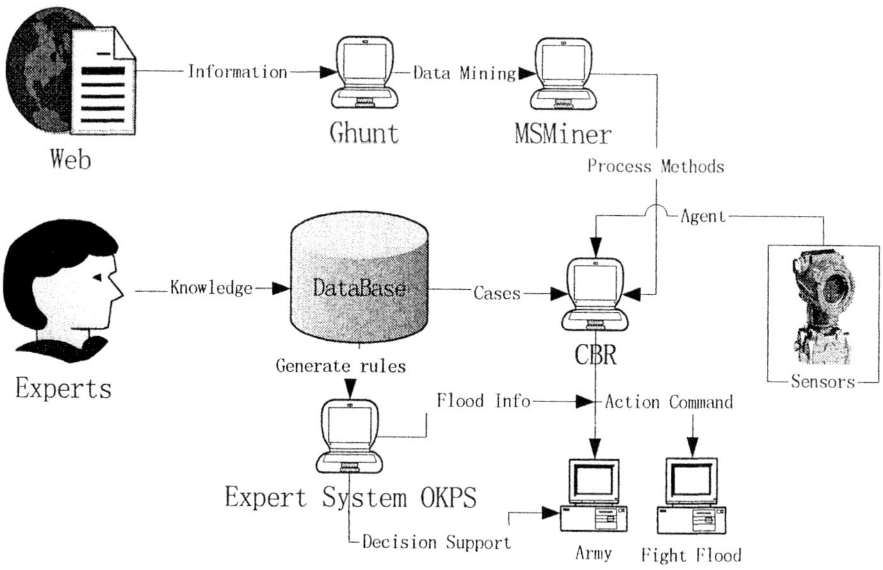

Figure 6. Agent-based flood decision support system

6. CONCLUSIONS

In this paper, we describe VAStudio, a generic and user-friendly tool for developing multi-agent applications. It has a hierarchical structure and visual programming environment. In order to support rapidly developing various applications, we build a basic library, which includes legacy components.

Though the application, we can see it an idea development environment. In the next step, we will continuously enrich the basic library and provide more useful and mature components for user developing multi-agent applications.

ACKNOWLEDGMENTS

This work is supported by the National High-Program of China (Grant No. 2003AA115220) and the National Basic Research and Development Plan of China (Grant No. 2003CB317000).

REFERENCES

[1] Zhongzhi Shi, Haijun Zhang, Yong Cheng, Yuncheng Jiang, Qiujian Sheng, Zhikung Zhao: MAGE: An Agent-Oriented Programming Environment. IEEE ICCI 2004: 250-257

[2] Zhongzhi Shi, Youping Huang, Qing He, Lida Xu, Shaohui Liu, Liangxi Qin, Ziyan Jia, Jiayou Li. MSMiner-A Developing Platform for OLAP. Decision Support Systems, 2005

[3] Zhongzhi Shi, Qing He, Ziyan Jia and Jiayou Li. Intelligence Chinese Document Semantic Indexing System. International Journal of Information Technology and Decision Making, Vol.2, No.3, 2003: 407-424.

[4] Zhikung Zhao, Research on Agent Unified Modeling Language, Ph.D. Thesis, Institute of Computing Technology, CAS, 2003

[5] http://www.cs.waikato.ac.nz/ml/weka/

[6] Intelligent science website www.intsci.ac.cn

A STUDY ON THE ANN-BASED CREDIT RISK PREDICTION MODEL AND ITS APPLICATION

Yan PENG[1] Xuyan TU[2]
[1]College of Information Engineering, Capital Normal University, Beijing 100037, China

[2] College of Information Engineering, University of Science and Technology Beijing, 100083, China

Abstract: Credit risk early warning system must provide precise support information to the bank managers for decision-making. So the risk prediction model is critical and regarded as the core part of the whole risk early warning system. Compared with other traditional prediction models, the neural network model has the advantages of self-studying, self-organizing as well as self-adapting. This dissertation puts forward an ANN-based risk prediction model, which combines the Self-Organizing Map Neural Network and the Probabilistic Neural Network together. Furthermore, the improved iteration ways in constructing and training the model are also presented, which includes the SOM boundary effect processing and the rare samples handling. The established model is trained with financial ratios for a specific credit risk early warning experiment. The preliminary experimental result demonstrates that the SOM-PNN model performs better than some traditional ones in the rates of prediction accuracy and efficiency.

Key words: Credit Risk; ANN; Prediction Model

1. INTRODUCTION

The Risk Early Warning is a complicated process. It discovers and distinguishes the risk sources, risk scopes, risk levels and risk trends in advance through a variety of techniques, and then generates the corresponding risk warning signals. This process could provide support information to the management for decision-making, which could in turn avoid or reduce the risk of loss over time. Obviously, the risk which could in turn avoid or reduce the risk of loss over time. Obviously, the risk prediction model is very important in the early warning system, which is regarded as the core part of risk early warning activity.

However, there are a few technical difficulties in modeling the risk early-warning system with the traditional statistics-based methods. First of all, various properties or different regional possibility would require different models. Secondly, the supporting data for the model is generally very difficult to acquire and some information may be incomplete. Finally, the credibility of the model has to be verified through a long period of time. Practically, most of the processes depend largely on the subjective decisions.

Different from the traditional methods, the Artificial Neural Network (ANN) solves certain problems by training the network. Training an ANN is to input a series of samples that can generate the ideal output, which enables the ANN to learn the fundamental principle behind the "solution". The ANN is analogous to the central nervous system of the living creatures. The ANN has the advantages of self-studying, self-organizing as well as self-adapting. It is suitable for handling fuzzy data and is capable of reapplying its evaluation specialty through the learned experience and knowledge, which ensures the objectivity of the predicted result.

The ANN system avoids the complexity and difficulty existing in the traditional analysis processes. The ANN model is established in a non-linear and natural way, and does not require extracting the exact linear relationship, which makes it convenient for analyzing and model generating.

The main contribution of this paper is presented, i.e., establishing a SOM-PNN neural network model in the risk early warning system as well as the improvement of constructing and training the prediction model. The remainder of this paper is outlined as the following: the SOM-PNN based risk prediction model is generated after analyzing the SOM and PNN characteristics; each critical link of the model training and constructing process is finalized; the generated model is trained with financial ratios for a credit risk early warning experiment; the benefits of using this model in risk early warning are discussed; finally, the conclusion is made with an outlook of future works.

2. SOM&PNN NEURAL NETWORK

In this section, the Self Organizing feature Map Neural Network and the Probabilistic Neural Network are briefly introduced.

2.1 Kohonen Self -Organizing Model

T. Kohonen presented a neural network model called Self-Organizing feature Map(SOM) in 1993[1].

The SOM model is made up of two neural layers. The input layer has the same number of neurons as that of the variables, and its function is simply to capture the information. The output layer is organized in a rectangular pattern with *x* rows and *y* columns, which is called 'the map' [2]. The SOM projects the multidimensional input space into the output space. Through this process, the variables presenting a similar value are arranged close to one another in the input pattern on the created map. In order to achieve this target, the SOM uses a competitive algorithm known as "winner takes all". The minimum distance determines the superior match neuron,

$$\|X - W_c\| = \min_{j=1}^{p} \|X - W_j\| \qquad (1)$$

where Wc is the synaptic weights of *C*,
$\|X - W_j\|$ is the Euclidean distance,

$$\|X - W_j\| = \sqrt{\sum_{i=1}^{n} (X_i - W_{ij})^2} \qquad (2)$$

where X*i* is the input signal, and W*ij* is the synaptic weight between the input neuron i and the output neuron j[3].

In this way, the essential topology of the input space is projected into the output space. This paper utilizes the standard non-directional SOM algorithm.

2.2 Probabilistic Neural Network (PNN)

The Probabilistic Neural Network[4] was introduced in 1990 by Specht. The benefit of using the PNN is that it can represent the architecture of a network in the form of *probability density functions*. In addition, most of the training algorithms for the PNN are easy to use.

The PNN network usually consists of four layers. The first layer is the input layer, which simply distributes the input signals to the pattern units, and its transmission function is linear. The second layer is the pattern unit layer, and each pattern unit is connected to the input layer with its weight W_{ij}. The activation function is used to construct the estimations of the population density function. The third layer is the summation unit layer, which has a linear summation function. The summation layer has one neuron for each class. Each summation neuron dedicated to a single class sums the pattern layer neurons corresponding to the number of that particular class. The fourth layer is the output layer. The output neuron is a threshold discriminator, which determines the maximum value of the summation unit outputs corresponding to its inputs.

3. PREDICTION MODEL BASED ON SOM- PNN

3.1 SOM-PNN Early-Warning System

It is innovative and worthwhile to develop the SOM-PNN model application in the early warning system, since there are few precedents in this field. The architecture of the SOM-PNN Early-Warning System is illustrated in Fig.1.

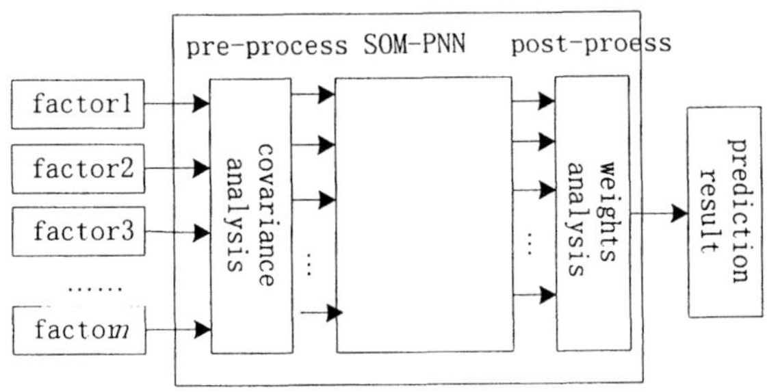

Fig.1 The Architecture of SOM-PNN Early Warning System

There are three primarily parts of the model:

(1) Pre-process: the target of this part is to transform the risk data into the ratios that would be used as the network's inputs. Due to the limitation of the pages, this problem will not be addressed in detail.

(2) SOM-PNN neural network: the core part of the model which addresses the prediction process.

(3) Post-process: the task of this part is to analyse the predicting results. The weight analysis method is used to represent the influence of each factor.

The SOM model can yield high identification rate, however can't generate the classification result directly. The PNN is integrated with SOM to analyse the output of the SOM, then generates the classification result explicitly.

The SOM extracts the characteristic of the original data, i.e., 'compress' the data. Therefore this method increases the training efficiency of the PNN. The SOM is integrated with the PNN as the following [5]:

(1) The SOM network is trained with the sample data first. Then the SOM MAP, which is acquitted through training and labelling, is used as the training sample of the PNN.

(2) The testing sample set is used to test the whole network as shown in Fig.2.

(3) The advantage of the integrated SOM-PNN model is that the trained SOM characteristic vector rejects the "noise" in the training samples. Therefore the precision and the efficiency of the PNN classification are increased significantly. Besides, the PNN generates the classification results explicitly.

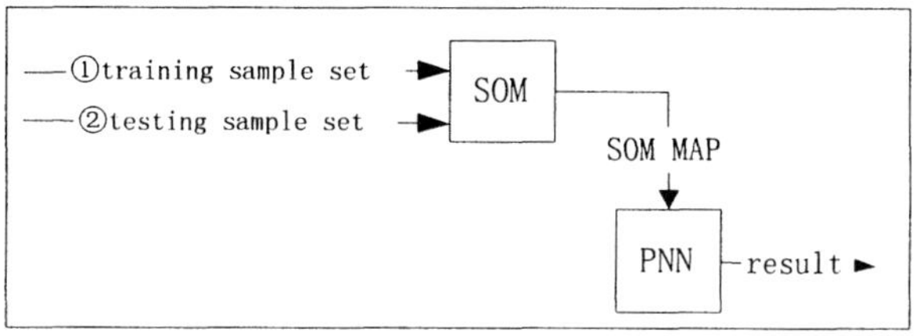

Fig.2 SOM- PNN model

3.2 Improvement of the Iteration Method

3.2.1 Handling the Rare Samples

In some cases, some risk data are either difficult to acquire or not under the estimated conditions. Then the specific input sample can not be trained sufficiently during the model training process. If the training frequency is very low, it can cause the classification result of the specific kind of input generating deviation, and decreasing the prediction precision. However, an increased overall training frequency could significantly increase the training time. Therefore, a specific method is used to identify the samples with less probability in order to improve the training process.

After the model has been trained for certain iterations, some input patterns innervate fewer neurons within the scope of its iteration radius in the preliminary MAP. Since the SOM MAP reflects the feature of the training samples, the following definition is introduced:

Definition: within the SOM MAP, if the number of innervated neurons in the iteration radius is less than the average value, this kind of sample is called the rare sample, i.e., the sample with the characteristic less needed than average. The expression is,

$$Z < \frac{S}{n \times m} \qquad (3)$$

where S is the total sample number, $n \times m$ is the number of output neurons and Z is innervated neurons in the iteration radius scope of certain input sample A, .

Sample A is automatically selected in the program to strengthen the training frequency, so that this particular kind of samples can be trained sufficiently. In doing so, the model prediction precision can be improved and the training efficiency can be increased.

3.2.2 Processing the Boundary Effect

The Boundary Effect is an existing problem of SOM itself, because the density of the neurons at the boundary is higher than that in the other regions in MAP (as shown in Fig.3). Kohonen presented a solution in 1993, which assigns some special samples with special weights. The disadvantage of this method is that it needs some personal subjective experiences. Another kind of method is to increase the iteration frequency, which would increase the network training time.

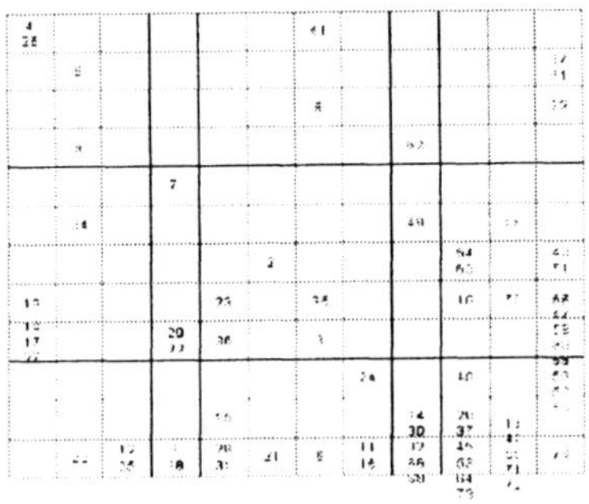

Fig.3 SOM MAP1

In this paper, the method of edge connection is proposed, which links the top and bottom edges as well as the left and right edges of the MAP. This makes the output similar to a sphere, thus every point in the MAP is adjacent to 8 neighbour points. Therefore, the boundary problem is eliminated, and the overall training efficiency of the network is improved.

4. CREDIT RISK PREDICTION EXPERIMENTS

The credit loan is the main income of a bank, which is also the most risky product[6]. In practice, the loans have been divided into *normal* and *concern* before they are granted. This kind of previous classification, in fact, is a risk analysis process. It provides the decision support for loaners. The Bank management can then use a series of methods to avoid or reduce the potential loan loss over time.

A particular characteristic of the credit early warning is that, the debtor's capability of repayment is the most important factor to be concerned about[7]. This paper primarily studies the early warning signals associated with certain financial situations, since the finance factors and its profit ability are closely related to the capabilities of making use of substance, capital structure as well as cash flows. This paper starts with the analysis of the financial ratios, and pays close attention to the debtor's current and future capability of repayment.

4.1 Sample Data

The sample data used in this paper are from 129 firms, among which 65 firms are bankrupt and the others are solvent. In order to satisfy both the modelling and verification practises, the sample data are randomly divided into two groups. The first group data are used for model training, which are from 74 firms and among which 36 firms are solvent and 38 firms are bankrupt. The second group data are used for model testing, which are from 55 firms and among which 28 firms are solvent and 27 firms are bankrupt.

The data contain four financial ratios taken from [8] for prediction experiments.

4.2 Constructing and Training of SOM and PNN

The SOM model has a two-dimensional topology, i.e., the model is made up of two neural layers. According to the finance ratios selected, the SOM network is constructed with 4 neurons at the input layer and 144 neurons at the output layer, and is arranged in a 12*12 square grid.

The training process of the SOM network is as the following:

The input financial ratios are located at the input layer once a single company is separated. Given that R_{ik} is the value of k company's ratio i and this ratio will be read by a neuron, the algorithm takes one neuron at a time at the output layer, and calculates the *Euclidean distance* as the similarity estimation. The "win neuron" is with the minimum d(j, k) and is named neuron k*. The algorithm now reduces the distance of d(j, k*) in order to change the Synaptic Weight Wij (synaptic weights between the input neuron i and the output neuron j). This process is repeated until all trainings have been completed. The weights are fixed upon the training completion, then the network is ready to use.

The label method of the SOM Map is as the following:

Compare the *Euclidean distance* of the input vector $X(x_1,x_2,\ldots, x_n)$(in this case, it could be the financial information of any firm) with every neuron connection vector Wj, then take the nearest node and mark it for this firm. After carrying out certain SOM calculations, generate a 2- dimensional Map. Each node is now representing one firm.

The PNN training can be accomplished in a number of ways. Generally, two methods are frequently used. One approach relies on defining the network topology with a large training set in advance. Another approach is to introduce one neuron for each training pattern. Each class of the training samples is then used as a centre vector of the hidden nodes. However, this particular approach is not feasible for large datasets and small parameter changes could impact the network performance significantly. The training method introduced in reference [9] is used in this paper, which automatically constructs the PNN network.

The SOM is trained initially, and then the MAP is derived (as shown in Fig.5). Two large zones can be recognized after this process. One corresponds to the solvent firms (1 to 36), and the other corresponds to the bankrupt firms (37 to 74) appeared with circular labels.

Upon the completion of the SOM, the PNN is then trained with each node of vector in Fig.4. Finally, the testing data set is used for the whole model testing.

The overall steps are as the following:

(1) Import 55 testing samples into the SOM to form the input layer, then get the prediction result form the output layer of the PNN ***('1' indicates solvent and '0' indicates bankrupt).***

(2) Use the PNN Model to predict solvent and bankrupt only.

(3) Compare the results of the two models

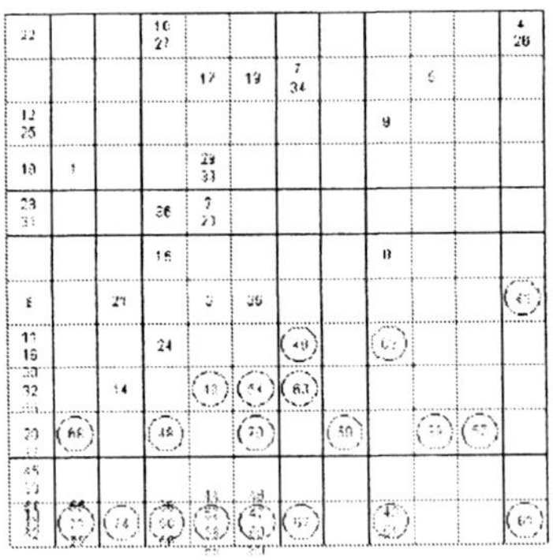

Fig.4 SOM MAP2

4.3 Predict Result Discussion

Table 1 compares the results with the SOM-PNN model and the PNN model only.

Table 1

No.	Sample data	SOM-PNN Result	PNN Result	No.	Sample data	SOM-PNN Result	PNN Result
1	1	1	1	29	0	0	0
2	1	1	1	30	0	0	0
3	1	1	1	31	0	0	0
4	1	1	1	32	0	0	0
5	1	1	0	33	0	0	0
6	1	1	1	34	0	0	0

7	1	0	1	35	0	1	0
8	1	0	0	36	0	0	0
9	1	1	1	37	0	0	0
10	1	1	1	38	0	0	0
11	1	1	1	39	0	0	0
12	1	1	1	40	0	0	0
13	1	1	0	41	0	0	0
14	1	1	1	42	0	0	0
15	1	1	1	43	0	0	0
16	1	0	0	44	0	0	0
17	1	0	0	45	0	0	1
18	1	0	0	46	0	0	0
19	1	1	1	46	0	0	0
20	1	1	0	47	0	0	0
21	1	0	0	49	0	0	0
22	1	1	1	50	0	0	0
23	1	1	1	51	0	0	1
24	1	0	0	52	0	0	1
25	1	1	1	53	0	0	0
26	1	1	1	54	0	0	0
27	1	1	1	55	0	0	1
28	1	1	1				

The following conclusion can be presented from the experiments:

(1) The precision by using the SOM- PNN model is 83.63%; and the precision by using the PNN model is 74.55%.

(2) A visual result and a direct classification can be achieved by using the SOM-PNN model.

(3) Reasons for the error classification:

Some bankrupt or solvent corporations are mistakenly classified in the experiment. The main reason is that the data used for classification in this experiment are raw finance data. However, the factors affecting a corporation's condition could be well beyond this. Some corporation's success or failure in the management could be determined by some special factors, such as a particular market condition, nature disasters and the termination of a certain manager, etc. These factors could all quickly change the condition of a corporation.

5. CONCLUSIONS

In this paper, a SOM-PNN model is introduced into the credit risk early warning system. The advantage of this model is that it combines the benefits of the SOM and the PNN, which in turn increases the accuracy and the efficiency of the risk prediction. This model can be a useful tool for various kinds of applications, such as tax paying grade evaluation, customers grade evaluation, insurance, risk investment, etc. One potential improvement is to identify and synthesize the factors associated with the risk prediction, and makes this risk early warning model even more practical and accurate.

ACKNOWLEDGEMENT

This work is supported by Scientific Research Common Program of Beijing Municipal Commission of Education. Under contract NO. KM200410028012.

REFERENCES

[1].T. Kohonen , Automatic Formation of Topological Maps in Self-Organizing systems: Proceedings of the 2nd Scandinavian Conf. On Image Analysis,1981:214 ~220

[2].Carpenter Gail A, Grossberg Stephen, The ART of Adaptive Pattern Recognition Self-Organizing Neural Network. Trans. IEEE on Computer, March 1988,77~88.

[3]. T. Kohonen, The Self Organizing Map, Proc. of the IEEE, (1990), Vol 78, 9; 1464-1480

[4]. Sprecht D F. Probabilistic Neural Network for Classification, Mapping and Associative Memory. IEEE ICNN San Dieg CA, 1988. I 525~532

[5]. F. Ma, W. Wang, W.W. Tsang, Z. Tang, S. Xia and X. Tong, Probabilistic segmentation of volume data for visualization using SOM-PNN classifier, *Proceedings of the 1998 Symposium on Volume Visualization*, Pages 71-77

[6]. Xi-wen Li, Zh-hong Zhao, Jian Wu. Establish the Risk Early-Warning System of Commercial Bank. Chinese financial, 2001,5: 37-38.

[7]. Wen-Bo Pan. Research Papers for Commercial Bank Risk Classification. The Investment Studies, 2001,1:22-26

[8]. Serrano, C. Self Organizing Neural Networks for Financial Diagnosis, Decision Support Systems, Vol 17, julio, 1996, 227-238,

[9] Michael R. Berthold. Constructive Training of Probabilitic Neural Networks, Neurocomputing 19(1998) 167-183.

A UNIVERSAL VECTOR GRAPHICS EDITING SYSTEM BASED ON DESIGN PATTERN AND JAVA

Limin Ao [1,2], Pingping Xia [2], Yanfeng Jia [2], Yongchun Wang [2]

[1] *College of Information and Electrical Engineering, China Agricultural University, Beijing 100083, China*

[2] *Department of Information Engineering, Northeast China Institute of Electric Power Engineering, Jilin Jilin 132012, China*

Abstract: Design patterns capture successful solutions to recurring problems that arise when building software systems. Firstly, this paper presents how to design a vector graphics editing platform using design pattern. At last, on the base of summarizing all kinds of vector graphics editing systems at home and abroad, this paper presents a new idea on how to develop a universal vector graphics editing system.

Key words: Design Patterns, Vector Graphics, Mediator Pattern, Strategy Pattern

1. INTRODUCTION

The main function of vector graphics editing system is to support all kinds of special graphics' input and output. On the base of summarizing all kinds of vector graphics editing systems at home and abroad, we absorb the merits of others during the development of the vector graphics editing system [1]. Meanwhile, considering all kinds of different and flexible requirements for graphics and symbols in many aspects, such as metallurgy, architecture, power system, etc, a new idea is introduced on how to develop a universal vector graphics editing system.

We developed the system using design patterns. Software design patterns became popular with the wide acceptance of the book (《Design Pattern-elements of reusable software》) by Gamma et al. (1995) [2]. They are successful design paradigms that have been summarized during practice. The rational use of design patterns can help software developers to comprehend design routes easily, perfect their solution, and accomplish the development of software better.

2. THE DESIGN AND IMPLEMENTATION OF MAIN PLATFORM

We developed the platform based on Java in the environment of IBM Eclipse3.0.1. The main components of vector graphics editing system are presented below Fig.1 [3]. *WinApp* defines the drawing interface and acts as a mediator among components. *ViewPanel* is an area that can show figures and accept user input. The *FigureSet* consist of *Figure*s, which in turn can be containers for other *Figure*s. Changes in the *FigureSet* are propagated to the *ViewPanel* that is responsible for updating any *Figure*s. Each *Figure* has *Handle*s, which define access points and determine how to interact with the *Figure*. In *ViewPanel*, you can select several figures and handle them. There are many *Tool*s in Toolbar, which are used to create or handle *Figure*s.

3. THE VECTOR GRAPHICS EDITING SYSTEM AND ITS DESIGN PATTERNS USED

3.1 The Application of Mediator Pattern

Object-Oriented Programming advocates distributing behavior over objects. However, as more of these isolated objects are developed in a program, the problem of communication between these classes becomes more complex. The more each class needs to know about the methods of another class, the more tangled the class structure can become [4]. This makes the program harder to read and harder to maintain. Furthermore, it can become difficult to change the program, since any changes may affect code in several other classes.

In vector graphics editing system objects, including *Command*, *Tool*, *ViewPanel* and their own subclasses, etc, interact with each other. If their interactions are dealt with general measures, it may lead to a pretty intricate network. At the same time, the maintenance and ability to change the system are difficult to expand. As a result, the reusability of the system is weakened.

The Mediator pattern resolves the problem by promoting loose coupling between these classes. Mediator accomplishes this by being the only class that has detailed knowledge of the methods of other classes. Classes send information to the Mediator when changes occur and the Mediator passes them on to any other classes. Therefore, Mediator pattern is used in the system (UML class diagram refer to Fig. 2). The *DrawingEditor*, as a mediator, takes charge of the interactions among Colleagues. These Colleagues consist of *Command*, *Tool*, *ViewPanel* and so on. The advantage of the Mediator is obvious—it is the only class that knows of the other classes, and thus the only one that would need to be changed if one of the other classes changes or if other interface-control classes are added [4].

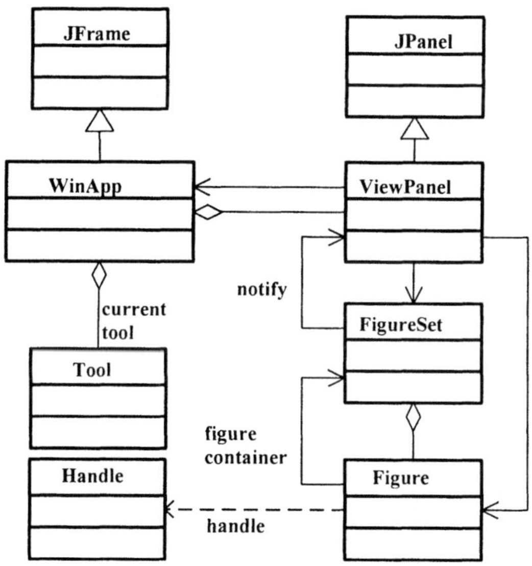

Figure 1. Main Framework

3.2 The Application of Strategy Pattern

The operation of a figure is actually to operate its many special points of the figure, which is updated itself according to these points. Then, how do we get these special points? The problem involves particular algorithms. On account of different special points of a figure, there are many differences among these calculating methods. For example, the algorithms are totally different when getting the middle point and end point of a line. Moreover, for different figures, even if getting the middle point or end point, the algorithm is also different. Therefore, we should define different algorithms on every special point to meet different responsibilities.

The Strategy pattern consists of a number of related algorithms encapsulated in a driver class called the *Context*. The client's program can select one of these differing algorithms or in some cases the *Context* might select the best one for you. The intent is to switch easily between algorithms without any monolithic conditional statements [4]. Strategy lets the algorithm vary independently from the clients that use it.

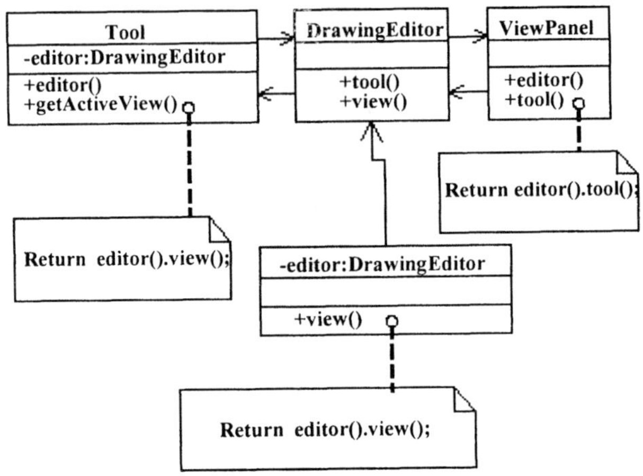

Figure 2. Mediator design pattern

In the system, the problem about how to choose algorithms of special point could be resolved just by using the Strategy pattern. Firstly, we define an interface *Locater* which has a method *locate*() implemented by *Locator's* subclass [5]. For instance, we get the middle point of line by subclass *CenterLocator*. The concrete algorithm is encapsulated in method *locate*().

The definition of interface *Locator* as follows:

```
public interface Locator{

  public Point locate(Figure owner){    }

}
```

The definition of subclass *CenterLoator* which get middle point is as follows:

```
public class CenterLocator implements Locator{

  public Point locate(Figure owner){

    Rectangle r=owner.displayBox();

    return

       new Point(r.x+r.width/2,r.y+r.height/2);
```

```
        }

    }
```

The contents mentioned above introduce several main patterns for the design of vector graphics editing system. These patterns can improve largely the reusability and expansibility of the system. Meanwhile, other design patterns, such as State pattern, Factory pattern, Composite pattern, etc, also have been used in the system. Their introduction is omitted because of the restrictions on the paper's length [7].

4. THE PRINCIPLE OF UNIVERSAL VECTOR GRAPHICS EDITING SYSTEM

Any graphics are composed of dots, lines and circles, so we define these graphics' Class as basic Class whose constructed functions have no parameters. Graphics' Class is the key to implement a universal vector graphics editing system [6]. We define a class *DynamicFigure* whose constructed function has a parameter (*int ID*). Using the class *DynamicFigure*, we can draw all kinds of different figures according as the difference of its ID value. Looking from the point of Object-Oriented Programming, we consider two factors: One is object's state; the other is object's behavior. As far as the object's state is concerned, the Class *DynamicFigure* has graphics' all kinds of properties, such as graphics' ID value, coordinates, size, color, stroke and so on. As far as the object's behavior is concerned, Class *DynamicFigure* have graphics' all kinds of methods, such as *public void move (int x, int y)* (whose function is to move a figure to a new place) and *public void drawFrame(Graphics g)* (whose function is to draw a figure using Java2D). After we draw a compositive graphics using basic graphics, clicking the Mouse right-button to show a Pop-Menu (See Fig.3.) and selecting the "composite" Menu-Item, then the system computes the smallest rectangle which encircles the selected basic graphics. Finally, the system connects database SQLServer2000 by JDBC driver and stores the selected basic graphics' properties, such as the basic graphics' ID value, the distance from basic graphics to the smallest rectangle, color(R,G,B), stroke, compositive graphics' ID value and the smallest rectangle's left X and top Y coordinate. In this way, when we select a *DynamicFigure* in the left Toolbar(See Fig.3.), even if we handle the same Class *DynamicFigure*, the system reads properties fields values from database according as the difference of graphics' ID value, we can draw different compositive graphics using the method *public void drawFrame(Graphics g)*.

Meanwhile, after we create a vector graphics, the system must build automatically a little icon whose shape is same to the compositive graphics in the left toolBar. We analyze the interface java.swing.Icon's code, implement the interface *Icon* and override the method *paintIcon(Component comp, Graphics g ,int x, int y)* to display the icon in the left toolBar [7] .In this way, we can create automatically any vector graphics what we want.

If we double click the little icon in the left toolBar, the compositive graphics will be deleted from SQLServer2000 and the icon will also be deleted from the toolBar.

The result can be seen in Fig. 3.

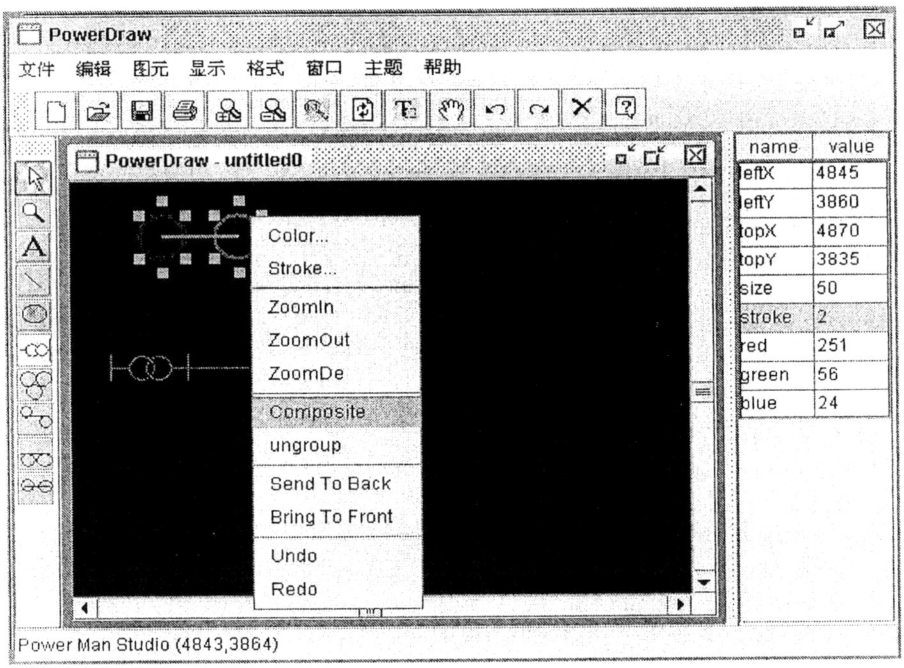

Figure 3. The Main interface of the editing system

5. CONCLUSIONS

Improving software adaptability is a formidable task in reality. One rather intriguing concept that strongly promotes adaptability is design patterns. This paper presented a new idea that aims to help software developers using design patterns. In particular, this paper has presented how to analyze and use design patterns as potential adaptability enhancers in developing software systems [8].

Meanwhile, in virtue of Java' merit, the system's maintenance and reusability are improved largely.

Based on the universal vector graphics editing system, we can shorten the designing time and reduce costs largely during the development of vector graphics system. The software developer can quickly design new drawing diagram software that accords with special industry need. Moreover, it also can be used in mechanization, manufacture, chemical plant, and so on. The application fields are very extensive.

REFERENCES

[1] Gardner, John A.; Bulatov, Vladimir: Directly Accessible Mainstream Graphical Information, In: Klaus, Joachim; Miesenberger, Klaus, Burger, Dominique; Zagler, Wolfgang (Eds.): Proceedings of the 9th International Conference on Computers Helping People with Special Needs (ICCHP), Springer, Berlin, 2004

[2] Eric Gamma, Richard Helm. Design Patterns-elements of reusable object-oriented software [M].Addison Wesley Publishing Company, 1995

[3] http://www.di.uniovi.es/~cueva/investigacion/lineas/patrones/JHotDraw.pdf

[4] James W. Cooper. Java Design Patterns: A Tutorial [M].USA: Pearson Education, 2003.

[5] J.Mylopoulos, L.Chung, S.S.Y.Liao et al., Extending object-oriented analysis to explore alternatives, IEEE Software (2001 January/February) 2-6

[6] Rotard, Martin; Otte, Kerstin; Ertl, Thomas: Exploring Scalable Vector Graphics for Visually Impaired Users, In: Klaus, Joachim; Miesenberger, Klaus; Burger, Dominique; Zagler, Wolfgang (Eds.): Proceedings of the 9th International Conference on Computers Helping People with Special Needs (ICCHP), Springer, Berlin, 2004

[7] D.C.Schmidt, M.Stal, Pattern-oriented Software Architecture: Patterns for Concurrent and Networked Objects, Wiley, New York, NY, 2000.

Limin Ao was born in 1956. She is a Ph.D. student at College of Information and Electrical Engineering, China Agricultural University, where she has studied for the last four years. She is currently Professor in the Department of Information Engineering at the Northeast China Institute of Electric Power Engineering. Hers research interests include Software Engineering, with application of computer in electric power system.

Pingping Xia was born in 1975. He is a postgraduate student at department of Information Engineering of Northeast China Institute of Electric Power Engineering. His research areas include design pattern, software engineering.

AN NOVEL NEURAL NETWORK TRAINING BASED ON HYBRID DE AND BP

Xiaohui Yuan [1], Yanbin Yuan [2], Cheng Wang [1]
1 Huazhong University of Science & Technology, 430074 Wuhan, China 2 Wuhan University of Technology, 430071 Wuhan, Chnia

Abstract: This paper proposes a new approach for training FNN by hybrid DE and BP. It combines the advantages of the global search performed by DE over the FNN parameter space and the local search of BP. Using a function approximation as an illustration, we compare the HDEBP and BP for effectiveness and efficiency for training FNN. It shows that the use of new method can provide better results than BP.

Key words: neural networks, differential evolution, BP algorithm

1. INTRODUCTION

It has been shown that multilayer feed-forward networks(FNN) can be used with great success to solve nonlinear optimization problems. The main difficulty in using FNN is the training phase, which can be error prone and slow, due to its nonlinear nature. Supervised NN training has been widely researched and many optimization algorithms have been devised, most of which have been based on the gradient descent techniques. Typically a variation of BP have been developed to train them, such as the gradient descent BP and Levenberg-Marquardt BP etc.

However, as pointed out by Curry and Morgan[1], BP based on gradient algorithm do not provide the best and fastest way to train NN, because NN

This work was supported by National Natural Science Foundation of China under Grant No. 50409010 & 50309013 generate complex error surfaces with multiple local optima, even for simple functions being estimated, BP tends to become trapped in local solutions that are not global. Since BP converges locally, the solutions found by this gradient technique are highly dependent on the initial random draw of weights, which are rather sensitive to their initial weights in the error space. Therefore, it should be clear that the precise starting position could affect the speed and accuracy with which the algorithm will find the minimum. The problem of local minima can be efficiently avoided by using better initial weight values instead of randomly values. So one possibility could be a hybrid of global optimization algorithm that provides the best initial weight values and BP method for training FNN.

DE is one of the recent population-based techniques. It was invented by K. Price and R. Storn in 1995 as an heuristic method for minimizing nonlinear and non-differentiable functions. It is successfully applied to many optimization problems, such as aerodynamic shape optimization, automated mirror design and mechanical engineering design.

To overcome BP local convergence for training FNN, this paper proposed a new hybrid DE and BP(HDEBP) which used DE to initialize the weights values of FNN. Finally function approximation problem have showed the feasibility and effectiveness of the method for training FNN.

2. DIFFERENTIAL EVOLUTION

DE is a population-based algorithm that creates new individuals one at a time. It is a greedy algorithm in which the new individual replaces the poorest member provided the new individual outperforms it.

DE utilizes NP D-dimensional parameter vectors $x_{i,G}$, (i =1,2,... NP as a population for each generation G). DE works as follows: First, all individuals are randomly initialized and evaluated using the fitness function. Afterwards, the following process will be executed as long as the termination condition is not fulfilled. DE generates new parameter vectors by adding the weighted difference between two population vectors to a third vector, which called mutation. The mutated vector's parameters are then mixed with the parameters of another predetermined vector, the target vector, to yield the trial vector, which called crossover. If the trial vector yields a lower cost function value than the target vector, the trial vector replaces the target vector in the following generation, which called selection.

Mutation

For each target vector $x_{i,G}$, a mutant vector is generated according to:

$$v_{i,G+1} = x_{r1,G} + F \cdot (x_{r2,G} - x_{r3,G}) \qquad (1)$$

where: $r_1, r_2, r_3 \in \{1,2,...NP\}$ are mutually different; F is a real constant factor between [0, 2]

Crossover

The trial vector $u_{i,G+1} = (u_{1i,G+1}, u_{2i,G+1}, ...u_{Di,G+1})$ is formed according to:

$$u_{ji,G+1} = \begin{cases} v_{ji,G+1} & if(rand(j) \le CR)\ or\ j = rnb(i) \\ x_{ji,G} & if(rand(j) > CR)\ and\ j \ne rnb(i) \end{cases} \qquad (2)$$

where rand(j) is a uniform random number between [0,1]. CR is the crossover constant between [0,1]. rnb(i) is a randomly index from 1,2,..D.

Selection

To decide whether or not it should become a member of generation G+1, the trial vector $u_{i,G+1}$ is compared to the target vector $x_{i,G}$ using the greedy criterion. If vector $u_{i,G+1}$ yields a smaller cost function value than $x_{i,G}$, then $x_{i,G+1}$ is set to $u_{i,G+1}$; otherwise, the old value $x_{i,G}$ is retained.

3. THE FNN TRAINING BY HDEBP

Since error surfaces for even simple problems can be quite complex with many local optima, the DE seems to be better suited for this type of search. It can be applied to global searches within the weight space of the FNN.

It is clear that the precise initial weights of the network can affect the speed and accuracy with which the BP will find the minimum. So this paper adopts DE training FNN to obtain optimal initial weights firstly. Then BP was used to train FNN, it can be furthermore improved significantly the performance for FNN training. This HDEBP works well for training FNN.

Output of a FNN is a function of synaptic weights W and input values x, i.e. y=f(x,W). In standard training processes, both the input vector x and the output vector y are known, and the synaptic weights in W are adapted to obtain appropriate functional mappings from the input x to the output y. Generally, the adaptation can be carried out by minimizing the network error function E which is of the form:

$$E(y, f(x,W)) : (y^{D1}, x^{D2}, W^{D3}, f) \to R \qquad (3)$$

The optimization goal is to minimize function E(y,f(x,W)) by optimizing the values of the network weights (now D=D3):

$$W=(w_1,w_2, \dots w_D) \qquad (4)$$

DE operates on a population P_G,of candidate solutions. These candidate solutions are the individuals of the population. DE maintains a population of constant size that consists of NP, real-value vectors, $W_{i,G}$, wher i is index to the population and G is the generation to which the population belongs.

$$P_G = (W_{1,G}, W_{2,G}, \dots W_{NP,G}) \qquad (5)$$

Additionally, in network training each vector contains D network weights:

$$W_{i,G} = (W_{1,i,G}, W_{2,i,G}, \dots W_{D,i,G}) \qquad (6)$$

For a FNN implementation, DE generates potential solutions using a forward propagation through FNN to obtain the value of the error function $E(y, f(x,W))$ for each individual in population at each generation. This error value is then used directly as the individual fitness. So, constructing an individual with a lower fitness is synonymous with training in the FNN. When the DE is finished, the global best individual serves as the high precise initial weight values of the FNN. Then we can use BP to train FNN directly. So, training performance of FNN can be improved significantly.

4. EXPERIMENTAL RESULTS

The HDEBP performance for training FNN is evaluated by experiment. In order to comparison of how well HDEBP and BP training FNN, function approximation problem was conducted using the sample data. The experiment was carried out using three-layer FNN and training function approximation problem, for example y=sin(x), x between [0,2π].

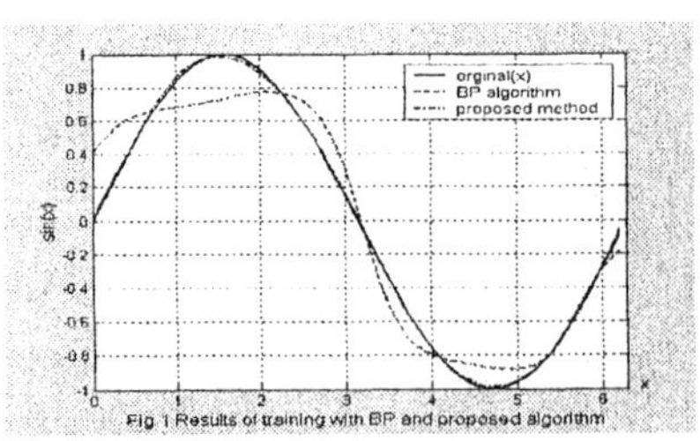

Figure 1.

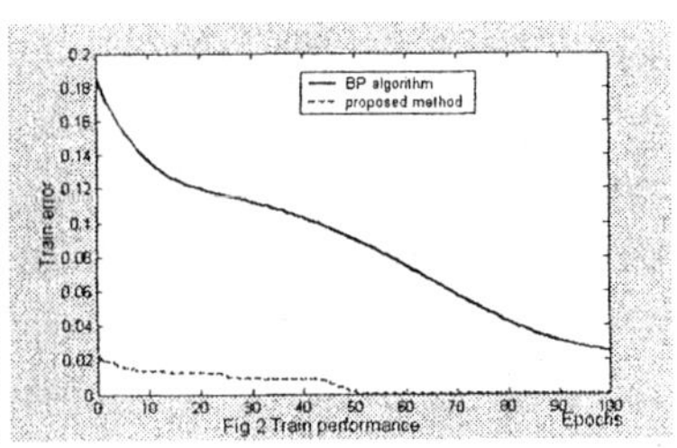

Figure 2.

In the experiment, 63 sample points of sin(x) for x =[0,2π] and three layer FNN 1 – logsig(5)- pureline(1), where logsig(5) means 5 neurons with a sigmoid transfer function and pureline(1) means 1 neuron with a pure linear transfer function, were used. Both BP and HDEBP were applied to train the network with 5 hidden layer units. Fig 1 shows the original training data (y=sin(x)) and network output after training with the BP and HDEBP. From Fig. 1, it is clear that HDEBP approximation effect is much higher than BP. This intuitively makes sense because BP may converge upon local solutions, while HDEBP can find global solutions.

The effectiveness of HDEBP was estimated by measuring the mean squared error for a training period of restricted max epochs 100 for sample. In the experiment, the HDEBP training was compared to BP. As shown in Fig2, we can find that HDEBP precision is much higher than BP. At the same time HDEBP had a faster convergence rate than BP. These comparisons also show that HDEBP captures the underlying function for the approximation problem rather very well. The FNN is trained by HDEBP, which speeds up convergence and overcomes local minima.

5. CONCLUSIONS

In this paper, a new HDEBP method based on hybrid DE and BP is proposed to train FNN. The performance of the HDEBP appeared to be comparable to that of BP for the function approximation, our simulation results show that the HDEBP is accurate and fast than BP for training FNN, which is much simpler to implement and yield overall better performance.

REFERENCES

1. Curry, B., Morgan, P.: Neural networks: a need for caution. Omega, International Journal of Management Sciences 25(1997)123-133
2. D. Patterson.: Artificial neural networks, theory and applications. Prentice Hall(1996)
3. P. Baldi.: Gradient descent learning algorithm overview: a general dynamical systems perpective. IEEE Trans. on neural networks,6(1)(1996)182-195
4. Moller m.: A scaled conjugate gradient algorithm for fast supervised learning. Neural networks,6(1993)525-533
5. Hagan, M., Menhaj, M.: Training feed-forward networks with the Marquadt algorithm. IEEE Trans. on Neural networks,5(6)(1994)152-157
6. R., Storn, K., Price.: Differential Evolution – A Simple and Efficient Heuristic for Global Optimization over Continuous Spaces. Journal of global optimization,11(1997)341-359

AUTOMATED IDENTIFICATION OF MOSQUITO (DIPTERA: CULICIDAE) WINGBEAT WAVEFORM BY ARTIFICIAL NEURAL NETWORK**

Zhenyu Li [1, 2], Zuji Zhou [1], Zuorui Shen [2*] and Qing Yao [2]

1 College of Agronomy,Sichuan Agricultural University, No.23 Xinkang,Ya'an,Sichuan

2 College of Agronomy and Biotechnology,China Agricultural University,No.2 Westroad Yuanmingyuan, Beijing, China

Abstract: The wingbeat waveforms of *Aedes albopictus* (Skuse), *A. aegypti* (Linnaeus), *Culex pipiens pallens* (Coquillett), *C. pipiens quinquefasciatus* Say, and *C. pipiens molestus* Forskal were recorded by a photosensor and WfRer system. Wingbeat frequencies were extracted from the wingbeat waveform. Back Propagation artificial neural network classifiers were built to identify automatically the species of mosquitoes by wingbeat waveform, wingbeat frequencies, and combining them as input variables. The most accurate classifier tested was an artificial neural network by wingbeat frequencies as input variable. The accuracy was average 72.67% and highest 89.00%. It also demonstrated that it was possible to identify automatically the species of mosquitoes. Meanwhile, it probably depended on the characteristic of frequencies for identifying each other among different mosquitoes.

Key words: mosquito, wingbeat frequency, artificial neural network, automated identification

* Communication author, email address: ipmist@cau.edu.cn

**National Priority Program of Innovative Technology (863) No. 2002AA243031 and 2003AA2090.

1. INTRODUCTION

With the rapid development of entomological taxonomy, artificial neural network theory and wingbeat frequencies of flying insects, which had been used to identify the species of insect, were more efficient, convenient and prompt than traditional morphology ways which needed necessary expert and special apparatus. Many animals, including grasshopper (David, 2004), spiders (David Reby et al., 1997), and bat (Parsons & Jones 2000) etc., had been identified automatically by artificial neural network. Wingbeat frequencies of flying insects might play significant role in insect behavior. The wingbeat frequencies were complicated, which were produced by wing beat, and formed all kinds of wingbeat waveforms. Lots of them what were caused by physical characteristics of the wings and their motion through the air provide much complex information, which might be used to communicate among insects (Williams et al. 1950). Peter & Robert (1979) measured the wingbeat frequencies of two species of mosquitoes and found median value were within 5 Hz of each other under the same condition. Different species of mosquitoes could mate (Taylor & Brust 1974), which proved the role of sounds in mosquito behavior. It was possible to communicate information between the female and the male through identifying fundamental wingbeat frequency of each other though the wingbeat frequencies of some species of mosquitoes were partly overlapped (Christophers 1960 & Clements 1963). It would be remarkable to identify the wingbeat frequencies of species of mosquitoes by artificial neural network, which had the ability of simulating human brain to distinguish difference of wingbeat frequencies between different mosquitoes with amount of nerve cells. After many years quantifying the wingbeat frequencies by processing the flying sound, which was recorded in the recorder, a photosensor what was designed to record the wingbeat waveform of two species of mosquitoes (Moore ea al. 1986) was based on the discovery that the wings of individual insects could reflect the transient waveform by an exposed photocell (Richards 1955). An optical sensor and data acquisition software for automated monitoring of flying insects were developed (Moore 1998), which could automate to record the transient waveform, and had been put into practice of automated identification. In this paper, it was by building and training an artificial neural network that the wingbeat waveforms of mosquitoes were identified in order to classify species of mosquitoes.

2. MATERIAL AND METHODS

2.1 Mosquitoes

Five species of mosquitoes including Aedes albopictus (Skuse), A. aegypti (Linnaeus), Culex pipiens pallens Coquillett), C. pipiens quinquefasciatus Say and C. pipiens molestus Forskal were provided by Institute of Microbiology and Epidemiology, Academy of Military Medical Sciences, China. All mosquitoes fed 5% glucose solution and maintained in the laboratory at 24 ℃ for a maximum of 2 days. Due to different wingbeat frequencies of male and female in the same species, female and male were distinguished.

2.2 Recording of Wingbeat Waveforms

For each recording session, only one mosquito was transferred into a transparent plastic jar measuring 17cm×14 cm×14 cm and fitted with a fine muslin top (Fig. 1). Females and males were recorded separately in each colony. The jar was covered black cloth for shield the flashes of AC power room light and placed between a DC power lamp and an optical sensor (Qubit Systems, Kingston, Ontario, Canada 2001). The optical sensor was connected to the microphone input port of a 16-bit sound card installed in the computer (Pentium Ⅳ 2.0G, 256 MB RAM). During recording waveforms, temperature was maintained in 24°C(± 0.5°C)in the jar. A transient waveform recorder program (WfRec, Qubit Systems 2001) was used to sample data and the sampling rate was 4,000 Hz. Wingbeat waveform recordings were separated into two groups. The first group (training data) was used for training artificial neural network classifiers. The second group (evaluating data) was used only for evaluating the classifiers.

2.3 Data processing

The raw data recorded by WfRec were processed and devided into three groups of variables. Fist, wingbeat waveform time series x1, x2 ......x300, which contains the signal amplitude at discrete time steps of 1/4000 s. Second, the spectral information of wingbeat waveforms f1, f2, f3, and f4. The f1 is the fundamental frequency that was wingbeat frequency, and f2, f3, and f4 represented the double frequency, triple frequency, and fourfold frequency harmonics within frequency band of each waveform (Fig. 3).

Third, data included x1, x2, ...,x300 and f1, f2, f3, f4. All data were normalized so that the values of each variable ranged between zero and one.

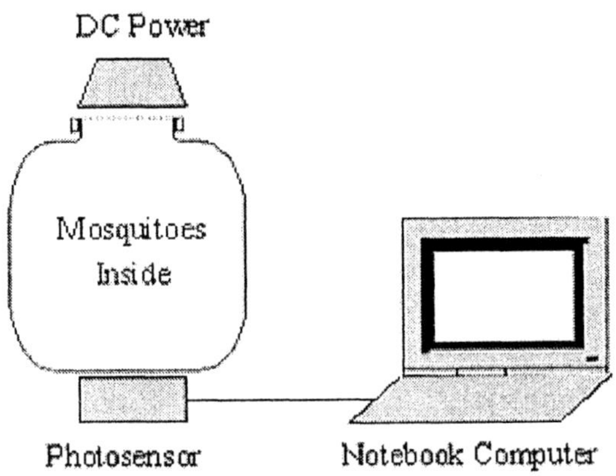

Figure.1 Apparatus for digital recording of insect wingbeat waveforms

2.4 Artificial neural network automated classification

Three BP artificial neural networks were built respectively to accept input data in the form of a wingbeat waveform time series, signature harmonics and their combination. These networks had all 100 input neurons and 9 output neurons, one output for each mosquito species. There were also five hidden layers with 10 neurons each layer. During training, the network was presented with three groups of variables as input respectively and a nine-digit vector consisting of a 1 and eight zeros to indicate the species of mosquito that produced the signature (e.g., male Aedes albopictus represented by 1 0 0 0 0 0 0 0 0). Convergence goal was 0.0001, value of logic judging is 0.5. After training, evaluating data were presented to the artificial neural network having been trained. Each output vector was classified as one species of mosquito.

3. RESULTS

Fig.2 showed the result of recording wingbeat waveform. According to the figure, automated classification waveforms of each species of mosquito were so similar sine wave that it was difficult to identify individual by waveform data alone. As a result of identification in Table1, only accurate 39% met by artificial neural network, which built with wingbeat waveform signature. The most accurate classification model tested was an artificial neural network that was constructed by using variable of wingbeat frequency with mean 72.67% and highest 89%, ranging from 89% for male Aedes aegypti (Linnaeus) down to 33% for female Aedes albopictus (Skuse). Male Aedes aegypti (Linnaeus) was low, which attributed to not evident fourfold frequency. If wingbeat waveform and wingbeat frequency were used as characteristic value of recognition to build artificial neural network, the accuracy had a drop.

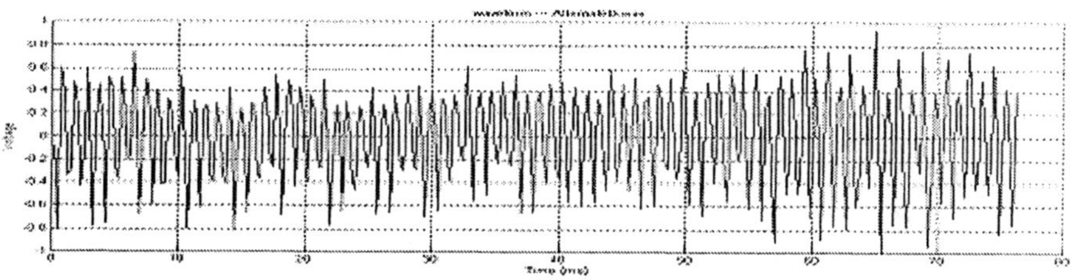

Figure2. Wingbeat waveforms of mosquitoes. Digital processing for calculation of a waveform signature starts with a time series of data point sampled at 4,000 samples per second.

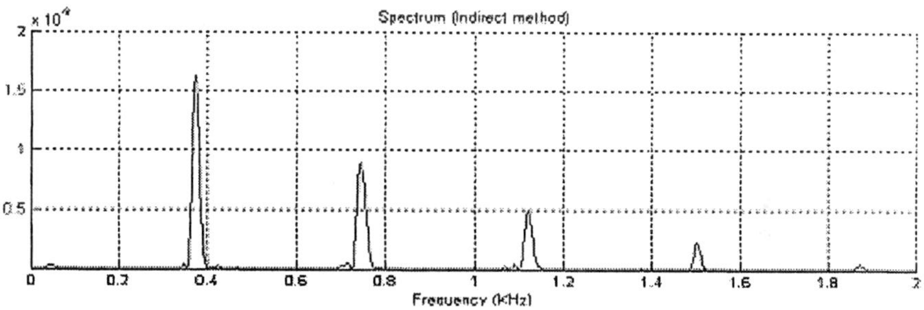

Figure 3. Wingbeat frequencies of mosquitoes. A frequency spectrum was produced by Fourier transform and contained a harmonic series

Table1.Automated identification by artificial neural network

Species of mosquitoes		Characteristic vector of inputting ANN: Data of wingbeat waveform	Data of wingbeat frequencies	Data of wingbeat frequencies and wingbeat waveform
A. albopictus	♀	39%	33%	59%
	♂	50%	89%	67%
A. aegypti	♀	28%	72%	56%
	♂	33%	89%	72%
C.pipien spallens	♀	39%	67%	71%
	♂	22%	83%	58%
C.pipiens quinquefasciatus	♀	44%	61%	55%
	♂	28%	83%	48%
C. pipiens molestus	♀	33%	77%	52%
Average accuracy		35.11%	72.67%	59.77%

4 DISCUSSION

The result of automated identification was 72.67% average accurate by building the artificial neural network with the wingbeat frequency. As a characteristic, the wingbeat waveform alone was not very useful to automate identification with 35.11% average accurate by constructing the artificial neural network since all these wingbeat waveforms were very similar sine waves， it was probably the reason of un-efficient identification. The result directly demonstrated that it was feasible to identify wingbeat frequencies of mosquitoes by artificial neural network, while wingbeat waveform was not efficient. Meanwhile the research validate that Roth (1948) observed the sexual behavior of mosquitoes, which had been generally accepted that in most species the fundamental frequency of the flight sound of the female attracts males from far distances (Gillett, 1971).

Moore (2002) built artificial neural network to automated identification wingbeat waveform of aphids with 67% average accurate arrange from 41% to 94%, the mean reasons included that there was no information communication between different species of aphids, it was more important that flying of aphids was in-continuous. Farmery (1981) showed that the wingbeat frequency stayed constant, the harmonic pattern of optically sensed wingbeat waveforms changes radically when the orientation of the insect with respect to the sensor was varied. So there were still many interesting fields to research on automated identification of species of insects in the future.

ACKNOWLEDGEMENTS

This research was granted by the National Priority Program of Innovative Technology (863) No. 2002AA243031and 2003AA2090. The author would like to extent sincere appreciation professor Yu yixin and professor Gu tao for their constructive advice.

REFERENCES

[1] Christophers S. R. *Aedes aegypti*(L). The yellow fever mosquito: its life history , bionomic and structure .Cambridge University Press, London and New York. 1960, 739pp

[2] Clements A. N. The physiology of mosquitoes. Pergamon Press, Oxord. 1963, 393pp

[3] David Chesmore. Automated Bioacoustic Identification of species. Annals of the Brazilian Academy of Sciences, 2004, 76(2): 435~440

[4] Do M.T, el al. A test of a pattern recognition system for identification of spiders. Bulletin of Entomological Research, 1999, 89:217~224

[5] Farmery M.J. Optical studies of insect flight at low altitude. Ph. D. dissertation. York University, York, UK. 1981

[6] Gillett J. D. Mosquitoes Weidenfeild and Nicholson. London. 1971, 274pp

[7] Moore A. Development of a data acquisition system for long-term outdoor recording of insect flight activity using a photosensor. 13th Conference on Aerobiology and Biometeorology, American Meteorological Society, Albuquerque, New Mexico.1998

[8] Moore A, el al. Automated identification of flying insects by analysis of wingbeat frequencies. J. Econ. Entomol. 1986, 79: 1703~1706

[9] Moore A, el al. Automated Identification of Optically Sensed Aphid (Homoptera: Aphidae) Wingbeat Waveforms. J. Econ. Entomol. 2002, 95(1): 1~8

[10] Qubit Systems. WfRec Transient Waveform Recorder. Kingston, Ontario, Canada. 2001

[11] Peter Belton, el al. Flight sounds of the females of some mosquitoes of western Canada. Ent. Exp. & appl. 1979, 26:105~114

[12] Parsons S, el al. Acoustic identification of twelve species of echolocating bat by discriminate function analysis and artificial neural networks. J. Exp. Bio. 2000, 203: 2641~2656.

[13] Roth L.M. A study of mosquito behavior. An experimental laboratory study of the sexual behaviour of *Aedesaegypti*(L).Amer. Mid. Nat. 1948, 40*:265~352*

[14] Taylor B. W, el al. Laboratory mating of *Addes vexans* (Diptera: Culicidae). *Ann. Ent. Soc. Amer.* 1974, 67: 137~138

[15] Williams C.M, el al. Oscilloscopic and stroboscopic analysis of the flight sounds of Drosophila *Bol. Bull. (Wood's Hole)* 1950, *99:300~307*

DATA MINING TECHNIQUES FOR SLOPE STABILITY ESTIMATION WITH PROBABILISTIC NEURAL NETWORKS

Shouju Li and Yingxi Liu
State Key Laboratory of Structural Analysis for Industrial Equipment, Dalian University of Technology, Dalian, 116024, China

Abstract: Probabilistic neural networks are applied to facilitate slope stability estimation by making use of data mining techniques and an intelligent system. Data mining can draw attention to meaningful structures in the archives of such slope stability data. The soil mechanical characteristics and the slope shapes with significant influences on slope stability are used to train and test the neural networks. Validation is performed to show the efficiency of probabilistic neural networks for estimation of slope stability. The simulation results show that probabilistic neural network models generate higher predicting precision than the conventional linear regression, limit equilibrium method and maximum likelihood estimation.

Key words: neural network; data mining; slope stability; state estimation

1. INTRODUCTION

The stability of slopes has been received wide attention to its practical importance in the design of excavations, embankments, earth and rockfill dams, and tailing dams. Generally, limit equilibrium techniques are commonly used to assess the stability of the sloped, as complex geological subsoil profiles, seepage, and external loads can be easily dealt with.[1] A difficulty with all the equilibrium methods is that they are based on the assumption that the failing soil mass can be divided into slices[2]. This in turn necessitates further assumption relating to side force directions between slices, with consequent implications for equilibrium. The economic and social values of slope stability analysis are very high. As a result, the problem has attracted many researchers in the area of computational intelligence recently.

Data mining, also known as "knowledge discovery in databases", is the process of discovering interesting patterns in databases that are useful in decision making[3]. Data mining is a discipline of growing interest and importance, and an application area that can provide significant competitive advantage to an organization by exploiting the potential of large data warehouses. The central focus of the data mining enterprise is to gain insight into large collections of data. Often, achieving this goal involves applying machine learning methods to inductively construct models of the data at hand[4]. A number of algorithms have been developed in domains, such as machine learning, statistics, and visualization, to identify patterns in data[5]. Of these, statistical modeling approaches are the oldest. The data set must conform to rigid distribution criteria to employ statistical modeling methods. Pattern discovery algorithms based on machine learning techniques, however, impose fewer restrictions and produce patterns that are easy to understand.

Recently, intelligent systems specifically ANNs, have been applied as a novel approach for modeling of complex, highly nonlinear dynamic systems. The main advantage of ANNs is in cases where intrinsic nonlinearities in the dynamics prevent the development of exactly solvable models. All of these criteria are present in the sense that the dynamics are inherently nonlinear, and prediction is one of the main goals. An ANN is a computational method inspired by studies of the brain and nervous systems in biological organisms. An ANN is constructed of a highly interconnected network of many basic computing processors named as neurons. Two of the characteristics of ANNs are their capability of self-organization and autonomous learning ANNs are well suited to problems involving matching input pattern to a set of output patterns where deep reasoning is not required. The ANN approaches have been applied to many problem domains in the civil engineering field with the main objective of assisting project engineers in decision making[6]. The objective of the paper is to propose an intelligent procedure for estimation of slope stability with probabilistic neural networks.

This paper is organized as follows: Section 2 describes the basic features of ANN, the principles of data mining with ANN, and the training process of probabilistic neural networks. In section 3, the applications of probabilistic neural networks to slope stability forecasting are executed and some comparisons with different methods for estimating slope stability are shown.

2. DATA MINING TECHNIQUES WITH PROBABILISTIC NEURAL NETWORKS

Data mining refers to the application of machine learning methods, as well as other automatic knowledge acquisition methods, to the generation of potentially useful knowledge from the organization and analysis of raw data. In overview, the implementation steps of data mining for slope stability analysis are:1) objective determination. The slope stability estimation is divided into two categories, which is stable or failed state.2) data preparation. Prior to a pattern recognition analysis, making a principal components plot gives a good idea of how difficult the classification will be and consideration of the loadings of principal components usually gives a preliminary idea of the importance of variables. 3) data transformation; data mining; and analysis of results. Making use of intelligent algorithms, for examples, genetic algorithm, neural networks, and other machine learning techniques; the classification and forecast problem for slope stability can be estimated. .

Several machine learning techniques have been proposed to acquire knowledge in soil and rock engineering. Some of them are symbolic learning, case-based learning, and ANN. The factors that influence the applicability of machine learning techniques include comprehensibility of knowledge, the complexity of representing input data and knowledge, the ability to handle missing values or noisy data, and so on. The comprehensibility of knowledge of the relation between slope stability and input parameters i.e., rock mechanical characteristics and the slope shape is opaque. Therefore, ANN is an appropriate machine learning technique in this case.

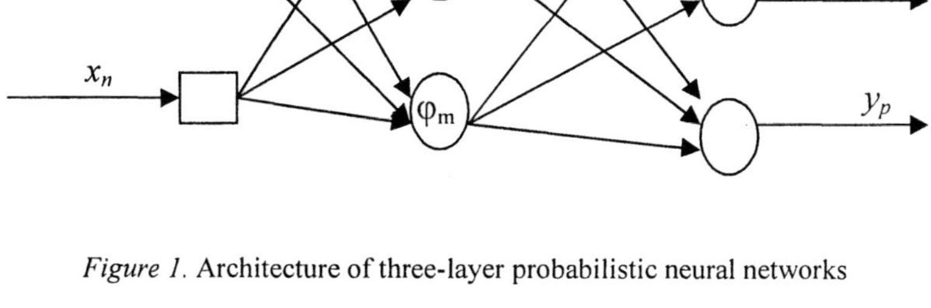

Figure 1. Architecture of three-layer probabilistic neural networks

Probabilistic neural networks(PNNs) are a kind of radical basis networks suitable for classification and will be used for modeling the data sets. The Architecture of three-layer probabilistic neural networks is shown in Fig.1. It has the three layers, including an input layer, which has as many elements as there are separable parameters needed to describe the objects to be classified. It has a hidden layer, also called a pattern layer, which organizes element represents each input vector. And finally, the network contains an output layer, called the summation layer, which has as many processing elements as there are classes to be recognized. Each element in this layer combines via processing elements within the pattern layer which relate to the same class and prepares that category for output.

PNNs are known for their ability to be trained quickly on sparse data sets by separating data into a specified number of output categories. PNNs are three-layer networks wherein the training patterns are presented to the input layer and the output layer has one neuron for each possible category. The number of neurons in the hidden layer must be equal to the number of training patterns. PNN determines which category that one pattern belongs to. It measures how far a given sample pattern is from patterns of the training set in the R-dimensional space, where R is the number of inputs in the problem. These layers of neurons in the input, hidden and output layers constitute a number of sensory units. The information passes from the input layer through the hidden layer to the output layer, that is, the signal processing from neurons of a layer to the neurons of the succeeding layer.

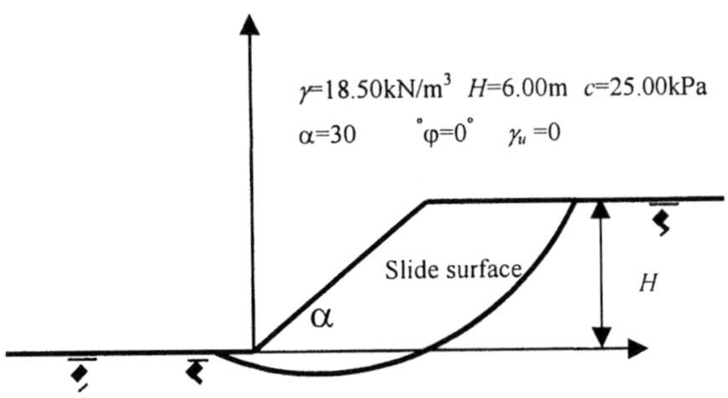

Figure 2. Basic description of slope stability analysis

As shown as Fig.2, the main factors of impact on slope stability are listed as follows: the unit weight of the soil γ; cohesion of soil c; internal fraction angle φ; slope angle α; slope height H; pore pressure ration γ_u. The main role of the input layer is to map all the external signals into the hidden layers. Thus, it requires a scaling function for each input neuron to normalize the range of external signals into a specific range that the neural network can process. The neurons in the hidden layer enable mapping of the non-linearity relations between the input and output values and thus give PNN models a better performance over others. The final output classifications are determined by values of the output layer generated by the PNN model. The network produces activation in the output layer, corresponding to the probability density function estimated for each category. The highest output represents the most probable category. The number of neurons in the input layer is the number of inputs to the problem, and the number of neurons in the output layer corresponds to the number of categories. As the purpose of a PNN network is to separate outputs into different categories, two or more output neurons are normally required, with output values normalized to fall within 0 and 1.

The output of the pattern layer is expressed as follows:

$$\varphi_j(x) = \exp(-\frac{(x - c_j)^2}{2\sigma_j^2}) \tag{1}$$

Where x is the input vector of for an input pattern; c_j is the center of j-th basis function; σ_j denotes a smooth parameter and is the deviation of radial basis function; φ is the radial basis function. Probabilistic neural networks can be used for classification problems. When an input is presented, the first layer computes distances from the input vector to the training input vectors, and produces a vector whose elements indicate how close the input is to a training input. The second layer sums these contributions for each class of inputs to produce as its net output a vector of probabilities. Finally, a competitive transfer function on the output of the second layer picks the maximum of these probabilities, and produces a 1 for that class and a 0 for the other classes.

The expression for the net input of a radial basis neuron is different from that of neurons in back propagation. The net input to the radial basis transfer function is the vector distance between its center vector c and the input vector x. The radial basis function has a maximum of 1 when its input is 0. As the distance between c and x decreases, the output increases. Thus, a radial basis neuron acts as a detector that produces 1 whenever the input x is identical to its center vector c. The output of the probabilistic neural network, $y(x)$, which is a model based on linear regression, is expressed as follows

$$y_i(x) = \sum_{j=1}^{m} w_{ij}\varphi_j(x, c) \qquad i = 1, 2, \ldots, p \tag{2}$$

Where p is the number of neurons in the output layer; w_{ij} is the weight linking the i-th neuron in the output layer to the j-th neuron in the hidden layer. The outputs of the summary layer are binary values. If y_i is larger than input of other neurons, y_i is set to 1, otherwise it is set to zero.

The learning process of probabilistic neural network is divided into two stages. The first stage is non-supervised learning, which Euclidian distance, d_j, is formulated as

$$d_j(t) = \|x - c_j(t-1)\| \qquad j = 1,2,...,m \tag{3}$$

Where t is the number of iteration. The center is adjusted as follows

$$c_j(t) = \begin{cases} c_j(t-1) + \xi[x(t-1) - c_j(t-1)] & j = \min d_j(t-1) \\ c_j(t-1) & others \end{cases} \tag{4}$$

The second stage is the supervised learning, in which the W is adjusted by using LMS method. In matrix notation, Eq(2) becomes

$$Y = W\Phi \tag{5}$$

Where Y is the real output matrix, W and Φ are the weight matrix and radial basis matrix, respectively. The weight matrix can be computed by using pseudo inversion method

$$W = \Phi^+ D \tag{6}$$

Where Φ^+ is the pseudo inversion of matrix Φ, and D is the expected output response matrix. The pseudo inversion can be expressed as

$$\Phi^+ = (\Phi^T \Phi)^{-1} \Phi^T \tag{7}$$

3. ESTIMATION OF SLOPE STABILITY WITH PROBABILISTIC NEURAL NETWORK

As shown as Figure 1, the factors influencing slope stability includes the unit weight of the soil γ, cohesion c, internal fraction angle φ, slope angle α, slope height H and pore pressure ration γ_u. As a result, there were six neutrons in the input layer of ANN, 46 neutrons in the hidden layer and 2 neutrons in the output layer. Designing network architecture requires more than selecting a certain number of neurons, followed by training only. Especially phenomena such as over-fitting and under-fitting should be recognized and avoided in order to create a reliable network. And 46 input-output samples were gotten from reference[7].

Preprocessing is numerically operating on the data in order to increase the useful information for pattern recognition.

$$\hat{x}_k = \frac{2(x_k - x_{k\min})}{(x_{k\max} - x_{k\min})} - 1 \tag{8}$$

Where $\hat{x}_k$ is the normalized network input, x_{kmin} and x_{kmax} are respectively minimum and maximum of the k-th property of soil parameters in all training pairs.

Table 1. Basic mechanical parameters of soil slopes

Case No.	γ/kN·m^{-3}	c/kN	φ/°	α/°	H/m	γ_u
E1	18.50	25.00	0.00	30.0	6.00	-
E2	12.00	0.00	30.00	35.0	4.00	-
E3	18.84	0.00	20.00	20.0	7.62	0.45
E4	14.00	11.97	26.00	30.0	88.0	0.45
E5	22.40	10.00	35.00	45.0	10.0	0.40

The basic mechanical parameters of soil slopes are listed in Table1. After training ANN with the practical engineering samples, the prediction of slope stability for the other 5 cases of the slope failure or stable are done with well trained ANN. Table 2 gives the comparison between the estimated and practical states of slope safety with different search methods. The practical application of proposed intelligent forecast procedure for slope stability shows that a well trained artificial neural network reveals an extremely fast convergence, a better generalization and a high degree of accuracy.

Table 2. Comparison between the estimated and practical states of slope safety with different methods

No.	Limit equilibrium method	Maximum likelihood estimation	Neural network	Practical states of slopes
E1	stable	stable	failed	failed
E2	stable	stable	stable	stable
E3	stable	failed	failed	failed
E4	failed	failed	failed	failed
E5	failed	failed	failed	failed

4. CONCLUSION

Probabilistic neural networks (PNN) can be used for classification problems. Their design is straightforward and does not depend on training. A PNN is guaranteed to converge to a Bayesian classifier providing it is given enough training data. These networks generalize well. Neural networks have a more suitable inductive bias than other commonly used data mining methods. This paper describes the application of a data mining technique, probabilistic neural networks, to tackle a commonly faced problem in a slope stability project: estimation of slope stability based on the soil mechanical properties and geotechnical slope shapes. The study demonstrates the ability of data mining to deliver new project insights in areas where traditional techniques had not been so successful.

ACKNOWLEDGEMENTS

This research is funded by the National Natural Science Foundation of China(No. 10472025).

REFERENCES

1. Goh A T. C.: Genetic algorithm search for critical slip surface in multiple-wedge stability analysis. Can. Geotech. J. 36(1999)382-391
2. Al-Karni A.: Study of the effect of soil anisotropy on slope stability using method of slices. Computer and Geotechnics. 26(2000):83-103
3. Business I B.: Data mining-a machine learning perspective. Information & Management. 39(2001) 211-225
4. Craven M W.: Using neural networks for data mining. Future Generation Computer systems. 13(1997) 211-229
5. Leu S S., Chen C N., Chang S L.: Data mining for tunnel support stability: neural network. Approach Automation in Construction 10(2001) 429-441
6. Tam C.M., Tong T K.L. Diagnosis of prestressed concrete pile defects using probabilistic neural networks. Engineering Structures. 26 (2004) 1155-1162
7. Sah N K.: maximum likelihood estimation of slope stability. Int. J. Rock Mech. Min. Sci. & Geomech. Abstr. 31(1994)47-53

DESIGN OF INTEGRAL VARIABLE STRUCTURE CONTROL FOR NONLINEAR SYSTEM BASED ON CMAC NEURAL NETWORK AND REFERENCE MODEL

Lin Lei, Houjun Wang, Shuchun Zhou
School of Automation Engineering, University of Electronic Science and Technology of China, Chengdu, Sichuan, China

Abstract: Because mismatch of models of uncertain nonlinear control system and external disturbance etc., these will make effects of controller designed badly in uncertain nonlinear system. In this paper, we put forward a method, which can improve performance of uncertain nonlinear control system. We divide nonlinear control system into reference model and uncertain parts two respectively design and last synthesize control law of two parts. We build up approximate reference model through information known, make use of integral variable structure control of exponential approach method, and adopt to integral variable structure control based on CMAC neural network for uncertain part. We make use of method of extension controller's design based on extension set theory while uncertain boundary unknown. The simulate experiment validate this control method can improve control quality in an extent.

Keywords: CMAC neural network; integral variable structure control; uncertain nonlinear system; robust control; reference model

1. INTRODUCTION

Because there are uncertainty and nonlinear property of system when design actual engineering controller, which makes design become difficult. We make use of method of Integral Variable Structure Control (IVSC)[1], while we have known estimative parameter and uncertain boundary of system model; we may make use of method of extension controller's design [2] based on extension set theory while uncertain boundary unknown. We both suppose that system model completely cannot be determined and design controller above two control method. In fact, sometimes we may make full use of information known to build up approximate system model. Although mismatch of model with actual system may be comparatively big, it can reflect some effective characteristic of actual system more or less. We call approximate system model to build up as reference model [3]. In this paper, we put forward integral variable structure control method of nonlinear system based on CMAC neural network and reference model. We confirm its validity through simulate and experiment.

2. THE THEORY AND SYSTEM DESCRIPTION OF NONLINEAR CONTROL SYSTEM

Define nonlinear system as: $x^{(n)} = f(\underline{x}) + bu$ (1)

In formula (1), $\underline{x} = (x_1, x_2 \dots x_n)^T = (x, \dot{x}, \ddot{x}, \dots x^{(n-1)})^T$ is state vector, f is continuous bounded function, b is unknown time-varying positive real even $0 < b_{\min} \le b \le b_{\max}$, and $u \in R$ is input. Object of control is to supply an appropriate control input u that it makes distance of error vector $\underline{e} = \underline{x} - \underline{x}_d = (e_1, e_2, \dots, e_n)^T = (e, \dot{e}, \ddot{e}, \dots, e^{(n-1)})^T$ and zero vector become minimum. In this formula, $\underline{x}_d = (x_{d1}, x_{d2} \dots x_{dn})^T = (x_d, \dot{x}_d, \dot{x}_d, \dots x_d^{(n-1)})^T$ is state vector of anticipant object.

Define reference model of nonlinear system built as follow:

$$x_m^{(n)} = f_m(\underline{x_m}) + b_m u_m \tag{2}$$

Describe mismatch of model and actual system as follow:

$$x_\Delta^{(n)} = f_\Delta(\underline{x_\Delta}) + b_m u_\Delta \tag{3}$$

In above two formulas, b_m is parameter estimate of b, let $b_m = \sqrt{b_{\min} . b_{\max}}$, $\underline{x_m}$ is state variable of reference model, and $\underline{x_\Delta}$ is dispersion between state variable of reference model and state variable $\underline{x}$ of actual system. Also, suppose that the relations as follows are tenable.

$$\underline{x_\Delta} = \underline{x} - \underline{x_m} \tag{4}$$

$$f_\Delta(\underline{x_\Delta}) = f(\underline{x}) - f_m(\underline{x_m}) \tag{5}$$

In condition of suppose, nonlinear system may be divided into two respective parts: reference model as formula (2) and model mismatch as formula (3). We may use different control law u_m and u_Δ for two parts to get optimal effect of control.

3. STRUCTURE OF CONTROL SYSTEM

P When f_m is known and f_Δ is uncertain, we may use approach method to resolve Integral Variable Structure Control (IVSC) u_m, use method of extension controller design u_Δ, and finally combine both as the ultimate control law. The control system structure is shown in figure 1[4]. The model controller makes state input $\underline{x}_m$ of reference model trace anticipant state vector $\underline{x}_d$. That is to make error vector $\underline{e}_m = \underline{x}_m - \underline{x}_d$ full approach to zero. If f_m known, we may directly use exponential approach method to resolve IVSC u_m

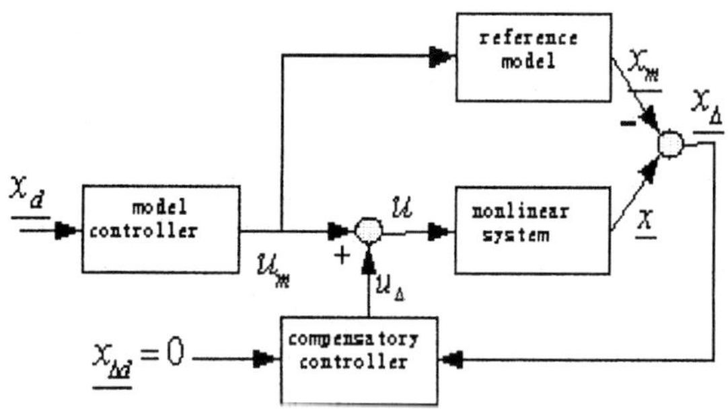

Figure 1. Structure of control system

4. DESIGNING CONTROL LAW OF NONLINEAR CONTROL SYSTEM

The switching function usually select linear function:

$$S_m(e_m)=e_m^{(n-1)}+a_1e_m^{(n-2)}+.....+a_{n-1}e_m+K_{\mathrm{Im}}Z_m \tag{6}$$

In above formula, define $Z_m = e_m$. Resolve derivative for (6) and get:

$$\dot{S}_m(e_m)=e_m^{(n)}+a_1e_m^{(n-1)}+.....+a_{n-1}\dot{e}_m+K_{\mathrm{Im}}e_m \tag{7}$$

Let $\dot{S}_m$ and exponential approach law identical:

$$\dot{S}_m=-\varepsilon\,\mathrm{sgn}(S_m)-kS_m \tag{8}$$

We may get u_m from (7), (8) and (2) formula as follows:

$$e_m^{n}+a_1e_m^{(n-1)}+.....+a_{n-1}\dot{e}_m+K_{\mathrm{Im}}e_m=-\varepsilon\,\mathrm{sgn}(S_m)-kS_m \tag{9}$$

$$x_m^{(n)}-x_d^{(n)}+a_1e_m^{(n-1)}+.....+a_{n-1}\dot{e}_m+K_{\mathrm{Im}}e_m=-\varepsilon\,\mathrm{sgn}(S_m)-kS_m$$

$$f_m(\underline{x}_m)+b_mu_m-x_d^{(n)}+a_1e_m^{(n-1)}+.....+a_{n-1}\dot{e}_m+K_{\mathrm{Im}}e_m=-\varepsilon\,\mathrm{sgn}(S_m)-kS_m \tag{10}$$

Get from above formula as follows:

$$u_m=b_m^{-1}\left\{u_m-f_m(\underline{x}_m)-\varepsilon\,\mathrm{sgn}(S_m)-kS_m\right\} \tag{11}$$

$$\hat{u}_m = x_d^{(n)} - a_1 e_m^{(n-1)} - \ldots\ldots - a_{n-1} \dot{e}_m - K_{\mathrm{Im}} e_m$$

Designing compensatory controller may adopt method to design extension controller [2]. The designing object of control law u_Δ is to compensate for dispersion between model's state vector $\underline{x}_m$ and actual system's state vector $\underline{x}$, which is to make $\underline{x}_\Delta$ full closer to anticipant value $\underline{x}_{\Delta d} = 0$. According to Integral Variable Structure principle, define switch surface as follow:

$$S(\underline{e}_\Delta) = e_\Delta^{(n-1)} + a_1 e_\Delta^{(n-2)} + \ldots\ldots + a_{n-1} e_\Delta + K_I Z_\Delta \quad (12)$$

$\underline{e}_\Delta = \underline{x}_\Delta - \underline{x}_{\Delta d}$, $\dot{Z}_\Delta = e_\Delta$ in the above formula. The control input u_Δ designed must satisfy sliding condition: $S\dot{S} \le -\eta|S|$ (13)

In the above formula, η is a positive definite constant. We may design control law u_Δ of compensatory controller from invariable structure control law. Define Lyapunov function as $V = 0.5S^2$. Thus

$$\begin{aligned}
\dot{V} &= S\dot{S} \\
&= S \cdot (e_\Delta^{(n)} + a_1 e_\Delta^{(n-1)} + \ldots\ldots + a_{n-1} \dot{e}_\Delta + K_I e_\Delta) \\
&= S \cdot \{f_\Delta(x_\Delta) + bu_\Delta - x_{\Delta d}^{(n)} + a_1 e_\Delta^{(n-1)} + \ldots\ldots + a_{n-1}\dot{e}_\Delta + K_I e_\Delta\} \\
&= S \cdot \{f_\Delta(\underline{x}_\Delta) + bu_\Delta - \hat{u}\} \qquad (14)
\end{aligned}$$

Suppose $u_\Delta = u_{\Delta eq} + u_{\Delta s}$. In formula (14), $u_{\Delta eq}$ is equivalent control and $u_{\Delta s}$ is striking control. While $\dot{V} = 0$, we may get a optimal equivalent control $u_{\Delta eq}$:

$$u^*_{\Delta eq} = b^{-1}(\hat{u} - f_\Delta(\underline{x}_\Delta)) \quad (15)$$

Because b is unknown, we use b_m as an approximate of b and get an equal control $u_{\Delta eq}$:

$$u_{\Delta eq} = b_m^{-1}(\hat{u} - f_\Delta(\underline{x}_\Delta)) \quad (16)$$

Thereinto, $\hat{u} = -(a_1 e_\Delta^{(n-1)} + a_2 e_\Delta^{(n-2)} + \ldots\ldots + a_{(n-1)} \dot{e}_\Delta + K_I e_\Delta)$

Determinate striking control $u_{\Delta s}$ through Lyapunov theory and method as follows:

$$\begin{aligned}
\dot{V} &= S\dot{S} \\
&= S \cdot \{f_\Delta(\underline{x}_\Delta) + bu_\Delta - \hat{u}\} \\
&= S \cdot \{f_\Delta(\underline{x}_\Delta) + bu_{\Delta eq} + bu_{\Delta s} - \hat{u}\} \\
&= S \cdot \{f_\Delta(\underline{x}_\Delta) + (bb_m^{-1} - 1)\hat{u} - bb_m^{-1} f_\Delta(\underline{x}_\Delta) + bu_{\Delta s}\} \qquad (17)
\end{aligned}$$

Let $u_{\Delta s} = b_m^{-1}(f_\Delta(\underline{x}_\Delta) - G^* \operatorname{sgn}(S))$ and expression of G^* is as follows:

$$G^* = b_m b^{-1}\eta + \left|b_m b^{-1} f_\Delta(\underline{x}_\Delta) + (1 - b_m b^{-1})\hat{u}\right| \quad (18)$$

We may confirm $\dot{V} = S\dot{S} \leqslant -\eta|S| \leq 0$ if we induce $u_{\Delta s}$ and G^* into the formula $\dot{V} = S\dot{S}$.

We find that $u_{\Delta s} = b_m^{-1}(f_\Delta(\underline{x_\Delta}) - G^* \operatorname{sgn}(S))$ can satisfy sliding condition. So synthesis control law from equivalent control and striking control is as follows:

$$\begin{aligned} u_\Delta &= u_{\Delta eq} + u_{\Delta s} \\ &= b_m^{-1}(\hat{u} - f_\Delta(\underline{x_\Delta})) + b_m^{-1}(f_\Delta(x_\Delta) - G^* \operatorname{sgn}(S)) \\ &= b_m^{-1}(\hat{u} - G^* \operatorname{sgn}(S)) \end{aligned} \tag{19}$$

Because b is unknown and f_Δ is completely uncertain, G^* cannot implement. We use CMAC neural network and make it full approach G^* through study and training.

Suppose that input of CMAC network is as follows [5]: $G_N(\underline{e_\Delta} \mid \underline{w}) = \underline{w}^T \underline{\mu}(\underline{e_\Delta})$. In above formula, $\underline{w}$ is a weighted vector and $\underline{\mu}(e_\Delta) \in R^{n\times 1}$ is a basis function of network. Suppose there is an optimal weight value $\underline{w}^*$ that makes $\varepsilon = G_N(\underline{e_\Delta} \mid \underline{w}^*) - G^*$ minimum. A renewed law of weighted vector may be determined by Lyapunov theory for guaranteeing stability of system.

Suppose Lyapunov function as $V = 0.5(S^2 + bb^{-1}\lambda^{-1}\underline{\xi}^T\underline{\xi}), \underline{\xi} = \underline{w} - \underline{w}^*$.

$$\begin{aligned} \dot{V} &= S\dot{S} + bb^{-1}\lambda^{-1}\underline{\xi}^T\underline{\dot{\xi}} \\ &= S\cdot\{f_\Delta(\underline{x_\Delta}) + (bb_m^{-1} - 1)\hat{u} - bb_m^{-1}(G^* \operatorname{sgn}(S))\} + bb_m^{-1}|S|\varepsilon \\ &\quad + \underline{\xi}^T|S|\underline{\mu}(\underline{e_\Delta}) - \lambda^{-1}\underline{\xi}^T\underline{\dot{w}}) \\ &\leq -\eta|S| - bb_m^{-1}(|S|\varepsilon + \underline{\xi}^T|S|\underline{\mu}(\underline{e_\Delta}) - \lambda^{-1}\underline{\xi}^T\underline{\dot{w}}) \\ &= -|S|\cdot\{\eta + bb_m^{-1}\varepsilon\} + bb_m^{-1}\underline{\xi}^T\{-|S|\underline{\mu}(\underline{e_\Delta}) + \underline{\dot{w}}\lambda^{-1}\} \end{aligned} \tag{20}$$

$\underline{\dot{w}} = \lambda|S|\underline{\mu}(\underline{e_\Delta})$ is tenable, we may get that an inequality (19) is tenable.

$$\dot{V} \leq -|S|\{\eta + bb_m^{-1}\varepsilon\} \tag{21}$$

Only if ε is full closer zero, we must get $\eta + bb_m^{-1}\varepsilon \geq 0$, thus $\dot{V} \leq 0$. According to above deduction, choose study equation of CMAC network as follow:

$$\underline{\dot{w}} = \lambda|S|\underline{\mu}(\underline{e_\Delta}) \tag{22}$$

According to literature [2] discussion, we divide movement space of system into eligible region and ineligible region by size of S and adopt different control in the different regions. Furthermore, we transfer sign function sgn(•) into saturation function sat(•) for reducing phenomenon of vibration. Thus, the control law of compensatory controller may modify as follows:

$$u_\Delta = \begin{cases} -b_m^{-1} G \cdot sat(S), S \geq 1 \\ b_m^{-1} (\hat{u} - G \cdot sat(S)), S < 1 \end{cases} \tag{23}$$

We sum formula (9) and formula (21), get a final control law of system as follows:

$$u = u_m + u_\Delta \tag{24}$$

5 SIMULATION AND DISCUSSION

Confirming actual example is to use nonlinear system equation as follows:

$$\ddot{x} + (0.5 + 0.2\sin(t))\dot{x} + 3.2\cos(x) = (1 + 0.2\sin(t))u \tag{25}$$

Suppose that reference model built is as follows:

$$\ddot{x} + 0.5\dot{x} + 3\cos(x - 0.5) = b_m u \tag{26}$$

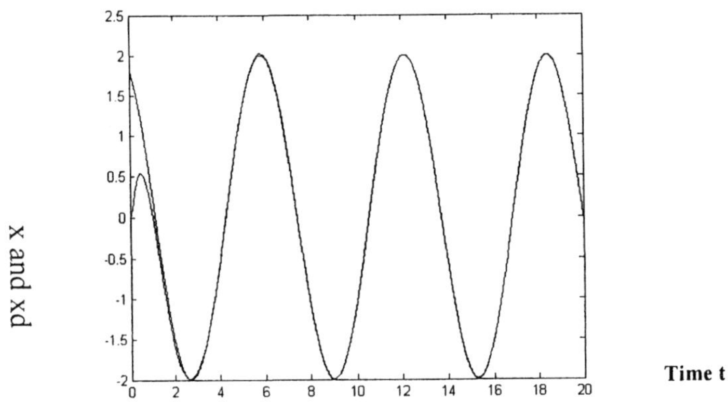

Figure2 output response of state vector

Evidently, $b = 1 + 0.2\sin(t)$, estimative value of b is $b_m = 0.98$. Suppose that the anticipant state of system or instruction input is as follows: $x_d = 2\sin(t + 2)$, $a_1 = 1, a_2 = 2$. In the formula (8), let $\varepsilon = 1, k = 10$. A simulative result is shown in figure 2 and figure 3. We find through simulation that inducing the project can more improve system performance of dynamic state and static state, make system steady, make system strong adaptability, make parameter definite easier, make effect of each parameter little, not demand more precise for parameter in arithmetic, make one-off determination. Also it confirms that controllable method in the paper has a good performance of track.

6 CONCLUSIONS

In this paper, we put forward an designing method of uncertain nonlinear systemic controller that can eliminate phenomenon of integral saturation, decrease overshoots, make system adaptability strong and steady, make parameter definite easier, make effect of each parameter little, make one-off determination for parameter in arithmetic. Also we find through simulation that inducing the project can more improve sy

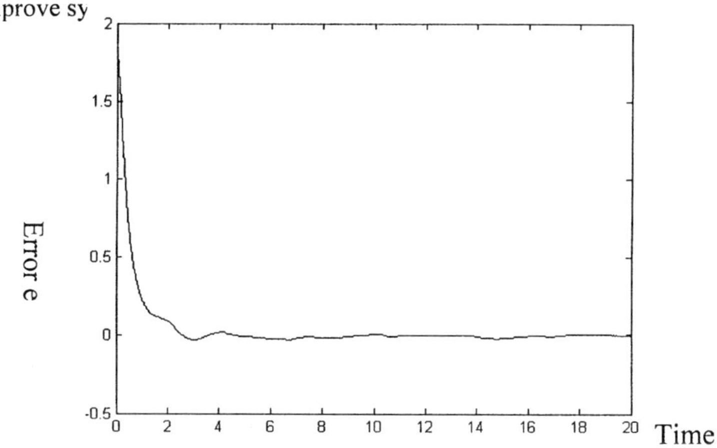

Figure 3 the error curve of reference model

REFERENCES

[1] Chin-Pao Hung. Integral Variable Structure Control of Nonlinear System Using a CMAC Neural Network Learning Approach. IEEE Trans. Syst., Man, Cybern.B, 2004, vol.34, no.1, pp. 702~709

[2] Chen Jenyang, Wong Chingchang. Extension Controller Design via Sliding Mode Control. Engineering Science, Sep. 2001, Vol.3, No.9, PP: 48~51

[3] Li Xinzhong, Jian Linke, Heyue. Neural Network Control for Nonlinear System Model Reference. Information and Control. Vol.25, No.6, 367~372, 1996

[4] David E, Kwon S. Neighborhood Sequential and Random Training Techniques for CMAC. IEEE Tran. Neural Networks, 1995, 6(1): 196~202.

[5] King-Lung Huang etc. Cascade-CMAC Neural Network Applications on the Color Scanner to Printer Calibration. Proceedings of the 1997 IEEE International Conference on Neural Networks, 1997.10~15

FORECASTING RUNOFF WITH HIGHER-EMBEDDED DIMENSIONS USING DMEP-BASED ARTIFICIAL NEURAL NETWORKS

Chuanwen Jiang *, Shuai Li *, Songhuai Du **

** Department of Electrical Engineering, Shanghai Jiaotong University*
Huashan Road 1954, PR China, 200030 ***(email:** jiangcw@sjtu.edu.cn**)***
*** Department of Electrical Engineering, China Agricultural University*
Beijing Tsinghua East Road 17, PR China, 100083

Abstract: The runoff series always presents complex chaos phenomenon with higher embedded dimensions because of the influence of many complicated facts. Generally, it is an effective method to combine phase space restructures theory with artificial neural networks (ANN) model for runoff forecasting. The traditional methods that not consider the variations of the character of full Lyapunov exponential spectrum in restructure space, are proved of high precision to forecast time series with low-embedded dimension. But, they are not so effective to forecast attractors with high-embedded dimension. The paper proposes a new method, which improves the character of full Lyapunov exponential spectrum in a restructure space with high dimensions. In the mean time, an artificial neural networks model based on determinate mutation evolutionary programming (DMEP) learning algorithm is presented for chaotic runoff series forecasting. DMEP introduces chaos mapping into the mutation operation of EP, which aim to increase its convergence rate and results' precision. The test result of runoff forecasting series shows that the precision of runoff forecasting is improved by means of the new method when the embedded dimension is high.

Key words: Chaos, runoff forecasting, ANN, evolutionary programming

1. INTRODUCTION

Forecasting runoff process is always a difficult task in simulation of the whole hydrological cycle, because the runoff process refers to hydrology, aerography, mechanics and so on. Nowadays, more and more scholars think that considering the nonlinear factors in the runoff forecasting modeling is the key to improving the runoff forecasting level. Recently, the theory of nonlinear chaos dynamics which links the determination and randomicity has become the foreland of hydrology study, many scholars do lots of useful explore for hydrology runoff modeling and forecasting[1]-[4]. Specially, combining phase space restructures theory with neural networks is considered as one of the most effective methods[5][6]. However, the embedded dimension will be relatively high, because runoff is influenced by various intricate facts. The traditional chaos methods are proved of high precision to forecast time series with low-embedded dimension. But, they are not so effective to forecast attractors with high-embedded dimension [7][8][9]. On the other hand, it is attractive to find a fast network convergent arithmetic for attractors with high-embedded dimension. The paper proposes a new method, which improves the character of full Lyapunov exponential spectrum in a restructure space with high dimensions. In the mean time, an artificial neural networks model based on determinate mutation evolutionary programming (DMEP) learning algorithm be presented for chaotic runoff series forecasting. DMEP introduces chaos mapping into the mutation operation of traditional evolutionary programming, which aim to increase its convergence rate and results' precision. The test result of runoff forecasting series shows that the precision of runoff forecasting is improved by means of the new method when the embedded dimension is high.

The paper was organized as follows: section 2 describes a artificial neural networks forecasting model based on phase space restructures theory; an improved ANN model with determinate mutation evolutionary programming learning algorithm is shown in section 3; followed by numerical examples in section 4, and conclusion in section 5.

2. ARTIFICIAL NEURAL NETWORKS FORECASTING MODEL BASED ON PHASE SPACE RESTRUCTURES THEORY

The basic theory of runoff forecasting making use of nonlinear chaos dynamics is phase space restructures theory proposed by Takens in 1981.

Consider a chaos system:

$$Y_{t+1} = f(Y_t) \qquad Y_t \in R^m \tag{1}$$

where: $f : R^m \to R^m$ is a continuous smooth function.

If the system can be observed through an observer: $g: R^m \to R^L \quad (L \le m)$, then:

$$x_t = g(Y_t) \qquad x_t \in R^L \tag{2}$$

To simplify the presentation, let L=1, then:

$$X_t = (x_t, x_{t-1}, \cdots, x_{t-d+1}) \tag{3}$$

where X_t is one state in the d-order state space. According to the famous Takens Theory [10], when $d \ge 2m+1$ (m is the order of the attractor), there exists a deterministic mapping with dimension being d: $F^{(d)}: R^d \to R^d$. It describes the evolving track of X_t in the state space and the mapping has the same geometric structure and topology with the original system. So:

$$X_{t+1} = F^{(d)}(X_t) \tag{4}$$

(4) can also be presented as:

$$x_{t+1} = \widetilde{F}^{(d)}(x_t, x_{t-1}, \cdots, x_{t-d+1}) \tag{5}$$

The state space described by $\widetilde{F}^{(d)}$ is called as the restructured state space. d is called as the embedded dimension, which is the dimension of the minimal state space that can completely contain the attractor sets comprised by state transition. Because $\widetilde{F}^{(d)}$ is deterministic, we are only needed to made an estimate on $\widetilde{F}^{(d)}$ in order to forecast x_{t+1}. Currently, fitting methods to $\widetilde{F}^{(d)}$ are local linear model, artificial neural networks model and so on. The forecasting model combining phase space restructures theory and artificial neural networks as follows:

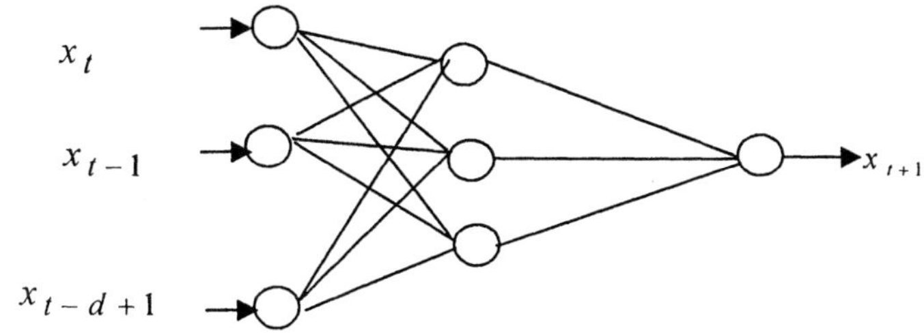

Figure 1. ANN Forecasting Model

By selecting a suitable set of weights and transfer functions, it is known that the ANN can approximate any smooth, measurable function between the input and output vectors. In this paper, a output mean squared error (MSE) of ANN is considered and defined as:

$$MSE = \frac{1}{N}\sum_{s=1}^{N}\left[\sum_{k=1}^{M}(o_{sk} - l_{sk})^2\right] \tag{6}$$

where o_{sk} is the expected output, l_{sk} is the predicted output, M is the number of output neurons, and N is the number of training set samples.

The above-mentioned method is very easy and feasible, but it still has two disadvantages: firstly, the current forecast methods have good forecast precision when the embedded dimension is low. However, when the dimension is high, the result is not satisfied. Secondly, the networks will converge very slowly when using common training arithmetic, especially, when the dimension d becomes enough large, the phenomenon is obvious. The following of this paper will mainly discuss the two problems.

3. AN IMPROVED ANN MODEL FOR RUNOFF FORECASTING

3.1 Improvement Of The Global Lyapunov Exponent Spectrum Of High Embedded Dimension Reconstructed State Space

Generally, the more information used for forecasting, the higher the forecasting precision. When using the current chaos forecasting methods to forecast, it is found that the forecasting precision will decrease with the increase of the embedded dimension after it reached some dimension. The reason for such phenomena lies in the change of the global Lyapunov exponent spectrum of the reconstructed state space[8]. According to the definition of Lyapunov exponent spectrum, it is known that the global Lyapunov exponent spectrum of the reconstructed state space will change with the change of embedded dimension. With the increase of the embedded dimension, the elements with small subscripts in the reconstructed state space have positive larger Lyapunov exponents which make the global Lyapunov exponent spectrum of the reconstructed state space increase. One way to decrease the global Lyapunov spectrum of the reconstructed state space is to let the nearby two tracks and time into the exponential separation relationship by taking the following form:

$$(e^{-\lambda d\tau} x_{t-d+1}, e^{-\lambda(d-1)\tau} x_{t-d+2}, \cdots e^{-\lambda\tau} x_1) \tag{7}$$

When the embedded dimension d is large enough,

$$\sum_{i=1}^{d} e^{-\lambda\tau i} \approx \frac{e^{-\lambda\tau}}{1-e^{-\lambda\tau}} = 1 \tag{8}$$

So: $\lambda\tau = \ln 2 \rightarrow e^{-\lambda\tau} = \frac{1}{2}$.

This means that we can introduce the effect of $(\frac{1}{2})^{d(t)}$ in the reconstructed state space. The reconstructed state space is transformed to:

$$X_t = ((\frac{1}{2})x_t, (\frac{1}{2})^2 x_{t-1}, \cdots, (\frac{1}{2})^d x_{t-d+1}) \tag{9}$$

This method can improve the forecasting error problem caused by the increase of embedded dimension.

3.2 A Deterministic Mutation Evolutionary Programming (DMEP) Algorithm For ANN

Evolutionary programming methods whose search direction was based on survival of the fittest were becoming a widely used method for complex optimal problems. EP seeks the solution of an optimization problem by evolving a population of candidate solutions over a number of generations or iterations. A new population was generated from an existing population through the use of a mutation operator. Assuming the EP population size is m, x_i is the i_{th} individual before mutation, x'_i is the i_{th} individual after mutation, they are related to a vector with n components, $x_i(j)$ is the j_{th} component of x_i, $x'_i(j)$ is the j_{th} component of x'_i, $\sigma_i(j)$ is the approximate mutation scale of the j_{th} component. CEP with Gaussian mutation can be expressed as:

$$x_i'(j) = x_i(j) + \sigma_i(j)N_j(0,1) \quad j = 1,2,\cdots,n \qquad i = 1,2,\cdots,m \tag{10}$$

Where, $N(0,1)$ indicates a random Normal Distribution value with a mean value 0, variances 1.

FEP with Cauchy mutation can be expressed as:

$$x_i'(j) = x_i(j) + \sigma_i(j)C_j(0,1) \quad j = 1,2,\cdots,n \qquad i = 1,2,\cdots,m \tag{11}$$

Where, $C(0,1)$ indicates a random Cauchy-distribution value with a center 0, scale 1.

MFEP with mean of Gaussian and Cauchy mutations can be expressed as:

$$x_i'(j) = x_i(j) + \frac{1}{2}\sigma_i(j)[C_j(0,1) + N_j(0,1)] \quad j = 1,2,\cdots,n \qquad i = 1,2,\cdots,m \tag{12}$$

The above three algorithms adopt a fixed-distribution random for mutation. These mutations cannot guarantee that the new individuals are all in the solution space. To avoid the illegal solutions, this paper implements a new chaos mutation operator considering the inner random and ergodic properties of a chaos dynamics system. It is well known that a chaotic motion can traverse every state in a certain region by its own regularity, and every state is visited only once therefore no precise periodicity. The unique ergodicity and the irregularity of the series generated by chaos make the chaotic dynamics a potential candidate in the field of global optimization [11]-[14]. The new mutation formula is:

$$x_i'(j) = x_i(j) + \frac{1}{2}\sigma_i(j)[R^{(1)}(j) + R^{(2)}(j)] \quad j = 1,2,\cdots,n \qquad i = 1,2,\cdots,m \tag{13}$$

$$\begin{aligned} R^{(1)}(j+1) &= 4.0y(j)\ (1 - y\ (j)) \qquad y(j) \in (0,1) \\ R^{(2)}(j+1) &= \sin(2 / y'\ (j)) \qquad y'\ (j) \in (0,1] \end{aligned} \tag{14}$$

Where, $R^{(1)}$ and $R^{(2)}$ are two famous chaos expressions.

It is assumed that the three-layered perceptrons are chosen for all application cases in this study. W_1 is the connection weight matrix between the input layer and the hidden layer, W_2 is the connection weight matrix between the hidden layer and the output layer.

The performance of each individual is measured according to a fitness function. The fitness function can be calculated by

$$f(W_1, W_2) = MSE(W_1, W_2) \quad (15)$$

The DMEP procedure for (15) can be described as follows:

Step 1 Initiation: Let $X_i = \{W_1^i, W_2^i\}$ be an individual set, create an initial group with m individuals. All individuals are set between the lower and upper bonds and then calculate fitness J.

Step 2 Mutation: every father individual X_i generates a child individual X'_i by using (13).

Step 3 Calculate fitness: all father and child individuals form a group with $2m$ members. For each member A, select q members from the group with a certain probability and compare them with the individual A; if A's fitness is smaller than that of the counterpart individual (for minimal questions), A wins. Here q is a prescribed integer which is called competition scale.

Step 4 Selection: select m individuals with the most winnings from the group to be the next father generation.

Step 5 Stop criteria: if the stop criteria be satisfied, the steps are stopped, else, go to step 2.

4. NUMERICAL EXAMPLES

To forecast runoff using chaos theory, it is necessary to examine the chaos characteristics of runoff. Chaos has three apparent characteristics: (1) sensitive dependence on initial conditions; (2) having non-cyclic characteristics; (3) strange attractors. In order to identify the numerical characters of chaos, many methods are proposed based on the above three characteristics. For example, the reconstructed state space theory and Poincaré section methods were used to describe the strange attractor of chaos movement; Lyapunov exponent was introduced to describe the sensitivity on initial state; several kinds of dimensions can be defined to describe the non-cyclic property.

Case studies for the proposed method were carried out for runoff forecasting using different historical data of Ge-Zhou Dam of Yangtze River in China based on modifying Takens restructure theory that showed in Equation (9). Dimensions of attractors are calculated by means of G-P algorithm which is put up by Grassberger and Procaccia, and the method which is put up by Wolf[15] to calculate Lyapunov exponential is also utilized.

Case I: Daily runoff data of Ge-Zhou Dam of Yangtze (From 1960/1/1 to 1969/12/31) is shown in Figure 2.

Maximum Lyapunov exponential: $\lambda_{\max} = 0.004883362$
Embedded dimension: $d = 6$
Time delay: $\tau = 1$

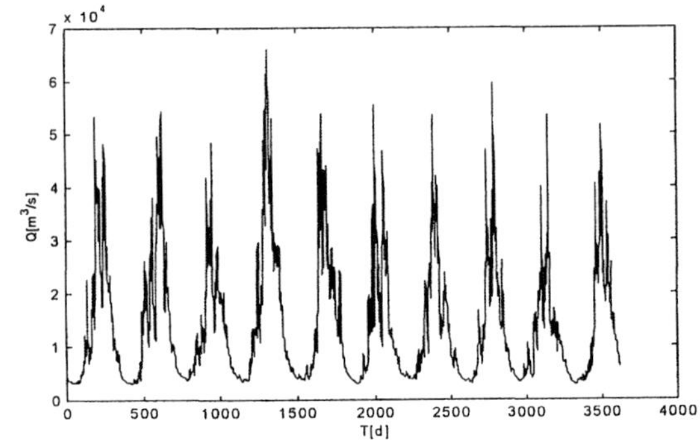

Figure 2. Daily runoff Poincare section of Ge-Zhou Dam (From 1960/1/1 to 1969/12/31)

The Poincare section of daily runoff is shown in Figure 3.

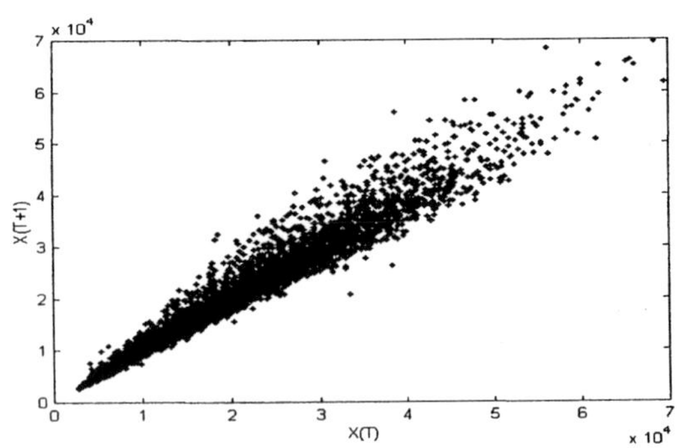

Figure 3. Daily runoff Poincare Section of Ge-Zhou Dam

(From 1960/1/1 to 1969/12/31)

Case II: Daily runoff data of Ge-Zhou Dam of Yangtze (From 1985/1/1 to 1998/12/31) is shown in Figure 4, the Poincare section of daily runoff is shown in Figure 5.

Maximum Lyapunov exponent: $\lambda_{max} = 0.002814374$
Embedded dimension: $d = 6$
Time delay: $\tau = 1$

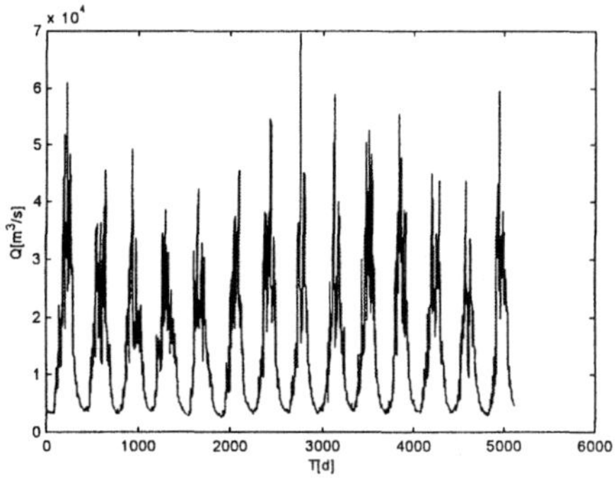

Figure 4. Daily runoff curve of Ge-Zhou Dam of Yangtze (From 1985/1/1 to 19998/12/31)

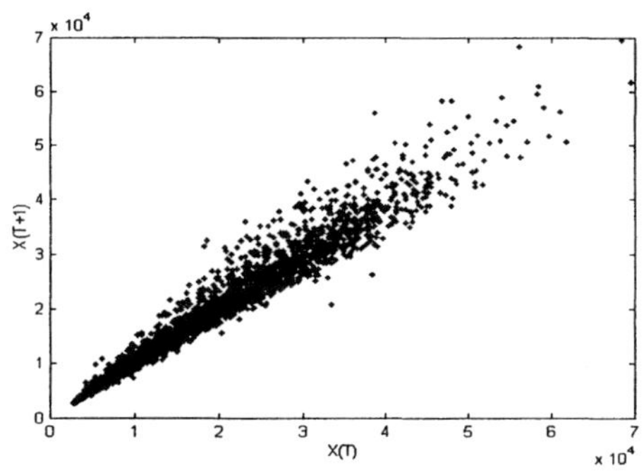

Figure 5. Daily runoff Poincare Section of Ge-Zhou Dam (From 1985/1/1 to 1998/12/31)

The demonstration of computing the Lyapunov exponent of Case 1 and Case 2 proves that there are chaos in these runoff time series.

Applying the data of Case 1, the paper forecasted for 24 consecutive days based on the above three methods in different embedded dimension. The results were analyzed based on the Relative Percentage Error Index (RPEI):

$$\mathrm{RPEI} = \frac{1}{N}\sum_{i=1}^{N}\frac{\left|x_t^i - \hat{x}_t^i\right|}{x_t^i}\times 100 \qquad (15)$$

The relative percentage forecasting errors are shown in Table 1.

Table 1 Forecasting Results

Embedded Dimension	*D=5*	*D=6*	*D=8*	*D=10*
Chaos model(local linear)	5.85%	5.51%	5.68%	6.31%
Phase space+BP	5.74%	5.43%	5.47%	5.80%
New method	5.70%	4.27%	4.50%	5.05%

The iteration performances of the DMEP and CEP are showed in figure 6.

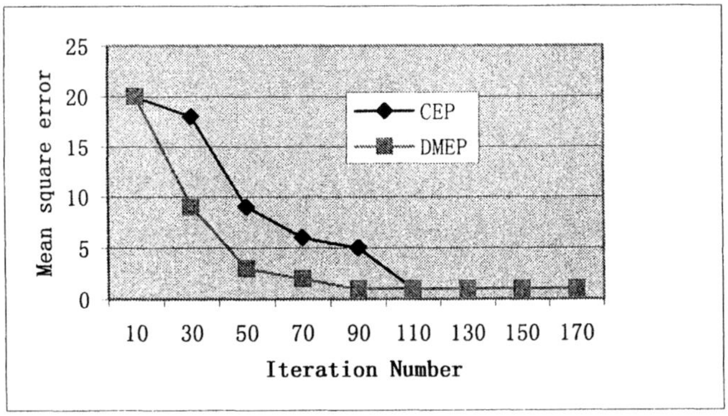

Figure 6. Iteration performances of the DMEP and CEP

Analysis of different historical runoff time series found that the forecasting precision for the method proposed in this paper is better than that for the traditional methods.

5. CONCLUSIONS

The chaotic runoff time series with high-embedded dimension is very common in the nature. Therefore it is useful to study the forecasting methods of high-embedded dimension. The paper proposes a new method, which improves the character of full Lyapunov exponential spectrum in a restructure space with high dimensions. In the mean time, an artificial neural networks model based on determinate mutation evolutionary programming (DMEP) learning algorithm be presented for chaotic runoff series forecasting.

DMEP introduces chaos mapping into the mutation operation of traditional evolutionary programming, which aim to increase its convergence rate and results' precision. The results show that the method plays an important role to improve the precision of forecasting of runoff series with higher embedded dimensions.

REFERENCES

[1] M.N Islam, B.Sivakumar. Characterization and prediction of runoff dynamics: a nonlinear dynamical view. *Advances in Water Resources.* (25), 2002:179-190

[2] Wang Wenjun, Ye Min, Chen Xianwei. The quantitative analysis of chaotic character for runoff time series of Yangtze River. *Advances in Water Science.* 5(2),1994:87-94

[3] Lin Shuzhen, Liu Changling, You Baoshan. The chaos dynamics research of daily runoff time series. *Taiwan Hydraulic.* 44(2),1996:13-23

[4] Jiang Chuanwen, Quan xianzhang, Zhang Yongchuan. A Research on the chaos dynamic model of runoff. *Journal of Hydrodynamics.* Ver B 12(2): 2000, 85-91

[5] Tsung-yi Pan, Ru-yih Wang. State space neural networks for short term rainfall-runoff forecasting. *Journal of hydrology*,297,pp34-50,2004

[6] Coulibaly P, Anetil F, Bobee B. Daily reservoir inflow forecasting using artificial neural networks with stopped training approach. *Journal of hydrology*, 230,pp244-257,2000

[7] Jiang Chuanwen, Hou ZhiJian, Zhang Yongchuan. One high embedded dimensions chaotic forecasting method based on degree of incidence. *Systems Engineering and Electronics.* vol.24, no.12 : 65-103 , Dec. 2002

[8] Hou Yuexian. Reconstructing high dimension phase space an improved approach to chaotic time series forecasting. *Journal of Tianjin University.* 32(5): 1999, 594-59

[9] Jiang Chuanwen, Li Tao. Forecasting method study on chaotic load series with high embedded dimension. *Energy Conversion and Management*, 46(5), 2005, 667-676

[10] Takens. F. Detecting strange attractors in turbulence, in: Dynamical systems and turbulence, Warwick 1980, *Lecture Notes in Mathematics*, No.898, edit by D.A.Rand and L.-S.Yong, springer-verlag, Berlin, 1981: 366-381

[11] Jiang Chuanwen, Etorre Bompard. A hybrid method of chaotic particle swarm optimization and linear interior for reactive power optimization. *Mathematics and Computers in Simulation*, 68(1), 2005, 57-65

[12] Kohata N, Sato M, Yamaguchi T, Baba T, Hashimoto H. Evolutionary computation for intelligent agents based on chaotic retrieval and soft DNA. *Lecture Notes In Artificial Intelligence.* 1585: 251-259 1999

[13] Jiang Chuanwen, Wang Chengmin. Improved evolutionary programming with dynamic mutation and metropolis criteria for multi-objective reactive power optimization. *IEE Proceedings-Generation Transmission and Distribution*, 152 (2): 291-294 MAR 2005

[14] Jiang Chuanwen, Etorre Bompard. A self-adaptive chaotic particle swarm algorithm for short term hydroelectric system scheduling in deregulated environment. *Energy Conversion and Management.* 46(17), 2689-2696, 2005

[15] Wolf A. Determining Lyapunov exponents from a time series, *Physica D.*16, 1985:285-317

RESERVOIR SYSTEMS OPERATION MODEL USING SIMULATION AND NEURAL NETWORK

Jianxia Chang [1,2] Yimin Wang [1] Qiang Huang [1]
1 Xi'an University of Technology, 2 Xi'an University of Architecture and Technology, *Shaan xi, Xi ' an , 710048*

Abstract: For multi-reservoir operating rules, a simulation-based neural network model is developed in this study. In the suggested model, multi-reservoir operating rules are derived using a neural network from the results of simulation. The training of the neural network is done using a supervised learning approach with the back propagation algorithm. The Yellow River upstream multi-reservoir system is used for this study. This paper presents the usefulness of the neural network in deriving general operating policies for a multi-reservoir system.

Key words: reservoir operating rules, simulation model, neural network, the Yellow River

1. LITERATURE REVIEW

Simulation models for reservoir operation studies generally permit detailed and realistic representation of the complex characteristics of a reservoir system. The concepts are easier to understand and communicate than other modeling concepts. The first publications documenting research in developing reservoir system simulation were produced by the Harvard Water Porgram (Maass et al. 1962). Examples of current state of the art include HEC-3 and HEC-5 models developed by the Hydrologic Engineering Center and described by Feldman(1981).

Application of artificial neural networks in water resources system analysis is fast growing. An artificial neural network is a model inspired by the structure of the brain that is well suited for complicated tasks. Ranjithan et al. (1993) used neural networks as screening models for a groundwater reclamation problem. Karunanithi et al. (1994) used neural networks for flow predictions. Zhang & Govindaraju (2000) used a modular neural network for a watershed runoff model. Different modules within the network were trained to learn subsets of the input space in an expert fashion. Chandramouli & Raman (2001) developed a multi-reservoir operation model using dynamic programming and a neural network. They used a three state variable dynamic programming algorithm in a constrained manner. In that dynamic programming model the three releases from the reservoirs considered were the decision variables.

In this study, a backpropagation neural network model is trained to derive reservoirs operation rules. To train the neural network, exemplars are required and obtained through a simulation model.

2. SYSTEM CONSIDERED

The system considered for the case study is the Yellow River upstream project in China. This is a multipurpose, multireservoir project. Operation of this system is monitored by the Yellow River Conservancy Commission. The system consists of three reservoirs, Long yangxia reservoir, Li jiaxia reservoir and Liu jiaxia reservoir, as given in Table 1. Among these reservoirs, Longyangxia is a yearly regulation reservoir, Li jiaxia is runoff reservoir, and Liu jiaxia is a annual regulation reservoir. The objectives for reservoir operation of this system include municipal, industrial, irrigation water supply, power generation and ecological purposes.

Table 1. Reservoir system characteristics

Reservoir	Inflow (m^3/s year)	Total Storage (10^9m^3)	Normal Reservoir Level(m)	Flood Control Level(m)	Power Plant Capacity (10^3kW)
Longyangxia	650	24.7	2600	2594	1280
Li jiaxia	664	1.65	2180		2000
Liujiaxia	877	5.7	1735	1726	1160

3. SIMULATION MODEL

The simulation model of a reservoir system is based on water balance of reservoirs. Figure. 1 is a schematic representation of a reservoir system. For reservoir i in period t, the water balance can be written as:

$$V_{i,t} = V_{i,t-1} + I_{i,t} - P_{i,t} - W_{i,t} - G_{i,t} - EV_{i,t} + \sum_{k=1}^{m} A_{i,k} D_{k,t} \tag{1}$$

where $V_{i,t}$ - the storage level of reservoir i at the end of period t, $I_{i,t}$ - random inflow into reservoir i during period t, $P_{i,t}$ - water release through power plant from reservoir i during period t, $W_{i,t}$ - water release for water supply from reservoir i during period t, $G_{i,t}$ - release to maintain the maximum allowable storage in reservoir i during period t, $EV_{i,t}$ - evaporation from reservoir i during period t, $D_{i,t}$ - downstream flow from reservoir i during period t, $A_{i,k}$ =1 if reservoir k releases flows into reservoir i, and 0 otherwise, m - number of reservoirs in the system.

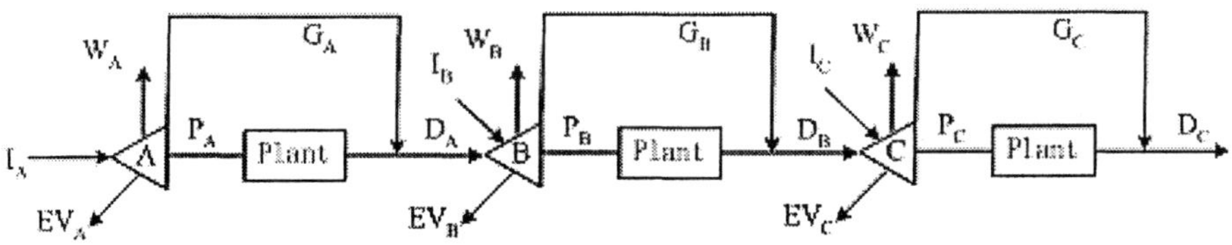

Figure 1. Schematic representation of a reservoir system

On the basis of equation (1), operation statuses can be simulated for each reservoir. In the case study, A denotes reservoir Long yangxia, B denotes reservoir Li jiaxia, and C denotes reservoir Liu jiaxia.

3.1 Simulation Constraints

The model constraints includes:

(1) water balance between reservoirs

Some factors such as the time of flow transmitting, water diversion, water loss, returning water, and inflow between up reservoir and down reservoir are considered in the water balance equation.

$$Q_{down,t} = Q_{up,t-1} \times \frac{t}{T} + Q_{up,t} \times \frac{(T-t)}{T} + q_{add,t} + q_{return,t} - q_{divert,t} - q_{loss,t} \tag{2}$$

Where $Q_{down,t}$-average discharge of period t at downstream reservoir(m^3/s); $Q_{up,t}$, $Q_{up,t-1}$ -average discharge of period t and t-1 at upstream reservoir(m^3/s); t- time of water transmission from upstream to downstream reservoir(day); T- number of days in the month(day); $q_{add,t}$, $q_{return,t}$, $q_{divert,t}$, $q_{loss,t}$-average inflow, return, divert, and water loss between upstream and downstream reservoir (m^3/s).

(2) reservoir water balance

$$V(m,t+1) = V(m,t) + (QRu(m,t) - QRc(m,t)) \times \Delta T(t) - LW(m,t) \tag{3}$$

Where m-reservoir number, m=1 denote Longy angxia, m=2 denote Li jiaxia, m=3 denote Liu jiaxia; $V(m,t+1)$, $V(m,t)$- the reservoir storage of number m at the end and begin of period t; $QRu(m,t)$, $QRc(m,t)$, $LW(m,t)$- the inflow, outflow and water loss of number m reservoir during the period t.

(3) other constraints

$$V\min(m,t) \leq V(m,t) \leq V\max(m,t) \tag{4}$$

$$q\min(m,t) \leq QRc(m,t) \leq q\max(m,t) \tag{5}$$

$$N\min(m,t) \leq N(m,t) \leq N\max(m,t) \tag{6}$$

Where $N(m,t)$- the reservoir output of number m during period t; $Vmin(m,t)$, $Vmax(m,t)$- the minimum and maximum reservoir storage values in time t; $qmin(m,t)$, $qmax(m,t)$- the minimum and maximum reservoir discharge in time t; $Nmin(m,t)$, $Nmax(m,t)$- the minimum and maximum output values in time t.

(4) ice-jam prevention constraint

Ice prevention requires certain discharge from Liujiaxia reservoir, and the discharge inversion is used in computation, i.e. the flow requirement is computed from Lanzhou to Liujiaxia.

3.2 Simulation Principle

The principle of simulation model operation is as follows:

1. The priority order for water supply is, ecological, municipal and industrial, agricultural, and power generation requirement.
2. The reservoir storage must satisfy the requirement of flood control and ice-jam prevention. Ice-jam occurred in Lanzhouin in the period of November till next March, thus the discharge from Liujiaxia reservoir must comply with the flood control limitation in the November till next March.
3. The water demand from Liujiaxia is satisfied by the joint operation of Longyangxia and Liujiaxia reservoir.
4. In terms of historical data statistics, the water transmission period in channel is considered.

During the simulation procedure, extensive knowledge and experiences of operators are required to set constraint limits, such as the ice-jam control flow and ecological base flow etc. while using the simulation model, the operator first interactively determines the constraint limits, and then alternative for reservoir operation can be acquired automatically.

3.3 Simulation Results

For the considered system, 49 years of flow records from 1951 to 1999 are available, and computation time period is month. The operation results for typical dry year 1970-1971 are shown in Table 2.

Table 2. Operation Results for typical dry year

month	Long yangxia				Liu jiaxia			
	Inflow (m^3/s)	Release Flow (m^3/s)	Reservoir Level (m)	Power Output (10^4 kW)	Inflow (m^3/s)	Release Flow (m^3/s)	Reservoir Level (m)	Power Output (10^4kW)
7	727	526	2588.7	59.1	715	1065	32.0	90.6
8	1180	513	2593.6	59.0	953	863	34.3	71.5
9	569	503	2594.1	59.0	944	731	40.0	62.9
10	614	504	2594.8	59.4	798	652	43.8	58.3
11	349	502	2593.7	59.0	630	646	43.4	58.2
12	177	511	2591.4	59.4	574	650	41.4	58.3
1	139	517	2588.5	59.0	588	660	39.5	58.4
2	135	532	2585.5	59.4	611	669	38.0	58.4
3	201	545	2582.8	59.5	603	446	42.1	39.6
4	336	545	2581.2	58.5	584	656	40.2	58.3
5	487	554	2580.7	58.9	632	661	39.5	58.2
6	639	558	2581.3	59.4	623	1252	22.9	101.6

4. NEURAL NETWORK FOR CONSIDERED SYSTEM

4.1 Neural Networks (NN)

NN performs two major functions, learning and recall. Learning is the process of adapting the connection weights or structure in an NN to produce the desired output in response to a stimulus presented to the input buffer. Recall is the process of accepting an input stimulus and producing an output response in accordance with the network weight structure. The back-propagation learning algorithm (BPL) is among the well-known algorithms used to train a given neural network. This learning algorithm is applied to multilayer feed-forward network consisting of processing neurons with differentiable activation functions. For a given input–output pair (x_k, d_k), the BPL performs two phases of data flow. First, the input pattern x_k is propagated from the input layer to the output layer and, as a result of this forward flow of data, it produces the actual output y_k. The error signals, resulting from the difference between the target output d_k and the actual output y_k, are then back-propagated from the output layer to the previous layers to update their weights.

The procedure for training the network is embodied in the following steps:

1. Apply an input vector to the network and calculate the corresponding output values;
2. Compare the outputs from the model with the target outputs and determine a measure of the errors;
3. Determine to increase or decrease the weights or find in which direction to change each weight in order to reduce the error;
4. Determine the amount by which to change each weight;
5. Apply the corrections to the weights;
6. Repeat items 1 to 5 with all the training vectors until the error for all vectors in the training set is reduced to an acceptable value.

In order to obtain the operating policy of the Yellow River upstream reservoirs system, a neural network is designed, which has three layers. The input and output patterns are derived from simulation results. The neural network considered has eight input nodes and three output nodes. Figure. 2 shows the proposed neural network. Release from reservoirs Long yangxia, Li jiaxia and Liu jiaxia during time period t are the outputs from the neural network. During time period t, initial storage of reservoir Long yangxia, inflow into reservoir Long yangxia, demand from reservoir Long yangxia, inflow into reservoir Li jiaxia, demand from reservoir Li jiaxia, initial storage of reservoir Liu jiaxia, inflow into reservoir Liu jiaxia, demand from reservoir Liu jiaxia are input patterns. The input patterns are decided by considering the variables that are influencing the reservoirs release. These dates are given to the neural network module for training. The neural network is trained with these patterns using back-propagation algorithm to derive the operating rules.

4.2 Measure of Errors

Square error (MSE) and relative error (MRE) are used for deciding the best network. MSE and MRE are defined as follows:

$$MSE = \frac{1}{2}\sum_{q}\sum_{j=1}^{p}(y'_j - y_j)^2 \tag{7}$$

$$MRE = \frac{1}{pq}\sum_{q}\sum_{j=1}^{p}\left|\frac{y'_j - y_j}{y'_j}\right| \times 100 \tag{8}$$

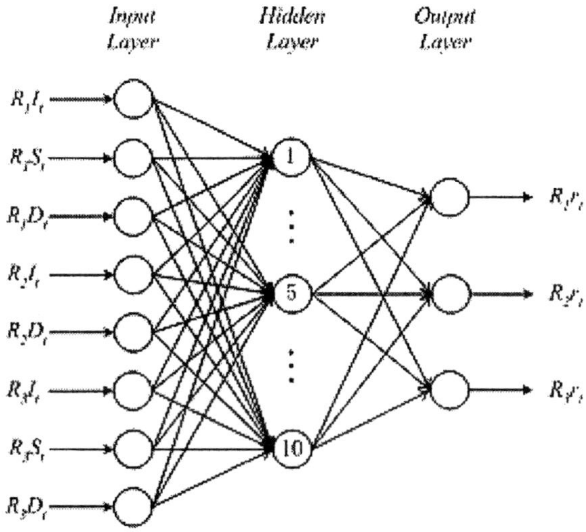

Figure 2. Neural network model for considered system

where p-number of patterns used for training; q-number of nodes in the output layer; y_j'-target output pattern value; and y_j-output from neural network model. The MSE value indicates the goodness of fit at high output values and MRE value indicate the goodness of fit for moderate output values.

4.3 Backpropagation Network Performance

The two strategies adopted for testing the applicability of the neural network in the present work are (1) to test the capability of the neural network to correctly predict the output for the given input set originally used to train the network (accuracy performance); and (2) to test the capability of the neural network to correctly predict the output for the given input sets that were not in the training set (generalization performance).

The network architecture, learning rate η, and momentum factor α values were adjusted to speed up the convergence. In this study, only one hidden layer was used in all the cases. The optimal architecture considered has 10 neurons in the hidden layer. The trial for this study is started with 2 neurons in the hidden layer and the network is studied up to a model with 14 neurons in the hidden layer. The architecture with 9 nodes in the hidden layer was faster in computation, but the convergence was very slow. The architecture with 11 nodes in the hidden layer was converging equally well as with 10 nodes in the hidden layer but relatively slower than that. So the architecture with 10 nodes in the hidden layer was selected. Learning rate η, which is the step size of the steepest gradient descent algorithm, is taken as 0.7. If it is too high, the search may miss a valley in the error surface. On the other hand, if it is too small, the convergence will be very slow. The α value for this study is kept at 0.5. Since sigmoidal function is used in the output layer, the output value form the network lies between 0 and 1. Hence normalization of the data is essential. Input patterns are normalized based on MSE and MRE values for the given data set. The interconnecting weights are initialized by random numbers between -1 and 1. The weights are re-adjusted while training using the back propagation algorithm for the supplied patterns.

5. CONCLUSION

An important notion tested in this research was that artificial NN have a potential to mimic, to a large extent, the high level information processing performed by human operators. This paper presents the usefulness of the neural network in deriving operating policies for a multireservoir system. From simulation results, to derive general operating policies, NN can be used. Generating the examples requires the conventional simulation model, and the training process requires considerable time. The method suggested is a baseline and is flexible to adopt in many problems. These results indicate the ability of the NN to capture knowledge from more complex system.

REFERENCE

[1] Simonovic S. P.: Reservoir systems analysis: Closing gap between theory and practice. Journal of Water Resources Planning and Management, Vol. 118. (1992) 262-280

[2] Yeh W W-G.:Reservoir management and operations models: a state-of-the-art review. Journal of water Resources Research, Vol. 21. (1985) 1797–1818

[3] Wurbs R A.: Reservoir-system simulation and optimization models. Journal of Water Resources Planning and Management, Vol.119. (1993) 455-472

[4] HEC-5 simulation of flood control and conservation systems user's manual. (1982), U.S. Army Corps of Engineers, Hydrologic Engineering Center, Davis, Calif.

[5] Ranjithan, S., Eheart, J. W., and Grarrett, J. H.:Neural network based screening for groundwater reclamation uncertainty. Journal of Water Resource Research, Vol.29. (1993)563-574

[6] Karunanithi, N., Grenney, W. J., Whitley, D., and Bovee, K.:Neural network for river flow prediction. J. Comp. in Cic. Engrg., ASCE, VOL.8. (1994) 201-220

[7] Zhang, B.,Govindaraju, R.S. : Prediction of watershed runoff using Bayesian concepts and modular neural networks, Journal of Water Resources Research, Vol. 36. (2000) 753–762

[8] Chandramouli, V. & Raman, H.: Multi reservoir modeling with dynamic programming and neural network. Journal of Water Resources Planning and Management, Vol.127. (2001) 89–98

ROTATING MACHINERY FAULT DIAGNOSIS BASED ON WAVELET FUZZY NEURAL NETWORK

Bin Peng[1] Zhenquan Liu[2]

1.College of Mechanical-Electronic Engineering, Lanzhou University of Technology, Lanzhou 730050, China;

2.College of Petrochemical Technology Lanzhou University of Technology, Lanzhou 730050, China

Abstract: According to complicated fault characteristic of rotating machinery, its fault diagnosis based on wavelet fuzzy neural network (WFNN) which combines wavelet packet analysis and fuzzy neural network is put forward. By using it, the fuzzy fault diagnosis of rotating machinery is realized. All the arithmetic process of WFNN is realized through the computer. The results of simulation and test indicate that this method has obvious advantage for dealing with multi-coupled fault situation, the diagnosis method is simple, quick and has high correctness of fault diagnoses, proving that the diagnosis method is effective and providing a theoretical basis and new way for the fault diagnosis of rotating machinery.

Key words: Wavelet packet analysis, Fuzzy neural network, Rotating machinery, Fault diagnoses

Modern rotating machines are apt to appear faults because of their complexity and high speed. The complexity hampers the operator's ability to diagnose and eliminate equipment failures before their occurrence, so many systems are furnished with the intellectual monitoring system, fault diagnosis are the main embodiment of intellectual monitoring system, so the level of diagnose technology influences the function of intellectual monitoring system, it also has important meanings to keep normal running, reduce the product cost, raise product efficiency and ensure product safety for whole system.

The fault diagnosis includes two steps: characteristic signal extraction and diagnose task. The first step is to draw the fault sign, the sign abstraction can adopt many kinds of techniques; the second step is really diagnose task which includes the type and severity of fault. Only the two steps have been confirmed, it could obtain overall fault description of rotating machinery. At present people carry on research just in a certain aspect and seldom combine the two sides to synthetically analyse, the text puts forward a new fault diagnoses method based on WFNN, all algorithms of WFNN are realized through the computer, WFNN can not only discern the correct type of fault but also get the serious level and development trend of fault[1].

1. FAULT DIAGNOSIS OF ROTATING MACHINERY

When rotating machinery appears fault, its vibration signal correspondingly changes, fault characteristics and types of vibration are reflected by these changed characteristic frequency band. The signal analyses is the main way as understanding equipment operation state and

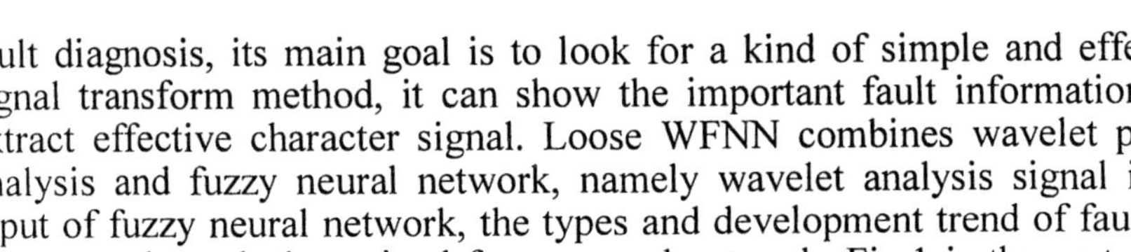

Figure1. The systematic diagram of rotating machinery fault diagnosis

fault diagnosis, its main goal is to look for a kind of simple and effective signal transform method, it can show the important fault information and extract effective character signal. Loose WFNN combines wavelet packet analysis and fuzzy neural network, namely wavelet analysis signal is the input of fuzzy neural network, the types and development trend of fault can be gotten through the trained fuzzy neural network, Fig.1 is the systematic diagram of rotating machinery fault diagnosis[2][3].

2. WAVELET PACKET TRANSFORM

Up to now, many kinds of signal transform have been applied to fault diagnose. Spectral analysis is the ripest method to draw signal characteristic of vibration, but FFT analyses have serious defects, firstly time information is lost while transforming from the time domain to spectral domain, FFT sets up on the basis of the steady signal, only suits to analyse steady signal. Secondly FFT is a kind of linearly method in essence, when the signal shows the strong nonlinearity, FFT can't deal with it, in addition anti-interference ability of FFT is relatively bad. Rotating machinery will be affected by various kinds of factors while running, it includes the non-steady composition in the output signals, especially when rotating machinery appears fault, its dynamics characteristic usually demonstrates complexity and non-linear, vibration signal also demonstrates nonstationarity, so it is very important to analyse this part signal. In order to overcome shortcoming of FFT, wavelet technology is put forward to deal with vibration signal and have made gratifying progress. The wavelet transform has the good characteristic in part, can realize the signal separation and don't lose any information. The wavelet transform can be applied to not only the steady signal but also the non-steady signal, so it is more suitable for vibration characteristic of signal than FFT. The article adopts wavelet packet to draw

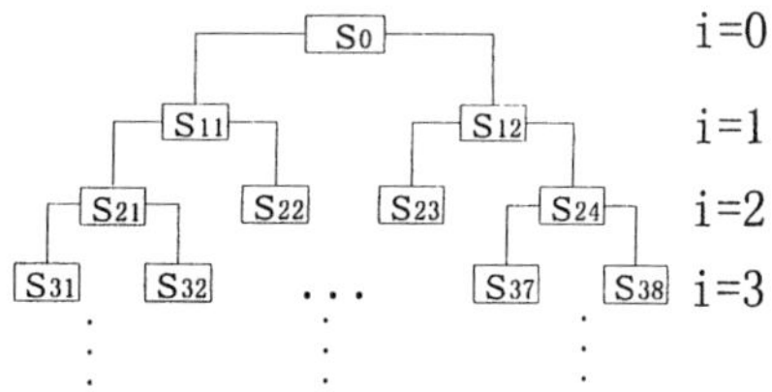

Figure2. The wavelet packet transform of signal

fault characteristic, wavelet packet is extension of wavelet, the defect of "a low resolving power of high frequency" is solved by wavelet packet transform, signal is divided into more careful frequency, different frequency weight has the corresponding node, those weights have different frequency characteristic, the relation of resolving coefficient is different too, the coefficient which relates to trouble information is kept among every node, interferential data are removed, it can reduce uproar, greatly compress the data, benefit real-time processing. Wavelet packet transform of signal is realized through Quadrature Mirror Filter, $s_0(t)$ is input signal, the transform expression is:

$$\begin{cases} s_{2m}(t) = \sqrt{2}\sum_{n\in z} h(n)s_m(2t-n) \\ s_{2m+1}(t) = \sqrt{2}\sum_{n\in z} g(n)s_m(2t-n) \end{cases} \quad t \in R$$

$h(n)$、$g(n)$ express lowpass and band-pass filter, function $\{s_m(t)\}\ m \in Z^+$ is orthogonal wavelet packet. Wavelet packet transform is the fine time-frequency analysis of signal, it is the all frequency band decomposition result of primitive signal in all kinds of yardstick, it can effectively obtain time-frequency characteristic. Multistage decomposition signal about the original subset s can get through wavelet packet transform. It can realize the signal separation at different frequently band, it composes every frequency band of the resolved vibration signal, but these frequency bands are not all useful to discern the fault, it must filtrate characteristic frequency band, usually 0.5f (f expresses work frequently), f and multiple of f have closer relation with fault, so these characteristic frequency bands are chosen as the characteristic frequency band. The energy value forms a vector in every frequency band, this vector has different value for different fault, therefore it can draw relevant fault information, offer a effective way for the fault diagnosis. Fig. 2 is the wavelet packet transform of the signal[4][5].

3. FUZZY NEURAL NETWORK

3.1 The Structure of Fuzzy Neural Network

The characteristic of extraction signal in wavelet packet is a vector which makes up of a lot of characteristic elements, the corresponding relation between it and fault is a kind of complicated nonlinearity mapping transformation, it is difficult to realize through the routine categorised method, the artificial neural network has unmatched conditions in this aspect,

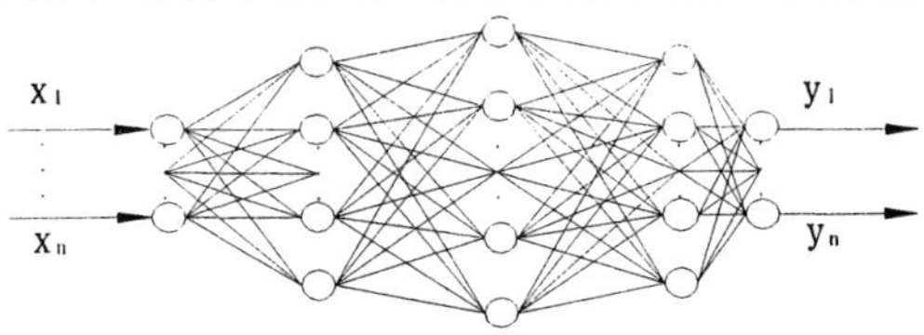

Figure 3. The structure of fuzzy BP neural network

it is a kind of ideal classification device. The second step of the fault diagnosis is a continuous mapping transformation course from fault sign vector U to the fault reason vector V, the element of vector V fetches continuous value between credibility area [0,1]. Because some faults or signs are fuzzy in rotating machinery, it is difficult to go on strict demarcation and can't use two value logic to describe and judge them briefly, at the same time the relation between some faults and signs is fuzzy, it is difficult to describe explicitly, so it can use the fuzzy law to realize continuous course of mapping transformation from sign vector U to fault vector V. Fuzzy neural network which combines fuzzy logic system and neural network not only has the advantage of fuzzy message but also has the characteristic of self-organize and self-study of neural network. The fuzzy neural network can get the realistic fuzzy rule through studying and overcome the subjectivity of the fuzzy logic system in a certain extent, it will more suitable for the fault diagnosis of rotating machinery. The article uses a kind of serial structure fuzzy BP neural network, this network has five layers structure in Fig. 3. The first layer is input floor, input signal decides nodes of input layer, the main sign value can be confirmed according to the relation of shown signs and common fault of rotating machinery. The input value $x_1, x_2 ... x_n$ don't change when reach the next layer in Fig.3. The second layer is to value input layer, its function is fuzzy value. The third layer is imply floor, its node is confirmed according to the actual studying conditions in the network, imply layers apply sigmoid function, this layer node is used to realize mapping transformation from input variable fuzzy value to output variable fuzzy value, The fourth layer is output floor, every node represents one fault of rotating machinery, each fuzzy value represents fault degree, the fifth layer is weighting exported layer, it can realize clear output. It is apt to know that above five layers fuzzy neural network can realize mapping transformation from input to output, it can realize fault diagnosis for the input vector characteristic through the trained neural network.

3.2 Membership Degree Function

The main difference between fuzzy BP neural network and traditional BP neural network lies in its input and output expressing fuzzy membership degree, the network can deal with the digital input form and the semanteme input form through the proper membership degree function, its output is not a single categorised result but all kinds of membership degree. The key of fuzzy BP neural network is to ensure membership degree function, the distributed amplitude of every frequency is most sensitive to reflect the machine working state, so the input adopts the distributed amplitude of every frequency band in vibration frequency spectrum. For the semanteme form with value, the membership function can be expressed as trapezoid function, for the semanteme form with no value, the membership function can be expressed as:
("H" represents "very obvious", "M" represents "obvious", "L" represents "not obvious") $H = \{0.05/L; 0.5/M; 0.95/H\}$;
$M = \{0.5/L; 0.95/M; 0.50/H\}$; $L = \{0.95/L; 0.50/M; 0.05/H\}$; if the input character value is numerical the membership function can be expressed as π function, gauss function, in the practice project, different parts and points of machine have different vibration frequency spectrum, considering adaptability of network, membership degree function adopts the ratio of each frequency band amplitude in characteristic frequency band and total of amplitude, namely:

$$\mu(x_i) = \frac{x_i}{\sum_{j=1}^{n} x_j} \qquad i = 1,2,\cdots,\ n$$

in formula, x_i, x_j represents spectral maximum of characteristic frequency band of i and j, n is the number of characteristic frequency band.

3.3 Fuzzy Neural Network Algorithm

Traditional BP algorithm is a kind of simple steepest descent static behavior and seeking the excellent algorithm in fact, it will often make the learning process shake, convergence slowly. The first several steps are dropping very fast for the gradient algorithm, but with closing to optimum value, the gradient tends zero, it causes goal function drop slowly, but Newton rule can produce an ideal search direction near optimum value. In order to accelerate the speed of convergence of BP network, the article adopts Levenberg-Marquart (L-M) algorithm, L-M algorithm is the combination of gradient descent method and Newton method, its advantage lies in having both some characteristic of Newton method and overall characteristics of gradient method, it is convergence very fast when the weights of the network is small. Generally L-M method can obtain better result for most rotating machinery questions. Fault factor and fault exist fuzzy, so it is difficult to confirm the severity of the fault using accurate describe method, fuzzy discern offers the powerful means for solving this problem [6][7].

4. APPLICATIONS

In order to validate the effect of WFNN in fault diagnosis, the article compares WFNN and traditional BP neural network with a certain rotating machinery.

The vibration signal which gets from the sensor on the rotor laboratory system regards as the sample signal, signal is separated in every characteristic frequency band through wavelet packet transform, it is used to draw fault signal characteristic, the whole frequency band is divided into nine sections: $0.01 \to 0.39f, 0.4 \to 0.49f, 0.5f, 0.51 \to 0.99f, f, 2f, 3 \to 5f, oddf, > 5f$. The article uses the vibration signal energy of nine frequency bands as diagnosing vector, while diagnosing, the output of network expressed the close degree of inputs vector and standard, namely it is the membership degree of various kinds of fault. The network input node is fault signs 9, the fuzzy value layer node is 27, output node is fault modes 5, it can get the third layer node (imply layer) through trained and synthetically compared, latent node h is 10 in the article. Fuzzy BP neural network is trained according to L-M algorithm, the stop error is 0.0001. The test adopts the common fault of the rotating machinery: Oil-film Whirl fault, initial imbalance, rotor rub-impact, rotor bend, rotor crack, rotor misalignment and bearing house's looseness etc., 5 kinds of fault modes are summarized from a lot of fault cases, each kind of fault mode has been trained through fuzzy BP neural network, also trained through BP neural network. Through contrast, it proves that fault diagnosis ability of fuzzy neural network is higher than general BP

Table 1. Fault input of rotating machinery

Measure point	The input character of fuzzy neural network								
	0.01 - 0.39f	0.40 - 0.49f	0.50f	0.51 - 0.99f	1f	2f	3 - 5f	odd f	>5f
1	0. 000	0. 000	0. 345	0. 000	0. 582	0.074	0. 000	0. 000	0. 000
2	0. 000	0. 000	0. 079	0. 079	0. 596	0. 180	0. 067	0. 000	0. 000
3	0. 000	0. 061	0. 136	0. 180	0. 236	0. 149	0. 175	0. 000	0. 063

Table 2. The diagnosis result of WFNN

Measure point	F_1	F_2	F_3	F_4	F_5
1	0.887	0.028	0.136	0.256	0.975
2	0.930	0.261	0.001	0.962	0.184
3	0.013	0.968	0.066	0.114	0.212

Table 3. The fault diagnosis result of BP neural network

Measure point	F_1	F_2	F_3	F_4	F_5
1	0.101	0.002	0.003	0.005	0.879
2	0.062	0.000	0.028	0.163	0.034
3	0.000	0.805	0.025	0.000	0.014

F1-F5 represent: Imbalance, Rub-impact, Rotor crack, Misalignment, Oil-film Whirl fault

neural network. Table 1 is the input fault of the rotating machinery, measure point 1 is very obvious imbalance fault and oil-film Whirl fault, measure point 2 is very obvious imbalance fault and misalignment fault, measure point 3 is very obvious rotor rub-impact fault, Table 2 is the diagnosis result of fuzzy neural network, it is very apt to find out that the fault diagnosis result is correct, can also get the developing direction of fault from the result. Table 3 is the fault diagnosis result of BP neural network, it can find out that only the third group fault diagnosis result of BP neural network is right, it also has mistake diagnosis (imbalance fault and misalignment fault) in the measure point 2. Its main reason is that BP network usually adopts the single fault sample to train, therefore it can not clearly or wrongly classify for many faults, but fuzzy BP neural network avoids this wrong through input and output membership degree to classify fault, the advantage is being more outstanding especially for dealing with multi-coupled faults.

5. CONCLUSION

The article puts forward a kind of new fault diagnosis method based on wavelet fuzzy neural network which combines wavelet packet analyse, fuzzy theory and neural network. It uses wavelet packet transform to draw the rotating machinery characteristic signal and offers the input characteristic of fuzzy neural network, it can get fault type and severe level according to the input characteristic through the trained fuzzy neural network, at the same time it also can get the developing direction of the output fault. The result of simulation proves that wavelet fuzzy neural network which integrates the merit of wavelet packet, fuzzy theory and neural network has very strong pattern-recognition and judgement as fault diagnosis method, it is a kind of extremely potential method in fault diagnosis of rotating machinery system.

REFERENCES

[1] Xu Feiyun, Jia Minping, Zhong Binglin, Huang Ren. Study on Fuzzy Neural Network for Fault Diagnosis of Rotating Machinery [J]. Journal of Vibration Engineering, 1996, 3(9), 21~219.

[2] Zhang Ji-xian, Zhong Qiu-hai, Dai Ya-ping. Fault Diagnosis of Rotating Machinery Using RBF and Fuzzy Neural Network [J]. Journal of System Simulation, 2004, 16(3), 560~563.

[3] HOU Xin-guo, XIA Li, WU Zheng-guo, ZHAO Yong-ling. Fault Diagnosis Method for Induction Motor Based on Wavelet Transformation and Neural Network [J]. Journal of Data Acquisition& Processing, 2004, 19(1), 32~36

[4] Hou Xiaomei, Mao Zongyuan. The Application of Artificial Neural Network on Turbogenerators' Fault Diagnosis[J]. Journal of South China University of Technology (Natural Science), 1999, 27(8), 47~49

[5] Zhao Hong, Zhou Rui xiang, Lin Tingqi. Neural Network Supervised Control Based on Levenberg—Marquardt Algorithm [J].JOURNAL OF XI AN JIAO TONG UNIVERSITY. 2002, 36 (5), 523~527.

[6] Zhou Shouqin, Xie Youbai. Research on Machine Fault Diagnosis Based on Fuzzy Neural Networks [J]. Turbine Technology, 1999, 44 (4), 216~202.

[7] Dong Tong. Study of Fuzzy Neural Network for Fault Diagnosis of turbine [J]. Techniques of Automation and Applications, 2001, 314~16.

A NOVEL DYNAMIC KNOWLEDGE EXTRACTION METHOD IN COOPERATIVE MULTIPLE ROBOT SYSTEM USING ROUGH SET

Hua Xu and Peifa Jia
State Key Laboratory of Intelligent Technology and Systems, Tsinghua University, Beijing, 100084, P. R. China

Abstract: Dynamic knowledge extraction is one of the critical problems in dynamic systems especially in cooperative multiple robot systems (CMRS).The knowledge may be fuzzy, because the information from dynamic environments is incomplete and uncertain. So it is difficult for traditional methods to extract dynamic knowledge effectively. According to the dynamic knowledge extraction requirements in CMRS, this paper proposes a novel dynamic knowledge extraction method in CMRS on the base of KANG's rough set based rules generation method. It has been demonstrated effective in our CMRS.

Key words: Rough sets, Fuzzy sets, Robotics, Knowledge extraction

1. INTRODUCTION

In cooperative multiple robot systems (CMRS), dynamic knowledge extraction is one of the critical problems in dispatching robots for cooperation requirements. The scheduling is conducted by the decision making modules distributed in every robot. According to the environment information, system states and task aims, the decision making module dispatches robots periodically and effectively. However, under different dynamic environments, the knowledge about the environments and tasks is various. At the instance of decision making, dynamic production rules generation is required for achieving the dynamic knowledge. That is to say, dynamic knowledge needs to be extracted. Then the extracted dynamic knowledge can be used in the decision making module and the system schedule can be conducted. On the other hand, the knowledge of dynamic environments may be incomplete or uncertain. So the knowledge may be fuzzy and the corresponding inference may be fuzzy reasoning. Above all, it needs a new method to extract dynamic knowledge in CMRS.

Compared with existing methods [6-9], the rough set (RS) theory [1, 2] has been proved to be a useful mathematical tool for the analysis of vague description of objects. In order to analyze vague information and get optimal fuzzy production rules, KANG, etc al [3], propose a rules generation method on the base of fuzzy sets (FS) [4,5] and RS [1,2].

This paper proposes a dynamic knowledge extraction method on the base of KANG's RS method. KANG's rules generation method [3] is used to generate dynamic knowledge of CMRS from the practical decision data. The forms of the extracted dynamic knowledge are certain production rules or fuzzy ones

This paper is organized as the following. In section 2, the preliminary notions are quickly reviewed. Section 3 illustrates the decision making subsystem in our CMRS. Then in section 4, the rules generation of the decision making system is discussed. Finally, the conclusion and future work is summarized in section 5.

2. PRELIMINARY NOTIONS OF FS AND RS

2.1 FS

In set theory [4], crisp sets are characterized by a Boolean membership function: an element x of the universe of discourse U (say, an interval of real numbers) is either a member of the set or it is not. FS [4], [5] are characterized by a continuous membership function $\mu(x)$ which maps x to a "*membership degree*" taking values in the interval [0, 1].

Definition 2.1: Let $\boldsymbol{U}$ be a set called universe and let $\boldsymbol{A}$ be a fuzzy subset of $\boldsymbol{U}$. For any member ($\boldsymbol{X}$) of $\boldsymbol{U}$, there exists a mapping function: $\boldsymbol{X} \rightarrow \mu_A(\boldsymbol{X})$, where $\boldsymbol{X} \in \boldsymbol{U}$ and $\mu_A(\boldsymbol{X}) \in [0, 1]$. $\mu_A(\boldsymbol{X})$ is called the member function of A and is continuous on the interval [0, 1]. □

Definition 2.2: For the fuzzy subset $\boldsymbol{A}$, if $\mu_A(\boldsymbol{X}) \in \{0, 1\}$, then the subset is a common subset. □

Definition 2.3: Let ***F(U)*** be the set of all the fuzzy subsets of ***U*** and let ***P(U)*** be the set of all the subsets of ***U***. They satisfies the following proposition: ***F(U)*** $\supset$***P(U)***. □

Definition 2.4: If ***A***$\subseteq$***F(U)***, then ***A*** is a proper fuzzy set of ***U*** and there exists a member x_0 which satisfies $x_0 \in A$ and $\mu_A(x_0) \subseteq \{0,1\}$. □

Definition 2.5: If the number of fuzzy sets in ***U*** is ***m*** and these fuzzy subsets represent as ***A1***, ***A2***, … and ***Am***, then

$$\mu_{A1}(X)+ \mu_{A2}(X)+\ldots+\mu_{Am}(X)=1 \tag{1}$$

The nature of FS makes it possible to define partially overlapping classes, thus making it possible a gradual classification of elements in the universe of discourse. By contrast, a model based on crisp sets (intervals) shows abrupt changes when the real value falls in the close interval, due to noise. Imperfect learning and adaptation may affect the quality of the resulting model, and the intrinsic robustness of a fuzzy model plays an important role to smooth this effect.

2.2 RS

In RS [1], [2], a rough set can be replaced by two precise sets. One is the lower approximation, while the other is the upper one. The difference between these two approximations is the boundary region (indiscernible region) of the rough set.

Suppose ***U*** is a non-empty set as a universe (feature space) and ***R*** is an equivalence relation defined by the input features in ***U.*** According to the equivalence relation ***R***, the set ***U*** can be partitioned into several basic equivalence classes which do not overlap with each other. Suppose **e** is an object of **U.** Then $[e]_R$ represents a set (an equivalence class) consisting of all the objects which can not be differentiated by the relation ***R.*** For any subset ***X*** of ***U,*** the lower approximation ***R*(X)*** and the upper approximation ***R*(X)*** of ***X*** by the relation ***R*** are defined by:

$$R^*(X) = \{e \in U : [e]_R \subseteq X\} \tag{2}$$

$$R^*(x) = \{e \in U : [e]_R \cap X \neq \varnothing\} \tag{3}$$

The crisp set ***R*(X)*** consists of all the objects which surely belong to the set ***X*** according to the knowledge provided by ***R.*** The set ***R*(X)*** is the union of all the equivalence classes $[e]_R$ whose intersection with the set ***X*** is non-empty, that is, ***R*(X)*** consists of all objects possibly belonging to the set ***X*** based on the knowledge given by ***R.*** The boundary region of ***X*** by ***R*** is defined by:

$$BN_R(x)=R^*(x) - R_*(x) \tag{4}$$

If $BN_R(X)$ is empty, the set X is crisp by R; otherwise X is a rough set by R. $BN_R(X)$ contains all the objects which are not classifiable to the set X based on the knowledge given by R in U. The basic concept for lower and upper approximations of a rough set is illustrated in Fig. 1

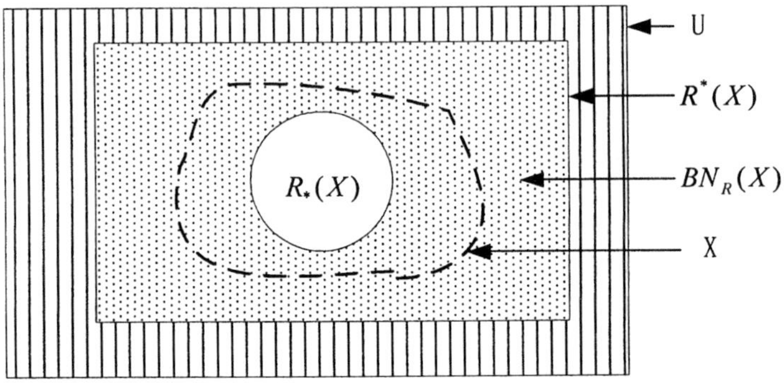

Figure 1 Lower Approximation and Upper Approximation and Boundary Region of A Rough Set X

2.3 The Rules Generation Method on the Base of FS and RS

On the base of fuzzy set [4, 5] and RS theory, KANG [3] presents a rule generation method, which has been discussed in detail in Ref [3]. Its main ideas are reviewed in the following. Some necessary concepts are discussed beforehand.

Definition 2.6: The fuzzy equivalence class $\boldsymbol{R}$(k) on the universal $\boldsymbol{U}$ is defined as $\boldsymbol{R}(k)=U/ind^*(\boldsymbol{R})$, where ind($\boldsymbol{R}$) is the equivalence relation set on the universal $\boldsymbol{U}$.

Definition 2.7: The fuzzy lower approximation $R_*(X)$ is defined as:

$$R_*(X)=\{(R_k(x),\mu_{Rk}(x)) \mid x\in U,\ R_k(x)\subseteq X,\ 1\leq k \leq|R(X)|\}$$

where $\mu_{Rk}(x)$ is the member function.

Definition 2.8: The fuzzy upper approximation $R^*(X)$ is defined as:

$$R^*(X)=\{(R_k(x),\mu_{Rk}(x)) \mid x\in U,\ R_k(x)\cap X\neq\varnothing,\ 1\leq k \leq|R(X)|\}$$

where $\mu_{Rk}(x)$ is the member function.

On the base of FS and RS theory, the KANG's rules generation method is just like the following:

1) Suppose the discussion object set is U (i=1 to m). The conditional property set is A (j=1 to n). The decision property set is C.

2) Decide the member function and language variable (the number of fuzzy intervals) of every conditional property.
3) Depict the member function result figure of the language variable of every conditional property.
4) for i = 1 to m
   for j = 1 to n
   Transform the conditional property values like the following:

$$\frac{f_{j1}^{i}}{R_{j1}} + \frac{f_{j2}^{i}}{R_{j2}} + \cdots + \frac{f_{jl}^{i}}{R_{jl}} \quad \textbf{(4)}$$

where R_{jk} is the kth fuzzy interval of the conditional property A_j. f_{jk}^{i} is the member function value of the object U^i on the fuzzy interval R_{jk}^{i}. $l = |A_j|$ is the number of language variable of the conditional property A_j.

5) Transform the original data table to the decision table with member function values. And calculate the fuzzy equivalence matrix.

6) for i = 1 to m
   for j = 1 to n
   Set $f_{jk}^{i}=\max(f_{j1}^{i},\ldots, f_{jl}^{i})$, where $1 \le k \le l$
   $R'_j = R_{jk}$
   Then the new decision table can be got.

7) Simplify the new decision table using the RS simplifying algorithm, then the reduction rules can be got.

8) The uncertain rule table can be got, which is made up of the incompatible decision and the decision conflicted with the incompatible decision.

9) List the equivalence class of conditional properties in the uncertain rule table. According to its fuzzy equivalence class, the fuzzy equivalence class $A'(k)$ can be got.

10) Calculate the $A'^{*}(k)$.

11) Suppose

$$D_p = A'^{*}(C) \cap (U/ind(C)) \quad \textbf{(5)}$$

where $1 \le p \le |A'^{*}(k)|$.

The selection function of D_p^d is defined as the following:

$$F(D_p^d) = \sum_{k=1}^{|D_p^d|} \frac{\min(f_j^{i*})}{\sum_{j=1}^{n} f_j^{i*}} \times \frac{D_p^d}{|U / ind^*(C)|} \quad \textbf{(6)}$$

where $1 \le d \le |D_p^d|$. f_j^{i*} is the fuzzy interval value of $A'(k)$. $|U / ind^{*}(C)|$ is the umber of decision equivalence class of D_p^{dk}.

12) Select the maximum $A'^{*}(C)$ in $F(D_p)$ as the final decision, where $1 \leq p \leq |A'^{*}(C)|$.

13) Combine the results in step 7) with those in step 12), the final decision rules can be got.

3. THE DECISION MAKING IN OUR CMRS

In CMRS, decision making is one of the important parts. However, this kind of robot systems always works in dynamic environments. The dynamic knowledge can not be summarized accurately beforehand. Usually it is fuzzy, incomplete or uncertain. What's more, decision making rules in dynamic environments stem from practical data in dynamic states. In order to generate the decision making rules from practices, the FS and RS based rules generation method [20] is used to get decision rules.

Our cooperative multiple robot system is a kind of distributed cooperative multiple robot system. It has a two-level system structure in every robot sub-system. The higher level is decision making layer. The lower level is control layer. According to the robot work state, velocity, movement direction and aim distance, decisions of every robot are made respectively, when a new task needs to be performed.

4. RULES GENERATION IN OUR CMRS

In decision making sub-system of CMRS, the form of dynamic knowledge represents as production rules. In order to generate decision making rules, a set of practical decision data have been got, which is shown in Table.1. In Table.1, Y means that the object will be scheduled to perform the task. W means that it will be regarded as an alternate. N means that it will not be scheduled. Then KANG's rules generation method [20] can be used.

Table 1. Data for Objects

Object	Velocity(VE:m/s)	Direction Angle(DA: Degree)	Aim Distance(AD:m)	Perform(PE)
1	0.5	30	1	Y
2	2	110	3	N
3	1	100	2	Y
4	2	80	2	N
5	0.5	45	3	N
6	1	90	2	W

1) From the object data, it is clear that VE, DA and AD are the condition properties set ***A***, while PE is the decision property set ***C***.

2) The number of selected fuzzy interval of VE, DA and AD is 3. They are represented as L (low-level), M (middle-level) and H (high-level).

3) The member function for VE, DA and AD is the same, which is the triangle function depicted in Fig.2.

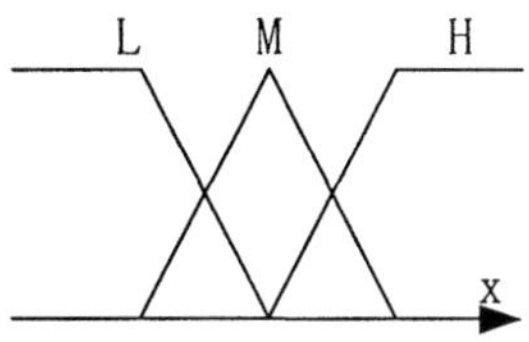

Figure 2. Member Function

4) According to the member function, the properties can be transformed into the following form in Table.2.

Table 2. Data Transformed From Member Functions

Object	VE	DA	AD	PE
1	0.5/L+0.5/M	0.67/L+0.33/M	0.5/L+0.5/M	Y
2	1/H	0.67/M+0.33/H	0.5/M+0.5/H	N
3	1/M	0.78/M+0.22/H	1/M	Y
4	1/H	.11/L+0.89/M	1/M	N
5	0.5/L+0.5/M	0.5/L+0.5/M	0.5/M+0.5/H	N
6	1/M	1/M	1/M	W

5) The fuzzy equivalence class matrix can be got from Table.2. It is listed in Table.3.

Table 3. The Fuzzy Equivalence Class Matrix

	(L,L)	(L,M)	(L,H)	(M,L)	(M,M)	(M,H)	(H,L)	(H,M)	(H,H)
L	(1)		(5)	(1)		(5)			
M	(1)		(5)	(1)	(1,3)	(5)		(3)	
H		(4)			(2,4)	(2)		(3)	(2)

6) The decision table (Table. 4) can be got from Table.2 on the base of the former algorithm.

Table 4. Decision Table

Object	VE	DA	AD	PE
1	L(or M)	L (or M)	L(or M)	Y
2	H	M(or H)	M(or H)	N
3	M	M (or H)	M	Y
4	H	L(or M)	M	N
5	L(or M)	L(or M)	M(or H)	N

Object	VE	DA	AD	PE
6	M	M	M	W

Simplify the Table.4 and the certain rules can be got.

Rule 1: IF (VE=H) and (DA=M) and (AD=M) THEN N

Rule 2: IF (VE=H) and (DA=M) and (AD=H) THEN N

Rule 3: IF (VE=L) and (DA=L) and (AD=L) TEHN Y

Rule 4: IF (VE=L) and (DA=L) and (AD=M) TEHN Y

Rule 5: IF (VE=M) and (DA=L) and (AD=L) TEHN Y

Rule 6: IF (VE=M) and (DA=L) and (AD=M) TEHN Y

8) According to the results of step 7), the uncertain decision table (in Table.5.) can be got.

Table 5. Uncertain Decision Table

Object	VE	DA	AD	PE
1	M	M	M	Y
3	M	M	M	Y
6	M	M	M	W

9) The property equivalence class: K={(M,M,M)}

The fuzzy equivalence class: A'(K)={(1,3,6)}

10) U / ind(C)={(1,3), (2,4,5),(6)}

$A^*(C)$= {(1,3,6)}

11) From the formula in KANG's method, the following results can be got.

D_1={(1,3),(6)} ; $F(D_1^1)$=0.18; $F(D_1^2)$=0.17.

So the uncertain rules can be got.

Rule 7: IF (VE=M) and (DA=M) and (AD=M) THEN Y (CF=0.18)

Rule 8: IF (VE=M) and (DA=M) and (AD=M) THEN W (CF=0.17)

12) From the results of Step 7) and 11), the rule set of our decision system can be got.

Rule 1: IF (VE=H) and (DA=M) and (AD=M) THEN N (CF=1)

Rule 2: IF (VE=H) and (DA=M) and (AD=H) THEN N (CF=1)

Rule 3: IF (VE=L) and (DA=L) and (AD=L) TEHN Y (CF=1)

Rule 4: IF (VE=L) and (DA=L) and (AD=M) TEHN Y (CF=1)

Rule 5: IF (VE=M) and (DA=L) and (AD=L) TEHN Y (CF=1)

Rule 6: IF (VE=M) and (DA=L) and (AD=M) TEHN Y (CF=1)

Rule 7: IF (VE=M) and (DA=M) and (AD=M) THEN Y (CF=0.18)

Rule 8: IF (VE=M) and (DA=M) and (AD=M) THEN W (CF=0.17)

5. CONCLUSIONS AND FUTURE WORK

Dynamic knowledge and uncertain rules are usual phenomena in dynamic systems, especially in cooperative multiple robot systems. So, dynamic knowledge extraction is the critical problems to be solved in the modeling and analysis of dynamic systems. This paper presents a novel method on the base of KANG's rules generation method [4] to extract dynamic knowledge in our CMRS. The validity of this method has been demonstrated by using it in our cooperative multiple robot system.

In the future, a combined method of extraction, representation and inference method in CMRS will be studied deeply, because the aim of dynamic knowledge is to reason and get the results. Recently, adaptive fuzzy Petri net [10] has been presented. It may be a feasible way to reach our goal.

ACKNOWLEDGEMENTS

This work is jointly supported by the National Nature Science Foundation for Youth Fund (Grant No: 60405011) and China Postdoctoral Foundation for China Postdoctoral Science Fund (Grant No: 20040350078).

REFERENCES

1. Pawlak Z. Rough Sets: Theoretical Aspects of Reasoning About Data[M]. Kluwer Academic Publisher, 1994.
2. X.P. Gu S. K. Tso, APPLYING ROUGH-SET CONCEPT TO NEURAL-NETWORK-BASED TRANSIENT-STABILITY CLASSIFICATION OF POWER SYSTEMS, Proceedings of the 5th International Conference on Advances in Power System Control, Operation and Management, AF'SCOM 2000, Hong Kong, October 2000, pp.400-404
3. KANG Shengwu1 ,WANG Yingming ,CAI Zhifeng, An Approach to Generating Rules Based on Rough and FSs Theories, Journal of Xiamen University (Natural Science), Vol. 41 No. 2:173-176, Mar. 2002, (See http://www.cd.cnki.net/index.htm)
4. L. A. Zadeh. Fuzzy sets. *Information and Control*, 8:338-353, 1965.
5. Andrea Bonarini, An Introduction to Learning Fuzzy Classifier Systems, LCS '99, LNAI 1813, pp. 83-104, 2000.
6. Sugeno M, Kang G T. Structure identification of fuzzy model, [J] . Fuzzy Sets and System , 1988 , 28 : 15 - 33.
7. Jang J . ANFIS: Adaptive2network2based fuzzy inference system, [J] . IEEE Trans. On SMC , 1993 ,23(3) :665 - 685.
8. Yinghua L , et al. Nonlinear system input structure identification : two stage fuzzy curves and surfaces[J] . IEEE Trans. On SMC part A , 1998 , 28(5) :678 - 684.
9. Magne S , Huns R. Transparent fuzzy modeling using fuzzy clustering and GA' s [J] . IEEE Trans. Part C , 1999 :198 -202.
10. X. Li, F. Lara-Rosano, Adaptive fuzzy petri nets for dynamic knowledge representation and inference, Expert Systems with Applications 19 (2000) PERGAMON 235–241

A ROUGH SETS BASED EVALUATION MODEL FOR BOT PROJECTS BIDDERS

Yonghe Yu[1,2], Miyuan Shan[1]
1.School of Management, Hunan University, Changsa 410082, China
2.Department of Civil Engineering, Guangxi University of Technology,Liuzhou 545006,China

Abstract: Bidding has been used as an optimal means in selecting investor of build, operate and transfer (BOT) projects in recently. An accurate evaluation on bidders is the key point of a successful bidding. However, evaluation on bidders is a tough and comprehensive work and the result of the evaluation is always affected by evaluators' understanding on standards set for evaluation, evaluators' expertise, experience and preference. In this paper, a hybrid and rough sets based method is presented to facilitate the discretization for continuous attributes and feature selection in evaluation. After a quick review on basic notions of rough sets, general procedures of the method are illustrated by an example, which shows the method's validity.

Key words: Evaluation Model, BOT Projects, Rough Sets

1. INTRODUCTION

The build, operate and transfer (BOT) concession model has been seen as a major trend during the recent two decades in the privatization of public sector infrastructure projects. This is particularly so in the rapidly developing regions. Though the recent financial and currency turmoil in Asia have caused a slowdown in their economies, most promoters and lenders of BOT projects are still confident of the role of the private sector in funding infrastructure projects. This is because the BOT mechanism offers host governments an opportunity to accelerate infrastructure development without incurring large public expenditure and borrowing. At the same time it also creates new business openings for the private sector, especially the construction industry, to participate more positively in the world economic development and contribute to the quality of life of the community. However, the road to winning a BOT concession is by no means easy. Pre-award negotiation is often protracted and arduous. Post-award implementation is usually subjected to unforeseen uncertainties. In the recent financial crisis, a few mega-sized infrastructure projects, such as the Bakun Dam in Malaysia and power plants in Indonesia, were canceled or suspended indefinitely due to funding difficulties [1].

The host governments must take a long view in such contract negotiation, because of the long duration and high capital costs of infrastructure projects and changing priority of the bidders. Upon successful construction of the projects, the actual concession period can last for 10-50 years depending on the type of project. During these operational phases, the maintenance of throughput and tariff rates in line with original forecast remains an area of great uncertainty and challenge to the promoters. BOT projects are a high-risk and high return business.A substantial risk premium, significantly exceeding the normal minimum attractive rate of return, is usually expected by both host governments and bidders.

Evaluation of tender proposals for privatized infrastructure projects that are let under the build, operate and transfer (BOT) concept involves decision making by different government officials from different departments and by their consultants. Choosing the best proposal would depend on the three elements: the quality of the definition of specific criteria, the quality of evaluation of the available alternatives, and the quality of the understanding of what these alternatives can produce. The purpose of the evaluation and selection process is to identify what needs to be done, develop the specific criteria for its accomplishment, and identify the advantages [2].

Many factors should be considered when making decisions on selecting the final contractor. During the decision-making, many factors concerning bidders cannot be measured by tenderee directly and some of them are incomplete and irrelevant, which makes it difficult for tenderee to judge. Even though, an evaluation indicator can be set up but the attributes values are difficult to deal with. Some values are continuous, which makes it more difficult to input the model to calculate and judge.

Our research focuses on a hybrid rough sets based evaluation model to help the hosts governments to evaluate the bidders in a comprehensive and high efficiency way. This paper consists of five sections. Section 2 proposes the evaluation model including the motivation, relevant theories and general algorithms and procedures of the model. An instance is presented to illustrate how to use the model in details in Section 3. Conclusions and discussion for further research hints are included in the last section.

2. PROPOSED METHODOLOGIES

2.1 Motivations

Due to the difficulties encountered in calculating the evaluation value for bidder of BOT projects, our proposed model cuts to the points from the perspective of two basic data mining issues: discretization and feature selection.

Defining classification rules is an important procedure in data mining. Discretization and feature selection are effective techniques in dealing with continuous attributes for rule generating. Many classification rule generation systems can only deal with discrete data, such as AQ, ID3. But continuous attributes seem to be common when mining data. Efforts have been made on discretization methods by using some novel techniques such as fuzzy theory, entropy, genetic algorithm and so on.

Generally, most of the discretization methods fall into two categories: local and global[3]. Local methods discretize only one attribute at a time, while the global ones discretize all attributes simultaneously. In general local discretization is relatively easy to implement and has been adopted in many applications. However, it is considered as a sub-optimal approach because of the lost of valuable information of other attributes[4, 5]. On the other hand, global discretization can usually get better results than the local one for taking interact of all attributes into account. But the costly computation limits its widely application in practice.

Another issue related to data mining is concerned with feature selection. Generally, a lot of features (attributes, variables) about the target object are stored and kept for later analysis. However, these features gathered to identify objects are often not all useful or equally informative: some of them may be redundant or irrelevant for the identification. Many candidate features are included since the relevant features are unknown. Unfortunately, the presence of more information in the form of additional features does not always result in a better revelation of the hidden natural patterns in the data. On the contrary, the presence of irrelevant features can mask the underlying natural patterns in the data, and the operators will have to look through all the data to ascertain the quality of objects during data mining. This kind of job is normally tedious, and will remarkably reduce the quality of data mining. Under such a situation, a feature selection technique can help discover those important features that best describe the target object and thus can simplify the mining procedure. Feature selection addresses this concern by the selection of a subset of features that is relevant. The importance of feature selection in a broader sense is not only to simplify the procedure of data mining, but also to reduce the search space and save future computation time and costs. Hence, to some extent, feature selection can be viewed as a pre-pruning process to choose minimally sized features that are necessary and sufficient to describe target concepts [6]. In recent decades, many feature selection methods have been developed (overviews can be found in Refs.[7,8]). These methods have different strengths and drawbacks, based on the specific feature selection criterion.

2.2 Rough sets

The rough sets philosophy is founded on the assumption that with every object of the universe of discourse we associate some information (data, knowledge). Rough set theory overlaps with many other theories, especially with fuzzy set theory, evidence theory and Boolean reasoning methods, discriminant analysis, which was first proposed by Poland scholar Z. Pawlak in 1982 and is regarded as a new soft computing method to deal with imprecise, vagueness and uncertainty data. Due to its advantage, which include the elimination of the need for additional information about data and the ability to extract rules directly from data itself, this theory has been used in more and more domains in less than two decades, such as medical diagnosis, stock market forecast, pattern recognition, machine learning, decision making and etc [9, 10].

A decision table is the basic kind of knowledge in Rough set theory. Let $S=(U, A \cup \{d\})$ be a decision table with n objects, where U is a non-empty, finite set called the universe and A is a non-empty, finite set of condition attributes, i.e. a: $U \rightarrow v_a$ for $a \in A$, where v_a is called the value of a, and $d \notin A$ is a distinguished attributes called decision. And the other concepts of rough set theory such as equivalence class, indiscernibility relation, approximation of sets, can be found in Refs [9,10,11].

2.3 Discretization

General discretization could be described as follows:

Let [a, b] be the value domain of an continuous attributes A. Discretization of A is a process of searching for an optimal (with respect to a given evaluation measure) cut points set {cl, c2,......,cm}, where a<c1<c2...<cm<b, which divides [a, b] into m disjoin intervals [a, c1], [c1 , c2],..., [cm, b]. Then the continuous values of A are transformed into m different discrete values v_1 , v_2 ... v_m .

$$DV(obj) = \begin{cases} v_1 & if \quad a \le V(obj) \le c_1 \\ v_i & if \quad c_{i-1} < V(obj) \le c_i \\ v_m & if \quad c_{m-1} < V(obj) \le c_m \end{cases}$$

i=2,3...m-1.V(obj) is the original continuous value of an object on A and DV(obj) is the discretized value of A.

The Rough Sets Theory cannot be used to deal with the continuous attributes, which is the disadvantage of this method[12]. The crucial problem now is how to discretize them therefore. Usually, the value of attribute changes monotonically with deterioration of the state. Boundary values to divide its domain into intervals corresponding to different state are selected by experience. However, when experience to discretize the domain is not present, other discretization methods have to be used. There are many discretization methods, such as equal-width-intervals, equal-frequency-intervals and Minimal Entropy Method. In this paper, MD-discretization method is used to discretize the attributes . The algorithm is presented below.

A continuous attribute a∈A defines a sequence $v_1^a < v_2^a \cdots < v_{n_a}^a$, where $\{v_1^a, v_2^a, v_{n_a}^a\} = \{a(x) : x \in U\}$ and $n_a \le n$.

Then the set of all possible cuts on a is denoted by

$$C_a = \{(a, \frac{v_1^a + v_2^a}{2}), (a, \frac{v_1^a + v_2^a}{2}), \cdots, (a, \frac{v_1^a + v_2^a}{2})\}$$

The set of possible cuts on all attributes is denoted by

$$C_A = \bigcup_{a \in A} C_a$$

.

Algorithm 1 MD-discretization
Input: the consistent decision table S =(U, A ∪ {d}), A={a1, a2···, am}
Output: the semi-minimal set of cuts D consistent with S
Method:

D = Φ; CA= initial set of cuts on S;
L = {(x, y)∈U2: d(x)≠d(y)};
While (L≠Φ) do

Begin

Choose the cut $C_{max} \in \mathbf{C_A}$ that discerns the largest number of pairs of objects in **L**.(i.e. the cut corresponding to the column with the largest number of "1")

Insert C_{max} into **D** and remove it from $\mathbf{C_A}$.

Remove all pairs of objects from **L** discerned by C_{max}.

End

2.4 Feature selection

In this section, the computation of feature selection in decision table is discussed. The resulting selection is a minimal set of attributes that enable to represent the whole set of attributes in a decision table to be considered when generation the rules from tables. The problem of computing all features from a decision system has been proved to be NP-Hard. Several new methods have been proposed such as MIBARK algorithm, feature selection-based algorithm and etc to improve the efficiency of basic feature identification. In this paper, a more effective algorithm is used.

Definition1 Let $\Psi=\{Y_1,Y_2,\cdots,Y_k\}$ be a partition of U, $P\subseteq A$.

$$\gamma_P(\psi)=\frac{\sum_{i=1}^{k} card(\underline{P}Y_i)}{card(U)}$$

The coefficient is called the quality of approximation of partition Ψ by set of attributes P, or in short, quality of sorting. It expresses the ratio of all P-correctly sorted objects to all objects in the system.

Definition2 Let $R\subseteq A$, $\gamma_R(\psi)=\gamma_A(\psi)$ if not exist another set $R'\subset R$, where $\gamma_{R'}(\psi)=\gamma_R(\psi)$, then R is a reduction of A. The core of A denoted by CORE(A), is the set attributes, which appears in all reduction of A.

Algorithm 2 Feature-Selection

Input: the consistent decision table S =(U, A∪{d}), A={a1, a2⋯, am}, $\Psi=\{Y_1,Y_2,\cdots,Y_k\}$ is a partition U/{d}

Output: a set of reduction P covering U

Method:

Step1: For i=1 to m do

Begin

Compute $\gamma_{ai}(\psi)$, $Q = CORE(A), P = Q, T = A \setminus P$.

If $\gamma_R(\psi)=\gamma_A(\psi)$ **then** P is a reduction P covering U, return **end**.

End

Step2: Compute $\gamma_{ag}(\psi) = \max(\gamma_{ai}(\psi) : a_i \in T)$,

Let $P = P \bigcup \{a_g\}$, $T = T \setminus \{a_g\}$, go to step3.

Step3:If $\gamma_R(\psi) = \gamma_A(\psi)$ **then** go to step4 **else** $\gamma_R(\psi) < \gamma_A(\psi)$,go to step2 **end.**

Step4:If $P = CORE(P)$ **then** P is a reduction P covering U, return **else** go to step5 **end.**

Step5: For any condition attribute $a_j \in P \setminus CORE(P), P = P \setminus \{a_j\}$, go to step4.

2.5 Inconsistency checking

To assure the effectiveness of discretization and feature selection, inconsistency checking is a necessary procedure, which was used in many literatures. The followings are the general procedures of inconsistency checking and its relationship with decision tables under the context of rough sets.

Let a decision table S=(U, A ∪ {d}), U={U_1, U_2...U_m} is the universe which consists of a finite set of objects, A={ A_1, A_2...A_n } is the set of conditional attributes and d is the decision attribute (this is also called the class of objects). $A_i(U_j)$ denotes the value of object Uj on attributes Ai and $d(U_j)$ is the class of U_j.

An object $U_i \in U$ is called inconsistent in S if an object $U_j \in U$ can be found which satisfied the following conditions:

$A_k(U_i) = A_k(U_j)$ and $d(U_i) \neq d(U_j)$, i,j ∈ {1,2,...,m}, k=1,2,...,n.

We define Iobj(S) as the set of all inconsistent objects in S, and then inconsistency of S can be defined as

$$INC(S) = \frac{|Iobj(S)|}{|U|}$$

A given δ is the criteria to judge the inconsistency of discretization and feature selection.

3. AN INSTANCE

3.1 Inconsistency checking

To accelerate the economic development of Guangxi, the local government invested more than 4 billion on constructing highway to connect the Guangxi with Guangdong province, Hunan province and Yunnan province. In order to improve the investment efficiency and guarantee the fairness of competition, bidding is employed as a common method to select the contractors.

3.2 Attributes of Evaluation Model

Attribute 1: project cost (measured in million yuan) U(1) ——includes the cost of labors and facilities;

Attribute 2: time limit for project (measured in days) U(2) ——indicates how long the project will take;

Attribute 3: scheme of technology U(3) ——refers to methodology and experiment routines used in construction;

Attribute 4: sets of rules for quality control U(4) ——to judge whether it is convincible to guarantee the project's quality;

Attribute 5: time needed for preparing the materials and staffs (measured in days) U(5);

Attribute 6: proportion of senior engineers U(6) ——indicates the proportion of senior engineers among all the professionals involved;

Attribute 7: capacity to prepay by cash U(7) ——to judge the financial situation of the bidders;

Attribute 8: history record and experiences U(8) ——to be judged by how many similar contracts the bidders have taken;

Attribute 9: expertise of management and professionals U(9) ——to judge the qualification of the bidders' human resources.

3.3 Calculus

In order to test our method, we performed an instance. Suppose S=(U, A ∪{d}) (as shown in table 1)is a decision table for evaluation, where A={ a1 a2 ⋯ a4} and U={u1, u2, ⋯ u9}. Attributes a2 and a4 are continuous attributes, and a1 and a3 are discrete attributes.

*Table 1.*The decision table

U	a1	a2	a3	a4	d
U1	3	1.1	3	2.5	1
U2	1	1.1	2	3.5	0
U3	2	1.8	2	1.5	0
U4	2	1.5	1	1.5	1
U5	3	1.5	1	2.5	0
U6	2	1.6	2	3.5	1
U7	3	1.6	1	3.5	1
U8	3	1.3	2	0.5	1
U9	1	1.3	1	0.5	0

The set of all cuts consists of four cuts on the attribute a2 and three cuts on the attribute a4.

$C_A=\{(a_2,1.2),(a_2,1.4),(a_2,1.55),(a_2,1.7)\}\cup\{(a_4,1),(a_4,2),(a_4,3)\}$.

Table 2 The new decision table S_1

L	f(a2,1.2)	f(a2,1.4)	f(a2,1.55)	f(a2,1.7)	f(a4,1)	f(a4,2)	f(a4,3)
(u1,u2)	0	0	0	0	0	0	1
(u1,u3)	1	1	1	1	0	1	0
(u1,u5)	1	1	0	0	0	0	0
(u1,u9)	1	0	0	0	1	1	0
(u2,u4)	1	1	0	0	0	1	1
(u2,u6)	1	1	1	0	0	0	0
(u2,u7)	1	1	1	0	0	0	0
(u2,u8)	1	0	0	0	1	1	1
(u3,u4)	0	0	1	1	0	0	0
(u3,u6)	0	0	0	1	0	1	1
(u3,u7)	0	0	0	1	0	1	1
(u3,u8)	0	1	1	1	1	0	0
(u4,u5)	0	0	0	0	0	1	0
(u4,u9)	0	1	0	0	1	0	0
(u5,u6)	0	0	1	0	0	0	1
(u5,u7)	0	0	1	0	0	0	1
(u5,u8)	0	1	0	0	1	1	0
(u6,u9)	0	1	1	0	1	1	1
(u7,u9)	0	1	1	0	1	1	1
(u8,u9)	0	0	0	0	0	0	0

The new decision table S1 consists of 7 attributes and 20 objects(table 2). The MD-discretization algorithm choose the cut (a2,1.4) first because it discerns 10 pairs of objects, then it chooses the cuts (a2, 1.2) , (a2, 1.55), (a4, 2) and (a4, 3). The result of discretization is the set of cuts S={(a2, 1.2), (a2, 1.4), (a2, 1.55), (a4, 2) , (a4, 3)} using algorithm1.

$$\psi = \{Y_1, Y_2\} = \{\{u_1, u_4, u_6, u_7, u_8\}, \{u_2, u_3, u_5, u_7\}\}$$

A={A1, A2, A3, A4}={{a1}{a2}{a3}{a4}}

A1Y1 = Φ, A2Y1 = {2, 9}

$$\gamma_{a1}(\psi) = \sum_{i=1}^{2} card(\underline{A_1}Y_i) \Big/ card(U) = 2/9$$

Using the same method to compute $\gamma_{a2}(\psi)$, $\gamma_{a3}(\psi)$ and $\gamma_{a4}(\psi)$. The result of feature reduction is the set of P={a1, a3, a4,} using the algorithm2, and the fitting rate of condition attribute is 20%. The result shows that condition attribute a2 is redundant or irrelevant for the evaluation system.

4. CONCLUSION

We have presented a hybrid and rough set based discretion and feature selection method with an inconsistency checking for evaluation. By employing rough set, the efficiency of discretion and feature selection is improved and more valuable information in raw data are reserved. An instance is raised to illustrate the method's validity, which implies further application of this method.

ACKNOWLEDGEMENTS

This research is supported by the National Nature Science Foundation of China(No. 70372039) and Guangxi Nature Science Foundation (No. 0481005).

REFERENCES

[1] Neal J. Financing of BOT projects. M.Sc. lectures, Nanyang Technological University, Singapore, 1993.

[2] Robert L.K Tiong, Jahjdul Alum. Evaluation of proposals for BOT projects. Int. J. project management, 1997,15(2): 67-72.

[3] R Susmaga, Analyzing. Discretizations of continuous attributes given a monotonic discrimination function. Intelligent Data Analysis, 1997,1: 157-179.

[4] S.D. Bay. Multivariate discretization of continuous variables for set mining. Proceedings of the sixth ACM SIGKDD International Conference on Knowledge Discovery and Data Mining (Boston, MA, August), 2000: 315-319.

[5] S.J. Hong. Use of contextual information for feature ranking and discretization. IEEE Transactions on knowledge and data engineering, 1997,9: 718-730.

[6] Lian Yin Zhai et al, Feature extraction using rough set theory and genetic algorithms — an application for the simplification of product quality evaluation, Computers & Industrial Engineering, 2002: 43.

[7] B. Walczak, D.L. Massart, Chapter calibration in wavelet domain, in: B. Walczak (Ed.), Wavelets in Chemistry, Elsevier, Amsterdam, 2000: 323–349.

[8] R. Kohavi, G. John. Wrappers for feature subset selection. Artificial Intelligence. 1997: 273–324.

[9] Z. Pawlak, Rough Sets, Theoretical Aspects of Reasoning about Data, Kluwer Academic Publishing, 1991.

[10] R. Slowinski, Intelligent Decision Support, Handbook of Applications and Advances of Rough Sets Theory, Kluwer Academic Publishing, 1992.

[11] S. Tsumoto, H. Tanaka, Automated discovery of medical expert system rules from clinical databases based on Rough Sets, in: Proceedings of the Second International Conference on Knowledge Discovery and Data Mining KDD'96 , AAAI Press, Menlo Park, 1996.

[12] Yao, Y. Y., Wong, S. K. M., & Lin, T. Y, A review of rough sets models. In T. Y. Lin, & N. Cercone (Eds.), Rough sets and data mining—Analysis for imprecise data, Boston, MA: Kluwer, 1997.

[13] Ye dongyi, An improvement to Jelonek's attributes reduction algorithm, Acta electronica sinica, 2000,28(12).

A CASE-BASED REASONING APPROACH TO ENHANCE WEB-BASED TRAINING ON INTERNET MARKETING

Duan, Y.[1], , Burrell, P.[2], Mullins, R.[3] and Jin, H.[3]
1-University of Luton, UK, 2 - South Bank University, UK, -University of Wales Lampeter, UK,

Abstract: Lack of knowledge and skills among small business managers has been well recognised, but how to effectively support small business managers in their knowledge acquisition and decision making with emerging information and communication technologies is still a challenge. This paper describes an application attempt to develop an intelligent web-based training system for SMEs to aid their learning and decision-making regarding the use of the Internet as a new marketing medium. Based on the training needs analysis carried out by a EU-funded research project TRIMAR, a case-based reasoning (CBR) approach is adopted as an effective tool to help small business managers to learn and to make better decisions. Over seventy small business Internet marketing cases were collected and processed. They form a case base for CBR in the system. The initial feedback from users proves using case base reasoning approach is effective, but the quality and the comprehensiveness of case base are key factors for the usefulness of the system.

Key words: Case-based reasoning, case based learning, intelligent web-based training, Internet Marketing, SMEs.

1. INTRODUCTION

Development of information and communications technologies has resulted in the emergence of new directions in marketing policies and activities. The Internet has become an attractive tool of marketing (Chaffey, 2002; Coupey, 2001; Dann, 2001). Decision makers from Small and Medium Enterprises (SMEs)[1] have to face difficulties while implementing and utilising the Internet marketing. The lack of knowledge and skills that

[1] SMEs are defined as those enterprises, which have 10-249 employees.

are necessary to introduce and carry out Internet marketing is one of barriers contributing to the difficulties. The situation was reflected in a survey conducted within EU funded pilot project TRIMAR[2]. TRIMAR attempts to contribute to the wider debate on the content and style of training most suitable to small businesses. It aims to identify the training needs of the small businesses for Internet Marketing at a pan-European level and to seek the most effective way to address the training and support needs with web-based systems. The findings from project Pan-European survey reveals the necessity to provide decision makers with up to date knowledge on Internet marketing and to develop skills that are indispensable. This paper reports the application attempt to address the training and decision support needs using Case Based Reasoning approach.

2. INTERNET MARKETING CHALLENGES IN SMES

The Internet provides exciting new opportunities for SMEs to extend their business to the global market place. However, introducing Internet marketing into SMEs and combining both off-line and on-line marketing campaigns is not an easy process. This process requires that decision-makers and marketing specialists acquire new skills.

Surveys and focus groups conducted at the University of Luton, with SMEs revealed that:

- SMEs are not equipped with necessary expertise to deal with culture-based market differences such as consumer and market characteristics.
- They do not have experience of world market characteristics and do not know how to adapt their companies to the converging global market place in terms of products, promotion and distribution.
- They have no knowledge of how other SMEs are operating on the Internet and which Internet Marketing models they are adopting.

The managers would like to learn from the successful experiences of other SMEs and adopt best practices identified from Internet marketing case studies within their sector.

To further investigate the training and decision support needs on adopting the Internet marketing in SMEs. TRIAMR carried out questionnaire surveys in five countries in Europe (UK, Germany, Poland, Slovak Republic and Portugal). The surveys involved 190 enterprises. They

[2] TRIMAR, i.e. On-Line Intelligent **Tr**aining System for **I**nternet **Mar**keting by SMEs (UK/00/B/F/PP/129_110), is funded by the European Commission's Leonardo Da Vinci programme.

of Internet as a marketing tool. More than half of respondents evaluated their level of Internet marketing knowledge and skills as low and insufficient. Most respondents believed that lack of knowledge and in-house expertise were the major barriers to the effective implementation of Internet Marketing strategies and operations, and that training of managers and employees could considerably contribute to their marketing success. Managers expressed their interest in the provision of a web-based training system to aid their learning and knowledge acquisition.

Exploring the possibility of using case based reasoning to enhance training and learning, the survey asked "in what way would you prefer to learn about Internet Marketing?". 40% of respondents selected "presentation of case studies", and 54% selected "model Internet solutions". This evidence indicates the willingness of SMEs manager to learn from other businesses' previous experience and lessons, and shed light on adopting CBR approach in the project.

3. ARCHITECTURE OF TRIMAR SYSTEM

In responding to SMEs training and decision support needs, one of the major outcomes of TRIMAR project was the provision of a web-based intelligent training and support system using case based approach. The general architecture of the system is shown in figure 1 which consists of three major modules:

a) Self Assessment Tool (SAT).
b) Training Modules (TM).
c) Case Retrieval System (CRS).

Self Assessment Tool (SAT) – Since one of the basic elements of learning is control and self-assessment of knowledge and skills, SAT module was designed to assess the knowledge of users in the field of Internet marketing. The SAT module provides access to on-line tests, facilitates passing subsequent stages of the training and enables tracking, managing and reporting users self-assessment process and results. Web-based training has potential to provide users with personalised training materials, but first of all, preliminary determination of their levels of knowledge on any selected topic should be obtained. This enables the system to direct users to an appropriate lesson at an appropriate level. That is what SAT is responsible for within the TRIMAR system.

Training Modules (TM) – The basic function of TM is to provide SMEs with theoretical and practical knowledge that refers to introduction and utilisation of Internet marketing in business. Two levels of training are developed: basic and advanced levels. At the basic level, training is presented as a form of themed lessons. that correspond to the needs identified by SMEs in TRIMAR surveys.

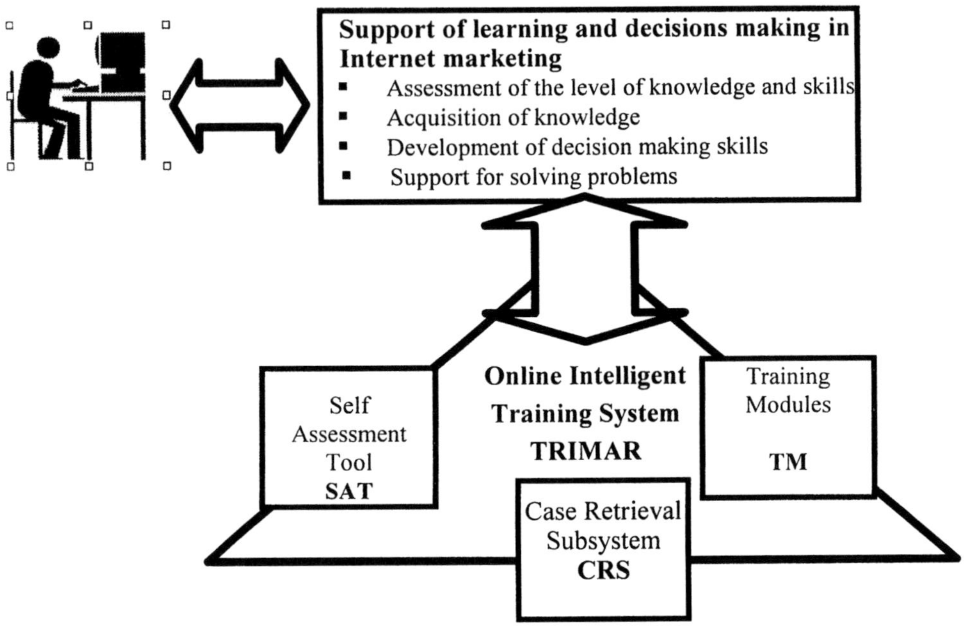

Figure. 1. Architecture of TRIMAR system

Advanced level comprises cases studies that allow for implementation of the case-based learning method and constitute practical examples of performing Internet marketing activities by enterprises. The aim of the case studies is to develop decision-making skills and to solve problems by reviewing appropriate cases. Case studies were developed in cooperation with SMEs that have already acquired experience in implementing and maintaining Internet marketing activities. Such co-operation includes those undertakings that were successful as well as those that failed. Each case study describes problems of SMEs in reference to three levels of management: strategic, tactical and operational. Each case study is summarised in a form of a "Case Study Report" and "Case Study Analysis".

Case Retrieval System (CRS) – CRS serves as a learning tool as well as a decision support subsystem. It contains 70 cases and incorporates case searching and matching activities underpinned by case based reasoning method. More details about this module are provided in the following sections.

4. DEVELOPMENT OF CRS SUBSYSTEM

Case Retrieval Subsystem aims to facilitate and enhance knowledge acquisition and learning by providing with relevant cases collected during TRIMAR project. The case retrieval is inferred from the case based reasoning technique. Case-based reasoning is one approach in the development of knowledge-based systems that is able to retrieve and reuse solutions that have worked for similar situations in the past (Sporl et al, 1999). A particular strength of CBR over most other methods is its inherent combination of problem solving with sustained learning through problem solving experience (Choy and Lee 2000). A case is therefore a contextualised piece of knowledge representing an experience. It contains two major parts: the lesson it teaches - the case抯 content, and the context in which it can teach its lesson – its indexes (Kolodner, 1993).

CBR technology has been successfully exploited in different application problems ranging from help desk applications, to planning and design (Choy and Lee, 2000, Choy et al., 2004; Mclvor and Humphreys, 2000). Applying CBR to a particular application problem requires identification of parameters relevant for decision making, acquiring cases that are described according to these parameters and maintaining the quality of the case-base over time.

Developing effective Internet marketing strategies and methods for competitive advantages in SMEs involves in making various decisions at operational, tactical and strategic levels. Empirical evidence collected from TRIMAR project indicates that when small business managers engaged in their learning and decision making activities on adopting the Internet marketing strategies and techniques, they would like to learn the lessons and experiences from other companies involved in similar situations. This evidence forms a strong base for adopting CBR approach in TRIMAR.

The initial stage of development was to review and to test known commercial CBR systems in order to ascertain their applicability for the intended TRIMAR project. The criteria used were that they had to be consistent with the way that cases were represented in the marketing domain, use some form of algorithmic search (such as nearest neighbour), be web enabled and to be within the budget of the project. A decision was made to use a bespoke system using a propriety database, Microsoft Access ©. This was able to represent cases effectively within the existing data structure, it was able to be accessed through a browser interface, and algorithmic search could be imbedded within the application and used to find the nearest matching cases.

4.1 Selection of Case Indexes

The critical part of any CBR system lies in the cases it possesses. Based on the domain knowledge of marketing and Internet marketing, a template was deigned for collecting and recording cases in five participating countries in the project. The template serves a base for the selection of indexes in the case base.

One of the major concerns with CBR is that of accurate case retrieval In order to facilitate this case retrieval, cases in the case library are assigned indexes. How efficient and successful the case retrieval is, depends mostly on choosing appropriate indexes to guide search for relevant cases in the case library. Good indexes should be truly relevant and generalised, but not over-generalised (Barletta & Mark, 1988).

The selection of the indexes in TRIMAR involved the collection of a small number of marketing cases from SMEs within the EU. This was achieved by providing these companies with a pro-forma with which to record past cases of a particular problem, the resolved solution to that problem and other aspects relating to the company's strategic, tactical and operational procedures. Initially, 10 cases were selected in order to analyse for appropriate case index fields. The analysis provided 7 initial fields which seem to provide the most appropriate description of the problems and their associated solutions. On the basis of the first findings, the pro-forma was modified in accordance with the selected index fields and distributed to a larger number of SMEs. There were 60 new cases returned for analysis, and from these, another 2 index fields were added to the initial 7. This made 9 index fields in total, which seemed to adequately reflect the general indexing for the system. The selected indexing fields are shown in table 1.

Table 1. Case indexing fields

Indexing Fields	Content
Company Category	The business function of the company. These were identified as different category groups. A company's business function would fall into one of these groups.
Problem Category	The problems the various companies seem to be experiencing. These were identified as different category groups. A company's problem would fall into one of these groups.
Business Strategy	The level of business strategy, as in the use of business models and planning, that a company was using for general business activities
Company Size	The size of the company as the number of employees employed
Website Strategy	The level of website strategy, as in website planning, that a company was using for the development and presentation of their website
IT Knowledge	The level of IT knowledge a company has at its disposal

Market Reach	The market in which the company was active
Management Structure	The type of management structure that exists within a company
Corporate Identity	The level of company visibility within its trading sector.

4.2 System Structure, Retrieval and Retention

The efficiency of case retrieval not only depends on the appropriately selected indexes, but also the chosen organisational structure of the case memory and the retrieval algorithms used.

In general, a case memory can be organised either sequentially (flat memory) or hierarchically. In a flat memory, cases are stored in a simple list. Hierarchical organisation involves clustering of cases in certain categories. Thus, hierarchical structures cluster together cases that share a number of features, where clustering has a priority over the discrimination of cases.

The retrieval algorithm relies on the indexes and the organisation of the memory to direct the search of potentially useful cases. Some of the well-known methods for case retrieval are: nearest neighbour, induction, knowledge guided induction and template retrieval (Watson, 1997).

The case memory in TRIMAR was organised as combined hierarchical and sequential structure. One level of hierarchy was employed in order to cluster the company categories, this being based on the assumption that a user would be more interested in accessing problems within their own business function. The system then employed a sequential structure for cases falling under each company category. This is shown in Figure 2.

Although the main method for retrieval was based upon clustered company categories, other options were provided to access similar problems under different company categories or to provide a search for different problems under similar company categories.

The retrieval mechanism was provided by a weighted, nearest neighbour type algorithm as shown in (1) (Kolodner, 1993), as this would allow cases to reside in unique regions of the case-space, thus providing a more accurate retrieval system.

$$\text{Similarity}(T,C) = \sum_{i=1}^{n} f(T_i, C_i) \times W_i \qquad (1)$$

The weightings were provided by analysis of the case studies available, this being based upon the collective, relative importance companies seem to place upon the various case fields. The nearest-neighbour search algorithms were implemented using VB and SQL routines embedded within the case-based data structure. The system provided the following functions for users:

- ***Add New Cases*** –to add new cases to the system.
- ***Review Cases*** - to view all the cases in the case base.
- ***Find the Nearest Case*** – to find cases that matched their problem.

These functions were provided through a browser interface, where the index fields were shown to the user via a set of drop-down menu (figure 3).

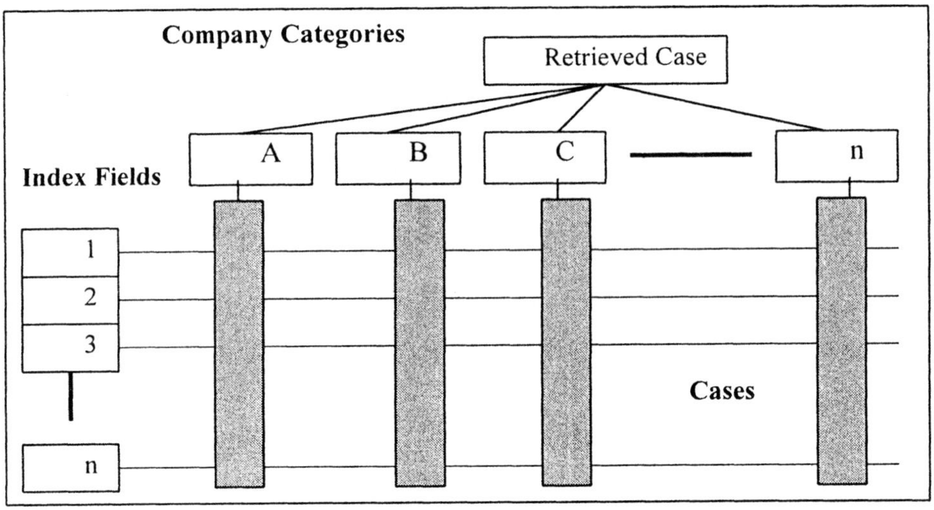

Figure 2. Case Memory Structure

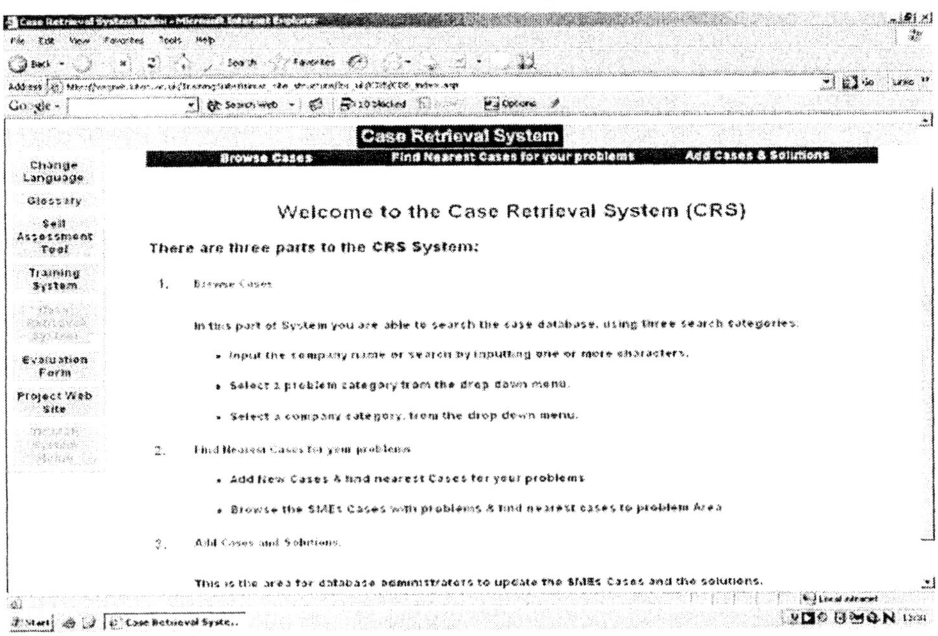

Figure 3. CRS browser interface

The result of the nearest neighbour search returned relevant case solutions, ranked in order of importance. The closest problem match being the most important. The solutions were presented in the form of a text solution and, if required, a full strategic, tactical and operational analysis associated with that solution.

A secondary data structure was used to capture each user抯 interaction with the system. The information retained in this data structure included a text description of the problem, together with related index fields, as provided. This information was retained in this data structure until the user provided a unique solution to their problem. A Null Adaptation technique (Watson, 1997) was used to provide the solution space for the new cases. These cases were then added to main case-based structure, thus providing additional cases for the system.

These functions were provided through a browser interface, where the index fields were shown to the user via a set of drop-down menus. The CRS Module collects knowledge acquired through the analysis of case studies. The module provides the basis for analysis of experiences (successes and failures) of SMEs in Internet marketing. Such experiences are extremely valuable for those companies that are now at the stage of implementing Internet marketing. CBR approach allows for resolving decision-making problems through adaptation of solutions that were implemented by other companies.

5. DISCUSSION AND CONCLUSION

TRIMAR system attempted to combine traditional way of delivering text-based learning materials with a case base to enhance knowledge acquisition and transfer. The strength of the system is its case base and the use of CBR. The case base serves two purposes in the system: 1. to help SMEs managers to learn theories and concepts with relevant case studies; and 2. to support the Internet marketing decision making by providing solutions from similar cases. TRIMAR system was tested and evaluated by various users via an online evaluation questionnaire. The feedback was positive and encouraging. For example, some users said:

"The system offers the possibility for an integrated theoretical and practical learning for companies."

"The examples shown in the case studies allow the user to find solutions for potential business problems without having to experience them. Problems

concerning cultural and social differentiation are evident through the case studies and solutions for the problems that are supplied."

However, the system抯 power, especially its capability to find solutions for existing problems is limited by its small case base. This was noted by some users, e.g.

"The idea of the system is very good – especially the case base. But at the moment the volume of the case base is too small to find matching problems. I hope that many SMEs will put in their cases so the case base will grow."

It is hoped that with the "add new cases" function provided in TRIMAR the case base can be extend to provide better services to SMEs.

ACKNOWEDGEMENT

The authors would like to acknowledge the project partners for their co-operation and contribution to the project. They are University of Munster; Karol Adamiecki University of Economics; Universidade Alberta, South Bank University, Technical University of Kosice .

REFERENCES

Barletta, R. and Mark, W. Explanation-based indexing of cases In Proceedings of the Seventh National Conference on Artificial Intelligence, California, (1988), AAAI Press.

Chaffey D. E-business and E-commerce Management, Strategy, Implementation and Practice Pearson Education Limited, Edinburgh Gate. (2002).

Choy, K.L. and Lee, W.B. Task allocation using case-based reasoning for distributed manufacturing systems. Logistic Information Management,13 (3), (2000), 167-176.

Choy, K.L.; Lee, W.B. and Lo, V., An enterprise collaborative management system – a cse study of supplier relationship management. The Journal Of Enterise Information Management. 17(3), (2004), 191-207.

Coupey E. Marketing and the Internet, Prentice-Hall, New Jersey, (2001).

Dann S. Strategic Internet Marketing, John Wiley & Sons. (2001).

Kolodner J.A Case-Based View of Case-Based Reasoning: What Have We Wrought? College of Computing, Georgia Institute of Technology, Atlanta, (1997).

Kolodner J. Case-Based Reasoning, Morgan Kaufmann Publishers, San Francisco, (1993).

Mclvor, R.T. and Humphreys, P.K. A case-based reasoning approach to the make or buy decision. Integrated Manufacturing Systems, 11(5), (2000). 295-310.

Sporl,B.B., Lenz, M. and Hubner, A. Case-based reasoning – A survey and future directions In: Puppe, P. (Ed.) Proceedings of the 5th Biannual German Conference on Knowledge Based Systems, W黵zburg, Germany, (1999).

Watson I. Applying Case-Based Reasoning: Techniques for Enterprise Systems, Morgan Kaufman Publishers, San Francisco, (1997).

A DECISION SUPPORT SYSTEM (DSS) FOR PRICE RISK MANAGEMENT IN VEGETABLE, CHINA

GUO Xiaomei[1,3], FU Zetian[2,3], MU Weisong[2,3], ZHANG Xiaoshuan[2,3,*]

([1] College of Economic & Management, China Agricultural University 209#, Beijing, P. R China, 100083)

([2] Key Laboratory for Modern Precision Agriculture System Integration, Ministry of Education, China, China Agricultural University, Beijing, P. R China, 100083)

([3] College of Engineering, China Agricultural University 209#, Beijing, P. R China, 100083)

** Corresponding author: Tel: +86-10-62736717 Fax: +86-10-62736717*

E-mail address: zhang_xiaoshuan@yahoo.com (ZH. Xiaoshuan)

Abstract: Vegetable industry plays a very important role in adjusting Agricultural structure and increasing farmers' income. But vegetable industry is characterized by a strong exposure to price risk, due to the increasingly volatility of vegetable price. Price volatility in vegetable markets has been wreaked havoc on the financial performance of producers and their customers. So it is important to develop decision aids that help manage the risks of the price fluctuate to vegetable growers and vegetable companies. A vegetable price risk management decision support system (DSS_PRM) was developed by China agricultural University. Based on questionnaire and interviews, we analyze the decision problems and user needs. Then the architecture and development of DSS_PRM were described. At last we discussed on problems we had encountered during development and promotion.

Key words: China, DSS, Price risk management, Vegetable

1. INTRODUCTION

In China, vegetable has been the fastest growing subsector within the planting economy over the past two decades. The share of cultivated vegetable in total production has increased substantially from 2.22% in 1978 to 11.78% in 2003. As far as export is concerned, the export deals of vegetable amount to 35.11 ten thousand kilogram in 2002. It can affirm that the vegetable industry has the important function in agriculture economy and agricultural product export trade in China. So the concerned national departments have been attached importance to the vegetable industry.

However, this rapid growth of the vegetable has been accompanied by fluctuating prices. Vegetable prices are notoriously volatile, which can wreak havoc on the financial performance of vegetable producers and their customers (David W Cox, 1998). Coping with market uncertainty and price volatility is a constant challenge for the Chinese vegetable industry.

This anticipated price volatility underscores the need for managing price risk (Wes Ishmael, 2004). But producer cannot mitigate price risk because they lack of the knowledge of risk management. So it is evident for providing the help or tools for farmers on vegetable price risk management. Decision support systems for price risk management in vegetable typically useful to aid in managing price risk.

In this paper we describe the decision support systems for price risk management in vegetable (DSS-PRM). The rest of the paper is set out as follows. We give in Section 2 a brief overview of the conceptual framework about price risk and risk management. Section 3 describes the decision problem and user needs. Section 4 shows the system architecture and discusses the system implementation. The results and conclusions are presented in Section 5.

2. PROBLEM DISCRIPTION

2.1 The process of price risk management

A simple definition of a "price risk" is a problem that could cause some loss or threaten the success of our project owes to price volatility (Karl E. Wiegers, 1998). The definition presented is applicable to vegetable producers. Price uncertainty makes planning difficult, yet essential. Producers should take effect measures to manage price risk.

Risk management is the process of identifying, addressing, and eliminating these potential problems before they can damage our benefits (Karl E. Wiegers, 1998). The process of managing the price risk involves several stages. The process of risk management includes the following steps.

The first step involves assessing risk. It consists of risk identification, risk analysis and risk prioritization. Risk identification carry on qualitative analysis to the price risk in order to find out the influence factor that may produce the risk. Risk analysis involves examining how outcomes might change with modification of risk input variables. Risk prioritization helps the project focus on its most severe risks by assessing the risk exposure.

The next step involves controlling risk. Risk control is the process of managing risks to achieve the desired outcomes. Risk management strategy produces a plan for dealing with each significant risk. Risk resolution is execution of the plans for dealing with each risk.

Finally, risk monitoring involves tracking your progress toward resolving each risk item.

2.2 User need and the questionnaire

To better meet the needs of vegetable grower and vegetable company, a questionnaire was designed to investigate their problems and needs. The questionnaires were sent to 120 farmers, 60 retailers from 13 regions in Shandong, Tianjin Provinces. Some interviews were also carried out afterwards to clarify the results collected. We learned that risks associated with price uncertainties turned out to be very important in the opinion of farmers (Jose, H Douglas, Valluru, Ram S K, 1994). Table 1 identifies the intended constituencies for the system along with samples of their decision making needs.

Table 1. Requirements for the ideal decision support systems

An effective DSS-PRM should have the potential to eliminate or mitigate price risk by
• Quantify the price risk
• Identify the most severe source of price risk of vegetable
• Offer the effective method of price risk management
• Be available at multi means and requires low skill and training, moreover, cost is affordable for users.
• Have a friendly and intuitive interface easy to use and communication method.

3. THE SYSTEM ARCHITECTURE

The problem description presented in the previous section indicates that the price risk management problem can be decomposed into four critical subproblems: price risk measure, the main source of price risk identification, price risk management method offering and user feedback. Therefore, the structure of price risk management consists of four main subsystems: measure subsystem, prioritization subsystem, management subsystem and response subsystem. Each of the subsystems contributes to the overall functionality of the system. It has different objectives and can be modeled and solved by different techniques appropriate for each. It is obviously that we do not absolutely obey the process of risk management above. In this system, we only consider the measure, prioritization, management of vegetable price risk because they are the most important needs to the users.

The user interface is responsible for the interaction between the system and its users, especially ascertaining user need and obtaining commands and management of the input/output data and their display. The more detail of each of the subsystems is described below.

3.1 The measure subsystem

The measure system is used to assess the level of price risk. It consists of data collection module and measure module.

1) Data collection module. The data collection module is responsible for gathering data from a multitude of producers and preparing the data sets for the measure module. The data is directly entered by hand. All the data are stored in database. The database plays an important role and is responsible for storing all the information needed for price risk quantification in DSS-PRM.

2) Measure module. The data measure module which quantifies the price risk is the key component of the subsystem. Actually, volatility can be indicated in a number of ways; here we use the measure of coefficient of variation (the standard deviation divided by the mean) (George Flaskerud; William Wilson; Bruce Dahl, 2002). The coefficient of variation is especially useful to measure the volatility of different commodity prices. It is a simple and effective method that quantifies price risk. Figure 1 shows the interface of price risk measure.

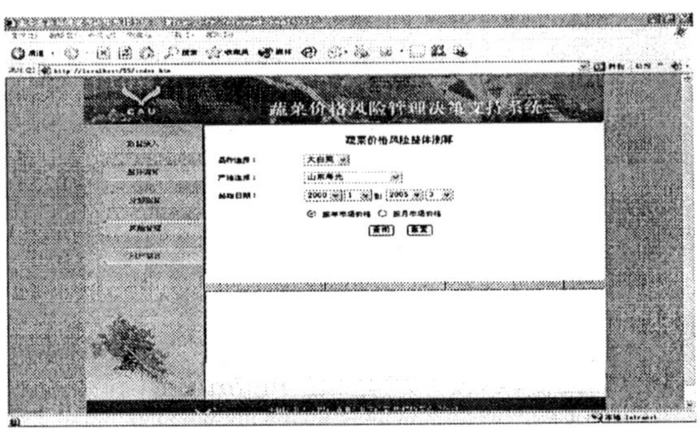

Figure 1. Interface of risk measure

3.2 The prioritization subsystem

This module is responsible for identifying the most severe price risk factor of vegetable. That is, focusing on the most important price risk factor by assessing the risk exposure. Once the exposures to several price risk factors have been identified and quantified, it is possible to analyze which ones represent the largest sources of price risk for the vegetable producer. Applying to factor decomposition model (Christopher Barrett, Winnie K.Luseno, 2004), it may be easier to estimate the probable degree of a variety of price risk factors. It also consists of data collection module and measure module. According the simple method of price risk decomposition, producer price risk is attributable to volatile inter-market margins, intraday variation, intra-week (day of week) variation, or terminal market price variability. They represent separately informational/institutional risk, local market risk, basis risk and terminal market risk.

3.3 The management subsystem

The management subsystem is responsible for offering the optimal method of avoid the price risk. It consists of a knowledge database. In the knowledge database, there are a plenty of price risk management strategies. In fact, vegetable producers have a wide variety of tools to manage price risk available to them. However, there is no clear-cut best strategy for all producers or one that works consistently over time. It is unlikely that one alternative will consistently be the best choice.

Selecting optimal risk management strategy of vegetable price should be based on a thorough comparison of available alternatives. In the risk management subsystem, we will offer the best risk mitigate strategy by fulfilling the operation.

3.4 The response subsystem

Cooperation and feed-back mechanism with the end users is also essential in this collaborative process to help improve the quality of information sought for remove price risk. We can receive the feedback information and opinions of the users by the response subsystem.

4. THE IMPLEMENTATION OF DSS-PRM

The structure of information system adopted B/S (Browser/Server/), which is able to better apply information system to network production. There are many solutions for developing the web-based systems. We adopted the solution by Microsoft, i.e. ASP (Actives server pages) + MS Access + IIS (Internet Information Server) due that it is prone to master by non-professional system developer.

5. DISCUSSION AND CONCLUSION

This paper reports a research attempt in developing a decision support system for price risk management in vegetable products market. The system is able to measure the degree of price risk and detect the most severe risk source in the vegetable products market via integration of risk measure and evaluation. The system is also offer the most effective price risk management method to the user.

However, there are still some shortages should be addressed, such as:

Internal problems relate to data update and deficiencies in the factor decomposition model. Even though we can obtain data from some vegetable product company, it proves difficult given that the research and development team is not an official governmental body. These factors resulted in slow adoption and willingness to participate in using the system.

On-going research is to integrate the proposed system with a decision support system that can assist participants in selecting the most effective plans.

ACKNOWLEDGEMENTS

This program is supported by EU Aided Asia IT&C under Grand No. CN/ASIA-IT&C/005(89099) and partly by NSFC (National Nature Science Foundation of China) under Grant No. 70133001. We also would like to thank many domain experts from China Agriculture University.

REFERENCES

[1] Christopher Barrett, Winnie K.Luseno, Decomposing producer price risk: a policy analysis tool with an application to northern Kenyan livestock markets, Food Policy, 2004, Vol.29, pp. 393-405.

[2] David W Cox, Paper company hedging programs uncomplicated to design, implement, Pulp & Paper, 1998.6, pp. 97-99.

[3] George Flaskerud; William Wilson; Bruce Dahl, Managing canola price risk, The Journal of the ASFMRA; 2002; ProQuest Agriculture Journals, pp. 53-63.

[4] Jose, H Douglas, Valluru, Ram S K, Insights from the Crop Insurance Reform Act of 1994, Agribusiness, 1997, Vol.13, Iss. 6, pp. 587-596.

[5] Karl E. Wiegers, Know Your Enemy: Software Risk Management, Process Impact, www.processimpact.com.

[6] Wes Ishmael, Manage your price risk, Beef, 2004.2, Vol.40, Iss. 6, pp. 6.

A DYNAMIC CONSTRAINT SOLVING SCHEME FOR SEMI ON-LINE SCHEDULING PROBLEMS

Juyang Zhang Jigui Sun Yonggang Zhang
College of Computer Science & Technology, Jilin University, 130012, Changchun, P.R.China
Key Laboratory for Symbolic Computation and Knowledge Engineering of Ministry of Education, 130012, Changchun, P.R.China

bstract: Most of real-life scheduling problems are semi on-line scheduling, where we do not know all the time variables of jobs in advance. Recently, solving such dynamic problems is a hot topic of research in Constraint Programming. In this paper we analyze the constraints in the semi on-line scheduling problems and introduce the concept of monotonic about constraints which appear in general dynamic constraint models. We designed a generic dynamic constraint solving algorithm for solving the scheduling problems. We give an example of its application to semi on-line discrete resource-constrained scheduling problem (ship-loading problem).

key words: Scheduling, Semi On-line, Constraint Solving, Monotonic

1. INTRODUCTION

Constraints are powerful tools for modeling many real-world problems. Constraint programming (CP) is based on the idea of describing the problem declaratively by means of constraints and, consequently, finding a solution satisfying all the constraints, i.e., assigning a value to each unknown from its respective domain. Scheduling is one of the strongest application areas of constraint programming [1]. The reason of such success can be found in a similar character of both scheduling problems and Constraint Satisfaction Problems (CSPs) [2]. In the constraint programming fiend, the constraint models of kinds of scheduling problems are based on CSPs. But the traditional formulation of CSPs is static in sense that all the variables and the constraints are known before we start to solve the problem. Nevertheless, many real-life scheduling problems such as (semi) on-line scheduling problems do not fit this static constraint model. In those dynamic scheduling problems, we do not know all the time variables of jobs in advance. The new variables are introduced as the schedule progresses, i.e., the original CSPs extend continually. Therefore, we require a more dynamic constraint modeling and solving scheme for those dynamic scheduling problems.

Operations Research (OR) has a long tradition in studying scheduling problems and many successful methods to deal with the dynamic problem were developed there. Recently, solving such dynamic problems is a hot topic of research in CP, however, not a new one. [3] proposed a concept of Dynamic Constraint Satisfaction motivated by problems in configuration. Since then the idea of using activity constraints and dummy variables is used in various concepts. This approach is useful when the number of dummy variables is not very large, i.e., when the number of alternatives is linear rather than exponential. Dynamic Constraint Satisfaction can deal with adding and removing variables and constraints to/from the problem. Addition and retraction can be done in arbitrary order and, thus, the concept must be implemented from scratch and it is hard (or impossible) to extend existing CSP packages to support it. In this paper, we designed a straightforward generic technique for making monotonic constraints in semi on-line scheduling problems dynamic. This scheme is easy to implement in the current scheduling systems, as it does not require a change of paradigm from CSP to Dynamic CSP and it can exploit directly the existing filtering algorithms for constraints.

In section 2, we first describe the semi on-line scheduling problem. The details about the generic dynamic constraint solving scheme including the concept of monotonic constraints and the dynamic constraint solving algorithm *Dyna-Solver* are showed in Section 3. In section 4, we give an example of its application to on-line discrete resource-constrained scheduling problem (ship-loading problem). Finally, we draw a conclusion on this new scheme.

2. SEMI ON-LINE SCHEDULING PROBLEM

Considering the information provided the task, scheduling falls generally into two categories[4], off-line and on-line. In the off-line scheduling all the information of tasks is known in advance, and this makes it possible to perform scheduling based on these given information. However in the on-line cases, the following two assumptions were made: (1) Information is given by sequence, i.e. the information about task T_{j+1} can only be announced after the scheduling of the tasks $T_1,\ldots,T_j$; (2) No changes are allowed to scheduled tasks, i.e. if a task is sent to some machine it is prohibited to re-schedule the task.

As described above, both off-line and on-line scheduling are idealized cases in terms of the quantity of knowledge provided. In case of off-line job scheduling, all the information required is given, so that an algorithm of high performance may be obtained by conducting operations on data, such as sorting, operating, and comparing. Considering an on-line scheduling no information, including the release-time, the amount of need and supply, and the number of the rest tasks, can be obtained in advance; the schedules made for former tasks are not allowed to be changed. In practice, however, few cases were found falling into these two idealized categories. Although the overall knowledge about tasks waiting to be scheduled may not be fully provided, it is generally possible for schedulers to have some information in advance, and/or to re-schedule the former tasks with higher degree of freedom than that in conventional on-line scheduling. Thus scheduling problems in practice will be solved by overcoming more difficulties than idealized off-line ones, however less effort might be taken to achieve a relative optimized algorithm than on-line scheduling. These scheduling problems, where the above two assumptions for on-line sorting can not fully apply, are so-called semi on-line scheduling problems. First reported in 1996, the studies based on semi on-line concept have been conducted in both practical and theoretical research fields for the last decade. Models being developed based on this concept, a new branch of scheduling was recognized as semi-on-line scheduling.

3. DYNAMISATION CONSTRAINT SOLVING SCHEME

In the semi on-line scheduling problem, we do not know all the time variables of tasks in advance. The new variables are introduced as the schedule progresses, i.e., the original constraint satisfaction problem extend continually. Consequently, we cannot post a constraint C(X) until we know all the variables X. Nevertheless, if the constraint is monotonic we can do better by posting a constraint over the known variables and when a new variable (or a variable set Y) arrives we can post a new constraint extended by the new variable and deactivate the old constraint. This is the basic idea behind a generic dynamisation scheme that we will describe in details now.

3.1 Dynamic constraint modeling

A *Constraint Satisfaction Problem*[5] P=(X,D,C) is defined as a set of variables $X=\{x_1,\ldots,x_n\}$, a set of domains $D=\{D(x_1),\ldots,D(x_n)\}$, where $D(x_i)$ is a finite set of possible values for variable x_i, and a set of constraints $C=\{c_1,\ldots,c_m\}$. A *constraint* c_i on the ordered set of variables $X(c_i)=(x_{i1},\ldots,x_{ik})$ is a subset of the Cartesian product $D(x_{i1}) \times\ldots \times D(x_{ik})$, it specifies the allowed combinations of values for the variables $x_{i1},\ldots,x_{ik}$. $|X(c_i)|$ is called arity of the constraint c_i.

Assume that $(v_1,\ldots,v_n)\downarrow(x_{i1},\ldots,x_{ik})$ is a standard projection operator, i.e., a projection of the tuple $(v_1,\ldots,v_n)$ to the variables $(x_{i1},\ldots,x_{ik})$: $(v_1,\ldots,v_n)\downarrow(x_{i1},\ldots,x_{ik}) = (v_{i1},\ldots,v_{ik})$. We call a complete instantiation $(v_1,\ldots,v_n)$ of the variables, such that $\forall i=1,\ldots,n$ $v_i\in D(x_i)$ and $\forall j=1,\ldots,m$ $(v_1,\ldots,v_n)\downarrow X(c_j) \in c_j$, a *valid tuple* or *solution*, i.e., the valid tuple is a complete instantiation of the variables satisfying all the constraints. Sol(P) is a set of all valid tuples, we call it a *solution set* of the constraint satisfaction problem P.

But the traditional formulation of a *CSP* is static in sense that all the variables and the constraints are known before we start to solve the problem. Nevertheless, the semi on-line scheduling problem does not fit this static constraint model and that require a more dynamic constraint modeling and solving scheme. Here we introduce the concept of monotonicity to tackle this problem. Monotonicity means that extending a constraint, i.e., adding new variables to the constraint, does not add new solutions. In the semi on-line problem, we can find there are some constraints which have this speciality. The following is the definition about monotonicity.

Definition 1: Problem P'=(X',D',C') is called an *extension of the problem* P=(X,D,C), if $X\subseteq X'$, $C\subseteq C'$ and $\forall x\in X$ $D(x)=D'(x)$. Briefly speaking, we extend the original problem P to problem P' if we add new variables and constraints to it.

Definition 2: *Constraint extension is monotonic*, if P' is an extension of P, then $Sol(P')\downarrow X \subseteq Sol(P)$, where X is a set of variables in P, i.e., every solution of the extended problem is also a solution of the original problem.

Let C(X) be a function that maps arbitrary finite ordered set of variables to a conjunction of constraints, which forms a sub-problem in the constraint satisfaction problem. Note, that the constraints in $C(x_1,\ldots,x_k)$ may contain variables other than $x_1,\ldots,x_k$ but these variables are local/hidden there, i.e., they do not appear in the rest of the problem. If we have a constraint conjunction C(X), we say that C(Y) is its extension if $X \subseteq Y$.

Definition 3: Let Sol(C(X), D(X)) be a solution set for the constraint C(X) and a set of variables X with domains D(X). *A constraint solving scheme/algorithm* is *monotonic*, if $Sol(C(X \cup Y), D(X \cup Y)) \downarrow X \subseteq Sol(C(X), D(X))$ for arbitrary sets X and Y of variables.

Generally speaking, monotony of constraint extension means that extending a constraint, i.e., adding new variables to the constraint, does not add new solutions. And monotony of constraint solving scheme means that if solving starts with larger domains then it does not achieve better pruning of the domains than when starting from smaller domains.

3.2 Algorithm Dyna-Solver

Our objective is to design a generic dynamisation constraint solving algorithm that allows extending the set of variables in the constraint scheme on fly while preserving consistency achieved by the solving algorithm for the static constraint. The dynamisation algorithm *Dyna-Solver* we designed is a dynamic extension of the static constraint solving algorithm *CB-Solver*[6], which maps a constraint C(X), domains D(X) and a new set of variables Y to domains $D'(X \cup Y)$ such that $Sol(G(X \cup Y), D(X \cup Y)) \subseteq D'(X \cup Y) \subseteq$ *CB-Solver*$(G(X \cup Y), D(X \cup Y))$.

Algorithm *Propagation* for the constraint C(X), which is wrapped in a trigger procedure *p* is a part of *CB-Solver*. In particular, procedure $p(x_1, \ldots, x_n)$ calls the filtering algorithm for the constraint C(X) every time a domain of any variable x_i is changed. We will use this procedure as the basic interface to the filtering algorithm for C(X). Our algorithm exploits the monotony property of the constraint in semi on-line scheduling problem. In particular, we can start with the previous solution (domains) to get a solution (restricted domains) of the extended constraint.

Compared with the static algorithm *CB-Solver*, *Dyna-Solver* has three improvements. The algorithm first handles the set of the extending variables (step 1). Variables can be removed from the constraint only upon backtracking, i.e. LIFO (last-in first-out) mechanism is applied for adding/removing variables to/from the constraint. Moreover, if we add a set of variables, the whole set is removed together upon backtracking. LIFO mechanism for adding/removing the variables may seem like a restriction but it simplifies significantly the implementation. Then, it deactivates the current propagation algorithm (step 2), note that it does not mean removing the constraint from the constraint store, it is just stopping propagation through it (the internal data structures are kept). Then, it saves domains of the variables to the stack (step 3), typically, the underlying constraint engine saves such information; we highlight it just to illustrate the track of the algorithm. The following is the detail of *Dyna-Solver*.

Dyna-Solver `(C(X1,…, Xk), Xk+1)`

```
1) Check the length of the variable stack, i.e.,
   judge the number of the variables is changed or
   not
2) Deactivate p(X1,…, Xk), i.e., push its internal
   data structures to the stack and stop propagation
   through this constraint (if k≥1, otherwise do
   nothing)
3) Push domains of X1,…, Xk, Xk+1 to the variable
   stack
4) Judge whether there is a variable in the variable
   stack. If no, skip to step(1)
5) Judge whether the domain of the variable is null.
   If yes, skip to step(9)
6) Select the variable that has the smallest domain
   and the most constraints to be the current
   variable
7) Judge the domain of current variable is null or
   not. If not, skip to step(9)
8) Check the constraint stack of current variable,
   i.e., judge whether any constraint propagation
   events happen. If the constraints are consistency
   (use the trigger procedure p to judge) then skip
   to step (4), else skip to step (5)
9) Backtrack. If success then skip to step (5), else
   terminate
```

When removing a variable upon backtracking, we simply reverse algorithm *Dyna-Solver*. It means: removing the extended constraint from the constraint store (now, it is real removing, not just deactivation), restoring domains of the variables (this is usually done automatically when the extended constraint is removed from the constraint store), and activating the former constraint again.

4. AN EXPERIMENTAL STUDY OF DYNA-SOLVER

Shop-loading scheduling is one kind of discrete resource-constrained scheduling problems, in which tasks require a discrete resource of capacity strictly greater than 1. In this context, two tasks which require the same resource may overlap in time, but the total capacity required at time t must not exceed the capacity available at time t. The problem is solved by assigning precise start an end times to each task in the schedule. The propagation of resource constraints is exploited to prune the search tree and to guarantee that the available capacity is never exceeded.

In the general/off-line shop-loading problem, the number of the tasks, the duration of tasks and the required amounts of resource capacity are fixed once and for all. The capacity of the resource (h) is also fixed. The goal is to minimize the makespan. Formally: task set *T*= { $T_1, T_2, \cdots, T_n$ } , duration set *Dur*={Dur_1, $Dur_2, \cdots, Dur_n$ } , required amounts of resource capacity set T(R)={$T_1(R)$, $T_2(R), \cdots, T_n(R)$}. A shop-loading scheduling problem can be encoded efficiently as a CSP:

- The time variable set X={$st_1, st_2, \ldots, st_n$}, time variable st_i is associated with each task T_i; it represent the start time of T_i.
- The domain D_i of st_i is initialized with $[0, \sum_{i=1}^{n} Dur_i]$.
- The constraint Set C:
  Temporal precedence constraint: Successors(T_i) =T_j means that $st_j \geq st_i + Dur_i$; Resource cumulative constraint: *Cumulative*(($st_1, \ldots, st_n$), ($Dur_1, \cdots, Dur_n$), ($T_1(R), \cdots, T_n(R)$), h). The constraint enforces the condition $\sum_{i=1}^{n} T_i(R) \leq h$, all t ($st_i \leq t \leq st_i + Dur_i$).

Consider the problem, which consists of 13 tasks (n=13) subject to precedence constraints, as indicated in the table1. The capacity of the resource R is 8 (h=8).

Table 1. Example of Ship-loading

T_j	T_1	T_2	T_3	T_4	T_5	T_6	T_7	T_8	T_9	T_{10}	T_{11}	T_{12}	T_{13}
Successors	T_2T_4	T_3	T_5T_7	T_5	T_6	T_8	T_8	T_9	T_{10}	$T_{11}T_{12}$	-	T_{13}	-
Dur_j	3	4	4	6	5	2	3	4	3	2	3	2	1
$R(T_j)$	4	4	3	4	5	5	4	3	4	8	4	5	4

Considering this example in off-line case, we solve it by using *CB-Solver*. The schedule results are displayed in the figure1. makespan=35.

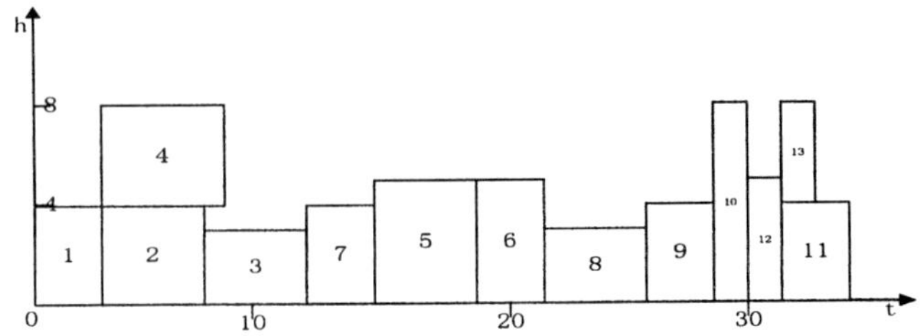

Figure 1. Schedule Results in Off-line Case

Considering this example in semi on-line case, we assume a new task is introduced at time t=20. We name the new task T_{14} (Dur_{14}=3, $T_{14}(R)$=1). The adding time variable set Y={st_{14}}. Extension constraints: Successors(T_8)= T_{14}, i.e., $V_{14} \geq V_8 + Dur_8$ and *Cumulative*(X∪Y, Dur∪Dur_{14}, T(R)∪T_{14}(R), h). The constraint solving scheme *Dyna-Solver* (*Cumulative*(X, Dur, T(R), h), Y) is monotonic because there are no local variables in the *Cumulative* constraint. The schedule results are displayed in the figure2.

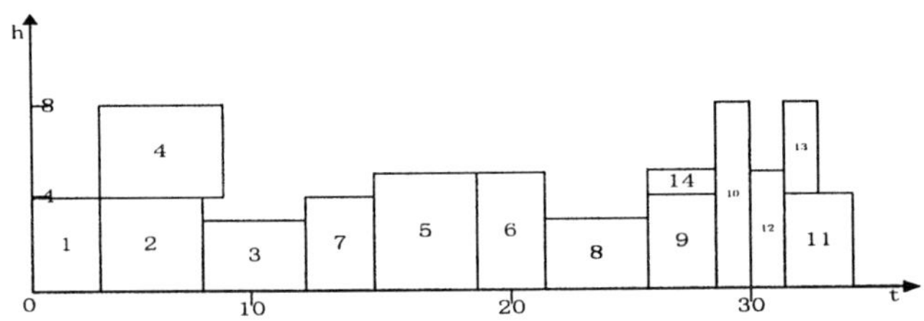

Figure 2. Schedule Results in Semi On-line Case

The results show that the adding variable st_{14} in the constraint *Cumulative* does not bring the new result to the original solution. So it is not essential for us to re-schedule the new problem because of the extension of monotonic constraints.

5. CONCLUSIONS

In the Operation Research field, the semi on-line scheduling problems are studied for a long time. But in the constraint programming field, the related research just begins. This paper presents the dynamisation of monotonic constraints solving in the semi on-line scheduling problems. We designed a generic dynamic constraint solving scheme, which adapts to arbitrary monotonic constraint appears in the semi on-line scheduling problem. In the highly dynamic problems, our approach is even more beneficial. However, there are also many non-monotonic constraints. These constraints cannot be dynamized using the scheme we proposed. The main obstacle here is that adding new variables to a non-monotonic constraint might add new solutions to the constraint. Consequently, to design a constraint solving scheme that can be used to solve real-life dynamic scheduling problems is also the biggest challenge of current constraint programming.

ACKNOWLEDGEMENTS

This paper is supported by the National Natural Science Foundation Key Project of China (Grant No.60273080, 60473003), the Program for New Century Excellent Talents in University and the Outstanding Youth Foundation of Jilin Province of China (Grant No.20030107).

REFERENCES

[1] Wallace, M.: Applying Constraints for Scheduling, in Constraint Programming, Mayoh B. and Penjaak J.(eds.), NATO ASI Series, Springer Verlag (1994)

[2] Tsang, E. P. K.: Foundations of Constraint Satisfaction, San Diego, Calif.: Academic (1993) 53-63

[3] Mittal, S., Falkemhainer, B.: Dynamic Constraint Satisfaction Problems, In Proceedings of AAAI-90 (1990) 25-32

[4] Sgall J.: On-line scheduling. In: Fiat, A. and Woeginger, G. eds. , On-line Algorithms: The State of Art, Lecture Notes in Computer Sciengces, 1442. Berlin: Springer-Verlag (1998)

[5] Tsang, E. P. K, Foundations of Constraint Satisfaction. San Diego, Calif.: Academic (1993) 5-10

[6] Juyang Zhang, Xin Li, Jigui Sun: Research On Constraint-based Scheduling and Its Implementation, Proceeding of CNCC'03, Beijing, The Tsinghua University Press (2003) 80-85

A WEB-BASED INTELLIGENT TUTORING SYSTEM

Zhiping Li, Yu Sun and Minkun Liu
[1]*Computer Center of Yunnan Normal University,* [2,3]*Institute of Computer Science and Information Technology, Yunnan Normal University, 650092, Kunming, China*

Abstract: A formal model of a web-based intelligent tutoring system composed of a user environment and a pedagogical environment is presented, which represents domain knowledge based on ontologies to improve the sharing and reusing of teaching materials. The system constructs the user environment based on users' knowledge levels, learning styles, psychology characteristics, etc. in order to improve the self-adaptability and pedagogical effects of the system. Furthermore, it distinguishes information about a user and what a pedagogical agent knows about the user. Based on the pedagogical agent's knowledge (represented by its cognitive state) about the user, a teaching process is designed for the user. Finally, the running process of the system is discussed in detail to show that the model is practicable.

Key words: intelligent tutoring system, ontologies, web, domain knowledge

1. INTRODUCTION

Intelligent Tutoring Systems (ITSs) is a branch of artificial intelligence and form an advanced generation of Computer Aided Instruction systems [1,2]. The key feature of intelligent tutoring systems is the ability to provide a user self-adapted presentation of the teaching material [9] by using artificial intelligence methods to represent the pedagogical decisions and the information about each user. The emergence of the WWW has increased the applications of such systems [3,4].

Although some tutoring systems have correct information and appropriate teaching strategies, a learner might still lack the motivation to complete a learning process [10]. The main reason is that these systems apply the same approach to all learners and do not consider users' different knowledge levels, learning styles, and demands. Our tutoring system constructs the user model based on users' knowledge levels, learning styles, psychology characteristics, etc. in order to improve the self-adaptability and pedagogical effects of the system. Furthermore we use ontologies for domain knowledge representation to improve the sharing and reusing of materials; and use multimedia materials obtained from web to improve teaching effects.

Even if some systems take a user's characteristics (e.g. knowledge levels, learning styles, etc.) and needs into account, a gap between the estimation of users' characteristics and the users' real characteristics may make these systems fail to reach the desired effects. To describe this gap, we distinguish information about a user and what a pedagogical agent knows about the user. The pedagogical agent transforms its perceptions about the user (e.g. knowledge levels, learning styles, etc.) into its knowledge. If this transformation is complete (no information loss), then there is no gap between the pedagogical agent's cognition of a user's characteristics and the user's real characteristics. Based on the knowledge about a user, a pedagogical agent designs a teaching process for the user.

The paper is organized as follows. Section 2 presents an overview of the system's architecture. Section 3 presents the user environments formalism of the system. Section 4 presents the representation of domain knowledge and the pedagogical environment formalism of the system. Section 5 describes the runs of the system in detail to show that the model is practicable. Finally, section 7 concludes the paper with conclusion and future works.

2. A WEB-BASED INTELLIGENT TUTORING SYSTEM

In this section, we propose the formal model of a web-based intelligent tutoring system showed in figure 1. The model consists of two parts: user environment (*PE*) and pedagogical environment (*PE*).

Our intelligent tutoring system contains one pedagogical agent with a set of cognitive states which records its cognition or knowledge of the user agent and one user agent with a set of user states (user models) recording basic information such as personal data, user characteristics, etc. about the user. The user agent updates its state after finishing a learning process.

The cognitive process of the pedagogical agent include two steps: (1) dividing user states into disjoint set; the pedagogical agent cannot distinguish two user states in a same partition; and for two user states in a same partition, the pedagogical agent adopt the same teach process; (2)

perceiving the user state; the perceptions of two user states in a same partition is the same. Then, according to what perceived from a user state, the pedagogical agent transforms the perceptions into its knowledge and changes its cognitive states. Since there may be information loss in the perceiving step and transformation process, what the pedagogical agent knows about a user state cannot completely reflect the user state.

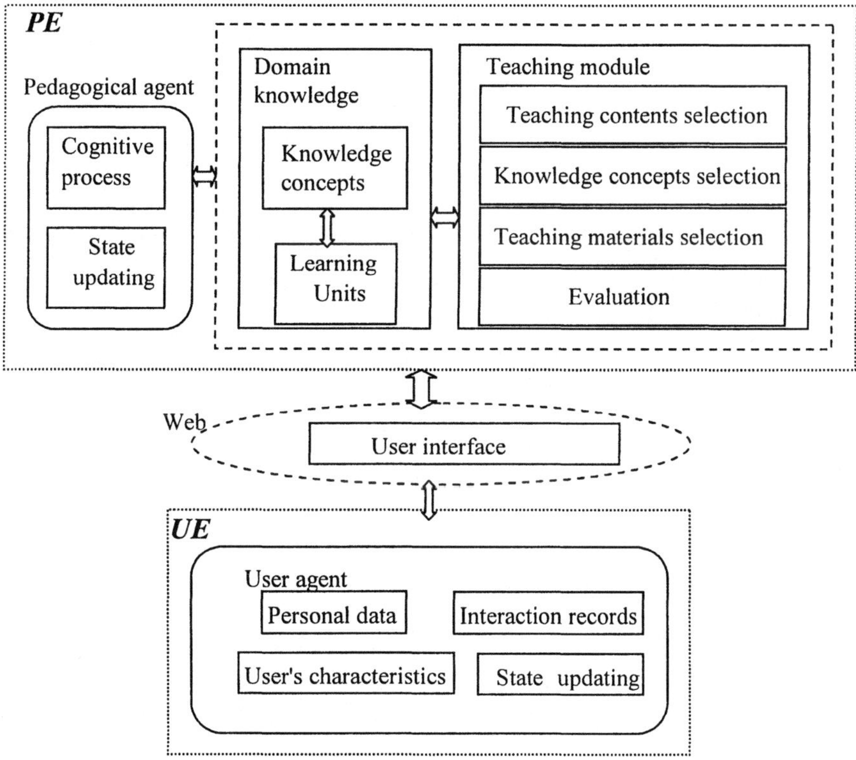

Figure 1: Intelligent Tutoring System

Finally, the pedagogical agent makes use of the domain knowledge and teaching module to design a teaching process based on its cognition or knowledge about the use agent. We discuss in detail the user environment and pedagogical environment in the following sections.

3. USER ENVIRONMENT

In this section, we introduce the user environment (*PE*) and give its formal definition.

Comparing with traditional pedagogical system, the most salience character of ITSs is self-adaptability [5]. ITSs construct user model based on users' knowledge levels, cognitive abilities, psychology characteristics, etc. and then makes a teaching plan for each user according to its user model. Furthermore, ITSs can instruct a user in person with pertinence; and adjust teaching contents and strategies dynamically in the process of teaching in order to optimize teaching materials and strategies and to improve the self-adaptability and pedagogical effects of the system.

The goal of user model is to guide intelligent tutoring systems to adopt the most suitable teaching content and strategies. Most of web-based systems cannot adjust learning materials on demands [6]. At the same time, even if there is correct information, users may lack the motivation to accomplish the whole learning process, for example, users may dislike current learning styles. These systems haven't considered that users have different levels in knowledge levels, learning styles and demands. Hence, they adopt a same teaching content and teaching methods for all the users.

Based on multiple domains and multiple applications, we study user environment in terms of learning styles, knowledge levels, learning motivations and psychology characteristics, etc.

Formally, a user environment *UE* is defined as follows:

UE=< *U, L,I, vis, perc, trans, inter, update*>, where

- $U=\{u_1, u_2,\ldots\}$ is a set of user states; each u represents a user model;
- $L=\{l_1, l_2,\ldots\}$ is a set of cognitive states of the pedagogical agent which represent the internal structure of the pedagogical agent, that is, the knowledge of the pedagogical agent about the user agent;
- $I=\{i_1, i_2,\ldots\}$ is a set of interaction states of a user agent with an intelligent tutoring system; interaction states contain information recorded from the interaction between a user and a system such as things like, the type and amount of help asked, the correct and wrong answers to exercises, the marks obtained from exercises, etc.
- *vis*: $U \rightarrow 2^U$, is a user state partition function; it divides the elements in U into disjoint sets such that $\forall u \in U$, we have $u \in vis(u)$. We say *vis* is transparent if $\forall u \in U$, $vis(u)=\{u\}$, that is, every user state is visible to a pedagogical agent; a pedagogical agent cannot distinguish two user states if they belongs to one partition, that is, it regards the two user states to be the same;
- *perc*: $vis(U) \rightarrow P$, is a user state perception function, where the set of user state perceptions P consists all the information that is perceived by a pedagogical agent in a user state; we say *perc* is perfect if it is an injection, that is, a pedagogical agent can perceive all the information that is visible to it;
- *trans*: $L \times Perc \rightarrow L$, is a cognitive state transformation function; it changes the cognitive state of a pedagogical agent according to its perception of a user state, that is, after a perception process of a user

state, a pedagogical agent translates what it perceives into knowledge and update its cognitive state; if *trans* (l, p)= *trans* (l', p') when $p= p'$, then *trans* is complete, that is, there is no information loss;

- *inter*: $I \rightarrow I$, is an interaction state transformation function; it updates the interaction records of a user agent with a system;
- *update*: $U \times I \times E \rightarrow U$, is a user state updating function; it changes the state of a user agent according to the pervious user state; the evaluation of the user's performance in a learning process (of a teaching content); and the interaction records between the user and the system.

A user state used to record information about the user is vital for the system's user-adapted operation. It includes the following information:

(1) Personal data: The personal data concerns information necessary for the creation and management of the user's account (e.g. name, email). It is used for the identification of the user.

(2) User's characteristics: cognitive abilities (e.g., attention, memory, etc.); learning styles (e.g., preferences of multimedia type such as text, image, etc.); experience concerning the use of computer and intelligent tutoring system and availability of Internet resources; expectations (e.g. the knowledge and skill that a use desires to learn; and teaching strategies preferences.

(3) Knowledge level such as novice, beginner, intermediate, advanced, etc. of the sub-domains and the whole domain.

(4) Interaction records which record the interaction of a user with a system.

User characteristics and knowledge levels directly affect the teaching process whereas most of the interaction information indirectly.

4. PEDAGOGICAL ENVIRONMENT

In this section, we discuss the pedagogical environment (*PE*) and give its formal definition.

The pedagogical environment provides the knowledge infrastructure in order to tailor presentation of the teaching material according to the cognitive states of the pedagogical agent. It dynamically produces personalized teaching web pages (learning units) to optimize teaching effect.

First, we discuss the representation of domain knowledge based on ontologies. The introduction of ontologies is to overcome the general problem in existing teaching systems [7]. At the same time, web introduces rich multimedia teaching materials by texts, images, audios, videos, examples, etc. to make the dynamic interaction between systems and users and between users available [8]. Besides effective communication, dynamic interaction improves the abilities of problem solving and learning.

Hence, we construct the representation frame of domain knowledge based on ontologies to improve the sharing and reusing of teaching materials; and we fuse the rich teaching materials provided by web into the frame. We adopt three-level frame to represent domain knowledge: subject level (the subject content of learning and teaching); knowledge concept level (knowledge concepts and the relations between these concepts such as part-of, is-a and prerequisite, etc.); and teaching material level (multimedia materials, e.g. text materials, image materials, example materials, exercise materials, video materials and audio materials). In the above three level frame, a subject corresponds to a set of knowledge concepts used to teach the subject; a knowledge concept corresponds to a set of multimedia materials used to teach the concept. We extract part of the materials from the multimedia materials according to user's learning styles, etc. and organize these materials based on some specific teaching strategies to form a learning unit of the knowledge concept. This learning unit is presented to users when teaching the knowledge concept.

Due to the differences among uses' teaching strategy preferences, learning styles, memory and knowledge levels, etc. and the richness of materials, same knowledge concept may correspond to several learning units.

Then, we discuss the process of teaching. In the process of teaching, the pedagogical agent must perform the following tasks: (i) Select teaching contents (sets of knowledge concepts) to be taught according to the cognitive state of the pedagogical agent; (ii) Select a knowledge concept that will be taught currently according to the relations between the knowledge concepts (of a teaching content) and the evaluation of the learning effect of the previous knowledge concept; (iii) Select a learning unit to be presented from the set of learning units corresponding to the knowledge concept selected in (ii) according to the cognitive state of the pedagogical agent; (iv) Evaluate the user's performance and update the user's state.

Selection of a set of knowledge concepts in (i) is based on the user's knowledge of the domain, links between knowledge concepts, and user's desired detail level of the presented educational content. Evaluation of the user's performance updates the inferable user characteristics and may create a feedback for tasks (iii) and (iv).

From what has been discussed above, we give the definition of pedagogical environment $PE = \langle K, C, E, csel, ksel, teach, eval \rangle$, where,

- $K=\{k_1, k_2, \ldots\}$ is a set of knowledge concepts;
- $C=\{c_1, c_2, \ldots\}$ is a set of learning units;
- $E=\{e_1, e_2, \ldots\}$ is a set of evaluation states of learning units;
- $csel$: $L \rightarrow 2^K$, is a teaching content selection function; it selects the set of knowledge concepts to be taught according to the cognitive state of the

pedagogical agent (especially about user's domain knowledge levels and expectations);

- *ksel*: $L \times E \times csel(L) \rightarrow K$, is a knowledge concept selection function; it selects the most suitable knowledge concept to be taught currently according to the cognitive state of the pedagogical agent; the relationships between knowledge concepts and the evaluation of the learning effect of the previous taught knowledge concept, for example, in teaching process, if there is a priority order between two knowledge concepts, then the system will not teach the user the next knowledge concept unless the evaluation of the learning effect of the previous taught knowledge concept reaches the lowest standard.
- *teach*: $L \times K \rightarrow C$, is a learning unit selection function; it selects the most suitable learning unit to be presented according to the cognitive state of the pedagogical agent (about user's cognitive abilities, learning styles, knowledge levels, etc.) and the knowledge concept to be taught;
- *eval*: $L \times I \times C \rightarrow E$, is a learning unit evaluation function; it evaluates user's performance in a learning unit according to the cognitive state of the pedagogical agent; the learning unit to be taught; and the interaction records between user and the system (the type and number of learning units accessed, the type and amount of help asked, the correct and wrong answers to exercises, the marks obtained from exercises, etc.).

5. RUN OF THE SYSTEM

A web-based intelligent tutoring system S=<*UE,PE*> consists of user environment and pedagogical environment and a set of its global states $S = \{s_0, s_1, \ldots\}$ is a sub-set of $U \times L \times C \times E$. A global state s composed of a user state u, a cognitive state l, a learning unit c, and an evaluation state e, that is, $s=(u, l, c, e)$.The goal user state $s_g = (u_g, l_g, c_g, e_g)$ represents the goal state that is expected by a user agent and a pedagogical agent; and $s_1= (u_1, l_1, c_1, e_1)$ is an initial global state composed of an initial user state u_1, an initial cognitive state l_1, an initial learning unit c_1 and an initial evaluation state e_1.

The run of an intelligent tutoring system can be viewed as a sequence of global states. A sequence $(s_1, s_2,\ldots)$ of S is a run of system S=<*UE,PE*> if and only if:

- the initial global state $s_1= (u_1, l_1, teach_1(l_1, ksel_1(l_1, e_0, csel_1(l_1))), e_1)$;where $l_1=trans_1(u_1, perc_1(vis_1(u_1)))$; $e_1= eval_1(l_1, i_1, teach_1 (l_1, ksel_1(l_1, e_0, csel_1(l_1))))$; and e_0 is the evaluation of the domain knowledge level of user agent;
- for every k, if $s_k=(u_k, l_k, c_k, e_k)$, $s_{k+1}=(u_{k+1}, l_{k+1}, c_{k+1}, e_{k+1})$, then $l_{k+1}= trans_k (u_k, perc_k (vis_k (u_k)))$; $u_{k+1}= update_k (l_k, i_k, eval_k(l_k, i_k, teach_k(l_k,$

$ksel_k(l_k, e_{k-1}, csel_k(l_k)))))$; $c_{k+1} = teach_k(l_k, ksel_k(l_k, e_{k-1}, csel_k(l_k)))$; and $e_{k+1} = eval_k(l_k, i_k, teach_k(l_k, ksel_k(l_k, e_{k-1}, csel_k(l_k))))$.

The run of system S can be described as follows: first, a pedagogical agent observes an initial user state u_1 in its cognitive process (using partition function *vis*, perception function *perc*) and change its state to l_1; then the pedagogical agent does the following tasks: (1) Select the set of knowledge concepts used to represent a teaching content according to its state via function *csel*; (2) Select the knowledge concept to be taught via function *ksel*; (3) Select a learning unit to teach the user agent via function *teach* and get c_1; and (4) Evaluates the performance of the user agent after the learning unit has been taught via function *eval* and get e_1. Thus we get the initial global state of the system s_1。

If s_1 is not in accordance with the goal state s_g (e.g. user agent haven't finish the learning of all the knowledge concepts in a teaching content; the performance of user agent haven't reach the expectations of the user agent or the pedagogical agent, etc.), then repeat the above process to get the next global state s_2 until there is some s_j such that it is in accordance with the goal state s_g.

6. CONCLUSION AND FUTURE WORKS

A formal model of a web-based intelligent tutoring system is presented with the following properties:

- ✧ The system represents domain knowledge based on ontologies to improve the sharing and reusing of domain knowledge.
- ✧ The system constructs the user environment based on users' cognitive abilities, knowledge levels, learning styles, psychology characteristics, etc. in order to improve the self-adaptability and pedagogical effects of the system.
- ✧ The model distinguishes the information about a user and what a pedagogical agent knows about the user agent.
- ✧ The running process of the system is defined and discussed in detail to show that the model is practicable.

The system discussed in this paper has only one user agent and the extension of the model to include multiple users are part of our future works. Furthermore, the lacking of face-to-face communication in web-based intelligent tutoring systems reduces users' learning motivation. Hence, the utilizing of the communication, interaction and self-adaptability of agents to improve the interaction between users and between users and the system in order to strengthen the learning motivations of users and to improve teaching effects is also our future works.

NOTES

The work is partially supported by the Natural Science Fund (NSF) of Yunnan Province (No.2004F0017Q), the key project of NSF of Yunnan Province (No. 04F00062), and the Education Bureau Youth Fund of Yunnan Province (No. 03Y312D, No.04Y769D).

REFERENCES

[1] J.M. Fritz, Provides Intelligence in Web-based Tutors. *North American Web Developers Conference,* October 1998.

[2] G. Katerina, The design of a 'motivating' intelligent assessment system, In *Proceedings of Lecture Note in Computer Science* 1839, pages 208-218, 2002.

[3] R. Reddy: Three open problems in AI. *JACM* 50(1): 83-86, 2003.

[4] M. Specht, R. Oppermann, ATS-Adaptive Teaching System: a WWW-based ITS, In U. Timm (Eds.), *Proceedings of Workshop Adaptivität und Benutzer modellierung in Interaktiven Software systemen:* ABIS 1998.

[5] P. Brusilovsky, Adaptive and Intelligent Technologies for Web-based Education. In: Rollinger, C., Peylo, C. (eds.) *Kunstliche Intelligenz, Special Issue on Intelligent Systems and Teleteaching*, 1999.

[6] N.Manouselis & D.Sampson: Dynamic Knowledge Route Selection for Personalised Learning Environments using Multiple Criteria Analysis, In *Proceedings of the 20th IASTED International Multi-Conference on Applied Informatics*, 2002.

[7] J. Lim, Theoretical bases on web-based instruction from a viewpoint of interactivity, In *Journal of Educational Technology*, 5(1):29-54,1999.

[8] Georgouli, K.: Modelling a Versatile Mathematical Curriculum for Low- attainers. In *Proceedings of the 8th Panhellenic Conference in Informatics*, pages 463-472, 2001.

[9] Vassileva, J.: Dynamic Courseware Generation. In *Journal of Computing and Information Technology*, 5: 87-102,1997.

[10] Angelides, M., Garcia, I.: Towards an Intelligent Knowledge Based Tutoring System for Foreign Language Learning. In *Journal of Computing and Information Technology*, 1:15-28, 1993.

[11] Aïmeur, E., Frasson, C., Dufort, H. "Co-operative Learning Strategies for Intelligent Tutoring Systems". In Journal of Applied Artificial Intelligence, 14 (5): 465-490, 2000.

[12] M. Wooldridge and A. Lomuscio. A Computationally Grounded Logic of Visibility, Perception, and Knowledge, in *Logic Journal of the IGPL*, 9(2):273-288, 2001.

AN APPROACH TO AUTOMATED KNOWLEDGE DISCOVERY IN BIOINFORMATICS

Junjun Ouyang[1], A. Fazel Famili[1], Weiling Xu[2]
[1]Institute for Information Technology, National Research Council Canada, 1200 Montreal Road, Ottawa, ON K1A 0R6 Canada; [2]118 Shady Grove Street, Nepean, ON K2G 6Z5 Canada (a co-op student with National Research Council Canada)

Abstract: Extensive data mining applications to bioinformatics research have shown that knowledge discovery requires repeated manual interventions, and that conglomerating and summarizing the results would be time consuming and sometimes error prone. To assist in efficiently applying data mining technologies in bioinformatics, we have developed Automation facilities in our data mining software suite. Experiences gained from case studies are extracted and presented as scenarios, which are sets of data processing and analysis operations for specific data mining objectives. Built as sequences of these predefined scenarios, procedures apply previously established data mining strategies to new data sets in an automated way. Automation also highlights the results particularly related to researchers' own areas of interest. We present insights into our automated knowledge discovery and two example scenarios extracted from one case study to demonstrate the usefulness of our approach.

Key words: data mining; bioinformatics; automation

1. INTRODUCTION

Advances in molecular biomedical technologies, e.g. large scale gene expression profiling[1,2] and high throughput sequencing[3,4], are producing enormous amount of data. Various knowledge discovery tools, techniques and algorithms have been applied to expression profile clustering[5], disease pattern classification[6], and DNA/protein sequence analysis[7].

How to efficiently apply various knowledge discovery technologies and strategies, however, is a challenge to bioinformatics researchers. As a solution, some tools or services that are used for sequence analysis and annotation[8,9], or for microarray data management and analysis[10-12] have developed automated pipelines, or provided the flexibility to build workflows based on specific analysis protocols. These developments focused mainly on building a workflow/pipeline as a connection of basic function modules. The knowledge discovery process, however, often involves interactive and iterative applications of complex computational operations, e.g. clustering analysis and various data transformation. Moreover, many biomedical researchers do not have enough knowledge and experience applying data mining techniques, while computer scientists usually lack the required expertise in biomedical research.

In our data mining software suite, BioMiner (http://iit-iti.nrc-cnrc.gc.ca/projects-projets/biomine_e.html), we are developing Automation facilities to encapsulate data analysis strategies, automate some operations, and highlight the most interesting discoveries. This approach involves: capturing real research experiences from case studies; structuring and presenting them as building blocks of knowledge discovery processes for new data sets.

2. DEVELOPMENT OF AUTOMATION

2.1 Motivation

To support knowledge discovery in our bioinformatics research, we have in-house developed a data mining software suite, BioMiner. Integrated into one environment, there are thirteen functional modules in data processing and analysis layers. These modules, e.g. statistics, visualization, clustering, and pattern recognition, are collections of data mining algorithms and tools. More specifically, clustering module has various clustering algorithms, e.g. hierarchical, K-Means and SOM; and pattern recognition module contains algorithms of decision trees, association rules, and so on. These modules are not only the units of software development, but also those of data analysis.

Working with biomedical researchers, we have applied BioMiner to microarray and sequence data analyses[13-18]. These case studies required well-defined data mining strategies and various functional modules. Results were reported in tables and displayed in, e.g. histograms and cluster centroid plots. One functional module may have been applied to a data set many times but with different settings. We then compared all the results to find common patterns and important discoveries. In these studies, the repeated manual operations and result summarization were usually time-consuming and error-prone. We, nevertheless, treasure the analysis strategies established in these studies and believe that preserving and reusing them in the future is a way to cope with the complexity of biomedical knowledge discovery.

2.2 Design

Designing any automated facility requires an in-depth understanding of the task(s) for which the system is built. Based on completed case studies, sets of operations of usually one functional module are identified and generalized as Scenarios for specific data mining objectives or tasks. A scenario relies on running one module and summarizing the outputs. This helps researchers use the module appropriately and focus on important results. Different applications of the same module may be designed as different scenarios (Figure 1a). These scenarios, sets of data mining operations, are building blocks for a Procedure, or components of a knowledge discovery process (KDP). Figure 1b shows a procedure as a sequence of one or more scenarios. For instance, a procedure of a microarray data analysis could consist of the following scenarios in sequence: characteristic checking, clustering analysis, and pattern recognition.

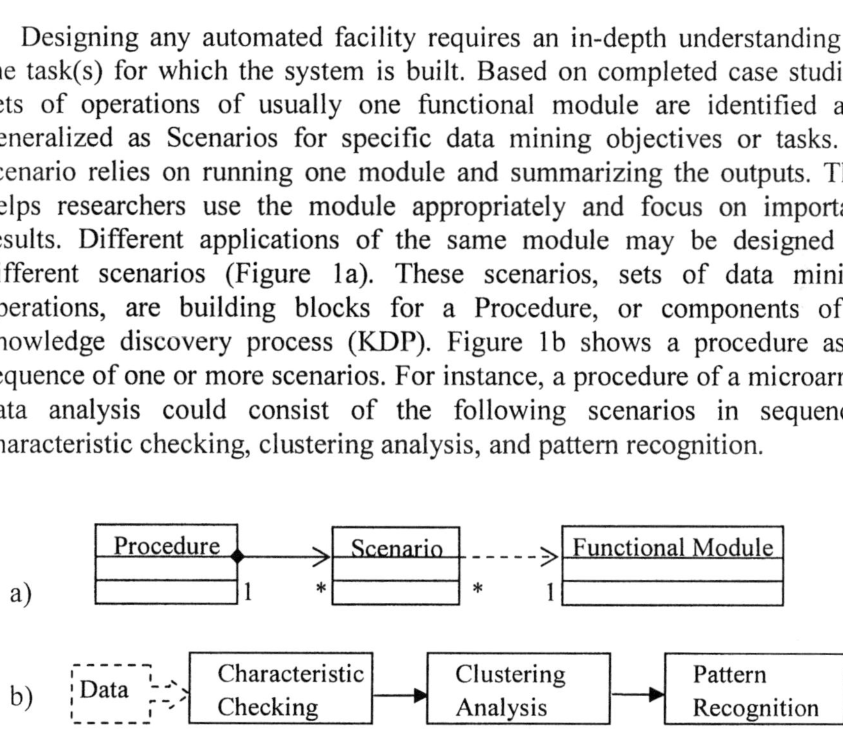

Figure 1. a). Object-oriented design: relationships between Procedure and Scenario, and between Scenario and Functional Module. b). A knowledge discovery process.

Other Automation features are also designed for creation, execution, and management of KDP's. Researchers may build a procedure consisting of several scenarios, set up appropriate parameters, and invoke the procedure. Automation executes scenarios in sequence, monitors the progress, and summarizes the outputs. Researchers then collect and study the results with highlighted discoveries.

Here, we use one of our genomics case studies to demonstrate what experiences are captured and how they are abstracted into Automation scenarios.

2.3 Case-Study-Based Scenario Design

In one case study on breast cancer[19], biologists isolated and characterized a murine mammary epithelial tumor cell line, which undergoes an epithelial-to-mesenchymal transition (EMT) as a result of a transforming growth factor (TGF-β1) exposure. We analyzed gene expression experiments to investigate TGF-β1 induced EMT and the role of p38 mitogen-activated protein kinase (p38MAPK). The expression data consisted of 331 genes (selected from a list of 15264 genes) obtained from cells treated with TGF-β1, or the p38MAPK inhibitor SB203580 (SB), or both of them (TGF-β1+SB). There were 6 experimental repeats for each treatment. In the next two subsections, we describe our data analyses and the designs of two scenarios accordingly.

2.3.1 A Pattern Recognition Scenario

We were interested in genes differentially expressed between two classes (treatments): (a) between TGF-β1+SB and SB; or (b) between TGF-β1+SB and TGF-β1. Two data sets were constructed that contained data for (a) or (b). Both expression data sets contained 331 genes (attributes) in 2 treatments (12 cases) respectively.

We used the pattern recognition module to generate decision tree models. A tree model consisted of one or more genes (nodes) that contain a particular threshold to discriminate between the classes in certain accuracy. These genes are considered informative as to the classification task. We removed (masked) these genes from the data and reran the algorithm to generate a new model involving some other genes. This operation of "discover-and-mask" was repeated until no more tree models could be built from the remainder of the data. With this approach, we highlighted informative genes in data set (a) and (b), respectively.

We captured operations of "discover-and-mask" into an Automation scenario, called EPR (Exhaustive Pattern Recognition). EPR automatically builds all possible models and identifies informative genes for the classifications. EPR also summarizes in a table the genes involved, discriminating threshold, class assignments and accuracy for each model. To assess the importance and informativeness, the models and involved genes can be ranked by their classification accuracies.

2.3.2 A Clustering Scenario

We also applied K-Means algorithm in the clustering module to select genes based on their expression profiles under the three treatments: TGF-β1,

TGF-β1+SB and SB. Here genes are objects and their expression levels in 18 experiments (3 treatments with 6 repeats for each) are attributes.

Our analysis started with running a series of K-Means clustering with different K (the number of clusters). Quality Measure (QM) facility[13] then helped us to determine the appropriate number of clusters for the 331 genes. With the aid of visual plots, we identified clusters of genes with interesting expression patterns. The expression pattern of one cluster is down regulated from TGF-β1 to TGF-β1+SB and to SB, while those of other clusters appeared relatively flat. We highlighted this cluster of genes for further biological validations.

We captured operations of this approach into an Automation scenario, called CQC (Clustering Quality Comparison). CQC automatically runs a series of clustering with different numbers of clusters. To help determine the most appropriate data division and choose interesting clusters, QM reports qualities for each clustering operation and for the generated clusters.

Additional EMT biological analysis brought the attention to some of the EPR and CQC highlighted genes for their modulation by TGF-β1 and the role of p38MAPK activities[19].

2.4 Implementation

Automation facilities are implemented within the BioMiner suite. When invoked from menu, Automation graphic user interface (GUI) is displayed next to the BioMiner main interface. Users therefore may easily switch between regular and automated data mining research activities.

Automation GUI has three components (Figure 2): Scenario List, Procedure Editor and Procedure List. Users drag an available scenario from Scenario List, and drop it to the panel of Procedure Editor. A procedure is built as a connected sequence of the selected scenarios. Users may set up or modify the parameters, if any, in a dialog box specific for each scenario. Users may also edit a procedure by adding and deleting scenarios, or cancel the editing and restore a procedure to its previous setting.

A procedure can be saved to a file and later reloaded into Automation for editing. Automation only saves the sequence of scenarios of a procedure and associated parameter settings, which do not require much storage space. Java serialization is the technology for saving and loading procedures. With graphic Procedure Editor in Automation, it is unnecessary to manually edit a text version of a procedure and its scenarios.

Once a procedure is started, Automation will execute embedded scenarios in sequence. In the case of extremely computation-intensive applications, we rely on a parallel (a computing cluster) version for the scheduling and allocation of the computing resources. Automation reports the outcome and summarizes the results of each scenario and the procedure. A procedure can be applied to different data sets, and the same procedure on the same data may have different outputs that for instance may result from random initial seeds in K-Means clustering. Automation, therefore, saves the output files in a new folder for each run of a procedure.

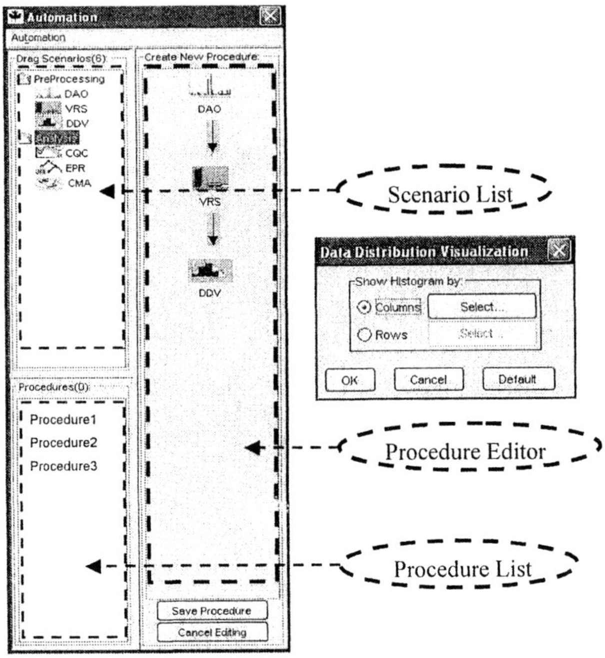

Figure 2. Automation interface: Scenario List; Procedure Editor; and Procedure List. A scenario's settings may be edited the left dialog box.

In case studies[13,17], the CQC based strategy helped to identify clusters of genes with targeted patterns. The EPR based technique generated lists of genes highly related to classification tasks in case studies[15,17,18]. Other scenarios were also developed for data quality examination and DNA sequence analysis. The more studies are carried out, the more experiences are accumulated as scenarios in Automation. In this way, Automation not only reduces manual intervention in the knowledge discovery processes, but also lowers the learning curve for biomedical researchers to plan advanced data analysis.

3. DISCUSSIONS

Production of high throughput genomics data and rapid advancements of biomedical research call for various data analysis technologies and application strategies. We introduce a novel approach to the research and development of automated data mining in bioinformatics. Processing operations and analysis strategies in case studies are abstracted and designed into Automation to reduce user's intervention and more importantly to lead the knowledge discovery activities in bioinformatics.

The development of Automation is an evolving process, as new scenarios are identified as a result of more case studies. A scenario editor would offer users the tool to create scenarios based on their own research experiences. More features for workflow management and results summarization will also be designed and implemented as our research and development advance.

Scenarios in Automation play a key role in transforming research experiences into powerful methods for later applications. The advantage of our approach is to guide bioinformatics researchers on how to plan and apply knowledge discovery processes. Other researchers and developers may wrap various data analysis experiences in the forms of scenarios or agents in order to automate their own technology workbenches.

ACKNOWLEDGEMENT

For biological experiments and analysis in the EMT case study, we would like to thank Dr. Maureen O'Connor-McCourt and Dr. Anne Lenferink (Biotechnology Research Institute, National Research Council Canada) for their special contributions. We would like to thank Dr. Youlian Pan for the valuable comments on an earlier version of this paper. We also acknowledge the contributions of all members of the BioMine project from the Institute for Information Technology and the Institute for Biological Sciences, National Research Council Canada.

REFERENCES

[1] Lockhart, D. J., Dong, H., Byrne, M. C., Follettie, M. T., Gallo, M. V., Chee, M. S., Mittmann, M., Wang, C., Kobayashi, M., Norton, H., Brown, E. L. Expression monitoring by hybridization to high-density oligonucleotide arrays. *Nat. Biotechnol.*, 1996, 14: 1675-1680.

[2] Velculescu, V. E., Zhang, L., Vogelstein, B., and Kinzler, K.W. Serial analysis of gene expression. *Science*, 1995, 270: 484-487.

[3] Lander, E.S., et al. Initial sequencing and analysis of the human genome. *Nature,* 2001, 409: 860-921.

[4] Venter, J. C., et al. The sequence of the human genome. *Science,* 2001, 291: 1304-1351.

[5] Eisen, M. B., Spellman, P. T., Brown, P. O., and Botstein, D. Cluster analysis and display of genome-wide expression patterns. *Proc. Natl. Acad. Sci. USA,* 1998, 95: 14863-14868.

[6] Golub, T. R., Slonim, D. K., Tamayo, P., Huard, C., Gaasenbeek, M., Mesirov, J. P., Coller, H., Loh, M. L., Downing, J. R., Caligiuri, M. A., Bloomfield, C. D., Lander, E. S. Molecular classification of cancer: class discovery and class prediction by gene expression monitoring. *Science,* 1999, 286: 531-537.

[7] Zhu, Z., Pilpel, Y., and Church, C. M. Computational identification of transcription factor binding sites via a transcription-factor-centric clustering (TFCC) algorithm. *J. Mol. Biol.,* 2002, 318: 71-81.

[8] Rowe, A., Kalaitzopoulos, D., Osmond, M., Ghanem, M., Guo, Y. The discovery net system for high throughput bioinformatics. *Bioinformatics,* 2003, 19 (Suppl. 1):i225-231.

[9] Shah, S. P., He, D. Y., Sawkins, J. N., Druce, J. C., Quon, G., Lett, D., Zheng, G. X., Xu, T., Ouellette, B. F. Pegasys: software for executing and integrating analyses of biological sequences. *BMC Bioinformatics,* 2004, 5: 40.

[10] Grant, J. D., Somers, L. A., Zhang, Y., Manion, F. J., Bidaut, G., Ochs, M. F. FGDP: functional genomics data pipeline for automated, multiple microarray data analyses. *Bioinformatics,* 2004, 20: 282-283.

[11] Hokamp, K., Roche, F. M., Acab, M., Rousseau, M. E., Kuo, B., Goode, D., Aeschliman, D., Bryan, J., Babiuk, L. A., Hancock, R. E., Brinkman, F. S. ArrayPipe: a flexible processing pipeline for microarray data. *Nucleic Acids Res.,* 2004, 32: W457-9.

[12] Knudsen, S., Workman, C., Sicheritz-Ponten, T., Friis, C. GenePublisher: Automated analysis of DNA microarray data. *Nucleic Acids Res.,* 2003, 31: 3471-3476.

[13] Famili, A. F., Liu, G., Liu, Z. Evaluation and optimization of clustering in gene expression data analysis. *Bioinformatics,* 2004, 20: 1535-1545.

[14] Famili, A. F., Liu, Z., Ouyang, J., Walker, R. R., Smith, B., O'Connor, M., and Lenferink, A. A novel data mining technique for gene identification in time-series gene expression data. presented at the 16th European Conference on Artificial Intelligence, 2004, Valencia, Spain.

[15] Famili, A. F., Ouyang, J. Data mining: understanding data and disease modeling. *Applied Informatics,* 2003: 32-37.

[16] Famili, A. F., Ouyang, J., Kryworuchko, M., Alvarez-Maya, I., Smith, B., and Diaz-Mitoma, F. Knowledge Discovery in Hepatitis C Virus Transgenic Mice. *IEA/AIE,* 2004: 29-39.

[17] Pan, Y., Pylatuik, J. D., Ouyang, J., Famili, A. F., and Fobert, P. R. Discovery of functional genes for systemic acquired resistance in *Arabidopsis Thaliana* through integrated data mining. *J. Bioinform. Comput. Biol.,* 2004, 2: 639-655.

[18] Walker, P. R., Smith, B., Liu, Q. Y., Famili, A. F., Valdes, J. J., and Liu, Z. Data mining of gene expression changes in Alzheimer brain. *Artif. Intell. Med.,* 2004, 31: 137-154.

[19] O'Connor-McCourt, M., Lenferink, A., Nantel, A., Cantin, C., Magoon, J., Ouyang, J., Lui, Z., and Famili, A. F. Analysis of Transforming Growth Factor (TGF)-ß Modulated Genes Involved in the Epithelial to Mesenchymal Transdifferentiation of Murine Mammary Epithelial Cells. Poster presentation at the 94th Annual Meeting of the American Association for Cancer Research, 2003, Washington, USA.

AN EXPERT SYSTEM FOR DEFICIT IRRIGATION IN THE NORTH CHINA REGION BASED ON PDA

Jianhui Lin [1], Yurui Sun [1※], Shaoyun Feng [2], Risheng Ding [2], Qiushi Hou [1]

1 College of Information and Electronic Engineering, China Agricultural University, Beijing, 100083, People Republic of China

2 College of Water Conservancy and Civil Engineering, China Agricultural University, Beijing, 100083, People Republic of China

Abstract: Deficit Irrigation (DI) is an advanced method of irrigation and this method was used in the north region of China more and more. But it is also a complex method for using. To allow this method to be used facilely, especially in field, an expert system (ES) for deficit irrigation based on Personal Digital Assistant (PDA) has been developed. The system structure and components such as database, knowledge base and their functions are described. This expert system is suitable for north of China and it also will be used in other regions by adding corresponding data to the knowledge bases.

Key words: Expert System, Deficit Irrigation, Personal Digital Assistant, North China

1. INTRODUCTION

It is known that agriculture is the major user of water resource which account for 70% of total water use and irrigation water use account for more than 90% of agriculture water use (Ma, 1998). But in some places where water resources are limited, available water is the most important factor limiting crop yields. For example in the Northwest China region, because of the severe lack of water, this region which account for 30% of Chinese total area only yields 7.4% of national grain output, and the water use efficiency is only 30% to 40% (Shangguan, Shao and Xue, 2001). When the available water supply is severely limited, water deficit will be unavoidable during some periods of crop growth. How to improve water use efficiency and to maintain crop yield under water deficit have become cosmopolitan problems. And just for these reasons, since 1960s, deficit irrigation which also was named Limited Irrigation has been studied in America. In a short time, this method has been studied and applied around the world. Deficit irrigation means that the soil water deficit is controlled at certain stages of crop growth. Studies on the effects of deficit irrigation on crop yield and water use efficiency show that crop yield can be largely maintained and product quality can, in some cases, be improved while substantially reducing irrigation volume. But in these cases, scheduling of irrigation timing and volume then becomes more complex, because irrigation decisions have to be based not only on the relationships among grain yield, crop growing phase and crop water use, but also on water availability (Kang, Shi and Zhang, 2000, Kang et al., 2002). It poses a major challenge for any attempt in developing a computer-based system capable for providing accurate decision.

The rapid increase of PDA application and the cost-effective growth of its key enabling technologies are revolutionizing information technology and creating unprecedented opportunities for developing small portable application. Advantages of PDA technologies have offered new opportunities for enhancing traditional decision support system and expert system. With the development of Expert System and Embedded technology, PDA is able to play some important roles that normally require human actions. A few of expert systems based on PDA are reported in literature. It appears that the research and development of expert system based on PDA are still in their early stage (Tu, Wang and Zhao, 2000, Chen et al., 2002,).

Most of the existing agricultural expert systems are developed for personal computers, such as CIMIS, an expert system for irrigation evaluation developed by California State University, U.S.A (Xie et al., 1992), and WRMDSS, an expert system for water resource management developed by Carolina University, U.S.A (Johuson, 1986). All of these systems have a disadvantage that they can not be used in field facilely. A portable expert system for deficit irrigation based on PDA called ESDI has been developed by Information and Electronic Engineering College of China Agriculture University. This expert system is suitable for farmer, agriculture technician or manager to come to a decision on-the-spot field with a user-friendly interface. It contains a large amount of weather data, hydrology data, crop water needed data and water resource data, which are used to make an irrigation decision. At the end of this paper, some experiments of developing portable expert system and suggestions of improving the development are discussed.

2. DEFICIT IRRIGATION METHOD

With increasing municipal and industrial demands for water, the allocation of water for agriculture is decreasing steadily. The major agricultural use of water is for irrigation, which, thus, is affected by decreased supply. Therefore, innovations are needed to increase the efficiency of use of the water that is available. Deficit (or regulated deficit) irrigation is one way of maximizing water use efficiency (WUE) for higher yields per unit of irrigation water applied: the crop is exposed to a certain level of water stress either during a particular period or throughout the whole growing season. The expectation is that any yield reduction will be insignificant compared with the benefits gained through diverting the saved water to irrigate other crops (Kirda, 2002). The research of the model of crop response to water is the core of the deficit irrigation, which is significant for the application of deficit irrigation. Early in the 1968, Jensen gave the Jenson model which not only presents the relationship between crop yield and water, but also confirm the effect of water supply to crop yield. After then, more models were studied such as Hiler & Clark model, Minhas model, Stewart model, Doorenbos & Kassam model and Sudar model et al (Zhao, Cai and Zhang, 2004). Among these models, Jensen model is the most suitable model for north China region according to more than three decades research. Jensen model is shown as (Chen and Kang, 1994):

$$\frac{Y_a}{Y_m} = \prod_{i=1}^{n} \left(\frac{ET_{ai}}{ET_{mi}}\right)^{\lambda_i} \qquad (1)$$

where Y_a and Y_m are expected and maximum crop yield, corresponding to ET_{ai} and ET_{mi}, actual and maximum evapotranspiration in stage i, respectively; λ_i is the sensitivity index of water lack in stage i.

3. DATA COLLECTION

In resent years, many techniques have been developed for data collection and knowledge acquisition. Some commonly used approaches are interviews, observations, finding from literature, taking experts through case studies and rule inducting by machines. In the development of ESDI, a multiple data collection method has been used. The data collection process consists of user surveys and interviews, expert interviews, finding data from literature and data transform by computer.

User surveys and interviews: A large number of data have been collected from farms then the needs of farm have been understood.

Expert interviews: Some irrigation experts from Beijing, Henan province and Shanxi province took part in interviews. They provided the basic rule of knowledge base.

Finding data from literature: All of the weather data, hydrology data, crop water need data and water resource data were collected from literature which located in water conservancy, weather bureau and bureau of agriculture et al. It can ensure the accuracy of the data.

Data transform: At first data were collected with Excel spreadsheets or word documents. But in expert system the database would use MS Pocket Access. A special program was developed for transforming data into suitable format.

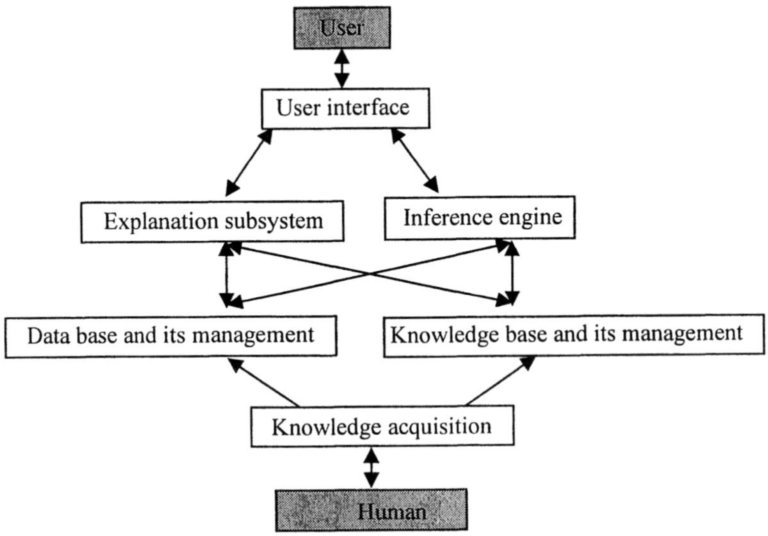

Figure 1. System Architecture

4. SYSTEM DESIGN AND DEVELOPMENT

The expert system for deficit irrigation consists of a data base, a knowledge base, inference engine, explanation subsystem, knowledge acquisition and user interface. The system architecture is showed in Figure 1.

4.1 Software Selection

Traditional ESs were developed for stand-alone computers and a number of development tools are available for developing traditional ESs. With the rapid development of the PDA, more ESs based on PDA are beginning to emerge. At the time when the expert system for deficit irrigation was developed, no suitable tool for ESs based on PDA was available. And during the development of the expert system based on PDA, it must be considered that the limited hard ware resource is available. Thus ESDI was developed using a mixture of embedded technique and visual programming language. So that MS WinCE, MS eMbedded Visual C++ 4.0, MS Pocket Access are selected in the developing.

4.2 Data Base

Database plays an important role in the development of ESDI. It is used for storing all the information needed for irrigation decision. The database is mostly designed with MS Pocket Assess which is only used on PDA. Most of the data were initially collected from irrigation experts, books and documents of water bureau et al. with Excel spreadsheets or Word documents. These Excel spreadsheets and Word documents were translated into Pocket Assess by system developers. The database includes weather database, hydrology database, crop water need database and water resource database.

4.3 Knowledge Base

The knowledge base contains all the rules for the irrigation decision. Each rule has two sections—a field or crops case selection and a corresponding data selection in the form of "IF field or crop case THEN selected corresponding data". For example if the crop is cotton then the number of Jensen model stages is four.

4.4 Inference Process

The inference process is showed in Figure 2. After user inputs some basic parameters, such as crop type, region and available water for irrigation, ESDI will find matched data from database. First, number of irrigation stage, sensitivity index and intending depth of wetted soil will be determined from crop water need database. Second, the max evapotranspiration will be calculated according to weather database and crop water need database.

Third, according to the knowledge base the model will be selected. At last, the model will be resolved using the algorithm of dynamic programming. With the output of the irrigation schedule, some detail interpretation will be given to the user, such as why irrigation water should be limited in a certain irrigation stage.

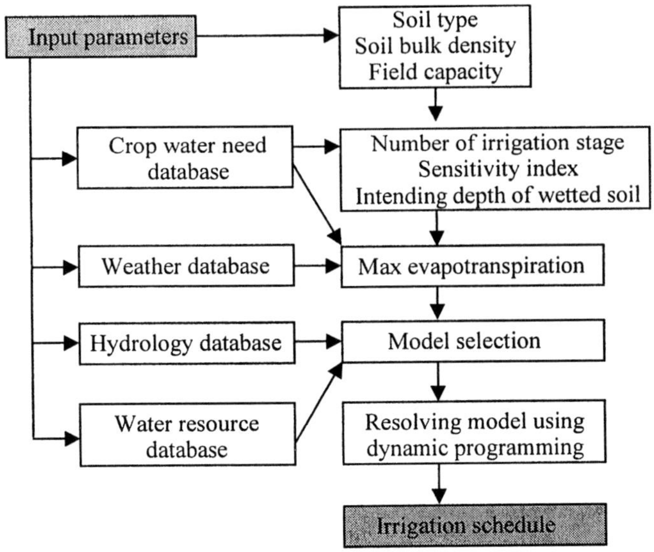

Figure 2. Inference Process

4.5 User Interface

Because the screen of PDA is so small, user interface can not display as many information as personal computer in one screen. The model of display was designed as multi-layer screens. Most of the information was displayed by text, table or picture. The displayed information includes irrigation schedule, max evapotranspiration of every stage and the proportion between actual production and potential production. Some detail explanations of result are also displayed for user.

5. CONCLUSION

ESDI is an expert system that presents the result schedule of deficit irrigation to a farm or field manager. In our opinion, it provides us a more extended environment to use this expert system in the irrigation decision process. And as a try to develop expert system based on PDA, we can draw the following conclusions from our experiments and the learning of the development of ESDI :

- PDA is an embedded system whose hardware resource is limited, so how to use available hardware resource effectively must be considered during the process to develop expert system. For example, how to design the format of display to suit the small screen and how to display the picture clearly.
- As an expert system for irrigation, the collection of credible data is very important. How to increase new data into the system is a challenge in the use of ESDI. A subsystem for increasing new data could be integrated for data update. This subsystem could transmit data between PDA and personal computer with suitable format.
- How to improve the speed of the system is a difficult problem because the algorithm of dynamic programming is very complex and the arithmetic speed of the microprocessor of PDA is more lower than personal computer.

In summary, the rapid development of PDA technology has changed the way in which an expert system can be developed and distributed. The essence of an expert system is to simulate experts and distribute expert knowlcdgc without experts. These benefits have been greatly enhanced with the emergence of PDA. However, the development of expert system based on PDA has also brought some challenges in the methodological and technological aspect. More researches should be carried out to address the challenges posted by developing and implementing expert system based on PDA.

ACKNOWLEDGEMENTS

The research was funded by the National High Science and Technology Development Plan (863 Plan) in China (project number: 2002AA2Z4031). We would like to thank many domain experts from Beijing, Henan and Shaxi province, for their cooperation and support.

REFERENCES

[1]. Chen Liping et al., 2002, Research and development of a development platform on handheld personal computer for agriculture expert system (in Chinese), Transaction of CSAE, 18(3): 142--145

[2]. Chen Yaxian, Kang Shaozhong, 1994, The theory of deficit irrigation (in Chinese), Beijing, Water and Hydropower Press.

[3]. Johuson L. E., Water resource management decision support system, Journal of water resource planning and management, 112(3): 308—325

[4]. Kang Shaozhong, Shi Wenjuan, Zhang Jianhua, 2000, An improved water use efficiency for maize grown under regulated deficit irrigation, Field crops research, 67: 207--214

[5]. Kang Shaozhong et al., 2002, Effects of limited irrigation on yield and water use efficiency of winter whet in the loess plateau of China, Agricultural water management, 55: 203—216

[6]. Kirda C., 2002, Deficit irrigation scheduling based on plant growth stages showing water stress tolerance, in FAO, Deficit irrigation practices, Rome, 3—10

[7]. Ma Zhongming, 1998, Studies on the Relationship between crop and water under limited irrigation (in Chinese), Agricultural Research in the Arid Areas, 16(2): 75—79

[8]. Shangguan Zhouping, Shao mingan, Xue Zengzhao, 2001, Decision support system of water requirement forecast for dryland crop (in Chinese), Transactions of CASE, 17(2): 42—46

[9]. Tu Yunhua, Wang Donghui and Zhao Chunjiang, 2000, The research and development of a development platform on HPC/PDA for agricultural expert system based on Windows CE (in Chinese), High Community Technology, 10: 28--31

[10]. Xie Guixu et al., 1992, Study of agriculture water save and management in American California (in Chinese), Irrigation and water conservancy and mini hydro, 2: 40—43

[11]. Zhao Yong, Cai Huanjie, Zhang Chaoyong, 2004, The status and problems of deficit irrigation research (in Chinese), China Rural Water and Hydropower, 4: 1—4

ARTIFICIAL INTELLIGENCE IN REAL-TIME EVALUATING ELECTRICAL CONDUCTIVITY OF GREENHOUSE SUBSTRATE

Junning Zhang, Minzan Li, Dexiu Kong, Qizhang Zou
Key Laboratory of Modern Precision Agriculture System Integration Research, China Agricultural University, Ministry of Education, P. R. China
No.17 Qinghua Donglu, Beijing, P. R. China, 100083
limz@cau.edu.cn

Abstract: To support decision-making in precision management of greenhouse cultivation, a portable electrical conductivity detector was developed to real-time measure substrate in greenhouse. It mainly included three units, probes, controlling and monitoring unit, and data processing and displaying unit. The probes were designed based on Four-electrode method. The controlling and monitoring unit provided a constant current into substrate and then measured the voltage drop between two points of substrate. Performance experiments under different conditions were conducted. The result revealed that, when water content was lower than 50%, the substrate electrical conductivity would be affected by both salinity and moisture in substrate. Therefore it was necessary to consider the factor of moisture when evaluating substrate property by substrate electrical conductivity. When water content was higher than 50%, substrate electrical conductivity was mainly affected by substrate salinity, and the effect of moisture could be ignored.

Key words: greenhouse; substrate; electrical conductivity; four-electrode method; digital agriculture

1. INTRODUCTION

Substrate cultivation is a common type in greenhouse. Greenhouse substrate has several good properties for crop growth. It not only can well hold water and nutrition to provide nice conditions for growth of plant's root, but also posses next advantages such as cheaper, rich resource, ventilating, easy management, and anti-disease. In recent years, many studies have indicated that substrate electrical conductivity (EC) included plenty of information reflecting substrate properties [1,2]. As the introduction of precision farming, it has become more important to understand the condition of substrate EC in a greenhouse. It would help us to know the status of plant growth, and then to perform precision management for the crops in greenhouse. Hence, we developed a portable substrate EC detector, and then used it to evaluate substrate properties in greenhouse, and investigated the effect of water content and salinity on substrate EC.

2. DEVELOPMENT OF A PORTABLE SUBSTRATE EC DETECTOR

Figure 1 shows the structure of the portable substrate EC detector. It was based on four-electrode method [3,4]. When using this detector to measure substrate EC, it was unnecessary to sample and stir substrate, and was able to continuously measure at some site. The detector included four electrodes, two electrodes connecting with a constant electrical current source and other two electrodes connecting with a voltage meter. The current electrodes injected a steady current into substrate, and then the voltage electrodes detected the output voltage drop between two points of the substrate. Finally, the substrate EC could be calculated according to the voltage drop.

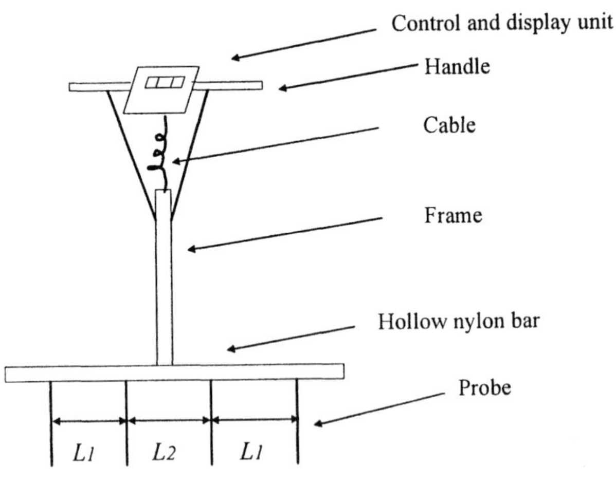

Figure.1 The structure of the portable substrate EC detector

Designed structure of the detector was suitable to expediently using in greenhouse. The probes were made from stainless steel, and were fixed in a frame made of a hollow nylon bar with a bundle of wire inside. The probes were connected to the control and display unit by this bundle of wire. Both L_1 and L_2 were the optimized structure parameters of the detector, L_1=15cm and L_2=20cm. The weight and height of the EC detector were 4Kg and 112cm, respectively. The control and display unit was placed on the top of the detector. It performed next functions: providing a constant electrical current to probes, acquiring substrate EC data, processing measurement data, recording the data in RAM, and displaying the measured result.

3. PERFORMANCE TEST OF THE DETECTOR

3.1 Materials and methods

The used substrate was a kind of mixture of vermiculite and straw charcoal. The vermiculite, a kind of inert mineral material, is a compound of Al, Mg, Fe and Si. It is light and can form many big holes when used in greenhouse cultivation so that it has good quality of water-sopping, water-holding, and ventilating. The straw charcoal is composed of semi-decomposed vegetables. The texture of the vegetable charcoal is delicacy. It also has rich organic material and nutritional which is necessary for plant growth. The substrate used in this greenhouse test was mixture of vermiculite and straw charcoal with the proportion of 1:1.

As the contrast, the EC of the substrate's solution was also measured with a portable EC tester (DDB303A, Shanghai Precision Scientific Instrument Co.LTD) since there was a linear relation between substrate bulk EC and substrate solution EC. In order to obtain substrate samples with different EC level, KCL solution was added into test substrate gradually to change its EC level.

3.2 Performance test

In order to establish standard method to real-time measure substrate EC, and to evaluate the performance of the portable detector under the different conditions, three kinds of tests were designed.

(1) According to the reference 4, when the culture medium material was soil, 30% of water content was a turning point. When the soil water content was below 30%, it had a remarkable effect on soil EC; while when the soil

water content exceeded 30%, the effect decreased distinctly. Therefore, we could conclude that there might be a similar turning point in substrate. Hence, in the first test we planed to change the water content of the substrate with unchanged salinity to find out the relationship between water content and substrate EC, and then to investigate the measurable range of the portable detector.

(2) When the substrate water content was above the turning point, that is when the water content had little effect on the substrate EC, we would add KCl solution into the substrate to change its EC level to establish the estimation model of the substrate EC based on the detector output voltage.

(3) When the substrate water content was below the turning point, that is when the water content had greater effect on the substrate EC, we would add KCL solution into the substrate to change its EC value and then to reveal the relationship between substrate EC and detector output voltage.

3.3 Result and discussion

Figure 2 shows the result of the test 1. The salinity content was 0.326%. Sixteen Experiments in different level of water content were performed. The output voltage of the sensor changed regularly with the change of substrate water content. Due to the output voltage represents the substrate EC value, it was observed that the 50% of water content was the turning point. It implied that when the substrate water content was below 50%, it would have a remarkable effect on substrate EC. However, when water content was above 50%, the effect of substrate moisture on substrate EC would become very weak. When substrate water content was below 50%, it was necessary to consider the effect of both salinity and water content on substrate EC when using EC to evaluate the physical and nutritional properties of substrate. When substrate water content was above 50%, the substrate EC value measured by developed portable detector was affected only by ion amount in substrate, and the contribution of water content could be ignored.

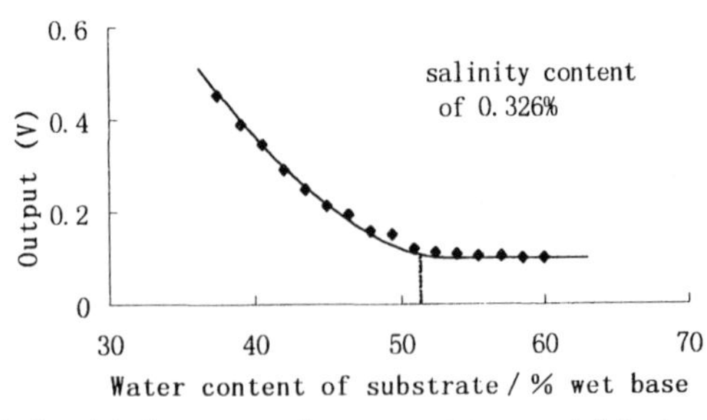

Figure.2 Relationship between substrate moisture and detector output voltage

In test 2, keeping substrate water content unchanged and in higher level (about 65%), and adding KCl solution to the substrate to change substrate EC level. Twenty-five Experiments in different EC levels were executed. Figure 3 shows the test result. The X axis is the output voltage measured by the detector. The Y axis is the substrate solution EC. The voltage output increased regularly as the substrate solution EC decreased. In order to further analyze the correlation between the output voltage and EC of soil solution, a power function model was attempted. It was observed that almost all the data points distributed closely around the curve. The coefficient of determination (R^2) reached 0.970. It indicated that the developed detector could estimate substrate electrical conductivity with high accuracy.

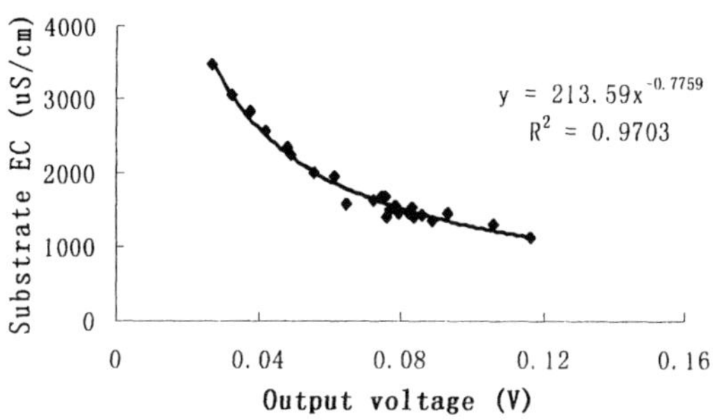

Figure.3 The relationship between voltage drop and substrate EC in test 2

The objective of the test 3 was to further investigate the performance and precision of the developed EC detector under the lower water content condition. Keeping substrate water content unchanged and in the level of about 45%, and adding KCl solution to the substrate to change substrate EC. Thirty-two experiments in different EC levels were conducted. Figure 4 shows the result of the test. A power function model was introduced in Figure 4. It was observed that the distribution of the data points in this test was similar to test 2, and all the data points distributed closely around the curve. The coefficient of determination (R^2) reached 0.875. It indicated that the developed detector was also practical to measure substrate EC under the lower water content condition.

Comparing Figure 3 with Figure 4, it could be find out that when the substrate water content was below 50% although the correlation between substrate EC and output voltage still conformed to the power function relation, the curvature was much less than the situation when substrate moisture content was above 50%. It seems better to use linear model to describe the points shown in Figure 4. The coefficient of determination still reached 0.83 when using linear model, and the precision met the requirement of the greenhouse planting. The difference between Figure 3 and Figure 4 could be attributed to different water content. When the water content was below 50%, the substrate EC would be influenced by both water content and total ion amount. It was necessary to design much more performance experiments to find out the variation law of the substrate EC, and further to expand the measurable range of the developed detector.

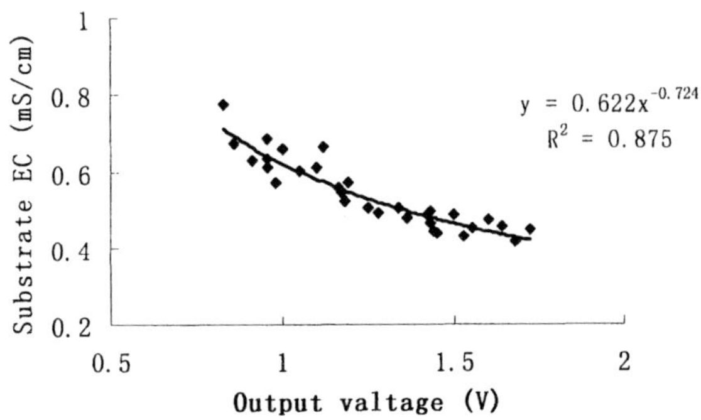

Figure.4 Relationship between voltage drop and substrate EC in test 3

In a word, all results showed that the developed real-time detector was satisfactory in both accuracy and practicality, and it was able to provide a base for modeling the substrate EC.

4. CONCLUSIONS

A portable EC detector was developed. And then it was used to investigate the correlations between substrate EC and two substrate parameters, water content and salinity in greenhouse. The obtained conclusions are as follows:

(1) Developed detector was reliable and easy to operate, and had high precision. It was valuable in precision management of greenhouse cultivation.

(2) Keeping the salinity (ion amount) unchanged and changing the substrate water content, the correlation between substrate water content and substrate EC was analyzed. The result shows that, when the substrate water content was below 50% the substrate EC was affected by both ion amount and water content. Thus it was necessary to consider the influence of the

water content when using substrate EC to evaluate the physical and nutrition properties of the substrate. While the influence could be ignored and the EC was mainly affected by the total ion amount when the water content was above 50%.

(3) Keeping the substrate water content unchanged at about 65% and changing substrate EC, the output of the developed detector was observed. The result shows that, there was a power function relationship between the output and the substrate EC, and the coefficient of determination reached to 0.970. When substrate water content was above 50%, the developed model could be used in practice directly.

(4) Keeping the substrate water content unchanged at about 45% and changing the substrate EC, the output of the detector was also observed. A power function model and a linear function model were used to describe the relationship between the output and the substrate EC, respectively. All models showed significant.

ACKNOWLEDGEMENT

This study was supported by National High Technology Research and Development Program of China (863 Program): Research and Demonstration for Digital Agriculture (2003AA209040).

REFERENCES

[1] Naiqian Zhang, Kyeong-Hwan Lee, et al. Simultaneous Measurement of Soil Water content and Method Salinity Using a Frequency-Response, 2004 CIGR International Conference.11- 14 October 2004, Beijing, China.

[2] Kitchen N R,Sudduth K A,Drummond S T. Soil electrical conductivity as a crop productivity measure for clay pan soils[J]. J Prod Agric, 1999, 12: 607-617.

[3] Li Minzan, Wang Qi, Wang Maohua. Testing and modeling of soil EC sensor[J]. Transactions of the CSAE, 2004, 20(1): 51-55.

[4] Sun Yurui, Wang Maohua. A Mathematical Model and Its Experimental Study for a Kind of Measurement Method of Soil Electric Conductivity.
Transactions of the CSAE (in Chinese), 2001, 17(2): 20-2.

[5] Corwin D. L. and S. M. Lesch. 2003. Application of Soil Electrical Conductivity to Precision Agriculture --Theory, Principles, and Guidelines. Agronomy Journal 95(3): 455-471.

AUTOMATIC GUIDANCE OF AGRICULTURAL VEHICLES BASED ON GLOBAL POSITIONING SYSTEM

Lan Yao, Li Li, Miao Zhang, Li Minzan

Key laboratory of Modern Precision Agriculture System Integration Research, Ministry of Education, China Agriculture University, Beijing 100083, China. Email: limz@cau.edu.cn

Abstract: The need for automatic guidance of farm vehicles has been recognized for a considerable time. Automatic guidance of agricultural vehicles must have some effective method for determining their position in the working environment in order to operate appropriately. Recently, Global Positioning System (GPS) receivers have become available for world-wide and all-weather outdoor localization. This paper presents a review of automatic guidance of agricultural vehicles based on stand-off Global Positioning System (GPS) or the integration of GPS and dead-reckoning system.

Key words: Automatic guidance , Global Positioning System, Dead-reckoning system

1. INTRODUCTION

Automatic vehicle guidance was defined as 'accurate automatic control of the vehicle or implement along a predefined trajectory' [1]. Over the past century, many changes have occurred in agricultural field production machinery [2]. The need for automatic guidance of farm vehicles has been recognized for a considerable time.

Automated guidance systems attempt to relieve the operator from many, if not all, of the tasks involved in guiding a vehicle.

There are several benefits of automatic guidance systems in agriculture. One major benefit of automatic guidance systems is a reduction in machine operator fatigue by automating repetitively monotonous steering tasks. And it will also complement and augment the farmer's abilities and skills to increase the volume and quality of produce, while production costs (particularly labor costs) are decreased and the working conditions improved.

Another benefit of automatic guidance systems is a potential improvement in the placement of agricultural inputs. With larger equipment, human operators often overlap previous paths in field operations, subjecting parts of a field to a double application of farming inputs (Nieminen and Sampo, 1993) [2].

Furthermore, the potential for vehicle automation in agriculture has increased by the advent of precision agriculture. Precision agriculture has helped advance vehicle guidance firstly in terms of providing position information that is required for vehicle guidance. Secondly, precision agriculture has placed the notion of vehicle automation within the conceptual boundary of equipment manufacturers and agricultural producers [3].

Developing a vehicle that can navigate autonomously in outdoor changing and dynamic agricultural environments is a challenging and difficult task and is crucial to any Intelligent Farm Vehicle developed for farming [4].Covering a large spectrum of different technologies, as well as some of the most advanced space science and engineering [5].

The key element of automatic guidance is navigation sensors to detect vehicle position, vehicle heading, and the current state of the vehicle (speed, wheel position, etc.), respectively. Some guidance sensors provide information for absolute positioning. Others only provide relative positioning (e.g. mechanical feelers and machine vision) between the vehicle and the guidance directrix. The usually used position sensors are mechanical feelers, machine vision and GPS sensors. And the usually used heading sensors are machine vision, GPS, with some work taking place with geomagnetic direction sensors (GDS) and inertial sensors [3].

Patterson et al. (1985) developed a dead reckoning system for used on a towed planter with wheel encoders [6]. A Japanese company, Kubota, has developed a method of guidance by photocells in order to exploit the presence of the crop edge left by the previous passage of the vehicle (Yoshida et al., 1988) [7]. Freeland et al. (1992) experimented with a low cost electronic compass used together with wheel encoders to provide dead-reckoning posture information [8]. Stanford University demonstrated high accuracy carrier phase differential GPS for the guidance of a John Deere 7800 series tractor [9]. An autonomous tractor using an optical surveying device and a terrestrial magnetism sensor for ploughing was developed (Yukumoto and Matsuo, 1995; Masuo et al., 2002) [10][11]. Carnegie-Mellon Robotics Institute developed an autonomous New Holland 2550 Speedrower for cutting forage using vision-based perception on the cut and uncut regions of the crop [12]. The University of Illinois, with international cooperation with

Hokkaido University in Japan, has a research program for both automatic and autonomous guidance of agricultural vehicles based on two Case 8920 2WD and MFD tractors [13]. Research is considering automation in terms of various posture sensors (global positioning systems, machine vision, inertial, and geomagnetic direction sensors).

Each of the approaches has its own advantages and disadvantages, which are limited by the application requirements as well as the environment where the method is going to be used.

As the fundamental element of agriculture technology, the global positioning system (GPS) signal can be used for agricultural vehicle guidance. It can provide the location, in degrees of longitude and latitude, of a receiver anywhere in the world (Langley, 1997) [14].

Global positioning systems, although new to agriculture, have generated much of the potential growth in agricultural equipment automation by enabling the agricultural equipment industry and producers to see beyond the limitations of other navigation sensors [3].

In this paper, give a review of previous research on automatic vehicle guidance based on GPS only or combined with local sensors.

2. METHODS

GPS technology has extremely important positions in the application of agriculture. By combining information collection with time, space and combining control technology and spacetime positioning, GPS has become the essential bridge between the information system and intelligent device of agricultural machinery [15].

The Global Positioning System (GPS) is a satellite-based radio positioning navigation and real-time ranging system developed by US Department of Defense. It is a highly accurate, full-time and rapid satellite navigation positioning system built for meeting the demand of military and business application. The whole GPS system consist of 24 satellites allocated in six orbital planes. Each satellite transmits carrier wave radio signals on the L1 (1575.42MHZ) and L2 (1227.6MHZ) frequencies. The GPS satellite transmits two kinds of positioning signals: P code and C/A code. A GPS receiver tracks these GPS satellites and receives signals (ranges to the satellites and the satellites orbit parameters) on the basis of the work conditions of GPS visible satellites in the sky.

The main principle behind a satellite navigation system is the creation of a trilateration from any point on the earth's surface to the satellites in view. In principle, three satellites must be available to determine a three-dimensional position [17]. All points, which have the same distance to one satellite, form a spherical surface with the satellite in the centre. Three spherical surfaces intersect in two points. One point can be disregarded, because its position is located too far from the earth.

High-level accuracy of several centimeters is necessary for machine guidance applications. The accuracy of GPS can be improved with selective availability (SA) down to a few meters with differential GPS (DGPS). The most commonly used form of DGPS is code-differential GPS. In code-differential GPS, the GPS receivers at the vehicle and reference station take phase measurements of the GPS pseudo-random noise (PRN) signal. The reference and vehicle measurements are then differenced to provide a relative position measurement. Code-differential systems offer 1 to 2m accuracy and corrections are valid for a large radius, usually on the order of 100 km (Parkinson and Spilker, 1996b) [16].

It is even possible to achieve centimeter accuracy with high-precision receivers working with carrier phase tracking techniques. A type of ultra-precise GPS positioning is known as Carrier-Phase Differential GPS, CPDGPS is based on measuring the phase of the GPS carrier signal. Because the L-band GPS carrier signal has a wavelength of approximately 19cm and GPS receivers can track that carrier signal to within roughly 1cm [1].

In the meantime, the measurement of the attitude of a vehicle with accuracy of up to 0.1° is possible with multiple antenna arrangements. Such accuracy is needed for autonomous guidance (Bell, 1999) to measure and compensate vehicle movements caused by rough terrain and slopes.

Although some accurate GPS receivers are available for providing centimeter accuracy in position measurement, most low-cost GPS receivers used in agricultural vehicles normally only have meter range positioning accuracy and could not meet the navigation accuracy requirement for many precision agricultural operations and the GPS performs poorly in highly dynamic environments due to the shadowing of satellites and high rates of changes in doopler. To solve these problems, the integration of two positioning methods, relative positioning using a dead-reckoning system(odometry, inertial sensors and other sensors which measure the rotation of vehicle or implement wheels, combination of travelled distance with the measured heading or steering angle is used to estimate position from a known starting point [3]), and absolute positioning using a global positioning system (GPS), can be used to provide improved navigation accuracy for agricultural vehicles.

Although receiving less attention, odometery is probably the most widely used navigation sensor. The rotation of one or more ground wheels is used to measure vehicle motion. The appeal of odometry is that is simple and low cost. The disadvantage is susceptibility to errors from a variety of sources, including wheel slippage and variation in the effective wheel rolling radius and the track width of the wheels. These errors are cumulative, giving a rapid loss in positional accuracy.

Inertial sensors, i.e. accelerometers and gyroscopes, have been used in a number of vehicle applications as an alternative to odometers for dead reckoning. Inertial systems have the advantage that they can be produced in an encapsulated and robust package, can supply not only continuous vehicle position and velocity information but also three axes attitude [17].

Unfortunately, both the zero point and the output scale of these types of sensor are prone to thermal drift (Barshan and Durrant-Whyte, 1993) [20] to a varying degree depending upon the type of the sensor (and inevitably linked to cost). Moreover, accelerometers are sensitive not only to accelerations of the vehicle, but also to the gravitational acceleration; therefore estimation of attitude for the full three rotational degrees of freedom is necessitated.

The use of a geomagnetic compass is also possible, a three axis fluxgate magnetometer allows an implementation with no moving parts.

In summary, dead reckoning, which determines machinery position by calculating the travel distance in the direction of machinery moving accumulatively, can provide a robust and accurate position measurement over a short period of time, improved navigation accuracy especially when GPS is degraded or interrupted because of jamming or interference [18]. But will always result in substantially accumulated positioning errors as the measurement time increases due to sensor drifting and machinery slippage. As comparison, in the GPS measurements, there is no accumulated positioning error because each measurement is independent to the previous measurement. The integration of GPS and inertial positioning can provide a complementary correction to improve both the accuracy and robustness in mobile positioning and navigation for agricultural machinery applications [19].

3. APPLICATIONS

Several studies have explored the use of high accuracy GPS or the integration of GPS and dead reckoning for vehicle guidance.

Researchers at the University of Illinois (Stombaugh et al., 1998) [2] utilized a 5Hz real-time kinematic (RTK) GPS for guidance of a 2WD Case 7720 tractor. In order to eliminate lag in the system responses the GPS was mounted in front of the front wheels on a mast extending to a height above the cab. Vehicle response in tracking a 3-m step change in position showed that the lateral position error at 4.5m/s was within 16cm (95% confidence).

Benson et al. (1998) used GDS and GPS together for vehicle guidance based on dead reckoning as a simple path planner. The system was tested at slow speeds (1.12 m/s) and had an average error of less than 1cm, which compared favorably to GPS-based guidance. When implementing a 3-m step change in responses the sensor fusion system had a maximum overshoot of 12%. Under GPS-under mode the system experienced a 50% overshoot [21].

A low-cost integrated positioning system, consisting of a Garmin GPS and a set of solidstate inertial sensors, was developed for autonomous agricultural vehicle applications. Based on a position-velocity-attitude (PVA) model of the vehicle, a PVA model-based Kalman filter was designed to integrate data from all sensors to provide accurate and robust vehicle positioning data. Figure 1 shows the block diagram of the PVA model-based fusion algorithm for the integrated position sensing system.

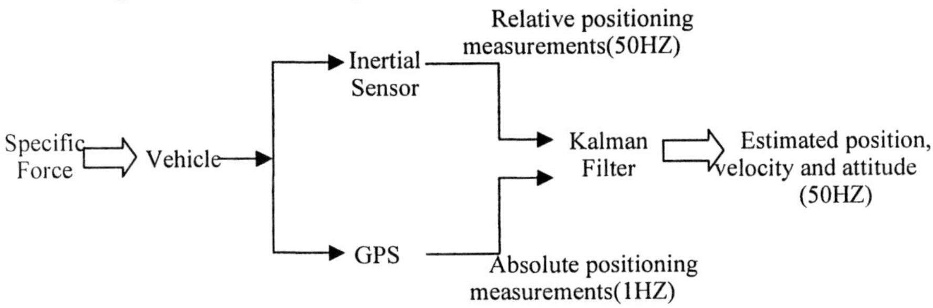

Figure 1. PVA model-based GPS/Inertial sensor fusion

This integrated positioning system was evaluated in different test sites. Test results showed that the maximum positioning error was 0.50m while the vehicle was traveling on a known path (determined based on static RTK-DGPS measurements) on a paved road nearby buildings and partially under trees. When the vehicle was traveling on open field, the maximum error was 0.30m.The accuracy of this low-cost integrated positioning system can meet most tasks in precision farming applications[22].

4. CONCLUSIONS

Current research has proven the basic concept of vehicle automation for agriculture and an overview has been presented of the subject of agricultural vehicles navigation using GPS signals. From successful experiments of past and on-going projects, it can be concluded that GPS may be successfully used as absolute positioning sensor on agricultural vehicles. However, the accuracy will in general not be high. For highly accurate and robust real time attitude determination, GPS equipment needs additional low-cost relative positioning sensors to assist in increasing the data rate and robustness. The future of automation and robotics in production agriculture is entering an exciting era. The potential for automatic and autonomous agricultural machines continues to grow at a rapid pace. The use of differential techniques, important for applications of machine guidance, as well as for attitude measurement will be possible, the on-going activities in GPS will improve the use of satellite navigation in Agriculture, the paths of university research, industrial development and government policies are on a course that will lead to increased opportunities for automation in agriculture [23][24].

ACKNOWLEDGEMENTS

This study was supported by National High Technology Research and Development Program of China (863 Program): Research and Demonstration for Digital Agriculture (2003AA209040).

REFERENCES

[1] Thomas Bell, 1999. Automatic tractor guidance using carrier-phase differential GPS. Computers and Electronics in Agriculture : Special Issue Navigating Agricultural Field Machinery. 25 (2000) 53–66

[2] T. S. Stombaugh, E. R. Benson, J. W. Hummel,1998. AUTOMATIC GUIDANCE OF AGRICULTURAL VEHICLES AT HIGH FIELD SPEEDS. ASAE Paper UIUC-ENG 98-7002. St. Joseph, MI

[3] . John F. Reid a, Qin Zhang a, Noboru Noguchi b,Monte Dickson. Agricultural automatic guidance research in North America. Computers and Electronics in Agriculture 25 (2000) 155–167

[4] . HANI HAGRAS, MARTIN COLLEY AND VICTOR CALLAGHAN, Online Learning and Adaptation of Autonomous Mobile Robots for Sustainable Agriculture. Autonomous Robots 13, 37–52, 2002

[5] agarajan Ramalingam, Timothy S. Stombaugh, and Jonathan Mirgeaux Ramalingam, N., T. S. Stombaugh, J. Mirgeaux. 2000. DGPS-Based Automatic Vehicle Guidance. ASAE Paper No. 001068. Annual International Meeting, Midwest Express Center, Milwaukee, Wisconsin, July 9-12.

[6] Patterson, R.J., Fehr B.W., Sheets. L.P., 1985. Electronic guidance system for a planter. ASAE Paper No. 85–1587. St. Joseph, MI:ASAE.

[7] Yoshisada Nagasaka, Naonobu Umeda, Yutaka Kanetai, Ken Taniwaki, Yasuhiro Sasaki, Autonomous guidance for rice transplanting using global positioning and gyroscopes. Computers and Electronics in Agriculture 43 (2004) 223–234

[8] Freeland, S.R., Wilkerson B.J., Hart. E.W., 1992. Instrumentation for measurement of tractor yaw. ASAE Paper No. 92-3552. ASAE, St. Joseph, MI.

[9] O'Connor, Michael, Thomas Bell, Gabe Elkaim, and Bradford Parkinson. 1996. Automatic steering of farm vehicles using GPS. 3rd International Conference on Precision Agriculture, Minneapolis, MN, June 23–26.9.

[10] Yukumoto, O., Matsuo, Y., 1995. Research on autonomous land vehicle for agriculture. in: Proceedings of the International Symposium on Automation and Robotics in Bioproduction and Processing, vol. 1, JSAM, Kobe, pp. 41–48.

[11] .Masuo, Y., Yamamoto, S., Yukumoto, O., 2002. Development of tilling robot and operation software.in: Proceedings of the Automation Technology for Off-road Equipment, ASAE, Chicago, IL, pp. 184–189.

[12] Ollis, M. and A. Stentz. 1997. Vision-based perception for an automated harvester. IROS'97.

[13] Will, J., T. Stombaugh, E. Benson, N. Noguchi, and J.F. Reid. Development of a flexible platform for agricultural guidance research. ASAE paper 983202. St. Joseph, MI.

[14] Langley, R.B. 1997. GLONASS: review and update. GPS World 8(7):46–55.

[15] Zhang XiaoChao, Wang Yiming, Ma Zhiyuan, Li liang. The Study of GPS Based Irrigation System for Precision Agriculture Technology. Transaction of the CIGR 2004 Paper No.30-109

[16] .Parkinson, B.W., Spilker, J.J. (Eds.), 1996a. Global Positioning System: Theory and Applications, American Institute of Aeronautics and Astronautics, Vol. I. 1996b. Global Positioning System: Theory and Applications,American Institute of Aeronautics and Astronautics, Vol. II.

[17] Lin Ninmin, Fang Jiancheng , Gan Guojian. A NEW COMPOSED CORRECTING KALMAN FILTERING METHOD FOR GPSISINS IN TEGRATED NAVIGATION SYSTEM

[18] Ma ruiping, Zhang minglian. A NEW ADAPTVIE KALMAN FILTER FOR GPS/INS INTEGRATED SYSTEM.

[19] T. Hague, J.A. Marchant, N.D. Tillett. Ground based sensing systems for autonomous agricultural vehicles. Computers and Electronics in Agriculture 25 (2000) 11–28

[20] Barshan, B., Durrant-Whyte, H.F., 1993. An inertial navigation system for a mobile robot. In:IEEE:RSJ International Conference Intelligent Robot Systems, pp. 2243–2248.

[21] Benson, E., Stombaugh T., Noguchi N., Will J., Reid. J.F., 1998. An evaluation of a geomagnetic direction sensor for vehicle guidance in precision agriculture applications. ASAE paper UILU 98-7011. St. Joseph, MI.

[22] L.S. Guo, Q. Zhang,L. Feng. A Low-Cost Integrated Positioning System of GPS and Inertial Sensors for Autonomous Agricultural Vehicles. ASAE Paper Number: 033112, St. Joseph, MI

[23] Dr. John F. Reid .A Status Report on Autonomous Guidance of Agricultural Vehicles in the US: New Frontiers in the 21st Century. UILU-ENG-987026

[24]Q.P.Chu,P.Th.L.M.vanWoerkon. GPS for Low-Cost Attitude Determination. Acta Astronautica Vol.41,Nos 4-10,pp.421-433,1997

BESTCITY: DEVELOPING CLEAN CITIES

By Intelligently Management of Information

L.C. Jayawardhana1*, Ajith de Alwis1, Sumith Pilapitiya2, Malik Ransinghe3

1Department of Chemical & Process Engineering, University of Moratuwa, Sri Lanka
2The World Bank (Colombo Office), Sri Lanka
3Department of Civil Engineering, University of Moratuwa, Sri Lanka

Abstract: Artificial Intelligence applications have immense potential to fill the knowledge gaps that exist in developing countries. During the past decades, many AI applications have developed to solve structured problem domain and less concern about complex problem domain such as solid waste management. Hence, solid waste management is a burning environmental issue in developing countries due to lack of expertise and information assimilation paths. To fill this knowledge gap a user-friendly decision support system (DSS), BESTCity is developed. This paper describes the techniques used for the development stage and robustness of BESTCity DSS. Much evident clean cities in developed economies with the huge amount of knowledge available could be intelligently managed to solve issues in developing countries, which is the main objective of BESTCity.

Key words: Knowledge-based system, Decision Support System, Solid Waste Management

1. INTRODUCTION

During the past decades, many Artificial Intelligence (AI) Applications have been developed and successfully used in different fields. In literature, it is highlighted that expert systems in environmental engineering have appeared after fifteen years after the first expert systems were pioneered. One key reason for the delayed involvement was that the behaviour of environmental processes was not well understood and environmental science is of multidisciplinary nature. Furthermore, it is often need to involve chemists, geologists, toxicologists, microbiologists and experts of other disciplines (Basri and Stentiford, 1995). Solid Waste Management (SWM) is also such a difficult problem domain to develop AI applications because of its complexity and being a politically and an emotionally charged issue.

Today, in most developing countries like Sri Lanka, SWM has become a grave problem due to knowledge inertia, scarcity of expertise, stagnant knowledge sources and use of routine problem solving procedures. Thus, Rubenstein-Montano (2000) stated that solid waste planning is also a problem domain well suited for a knowledge-based approach. It has been proved by developing AI tools such as Decision Support Systems (DSS) to assist waste planners since 1940s (McHenry et al., 2002). As access to human experts at the field and operational levels is not always easy in developing countries, particularly in rural cities, it is clear that AI tools can be used to assist in filling the knowledge gaps that exist in the SWM hierarchy. However, Wilson's (1981) review showed that no completely satisfactory modelling approach was available, and concluded that such models offer little scope for further development as practical aids to waste management planning (Basri and Stentiford, 1995). In literature, it is found that past developments have been concerned as a series of small problems such as routing, processing, disposal, marketing etc without considering the relationship between each. McDougall (2001) emphasised that integrated waste management takes an overall approach to waste management, it combines a range of collection and treatment methods to handle all materials in the stream in an environmentally effective, economically affordable and socially acceptable way. Hence, this research focused on developing a DSS, BESTCity to assist decision makers and solid waste planners to run an effective integrated SWM system.

2. METHODOLOGY

2.1 Problem Identification

Problem domain is identified as flow-through systems in various stages such as waste collection, recycling, treatment, and disposal. All the problems were thoroughly analyzed and the knowledge required is clearly identified by doing case studies. Imported elements of integrated SWM such as the concept of 3R's (reduce, reuse, recycling) have been included.

2.2 System specification & development tool selection

As programming the inference engine is laboriously time-consuming, a commercially available high-level expert system shell , Acquire® 2.1 is used for developing the decision support tool. Acquire® was selected as system development tool as it provides a step-by-step method for acquiring and structuring knowledge that lets developer without programming skills develop knowledge-based applications. Such direct involvement by subject matter experts improves quality, accuracy and usability and lowers development and maintenance time and cost (Internet,1). Acquire SDK is used to develop applications with custom user interfaces, to create additional computational functionality for Windows and to deploy Acquire knowledge bases in a user environment.

2.3 Knowledge Acquisition

Even though here is no formal methodology, which is applicable universally for knowledge acquisition, it is the main bottleneck during the development of the AI tool, not because expertise in the field is scarce but also 'paradox of expertise'. They look at the problem in different ways and suggest different solutions. The techniques to elicit and acquire knowledge are shown in figure 1. Dynamic data mining is a significant research activity in itself.

2.4 Knowledge Representation

A knowledge representation (KR) is most fundamentally a surrogate, a substitute for the thing itself, used to enable an entity to determine consequences by thinking rather than acting, i.e., by reasoning about the world rather than taking action in it (David et al., 1993). In BESTCity DSS, knowledge representations including production and action rules, cases, reports and objects are being utilized. It can provide a qualitative representation of tacit assessment knowledge (Mitri, 2003).

3. BESTCITY FOR ISWM

The national strategy for SWM introduced by the Ministry of Forestry and Environment in 2000 for Sri Lanka for sustainable waste management emphasizes the need to minimize waste production, increase waste recovery and reduce the use of landfill (NSSWM, 2000). The aim of developing

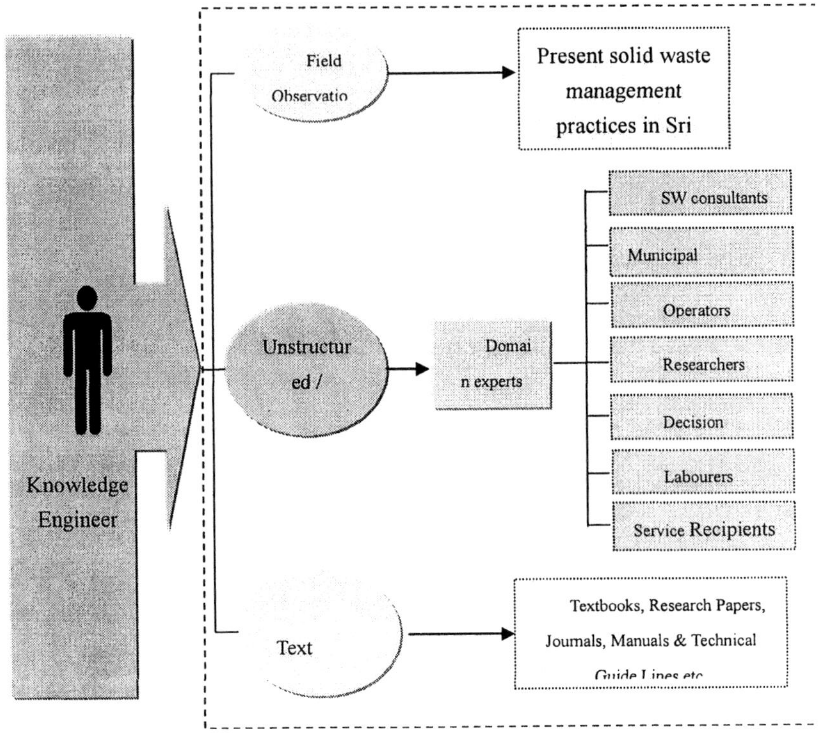

Figure 1 : Knowledge Acquisition Techniques used for BESTCity DSS

BESTCity DSS to provide expert knowledge to implement national strategy as Local Authorities typically lack knowledge, information, resources and expertise.

As solid waste management is a complex problem, one problem is chosen for the initial prototype development. The performance of developed BESTComp prototype expert system demonstrates the usability of a knowledge–base tool for integrated solid waste management. BESTCity DSS is embedded with sub-modules such as BESTComp, BESTBio, BESTFill, BESTCycle, BESTherm, BESTMove and BESTPractices. BESTComp is to guide how to make quality compost. BESTBio is to fill the knowledge gap of anaerobic digestion. BESTFill will address issues that can arise from landfilling site selection to landfill closure. BESTCycle is a info desk which provides recycling opportunities and linkages among manufacturers. BESTherm will guide incineration processes. BESTMove enables decision makers to allocate trucks from waste collection points to disposal site so as to reduce travelling cost covering basically the logistic aspects of waste collection and transport. BESTPractices is a compilation of success stories, lessons learnt and so on, for drawing ideas for better design when implementing SWM systems. In this manner, each module clearly defined within a narrow domain and has available sources of expertise for solid waste management hierarchy.

Graphical user interfaces are certainly more use-friendly than command language interfaces (Virvou and Kabassi, 2004). Further more, Mitri (2003) highlighted that natural language and speech understanding front ends improve query tools for knowledge management systems. Hence, the BESTCity DSS interface is designed to include the specific features of changeability, traceability, plenitude, and qualitative description. To make the computer as easy for the user to operate as possible, the BESTCity offers the capacity to interact with the system through text, pictures and graphics.

4. BRIDGING THE COMMUNICATION GAPS

Even though DSSs' contain enormous amount of information and knowledge, many decision makers and users in rural areas of the developing world will be denied the benefits of DSSs, if the information is available only in English. It is necessary to consider the wide range of users and their cognitive capabilities (Mikolajuk and Gar-On-Yeh, 1999). Decision-making using DSS occurs in all countries and is undertaken by people who are not necessarily fluent in any language other than their mother tongue (Hall, 1999). However, Lee et al., (2005) argued that decision support systems could be used to provide the right knowledge in the right form to the right persons at the right time. Hence, AI tools in local languages can make a significant impact on rural local authorities and other users. When users can get the required information in their native language, it would naturally motivate them to seek the powerful benefits of knowledge-based tools. The BESTCity DSS is embedded with multilingual natural language interfaces that users can formulate queries in their native languages.

5. SINHALA - ENGLISH ENVIRONMENTAL GLOSSARY

Even though the majority of people in Sri Lanka (79% of the population is Sinhalese) communicate in the Sinhala language, there is a remarkable absence of Sinhala lexicon for the technical and scientific words. Therefore, in order to ensure wide use of the BESTCity DSS, a Sinhala- English environmental glossary has been developed. The glossary consists of more than 1000 technical and scientific words, which are related to solid waste management. It describes each word both in English and Sinhala languages.

One of the principal impediments encountered while selecting the font in developing the glossary, is the lack of a standard Sinhala (or Tamil) font (character encoding). Although there are many Sinhala fonts available, none of them are ubiquitous (Sri Lanka – Country Report, 2003). Thus, the freely available "Dimuthu" font (Internet, 2) is selected for Sinhala language interface development (Figure 2).

w b W t T 1 . g o k m n u h r , j i

Figure 2 : Dimuthu Font

6. CONCLUSION

As technology does not always need to be high-end state-of-the art technology, in this research AI applications are used in simple user-friendly ways, keeping the end user, the Local Authority, and its technical capabilities in mind. This research covers both the extraction of information from knowledge bases (including active computer systems such as expert systems) and manipulation of information (to solve particular problems or to present data in an easily comprehensible manner). Thus, BESTCity is not only a decision support tool but also a training tool for novices.

ACKNOWLEDGEMENT

The funding provided by the University of Moratuwa, National Science Foundation for this research, continuing support and facilities provided by the Department of Chemical & Process Engineering, University of Moratuwa to carry out this research are gratefully acknowledged.

REFERENCES

[1]. Basri, H.B., Stentiford, E.I. (1995), Expert Systems in Solid Waste Management, Waste Management & Research, 13, 67-89.

[2]. Davis, R., Shrobe H., Szolovits P. (1993), What is a Knowledge Representation? *AI Magazine*, 14(1):17-33.

[3]. Hall, P.A.V., (1999), Software Internationalization Architecture for Decision Support Systems, in Decision Support Systems for Sustainable Development: A Resource Book

of Methods and Applications, eds, Kerson G.E., Mikolajuk Z., Gar-On-Yeh A., International Development Center, Canada.

[4]. Internet, 1 (2005), www.aiinc.ca

[5]. Internet, 2 (2004), www.manamala.com/download/fonts/index.asp

[6]. Lee K. C., Lee S., Kang I.W. (2005), KMPI : measuring knowledge mnagement performance, Information and Management, 42, 469-482.

[7]. McDougall, F.R. (2001), Life Cycle Inventory Tools : Supporting The Development of sustainable Solid Waste Management Systems, Corporative Environmental Strategy, 8, 142-147.

[8]. McHenry, P., Longhurst P., Lowe M., Seaton R. (2002), Evaluating Opportunities for Innovation in the Waste Industry - The Development of a GIS Based Decision Support Tool for Waste Strategy Planning, 5th International Conference on Solid Waste Management, International Solid Waste Association - ISWA, February, Istanbul, 1, pp.185-193.

[9]. Mikolajuk, Z., Gar-On-Yeh A. (1999), Sustainable Development and Decision Support Systems, in Decision Support Systems for Sustainable Development : A Resource Book of Methods and Applications, eds, G.E Kerson., Z. Mikolajuk, A. Gar-On-Yeh, International Development Center, Canada.

[10]. Mitri, M. (2003), Applying tacit knowledge management techniques for performance assessment, Computers & Education, 41, 173-189.

[11]. NSSWM, (2000) National Strategy for Solid Waste Management, Ministry of Forestry and Environment, Sri Lanka.

[12]. Rubenstein-Montano, B. (2000), A survey of knowledge-based information systems for urban planning : moving towards knowledge management, computers, environment and urban systems, 24, 155-172.

[13]. Sri Lanka – Country Report, (2003) Sri Lanka – Country Report, *Asian Forum on ICT Policies and e-strategies*, Kuala Lampur, Malasia, 20-22 October, retrieved from www.apdip.net/asain-forum

[14]. Virvou, M., Kabassi, K. (2004), Evaluating an intelligent graphical user interface by comparison with human experts, Knowledge-Based Systems, 14, 31-37.

[15]. Wilson D.C. 1981, Waste Management – Planning, Evaluation, Technologies, Oxford University Press, Oxford, UK

DETERMINING OF THE DELAY TIME FOR A HEATING VENTILATING AND AIR-CONDITIONING PLANT USING MULTI-WEIGHTS NEURONS APPROACH

Mengdi Hu [1], Hao Feng[2], Wenming Cao [3] , Shoujue Wang [4]

[1]Department of Civil Engineering, Zhejiang University Of Science and Technology , Hangzhou, China, Email: humengdi1958@163.com ,[2]Jiaxing College,Jiaxing,Zhejiang,China [3]Information College, Zhejiang University of Technology, Hangzhou 310014,China,[4]Institute of Semiconductors, Chinese Academy of Science, Beijing 100083,China

Abstract: This paper presents an Multi Weights Neurons approach to determine the delay time for a heating, ventilating and air-conditioning (HVAC) plan to respond to control actions. The Multi Weights Neurons is a fully connected four-layer network. An acceleration technique was used to improve the General Delta Rule for the learning process. Experimental data for heating and cooling modes were used with both the Multi Weights Neurons and a traditional mathematical method to determine the delay time. The results show that Multi Weights Neurons can be used effectively determining the delay time for HVAC systems.

Key words: Multi Weights Neurons , HVAC , Delay time

1. INTRODUCTION

Since Wang shoujue proposed Multi Weights Neurons[1,2,3,4,5,6], it have widely applied pattern recognition[7,8,9,10,11,12,13,14] 、 control theory[15,16,24] and approximation theory[17] . In my paper, we will apply Multi Weights Neurons approach to determine the delay time for a heating, ventilating and air-conditioning (HVAC)[25,26,27,28] plan to respond to control actions.

Figure 1 denotes the control system of a general heating, ventilating and air-conditioning. $u(t)$, $y(t)$, $r(t)$, $e(t)$ denote the controlling parameter, controlled parameter, defining parameter and error. Given a signal (as figure 2), the system will responds as figure 2. In this figure, the interval BC at which y(t) ascending from 5% to 95% is defined as ascending time (Ts). And the interval AB at which system does not respond is defined as delay time (Td). The interval AC is defined as responding time (Tr). Ascending time is relevant with system and controller, but delay time is only relevant with system.

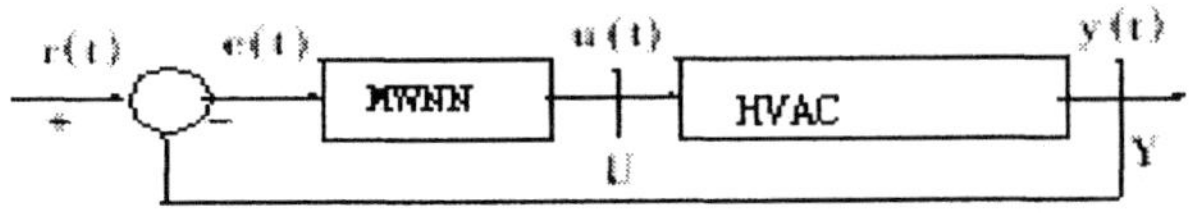

Fig.1. Multi-weighted neural networks feedback control system.

Delay time can also be defined by Dirac pulse. In theory, a Dirac pulse would respond at Y when a Dirac pulse happened at U (as figure 3b). But, in fact, the system responds as figure 3c. The interval of the pulse is defined as delay time. In general, the output of a controller can be parsed as a serial of Dirac pulse (as figure 4a). The system will produce a responding curve $y(t)$, which looks like $u(t)$ (as figure 4b). Every response has its own delay time. The comprehensive response of linear system to continuous control signal has the same delay time. Then, we can determine the delay time by comparing $u(t)$ and $y(t)$.

In this paper, we use neural network to determine the delay time of system. At first, get some control signal:

$u(0), u(Tc), u(2Tc), \cdots, u(nTc), \cdots$, and the corresponding responses:

$y(0), y(Tc), y(2Tc), \cdots, y(nTc), y([n+1]Tc), y([n+2]Tc), \cdots, y([n+k]Tc), \cdots$,

(Tc is the sample interval). If the response of control signal $u(nTc)$ is $y([n+k]Tc)$, then the delay time T_d is the product of sample times and sample interval Tc:

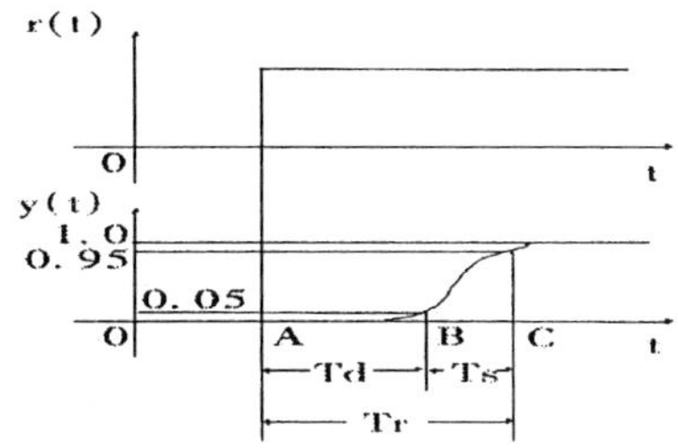

Fig. 2. The response of system

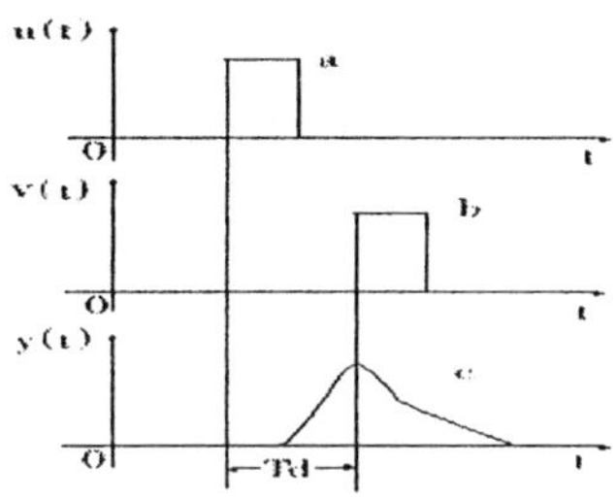

Fig. 3. The response of Dirac pulse.Dirac pulse (b)Ideal response (c)Practical response

$$T_d = K \bullet T_C \quad . \tag{1}$$

The array $u(Tc), u(2Tc), \cdots, u(nTc), \cdots$ is much is the array $y([k+1]Tc), y([k+2]Tc), \cdots, y([k+n]Tc), \cdots$. We can determine the delay time by check whether $u(iTc)$ resemble $y([k+i]Tc)$ $(i = 1,2,\cdots,n)$. Shown as Figure 5, when $u(iTc) = y([k+i]Tc)$, the output of z is 1, else the output of z is less than 1.0. The more $u(iTc)$ resembles $y([k+i]Tc)$, the more the value of z approaches 1.0. Here, we define z as resemble coefficient. In the paper, Multi Weights Neurons has two inputs, the one is $u(iTc)$, and the other is $y([k+i]Tc)$. The time corresponding to k which make the largest output of Multi Weights Neurons is delay time (as formula (1)).

2. THE THEORY OF MULTI WEIGHTS NEURONS

The present neurons are based on single-weight vector which can only reach the simple and regular shapes. In fact, the real shapes of some a pattern in the feature space, such as a given person's face images, are irregular and complicated, so we developed a novel theory of multi-weight vector neurons .

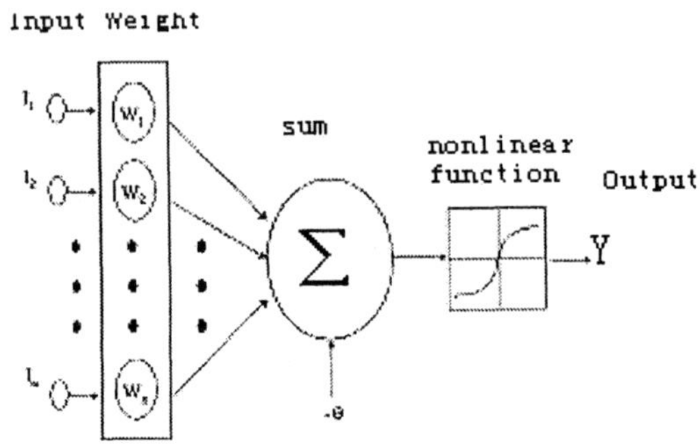

Single weight neuron model

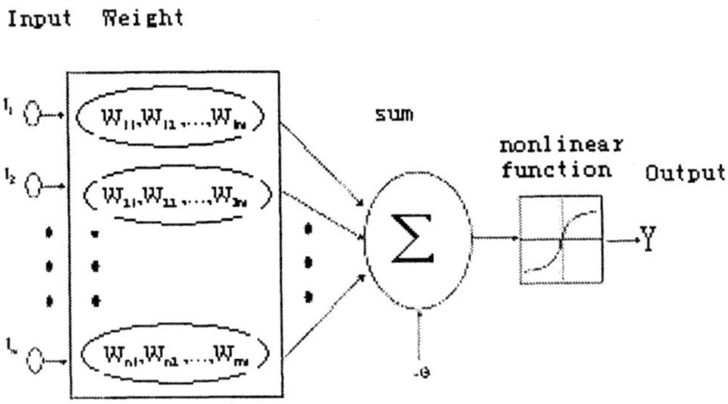

Fig 5. Multi Weight Neuron Model

Mathematic expression of the shape by this neuron is:

$$| \overrightarrow{X} - \overrightarrow{W} |^2 = k$$

hyper-sausage is the topologic product of a line segment(1-dimensional manifold) and a hypersphere, this line segment's endpoints are decided by study samples A and B, and it is actualized by a two weights neuron.(The two weights are decided by A and B). The shape by this neuron is made of three parts: S_1 is the set of points whose distances to the line segment equal a certain constant k.; S_2 is the set of points whose distances to a sample point A equal k; S_3 is the set of points whose distances to a sample point B equal k. the mathematic expressions of them are:

$$S_1 : |\overrightarrow{X} - \overrightarrow{W_1}|^2 - \left[(\overrightarrow{X} - \overrightarrow{W_1}) \bullet \frac{\overrightarrow{W_2} - \overrightarrow{W_1}}{|\overrightarrow{W_2} - \overrightarrow{W_1}|}\right]^2 = k$$

$$S_2 : |\overrightarrow{X} - \overrightarrow{W_1}|^2 = k$$

$$S_3 : |\overrightarrow{X} - \overrightarrow{W_2}|^2 = k$$

According t the theory of high-dimension space geometry[4], the volume of a hypersphere in k dimensions is :

$$V_1 = \begin{cases} \dfrac{\pi^{\frac{k}{2}}}{(\frac{k}{2})!} r_1^{\,k}, k = 2m \\ \dfrac{2^{\frac{k+1}{2}} \pi^{\frac{k-1}{2}}}{k!!} r_1^{\,k}, k = 2m+1 \end{cases}$$

r_1 is the radius of the circle.

and the volume of a hypersausage(hyper cylinder) is

$$V_2 = \begin{cases} \dfrac{2^{\frac{k}{2}} \pi^{\frac{k-2}{2}}}{(k-1)!!} r_2^{\,(k-1)\times h,}, k = 2m \\ \dfrac{\pi^{\frac{k-1}{2}}}{(\frac{k-1}{2})!} r_2^{\,(k-1)} \times h, k = 2m+1 \end{cases}$$

r_2 is the radius of the cylinder's bottom, which is (k-1) dimension hypersphere; h is the altitude of it.

3. TOPOLOGY STRUCTURE OF MULTI-WEIGHTED NEURAL NETWORK.

The multi-weighted neural network.'s topology is shown in figure 6. The first layer is input layer which has two input node. The forth layer is the output layer which only has one neuron. The second and third layer both has five neurons. The output of controller and the response (temperature) which is normalized is the input of the Multi Weights Neurons. Every neuron is a Sigmoid function. The output ofMulti Weights Neurons is between 0 and 1. The weights of the multi-weighted neural network were adjusted by the multi-weighted neural networks algorithm[20].

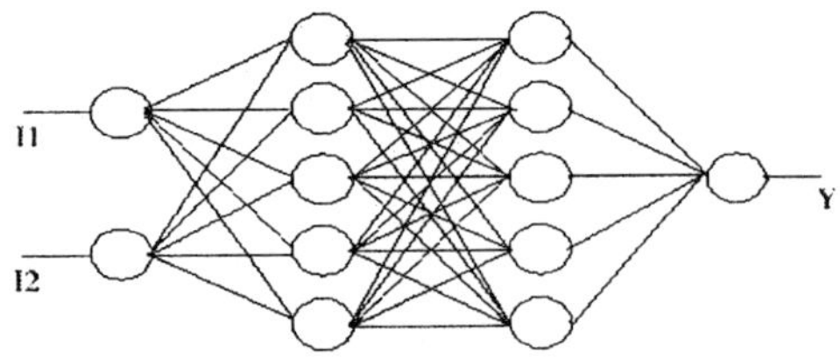

Fig. 6. The topology of the multi-weighted neural network.

We adapt Multi Weights Neurons in our experiment, one of them has three layers, and the other has four layers. Every hide layer of the Multi Weights Neurons both has five neurons. The simulation was shown in figure 7 and figure 8. The two criterions, mean square error (Ea) and the largest error (Em), are used to assess our Multi Weights Neurons. The criterions were defined as follows:

$$E_a = \frac{1}{N_b} \sum_{b=1}^{N_b} (D_b - Y_b)^2 \tag{2}$$

$$E_m = \max\{abs(D_b - Y_b)\} \tag{3}$$

D_b is between 0 and 1 which is the expect output of input state b in one circle of study; Y_b is the actual output, which is between 0 and 1. N_b is the number of input state in one circle of study. The learning algorithm also has a powerful influence on the multi-weighted neural network.[4].

4. EXPERIMENT

The HVAC in our experiment was composed with 2000-cfm fan-winding-pipes, refrigeration, cold water, hot water and steam-winding-pipes, a controller used to control the temperature of return wind. When heating, air is heated by steam; when cooling, air is cooled by cooler. Different operation has different delay time.

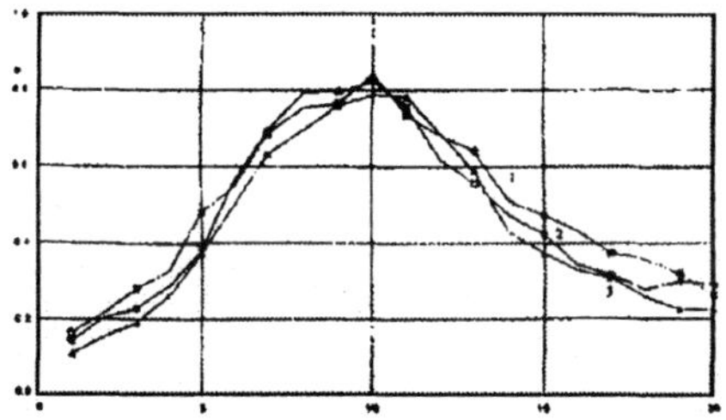

Fig. 7. The mean resemble coefficient of heating.

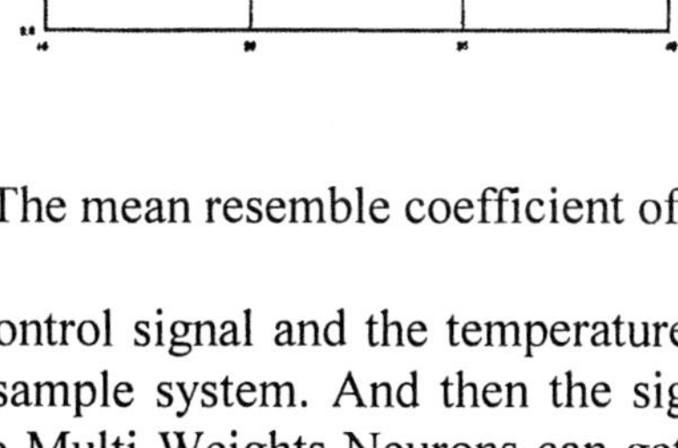

Fig. 8. The mean resemble coefficient of cooling

We get signals (control signal and the temperature of return wind) from controller with data sample system. And then the signals were normalized between 0 and 1. The Multi Weights Neurons can get resemble coefficients with interval K. In figure 7, curve 1 depicts the result of heating. In figure 10 curve 1 depicts the result of cooling. In figure 7, the largest resemble coefficient is 0.5 at $k = 18$, the interval of sample is 2.12 minute, so, the delay time of heating is 86. 1 minute. In figure 8, the largest resemble coefficient is 0.84 at $k = 15$, so the delay time of cooling is 50 minute.

5. CONCLUSION

In this paper, a Multi Weights Neurons with four layers was used to determine the delay time of HVAC system. The simulation and experiment denote that Multi Weights Neurons is efficient in determining the delay time of HVAC system. Compared with conventional algorithm, Multi Weights Neurons can eliminate the interrupt of input noise by adopting the bias and coefficient of the neuron. Then, Multi Weights Neurons is more precise than conventional algorithm. It can be used on controller to predict system delay time. When learning, the acceleration algorithm can improve the conventional learning algorithm, it lower the output error and accelerate the convergence.

REFERENCE

1 .Wang ShouJue etc., "Discussion on the Basic Mathematical Models of Neurons in General Purpose Neuro computer", ACTA ELECTRONICA SINICA, Vol.29 No.5, 2001

2. Wang Shoujue etc., "The Sequential Learning Ahead Masking (SLAM) model of neural networks for pattern classification", Proceedings of JCIS98. Vol.IV. pp199-202. Oct. 1998. RTP. NC. USA

3. Caoyu,Wang shoujue, multi-weighted neural network.s and its approximation, thesis , Institute of Semiconductors, Chinese Academy of Science, Beijing ,China,2000

4. Wang ShouJue, Bionic(Topological) Pattern Recognition——A New Model of Pattern Recognition Theory and Its Applications, ACTA ELECTRONICA SINICA, 2002, 30(10): 1417-1420

5. Wang ShouJue, Wang Bianan, Analysis and Theory of High-Dimension Space Geometry for Artificial Neural Networks, ACTA ELECTRONICA SINICA, 2002,30(1): 1-4

6. Wang ShouJue, A new development on ANN in China – Biomimetic pattern recognition and multi weight vector neurons, LECTURE NOTES IN ARTIFICIAL INTELLIGENCE 2003,2639: 35-43

7. Wang Shoujue, Xu Jian, Wang Xianbao, Qin Hong, Multi-camera Human-face Personal Identification System Based on the Bionic Pattern Recognition, ACTA ELECTRONICA SINICA,2003,31(1): 1-3

8. Cao WM, Hao F, Wang SJ, The application of DBF neural networks for object recognition, INFORMATION SCIENCES, MAR 22 2004, 160 (1-4): 153-160

9. Shi Jingpu, Chen Ji, Chen Xiaodong, Chen Chuan, Wang Shoujue, The Speaker Verification System Based on Neurocomputer and Its Application, ACTA ELECTRONICA SINICA, 1999,27(10):27-29

10. Wang Shoujue, Li Zhaozhou, Wang Bonan, Deng Haojiang, Feed-forward Neural Network Modeling for Noise Rejection, JOURNAL OF CIRCUITS AND SYSTEMS, 2000, 5(04):21-26

11. Deng Haojiang, Wang Shoujue, Xing Cangju, Li Qian, Research of Text-Independent Speaker Recognition Using Clustering Statistic, JOURNAL OF CIRCUITS AND SYSTEMS, 2001, 6(03):77-8

12. Xing Cangju, Qu Yanfeng, Wang Shoujue, Face Detection on Gray-Scale Static Image with Complex Background, JOURNAL OF COMPUTER-AIDED DESIGN & COMOPUTER GRAPHICS, 2002, 14(05):401-403
13. Qu Yangfeng, Li Weijun, Xu Jian, Wang Shoujue, Fast Multi-Pose Face Dection in A Complex Background, JOURNAL OF COMPUTER-AIDED DESIGN & COMOPUTER GRAPHICS, 2004, 16(01):45-50
14. Deng Haojiang, Wang Shoujue, Du Limin, Text-Independent Speaker Verification on Using Priority Ordered Radial Basis Function Networks, JOURNAL OF ELECTRONICS AND INFORMATION TECHNOLOGY, 2003, 25(09):1153-1159
15. Wenming Cao Feng hao and Shoujue Wang, An adaptive controller for a class of nonlinear system using direction basis function. ACTA Journal Of Electronics 2002, 23: 43-48.
16. Cao, Wenming, Wang, Shoujue, Fenghao, Approximation with direction basis function neural networks, IEEE Region 10 Annual International Conference, Proceedings/TENCON, 2002,3:1290-1293
17. Xu, Jian, Li, Weijun, Qu, Yanfeng, Qin, Hong, Wang, Shoujue, Architecture Research and Hardware Implementation on Simplified Neural Computing System for Face Identification,Proceedings of the International Joint Conference on Neural Networks, 2003, 2:948-952
18. Ji Yongqiang, Geometry of Submanifolds, Science Press, 2004.1
19. Xue Senlin, Manifold and STOKES Theorem, People's Education Press, 1983.69(1): 1-132
20. Hao Feng, The theory and application of multi-weighted neural network, PHD thesis,2004.
21. Shoujue Wang, Direction-Basis-Function neural networks, Proceedings of IJCNN'99, 10–16 July,Washington, DC, USA, 1999:1251–2171
22. Shoujue Wang, Priority ordered neural networks with better similarity to human knowledge representation. Chinese Journal Of Electronics, 1999, 8(1):1–4.
23. Wang Shoujue, Artificial Neural Network, Neural Computer and Its Application, Measurement & Control Technology, 1999, 18(08):1-5
24. Li Yujian, Wang Shoujue, Direction-basis-function Neural Network and Its Approximation Capabilities, JOURNAL OF BEIJING UNIVERSITY OF TECHNOLOTY, 2003, 29(03):372-376
25. Xu Qing Qu Ruigui, Study and Analyze on Temperature Parameters Used in HVAC, Refrigeration & Air-Condition ,2004,(4),15-17 (In Chinese)
26. L I Hongxin, SELECTING FANS IN THE HVAC SYSTEM DESIGN, Refrigeration & Air-Condition,2004,(5),82-85 (In Chinese)
27. Graham ,J .B. Fan selection by computer techniques [J] . Heating ,Piping and Air Conditioning (April) :168. 1966.
28. System and equipment ,fan [M] . ASHRAE Fundamentals Handbook ,2000 ,15. 1215. 17.

DEVELOPMENT OF AN EXPERT SYSTEM FOR LANDFILLING APPLICATIONS IN SRI LANKA

ASANGA MANAMPERI[1], L.C. JAYAWARDHANA[2], AJITH DE ALWIS[3], SUMITH PILAPITIYA[4]

[1,2,3]*Department of Chemical & Process Engineering, University of Moratuwa, Sri Lanka*

[4]*The World Bank (Colombo Office), DFCC Bldg., Galle Road, Colombo 03, Sri Lanka*

Abstract: An expert system was developed to assist proper implementation of landfill technology in Sri Lanka. The knowledge base was acquired through text books, manuals, technical reports, research publications and domain experts. An object oriented expert system shell, ACQUIRE 2.1 was used as the building tool for the prototype development. BESTFill expert system contains several sub modules by which the user can obtain a comprehensive background of the domain. The output is expected to support effective integrated solid waste management.

Key words: Expert system, Landfilling, Decision support tool

1. INTRODUCTION

Solid waste management has long been a problem area for local authorities in Sri Lanka. Uncontrolled dumping and burning is being practiced at large scale due to lack of proper guidance and awareness. The solid waste practices after the recent Tsunami event demonstrates how bad these practices were (Draft Field REA Report-Sri Lanka Tsunami, 2005). The main reason attributable to this deficiency is the lack of expertise in the solid waste management domain. The aim of this research is to address one of the main areas of solid waste management, the landfilling technology, in order to cater to the need of expertise in this area, by providing an expert system called BESTFill. Currently there are two operating landfill sites in Sri Lanka, with minimum facilities for treatment of leachate and landfill gas. However there are hundreds of other potential sites (currently used for open

However there are hundreds of other potential sites (currently used for open dumping) which could be converted to sanitary landfills. To guide the proper implementation of this technology, the need of expertise, in the form of a human expert or a written program such as an expert system is a crucial factor. However in Sri Lanka, the human experts are extremely scarce for landfill technology, and are restricted to the few universities in the country. In order to convey the expert knowledge to the operational level personnel, the most convenient and cost effective means is an expert system.

1.1 Expert Systems

Solid waste management area has been a target for the development of expert systems in many countries. Expert systems were developed for many different sub divisions of solid waste management such as waste minimization, recycling, optimal transportation, optimal land use, designing of landfilling, composting and biogas facilities etc.

SWIM (Wang et al., 1998) was developed to provide a structure for systems analysis of solid waste management problems at the municipal level. The SWIM model identifies the costs for collection and transportation of waste/ recyclables and adverse environmental impacts associated with these operations. Waste Plan (http://www.epa.gov/opptintr/acctg/rev/8-13.htm) is a commercial model that has been developed as a policy analysis tool. The model allows users to build integrated solid waste management plans. HMA (Helsinki Metropolitan Area) model (Tanskanen, 2000) is for integrated analysis of separation strategies and their effects on recovery rates, waste streams, costs and emissions of regional municipal solid waste management. ORWARE (Organic Waste Research) model (Sonesson, 1998, Sonneson, 2000) is a simulation model for organic waste management systems. The objective is to facilitate studies of waste management systems. MSW-Xpert (Mc. Cauley-Bell and Reinhart,1997) was developed to assist in the planning and analysis phases of a waste composition study and to produce consistent results from country to coutry by controlling the variance in planning techniques. However this system has been developed only for users who are experienced in development of waste composition studies.

Leachate Management Advisor (LMA) (Basri, 2000), Landfill Design Advisor (LDA) (Basri & Stentiford,1994), Landfill Restoration Plan Advisor (LRPA) (Basri,1998) and Visual Help (www.scisoftware.com/products/ visual_help_demo.html) have been designed to address different areas of landfilling applications.

Compost Design Consultant (CDC) (Basri,1999) was developed to aid the preliminary design of composting facilities in treating municipal solid waste for developing countries.

The knowledge based system called ENVOP Expert (Environmental Optimization) has been first used to identify possible waste minimization alternatives and later extended for waste minimization analysis in chemical processes (Halim and Srinivasan, 2002).

These systems have proved their reliability and usefulness in their respective domains throughout the world. Therefore as a developing country, Sri Lanka too can benefit from the developed expert system for landfilling applications.

Among the many advantages of the expert systems, it could be highlighted for a country like Sri Lanka, that its ability to provide training facility for the key personnel in the solid waste management hierarchy. This can be easiliy achieved since expert systems contain the necessary knowledge and the ability to explain their reasoning process (Waterman,1986). By incorporating user-friendly interfaces and knowledge about teaching methods and user modeling, a smooth learning and training process between the trainee and the expert system could be achieved. As a training device the expert system provides new staff members with a vast reservoir of experience and strategies from which to learn about recommended policies and methods. The system can also be adapted to train novices in specific tasks such as, site selection, site preparation, leachate management, surface water management, usage of landfill machinery accepting and control of incoming waste, handling unusual wastes, record keeping, financial planning and so on. The experience from the two operating landfill sites shows that this type of training is a crucial factor for the better management of the sites. Since the planners and designers have been unable to convey their design and operational goals to the site managers and workers, the expected quality is hardly achieved. Expert systems can be used to bridge this knowledge gap, thus improving the quality of the project, dramatically.

The nature of the domain of landfilling technology provides many reasons for its suitability for the development of an expert system. There are no hard and fast solutions for most of the issues arising in this area. The knowledge base consists of the experience gathered through many human years of study or practice through trial and error. Therefore approximate methods, heuristics and rules-of-thumb makes up the entire knowledge base, except for a few exceptions. An expert system could be the only way to tackle a domain such as landfilling with so many ill defined concepts, over abundance of possibilities, difficulty of gathering information, uncertainty and unreliability of data, cost of gathering information and so many inconsistencies.

The domain of landfilling is essentially multi disciplinary in nature. It requires substantial contributions from geologists, engineers, biologists, economists etc. When the expert is in the form of an expert system, it would be much easier to gather information from various disciplines and incorporate into a one body. Problem solving becomes much easier when the system posses information from various disciplines involved with the issue.

Transferability (or reproducibility) of expertise is an essential factor when considering the substantial time, effort and cost involved in building up an expertise. Unlike transferring the human expertise, which is a lengthy, laborious and expensive process, the transferring of artificial expertise is a trivial process of copying or cloning programs or data files. The importance of this feature is highlighted when similar expertise is required at different locations. According to this scenario, when considering the hundreds of potential landfill sites and thousands of potential users, the developed expert system would be a very useful tool for the local authorities in Sri Lanka which numbers to 297.

2. METHODOLOGY

2.1 Knowledge Acquisition

Knowledge acquisition is the lengthiest process in building of an expert system. However it is the single most important process of the knowledge engineer upon which the quality of the expert system depend on. The central core of the knowledge base was acquired from the published text books and manuals. This knowledge consists of well established facts, rules, theory and guidelines that had been practiced over many years. Technical reports such as Environmental Impact Assessment reports, Initial Environmental Examination reports related to proposed, operated and abandoned landfill projects in Sri Lanka, have provided very valuable sources of information on applicability and suitability of landfill technology for Sri Lanka. This source of information provided a means to build a unique knowledge base for BESTFill expert system.

Domain experts provided the valuable source of expertise related to problem areas of landfill technology in Sri Lanka. Since most landfills in Sri Lanka have failed, abandoned or poorly operated, it could be traced from these human experts the deficiencies involved in these projects and what really went wrong. Also human expertise was helpful in organization and refinement of the knowledge base of the expert system, acquired from other sources. Most of the experts, however, were concentrated around the universities in the country, rather than involved with actual projects.

Knowledge acquisition has now become relatively easy than two decades ago, due to the advancement of Internet facilities. Much valued information about landfill operating procedures, organizations, experts and so on, were acquired through the Internet. These were helpful in building the sub modules of the BESTFill expert system.

2.2 Building tool

For the development of BESTFill,an expert system shell, ACQUIRE 2.1 (www.aiinc.ca), was preferred over conventional programming languages. Expert system shells are high level programming tools which has a built in inference engine. This feature improves productivity since the knowledge engineer needs only to add the knowledge base. ACQUIRE was preferred because of its object oriented approach which combines the two main knowledge representation techniques for expert systems, i.e. production rules for inferential knowledge, and objects (or frames) for static knowledge. ACQUIRE was selected because of its proven reliability and availability of its support facilities and documentation.

2.3 User interface

Proper organization of the user interface is important since it is the part of the expert system that interacts with the user. The presence of a standard user interface framework not only simplifies development efforts, but also reduces user training and support requirements for users (Grove,2000). In the BESTFill expert system, the knowledge base was divided into four categories as site, technology, safety and post closure, as shown in the figure1. Once the user type a keyword related to the desired area and activate the system, the system will display an entire list of questions related to that area. If the user finds it superfluous, he has the option to add on more keywords in order to narrow down the problem area. If the system requires more specifications or clarifications, it will prompt the user to input more data, instead of producing the answer in a one frame. The user can select the option "unknown" or give an approximate answer, if he is uncertain about an issue. Then the system may either ask for other inputs relevant to the issue, or else it will formulate the answer based on given data indicating all the uncertainties and assumptions. If the question is straight forward, the system will produce the answer through texts, charts or tables within a single frame. If the user wants additional information on landfilling, he can select one of the eight sub modules as shown in the figure1.

2.4 Inference engine

Inference engine contains the general problem solving knowledge. It processes the domain knowledge (located in knowledge base) to reach new conclusions. The inference engine acts upon the rules and other data related to landfilling to solve the problem and applies the rules as encapsulated in the knowledge base and draw inferences and records conclusions in the database (Beerel, 1993). The production rules were applied for the site related questions (site selection etc.) and objects or frames were used for other divisions, namely technology, safety and postclosure.

Figure1. Main user interface of BESTFill expert system

2.5 Sub modules

A unique feature of BESTFill expert system is that it contains several submodules by which the user can obtain a comprehensive background understanding. The submodules were named as literature, info desk, training tool, photo gallery, landfill rapid assessment tool, economics & costing, regulations and reports as shown in the figure 1.

The literature module consists of information about the relevant books, journals, research papers and websites (figure 2).

Figure2: Literature module

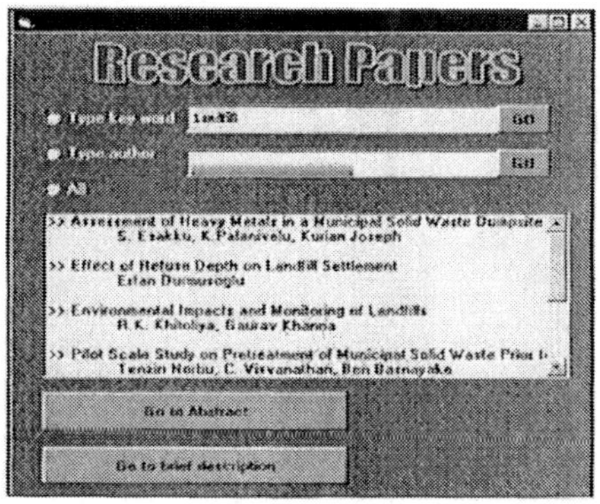

Figure3. Interface for Research Papers module

Books were categorized by the title and given with the information of authors, publishers, year, ISBN and a brief description. Similarly the journals were classified by the name and provided with the information such as publisher, address and a description. Relevant websites were downloaded and made accessible to the user, off line, and displayed in a screen similar to a search engine. Research papers related to landfilling were listed as shown in figure3 and provided with the abstract and a brief summary.

Info desk is a module from which the user can obtain contact details of all the relevant experts, institutions and organizations involved in landfill applications (figure 4). Information of experts were given in the form of name, institution, country, address, email, telephone and personnel website (figure 5). The details of institutions and organizations were provided with similar interfaces with similar information.

Figure 4: Info Desk module

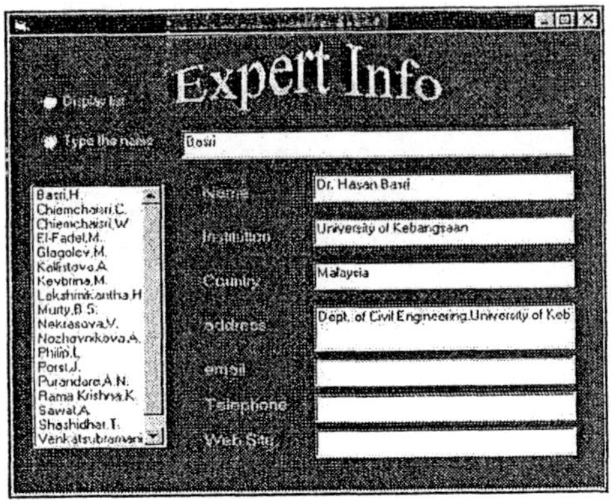

Figure 5: Interface for Expert Info

Landfill rapid assessment tool is embedded with technical details such as terminology, calculations and examples (Figure 6). If the user come across an unfamiliar term, he can go to the terminology section of the landfill rapid assessment tool module and type the word as shown in the figure 7. In the "calculations" module, the user can simply input the values for the variables and get the answer for all the calculations associated with landfill processes, in no time. Examples module is a further extension of the calculations module and also provided with a detailed example with all the relevant maps, tables, charts etc.

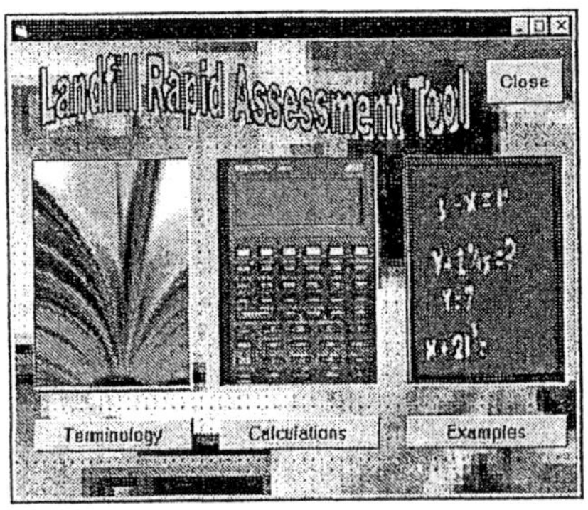

Figure 6: Landfill Rapid Assessment Tool Module

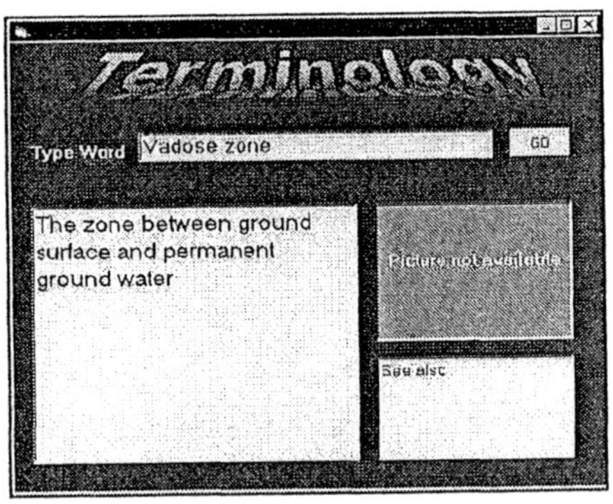

Figure 7: Interface for Terminology

Training tool module has been designed for the use of the novices to the field (Figure 8). It has been provided with six power point presentations highlighting the adverse effects of open dumping, adverse effects of improper planning of a landfill, necessary items of a landfill, benefits of a properly managed landfill, Hazardous waste secure landfills and an example of a well run and managed system of a developed country.

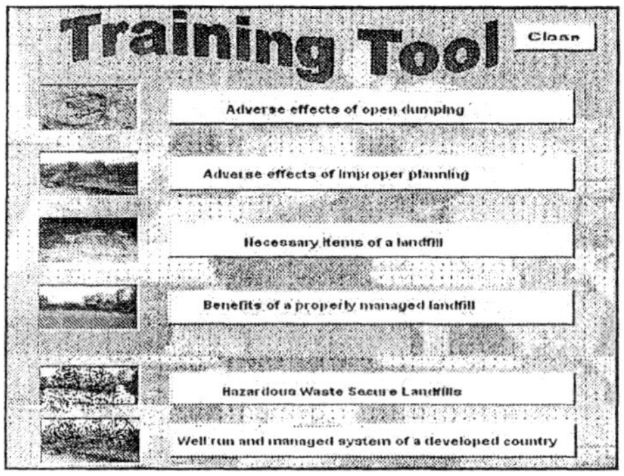

Figure 8: Training Tool module

Figure 9: Photo Gallery module

Photo gallery consists of a huge collection of pictures and was divided into six areas as landfill sites, containment facilities, treatment facilities, environmental monitoring, operations and machinery and a separate collection of pictures of projects in Sri Lanka (Figure 9). Pictures were displayed as thumbnails and once selected, were provided with full picture and a brief description.

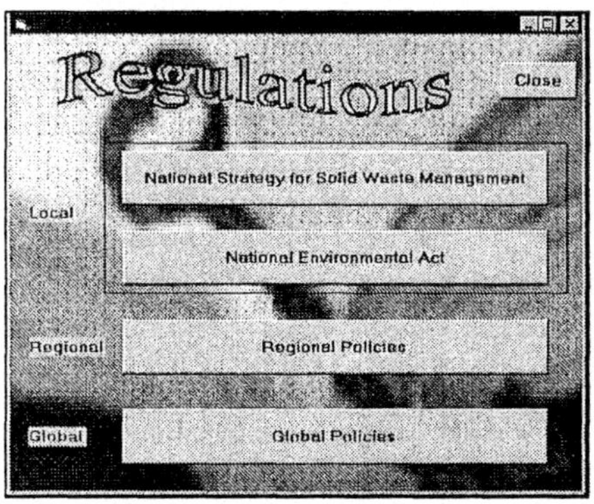

Figure 10: Regulations module

Figure 11: Reports module

Regulations module was incorporated in order for the user to obtain a background knowledge on legal framework associated with solid waste management. Regulations module was subdivided into local (legislation relevant to Sri Lanka), regional (environmental policies pertaining to each South Asian country) and international (other important international policies)(Figure 10). Specific landfill directives such as of European Union are also included.

Reports module provides the user with Environmental Impact Assessment reports, Initial Environmental Examination reports, technical reports on landfilling and case studies carried out in landfill sites (Figure11).

3. CONCLUSION

The BESTFill expert system has been developed to cater to the need of expertise in landfill technology. The development has been carried out in several phases, including problem identification, knowledge acquisition, knowledge representation, programming, testing and validation. It has incorporated several user interfaces in order to make the system user friendly as much as possible. Among the potential users are local authorities, consulting firms, constructors, researchers and students. The output is expected to support effective integrated solid waste management.

ACKNOWLEDGEMENT

The funding provided by the University of Moratuwa, National Science Foundation for this research, continuing support and facilities provided by the Department of Chemical & Process Engineering, University of Moratuwa to carry out this research are gratefully acknowledged.

REFERENCES

[1] ACQUIRE 2.1 ActiveX Control, Programmer's Guide, Acquired Intelligence Inc., #205-1095 McKenzie Ave., Victoria, BC, Canada.

[2] Basri, H.B., An Expert System for Landfill Leachate Management, Environmental Technology, 2000, 21: 157-166.

[3] Basri, H.B., Stentiford, E.I., Expert Systems in Solid Waste Management, Waste Management & Research, 1994, 13: 67-89.

[4] Basri, H.B., (1998), An Expert System for Planning Landfill Restoration, Wat. Sci. Tech., 1998, vol.37,No. 8: 211-217.

[5] Basri, N.E.A, Stentiford, E.I., Basri, H., Development of an expert system for the design of composting facilities for municipal solid waste, Proceedings World Engineering Congress (Civil Engineering) 1999 (24-26 November), Kuala Lumpur, ISBN 967-960-086-6, 1999: 13-20

[6] Beerel, A., Expert Systems in Business (Real World Applications), Ellis Harwood Limited, 1993: 245-248.

[7] Draft Field REA Report-Sri Lanka Tsunami , Draft Field Report: Rapid Environmental Impact Assessment- Sri Lanka Tsunami, 2005.

[8] Grove R., Internet-based Expert Systems, Expert Systems, 2000, 17(3), 129-135.

[9] Halim, I., Srinivasan, R., Integrated Decision Support System for Waste Minimization Analysis in Chemical Processes, Environ. Sci. Technol., 2002, 36, 1640 – 1648.

[10] McCauley-Bell P., Reinhart D., Development of a Waste Composition Study Planning and Analysis Tool – MSW_Xpert, Florida Center for Solid and Hazardous Waste Management,1997, Report # 97-3.

[11] Sonneson U., Calculating Transport Labour for Organic Waste from Urban to Rural Areas, Resources, Conversation and Recycling, 1998, 24 a: 335-348

[12] Sonneson U., Modeling of Waste Collection- A General Approach to Calculate Fuel Consumption and Time, Waste Management and Research, 2000,b: 115-123.

[13] Tanskanen J.H., An approach for Evaluating the Effects of Source Separation on Municipal Solid Waste Management, Helsinki University of Technology, Doctoral Thesis, Helsinki, 2000.

[14] Wang F.S., Richardson A.J., Roddick F.A., SWIM-Modeling Approach and its Applications, System Engineering Models for Waste Management, International Workshop in Gothenburg, Sweden, 1998.

[15] Waterman, D.A., A Guide to Expert Systems, Addison Wesley Longman ,Inc., New York, 1986.

[16] www.aiinc.ca

[17] www.scisoftware.com/products/ visual_help_demo.html

[18] http://www.epa.gov/opptintr/acctg/rev/8-13.htm

DEVELOPMENT OF AN INTELLIGENT ADAPTER FOR FIELD COMPUTER

Wei Yang, Minzan Li, Hui Liu
Key laboratory of Modern Precision Agriculture System Integration Research, Ministry of Education, China Agriculture University, Beijing 100083, China. Email: limz@cau.edu.cn

Abstract: A kind of intelligent adapter between CAN bus network and PC104 system was developed. The adapter is made up of an interface of CAN bus network, a CAN receiver connecting with the interface, a CAN controller, a PC104 bus-slot, a high speed opt coupler, a microprocessor and a parallel interface circuit. PC104 system can just take charge of transmitting and receiving data without performing maintenance of CAN bus because of using the microprocessor. Thus the system resource can be saved for other tasks. The adapter uses parallel communication mode and has high data transmission rate. The drive VxD of the adapter and the functional module of the PC104 system were programmed. Debugging shows the adapter works stably and satisfactorily.

Key words: PC/104, CAN bus, Field computer, parallel communication mode

1. INTRODUCTION

The Controller Area Network (CAN) is a serial communications protocol, which efficiently supports distributed real-time control with a very high level of security. It has been used from high speed networks to low cost multiplex wiring, such as automotive electronics, engine control units, sensors, anti-skid brake systems, etc. PC104 system is a new kind of embedded system. It has two bus hubs, P1 and P2. P1 has 64 pins and P2 has 40 pins so it is called PC104 system. The size is very small just 90mm×96mm, and the drive current is low. Thus it fits for using in commercial installation.

In a word, field computer based on PC104 system and farmland data collection control system based on CAN Bus have been developed. In order to use the field computer as an independent application unit or an independent CAN node for precision agriculture, it is necessary to build a kind of bridge between CAN Bus and PC104 system. Hence, we decided to develop an intelligent adapter between CAN Bus and PC104 system.

2. MATERIALS AND METHODS

The development of the intelligent adapter was based on a developed field computer. The field computer was an embedded mobile computer system fixed on farm machinery. It can be used as a real-time information management tool for precision agriculture, such as field data acquisition, variable rate controlling, and so on.

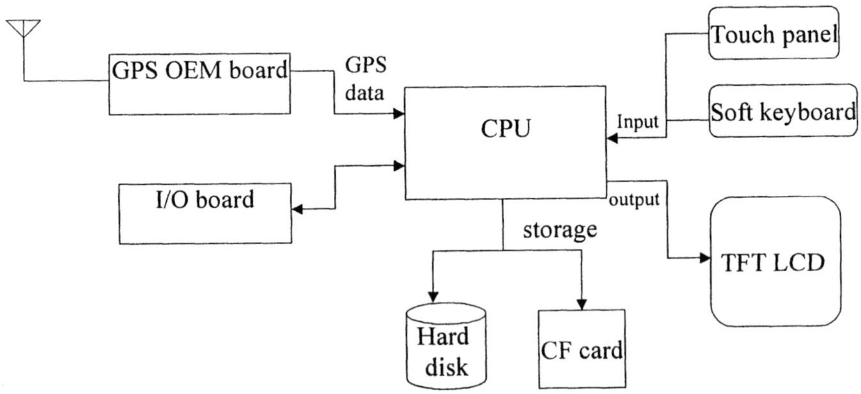

Figure 1. The structure of the field computer

Fig.1 shows the structure of the field computer. It consisted of a CPU, a GPS OEM board, a I/O board, a touch panel, a soft keyboard, a TFT LCD, a hard disk, and a driver of Compact Flash Card. PCM-3350, a kind of industrial PC/104 motherboard, was chosen as the core of the field computer. A TFT LCD and a tough panel were selected as the output device and the input interface respectively, and a hard disk was taken as storage device. The Field Computer supported RS-232 and USB serial ports. It also supported Compact Flash Card as a mobile storage medium. A GPS-OEM board was embedded, which made the Field Computer have more options on GPS.

The software needed by the computer was programmed. It could meet the field operation demands of precision agriculture. Map Objects 2.0, a kind of

GIS Active X control from ERST, was chosen as the base of the software to aim at the integration of GPS and GIS in agriculture. The software was developed under the Visual C++6.0 with friendly interface and abundant functions. The software could perform the functions such as GPS data receiving and processing, field mapping, grid sampling, feature logging, parallel swathing, and so on.

3. DEVELOPMENT OF THE INTELLIGENT ADAPTER

The adapter based on field computer was made up of an interface of CAN bus network, a CAN receiver connecting with the interface, a CAN controller, a PC/104 bus-slot of the industrial PC/104 motherboard, a high speed opt coupler, a microprocessor, and a parallel interface circuit. Below will introduce the whole design and the working principle of the adapter.

3.1 Hardware of the adapter:

The main function of the adapter was to build a bridge between CAN Bus and PC104 system. Thus the adapter was needed to incept data from CAN and then transfer to PC104 system, and to transfer data from PC104 system to CAN. In order to meet the demand of the real-time control with a very high level of security in farm data collection, the adapter must have high receiving and transmitting data speed. In order to make the data receiving and data transmitting accurate, the hindrance between PC104 and CAN should be avoided. In the hardware development, a microprocessor was used as the control unit of the adapter, which made the adapter intelligent.

Fig.2 shows the operational principle of the intelligent adapter. The adapter included: A CAN bus interface used to connect CAN, a CAN BUS receiver 82C250 used to transmit and receive data from CAN, a CAN controller used to process data and then transmit it to CAN BUS receiver, or to transmit and receive data from CAN BUS receiver, a PC/104 bus-slot used to connect with mainboard, a MCS51 microprocessor (MCU) used to maintain CAN serial, a Parallel interface circuit (8255A) used to transmit data in parallel mode, and a opt coupler used to enhance the anti-jamming of the system.

3.2 Design of the Parallel interface circuit

Since the low speed of the serial communication was not able to match the CAN bus speed reached 1MbPs, the parallel communication mode was

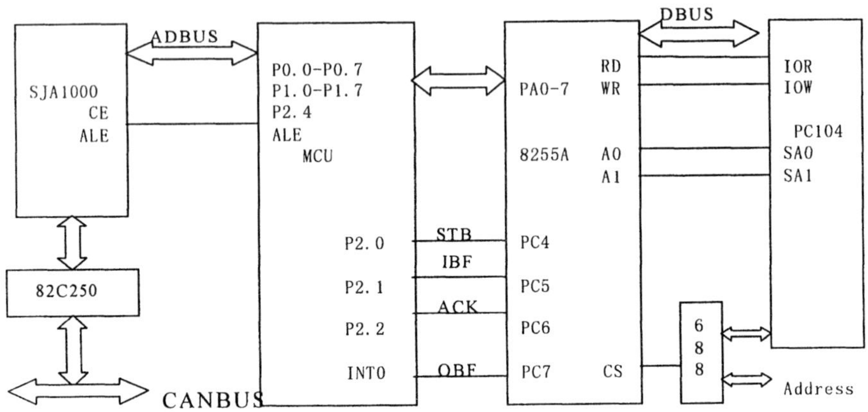

*Figure 2.*The operational principle of the adapter

used by the adapter. And an 8255A was used to directly read and write I/O port under the bus timing of PC104.

8255A has three kinds of working modes. Mode 2 was used in data communication, which was bi-directional communication mode and only fit for the port A. Port A was connected with port P1of the MCU to transmit data between 8255A and MCU. Port C of 8255A provides control signals to port A. The data bus of the 8255A was connected with the data bus of the PC104, so that it could transmit data to PC104 serial, and could also receive data from PC104 serial. On addressing selection, PC104 could provide 64K I/O ports for data communication. We only used four of those to control 8255A, address 280H-283H. When the field computer wanted to transmit data to adapter, PC104 serial port sent address signal 282H firstly, then read port C to judge if IBF bit was in effect, in aims to judge if there were data in buffer. If yes, delaying for a moment and sending 282H again. Otherwise sending addresses signal 280H and then sending data to port A of 8255A. At the same time, 8255A sent OBF signal to INT0 of MCU. When MCU received the signal, it would send ACK signal to 8255A, and 8255A would make output buffer in effect and then send data to the buffer.

When data were transmitted to the field computer, MCU received the data from CAN controller and judged if IBF was in effect. If input buffer was full, sending data to port A of 8255A, and at the same time sending STB signal. The computer queried IBF bit of port C to judge if IBF bit was in effect. If yes it would take the data from input buffer of 8255A.

3.3 Design of CAN controller interface

A CAN controller SJA1000 and a CAN receiver 82C250 were used as the CAN interface of the adapter. In order to enhance the ability of anti-disturbance, the adapter adopted two high-speed opt couplers installed between SJA1000 and 82C250 and a DC/DC power supply for the opt couplers. MCU was the key of the whole adapter since it took charge of the communication between 8255A and CAN controller.

3.4 Software of the adapter

The adapter mainly took charge of data translating between PC104 and CAN node. The designed software included two parts. One was the adapter driver VxD and the initialization of CAN interface. The other was MCU control program.

a) Adapter driver VxD

The driver mainly included interface function to take charge of the communication between the field computer and 8255A. The programming of the driver was based on Visual Basic 6.0. The adapter must compile VxD (virtual device driver) to call the low-level hardware of the computer. We used DLL to encapsulate VxD so that users could use VxD more conveniently. The DLL provided several functions such as port setting, port closing, port writing, and port reading.

b) Initialization of CAN interface and MCU control program

The MCU control program was used to take charge of the communication between 8255A and CAN controller. It was finished by ASM51 assemble language. The main tasks of the software were: translating the commands of the computer to the CAN controller, and then transmitting them to CAN Bus; and transmitting all kinds of state from CAN to 8255A.One of the key points of the software was the initialization of the CAN controller SJA1000.

4. DEBUGGING AND CAPABILITY EVALUATION

Using a base CAN node the adapter was tested for simulation debugging and capability evaluation. Simulation debugging included two procedures: self-transmitting and self-receiving test and node-to-node test.

a) Self-transmitting and self-receiving test

CAN controller SJA1000 has the function of self-transmitting and self-receiving data. When setting the special bit of SJA1000, it would be possible to conduct self-transmitting and self-receiving data test. The CAN part of the adapter followed CAN 2.0B protocol, and could work on PELICAN mode. The result showed that the data in output buffer of SJA1000 was the same as the data in input buffer of SJA1000. It proved that the CAN mode could work up to snuff.

b) Node to node test

Using an independent CAN node to communicate with the adapter, the node-to-node test was executed. Figure 3 shows the interface of the test. 【input port address】 was the CS of 8255A. 【querying state port】 displayed input address of state port. 【output data】 and 【input data】 showed the data received from CAN bus and the data from PC104 system respectively. 【input data show】 and 【output data show】 showed the data has been received or transmitted.

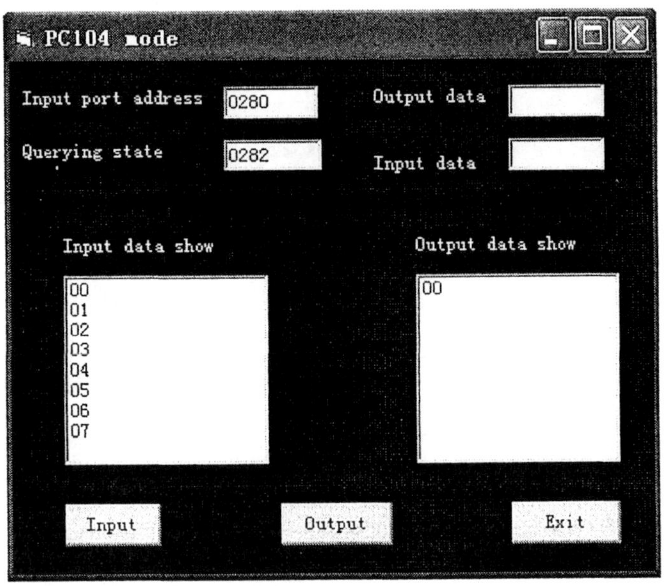

Figure3. Interface of node-to-node test

The test result proved that the adapter could perform the communication between CAN Bus and PC104 system accurately and rapidly. The test result was satisfactory

5. SUMMARY

An intelligent adapter between CAN bus network and PC/104 system was developed. It has following characteristics: (a) The adapter did not impropriate main board MAB. It only needed four free port-settings so that it would not appear the problem of the resource disturbance. (b) Since the adapter used parallel communication mode the data transmission speed was very high. (c) The MCU of the adapter made it intelligent to transmit and receive CAN-data packets. It not only could minimize the adapter's size and power consumption, but also could reduce the tasks of the PC104, which was only needed to take charge of transmitting and receiving CAN-data packet without conducting maintenance works

ACKNOWLEDGEMENTS

This study was supported by National High Technology Research and Development Program of China (863 Program): Research and Demonstration for Digital Agriculture (2003AA209040).

REFERENCES

[1] Wu bin, Yang xueyou, Chang jie. The Research of Auto car-Body Visual Inspection Station Based on CAN. Computer Automated Measurement& Control.1999, 7(3): 16～17

[2] .Scarlet A. Integrated control of agricultural tractors and implements: a review of potential opportunities relating to cultivation and crop establishment machinery. Computers and Electronics in Agriculture, 2001, 30： 167-191

[3] .Hu gungbin, Hu yunan. A Temperatures-Measuring System with Multi-drop Capability Based on CAN. Automation & Instrumentation.1999, 14(5)： 27～29

[4] Yang gongxun, Zhou chunliang, Yang yancong. Design of an Embedded DC Control and Monitoring Device Based on the PC104 Industry Controller. Industry and Mine Automation.2002 (2)： 25～27

[5] .Liuhui. Research and Development on a Field Computer used in Farm Machinery. [Master's thesis]， Beijing： China Agriculture University, 2003

[6] Wu chunxue, Hong kui, Lei Ming. The Vehicular Automatic Van Blender System Based on PC104 Computer. Computer Development & Applications, 2003,16(5)： 21～22

[7] Liu wei. The application of CAN controller SJA1000. Nanjing engineering institute.2002, 2(1): 32～35

[8] .Philips semiconductors SJA1000 stand-along CAN controller. DATA SHEET.1997

DEVELOPMENT OF AN INTELLIGENT YIELD MONITOR FOR GRAIN COMBINE HARVESTER

Minzan Li, Peng Li, Qi Wang, Jianqing Fang, Maohua Wang
Key laboratory of Modern Precision Agriculture System Integration Research, Ministry of Education, China Agriculture University, Beijing 100083, China. limz@cau.edu.cn

Abstract: An intelligent yield monitor for grain combine harvester was developed. The harvested crop was wheat, and the harvesting combine used to equip the monitor was JL1065, a typical machine with 4-meter swath width in northern China. The monitor can collect four analog signals, grain flow, grain moisture content, grain temperature, and header up/down signal, and two digital signals, ground speed and elevator speed. Two digital signals were sensed by Hall effect elements. The monitor can also synchronously receive DGPS signal. A liquid crystal display and a touch screen were integrated as an I/O interface. Field tests showed a linear relationship between actual yield and the output of the yield monitor. The error between measurement and prediction was less than 3%. It is concluded that the developed intelligent yield monitor is practical.

Key words: artificial intelligence, yield monitor, yield mapping, precision agriculture

1. INTRODUCTION

Yield monitor is an important component of precision agriculture [1, 2]. Yield maps provide feedback for determining the effects of management inputs such as fertilizer and lime, seed and pesticides, and cultural practices such as tillage, irrigation and drainage [3, 4]. Some commercial yield monitors are available, such as Greenstar®, Fieldstar®, Ag Leader® and AFS® [5, 6]. However, all these systems were designed for large combine harvester used by American or European farmers. It is difficult to apply this type of monitors to typical small Chinese machine. In addition, their high price is another obstacle for their application in developing countries like China. Thus it is necessary to develop an intelligent yield monitor for grain combine harvester in China [7].

This paper describes a new impact type of grain yield monitor used for small combine harvester with the swath width less than 4 meters, and reports the results of performance test and field test, and finally gives an evaluation of its practicability.

2. DEVELOPMENT

In order to obtain correct grain yield information and yield map, except for grain weight sensor or grain bulk sensor, some other sensors are necessary. Figure 1 shows the yield monitor system developed. It includes six sensors (grain flow sensor, header height sensor, elevator speed sensor, ground speed sensor, grain moisture and temperature sensor) and some other components, such as a GPS receiver, a liquid crystal display (LCD), a touch screen, and an intelligent controller.

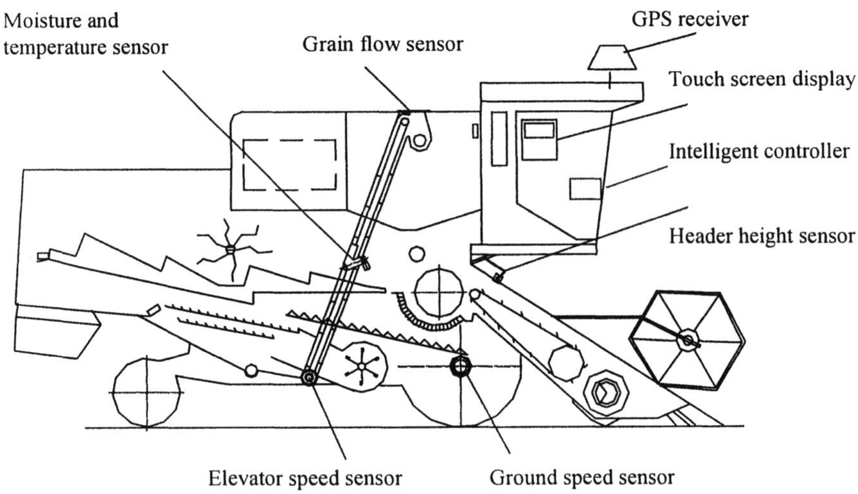

Figure 1. Components of the grain yield monitoring system developed

The yield monitor collected four analog signals (grain flow, header height, grain moisture, and grain temperature), two pulse signals (ground speed and elevator speed), and DGPS data at the same time. After a series of process, the system stored all data on a CompactFlash® (CF) card once per second. The yield monitor also included a liquid crystal display (LCD) and a touch screen as the Man-Machine interface [8].

Figure 2 shows the diagram of the yield monitor developed. It used a P80C592 manufactured by Philips Semiconductors as the microcontroller. It had a 10-bit analog-to-digital converter (ADC) with 8 multiplexed analog inputs and 15 interrupt sources with 2 priority levels [9].

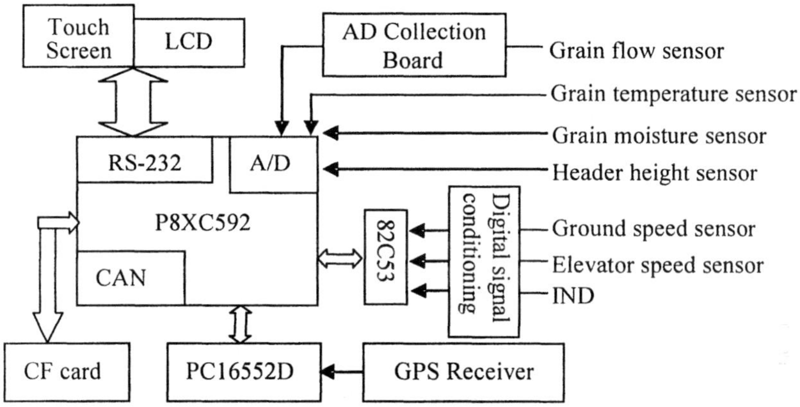

Figure 2. Diagram of the yield monitor system developed

For each analog signal, the microcontroller used an analog channel to collect it. Then these signals were converted into digital. Two Hall effect sensors were individually mounted in the drive shaft of the front wheel and the shaft of elevator to measure ground speed and elevator speed respectively. Each of them was able to generate a square wave with a frequency in direct proportion to the measured speed. Data storage device was a necessary part of the system. Storage media should be large enough and safe enough to save all the data mentioned above once per second for several days or even a whole harvest season. CompactFlash® card was chosen as the storage media. The user interface consisted of a touch screen and a LCD. The touch screen was used to input some parameters and settings for system configuration. The LCD was used to show the data related to yield. Microcontroller operated these two devices through RS-232 serial port.

3. TESTING AND MODELING

3.1 Lab Test and Modeling

Grain flow sensor is the most important part of yield monitor system. It was performance-tested on a special test-bed in laboratory. The test-bed was made by a elevator of combine harvester, a driving motor and a adjustor to change RPM of the motor, a hopper to input grain to the elevator, and a chamber. The grain flow sensor was fixed in the chamber near the outlet of the elevator so that it can monitor the grain flow and then change the grain impact to an electric signal.

Firstly, the sensitivity of the grain flow sensor was tested. Figure 3 shows an example of the test result. It is obvious that when grain was input to the test-bed the output signal of the sensor jumped remarkably and kept stable in high level. A linear estimation model was proposed to transform the output of the flow sensor to grain weigh (wet):

$$W = kU \tag{1}$$

where, U was the output of flow sensor (V); k was a coefficient obtained from sensitivity test (calibration) as shown in Figure 3; W was the grain weight. The frequency of sampling and transforming was 1 Hz, so that W also meant the grain flow. Table 1 shows the test result.

Table 1. Result of repeatability test for grain flow sensor

Number	Estimated Weight (kg)	Scale Weight (kg)	Error
1	277.1	277	0.04%
2	328	324.3	1.14%
3	311	341.1	8.82%
4	309	318.4	2.95%
5	311	315.7	1.49%
Sum	1536.1	1576.5	2.56%

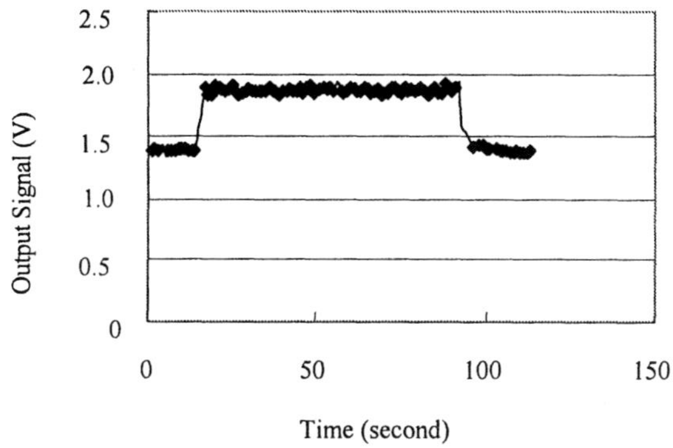

Figure 3. Result of sensitivity test for grain flow sensor

Five tests were executed and the estimation errors were calculated based on equation (2):

Error = (Estimated Weight - Scale Weight) / (Scale Weight) × 100% (2)

Except for test 4, all other errors were smaller than 3%. If calculated the sum of grain weight for all five tests, the relative error between estimated weight and scaled weight was 2.56%. All these showed that the repeatability of the flow sensor was practical.

3.2 Field Test

3.2.1 Calibration method

In field test, the flow sensor was calibrated again to correct the coefficient k obtained from equation (1). The calibration steps were listed below:

(1) Harvesting a piece of field, then calculating the grain weight (wet) with equation (1). The coefficient k was initially set as the system default value (0.9) obtained from lab test.

(2) Measuring the actual weight of the harvested grain (wet).

(3) Inputting the actual weight to the system through touch screen.

(4) System automatically calculated the new k according to equation (3):

$$k = k_1 \times W_1 / W_2 \qquad (3)$$

where W_1 was the actual weight of the harvested grain; W_2 was the weight calculated by system; k_1 was the value of the coefficient k, which was just used in the harvest. The calibration can be repeated several times to improve sensor accuracy.

3.2.2 Calibration in field

First field test with total six loads was performed on June 11, 2004. The data of the six loads are shown in Table 2. Calibrations were conducted in the first three loads, and then validation was executed in the last three loads. System used the default value of k (0.9) for the first calibration. The huge error of 45.55% showed that the default value obtained from the simulation test was not fit for real harvests. Calibration changed the value of k to 0.618, and the errors in the second and third loads were greatly decreased. After the third calibration, the value of k was modified to 0.613; and then it was not changed in last three loads (validation test). The errors of the last three loads were all less than 3%. Therefore, the flow sensor performed well in linearity and stability.

Table 2 Data and result of the field test on June 11, 2004

Load number	Value of k	Actual grain weight (wet) (kg)	Grain weight (wet) measured by system (kg)	Error
1	0.900	366.2	533	45.55%
2	0.618	277.1	277	-0.04%
3	0.618	383.1	380	-0.81%
4	0.613	421.7	426	1.02%
5	0.613	406.6	416	2.31%
6	0.613	375.4	381	1.49%

Second field test was taken on June 13, 2004. The data are shown in Table 3. The k value of 0.613 from the last test was used for calibration in the first load. After the calibration, the errors of the second and third loads decreased significantly. However, the error in the first load of the test was much bigger than the errors in the second and third loads of the previous test. The possible reason was thought to be environmental temperature. The environmental temperature increased greatly between the two days, and the grain moisture decreased greatly. So the ground speed and grain flow would both increase in the second test. The several changed conditions contributed to the increase in error.

The difference between the two tests shows that the system calibration method should be improved, so that the system can work with a high accuracy for a relatively long period of time.

Table 3 Data and result of the field test on June 13, 2004

Load number	Value of *k*	Actual grain weight (wet) (kg)	Grain weight (wet) measured by developed system (kg)	Error
1	0.613	418.4	367	-12.28%
2	0.705	324.3	328	1.14%
3	0.705	362.5	367	1.24%

4. SUMMARY

An intelligent yield monitor for grain harvester based on an 8-bit microcontroller was developed. A long time of laboratory and field tests showed that the monitor was in high accuracy and practicability.

Modeling of the grain flow sensor in both laboratory and field tests showed that the sensor had a high linearity and worked steadily. Field test showed that the system had the capability to predict accumulated grain mass with an error less than 3% under the given harvest conditions. More filed tests are needed to improve the calibration method and to reduce the effect of the harvest conditions on measurement accuracy of the monitor system.

ACKNOWLEDGEMENTS

This study was supported by National High Technology Research and Development Program of China (863 Program): Research and Demonstration for Digital Agriculture (2003AA209040).

REFERENCES

[1] Blackmore, S, Moore, M, 1999. Remedial correction of yield map data, Precision Agriculture, 1, 53-66.

[2] Blackmore, S, 2000. The interpretation of trends from multiple yield maps. Computers and Electronics in Agriculture, 26, 37-51.

[3] Dobermann, A, et al, 2003. Processing of yield map data for delineating yield zones, Precision Agriculture, Wageningen Academic Publishers, Wageningen, 177-185

[4] MU Extension. 1998. Precision Agriculture: Yield Monitors: University of Missouri Extension. Available at: http://muextension.missouri.edu/. Accessed 29 July 2004.

[5] GreenStar, 1997. Combine yield mapping system, Operator's Manual, Deere and Company, Moline, Illinois.

[6] Shearer, S, 1999. Elements of precision agriculture: basics of yield monitor installation and operation, Cooperative Extension Service, University of Kentucky, Lexington.

[7] Wang M, 2003. Practical practise of precision agriculture and priorities to promote technological innovation in P. R. China, Precision Agriculture, Wageningen Academic Publishers, Wageningen, 705-709.

[8] Zhang, W. G., P. Li, and Q. Wang. 2003. Design and Development of yield monitor. Progress of Information Technology in Agriculture, China Agriculture Press, Beijing, 332-334.

[9] Philips Semiconductors. 1996. Product specification: P8xC592 8-bit microcontroller with on-chip CAN.

FEATURE FUSION WITH NEIGHBORHOOD-OSCILLATING TABU SEARCH FOR ORIENTED TEXTURE CLASSIFICATION

Yindi Zhao, Liangpei Zhang, and Pingxiang Li
LIESMARS, Wuhan Univiersity, Wuhan 430079, China

Abstract: This paper develops two techniques of oriented texture analysis: the modified Gabor filters (MGF) and the Gaussian Markov random field model with circular neighborhoods (CGMRF). The neighborhood-oscillating tabu search algorithm (NOTS) is proposed to solve the MGF/CGMRF feature fusion problem, and compared with classical algorithms, such as sequential forward selection and sequential forward floating selection methods. Based on the experimental results, NOTS is shown to be a promising tool for feature fusion, and the MGF/CGMRF fused features achieved by NOTS perform better than either MGF or CGMRF alone according to the Fisher criterion and classification accuracy.

Key words: Gabor filters, Gaussian Markov random field, tabu search, feature fusion

1. INTRODUCTION

With the increased demand for automatic inspection of industrial application, oriented texture analysis has received great attention in machine vision. Oriented textures are characterized by a dominant orientation at each point of the texture, and can be summarized by images encoding these dominant orientations. Many approaches of extracting texture features have been proposed over recent years, including spatial frequency based techniques such as multi-channel Gabor filters [1], stochastic models such as Markov random fields (MRF) [2] , and statistical analysis methods. Gabor filters can obtain multi-scale texture information corresponding to different scales and orientations. And MRF can capture the local spatial texture information assuming that the intensity in an image depends on the intensities of only the neighboring pixels. Based on traditional techniques, this paper develops two schemes of oriented texture analysis: the modified Gabor filters (MGF) and the Gaussian Markov random field model with circular neighborhoods (CGMRF).

MGF and CGMRF features extracted from an input oriented texture image are quite different in nature and have low inter-feature correlations [3]. The combined MGF and CGMRF features are expected to provide richer texture information than either MGF or CGMRF features alone. However, the combined features without selection give more dimensions, which may affect the performance of designed classifiers and result in even worse classification accuracy than the pure features. In order to reduce data quantity and improve data quality, the combination of different features should be processed by feature selection. In this paper, the neighborhood-oscillating tabu search algorithm (NOTS) is proposed to select an optimal feature subset from the pooled set of MGF and CGMRF features. The performance of NOTS is compared with some classical algorithms, such as sequential forward selection and sequential forward floating selection methods.

The rest of this paper is organized as follows. In the following section, MGF and CGMRF texture features are presented. In Section 3, NOTS is proposed to solve the MGF/CGMRF feature fusion problem. Experimental results are given in Section 4 and conclusions drawn in Section 5.

2. ORIENTED TEXTURE FEATURE EXTRACTION

2.1 Multi-Channel Gabor Filters

Each texture can be thought of as containing a narrow range of frequency and orientation components. By filtering an input texture image with multiple band-pass filters tuned to the dominant frequency and orientation component of the textures, it is possible to locate each texture. Due to its appealing simplicity and optimum joint spatial/spatial-frequency localization, the Gabor filter is attractive for texture analysis. The Gabor function takes the form of a 2-D Gaussian modulated complex sinusoidal grating in the spatial domain [1]:

$$h(x,y) = \frac{1}{2\pi\sigma_1\sigma_2} \cdot \exp\left\{-\frac{1}{2}\left[\left(\frac{x'}{\sigma_1}\right)^2 + \left(\frac{y'}{\sigma_2}\right)^2\right]\right\} \cdot \exp[2\pi j(Ux + Vy)] \quad (1)$$

where σ_1 and σ_2 characterize the spread in the x and y directions, $(x',y') = (x\cos\theta + y\sin\theta, -x\sin\theta + y\cos\theta)$ represents rotated spatial-domain rectilinear coordinates, (U,V) defines the position of the filter in the frequency domain with a center frequency of $F = \sqrt{U \times U + V \times V}$ and an orientation of $\phi = \arctan(V/U)$.

In order to maximize the coverage of the frequency domain while minimizing the overlap between filters, there are another two important aspects, namely the frequency bandwidth B_F (measured in octave) and the angular bandwidth B_θ (measured in radian). For more details on the frequency and angular bandwidth, the reader is encouraged to refer to [1, 4]. The frequency and angular bandwidth can be set to constant values that match psychovisual data. Jain and Farrokhnia [1] implemented Gabor filters for texture segmentation using frequency bandwidth (B_F) of one octave, center frequency spacing (S_F) of one octave, angular bandwidth (B_θ) of $45°$ and angular spacing (S_θ) of $45°$. For a $N \times N$ texture image, the center frequencies F (normalized by N) are selected as follows:

$$F = \sqrt{2}\{1,\ 2,\ 4,\ 8,\ \cdots,\ N/4\}/N \text{ cycles per pixel (cpp)} \quad (2)$$

When the image width and height are not equal, in order to guarantee that the passband of the filter with the highest center frequency falls inside the image, the values of F should be set based on the smaller side. On the other hand, due to the symmetry of Fourier spectrum, only half part $[0°, 180°]$ is considered. Thus 4 equally spaced orientations are used: $0°$, $45°$, $90°$, and $135°$. For the sake of simplicity, we call the above designed Gabor filters as traditional Gabor filters (TGF).

Unit octave spacing matches the experimentally determined human visual system ability; however, the $45°$ angular bandwidth is not in agreement, and the $30°$ angular bandwidth is argued to have stronger capability of capturing texture features [4]. In this paper, a smaller bandwidth of 22.5° is used in order to detect oriented textures effectively. Finer quantization of orientation may be needed in general. And a bigger one will bring about negative impacts on the discrimination performance for oriented textures when there are texture orientations to which none of the channels of the filter bank will respond sufficiently. Furthermore, for an input oriented texture image of size

$M \times N(M \neq N)$, the center frequencies determined by Equation 2 cannot cover the entire frequency domain because of frequency leakage. From this point we propose a new frequency selection scheme. First radial directions are defined corresponding to the angular bandwidth and angular spacing. Then draw a radial line from the image center along each radial direction, and compute the distance (L) between the image center and the point of intersection of the radial line with the image side. For each direction, the center frequencies F are set by the similar way of Equation 2:

$$F = \sqrt{2}\{1, \quad 2, \quad 4, \quad 8, \quad \cdots, \quad L/2\}/L \text{ cpp} \tag{3}$$

We denote the Gabor filters with 8 equidistant preferred orientations ($0°$, $22.5°$, $45°$, $67.5°$, $90°$, $112.5°$, $135°$, and $157.5°$) and center frequencies selected using the proposed new scheme as modified Gabor filters (MGF). However, Filter outputs by default are not appropriate for identifying key texture features. Each filtered image is subjected to a sigmoidal non linear transformation that is interpreted as a blob detector [1].

2.2 MRF Model

MRF can specify the local dependence of image regions by defining a neighborhood system on the pixels of an image and a probability density function on the spectrum distribution of the pixels. A typical MRF model is the Gaussian MRF (GMRF) model, which is widely used for modeling image textures. Let $i(s)$ represent the gray level intensity of a pixel s, the GMRF model is defined by the following equation:

$$i(s) - u = \sum_{r \in \eta} \theta(r) \times \left(i(s+r) - u\right) + e(s) \tag{4}$$

where u is the mean of variable $i(s)$, $\theta(r)$ s are the model parameters and η is a neighbor set, and $e(s)$ is a zero-mean Gaussian noise sequence with the variance of v .Since GMRF models are defined only for symmetric neighborhood sites, often η is equivalently characterized using an asymmetrical neighbor set $\overline{\eta}$, i.e. if $r \in \overline{\eta}$ then $-r \notin \overline{\eta}$ and $\eta = \{r : r \in \overline{\eta}\} \cup \{-r : r \in \overline{\eta}\}$. Therefore, Equation 4 can be rewritten by

$$i(s) - u = \sum_{r \in \overline{\eta}} \theta(r)\left((i(s+r) - u) + (i(s-r) - u)\right) + e(s) \tag{5}$$

There are many existing methods for estimating the GMRF model parameters. The choice of the least squares method [5] is motivated by this simplicity-stability tradeoff. Then the least square estimates of the parameters are:

$$\hat{\boldsymbol{\theta}} = \left[\sum_{s \in R} \mathbf{q}(s) \mathbf{q}^{\mathrm{T}}(s) \right]^{-1} \left[\sum_{s \in R} \mathbf{q}(s) (i(s) - u) \right] \tag{6}$$

where $\mathbf{q}(s) = col[(i(s+r) - u) + (i(s-r) - u) \mid r \in \overline{\eta}]$, R is an interior of the image, $\hat{\boldsymbol{\theta}} = col[\hat{\theta}(r) \mid r \in \overline{\eta}]$, and the hat $\wedge$ over a quantity indicates an estimate of that quantity. The estimate $\hat{\nu}$ of the noise variance is

$$\hat{\nu} = \frac{1}{M} \sum_{s \in R} \left[(i(s) - u) - \hat{\boldsymbol{\theta}}^{\mathrm{T}} \mathbf{q}(s) \right]^2 \tag{7}$$

where M demotes the number of elements in R. According to the GMRF model parameters $\hat{\theta}(r)$ s, a new different set of texture features, $f(r)$ s are derived by [2]

$$f(r) = \frac{1}{M} \sum_{s \in R} \left[(i(s) - u) - \hat{\theta}(r) \big((i(s+r) - u) + (i(s-r) - u) \big) \right] \tag{8}$$

Due to the similarity between Equation 7 and 8, $f(r)$ s behave like variances in different directions defined by r. Because of directionality, $f(r)$ s can strengthen the orientation selectivity in texture feature detection, and have been proved to be more discriminatory than $\hat{\theta}(r)$ s [2]. Hereby $f(r)$ s and the variance $\hat{\nu}$ are employed as MRF features.

The performance of the GMRF approach depends very much on the neighbor set used. In Figure 1(a), up to 6th order traditional neighbors are depicted. For example, a 2nd order GMRF model centered on image cell S would include those cells marked 1.x and 2.x. Traditional GMRF features are not effective for oriented texture classification, since there are limited directions defined. In order to obtain more orientation information of textures for any order model, we use a new neighbor set via the circular neighborhood system, which has been used by Kashyap and Khotanzad to achieve rotation-invariant features [6]. The circular neighbor sets for a 1st, 2nd, and 3rd GMRF model with 16 orientations are shown in Figure 1(b). An angular interval between two nearest neighbors in the same concentric circle is defined as $\theta = 2\pi/\tau$, where τ is the number of neighbors in one concentric circle. Note that the angular spacing of different concentric circle need not be the same, and the angular spacing of outer concentric circles can be smaller than that of inner circles. In this paper, we use the same angular spacing 22.5° for all concentric circles. Finer quantization of orientation may be needed in some cases.

For simplicity, this paper refers to the GMRF model defined with traditional neighbors as a traditional GMRF (TGMRF) model while the GMRF model with circular neighbors as a circular GMRF (CGMRF) model. The CGMRF features can be computed using Equation 6-8, which is exactly the same as that of TGMRF features. The values of the neighbors that are not located on the image grid can be calculated by interpolation.

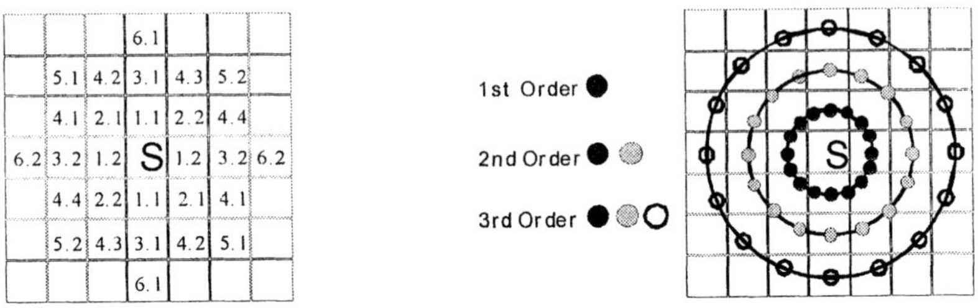

(a) traditional neighbor set (b) circular neighbor set

Figure 1. Neighbor sets of GMRF models

3. FEATURE FUSION WITH NEIGHBORHOOD-OSCILLATING TABU SEARCH (NOTS)

The correlation relationship between MGF and CGMRF features is investigated. A low correlation coefficient (e.g., closer to zero), which suggests that the relationship between MGF and CGMRF features is weak or non-exist, shows the potential to produce an improved classification result by MGF/CGMRF feature fusion. In this section, the neighborhood-oscillating tabu search algorithm (NOTS) is proposed to solve the MGF/CGMRF feature fusion problem.

The strategy of feature fusion is first to combine various features and then perform feature selection to choose an optimal feature subset. A number of feature selection methods have been developed [7]. Tabu search has been proved to be a promising tool for feature selection in respect to the quality of obtained feature subset and computation efficiency, compared with classical algorithms, such as sequential forward selection (SFS) and sequential forward floating selection (SFFS) methods. The SFFS method yields better results than SFS, but it is still likely to trap into a local optimal solution.

Tabu search differs from classical techniques, in that it allows the search to move away from the local minima in order to search more extensively in the feasible domain. There are some parameters which should be selected carefully, such as neighborhood size, tabu list's length and initial solution. An adaptive tabu tenure strategy has been proposed [8], and here we emphasize on the problem of the search neighborhood size. The classification process is based on the widely used multivariate Gaussian Bayes classifier and the Kappa coefficient (κ) is used as the criterion of feature selection.

Traditional neighborhoods have constant sizes, for example, a 2-neighborhood is generated by reversing one or two features' states [7]. When the neighborhood size is smaller, the computational efficiency is raised while the access to the neighborhood is limited. Alternatively, when the neighborhood size is bigger, the high-ration access to the neighborhood is maintained while computational cost is increased tremendously. Thus, we propose an oscillating neighborhood scheme by introducing the idea of the oscillating search algorithm [9]. The oscillating search is based on repeated of the current subset, which is achieved by alternating the down- and up-swings. And the neighborhood size during tabu search is determined by the oscillation cycle depth. We call the tabu search method with the oscillating neighborhood scheme as neighborhood-oscillating tabu search (NOTS). Let G denote the global best solution so far, C the current best solution , TL the tabu list, o the oscillation cycle depth, Δ the used-specified limit of oscillation cycle depth, t the number of none improvement at the current move and T the maximum of consecutive rejections. Below is a detailed description of the NOTS algorithm.

Step 1. Initialization: generate the initial set X of d features by means of the SFS method. Let $G = X$, $C = X$, and $t = 0$.

Step 2. Tabu moves: pick the best non-tabu neighbor in the dynamic neighborhoods using the oscillating search method. In the oscillating search, if the current feature set is better than C but belongs to TL, we consider that the present search does not bring any improvement. The oscillating search algorithm stops if C is better than G or the value of o exceeds Δ.

Step 3. Output: If C is better than G, let $G = C$ and $t = 0$; or else let $t = t + 1$. If $t \geq T$, the termination condition is satisfied, stop and output the global best solution G. Otherwise, let $TL = TL \cup C$ then go back to Step 2.

4. EXPERIMENTAL RESULTS

The experiment is set up on the following issues. First, we use NOTS to solve the MGF/CGMRF feature fusion problem, and compare the performance of NOTS with that of SFS and SFFS algorithms. Second, we test and compare the developing approaches with the traditional ones, namely TGF vs. MGF, and TGMRF vs. CGMRF, in a quantitative manner. It is expected that MGF and CGMRF features would respectively outperform TGF and TGMRF features. For both TGF and MGF, the filters with the two lowest frequencies are left out as they capture spatial variations that are too large to be considered texture. Third, the fused MGF/CGMF features achieved by NOTS are expected to achieve higher classification accuracy than either MGF or CGMRF features alone. All the extracted texture features should be normalized so that each measurement has zero-mean and unit standard deviation before performance comparison.

(a) (b) (c) (d)

Figure 2. A comparison of classification results using SFS, SFFS, and NOTS methods to solve the MGF/CMGF feature fusion problem: (a) input image, (b) classification results using SFS, (c) classification results using SFFS, (d) classification results using NOTS.

Brodatz texture D49 (straw screening) is selected as the original texture. Figure 2(a) with size 128×256 is composed of 8 samples by rotating the texture with 8 angles ($0°$, $22.5°$, $45°$, $67.5°$, $90°$, $112.5°$, $135°$, $157.5°$) in the counterclockwise direction. First, Texture features are extracted from Figure 2(a) using MGF and the 2nd order CGMRF model. For the 128×256 image, the MGF bank comprises 19 channels, resulting in a 19-dimensional MGF feature vector for each image pixel. And the 2nd order CGMRF model corresponds to a 17-dimensional CGMRF feature vector for each point of the input image. Then SFS, SFFS, and NOTS methods are implemented to solve the MGF/CGMRF feature fusion problem, respectively. Figure 2 shows the graphical results for the three above algorithms while Table 1 lists the corresponding tabular results. The first column of Table 1 gives the dimensions of selected features (SD). The following columns give the Kappa coefficient (k) and overall accuracy (OA) using that selected features. From Table 1, we can see that the NOTS method outperforms SFS and SFFS by yielding the Kappa coefficient of 0.9533.

Table 1. Results using three feature selection algorithms for MGF/CGMRF feature fusion. SD- dimension of selected features, k - Kappa coefficient, and OA – overall accuracy.

Feature Selection	SD	k	OA
SFS	16	0.9389	94.64%
SFFS	10	0.9348	94.29%
NOTS	11	0.9533	95.92%

Table 2. Performance evaluation of different features. D - dimension of features without selection, SD - dimension of selected features using NOTS, k - Kappa coefficient, OA – overall accuracy, Max. J and Min. J - maximum and minimum Fisher criterion.

Feature type	D	SD	k	OA	Max. J	Min. J
TGF features	12	6	0.8838	89.83%	54167.24	744.58
MGF features	19	10	0.9040	91.60%	200481.95	710.80
TGMRF features	5	3	0.7845	81.15%	297.17	0.15
CGMRF features	17	8	0.9398	94.73%	6919.36	379.77
MGF & CGMRF features	36	11	0.9533	95.92%	161218.65	1251.29

For the sake of comparison, we also use TGF which comprises 12 channels and the 2nd order TGMRF model, yielding a 12-dimensional TGF feature vector and a 5-dimensional TGMRF feature vector for each image pixel, respectively. Performance is assessed by the criterion of classification accuracy with the multivariate Gaussian Bayes classifier and NOTS. And the minimum and maximum Fisher criterions, which can express the separation ability between classes in the selected feature space, are recorded simultaneously. Table 2 shows that, as expected, the Kappa coefficient by MGF features is improved from 0.8838 to 0.9040 with respect to that by TGF features, and the Kappa coefficient by CGMRF features is increased from 0.7845 to 0.9398 with respect to that by TGMRF features.

Furthermore, the correlation relationship between the MGF and CGMRF features is investigated. The correlation coefficient between the two different types of features extracted from Figure 2(a) is 0.0473. The low correlation coefficient indicates that CGMRF features are not well correlated with MGF features, and the combined features are expected to offer more texture information than the pure features. From Table 2, we can clearly see that the fused MGF/CGMRF features achieved by NOTS perform better than either MGF or CGMRF features alone.

5. CONCLUSIONS

Based on traditional methods, this paper develops MGF and CGMRF techniques for oriented texture analysis. NOTS is proposed to solve the MGF/CGMRF feature fusion, and compared with SFS and SFFS methods. There are three important remarks made. First MGF and CGMRF features for oriented texture classification respectively outperform TGF and TGMRF features. Second NOTS, which would not trap into a local optimal solution, can find an optimal feature subset effectively, and its performance is better than that of SFS and SFFS methods. Finally according to classification accuracy, the MGF/CGMRF fused features achieved by NOTS perform better than either MGF or CGMRF features alone. The experimental results indicate that the proposed algorithm of MGF/CGMRF feature fusion with NOTS for oriented texture classification is stable and reliable and efficient to improve classification results.

ACKNOWLEDGEMENTS

This work was supported by the 973 Project of the People's Republic of China (Project Number 2003CB415205), and the National Natural Science Foundation of China (Project Number 40471088).

REFERENCES

[1] Jain A.K, et al. Unsupervised texture segmentation using Gabor filters. Pattern Recognition, 1991, 24(12): 1167~1186

[2] Cesmeli E, et al. Texture segmentation using Gaussian-Markov random fields and neural oscillator networks. IEEE Transactions on Neural Network, 2001, 12(2): 394~404

[3] Clausi D.A. Comparison and fusion of co-occurrence, Gabor, and MRF texture features for classification of SAR sea ice imagery. Atmosphere & Oceans, 2001, 39(4): 183~194

[4] Clausi D.A, et al. Designing Gabor filters for optimal texture separability. Pattern Recognition, 2000, 33(11): 1835~1849

[5] Chellappa R, et al. Classification of textures using Gaussian Markov random fields. IEEE Transaction on Acoustics, Speech, and Signal Processing, 1985, 33(4): 959-963

[6] Kashyap R.L, et al. A model-based method for rotation invariant texture classification. IEEE Transactions on Pattern Analysis and Machine Intelligence, 1986, 8(4): 472~481

[7] Zhang H, et al. Feature selection using tabu search method. Pattern Recognition, 2002, 35(3): 701~711

[8] Korycinski D, et al. Adaptive feature selection for hyperspectral data analysis. SPIE - The International Society for Optical Engineering, 2004, 5238: 213~225

[9] Somol P, et al. Oscillating search algorithms for feature selection. ICPR 2000: 406~2409

FUZZY RELATIONSHIP MAPPING INVERSION AND AUTOMATIC REASONING OF CRIME DETECTIVE

Ping He
Liaoning Police Academy Dalian 116033

Abstract: In the paper, fuzzy relationship mapping inversion principle (FRMI) application in the criminal investigate inference. To put forward fuzzy fixing structure of automatic inversion and the fuzzy theory is combined with a FRMI to found a learn system of fuzzy inversion mapping. By means of the FRMI principle, the paper describes the processes which criminal investigate inference and the fuzzy system structure of information's in criminal investigate inference.

Key words: FRMI, Fuzzy Fixing, Investigate automatic inference heading

1. INTRODUCTION

To image human's intelligence is one of the manual intelligence study aims. Though the study of manual intelligence has been progressing rapidly for more than a decade, there still be considerable difference than our wish. The basic cause lies that we pay too much attention to the detailed and calculating studies, so as to we are far lagged off. The practice of scientific studies shows that mathematical deduction and proving play a vital role in scientific studies. But, we must admit that the conceptualizing and digital featuring of practical problems are the requirements of the math & computer use and development. What is the genuine attribute of human's intelligence? Could it be depicted with mathematical method? Frankly, the models of man' thinking, imagining, and memorizing by the researcher of manual intelligence are founded under certain conditions. While, after you have studied the policy making process by the computer, you'll find that the suppositions are not really in existence. Nevertheless, people are stepping forward on the way in order to find better solutions.

Formerly, in detective practice, the job revolves around reasoning. Under the circumstance that the case has been known, with theory and experience, we judge the fact, phenomenon upon the incident, and find new judgment based on the known fact and affirmed judgment. Thus we can disclose the deep aspects regarding the case. Founding the reasoning system in the detective could not go beyond the detecting practice. That is to say, with sufficient use of current manual intelligence and professional system, and uncertainty reasoning method helps to found effective reasoning regulations. This is the cooperation regulation. It means the combination of intuition, knowledge and experience. First, we start with the analysis of detection reasoning. Formerly, the inspectors and judges themselves gain the direct experience with limitation. Sometimes we judge by our personal experience about which is essential to the detective. Or, there are all kinds of symptoms in a certain detective, these are not only imagination, they are the combination of knowledge and experience, and the comprehension of intuition. On more occasions, mostly for the judge, he or she must reason based scientific theory and knowledge. We call the former experimental intuition reasoning and the latter knowledge-based reasoning. Currently, more often we use the knowledge-based one. However, knowledge has its limitation in certain field, if we emphasize this reasoning model too much, we'll encounter considerate frustration in solving practical cases.

The article poses the FRMI principle upon the detective reasoning practice, and founds fuzzy cooperation automatic reasoning method.

2. FUZZY RELATIONSHIP MAPPING INVERSION PRINCIPLE

Fuzzy relationship mapping inversion principle refers to a general method or criterion in problem solving. It belongs to a working principle of general methodologies.

In founding the professional detective system, the focus is finding the proper methodology in realizing the detective aims. Then it may embody the intellectual aspect in the professional detective system. By analysis, we find that FRMI is a useful tool in constructing this intellectual behavior. Here firstly we give a supposition. In detective practice, by analyzing the attribute of the case, the detector can construct a crime model. Thus, we may found a similar image model of the initial case. Normally, the detector could not see the crime procedure on spot. After crime happened, people will never experience the scene again. Consequently, only by mocking and recognizing could people realize and grasp its changing regular patterns. The happening of a case composes a specific commitment shaping in a certain space. It is determined by the initial crime construction. Here, we call the suspect relationship former image, the case shaping from the spot reflecting relationship. Supposedly, by this kind of relationship, we can confirm the specific shaping. So we get the specific initial image. Encouragingly, this initial image is to be the suspect. This running principle is being called detective relationship mapping inversion principle.

However, in reality, there are fuzzy relations. Thereafter, to found the fuzzy relationship mapping inversion has practical significance. Simply to say, we shorten this into FRMI. Firstly, here's the description of this principle:

Say R represents the fuzzy relationship construction, which include certain problems (the initial image) x, say M represents a kind of mapping. By this function suppose the fuzzy relationship of the initial image R be inversed into the fuzzy relationship of shaping R^*. In the latter relationship there is unknown problem (the initial image) x which lead to shaping x^*. We firstly find x^*, then with the inversion i.e. function we find x. This is called FRMI principle.

In study practice, general meaning may be vested to mapping inversion. For instance, the brain forms fuzzy concepts as one in face of fuzzy things. It is the representation of fuzzy feature or fuzzy relationship. Just take the process of fuzzy concept forming as the mapping of the brain's action. So, the fuzzy concept is the fuzzy thing's shaping of its initial image. Using thinking of fuzzy concept helps to conclude and to resolve problems on the basis of the former models. This procedure could be called inversing process. See table 1, at the beginning, we talk about the realistic problem reflect by initial image system S and shaping system S^*. Suppose in a certain problem x there is the fuzzy relationship R which could be got. But, we can hardly find x with R. On the other hand, if S^* and R* are known to us, or we can find S^* and R^* with S, then we can solve problems with the help of FRMI principle.

Suppose S_m the social crime system, between this, there are all kinds of crime relationships,

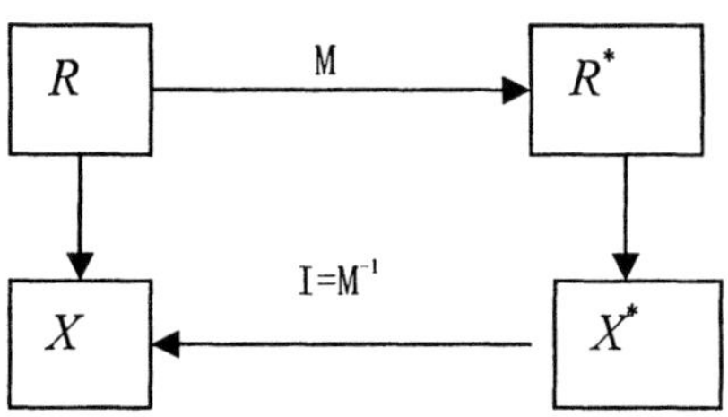

Fig 1 Fuzzy relationship mapping inversion

These relationships are posed by varies commitments. That is to say, different people commit on different scales. It could be gained by the analysis of probability. The sorting of the former statistics of cases composes the crime model space, which may be input the computer as the initial image system for recognizing suspects.

We all know, each case is mutation-characterized, and unrepeatable, they are not mutual constructive but mutual stated. Consequently, through the crime model space of the initial image system we can forward all kinds of crime models. These models were gained by fuzzy relationship analysis so inevitably subjective. In addition, when a specific case occurs, it shows a relationship R*m in the social crime system. By the information of the spot and other surroundings, we can confirm the shaping of this case. Further, as the relative information is fuzzy, R*m is too. In fact, R, which determines the fuzzy construction of crime model, is not a static relationship construction, but a never-ending changeable and new-sense creative fuzzy one. More over, only if the specific information is input to the initial image can the suspect be made sure. Thereafter, R_m may be thought as the primary-state fuzzy relationship construction, R^*_{m}, the shaping of this construction. Notwithstanding, for the uncertainty of the social crime actions, the mapping provided by the initial image relationship i.e. crime model could no longer reflect the attribute of each case. That's to say, R*m is insufficient to confirm the shaping of the suspects. Only by adding the specific information C^*_m to the certain cases based on R^*_m ,this information should be input the initial fuzzy relationship system thus R_m is learned . we gain new shaping relationship. By this means, we can confirm the shaping of the suspect and the suspect respectively. See fig 2:

Here we depict FRMI mathematically: suppose φ is a mapping, it maps the element from the fuzzy set $S=\{a\}$ into another one $S^*=\{a^*\}$. In this, a* represents the shaping of a, a is called the initial image. Thus,

$$\varphi: \ S \rightarrow S^*, \ \varphi\{a\} = a^*.$$

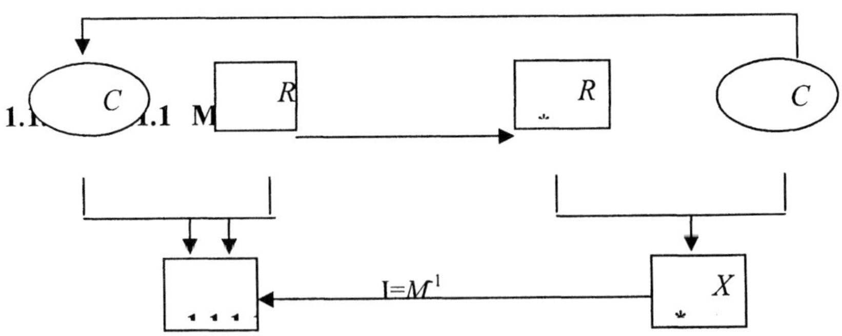

Fig 2 The inversion construction of mapping

If S is a fuzzy relationship construction, with , S may get a full mapping of S^*, then take $S^* = \varphi(s)$, and call S^* the shaping fuzzy relationship construction. Especially, if *S* includes an unknown x in the fuzzy relationship construction and *x* is to be certified, then we call *x* the objective initial image. With the function of $x^* = \varphi(x)$ objective shaping.

If the objective shaping could be gained from the shaping fuzzy relationship construction *S** with automatic reasoning method, we can say φ is fuzzy confirmative mapping. To conclude, we depict the FRMI principle this way:

For a given fuzzy relationship construction *S* which including an objective initial image *x*, if a confirmative mapping φ *S* to *S** could be found, then we can confirm the objective shaping with a certain reasoning method, so as to make sure *x* with the tool of inversion.

3. THE AUTOMATIC REASONING IN FIXED MAPPING CONJUNCTION

The main construction within system of crime relation lies in case cracking: the clues and suspect-to-make-sure, and can think from clues to the suspect type is the constancy of the two mappings the initial shaping and shape mapping. Firstly, the main mapping to suspect-to-make-sure. Secondly, the auxiliary clues to suspects. The auxiliary clue means the conjunction of the spot information and the similar case information. Thus, the automatic reasoning system could be founded. Primarily, the following two mappings are to be founded.

$$F_{\text{I}}:\ S \to D, F_{\text{II}}:\ A \to K$$

Notes: $S = \{s_1, s_2, \cdots, s_m\}$ is the total collect of the main clues, $s_m (m = 1,2,\cdots, g)$ is the total collect of the specific clues, D={ $d_1, d_2, \cdots, d_n$} d_j {j=1,2,⋯,n} is the specific suspect-to-make-sure, C $=\{c_1, c_2, \cdots, c_u\}$ is the total collect of the auxiliary clues, c_u {u=1,2,⋯,r}are the specific auxiliary clues, $K = \{k_1, k_2, \cdots, k_v\}$ } is the total collect of the suspects, k_v {v=1,2,⋯,l} are the specific suspects.

If we represent the total collect with $W = \{S, A\} = \{W_1, W_2, \cdots, W_{g+r}\}$, when we input a series of clues $W_i \subseteq W$ we accordingly get the output of the function of the two mappings: suspect-to-make-sure $d_j \in D$ 与 and suspect-to-make-sure $k_j \in K$.

3.1 The departure of the clue groups

Before making sure the two mappings' characteristics, we should divide the statistical clue groups into main clue groups and auxiliary groups. The principle depends on the amount of the information for identifying the suspect-to-make-sure. Let

$$P(d_j \mid w_i) = \frac{N_{d_j}}{N_{w_j}}$$

to be the probability of the suspect-to-make-sure d_j were the suspect , note: N_{w_i} is the number of the clue w_i occurs, N_{d_j} is the number of the suspect-to-be-sure d_j were the suspect w_i. In addition,

$$P(w_i) = \{P(w_1), P(w_2), \cdots, P(w_{m+r})\}$$

is the probability distribution of the clue w_i, i.e.

$$P(w_i) = \frac{N_{w_i}}{N_w}$$

N_w is the number of the general clues occur, N_{w_i} is the number of a certain clue i occur. The mentioned N_{d_j}, N_{w_i}, N_w could be gained from statistical material. Thus, the according function of the crime entropy is $P(Dw_i)$ and the according average entropy is

$$H(D| \; w_i) = -\sum_{j=1}^{n} P(d_j|w_i) \log 2 \, P(d_j|w_i)$$

$$H(D| \; W) = \sum_{i=1}^{m+r} P(w_i) H(D|w_i)$$

Choose a reliable level β, in order to make

$$\frac{H(D|w_i)}{H(D|W)} \le \beta \, ,$$

the required main clues, i.e. the multi-information for judging the suspect-to-make-sure d_j , the less-information clues the auxiliary ones. For the corresponding clues w_i, w_g,

$$H(D|w_i) = H(D|w_g)(i \ne g) \, ,$$

w_i, w_g unite to be auxiliary clues.

From the detected case database, we can get the relative collect of the clues and number them. For instance, regarding economical crimes, let the main clues be membership, then we can go on reasoning following a certain regulations.

3.2 Making sure of the first type mapping characteristics

Choose a group of typical cases from the material, depict each case with a "fuzzy" if sentence. For example, the changing of living habits, sudden incomes, and economical crimes. The main clue is: the changing of living habits, sudden incomes. The auxiliary clue is: economical crimes. Thus,

IF S_1 S_2 THEN d_1

and the according series of if-sentences are

IF C_1 C_2 THEN k_1

IF $\{S_1\ S_2\} \cup \{C_1\ C_2\}$ THEN $d_1 \cap k_1$

IF $S^j_{m_i} \subseteq S$ THEN $d_j (j = 1,2,3,4)$

IF $C^v_u \subseteq S$ THEN $k_v (1,2,\cdots,l)$

here, j in d_j is the corresponding sets of clues, i means the I if-sentence, m is its series number.

For the consideration that for a certain clue, the judging effect for the suspect-to-make-sure is unequal, i.e. the unequal of S_m and d_j membership degree Its membership function is

$$\mu^j_m = \mu_{m_j},\ (s_m = s^j_{m_i,}), \mu^j_m = 0$$

Apparently, the much the clue $s_m \in S$, contributes to the suspect-to-make-sure, the bigger its relative membership degree. To determine the membership degree, there are a lot of elements to be considered. First of all, the statistical material. Second, to supplement the limitation of the material, the crime functional analysis element, the apparentness of the clue occurs, the difficulty of gaining the clue on-spot, etc. must be considered. For these elements, we can get the relative powers, and then the power contribution collect regarding the above elements may be scored, thus the collect of fuzzy scoring.

$$Ks_{m_j} = (K^{l_1}_{s_{m_j}}, K^{l_2}_{s_{m_j}}, K^{l_3}_{s_{m_j}}, K^{l_4}_{s_{m_j}})\quad m=1,2,\cdots,n,\ j=1,2,3,4,$$

take

$$\mu_{m_j} = \max\{K_{s_m} \oplus L\}$$

note: the definition of the operator $\oplus$ is $a \oplus b = a + b - ab$. For a certain scoring of the specific clues, the first element scoring could be got from the statistical material, i.e.

$$K^{l_1}_{s_{m_j}} = P(s_{m_j} | d_j) = \frac{N_{s_{m_j}}}{N_{d_j}}$$

N_{d_j} and $N_{s_{m_j}}$ refer to the total number of the suspect-to-make-sure s_{m_j} to be suspects d_j. The second, third, and fourth elements scoring may be got by corresponding membership degree

By calculating the membership degree μ_{m_j} of a certain clue, we can get the matrix of suspect-to-make-sure judgment $R_d = (\mu_{m_j})$. This is the number one sort of mapping characteristics.

Suppose $P_j = (\mu_{1j}, \mu_{2j}, \cdots, \mu_{gj}), j = 1,2,3,4$ as the line vector of the matrix, during a case detection reasoning, when input the collect of clues $S = (s_1, s_2, \cdots, s_n)$ if $S_m = 1$, then a clue occurs, if $S_m = 0$, then the clue doesn't occur, thus,

$$\mu_{d_j} = S \circ P_j = \max\{\min(s_m, \mu_{m_j})\}$$

the corresponding

$$X_{d_j} = \max\{\mu_{d_j}(s); j = 1,2,3,4\}$$

is to be the deduced suspect-to-make-sure.

3.2.1 Making sure the second type mapping characteristics

For instance, in the case analysis, a certain case has 20 clues and the STMS has 15. With the above method, to calculate how each clue affects a certain suspect k_v i.e. membership function μ_{uv}, we find the suspect judging matrix $R_k(\mu_{uv})$ (row 20, line 15), store it into the computer. This is the second type mapping characteristics, give a certain input of this mapping, we get a corresponding suspect output.

Consider the fact that the number of the clues is large 20, i.e. the clue region is $C = \{c_1, c_2, \cdots, c_{20}\}$, when make a judgment, one couldn't get the details of the 20 clues simultaneously, but only some of them, i.e. a series of clues $C_o = \{c_1, c_2, \cdots, c_q\}$. Thereafter, its not easy to work out the problem with formulas, we change to follow the principle of max membership, let

$$\mu_{k_v}(C_o) = \frac{\mu_{1v} \circ \mu_{2v} \circ \cdots \circ \mu_{qv}}{\sum_{v=1}^{20} \mu_{1v} \circ \mu_{2v} \circ \cdots \circ \mu_{qv}}$$

use μ_{k_j} as the suspect C_o's membership function toward a given set of clues k_v

$$\mu_{k_j}(C_o) = \max\{\mu_{k_v}(C_o), j_v = 1,2,\cdots,20\}$$

is the given input C_o and the output of the judged suspect k_j.

3.2.2 The automatic judgment and reasoning

When to recognize a crime, the given information may be not unanimous, so as to computer may find difficult to tell it apart. To solve the problem and enable the computer to reason automatically and find the most valuable clues, then use the man-computer system to go on with the judgment. Automatic checking function:

When input a series of clue $C_o = \{c_1, c_2, \cdots, c_q\}$, if the computer reads

$$\mu_{k_j} = \text{Max}\{\ \mu_{k_v}(C_o), j = 1,2,\cdots,20\}$$

let

$$\varepsilon = \frac{\mu_{k_j}(C_0) - \mu_{k_i}(C_o)}{\mu_{k_j}(C_o)}(i \neq j)$$

if $\varepsilon < \rho$ should be adjusted, here ρ is the region value, $0 < \rho < 1$ the affirming method could be as following:

Choose a group of cases from the material (the more the better, and not necessarily typical ones, and the clues are not complete), i.e. each case's clue C_o and k_o each suspect is known. Input C_o to the computer, we get

$$\mu_{k_j}(C_o) = \max\{\ \mu_{k_v}(C_o), j = 1,2,\cdots,20\}$$

if $k_j = k_c$, then the recognizing is over. Or if

$$k_i = k_c(i \neq j), \mu_{k_j}(C_o) > \mu_{k_i}(C_o)$$

then error occurs. With the former method, we can find the corresponding value ρ $(0 < \varepsilon < 1)$. Choose λ for a certain section $(\varepsilon_i, \varepsilon_{i+\lambda})$ find the statistical number N_i, design the total number to be N_i,

let

$$P(\varepsilon_i < \varepsilon < \varepsilon_{i+\lambda}) = \frac{N_i}{N_\Sigma}$$

be a corresponding section's judging probability, with its distribution we can find the distributions function:

$$F(\varepsilon) = P\{\varepsilon \leq \varepsilon_i\} = \sum_{\varepsilon \leq \varepsilon_i} P\{\varepsilon = q_i\}$$

Choose the judgment rate α, then the threshold value is ρ

What kind of clue is to be posed depends on the given clue collect C_o input. Thus, it is more likely to find the suspect. I.e. this clue is evaluated by its effect for suspect judging.

Suppose C_o's clue series number collect as I we get

$$\frac{\mu_{k_j}(C_o) - \mu_{k_i}(C_o)}{\mu_{k_j}(C_o)} \leq \rho(i \neq j)$$

Then, for the two lines C_o, calculate the difference of the *membership* function regarding the not-occurred clues k_i and k_j Take

$$X_b = \max\{\ \mu_{rj} - \mu_{ri}, r \notin I\}$$

again question the corresponding clue of C_b, so as to judge once more.

4. CONCLUSION

As a matter of fact, the key of founding the system of fuzzy automatic crime detect reasoning is to make good use of the FRMI principle. However, it requires good man-computer functions. Meanwhile, the statistical information function is also needed. The studies and practices show that, the using of FRMI principle combining Fuzzy automatic reasoning surely has a promising future.

REFERENCES

[1] He Ping Research about Criminal Investigation Specialist Expert System. *Advances in Management Information System About China.*1985:355-358.

[2] Lang Yanhuai He Ping. The Self-Organized Fuzzy Neural Networks and Crack a Criminal Case Fuzzy Reasoning. *Advances in Systems Science and Application.*2000:(2)200-203.

[3] He Ping. Fuzzy Neural Networks and Reasoning. Automation Theory, Technology and Application. 1995:155-168

[4] He Ping. Fuzzy relationship mapping inversion and the automatic reasoning of crime detective. *Pattern Recognition and Artificial intelligence.*2003,16(1):58－62

[5] Wen Cai. Extension management engineering and applications. *International Journal of Operations and Quantitative Management*, 1999, 5 (1): 59-72

[6] He Ping. The fresh means of economic system acquirement. Dalian : Dalian University of Technology press, 1989

[7] He Ping. The system is non-optimum distinguished the direction system. *The dominates together with the decision*, 1989 (4): 18～21

[8] Yichuiciang, Non-lineal Science and its use in geology. Meteorology Press,

GENERIC BI-LAYERED NET MODEL

General Methodology for Process Simulation

Gyöngyi Bánkuti, Béla Csukás

Institute of Mathematics and Information Technology, University of Kaposvár, Guba S. u. 40., Kaposvár, 7400, Hungary; Process Information Techn. Ltd., Bárd u. 26., Bárdudvarnok, 7478, Hungary csukas@matinf.gtk.u-kaposvar.hu; bankuti@matinf.mail.gtk.u-kaposvar.hu

Abstract: The recently developed Generic Bi-layered Net model provides a common framework for the simulation of the hybrid (continuous and discrete, quantitative and qualitative) balance-based and/or rule-based processes. The common features of the process models are represented by a bi-layered net of variable structure also determines the network (ring) structures of thc influence routes and flux routes, as well as the Gantt Chart view of the process. The advantage of the new methodology is that the computational model is specified by the very structures and building elements of the process to be modeled. Using this approach, the qualitative complexity of the usual mathematical models can be transformed into the multiplication of the building elements of four types.

Key words: net and network (ring) structures, conservational and informational processes, Direct Computer Mapping, Generic Bi-layered Net, hybrid dynamic simulation, cybernetics

1. INTRODUCTION

The computer simulation of the continuous processes is usually based on the numerical solution of a set of algebraic, differential and/or integro-differential equations (IPDAE). The discrete simulation models are represented by various structures. Many net models, like the pioneering Petri Net [1], as well as, the various State Transition Nets belong to the family of General Nets [2]. Recently Quantitative Petri Nets offer a combined approach for modeling of the various systems [3]. Kalmans' State Space Model [4] established a general framework for the description of formal models, while this approach does not describe the knowledge about the structure. Artificial Intelligence developed various knowledge representation and search methods, without the explicit consideration of domain specific structures and of fundamental conservation laws. The tools of Computational Intelligence (neural networks, genetic algorithm, fuzzy sets) were derived from the simplified pattern of the biological systems, as well as from the human reasoning. Regardless to the existing combined methods, there is no single unified methodology that covers all aspects of process simulation.

2. THE GENERIC BI-LAYERED NET MODEL

Direct Computer Mapping [5,6] of Generic Bi-layered Net model [7] integrates the structural capabilities of the general net models with the functional abilities of the state space model. The formal description determines a general skeleton for the adequate software implementation of a model-driven and model specific computing architecture.

2.1 Formal Description of the Generic Bi-layered Net

The basic notions and the inherent feedback structure of the process models are shown on Fig. 1 (left), while a simplified example for the structure of a fictitious process is illustrated on the right hand side.

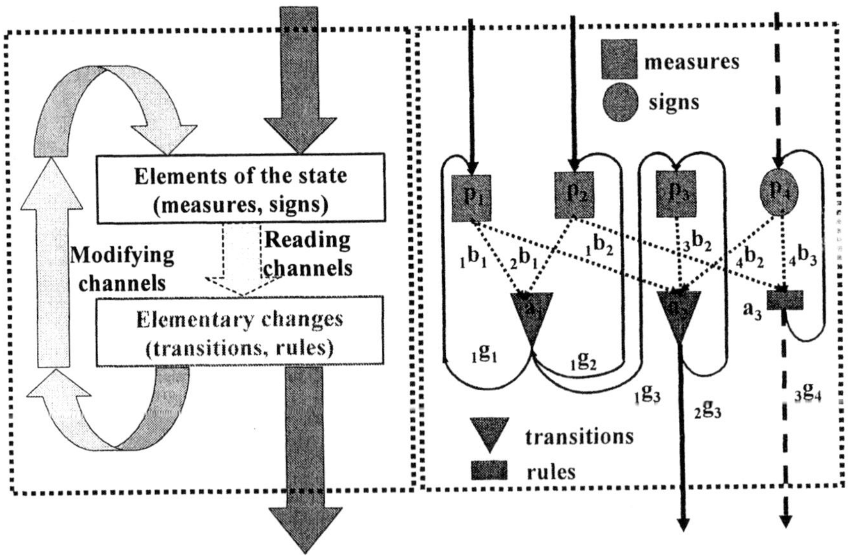

Figure 1. Simplified generic bi-layered structure of process models

The ***generic, bi-layered net model*** can be defined by the ten-tuplet of

$$\langle P, A, B, G, X, Y, \Phi, \Psi, \underline{r}, t \rangle \tag{1}$$

The communication channels B and G determine the passive→active

$$B(\tau) \subset P(\tau) \times A(\tau) \tag{2}$$

$$_j b_i(\tau) = (p_j(\tau), a_i(\tau)) \in B(\tau) \tag{3}$$

$$\exists_j \underline{b}(\tau) \mid \forall_i (p_j(\tau), a_i(\tau)) \in {}_j\underline{b}(\tau) \tag{4}$$

$$\exists \underline{b}_i(\tau) \mid \forall_j (p_j(\tau), a_i(\tau)) \in \underline{b}_i(\tau) \tag{5}$$

and active→passive data flows

$$G(\tau) \subset A(\tau) \times P(\tau) \tag{6}$$

$$_i g_j(\tau) = (a_i(\tau), p_j(\tau)) \in G(\tau) \tag{7}$$

$$\exists_i \underline{g}(\tau) \mid \forall_j (a_i(\tau), p_j(\tau)) \in {}_i\underline{g}(\tau) \tag{8}$$

$$\exists \underline{g}_j(\tau) \mid \forall_i (a_i(\tau), p_j(\tau)) \in \underline{g}_j(\tau) \tag{9}$$

respectively. Index j designates the ordered sets of the existing output (${}_j\underline{b}$ (4)) and input ($\underline{g}_j$ (9)) connections for the j-th passive element. Similarly, index i defines the ordered sets of the existing output (${}_i\underline{g}$ (8)) and input ($\underline{b}_i$ (5)) connections for the i-th active element. Variable τ denotes the optional points or intervals of the continuous or discrete time t, declaring the existence of the respective elements and connections.

The ***passive elements*** P are associated with state variables X_j and with an operator, describing the change of the state:

$$\forall_j p_j \to X_j \in X; \quad \psi_j \in \Psi; \quad \psi_i = \begin{bmatrix} \underline{y}_j[\underline{g}_j] \\ {}_j\underline{x}[{}_j\underline{b}] \end{bmatrix} \tag{10}$$

where X_j contains any structured data set, and operator ψ_j describes how y_j changes the state via the channels $\underline{g}_j$.

The ***active elements*** A are characterized by the operators φ_i, providing a mapping. This determines how the output changes ${}_i y_j \in {}_i\underline{y}$, carried by ${}_i\underline{g}$ are calculated from the coordinated input readings ${}_j x_i \in \underline{x}_i$ that comes from the passive elements through the channels $\underline{b}_i$:

$$\forall_i a_i \to \varphi_i \in \Phi; \quad \varphi_i = \begin{bmatrix} \underline{x}_i[\underline{b}_i] \\ {}_i\underline{y}[{}_i\underline{g}] \end{bmatrix} \tag{11}$$

The operators $\psi_i \in \Psi$ and $\varphi_i \in \Phi$ ***may be anything from a simple input/output mapping to a brief program***, calculating the elementary process or the rule.

Variable $\underline{r}$ designates the geometrical and/or the property coordinates of the distributed systems and/or population balances.

In the network view of the net we can interpret the alternating, connected, ordered set of the communication channels

$$\left\{ {}_{j_1}b_{i_1},\ {}_{i_1}g_{j_2},\ {}_{j_2}b_{i_2},\ {}_{i_2}g_{j_3}, \ldots\ {}_{j_n}b_{i_n},\ {}_{i_n}g_{j_{n+1}} \right\}. \qquad (12)$$

They are called ***influence routes***, which determine a special network structure. The influence routes carry the influence. E.g. the perturbation of the content X_{j_1} of the element p_{j_1} affects the content $X_{j_{n+1}}$ of the element $p_{j_{n+1}}$, according to the influence:

$$\left\{ {}_{j_1}\Delta x_{i_1}(t_1),\ {}_{i_1}\Delta y_{j_2},\ {}_{j_2}\Delta x(t_2)_{i_2}, \ldots, {}_{i_n}\Delta y_{j_{n+1}} \right\} \qquad (13)$$

where ${}_j\Delta x_i$ and ${}_i\Delta y_j$ refer to the perturbation of the state and the change, respectively. The sensitivity and its special forms, such as observability and controllability can be studied by means of the influence route network. The minimal (generating) influence routes are the basic edges. The maximal influence routes are the transferring routes and the complete loops. The simplified structure of the influence routes is a special ring, where the two algebraic operations are the concatenation and the common part.

2.2 GBN model of problems with increasing complexity

The detailed features of the GBN model are illustrated in Fig. 2 by the example of an isothermic chemical reaction in a perfectly mixed volume. Expanding the model for a continuous vessel, equipped with control devices the homogeneous ODE should be replaced for an inhomogeneous DAE system. However in the GBN model this change can be solved of introducing passive and active elements of informational type, as well as by new connections (see Fig. 3).

When modeling a tubular reactor of distributed parameters (Fig. 4), the mathematical complexity increases for the system of inhomogeneous partial differential equations of second order. In the GBN it means the simple multiplication of the elements and of the (mainly local) connections, along the actual coordinate $\underline{r}$. (accompanied with compensation of the numerical dispersion).

Furthermore, in the case of a, say, fuzzy controlled side flow reactor (Fig. 5) the mathematical construct becomes extremely complex (IPDAE), but in the GBN model we have to add passive and active elements of new functionalities, as well as, the respective new connections simply.

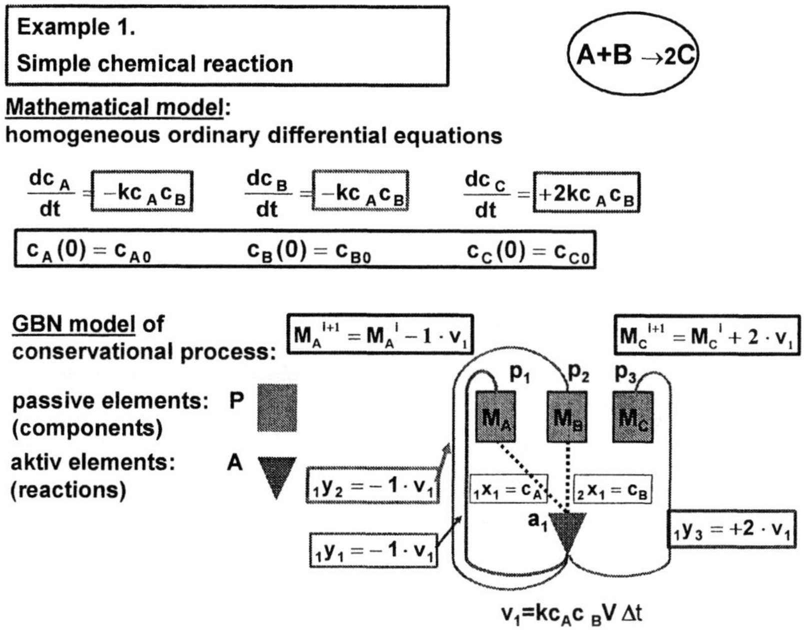

Figure 2. Mathematical and GBN models of a simple reaction

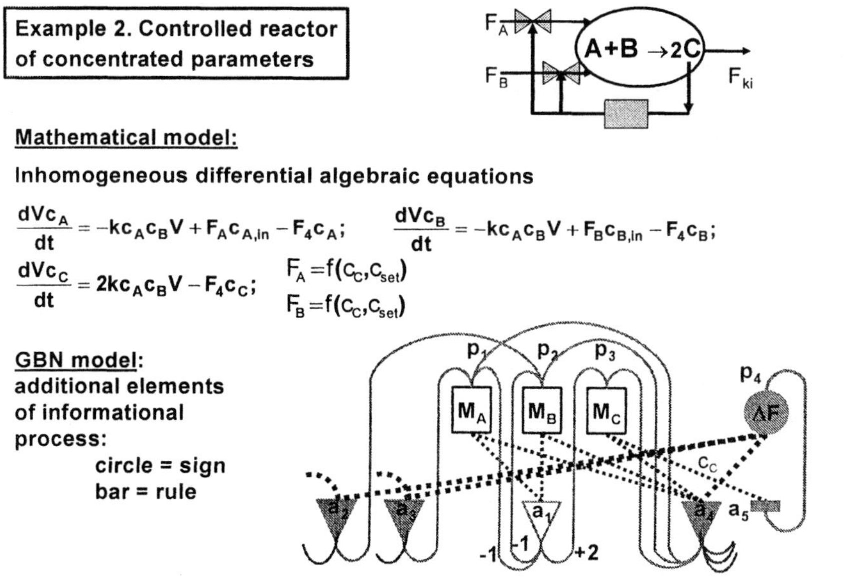

Figure 3. Effect of controlled flows on the mathematical and GBN models

Example 3. Continuous tubular reactor of distributed parameters

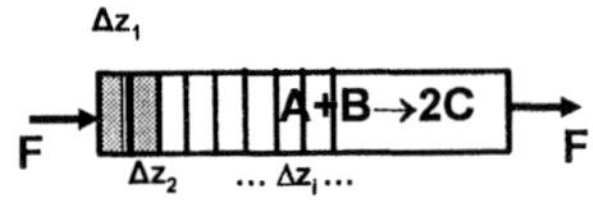

Mathematical model:

Inhomogeneous partial differential equations of second order

$$\frac{\partial c_A(z,t)}{\partial t} = u\frac{\partial c_A(z,t)}{\partial z} - D\frac{\partial^2 c_A(z,t)}{\partial z^2} - kc_A(z,t)c_B(z,t); \quad \text{etc.}$$

$$c_A(z,0) = c_{A,0}; \quad Fc_{A,in} = Fc_A(0,t) - DS\frac{\partial c_A(z,t)}{\partial z}; \quad \left[\frac{\partial c_A(z,t)}{\partial z}\right]_{z=Z} \approx 0$$

GBN model: multiplication of the elements

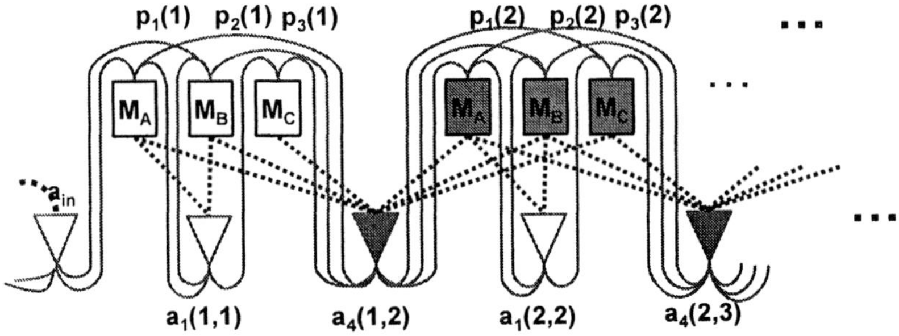

Figure 4. Effect of distributed parameters on the math and GBN complexity

Example 4. Tubular reactor with fuzzy controlled side inflows

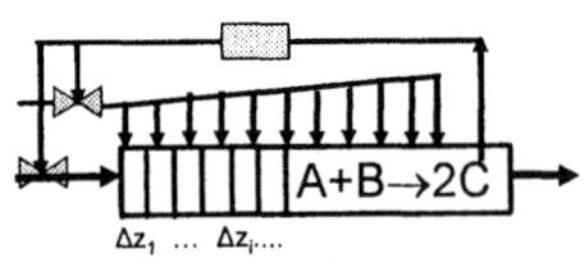

Mathematical model:

Inhomogeneous hibrid integro-partial differential equations

$$\frac{\partial c_A(z,t)}{\partial t} = \left(u_1 + \int_0^z u_2(z,t)\partial z\right)\frac{\partial c_A(z,t)}{\partial z} - D\frac{\partial^2 c_A(z,t)}{\partial z^2} - kc_A(z,t)c_B(z,t);...$$

$$u_2(z,t) = \Omega\left[u_2(z,0), c_C(Z), \left[\frac{\partial c_C(z)}{\partial t}\right]_{z=Z}\right]; \quad u_2(z,0) = u_2^*(z); \quad u_2(0,t) = u_1^*(t);$$

GBN model: additional signs, rules and communication channels

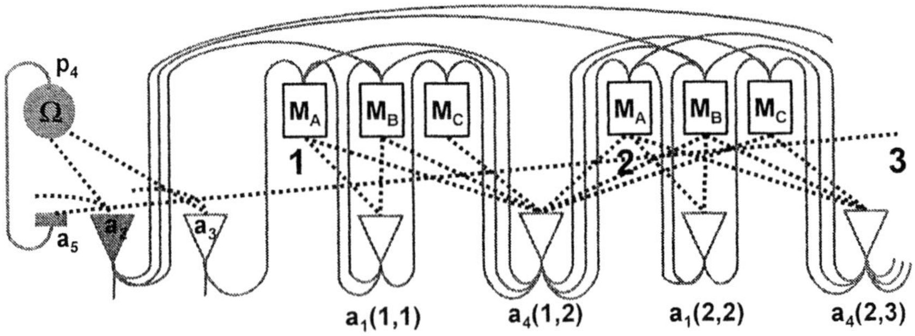

Figure 5. GBN representation of a hybrid IPDAE model

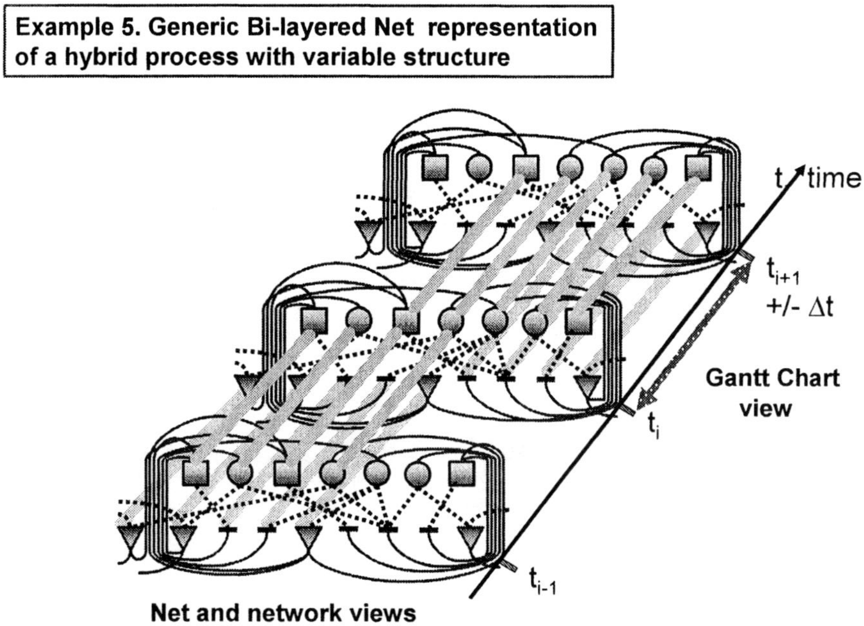

Figure 6. Network and Gantt Chart views of a model with variable structure

Finally, the methodology supports also the adequate description of hybrid processes with variable structure. As it can be seen in the Gantt Chart view of the GBN model (Fig. 6), the existence of the respective passive and active elements can be changed in time t.

An important special case of net (1) is the class of ***balance processes***, where the basic part of the state X_j is a measure and, the operator ψ_j summarizes the simultaneous rates. Depending on the discrete or continuous time, operator ψ_j generates also the appropriate

$$\psi_j(\underline{y}_j) = \frac{dX_j[p_j]}{dt} \approx \frac{\Delta X_j[p_j]}{\Delta t} = \sum_i {}_i y_j \tag{14}$$

difference or differential equations, called balance equations. In the balance model the descendent of the mappings, φ_i can be divided into two disjunct parts, corresponding to the increases (+) and decreases (-) of the characteristic measures:

$${}_i\underline{y}[{}_i\underline{g}] = {}_i\underline{y}^+[{}_i\underline{g}^+] \cup {}_i\underline{y}^-[{}_i\underline{g}^-] \tag{15}$$

The active elements of the balance process models describe the various transportations and transformations. In the balance process models the alternating, connected, ordered set of the communication channels

$$\left\{ {}_{j_1} g^{-}_{i_1},\ {}_{i_1} g^{+}_{j_2},\ {}_{j_2} g^{-}_{i_2},\ {}_{i_2} g^{+}_{j_3}, \ldots, {}_{j_n} g^{-}_{i_n},\ {}_{i_n} g^{+}_{j_{n+1}} \right\} \tag{16}$$

is called flux route. Flux routes determine another network structure, which carry the conservational measures. For example, if we modify the value of measure X_{j_1} in element p_{j_1}, then this change effects on measure $X_{j_{n+1}}$ of the element $p_{j_{n+1}}$, i.e.:

$$\left\{ {}_{j_1} \Delta y^{-}_{i_1}(t_1), {}_{i_1} \Delta y^{+}_{j_2}(t_2), {}_{j_2} \Delta y^{-}_{i_2}(t_1), \ldots, {}_{i_{n-1}} \Delta y^{+}_{j_n}(t_n) \right\} \tag{17}$$

The $\Delta y^{+/-}_{j_i}$ values refer to the dispersion of the changes in the rate of subsequent processes (multiplied by the stoichiometric coefficients). The minimal (generating) flux routes are the basic edges. The maximal flux routes are transferring routes and the complete loops. Similarly to influence routes, the simplified structure of the flux routes the is a special ring, where the two algebraic operations are the concatenation and the common part.

Conservational measure is a special case of the balance measure, where there are constant measures $\underline{C}$ determined by the model specific conservation laws. All of the conservational measures $\underline{M}$ can be combined from constant measures, according to the respective stoichiometry $\underline{\underline{S}}$, i.e.:

$$\exists \underline{C} \quad \exists \underline{\underline{S}} \quad | \quad \underline{M} = \underline{\underline{S}} \cdot \underline{C} \tag{18}$$

For the conservational processes

$$\underline{0} = \underline{\underline{\Gamma}} \cdot \underline{M} = \underline{\underline{\Gamma}} \cdot \underline{\underline{S}} \cdot \underline{C} \tag{19}$$

is fulfilled, where $\underline{\underline{\Gamma}}$ is the process rate matrix [8].

2.3 Properties of the GBN Model

GBN architecture offers a general tool to develop robust case specific simulators for any conservational and/or informational process rapidly. When building a simulator for a completely new class of problems, only the respective new dynamic partitions have to be added. The most important useful features of the GBN based generic tools are the following:

Complexity is rather quantitative than qualitative. To move from a lumped balance model to another one of distributed parameters and further to the population balance, usually means the change of complexity from ordinary differential equations to partial differential equations and furthermore to integro-differential equations. In GBN models the above changes can be replaced for declaring the respective new dimensions, while the model generator prepares more elements that will be executed by the same kernel during a longer time.

Easy supplement of new add-on modeling capabilities. In a conventional simulator expert has to write new module with the respective interface. In GBN, the problem specific knowledge can be contained in the expert defined new program partitions, communicating with the generalized dynamic database.

Full runtime modification. When running the user can pause the simulation and all of the programs and parameters can be modified easily. Afterwards the execution can be continued with the modified structure and parameters.

Macrogranular parallelism: combining generic simulation with genetic algorithm in evolutionary problem solving [7]. First the user must define the so-called possibility space of the given problem of synthesis type. The possibilities can be declared either directly by the full set of the possible active and passive generic elements, or indirectly by the alternative "surface" features and variables. Next the objective(s) have to be declared that can be formulated by an aggregated goal function or by a number of evaluations. The genetic algorithm prepares an initial population. Next the model synthesizing program generates and simulates the variants one after the other, followed by the evaluation of the prescribed objectives. With the knowledge of these evaluations the genetic algorithm proposes a new population to be studied while the new variants will be tendentiously better. The principle is that similarly to the engineering way of thinking, modeling is based on the *a priori* knowledge of the essential features, while the final evaluation is made with the most versatile consideration of the best detailed experiences. Because of the very limited communication between the genetic algorithm and the simulations, the method can be executed by macrogranular parallel architectures (cluster, GRID) effectively.

Microgranular parallelism: possible model-based hardware architectures. The direct mapping of process models onto adequate software architecture gives an idea also for a corresponding hardware implementation. In this hypothetical machine, programming means the configuration of the processors and the communication network, as well as the distribution of data and of brief programs amongst the processors.

3. CONCLUSIONS ABOUT THE "NATURAL INTELLIGENCE" OF PROCESS MODELS

Having studied various process models, coming both from the nature and from the engineer-made artifacts, the following general conclusions can be derived:

a) The natural processes are conservational processes. This means that the state of the natural processes is determined by additive quantities, called measures, while the majority of these measures can be derived from the model specific constant measures (that cannot be formed or decomposed further within the modeled system). In the feasible formulation of the programs the rate of the processes is controlled by the specific measures, therefore the driving force of the processes converges to zero, if the input measures are exhausted.

b) The analysis of the complex conservational GBN models leads to a new interpretation of the informational process, as a simplified and idealized part of conservational processes. A given subsystem behaves as an informational process with respect to its complement if it consumes and produces significantly less conservational measures than the complementary process, while the informational subprocess affects more influence on the complement than the completing part on it.

ACKNOWLEDGEMENTS

The work was supported by Hungarian Scientific Research Fund T 037-297 and by the Grant of Hungarian Ministry of Economy and Transport GVOP-3.3.1 200404-0091/3.0.

REFERENCES

1. Petri, C. A., Kommunikation mit Automaten, Schriften des Institut für Instrumentelle Mathematik, Nr. 2, Bonn, 1962.
2. Brauer, W. Ed., Net Theory and Applications. Springer Lecture Notes in Computer Science, (84) 1980.
3. Chen, M., Hofestaedt, R.: Quantitative Petri Net Model of Gene Regulated Metabolic Networks in the Cell, In Silico Biology, 3, 0029, 2003.
4. Kalman, R., Falb, P., Arbib, M., Topics in Mathematical System Theory, McGraw Hill, 1969.
5. Csukas B.: Direct Computer Mapping of Conservational and Informational Processes, DSc Thesis, Manuscript in Hungarian, 2001.
6. Csukas B., Bankuti Gy.: Direct computer mapping of process models, In: Foundations of Computer Assisted Process Operations, A View to the Future Integration of R&D, Manufacturing and the Global Supply Chain. I. E. Grossmann and C. M. MacDonald, Eds., AIChE INFORMS, pp. 577-581, 2003.
7. Csukas B. Bankuti Gy.: Generic Bi-layered Net model of conservational and informational proceasses. In: C. H. Dagli, A. L. Buczak, J. Ghosh, M. J. Embrechts and O. Ersoy Eds., Intelligent Engineering Systems through Artificial Neural Networks, Volume 13, Smart Engineering System Design: Neural Networks, Fuzzy Logic, Evolutionary Programming, Data Mining and Complex Systems and Artificial Life. ASME Press, New York, 2003, pp. 769-774.
8. Csukás B., Bánkuti Gy.: Generic Bi-layered Net, as the Natural Computational Model of the Conservation and Information Processes, Journal of simulation, Systems, Science & technology, 2005 (in press).

GENERIC BI-LAYERED NET PROGRAMMING

General Software for the Simulation of Hybrid Processes

Béla Csukás, Sándor Balogh, Gyöngyi Bánkuti

Institute of Mathematics and Information Technology, University of Kaposvár, Guba S. u. 40., Kaposvár, 7400, Hungary; Process Information Techn. Ltd., Bárd u. 26., Bárdudvarnok, 7478, Hungary; csukas@matinf.gtk.u-kaposvar.hu; bankuti@matinf.mail.gtk.u-kaposvar.hu; balogh@matinf.gtk.u-kaposvar.hu

Abstract: Based on the Generic Bi-layered Net model, an effective software architecture has been developed for the Direct Computer Mapping of process models. The novel, model-driven programming technique makes possible the natural, model-driven software generation for the simulation based problem solving. The PROLOG implementation of the GBN model has been applied for the solution of various difficult practical problems. The solution supports the parallelism of different granularity.

Key words: programming technique, software architecture, Direct Computer Mapping, Generic Bi-layered Net, hybrid processes, dynamic simulation, Prolog

1. INTRODUCTION

Many recently used engineering methods had been established before the onset of powerful computers. Modeling starts either from the consideration of changes in characteristic measures, or from the rules and signs. Next this is transformed into mathematical construct. It usually cannot be solved, should be discretisized and, finally, the computer executes simple arithmetical steps. However, mostly there is not a plausible connection between the final computer operations and the primary functioning of the building blocks, directly.

In ***Direct Computer Mapping*** [1] we can map the simple building blocks of the conservational and informational processes onto the generic "active" and "passive" elements of an executable program. The balance elements and the signs, as well as the elementary transitions and the rules can be described by brief uniform programs, executed by the same kernel algorithm. Direct Computer Mapping of process models allows the computer to know explicitly about the very structures and bounds of the physical world. In this knowledge representation, the model is organized rather by the transitions, than by the state. ***The key issue is that the computational software (and/or optional hypothetical hardware) can copy the natural structure and building elements of the investigated problem.***

2. THE GENERIC BI-LAYERED NET SOFTWARE ARCHITECTURE

In the software implementation of the $\langle P, A, B, G, X, Y, \Phi, \Psi, \underline{r}, t \rangle$ ten-tuplet of the Generic Bi-layered Net model [2], the dynamic partitions of the elements and connections are executed by a general and optionally extendable kernel.

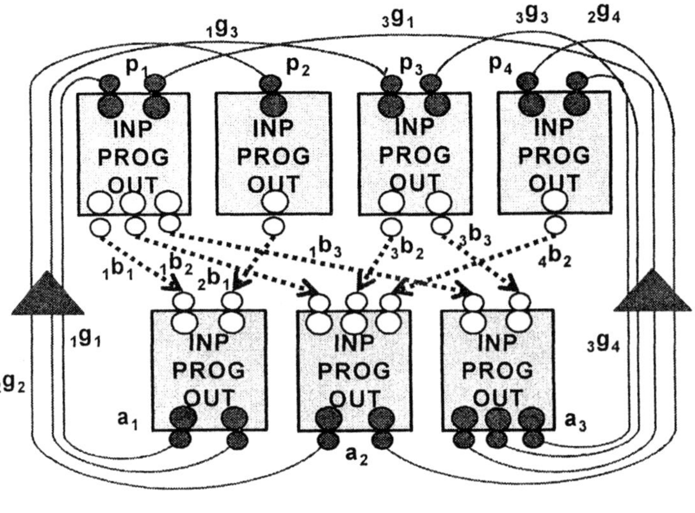

Figure 1. The GBN model based software architecture

According to Fig.1, the execution consists of four, cyclically repeated consecutive steps, as follows:

(1) active elements A read the content X from the associated passive elements according to the reading channels B;

(2) programs Φ, associated with elements A calculate the changes;

(3) passive elements P are changed according to Y changes carried via modifying channels G;

(4) operators Ψ, associated with the elements P calculate the new state.

The first complete implementation of GBN architecture is written in PROLOG, where the free unification of the high level structures contained in dynamic partitions supports the methodology.

In the PROLOG representation, the elements of sets P, A, B and G correspond to the automatically generated dynamic partitions, describing the actual detailed state, the changes, the readings and the modifications of the modeled process. Accordingly variables X and Y correspond to the freely determined possible set of signs transported via the communication channels B and G. The fundamental predicates are the following:

p (PID, Name, Space, Time, Glist, PassiveID, State, Blist)
b (BID, PID, X, AID)
a (AID, Name, ISpace, OSpace, Time, Blist, ActiveID, Process, Glist)
g (GID, AID, Y, PID)

where:

PID, BID, AID, GID = the identifiers of the passive elements, reading channels, active elements and modifying channels, respectively;

Name {stringlist}= the name of the element (in hierarchical models the name describes the subsequent elements of the tree);

Space {integerlist}= the spatial and property coordinates in the case of the processes with distributed parameter);

Time {tlist} = the temporal existence of the elements according to variable τ, declared by the Time=[tk(S,E,[T1,...,TN],DT,0),...] data structure, where S and E are the starting and ending points of the time intervals, as well as T1,...,TN are the discrete points of time, when the given element is to be taken into consideration, while DT is the optional time step of the repeated execution;

Blist {blist} = the list of (feedback) readings, determining the input data for the functioning of the active elements, i.e. blist=b*;

Glist {glist} = the list of changing, corresponding to the output data of the active elements, i.e. glist=g*;

X {sign} = a user configured data set about the state (e.g. integers, reals, strings, tables, fuzzy variables, optional records, etc.);

Y {sign}= a user configured data set describing an individual change (increase, decrease, overwriting, modification, etc.);

State {state_data} = a user configured static and/or dynamic data set characterizing the state of a given class of passive elements;

Process {process_data} = a user configured static and/or dynamic data set, associated with a given class of active elements;

PassiveID = identifier of the dynamic clause partition ψ that executes the functionality associated with the given passive element;

ActiveID = identifier of the dynamic clause partition φ that executes the functionality associated with the given active element.

The Ψ and Φ functionalities are described by the dynamic partitions of clauses

passive(PassiveID, Glist, State, Blist) if
... and
active(ActiveID, Blist, Process, Glist) if
..., respectively.

3. APPLICATIONS OF THE METHODOLOGY

All of the listed adaptations run with the same kernel program, supplied with the respective domain specific interpreter module. Actually only a single one of the 12 modules has to be modified when moving from one application to the other. As an actual challenge, the present efforts are concentrated on developing a platform independent code for any, arbitrary application, where the domain specific structures and functionalities can be edited by the field expert, using the so-called expert's interface.

3.1 Model Based Design and Control of Cyclic, Pseudo-steady State (SMB) Separation Processes

Practical problem to be solved: Design and control of the countercurrent separation processes, realized in the so-called Simulated Moving Bed (SMB) system. The key idea of SMB is to "simulate" the solid phase motion by periodic switching the inlet and outlet ports of the unit.

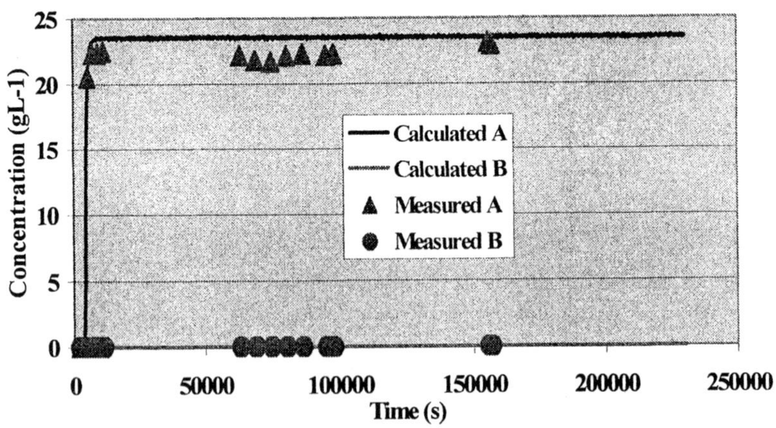

Figure 2. Measured and calculated data of an SMB fraction

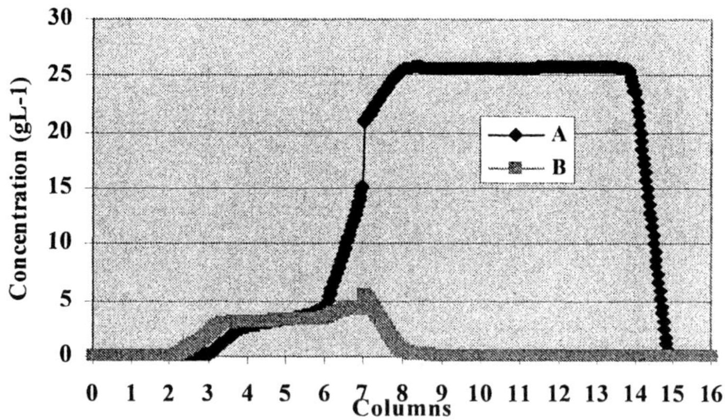

Figure 3. Calculated concentration profile of the SMB

Passive elements (P) Individual competitive components in the given phase at a given compartment along the length of the respective column.

Active elements (A): The terminal elements designate the architecture of the elementary transformations, transportations, and rules (control actions).

State functionalities (Ψ): These brief dynamic program partitions define the calculation of the intensive properties from the extensive ones.

Transition functionalities (Φ): These brief dynamic program partitions declare the calculation of the component transfer, of the liquid flow, etc. for the conservational processes, as well as the execution of the diagnostic, control and evaluating rules.

Input data: The user has to define the configuration of the system, the data of the columns, the initial state, the equilibrium and the process parameters (flow rates, column switch time, etc.). The kinetic and mixing parameters have to be identified from elution tests, using the simulator itself.

Output results: There are detailed time functions for the instantaneous and column step averaged concentrations (see Fig. 2.), as well as for the concentration profiles (see Fig. 3.) along the length of the column series.

Experiences: There is a good agreement between the measured and calculated results (see Fig. 2.). The simulator helped in the successful design and control of SMB processes in the pharmaceutical industry [3].

3.2 Identification of Cellular Metabolic Processes

Practical problem to be solved: There is a gap between the genomic information discovered by bioinformatics and the organization & functioning of the metabolic processes. The efforts to synthesize the major cellular functions from the in vitro measured individual enzyme kinetics failed. Biosystem engineers need large, complex models, built from the elementary steps. The models must be able to be supplemented with any new interaction (e.g. in drug discovery or in toxicology). These models have to connect the metabolism with the polypeptide formation and degradation, too.

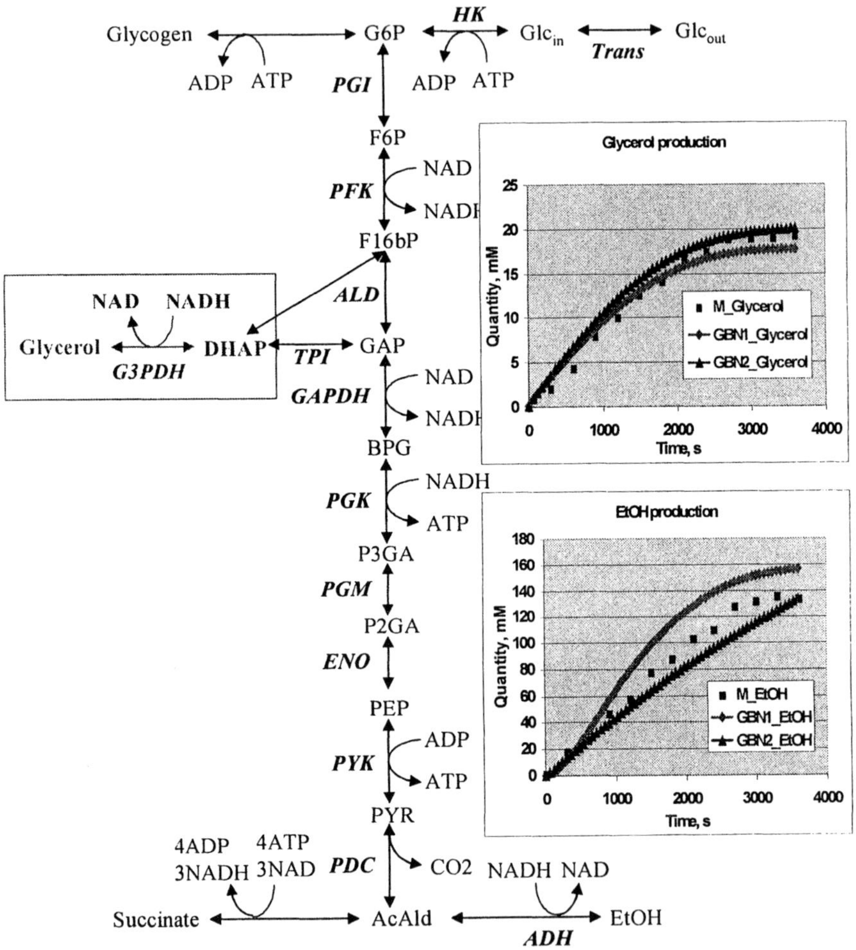

Figure 4. Measured and calculated data of glycolysis

Special difficulties of the simulation: Regardless to the equilibrium reaction kinetic approach of biochemistry, the chemical engineer's way of thinking has to be combined with the discrete cellular machineries, working as the production lines in mechanical engineering. The biosystems are highly underdetermined and, the useable models need special identifying abilities to treat the missing or uncertain knowledge.

Passive elements (P) All of the possible, more or less freely moving compounds and complexes, as well as the structured, located sites that may have any functionality in the various compartments.

Active elements (A): All of the possible elementary transformations inside the compartments, and transportations between the compartments.

State functionalities (Ψ): These brief dynamic program partitions define the calculation of the intensive properties from the extensive quantities, as well as the evaluation of the signs for the control systems.

Transition functionalities (Φ): These brief dynamic program partitions declare the calculation of the transformations and transportations of the conservational processes, as well as the execution of the control functions in the signaling processes.

Input data: The available quantities and concentrations, as well as the estimations of the process parameters. The detailed equilibrium, kinetic, transporting and signaling parameters have to be identified from possible measurements, using the simulator combined with a genetic algorithm [4].

Output results: The calculated change in the amount and concentration of the various metabolites and macromolecular complexes, as well as the state of the keynote cellular elements.

Experiences: There is a good agreement between the measured and calculated results (see Fig. 4.) of the yeast glycolysis [5].

3.3 Quantitative Health Risk Analysis of Multiproduct Batch Plants

Practical problem to be solved: Health risk management at multiproduct workplaces is a typical field, where computer simulation can help to cope with strict and sometimes ambiguous regulations. Standards do not contain proper methodologies for handling the presence of multiple inhalative risk sources, distributed in space and time, according to the dynamic changes in production demand and schedule.

Special difficulties of the simulation: The various sources are allocated in interconnected workplaces with multiple ventilation inputs and outputs, while employees are working in the vicinity of different sources of potential inhalative risk.

Passive elements (P) Various compounds in the compartments of the plant building, equipments, ventilation units, workers, etc.

Active elements (A): Loss of solvents, sources of the dangerous compounds, input / output arrangement of the risk factor calculation, etc.

State functionalities (Ψ): Calculation of balances, intensive parameters, equilibrium properties, etc.

Transition functionalities (Φ): Calculation of the losses, flows, risk factors, etc.

Input data: First the equipments, the partially open ceilings and walls, as well as the ventilation system must be allocated in the simplified, discretisized 3D representation of the plant building, where the various batch technologies are running simultaneously. Next, with the knowledge of the actual (daily, weekly) schedule, the elementary models of the events, associated with potential sources of inhalative exposure risk are generated from the SQL database, comprising all of the data related to equipments, process steps and materials. Finally, considering the shift schedule, the employees are allocated to the safe and potentially risky places, while the use of personal protective equipment may be also taken into account.

Output results: The method makes possible the detailed calculation of the risk factors of the employees. The tool is also able to simulate the effect of any feature (e.g. modified ventilation characteristics, changed substances or duration of different procedures) on the inhalative risk. A simplified illustration [6] can be seen in Fig. 5.

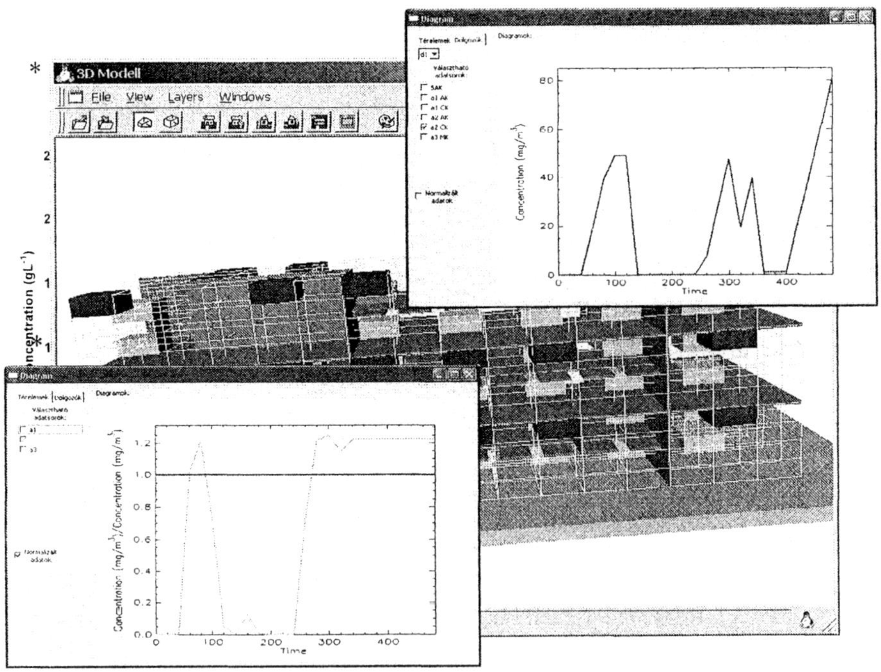

Figure 5. Illustration of the simulation model

Experiences: Detailed characterization of the losses and risk can be solved with considerably less number of expensive analytical measurements.

3.4 Simulation Based Cash Flow Analysis of an Agricultural Farm

Practical problem to be solved: Planning and scheduling of an agricultural farm, including the liquidity (cash flow) analysis.

Special difficulties of the simulation: There is a lot of elaborated data in form of statistical correlations, but the consistent system of the first principle expressions for the appropriate balance equations has not evolved yet. In addition, the qualitative knowledge of the field expert has not collected in a systematic way.

Passive elements (P) There are various groups of realistic and fictitious storage volumes at vendors, inside the farm, as well as at the consumers, containing seeds, crops, fertilizers, etc. Another class of passive elements declares the manpower, the machine resources and the economic properties.

Active elements (A): Describe the structure of the possible purchases, sales, as well as of the agricultural processes (e.g. ploughing, harrowing, sowing, harvest, etc.).

State functionalities (Ψ): Describe the calculation, associated with the storages and evaluation of the signs for the control system.

Transition functionalities (Φ): Determine the simulation of the agricultural processes (consumption of land, seeds, crops, fertilizers, chemicals, machines, manpower and the productions, as well as calculate the economic characteristics.

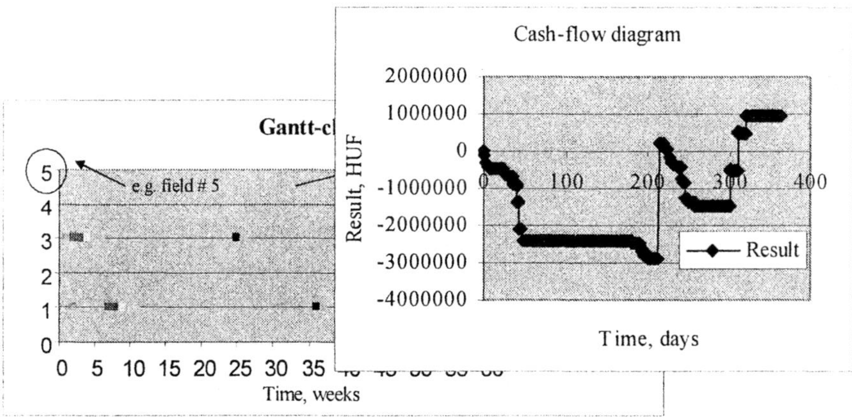

Figure 7. Simulation of an agricultural farm

Input data: The user has to define the initial state of the agricultural system, the estimated (optionally changing) economical parameters, as well as the possible, alternative agricultural activities, described by the sequence of the respective operations.

Output results: The simulated output describes the detailed change of the characteristic materials, energy, manpower and machine consumption, as well as the cash-flow of the alternative plans. In addition, the Gantt-chart of the allocated resources can also be generated (see Fig. 7).

Experiences: The calculated results are in good agreement with the practical experiences and, having connected the simulator with a genetic algorithm, feasible propositions for more favorable rotations of crops have been suggested [7].

ACKNOWLEDGEMENTS

The work was supported by Hungarian Scientific Research Fund T 037-297, by the Gedeon Richter Ltd., and by the Grant of Hungarian Ministry of Economy and Transport GVOP-3.3.1 200404-0091/3.0.

REFERENCES

1. Csukas B.: Direct Computer Mapping of Conservational and Informational Processes, DSc Thesis, Manuscript, 2001 (in Hungarian).
2. Bánkuti Gy., Csukás B.: Generic Bi-layered Net Model – General Methodology for Process Simulation, Proceedings of the Second IFIP Conference on Artificial Intelligence Applications and innovations, Beijing, China, September 7-9, 2005.
3. Temesvári K., Aranyi A., Csukás B., Balogh S.: Simulated Moving Bed Separation of a Two Components Steroid Mixture. (Accepted manuscript for Chromatographia, 2003).
4. Csukás B., Balogh S.: Combining Genetic Programming with Generic Simulation Models in Evolutionary Synthesis. Computers in Industry, 36, 181-197 (1998).
5. Csukás B., Debelak, K. A., Prokop, A, Balcarcel, R. R., Tanner, R. D., Bánkuti Gy, Balogh S.: Generic Bi-layered Net Model Based Discrimination of Chemical and Biological Warfare Agents, AIChE Annual Meeting, San Francisco, November 16-20, 2003, Manuscript 474f.
6. Balogh S., Négyesi Gy., Budai M., Sógor A., Csukás B.: Measurement and Dynamic Simulation of Solvent Exposure in Multiproduct Batch Plants. Process Engineering Days' 2003, Veszprém, April 8-10, pp. 284-290, 2003 (in Hungarian).
7. Bosnyák B., Balogh S., Csukás B.: Planning and Scheduling of a Plant Cultivating Farm by means of Generic Simulation and Genetic Algorithm, 4-th Conference on Applied Informatics, Kaposvár, May 27, 2005 (in Hungarian).

LEAF IMAGE RETRIEVAL USING A SHAPE BASED METHOD

Yangcheng Shen[1], Changle Zhou[2], Kunhui Lin[1]
[1] *1275#, Software school, Xiamen University, Xiamen, Fujian 361005, China (email: shenyangcheng@sina.com)*
[2] *Information Science and Technique School, Xiamen University, Xiamen, Fujian 361005, China (email: dozero@xmu.edu.cn)*

Abstract: For content-based image retrieval, shape information is of great importance. This paper presents a shape descriptor of imaged leaf objects according to their boundaries for image retrieval. We take picture of leaves, exact the sketch from original images and produce a low dimensional feature vector to describe the shape. By comparing the similarity of the query image with those in database, a set of images with shape similarity are retrieved. The experiment shows that the method has high reliability and less time consuming.

Keywords: CBIR, shape, leaf image retrieval, image representation

1. INTRODUCTION

Chinese tradition medicine is becoming more and more popular all over the world. But it is difficult to identify and classify the herbal medicine. If a non-skilled doctor or a student wants to know the name of an unknown species of herbal medicine, a book about herbal medicine is needed. It would be useful if we take a picture of a sample, input it into a computer and a computer-aid process may help recognize it.

Most herbal medicine are plant leaves or flowers, leaves or flowers are usually distinguished by their shapes and colors, but the color of a leaf usually green, and shades and the background light always make the color feature low reliability. Therefore, we decided to research their shape feature based on 2D images for our purpose.

Klassen et al. [13] consider the shapes of continuous, closed curves. Shapes are often encoded by a set of sampled points of objects' boundaries. Our goal is to develop mathematical approach to represent the continuous boundaries of high accuracy and efficiency.

Some recent work has focused on shape feature extraction. [7][8][9] describe the shape of an object by contour points which are represented by their distance and angel to the centroid points. In some special applications, they show good results, but their process is often time consuming. [11][12] use the region-based feature to represent the shape. Consider their advantages and disadvantages, we propose an improved contour based algorithm that is more efficient and easily implemented.

An important step before shape representation is edge detection. We will assume that the boundary of the shape have been extracted from training images or using a standard edge detector. There are many robust edge detection methods such as Sobel operation, Roberts operation and Laplacian operation. In our prototype system, we choose Sobel operation to detect the edge of an object.

This paper is organized as follows: Section 2 describes in detail the methods we proposed, followed by the experiment we implemented in Section 3. Conclusions and future work is given in Section 4.

2. SHAPE REPRESENTATION

In this section, we introduce our shape descriptor which is invariant to translation, scaling and rotation and how to measure the similarity between images based on the shape descriptor. Global shape parameters are extracted from the entire image, like area, contour points, and shape feature are calculated like centroid, orientation and curvature. A combination of global features is used in our approach.

2.1 Centroid and Contour representation

The sketch extracted from an original image can be characterized by a sequence of points belonging to its boundary. The base idea is as follows:

(1) The centroid

The first step is to determine the centroid C of an object, its coordinates (x_0, y_0) is computed by:

$$x_0 = \frac{\sum_{\forall pixel \in image} x \cdot S(x,y)}{m}, \quad y_0 = \frac{\sum_{\forall pixel \in image} y \cdot S(x,y)}{m} \tag{1}$$

$$m = \sum_{\forall pixel \in image} S(x,y)$$

where

$$S(x,y) = \begin{cases} 1 & \cdots\cdots if \quad pixel\,(x,y) \in contour \\ 0 & \quad\quad\quad\; pixel\,(x,y) \notin contour \end{cases}$$

(2) Boundary representation

Here, we have taken the centroid $C(x_0, y_0)$ of an object, and then the contour can be described by the following equations:

$$d = \sqrt{(x - x_0)^2 + (y - y_0)^2} \tag{2}$$

$$\theta = \begin{cases} \arctan(y - y_0 / x - x_0) & y - y_0 > 0, x - x_0 > 0 \\ \pi/2 & y - y_0 > 0, x - x_0 = 0 \\ \pi + \arctan(y - y_0 / \; x - x_0) & x - x_0 < 0 \\ 3\pi/2 & y - y_0 < 0, x - x_0 > 0 \\ 2\pi + \arctan(y - y_0 / \; x - x_0) & y - y_0 < 0, x - x_0 > 0 \end{cases} \tag{3}$$

The value of θ ranges from 0 to 2 π .

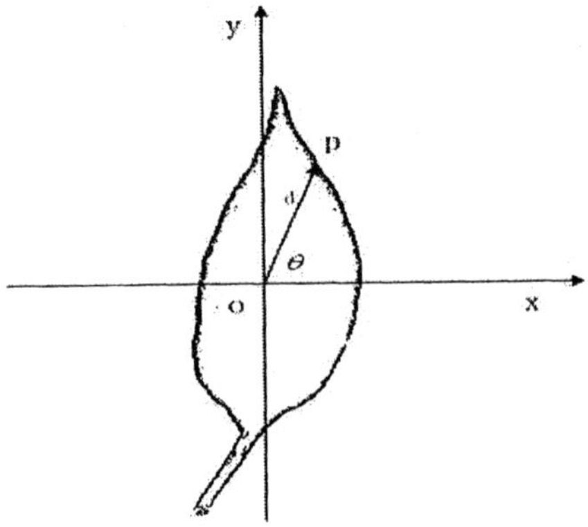

Figure 1

Consider the boundaries of the object as closed, the point P(x, y) on contour is determined by the centroid $C(x_0, y_0)$, the distance *d* between C and P, and the angel θ of the two points. Obviously, it is translation invariant. Finally, we can describe the object by the vector $< x_0, y_0, d_1, \theta_1, d_2, \theta_2 \cdots\cdots d_n, \theta_n >$.

2.2 Feature vector

As the method mentioned above is neither scaling nor rotation invariant, it can not be used for image retrieval effectively. The essential of achieving rotation invariant is to find the start point of the curve. Generally, the shape of a leaf is usually symmetrical. We choose the $\max\{d_1, d_2 \cdots d_n\}$ as the start point.

In a content based image retrieval system, the shape matching process efficiency is very essential, so a low dimension feature vector is needed. We can select fixed *k* pixels on a contour as the feature vector of an image.

The procedure of the algorithm is as follows:

1. Select the d_{max} as the start point, the corresponding angel of d_{max} is θ_{max}.
2. let $\Delta\theta = 2\pi / k$
3. SV[0] = d_{max};
   ```
   for(j=1; j<k; j++)
       SV[k] =0.0;
   ```
4. ```
   for(each (d_i, θ_i)) {
           for (j=1; j<=k; j++) {
            if (θ_i < θ_max) {
              if ((2π + θ_i - θ_max - j·Δθ)<0.01 ) {
                if(SV[j]!=0)
                   SV[j] = d_i;
   ```
   ```

```
            }
        }
        if (θi>θmax) {
            if ((θi - θmax- j·Δθ)<0.01 ) {
                if(SV[j]!=0)
                SV[j] = di;
            }
        }
    }
}
```

To improve efficiency, we reduce the *k* vertices to a lower dimensional vector. The least important sample point is removed every time, the process is repeated unless we get the desired shape representation. The importance of a sample point *p* is determined by:

$$K_p = \left|\frac{k_1 - k_2}{1 + k_1 k_2}\right| \cdot \frac{l_1 l_2}{l_1 + l_2} \tag{4}$$

Let p_1, p_2 be the neighbor point of *p*. k_1 is the slope of curve p_1p, l_1 is the length of p_1p, k_2 is the slope of curve pp_2, l_2 is the length of pp_2. The lower of the value of K_p, the less the point is important to the shape. For a closed contour, this method can generate a set of sampled points with the value {d, θ } that represents the boundary.

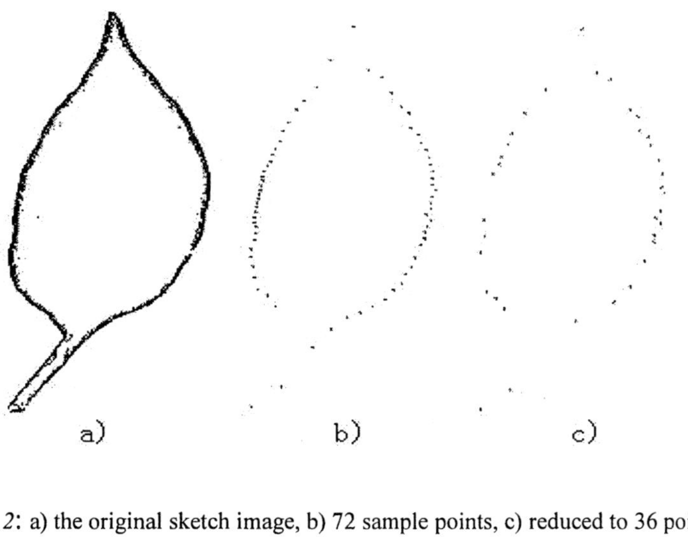

Figure 2: a) the original sketch image, b) 72 sample points, c) reduced to 36 points

2.3 Strategy before image matching

A query image Q and a database image D which is the same species of leaf may be different in size. We can normalize the curve value to range [0, 1] to make scaling invariant. The distance vector $SV[k]$ will be normalized to $SV'[k]$ by:

$$SV'[i] = \frac{SV[i]}{\max\{SV[0], SV[1] \cdots SV[k]\}} \qquad 1 \le i \le k \qquad (5)$$

Because image matching is a time-consuming task, we can use some simple feature to index the database images to be compared.

We use a shape feature, the ratio of d_{max} over d_{min}. The feature is calculated by:

$$R = \frac{d_{\max}}{d_{\min}} \qquad (6)$$

And the distance between image Q and D is computed by:

$$d_r(Q, D) = |R_Q - R_D| \qquad (7)$$

It is easy to verify that the ratio is translation, scaling and rotation invariant. This method can be used to score the similarity before the matching process. By this method, the whole database can be pruned to a small candidate set. This can significantly improve the matching efficiency.

2.4 Shape matching

The similarity between two images can be defined as the distance between their feature vectors, so that we can use the Euclidean distance function to measure their similarity. The function is as follows:

$$d_c(Q, D) = \sqrt{\sum_{i=1}^{k} (SV_Q{}'[i] - SV_D{}'[i])^2} \qquad (8)$$

where Q is the query image and D is the database image, k is the number of sample points.

But the method mentioned above does not guarantee if there is more than one maximum distance in the sample points. Motivated by the MCS method in [a study of shape-based image retrieval], we proposed a method to reduce this problem. The algorithm is described as follows:

1. select the top m maximum distances as the possible start points
2. calculate the $d_{ci}(Q,D)$, $1 \leq i \leq m$
3. the minimal distance $d_c = \min\{d_{c1}, d_{c2} \cdots d_{cm}\}$

3. EXPERIMENTS

We pluck leaves from plants, and then put a single leaf on a white panel and take photo of the leaf by a digital camera. In this way, the shape of a leaf will be presented and the background will be wiped off easily. Our image database includes 30 species, with 10 sample images in each species. Every image can be used as query. For every image, first the edge detector is adopted to get the sketch, then for every $2\pi / k$ (k = 72, 144, 216) orientation, k points on the contour are selected as the feature vector, finally the vector is reduced to a 36-dimentional vector by removing the unimportant points to the shape. Example is given in Figure 2.

For the image retrieval, give a query image and a value r of the number of the images to be ranked, let $r1$ be the number of images that are the same object with the query image and r_T be the number of images with same object in the database, the average precision is defined as $r/r1$, the average recall is defined as r/r_T. The system performs the similarity algorithm to recover the set of images that best match.

Fig.3 shows a good result with the query image at the left and the retrieved images at the right with 10 ranked images. Eight out of ten were the same with the query image.

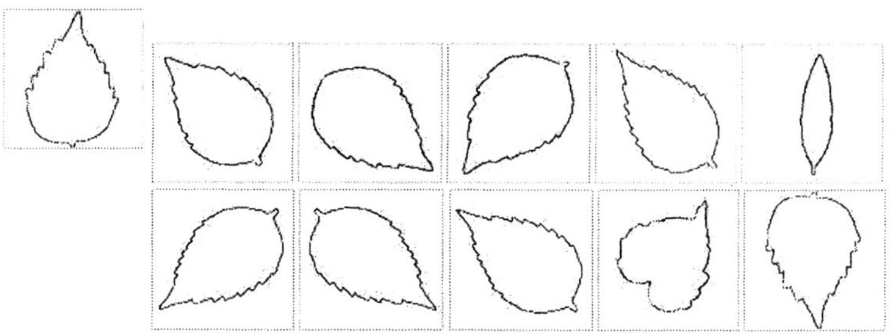

Figure 3

Table 1 lists the result compared with those of A. Hong in [9]. We can see that our proposed method is better. Table 2 shows the recall rate and precision with respect to different *k* sample points.

Table 1. Compared result

Feature	Return Images	Recall rate (%)
A.Hong's method	10	0.266
	30	0.533
Our Method	10	0.49
	30	0.65

Table 2. Recall rate and precision with different sample points

Number of Sample Points (10 return images)	Recall rate (%)	Precision (%)
72	0.43	0.72
144	0.51	0.74
216	0.54	0.78

4. CONCLUSIONS AND FUTURE WORK

This paper proposed a shape based method to retrieve leaf images. It discussed how to extract shape feature from sketch images and how to compare the feature vectors. The method is implemented and evaluated in order to analyze its effectiveness and efficiency.

Future work is to include more features to improve the performance of our method and extend our method to handle broken leaves.

ACKNOWLEDGEMENT

This research has been supported by the Academician Foundation of Xiamen University.

REFERENCES

[1] Marinette Bouet, Ali Khenchaf, Henri Briand, "Shape representation for image retrieval," Proceedings of the seventh ACM international conference on Multimedia (Part 2), pp: 1 – 4, 1999

[2] Hwei-Jen Lin, Yang-Ta Kao, Shwu-Huey Yen, Chia-Jen Wang, "A Study of Shape-Based Image Retrieval," 24th International Conference on Distributed Computing Systems Workshops, pp. 118-123, 03 23 - 03, 2004

[3] H Freeman, "On the encoding of arbitrary geometric configurations," IEEE Trans. Electron. Comput., vol. 10, no. 2, pp. 260–268, 1961.

[4] H Freeman and L S Davis, "A corner finding algorithm for chain coded curves," IEEE Transactions on computers, vol. 26, pp. 297–303, 1977.

[5] C T Zahn and R Z Roskies, "Fourier descriptors for plane closed curves," IEEE Trans. Comput., vol. C-21, no. 3, pp. 269–281, 1972.

[6] E Peerson and K S Fu, "Shape discrimination using Fourier descriptor," IEEE Trans. Syst., Man, Cybern., vol. SMC-7, no. 3, pp. 170–179, 1977.

[7] T. Bernier, J.A. Landry, A new method for representing and matching shapes of natural objects. Pattern Recognition 36(2003) 1711-1723.

[8] H. Nishida, Structural feature indexing for retrieval of partially visible shapes. Pattern Recognition 35(2002) 55-67.

[9] A. Hong, G. Chen, J. Li, Z. Chi, and D. Zhang, "A Flower Image Retrieval Method Based on ROI Feature," Journal of Zhejiang University (Science) Vol. 5, No. 7, pp.764-772, July 2004.

[10] Rui, Y., She, AC, and Huang, T.S. Modified Fourier Descriptors for Shape Representation - A Practical Approach. Proc. of First Int'l Workshop on Image Databases and Multi Media Search, Amsterdam, The Netherlands, 1996.

[11] D. Shen and H.H.S. Ip, "Generalized affine invariant image normalization," IEEE Transaction on Pattern Analysis and Machine Intelligence, vol. 19, no. 5, pp.431-440, 1997.

[12] C. S. Fuh and H. B. Liu, "Projection for Pattern Recognition," Image and Vision Computing, vol. 16, pp. 677-687, 1998.

[13] E. Klassen, A. Srivastava, W. Mio, and S. Joshi, "Analysis of Planar Shapes Using Geodesic Paths on Shape Spaces," IEEE Trans. Pattern Analysis and Machine Intelligence, vol. 26, no. 3, pp. 372-383, Mar. 2004.

PERFORMANCE COMPARISON OF LANGUAGE MODELS FOR INFORMATION RETRIEVAL

Shuaixiang Dai, Qian Diao and Changle Zhou
Department of Computer Science and Technology, Xiamen University, 361005, Xiamen, Fujian,China; Intel China Research Center, 100087, Beijing, China

Abstract: Vector Space Model (VSM), Statistical Language Model (SLM) and Inference Network are three distinguished language models. Instead of evaluating their performance directly, we estimate the information strategies founded on them using the known measures: precision and recall. What's more, we proposed the Sort Order Rationality (SOR) to make further performance comparison among different language models. All models are tested on a standard testing collection. Three important conclusions are attained:

(1). The IR model combining the statistical language modeling and inference network approaches is better than that only founded on statistical language modeling approach. What's more, it is also better than that based on vector space modeling approach.

(2). The performance of IR model based on VSM is similar to that based on SLM.

(3). The *Dirichlet priors* method often is a better option to smooth a statistical language model.

In some respects, these conclusions provide some experimental bases for constructing an efficient information retrieval system.

Key words: language model, language modeling approach, information retrieval

1. INTRODUCTION

While the language modeling approaches, or more simple the language models are more and more wildly used in nature language process, in particular, some new approaches to text information retrieval based on language modeling methods have emerged, which are quite different from traditional probabilistic approaches, and are fundamentally different from vector space methods, one of the attractive aspects of the language modeling approach is the potential for estimating the document model or document-to-query translation model in different ways. This paper supplies the performance comparison of the popular language models by means of evaluating the information retrieval strategies based on them. It's maybe beneficial to the search engine builder.

2. LANGUAGE MODELS FOR IR

There are a lot of language modeling approaches have been proposed such as vector space model (VSM), statistical language model (SLM), inference network and latent semantic analysis (LSA) etc. So there also occur lots of information retrieval (IR) strategies based on them. For example, tf*idf[1] approach and cosine similarity model founded on VSM, Okapi[2] and KL-divergence[3, 4] belonging to SLM, and Indri model[5] using inference network with statistical language modeling probabilities. Retrieval strategies on the basis of language modeling assign a measure of similarity between a document and a query. Commonly, the strategies are based on the notion that the more often terms occur in both the document and the query, the more "relevant" the document is deemed to be to the query.

A retrieval strategy is an algorithm that takes a query q and a set of documents $d_1, d_2, \cdots, d_n$, and scores the Similarity Coefficient of them by some $SC(q, d_i)$ $(1 \le i \le n)$ function for each of the documents. In general, any approach to the retrieval problem is decomposed into three basic components: (1) query representation; (2) document representation; and (3) matching of query representation and document representation.

2.1 TF*IDF

The vector space model has been widely used in the traditional IR field and most web search engines. Both documents and queries are represented by vectors, which are sets of terms with associated weights. A vector similarity function, such as the inner product, can be used to compute the similarity between a document and a query.

We assume each document and each query are represented by a term frequency vector $\bar{d} = (x_1, x_2, \cdots, x_n)$ and $\bar{q} = (y_1, y_2, \cdots, y_n)$ respectively, where n is the total number of terms or the size of vocabulary and x_i, y_i are the frequencies (i.e., the counts) of term t_i in d and q respectively. Given a collection C, where N is the total number of documents in C and n_t is the number of documents with term t. All terms in a query or a document are weighted by the heuristic TF*IDF weighting formula:

$$w_{t,d} = tf(x)idf(t)$$

Where $tf(x) = c(x)$ and $idf(t) = \log\frac{N}{n_t}$.
So the weighted vectors for $\overline{d}$ and $\overline{q}$ are:

$$\overline{d} = (tf_d(x_1)idf(t_i), tf_d(x_1)idf(t_i), \cdots, tf_d(x_n)idf(t_n))$$

$$\overline{q} = (tf_q(y_1)idf(t_i), tf_q(y_1)idf(t_i), \cdots, tf_q(y_n)idf(t_n))$$

The score of document $\overline{d}$ against query $\overline{q}$ is given by

$$s(\overline{d},\overline{q}) = \sum_{i=1}^{n} tf_d(x_i)tf_q(y_i)idf(t_i)^2$$

2.2 Cosine similarity model

Cosine similarity measures the cosine of the angle between two vectors. Thinking of a document or a query as a vector, similarity is the angle between two vectors. The bigger angle indicates less similarity. In this case long documents do not have an unfair advantage any more. The similarity depends on pattern of word use but not on document length; every document is most similar to itself. Cosine similarity between vectors for document $\vec{d_j}$ and query $\vec{q}$ is:

$$w(\vec{d_j},\vec{q}) = \frac{\vec{d_j} \bullet \vec{q}}{\left|\vec{d_j}\right| \cdot \left|\vec{q}\right|} = \frac{\sum_{i=1}^{n}(w_{i,j}w_{i,q})}{\sqrt{\sum_{i=1}^{n} w_{i,j}^2 \sum_{i=1}^{n} w_{i,q}^2}}$$

Where $w_{i,j}$ is the weight of term i in document j. The inner product is often used to normalize the term weight. If the $w_{i,j}$ is the unnormalized weight, the normalized weight $w'_{i,j}$ is given by

$$w'_{i,j} = \frac{w_{i,j}}{\sqrt{\sum_j w_{i,j}^2}}$$

2.3 Okapi

Okapi is the name given to a family of experimental retrieval systems [6, 7]. It is based on the Robertson-Sparck Jones probabilistic model of searching [8]. A detailed summary of the contributions to TREC-1~9 by the Okapi system is presented in [9, 10]. Unlike TF*IDF, the Okapi method not only considers the frequency of the query terms, but also the average length of the whole collection and the length of the document under evaluation. The similarity can also be described as the inner product of the query vector and the document vector. The Okapi weighting function is based on the Robertson-Sparck Jones weight [8]:

$$w^{(idf)} = \log \frac{(r+0.5)/(R-r+0.5)}{(n-r+0.5)/(N-n-R+0.5)}$$

where N is the number of documents in the collection, n is the number of documents containing the term, R is the number of documents relevant to a specific topic, and r is the number of relevant documents containing the term. This weight reduces to an inverse document frequency (IDF) weight without relevance information (when $R = r = 0$).
The Okapi TF formula is implemented as

$$w^{(tf)} = \frac{(k_1+1)tf}{(K+tf)}$$

$$K = k_1((1-b)+b\frac{dl}{avdl})$$

The TF formula with query modification as relevance feedback is

$$w^{(tf)} = \frac{(k_1+1)tf}{(K+tf)} \cdot \frac{(k_3+1)qtf}{(k_3+qtf)}$$

where tf is the frequency of occurrence of the term within a specific document; qtf is the frequency of occurrence of the term within a specific query; dl and $avdl$ are respectively the document length and the average document length measured in arbitrary units, such as word or a sequence of words; and k_i, b are the constants used in BM functions(Best-match weighting function).
The Okapi weighting function (BM25) is

$$w_{t,d} = w^{(tf)} w^{(idf)}$$

which describes the contribution of term t to the relevance of document d.

2.4 KL-divergence retrieval model

The KL-divergence retrieval model essentially scores a document by computing the KL-divergence between the query language model and the document language model, in fact, which is the relative entropy of the query model with respect to the document model. The KL-divergence retrieval model was introduced in [11] as a special case of the more general risk minimization retrieval framework. Interestingly, it is similar to the vector space model, except that it uses probabilistic models, rather than ordinary term vectors to represent a document or a query.

Given two probability mass functions $p(x)$ and $q(x)$, the Kullback-Leibler divergence (or relative entropy) between p and q, denoted $D(p \| q)$, is defined as

$$D(p \| q) = \sum_x p(x) \log \frac{p(x)}{q(x)}$$

The relevance value of a document with respect to a query can be measured by the following KL-divergence function:

$$D(\hat{\theta}_Q \| \hat{\theta}_D) = -\sum_{\omega} p(\omega | \hat{\theta}_Q) \log p(\omega | \hat{\theta}_D) + cons(q)$$

$$cons(q) = -\sum_{\omega} p(\omega | \hat{\theta}_Q) \log p(\omega | \hat{\theta}_Q)$$

where $\hat{\theta}_Q$ and $\hat{\theta}_D$ are the estimated query and document language models respectively; $cons(q)$ is the entropy of the query model, which is a document-independent constant, can be dropped.

To avoid simple counting zero probabilities, we can introduce some smoothing methods to smooth the language model. Assume the general form of a smoothed model to be the following:

$$p(\omega | d) = \begin{cases} p_s(\omega | d) & \text{if word } \omega \text{ is seen} \\ \alpha_d p(\omega | C) & \text{otherwise} \end{cases}$$

where $p_s(\omega | d)$ is the smoothed probability of a word seen in the document is, $p(\omega | C)$ is the collection language model, and α_d is a coefficient controlling the probability mass assigned to unseen words, so that all probabilities sum to one. The representative smoothing methods include *the Jelinek-Mercer method*, *Bayesian smoothing using Dirichlet priors* and *absolute discounting*, which are detailed in [12].

2.5 Indri model

Unlike above statistical language models, Indri model combines the statistical language modeling [14, 15] and inference network [16] approaches to information retrieval. The resulting model allows structure queries similar to those used in INQUERY to be evaluated using language modeling estimates within the network, rather than *tf*idf* estimates. Figure 1 shows a graphical model representation of the network. As in the original inference network framework, documents are ranked according to $P(I | D, \alpha, \beta)$, the belief the information need I is met given document D and hyperparameters α and β as evidence.

Typically, in the statistical language modeling framework, a document is represented as a sequence of terms (tokens). Based on this sequence, a multinomial language model over the vocabulary is estimated. However, In Indri model, documents are represented as multisets of binary feature vectors. Each document is estimated by a multiple-Bernoulli model [17]. The multiple-Bernoulli model imposes the assumption that the features (r_i's) are independent, which of course may be a poor assumption depending on the feature set.

Indri model takes a Bayesian approach and imposes a multiple-Beta prior over the model (θ). The Beta is chosen for simplicity, as it is the conjugate prior to the Bernoulli distribution. Thus, $P(D \mid \theta) \sim MultiBernoulli(\theta)$ and $P(\theta \mid \alpha, \beta) \sim MultiBeta(\alpha, \beta)$. The belief at node θ is given by

$$P(\theta_i \mid D, \alpha, \beta) = \frac{P(D \mid \theta_i) P(\theta_i \mid \alpha_i, \beta_i)}{\int_{\theta_i} P(D \mid \theta_i) P(\theta_i \mid \alpha_i, \beta_i)} = Beta(\#(r_i, D) + \alpha_i, |D| - \#(r_i, D) + \beta_i)$$

for each i, $\#(r_i, D)$ is the number of times, feature r_i is set to 1 in document D's multiset of feature vectors.

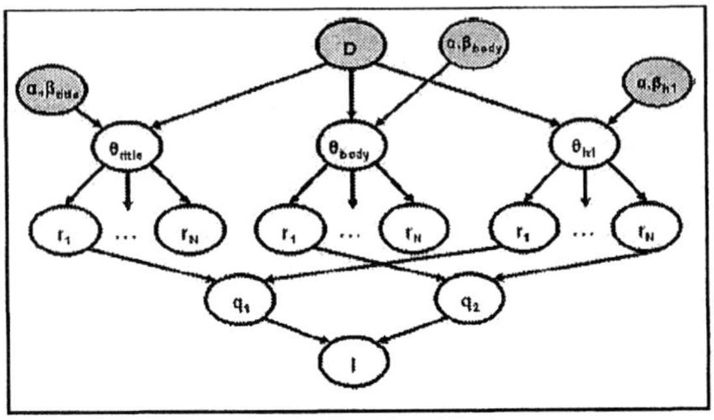

Figure 1. Indri's inference network retrieval model

3. EVALUATIONS AND COMPARISONS

To estimate a statistical language modeling approach for IR, In 1998 Ponte and Croft proposed using a smoothed version of the document unigram model to assign a score to a query, which can be thought of as the probability that the query was generated from the document model. This simple approach was remarkably effective. As developed further in [13]. In our experiments, we use three smoothed versions of KL-divergence and evaluated them respectively. Some known measures are taken, as well as a new but effective evaluation criterion.

3.1 Experimental Setup

We develop the evaluating programs based on Lemur Toolkit [18] and carry out a series of experiments. The English testing collection is CACM database (3204 documents, 64 queries and their answer set) that comes from Lemur downloading package. Sixty four queries with the right answers are also included and put to evaluate above language models. The following performance measures are considered in our evaluation:

- Non-interpolated average precision
- Interpolated precision at different recall levels
- Sort order by score of relevant document

Because some models are very similar in principle, their retrieval results are also very alike in precision. To distinguish the performance of these models clearly, we introduce the sort order by score of relevant documents to evaluate their retrieval performance at a different angle. Assuming a query q and a set of documents D, the Similarity Coefficient of q and d_i $(d_i \in D, 1 \le i \le n)$ is represented by $SC(q,d_i)$, we normalize the similarity coefficient by

$$s(q,d_i) = \frac{SC(q,d_i) - Min_{sc}}{Max_{sc} - Min_{sc}}$$

where Max_{sc} is the maximum in all $SC(q,d_i)$ $(1 \le i \le n)$, Min_{sc} is the minimum. The Sort Order Rationality (SOR) is defined as

$$SOR(q,D) = \frac{\sum_{j=1}^{R} s_j}{M}$$

For each j, s_j is the normalized similarity coefficient between q and one of its relevant documents $d_j (1 \le j \le n)$. R is count of relevant documents in retrieval result set. M is the count of documents relevant to query q in document collection.

The Sort Order Rationality (SOR) indicates the rational degree of sort order of relevant documents in retrieval result set. It also reflects the performance of IR model to some extent. If the relevant documents line in the front of all retrieval result documents, i.e. only retrieval less documents we can attain all relevant documents. If so, we think this kind of result is better. Thus the bigger the SOR value is, the more rational the result is, and the better performance the model shows.

For getting the true performance of above models, we use the simplest form of each model; don't consider feedback and other improvements over parameters. Especially, to Okapi, we set k_1=1.2, b=0.75 and k_3=7, which are suggested by Robertson in [19].

When using Indri to retrieval information, we also take *Dirichlet priors* to smooth the probabilistic model.

3.2 Results and Discussions

To every query, we compute all precisions and recalls when returning different number of result documents, for example from 1 to 1000. We attain the non-interpolated average precisions of all models, as follows.

Table 1, Comparison of average precisions

Models	Indri	KL-Dir	KL-JM	Okapi	TF*IDF	Cosine	KL-Abs
Average Precision	0.3481	0.3354	0.3207	0.3095	0.3057	0.2532	0.2459

From all recall-precision pairs computed above, we calculate 11 interpolated precisions when recall equals 0, 0.1, 0.2,···, 1 respectively, and attain the following diagram.

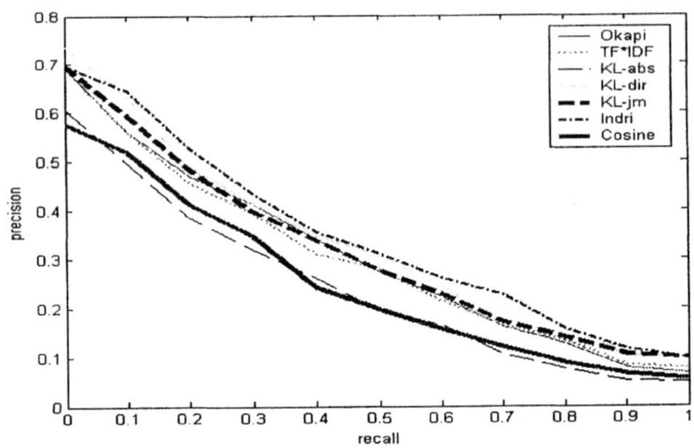

Figure 3. Interpolated recall-precision curves

From table 1 and figure 3, we can see that Indri model displays the best performance, but the Cosine and KL-Abs are contrary, they have the worse performance. The precisions of the TF*IDF, Okapi, KL-divergence smoothed by *Dirichlet priors* and KL-divergence smoothed by *Jelinek-Mercer method* are close, so are their performances.

In fact, whether TF*IDF, Okapi or KL-divergence smoothed by *Dirichlet priors* or *Jelinek-Mercer* is based on how often the term appears or does not appear in relevant documents and non-relevant documents. The betterment of weighting function can't bring essential improvement of performance, little if anything. This is why these models all return the similar precisions.

Indri not only use inference network but also add statistical language modeling probabilities, as compare with other models, it gives more information when retrieval. This may be one of the reasons why the performance of Indri model is best in our experiments.

To KL-divergence, different smoothing method brings different performance. It's obvious that *Dirichlet priors is* the best option to smooth a model.

Since the TF*IDF, Okapi, KL-divergence smoothed by *Dirichlet priors* and KL-divergence smoothed by *Jelinek-Mercer method* display the similar performance, we use average SOR to make further comparison. The average SOR of these models are given by Table 2.

Table 2, Average sort order rationalities when returning 1000 result documents

Models	KL-Abs	Okapi	KL-Dir	Indri	KL-JM	TF*IDF	Cosine
Average SOR	0.4309	0.4032	0.3977	0.3847	0.3582	0.3159	0.2819

From the table 2, we can see the average SOR values of Okapi and KL-Dir are close; in addition their precisions are also close, so we can consider their performances are alike. But their performances are better than those of KL-JM and TF*IDF, because SOR values of the former are bigger than those of the latter.

4. CONCLUSION

Lots of Language models are proposed and used in natural language process, especially in information retrieval. What's more, previous works showed all the models are effective respectively. However, these works did not tell us which one of them was better than other. In this paper, we selected five representative language models and designed a serious of experiments to compare the performance between them. The following points are concluded after the experiments:

The Indri model which combines the statistical language modeling and inference network approaches is better than that only founded on statistical language modeling (SLM) approach. What's more, it is also better than that based on vector space modeling (VSM) approach.

The performance of IR model based VSM is similar to that based on SLM.

The *Dirichlet priors* method often is a better option to smooth a statistical language model.

In some respects these conclusions are important to construct a high-powered information retrieval system; they also provide experimental bases for designing an efficient search engine.

ACKNOWLEDGEMENTS

Most of this work was done while the author was visiting Intel China Research Center; we thank Liu Juan and Zhang Yiming who is leader of

Scalable Statistical Computing Group at Intel China Research Center for discussing some issues about this paper.

REFERENCES

[1] Gerard Salton and M. J. McGill (1983): *Introduction to Modern Information Retrieval*, New York: McGraw-Hill.
[2] Robertson, S. et al. Okapi at TREC-3. Proceedings of the 3rd Text Retrieval Conference, 1994, pp 109-126.
[3] Zhai, C. and Lafferty, J. *Model-based feedback in the KL-divergence retrieval model*. In Tenth International Conference on Information and Knowledge Management (CIKM 2001), pages 403–410.
[4] C. Zhai and J. Lafferty, Model-based feedback in the language modeling approach to information retrieval, Tenth International Conference on Information and Knowledge Management (CIKM 2001), 2001.
[5] Metzler, D., Strohman T., Turtle H., and Croft, W.B., "Indri at TREC 2004: Terabyte Track" in the Online Proceedings of 2004 Text Retrieval Conference (TREC 2004).
[6] Special issue of Journal of Documentation 53 (1), 1997.
[7] Okapi projects home page. Available at http://web.soi.city.ac.uk/research/cisr/okapi/okapi.html.
[8] Robertson, S.E. and Sparck Jones, K. Relevance weighting of search terms. *Journal of the American Society or Information Science 27,* 1976, 129-146.
[9] Robertson, S.E. and Walker, S. (1999). Okapi/Keenbow at TREC-8. In TREC-9.
[10] Robertson, S.E. and Walker, S. (2000). Microsoft Cambridge at TREC-9: Filtering track. In TREC-9.
[11] J. Lafferty and C. Zhai. Document language models, query models, and risk minimization for information retrieval. In 24th ACM SIGIR Conference on Research and Development in Information Retrieval (SIGIR'01), 2001.
[12] C. Zhai and J. Lafferty. A study of smoothing methods for language models applied to ad hoc information retrieval, In *24th ACM SIGIR Conference on Research and Development in Information Retrieval* (SIGIR'01), 2001.
[13] A. Berger and J. Lafferty, Information retrieval as statistical translation, in Proceedings of the *1999 ACM SIGIR Conference on Research and Development in Information Retrieval*, pages 222-229, 1999.
[14] W. B. Croft and J. Lafferty. *Language Modeling for Information Retrieval*. Kluwer, 2003.
[15] J. M. Ponte and W. B. Croft. A language modeling approach to information retrieval. In *SIGIR 1998*, pp. 275–281.
[16] H. Turtle and W. B. Croft. Evaluation of an inference network based retrieval model. *TOIS*, 9(3):187–222, 1991.
[17] D. Metzler, V. Lavrenko, and W. B. Croft. Formal multiple Bernoulli models for language modeling. In *SIGIR 004*, pp. 540–541.
[18] http://www.lemurproject.org/.
[19] S.E. Robertson, and S.Walker (2000), "Okapi/Keenbow at TREC-8," in E. Voorhees and D.K. Harman (editors), The Eighth Text REtrieval Conference (TREC-8), NIST Special Publication 500-246.

RESEARCH ON PREDICTION ABOUT FRUIT TREE DISEASES AND INSECT PESTS BASED ON NEURAL NETWORK

Gang Liu[1], Hongyan Shen[1], Xuehong Yang[1], Yinbing Ge[2]
1 China Agricultural University, Beijing, P.R. China pac@cau.edu.cn

2 Currently study in Utah State University, Logan, UT, USA

Abstract: Fruit tree diseases and insect pests always occur which are related to weather. According to weather information and occurrence status of fruit tree diseases and insect pests in orchards of the Qixia county for 11 years, the MATLAB neural network toolbox was used to build up the prediction system about fruit tree diseases and insect pests based on Back Propagation (BP) neural network. Then the system was trained by the history record data. Finally, the ring spot, a fruit tree disease, was chosen as the research object to compare the predicted value with the actual value. The results indicate that the system can predict accurately, run fast, and function robustly. The system can be applied for prediction about fruit tree diseases and insect pests.

Key words: neural network, MATLAB, diseases and insect pests prediction

1. INTRODUCTION

Since the 90s of the 20th century, fruit tree diseases and insect pests in our country has occurred frequently, disaster area has increased by 30% compared with the status of the 80s, and the average yield loss per year has been more than 25%. In recent years, pesticide is used mainly to control fruit tree diseases and insect pests and is used superfluously and abusively. It has influenced the fruit quality badly and endangered the human health. Every country in the world has started to pay more and more attention to it. During the "ten$_{th}$ five-year plan" period, our country put forward the policy of "prevention is primary combining with management" to control the agriculture disaster. A lot of plant disaster monitor and forecast stations have been established in many areas. However, the prediction function of these stations did not work well because the prediction technique was behindhand and the prediction accuracy was low. Therefore, the monitor, prediction, control and decision-making technology based on artificial intelligence have become the principal research direction in the prediction about fruit tree diseases and insect pests in our country.

Yantai city is one of the important areas to plant fruit tree in the north of our country. There are a variety of fruit tree diseases and insect pests in a wide range of areas. Recently, intelligentized information technology has been applied in research and practice of plant protection. Because the weather conditions are important factors to the occurrence and development of fruit tree diseases and insect pests, most expert systems depend on probability analysis from the history data and lead to imprecise diagnosis and prediction.

Artificial neural network (ANN) can simulate, to some extent, how neural network in human brain deals with, searches and stores information. ANN can obtain knowledge expediently and quickly, organize and study by itself, be adapted to environment changes and deal with nonlinear problems. Based on Back Propagation (BP) neural network, MATLAB neural network toolboxes were used in this paper to establish a prediction system about fruit tree diseases and insect pests. The system can predict the occurrence of fruit tree diseases and insect pests according to the weather data from 1992 to 2002 and the occurrence situation of diseases and insect pests in Qixia county of Yantai city.

2. MATERIALS AND METHODS

2.1 Data Acquisition

There are many kinds of fruit tree diseases and insect pests such as foulbrood, fruit rotted disease, defoliated disease, ring spot, mite, lyonetid moth, aphide, fruit moth in Qixia county of Yantai city. Weather, biological, spatial data, etc. are mainly used in the diagnosis and prediction about fruit tree diseases and insect pests. The weather data including average temperature, rainfall, rainfall days, air humidity, wind speed and wind direction are obtained from April to August from 1992 to 2002 in Qixia county weather station. Correspondingly, fruit tree diseases and insect pests occurrence situation were obtained from May to September every year by searching data and consulting experts in plant protection. This research is completed with the cooperation of the agriculture information center in Yantai city.

2.2 The Construction of Artificial Neural Network

Three-layer ANN is the most widely applied in the field of diagnose and prediction. Figure 1 shows the ANN model. The standard three-layer network topological structure is made up of input layer, hidden layer and output layer. The nonlinear mapping from input to output is realized by using connective weight matrixes from input layer to hidden layer and from hidden layer to output layer. ANN always adopts BP algorithm. After the neural network is trained with samples, the connective weight values such as W_{ij} and W_{jk} among neural nodes are adjusted constantly according to errors between expectation and actual output. Eventually, the output of network, determined by W_{ij} and W_{jk}, come close to the expectation in desired precision. Hence, the self-study of ANN can be well solved.

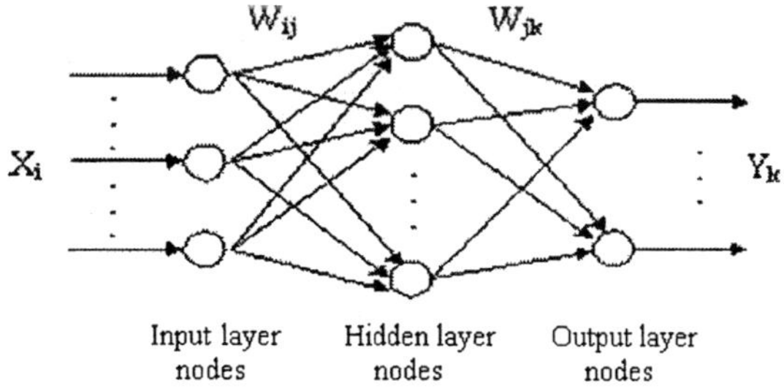

Figure 1 Artificial neural network model

2.2.1 The Study Algorithm of BP Artificial Neural Network

BP ANN study algorithm adopts gradient descent. The basic idea of this algorithm is to change the network weight values according to the minimum value of the sum-square error between expectation and actual output.

Error function J(W) is defined as follows :

$$J(W) = \frac{1}{2}(Y(k) - \overline{Y}(W,k))^2 \tag{1}$$

where, $Y(k)$ is the expectation, $\overline{Y}(W,k)$ is the actual output of the neural network, and W is the vector consisting of all weight values in the network. Gradient descent is to revise the value of $W(k)$ along the negative gradient descent of $J(W)$ till $J(W)$ reaches the minimum. It is expressed mathematically as:

$$W(k+1) = W(k) + p(k)(-\frac{\partial J(W)}{\partial W})\Big|_{W=W(k)} \tag{2}$$

where, $p(k)$ is the variable controlling the revised speed of weight values.

In the nth iterative output of BP ANN, $y_{j(n)}$ is the jth neural cell output, and $d_{j(n)}$ is the corresponding output (it can be provided by training sample). The error in this neural cell is:

$$e_j(n) = d_j(n) - y_j(n) \tag{3}$$

Square error in the neural cell j is $\frac{1}{2}e_j^2(n)$. The sum-square error in output is:

$$E(n) = \frac{1}{2}\sum_{j\in c} e_j^2(n) \tag{4}$$

where, c contains all of output neural cells, and n is the total number of training samples. The average of square error is:

$$E_{AV} = \frac{1}{N}\sum_{n=1}^{N} E(n) \tag{5}$$

where, E_{AV} is the study object function. The purpose of the study is to make E_{AV} minimum.

2.2.2 The Node Number in Hidden Layer

The node number in hidden layer is related to the complexity of problems and can directly influence the network nonlinear capability. It can be increased to improve the network training precision. This system uses experiential formula as follows to determine the node number in hidden layer:

$$p = \begin{cases} n + 0.618(n - m) & n >= m \\ m - 0.618(m - n) & n < m \end{cases} \tag{6}$$

where, n is the input node number, m is the output node number, and p is the hidden node number.

2.2.3 The Study Parameters in Artificial Neural Network

1. The Initialized Weight Values

Before study, the network must be initialized. Initialization is mainly to set random numbers less than 1 to all connective weight values between neural nodes in BP ANN model. Since the system is nonlinear, initialized weights have an effect on whether the study reaches partial minimum and converges and how long the training takes. Generally, it is expected that the output of every neural node comes close to 0 after the weights are added. In this way, it can ensure that the weight value of every neural node can be adjusted when their Sigmoid active functions change. Therefore, the initialized values are commonly random number within [-1, 1]. The research and experiment have shown, if the initialized values are mostly selected around 0, the network might not converge. In this system, the initialized weight values within [-5, 5] are set so as to accelerate convergence.

2. The Learning Rate

The learning rate determines the variety of weight values produced in each cycle. Higher learning rate may lead to instability of the system. Lower learning rate may make the training longer and convergence rate slower. The learning rate is associated with the network size that indicates the node number of input and output in the network. Based on experiential formula, η_0 is chosen as the initialized value of learning rate η.

$$\eta_0 = \frac{1}{\sqrt{p}} \tag{7}$$

where, p is the node number in hidden layer.

During the study, the iterative times obviously decreases when η increases. Therefore, dynamic adjustment is utilized to control learning rate in this system. When learning rate lowers, η is increased slowly. When the network is emanative, η is decreased quickly. The algorithm is as follows:

When E(t)-E(t-1)>0.05E(t-1), the network converges quickly and each value keeps invariable;

When E(t)-E(t-1)<0, the network is emanative, and $\eta=\eta/2$;

When 0<E(t)-E(t-1)<0.05 E(t-1), the convergence rate of the network is slow, and $\eta=1.3*\eta$.

2.2.4 The Pretreatment of Sample Data

Since data are not always in the same dimension, they should be mapped within [-1,1] and normalized. This can improve the training speed of neural network. The algorithm is as follows:

$$x' = \frac{x_{max} - x}{x_{max} - x_{min}} \tag{8}$$

where x' are the data after normalization, x are the raw data, x_{max} is the maximum value of the raw data and x_{min} is the minimum value of the raw data.

Because many weather factors influence the occurrence of fruit tree diseases and insect pests, several weather factors well related to fruit tree diseases and insect pests are selected for neural network prediction model through research and data analysis. These weather factors are average temperature, rainfall, rainfall days and air humidity from April to August during 1992-2002 in Qixia county. Correspondingly, the main kinds of fruit tree diseases and insect pests are foulbrood, fruit rotted disease, defoliated disease, ring spot, mite, lyonetid moth, aphide, fruit moth from May to September. Table 1 shows the data after normalization for fruit tree disease of ring spot in Qixia county in 1992. According to the normal grade issued by national station of plant protection, fruit tree diseases and insect pests grades contain: bad, less bad, intermediate, light, lighter and the normalization data are: 0.9, 0.7, 0.5, 0.3, 0.1.

Table 1. Sample data after normalization

Month	Average Temperature	Rainfall	Rainfall Days	Average Humidity	Grades)
4	0.832	0.765	0.942	0.941	0.1
5	0.517	0.592	0.623	0.768	0.5
6	0.396	0.401	0.590	0.352	0.9
7	0.204	0.232	0.383	0.310	0.3
8	0.096	0.130	0.095	0.024	0.1

3. RESULTS AND ANALYSIS

In terms of different growth seasons of fruit tree, several occurrence periods of fruit tree diseases and insect pests are distinguished. These prediction models for fruit tree diseases and insect pests in these growth seasons are made respectively. Forty neural network prediction models may be established according to weather factors from April to August, 5 prediction periods from May to September for fruit tree diseases and insect pests and 8 kinds of diseases and insect pests. However, some kinds of diseases and insect pests always occur in some centralized months, for example, the ring spot disease in Qixia county mainly occurs in June. Hence, only 14 neural network models are built up in this system.

Neural network prediction system uses MATLAB neural network toolbox to establish training program database, neural network weight and threshold value databases. These weight and threshold values have been trained successfully. For each neural cell subsystem, the node number in input layer is 4 and the input x_i ($i = 1\ldots4$) represents average temperature, rainfall, rainfall days, and air humidity respectively. The node number in output layer is 1 and y is used to present the occurrence grades of fruit tree diseases and insect pests, such as bad, less bad, middling, light, lighter. BP network algorithm provided by MATLAB is as follows:

p = [average temperature, rainfall, rainfall days, air humidity];

t = [occurrence grades of diseases and insect pests];

Initialized function is newff:

net = newff(minmax(p), [a, 1], {'Transig', 'Purelin'}, 'Trainlm');

This is to establish a three-layer BP network data structure called 'net'. The node number in hidden layer is 'a', and the recursion function is 'Transig'. The node number in output layer is 1, and the recursion function is 'Purelin'. The training algorithm function is 'Trainlm'. In this system, 'a' is selected as 6 according to eq. (6).

Before training, the parameters as follows must be evaluated and the others are set as default:

Maximum of training times: net.trainParam.epochs = 20000;

Minimum of grads difference: net.trainParam.min-grad = 0.01;

Goal value of accuracy: net.trainParam.goal = 0.01;

Display interval: net.trainParam.show = 100;

Initialized learning speed: net.trainParam.lr = 0.4;

Network training function is:

[net, tr] = train (net, p, t);

This function is to train the network and save the network structure into the array 'net'.

With the input of the weather data in May and the ring spot disease in June in Qixia county, the network is firstly initialized and then trained by function "Trainlm" for 18546 times. Eventually, the sum-square error of the network reaches the requirement of goal error. Figure 2 shows the change of, sum-square error during training. The curve indicates that sum-square error decreases with the increase of training times. When the error reaches the expectation, the training stops.

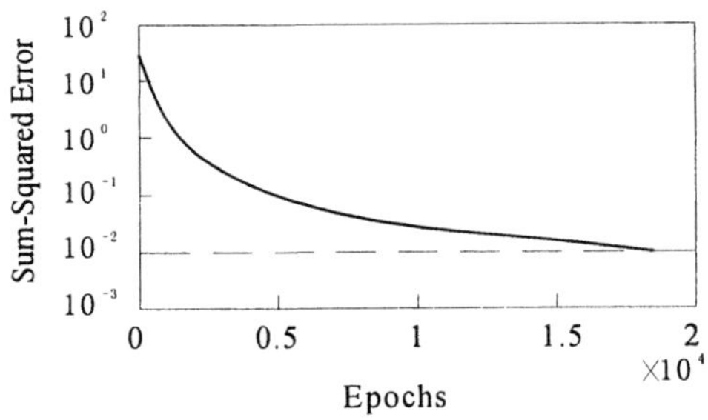

Figure 2 The change of sum-square error with training times

The data of weather and fruit tree diseases and insect pests from 1992 to 2000 are selected as the raw data of network training and the data from 2001 to 2002 are selected as validation data. Table 2 shows the comparison between the prediction value and the actual value about the ring spot disease in Qixia county in June 2001 and 2002.

Table 2 Comparison of Prediction Value with Actual Value

Month & Year	Prediction Value	Prediction Grades	Actual Value	Actual Value	Error Rate
2001.6	0.96427	Bad	0.9	Bad	7.14%
2002.6	0.76503	Less Bad	0.7	Less Bad	9.29%

Table 2 shows that the model error between the prediction value and the actual value is small. This indicates that the method is feasible in which MATLAB neural network toolbox is used to predict fruit tree diseases and insect pests based on BP network.

4. CONCLUSION

Based on the basic theory of artificial neural network, MATLAB neural network toolbox has been used to realize BP network algorithm in different conditions and to establish 14 neural network models. The prediction results are satisfactory from the comparison between the prediction value and the actual value of the ring spot disease in June 2001 and 2002. In this study, eight fruit tree diseases and insect pests are chosen as the research object and 4 weather factors are selected in every month as prediction condition. However, it is noteworthy to point out that the number of fruit tree diseases and insect pests increases with changes of climate and management of fruit tree in recent years. Different fruit tree diseases and insect pests are influenced by different weather factors. So the model in the research should be further improved correspondingly.

The prediction system about fruit tree diseases and insect pests takes the advantage of BP in prediction to avoid establishing complex mathematic models. After it is extended and improved, the system may be suitable for diagnosis and prediction of many kinds of crop diseases and insect pests and is valuable to be a reference.

ACKNOWLEDGEMENT

This program is supported by Chinese National Funded High Science and Technology Research Project (863 project) - the long-distance diagnosis platform of plant diseases and insect pests based on network 2002AA243031.

REFERENCES

[1] Mie Mie Thet Thwin, Tong-Seng Quah: Application of Neural Networks for Software Quality Prediction Using Object-Oriented Metrics. The Journal of Systems and Software. Vol. 76 (2005) 147-156

[2] D.Ashish, G.Hoogenboon, R.W.McClendon: Land-Use Classification of Gray-Scale Aerial Images Using Probabilistic Neural Networks. Transactions of the ASAS. Vol. 47(5)(2004) 1813-1820

[3] C.Yu, W.J.Northcott, G.F.McIsaac: Development of an Artificial Neural Network for Hydrologic and Water Quality Modeling of Agricultural Watersheds. Transactions of the ASAS. Vol. 47(1)(2004) 285-290

[4] L.O.Odhiambo, R.S.Freeland, R.E.Yoder, J.W.Hines: Investigation of a Fuzzy-Neural Network Application in Classification of Soils Using Ground-Penetrating Rader Imagery. Applied Engineering in Agriculture. Vol.20(1)(2004)109-118

[5] M.P.Bange, S.A.Deutscher, D.Larsen, D.Linsley, S.Whiteside: A Handheld Decision Support System to Facilitate Improved Insect Pest Management in Australian Cotton Systems. Computers and Electronics in Agriculture. Vol.43(2)(2004)131-148

[6] Lo.Tedeschi, D.G.Fox, P.J.Guiroy: A Decision Support System to Improve Individual Cattle Management. 1. A Mechanistic, Dynamic Model for Animal Growth. Agricultural System. Vol.79(2)(2004)171-204

[7] Mingyao Zhou, Hongwei Chen: Artificial Neural Network Model for Soil Moisture Forecast in Deficit Irrigation Rice Field. CIGR International Conference. Beijing, China (2004)

[8] Zailin Huo, Haibin Shi, Dongmei Qiao: Study on Artificial Neural Network Model for Crop Response to Soil Water-Salt. CIGR International Conference. Beijing, China (2004)

[9] Zhang X, Engel B. A., Benady N.: Locating Melons Using Artificial Neural Networks. ASAE Paper (1992)

[10] Muslim Abbas Zaidi, Haruhiko Murase: Evaluation of Seeding Vigour Using Neural Network Model under Clinostated Conditions. International Conference on Agricultural and Science and Technology. Beijing, China (2001) 504~507

[11] Xiumei Li, Xiaojun Qiao, Tao Ye: A New Fuzzy Neural Network Controller Applied in The Greenhouse. Progress of Information Technology in Agriculture. Beijing, China (2003) 546-549

[12] Hongchun Yuan, Fanlun Xiong: A Novel Approach For Extracting Rules from Trained Neural Network. International Symposium on Intelligent Agricultural Information Technology. Beijing, China (2000) 305~309

[13] S.T.Drummond, K.A. Sudduth, A.Joshi, N.R.Kitchen: Statistical and Neural Methods for Site-Specific Yield Prediction. Trans ASAE.(2003) 46(1):5-14

[14] Y.He, Q Zhang, L.Feng. Engine Real-time Fault Diagnosis Using Neural Networks. ASAE Paper No. 701P0502. Chicago, Illinois, (2002) USA:ASAE

[15] M.A Kramers, C.G.M. Conjin, C. Bastiaansen. An expert system for diagnosing flowerbulb diseases, pests and non-parasitic disorders. Agricultural systems, Vol58, No.1,PP 57-85, (1998)

RESEARCH ON PUBLISHING SYSTEM OF FRUIT TREE DISEASES AND INSECT PESTS BASED ON WEBGIS

Zhifang Yang [1], Gang Liu [2], Yongsheng Si [1]
1 Hebei Agricultural University, 071001, Baoding, China
2 China Agricultural University, 100083, Beijing, China

Abstract: A web publishing system of fruit tree diseases and insect pests was developed based on WebGIS. It can publish most of the new information of fruit tree diseases and insect pests with the spatial and zone features in the orchard. It can also make appropriate prevention and cure decision in time. This system provides many analysis methods, including spatial query, statistical analysis, buffer analysis, overlay analysis, predication analysis, expert diagnosis and so on. The system is developed as the B/S structure with Java Based on GIS platform ArcIMS.

Key words: publishing system, WebGIS, buffer analysis, ArcIMS

1. INTRODUCTION

The fruit tree diseases and insect pests in our country have occurred frequently in the past decade. The pesticide is the main means to control fruit tree diseases and insect pests, but it influences the fruit quantity badly and endangers the human health. Every country in the world has begun to pay more and more attention to it. In recent years, some expert systems for fruit tree diseases and insect pests were completed in our country. Because the occurrence and development of fruit tree diseases and insect pests have strong regionality, the expert systems did not work very well. Therefore, the technology based on '3S' has become the principal research direction in the management about fruit tree diseases and insect pests in our country.

Fruit tree diseases and insect pests firstly occur in some partial areas and then spread quickly and unevenly to neighborhood by the affect of weather conditions. These statuses of fruit tree diseases and insect pests are related to geography spatial position and are easily expressed by spatial analysis of GIS. The buffer analysis of GIS can help to analyze the spreading tendency and spatial distribution for fruit tree diseases and insect pests in a period. The overlay analysis model can help to analyze the spatial and temporal developing tendency for fruit tree diseases and insect pests in a district and find the main weather factors that are related to fruit tree diseases and insect pests.

The GIS platform ArcIMS was used to develop a publishing system of fruit tree diseases and insect pests based on the B/S structure with Java. The system can publish the most new information for fruit tree diseases and insect pests and can make appropriate prevention and cure decision in time. The system was demonstrated in Yantai city, Shandong Province.

2. SYSTEM DESIGN

2.1 System Framework

In recent years, the Internet has emerged as an extremely popular and effective means of sharing information, data, and technology. The tremendous growth in Internet use has resulted in an increased demand for the delivery of geographic data, maps, and applications over the Internet. A system is built on Windows 2000 operating system based on WebGIS technology to meet this growing demand. It is designed with a typical three-tier B/S (Browse/Server) and MVC (Model-View-Controller) design pattern and is particularly suitable for handling complicated user-interactive circumstance.

The typical three-tier B/S system structure (Fig.1) is composed of data layer, logic layer, and view layer, among which database oracle9i is used

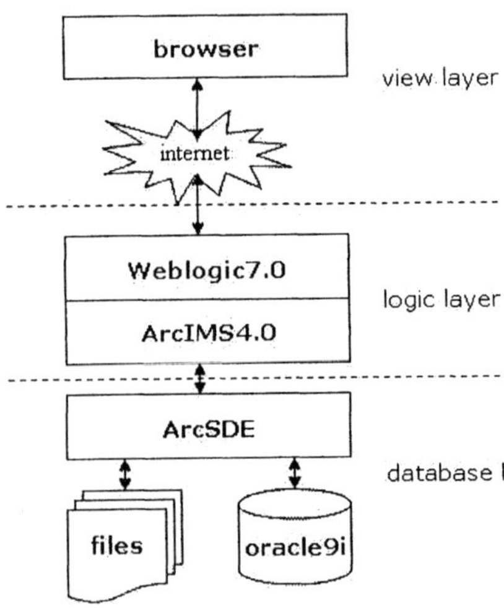

Fig.1 Three-tier system structure

for storing attribute data and spatial data and ArcSDE belongs to data layer. Logic layer includes ArcIMS server with Java technology and Weblogic used for Web server. ArcIMS is Internet Map Server software for building and delivering maps, data, designing, publishing, and administering mapping applications over Internet. It takes advantage of the Internet technology that makes it possible to share information and data with many users, either locally or around the world. With ArcIMS, large amounts of area map, data, and application service about fruit tree distribution of Yantai city can be built. ArcSDE works with oracle9i, it is the tool that allows to store and to manage spatial data related to fruit tree diseases and insect pests in orchard in the DBMS. It plays a fundamental role in a multi-user GIS, with which, ArcIMS can work directly with spatial data managed in DBMS.

Java MVC (Fig.2) design pattern allows the Web page to be mostly separated from the internal application code (Controller/Model) and makes it easier to focus on respective function. The Controller is responsible for allocating HTTP requests to the appropriate Model based on configuration mappings. The Model contains the business logic for the application. The Controller forwards the request to the appropriate View component, which is usually implemented by a combination of HTML with JavaScript and CSS. Java MVC design pattern is used to set up the system framework for data collecting, managing, analyzing and viewing.

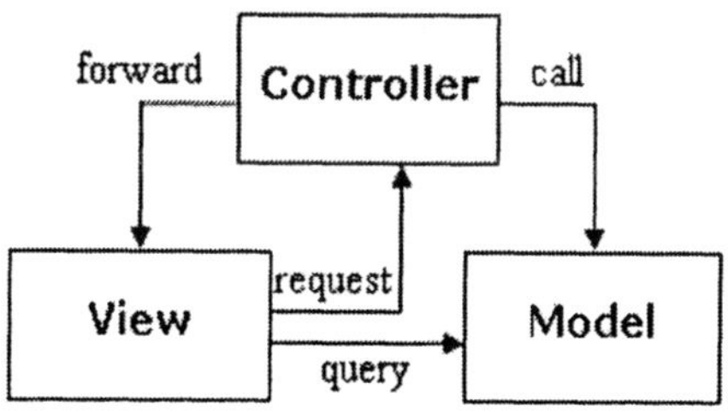

Fig.2 MVC design mode

2.2 System Main Function Modules

According to actual need, the system includes six big function models, shown as Fig.3:

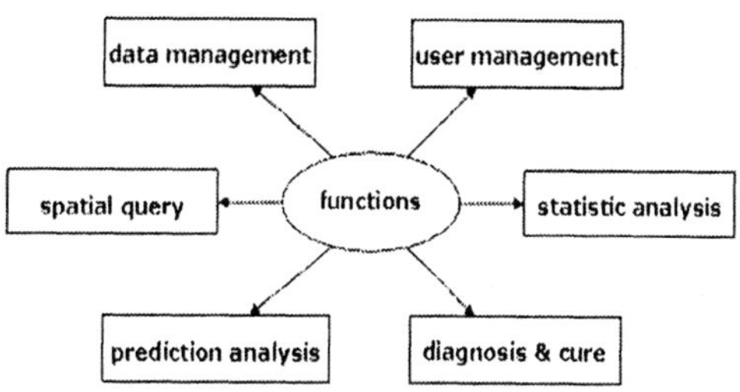

Fig.3 System functions

1. Data Management: the system needs the supports of multi-source data, which can be accessed from geographical spatial database, meteorological database, knowledge database of fruit tree diseases and insect pests and its real-time monitoring data.

2. User management: the users are classified as common users and administrators. The common users only have the browse right such as query, analysis, etc. But administrators not only have above right but also have right to manage data, including update, import, delete, and so on.

3. Spatial query: In this function model, map query is provided. A given zone is selected by clicking or drawing rectangle in map to get information for diseases and insect pests in orchard related to the selected zone. Besides, the attribute condition query is also included in this model. The information can be accessed after setting special conditions. The last query is the knowledge of fruit tree diseases and insect pests in orchard.

4. Statistics analysis: The aim of statistic analysis is mainly to sum up the statistics, which can create a geographical distribution map of different levels of infection, a statistic map of different infection categories and a bar-graph map of the development trend of infection. Figure 4 shows the statistics analysis results.

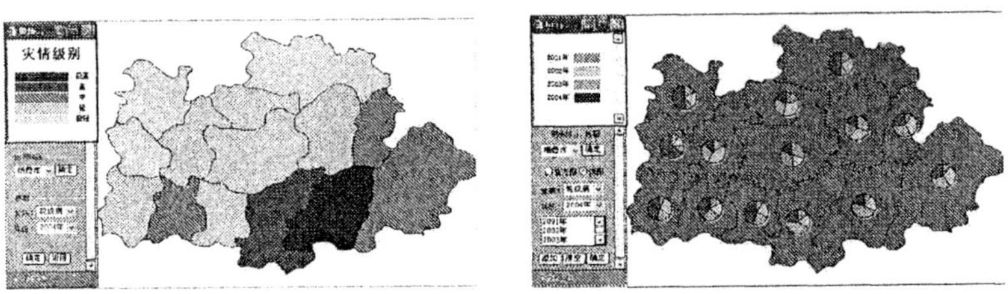

Fig 4: Statistics analysis (classification analysis and bar diagram statistic)

5. Spatial analysis: The spatial analysis for fruit tree diseases and insect pests was completed by Arc/Info. The buffer analysis model can create a zone area by the analysis of the entities of dot, line and polygon. The zone area can indicate the affect range or grade of these entities to their neighbors. Fruit tree diseases and insect pests firstly occur in some partial areas, then spread quickly and unevenly to neighborhood with the affect of weather conditions such as temperature, humidity, wind speed and wind direction etc.

The buffer analysis model can help to analyze the spreading tendency and spatial distribution for fruit tree diseases and insect pests in a period.

In buffer model, the basic idea is to give a spatial area, then ascertain its adjacent area which size is relative to radius B (Fig 5). So definition of buffer size is showed as follows:

$$B_i = \{x : D(x, O_i \leq d)\} \tag{1}$$

where $O = \{O_i : i = 1, 2, \cdots, n\}$

The spatial buffer area is aggregate values, as shown below:

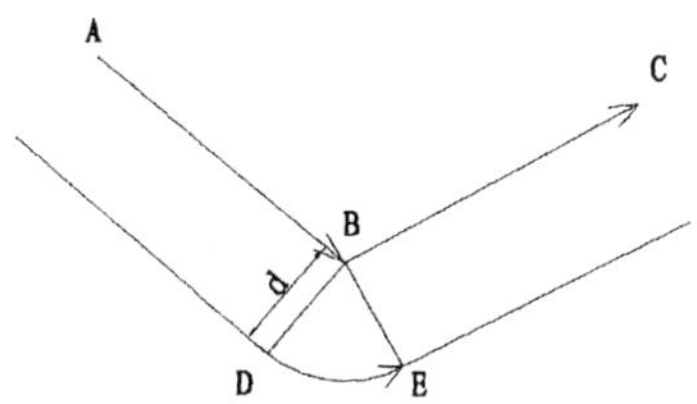

Fig 5: Salient buffer

$$B = \bigcup_{i=1}^{n} B_i \tag{2}$$

5. Prediction analysis: Some conditions such as weather data are the decisive factors that affect the occurrence of fruit tree diseases and insect pests. The real-time monitored weather data and fruit tree diseases and insect pests data are processed with forecasting models and GIS overlay analysis to give the prediction results. To ensure the precision of forecasting and decision-making, data should be real-time and the high-precision prediction models and decision-making models should be built.

6. Diagnosis and cure: The diagnosis of fruit tree diseases and insect pests is achieved remotely by using the knowledge database and diagnosis model by Internet. The position of fruit tree was firstly selected, the corresponding pictures and text was queried, the occurrence grade of the disease in a town was finally ascertained. Figure 6 shows the map of the occurrence grade of a disease of fruit tree.

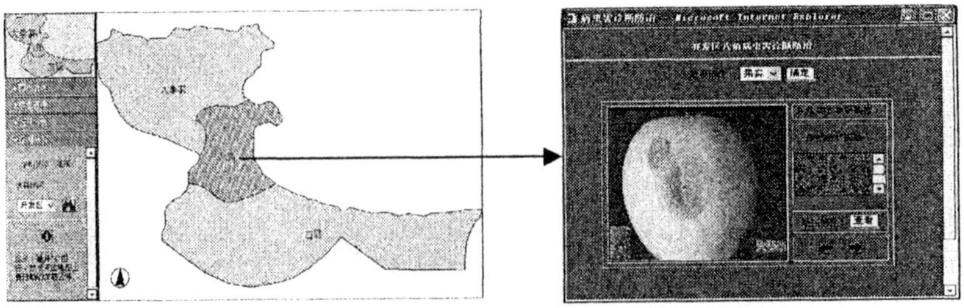

Fig 6: Diagnosis and cure

3. CONCLUSION

The system based on WebGIS are developed using GIS software (ArcIMS, ArcSDE, ArcInfo), Web server (Weblogic) and database management system (oracle9i). The system also integrates Java MVC design pattern technology, three-tier B/S structures, spatial analysis models, experts knowledge models and the information of fruit tree diseases and insect pests in orchard. It can solve some problem about fruit tree diseases and insect pests in orchard by applying incorporated WebGIS technology. The GIS and biologic geographical statistics are applied to describe the distribution pattern of fruit tree diseases and insect pests and to carry out spatial overlay analysis and so on.

The WebGIS technology is a promising mode to develop a control system for fruit tree diseases and insect pests, newer ArcIMS technology with more actual functions and analysis methods have been developed. It is necessary that some exact decision-making and prediction models should be researched and applied to ensure usability of the system.

ACKNOWLEDGEMENTS

The research project is founded by the 863 Program- the long-distance diagnosis platform of plant diseases and insect pests based on network 2002AA243031.

REFERENCES

[1]Wang Maohua. Possible adoption of precision agriculture for developing counties at the threshold of the new millennium. [J]. Computers and Electronics in Agriculture. 2001, 30:45-50.

[2]{0><}0{>Wu Lun, Liu Yu, Ma Xiujun, Wei Zhongya, and Tian Yuan. 2001.The Geographic Information System— Its Principle, Methods and Application. China,Beijing:The Science Press. <0}.

[3]{0><}0{>Mao Feng, Sheng Xiaohua, Ai Lishuang.2001.Development and Pracetice of ArcGIS 8, 193-217.China,Beijing: The Science Press.

[4]Liu Shuhua, Yang Xiaohong, Jiang Wenke and Cao Keqiang. 2003.GIS-based Decision Support System for Crop Pest Control. The Transaction of Agricultural Engineering. 19(4):147-150.

[5]Hardy Pundt, Klaus Brinkkotter-Runde. Visualization of spatial data for field based GIS. [J]. Computer & Geosciences. 2000, 26:51-56

[6]M.A Kramers, C.G.M. Conjin, C. Bastiaansen. An expert system for diagnosing flowerbulb diseases, pests and non-parasitic disorders. Agricultural systems, Vol58, No.1, (1998)PP 57-85.

[7] Lo.Tedeschi, D.G.Fox, P.J.Guiroy: A Decision Support System to Improve Individual Cattle Management. 1. A Mechanistic, Dynamic Model for Animal Growth. Agricultural System. Vol.79(2)(2004)171-204.

[8] M.P.Bange, S.A.Deutscher, D.Larsen, D.Linsley, S.Whiteside: A Handheld Decision Support System to Facilitate Improved Insect Pest Management in Australian Cotton Systems. Computers and Electronics in Agriculture. Vol.43(2)(2004)131-148

RESEARCH ON WHEAT DISEASES AND INSECT PESTS GEOGRAPHIC INFORMATION SYSTEM

Hongyan Shen[1] ,Gang Liu[1] and Yinbing Ge[2]
[1] *China Agricultural University, Beijing, P.R. China* shy0907@hotmail.com pac@cau.edu.cn
[2] *Currently study in Utah State University, Logan, UT, USA* geyinbing@hotmail.com

Abstract: A geographical information system for wheat diseases and insect pests is developed, which can provide valuable information for farmers to appropriately prevent diseases and insect pests so as to decrease the environment pollution, using the techniques of inference engine, BP network, etc.

Key words: GIS、 inference engine、 BP Network、 ODBC

1. INTRODUCTION

In recent years, the technique of wheat planting has been improved. However, how to prevent wheat diseases and insect pests is still a key problem. As most farmers do not understand rules of occurrence and popularity of wheat diseases and insect pests, they cannot prevent diseases and insect pests effectively and reasonably. Even though it can increase yield and cut the throat of the diseases and insect pests to use the pesticide widely, the environment has been polluted, the natural control has been lowered and so on. These series of problems have influenced the agricultural production of our country. To guide farmers to prevent diseases and insect pests appropriately, a geographical information system for wheat diseases and insect pests is developed.

The techniques used include Geographic Information System (GIS), Expert System (ES) and Artificial Neural Network (ANN). GIS is a software platform used to input, save, analyze, deal with, and express geographic space data. ES is one of the most mature techniques in Artificial Intelligence (AI) area. It emphasizes the effect of the special knowledge to intelligent behavior. It simulates the ways of thinking of and digests the knowledge like a human being. ANN is a nonlinear dynamics model which possesses strong memory, self-adaptation, self-study and is capable of dealing with complicated patterns. The system modules, such as consultation, graphic display and data management, contain massive information and provide higher reliability by combining GIS with ES. ES imitates human's logical thinking and ANN imitates human's experience thinking. Therefore, the prediction-decision module in the system is not only established with experts' experiences but also can be corrected automatically.

2. STUCTURE AND FUNCTION

Connecting GIS, ES, and ANN with object oriented knowledge representation method, a geographical information system for wheat diseases and insect pests is developed. Based on reports of wheat diseases and insect pests, diseases and insect pests prevention and cure are systematized and GIS platform in mode of controller is linked with application. It involves weather factors, plant-protection knowledge, scientific findings, expertise and GIS with computer technology. The GIS for wheat diseases and insect pests has five function modules to applied to the wheat growth process. They are predict-decision module, diagnoses module, history disaster map showing module, consultation module, and database management. The whole structure of this system is shown in figure 1.

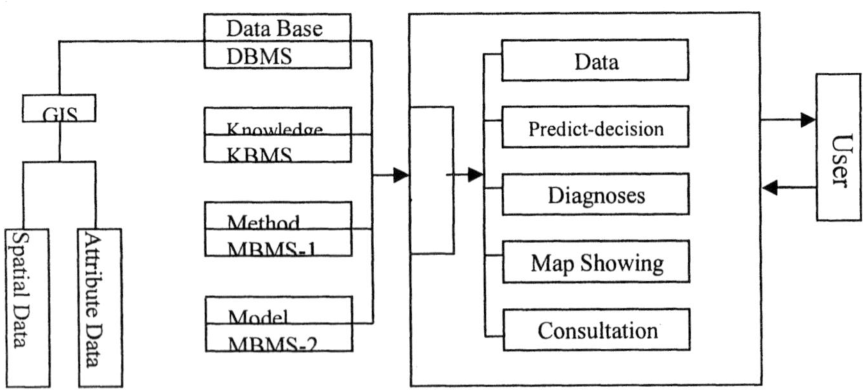

Figure 1: the Structure of the System

In figure 1, DBMS represents database management system ; KBMS represents knowledge database management system ; MBMS-1 represents method database management system; and MBMS-2 represents model database management system .

3. TECHNOLOGY ANALYSIS OF THE SYSTEM

3.1 Linking Modules with GIS

The Loose Coupling is used to link system modules to GIS . Via the Loose Coupling, the operation module can call some functions of GIS such as data input, data edit, data display, and database management. The operation module first reads data from GIS through the interface of ODBC (Open DataBase Connectivity). ODBC is a standard access method that can access DBMS from our system. It is based on the Call-Level Interface (CLI) specifications from X/Open and ISO/IEC for database APIs and uses Structured Query Language (SQL) as its database access language. After this, the operation module calculates data and writes new data back into database of GIS using the same format.

3.2 Inference Engine

Inference engine is the generic control mechanism that applies the axiomatic knowledge present in the knowledge base to diseases and insect pests to arrive at some diagnosis conclusion for farmers. It is the core component of all expert systems.

3.2.1 Inference Strategy

The system adopts the multi-level inaccurate reasoning method. Multi-level inaccurate reasoning means that expert system obtains relatively definite conclusion and goal by the uncertain algorithm, in terms of judgment in previous period, incomplete or uncertain knowledge and data. Reasoning result is the strategy to determine object and relevant value. The process of inference is to identify the reliability. The system utilizes the inheritance of object-oriented knowledge expression method to realize multi-level and inaccurate inference, to obtain reliability of the object through distribution weight of each property and the distribution reliability of user's choices 'yes', 'no' and 'uncertainty'.

3.2.2 Control and Search Strategy

The system uses Depth-First Search (DFS) algorithm. The ultimate goal is to find the answer. When the first conclusion is verified with a congruous symptom, the characteristics of this symptom need to be verified but not the others. If the characteristics are suitable, final conclusion can be made. Otherwise, other symptoms need to be verified. DFS is suitable for the inference of hierarchical structure knowledge expression. The process of inference is to calculate the reliability in terms of the user's choice. How to calculate the reliability is introduced as follows: first, choose an object; second, set the initial attribute parameter as Q_1, reliability as K_1, the second attribute parameter as Q_2, reliability as K_2......the Nth attribute parameter as Q_n, reliability as K_n; finally, the reliability of the diagnose structure is:

$$\frac{\sum_n Q_n K_n}{\sum_n Q_n} \qquad (1)$$

the value of K_n is: $$K_n = \begin{cases} 1 \\ 0 \\ 0.5 \end{cases}$$

if the user's choice is 'yes', $K_n = 1$; if 'no' , $K_n = 0$; if 'uncertainty', $K_n = 0.5$.

The following is the example how to use inference engine to diagnose the wheat rust disease. First, enter the main interface of system and click consultation button. Then, follow the voice instructions of system and answer the questions ("yes", "no", or "uncertainty). Items you have chosen are immediately displayed in the list box. If the information is not what you expect, double click the items to cancel it. Thereafter, you can find the diagnosis result including the name of diseases, reliability etc. Pictures are shown on the screen of the diseases, harm character, occurrence regulations, and prevention methods.

Table1. Diagnosis process of wheat rust diseases

Attribute & character	Weighted Value	Ve	Vs	Reliability
Are wheat diseases?	10	Yes	Yes	1
Are Leaf diseases?	10	Yes	Yes	1
White mycelia spot	20	No	No	0
Disheveled spore & henna	30	No	No	0
Disheveled spore & puce	30	No	Uncertain	0.5
Disheveled spore & orange	30	Yes	Yes	1
Prominent spore	20	Yes	Yes	0

The diagnosis reliability is 0.8.

3.3 BP Network

ANN is a nonlinear dynamics simulation model of a human nervous system, which contains a collection of neuron units communicating with each other via axon connections. ANN has been applied in many fields including speech synthesis, diagnostic problems, medicine, business and finance, robotic control, signal processing, computer vision and many other problems of pattern recognition. Moreover, neural models show promise in achieving human-like performance over more traditional artificial intelligence techniques.

Currently, dozens of neural networks have been developed. The parallel network structure is adopted in BP neural network model - one of the most popular networks. BP network concludes three layers: input layer, hidden layer, and output layer. The study of BP network primarily contains four steps:

1) Input mode forward pass (input mode forwards calculation to middle layers and then to output layer): This step is to calculate the actual output corresponding to input mode. The actual output of the tth unit in the output layer is defined as c_t

$$c_t = f(l_t) \quad (t = 1, 2, \ldots, q) \tag{2}$$

where, l_t is the activation value of the tth unit in the output layer. f is activation function of type S:

$$f(x) = \frac{1}{1+\exp(-x)} \tag{3}$$

The activation function of type S is closer than other types of function to the signal output form of the biology nerve center and it is consecutive and differentiable.

2) Output error backward pass: In the first step, the error between actual output and expectation is calculated. If the error goes beyond the limited value, the weights of network will be revised. It is called error backward pass because BP is revised from the back to the front. The calculation begins from the output layer to the middle layer and then to the input layer. The revised error of the output is:

$$d_t^k = (y_t^k - c_t^k) f'(l_t^k) \tag{4}$$

where, y_t^k is the expectation, c_t^k is the actual output, f'(.)is the derivative of the output layer function.

The revised error of each unit in middle layers is:

$$e_j^k = \left(\sum_{t=1}^{q} v_{jt} \cdot d_t^k\right) f'(s_j^k) \quad (j=1,2,\ldots,p \;\; k=1,2,\ldots,m) \tag{5}$$

It is caused by revised errors transferred from q output layers. After educing the revised error, the weighted value between the output layer and the middle layers and from the middle layers to the input layer can be adjusted conversely with the values of d_t^k and e_j^k

3) Circular memory training: Circular memory training is to make the output error of the network run to the minimum. At each training mode, the BP network should be trained circularly hundreds of times, maybe ten thousands, to remember it. This kind of circular memory training actually repeats the input mode forward pass and output error backward pass again and again.

4) Judgment of the learning result: After each circular memory training, the network should judge the learning result. The purpose of the judgment is to check whether the output error is in the limited area. If it is, the learning ends. Otherwise, the network goes on circularly training. The training is a process that the global error of the network tends to the minimum.

The initialization of BP network is to set up the topological structure (input layer, hidden layer, and the number of the nerve code in the output layer). After setting some main parameters of the BP network algorithm (learning rate, aim error, the maximum loop number, and times of display interval), the BP network starts the training.

The prediction module in the system is built by BP network. VB language is used to design the main interface, to realize the Human-Computer Interaction function, to establish the link with Matlab at the same time. The Matlab is applied to complete the network training and prediction. Example codes are as follows:

```
Dim Matlab As Object
Dim MReal1(5， 5) As Double
m MImag() As Double
SetMatlab=CreateObject("Matlab.Application")
Matlab.Execute("a=hilb(5)")
Call Matlab.GetFullMatrix("a","base", MReal1， MImag)
```

What the prediction function to produce and display is the grade of the diseases and insect pests in the region based on four parameters in the area: average temperature, lowest temperature, hours of sunshine, and rainfall. The module can also provide short-term prediction. The main purpose is to simulate the spread of diseases and insect pests in a short-term period and the corresponding result can be displayed in the map.

4. CONCLUSION

ES、oriented object method、ANN are utilized in this research to analyze GIS and the occurrence rules of wheat diseases and insect pests. Referring to the main diseases and insect pests, the system realizes prediction, consultation, diagnoses etc. The system not only deals with spatial data but also infers the result and makes decisions. It can transfer abstract data to compendious electronic maps and display distribution rules of the diseases and insect pests. In a word, the system aims to provide help for decreasing the cost of agricultural product, protecting environment, etc.

ACKNOWLEDGEMENTS

This program is supported by Chinese National Funded High Science and Technology Research Project (863 project) - the long-distance diagnosis platform of plant diseases and insect pests based on network 2002AA243031.

REFERENCES

[1] Xing Xianfang. Comprehensive Administration of Crop Diseases and Insect Pests Geographic Information System [D]. Bao Ding: Publishing Company of agricultural university of Hebei, 2004: 19-31.

[2] RAMANMC,LINERF.An expert advisory system for wheat disease management m [J].Plant Disease,1994(2):209-215.

[3] Kuang Pusheng ,Jiang Wenke, Liu Gang. Precision Agricultural Elements [M]. Beijing: Publishing Company of Agricultyre University of China, 1999.30-60.

[4] He Xingui . Knowledge Disposal and Expert System. Beijing: Publishing National Defence Industry, 1990.

[5] Wu Xincai. Geographic Information System Theory and Method. Beijing: Publishing House of Electronics Industry, 2002.

[6] Zhong Xinyi ,Pan Xinan, Yang Yixian. Beijing: Intelligence Theory and Technology – Artificial Intelligence and Neural Network. Publishing House of People Posting,1992.

[7] Robert P C, Rust R H, Larson W E. Preface. Proceeding of Site Specific Management for Agriculture Systems. The 2nd International Conference on Re-search and Development Issues in Site-Specific Crop Management, 1994.

SKFD-ISOMAP FOR FACE RECOGNITION

Ruifan Li[1], Cong Wang[1], and Xuyan Tu[2]
[1]*Beijing University of Posts and Telecommunications, Beijing, China*
[2]*University of Science and Technology Beijing, Beijing, China*

Abstract: Recently, neuroscientists emphasized the manifold ways of perception and proposed Isomap for manifold learning. Favorable results have been achieved using Isomap for data description and visualization. However, since the unsupervised Isomap is developed based on minimizing the reconstruction error with multidimensional scaling (MDS) without using the class specific information, it may not be optimal from the perspective of pattern classification. Therefore, an improved version of Isomap, namely SKFD-Isomap, is proposed using class information to construct the neighborhood, and kernel Fisher discriminant (KFD) to achieve the nonlinear embedding. A nearest neighbor classifier is then applied in the subspace for classification. Experimental results show the effectiveness of the proposed approach.

Key words: face recognition, manifold, Isomap (isometric feature mapping), KFD

1. INTRODUCTION

Recent years, a growing interest has been shown in subspace methods for face recognition [1-5]. As facial images, represented as high-dimensional pixel arrays, often belong to a subspace of intrinsically low dimension. Eigenfaces [2] and Fisherfaces [3] are two typical examples. Eigenfaces, based on Principle component Analysis (PCA), is an unsupervised learning algorithm. PCA performs dimensionality reduction by projecting the original N -dimensional data onto the d ($<<N$)-dimensional linear subspace spanned by the leading eigenvectors of covariance matrix of the original data. For linearly embedding manifolds, PCA is guaranteed to produce a compact

representation for data visualization. However, without using the class information this method may be not effective for pattern classification.

Fisherfaces is based on Fisher Linear Discriminant (FLD). Contrasted to PCA, which finds a projection direction that retains maximum variance, FLD finds the optimal projection direction that maximized the distances between classes and minimized the distances within classes. In general, the FLD-based methods perform better than those of PCA-based [4]. However, Fisherfaces are confronted with the singularity of with-class matrix caused by the small samples against their high dimensions. Moreover, they both search for a linear subspace for further classification, failing to deal with nonlinear changes in face images.

As enhancements for PCA and FLD, kernel Eigenfaces and Fisherfaces [6, 7] showed expressive results in face recognition, in which the samples are first implicitly mapped onto a high-dimensional feature spaces, then PCA or FLD is applied, equivalent to extracting the most discriminant nonlinear features in the original input space. These methods can discover the nonlinear structure in the face images. However, none of them explicitly considers the structure of the manifold on which the face images possibly reside.

Recently, neuroscientists emphasized the manifold ways of perception, and showed the face images may reside on a nonlinear manifold [8]. Some manifold learning methods, i.e. Isomap (or Isometric feature mapping) [9], Locally Liner Embedding (LLE) [10], and Laplacian eigenmaps [11] are proposed. Although these methods have demonstrated excellent results in finding the embedding manifolds that best describe the data points, they are suboptimal from the classification viewpoint.

In this paper, an improved version of Isomap, namely SKFD-Isomap, is proposed for face recognition. SKFD-Isomap utilizes class information to guide the construction of neighborhood graph, and then applies Kernel Fisher Discriminant (KFD) to find an optimal projection direction using geodesic distances as feature vectors. Experimental results demonstrated the effectiveness of SKFD-Isomap for face recognition.

The rest of this paper is organized as follows. In section 2, Isomap is briefly reviewed. In section 3, SKFD-Isomap is proposed. In section 4, experiments are reported. Finally, section 5 ends with some conclusions.

2. ISOMAP

For data lying on a nonlinear manifold, the true distance between two data points is the geodesic distance on the manifold, i.e. the distance along the surface of the manifold, rather than the straight-line Euclidean distance, as shown in Figure 1. Isomap [9] builds on Multi-Dimensional Scaling (MDS) but seeks to preserve the intrinsic geometry of the data, as captured in the geodesic manifold distances between all pairs of data points. The crux is estimating the geodesic distance between faraway points, given only input space distances. For neighboring points, Euclidean distance in input space provides a good approximation to geodesic distance. For faraway points, geodesic distance can be approximated by adding up a sequence of short hops between neighboring points.

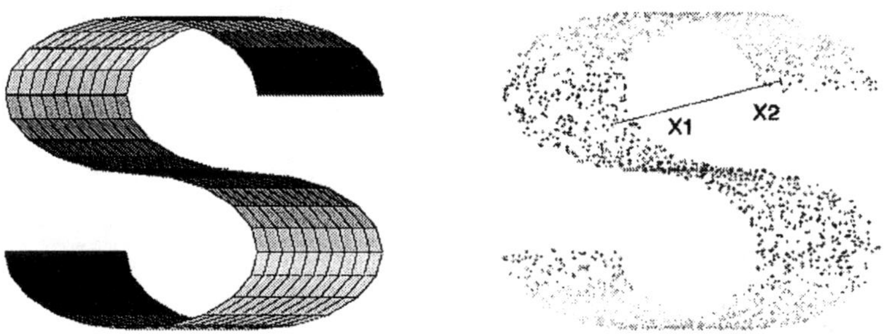

Figure 1. S-curve and geodesic distance

Given a set of n samples, $\{x_i\}_{i=1}^n$, each element $x_i \in \mathbb{R}^N$. Isomap can find an implicit mapping $f: \mathbb{R}^N \to \mathbb{R}^d (d < N)$ from the input space onto the feature space, generating the lower coordinate vector set $\{y_i\}_{i=1}^n$ of $\{x_i\}_{i=1}^n$. The procedures of Isomap are listed as follows:

Step 1, Construct neighborhood graph: First compute Euclidean distance, $d_X(x_i, x_j)$ between any two data points x_i and x_j in the input space. Next, define the graph G over all data points by connecting neighborhood points x_i and x_j, in which the neighborhood of any point can be defined either as the K nearest points or all the points within a fixed radius ε.

Step 2, Compute shortest paths: Initialize the element $d_G(x_i, x_j)$ of graph matrix G as $d_X(x_i, x_j)$ if x_i and x_j are linked by an edge; $d_G(x_i, x_j) = \infty$ otherwise. Then for each $k = 1, \cdots, n$ in turn, replace all entries $d_G(x_i, x_j)$ by $min\{d_G(x_i, x_j), d_G(x_i, x_k) + d_G(x_k, x_j)\}$. The matrix of final values $D_G = \{d_G(x_i, x_j)\}$ will contain the shortest path distances between all pairs of points in G.

Step 3, Construct d-dimensional embedding applying MDS to the matrix of graph distance D_G: Compute $\tau(D_G)$ with τ defined as $-HSH/2$, where S is the matrix of squared distance $S_{ij} = D_{ij}^2$, and H is the centering matrix $\{H_{ij} = \delta_{ij} - 1/N\}$. Let λ_p be the p-th eigenvalue (in decreasing order) of the matrix $\tau(D_G)$, and v_p^i be the i-th component of the p-th eigenvector. Then set the p-th component of the d-dimensional coordinate vector y_i equal to $\sqrt{\lambda_p} v_p^i$.

As for classification tasks, Isomap can be viewed as a feature extraction process. However, the mapping between input space and feature space is implicit. It should be learned by some nonlinear interpolation techniques, such as Generalized Regression Neural Network (GRNN) [15] for the new test samples. Moreover, MDS used in Isomap is based on minimizing the reconstruction error, thus, discriminant information cannot be extracted effectively. From this, Yang [12] proposed Ext-Isomap algorithm with FLD replacing the MDS used in the original Isomap for pattern classification. Nevertheless, in Ext-Isomap, when constructing the neighborhood graph no class-label information are used. Therefore, further modifications should be made on Isomap for pattern classification.

3. SKFD-ISOMAP

Consider a set of c disjoint subsets $X = \bigcup_{i=1}^{c} X_i$ with each element $x \in \mathbb{R}^N$, and each subset has n_i samples, i.e. $\sum_{i=1}^{c} n_i = n$. In SKFD-Isomap, the first step is to determine the neighbors of each sample x_i on the low-dimensional manifold M based on Euclidean distance metric $d_X(x_i,x_j)$. Whereas, contrasted to the unsupervised nature of Isomap, the SKFD-Isomap utilizes the class information by rescaling the Euclidean distance between two data points with a constant factor λ $(0 < \lambda < 1)$ if the class labels are the same. Then, the modified distance matrix between any two data points is utilized to determine whether two points are neighbors or not. These neighborhood relationships are represented in a weighted graph G in which $d_G(x_i,x_j) = d_X(x_i,x_j)$ if x_i and x_j are neighbors, and $d_X(x_i,x_j) = \infty$ otherwise.

The next step is to estimate geodesic distance $d_M(x_i,x_j)$ between any pair of points on the manifold M. For neighboring points, input space distance provides a good approximation to geodesic distance. For faraway points, geodesic distance can be approximated by a sequence of short hops between neighboring data points. In other words, $d_M(x_i,x_j)$ is approximated by the shortest path between x_i and x_j on G, which is computed by $min\{d_G(x_i,x_j), d_G(x_i,x_k) + d_G(x_k,x_j)\}$, for each $k = 1, \cdots, n$. The shortest paths between any two points are represented in a matrix D, where $D_{ij} = d_G(x_i,x_j)$.

Thus, each data point is represented as a feature vector of its geodesic distance to any points. In other words, the feature vector of data point x_i is an n-dimensional vector $f_i = [D_{ij}]$ where $j = 1, \cdots, n$ and $D_{ii} = 0$. We then apply KFD on the feature vectors find an optimal projection direction for classification.

In KFD, each vector f_i is projected to a high-dimensional feature space, $\mathbb{R}^f$, by a nonlinear mapping function, $\phi: \mathbb{R}^n \rightarrow \mathbb{R}^f$, $f > n$. Note that the dimensionality of the image space $\mathbb{R}^f$ can be arbitrarily large. Then, we formulate the FLD problem in the high-dimensional feature space only using dot products [13].

We assume the projection $\phi(f_i)$ are centered in $\mathbb{R}^f$, i.e. $\frac{1}{n}\sum_{i=1}^{n}\phi(f_i)=0$, which could be implemented as in [14]. The between-class and within-class scatter matrix are defined as

$$S_B^\phi = \sum_{i=1}^{c} n_i \mu_i^\phi (\mu_i^\phi)^T$$

$$S_w^\phi = \sum_{i=1}^{c}\sum_{j=1}^{n_i}(\phi(f_j)-\mu_i^\phi)(\phi(f_j)-\mu_i^\phi)^T$$

, where μ_i^ϕ is the mean of class i in $\mathbb{R}^f$. Applying FLD in feature in kernel space, we need to find eigenvalues and eigenvectors w^ϕ of

$$S_B^\phi w^\phi = \lambda S_W^\phi w^\phi$$

, which can be obtained by

$$W_{OPT}^\phi = \arg\max_{W^\phi} \frac{|(W^\phi)^T S_B^\phi W^\phi|}{|(W^\phi)^T S_w^\phi W^\phi|} = [w_1^\phi, \cdots, w_m^\phi]$$

, where $\{w_i^\phi\}_{i=1}^m$ is the set of generalized eigenvectors corresponding to the m largest generalized eigenvalues $\{\lambda_i\}_{i=1}^m$.

From the theory of reproducing kernels, any solution $w^\phi \in \mathbb{R}^f$ must lie in the span of all the mapping of training samples [8], and there exist coefficients α_i such that

$$w^\phi = \sum_{i=1}^{n} \alpha_i \phi(f_i)$$

We define the kernel function as $k(x,y)=\phi(x)\cdot\phi(y)$, thus the kernel matrix in high-dimensional space can be denoted as K, i.e., $K_{ij} = k(f_i,f_j) = \phi(f_i)\cdot\phi(f_j)$, which is a $n\times n$ symmetric matrix. We can also define a matrix Z: $Z=(Z_i)_{i=1,\cdots,c}$, where Z_i is a $n_i \times n_i$ matrix with terms all equal to $1/n_i$, i.e., Z is an $n\times n$ block diagonal matrix. Thus, the KFD problem becomes

$$\lambda KK\alpha = KZK\alpha$$

We can now project the vectors in $\mathbb{R}^f$ to a lower dimensional space spanned by the eigenvector. Let f be the feature vector of a test sample x, whose projection is $\phi(f)$ in $\mathbb{R}^f$, then the projection of $\mathbb{R}^f$ onto the eigenvectors as follows:

$$w^\phi \cdot \phi(f) = \sum_{i=1}^{n} \alpha_i k(f_i, f)$$

The above procedures can learn a subspace for further classification. To summarize, the SKFD-Isomap for classification has five steps as follows: S1, Compute original distances matrix between data points, and rescaling them with class information, i.e., $d_X(x_i,x_j) = \lambda\, d_X(x_i,x_j)$. S2, Compute shortest paths on the manifold, and feature can be denoted as f_i. S3, Compute projection direction with KFD applied to the matrix of shortest paths. S4, For new test sample use GRNN to approximate its mapping from input space onto the feature space. S5, Map the feature vector to kernel space and then predict its class-label using simple classier, such as K nearest neighbor.

4. EXPERIMENTS

In this section, SKFD-Isomap is compared with kernel Fisherfaces for face recognition using the Yale face database. In those two methods, the polynomial kernel functions with second or third order are selected. The parameters for most of the methods are determined empirically to achieve the best results. For SFKD-Isomap, different values of λ between 0.1 and 0.5 are tested. For kernel Fisherfaces, the samples are projected to a subspace spanned by the $c-1$ largest eigenvectors.

This Yale database contains 165 images, each size 320 by 243, of 15 subjects in a variety of conditions including with and without glasses, illumination variation, and changes in facial expression. Since the database has large background, to reduce the adverse effect, original images have been cropped without containing the facial contours with size 87 by 123. Furthermore, each image has been resized to 58 by 82 for computational efficiency. Figure 2 shows closely cropped images of a few subjects.

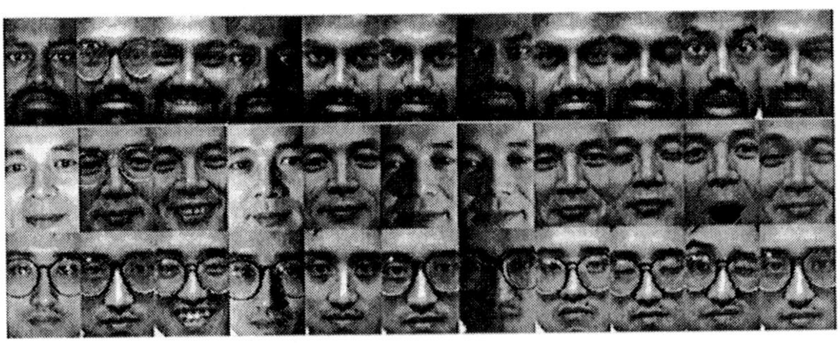

Figure 2. Some chopped face images from database

In this experiment, each image is represented as a raster scan vector of intensity values, and then normalized to be zero-mean unit-variance vectors. The training set and test set are selected randomly. When performing the experiment, for each subject, eight images are selected for training, and the other two samples are left as test samples. All the images are then projected to a reduced space and recognition is performed using a nearest neighbor classier. To reduce the fluctuation among the results as possible, the experiments are performed 400 times. The best experimental results with the order of kernel functions $d = 2$, $K = 40$, and $\lambda = 0.3$ are given in table 1.

Table 1. Performance comparison on the Yale Database

Method	Parameters	Dimension of Space	Error Rate (%)
Kernel Fisherfaces	$d = 2$	14	12.37
SKFD-Isomap	$d = 2, K = 40, \lambda = 0.3$	14	8.62

In addition, we test the performance of SKFD-Isomap with different values of and with different order of polynomial kernel function, i.e. d = 2 or 3. Figure 3(a) shows the results, where $K = 40$. The order of polynomial kernel, d = 2 performs better that higher order. This phenomena may caused by the overfitting with higher order. For the neighborhood parameter, K, its performance impact on SKFD-Isomap is also test. The results are shown in figure 3(b), where $d = 2$ and $\lambda = 0.3$. We can see that the proposed approach shows better compared with that of Ext-Isomap. We suppose that the class information used in SKFD-Isomap improved the feature extraction for further classification.

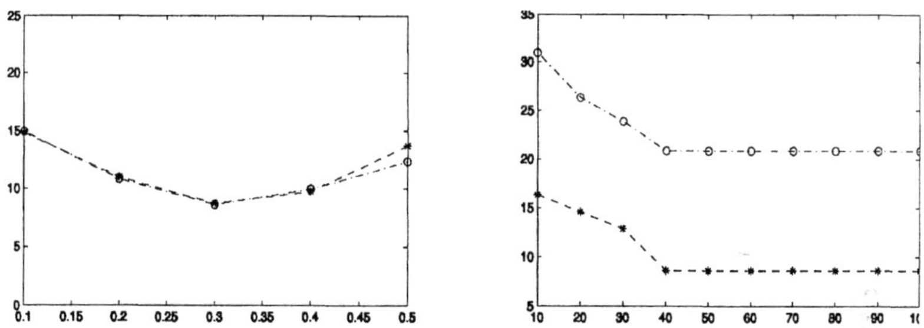

Figure 3. a) SKFD-Isomap with $d = 2$ or 3; b) performance of Ext-Isomap and SKFD-Isomap

5. CONCLUSION

In this paper, an improved version of Isomap, namely SKFD-Isomap, is proposed for face recognition. The SKFD-Isomap utilizes class information to guide the construction of the distances matrix between any two data points. Moreover, the geodesic distances between all pairs of points are applied as feature vectors replacing MDS with KFD to find an optimal projection direction for classification. In face recognition experiments, SKFD-Isomap serves as a feature extraction process compared with Ext-Isomap and Kernel Fisherfaces, combined with a nearest neighbor classier. Experimental results show that SKFD-Isomap excels kernel Fisherfaces and Ext-Isomap.

ACKNOWLEDGEMENTS

The authors would like to thank AT&T laboratory Cambridge and Center for Computational Vision and Control at Yale University for their devotion of face database for public research.

REFERENCES

[1] Zhao, W., Chellappa, R., Phillips, P., Rosenfeld, A.: Face recognition: A literature survey. ACM Computing Surveys, 35 (2003), 399~458

[2] Turk, M.A., Pentland, A.P.: Eigenfaces for recognition. Journal of Cognitive Neuroscience, 3 (1991), 72~86

[3] Belhumeur, P.N., Hespanha, J.P., Kriegman, D.J.: Eigenfaces vs. Fisherfaces: recognition using class specic linear projection. IEEE Transactions on Pattern Analysis and Machine Intelligence, 19 (1997), 711~720

[4] Martinez, Aleix M.; Kak, A.C.: Pca versus lda. IEEE Transactions on Pattern Analysis and Machine Intelligence, 23 (2001), 228~233

[5] He, X., Yan, S., Hu, Y., Zhang, H.: Learning a locality preserving subspace for visual recognition. In: Proc. IEEE Ninth International Conference on Computer Vision (ICCV03), Nice, France, (2003), 385~392

[6] Yang, M.H.: Kernel eigenfaces vs. kernel fisherfaces: face recognition using kernel methods. In: Proc. IEEE Sixth International Conference on Automatic Face and Gesture recognition (FGR02), Washington D.C. (2002), 215~220

[7] Liu, Q., Huang, R., Lu, H., Ma, S.: Kernel-based nonlinear discriminant analysis for face recognition. In: Proc. IEEE Sixth International Conference on Automatic Face and Gesture recognition (FGR02), Washington D.C. (2002), 788~795

[8] Seung, H.S., Lee, D.D.: The manifold ways of perception. Science, 290 (2000), 2268~2269

[9] Silva, V., Tenenbaum, J., Langford, J.: A global geometric framework for nonlinear dimensionality reduction. Science, 290 (2000), 2219~2223

[10] Roweis, S., Saul, L.: Nonlinear dimensionality reduction by locally linear embedding. Science, 290 (2000), 2223~2226

[11] Belkin, M., Niyogi, P.: Laplacian eigenmaps and spectral techniques for embedding and clustering. In: Advances in Neural Information Processing Systems, Vancouver, British Columbia, Cannada, (2001), 788~795

[12] Yang, M.H.: Face recognition using extended isomap. In: Proc. IEEE International Conference on Image Processing, Rochester, NY, (2002), 117~120

[13] Mika, S., Ratsch, G., Weston, J., Scholkopf, B., Muller, K.: Fisher discriminant analysis with kernels. In: Proc. IEEE Neural Networks for Signal Processing Workshop, Madison, Wisconsin, (1999), 41~48

[14] Scholkopf, B., Smola, A., Muller, K.: Nonlinear component analysis as a kernel eigenvalue problem. Neural Computation, 10 (1998), 1299~1319

[15] Specht, D.F.: A general regression neural network. IEEE Transactions on Neural network, 2 (1991), 568~576

SOLUTION OF MDPS USING SIMULATION-BASED VALUE ITERATION

Mohammed Shahid Abdulla and Shalabh Bhatnagar
Department of Computer Science and Automation, Indian Institute of Science, Bangalore – 560 012, India.

Abstract: This article proposes a three-timescale simulation based algorithm for solution of infinite horizon Markov Decision Processes (MDPs). We assume a finite state space and discounted cost criterion and adopt the value iteration approach. An approximation of the Dynamic Programming operator *T* is applied to the value function iterates. This `approximate' operator is implemented using three timescales, the slowest of which updates the value function iterates. On the middle timescale we perform a gradient search over the feasible action set of each state using Simultaneous Perturbation Stochastic Approximation (SPSA) gradient estimates, thus finding the minimizing action in *T*. On the fastest timescale, the `critic' estimates, over which the gradient search is performed, are obtained. A sketch of convergence explaining the dynamics of the algorithm using associated ODEs is also presented. Numerical experiments on rate based flow control on a bottleneck node using a continuous-time queueing model are performed using the proposed algorithm. The results obtained are verified against classical value iteration where the feasible set is suitably discretized. Over such a discretized setting, a variant of the algorithm of [12] is compared and the proposed algorithm is found to converge faster.

FRAMEWORK AND INTRODUCTION

We consider an MDP $\{X_t, t = 0,1,...\}$ where decisions are made at instants $t = 0,1,...$ using an associated control-valued process $\{Z_t\}$. Suppose $S \equiv \{1,2,...s\}$ is the (finite) state space and C is the control space. Suppose also that $U(i) \subseteq C$ is the set of all feasible controls in state i. Let $p(i,u,j), i,j \in S, u \in U(i)$ be the transition probabilities associated with this MDP. An admissible policy $\mu = \{\mu^0, \mu^1, \mu^2,...\}$ with

$\mu^t : S \rightarrow C, t \geq 0$, is such that $\mu_i^t \in U(i)$. An admissible policy μ is stationary if $\mu^t = \gamma, \forall t$. Suppose $K(i_t, u_t, i_{t+1})$ denotes the one-step transition cost when the current state is i_t, the action chosen is $u_t \in U(i_t)$ and the next state is i_{t+1}. The aim here is to find a stationary admissible policy π that minimizes for each state $i \in S$ the associated infinite horizon discounted cost $V_\pi(i)$, where

$$V_\pi(i) = E\{\sum_{t=0}^{\infty} \alpha^t K(i_t, \pi_{i_t}, i_{t+1}) \mid i_0 = i\} \tag{1}$$

and $0 < \alpha < 1$ is the discount factor. For any state $i \in S$, the minimum infinite-horizon discounted-cost V_i^* satisfies the *Bellman equation*

$$V_i^* = \min_{u \in U(i)} E\{K(i, u, \eta(i,u)) + \alpha V_{\eta(i,u)}^*\} \tag{2}$$

the random variable $\eta(i,u) \in S$ being the state to which the system transits upon application of control u in state i. The expectation above is over $\eta(i,u)$. To compute $V^* = (V_i^*, \forall i \in S)^T$ we may apply the Dynamic Programming algorithm recursively:

$$V_i(n+1) = \min_{u \in U(i)} E\{K(i, u, \eta(i,u)) + \alpha V_{\eta(i,u)}(n)\} \tag{3}$$

Note that here $V(n) = (V_i(n), \forall i \in S)^T$ are iterates unlike defined quantities V_π in (1). It is known that as $n \rightarrow \infty$, the iterates $V_i(n)$ converge to V_i^* exponentially. We may rewrite (3) as $V_i(n+1) = T_i(V(n))$ where $T : \Re^s \rightarrow \Re^s$ such that $T = (T_i, \forall i \in S)^T$ is the Dynamic Programming (DP) operator and the vector V^* is the unique fixed point of T. This method of continually applying T is termed as successive approximation or value iteration (cf. sec. 8.2 of [2]). The optimal policy π^* (where $V_{\pi^*} = V^*$) can be inferred from (2), in general, provided the system transition probabilities $p(i, \pi_i^*, \cdot)$ are known, which is not true in most real-life applications. When $p(i, \pi_i, \cdot)$ are available but not obtainable via a closed form expression, storing these values when $|S|$ is large is difficult. Even so, such a possibility is ruled out in the case where $U(i)$ are compact or countably infinite. Denote $\pi_i(n)$ as the 'greedy' policies w.r.t. the iterates $V(n)$ of (3), i.e.

$$\pi_i(n+1) = \arg\min_{u \in U(i)} E\{K(i, u, \eta(i,u)) + \alpha V_{\eta(i,u)}(n)\} \tag{4}$$

then we may infer that $\pi_i(n) \rightarrow \pi_i^*$ although tight bounds of the form $V_i(n) + \underline{c}_i(n) \leq V_i^* \leq V_i(n) + \underline{c}_i(n)$, where $\underline{c}_i(n) \leq \underline{c}_i(n)$, available in value iteration hold for $\pi_i(n)$ if $\pi_i(n)$ belong to a space with a well-defined metric topology, e.g. $\pi_i(n) \in \Re^s, \forall n \geq 0$. Therefore, we assume a compact action set $U(i) \in \Re^{N_i}, \forall i \in S$.

Simulation based approaches to value iteration in the literature go under the rubric *critic-only* algorithms. See, for example, sec. 1 of [9], where the drawbacks of such schemes are also identified. In a typical simulation based implementation of T_i, first the estimation of $E\{K(i,u,\eta(i,u)) + \alpha V_{\eta(i,u)}(n)\}$ is performed, for each action $u \in U(i)$. This procedure is not feasible when $U(i)$ is a compact or even a countably infinite set. This is followed by finding the minimum of such terms over $U(i)$, we call this minimum $\tilde{V}_i(n+1)$, and (possibly) storing the minimizing u as iterate $\tilde{\pi}_i(n+1)$. Note that this minimization step has computational complexity $O(\sum_{i=1}^{s} |U(i)|)$. An example of critic-only value iteration are the algorithms in sec. 6.2 and 6.3 of [12], that employ online TD(0) learning, both without and with exploration of $U(i)$, respectively. However, these algorithms use value function approximation whereas we target the look-up table case. An important difference in approach is that in [12], the system is simulated using a single endless trajectory to enable learning of the coefficients involved in value function approximation. As we shall show in sec. 4, this reduces to simulating single transitions out of each state $i \in S$ repeatedly. Further, the setting there is also somewhat different in that one does not have to use a simulator in order to estimate the minimizing $\tilde{\pi}_i(n+1)$. As a result, it is easy to find the resultant greedy policy $\tilde{\pi}_i(n+1)$ once the value function iterate $V_i(n)$ is identified. This property of such systems is what makes value iteration attractive to implement. Two examples of other systems where this property holds are to be found in [11] and [10].

In contrast, we use the actor-critic approach to approximate T_i. Gradient search is performed using a slower timescale recursion for finding the minimizing control in (3). Thus, given value function estimates $V(n)$, the iterates $\tilde{\pi}(n+1)$ represent an approximation to $\pi(n+1)$ of (4). To perform gradient descent we employ SPSA estimates of the true gradient $\nabla_u E\{K(i,u,\eta(i,u)) + \alpha V_{\eta(i,u)}(n)\}$ in a stochastic approximation recursion, similar to the policy gradient approach of [4] and [1]. Note that the difficulty here arises since it is not only the expectation $E\{\cdot\}$ that needs to be evaluated but also the value function itself, before the gradient is estimated. Clearly, the objective function here does not possess any analytically obtainable expression and hence needs to be estimated. In particular, to obtain control $\tilde{\pi}_i(n+1)$ we evaluate $E\{K(i,u^r,\eta(i,u^r)) + \alpha V_{\eta(i,u^r)}(n)\}$, $r = 1,2$ at two 'perturbed' actions, u^1 and u^2 that will be made precise later. A faster time-scale recursion estimates the two $E\{\cdot\}$ terms required above by independently simulating M transitions from state i using actions u^1 and u^2, respectively, thus permitting two `parallel' simulations. Note that in the normal course, given a control $u \in U(i)$, one would wait for convergence of iterates towards the $E\{\cdot\}$ terms required above. Instead we only perform a fixed M steps of averaging the random variables $E\{K(i,u^r,\eta^r_m(i,u^r)) + \alpha V_{\eta^r_m(i,u^r)}(n)\}, 0 \le m \le M-1, r = 1,2$, where η^r_m now stands for the two parallel M-element random processes having the law $p(i,u^r,\cdot)$. Note that in the above, the convergence analysis permits us to fix M at 1 - although better performance was obtained when a larger M was used. Convergence in the proposed algorithm is achieved because of the different step size schedules or timescales as with [1], [3], [4], [5], [8], and [9]. While in critic-only methods the resultant optimal policies are not explicitly computed, a highlight of the proposed algorithm is that due to its actor-critic structure, the convergence criteria can now be designed based on *both* the policy iterates $\tilde{\pi}$ and the value-function iterates V. This helps to accommodate problem-specific sensitivity to these quantities. Such a feature is achieved due to both these quantities being estimated in the algorithm.

ALGORITHMS

Suppose $U(i), i \in S$ are of the form $U(i) = \prod_{j=1}^{N_i}[a_i^j, b_i^j]$, where $a_i^j, b_i^j \in \Re$. We make the assumption that $\forall i, j \in S, u \in U(i)$, both $K(i,u,j)$ and $p(i,u,j)$ are continuously differentiable in u.

Let $P_i^j(y) = \min(b_i^j, \max(a_i^j, y)), y \in \Re$ be the projection of y onto the interval $[a_i^j, b_i^j], 1 \le j \le N_i$. Further, for $y = (y_1, y_2, \ldots, y_{N_i})^T \in \Re^{N_i}$, let $P_i(y) = (P_i^1(y_1), P_i^2(y_2), \ldots, P_i^{N_i}(y_{N_i}))^T$. Then $P_i(y)$ denotes the projection of $y \in \Re^{N_i}$ to the set $U(i), i \in S$. Also define an operator $P(\cdot)$ as $P(x) = (P_1(x_1), P_2(x_2), \ldots, P_s(x_s))^T$ where $x_j \in \Re^{N_j}, 1 \le j \le s$, and $x = (x_1, x_2, \ldots, x_s)^T$.

The recursion that tracks (3) is the following: For all $i \in S$ and $n \ge 0$:

$$V_i(n+1) = V_i(n) + a(n)(\tilde{V}_i(n+1) - V_i(n)) \tag{5}$$

where $\tilde{V}_i(n+1) = \left(\tilde{V}^1{}_i((n+1)M) + \tilde{V}^2{}_i((n+1)M)\right)/2$ is an approximation to $T_i(V(n))$ and $a(n)$ is a diminishing step size. Here, M is the number of instants over which additional averaging in recursion (7) is performed. The iterate $\tilde{V}$ will be made precise below in the description of (7). Recursion (6) updates $\tilde{\pi}(\cdot)$:

$$\tilde{\pi}_i(n+1) = P_i(\tilde{\pi}_i(n) + b(n)\frac{\tilde{V}_i^1((n+1)M) - \tilde{V}_i^2((n+1)M)}{2\delta\Delta_i(n)}) \quad (6)$$

Here, $\Delta_i(n)$ are deterministic normalized Hadamard-matrix based perturbations generated according to the method in sec. 2.2.1 of [3] (see also [5] where Hadamard matrix based perturbations were first introduced) whereas $\delta \geq 0$ is a small constant. To produce the iterates $\tilde{V}_i^1((n+1)M)$ and $\tilde{V}_i^2((n+1)M)$ consider perturbed policies $\tilde{\pi}_i^1(n) = P_i(\tilde{\pi}_i(n) - \delta\Delta_i(n))$ and $\tilde{\pi}_i^2(n) = P_i(\tilde{\pi}_i(n) + \delta\Delta_i(n))$. Now perform the following iterations for $r = 1,2$ and $m = 0,1,\dots,M-1$:

$$\tilde{V}_i^r(nM+m+1) = \tilde{V}_i^r(nM+m) + c(n)\begin{pmatrix} K(i,\tilde{\pi}_i^r(n),\eta_{nM+m}^r(i,\tilde{\pi}_i^r(n))) \\ +\alpha V^r_{\eta_{nM+m}^r(i,\tilde{\pi}_i^r(n))}(nM+m) \\ -\tilde{V}_i^r(nM+m) \end{pmatrix} \quad (7)$$

Here, we run two simulations corresponding to $r=1$ and $r=2$ in parallel. Note that in the above, η^1 and η^2 represent two stochastic processes with elements of the form $\eta_k^r(i,u), k \geq 0$ which are $S-$valued random variables, independently generated using $p(i,u,\cdot)$. The requirements on the step-sizes $a(n)$, $b(n)$ and $c(n)$ used in (5), (6) and (7), respectively, are as follows: $d(n) > 0$, $\sum_n d(n) = \infty$, $\sum_n d^2(n) < \infty$ where $d(n)$ represents all three sequences $a(n), b(n)$ and $c(n)$, alongwith:

$$a(n) = o(b(n)), b(n) = o(c(n)). \quad (8)$$

Thus $a(n) \to 0$ is the fastest and $c(n) \to 0$ is the slowest among the three step-size schedules. As a result, the timescale corresponding to $\{a(n)\}$ is the slowest while that corresponding to $\{c(n)\}$ is the fastest. This is because beyond some finite $N_0 > 0$ (i.e., for $n > N_0$), the increments in the recursion governed by $\{a(n)\}$ are uniformly the smallest while those in recursion governed by $\{c(n)\}$ are uniformly the largest among the three. Hence recursions governed by $\{c(n)\}$ converge the fastest (even though they exhibit higher variability in their iterates) amongst the three recursions. Note that we could replace (5) with the direct-assignment recursion $V_i(n+1) = \tilde{V}_i(n+1)$. However, using stochastic averaging with step-size $a(n)$ results in graceful convergence properties in our experiments. Such a choice between the averaging of (5) and direct-assignment is an example of the *bias-variance* dilemma.

OUTLINE OF PROOF

We explain briefly the intuition behind the algorithm, using the Ordinary Differential Equation (ODE) approach for easy illustration and only supply pointers to related proofs already in the literature.

Suppose we define the $\Re-$valued function $\overline{V}_i(W,u)$ (for any $W \in \Re^s$ and $u \in U(i)$) as follows: $\overline{V}_i(W,u) = E\{K(i,u,\eta(i,u)) + \alpha W_{\eta(i,u)}\}$ .It is easy to see that, for a given stationary admissible policy π, the vector function $\overline{V}(W,\pi) = (\overline{V}_1(W,\pi_1), \overline{V}_2(W,\pi_2),...,\overline{V}_s(W,\pi_s))^T$ is in fact the appropriate constrained DP operator T_π. Also, (3) may be written as $V_i(n+1) = T_i(V(n)) = \min_{u\in U(i)}\{\overline{V}_i(V(n),u)\}$. Recall that the fixed point of the operator T_π, $V_\pi = T_\pi(V_\pi)$ is the solution of the Poisson Equation: $V_\pi(i) = E\{K(i,\pi_i,\eta(i,\pi_i)) + \alpha V_\pi(\eta(i,\pi_i))\}$, where $V_\pi(k)$ represents the $k-$th element of the vector V_π.

Using a proof technique resembling that of Corollary 4.2 of [4], for any $n \geq 0$ the asymptotically stable ODE that the faster recursion (7) tracks is, for $t \geq 0$

$$\dot{\widetilde{V}}_i^r(t) = \overline{V}(V(t), \pi_i^r(t)) - \widetilde{V}_i^r(t) \tag{9}$$

Note that the terms $\widetilde{\pi}_i^r(t)$ and $V(t)$ are quasi-static at the time scale corresponding to (7) as recursions (6) and (5) proceed on slower timescales (cf. (8)). Hence we may replace $\pi_i^r(t)$ with π_i^r and $V(t)$ with V, respectively. The asymptotically stable equilibrium point of (9) would be $\widetilde{V}_i^r = \overline{V}(V, \widetilde{\pi}_i^r)$. By virtue of (8) again, (7) would be seen by (6) (and (5)) as having converged. Using the iterates $\widetilde{V}_i^1((n+1)M)$, a better estimate $\widetilde{\pi}(n+1)$ to the policy $\pi(n+1)$ of (4) will be produced via the SPSA update rule of (6).

For the time being, we assume that the SPSA based estimate in (6) performs correct gradient descent towards $\pi_i(n+1)$ (the proof technique for such a claim resembles that of Lemma 4.10 of [4]). This implies that (6) tracks the asymptotically stable (projected) ODE:

$$\dot{\widetilde{\pi}}_i(t) = \hat{P}_i(-\nabla_u \overline{V}_i(V,u)), \tag{10}$$

whose equilibrium point is the desired minimum. Here, $\hat{P}_i = (\hat{P}_i^j, 1 \leq j \leq N_i)^T$ and $\hat{P}_i^j(v(y)) = \lim_{\eta\to 0}\left(P_i^j(y+\eta v(y)) - y\right)/\eta$ for any bounded, continuous and real-valued function v. Further, (5) views recursions (6) and (7) as having converged and so considers an estimate to

$V_i(n+1) = T_i(V(n))$ as available at its $(n+1)-$ th update. Note that recursion (5) has no direct use for the $\widetilde{V}_i^r((n+1)M)$ terms of (7) and instead requires an approximation to $T_i(V(n))$. However, we can employ the iterates $\widetilde{V}_i^r$ in (5), as we describe below. The novelty is that this role of iterates $\widetilde{V}^r$ is in addition to the role played as `critic' for recursion (6).

Note that iterate $\widetilde{\pi}(n+1)$ does approximate $\pi(n+1)$ (by virtue of (10)), and we may use $\overline{V}(V(n), \widetilde{\pi}(n+1))$ as $V_i(n+1)$ in (5). However, we would need additional simulation to estimate the former term. This we can avoid by considering the quantities $\overline{V}_i(V(n), \widetilde{\pi}_i^r(n))$, for $r = 1,2$, approximated by the iterates $\widetilde{V}_i^r((n+1)M)$. Using Taylor series expansion (as in the proof of Lemma 4.10 of [4]), we see that $V_{\widetilde{\pi}^1(n)}(i) + V_{\widetilde{\pi}^2(n)}(i) = 2V_{\widetilde{\pi}(n)}(i) + O(\delta)$ and use this fact in (5). Note that no properties of the perturbations Δ_i are used in the above equality. Further, it is an estimate of $\overline{V}_i(V(n), \widetilde{\pi}_i(n))$ that is available to us and not the more recent $\overline{V}_i(V(n), \widetilde{\pi}_i(n+1))$. This represents the loss in accuracy due to *not* estimating $\overline{V}_i(V(n), \widetilde{\pi}(n+1))$ by simulation.

NUMERICAL RESULTS

We consider a continuous time queuing model for flow control in communication networks as in [4]. A single bottleneck node is fed with two arrival streams, one an uncontrolled Poisson stream and the other a controlled Poisson process. Service times are assumed i.i.d., with exponential distribution. We assume that the node has a buffer size $B < \infty$. Given a constant $T > 0$, we assume that the continuous-time queue length process $\{q_t, t > 0\}$ at the node is observed every T instants and on the basis of this information the controlled source tunes the rate at which it sends packets so as to minimize a certain cost. Suppose q_n denotes the queue length observed at time $nT, n \geq 0$. The controlled source thus sends packets according to a Poisson process with rate $\lambda_c(q_n)$ during the time interval $[nT, (n+1)T]$. The rate is then changed to $\lambda_c(q_{n+1})$ at instant $(n+1)T$ upon observation of state q_{n+1} - we assume for the present that there is no feedback delay. The aim then is to find a stationary optimal rate allocation policy that minimizes the associated infinite horizon discounted cost. We choose $B = 50$ and take the compact action set $U(i)$ (where $\lambda_c(i) \in U(i), \forall i \in S$) to be the interval $[0.05, 4.5]$. The discount factor α is 0.9.

The uncontrolled traffic rate λ_u is chosen as 0.2 and the service rate μ for incoming packets is set to 2.0. For a system operating under a stationary policy π, we use the cost function $K(q_n, \pi_{q_n}, q_{n+1}) = |q_{n+1} - B/2|$ Note that while the source rate chosen, $(q_n) \equiv \pi_{q_n}$, does not directly enter into the cost function above, it has an impact on the queue length q_{n+1} observed T seconds later, which in turn affects the cost. A cost function of this type is useful in cases where the goal is to simultaneously maximize throughput and minimize the delay in the system.

The value of δ needed in (6) is set to 0.1. We arbitrarily set the initial value function iterate $V_i(0) = 0, \forall i \in S$ and policy iterate as $\tilde{\pi}_i(0) = 2.275, \forall i \in S$ for the proposed algorithm. The value of M needed in (7) is taken to be 100. As a metric to characterize the convergence of all algorithms, we measured a quantity $err_V(n)$ at value function update n in the following manner: $err_V(n) = \max_{i \in S, 1 \le k \le 50} \{|V_i(n) - V_i(n-k)|\}$. Similarly, convergence in terms of policy is obtained using $err_{\tilde{\pi}}(n) = \max_{i \in S, 1 \le k \le 50} \{\tilde{\pi}_i(n) - \tilde{\pi}_i(n-k)\}$ The step-size sequences $\{a(n)\}$, $\{b(n)\}$ and $\{c(n)\}$ needed in (5), (6) and (7), respectively, were chosen as $a(0) = b(0) = c(0) = 1$, $a(n) = n^{-1}, b(n) = n^{-0.9}, c(n) = n^{-0.55}$ respectively.

Convergence of the form $err_V(n) \le 0.1$ and $err_{\tilde{\pi}}(n) \le 0.1$ is achieved within 150 and 300 updates of (5), respectively. In Figure 1a, we plot the converged source rates for $T = 5,10$ and 15 respectively. Similarly, converged value functions (using the err_V criterion) are shown in Figure 1b. We observe that for given T, the source rates are inversely related to the queue length values since the cost function imposes a high penalty for states away from $B/2$. Further, the difference between the highest and lowest rates decreases as T increases since for lower values of T, the controller has better control over the system dynamics than when T is large.

Convergence for the classical value iteration algorithm (3) for $err_V(n) \le 0.1$, is achieved within 100 $V(n)$ updates for all T. The value functions obtained therein are shown in Figure 2a, which match the corresponding results of the proposed algorithm shown in Figure 1b. We made some modifications to $U(i)$ in order to compute the transition probabilities $p(i,u,j), \forall i,j \in S, u \in U(i)$ needed in the RHS of the Poisson Equation $\sum_{j=1}^{s} p(i,u,j)(K(i,u,j) + \alpha V_j(n))$. The discrete action set $U(i), \forall i \in S$, consists of actions spaced at roughly 0.005 within the compact interval $[0.05, 4.5]$, thus making for $|U(i)| = 225, \forall i \in S$. The transition probabilities were computed in a method similar to that in [3]. On a Pentium 4 computer, classical value iteration (for the above discretized set) took 2 seconds whereas the proposed algorithm took 12 seconds (over the compact action set). This is due to the time required for simulating transitions, and a faster simulator will bring such a comparison closer.

For purposes of comparison, we propose a variant of the algorithm in sec. 6.2 and 6.3 of [12] for the current situation of a look-up table. We first present the algorithm and then its proposed variant to suit our framework. The algorithm proposed in [12] simulates a single endless trajectory, i.e. $i_{n+1} = \eta_n(i_n, u_n(i_n))$ and updates a coefficient vector that helps approximate the value function for each state $i \in S$. This coefficient vector is $r(n) \in \Re^K$ where $K << s$, and the approximate value function is given by $\tilde{V}_i(n) = (\Phi r(n))(i), \forall i \in S$. Here, the $s \times K$ matrix Φ consists of the feature vectors $\phi(i), \forall i \in S$ as the rows and is of full rank. The $i-$th element of the $s \times 1$ vector $\Phi r(n)$ is indicated by $(\Phi r(n))(i)$. Below is the algorithm of sec. 6.2 of [12]:

$$r(n+1) = r(n) + a(n)\phi(i_n)\begin{pmatrix} K(i_n, u_n(i_n), i_{n+1}) + \alpha(\Phi r(n))(i_{n+1}) \\ -(\Phi r(n))(i_n) \end{pmatrix}, \quad (11)$$

where the decision $u_n(i_n)$ is the `greedy' decision, i.e.,

$$u_n(i_n) = \arg\min_{u \in U(i_n)} E\{K(i_n, u, \eta(i_n, u)) + \alpha(\Phi r(n))(\eta(i_n, u))\}. \quad (12)$$

Now, consider the value function iterates $V(n)$ in place of the coefficient vector $r(n)$ in (11). Also make the feature vector $\phi(i), \forall i \in S$ equal to the unit vector $e_i \in \Re^s$, then the algorithm (11) reduces to:

$$V(n+1) = V(n) + a(n)\begin{pmatrix} \sum_{i=1}^{s}\{K(i, u_n(i), \eta(i, u_n(i))) + \alpha V_{\eta(i, u_n(i))}(n)\}e_i \\ -V(n) \end{pmatrix}, \quad (13)$$

where recall that $u_n(i)$ is just the $\pi_i(n+1)$ in (4). Note that whereas (13) requires $u_n(i)$ for all $i \in S$, (11) uses only $u_n(i_n)$. Using the fact that $\Phi^T \Phi$ is the identity matrix, one can see that (13) is a variant for the more recent algorithm for approximate fixed point computation given in [6] as well, which employs a Kalman filter approach. In most simulation based settings, the term $u_n(i)$ can only be identified by simulating transitions out of i using all $u \in U(i)$, possibly averaging over multiple transitions for the same action $u \in U(i)$. Note that (13) corresponds to a stochastic approximation implementation of the operator T, using the diminishing stepsize $a(n)$. In [12], sec. 6.3 suggests that a greedy selection like (12) does not work in practice and exploration of $U(i)$ is employed. Further, [7] theoretically formalizes this using a T_δ operator which employs a Boltzmann distribution to select $u_n(i_n)$ from $U(i_n)$. We implement the variant of the algorithm of [12], using the exploration suggested in [7], and discretizing each $U(i)$ into 45 equally spaced actions. The algorithm uses $a(n) = n^{-0.6}$ and requires roughly 4000 updates and almost 800 seconds in all cases of T for the $V(n)$ vector to converge to $err_V(n) \leq 0.1$. Figure 2b plots the value function iterates obtained after convergence.

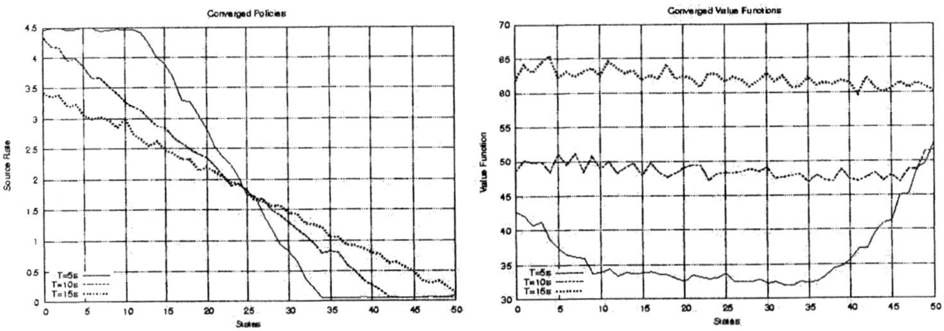

Figure 1: Plots of (a) converged policies and (b) value functions

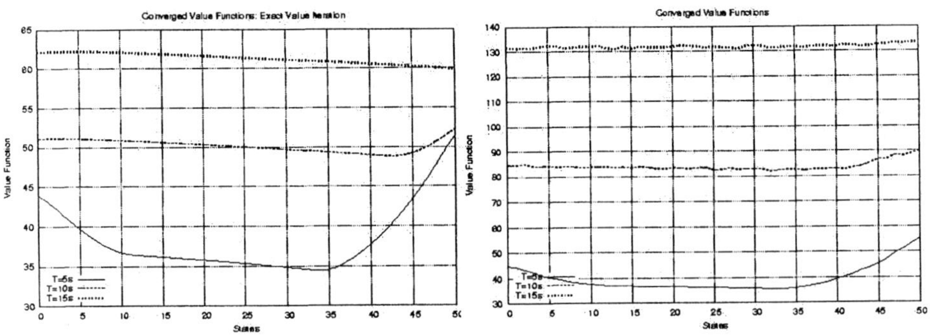

Figure 2: V iterates obtained using a) classical VI b) algorithm in [12]

ACKNOWLEDGEMENTS

This work was supported in part by Grant No. $SR/S3/EE/43/2002-Engg$ from Department Of Science and Technology, Government of India.

REFERENCES

[1] Abdulla, M.S., and Bhatnagar, S. Reinforcement Learning Based Algorithms for Average Cost Markov Decision Processes. *Submitted.*

[2] Bertsekas, D.P. *Dynamic Programming and Stochastic Control*, 1976 New York: Academic Press.

[3] Bhatnagar, S., and Abdulla, M.S. Reinforcement Learning Based Algorithms for Finite Horizon Markov Decision Processes. *Submitted.*

[4] Bhatnagar, S., and Kumar, S. A Simultaneous Perturbation Stochastic Approximation-Based Actor-Critic Algorithm for Markov Decision Processes. IEEE Trans. on Automatic Control, 2004, 49(4):592~598.

[5] Bhatnagar, S., et al., Two-timescale simultaneous perturbation stochastic approximation using deterministic perturbation sequences. ACM Trans. on Modeling and Computer Simulation, 2003, 13(4):180~209.

[6] Choi, D. S., and Van Roy, B. A Generalized Kalman Filter for Fixed Point Approximation and Efficient Temporal-Difference Learning, *Submitted to Discrete Event Dynamic Systems.*

[7] De Farias, D.P., and Van Roy, B. On the Existence of Fixed Points for Approximate Value Iteration and Temporal-Difference Learning. Journal of Optimization Theory and Applications, June 2000, 105(3).

[8] Konda, V.R., and Borkar, V.S. Actor-Critic Type Learning Algorithms for Markov Decision Processes. SIAM J. Control Optim., 1999, 38(1): 94~123.

[9] Konda, V.R., and Tsitsiklis, J.N. Actor-Critic Algorithms. SIAM J. Control Optim., 2003, 42(4): 1143~1166.

[10] Singh, S., and Bertsekas, D. Reinforcement Learning for Dynamic Channel Allocation in Cellular Telephone Systems. Advances in Neural Information Processing Systems (NIPS), 1997, 9: 974~980.

[11] Tsitsiklis, J. N., and Van Roy, B. Optimal Stopping of Markov Processes: Hilbert Space Theory, Approximation Algorithms, and an Application to Pricing High-Dimensional Financial Derivatives. IEEE Trans. on Automatic Control, 1999, 44(10): 1840~1851.

[12] Van Roy, B., et. al., A Neuro-Dynamic Programming Approach to Retailer Inventory Management, 1997, Proc. of the IEEE Conf. on Decision and Control..

STUDY ON APPLICATIONS OF WEB MINING TO DIGITAL LIBRARY

Baoji Wang, Ruiqing Xu, Jinnuo Zhu, Qingsheng Luo, Guoming Cheng, Wenli Yang, Zhihua Xin, Luyan Wang, Qingshui Liu
China Agricultural Univeristy Library, 17 Tsinghua East Road, Beijing,100083, P.R.China

Abstract: Based on the discussion of the technology properties of Data Mining and Web Mining, the types of Web mining were analyzed, the applications of Web mining to digital library and the Agricultural Engineering Digital Library (AEDL) based upon modern network, information and web mining technology were introduced.

Key words: Digital library, Data Mining, Web Mining, Information Service

1. INTRODUCTION

Digital library is a data information system, which contains abundant and diverse digital information resources, and depends on the support of modern technologies. It meets the need of users effectively by adopting modern new advanced technology and organizing resource orderly. At present, the information content of digital library comprises large number of digital library collection, various databases, full-text Web resource link and a mass of information in Internet. These considerable data must be organized, analyzed and mined to find out the valuable information, which the user need really. This is also the problem that the Web data mining technology wants to resolve. Web data mining technology is adopted and applied in the whole process of information discovery and supply of information in digital library to provide optimized information service and meet the individual need of user. Therefore, the Web data mining has expensive application space in several aspects as the optimum building of digital library information, information automated handling, advancing of information service quality and extension of obligation. And Web data mining will play an important role in the development of digital library to automation, networking and intelligence.

1.1 Web Mining and Data Mining (DM)

1.1.1 Data Mining

Data mining is a process of extracting connotative and unknown but useful information and knowledge from the vast, incomplete, noisy, fuzzy and stochastic data. DM brings the database technology into a more advanced phase. It cannot only inquiry the departed data, but also can find out the potential relationship between the old-time data, thereby DM can promote the information transfer. Briefly, DM is an advanced handing process that screens out connotative, believable, novel and effective information from a mass of data.

DM syncretizes statistic methods, computer technology and artificial intelligence technology, and extracts mode, amend, relationship, abnormity, regularization from the vast databank and statistic important structure and event.

DM was achieved mainly by followed methods: classification, regression, clustering, summarization, change and deviation detection and association rules.

1.1.2 Web Mining

Web data mining is the application of data mining technology to net information handing. It is the process that extracts the useful information or knowledge from web resource and distills the unknown mode, which contained in Web resource and has potential application value. Considered as integrated technique, Web data mining technology relates to multi-fields as Web technology, artificial intelligence, computer linguistics, informatics and statistics.

1.1.3 Distinguish betw Web Content Mining een Web mining and data mining

Web mining grows out of data mining, compared to data mining, Web mining has own characteristic as followed: firstly, the objects of Web mining are large number of heterogeneity distributing Web documents, and each data source is isomerous. The mining work towards the databank with Web as middle-piece, as well as towards the data of log and user information in Web server still belongs to traditional data mining. However, these types of data mining are considered as Web mining in most literatures presently. Secondly, Web is a logic diagram consists of document node and hyperlink. Therefore, the mode obtained from Web mining may be about Web content, and also can be about Web structure. Thirdly, Web is unstructured, semi-structure and lack of semantic that machine can understand, and the objects of traditional data mining are limited in structural data of database. Thereby, many data mining technologies cannot apply to Web mining, although Web document need pretreatment.

2. CHARACTERISTICS OF WEB DATA MINING

Web is a distributed information system based upon hypertext. At present, Web involves many information service fields, such as news, advertisement, consumption information, finance management, education, government, electronic business. These information services provide abundant resource to data mining. The characteristics of Web data mining were listed as followed:

(1) Most data of Web is HTML format, and the information about some subject is distributed desultorily in multi-directories of Web site. In this way, a strong search engine is needed, by searching keywords to locate the hypertext. And an intelligentized system is also needed to understand the data described by natural language. It was difficult to understand these data completely, due to the immature natural language understanding technology presently. At the same time, there are redundancy, inconsistency and even contradictory between data source.

(2) Web seems to be too large to effective data storage and data mining. At present, web data is calculated by millions megabyte, and still increases rapidly, and has following two characteristics:

① Data source has very strong dynamic. Internet is a system that updates and changes momently. Therefore, it need use some technologies of data storage to save the renewed date of Web.

② The date has diversity. After filtrated, Web data has numeric data (integer, real), Boolean data, classified data, property metadata and proper Web data (URL and Email address et al). The new data type must generate new characteristic, and intrinsic mining method need to be improved and expended.

(3) The aim of user is fuzzy. Data mining user based on Internet always has a passing acquaintance with the mining object and has not a specific aim. So the data mining system need to has some intelligence and learning mechanism, tail the interests of user continuously, and expatiate on the results of mining distinctly and detailedly.

Based upon the above characteristics, Web data mining is a challenge subject, refers Web access mode, Web structure and regulation, and dynamic Web content research.

3. TYPES OF WEB DATA MINING

The tasks of Web mining are diverse due to the complexity of Web information. Based on the different mining objects, Web data mining can be divided into following types: Web Content Mining, Web Structure Mining and Web Usage Mining. The classified structure is shown in Fig.1.

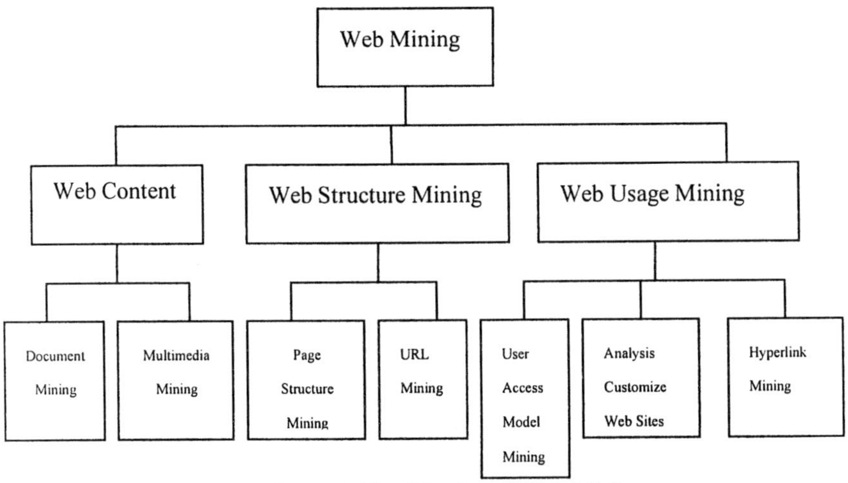

Figure 1. Classification of Web Mining

3.1 Web Content Mining

Web content mining is a process that obtains potential and valuable knowledge or mode from the file content and information of Web. Web content mining is divided into Web text mining and Web multimedia mining, and the mining objects are Web text information and Web multimedia information, respectively.

(1) The mining towards text document (including Txt, PostScrip, PDF, HTML and so on) is considered as text mining. Web text mining can summarize, classify, cluster and relation associate analysis the content of vast document aggregate in Web, as well as can use Web document to analysis the trend.

The general treatment process of Web text data mining is described in Fig.2. Most document data of Web is html document and lack of structure characteristic as databank planar table. Thereby, characteristic information of html document aggregate that expressed as VSM generally must be extracted firstly. In this way, the document eigenvector has stupendous dimension, therefore, characteristic aggregate must be curtailed. Then, knowledge mode faced to specific application purpose is extracted by the method of machine learning. Finally, the gained knowledge mode is evaluated.

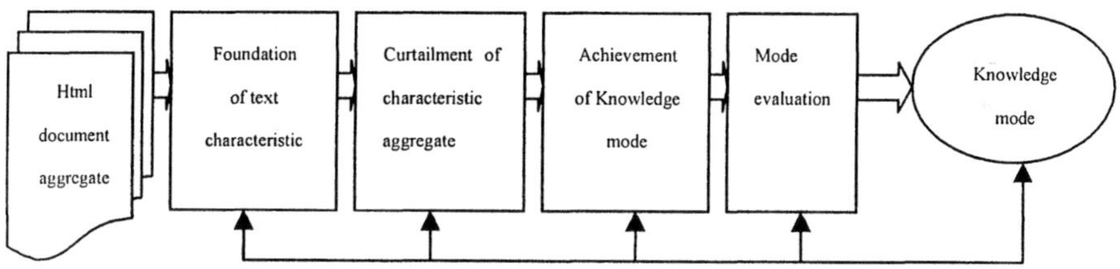

Figure 2. The general process of Web text data mining

(2) To mine the multimedia document (Image, Audio, Video) is called multimedia mining. The process of multimedia information mining is that pre-treats the audio-data, video data and image in Web firstly, and then mines the potential and significant information and mode by applying mining technology.

3.2 Web Structure Mining

Web structure mining is to infer the knowledge out of Web content by using organization structure and hyperlink relationship of Web page and institution information of Web document (Title, Heading, Anchor sign), it comprises hyperlink mining, inter structure mining and HTML mining. The hyperlink between documents reflects some affiliation of documents, such as inclusion, affiliation, correlativity, citation. Web page is analyzed by HTML tree logic structure to attain the characteristic of inter structure. Moreover, the HTML of Web page may reflect the type of page or directory structure relationship between pages. Web structure mining can summarize the structure of website and web page, and generates information of comparability and relationship between websites. It also can sort and cluster the web pages, and find the association between the web pages, then, judge the importance of pages and find the authoritative site of the correlative subject. Page Rank method and Key Page or Scripture method are the common methods. The new position of shifted Web Page is found by constructing heuristic regulation about Web Page HTML. The mining based on link can resolve the problem of network wander, and it can improve the using efficiency of Page by optimizing and recomposing dynamically the hyperlink.

3.3 Web Usage Mining

To mine the log left by the users when they accessed Web server is Web usage mining, and it is also called Web log mining. Web log mining discovers the browse mode of access site of users by analyzing log file of Web serve to provide multifarious information which profits the improvement of Web sites to the site administrators, such as the navigation function of Web sites and system design of Web application. Accordingly, Web usage mining benefits users, improves the performance of Web server and increases individual service.

The data treated by Web log mining contains: server log (access log, citation log and agency log), choice data as the structure of Web sites and login number. The basic processes of Web mining shown in Fig.3 consist of pretreatment, transaction recognition, mining arithmetic actualization and mode analysis.

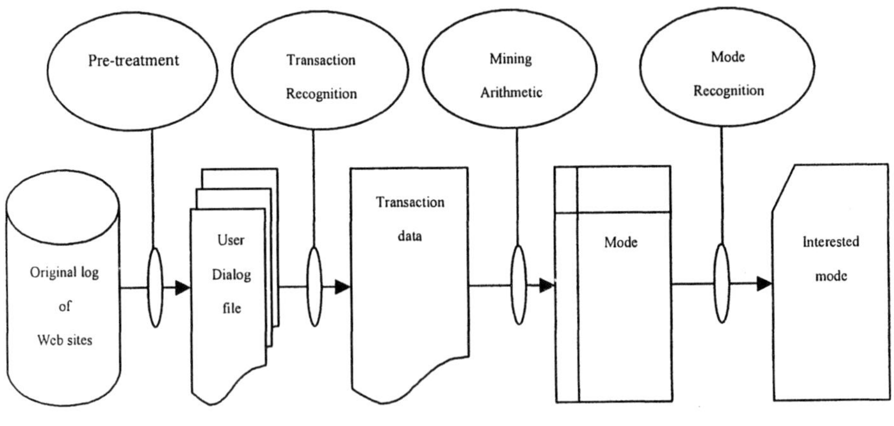

Figure 3 The basic process of Web log mining

4. APPLICATIONS OF WEB DATA MINING TO DIGITAL LIBRARY

4.1 Applications of Web data mining to information discovery

The applications of Web data mining to information discovery comprise Web data exploitation techniques, multilingual information discovery and interdisciplinary coordinated searches. Web data exploitation technology is developed due to the difficulty of gaining the information from Internet, the realization process consists of information collection, document identification, document classification and others. Network intelligence and intelligent information catcher are the two realization manners. Multilingual information discovery is a research project developed for the geographical and lingual obstruction of globalization information. And the study involves several aspects as followed: multilingual electronic document getting, integrated machine translate and multilingual information searches system. Interdisciplinary coordinated search can send concurrent request to several even tens of databanks, and links with OPAC, interlibrary loan, document submission and electronic source. It provides uniform searches interface to users and returns to uniform results after interdisciplinary querying.

4.2 Applications of Web data mining to service improvement

User information and user access log are the two types of user access data that can be recorded when the user accesses digital library with browser. The user information includes user name, user access IP address, profession, age and hobby and so on. User name is inputted by user when the user enters into the library. The profession, age and hobby and other information of user are filled in when the user register the library. The user access IP address can attain via program. User access record embodies the click record of classified browse item and keywords and mode of search. The user access record also can obtain from program. To analysis the user access data, it can help the digital library understand well the user requirements in following aspects:

(1) To guide the collection of digital library information source. The default of information source can be discovered by analyzing the data of fail demand of user in server and integrating the assemble arithmetic to direct the collection of information source, then it makes the information source systems of digital library rational. The data of online investigation, message

note, reading guide slip and others in digital library system can be transformed into normal structure database by collecting, clearing up and reconstructing. The data mining methods can be used to discover the interest mode of user and even pre-detect the interest vicissitude of user colony, adjust the direction of library collection, and do a collection plan of information source ahead.

(2) To improve the design of library site structure. The information demand and action rule of user can be found by using Web mining to provide reference to network site structure optimization. Sequentially, it makes the source configuration rational and the speech that user finds out the demanded information quicker. The measures that improve the design of library site structure include following aspects:

Investigating the user address in high access rate resource;

Making mirror image in concentrated region of user (obtaining by analyzing IP address);

Mining, catching and confirming the frequent browser and access path by using path analysis mode, adjusting the site structure;

Appending advertisement or reading guide slip in suited place.

4.3 Applications of Web data mining to information supply

One of the applications of Web data mining to information supply is to individual service, supplying actively the user with integrated and relative intact information or knowledge aggregate to meet the special demand of user. There are three types of individual service: ① according to the specific user demand, providing customizing Web page and information channel or information item to user, putting the query agent service in practice; ② according to specific subject, to direct literature source or supply literature full text, and to bring the individual literature information service into effect; ③ according to specific subject, offering relative intact project knowledge and carrying individual decision-making support service. These processes as followed must be experienced to actualize the individual service: Constructing individual user dynamic demand model; Searching and mining correlative information toward specific demand; According to specific subject, filtering, processing and assembling the gained information to integrate the relative intact information aggregate, and sending it to the user or service agent online or offline to realize information support. According to specific subject, syncretizing and activating the relative intact information aggregate to generate new project knowledge, and sending it to the user online or offline to realize decision-making support. The mining of Web usage log is the best method to realize this process in Web data mining technology.

Another application is information intelligent pusher, on the basis of the keyword that the user inputs, it can identify and forecast the interest and fancy of user, thereby, it pushes relative knowledge and up to date information to user in time. The form of push has channel push, mail push, web page push or special push.

The third application is interactive service, it emphasizes the building of uniform information supply platform, and let the different group that has different type of information and technology actualize information sharing. Based on these, the new information is generated by clustering and calculating.

5. TO BUILD AN AGRICULTURAL ENGINEERING DIGITAL LIBRARY

In order to supply agricultural engineering information more efficiently, accurately and completely for agricultural technician, we are making use of modern network, information and web mining technology to build an Agricultural Engineering Digital Library (AEDL).

AEDL has seven subsystems as followed:

Data source collection system, it has several functions as information collection on the web, existing electronic document format transition and metadata system transition.

Data source processing system, it is used to complete the digital processing and indexing classification of traditional source.

Database issuance and search system: to actualize various search service (full text retrieval, heterogeneous database uniform retrieval and distributed retrieval), and to realize subscription push, content issuance, full text transmission and Compact Disc publication.

Data source management system, it can actualize user purview management, databank maintenance, statistic and meterage.

Data reference consulting system: including such modules, such as FAQ consultation, MAIL consultation, QQ character interactive consultation, audio and video frequency real time reference and BBS.

User education system on the web, it consists of multimedia schoolteaching learning system, multimedia homework and examination system, online reference and tutorship system and courseware make tools, and can realize interactive distance learning based on network real time interactive technology.

Personal digital library system, which actualizes individual personal source storage, management and collection, and the personal resource bank is divided into document data section, work and study section and entertainment section.

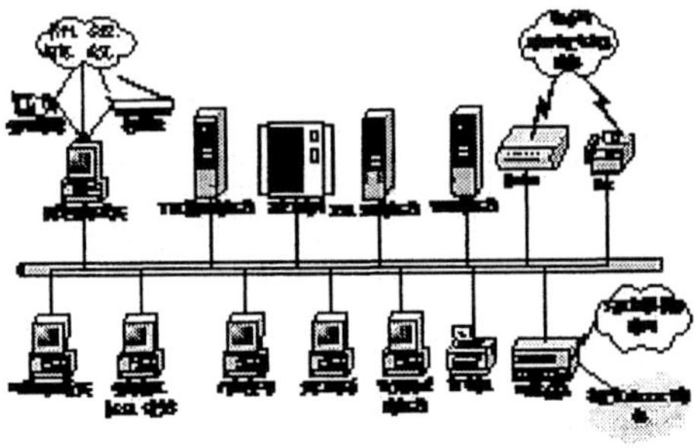

Figure 4 AEDL system structure

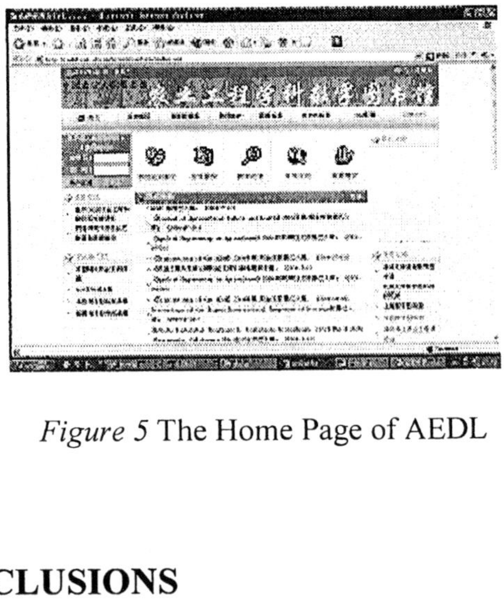

Figure 5 The Home Page of AEDL

6. CONCLUSIONS

Presently, there are many fruits in various aspects of knowledge discovery research. The study of Web data mining in digital library not only can utilize the exiting artificial intelligence theory well and can develop knowledge discovery research deeply, but also can obtain study fruits with comprehensive application foreground. Thereby, it has great value of research and application. Thus it can be seen that comprehensive integrated applications of knowledge discovery technology can resolve many problems of digital library currently, and it will accelerate the development of digital library radically by integrating the knowledge discovery applications into digital library system.

REFERENCE

[1]Arms W Y. Digital Libraries. Massachusetts, London: The MIT Press Cambridge, 2000

[2]Wang Yan. The Application of Data Mining in Digital Library. Information Science, 2003(2)

[3]Zhou Tao, Li Jun. The Research of Web Data Mining Technology, Journal of HanZhoug Teachers College (Natural Science), June, 2004

[4]Liu Wenqing, Bao Juejie. Research on Web-based Data Mining Technology and Its Application, Journal of Chongqing Three Gorges University, 2004(3)

[5]Bao Junjie. Research on Web Data Mining, Journal of Chongqing College of Education, May, 2004

[6]Wang Baoji. Study and Practice on Agricultural Engineering Digital Library Based on TPI, New Technology of Library and Information Service, 2003(5)

[7]He Shaozhuo. A few words about Data Mining and its Application to Library, Library World, sep., 2004

STUDY ON CONTROLLER WITH ONLINE DECISION SUPPORT SYSTEM FOR LASER-CONTROLLED LEVELING

Yongsheng Si [1], Gang Liu [2], Yuliang Chen [1]

1 Hebei Agricultural University , 071001, Baoding, China siyongsheng@yahoo.com

2China Agricultural University, 100083, Beijing, China pac@cau.edu.cn

Abstract: A controller and its hardware structure for laser-controlled field leveling was developed that has online decision support function. S3C44B0X and μC/OS-II were adopted as the CPU and operating system respectively. The controller has three main functions: course determination, rough/precision leveling switch and earthwork calculation. The purpose of course determination is to find the shortest transport distance and minimize the cost. The rough/precision leveling switch can increase working efficiency and reduce the wearing and tearing of the equipments. And the function of earthwork calculation is used to estimate the workload of the leveling system. Experiments showed that the online support system made the field leveling quite efficient and intelligent.

Key words: decision support system, laser leveling, ARM, μC/OS-II, controller -

1. INTRODUCTION

Laser leveling is an important technique widely used in many fields of industry and agriculture. It provides precise measurement for horizontal, vertical, aligning or measuring in different applications. In agriculture, this technique is effectively used to improve the irrigation quality and planting conditions that can save water and increase yields.

In this paper, the laser leveling system consists of five parts: laser transmitter, laser receiver, controller, hydraulic device and bucket. The operation principle of the system is as follows: Laser transmitter is fixed at the building site with tripod, and it can automatically rotate to form horizontal laser plane as a reference to land leveling above the field. The laser receiver is installed on the backstay of the bucket. Thus, the height of the field can be measured and the signals can be sent to controller. After receiving the signals, the controller will adjust the height of the bucket through the hydraulic device.(Figure 1)

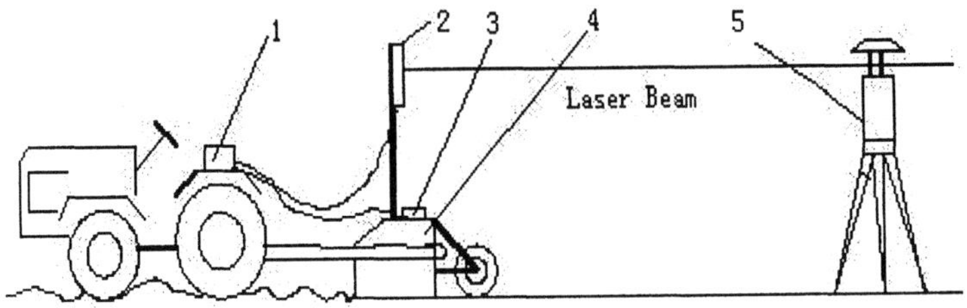

1 controller 2 receiver 3 hydraulic device 4 bucket 5 transmitter

Figure 1 Schematic diagram of the laser leveling system

Many laser leveling systems have been developed in China, For example, China Agricultural University (CAU) developed a laser leveling sample device in 2002. All laser leveling systems can work efficiently with the help of experienced operators. The operators need to draw a 'cut/fill' map and make a plan to effectively move soil from high to low areas. The operators also need to measure distance of the field as many of the critical decisions are based on the accuracy of distance. The workload can be estimate by calculating the volume of soil to be moved. To make the laser leveling system more efficient and more intelligent, a controller with online decision support system was developed based on the laser leveling sample device designed by Research Center for Precision Agriculture, China Agricultural University (CAU). The online decision support system has four main functions:

1. Automatically record the height of the field with the GPS data
2. Calculate the mean height of the field and determine a course to effectively move soil from high to low areas
3. Calculate the volume of soil shifted
4. Switch Rough/Precision leveling

2. HARDWARE STRUCTURE

The key step for the system design is to choose CPU. Considering the requirements for agriculture and low-cost, the CPU should have some important features such as integrated LCD controller, high clock rate, etc. In recent years, the ARM (Advanced RISC Machines) is popularly used as embedded processor because it is a high-capability and low-cost RISC microprocessor. The SAMSUNG Company provides a kind of ARM processor: s3c44b0x. It is a 16/32-bit RISC microprocessor with LCD controller and 66MHZ clock rate. The LCD controller has 256-color DSTN with 1-ch LCD dedicated DMA. In addition, the s3c44b0x has 2-ch UART that can be used to receive the GPS signals. The system architecture is shown in detail in Figure 2.

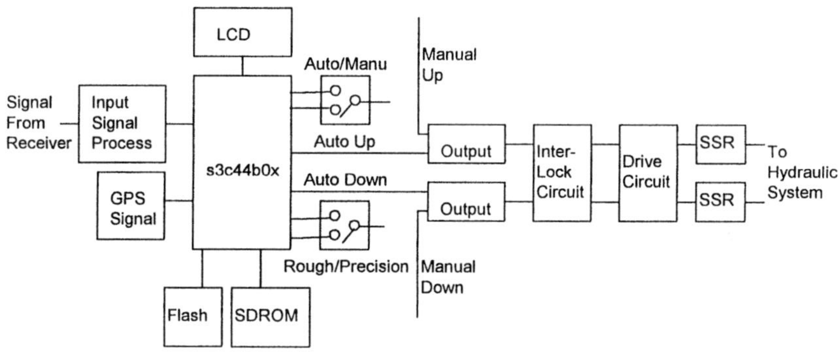

Figure 2 System Architecture

3. ONLINE DECISION SUPPORT SYSTEM

The online decision support system is developed based on µC/OS-II operating system. It has three main functions: course determination, rough/precision leveling switch, and earthwork calculation. The online decision support system can receive the GPS and field height data from the controller in real-time. By analyzing the data, the system will output the optimal course scheme, calculate workload and automatically adjust the leveling.

3.1 Course Determination Based on Quadtrees Environment Model

Transportation distance is one of the key factors that affect total budget of field leveling project. The cost of field leveling project is calculated as (Liu Changshun, Liu Gang, 2004):

$$C = \frac{Wa}{P} \square F = \frac{V \square \overline{D}}{P} \square F$$

where W_a represents the work done in field leveling, P is the power, F is the fee per unit time, V is the volume of soil to be moved and $\overline{D}$ is the transport distance. P and F will be changed to constant values after a period of time. And then, the cost is determined by $V \cdot \overline{D}$. In some field conditions, V is a constant. If so, the cost is determined by $\overline{D}$.The purpose of course determination is to find the shortest transport distance and to minimize the cost. Hence, the tractor should be driven in a circular or elliptical direction from the high areas to the nearest lower areas in the field. And the minimal turn-around radius of the tractor should also be considered. The optimal course will be displayed in the LCD to guide the operator to control the tractor.

To achieve this function, a grid map is created to visually represent the field information that includes the field height data and GPS data. To calculate the mean height, all of the measured points are added up and divided by the number of measurements. Similarly, the height of each grid can be calculated. Then all the data are input into the controller. To improve operational efficiency, an intelligent measurement device for field topographic survey was developed by China Agricultural University (Liu Zhichun, 2004). The height data and GPS data are stored in quadtrees structure. In the course determination, environment model of the leveling system is square area consisting of 2×2 basic elements (Figure. 3). The basic elements are also squares of which the length of the side should be longer than the width of bucket and the minimal turn-around radius of tractor. The value of the basic elements can be 0, 1 or 2 which indicates the height of the grid is lower than, equal to, or higher than the reference height respectively. The reference height for the rough leveling mode is different from that for the precision mode. If the heights in one grid are all higher or all lower than the reference height, this grid does not need to be divided and should be marked with 2 or 0. If some of the recorded heights in one grid are higher than the reference height while the others are lower, this grid should be divided into 4_subspaces. Divide the subspace by the same principle. Generally, the grids marked with 2 are named 'cut grid' and the grids marked with 1 are named 'fill grid'. The first two highest and lowest areas will be displayed on LCD with the guide course (Figure 4). The height data will be updated while the system is working.

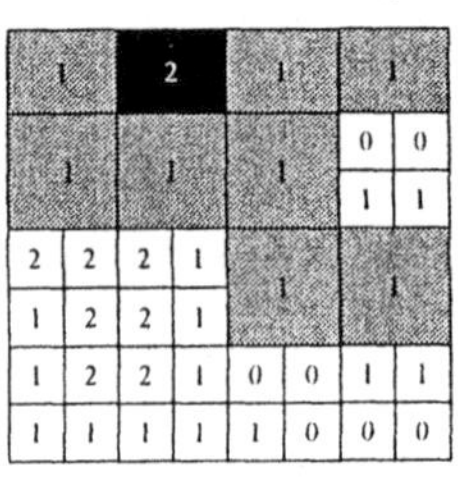

Figure 3 Environment Model

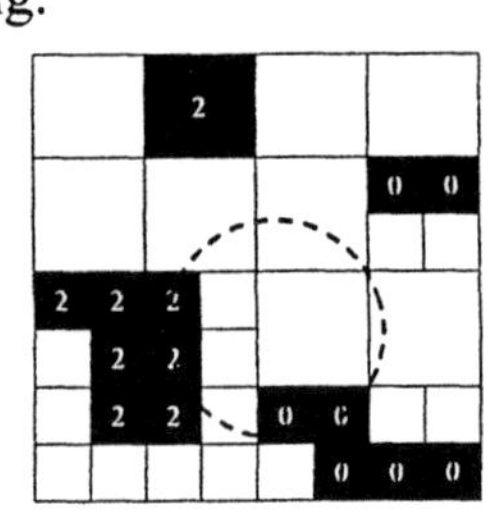

Figure 4 Course Displayed on LCD

3.2 Rough/Precision Leveling

The rough/precision leveling switch function of the online decision support system is to increase working efficiency and reduce the wearing and tearing of the equipments. Two leveling modes (rough and precision) are used to switch during the processing of operation. Generally, the rough leveling mode is used in the beginning. First, the field height data are collected by the laser receiver and translated to controller. Then, the online decision support system outputs the signals to the controller. When all the data inputted are distributed within certain area, the system will indicate on the control panel that the operator should switch leveling mode to precision leveling. At the same time, the system outputs different signals according to the rising/falling speed of the bucket, the switch frequency of the valve, the rotating speed of the laser transmitter. The output signals are different in different modes.

There are nine kinds of input signals accepted and processed from the receiver that indicate different positions of the bucket. The controller will output corresponding signals according to input signals and rough/precision leveling mode. Moreover, the controller has memory function. It can judge the position of the bucket when the laser beam above or below the receiver and adjust the bucket accordingly. (Table 1)

Table 1. Input and output signals

Input Signals	Elevation Indicated	Output Signals (positive pulse in 200ms period)			
		Precision Leveling		Rough Leveling	
		Channel 1 (up)	Channel 2 (down)	Channel 1 (up)	Channel 2 (down)
10000	very high	200ms	0 ms	200 ms	0 ms
11000	very high	200 ms	0 ms		
01000	high	80 ms	0 ms		
		Output Signals (positive pulse in 200ms period)			
01100	high	80 ms	0 ms	0 ms	0 ms
00100	even	0 ms	0 ms		
00110	low	0 ms	80 ms		
00010	low	0 ms	80 ms	0 ms	200 ms
00011	very low	0 ms	200 ms		
00001	very low	0 ms	200 ms		

3.3 Earthwork Calculation

There are different ways to calculate the earthwork. Square grid is a common method to estimate the quantity of earthwork (Wang Yujuan, Chen lijuan, 1995). Two algorithms are used to calculate the mean height: weighting average algorithm and arithmetic average algorithm. The former is higher in precision (Lin Weiqi, 2001) and was adopted in the support system. The volume of soil to be cut or filled in the grid can be calculated as (Li Fuxiang, et al., 2000):

$$V_{Ci} = \frac{A_i\left[\sum C(x,y)\right]^2}{4\square\left\{\left|\sum C(x,y)\right| + \left|\sum F(x,y)\right|\right\}}$$
$$V_{Fi} = \frac{A_i\left[\sum F(x,y)\right]^2}{4\square\left\{\left|\sum C(x,y)\right| + \left|\sum F(x,y)\right|\right\}} \tag{2}$$

where V_{ci} and V_{Fi} represent the volume of soil to be cut or filled in the grid, respectively. C(x, y) and F(x, y) indicate the heights need to be cut or filled at the 4 corners of the grid. A_i is the area of the grid.

4. EXPERIMENT RESULTS

Experiments have been conducted in Beijing Xiaotangshan Precision Agriculture Demonstration Base to check if the online support system can work normally. There are two parameters to evaluate the quality of field leveling. One is s_d (standard deviation):

$$S_d = \sqrt{\sum_{i=1}^{n}(h_i - \bar{h})^2 / (n-1)} \tag{3}$$

where hi represents the ith height measured, $\bar{h}$ is the mean height and n is the number measured. The other parameter is P (percentage)

$$P = n_c / n \tag{4}$$

where n_c represents the number of points whose absolute difference, between the measured height and the mean height, is less than a certain value. The results of the experiments are shown in Table 2.

Table 2. Results of the two experiments

	Efficiency (ha/h)	S_d (before) (cm)	S_d (after) (cm)	P (value=1.5cm)
No support system	0.16	7.0	2.4	0.81
With support system	0.18	7.1	2.1	0.85

Figure 5 and 6 are the figures drawn by the software SUFER based on the data before and after the leveling. From the two figures we can see that the use of online support system resulted in better leveling quality.

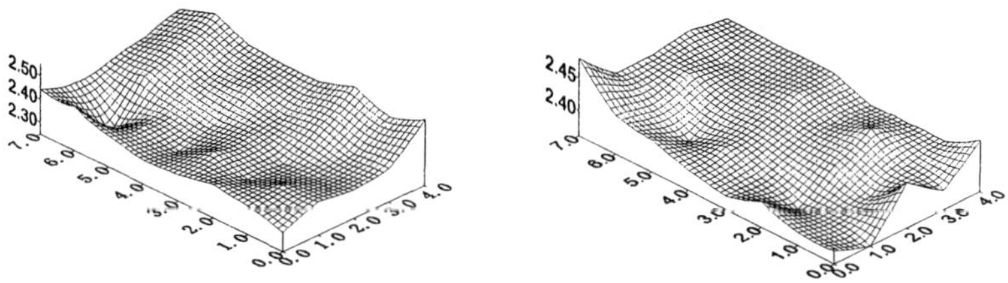

Figure 5 Before and after leveling without support system

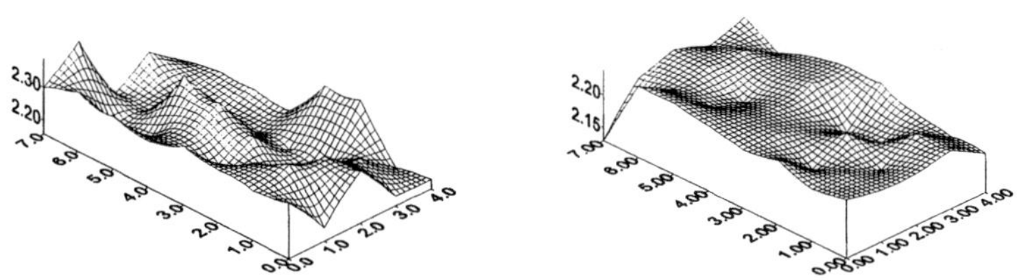

Figure 6 Before and after leveling with support system

5. CONCLUSIONS

Two experiments were conducted by the same operator. The results clearly showed that both the working efficiency and the leveling quality were improved by the online decision support system. To make the prototype more credible for users, it is necessary to work for long period to check and improve its stability and reliability.

ACKNOWLEDGEMENTS

The research project is funded by the 863 Program "Research of Precise Irrigated Technique - Research and Development of Laser Leveling System" (2002AA6Z3041).

REFERENCES

[1] Liu Zhichun, Liu Gang, An Intelligent measurement system of the field landscape for laserleveling, 2004 CIGR International Conference,Beijng:III-195

[2] Wang Yujuan, Chenlijun, Computational Program for Earthwork Quantity with Square Grid, J. OF HLJ. Hydr. Eng. Col, NO.1 1995, 21~25

[3] Lin Weiqi, Method of measure and count and analysis on precision of earthwork, Southern Metals, 2001, 49~52

[4] Li Fuxiang, Xudi, Li Yinong, Effectiveness Evaluation and Application of Land Leveling Technology, Transactions of the Chinese Society of agricultural Engineering, 2002, 50~53

STUDY ON KNOWLEDGE REASONING BASED ON EXTENDED FORMULAS

Chunyan Yang, Guanghua Wang, Yang Li, Wen Cai
Research Institute of Extension Engineering, Guangdong University of Technology, Guangzhou, P.R. China 510090

Abstract: In artificial intelligence, knowledge representation and knowledge reasoning are very important problems. There are different reasoning rules for different knowledge representation methods. In this paper, extended formulas are established based on the extended analysis principle of basic-element , and the new knowledge representation methods and knowledge reasoning modes with extended formulas are put forward. Accordingly extended reasoning modes are established. The study will provide new formalized tools for knowledge mining and new reasoning technique for solving contradiction problems.

Key words: extended formula, knowledge reasoning, basic-element, knowledge representation, problem solving

1. INTRODUCTION

Extenics studies the extensibility of things, the rules and methods for opening up things, and then uses them to solve contradiction problems with formalized models.[1] Its study objects are contradiction problems in the real world and its logic cells are basic-elements, including matter-element, affair-element and relation-element. Its logic base is extension logic.[2] Its fundamental theory is extension theory, containing three pillars— basic-element theory, extension set theory and extension logic.

Extenics has a special method of its own called extension method, containing extension analysis method, extension transformation method, conjugate analysis method and extension set method. The technology applying extension theory and extension method to different special fields is called extension engineering[3]. *Extenics* has been in great progress, which has been made in both basic theory and application research. Not long after the birth of extension theory, many experts point out that "extension theory has very strong relation with AI"[4] and "it must penetrate into AI and its related subjects". [5] AI and *Extenics* are interrelated, which can be seen from their development process.

In AI, knowledge representation and knowledge reasoning are very important problems. There are different reasoning rules for different knowledge representation methods[6]. In this paper, extended formulas are established based on the extended analysis principle of basic-element, and the new knowledge representation methods and knowledge reasoning modes with extended formulas are put forward. Accordingly extended reasoning modes are established. The study will provide new formalized tools for knowledge mining and new reasoning technique for solving contradiction problems.

2. BASIC-ELEMENTS AND KNOWLEDGE REPRESENTATION

Basic-elements, including matter-element, affair-element and relation-element, are logic cells of *Extenics*. They can be used to express varied knowledge and get the form of knowledge representation standardization.

2.1 The concepts of basic-elements

The world is formed by all things. The reciprocity among things is called affairs. Things, affairs and their relations make up of the real world. In order to describe things, affairs and their relations with formalized methods, The conceptions of matter-element, affair-element and relation-element are provided.

Matter-element is a basic element to describe a matter. The ordered three-dimensional group $R = (N, c, v)$ is called a matter-element. A matter' s name N, its characteristic c and the measure v about c are three key elements of a matter- element.

A matter can have more than one characteristic. If we express a matter N with its n characteristics $c_1, c_2, \cdots, c_n$ and the corresponding measures $v_1, v_2, \cdots, v_n$; the matter-element can be denoted by

$$R = \begin{bmatrix} N, c_1, v_1 \\ c_2, v_2 \\ \cdots\cdots \\ c_n, v_n \end{bmatrix} = \begin{bmatrix} R_1 \\ R_2 \\ \cdots \\ R_n \end{bmatrix}$$

R is called a n-dimensional matter-element, where $R_i = (N, c_i, v_i)$ is called *R*'s component matter-element.

Affair-element is a basic element to describe an affair. The ordered three-dimensional group $I = (d, b, u)$ is called an affair-element. A verb' s name *d*, its characteristic *b* and the measure *u* about *b* are three key elements of an affair-element.

Be similar to a n-dimensional matter-element, a n-dimensional affair-element can be denoted by

$$I = \begin{bmatrix} d, b_1, u_1 \\ b_2, u_2 \\ \cdots\cdots \\ b_n, u_n \end{bmatrix} = \begin{bmatrix} I_1 \\ I_2 \\ \cdots \\ I_n \end{bmatrix}$$

Relation-element is a basic element to describe a relation. The ordered three-dimensional group $Q = (s, a, w)$ is called a relation-element. A relation's name(or relation's symbol) *s*, its characteristic *a* and the measure *w* about *a* are three key elements of a relation-element.

2.2 The knowledge representation methods based on basic-element

The traditional artificial intelligence(AI), based on symbol and logic, solves problems by knowledge representation and knowledge reasoning[6]. There are many different representation methods for the same problem, and they have different representation space. Whether the representations of a problem are good or not has great influence to the results and workload of solving the problem. Therefore, it will greatly improve the efficiency of problem solving in AI that properly selecting and correctly using knowledge representation methods.

There are many kinds of knowledge representation methods, such as predicate logic method, semantic network, frame representation, production rule and process representation, etc.. All of them have their own advantages and disadvantages[6]. Basic-elements, their operation formulas and compound-elements can give the representation methods a united form. That is to say, we can use basic-elements to represent predicate, production rule, semantic network and frame, etc[2]. Representing knowledge with basic-elements, we can use transformation and reasoning to generate new knowledge and form new knowledge reasoning methods. It will raise the feasibility of problems solving, especially contradiction problems.

3. EXTENDED FORMULAS OF BASIC-ELEMENT

Basic-elements have extensibility. According to their extensibility, the document [2] studies the extended analysis principles, including divergent analysis principle, correlative analysis principle, implication analysis principle and opening-up analysis principle. Take matter-element as example, according to these principles, we can get the following extended formulas, which are the "knowledge" in AI.

(1) divergent formulas of matter-element

Given a matter-element $R=(N, c, v)$, then

$$R\dashv \{R_i \mid R_i = (N,\ c_i,\ v_i),\ i = 1,\ 2,\ \cdots,\ n\}$$
$$\text{or } R\dashv \{R_i \mid R_i = (N_i,\ c,\ v_i),\ i = 1,\ 2,\ \cdots,\ n\}$$
$$\text{or } R\dashv \{R_i \mid R_i = (N_i,\ c_i,\ v),\ i = 1,\ 2,\ \cdots,\ n\}$$
$$\text{or } R\dashv \{R_i \mid R_i = (N,\ c,\ v_i),\ i = 1,\ 2,\ \cdots,\ n\}$$
$$\text{or } R\dashv \{R_i \mid R_i = (N,\ c_i,\ v),\ i = 1,\ 2,\ \cdots,\ n\}$$
$$\text{or } R\dashv \{R_i \mid R_i = (N_i,\ c,\ v),\ i = 1,\ 2,\ \cdots,\ n\}$$

They can be denoted by $R\dashv\ R_i = (N_i,\ c_i,\ v_i)$ for short, and be called divergent formulas. When $N=N_i$, we call R and R_i matter-elements with the same matter. When $c=c_i$, R and R_i are called matter-elements with the same characteristic. And when $v=v_i$, R and R_i are called matter-elements with the same maesure. The same below.

(2) correlative formulas of matter-element

Given a matter-element $R=(N, c, v)$, if there exist matter-elements $R_i = (N_i,\ c_i,\ v_i)$, (i=1,2,…,n), and $v_i=f(v_1)$, then $R \sim R_i$(i=1,2,…,n), which are called correlative formulas.

(3) implication formulas of matter-element

Given a matter-element $R=(N, c, v)$, to certain matter-elements $R_i = (N_i,\ c_i,\ v_i)$, (i=1,2,…,n), if R@, there must be R_i@, then $R \Rightarrow R_i$(i=1,2,…,n), which are called implication formulas.

(4) opening-up formulas of matter-element

Given a matter-element $R=(N, c, v)$, if there exist matter-elements $R_i = (N_i,\ c_i,\ v_i)$, (i=1,2,…,n), so that

$$\begin{bmatrix} N \oplus N_i, & c, & v \oplus c(N_i) \\ & c_i, & v_i \oplus c_i(N) \end{bmatrix} \quad @$$

then $(R \oplus R_i)$@, denoted by

$$R \oplus R_i = \begin{bmatrix} N \oplus N_i, & c, & v \oplus c(N_i) \\ & c_i, & v_i \oplus c_i(N) \end{bmatrix}$$

And we call them combined formulas.

Given a matter-element $R=(N, c, v)$, if there exist matter-elements $R_i=(N_i, c_i, v_i)$, (i=1,2,...,n), so that $R=R_1 \oplus R_2 \oplus \cdots \oplus R_n$, then

$$R/\{R_1, R_2, \cdots, R_n\}.$$

And we call it decomposition formula.

4. EXTENDED REASONING MODES-----THE KNOWLEDGE REASONING MODES BASED ON EXTENDED FORMULAS

According to the above-mentioned extended formulas, we can get the following knowledge reasoning modes:

(1) divergent reasoning modes

$$(N, c, v) \wedge [(N, c, v) \dashv (N_i, c_i, v_i)] \models (N_i, c_i, v_i)$$

The formula means that $(N, c, v) \dashv (N_i, c_i, v_i)$ are divergent formulas. If (N, c, v) is a fact, then (N_i, c_i, v_i) are facts. In the formula, (N_i, c_i, v_i) can be the matter-elements with the same matter, the matter-elements with the same characteristic, or the matter-elements with the same measure, etc..

(2) correlative reasoning modes

$$(N, c, v) \wedge [(N, c, v) \sim (N_i, c_i, v_i), v_i = f(v)]$$
$$\models [(N_i, c_i, v_i), v_i = f(v)]$$

(3) implication reasoning modes

$$(N, c, v) \wedge [(N, c, v) \Rightarrow (N_i, c_i, v_i)] \models (N_i, c_i, v_i)$$

(4) opening-up reasoning modes

$$(N, c, v) \wedge (N_i, c_i, v_i) \wedge$$
$$\left\{ (N, c, v) \oplus (N_i, c_i, v_i) = \begin{bmatrix} N \oplus N_i, & c, & v \oplus c(N_i) \\ & c_i, & v_i \oplus c_i(N) \end{bmatrix} \right\}$$
$$\models \begin{bmatrix} N \oplus N_i, & c, & v \oplus c(N_i) \\ & c_i, & v_i \oplus c_i(N) \end{bmatrix}$$

$$(N, c, v) \wedge [(N, c, v)/\{(N_1, c_1, v_1), \cdots, (N_n, c_n, v_n)\}]$$
$$\models \{(N_1, c_1, v_1), (N_2, c_2, v_2), \cdots, (N_n, c_n, v_n)\}$$

Taking advantage of the above knowledge reasoning modes, we can provide many kinds of formalized, operative thoughts and approaches for problems solving. It is especially more effective to contradiction problems solving.

5. CASE STUDY------SOLVING CONTRADICTION PROBLEMS WITH EXTENDED REASONING

[A monkey picks bananas] A room has the height of 2.8m. At 1.8m above the ground, a handful of bananas *B* hang. The monkey *A* wants to pick *B*. But when standing up, its body height is 0.5m, and its touching height is 0.7m. There are an estrade, which is 1.4m high and has a weight of 15kg, a chair, 0.5m high and a weight of 5kg, a cabinet, 1.8m high and a weight of 50kg, and a table, 1.2m high and a weight of 20kg. Suppose these objects are mobile(can be moved or be pushed), and the biggest impetus of *A* is 25kg(that it is, *A* can push the objects under 25kg weights).

Now we use the knowledge representation methods based on basic-element and extended reasoning to solve the contradiction problem. Therefore, we should formulate the problem and its core problem with formalized method.Suppose the goal is

$$G=\begin{bmatrix} obtain, & subjection\ \ object, & bananas\ B \\ & executive\ \ object, & monkey\ \ A \\ & position, & 1.8m\ \ height \end{bmatrix}=\begin{bmatrix} d, & b_1, & B \\ & b_2, & A \\ & b_3, & 1.8m \end{bmatrix}$$

the condition is

$$L=(A,\ \text{height},\ 0.5\text{m})=(A,\ c_0,\ 0.5\text{m})$$

the problem is denoted by $P=G*L$.

Assume the appraisal characteristic c_0=height. c_{0s}, whose domain of value-measures is $X_0=<1.8,\ 2.8>$, is the needed height for realizing the goal G. c_{0t} is the height which is provided by z_0 in condition L. In this case, $z_0=L=(A,\ c_0,\ 0.5\text{m})$, then $c_{0t}(z_0)$=0.7m(touching height).

Let $W=\{g|g=(z,\ c_{0t},\ c_{0t}(z))=(z,\ c_{0t},\ x),z\in\{z_{0\dashv},z_{0\sim},z_{0\oplus},z_{0\Rightarrow}\}\}$,
then the core problem of the original problem P is

$$P_0=g_0*l_0=(z_0,\ c_{0t},\ c_{0t}(z_0))*(z,\ c_{0s},\ X_0).$$

According to the actual problem, we can establish the dependent function

$$k(x)=\frac{x-\mathbf{1.8}}{\mathbf{2.8}-\mathbf{1.8}}=x-\mathbf{1.8}$$

To $\forall g=(Z,\ c_{0t},\ x)\in W,Z=(N,c,c(N)),c=c_0$ or c and c_0 is the characteristics with the same domain of measures, let

$$\widetilde{A}(T) = \{(g,y,y') | g \in T_W W, y = K(g) = k(x), y' = T_K K(T_g g)\}$$

then

$$K_0(P) = K(g_0) = k[c_{0t}(Z_0)] = \frac{\mathbf{0.7 - 1.8}}{\mathbf{2.8 - 1.8}} = \mathbf{-1.1 < 0}$$

So the problem P is an incompatible problem. The reason is the value of c_{0t} (touching height) cannot fulfill the request of the problem.

Now we take advantage of the extended reasoning modes to solve this incompatible problem. To be simple, we only show the application of divergent reasoning mode and expansile reasoning mode.

(1) Making use of divergent reasoning modes

$$(Z_0) \wedge (Z_0 \dashv (A_i, c_0, c_0(A_i)) = Z_i) \models Z_i, (i=1,2,\cdots,n)$$

Let

$$g_i = (Z_i, c_{0t}, c_{0t}(Z_i)) \triangleq (Z_i, c_{0t}, x_i)$$

According to the definition of dependent function, to make $y = K(g_i) > 0$, we need $k(x_i) > 0$, that is $k(c_{0t}(Z_i)) = c_{0t}(Z_i) - 1.8 > 0$. Therefore, we can get $c_{0t}(Z_i) > 1.8$.

Then make a transformation ,

$$T_1 = \begin{bmatrix} replace, & b_1, & A \\ & b_2, & A_i \end{bmatrix}$$

That is, we can use a life-form A_i, whose touching height is over 1.8m to replace A. So

$$T_1 g_0 = (T_{1Z_0} Z_0, c_{0t}, c_{0t}(T_{1Z_0} Z_0)) = ((A_i, c_0, c_0(A_i)), c_{0t}, c_{0t}(z_i))$$

$$K(T_1 g_0) = k(c_{0t}(Z_i)) > 0$$

Now the incompatible problem is transformed to a compatible one.

(2) Making use of opening-up reasoning modes

$$(Z_0) \wedge (Z_i) \wedge (Z_0 \oplus Z_i = (A \oplus A_i, c_0, c_0(A) \oplus c_0(A_i)) = Z_i') \vdash Z_i', (i=1,2,\cdots,n)$$

Let

$$g_i' = (Z_i', c_{0t}, c_{0t}(Z_i')) = (Z_i', c_{0t}, 0.7 \oplus c_{0t}(A_i)) \triangleq (Z_i', c_{0t}, x_i)$$

According to the definition of dependent function, there is $k(x_i) > 0$, that is

$$0.7 \oplus c_{0t}(A_i) - 1.8 > 0$$

so that $c_{0t}(A_i) > 1.1$. That is to say, we can look for an object A_i, which is over 1.1m high, to combine with monkey A to solve the incompatible problem.

For example, we can use Z_1=(estradeA_1,c_0,1.4m), Z_2=(chairA_2,c_0,0.5m), Z_3=(cabinetA_3,c_0,1.8m), Z_4=(tableA_4,c_0,1.2m),$\cdots$ to combine with A.

So we can make transformation

$$T_2 = \begin{bmatrix} add, & b_1, & g_0 \\ & b_2, & g_1 \\ & b_3, & g_0 \oplus g_1 \\ & b_4, & push\ \ A_1 \\ & b_5, & manual \\ & b_6, & beneath\ the\ bananas \end{bmatrix}$$

where the character b_4 expresses the mode of "*add*", b_5 expresses the tool and b_6 expresses the place. T_2 shows A pushes the table A_1 to the underside of the banana and stands on A_1, which is 1.4m high. At this time,

$$T_2 g_0 = g_0 \oplus g_1 = ((A\ ,c_0,\mathbf{0.5}\text{m}), c_{0\prime}, 0.7m) \oplus ((A_1,c_0,\mathbf{1}.4\text{m}), c_{0\prime}, \mathbf{1}.4\text{m})$$
$$= ((A \oplus A_1, c_0,\ \mathbf{1}.9\text{m}), c_{0\prime}, \mathbf{2}.1\text{m})$$

$$K(T_2 g_0) = k(2.1) = 2.1 - 1.8 = 0.3 > 0$$

Now we have changed the incompatible problem to a compatible one.

Similarly, we can make transformations T_3, T_4, T_5, so that

$$K(T_3 g_0) = k(1.2) = 1.2 - 1.8 = -0.6 < 0$$
$$K(T_4 g_0) = k(2.5) = 2.5 - 1.8 = 0.7 > 0$$
$$K(T_5 g_0) = k(1.9) = 1.9 - 1.8 = 0.1 > 0$$

Apparently, T_4, T_5 can change the incompatible problem to a compatible one, but T_3 cannot.

It can be seen from the above case that through establishing the extension model of contradiction problems and using extended reasoning mode and extension transformation, we can get many transformations, such as T_1, T_2, T_4, T_5, for solving contradiction problems. But their degrees of superiority are not same. We must do superiority evaluation according to the feasibility(c_1), cost(c_2) and effect(c_3), and then select the transformations with higher superiority degree to put in practice. In this case, we can know the superiority degree of T_2, T_5 are higher through simulating in computer and superiority evaluation calculation. Limited to space, they are omitted.

6. CONCLUDING REMARKS

The objective of knowledge representation and knowledge reasoning is problem solving[7]. In this paper, through the approach to knowledge reasoning modes based on extended formulas, we attempt to apply them to solve contradiction problems, and the case analysis has proved it is feasible. The study will provide new tools for knowledge representation and knowledge reasoning of AI, and advance the study of knowledge reasoning.

Moreover, it will probe new ways for intelligentizing the process of solving contradiction problems.

ACKNOWLEDGEMENTS

The research is supported by National Natural Science Foundation of China 70271060 and 70140003 and Guangdong Province Natural Science Foundation 010049.

REFERENCES

[1] W. Cai. Extension Theory and its application. Chinese Science Bulletin, Vol. 44, No. 17(1999) 1538-1548.

[2] Cai Wen, Yang Chunyan, He Bin. Preliminary of extension logic[M]. Beijing: Science Press,2003(in Chinese).

[3] Cai Wen, Yang Chunyan and Lin Weichu. Methods of Extension Engineering. Beijing: Science Press,2003

[4] P. Z. Wang. My Tentative Knowledge to Matter-element Analysis, From Matter-element Analysis to Extenics (Science and Technology Documentation Pub., Peking, 1995). (in Chinese)

[5] S. G. Hong. A New Study Orientation. From Matter-element Analysis to Extenics (Science and Technology Documentation Pub., Peking, 1995). (in Chinese)

[6] Cai Zixing, Xu Guangyou. Artificial intelligence and its application[M]. Beijing: Tingshua University Press,2004(in Chinese).

[7] George. F. Luger. Artificial intelligence—structures and strategies for complex problem solving[M]. Beijing: China Machine Press, 2003

STUDY ON PHOTOELECTRIC AND DYNAMICAL CONTROL SYSTEM FOR FRUIT SIZING

Dongxing Zhang and Jing Li
College of Engineering, China Agricultural University P.O. Box 46, Beijing 100083

Abstract: A fruit sizing system based on photoelectric sensor is developed. The system uses AT89C51 microcomputer as its core, and a signal gathering circuit, a processing circuit, an output circuit and a display/keyboard unit are also provided. When it works, the system receives digital signals produced by fruits that shadow the light from a photoelectric sensor. After digital signals processed by the system software, every fruit's sizing level is deduced. Then, the system will output switch signals to open the sorting switches according to fruits' size, and fruits are dynamically measured and sorted in real time. Experiment results indicated that the system works well and can be easily controlled; meanwhile it is multipurpose by setting sizing levels to sort different kinds of fruits.

Key words: microcomputer, photoelectric sensor, fruit sorting

1. INTRODUCTION

Fruit production are developing very fast In China in recent years, and the increased consumers' awareness of fruit quality has made fruit production and marketing very competitive. Although growers always try to select optimal fruit varieties, and use the correct practices, they do not have absolute control over their products and therefore, unlike other industries, the "production line" of fruit will produce very non-uniform products. There has been an increasing demand for tools to sort and grade those products by various criteria. Such tools will enable the growers to grade their products and to predict the shelf life and direct the various grades to different markets according to their transportation schedule or predicted revenues.

Meanwhile, huge quantities of fruits are used by food industry. Food processing plants manufacture more than one product and use fruits of different quality for different products. For example, peach-processing plant may use firm peaches for its canning production, and soft and overripe ones for its juice and paste line. Sorting and grading the fruits will enable the processors to direct their optimal use and save a great deal of money.

When fruits are harvested, they must be cleaned, sorted, sized, graded, and packed according to its destination. Those operations are likely to be done as close as possible to the field. Quite often preparation of the products for marketing includes additional steps such as wax coating, disinfection, or drying. All these operations are performed to increase the value and marketability of the products, and in many cases some of these operations are required in order to conform to marketing regulations and standards.

Fruits are usually sorted according to their "Quality". Two main quality categories are widely used: external and internal. The "external" attributes include size, weight, shape, and color; the "internal" attributes include sugar, water content, acidity, firmness and tissue structure, bruise, tissue breakdown, internal color, etc.

Though external attributes are generally used to sort fruits, but in most cases the internal and external quality attributes are closely related. For example, an overripe fruit may change in color, sugar content, firmness and may show rot spots on the peel. A small fruit is normally not to be mature enough. A bruised fruit may show external color changes.

2. INTRODUCTION

2.1 Sizers

Belts: It uses diverging belts on which fruits travel until the gap between the belts is wide enough for the fruits to pass through. Another version is the belt-and-bar sizer. On this one, the belt conveyor is inclined at a side angle so that fruits are forced to roll against a fixed bar which creases a gap, increasing in size. When the gap is large enough the fruit rolls under the bar and into a bin. Fruit may be sized by any of its dimension. The result may be poor sizing accuracy.

Bars: Parallel bars are used to rotate the fruits about their axis and cause orientation of the fruits. This method is good with fruits such as lemons or oranges. The rotation of the fruits is achieved by rotating the parallel bars. In some cases the bars are fixed in their position and the fruits are pushed forward by incoming fruits and thus progress along the sizer. Alternatively, the bars are linked into an infinite chain that is driven as a conveyor.

Cylinders: There are 3 or 4 cylinders on the sizer, different diameter holes are allocated on each cylinder. Fruits are driven to pass the cylinders. If the size of a fruit is smaller than the holes on a cylinder, this fruit will pass the hole falling into to a tray. Otherwise, it will move to next cylinder, and so on.

2.2 Weight sortor

Apples, pears, tomatoes, and other sensitive fruits are sometimes weighted rather than sized. Fruits are placed in individual trays on a tray-conveyor, which slide over a weighing sensor monitored by a computer, which controls the discharge of the fruits into weight groups. Mechanical system is sometimes used instead of electrical system, but less accurate.

2.3 Mchine vision

Machine vision, also named computerized vision or artificial vision, is a sensing method in replacing the human visual inspection. Cameras and sensors are used for fruits features extraction and classification, algorithms for images processing and analysis. Although machine vision methods detect external visible quality attributes, some of the measurements may give indications of the overall quality of the products.

Machine vision system will have a bright future as fruit sorters, since hardware costs are declining rapidly, and the advantages of a combined inspection result of other quality attributes such as size, shape and col

3. PHOTOELECTRIC AND DYNAMICAL CONTROL SYSTEM FOR FRUIT SIZING

3.1 System Hardware

Signal Gathering System: 2 infrared transducers are oppositely positioned on the fruit sorting unit, one to sent light signals, well the other receives signals.12~36 voltage input, and high & low switch signals output.

Signal processing System: Signal and data processing system is the core for the sizer. It will control all the activity of the machine. Its performance will affect working speed, accurate, reliability and efficiency. Ether a PC or a single chip can be used, but PC will be cost and complicate to operate. Single chip AT89C51 is selected due to its advantages: low cost, high reliability, simple to program & erase, easy to expand, small in size etc.

Signal Output System: LED and LCD are used to display the output results, and executive orders will be sent to electromagnetic valves.

3.2 System Software Modules

Figure 1 Infrared sensors

Working principle of the sizer: When a fruit passes through the 2 sensors (figure 1), it will shade the light signal sent by one of the 2 sensors, so the other sensor could not get the light signal, makes the sensors output voltage changes, resulting single chip outside interrupt, entering into data processing system. When interrupt happens, timing program of the single chip is initiated, which will inspect the system intermittently. Meanwhile, the data processing system will start to grade the fruit into a "group" according to fruit "size", sending an executive order to the relative electromagnetic valve to open for discharging this fruit to that group.

Signal Gathering program Module: As descript above, shading light will make the sensors output voltage changes. In reverse, when fruit left the sensors, it will also cause voltage changes, and the timer will stop working. According to the time it takes for shading light, and the belt velocity, fruit' "size" could be calculated:

$$S = V \times T$$

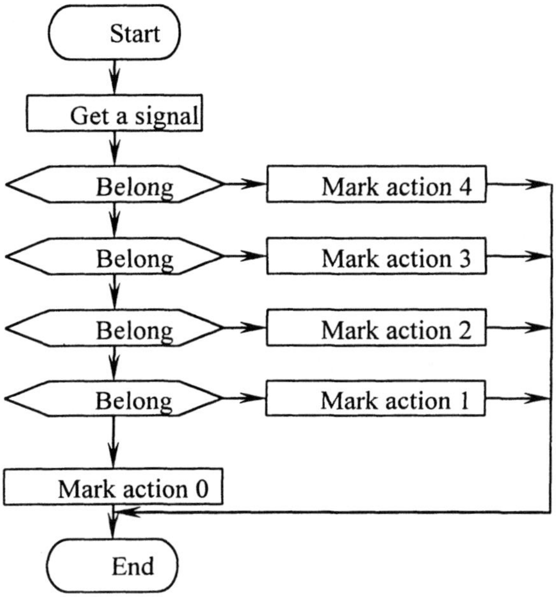

Flow chart 1 *Data Processing chart*

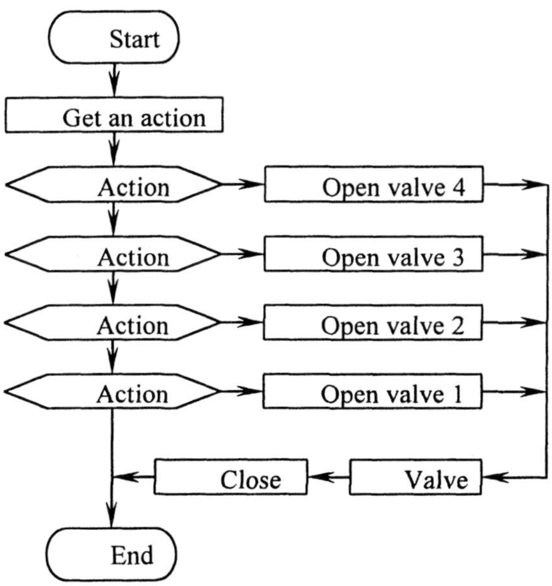

Flow chart 2 execute control chart

Signal Processing program Module: Before starting the system, the number of grades for fruit sorting must be preset first. It is completely artificial, you can set as many grades as you like, but 4 grades are popular in practice.

When processing program runs, it will compare a gathered signal with the 4 presetting grades one by one. If this signal belongs to grade 4, an action 4 will be marked. If the signal is smaller than grade 4, then it will be compared with grade 3, and so on, till the equivalent grade for this signal is found (flow chart 1). After calculation and comparison done by the processing program, all the gathering signals can be marked with action numbers, so all fruits can sorted into relative grades.

Executive control program Module: When the system works, the program will send discharge orders to the relative electromagnetic valves according to the different action marks (flow chart 2).

Man-Machine communication function: This makes it possible for one to preset the number of grades, and it will also display the sorting results, so one can directly look at the operation status.

4 ORIENTING SYSTEM

In order to get higher sorting accuracy, an orienting unit is developed. When it works, the orienting wheel is turning vertically while the cup is turning horizontally. Once the stem or calyx area touched the orienting wheel, the fruit was in a strait up & down position. Then the sensors could measure the maximal diameter of a fruit.

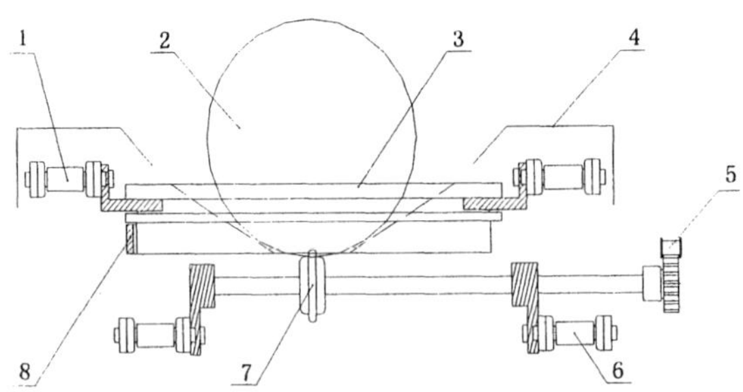

Fig.2 The Apple Orientation Unit

5. CONCLUSION

Infrared sensors and single chips are used for the system instead of weighing sensors and PC, that reducing the system cost and making the system simplified significantly, experiment results indicate that there is no compromising of fruit sorting quality.

ACKNOWLEDGEMENTS

The authors would like to thank Mr. Wang Xinting, Mr. Zhang Hailiang, Mr. Xie Feng and Miss Zhou Qinghong for their significant contribution to the machine system

REFERENCES

[1] Jose Campins, James A. Apple Stem and Calyx Indentification for Automatic Sorting. ASAE Paper, No.373079, 1997

[2] Dr.Boaz Zion. Principles of Sorting, Sizing and Grading. Postharvest Technology, 1994

[3] Wang Xinting, Zhang Dongxing. Study on Single Chip Control and Measurement System for Fruit Sorter, Journal of China Agricultural University, No.4 Vol.8, 2003

STUDY ON WEB-BASED AGRICULTURAL MECHANIZATION DECISION SUPPORT SYSTEM

Minli Yang, Feng Yang, Lijuan Shi, Jieqiang Zhuo

College of Engineering, China Agriculture University, No. 17 Qinghua Donglu, Haidian District, Beijing, China

Abstract: The paper discussed the background and meaning of research on Agricultural Mechanization Decision Support System (AMDSS). The exploitation idea of AMDSS based on web was brought forward. The data mining technique was put into the system in order to make its functions stronger and realization easier. Also designs were proposed on general framework and modules for AMDSS.

Key words: Agricultural Mechanization, DSS, Web, Data Mining

1. FOREWORD

Decision Support System (DSS) is the newest developing stage in the information system research. It is a decision-supported knowledge and information system, which bases on the computer technology and is used for dealing with the semi-structured and unstructured problems during the decision process. The research of DSS started at the beginning of the seventies of the 20th century. After more than 30 years of development, DSS and it's relevant technologies have been regarded as the accessorial support tool of administrative decision, widely used in such aspects as agriculture, industry, commerce etc., and become the important research subject in the system engineering and computer field. [1] The rapid development of the computer technology plays a strong role to DSS technology. The fast popularization of WWW technology, the mode of calculation taking network as the centre becomes the mainstream, the combination of various kinds of advanced communication technology and DSS is the inevitable trend of DSS development.

The agricultural mechanization system is a complicated system based on the regional natural resources and the social economic condition, and its macroscopical decision is a complicated course. The agricultural mechanization department as the policymaker should fully consider the social economic and natural conditions in a certain area. Also it should utilize the high-quality information effectively and in time in order to serve for adjusting the market and macroscopical decision of rural economy. So, it is urgent to establish an open Agricultural Mechanization Decision Support System (AMDSS), which regards aid decision as object. This AMDSS can offer various kinds of integrated data information, suitable models and analytical methods to support the agricultural administrative staffs to solve various kinds of decision problems or make relevant development plans.

2. DESIGN FOR THE GENERAL FRAMEWORK

The problems, which the staffs meet during the agricultural mechanization decision-making process, belong to semi-structured and unstructured problems. So-called structured degree means that the environment and law of a certain process could be offered clear explanation or description by the specific language (mathematics or logic, formal or informal, quantitative or rational). If they can be described clearly, they are called the structured problems; if they can't describe clearly, and only can be judged by intuition or experience, they are called unstructured problems; other problems lie between the two, are called semi-structured problems. [2]

As AMDSS involves an amount of the data and economic information of agricultural mechanization, and involve a wide range, including the area, the affiliated province and whole China, and according to the latest direction of DSS development at present, the Data Warehouse, the On Line Analytical Process and Data Mining technology were adopted into AMDSS to form a comprehensive DSS. Also the information of agricultural mechanization information net and economic information used in AMDSS to make the whole AMDSS connect with INTERNET. AMDSS is divided into 3 modules: Data Warehouse Management System, Data Mining System and Model Management System. AMDSS structure is as Fig.1.

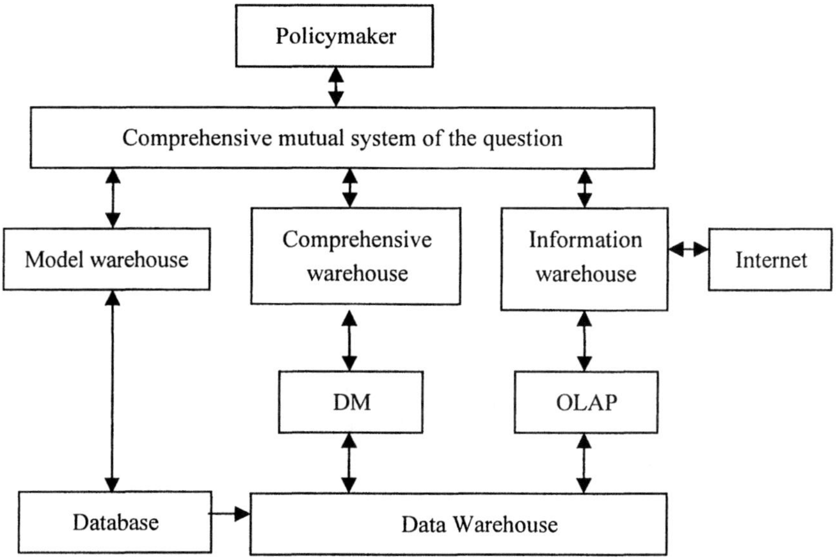

Figure1 AMDSS structure on the basis of the data warehouse

3. CHOOSING AMDSS DEVELOPING PLATFORM

There must be a good developing tool to popularize the DSS. It requires a language system to combine the data module, model module and dialogue module together. Data module and model module has separate riper language systems each other. The traditional algorithmic language such as FORTRAN, PASCAL, etc., suits the realization of the mathematics model very much, but does not support the operation of the database.[3] Various kinds of DBMS language are suitable for the management and operation of the database, but not suitable for number value operation. Integrated language should synthesize the calculate language and the database language. Statistical analysis system (SAS) is the most famous data analysis software system nowadays in the world. In latter sixties of the 20th century, SAS was developed by Prof. A. J. Barr and Prof. J. H. Goodnight in U.S.A. North Carolina State University. They established U.S.A.SAS research institute in 1975, and then put out SAS system. SAS was world-famous for leading technology and reliable support all the time. Through the constant development and improving of more than 30 years, SAS have already become the large-scale integrated application software system at present. After 1990s, SAS was devoted to develop the data warehouse, the on-lined analyze and process system, data mining and DSS. And now, the more successful large-scale software SAS8.0 integrates calculating language with database language to be simpler and more direct than other language such as FORTRAN etc. in calculating in number value. [4] So, we choose SAS8.2 as the platform to develop the whole system.

4. DESIGN OF EVERY MODULE

4.1 Setting-up the Data Warehouse System

The data warehouse is a theme-oriented, integrated and steady data collection in different time, which is used to support the decision formulation process in management. The data in warehouse faces theme correspond to traditional database face applying. Theme is a standard which classify the data in higher level, and every theme corresponds to one macroscopic analysis field. The integrated characteristic of the data warehouse refers to the process that before entering the data warehouse, the data must be processed and integrated. It is the key step of setting up data warehouse to unify the contradiction of the initial data and to make the data structure a change from face applying to face theme. The stability of the data warehouse means the data warehouse reflects the content of the historical data, but not the data produces in daily transaction processing, the data are seldom revised or not revised at all after processing and integrating and entering the data warehouse. Data warehouse is the collection of data in different time. It requires the data saved in warehouse to keep enough time in order to meet the requirement to carry on decision analyses. The data in warehouse should show its historical periods. [5]

Meta-data is another important concept in the data warehouse. It is usually defined as data that is related with others. Meta-data refers to data that describes other objects. These descriptions are used to define tabulation, database, view and other objects in relational database. Generally, Meta-data represents anything that is used to define the objects of data warehouse, and the objects may be tabulation, a list, a query, a commerce rule or metastasis in the data warehouse. The definitions of meta-data help us finish the definition of the entire significative object in the data.

The purpose of studying AMDSS is solving management and decision problems during the development of agricultural mechanization. However, the agricultural mechanization system is an open system, which is influenced by the external population, resource, environment, economic development, agricultural production, technological progress and market demand, etc.. In order to meet the research requirement, the data warehouse should embody the data of agricultural production, industrial structure, agricultural workforce proportion, agricultural output value etc. in every region in China and all over the country. The researching content is mainly to solve the problems of agricultural mechanization development management and decision. So, the setting-up of the data warehouse is mainly around these respects. Its themes are chosen according to the content of the data but not the difference of the area. The same content data is belonged to the same theme. The same data in different areas is gathered into the collection, and then compared and analyzed. Processed data is put into the information market. Also it sets up several data markets in the warehouse in order to meet the demands of the different levels' managers for data.

4.2 The Development of Data Mining System

Data Mining (DM) is getting the knowledge that people are interested in from the large-scale database. The knowledge is connotative, potential useful information which is not known in advance. And the drawn knowledge is expressed as concept, rule, law, mode, etc.; it means looking for the mode of decision support process in the aggregation of facts and data. [6] The target that the data mining is not only the database, but also file system, or other data aggregations, such as WWW information resources.

All the research of data mining is base on the data warehouse which we have set up, and it form a structure with data warehouse, manager and decision tools as Fig. 2. It has the following functions: (1) Simple— data sampling; (2) Explore — exploring, analyzing and pre-treating the characteristics of the data; (3) Modify—defining the problems, adjusting the data and choosing the technology; (4) Model—researching the model and discovery the knowledge; (5) Assess — comprehensive explaining and appraising of the model and knowledge.

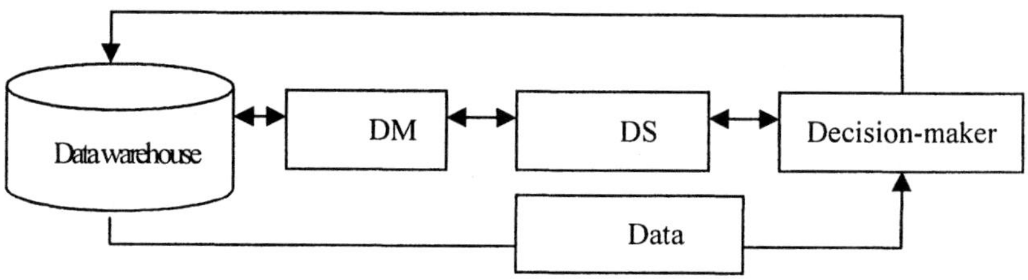

Figure 2 Data Mining under data warehouse environment

4.3 The Model Warehouse and Managment System

The model is the description of the essential characteristics of a system in a certain form to describe the function, behavior and the rules of change of the system. Generally, we have 3 kinds of methods, including logical oreganos method, experiments method and models method, to understand and research the objective world. The model method is the most capable, convenient and effective way to understand and explore the objective world. And it erects a bridge between the objective world and the scientific theory to analyze all aspects of the system. The multiformity and complexity of agricultural mechanization bring a lot of difficulties to research its development. The foundation and analyses of model is helpful to its development. And the operation of the model is help to optimize its structure.

The model warehouse is the computer system to offer storage and express, which is named "the model management system". There is over one proper memory mode to acquire, visit, refresh and synthesize the model in it. In this system, the first thing we should think over is take a propel express and storage way in order to manage the model, connect in a flexible way and participate illation. The express way of model tends to disassemble to the basic cell so as to strengthen management flexibility and reduce the storage redundancy. AMDSS adopts data mining technology under SAS platform. So, the model can realize in the data mining in general DSS. This reduces the model quantities in the storehouse and developing difficulties of management system and the whole system.

The OR model in SAS system includes the common planning method. This kind of question can be considered as a problem of solving the maximum of a goal function under a group of restrictions. If the restrictions and goal functions are linear function, it is the Linear Programming (LP). If the variable must be the integer, it is the Integer Plan (IP). Process LP in the OR model can be solved by the LP, which includes the integer plan and mixed integer plan. Generally, planning that are used in AMDSS is linear programming. The restraint terms, parameters and goal function of the LP can be stored in the database, and some of parameters can directly get from the database. Operation only need to transfer LP program and input the data from the database. When the model changes, it can finish the operation and management at the same time through the parameters in the data file only are revised. It simplifies the workflow of the model management system, and improves working efficiency. As follow Fig. 3.

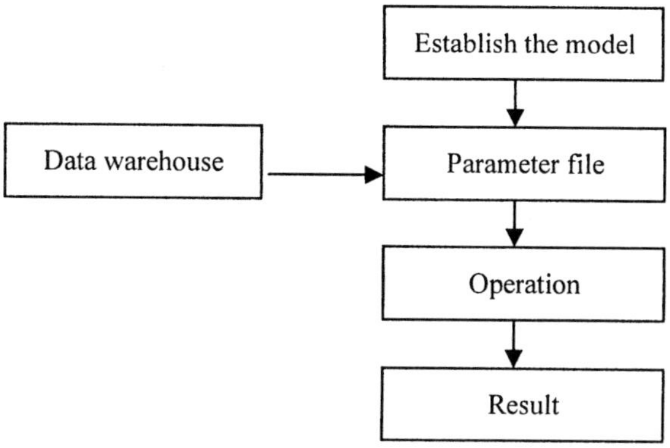

Figure 3 The development of the model administrative system on the basis of SAS system

5. INTEGRATING OF AMDSS SOFTWARE SYSTEM

Because the data warehouse system, data mining system and model administrative system of AMDSS are developed under the systematic platform in SAS, and the source of the data mining is the data warehouse. So, the data mining and the establishment of data warehouse link seamlessly. (Fig. 4) In the model management system, the process of AMDSS developing is: (1) obtaining the data from the data warehouse through the data file of the model; (2) finishing the development of every module and the module interface in the data warehouse. Integrating research results is as Fig. 5.

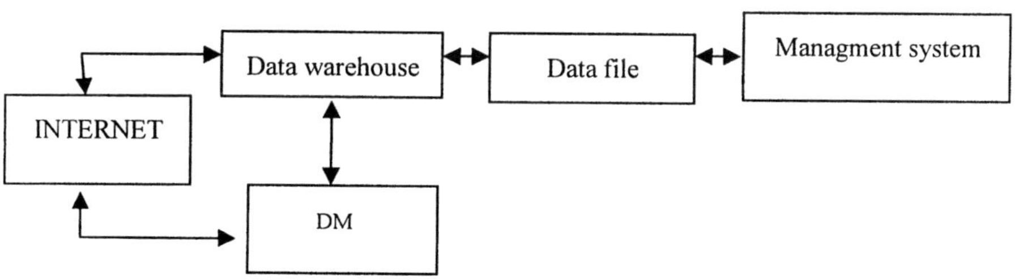

Figure 4 Connection of the module in AMDSS

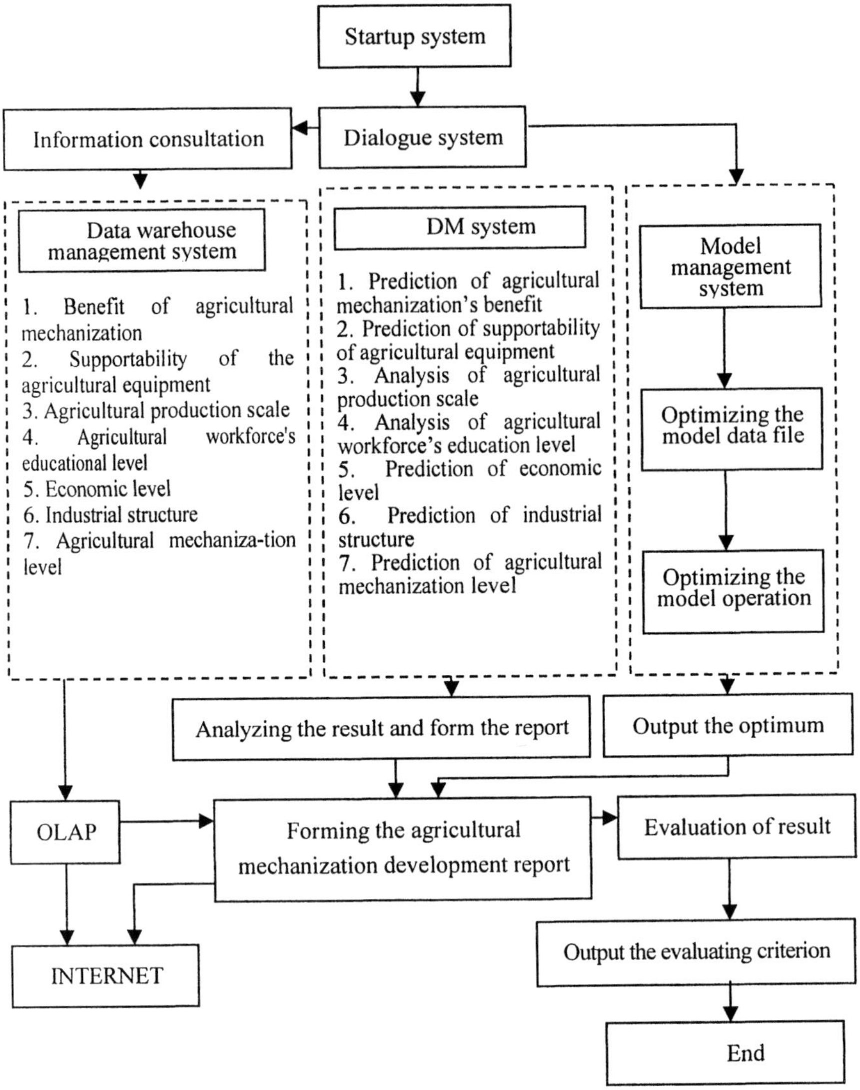

Figure 5 AMDSS operation structure

6. CONCLUSIONS

AMDSS has used in China every province and all over the country to appraisal and make policy of the agricultural mechanization development. Some decisions have been implemented. Agricultural information is one of the developing directions of future agriculture, and AMDSS is an important part of it. AMDSS is sure to play more and more important role in the agriculture development in future.

REFERENCES

[1] Liu Yao. On Application and Development of the Decision Support System. Computer and Modernization, 2000(2): 41~47

[2] Meng Ju, Yang Guanglin. The Research of Agricultural Producing Macro Decision Support System. System Sciences and Comprehensive Studies in Agriculture, 2002, 18(4): 293~297

[3] Cheng Weiwen. Decision Support System and its Development. Beijing: Tshinghua University Press, 2000

[4] Gao Hongshen. Theories, Methods and Cases for DSS. Beijing: Tshinghua University Press, 2000

[5] Weston J., author; Chen Shuoying, etc., translater. Decision Support in the Data Warehouse. Beijing: Beijing Institute of Technology Press, 2000

[6] Jiawei Han, Micheline Kamber, author; Fang Ming, Meng Xiaofeng, translater. The Concept and Technology of Data Mining. Beijing: China Machine Press, 2001

THE COMPLEX FUZZY CONTROL

Enhancing tractor automatic steering precision

Song Zhenghe, Lü Antao, Mao Enrong

College of Engineering, China Agricultural University, Beijing 100083, P.R. China

Abstract: This paper mostly introduces that it is necessary to apply autonomous tractor in agriculture and how to select control parameter, tractor automatic steering dynamic model is set up and a complex fuzzy control technique is put forward. In addition, fuzzy control formula is designed, which is evaluated by the simulink software. The simulating result reveals that the complex fuzzy control technique produces the behaves similar to the tractor driver, and, it is suitable for tractor automatic steering system.

Key words: tractor; autonomous driving; fuzzy control; PID

1. INTRODUCTION

Autonomous tractors are believed to be one of the driving forces for precision farming, since they can perform farming operations accurately and automatically. At the same time, it can assure the precision task, such as holding space of ridge in a field. In addition, it can take from the technique request of operator, decrease the overlap operation, and accelerate the rate of progress and economize cost. Document [1] indicates proficiency tractor driver can plough in 10cm precision, but after a day's work, precision will recede much more. Whereas, autonomous tractors based on GPS, which cost is 42% more than general tractors', can maintain operation in 3cm precision all time, avoid overlap operation, save fuel consume and cut down dosage of pesticide. So, they can enhance 40% profit of farm. The study about autonomous tractors have been reached in the worldwide, and the research keystone of it is autonomous steering, namely yaw control of the tractor.

Navigation control, which will firstly be designed based on control point, in according to operating mode, is sticking point of autonomous tractor. For example, it is selected in front when tractor used in reaping which dead stocks are equipped, it is selected in rear when tractor used in plough which dead stocks are equipped. Front control point that may be select at front axes and rear control point may be select at rear axes herein putting up vehicle dynamic model. Although there are many navigation control methods, control parameters are all yaw error and yaw angle error, which are limited in permit bound in order that autonomous tractor runs along desire route[2,3]. At the same time, data fuse that can make two parameters change into one parameter reinforces data nicety, and the last navigation control is confirmed. In the context vehicle dynamic model based on center of mass is putted up, and a sort of complex fuzzy control technique of tractor automatic steering is put forward, which suits for autonomous tractors.

2.MODEL OF TRACTOR DYNAMICS

There are 6 free degrees when tractor runs, H-P Willumeit, who assumed that vehicle was running on a level frictional surface but including vehicle run in plane and tyre sideslip angle, suppose 4 items [4]:

(1) There are 3 free degrees without uprightness movement, pitching movement roll y shaft and list movement roll x shaft;

(2) The two wheel on each axle collapse into a single wheel located at the center of the axle, axis load of front and rear only lie in center of axis;

(3) Front wheel sideslip angle, which change is small, and it is directly input losing sight of steer system infection, so model is linearity.

(4) Side force of COM (in this article, COM means the center of mass) equal side force of wheel which lead to wheel side departure, namely angle of wheel plane and wheel onward, and the tyre characteristic change is neglected.

So, a bicycle model was used to describe the tractor dynamic responses, the bicycle model of the tractor should be defined in field coordinates (Fig.1).

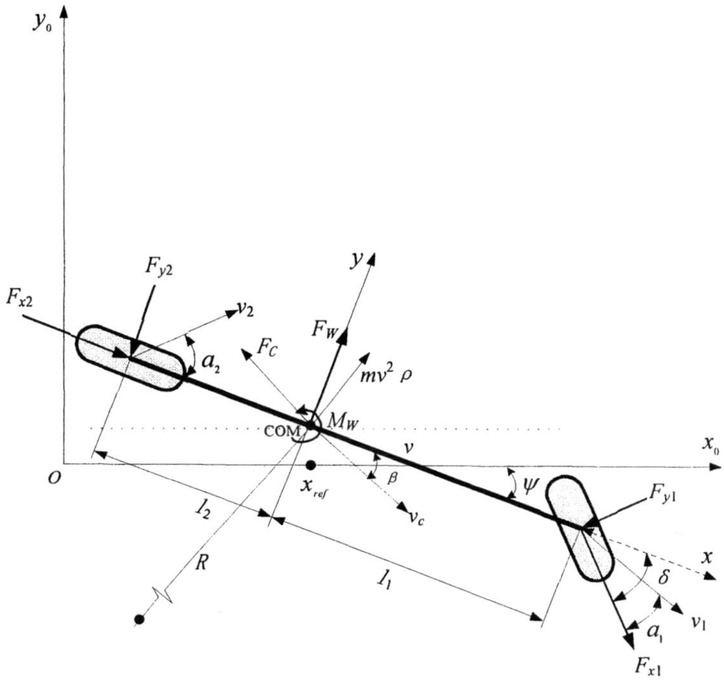

Figure 1. Bicycle model of tractor in field coordinates and tractor-body coordinates

Dynamics equation of the bicycle model about slip angle of tractor and tractor yaw angular acceleration can be defined by the following equations without considering the influence of the side wind:

$$\dot{\beta} = A_{11}\beta + A_{12}\dot{\psi} + B_1\delta$$
$$\ddot{\psi} = A_{21}\beta + A_{22}\dot{\psi} + B_2\delta$$

Where, $A_{11} = -\frac{k_1 + k_2}{mv_c}$; $A_{12} = -1 + \frac{k_2 l_2 - k_1 l_1}{mv_c^2}$; $A_{21} = \frac{k_2 l_2 - k_1 l_1}{M}$; $A_{22} = -\frac{k_2 l_2^2 + k_1 l_1^2}{Mv_c}$; $B_1 = \frac{k_1 - F_{x1}}{mv_c}$; $B_2 = \frac{l_1(k_1 - F_{x1})}{M}$; m is the mass of tractor, kg; M is the turning inertia with regard to tractor COM, kg • m^2; l_1 and l_2 are the distance of the front and rear wheel to tractor COM respectively, m; v_c is the velocity of tractor-body, km/h; F_{x1} and F_{x2} are the resistance of the front and rear wheel respectively, N; F_{y1} and F_{y2} are the side forces at the front and rear wheel respectively, N; F_W is the side force of side wind, N; M_W is the moment of side wind, N • m; ρ is the curvature of tractor steering, m^{-1},

$R=\frac{1}{\rho}$; ψ is the yaw angle, rad; β is the slip angle of tractor, rad; δ is the steering angle of tractor, rad.

Because lateral speeds of the tractor play important roles in calculating yaw error (distance between COM and x_{ref}), the speed can be determined using the following equations:

$$\dot{y} = v_C \sin(\beta+\psi) \approx v\ (\beta+\psi)$$

If steering machine is predigested by first-order inertia system, the tractor yaw angle was chosen as a state variable in order to compare it for emulation. The tractor dynamics is then represented in matrix form to determine the slip angle, the yaw rate, the steer angle and the yaw angle of the tractor as following:

$$\begin{bmatrix}\dot{\beta}\\ \dot{\omega}\\ \dot{y}\\ \dot{\psi}\\ \dot{\delta}\end{bmatrix} = \begin{bmatrix}A_{11} & A_{12} & 0 & 0 & B_1\\ A_{21} & A_{22} & 0 & 0 & B_2\\ v & 0 & 0 & v & 0\\ 0 & 1 & 0 & 0 & 0\\ 0 & 0 & 0 & 0 & -\frac{1}{\tau}\end{bmatrix}\begin{bmatrix}\beta\\ \omega\\ y\\ \psi\\ \delta\end{bmatrix} + \begin{bmatrix}0\\ 0\\ 0\\ 0\\ \frac{1}{\tau}\end{bmatrix}\delta_d$$

Where, τ is the inertia time constant of the steering system; δ_d is the expectation steering angle of the tractor.

3. YAW COMPLEX FUZZY CONTROL

Since the action of the tractor wheel is complex in allusion to characteristic of tractor tasks: low speed and no way, and a precision tractor model is not mostly putted up, besides speed change of tractor-body impact the frequency region response, tractor navigation control will avoid depending on tractor dynamics model. However, expert knowledge can be expressed by the fuzzy rule, which can judge state of controlled object real time without precision math model. And, fuzzy control has the characteristic of robust and applicability spontaneously. In this paper, the fuzzy control is introduced into the yaw control of the tractor. PID control is in common used in the industry field, about 84%, which not depends on model and includes proportion, integral and differential coefficient.

There is strongpoint and shortcoming for PID control and fuzzy control separately. For example, PID control is simple but no good adaptability, the fuzzy control is good adaptability but no control effect when language variable is small. Complex fuzzy control, which fits PID control and fuzzy control together (Fig 2), has strong control function, its principle is that when language variable is small than zero section, fuzzy is disconnection, PID work alone, in order to enhance system stabilization performance.

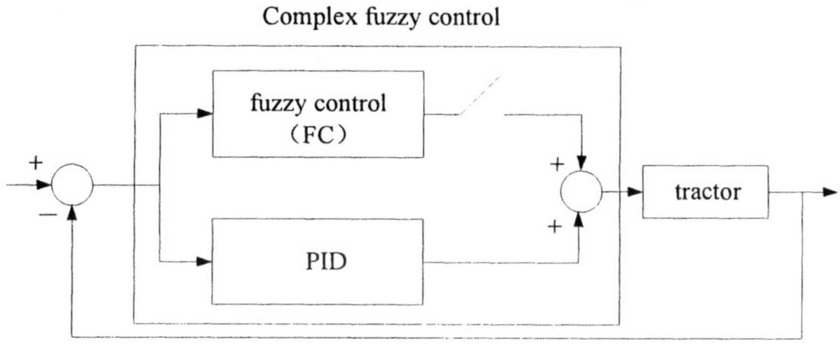

Figure2. Complex fuzzy control system

In this research, a fuzzy controller is selected, which there are two input, yaw error (y) and yaw angle (ψ), and one output (δ). $y \in [-1 \quad 1]$ and y={ *NB NM NS 0 PS PM PB* }; $\psi \in [-1.57 \quad 1.57]$ and ψ={ *NB NM NS 0 PS PM PB* }; $\delta \in [-0.5233 \ 0.5233]$ and δ={ *NB NM NS 0 PS PM PB* }; Mamdani rule is used, subjection function of language variable is trapezium and triangle, then control rule is showed in table 1, and relation between input and output is show in figure 3.

Table 1. Fuzzy control rule

ψ / δ / y	*NB*	*NM*	*NS*	*O*	*PS*	*PM*	*PB*
NB	*NB*	*NB*	*NB*	*NB*	*NB*	*NB*	*NB*
NM	*NB*	*NB*	*NB*	*NB*	*NB*	*NB*	*NB*
NS	*NB*	*NB*	*NM*	*NM*	*NM*	*NS*	*NS*
O	*NB*	*NM*	*NS*	*O*	*PS*	*PM*	*PB*
PS	*PS*	*PS*	*PM*	*PM*	*PB*	*PB*	*PB*
PM	*PM*	*PM*	*PM*	*PB*	*PB*	*PB*	*PB*
PB	*PM*	*PM*	*PB*	*PB*	*PB*	*PB*	*PB*

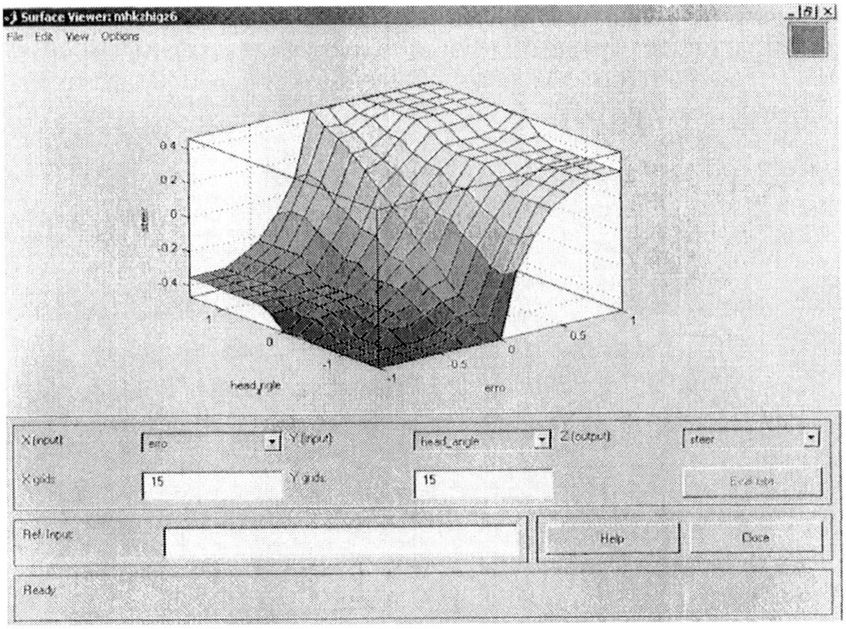

Figure3. Relation between input and output

4. RESULTS AND DISCUSSION

A tractor character parameter, such as l_1 = 1.575m, l_2 = 0.86m, k_1 =80kN/rad, k_2 =100kN/rad, v = 3m/s, M=4834kg·m^2. Firstly, the tractor dynamics model is founded, parameter of PID control is estimated by simulink, k_p=10, k_I=1, k_D=5; then Complex fuzzy control system is set up according to configuration(fig2), valve of fuzzy control is: yaw error is 0.2 and yaw angle is 0.157; when yaw error and yaw angle are more than valve, fuzzy control and PID will work together, which will enhance output but it can not exceed max output(±0.5233rad) ; when yaw error or yaw angle is less than valve, fuzzy control will be cut down, and then, PID work by oneself. Since at this time tractor has been running along expectation route, it is viable that PID control yaw error alone. Original yaw error is 0, finally yaw is 1, and original yaw angle is 0, in order that change route of tractor is simulated. Results are shown in figure 4, and the results that fuzzy control working alone is shown in figure 5. The simulation results indicate that representation of complex fuzzy control is better than single fuzzy control, and embodiment driver knowledge which is suitable for tractor automatic steering system.

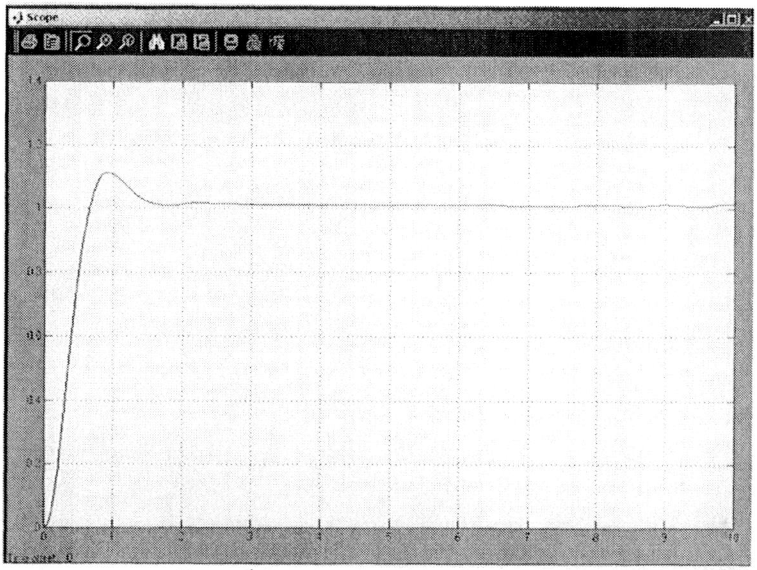

Figure4. Results of complex fuzzy control

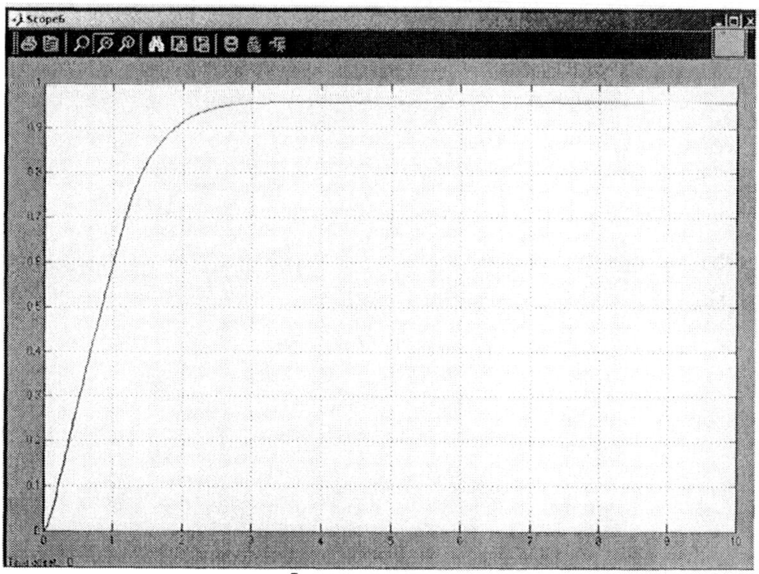

Figure5. Results of fuzzy control

5. CONCLUSIONS

The main goal of this study is to develop a new method that can enhance navigation capable of autonomous tractor. Such a complex fuzzy control is put forward based on fuzzy control and PID, and tractor dynamics model is set up, which is base for simulation. Computer simulation analyses demonstrate that the complex fuzzy control can enhance control performance, such as reducing stabilization error and improving response speed besides realizing personification drive.

REFERENCE

[1] Chen tan. Cultivation manner changed by autonomous driving tractor. Science development and prospect, 1997, (3)

[2]Noboru Noguch, John F.Reid, Qin Zhang et al. Development of robot tractor based on RTK-GPS and gyroscope.ASAE paper:01-1195

[3]Simon Blackmore, Hans Werner Griepentrog, Henning Nielsen et al. Development of a deterministic autonomous tractor . Beijing : 2004 CIGR International Conference·Beijing, 11-14 October 2004

[4] Hans-peter Willumeit. Vehicle dynamics simulation and method[M]. Beijing: Beijing science and engineering university. 1998

[5] Yi jikai, hou yuanbin. Intelligent control technology[M]. Beijing: Beijing industry university. 2002.

[6] Wu xiaoli, lin zhehui. Matlab assistant fuzzy control[M]. Xi'an: Xi'an electron science and technology university,2001

ICT SUPPORTED KNOWLEDGE TRANSFER FOR AGRICULTURAL EXTENSION

A Case in China

Weizhe Feng [a], Yanqing Duan [b,*], Zetian Fu [a], Brian Mathews [b]

[a] *China Agricultural University, 100083, Beijing, China*

[b] *University of Luton, LU1 3JU, Luton, UK*

[*] Corresponding author. Tel.: 0044 1582 743134; fax: 0044 1582 743926
Email address: yanqing.duan@luton.ac.uk.

Abstract: This paper offers a qualitative study of the applications of ICT in supporting knowledge transfer for the enhancement of modern agricultural extension. To address the challenge, this paper applies an inter-disciplinary approaches to review, analysis and develop a knowledge transfer model, and to conducts an empirical verification of it. A framework is proposed to illuminate the knowledge transfer process, and its associated channels.

Key words: Information and communication technology (ICT), knowledge transfer, knowledge brokering, agricultural extension, P.R. China

1. INTRODUCTION

Information and communication technology (ICT) is seen as a powerful means of catalysing the formation of knowledge societies in rural areas of the developing world (Meera et al. 2004). As ICT has a growing role in agricultural extension, more systematic research is called for in the exploration and analysis of ICT applications. A review of the literature found that in the context of knowledge management there is no commonly accepted framework for the analysis of ICT supported knowledge transfer for agricultural extension . This paper aims to apply knowledge management theories for a development of an ICT-based knowledge transfer framework.

In the perspective of social research methods, epistemological and ontological views are two of major influences on study (Bryman, 2004). In knowledge management study, an epistemological approach investigates the nature of knowledge itself and looks at knowledge as an entity with discrete and relevant attributes. An ontological approach views knowledge as a 'black box' and defines it through relationships, with a systematic account of existence. This view is further extended that epistemological and ontological perspectives have a high potential for synergy (Gebert, et al. 2003). The strategy of this study is to adopt this approach to evaluate knowledge transfer with dynamic changes of knowledge itself and involving relational interactions.

The paper starts with critical review on concepts and theories related to knowledge transfer. With the support of communication theories further classification of tacit knowledge is given. With the incorporation of transfer process and channels a conceptual framework is theoretically constructed using flow charts and a matrix representing processes and channels. On the basis of the evidence collected in a case study in China, the framework is empirically tested. The final conclusion highlights the implications related to the framework and its limitations.

2. Transferring tacit knowledge with ICT

A well accepted classification of knowledge is given by Polanyi (1962:) who divides knowledge into the explicit and the tacit. Explicit knowledge could be codified and communicated in human created scientific or linguistic symbols, Tacit knowledge can be very difficult to articulate but may be communicated through direct human interactions. Researchers may have no doubts about the ability and efficiency of ICT in facilitating explicit knowledge transfer, but they may debate on the transferability of tacit knowledge through ICT.

Bolisani and Scarso (1999) studied cases of ICT applications implemented in Italy and argued that ICT can accomplish all sorts of knowledge transfer tasks, including the transfer of tacit knowledge. Blumentritt and Johnston (1999) and Boutellier et al. (1998) argue that ICT is not able to transfer knowledge directly, but can assist the transfer process. They believe that ICT actually transfers the information but information will be decoded into knowledge by the receiver. Empirical evidence from ICT supported international virtual NPD projects by, Cummings and Teng (2003) led them to argue that ICT is effective at facilitating codified knowledge transfer but could not transfer related 'sensory information', such as feelings, intuition, and non-verbal communications. Roberts (2000) predicts that future advanced ICT may provide the context at the same as richness of face-to-face contact, which may really see the 'death of distance'.

In the context of studying ICT supported knowledge transfer, it is argued that importance needs to be attached to both information and communication. From one perspective the knowledge transfer process could be regarded as the process of communication (Shin, 2001). Furthermore, communication is fundamental to knowledge transfer (Riusala and Suutari, 2004) and to all knowledge management process (Quintas, 2002). The theoretical basis of communication study should therefore not be undervalued in the context of in information and dknowledge management.

In conventional theory, human communication could be defined into verbal and non-verbal communication. The former is affected by words both oral and written and the later by means without codes of linguistic symbols (Knapp and Hall, 1997). For the success of non-verbal communication, three primary factors are regarded as important. They include (1) physical environment, e.g. lights, temperature, additional noises etc., and spatial environment or proxemics; (2) communicators' physical appearances, e.g. smell, hair, skin colour, tones etc.; (3) body movement and position, e.g. gestures, posture, touching behaviour, facial expressions, eye behaviour, etc. (Knapp, and Hall, 1997). It is quite clear that electronic transmission might have no way to transfer fully all such elements nor any closely associated instinctive feelings.

In the electronic communication school, media richness theory predominantly explains the transferability of ICT in support of human communication (Daft and Lengel, 1984, 1986). Employing the theory, DeRosa et al. (2004) further classify ICT supported human communication into seven categories that are adapted into figure 1. The layers in two triangles are constructed to explain the richness of communication means between two communicators. The overlapping areas in the middle demonstrate a shared context, or face-to-face communication. This model has the advantage of representing the richness of the communication means with areas of each layer within the triangle.

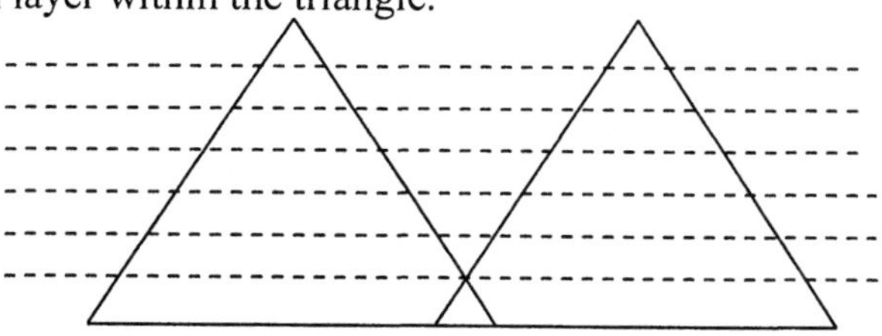

Figure 1. The richness of communication means adapted from DeRosa et al. (2004)

Some knowledge management literature has also attempted to classify the knowledge in accordance with its richness. Sunaoshi et al. (2005) recommend two constructs that affect the transfer of tacit knowledge. They include (1) drawability, for encoding knowledge into two-dimensional representations (signs, pictures, diagrams etc.) which might be difficult to be articulated in a language; and (2) demonstrability for doing 'on the floor' or performing the task together simultaneously. More specifically McCreadie and Rice (1999) draw a distinction between electronic medium transferable knowledge and all other knowledge dimensions. The ICT transferable knowledge is classified with those being represented on video-or audio-tape, videodisc, CD-ROM, internet or other electronic and computer media.

Knowledge transfer may be conducted with direct or indirect human interactions (Sveiby, 1996; Hlupic et al. 2002). In terms of direct knowledge transfer, it indicates the direct face-to-fact interaction (FTF) between people and indirect transfer where no such interaction has taken place. Based on the communication richness theory, together with suggestions on classification of knowledge transfer into direct and the indirect, one may be able to further classify tacit knowledge into indirect-tacit (pictorial knowledge transferable with ICT) and direct-tacit (transferable only with co-presence and co-location, or FTF). With this classification it may be possible to better explain the questions raised previously on the capability of ICT in transferring tacit knowledge.

3. Knowledge transfer, creation and conversion

In cognitive research, researchers recognise that knowledge transfer is a cognitive process and claim that knowledge creation and transfer can occur simultaneously. It is argued that new knowledge is dynamically created by the receiver when interpreting the transferred knowledge with his personal perception (Holden and Kortzfleisch, 2004; Garavelli et al. 2002).

Nonaka's knowledge creation/conversion theory (Nonaka 1991, Nonaka et. al., 1996; Nonaka et. al., 1998; Nonaka et. al., 2000) is also adopted by other researchers (e.g. Bolisani and Scarso, 1999; Dayasindhu, 2002; Holden and Kortzfleisch, 2004) as knowledge transfer theory. The former illustrates that the knowledge creation process calls for dynamic conversion between the explicit and the tacit. The later claims that the process of knowledge creation/conversion is also taking place when knowledge is being transferred, that is, the transfer and creation/conversion are inseparable. This point of view coincides with the position of Sparkes and Miyake (2000), who argue that knowledge transfer, absorption and assimilation take place sequentially but as a continuous process.

Based on the new contributions and accounts of the sub-division of tacit knowledge, direct and indirect tacit knowledge, Nanaka's knowledge creation/conversion theory could be further modified into a transfer-creation/conversion process, shown in a matrix in Table 1.

Table 1. The matrix of knowledge transfer-creation/conversion process

Transfer-conversion	Explicit	Indirect tacit	Direct tacit
Explicit	Explicit-to-explicit	Explicit-to-indirect tacit	Explicit-to-direct tacit
Indirect tacit	Indirect tacit-to-explicit	Indirect tacit-to-indirect tacit	Indirect tacit-to-direct tacit
Direct tacit	Direct tacit-to-explicit	Direct tacit-to-indirect tacit	Direct tacit-to-direct tacit

4. Towards developing a knowledge transfer framework

Between the knowledge source and receiver, a third party may be called as intermediary, bridge-maker or negotiator (individuals and/or organizations) for initiating, facilitating, channelling and even participating in interactions (Sverrisson 2001; Hargadon 2002; Matson et al. 2003).

In the context of transferring scientific knowledge in the agriculture sector, it is evident that in a growing number cases research knowledge based on science alone may not necessarily be accepted as correct knowledge by farmers (Burgess et al. 2000). The extensionist is the major source of knowledge and a crucial link to rural knowledge community (Rees et al. 2000; Rivera and Qamar 2003). Therefore, when scientific knowledge is transferred through ICT to the local farmers, field extensionists may act as local decoders and interpreters for knowledge retrieved from ICT. Such an approach was found by Cecchini and Scott (2003) who reviewed major ICT projects in India and Weiss et al. (2000), who studied transfer of agro-meteorological information and knowledge projects world wide.

In addition to the extensionist, all ICT supported knowledge transfer may call for knowledge engineers to acquire and encode domain expert's knowledge for ICT embededdness and transmission. For example, when developing an agricultural expert system, surveys, interviews and case studies are adopted by knowledge engineers for knowledge acquisition from experts. The knowledge base contains text, images, graphics, sound and video sequences (Carrascal et al., 1995). For such knowledge acquisition processes, a broad agreement is that it is impossible to articulate all of the knowledge of an expert explicitly (Wu 1998). However, it is argued that the more indirect tacit knowledge encoded into ICT, the better quality of knowledge being transferred.

In literature, channels of communication are frequently applied in knowledge transfer studies (e.g. Cohen et al. 2002; Holsapple and Joshi 2002). More specifically, channels of knowledge transfer are applied for analysing inter-organisational knowledge transfer activities (e.g. Deardorff and Djankov 2000, Kim et al. 2003). In developing the conceptual framework of this study, the same term is adopted for representing the means by which different dimensions of knowledge being transferred across different knowledge systems. In accordance with the previous classification of tacit knowledge, three channels may appear in an ICT supported knowledge transfer context, namely, the channels for the explicit, the indirect tacit and the direct tacit knowledge.

Nonaka et al. (2000) use two overlapped triangles to demonstrate organisation interactions with business constituents for knowledge creation. With appropriate modifications, two overlapped triangles may be used to illustrate the knowledge transfer-creation/conversion between two immediate interactions. In the case scientific knowledge transfer through ICT for agricultural extension, two sorts of immediate interactions may take place: between expert and knowledge engineer and between extensionist and farmer. Two sorts of knowledge transfer are illustrated in figure 2 and 3 with respective three transfer channels.

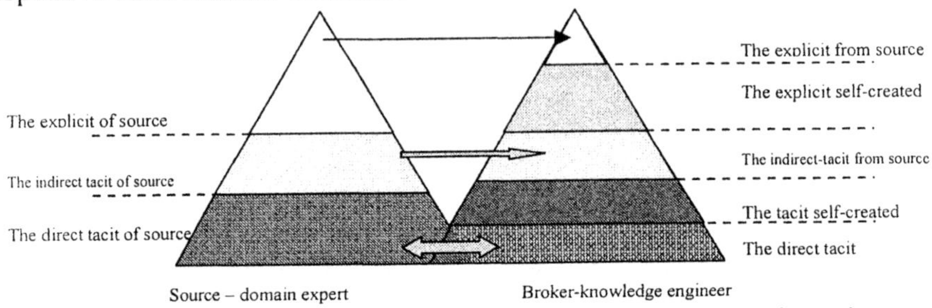

Figure 2. **Transfer-creation/conversion process between source and knowledge engineer**

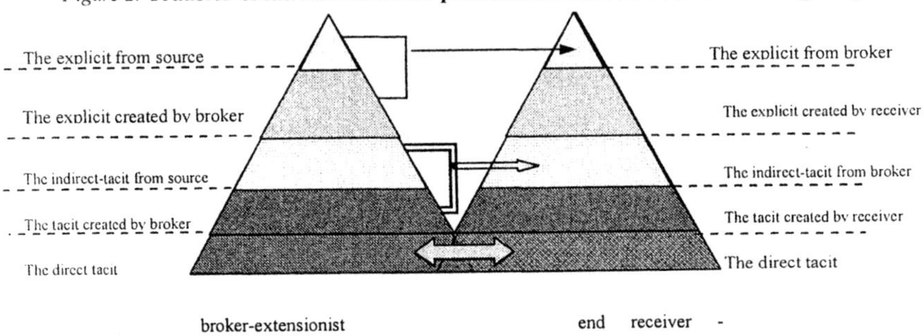

Figure 3. **Transfer-creation/conversion process between extensionist and farmer**

According to the conceptual development, a framework of ICT supported knowledge transfer for agricultural extension could be defined as two stages of transfer, through which the scientific knowledge is acquired and encoded by the knowledge engineer firstly, and then being decoded and interpreted to farmer by the extensionist. The ICT acts in the middle with a crucial role in linking knowledge engineer and extensionist effectively and efficiently.

To analyse the creation/conversion of different knowledge dimensions, the modified Nonaka's knowledge transfer-creation/conversion process is adopted into the framework. To have synergic link of the ontological and epistemological approaches, previously developed knowledge transfer channels are adopted into the framework as well. The framework is shown in Figure 4. Two spirals below the triangles are used to represent the transfer-creation/conversion process with three dimensions of knowledge, the explicit, the indirect tacit and the direct tacit.

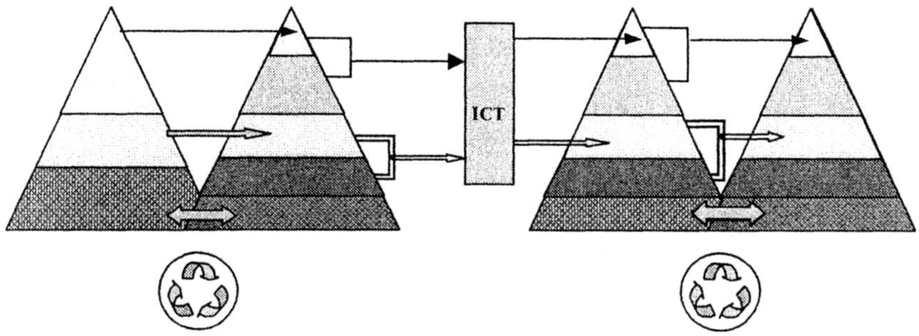

Figure 4. The framework of knowledge transfer for agricultural extension

5. A case study

The case study methodology is employed since it best fits empirical inquiry that investigates bounded contemporary phenomena based on the real life context (Yin 2003). The methodology made it possible to examination of the ways a conceptual framework is shaped in accordance with the specific circumstances of applications over similar projects.

To reach a triangulation analysis in the findings, this research is based on information collected from three major sources in the case: in-depth interviews, project review documents and direct observation.

Compared with the vast population engaged in agricultural production in China, the supply of agricultural extension service is fairly low. It is reported that the average ratio of extensionist to farming households in service is about 1: 1200 (Yan et al., 2000). In coping with an insufficient supply in the area of agricultural extension services, the government attaches a great importance in the development of ICT technology toward developing greater efficiency in agricultural extension. Projects are launched by one of the leading state organisations in Beijing for conducting ICT supported extension projects around the country.

The web-based expert systems projects initiated by the organisation demonstrate a dynamic integration of exogenous scientific knowledge and endogenous local knowledge for agricultural extension. A web-based expert system is designed with the target of high performance of local internet infrastructure together with high capability of local extension agency in their continuing building and operating the system. A great advantage of the system is that it allows local extensionist to further modify and upgrade the knowledge base through the Platform of Agricultural Information Development (PAID), a built-in tool of the extension system, in accordance with local farming context. With the support of the government, the project has been implemented in more than fifty provincial project sites around the country. The localised expert systems can provide knowledge and help to various farming production such as grains, fruits, vegetables and husbandries. The projects structure and knowledge flow are shown in Figure 5.

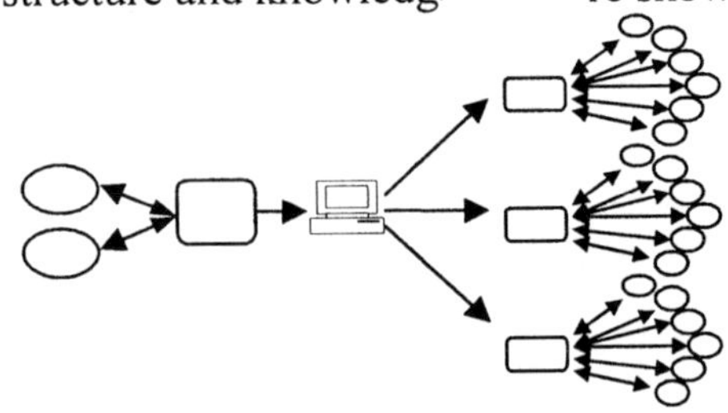

Figure 5. Web-based expert system projects

In the project, the knowledge engineers determines the flexibilities of domain knowledge being embedded into the knowledge base of the system with consideration of the local context. The system differs in the various areas of agricultural production, each system also varies in accordance with related domains. The role of extensionist in such project is very challenging, because considerable computer skills are required to further develop the system toward localisation.

The knowledge transfer-creation/conversion process and channels of knowledge transfer are analysed in table 2 and 3.

Table 2. Knowledge transfer-creation/conversion process

Process	Conducted by knowledge engineer	Conducted by extensionist
Explicit to Explicit	• It is most signification process to be studied. In the knowledge base of the expert system built by engineer, the majority of terms, definitions, descriptions, explanations can be traced back in the source of explicit knowledge, such as books, working papers and notes from expert and other published references.	• Text in the original knowledge base is translated into more localised folk terms. Sometimes it is printed for distribution, which is called by farmer the 'plain paper'. • Local farmer's agricultural adages are also incorporated into the relevant knowledge base of the system by extensionist.
Direct tacit to Explicit	• There is great endeavour given by a knowledge engineer to write down what he learned during the interviews, meetings and laboratory observations. This part of the answers may never been stated explicitly in text by others.	• Extensionist corrects and adds a certain amount of text based knowledge into the original knowledge base according to his knowledge and understanding of the local context. This part counts for the largest amount of the contents of modifications and additions to the original knowledge base.
Explicit to Direct tacit	• In case agricultural domain experts raising different opinions to a question, or a less favoured topics to experts, knowledge engineer has to search information and data and relevant domain knowledge by himself elsewhere and to finally reach his own understandings.	• Extensionist reads text based knowledge in the original knowledge base of the expert system and also actively acquires knowledge from the accessible books, notes in a specific topic in learning the scientific knowledge introduced through the expert system..
Direct tacit to Direct tacit	• Due to reasons of incentives, domain language difficulties, and the complexity of agricultural production conditions, many blank knowledge	• Extensionist frequently communicates with farmers with interested topics and teaches farmer the related scientific knowledge that he has learned through the expert system. He

	areas need to be well understand by knowledge engineer himself through site visits, interviewing people and discussion with colleagues • All agricultural domain knowledge has to be finally interpreted in a rule-based computing language. On the other hand, a large amount of personal experience and inductive knowledge acquired from the domain expert may not be reflected rigorously in the rule based system. For such-cross discipline integration of two knowledge systems the issues have to be considered over and addressed in the mind of the knowledge engineer before the construction of the system.	may also empirically evaluate the effectiveness of the expert system based on farmer's opinions and practices. • Supported with some computing skills, the extensionist also conducts some simple programming to encode his local exogenous knowledge into rigorous rule-based knowledge. For such-cross disciplines integration of two knowledge systems has to be well addressed in his mind before his physical modifications of the expert system.
Indirect tacit to Explicit	• Academically derived charts, diagrams, pictures, animations and videos sometimes need to be simplified into less academic based text by knowledge engineers.	• Extensionist sometimes find it necessary to interpret those charts, diagrams, pictures, animations and videos in the expert system with local folk terms orally or producing 'plain paper'.
Explicit To Indirect tacit	• Descriptive text is understood and is developed into Charts, diagrams, pictures, animations and videos.	• Difficult concepts and process are interpreted into cartoons, charts and diagrams for the ease of farmer's understanding.
Direct tacit to Indirect tacit	• Observed diagnostic phenomena or best practices are explained or demonstrated in charts, diagrams, pictures, animations and videos into the system	• Observed local best practices are explained or demonstrated in charts, diagrams, pictures, cartoons and videos in the modification of the expert system
Indirect tacit to Direct tacit	• Charts, diagrams, pictures, animations and videos acquired help engineer to understand the domain knowledge	• Charts, diagrams, pictures, animations and videos in the expert system help the extensionist to understand the domain knowledge
Indirect tacit to Indirect tacit	• Charts, diagrams, pictures, animations and videos acquired are re-edited or modified by knowledge engineer	• Charts, diagrams, pictures, animations and videos in the original knowledge base are further re-edited or modified by extensionist

Table 3. Knowledge transfer channels

Channels		**Description**
Channels for transfer explicit knowledge	Expert to knowledge engineer (KE)	• A large amount of text based knowledge on books, notes are collected by domain expert for knowledge engineer
	KE to extensionist	• A large amount of text based knowledge on books, notes are retrieved and edited into the knowledge base by knowledge engineer during web-based expert system building • Knowledge engineer has to derive rules and process explicitly that have never been done before for building the web-based system • Both categories of text based knowledge in the system are electronically transmitted to and retrieved by extensionist
	Extensionist to farmer	• All text based built-in knowledge in the web-based knowledge system is retrieved by extensionist according to farmer's request or retrieved by farmer directly. • The extensionist has to modify some text in the knowledge base in accordance with the local context. The extensionist also use his integrated exogenous and indigenous knowledge to produce a piece of 'plain paper' for farmers' convenient use
Channels for transfer	Expert to KE	• Charts, diagrams, pictures, animations and videos are collected by domain expert for the knowledge engineer

indirect-tacit knowledge	KE to extensionist	• Charts, diagrams, pictures, animations and videos are retrieved and edited into the knowledge base of the system by knowledge engineer • Knowledge engineer has to produce a certain amount of charts, diagrams, pictures, animations and videos that were not available but important for the knowledge base building • Both categories of charts, diagrams, pictures, animations and videos based knowledge in the system are electronically transmitted to and retrieved by extensionist
	Extensionist to farmer	• All charts, diagrams, pictures, animations and videos in the expert system are retrieved by extensionist according to farmer's request. • The extensionist has to modify some charts, diagrams, pictures and videos in the knowledge base in accordance with local context.
Channels for transfer direct-tacit knowledge	Expert to KE	• Intensive face-to-face interactions between agricultural experts and knowledge engineer throughout the system development
	KE to extensionist	• Some intensive fact-to-face training programmes delivered by knowledge engineer in helping extensionist get familiar with the knowledge base and operation of the system
	Extensionist to farmer	• Intensive FTF interactions between extensionist and farmer for integration of exogenous and indigenous during the application of the web-based expert system

6. Conclusions and implications

A framework of the ICT supported knowledge transfer for agriculture extension is proposed in this study. It offers an analytical tool for designing, explaining, analysing and evaluating how ICT applications can support scientific knowledge transfer to farmers. The framework is based on synergic incorporation of epistemological and ontological approaches. The transfer-creation/conversion process may help expert system designers to project, trace and assess the different dimensions of knowledge in terms of its quantity, quality and dynamic changes. The transfer channel formulates the structure of knowledge base and applications of ICT means.

With the proposed classification of tacit knowledge into the indirect and direct, the framework facilitates channels for their respective transferring Transferring indirect knowledge remains ignored by many researchers. Such ignorance, to some extent, misleads the attention of ICT applications towards developing more effective computing systems. Although the relevant research interests has appears in literature and pilot application (e.g. Duan et al. 2003; Carrascal et al. 1995), indeed, other indirect tacit knowledge transfer channels, e.g. mass media like TV that are popularly available in the rural areas, have not yet drawn enough attention in both academic and practical world. In China, interactive TV programmes via internet or text-message of mobile phone are very popular. But there is no agricultural extension projects have been initiated to adopt this advance technology. It is suggested by Weiss et al. (2000) that 'multiplier effects' may be achieved by linking the internet based knowledge transfer with mass media toward a more effective result.

The limitation of the framework is its focus on knowledge transfer process and channels. In terms of knowledge transfer, use of advanced ICT technology can not guarantee an effective knowledge interpretation, assimilation and application (Bolisani and Scarso 1999, Meera et al., 2004). This argument implicates that further study of the knowledge transfer context and influential factors are called for. The second limitation of this framework rests its coverage on implementation of knowledge transfer by knowledge engineer and extensionist rather than knowledge absorption process by farmers. If the knowledge transfer process is considered as two-stages, knowledge transmission by source and absorption by receiver (Garavelli et al. 2002, Forsman and Solitander 2003), it may call for future research endeavour to be conducted in the learning process of farmers in absorbing knowledge from the ICT means directly or from an ICT equipped extensionist.

REFERENCES:

[1] Blumentritt, R. and Johnston R. (1999). "Towards a Strategy for Knowledge Management." Technology Analysis & Strategic Management Vol. 11, No. 3: 287-300

[2] Bolisani, E. and Scarso E. (1999). "Information technology management: a knowledge-based perspective." Technovation(19): 209–217

[3] Boutellier, R., Grassmann, O., Macho, H., Roux, M., (1998) Management of dispersed product development teams: the role of information technologies. R&D Management 28: 13-25

[4] Bryman, A. (2004). Social research methods, 2nd ed. New York, Oxford University Press. pp 21

[5] Burgess, J., Clark, J. et al. (2000). "Knowledges in action: an actor network analysis of a wetland agri-environment scheme." Ecological Economics 35: 119–132

[6] Carrascal, M., Pau, L. et al. (1995). "Knowledge and information transfer in agriculture using hypermedia: a system review." Computers and electronics in agriculture Vol. 12: 83-119

[7] Cecchini, S. and Scott C. (2003). "Can information and communications technology applications contribute to poverty reduction? Lessons from rural India." Information Technology for Development 10: 73–84

[8] Cohen, G., Salomon, I., et al. (2002). "Information–communications technologies (ICT) and transport: does knowledge underpin policy?" Telecommunications Policy 26: 31–52

[9] Cummings, J. and Teng B.S. (2003). "Transferring R&D knowledge: the key factors affecting knowledge transfer success." Journal of Engineering and Technology Management(20): 39–68

[10] Daft, R. L. and Lengel R. H. (1984). "Information richness: A new approach to managerial behavior and organizational design." Research in organizational behavior 6: 191-233

[11] Daft, R. L. and Lengel R. H. (1986). "Organizational information requirements, media richness, and structural design." Management Science Vol. 32, No.5: 554-571

[12] Dayasindhu, N. (2002). "Embeddedness, knowledge transfer, industry clusters and global competitiveness: a case study of the Indian software industry." Technovation 22: 551-560

[13] Deardorff, A. and Djankov S. (2000). "Knowledge Transfer Under Subcontracting: Evidence from Czech Firms." World Development Vol. 28, No. 10: 1837-1847

[14] DeRosa, D. M., Hantula, D. A. et al. (2004). "Trust and leadership in virtual teamwork: A media naturalness perspective." Human Resource Management Vol. 43, No. 2 & 3: 219–232

[15] Duan, Y., Fu, Z. et al. (2003). "Toward developing and using Web-based tele-diagnosis in aquaculture." Expert Systems with Applications Vol. 25: 247–254

[16] Forsman, M. and Solitander N. (2003). "Knowledge transfer in clusters and networks - An interdisciplinary conceptual analysis." Journal of international business studies-www.jibs.net-2003. http://copenhagen.jibs.net/LitReview/2003/2003_3_24.pdf

[17] Garavelli, C., M. Gorgoglione, et al. (2002). "Managing knowledge transfer by knowledge technologies." Technovation 22: 269–279.

[18] Gebert, H., Geib, M. et al. (2003). "Knowledge-enabled customer relationship management: integrating customer relationship management and knowledge management concepts." Journal of knowledge management Vol. 7, No.5: 107-123

[19] Hargadon, A. (2002). "Brokering knowledge: linking learning and innovation." Research in organizational behavior Vol. 24: 41-85

[20] Hlupic, V., Pouloudi, A., et al. (2002). "Towards an Integrated Approach to Knowledge Management: 'Hard', 'Soft' and 'Abstract' Issues." Knowledge and Process Management Vol. 9, No. 2: 90–102

[21] Holden, N. J. and Kortzfleisch H. F. (2004). "Why Cross-Cultural Knowledge Transfer is a Form of Translation in More Ways than You Think." Knowledge and Process Management Vol. 11: 127–136

[22] Holsapple, C. W. and Joshi K. D. (2002). "Knowledge manipulation activities: results of a Delphi study." Information & Management 39: 477–490

[23] Kim, S., Hwang, H. et al. (2003). "AProcess-based Approach to Knowledge-Flow Analysis: A Case Study of a Manufacturing Firm." Knowledge and Process Management Vol.10, No.4: 260-276

[24] Knapp, M. and Hall J. (1997). Nonverbal communication in human interaction, 4th ed. Fort Worth, TX, Harcourt Brace. pp 5, 11

[25] Li, D., Fu, Z. et al. (2002). "Fish-Expert: a web-based expert system for fish disease diagnosis." Expert Systems with Applications 23: 311–320

[26] Matson, E., Patiath, P. et al. (2003). "Stimulating Knowledge Sharing: Strengthening Your Organization's Internal Knowledge Market." Organizational Dynamics Vol. 32, No. 3: 275–285

[27] Maxwell, J. (1996). Qualitative Research Design, An Interactive Approach. Thousand Oaks, SAGE. pp17

[28] McCreadie, M. and Rice R. E. (1999). "Trends in analyzing access to information. Part I: cross-disciplinary conceptualizations of access." Information Processing and Management 35: 45-76

[29] Meera, S. N., Jhamtani, A. et al. (2004). "Information and communication technology in agricultural development: A comparative analysis of three projects from India." ODI: Agricultural Research & Extension Network, Network Paper No. 135

[30] Nonaka, I. (1991). "The knowledge-creating company." Harvard Business Review on Knowledge Management (paperback), Harvard Business School Press, Boston 21-46

[31] Nonaka, I., Umemoto, K. et al. (1996). "From Information Processing to Knowledge Creation: A Paradigm shift in Business Management." Technology In Society Vol.18, No.2: 203-218

[32] Nonaka, I., Reinmoeller, P. et al. (1998). "The 'ART' of Knowledge: Systems to Capitalize on Market Knowledge." European Management Journal(16): 673-684.

[33] Nonaka, I., Toyama, R. et al. (2000). "SECI, Ba and Leadership: a Unified Framework of Dynamic Knowledge Creation." Long Range Planning(33): 5-34.

[34] Polanyi, M. (1962). Personal knowledge. London, Routledge. pp. 92

[35] Quintas, P., Ed. (2002). Managing knoweldge in a new century. In Little et al. (ed.) Managing knowledge. An essential reader. pp1-14. London, Sage Publications

[36] Rees, D., Momanyi, M. et al. (2000). "Agricultural knowledge and information system in Kenya-implications for technology dissemination and development." Agricultural Research & Extension Network, Network Paper No.107, http://www.odi.org.uk/agren/papers/agrepaper_107.pdf. Retrieved on 16, Jan., 2004

[37] Riusala, K. and Suutari V. (2004). "International Knowledge Transfers through Expatriates." Thunderbird International Business Review Vol. 46 (6): 743–770

[38] Rivera, W. M. and Qamar M. K. (2003). Agricultural extension, rural development and the food security challenge. Rome, FAO. pp. ii

[39] Roberts, J. (2000). "From Know-how to Show-how? Questioning the Role of Information and Communication Technologies in Knowledge Transfer." Technology Analysis & Strategic Management Vol. 12, No. 4: 429-443.

[40] Shin, M., Holden, T. et al. (2001). "From knowledge theory to management practice: towards an integrated approach." Information Processing and Management(37): 335-355

[41] Song, J., Hu, R. et al. (1998). "An analysis of farmer's behaviour on agricultural technology." Agricultural Technology and Economics (6) : 36-44 (in Chinese)

[42] Sparkes, J. R. and Miyake M. (2000). "Knowledge transfer and human resource development practices: Japanese firms in Brazil and Mexico." International Business Review 9: 599–612.

[43] Sunaoshi, Y., Kotabe, M. et al. (2005). "How technology transfer really occurs on the factory floor: a case of a major Japanese automotive die manufacturer in the United States." Journal of World Business 40: 57–70

[44] Sveiby K.E. (1996). "Transfer of Knowledge and the Information Processing Professions." European Management Journal 14, No. 4: 379--388.

[45] Sverrisson, A. (2001). "Translation Networks, Knowledge Brokers and Novelty Construction: Pragmatic Environmentalism in Sweden." ACTA Sociologica 14: 313-327

[46] Weiss, A., Crowder, L. V. et al. (2000). "Communicating agrometeorological information to farming communities." Agricultural and Forest Meteorology 103: 185–196

[47] Wu, X. (1998). "Explicit schematic information in knowledge representation and acquisition." Expert Systems with Applications 15: 215–221

[48] Yan J., et al. (2000). " Agricultural Expert and the diffusion of knowledge in the agriculture sector." Journal of Tsinghua University-Philosophy and Social Sciences Vol.15, No. 1: 57-61 (in Chinese)

[49] Yin, R. (2003). Case study research design and methods, 3rd ed. Thousand Oaks, SAGE. pp 13, 116

REVIEW OF MODELING AND STIMULATING HUMAN IMMUNE SYSYTEM

Hongwei Mo
Automation College,Harbin Engineering University Harbin,150001,China

Abstract: The human immune system(HIS) is a self-adaptive, complex system. Many different components cooperate each other to emerge intelligence behavior. Many researches have been done in order to explore the nature of immune system and its intelligent behavior. Computational models and concept models are the main two approaches of modeling and simulating the HIS. They are reviewed in detail in this paper. Differential equation and cellular automaton are two ways of being used frequently in modeling and simulating the HIS. The advantages and disadvantages of them are discussed in order to inspire new ways of researching the intelligent behavior of it. The application of HIS modeling in AI is also introduced briefly .

Key words: Human Immune System, Modeling, Simulating

1. INTRODUCTION

The HIS is a complex set of cells and molecules distributed throughout the body. It provides a natural deference mechanism from the infection agents such as viruses, bacteria, fungi or other parasites. As explained in Jerne [14] the HIS has the ability to memorize the foreign substances that enter the body. The whole set-up represents a very complex and dynamic system that is distributed over billiards of elements but still maintaining effective communication.

The basic component of the HIS is lymphocyte (white blood cells). There are two types: B-lymphocyte (produced in bone marrow) and T-lymphocyte (trained in thymus). Then there are other elements such as antigen presenting cells (APC) identifying antigens, natural killer cells (NK cells), antibody molecules and message molecules (lymphokines). In the past decades, research in Artificial Intelligence has been inspired by phenomena observed in life. The HIS shares many properties with neural networks and genetic algorithms. Modeling and Simulating the HIS in a computer provides immunologists with a new way of testing immunological theories, experiments *in labs*. However,if we observe the HIS and models of the HIS from an artificial intelligence or a complex systems simulation point of view, a number of questions arise.

Are techniques from the HIS simulation applicable to artificial intelligence or scientific computing? What properties of the HIS make it particularly fit or unfit to use the HIS as a natural solver?

In the past years, artificial intelligence researchers have started using models of HIS as a base for developing new artificial intelligence techniques. In the paper, a review of approaches of modeling and simulating HIS in recent years is given in order to inspire new ways of designing intelligent system.

The paper is organized as follows. In section 2, many approaches of modeling and simulating the HIS are reviewed and analyzed. The applications of HIS models are given in section 3. Discussions and conclusions are given in section 4 and 5 respectively.

2. APPROACHES OF MODELING AND SIMULATING THE HIS

Some models are referred to identify the computational model, i.e. the algorithm or the code, while the other models to the conceptual model in term of logical statements describing the entities and their interaction rules in the following sections.

2.1 Computational His Models

2.1.1 Differential Equation

The earliest models of the HIS are differential equation based models. They have been very popular, and a wide range of immunological phenomena have successfully been simulated using differential equation based models. A list of titles and abstracts of publications using a differential equations based model of HIS is composed in[15].

Most of these models focus on one specific phenomenon observed in immunology. The outcome of the model is then compared to data of *in vivo* or *in vito* experiments. Differential equation models of the HIS have been very successful for immunologists. From the viewpoint of AI, the following properties make differential equation based models less appropriate.

- Only theories involving a small number of variables can be modeled
- The diversity of the HIS can not easily be modeled
- Incorporating theories about different phenomena in HIS in the same model is hard, because the relations between those parts are not easily expressed in differential equations

The operation of differential equation based models is very different from what happens in reality. While differential equation based models are used widely in all research areas that simulate complex systems, they are of little interest to artificial intelligence, since they depend on known relations between variables, while artificial intelligence focuses on areas where these relations are unknown.

2.1.2 BIT-String Based Models

In a real HIS, binding between for example a B-cell receptor and an antigen's B-cell epitope will take place through the matching of the amino acids string. It is possible to represent the amino acid string using an alphabet of m characters where each character corresponds to a given amino acid. Then, any of a number of string-matching algorithms can be used to determine the degree of complementarity. For a string of length N, the repertoire size is given by m^N such receptor's or epitope's idiotype was first introduced by Farmer et al[9] as a way to perform clever calculations for determining molecular complementarity and predict the optimal size of an epitope. But the greatest impact the string representation introduced by Farmer is in lattice gas simulations of the HIS. The typical lattice gas simulations chose to build the epitope and receptor strings using an alphabet containing only two characters, namely 0 and 1, and those models are consequently referred to as 'bit-string' models. Since the receptors and epitopes of a bit-string model are represented by a string of bits,i.e. a string of 0s and 1s, those models have a repertoire size of 2^N is the length of the bit string.

2.1.3 Genetic Algorithm

Another very interesting research is coming up with interesting results. The research is based on the work of the University of New Mexico and is mainly composed of Forrest et al. They have published very interesting papers using the bit-string representation where they explore evolution and somatic learning in V-region genes[21],and the use of genetic algorithms to explore pattern recognition in the HIS[10].In[21], they found that their 512-bits genome can encode information about 32 64-bits antigens, i.e.about 2048 bits. The organization of the resources by the HIS suggests that the system has the ability to recognize pattern in the antigens and exploits the HIS to maximize its recognition while minimizing its resources. In[10], they explored the HIS further using genetic algorithm and found that it was impressively good at recognizing patterns. Challenging the pattern recognition capabilities of the HIS, they found that the genetic algorithm together with clonal selection could evolve an antibody type that matched multiple antigens through the identification of common schemes among antigens. They also found that when the genetic algorithm was faced with 2 or 3 different antigens, i.e., multiple peaks in the antigen landscape, the genetic algorithm can discover all peaks and similarity among antigens does not prevent distinction by antibodies, no matter how similar the antigens are. Finally, they found that the number of antibodies exposed to any antigen will greatly affect the capacity of the HIS to recognize patterns. But perhaps even more interesting is the group's attempt at constructing a computer immune system to improve computer security[25].

2.1.4 Large Scale Simulation

Cellular Automata based models have proven capable of providing several new insights into the dynamics of the HIS response. A qualitative picture of the HIS behaviors can be obtained with small-scale simulations. However for a more detailed analysis and to further validate the models, large scale simulations are required.

One of the most prominent attempts to cope with the quest for biological fidelity is the IMMSIM (Immune Simulator or CS-model) automaton, developed by Seiden and. Celada in 1992[23]. It is also the first cellular automaton model using bit-strings to model the receptors and epitopes.

IMMSIM is a very interesting model as it is attempting to create a general HIS simulator rather than only a simplified toy model for answering a particular problem. The various authors who have used the model claim that the results obtained compared well with experimental data. The model has already been used to investigated various immunological questions[6][3][7][1]. Those results were obtained by the IMMSIM group based at Princeton University and their collaborators. This new approach is closer to the classical definition of cellular automata than the previous one. It has the advantage of achieving the same results obtained with the IMMSIM with a lower computational effort. IMMSIM belongs to the class of immunological cellular automata, but its degree of sophistication sets it apart from simpler CA in the Ising-like class[16][19].

Bernaschi and Castiglione came up with a parallel coded version of the latest IMMSIM entirely written in the C language that they called ParImm[2] and later CIMMSIM. CIMMSIM was designed according to criteria of openness and modularity to allow smooth upgrades and addition of new features (cells, molecules, interactions and so on) for future investigations. The current version of the code (version 4.3) is able to simulate both the humoral response described in[23][4]and the cellular response described in [5]. In the respect it is the most advanced parallel version of the IMMSIM.

In[18], Meier-Schellershiem and Mack present their own model, SIMMUNE. The model is run on a 3-D grid and can be made to comprise different compartments. It lets the user define the properties of the compartments with the simulation such as the dimension of the compartment, the diffusion rates of molecules and cells with the compartments and the initial concentrations of the different types of agents can be given. Further, the exchange of agents between the different compartments can be regulated. Interestingly, the model incorporates the ability of B-cells to respond to certain kind of antigens directly, i.e. without the assistance of T helper cells. One major drawback of the SIMMUNE model is that it is impossible to find any kind of precise description of its implementation.

2.2 Concept Models

2.2.1 Agent-Based Models

The goal of [22] is to present an agent-based, bottom-up approach to the HIS modeling. This approach is widely used in Artificial Life. The HIS is a suitable candidate for this kind of modeling because it has a structure of non-centralized system based on a high number of distributed elements. The set of local level activities results in a well working. It presents an example of bottom-up HIS model and discusses its advantages and disadvantages. The model is focused on visualizing the dynamic interactions in the system. A bottom-up approach is based on the synthesis of a complex system from the activities on a lower system level. The artificial models have a design of a computer environment with a set of simple autonomous entities on local a level. The activity of these entities is emerging into the behavior of a global system. A model with this kind of structure is easily implemented by using agents-based modeling. It offers us a direct "entity to agent" implementation of entities' features. An agent-based modeling, in general, offers a tool for biological systems modeling that is easy to understand and develop.

2.2.2 Swarm-Based Models

In[13], it presents a swarm-based, 3-dimensional model of the HIS and its response to first and second viral antigen exposure.The model utilizes a decentralized swarm approach with multiple agents acting independently—following local interaction rules—to exhibit complex emergent behaviour, which constitute externally observable and measurable immune reactions. The two main functional branches of the human immune system, humoral and cell-mediated immunity, are simulated in the model. It models the production of antibodies in response to a viral population. Antibody-antigen complexes are formed, which are removed by macrophages. This system also demonstrates reinforced reaction to a previously encountered pathogen, thus exhibiting realistic memory response.

2.2.3 Cellular Automaton

Many models of the HIS using a cellular automaton are based on the work of de Boer [8]. In 1992, de Boer et al. used a cellular automaton to model HIS. Their model is based on Jerne's network theory , which is a classic immunology theory described by differential equation, and simulated the activation of B-cells caused by injection of antigen.

According to Jerne's network theory, the main cause of immunity is the emergence of a network of interacting B-cell populations.

The cellular automata models [8][24][26][27] based on the theory, model the so called shape space of the B-cell receptors. In these models, B-cells with every possible receptor are represented as cells in a multidimensional grid. The shape of a receptor of a B-cell is represented by the vector denoting the grid position of the B-cell. Two B-cells have a matching receptor if their position vectors are opposite. A cell can be in two states, active or non-active.

In a cellular automaton, the state of a cell at time $t + 1$ depends only on the state of its most direct neighbours at time t, or earlier. Usually, if the position of a cell in the grid is denoted by a vector a, its neighbours are those cells with a position close to a. The cellular automaton models of HIS use a different concept of neighbourhood, that expresses the concept of affinity between two receptors. Many variants of the basic model have been constructed, some of which use more than two states, others using different numbers of dimensions. A serious problem with these cellular automaton based models is that they are still based on the immune network theory.

It may be worth mentioning the work in[29],which have developed simplistic CA toy models of HIS to answer specific questions. In [29] ,it uses a very simple celluar automaton of immunization and aging in the context of immune network. The cellular automaton model is such that rather than having different types of cells moving around on the grid(lattice gas model), every site of the CA grid in a d-dimensional space corresponds to the shape of a molecule(associated with a B cell or antibody) and can be in any of 3 states: $B_i = 0$ (or nonactivated) for low, $B_i = 1$ for immediate or $B_i = 2$ for high(activated). The authors then define a field, h_i that represents the concentrations of complementary receptors as $h_i(t) = \sum_{2d+1} B_i(t)$. The rule for the evolution of the system is then defined as

$$B_i(t+1) = \begin{cases} B_i(t)+1 \text{ if } \theta_1 \leq h_i(t) \leq \theta_2 \\ B_i(t)-1 \quad \text{otherwise} \end{cases} \tag{1}$$

But no change is made if it would lead to $B_i = -1$ or 3. This simplistic model has a transition region, between a stable and chaotic region, where the authors have observed emergent complex behavirour which they claim is appropriate to describe a self-regulated multiconnected network and possibly provides the much needed connections between the available experimental results and the Jerne's theory.

HIS models using a modified cellular automaton have several advantages[12]:

Firstly, it can estimate the distribution of behaviors more widely, not only the average because of stochastic characteristics.

Secondly, it is easy to modify the complexity of the interactions without introducing any new difficulties in solving the model because nonlinear is not intrinsically difficult to treat in cellular automata.

Lastly, the cellular automaton is able to represent the components and processes of interest in biological language. Thus can allow researchers to check the correctness of the model.

However, there are penalties to be paid. First we will always be dealing with a relatively small system. In reality , the HIS is gigantic, in humans involving 10^{12} cells of perhaps 10^9 possible specificities. The simulations will be always much smaller and researchers must pay constant attention that the results they see are not artifacts due to our restricted size. Second it will sometimes be hard to extract the essence of what is happening.

3. APPLICATIONS OF THE HIS MODELS

One hand,currently many applications can be found by using ideas derived from the HIS and its simulation in the field of medical science.

On the other hand, many properties of the immune system have been recognised as important features for a number of applications in the field of computer science or Aritifial Immune Systems(AIS). In the last few years, a number of applications of artificial immune systems had been developed.

Many applications have been in the field of computer security[25],robot control [28]or semiconductor production line[11]. Some applications use models based on Jerne's network theory. Other applications use general properties of the immune system that are considered useful for the problem that is being researched, and implement them in ways very different from the HIS.

If we observe the immune system from an artificial intelligence point of view, we can see it as a learning system that autonomously performs a number of tasks including pattern recognition, learning from examples, regulating actions based on sensor information, and optimization toward better solutions[12]. Thus, the immune system consists of several learning components. For artificial intelligence research, interesting properties of the immune system are the following.

- Classification: discrimination between self and non-self
- Regulation: Control of the reaction against antigen
- Parallelism: Distributed memory for known antigen
- Optimization: Adaptive recognition leading to a faster response

The Celada and Seiden model exhibits all of these properties. Since the model classifies data that is represented by bit strings, it could be used in various classification and pattern recognition tasks. Representing the problem data as bit strings in a way that is usable and meaningful in the CS model.

4. DISCUSSION

Computational modeling is of growing interest in a number of fields including biology, mathematics, physics and computer science.

We have to distinguish between two types of computer modeling, namely computational models[12][17], such as differential equation and concept models, such as cellular automaton. As mentioned above, the former is often a preferable way to model a complex system since more is know about differential equations. It is often the case that the differential equations will likely contain nonlinear and time-delays. The simplifications made are of mathematical concern and will most often distort the dynamics away from that of the real system. Of course, if one is to model the HIS using differential equations, common sense dictates that one has to first simplify the dynamics to no more than a few equations. It is not always a bad approach as it will, for a valid model, give an averaged estimate of the dynamics.

But when one's ultimate goal is to understand the full behavior of the system, in particular the characteristics of the local rules that give rise to the formidable array of complex behavior observed in HIS, it is necessary to resort to a more appropriate tool, namely cellular automata. Cellular automata and in particular lattice gas models are good candidates for studying HIS, which is one type of self organization systems(SOSs). A well known feature of CA computations is their ability to produce surprisingly complex behaviour from very simple rules. Nonlinear or time-delays is not intrinsically difficult to treat since they are either a consequence of the dynamics rather than a cause or are otherwise trivial to include in the context of the CA local rules. Another great advantage of CA is that its computational structure is inherently parallel and it can therefore be run on a parallel computer very efficiently.

5. CONCLUSIONS

The immune system can be seen as a parallel, information processing system that learns through examples and constantly adapts itself to new situations and possesses a distributive memory for patterns. It has many intelligent features from the point of view of AI. Many models and simulations had been established to explore its nature and its intelligent behavior. To the researchers in the field of AI, human immune system is an inspiring resource for designing new intelligent way for solving engineering problem. While to immunologists, by computer modeling and simulating, they can find new ways of improving medical approaches for people. So modeling and simulating the HIS will benefit more to both engineering and medical. The combination of them has been a trend both in the field of AI and medical, but there is still a lot of work to do.

ACKNOWLEDGEMENTS

This paper is supported by National Nature Science Foundation of China,No.60305007, and Nature Science Foundation of Heilongjiang Province, China, No.F0210 and Basic Theory Research Project Foundation of Harbin Engineering University,No.HEUF04076.

REFERENCES

[1] Bernaschi M.,Castiglione. F. Selection of escape mutants from immune recognition during HIV. Immunology and Cell Biology. Special issue devoted to Immuno-informatics. 80:307-312, 2002

[2] Bernaschi M., Castiglione F. and Succi.S. A parallel simulator of the immune response. 1401:163–172,1998

[3] Bezzi,M., Celada,F. Ruffo S. and Seiden. P.E. The transition between immune and disease states in a cellular automaton model for clonal immune response.Physica A. 245:145-163, 1997

[4] Castiglione F., Bernaschi M. and Succi S. Simulating the immune response on a distributed parallel computer.Int. J. Mod. Phys. C8:527–545, 1997

[5] Celada F.and Seiden P. A. Cmputer model of cellular interaction in the immune system. Immunology Today.13:56–62, 1992

[6] Celada F., Seiden P.E. Affinity maturation and hypermutation in a stimulation of the humoral response. Eur.J.Immunol,26(6):1350-1358, 1996

[7] Celada F., Seiden.P.E. Modeling immune cognition. Proceedings of the 1998 IEEE International Conference on Systems,Man and Cybernetics,San Diego,CA, 3787-3792,11-14 Oct.1998,

[8] De Boer,R. J., Segel L. A. and Perelson A. S. Pattern-formation in one dimensional and 2-dimensional shape space models of the immune-system. J. Theor. Biol., 155:295– 333, 1992.

[9] Farmer J. D., Packard N., and Perelson A. The immune system,adaptation and machine learning. Physica D **22**:187–204, 1986

[10] Forrest S., Smith R., Javornik E B and Perelson. A. S. Using genetic algorithms to explore pattern recognition in the immune system. Evolutionary Compuatation,1(30):191-211,1993

[11] Fukada T., Mori K. and Tsukiyama M. Immunity based management system for a semiconductor production line. Proc. of The 1998 International Conference on Evolutionary Computation, 1998.

[12] Hanegraaff W. Simulating the immune system.2001 http://www.lymenet.de/literature/hanegraaff.pdf

[13] Jacob C., Litorcol J. and Lee L. Immunity Through Swarms: Agent-Based Simulations of the Human Immune System .Giuseppe N., Vincenzo C., Peter J. Bentley et al. I Artificial Immune Systems, Third International Conference, ICARIS 2004.Berlin, Springer-Heiderberg, 2004,400-412

[14] Jerne. N. Towards a network theory of the immune system. Ann. Immunol.,125C:373– 389, 1974.

[15] Joachim G. Models of immune systems: The use of differential equations.http://www.lymenet.de/literatur/immundif.htm.

[16] Kaufman M., Urbain J., and Thomas R. Towards a logical analysis of the immune response. J. Theor. Biol. 114:527, 1985.

[17] Kleinstein S. H., Seiden P. E. Simulating the immune system. Computing in Science and Engineering, 4:69– 77, 2000

[18] Meier-Schellersheim M., Mack.G. Simmune: a tool for simulating and analyzing immune system behavior,1999,arXiv:cs.MA/9903017

[19] Pnadey R.,Tauffer D. Metastability with probabilistic cellular automata in an HIV infection. J. Stat. Phys. 61:235, 1990

[20] Perelson, A. S., 1989, Immunology Review. 110, 5-36.

[21] Perelson A.S.. Hightower R. Forrest. S. Evolution and somatic learning in v-region genes. Res.Immunol.,147:202-208,1996

[22] Peter Zvirinksy A. Bottom-up Approach to Immune System Modeling. Intelligent and Adaptive system in Medicine. Prague,20003

[23] Seiden P., Celada F. A model for simulating cognate recognition and response in the immune system. J. Theor. Biol. 158:329–357, 1992

[24] Smith D. J., Forrest S. Hightower,R. R. and Perelson A. S.. Deriving shape space parameters from immunological data. J. Theor. Biol., 189:141– 150,1997

[25] Somayaji, A. Hofmeyr,S. and Forrest.S. Principles of a computer immune system. New Security Paradigms Workshop, 1997

[26] Stauffer D., Sahimi. M. High-dimensional and very large cellularautomata for immunological shape space. Int. J. Mod. Phys. C-Phys. Comput.4:401– 408, 1993

[27] Stauffer D., Sahimi. M. High-dimensional simulation of simple immunological models. J. Theor. Biol., 166:289– 297, 1994.

[28] Watanabe Y. Ishiguro A. Shirai Y. and Uchikawa Y..Emergent construction of behavior arbitration mechanisms based on the immune system. Proc. of The 1998 International Conference on Evolutionary Computation.481– 486, 1998.

[29] Zorzenon dos Santos R.M., Coutinho S..Dynamics of hiv infection:A cellular automata approach. Physical Review Letters,87(16),2001

STUDY AND APPLICATION OF SOFTMAN COMMUNICATION MODEL

Zhonggui Ma[1] , Bin Ye [1,2] , Guangping Zeng [3] , Xuyan Tu[3]
[1] *The Department of Automatic Control, Beijing Institute of Technology, Beijing 100081;*[2] *Taiyuan University of Technology, Taiyuan 030024;*[3] *School of Information Engineering, University of Science and Technology Beijing, Beijing 100083*

Abstract: By analyzing present communication model of multi-agent and SoftMan's characteristics, a SoftMan communication model which combined centralized-decentralized mode with direct-indirect mode was presented base on multi-level hierarchical architecture of Large System Cybernetics. This model can assign task and deal with information logically. It can optimize scheduler, decentralize danger, and improve the speediness and security of communication of SoftMan system. Using this communication model can make system design more easily. A good application has been performed in digital gas field.

Key words: SoftMan Communication, DAI(Distributed Artificial Intelligence), Digital Gas Field, Multi-Agent System

1. INTRODUCTION

The term "SoftMan" was first put forward in the second bibliography. Its basic concept is developing a king of automated intelligent tool named "SoftMan" in the internet on the basis of Artificial Intelligence, Artificial Life and Distributed System, combined intelligent robot, intelligent net with Multi-Agent. This king of SoftMan can move freely, and deal with some tasks automatically using information push-pull technology. It can act as certain office clerk, such as safety policeman, garbage collector, information waiter in the internet, and so on.

In a SoftMan system, SoftMan can solve distributed problems by coordination and cooperation. However, communication is a bridge for coordination and cooperation. Communication in the SoftMan system includes communication between SoftMan and SoftMan platform, communication between SoftMan and SoftMan.

For this purpose, SoftMan communication language and communication protocols based on Speech Act theory must be built.

There are three main problems as follows need to be solved now:

1) Communication Management: After communication intention is produced, it usually can't be finished by one message; and there are logical relations between messages. The right understanding to a message relies on not only message contents and communication protocols, but also communication history. So it needs to manage communication process so as to combine communication content with cooperation.

2) Communication Language: Communication language is the media of message transferring and knowledge exchanging of SoftMan. All SoftMans share syntax, semantics and pragmatics of communication language.

3) Communication Protocols: The communication protocols refer to generalized communication protocols, which include high level communication protocols and low level transportation protocols. High level communication protocols describe basic processes of communication and all possible instances of corresponding messages, and they are usually described by finite state machine. Low level transportation protocols refer to transportation control in practical communication, such as TCP, SMTP and HTTP, and son on.

2. COMMON COMMUNICATION MODEL

Prof. Xuyan Tu has put forward three kinds of information structure of Multi-Agent System: Centralized Information Structure, Decentralized Information Structure and Hybrid Information Structure. Based on these structures, there are two common communication models: Client/Server Model(for short C / S Model) and Point-To-Point Model(for short P2P Model).

2.1 Client/Server Model(C / S Model)

Agent Communication is indirect in the communication system based on C/S Model. There is a central server in this model, all agents only communicate with the central server and can't communicate one another, so agent communication relies on the central server to achieve communicating one another and sharing resource. This model usually use "blackboard" as communication mode. Figure 1 shows the block diagram of this model.

The characteristics of C/S Model as follows:

(1) Centralized Information

All agents only communicate with the central server and can't communicate one another. The central server controls the access rights of all agents, only registered agents can exchange information and share resource, which is in favor of allotting information resource reasonably.

(2) Simple Structure

The structure of this model is simple, so it is easy to achieve, diagnose and maintain.

(3) Centralized Load

Because information is centralized, load is centralized. As the number of agents increase, storage space of the central server and communication load between all agents and the central server also increase. The performance of server and network bandwidth will be the bottleneck of multi-agent system.

(4) Centralized Danger

Because information is centralized, danger is centralized. When the central server fails to run, it will lead to crash of multi-agent system. So reliability of C/S Model is weak.

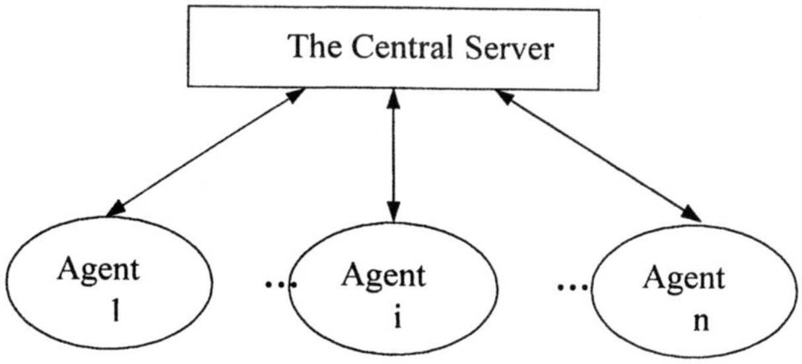

Figure 1. the block diagram of C/S Model

2.2 Point-To-Point Model(P2P Model)

Agent communication is direct in the communication system based on P2P Model, which need not transmit by the central server. This model uses decentralized communication structure and usually uses message as communication mode. Figure 2 shows the block diagram of this model.

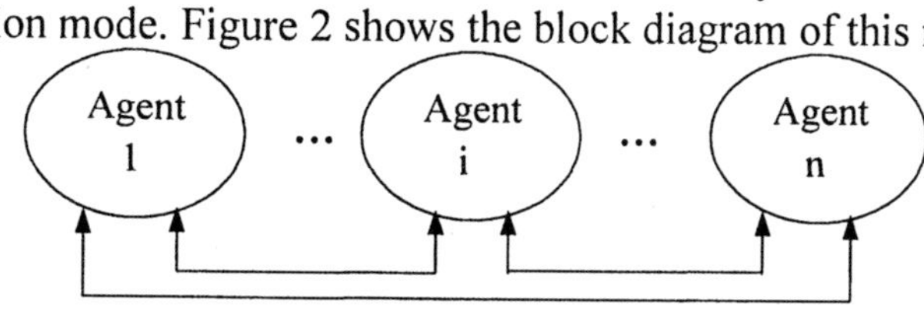

Figure 2. the block diagram of P2P Model

The characteristics of P2P Model as follows:

(1) Decentralized Information

There is not central server. All agents directly communicate one another with message. Any agent can be a sender or a receiver of message. This model seems like full interlinkage model of net model, so it is the same as peer to peer system. Because any two of agents have the direct access, they can communicate directly.

(2) Balanced Load

Multi-agent system doesn't depend on certain special node when it runs, so its load is balanced, and reliability of this model is strong.

(3) Harmonious Communication

Decentralized information structure needs to define communication protocols, formats of message, transmitted mechanism and communication language (including syntax and semantics).In this way, exchanging information and sharing resource can be easily done among agents.

(4) Difficult to Achieve

First, because each agent saves status information of all agents, it increases local storage load. Second, any inner status change of an agent must inform other agents, it increases communication load. Third, every agent must deal with correlative calculation of controlling and scheduler, so it increases calculating load of multi-agent system. Because all of these need perfect low level communication protocols, it is difficult to achieve.

3. SOFTMAN COMMUNICATION MODEL

From the two models discussed above, we can learn that the communication system can't satisfy the multitasking requirement of SoftMan only based on C/S Model or P2P Model. Therefore, this paper puts forward SoftMan communication model with multi-level hierarchical architecture on the basis of C/S Model and P2P Model. This model has the merits of the two models discussed above. Figure 3 shows the block diagram of this model.

The goal of SoftMan Design is to simulate behavior of human society, extend and prolong human intelligence, so SoftMan should be marked off according to role and ability of human society. Different SoftMan has different ability and plays a different role. We mark off one group with commonness, and each group assigns a group leader who manages other SoftMan of his group and communicates with other groups by the central server. In the SoftMan group of figure 3, we supposed that there are n groups of SoftMan, such as Group 1, Group 2, ……, Group n, the SoftMan number of each group is r, s,……, t accordingly, and the group leader of each group is GL_1, GL_2, ……, GL_n accordingly. Communication between group and group uses C/S Model, respectively group leader of each group is delegated to communicate with group leader of other groups, and the central server save name, address, ability and status of group leader of all groups, etc. Communication within one group uses P2P Model which harmoniously communicates with full interlinkage mode.

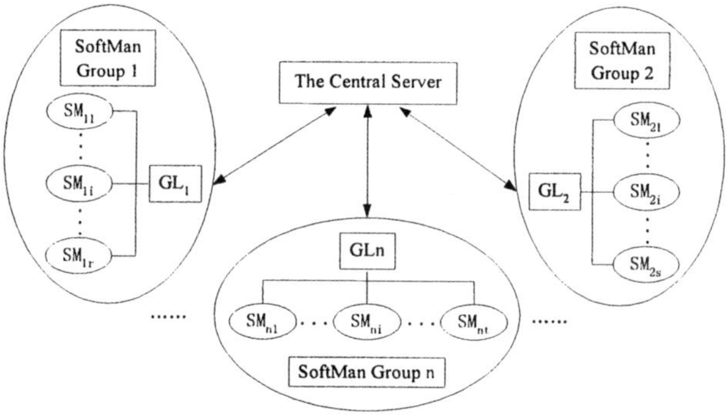

Figure 3. SoftMan Communication Model

Because SoftMan communication model combined centralized-decentralized mode with direct-indirect mode, it can learn from others's strong points to offset one's weakness, assign task and deal with information logically. It can also optimize scheduler, decentralize danger, and improve the speediness and security of communication of SoftMan system. Using this communication model can make system design more easily.

4. COMMUNICATION LANGUAGE AND COMMUNICATION PROTOCOLS OF SOFTMAN

In this paper, KQML(Knowledge Query and Manipulation Language) is used as communication language and is expanded in security. KQML is a kind of high-level and message-oriented communication language and communication protocols for agent, it supports knowledge-sharing of runtime and coroutine problem. KQML messages do not merely provide communication sentences, they are sent to recipients with an attitude about the content(assertives, directives, commisives, declaratives, and expressives). An attitude of content is conceptualized to primitives that are called performatives. It provides an extensible set of performatives, using it we can build high-level agent communication model, such as Contracts Nets. It uses facilitator to communicate with different agents, and facilitator is also a king of special agent.

KQML is a kind of hiberarchy language. Conceptually, KQML message can be viewed as being divided into three layers: the content layer, the message layer, and the communication layer. The KQML structure is illustrated in Figure 4. The content layer bears the real content of the message in the program's own representation language. KQML may use any form of languages(such as ASCII character strings, binary code), so its realization form is independent of meanings of the content layer. The message layer determines the kinds of interaction between KQML-speaking agents. The main function of the message layer is to identify the protocol to be used to deliver the message and to supply a speech act or performative that the sender attaches to the content. The speech act indicates whether the message is an assertion, a query, a command, or any other of a set of known performatives. The communication layer encodes a set of features to the message that describe the lower-level communication parameters, such as the identity of the sender and recipient, and a unique identifier associated with the communication.

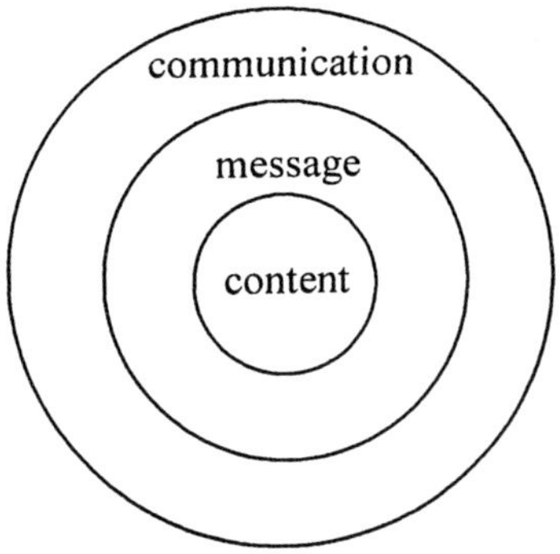

Figure 4. KQML structure

5. SOFTMAN APPLICATION IN DIGITAL GAS FIELD

The conformity of multi-source complex information is the core in the key technology of digital gas field, it directly restrict the success of production control, decision-making and data mining, and its purpose is to achieve the conformity of multi source and multilayer data, and make existing application exchange data one another. Because of lacking of standard data format, point-to point way is inefficient when every application get data from other applications. For example, as data formats of certain application have been changed, other applications using this data must change accordingly. One way to solve this problem is to build uniform data format in data exchanging center, and build corresponding relation between uniform data format and its own data format in every application accordingly.

Therefore, a kind of standard data format should be built. At the same time, there are many existing application software and many kings of database, such as text file, FoxBASE, Access, SQL Server, Sybase, Oracle, and so on, so many application interfaces and data interfaces should also be built. It is difficult to carry into execution. Thus we present the data exchange method using SoftMan technologies. The data exchanging structure is illustrated in Figure 5. Data exchanging center communicates and exchanges data (including uploading data and downloading data) by the interface SoftMan of data exchanging. First, the interface SoftMan of data exchanging decides to call certain SoftMan group by parsing message header. Second, the group leader of SoftMan group receiving message shares message by broadcasting. Third, query SoftMan queries data from corresponding database according to query condition and saves the data in the data cache. Fourth, validating SoftMan checks the validity and rationality of data and saves the result. Fifth, converting SoftMan generates standard data according to corresponding relation between uniform data format and data format of current application. Sixth, executing SoftMan packages the data and informs the group leader to transfer data. The data of different locations and different formats can access one another by the data exchanging center, and the data exchanging center integrates correlative application systems and forms the basic platform of digital gas field.

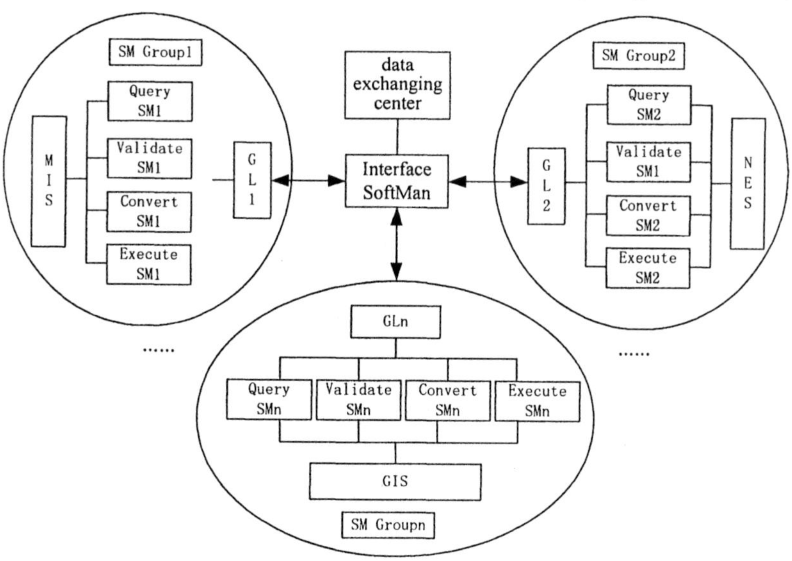

Figure 5. data exchanging structure

This structure belongs to LCN like stelliform net, and it is easy to expand in structure. It can build multilevel data exchanging center so as to support fargoing Wide Area Information Server. Using SoftMan technologies, greatly predigest design difficulty and it is easy to maintain. A good application has been performed in digital gas field.

6. CONCLUSION

With the development of computer and network technology, internet has been anywhere. However, more and more people need to provide safe, shortcut and humanity information services in tremendous amount ofvast net world. Many experts and scholars have done many predominant work, on the basis of these work, a SoftMan communication model which combined C/S Model with P2P Model was presented base on multi-level hierarchical architecture of Large System Cybernetics. This model can assign task and deal with information logically. It can optimize scheduler, decentralize danger, and improve the speediness and security of communication of SoftMan system. Using this communication model can solve communication problems of distributed system effectively.

NOTES

Foundation item: National Science Foundation of China (No.60375038)

REFERENCES

1. Xuyan Tu, Large System Cybernetics, Defense Industrial Publishing House, 1994, Beijing.
2. Guangping Zeng and Xuyan Tu, "SoftMan", < Progress of Artificial Intelligence in China>, Proceedings of 10th CAAI Conference, Beijing University of Posts and Telecommunications Publishing House, 2003, Beijing.
3. Zhongzhi Shi , Intelligent Agent and its Applications, Science Publishing House, 2000, Beijing.
4. Xuyan Tu and Junping Du etc., Multi-Agent System, Software World, Aug. 2000, Beijing.
5. Xinyu Feng and Xianping Tao etc., An improved mobile Agent communication algorithm, Chinese Journal of Computers, 2002, 25(4):357~364, Beijing.
6. Thome, M. Multi-tier communication abstractions for distributed multi-agent systems. Integration of Knowledge Intensive Multi-Agent Systems, 2003. International Conference on , 30 Sept.-4 Oct. 2003 Pages:209 – 214

THE ADAPTIVE WEB SERVER BASED ON ANT BEHAVIOR*

Ping Guo, Qin Xie
School of Computer Science, Chongqing University, Chongqing, 400044, P.R.China
E-MAIL: guoping@cqu.edu.cn

Abstract: This paper presents an approach to establish an adaptive Web site, which is inspired by the ant colonies foraging behavior. In this approach, artificial ants metaphorically guide users' activity and adaptively mark the most significant links, by means of the shortest route to target node. By the simulated experiment, we study those factors that influence Web user's behaviors, which can be useful for further theoretical research and algorithm realization.

Key words: ant colony algorithm, adaptive Web site, simulation

1. INTRODUCTION

Nowadays, World Wide Web has become the most dominant medium in these fields of information, communication and communion. The number of Web sites has increased rapidly, and the size of them has also enhanced. Consequently, it will be more difficult for the users to search from the large and complex information in the Web sites. Therefore, in the construction of Web sites, we should emphasize the importance of convenience and quickness.

One efficient solution is to establish adaptive Web sites through the study of user access pattern. The definition of an adaptive Web site is a site that automatically improves their organization and presentation based on user access pattern[1]. The adaptation can be realized in two ways. One is Dynamic Customization, which means it can adapt the site's presentation to

* This work was supported by National Natural Science Foundation of China, NO. 50378093.

the needs of individual visitors, based on information about those individual, such as path prediction. The other is Optimization, which means it can improve the site's structure based on interactions with all visitors so that they can be visited more easily and conveniently, including Promotion and Demotion, Highlighting, Link, and Clustering[2]. Dynamic Customization focuses on individuals and is for a single user, while Optimization is for all users, and it focuses on the improvement of the site's structure and contents, in order that all the users can access them facilely and advantageously.

Proposed by M. Dorigo, ant colony algorithm[3] imitates the action of ant colonies foraging behavior, which is a kind of bionic algorithm based on the natural environment, and is also for the adaptive problems. According to heuristic idea and through the inducement by pheromone, we can get the convergent and optimized solution. So far, ant colony algorithm has already been successfully applied in such fields as combinatorial optimization, computer network routing, continuous function optimization, robot path planning, data mining, and the optimization of electric network.

Based on the Web usage mining, this paper tries to apply the ant colony algorithm in the establishment of the adaptive Web site, and bring forward the Ant-based Adaptive Web site Algorithm (AAWA). Through the simulated experiment, we have studied the factors that influence the action of users, which include pheromone weight, pheromone evaporation coefficient, the number of Web users, and the amount of residual pheromone. The result can be significant to the further study and the realization of the algorithm.

2. AAWA (ANT-BASED ADAPTIVE WEB SITE ALGORITHM)

2.1 The introduction of ant colony's behavior

In nature, though the behavior of a single ant is extremely simple, when these ants act as a whole community, they are capable of solving complex problems in their daily life. Ethnologists have discovered that ants are capable of finding the shortest path from a food source to their nest without the use of visual information. And they are also able to adapt to the changes of the environment, for example, finding a new shortest path once the old one is no longer feasible due to a new obstacle. While walking from the food source to the nest, ants deposit on the ground a substance called pheromone, forming a pheromone trail. When a single ant moves at random and encounters those previously laid trails, it can feel the pheromone and is more likely to choose the thicker one and reinforces the trail with its own pheromone. The more the ants following a trail are, the more probability that this trail becomes attractive for the followers. The process is thus characterized by a positive feedback loop, where the probability that an ant chooses a path increases with the number of ants that chose the same path in the preceding steps.

In a sense, the process of surfing in Web is similar to that of the ant colonies foraging. In this paper, we consider users' visiting the Web as the ant colonies foraging process (the users are compared to the artificial ants, and the target node, the food source). Different from ants, visitors of Web do not have any communication. Each one obtains their own route to find their objective without the support of others that may have previously passed through the same path. So, in this article, we connect the users through imitating the ants' pheromone, which can make a single user find the target node more easily and quickly.

2.2 Basic theory

In the Web site, we can apply the ant colony theory to make Web users reach the target node through the shortest route (In this article, we name a Web site's page as a node and a link between pages as a route). The method is as follows: Within t, a Web user sets out from the homepage every Δt, and according to the staying time at each node and the pheromone density on each route, it selects the next node, and finally stops at the destination node. All users stop after t and we can update the amount of pheromone at all nodes that the users who have reached the target have passed. Through several times of simulation (a process of $t/\Delta t$ users' finding target node within t), the users gradually concentrate on an optimized route. The detailed theory is the following:

We suppose there is a user visiting the Web site every Δt. The iteration p is a number of the users visiting the Web site within t, namely, $p=t/\Delta t$. Here, t is the duration of a simulation. The amount of pheromone $\tau_{ij}(p)$ associated to a link (i,j) is intended to represent the learned desirability of the choosing node j when in node i. The initial amount of pheromone $\tau_{ij}(0)$, at iteration $p=0$, is set to a small positive constant value or zero for all links. In our case the initial probability value which a user (k) chooses from node i to node $j \in N_i$ is obtained from the Web usage mining.

A probability value p_{ij}^d expresses the goodness of choosing j as next node when the target node is d, it has the constraint:

$$\sum p_{ij}^d = 1, j \in N_i, N_i = \{neighbors\,(i)\} \tag{1}$$

We define the transition probability from the node i to the node $j \in N_i$:

$$p_{ij}^{d}(p)=[\tau_{j}^{d}(p)]^{\alpha}[\eta_{j}(p)]^{\beta}/\sum\{[\tau_{l}^{d}(p)]^{\alpha}[\eta_{l}(p)]^{\beta}\}\quad j\in N_{i},l\in N_{i}\quad (2)$$

Where $\tau_j^d(p)$ is the amount of pheromone trail at the node *j* at iteration *p* for destination *d*. N_i is the set of neighbors of the node *i*, and α and β are both parameters that control the relative weight of residual pheromone trail and heuristic value. $\eta_i = 1/wt_j$ is the heuristic value of moving to node *j*:

$$wt_j = lt_j + vt_j \quad (3)$$

Where wt_j is the estimated time at the node *j*, including lt_j, the estimated time to get all information of the node *j* to the browser at some velocity of the process; and vt_j, the estimated time to visit the node *j*.

In this paper, we define the distance between two neighboring nodes that users have passed as 1. For example, if a user reaches the target node 2 through a route as 1A→2A→3A→2B→2 (fig.1), then the distance between node 1A and node 2A is 1 and that between node 1A and node 2 is 4.

After a user has completed his visit, pheromone evaporation at all nodes is triggered, and then the user (k) deposits a quantity of pheromone $\Delta\tau_i^{d,k}(p)$ at each node that has been visited:

$$\Delta\tau_i^{d,k}(p)=\begin{cases}1/[(nl_i^{d,k}(p)+1)\sigma] & if\ i\in T^{d,k}(p)\\ 0 & if\ i\notin T^{d,k}(p)\end{cases} \quad (4)$$

Where $T^{d,k}(p)$ is a set of all the visited nodes by user (k) to get to the destination node *d*, and $nl_i^{d,k}(p)$ is the distance between node *i* and node *d* in the $T^{d,k}(p)$. σ is a parameter that can control and adjust the value of $\Delta\tau_i^{d,k}(p)$.

$$\Delta\tau_i^d(p)=\sum\Delta\tau_i^{d,k}(p)\qquad k=1,\cdots p, i\in T^{d,k}(p) \quad (5)$$

The addition of the new pheromone by users and pheromone evaporation is implemented by the following rule applied to all nodes.

$$\tau_i^d(p)\rightarrow(1-\rho)\tau_i^d(p)+\rho\Delta\tau_i^d(p)\quad \rho\in(0,1) \quad (6)$$

Where ρ is the pheromone trail decay coefficient.

2.3 The algorithm

At the beginning of the algorithm, all Web users are at the homepage of the Web site. There can be a user setting out from the homepage every Δt. When t=0, the first time of simulation begins, and when t=T, it ends. Therefore we can calculate the amount of pheromone at all the passed nodes that lead to the target node so as to update the pheromone of all nodes. Then the next similar simulation starts. If the times of simulation reaches the maximum $NC_{\max}$ set by us, or all the users choose the same path, the algorithm can be over. Ultimately, the optimized route that users have found is the optimized solution of the problem. The Steps are as follows:

(1) Applying the Web usage mining algorithm to get initial probability of the desirability of choosing the node j when in the node I ($j \in N_i$);

(2) Parameter initialization: Setting total time of a simulation as T, simulation times NC=0, the maximum of simulation times $NC_{\max}$ =N, $\tau_{ij}(0)$=C, $\Delta\tau_{ij}$=0 and t=0.

(3) At the homepage of the Web site, a user (k) is generated every Δt to find the destination node (in this paper, we limit ourselves to one destination node).

(4) Each user (k) at the node i choose the next node randomly as gambling at a rotary table until they find the target node. (The rotary table gamble way is that we add those choice probabilities to get some accumulative probabilities, and then generate a random number which is in the domain of some accumulative probability, and the node corresponded the accumulative probability is the next node that will be selected.)

(5) When the user (k) reaches the destination node, he stops and calculates, through the formula (4), the amount of pheromone $\Delta\tau_{ij}^{k}(p)$ that is deposited at each visited node.

(6) A time of simulation finishes when t=T. Resetting NC=NC+1 and t=0, through formula (5), we compute the total amount of pheromone at each visited node deposited by all the users that have reached the target node, and then update pheromone of all nodes according to formula (6).

(7) Recalculating the probability of choice from node i to node j ($j \in N_i$) by using formula (2), and replacing the existed probability.

(8) If $NC< NC_{\max}$ or no convergence phenomenon exists, then returning to step (3). Otherwise, inputting the shortest route and the algorithm is over.

3. SIMULATED EXPERIMENT AND THE ANALYSIS OF THE RESULT

In this experiment, we simulate the structure of the Web site as Fig.1. We set the duration of each simulation as t=100s and the interval between two users who are generated as Δt=5s, so p=t/Δt=20, meaning there are 20 users visiting the Web site in each simulation. The probability P(1A,2A) with which the users go along the route 1A→2A is fixed as 0.4, P(1A,2B) as 0.4, and P(1A,2C) as 0.2. Node 2 is the objective.

Through the simulated experiment, we select the representative data as follows:

(1) $\tau_{ij}(0)$=0, t=100s, Δt=5s, α=2, β=3, ρ=0.7, σ=2
(2) $\tau_{ij}(0)$=0, t=100s, Δt=5s, α=1, β=2, ρ=0.7, σ=1
(3) $\tau_{ij}(0)$=3, t=100s, Δt=5s, α=1, β=2, ρ=0.7, σ=1

Through the imitated experiment, we are able to observe that the third group of data is the best. From Fig. 2, we find the choices of the parameters have a great influence on the final performance of the algorithm. The parameters mainly include α, β, ρ, σ in this algorithm. α determines the relative importance of the remaining pheromone, β represents the relative importance of the heuristic information, ρ is the degree of pheromone evaporating, σ is the parameter that controls and adjusts the value of released pheromone at each node. The higher α is, the higher the probability will be, with which Web users choose the route that has been passed before. That makes the algorithm converge more quickly, but meanwhile the search may be stagnated much earlier, and even leads to the local optimal solution. The higher β is, the easier users will choose the node where the previous users have stayed shorter. When ρ is lower, pheromone usually decays more slowly, and the influence of pheromone increment will be weakened, so the function of positive feedback is reduced; when ρ is higher, some time later, pheromone on all routes is of the similar size. The accumulative knowledge cannot be utilized fully. When σ is higher, the effect of pheromone increment is not obvious, and the function of positive feedback is reduced, too. Therefore, studying the disposition of the parameters α, β, ρ and σ plays a very important role in solution of practical problems.

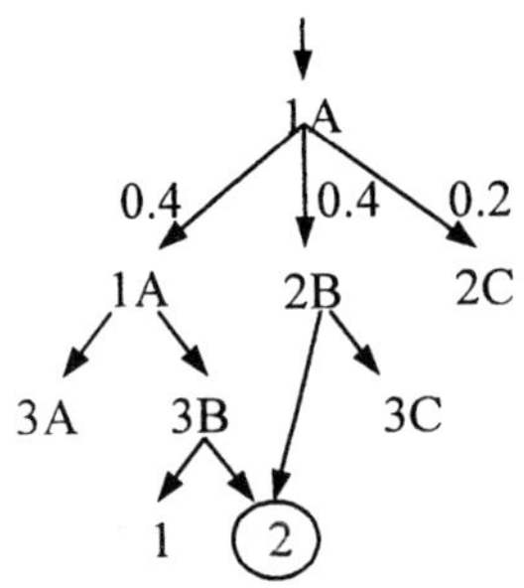

Figure1.The structure of a Web site with two routes to the same target node

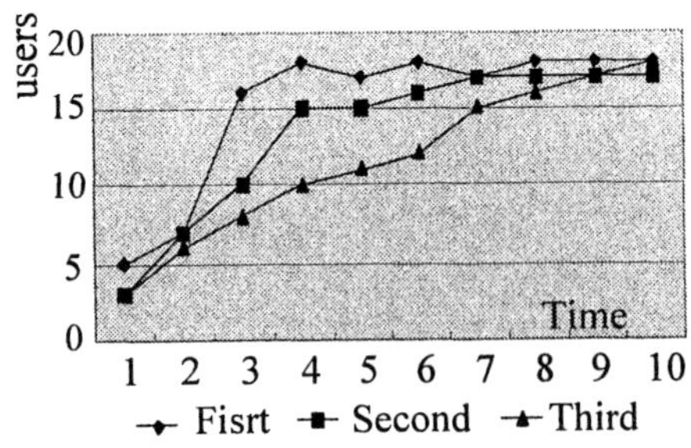

Figure 2. Evolution of the number of users reaching the target node through the shortest route

4. ALGORITHM IMPROVEMENT

In the above simulated experiments, from a large amount of experimental data we found that the algorithm converge when $NC \in [2,4]$, which easily leads to local optimal solution. Therefore, we improve AAWA algorithm in three aspects of the following:

(1) Improving the ways of counting the amount of pheromone

When ant colony algorithm is applied in TSP (Travelling Salesman Problem), it uses average method to compute the amount of pheromone, namely, the total length that the ant has passed divided by the total amount of pheromone. So, in this paper, we improve the formula (5) that is used for counting the amount of pheromone at every node:

$$\Delta\tau_i^{d,k}(p) = \begin{cases} \mathbf{1}/((L_k(p)+\mathbf{1})\sigma) & \text{if } i \in T^{d,k}(p) \\ \mathbf{0} & \text{if } i \notin T^{d,k}(p) \end{cases} \tag{7}$$

Where $T^{d,k}(p)$ is a set of all the nodes passed by the user(k) until reaching the target node *d*. $L_k(p)$ is the total length passed by user(k) until reaching the target node *d*.

The amount of pheromone at these nodes that all the users has passed for the target node is the same through the above formula, unlike the formula (5), in which the nearer to the target node, the larger the amount of pheromone is. Meanwhile it makes some pheromone too centralized and neglects other routes to the target node, which would result in reducing search space or bogging in local optimized solution.

(2) Strengthening the effect of the users that have passed the optimized routes to the target nodes

After every simulation, if every user's pheromone overlapped on the route, the users, who find the worse route, may give their effects on the pheromone's distribution of the system. Under this situation, the advantage of the best route will not be shown. And so we should find the feedback from the users who use thc shortest route in every simulation in order to avoid the useless information's interfere. We can change formula (6) into:

$$\tau_i^d(p) \rightarrow (1-\rho)\tau_i^d(p) + \rho\Delta\tau_i^d(p)^{Best} \tag{8}$$

(3) Limiting the pheromone density

For the existence of the positive feedback effect and pheromone's gradual evaporation, when the algorithm is bounded in the local optimal solution, the pheromone density on the route has the absolute advantage to other routes. In that case, it is hard for the algorithm to escape from the local optimized solution. Therefore, we must limit the maximum and minimum of the pheromone density on the route, such as [$\tau^d(p)_{\min}$, $\tau^d(p)_{\max}$]. If the amount of pheromone on any route is beyond the range, we should force the value to be the fixed maximum or minimum[4].

Based on the above three aspects, we have improved the AAWA algorithm and made the simulated experiment. The applied data is as follows:

$\tau_{ij}(0)=5$, $t=120s$, $\Delta t=4s$, $\alpha=1$, $\beta=2$, $\rho=0.7$, $\sigma=1$

The result is showed in Fig.3. We find that improved algorithm has an advantage in convergence, so the probability of being into the local optimal solution is relatively less.

Fig.2 and Fig.3 show that the number of users that reach the target node through the shortest route is an average value, not something individual. This is a result of the random feature: on the one hand, the algorithm itself is heuristic and random, and on the other hand, the staying time wt_j at every node is also generated in a random way. Therefore, to find the average of the several numbers of users that reach the target node through the shortest route can reduce the influence of the random feature.

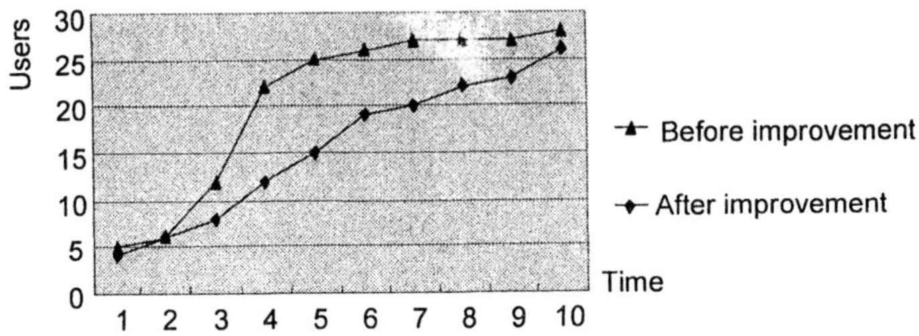

Fig.3. Evolution of the number of users reaching the target node through the shortest route

5. CONCLUSIONS

In this paper, we combine the ant colony theory to adaptive Web techniques as a new method under the scientific research of Web Intelligence. In this way, the users can get to the target nodes through optimized routes. However, either ant colony theory or adaptive Web techniques need further development, and the new method still wants to be studied, in order that it can play more important role in the building of adaptive Web sites.

REFERENCES

[1] Perkowitz, M., Etzioni, O. Adaptive Web sites: an AI challenge. Proceedings of the IJCAI-97. Nagoya, Japan, 1997, 23-29.

[2] Perkowitz, M., Etzioni, O. Adaptive Web sites: automatically learning from user access patterns. In Proceedings of the Sixth Int. WWW conference, 1997.

[3] Dorigo, M., Garnbardella, L. Ant colony system: a cooperative learning approach to the traveling salesman problem. 53-66 IEEE Trans. Evolutionary Computation 1997, Vol.1(1), 53-66.

[4] Thomas, S., Holger, H., MAX-MIN Ant System. Future Generation computer Systems. 2000, Vol.16(8), 889–914.

[5] Wesley, M.,TELES,Li, W.. AntWeb— The adaptive Web server based on the ants' behavior. Proceedings of the IEEE/WIC International Conference on Web Intelligence (WI'03). 2003, 558-561.

THE VALIDITIES OF PEP AND SOME CHARACTERISTIC FORMULAS IN MODAL LOGIC

Hong Zhang, Huacan He
School of Computer Science, Northwestern Polytechnical University,Xi'an, Shaanxi 710032, P.R. China

Abstract: In this paper, we discuss the relationships between some characteristic formulas in normal modal logic with their frames. We find that the validities of the modal formulas are conditional even though some of them are intuitively valid. Finally, we prove the validities of two formulas of Position-Exchange-Principle（PEP） proposed by papers 1 to 3 by using of modal logic and Kripke's semantics of possible worlds.

Key words: Characteristic Formulas, Validity, PEP, Frame

1. INTRODUCTION

Reasoning about knowledge and belief is an important issue in the research of multi-agent systems, and reasoning, which is set up from the main ideas of situational calculus, about other agents' states and actions is one of the most important directions in AI[1-3]. Papers [1-3] put forward an axiom scheme in reasoning about others(RAO) in multi-agent systems, and a rule called Position-Exchange-Principle (PEP) , which is shown as following, was abstracted .

$$C(\varphi \rightarrow \psi) \rightarrow (C\varphi \rightarrow C\psi) \quad (C \in \{B_1^{S_1}, \dots, B_m^{S_m}\})$$

When the length of C is at least 2, it reflects the mechanism of an agent reasoning about knowledge of others. For example, if C is replaced with $B_i^{S_i} B_j^{S_j}$, then it should be

$$B_i^{S_i} B_j^{S_j}(\varphi \rightarrow \psi) \rightarrow (B_i^{S_i} B_j^{S_j}\varphi \rightarrow B_i^{S_i} B_j^{S_j}\psi)$$

The axiom schema plays a useful role as that of *modus ponens* and axiom K when simplifying proof. Though examples were demonstrated as proofs in papers [1-3], from the perspectives both in semantics and in syntax, the rule is not so compellent. They had not developed systematic proof for RAO, and paper [1] only assumed that any single modal operator $B_j^{s_j}$ should satisfy the K45. From the point of intuitive view, the formula $K_a p \wedge K_a(p \rightarrow q) \rightarrow K_a q$ can be proved in epistemic logic systems[5], i.e. the logic subsequence of a epistemic proposition is also known. Thus the logic the omniscience problem is emerged[4-6]. From another point of view, because of many different factors such as agents' states both in physical and in mind, the understandings of agents' to PEP are also much different.

Researches in modal logic and the semantics of possible worlds have become a set of theories which are one of the most powerful formal tools in knowledge representing and reasoning or even in intelligent agent and Multi-Agent Systems[4]. As normal modal systems are formed by adding some axioms on the basis of System K, they are also called expansions of System K. If a new system S is obtained by adding an axiom, then the axiom is called the characteristic axiom of S, and in sometimes it is also called axiom S for simplifying.

We analyzed some characteristic axioms (or formulas) in the semantics of possible-worlds, and obtained their corresponding conditions, to which are met, the corresponding axioms are valid. Through analysis and proof, we find that some formulas are conditional valid even through they are valid from an intuitive view. As the validity problems cannot be solved formally in the Modal Logic[7], we prove them in a semantic view.

The rest of the paper is organized as following: Some of the theories, which including the semantics of the possible worlds, the concepts of frame, model and characteristics, etc., are related in Section 2. In Section 3, we prove the validities of some characteristic formulas, such as D,T,B etc., with the corresponding conditions of their frames. In Section 4, we present two corresponding modal formulas to prove the validity of PEP. Finally, we give our conclusions.

2. RELATED THEORIES

Modal Logic[7,9] is formed from the classical logic by adding the modal operators, such as $\Box$ and $\Diamond$ for 'necessity' and 'possibility', as well as the extensions of axioms and rules. Different modal logic calculus systems are formed by choosing different set of axioms.

The semantics of the possible-worlds[10] is also called relationship semantics. In the research to necessity or/and possibility of a proposition, we should make clear of the following two important contents:

(1) The proposition to be studied should be in a world, though under the idea of semantics of the possible worlds, its necessity and possibility are depended on the truth-values of other worlds.

(2) The relationships to those possible worlds. Because not all of the possible worlds are 'possible' accessible from the world to be studied, the possible worlds have some relations or conditions with each other. When we study the necessity and/or the possibility of a proposition in a world, we simply concern the "possible" worlds, called accessible worlds, not the un-accessible ones.

There are two opposite views in logic-philosophy school regarding the definitions of possible worlds. While there three famous points of view on how to regard possible worlds and practical ones[8]. The theoretical bedrocks of our researches are modal logic and Kripke's semantics of possible worlds, which was established from Leibnitz's theory of possible worlds.

DEFINITION 1: ISSUES RELATED TO THE THEORY OF POSSIBLE WORLDS

A possible world is one of the possible integration of all of the possible subjects, which are either practical or non-practical worlds. The worlds which are impossible in physics belong to the subset of possible world, while the possible worlds' set in physics are a true subset of all possible worlds' sets, which form a class of possible worlds, denoted by W.

The world an agent stays may be considered as a real world, which is make up of all of the subjects existed. An agent's possible world or state is the integration of its physical states and mental ones.

DEFINITION 2: FRAME AND MODEL

A frame is a kind of structures which describe the relationships among possible worlds. It can be denoted by a dual <W,R>, where the possible world W is a non-empty finite set, and R is a two-place relation $(R \subseteq W \times W)$ on the W. Usually , we call a frame a certain one according to the property of the R. For example, if R is reflexive, we call the frame a reflexive frame, while a symmetric frame if R is symmetric,..., and so on.

A model is a logically rigor explanation to a frame in some specific possible worlds. It is denoted by a dual <F, V> or a triple <W,R,V>, where W and R are the same to the corresponding frame F, and V is a dualistic function, which expresses a valuation or assignment of truth values true or false not to a formula but to pairs (w, P) consisting of an element w of W and a formula P in the possible world. Its value-domain is {true, false} or {0,1}.

DEFINITION 3: BASIC SEMANTIC DEFINITION

Let M= <W,R,V> be a model, P and Q are formulas, then the valuation $V_{M,w}(P)$ on a given M ,w∈W is defined as following:

(1) $V_{M,w}(p) = V_w(p)$, where p is a basic meta-proposition ;

(2) $V_{M,w}(\neg P) = true$, if and only if $V_{M,w}(P) = fasle$;

(3) $V_{M,w}(P \rightarrow Q) = true$, if and only if $V_{M,w}(P) = fasle$ or $V_{M,w}(Q) = true$;

Note that (3) also can be equally expressed as following:

(3)′ $V_{M,w}(P \rightarrow Q) = true$, if and only if if $V_{M,w}(P) = true$, then $V_{M,w}(Q) = true$;

(4) $V_{M,w}(\Box P) = true$, if and only if for every $w' \in W(wRw')$ we have $V_{M,w'}(P) = true$, please see figure 1(a) for reference;

(5) $V_{M,w}(\Diamond P) = true$,if and only if for some $w' \in W(wRw')$ we have $V_{M,w'}(P) = true$, please see figure 1(b) for reference;

figure 1 Necessity and Possibility

Because P can be a new formula by adding modal operators to the atomic propositions, we have the following deductions:

(4)′ $V_{M,w}(\Box\Box P) = true$, iff for all $w' \in W(wRw')$ we have $V_{M,w'}(\Box P) = true$, please see figure 2(a);

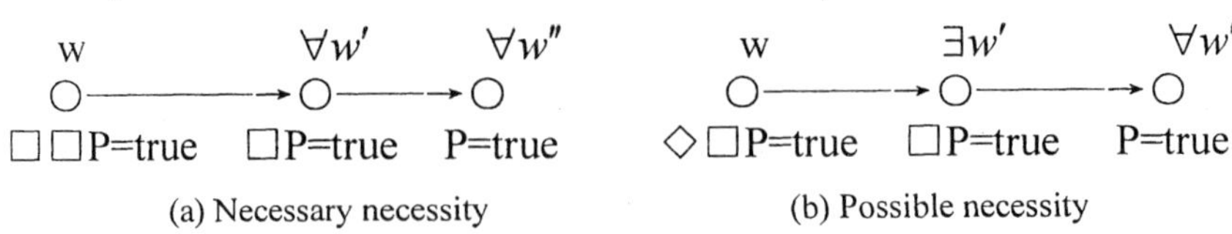

figure 2 Superposition of modal operators

(5)′ $V_{M,w}(\Diamond\Box P) = true$, iff for some $w' \in W(wRw')$ we have $V_{M,w'}(\Box P) = true$, please see figure 2(b).

DEFINITION 4: THE SATISFIABILITY AND THE VALIDITY OF A FORMULA

Let M=<W,R,V> be a model, w a given state in the W of M. For a arbitrary formula P, if there is a valuation V, such that $V_{M,w}(P) = true$, then we call that P is satiable in the w of the M, denoted by $M \models_w P$. Otherwise, P is un-satiable in the w of the M, denoted by $M \not\models_w P$.

If for all the possible worlds w(w ∈ W) on the M, we always have $V_{M,w}(P) = true$, then we call that P is valid on the M, denoted by $M \models P$. Otherwise, P is un-valid on the M, denoted by $M \not\models P$.

Furthermore, P is valid on a frame F if P is valid on a class of model based on F.

DEFINITION 5: THE PROPERTIES OF A FRAME

A frame (or model) usually has many properties, which can be strictly expressed by a formal way. For example, if a formula P is true under an arbitrary valuation V in all of the w(w∈W), i.e. P is valid on F, then for every w, it must has a accessible world w'. This case can be denoted by: $(\forall w)(\exists w')(wRw')$.

A relation which meets such kind of condition is called a serial one, and a frame with a R of serial relation is called a serial frame.

Four of other most frequently used properties of a frame are formally given as followings:

reflexivity	$(\forall w)(wRw)$
symmetry	$(\forall w)(\forall w')(wRw' \rightarrow w'Rw)$
transitivity	$(\forall w)(\forall w')(\forall w'')(wRw' \wedge w'Rw'' \rightarrow wRw'')$
Euclidean	$(\forall w)(\forall w')(\forall w'')(wRw' \wedge wRw'' \rightarrow w'Rw'')$

CHARACTERISTIC FORMULAS:

Formal systems of modal logic are established according to either a formula's validity or its non-contrariness. They are divided into normal systems and non-normal systems according to whether they contain axiom K and necessitation (another common name for it is generalization) rule. The followings are 5 of the most important characteristic formulas (or axioms) of modal logic.

D: □p→◇p

T: □p→p

B: p→□◇p

A: □p→□□p

E: ◇p→□◇p

Where, D and T are intuitively valid formulas. The mean of D is that if p is necessary, then it is possible. In some degree, D reflects the law of "The ought should be approved" in deontic logic. The mean of T is that if p is necessarily true, then p is true. Or in a nutshell, the necessary is the practical. T is called necessitation axiom as well.

B,A and E are the formulas which cannot be ascertained its validity on intuitively. The mean of B is that if p is true, then p is necessarily possible. The mean of A is that if p is necessary, then the necessity of p is necessary. The mean of E is that if p is possible, then the necessity of p is possible. Though these points of view are sounded, their validities are not so evident.

There are also some intuitively in-valid formulas, such as p→□p, ◇p→p, etc. which are also belong to modal logic formulas, because they can form theoretically meaningful systems according to non-contrariness rule.

If a characteristic axiom is to be valid on a frame, the R of the frame must meet a certain condition. We often ignore the corresponding conditions of some formulas which are not intuitively valid because of the intuitively validity of D and T. The followings are some of the proofs we give to the characteristic axioms on their frames.

3. THE VALIDITIES OF SOME CHARACTERISTIC FORMULAS ON THEIR FRAMES

We will discuss the relationships between the validities of the 5 characteristic formulas (or axioms) with the corresponding properties of their frames (or models), respectively.

PROPOSITION 1: AXIOM D IS SOUND AND COMPLETE FOR SERIAL MODELS

Proof. Let's prove the soundness first, i.e. D (□p→◇p) is sound for serial models. Because for every valuation V on a serial frame and to every possible world w, if $V_{M,w}(\Box p) = true$, as R is serial, there will be w, wRw', such that $V_{M,w'}(p) = true$. According to the definition of possibility

(Definition 3(5)), we get that when p is true on the accessible world w', ◇p is true on w. therefore $V_{M,w}(\Box p \rightarrow \Diamond p) = true$. Since V and w are both arbitrary, D is valid on the frame.

Now let's prove the completeness, i.e. D (□p→◇p) is complete for serial models. Let F=<W, R> be an arbitrarily given serial frame. For an arbitrary w from set w∈W, if $V_{M,w}(\Box p \rightarrow \Diamond p) = true$, then according to definition 3(3), we get

$$V_{M,w}(\Box p) = false \qquad (1)$$

or $$V_{M,w}(\Diamond p) = true \qquad (2)$$

We apply definition 3(4) to (1), there exists a w, wRw', and

$$V_{M,w'}(p) = false \qquad (3)$$

and we apply definition 3(5) to (2), there exists a w'', wRw'', and

$$V_{M,w''}(p) = true \qquad (4)$$

We can see from expressions (3) and (4) that if we wish w be true in w, there must be an accessible world $w*$, regardless either it is w' or w''. Because whether $w*$ is any of them, the proposition that p is true or false is always true in $w*$. i.e. (3) or (4) is always valid. According to the serial property of a frame, if D is desired to be valid on a frame, then the frame must be serial.

PROPOSITION 2: AXIOM T IS SOUND AND COMPLETE FOR REFLEXIVE MODELS

Proof. Let's prove the soundness first, i.e. T ($\Box p \rightarrow p$) is sound for reflexive models. Let M be a model with a reflexive relation. If in a possible world $w(w \in W)$, we have $V_{M,w}(\Box p) = true$, then for all $w'(wRw')$, we get $V_{M,w'}(p) = true$. As model M is reflexive, i.e. $(\forall w)(wRw)$, we have $V_{M,w}(p) = true$. Therefore we get $M \models_w \Box p \rightarrow p$. For w is arbitrary, we get $M \models \Box p \rightarrow p$. Furthermore, $\Box p \rightarrow p$ is valid in a frame with a reflexive relation.

Then we come to the completeness, i.e. T ($\Box p \rightarrow p$) is complete for reflexive models. Let's construct a counter-example of $M \models \Box p \rightarrow p$, which implies the frame is not reflexive. Let M be a model without the property of reflexive, i.e. there is a $w(w \in W)$ in which (wRw) is invalid. In other words, assume that F is a non-reflexive frame, then there must be a state $w(w \in W)$, such that (wRw) does not hold.

We will try to falsify $\Box p \rightarrow p$ in w. For this purpose we have to find a valuation V such that $V_{M,w}(\Box p) = true$ but $V_{M,w}(p) = false$, thus we get $V_{M,w}(\Box p \rightarrow p) = false$. i.e. we have indeed found a valuation V and a state w such that $\Box p \to p$ does not hold in w. Therefore T is not valid in F. This proves the completeness.

PROPOSITION 3: AXIOM B IS SOUND AND COMPLETE FOR SYMMETRIC MODELS

Proof. We prove the soundness first, i.e. B ($p \to \Box\Diamond P$) is sound for symmetric models. If $M \models_w p$, then for any $w'(wRw')$ we have $M \models_{w'} \Diamond p$, and $M \models_w \Box\Diamond p$ by symmetry $(\forall w)(\forall w')(wRw' \to w'Rw)$. Thus we get $M \models_w p \to \Box\Diamond p$. Furthermore, as w is arbitrary, we get $M \models p \to \Box\Diamond P$.

Then let's come to the completeness, i.e. B ($p \to \Box\Diamond P$) is complete for symmetric models. Assume $V_{M,w}(p \to \Box\Diamond p) = true$, i.e. if $V_{M,w}(p) = true$ then $V_{M,w}(\Box\Diamond p) = true$. The latter can be also interpreted as: for all w', if wRw' then $V_{M,w'}(\Diamond p) = true$. Applying the premise, we obtain if $V_{M,w}(p) = true$ then $V_{M,w'}(\Diamond p) = true$ .From the definition of possibility, we can see that w is accessible to w', i.e. $w'Rw$. Therefore we obtain $(\forall w)(\forall w')(wRw' \to w'Rw)$.

PROPOSITION 4: AXIOM A IS SOUND AND COMPLETE FOR TRANSITIVE MODELS

Proof. We prove the soundness first, i.e. A ($\Box$p→$\Box\Box$p) is sound for transitive models. If $M \models_w \Box p$, then for any $w'(wRw')$, $M \models_{w'} p$. And it is the case that for any $w''(w'Rw'')$ we have wRw'' by transitivity, and so $M \models_{w''} p$. Thus $M \models_{w'} \Box p$ for any $w'(wRw')$, and $M \models_w \Box\Box p$. Thus $M \models_w \Box p \to \Box\Box p$. Further, for w is arbitrarily given, we get $M \models \Box p \to \Box\Box p$.

Then we come to the completeness, i.e. A ($\Box$p→$\Box\Box$p) is complete for transitive models. Let wRw' if and only if whenever a formula $\Box$p is in w, the formulas $\Box$p and p are both in w'. Then R will be transitive. For if $(\forall w)(\forall w')(\forall w'')(wRw' \wedge w'Rw'' \to wRw'')$, then whenever $\Box$p is in w, $\Box$p and p will be in w', and since the former is in w' both will also be in w'', so we get wRw''.

PROPOSITION 5: AXIOM E IS SOUND AND COMPLETE FOR EUCLIDEAN MODELS

The reasoning procedures are same to the above, omitted.

4. THE VALIDITY OF PEP

Paper [1-3] presented a reasoning pattern regarding reason about knowledge of others in multi-agent systems ---- Position-Exchange-Principle, which is formalized as the following axiom schema:

$$C(\varphi \to \psi) \to (C\varphi \to C\psi) \qquad (5)$$

Where $C \in \{B_1^{S_1}, ..., B_m^{S_m}\}$, and the length of C is at least 2. When $C = \varepsilon$, (5) is a variant of the so-called *modus ponens* in propositional logic and predicate logic. When $C = B_i^{S_i}$, (5) is just the axiom (K) in knowledge logic. When the length of C is at least 2, (5) reflects the mechanism of one agent reasoning about knowledge of another agent. For example, if $C = B_i^{S_i} B_j^{S_j}$, then (5) should be

$$B_i^{S_i} B_j^{S_j} (\varphi \to \psi) \to (B_i^{S_i} B_j^{S_j} \varphi \to B_i^{S_i} B_j^{S_j} \psi)$$

Because equivalent propositions are not equivalent as belief[11], PEP, which makes the reasoning procedures of reasoning about others in MAS simple and clear, may probably imply a character which is counter-intuitive. Though paper[1-3] demonstrated examples to support their theories, we think it is not sufficed. From our analyzing in Section 3, many formulas are conditional valid even if they are valid on intuitions.

As the necessitation operator $\Box$ represents an agent's belief in the general BDI model[12], in the following, we will prove the validity of two basic modal formulas which support PEP.

PROPOSITION 6: FORMULA $\Box(p \to q) \to (\Box p \to \Box q)$ IS VALID FOR THE CLASS OF ALL MODELS

Proof. Let M be any model, w an arbitrarily given state in W. If $M \not\models_w \Box(p \to q)$, then $M \models_w \Box(p \to q) \to (\Box p \to \Box q)$. If $M \models_w \Box(p \to q)$ and $M \not\models_w \Box p$, then $M \models_w (\Box p \to \Box q)$, Hence $M \models_w \Box(p \to q) \to (\Box p \to \Box q)$. So we need only to prove $M \models_w \Box(p \to q)\ \&\ M \models_w \Box p \to M \models_w \Box q$.

(a) The necessity of an implication (b) The necessity of a proposition

Figure 3 The necessities of formulas

If $M \models_w \Box(p \to q)$ and $M \models_w \Box p$, then for any $w'(wRw')$ we have $M \models_{w'} (p \to q)$ (please see figure 3(a)) and $M \models_{w'} p$ (please see figure 3(b)). Hence $M \models_{w'} q$ for any $w'(wRw')$, and $M \models_w \Box q$. So $M \models_w \Box(p \to q) \to (\Box p \to \Box q)$.

Since M is any model, and w an arbitrarily given state in W, $\Box(p \to q) \to (\Box p \to \Box q)$ is valid for the class of all frames.

PROPOSITION7: FORMULA $\Box\Box(p \to q) \to (\Box\Box p \to \Box\Box q)$ IS VALID FOR THE CLASS OF ALL MODELS

Proof. Similar to the above, we only prove $M \models_w \Box\Box(p \to q) \;\&\; M \models_w \Box\Box p \to M \models_w \Box\Box q$.

For an arbitrarily given state $w'(wRw')$, if $M \models_w \Box\Box(p \to q)$, we get $M \models_{w'} \Box(p \to q)$; and for another arbitrarily given state $w''(w'Rw'')$, we also have $M \models_{w''} (p \to q)$ (please see figure 4(a) for reference). And by the some procedure, we have $M \models_{w'} \Box p$ and $M \models_{w''} p$ from $M \models_w \Box\Box p$ (please see figure 4(a) for reference). Hence $M \models_{w''} q$. Since w'' and w' are both arbitrary, we get $M \models_{w'} \Box q$; and as w' and w are both arbitrary possible worlds or states, we obtain $M \models_w \Box\Box q$. Thus $M \models_w \Box\Box(p \to q) \to (\Box\Box p \to \Box\Box q)$. Because M and w are both arbitrarily chosen, $\Box\Box(p \to q) \to (\Box\Box p \to \Box\Box q)$ is valid for the class of all frames.

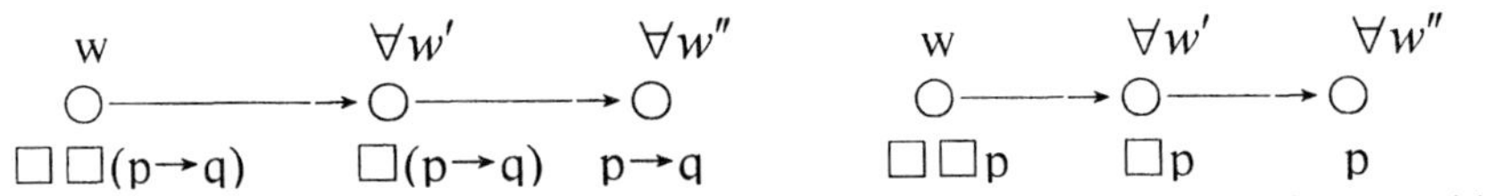

(a) The necessary necessity of an implication (b) The necessary necessity of a proposition

Figure 4 The necessary necessities of formulas

5. CONCLUSIONS

By analyzing the characteristic axioms using the possible-world semantics, we obtained some of their corresponding conditions, saying corresponding formulas. These formulas can be regarded as the formal explanations of the characteristic axioms. On the other hand, only when these conditions are met, are valid the corresponding formulas (or axioms). In this way, we can make it sure that which axioms are valid for the right thinking formulas at a specific condition. Through analyzing, we discover that some formulas, such as D and T, are conditional valid even through they are valid on intuition. As the necessitation operator □ represents an agent's belief in the general BDI model, we analyzed the validity of PEP proposed by papers [1-3], and proved the validity of PEP from the points of modal logic and Kripke's semantics of possible worlds.

PEP is very useful in multi-agent epistemic logic. It plays an important role in the knowledge research of MAS as that of *modus ponens* and axiom K do in propositional logic and knowledge logic. Though we have proved the validity of PEP on any frames, it is a reasonable reasoning of an agent reasoning about knowledge of others in the default of the premise that she knows the states and actions of herself and the agent about whom she reasons. If an agent doesn't know her states or actions (i.e. epistemic reflexive axioms are not met), or the epistemic states of the two agents are much different, then PEP is probably not so valid. Therefore, in practical, when we use PEP as a good tool to reason about others, it is wise to make sure or clear that any single modal operator satisfies the KD45.

REFERENCES

[1] SHI Zhongzhi,TIAN Qijia and LI Yunfeng. RAO Logic for Multi-agent Framework. Journal of Computer Science and Technology,1999,14(4):393-400

[2] WANG Wenjie,TIAN Qijia and SHI Zhongzhi.Reasoning About Others in MAS(In Chinese).Journal of Computer Research and Development.1998,35(11):971–974

[3] TIAN Qijia, SHI Zhongzhi and WANG Huaiqing. Reasoning About Actions and Knowledge in MAS(In Chinese). In: Proceeding of The Fourth Chinese Joint conference on Artificial Intelligence.Beijing:Tsinghua University Press,1996:74–79

[4] YANG Kun,CHEN Jianzhong,SUN Degang,LIU Dayou. Logic Omniscience Problem in Epistemic Logics and the Methods to Resolve It. Journal of Jilin University(Natural Sciences), 1999(3):40-43

[5] ZHOU Changle. A Introduction to Epistemic Logics(In Chinese). Beijing:Tsinghua University Press,2001

[6] LI Jinhou, JIANG Jinping. Two Blind Spots in Recent Logic-Based Agent Study Inferred from the Declaration of Logic Omniscience Problem(In Chinese). Journal of University of Science and Technology Beijing, 2004,26(2):215-218

[7] ZHOU Beihai. Modal Logics(In Chinese). Beijing: China Social Science Press,1997

[8] HU Zehong. The Philosophical reflectons of Logics(In Chinese). Beijing: Central Editorial Press, 2004:127-135

[9] Patrick Blackburn, Maarten de Rijke, Yde Venema. Modal Logic. Cambridge University Press, 2001

[10] S.Kripke. Semantic Analysis of Modal Logic Ⅱ: Non-Normal Modal Propositional Calculi. In:Symposium on the Theory of Models,North-Holland,Amsterdam, 1965

[11] Konolige,K. A Deduction Model of Belief. Pitman,London and Morgan Kaufmann,San Mateo,CA.1986

[12] LIU Yong,PU Shuzhen,CHENG Daijie,and CAO Zehan.Belief Characteristic's of BDI Model(In Chinese).Journal of Computer Research and Development.2005,42(1):54–59